W9-DDO-475

ÆLFRIC'S CATHOLIC HOMILIES

INTRODUCTION, COMMENTARY AND GLOSSARY

EARLY ENGLISH TEXT SOCIETY
S.S. 18
2000

ÆLFRIC'S CATHOLIC HOMILIES

INTRODUCTION, COMMENTARY AND GLOSSARY

BY

MALCOLM GODDEN

Published for
THE EARLY ENGLISH TEXT SOCIETY
by the
OXFORD UNIVERSITY PRESS
2000

OXFORD
UNIVERSITY PRESS

Great Clarendon Street, Oxford OX2 6DP

Oxford University Press is a department of the University of Oxford.
It furthers the University's aim of excellence in research, scholarship,
and education by publishing worldwide in

Oxford New York

Athens Auckland Bangkok Bogotá Buenos Aires Calcutta
Cape Town Chennai Dar es Salaam Delhi Florence Hong Kong Istanbul
Karachi Kuala Lumpur Madras Melbourne Mexico City Mumbai
Nairobi Paris São Paulo Singapore Taipei Tokyo Toronto Warsaw

and associated companies in Berlin Ibadan

Oxford is a registered trade mark of Oxford University Press

Published in the United States
by Oxford University Press Inc., New York

First published 2000

British Library Cataloguing in Publication Data
Data available

Library of Congress Cataloging in Publication Data
Data applied for

ISBN 0-19-722419-9

1 3 5 7 9 10 8 6 4 2

Typeset by Joshua Associates Ltd., Oxford
Printed in Great Britain
on acid-free paper by
Print Wright Ltd., Ipswich

PREFACE

This is the third and final volume in a project which began with the publication of my edition of the Second Series of Ælfric's Catholic Homilies in 1979 and continued with the publication of Peter Clemoes' edition of the First Series in 1997. It was originally conceived as a collaboration between Peter Clemoes and myself, and we mapped out the general content and structure together in the early 1970s, but Peter was in the end still embroiled in revising his edition of the text when he died in 1996, and this final volume was left to me. The extensive and complex manuscript tradition of the two series, together with Ælfric's continuous revision of the text and his reissuing of the homilies from time to time in different kinds of collections, is discussed in detail in the introductions to the previous two volumes. This volume provides a brief general introduction, dealing with the composition of the text and the treatment of sources, a commentary on each homily which summarises its main concerns and sources and gives all the source-passages I have been able to trace, together with comments on any necessary points of detail, and a glossary. An analysis of the language of the text, though long customary in EETS volumes, was excluded from the original plan since even then it seemed impractical: this is by far the longest extant text in Old English (some twelve per cent of the extant corpus of prose and verse in Old English), it has been available in print for 150 years and has been the focus of countless philological studies and textbooks, and although much remains to do, and the Royal MS which forms the basis for the text of CH I has been relatively little studied, it is clear that at least another lengthy volume, and many more years, would be needed to do justice to the language.

I first embarked on the work for this volume in 1970 and have acquired many debts to friends and colleagues over the years. I acknowledge with pleasure the support of Pembroke College, Cambridge, where I was a research fellow 1969–72; the University of Liverpool, where I was a lecturer 1972–5; the University of Oxford, where I have been a lecturer and subsequently professor since 1976, together with Exeter College where I held a tutorial fellowship 1976–91 and Pembroke College where I have held a professorial fellowship since 1991. The officers and council members of the Early English Text

Society have been their usual patient and supportive selves, from Pamela Gradon who was editorial secretary at the outset to her current successor Dr Helen Spencer, and Professor Janet Bately, who read the typescript for the Society and made countless suggestions for change and improvement. Of the work of others, I have profited especially from the work of Professor Mary Clayton of University College Dublin and Dr Susan Irvine of University College London, both former graduate students; and, it goes without saying, from the work of Professor J.E. Cross, who was a generous and supportive head of department at Liverpool. Gordon Whatley of Queen's College, New York, was extremely generous in giving me an advance copy of his massive work on the saints' lives known in Anglo-Saxon England, and my use of it will be evident throughout the volume. Professor Simon Keynes was prompt and generous in responding to my queries and arguments about the dating and background of Ælfric's work. Brad Bedingfield of Oxford University helped on the glossary, and his work on the relation of the homilies to the liturgy has much influenced my thinking. Other debts to colleagues and former students are noted in the text and footnotes. The biggest debt, however, is to Dr Rohini Jayatilaka, who made sure that I could and would access the latest electronic resources, found articles that I could not trace, checked endless references and quotations, queried dodgy arguments, and reduced an enormous variety of citations to order. The book would not have been finished without her.

My introduction to this project came from Peter Clemoes, who signed me up to it when I was an undergraduate in 1965. I hardly dare imagine that he would have liked the result; but his humanity and generosity is behind it all.

CONTENTS

ERRATA IN CH I AND CH II

CH I

Praef.120–1 For **oþþe þurh gewritu** read **oþþe þurh tungan oððe þurh gewritu.**

I.2.167 For **geswutelung. |** read **| geswutelung.**

I.3.65 For **gebodadon** read **gebodad on**

I.6.53 For **ætforeweardan** read **æt foreweardan**

I.7.119 For **þe ða** read **þa ða**

I.9.144 For **hi** read **his.**

I.10.159 For **þyrenum** read **þyrnenum**

I.10.164 For **heofonanrice** read **heofonan rice**

I.13.77 For **ofterwann** read **oferwann**

I.13 p. 283 app.crit.
For line numbers 66, 67, 68, 69, 70, 71, 74, 78, 79, 80, read 65, 66, 67, 68, 69, 70, 73, 77, 77, 79

I.15.153 For **þær on** read **þæron.**

I.19.186 For **þater** read **pater**

I.24.182 For **ðe** read **ða**

I.28.app.crit. on p. 411:
40 For **habeturø** read **habetur'**
42 For **$usend** read **þusend**
44 For **$a** read **þa**
45 For **£** read **7**

I.29.119 For **gehwa** read **ge hwa**

I.32.205 For **gif us** read **gif we us**

I.34.138 For **he** read **het**

I.35.55 For **beleafe** read **be leafe**

I.35.140 For **Gewuniað** read (probably) **Ge wuniað.**

I.38.25 For **woruld wisdom** read **woruldwisdom**

CH II

p. xcv foot: the last two signs (< and –) should be interchanged.

II.10.174 For **wæter æddre** read **wæteræddre.**

II.16.114 For **Gecnawan** read **Ge cnapan**

II.39.54 For **unlayfedlicum** read **unalyfedlicum.**

ABBREVIATIONS AND SHORT TITLES

(For works cited as sources for Ælfric, see the Summary of Sources below, and the headnote to each homily.)

Archiv	*Archiv für das Studium der neueren Sprachen und Literaturen*
ASE	*Anglo-Saxon England*
ASS	*Acta Sanctorum quotquot toto orbe coluntur* (Antwerp, etc., 1643–1894; 1925)
Assmann	B. Assmann, ed., *Angelsächsische Homilien und Heiligenleben*, BaP 3 (Kassel, 1889, repr. with suppl. by P. Clemoes, Darmstadt, 1964)
BaP	Bibliothek der angelsächsischen Prosa
Barré	H. Barré, *Les Homéliaires carolingiens de l'école d'Auxerre*, Studi e testi 225 (Vatican City, 1962)
Bately see OE Orosius	
Bazire and Cross	J. Bazire and J. E. Cross, eds., *Eleven Old English Rogationtide Homilies*, Toronto Old English Series 7 (Toronto, 1982)
Belfour	A. O. Belfour, ed., *Twelfth-Century Homilies in MS. Bodley 343*, EETS os 137 (1909)
Bethurum see Wulfstan	
BHL	*Bibliotheca Hagiographica Latina*, 2 vols., Subsidia hagiographica 6 (Brussels, 1898–1901); Supplement, Subsidia hagiographica 12 (Brussels, 1911); *Novum supplementum*, Subsidia hagiographica 70 (Brussels, 1986)
BL	London, British Library
Blickling Homilies	R. Morris, ed., *The Blickling Homilies*, EETS os 58, 63 and 73 (1874–80, repr. 1990)
Bodleian	Oxford, Bodleian Library
Bonnet see Lipsius and Bonnet	
Brotanek	R. Brotanek, ed., 'Sermo in dedicatione templi', in his *Texte und Untersuchungen zur altenglischen Literatur und Kirchengeschichte* (Halle, 1913), pp. 3–15

BT, BTS, BTA	J. Bosworth and T. N. Toller, *An Anglo-Saxon Dictionary* (London, 1898); T. N. Toller, *Supplement* (Oxford, 1921), with *Revised and Enlarged Addenda* by A. Campbell (Oxford, 1972)
CC	Cotton-Corpus Legendary (as analysed and described in Zettel 1979 and 1982, and Jackson and Lapidge 1996)
CCCM	Corpus Christianorum, Continuatio Mediaevalis
CCSL	Corpus Christianorum, Series Latina
CH I, CH II	Ælfric's Catholic Homilies, First and Second Series. *CH I* (in italics) refers specifically to P. Clemoes, ed., *Ælfric's Catholic Homilies: the First Series, Text*, EETS ss 17 (1997); *CH II* refers to M. Godden, ed., *Ælfric's Catholic Homilies: the Second Series, Text*, EETS ss 5 (1979). See also Thorpe (1844–6).
Clark Hall	J. R. Clark Hall, *A Concise Anglo-Saxon Dictionary*, 4th ed., with a supplement by H. D. Merritt (Cambridge, 1960)
Clavis Patrum Latinorum	E. Dekkers and A. Gaar, *Clavis Patrum Latinorum* (Steenbrugge, 1995)
Clayton 1983	M. Clayton, 'The Cult of the Virgin Mary in Anglo-Saxon England with Special Reference to the Vernacular Texts' (unpubl. D.Phil. thesis, Oxford Univ., 1983)
Clayton 1985a	M. Clayton, 'Homiliaries and preaching in Anglo-Saxon England', *Peritia* 4 (1985), 207–42
Clayton 1985b	M. Clayton, 'Ælfric's *De Virginitate*, lines 35–54', *Notes and Queries* 230 (March 1985), 8–10
Clayton 1990	M. Clayton, *The Cult of the Virgin Mary in Anglo-Saxon England*, CSASE 2 (Cambridge, 1990)
Clemoes 1959	P. A. M. Clemoes, 'The Chronology of Ælfric's Works', in *The Anglo-Saxons: Studies in some Aspects of their History and Culture presented to Bruce Dickins*, ed. P. Clemoes (London, 1959), pp. 212–47
De Cogitatione (Ælfric)	Printed by A. S. Napier, in 'Ein altenglisches leben des heiligen Chad', *Anglia* 10 (1888), 131–156, at 155

Cook 1898 — A. S. Cook, *Biblical Quotations in Old English Prose Writers* (London, 1898)

Crawford — S. J. Crawford, ed., *The Old English Version of the Heptateuch, Ælfric's Treatise on the Old and New Testament, and his Preface to Genesis*, EETS os 160 (1922, repr. with the text of two additional manuscripts transcribed by N. R. Ker, 1969)

Crawford see also *Hexameron* (Ælfric)

Cross 1963a — J. E. Cross, 'Bundles for burning: a theme in two of Ælfric's Catholic Homilies—with other sources', *Anglia* 81 (1963), 335–46

Cross 1963b — J. E. Cross, *Ælfric and the Medieval Homiliary: Objection and Contribution*, Scripta Minora Regiae Societatis Humaniorum Litterarum Lundensis 4 (Lund, 1963)

Cross 1968 — J. E. Cross, 'More Sources for Two of Aelfric's Catholic Homilies', *Anglia* 86 (1968), 59–78

Cross 1969 — J. E. Cross, 'Ælfric: mainly on memory and creative method in two Catholic Homilies', *Studia Neophilologica* 41 (1969), 135–55

Cross 1972 — J. E. Cross, 'The Literate Anglo-Saxon: on Sources and Disseminations', *Proceedings of the British Academy* 58 (1972), 67–100 [and separately, London, 1972]

Cross 1975 — J. E. Cross, 'Blickling Homily XIV and the Old English Martyrology on John the Baptist', *Anglia* 93 (1975), 145–60

Cross 1987 — J. E. Cross, *Cambridge, Pembroke College MS. 25: a Carolingian Sermonary used by Anglo-Saxon Preachers*, King's College London Medieval Studies 1 (London, 1987)

Cross 1996 — J. E. Cross *et. al.*, eds., *Two Old English Apocrypha and their Manuscript Source*, CSASE 19 (Cambridge, 1996)

CSASE — Cambridge Studies in Anglo-Saxon England

CSEL — Corpus Scriptorum Ecclesiasticorum Latinorum

Day 1974 — Virginia Day, 'The influence of the catechetical *narratio* on Old English and some other medieval literature', *ASE* 3 (1974), 51–61

EETS	Early English Text Society os = Original Series ss = Supplementary Series
EHD	D. Whitelock, ed. and trans., *English Historical Documents, Volume 1: c.500–1042* (2nd ed., London and New York, 1981)
Eliason and Clemoes 1966	Norman E. Eliason and Peter Clemoes, eds., *Ælfric's First Series of Catholic Homilies (British Museum Royal 7 C.XII, fols. 4–218)*, Early English Manuscripts in Facsimile 13 (Copenhagen, 1966)
Excerptiones Ps-Egberti	Printed in B. Thorpe, ed., *Ancient Laws and Institutes*, 2 vols. (London, 1840), II.97–127
Excerpts (Ælfric)	Ælfric's Excerpts from the *Prognosticon Futuri Saeculi* of Julian of Toledo, ed. Gatch 1977, pp. 129–46
Fábrega Grau	A. Fábrega Grau, ed., *Pasionario Hispanico, Monumenta Hispaniae Sacra*, 2 vols., Serie Litúrgica 6 (Madrid, 1953–5)
Fabricius (or Fab.)	J. A. Fabricius, ed., *Codex Apocryphus Novi Testamenti*, 2 vols. (Hamburg 1719, 1743)
Fehr	B. Fehr, ed., *Die Hirtenbriefe Ælfrics*, BaP 9 (Hamburg, 1914, repr. with suppl. by P. Clemoes, Darmstadt, 1966)
Förster 1892	M. Förster, *Über die Quellen von Aelfrics Homiliae Catholicae: I. Legenden* (Berlin, 1892)
Förster 1894	M. Förster, 'Über die Quellen von Aelfrics exegetischen Homiliae Catholicae', *Anglia* 16 (1894), 1–61
Frank 1994	R. Frank, 'Poetic Words in Late Old English Prose', in Godden, Gray and Hoad 1994, pp. 87–107
Gabrielson 1912	A. Gabrielson, 'Guischart de Beauliu's debt to religious learning and literature in England', *Archiv* 128 (1912), 309–28
Gameson 1995	R. Gameson, *The Role of Art in the late Anglo-Saxon Church* (Oxford, 1995)
Gatch 1966	M. McC. Gatch, 'MS Boulogne-sur-Mer 63 and Ælfric's First Series of Catholic Homilies', *JEGP* 65 (1966), 482–90
Gatch 1977	M. McC. Gatch, *Preaching and Theology in*

	Anglo-Saxon England: Ælfric and Wulfstan (Toronto 1977)
GCS	Die griechischen christlichen Schriftsteller der ersten drei Jahrhunderte
Glorieux 1952	P. Glorieux, *Pour revaloriser Migne: tables rectificatives*, Mélanges de science religieuse 9 (Lille, 1952)
Glossary (Ælfric) see	Grammar (Ælfric)
Gneuss 1968	H. Gneuss, *Hymnar and Hymnen im englischen Mittelalter*, Buchreihe der Anglia 12 (Tübingen, 1968)
Godden 1973	M. R. Godden, 'The development of Ælfric's Second Series of *Catholic Homilies*', *English Studies* 54 (1973), 209–16
Godden 1978	M. R. Godden, 'Ælfric and the Vernacular Prose Tradition', in *The Old English Homily and its Backgrounds*, ed. Paul E. Szarmach and Bernard F. Huppé (Albany, NY, 1978), pp. 99–117
Godden 1980	M. R. Godden, 'Ælfric's changing vocabulary', *English Studies* 61 (1980), 206–23
Godden 1985a	M. R. Godden, 'Anglo-Saxons on the Mind', in Lapidge and Gneuss 1985, pp. 271–98
Godden 1985b	M. R. Godden, 'Ælfric's Saints' Lives and the Problem of Miracles', *Leeds Studies in English* 16 (1985), 83–100
Godden 1990	M. R. Godden, 'Money, power and morality in late Anglo-Saxon England', *ASE* 19 (1990), 41–65
Godden 1994	M. R. Godden, 'Apocalypse and Invasion in Late Anglo-Saxon England', in Godden, Gray and Hoad 1994, pp. 130–62
Godden 1996	M. R. Godden, 'Experiments in Genre: The Saints' Lives in Ælfric's *Catholic Homilies*', in Szarmach 1996, pp. 261–87
Godden, Gray and Hoad 1994	M. Godden, D. Gray and T. Hoad, eds., *From Anglo-Saxon to Early Middle English: Studies presented to E. G. Stanley* (Oxford, 1994)
Grammar (Ælfric)	J. Zupitza, ed., *Ælfrics Grammatik und Glossar*, Sammlung englischer Denkmäler 1 (Berlin, 1880)
Grundy 1991	L. Grundy, *Books and Grace: Ælfric's Theology*,

	King's College London Medieval Studies 6 (London, 1991)
Grundy 1992	L. Grundy, 'God meditates: a model for the 'salvation histories' in three homilies of Ælfric and in his *Hexameron*', *Medium Ævum* 61 (1992), 189–205
Hecht	H. Hecht, ed., *Bischof Wærferths von Worcester Übersetzung der Dialoge Gregors des grossen*, BaP 5 (Leipzig, 1900–7, repr. Darmstadt, 1965)
Henel	H. Henel, ed., *Ælfric's De Temporibus Anni*, EETS os 213 (1942, repr. 1970)
Heptateuch (Ælfric) see Crawford	
Hexameron (Ælfric)	S. J. Crawford, ed., *Exameron Anglice, or the Old English Hexameron*, BaP 10 (Hamburg, 1921)
Hill 1992	J. Hill, 'Ælfric and Smaragdus', *ASE* 21 (1992), 203–37
Hom.	*Homilia, Homiliae*, Homily, Homilies
Interrogationes (Ælfric)	G. E. MacLean, 'Ælfric's Version of *Alcuini Interrogationes Sigeuulfi in Genesin*', *Anglia* 6 (1883), 425–73, and *Anglia* 7 (1884), 1–59
Irvine	S. Irvine, ed., *Old English Homilies from MS Bodley 343*, EETS os 302 (1993)
JEGP	*Journal of English and Germanic Philology*
Jackson and Lapidge 1996	P. Jackson and M. Lapidge, 'The Contents of the Cotton-Corpus Legendary', in Szarmach 1996, pp. 131–46
Jones 1998	C. Jones, ed., *Ælfric's Letter to the Monks of Eynsham*, CSASE 24 (Cambridge, 1998)
Jost	K. Jost, ed., *Die 'Institutes of Polity, Civil and Ecclesiastical'* (Bern, 1959)
Ker 1957	N. R. Ker, *Catalogue of Manuscripts Containing Anglo-Saxon* (Oxford, 1957, reissued with suppl., 1990)
Keynes 1980	S. Keynes, *The Diplomas of King Aethelred 'The Unready' 978–1016: A Study in their Use as Historical Evidence*, Cambridge Studies in Medieval Life and Thought, 3rd ser., 13 (Cambridge, 1980)
Kotzor see OE Martyrology	

Lapidge and Gneuss 1985	M. Lapidge and H. Gneuss, eds., *Learning and Literature in Anglo-Saxon England: Studies Presented to Peter Clemoes on the Occasion of his Sixty-Fifth Birthday* (Cambridge, 1985)
Leinbaugh 1980	T. H. Leinbaugh, 'The Liturgical Homilies in *Ælfric's Lives of Saints*' (unpubl. Ph.D. dissertation, Harvard Univ., 1980)
Leinbaugh 1994	T. H. Leinbaugh, 'Ælfric's *Lives of Saints* I and the Boulogne Sermon: Editorial, Authorial and Textual Problems', in *The Editing of Old English: Papers from the 1990 Manchester Conference*, ed. D. G. Scragg and P. E. Szarmach (Cambridge, 1994), pp. 191–211
Lenker	U. Lenker, ed., *Die westsächsische Evangelienversion und die Perikopenordnungen im angelsächsischen England*, Texte und Untersuchungen zur englischen Philologie, Bd. 20 (Münich, 1997)
Lewis and Short	C. T. Lewis and C. Short, *A Latin Dictionary* (1879, repr. Oxford, 1993)
Lipsius and Bonnet	R. A. Lipsius and M. Bonnet, eds., *Acta Apostolorum Apocrypha*, 2 vols. (Leipzig, 1891–1908)
Liuzza see *OE Gospels*	
LS	W. W. Skeat, ed., *Ælfric's Lives of Saints*, 4 vols., EETS os 76, 82, 94 and 114 (1881–1900, repr. in 2 vols., 1966)
Magennis 1994	Hugh Magennis, ed., *The Anonymous Old English Legend of the Seven Sleepers* (Durham, 1994)
Magennis 1996	H. Magennis, 'Ælfric and the legend of the Seven Sleepers', in Szarmach 1996, pp. 317–31
Menologium (verse)	E. van Kirk Dobbie, ed., *The Menologium* in *The Anglo-Saxon Minor Poems*, Anglo-Saxon Poetic Records 6 (New York and London, 1942), pp. 49–55
MGH	Monumenta Germaniae Historica
Mombritius 1910 (or Momb.)	B. Mombritius, ed., *Sanctuarium seu Vitae Sanctorum*, 2 vols. (2nd ed., Paris, 1910)
Morris	R. Morris, ed., *Old English Homilies*, EETS os 29 and 34 (1867–8, repr. 1988)
ODCC	F. L. Cross and E. A. Livingstone, ed., *Oxford*

	Dictionary of the Christian Church (2nd ed., Oxford 1974, repr. with corrections 1983)
OE Bede	T. A. Miller, ed., *The Old English Version of Bede's Ecclesiastical History of the English People*, EETS os 95 and 96 (1890–91)
OE Boethius	W. J. Sedgefield, ed., *King Alfred's Old English Version of Boethius De Consolatione Philosophiae* (Oxford, 1899)
OE Gospels	R. M. Liuzza, ed., *The Old English Version of the Gospels*, EETS os 304 (1994) [OE Gospels (not in italics) designates the Old English Gospel translations and glosses generally, including Rushworth and Lindisfarne.]
OE Martyrology	G. Kotzor, ed., *Das altenglische Martyrologium*, 2 vols., Bayerische Akademie der Wissenschaften, philos.-hist. Klasse ns 88.1–2 (Münich, 1981)
OE Orosius	J. Bately, ed., *The Old English Orosius*, EETS ss 6 (London, 1980)
OES	Bruce Mitchell, *Old English Syntax*, 2 vols. (Oxford, 1985)
Ogilvy 1967	J. D. A. Ogilvy, *Books known to the English, 597–1066* (Cambridge, Mass., 1967)
On the Old and New Testament (Ælfric) see Crawford	
Pastoral Care	H. Sweet, ed., *King Alfred's West-Saxon Version of Gregory's Pastoral Care*, EETS os 45 and 50 (1871–2, repr. 1996)
PD, PDM	Paul the Deacon's Homiliary; PDM is the expanded version printed PL 95
PG	J.-P. Migne, ed., *Patrologia Graeca*, 162 vols. (Paris, 1857–66)
PL, PLS	J.-P. Migne, ed., *Patrologia Latina*, 221 vols. (Paris, 1844–64); PLS: *Patrologia Latina, Supplementum*, 5 vols. (Paris, 1958–74)
Pope	J. C. Pope, ed., *Homilies of Aelfric: A Supplementary Collection*, 2 vols., EETS os 259 and 260 (1967–8)
Preface to Genesis (Ælfric) see Crawford	
Ps-Egbert Penitential	J. Raith, ed., *Die altenglische Version des Halitgar'schen Bussbuches (sog. Poenitentiale Pseudo-Egberti)*, BaP 13 (Hamburg, 1933)
RB	*Revue Bénédictine*

Raw 1990	Barbara Raw, *Anglo-Saxon Crucifixion Iconography and the Art of the Monastic Revival*, CSASE 1 (Cambridge, 1990)
Regularis Concordia	T. Symons, ed., *Regularis Concordia Anglicae Nationis Monachorum Sanctimonialiumque* (London, 1953)
SASLC 1990	F. M. Biggs, T. D. Hill and P. E. Szarmach, eds., *Sources of Anglo-Saxon Literary Culture: A Trial Version*, Medieval and Renaissance Texts and Studies 74 (Binghamton, 1990)
Sauer	H. Sauer, ed., *Theodulfi Capitula in England*, Texte und Untersuchungen zur englischen Philologie, Bd. 8 (Münich, 1978)
Scragg 1991	D. G. Scragg, ed., *The Battle of Maldon AD 991* (Oxford, 1991)
Scragg see also Vercelli Homilies	
Serm.	*Sermo, Sermones*, Sermon, Sermons
Sisam, *Studies*	K. Sisam, *Studies in the History of Old English Literature* (Oxford, 1953) [The chapter on Ælfric reproduces articles originally published in 1931–3.]
Smetana 1959	C. L. Smetana, 'Aelfric and the Early Medieval Homiliary', *Traditio* 15 (1959), 163–204
Smetana 1961	C. L. Smetana, 'Aelfric and the Homiliary of Haymo of Halberstadt', *Traditio* 17 (1961), pp. 457–69
Soliloquies	T. A. Carnicelli, ed., *King Alfred's Version of St. Augustine's Soliloquies* (Cambridge, Mass., 1969)
Surius	L. Surius, ed., *De Probatis Sanctorum Historiis*, 6 vols. (Cologne, 1576–81)
Szarmach 1996	P. E. Szarmach, ed., *Holy Men and Holy Women: Old English Prose Saints' Lives and their Contexts* (Albany, 1996)
De Temporibus Anni (Ælfric) see Henel	
Texte und Untersuchungen	Texte und Untersuchungen zur Geschichte der altchristlichen Literatur
Thorpe	B. Thorpe, ed., *The Homilies of the Anglo-Saxon Church: the First Part, containing the Sermones Catholici or Homilies of Ælfric*, 2 vols. (London, 1844–6)

Thorpe see also *Excerptiones Ps-Egberti*

Vercelli Homilies	D. G. Scragg, ed., *The Vercelli Homilies and Related Texts*, EETS os 300 (1992)
Warner	R. D.-N. Warner, ed., *Early English Homilies from the Twelfth Century MS. Vesp. D.xiv*, EETS os 152 (1917)
Whatley, *Acta* (forthcoming)	Gordon Whatley, volume on the *Acta Sanctorum* in Anglo-Saxon England, forthcoming in the SASLC project
Wilcox 1994	J. Wilcox, ed., *Ælfric's Prefaces* (Durham 1994)
Wordsworth and White	J. Wordsworth, and H. I. White, eds., *Nouum Testamentum Domini nostri Iesu Christi Latine, Pars prior: Quattuor Evangelia* (Oxford, 1889–98)
Wulfstan	D. Bethurum, ed., *The Homilies of Wulfstan* (Oxford, 1957)
Zettel 1979	P. H. Zettel, 'Ælfric's Hagiographic Sources and the Latin Legendary Preserved in B.L. MS Cotton Nero E. i and CCCC MS 9 and Other Manuscripts' (unpubl. DPhil. dissertation, Oxford Univ., 1979)
Zettel 1982	P. H. Zettel, 'Saints' Lives in Old English: Latin Manuscripts and Vernacular Accounts: Aelfric', *Peritia* 1 (1982), 17–37

Zupitza see Grammar (Ælfric)

Abbreviations for Books of the Bible

Gen = Genesis
Exod = Exodus
Lev = Leviticus
Num = Numeri
Deut = Deuteronomium
Jos = Iosue
Jud = Iudicum
1 Sam = 1 Samuel
3 Reg = 3 Reges
4 Reg = 4 Reges
Tob = Tobias
Job = Iob
Ps = Psalmi
Prov = Proverbia
Eccl = Ecclesiastes
Cant = Canticum canticorum
Sap = Sapientia
Sir = Sirach (Ecclesiasticus)
Is = Isaias
Jer = Hieremias
Lam = Lamentationes (Threni)
Bar = Baruch
Ez = Hiezechiel (Ezechiel)
Dan = Danihel
Os = Osee (Hosea)
Joel = Iohel

Amos = Amos
Jon = Ionas
Mich = Micah
Hab = Abacuc (Habbakuk)
Soph = Sofonias (Zephaniah)
Zach = Zaccharias (Zechariah)
Mt = Evangelium secundum Matthaeum
Mc = Evangelium secundum Marcum
Lc = Evangelium secundum Lucam
Jn = Evangelium secundum Iohannem
Acts = Actus apostolorum
Rom = Epistola ad Romanos
1 Cor = Epistola ad Corinthios I
2 Cor = Epistola ad Corinthios II
Gal = Epistola ad Galatas
Eph = Epistola ad Ephesios
Phil = Epistola ad Philippenses
Col = Epistola ad Colossenses
1 Thess = Epistola ad Thessalonicenses I
2 Thess = Epistola ad Thessalonicenses II
1 Tim = Epistola ad Timotheum I
2 Tim = Epistola ad Timotheum II
Tit = Epistola ad Titum
Hebr = Epistola ad Hebraeos
Jac = Epistola catholica Iacobi
1 Petr = Epistola I Petri
1 Jn = Epistola I Iohannis
2 Jn = Epistola II Iohannis
Jude = Epistola catholica Iudae
Apoc = Apocalypsis

INTRODUCTION

ÆLFRIC OF EYNSHAM

The general outlines of Ælfric's life, according to the traditional consensus, are as follows. He was born around 950; educated in the school of St Æthelwold at Winchester, where he became a monk; moved to the newly-established monastery of Cerne Abbas in Dorset around 987, as priest and probably school-master; in about 1005 moved to the new monastery at Eynsham, as abbot; and probably died around 1010.[1] The canon of his works was laid down by Peter Clemoes in 1959, and confirmed and refined by John C. Pope in 1967–8.[2] According to the tentative chronology suggested by Clemoes, at Cerne Ælfric wrote, in rapid succession, his two series of Catholic Homilies; the *De Temporibus Anni*; a pastoral letter for Wulfsige, bishop of Sherborne; the Grammar and Glossary; the collection of saints' lives, homilies and Old Testament paraphrases known as the Lives of Saints; the Colloquy (in Latin); and some further Biblical paraphrases (including Genesis, Judges, Joshua, Esther, Judith). In his final years at Cerne he also compiled and issued a new collection of homilies for the temporale, combining revised versions of items from the Catholic Homilies with newly composed items. At Eynsham he wrote pastoral letters for Wulfstan, archbishop of York and bishop of Worcester; a Latin life of St Æthelwold; and his letter for the monks of Eynsham. He also revised and reissued the first series of Catholic Homilies, with some new items, and revised and extended the temporale collection of homilies.

THE NATURE OF THE CATHOLIC HOMILIES

The Catholic Homilies represent Ælfric's first, and in many ways most ambitious, undertaking, and he continued revising and reissuing them to the end of his life. What the Catholic Homilies were for is surprisingly

[1] The most recent biographical account is in Wilcox 1994; an older but fuller biography is J. Hurt, *Ælfric* (New York, 1972); for the datings see Clemoes 1959.

[2] Clemoes 1959; Pope, pp. 136–46.

difficult to say.[3] In the preface to CH I Ælfric describes them as two books of forty discourses, which were to be read aloud in church by the clergy:

Quadraginta sententias in isto libro posuimus. credentes hoc sufficere posse per annum fidelibus. si integre eis a ministris dei recitentur in ecclesia. . . . Duos libros in ista translatione facimus. persuadentes ut legatur unus per annum in ecclesia dei. et alter anno sequenti.

Within individual homilies he often includes references to the context in which he presumably imagined them being recited, that is, in the course of the Mass, after the deacon has read the Gospel passage appointed for the day: 'Her is geræd on ðisum godspelle þe we nu gehierdon of þæs diacones muðe . . .' (I.10.3); 'Ic wolde eow trahtnian þis godspel þe man nu beforan eow rædde . . .' (I.11.3); 'Nu wylle we eow gereccan be ðam halgum godspelle þe man· æt ðyssere mæssan eow ætforan rædde' (II.29.5; see also I.7.3–8; 14.2; 17.3). In his pastoral letter written in English for Wulfsige, bishop of Sherborne, about the time he completed the Catholic Homilies (Wulfsige became bishop around 993), and addressed to the clerics of the diocese, he says the priest must 'secgan Sunnandagum and mæssedagum þæs godspelles angyt on englisc þam folce' and the Catholic Homilies clearly supplies that need, both in the simple sense that the homilies provide paraphrases of the Gospel readings for the day and in the larger sense that they expound the significance and doctrines of those readings. But the preface to CH I suggests that as well as such preaching use he had in mind individual readers (my italics):

. . . transtulimus hunc codicem . . . in nostram consuetam sermocinationem ob aedificationem simplicium qui hanc norunt tantummodo locutionem. *siue legendo. siue audiendo*. Ideoque nec obscura posuimus uerba. sed simplicem anglicam quo facilius possit ad cor peruenire *legentium. uel audientium*. . . .

Though the readers could include the learned who might chance to see the sermons (cf II.30.227–8) and the semi-learned who would read them over to themselves before reading them aloud to their congregations, the language here seems to identify readers as part of the target audience for the homilies. The reference in the English part of the preface to supplying the needs of unlearned people who have only unreliable books on the Gospels available to them, apart from those of them who

[3] The most useful recent discussions are in Gatch 1979 and Clayton 1985a. The latter has already made many of the points which I make here.

knew Latin and apart from those books translated by King Alfred (lines 50–56), also seems to suggest readers as part of the target audience; indeed the wording could even be taken to include among the unlearned some of those who knew Latin. The CH II preface refers to listeners, *auditoribus* (line 11), but apparently also to readers, 'þam mannum to rædenne þe þæt leden ne cunnon' (lines 30–31); but since Ælfric goes on to say that it would be less tedious to *hear* if one series were to be read in the course of one year and the other in the next, this could be construed as a reference to the Latin-less preachers who were to read the homilies aloud in church. The opening sentences of the *Excusatio Dictantis* in CH II (pp. 297–8), which apologise for the length of the collection, seem to envisage readers working their way through the whole series rather than listeners or preachers choosing items for use on particular occasions. Presumably Ælfric had in mind as potential *readers* either a substantial body of ordinary laity who could read English and had access to books, or the secular clergy, such as the unlearned priests whom he discusses in his preface to Genesis and those whom he addresses in authoritarian terms, through the voices of Bishops Wulfsige and Wulfstan, in the pastoral letters that he wrote at the bishops' request; or indeed he could be thinking of both categories. One might note in this context that in the preface to the Lives of Saints collection Ælfric similarly refers to both reading and hearing the text and identifies the laity as his expected readers or listeners; the ealdorman Æthelweard and his son Æthelmær were clearly his most important readers for this collection.

Ælfric evidently also anticipated that more learned people would read or hear his homilies, as is clear especially from the evidently authorial Latin notes which are scattered through the text in MS K and occasionally other manuscripts (cf II.4.129, for instance, or II.30.19). He imagines that such readers might question a point of interpretation or Biblical reading, or be irritated with him for rehearsing a Biblical narrative (II.4.129) or giving a literal interpretation of the Bible (II.30.227 ff); the latter kind of comment suggests that the learned might be reading the homilies for their own use, not just in order to approve their use for the ignorant or to preach them to the uneducated. One of these more learned readers was presumably Ealdorman Æthelweard, who had a special copy of CH I according to a note at the end of the preface (134, app. crit.) and whose learning is evident from his Latin *Chronicle*. In the text of the homilies Ælfric is remarkably consistent in directing second-person address to the uneducated laity, but he allows himself to address the learned and the clergy through the third person. The passage at II.30.227 ff illustrates the complexity of the issue. The comment is addressed to the unlearned laity but directed at the learned person who might 'overread' the homily or hear it read ('Gif hwilc gelæred man').

The question of voice is complicated. Ælfric seems to refer to himself both by first person singular and by first personal plural forms: see for instance the CH I preface lines 3–5, 128–31, or I.11.3–7. There is perhaps a tendency to use the plural form for his role as writer, but both forms are freely used. When the homilies were recited in church, many such references could perhaps be appropriately taken as the voice of the preacher, e.g. I.2.3 ff; I.3.186; I.5.183; I.6.200; I.11.3; in other cases the first person plural is clearly more general, referring sometimes to the monks or clergy as a body, sometimes to all Christians, as at I.3.3, 6.200. But some seem more personal. The addition to I.16 (App. B2.48–52) ends with a personal reference to travelling across the country or riding to the *hired* which looks rather specific to the author. The defensive comment at the end of II.30 seems to be a case of the author addressing a learned reader, as in the Latin notes, rather than something designed for the voice of a preacher addressing his congregation. Such details suggest that, however much he tried to cast his homilies in the voice of any preacher addressing a lay audience, his mind at times returned to the mode of personal address to a reader.

Peter Clemoes in his introduction to CH I (p. 65) offers the following statement on the origin of the homilies:

> Ælfric first composed the *Catholic Homilies* for his own use as masspriest at Cerne. Later he issued them in two Series for general circulation to furnish the clergy with a sufficiently comprehensive body of orthodox preaching material in the vernacular. This stage is marked by the composition of the prefaces . . . . Almost certainly A, as first written, did not contain the prefaces to CH I . . . so that probably the manuscript represents a stage between Ælfric's original composition of the homilies for his own use and his despatch of a copy to the archbishop.

Clemoes was here recalling the similar comment by Sisam in 1933, whom he cites in the same context in the facsimile edition (Eliason and Clemoes 1966, p. 29):

> We should think of the *Catholic Homilies* . . . as in the main a two years' course of sermons actually preached by Ælfric, and later revised and made available for other priests.

Yet, plausible though the assumption might be that the homilies were first devised for Ælfric's own use in preaching, there seems to be no evidence for it, and in his prefaces Ælfric is adamant in saying that he composed the homilies in the first place for general circulation as a book and for use by listeners and readers: ' . . . transtulimus hunc codicem ex libris latinorum scilicet sanctam scripture in nostram consuetam sermocinationem ob aedificationem simplicium qui hanc norunt tantummodo locutionem. siue legendo. siue audiendo. Ideoque nec obscura posuimus uerba. sed simplicem anglicam quo facilius possit ad cor peruenire legentium. uel audientium' (CH I. praef.5–10); 'þa bearn me on mode . . . þæt ic ðas boc of ledenum gereorde to engliscre spræce awende . . . for ðan ðe ic geseah and gehyrde mycel gedwyld on manegum engliscum bocum . . . and me ofhreow þæt hi ne cuðon ne næfdon ða godspellican lare on heora gewritum' (lines 47–54); 'ic . . . awende þas boc of ledenum bocum to engliscum gereorde þam mannum to rædenne þe þæt leden ne cunnon' (CH II.praef.29–31). His statements that he was still working on the second volume when he sent the first to Sigeric, and that he had subsequently hastened to finish it, confirm that the homilies did not exist, or at least did not all exist, before the project for general circulation began; the clear differences of style and language evident between the two series[4] indicate that something more than revision was being referred to. The replacement of the cancelled passage on the Exodus in I.12 by the fuller account in II.12 similarly suggests that some of the homilies of the Second Series were composed after a written version of CH I had been established. The apparently planned way in which the sequence of homilies at the beginning of CH I tell the Christian story (see below) seems also to belong to an organised programme of instruction rather than the products of ad hoc preaching. It is likely enough that Ælfric did give sermons to the laity himself, at least at Cerne, and that this experience influenced the way he designed and wrote the two series; but he seems to insist that the formally composed English texts were conceived and produced for the use of others to read and to read out, and it may well be that for any preaching to the laity that he did himself he was able to rely on his own reading in Latin texts, and notes or précis, and did not need a formally-composed vernacular text.

If this is right then the references within the text of the homilies to the liturgical context within which they will be heard are presumably

[4] On style see below p. xxxvi; on language see Godden 1980.

not left-overs from Ælfric's own preaching but quasi-dramatic devices reflecting his sense of how they might be used. In most cases this assumption causes no difficulty, and Ælfric's familiarity with such devices is evident from the introduction to his pastoral letter for Bishop Wulfsige, in which he says that he has written the letter 'as if coming from your mouth and as if you were speaking to your clerics' ('quasi ex tuo ore dictata sit et locutus esses ad clericos tibi subditos').[5] The only one which perhaps causes pause for thought is the comment originally at the end of I.38 (see App. A2) explaining his failure to include an account of the passion of St Andrew and his intention to cover it later. This could be a relic of Ælfric's own preaching, recalling, as Sisam put it, a dark day at the end of November when he was due to deliver the sermon himself and knew that time or daylight would not allow a long address; Ælfric clearly wrote it with oral delivery in mind, rather than as an address to a reader, and the parenthetic 'gif we gesundfulle beoð' does indeed look like a personal reference. But it could alternatively be a remark imaginatively designed for the voice of any preacher to cover Ælfric's omission as a writer, or to point forward to an already-planned account of the passion for the second series; and, given the mix of preacherly addresses to the congregation and authorial addresses to individual readers, within the text generally and within a single passage at the end of II.30, it would not be surprising if this comment too contained an element of both.

If the primary target audience was the laity and their ill-educated preachers, there is also much in the Catholic Homilies that reflects the specialist concerns of monks, the clergy and the more learned. The main sources, and precedents, for Ælfric's collection were homiliaries and legendaries made for the use of monks in their services. The Gospel exegesis which is the most frequent concern of his homilies reflects the practices of monastic devotion more than preaching for the laity. Some of the homilies are devoted to Old Testament readings which were part of monastic services not the Mass (e.g. II.12), or to saints whose feasts were celebrated only by monks (e.g. II.18b). The level of discussion often seems more appropriate to advanced understandings of theology than the ordinary laity, though there are also many occasions in which discussion is explicitly or implicitly directed at the meanest level of understanding. And there are times when the particular subjects of a

[5] Fehr I, preface. He would also have noted the device being used very similarly in Gregory the Great's homilies, e.g. Hom. 1, PL 76, 1077C, used as a source for CH I.40.26–31.

homily seem to be appropriate especially to monks (such as the second half of I.27, esp. 248–50). Much of this mixture no doubt reflects Ælfric's own situation as a monk of Winchester and a learned scholar setting out to mediate the world of Christian learning to the ordinary laity and clergy of his time. Others would no doubt have shared this position: Wulfsige was a monk and abbot of Westminster when he was appointed bishop of Sherborne about 993 and had to confront the clerics of his diocese—and to seek advice from Ælfric on their duties. Mary Clayton has persuasively argued that it also reflected his own experience of preaching, in situations where sermons would be addressed to both monks and laity, as in the Old Minster at Winchester or probably the church of his monastery at Cerne. As she points out, the surviving manuscripts of the Catholic Homilies are particularly associated with monastic cathedrals such as Canterbury, Winchester and Worcester, where monks would be heavily engaged in pastoral work with the laity.[6] It may well be, too, that the monks of Ælfric's time and later were less Latinate than monastic proponents liked to assume or admit, and that much of the writing was done with their needs in mind as well as the laity. And we should not forget that secular clergy too lived a community existence and were encouraged to maintain the same regime of daily offices as the monks. There would have been a continuous scale of Latinity and learnedness which would not always have coincided with the scale from monks through secular clergy to laity. (An example like II.22 shows that quite complex exegesis could be addressed to the laity.)

Although the homilies are primarily arranged according to the demands of the church year, in two cycles to allow for variety, there are also signs that Ælfric may have selected particular feastdays and topics in order to present a staged programme of teaching. The first few homilies at least of CH I seem to be designed to tell the basic Christian story sequentially from the beginning, as far as the constraints of the calendar would allow: the series begins with a simple and summary account of salvation history, then proceeds through Christ's nativity (2), the visit of the magi and the massacre of the Innocents (5), the circumcision (6), the magi again (7), the purification and presentation at the temple (9), the temptation in the wilderness (11), the entry into Jerusalem (14), resurrection (15), ascension (21), the coming of the holy spirit (22). The annunciation is covered in 13, inevitably outside its

[6] Clayton 1985a, pp. 235–9.

historical order, and Christ's ministry is selectively covered in other homilies, starting with 8, though perhaps without such a design. One sign of this purpose is the telling of the magi story in I.5 (ahead of its calendrical place) as a prelude to the main event, the massacre of the innocents. Ælfric's preface to CH I (lines 24–6) seems indeed to hint that he selected those Gospel readings which were of benefit to the uneducated, though one must suppose that the need to cover the major feasts would also have been a factor. The one striking omission is the absence from CH I of a detailed account of the passion; this is perhaps partly explained by the lack of an occasion for discussing it, once Ælfric had decided to use Palm Sunday for the entry into Jerusalem, but the first homily could have included a much fuller account than it does. The approach seems to assume virtually no prior knowledge in the reader or listener. Note especially the passage originally in I.12 but subsequently cancelled, which is explicitly written for those who do not know who Moses was.

The origin of the angels and of mankind and the story of the fall and its consequences, with a brief resumé of subsequent Old Testament history in so far as it affected redemption, are covered in the first homily of CH I, but otherwise Old Testament story is largely left to CH II: a survey of the six ages is given in 4, outlining the basic shape of Old Testament history and describing for the first time the stories of Cain and Abel, Abraham and Isaac, Saul and David, and the Babylonian exile; Exodus is covered in great length in 12, and discussed again in 13 and 15; material from Daniel is covered in 1 and 28; Job in 30; and the story of Solomon in 40. Though a very brief summary of Moses had originally been included in CH I.12, the deletion, and provision of a much fuller account in CH II.12, perhaps suggests some conscious plan of focusing coverage of the Old Testament in CH II. The programme is continued in the Lives of Saints collection, with the versions of Kings and Maccabees and more material from Exodus (and originally further Old Testament material in *De Falsis Deis*), and in the separate renderings of Genesis and other parts of the Pentateuch absorbed into the Heptateuch, Joshua, Judges, Esther and Judith, and more material from Exodus and Numbers in *De Populo Israhelo*.

There is no obvious principle behind the distribution of saints' days and topics between the two Series, apart from perhaps a tendency to cover the more important saints in CH I: of the apostles, CH I covers John (in the already crowded area of Christmastide), Peter and Paul, Bartholomew, Andrew; CH II has Philip and James, Peter again, the other James, Matthew, Simon and Jude. Of other saints, CH I has Stephen, Laurence, John the Baptist (twice), Clement, Michael, Mary (Assumption, as well as the Annunciation and Purification); CH II has Stephen and the Assumption of the Virgin again, Gregory, Cuthbert, Benedict, Invention, Alexander, Seven Sleepers, Martin.

THE DATE AND ORIGIN OF THE CATHOLIC HOMILIES

In his preface to CH I, addressed to Archbishop Sigeric of Canterbury, Ælfric identifies himself as a monk and masspriest, and a pupil of St Æthelwold, and says that he was sent to Cerne by Ælfeah bishop of Winchester. The outside dates for that move must be between 984, when Ælfeah became bishop, and 994 or 5, when Sigeric died; and we should probably look early in that span, since the two series of Catholic Homilies were apparently conceived at Cerne and completed before Sigeric's death. The foundation charter of Cerne is dated 987, which has generally been taken as also the date of Ælfric's move to Cerne. The surviving copy of the charter is late and the notion that Cerne was a new foundation at that date has been questioned,[7] but Ælfric's move to Cerne must have been around that time anyway, so it is reasonable to associate it with the (re)foundation. (If the date is right, then it is reasonable to suppose that the move was prompted by the needs of the new monastery, not by the death of Æthelwold and the advent of a new regime at Winchester.) Ælfric was a priest at the time of writing the preface, not necessarily at the time of the move, though it is a reasonable guess that his value to a small place like Cerne depended in part on his being a priest. He would then have been at least thirty, the canonical age for ordination to the priesthood, and that has presumably prompted the traditional guess of c. 955 or 957 as his year of birth.[8] But there is no reason to suppose that he was only thirty: he could have been a priest for a long time by then, or ordained priest later in life (there would have been no need at Winchester for all the monks to be priests) and the move to Cerne was evidently prompted by the foundation of that monastery, not by Ælfric's coming of age and ordination. Assuming

[7] See Barbara Yorke, 'Æthelmær: the Foundation of the Abbey at Cerne and the Politics of the Tenth Century', in *The Cerne Abbey Millennium Lectures*, ed. K. Barker (Cerne Abbas, 1988), pp. 15–25.

[8] See, e.g., Hurt, *Ælfric*, and Clemoes 1959.

that the CH I preface was written around 990 or soon after (see below), the latest possible date for his birth is 960, and more probably 957; but it could easily have been much earlier.

Jonathan Wilcox cites evidence from Ælfric's Grammar that points to hitherto unnoticed aspects of his life and an earlier date of birth.[9] Following a suggestion by Vivienne Law, he interprets the following model dialogue (given to illustrate the use of pronouns) as autobiographical and thus revealing that Ælfric was taught and ordained by archbishop Dunstan:

> Gif ðu cwest nu: hwa lærde ðe?, þonne cweðe ic: Dunstan. Hwa hadode ðe? He me hadode: þonne stent se he on his naman stede and spelað hine. (8.13–15).

He goes on to argue that the likeliest occasion when Dunstan could have taught Ælfric would have been before the former's exile in 956, indicating a date of birth for the pupil of 940 or 945. There are, though, some difficulties in reading the reference as autobiographical. If Ælfric had indeed been taught by Dunstan it seems unlikely that he would have repeatedly identified himself as a pupil of Æthelwold and never mentioned the link with the still more famous archbishop except so indirectly; one might note especially the preface to the Grammar itself,[10] where he refers to what he had learnt in the school of Æthelwold and goes on to mention Dunstan's role in reviving the knowledge of Latin without hinting at any closer contact. Besides, if we have to place his birth early enough to fit in teaching by Dunstan before 956, Ælfric would surely have been too old to receive his main education in Latin as a pupil of Æthelwold when the latter set up his school some time after 963, especially if we also have to allow for the period when, according to his preface to Genesis, he was taught by an ill-educated priest at a time when he himself knew little.[11] And since Ælfric was evidently educated at Winchester and was still there in 987 when he went to Cerne as priest and monk, the obvious person to have ordained him was Æthelwold or his successor Ælfeah.

The time when Ælfric was taught by an ill-educated magister presumably preceded his arrival at Æthelwold's school. That could either be because that school had not been established when he began his education, or because it was far away from Ælfric's home region, or because he was too young. Wilcox (8) points to faint evidence that

[9] Wilcox 1994, pp. 6–7.
[10] Wilcox 1994, pp. 114–6.
[11] Crawford, p. 76.

Ælfric was at Winchester in 970 but not in 964. From a comment in the *De Temporibus Anni* (6.17–18) it would appear that he spent some time in the north of England:

On Engla lande hæfð se lengsta dæg seofontyne tida; On ðam ylcan earde norðeweardan beoð leohte nihta on sumera. swilce hit ealle niht dagige. swa swa we sylfe foroft gesawon.

His similarly personal reference to having seen silk-worms suggests he may have visited Italy.[12]

If we assume that Ælfric was educated at Winchester and remained there as a monk until he went to Cerne, one might ask what he was doing between the completion of his education and his move to Cerne at the age of thirty or more, that is, in the ten to twenty years before 987. There was of course the daily round of prayer and study, but given the prolific rate of composition after 987 (the Catholic Homilies, the Lives of Saints, the Grammar and Glossary, the *De Temporibus Anni*, some Biblical translations all before 1001 at latest) it seems surprising that he was not writing before then. His CH I preface indicates that the Catholic Homilies project was conceived after he came to Cerne, and the CH II preface seems to confirm that the writing took place at Cerne. The one work which we could perhaps place with confidence in this pre-Cerne period is the Latin sermon based on Julian of Toledo's *Prognosticon*, which has been described as his earliest known work and is one of the sources for the Catholic Homilies.[13] If that is right, it perhaps suggests that some of his time at Winchester was spent composing Latin sermons and homilies for the monks and clerics and perhaps students, which may have provided a starting-point for the later vernacular work.

Whether or not this is so, there are signs that Ælfric had either established a significant reputation, or acquired powerful backers, or both, before the Catholic Homilies had made their mark. Though he addresses the Latin preface to CH I to the Archbishop of Canterbury and modestly asks for his correction and authority, the preface also makes it clear that he was anticipating widespread use and copying without depending on Sigeric's imprimatur or help in circulating the text, and it is striking that he takes full responsibility for his ambitious initiative, claiming no commissioning or requests from others (as he tends to in later prefaces). We might note also that when Wulfsige,

12 See CH I, App. B2.15–16, and the notes on this under I.16.
13 See Gatch 1966.

already abbot of Westminster, became bishop of Sherborne around 993, he promptly wrote to Ælfric for advice on his duties.[14]

Peter Clemoes, following arguments developed by Kenneth Sisam, proposed that CH I was sent to Sigeric in 991 and CH II in 992.[15] In the introduction to CH II, written in 1975, I argued that the second series was sent to Sigeric in 995, and the first series a year or so before.[16] Those dates have been more often dismissed than accepted since I wrote.[17] On returning to the subject my first instinct was to accept the authority of the historians, but on reviewing the material again it seemed to me useful to set out the evidence as it now stands—not least because it affects a number of other issues as well as the dating of Ælfric's first works.

Ælfric addressed both series to Sigeric, Archbishop of Canterbury, who was elected on 13 Feb 990 and died 28 Oct 994 or 995. In the preface to CH II he says:

> Et licet multis iniuriis infestium piratarum concutiebamur. postquam praefatum libellum tuae sanctitati transmisimus. tamen nolentes repperiri falsidici promisores. dolente animo hoc opus perfecimus.
> (And although we [*an authorial plural*] have been struck by many injuries of hostile pirates since we sent the aforesaid book [CH I] to your holiness, nevertheless, not wishing to be found a false promiser, with sorrowing heart we have completed this work [CH II].)

Though he may only mean mentally anguished rather than physically harmed, the wording seems to imply something more than a general anxiety about Viking raids elsewhere in England.[18] The only known attacks of Vikings in this period that are likely to have affected Ælfric's vicinity are those of late 994 in which, according to the *Chronicle*, after besieging London on 8 September and then devastating Kent, they

> did the greatest damage that ever any army could do, by burning, ravaging and slaying, both along the coast, and in Essex, Kent, Sussex and Hampshire; and finally they seized horses and rode as widely as they wished, and continued to do indescribable damage.[19]

[14] See Fehr I, preface.

[15] Eliason and Clemoes 1966, p. 35; *CH I*, p. 161.

[16] *CH II*, pp. xci-xciii.

[17] See Keynes 1980, pp. 249–51; Wilcox 1994, p. 11, n.39; Michael Lapidge, 'Ælfric's *Sanctorale*', in Szarmach 1966, pp. 115–29, at p. 127, n.13 (which egregiously misrepresents my arguments). I should add that the ensuing discussion owes a great deal to the generous help of Professor Keynes (whose own views have, nevertheless, not changed).

[18] *Concutio* is glossed *ic sceace oððe ic samod slea* in the Grammar (169.5), so *concutiebamur* presumably means 'we have been shaken'.

[19] The translation is that of Dorothy Whitelock in EHD, p. 235.

Confirmation is to be found in the treaty between Ethelred and the Vikings under Olaf, known as II Ethelred, which refers to 'the terms which Archbishop Sigeric, Ealdorman Æthelweard [of the western provinces] and Ealdorman Ælfric [of Hampshire] made when they obtained permission from the king to purchase peace for the areas which they had rule over, under the king.' (EHD, pp. 437–8). There now seems fairly general agreement that the negotiations to which this treaty refers are those made during the raids of late 994.[20] Æthelweard was a patron and close associate of Ælfric, who had his own copy of CH I; it would not be surprising if attacks which involved the ealdorman in negotiating truces for his own area and presumably collecting and paying tribute had also disturbed Ælfric at Cerne. Earlier suggestions that the attacks of 991 also affected the south-west, and that Ælfric could have been referring to these, depended entirely on attributing this treaty to 991 rather than 994, and that theory seems no longer to have any standing amongst historians.

The possibility that Ælfric was referring to the 994 attacks depends on the question of the year of Sigeric's death. It is agreed that he died on 28 October or thereabouts, in either 994 or 995; if it was 994, it is not really feasible that Ælfric could have completed the writing of CH II, revised it and sent a copy to Sigeric after the 994 raids, which must still have been in full force at the time of Sigeric's death. The evidence for Sigeric's year of death is full but frankly contradictory, and it is doubtful whether the contradictions can be satisfactorily resolved. The one new piece of evidence since I wrote in 1975 is the entry in the Easter Tables in BL, MS Cotton Titus D.xxvii, recording his death in 994, to which Keynes drew attention;[21] but since the manuscript belongs to the period 1023–35, some thirty to forty years after the event, I would see it as only one more piece of evidence, not the clinching argument that it has been seen as. (And since it was produced at Winchester, it is presumably not independent evidence but a reflex of the same tradition as the A *Chronicle*, which was probably kept at Winchester until some time in the eleventh century.) The chronicles are divided, the A version recording the death in 994 and the CDE and F versions in 995. There seems now a fair amount of agreement that the A annal for 993 really relates to 994, and that the annal for 994 is also a year out is the view of its editor, Janet

[20] Cf esp. the comments by various contributors to the 1991 collection of papers on the Battle of Maldon (Scragg 1991), at pp. 103 ff (Keynes), 132 (Lund), 145 (Abels).

[21] Keynes 1980, pp. 251–3; EHD, p. 236.

Bately.[22] It is the evidence of the charters that is most problematic. The earliest evidence is provided by a contemporary charter (Sawyer no. 1379)[23], dated 995 and witnessed by Sigeric as archbishop of Canterbury, next after the king himself. It records a grant of land at Cuxham in Oxfordshire by Æscwig bishop of Dorchester to his man Ælfstan, and there seems general agreement that the document is an original.[24] Keynes suggests that it was drafted by Æscwig himself or one of his entourage.[25] If Sigeric was not alive in 995, Æscwig must have made a curious mistake about the year in which he was operating. The contents of another charter (Sawyer no. 882), extant only in a fifteenth-century copy, seem to lend further support to a 995 date. It has the same set of witnesses and the same 995 date, though the indiction for 994. It records the negotiations which Sigeric made with the Vikings when they attacked Kent, apparently after the attack on London which took place according to the *Chronicle* on 8 September 994. The charter, which is generally agreed to be authentic, reports that when the Vikings were devastating Kent, they threatened to destroy the church in Canterbury unless Sigeric paid them the money he had promised them. Sigeric, not having any, sent messengers to Æscwig bishop of Dorchester to ask him for it, offering an estate in exchange. Æscwig sent the money, Sigeric paid it to the Vikings and gave the title-deed to Æscwig in the presence of the king and his chief men. The present charter, it reports, was drawn up in 995, with the consent of witnesses, who again begin with the king and Sigeric himself. The negotiations with the Danes described in the charter are presumably those mentioned in the general treaty II Ethelred, which refers to the terms which Sigeric and others had made for the areas under their control (so Keynes 1980). The language of the charter, like that of the treaty, seems to imply that the crisis is over at the time of writing, and that there has been time for a meeting of the witan and the handing over of title-deeds. Yet neither text hints at the death of one of the main participants, Sigeric, in the meantime, and Sigeric is firmly recorded as witness to the formal charter drawn up after the events. Whatever the accuracy of the date record in the

[22] See Bately in Scragg 1991, p. 47 and *The Anglo-Saxon Chronicle: MS A*, ed. J. Bately (Cambridge, 1986), p. lxii.

[23] P. Sawyer, *Anglo-Saxon Charters: An Annotated List and Bibliography* (London, 1968).

[24] See Sawyer, *Anglo-Saxon Charters*, p. 391 and Keynes 1980, p. 124.

[25] Keynes 1980, p. 124.

charter, it is difficult to see how all the negotiations which the two texts describe can have taken place if Sigeric was dead by 28 October 994.

The counter evidence from the charters is the existence of three charters dated 995 and witnessed by Sigeric's successor, another Ælfric, as bishop-elect or, in one case, bishop, of Canterbury. One is apparently contemporary. These would not in themselves rule out an October 995 date for Sigeric's death, if Ælfric was appointed late in the year, but a Canterbury tradition recorded around a century later in the F version of the *Chronicle* reports that Ælfric's election took place at Easter 995. Perhaps we should not place too much weight on this late tradition (it is mixed up in F with an extremely embroidered story of archbishop Ælfric's expulsion of clerics) and allow the possibility that there was some election or pre-election in late 995, at a meeting which also generated the three charters. We might note that Sigeric himself had been elected within two months at most of his predecessor's death in 990.[26]

It remains possible, of course, that Ælfric was referring to Viking raids that are not otherwise recorded, and we should keep an open mind on the precise dating of the two series within the period 990–5. The important point is that there is no reason to think that the 991 raids are at issue, and no need therefore to place the 'publication' of CH I in the narrow gap between Sigeric's consecration in 990 and the raids of August 991, and hence the completion of CH I and the near-completion of CH II in the short and no doubt unsettled period between the foundation of Cerne in 987 and early 991.

We can say then that somewhere between 990 and 994 Ælfric completed CH I, added the preface and sent a copy to Sigeric at Canterbury. The preface would suggest that copies were given or sent at the same time to ealdorman Æthelweard and to a number of other users (see further below, in the commentary on the CH I preface).[27] A year or so later he completed CH II (already 'in hand' when he despatched CH I), added the preface and admonition against drunkenness, and sent copies to Sigeric and presumably to Æthelweard and others who had been sent CH I. Either then or soon after[28] he combined CH I and II

[26] Keynes 1980, pp. 249–50.

[27] If the abbey at Cerne seems unlikely to have possessed the resources for such extensive book production, it may be that Ælfric was able to call on the resources either of the wealthy Æthelweard or of his alma mater Winchester.

[28] By the time that he produced K itself, or its antecedent, Ælfric had evidently had time to do some small-scale revision to CH I and to add the occasional Latin notes to the

into a single collection such as we find in MS K, still in two sets of forty homilies with their separate prefaces but furnished now with a closing prayer that refers to the two series, and presumably sent copies of this two-series set to others who had expressed interest. K itself contains not just the two series but a number of other texts by Ælfric: the *De Temporibus Anni*, some prayers, creeds and admonitions, and the pastoral letter which he wrote for Wulfsige bishop of Sherborne and addressed to his clergy. Since the end of the letter has been lost there may have been still other items following it. The linking sentence at the end of the prayer which concludes CH II suggests that it was Ælfric himself who added these texts as an appendix to the Catholic Homilies, and they would clearly have been appropriate to the kinds of clerics who are addressed in the pastoral letter and who were expected to use the homilies in their preaching. All these texts appear to be early compositions, closely associated in date with CH II itself, and it could easily be that Ælfric added them when he first created and circulated the two-series set.

ALLITERATIVE STYLE IN THE CATHOLIC HOMILIES

The distinctive rhythmical style which Ælfric developed in the course of his work on the Catholic Homilies and used for most of his work thereafter has been most fully described by John C. Pope in the introduction to his edition of Ælfric's supplementary homilies (pp. 105–36). Its characteristic feature is a regular pattern of two-stress phrases generally linked in pairs by alliteration, evidently modelled on the Old English verse line but preserving the word-order and clause structure and (usually) the diction of prose. The style is used extensively for II.10 (Cuthbert), the second half of II.12 (Mid-Lent Sunday), II.14 (Palm Sunday), II.17 (Philip and James), II.18 (Invention and St Alexander, all but the first sentence of each part), II.19 (Rogationtide), the second part of II.23 (3rd Sunday after Pentecost), and II.34 (Martin, all but the first 19 lines). It is also used for the conclusions (mostly single sentences) of II.11, 30, 32 and 38, and the first sentence of II.16, and in the last paragraph of I.38. It is often

two series, some of which seem to respond to queries from readers, but not apparently to do much more with CH II, whose text is much less revised than that of CH I in the same MS; but he may of course have produced copies of the two-series set prior to K.

accompanied in MS K by punctation marking the two-stress phrases, not by any means every one but nevertheless using a system clearly distinct from the normal punctation; cf e.g. II.10.171 ff. It is also accompanied at times by a sprinkling of poetic vocabulary or other unusual diction, e.g. *metod* (I.38.351, II.14.208, II.19.259, II.23.185, II.34.233); *folme*; *molde; rodor; unman.*[29] There are occasional examples of rhyme too, e.g. II.19.263–4.

One of the original functions of this style was evidently to produce a concluding flourish, as in the final paragraphs of I.38 and II.11 and the brief doxologies of II.30, 32 and 38. In more extended use, the style is primarily associated with narrative in the Catholic Homilies, especially hagiographic (II.10, 17, 18, 34) but also Biblical (II.12, 14, 23b); but it is also used for II.19, a sermon on the duties of society, and for the exegetical passages in II.12, 14 and 23b. The account of St Cuthbert, II.10, seems to be an early and experimental version of this style, with very marked rhythms and a more extravagant use of poetic and colourful language; since one of its main sources was Bede's metrical life of the saint, and it is indeed the first and perhaps only work by Ælfric that used a poem as its main source, it seems likely that the inspiration and model for the use of this style *in extenso* was the use of Latin verse for hagiographical narrative. After the Catholic Homilies it next appears in the narrative parts of the Lives of Saints collection, but then became his standard style for all writing, including exegetical. The beginnings of this style are clearly in part associated with genre therefore; but since Ælfric was from the outset prepared to use it occasionally for other genres, including Biblical exegesis, it seems reasonable to maintain the view[30] that the alliterative pieces in CH II are generally later than those in plain prose. Two of the three non-narrative examples in CH II (12 and 23) are in fact found in the second parts of two-part homilies, which perhaps supports this hypothesis. The one clear use of this style in CH I is in the closing passage of the homily on St Andrew, 38. The cancelled comment in MS A reveals that the second half of this homily, covering the passion of the saint, was in any case a later addition, and there is no great difficulty in supposing that it was written around the same time as the alliterative pieces in CH II, that is, after most of the pieces for CH II had been written; indeed, as I suggest below, it may originally have been intended for CH II.

[29] Cf Godden 1980 and Frank 1994.
[30] Cf Clemoes 1959, pp. 222–23.

ÆLFRIC'S SOURCES

The question of Ælfric's sources was in the first place a matter of paramount importance to Ælfric himself. 'I follow Augustine, Jerome, Bede, Gregory, Smaragdus and sometimes Haymo' he announces in the preface to his First Series of Catholic Homilies; 'their authority is willingly accepted by all the orthodox.' In a wonderfully simple but persuasive picture he contrasts the true faith to be found in their writings, which he claims merely to have translated, with the opposite extreme of *gedwyld*, folly or heresy, which is to be found in other kinds of books. In subsequent prefaces he recalls his debt in general terms to devout fathers and holy teachers, and often in individual texts names his sources: 'Bede the wise teacher of the English people wrote the life of this saint' (II.10.3–4); 'Gregory the expositor said that this gospel has a long interpretation' (II.5.34–5). Such statements and invocations reflect not just a concern for scholarly obligations but a claim to authority. It was a time of crisis and there were dangerous ideas abroad, as the first preface reveals. Ælfric knew what he wanted to say, but he also knew that he had to claim a higher authority than his own for it. Sources were authorities in the fullest sense, guarantors of the validity of Ælfric's views against the heresies and errors found in other writers and teachers. Yet the example of Chaucer and Malory should be warning enough that the citation of sources by authors is far from straightforward: it is frequently strategic, and often misleading. And it becomes clear from working with Ælfric's sources that the situation was much more complicated than he implies. It was partly that his authorities were often at odds with each other and that reconciling their positions was a major difficulty for him; it was also that Ælfric had views of his own to develop and frequently wanted to follow a different line from his authorities. He had an ambivalent attitude to his sources, grateful for their authority in the war against those contemporaries who thought differently, and often dangerously, grateful too for their help in interpreting the Bible and Christian tradition, but aware that they did not always answer his needs or those of his own time.

Something of that cautious discrimination is suggested by the terms in which he refers to them (CH I.praef.15–16). Augustine is mentioned first in Ælfric's list and was clearly the authority that he respected most (though also the one he differed from most); 'Augustine the wise' or

'Augustine the great' is how he habitually refers to him. Jerome appears next in the list, though his influence is slight. It is not for his exegetical and theological work that he figures but for the works mis-attributed to him in the Middle Ages—the *Historia Ecclesiastica* of Eusebius and Rufinus and the epistle on the assumption of the Virgin actually written by Paschasius Radbertus. Jerome is not quite the guarantor of good doctrine that he might appear from Ælfric's reference, and his prominence in second position perhaps reflects his value as an authority rather than his actual use by Ælfric. When he cites Jerome in support of an exegetical position at I.11.110, he seems in fact to be taking a different line from him. Bede comes next perhaps because of Ælfric's respect for him: the wise one or the teacher is how he refers to him (though the signs are that he had little enthusiasm for his style; there is seldom if ever the close imitation of Bede's wording that one can see so often with Augustine and Gregory). Gregory the Great was probably used more than any of these, but comes fourth and is referred to only as *se eadiga*, the blessed, or *se halga*, the holy. The distinction between him and Augustine is suggested by a remark in a CH II homily: 'Augustine the wise uncovered the deepness of this text, and the holy Gregory also wrote about it' (II.39.25–6). And the concluding phrase 'Smaragdus and sometimes Haymo' seems odd given the evidence that Haymo's work was much more important to him than that of Smaragdus, who scarcely wrote a line in his exegetic collection that was not taken verbatim from another source that Ælfric knew well; the name of Smaragdus perhaps had greater conjuring power, as the author of a commentary on the Rule of St Benedict and a standard guide to monasticism (*De Diadema Monachorum*).

Citations in individual texts are frequent: often he names a particular authority at the head of the text, perhaps as a routine assertion of the authority behind his argument, sometimes giving the impression that the whole homily is in the voice of one of the fathers (cf I.40.20–21, or II.38.38). In other cases the authority is cited in support of a particular detail. When he sets out the idea of the three grades of chastity, he prefaces it with the Latin note 'Augustinus magnus sic docet' and follows the first grade with the statement 'this is the rule for laymen according to the decrees of books' and reinforces the second with an appeal to a synod of 318 bishops (II.6.115–57). This was clearly difficult ground. Again, when he interprets Peter as a symbol of the church he interjects a Latin note citing Augustine in support (II.24.163–4); in his previous collection he had interpreted Peter as a type of the bishop, and presumably felt the need to call Augustine in in support of his shift of argument. Often such ascriptions give us good guidance, even if on occasion writers such as Jerome and Augustine and Hilary are cited for texts they did not actually write but were commonly thought to have written. Others are more problematic. There are the many occasions when Ælfric cites a single authority for a text when it actually draws on a variety of sources by different writers. Thus in CH I.28, on Christ weeping over Jerusalem, he three times cites Gregory as his authority and mentions no other source, but he was in fact using two different texts by Gregory as well as works by several other writers. Again, in CH II.24, one of his most sophisticated and ambitious homilies, digging deep into problems of Christological doctrine, he three times names Augustine as his authority, twice indeed quoting him in Latin, which is otherwise a very rare practice in the homilies. What he fails to tell us is that he is using material from probably three different texts by or attributed to Augustine, as well as several sources by other writers. Sometimes even the initial detail which is specifically attributed seems not to be from the source named. Thus he begins I.33 by citing Bede's interpretation of the place-name Naim: but that is virtually the one detail in his text which could not come from Bede. Or in I.32 he announces that he is following Bede and does indeed for much of the text agree closely with Bede's exposition; but when he introduces a passage on evil women with the words 'Now says the expositor' (line 172) he does not reveal that he is at that moment shifting to a quite different source, an anonymous and virulently misogynist text going under the name of St John Chrysostom. One might note the curious misrepresentation of St Augustine's views in the *Excusatio Dictantis* (CH II, pp. 297–8). One can readily conceive of possible reasons for such misleading information. He may have been using different versions of texts from ours, or texts with different ascriptions. He may have been drawing on his notes rather than a source in front of him, or he may often have produced a Latin draft comprising passages culled from his various sources and forgotten the origin of particular parts when he came to compose a polished English version. But there is a distinct impression of at least a willingness to allow his exposition to appear to be a translation from a single authority rather than the result of weaving together material from several authorities and his own ideas. A casual reader of the prefaces might indeed have supposed that the whole collection was simply a translation from Latin writings of the fathers.

Ælfric's main sources in writing the Catholic Homilies were three major collections of material: the homiliaries of Paul the Deacon and Haymo of Auxerre, both providing sermons and Gospel exegesis, and the anonymous collection of hagiographic narratives known as the Cotton-Corpus legendary.[31] Collectively these three may have made over 600 homilies and saints' lives available to him. Paul the Deacon (720—c. 799) was a monk of Monte Cassino who spent some time at the court of Charlemagne and compiled his homiliary apparently at the latter's direction, for reading in the course of the monastic offices.[32] In its original form it contained some 244 sermons and homilies written by, or assigned to, a variety of patristic authors, especially Augustine, Gregory the Great, Bede, Maximus, Leo and St John Chrysostom, and organised according to the church year. But its contents were continually revised, and especially expanded, over succeeding centuries; the later version printed by Migne in PL 95 has some 298 items. A number of copies survive from late Anglo-Saxon England, and C. L. Smetana convincingly demonstrated its importance as a source-book for Ælfric in 1959.[33] Ælfric used a number of texts that appear in later versions but not in the original and it is likely, therefore, that he was using an expanded and revised version, but its precise contents cannot be known. Altogether he used just under a hundred homilies from the collection in compiling the Catholic Homilies (and he continued to use it for his subsequent homiletic work), choosing mainly items by (or attributed to) Augustine (14–17), Gregory (33) and Bede (29). His frequent reference to those authors by name, when drawing on PD, indicates that his version included attributions, in the text or margins (as for instance in the surviving Durham copies from the eleventh century); this presumably explains why he did not mention Paul the Deacon as an authority in the preface but instead specified the original authors. The sermons attributed to Leo and Maximus are never used (with the possible exception of one in CH II.38); possibly they had been eliminated from the copy Ælfric knew.[34]

Haymo's homiliary was a collection of his own mainly exegetical

[31] Max Förster originally identified many of Ælfric's individual sources (see Förster 1892 and 1894), and many additional sources have been identified by J. E. Cross (see the long list of articles under his name in the list of abbreviations above).

[32] See esp. Smetana 1959, and Clayton 1985a, and also C. L. Smetana, 'Paul the Deacon's Patristic Anthology', in *The Old English Homily and its Backgrounds*, ed. Paul E. Szarmach and Bernard F. Huppé (Albany, NY, 1978), pp. 75–97.

[33] Smetana 1959.

[34] Cf Smetana 1959, p. 203.

homilies: he drew heavily on earlier patristic accounts, frequently the ones also used in PD, but generally expanded their treatments, especially with historical material and with supportive quotations from other parts of the Bible.[35] The version printed in PL 118, which runs to 153 homilies, is an augmented collection, containing at least 72 items not by Haymo himself; Ælfric certainly knew some of the interpolated items (see below and Pope) but how much his copy had been augmented one cannot tell. In his preface Ælfric only says that he used Haymo sometimes (*aliquando*), and he cites him as an authority only in the two homilies for which he was the main source; but Haymo's collection seems to have provided some ideas and information and phrasing in a further 33 homilies, drawing on 34 items.

The Cotton-Corpus legendary is, or was before additions were made, a collection of 165 mainly anonymous saints' lives and other hagiographic narratives, running from January to December. It survives only in manuscripts of English provenance, but is thought to have been originally compiled in northern France or Flanders, in the late ninth or early tenth century.[36] Its importance as a source-book for Ælfric's homilies for saints days and his Lives of Saints collection was demonstrated comprehensively by Patrick Zettel in an Oxford D. Phil. thesis in 1979. (The thesis has unfortunately never been printed, but the essence of the argument, and some detailed examples, are to be found in an article of 1982—see Zettel 1982.) The texts all survive in other manuscripts and in printed form, but Zettel showed that the manuscripts of this particular legendary not only contained virtually all the hagiographic sources used by Ælfric but also frequently showed the particular variant readings that he must have found in his sources. It is clear from his evidence that Ælfric must have used a version of this legendary; twenty-four of the items from it were used as sources in the Catholic Homilies, and a further number for the Lives of Saints. Citation of this source-material is difficult. The collection has not itself been printed, though Zettel has provided a detailed analysis of the significant differences from the standard editions, and in any case the surviving manuscripts are all later than Ælfric, they differ among themselves and contain many variations of detail and corruptions which cannot have been in the version which he used. Hagiographic texts in general seem to have been subject to a degree of textual

[35] See esp. Smetana 1961.
[36] See Jackson and Lapidge 1996, pp. 133–4.

variation and contamination that is not common amongst homiletic and exegetical texts. The standard editions are mostly very ancient, ranging from the sixteenth-century collection printed by Surius, the Acta Sanctorum series begun in 1643 and continued and revised through succeeding centuries, the eighteenth-century collection printed by Fabricius, down to the 1910 edition of the originally fifteenth-century collection by Mombritius and the 1953–5 edition by Fábrega Grau, and their versions of the same texts differ considerably in details of expression and often content. Even when, for individual items, a modern critical edition exists it can be less useful as a guide to what Ælfric saw than one of the older collections. I have therefore chosen for each homily whichever printed edition seems closest to what Ælfric saw and cited source-passages from that, but noted relevant variant readings from other editions or from manuscripts of the Cotton-Corpus legendary where necessary.

In addition to these three main collections of source-material, Ælfric evidently drew on a range of other texts. For Gospel exegesis, he also used another Carolingian homiliary, that of Smaragdus, whom he mentions in his preface; Augustine's Tractates on John; a substantial number of Augustinian and Ps-Augustinian sermons beyond those known to have been included in PD; perhaps Bede's commentaries on Luke and Mark; and a few other sermons. For other parts of the New Testament the homiliaries of Paul the Deacon and Haymo provided very little, and although Smaragdus provided a comprehensive set of commentaries on the epistles for the day Ælfric seems never to have used it; but he does seem to have known and used Bede's commentary on Acts and commentaries on the epistles by Bede, Ps-Hilary, Haymo and Pelagius.

For Old Testament exegesis the Carolingian homiliaries offered very little. Ælfric evidently knew Alcuin's short commentary on Genesis and probably Bede's, and seems also to have drawn on a commentary which went under the name of Isidore. For historical narrative and background, sometimes as an alternative to hagiographic texts, he mainly used the *Historia Ecclesiastica* of Rufinus, Haymo's *Historiae Sacrae Epitome*, and Bede's *Historia Ecclesiastica Gentis Anglorum*. Apart from the Cotton-Corpus legendary he was also able to draw on Bede's lives of St Cuthbert and the Lindisfarne Life, and the account of St Benedict in Gregory's *Dialogues*. The *Dialogues*, along with the *Vitae Patrum*, also provided him with occasional exempla. On matters of doctrine we can see the influence of Alcuin's *De Animae Ratione* and

Julian of Toledo's *Prognosticon*, both of which he also abridged and adapted in Latin form, and of the eucharistic treatise of Ratramnus of Corbie *De Corpore et Sanguine Domini*. Much of his thinking on major issues was clearly Augustinian and he sometimes cites Augustine as authority for such points, but it is curiously difficult to identify convincing parallels with the larger doctrinal works of the saint. His wording, and at times his thinking (for instance on the origin of the soul), on matters of doctrine seems to have been generally more independent than on matters of exegesis. For moral teaching he supplemented the homiliaries occasionally with Alcuin's *De Virtutibus et Vitiis*, Cassian's *Conlationes* and the Ps-Cyprian *De Duodecim Abusivis*. For scientific points he used Bede's *De Natura Rerum* and *De Temporum Ratione*. For matters of liturgy and church festivals his main authority was Amalarius of Metz.

BIBLICAL SOURCES

Ælfric reproduces the relevant Biblical readings for the day, from the Gospels or occasionally the epistles or Acts, in full at the beginning of most exegetical homilies, paraphrases at length Old Testament material in homilies such as II.12 (Exodus) and II.40 (Solomon and the building of the temple), and frequently quotes individual verses or passages in the course of his exegesis or argument. On a rough count there are something like 1135 separate Biblical citations or quotations in the Catholic Homilies, 550 of them derived from his other sources. Presumably he had access to a copy of the Latin Bible, but there would have been other sources for his quotations as well. His awareness of different translations or versions is evident from his comment at II.30.19, and his familiarity with variant readings in different manuscripts of the same version is evident from the Latin note at I.11.110. It seems likely that in other cases he silently chose the reading which supported his interpretation. His versions of the Gospel passage for the day often incorporate readings from parallel Gospels, and occasionally he acknowledges this. His incidental quotations sometimes do not tally with the Vulgate text, and occasionally not with any version of the Bible (most noticeably in II.1). The exegetical sources which Ælfric used quote the Bible repeatedly, and must have influenced the nature of his own quotations.

ÆLFRIC'S WORKING METHODS

The three main source collections could have amounted to five volumes in toto, and the further sources needed for the Catholic Homilies need not have come to more than a further ten volumes perhaps—not an enormous library for Cerne to be provided with, especially given Ælfric's expectations of the library of even an ordinary secular priest.[37] Though some of the material he uses could have been drawn from a good memory of earlier reading, his close renderings of many Latin passages, especially from Gregory and Augustine at times, confirms that he had direct access to the source-texts at the time of writing. He may have relied in some cases on his own Latin abridgements of works read elsewhere, but examples are hard to find. The Boulogne MS[38] contains abridged adaptations, almost certainly by Ælfric himself, of Julian of Toledo's *Prognosticon* and Alcuin's *De Animae Ratione* and he used both as sources for the Catholic Homilies; but he evidently had access to the full *Prognosticon* as well while writing the homilies, and both adaptations seem to have been devised as Latin sermons, not just as personal source material. The 'hagiographical commonplace-book compiled by Ælfric himself' which Michael Lapidge thought he had identified in 1991, as Ælfric's own source-collection, turns out to have little connection with his sources, at least for the one item in the Catholic Homilies (see commentary on II.10, esp. n.4). And while Ælfric liked to have the backing of the Fathers and could frequently follow Latin sources quite closely, there were certain topics which were evidently key concerns for him and which could almost be guaranteed to prompt an independent discussion, departing from his authorities and sometimes silently taking issue with them. The most striking are: the basic doctrine of the Trinity, which he repeatedly rehearses in his own words; the great numbers who will eventually be saved, a topic on which he begs to differ from Gregory the Great (see esp. CH I.8, I.24, I.35 and II.5, and notes); the doctrine of the soul, and especially its origins and the fact that animals do not possess souls (on this see Godden 1985a); the resurrection of the body (see especially I.8 and I.16); and the justification of the wealthy (on which see Godden 1990).

[37] See Fehr I, §52.

[38] Boulogne, Bibliothèque Municipale, MS 63. See Enid M. Raynes, 'MS. Boulogne-sur-Mer 63 and Ælfric', *Medium Aevum* 26 (1957), 65–73, and also Gatch 1966 and Leinbaugh 1980 and 1994.

SUMMARY LIST OF SOURCES USED BY ÆLFRIC IN THE CATHOLIC HOMILIES

(I have included here a few items which were probably not actual sources but furnish significant parallels from time to time.)

[PD = Paul the Deacon's Homiliary; PDM = PD as preserved in PL 95; CC = the Cotton-Corpus Legendary]

A. Latin

1. Named Authors

Adso of Montier-en-Der (d. 992)

De Ortu et Tempore Antichristi (ed. D. Verhelst, CCCM 45, Turnhout, 1976). See CH I preface.

Alcuin (735–804)

De Animae Ratione (PL 101, cols. 639–50). An abridged and adapted version forms the major part of a Latin sermon, probably by Ælfric, which occurs in Boulogne, Bibliothèque Municipale MS 63, ed. Leinbaugh 1980; two OE versions of the sermon, both by Ælfric, are printed as LS 1 and Belfour 9 (see Godden 1985a, esp. pp. 296–8, and Leinbaugh 1994). There are brief parallels at CH I.1.161–6, I.10.125–36 and I.20.177–85, 190–212. All three passages seem to derive from the adaptation rather than from Alcuin himself, and the last shows very close parallels with the version in LS 1. The Latin sermon as a whole, if by Ælfric, is probably a late composition, since the first part is almost certainly a translation of the corresponding part of LS 1, which refers back to CH I. But it is possible that Ælfric had made the Latin adaptation of Alcuin at an earlier stage, prior to the CH, and added the introductory section to form a sermon subsequently.

Commentaria in S. Ioannis Evangelium (PL 100, cols. 737–1008). Heavily dependent on Augustine's Tractates. The only possible uses noted are all passages that Ælfric could alternatively have found excerpted in Smaragdus; cf. I.12.102–6, I.16.44–6, II.16.186–90.

Expositio Apocalypsis (PL 100, cols. 1087–1156). Cf note on I.40.131–47.

Interrogationes et Responsiones in Genesim (PL 100, cols. 516–66). Adapted and translated by Ælfric separately (= *Interrogationes*). For possible points of influence see I.1.177, I.13.4–17, I.20.190–212, I.35.259–73, II.12.273–311.

De Virtutibus et Vitiis (PL 101, cols. 613–38). Used for the account of the chief sins and virtues at II.12.477–559, and a possible recall at I.17.209–34.

Vita Sancti Martini Turonensis (PL 101, cols. 657–64). Used for II.34, and probably found in CC.

Aldhelm (d. c. 709)

De Virginitate, prose (ed. R. Ehwald, MGH, Auctores Antiquissimi 15, Berlin, 1919, pp. 226–323). II.praef.9–13.

Amalarius of Metz (780–850)

Liber Officialis (ed. J. Hanssens, in *Amalarii Episcopi Opera Liturgica Omnia*, 3 vols., Studi e Testi 138–40, Vatican City, 1948–50, vol. 2). Mentioned as source on the significance of Septuagesima at II.5.237, and probably used for comments on other feast-days at I.18.5–11, I.22.1–3, 27–9, and II.13.1–10. Cf too II.3.262–72 and II.16.208–25. Ælfric probably knew the work in an abridged and adapted form; see M. McC. Gatch, 'The Office in late Anglo-Saxon Monasticism', in Lapidge and Gneuss 1985, pp. 341–62, and Jones 1998, pp. 62–5.

Ambrose (339–97)

Hexameron (ed. K. Schenkl, CSEL 32.1, Vienna, 1897, pp. 3–261). Possible source for analogies to the resurrection of the body in the late addition to I.16 (App. B2.1–8 and 25–34).

Ps-Ambrose

Sermones (PL 17, cols. 603–734). Sermo 24 provides the closest parallel to a commonplace used in I.8.180–94.

Augustine of Hippo (355–430)

De Bono Coniugali (ed. J. Zycha, CSEL 41, Vienna, 1900, pp. 187–231). Perhaps alluded to at II.6.117.

De Catechizandis Rudibus (ed. J. B. Bauer, CCSL 46, Turnhout, 1969, pp. 121–78). Probable source for the comments on Jerusalem and Babylon at II.4.239–67.

De Civitate Dei (ed. B. Dombart and A. Kalb, 2 vols., CCSL 47–8, Turnhout, 1955). Not apparently used by Ælfric. The account of the miracles of St Stephen used in II.2, ultimately from *De Civitate Dei*, came to him via an anonymous homily, and the brief point at I.40.131–47 derives from a reference in a commentary on the Apocalypse by

Remigius, probably via his own adaptation of Julian of Toledo's *Prognosticon*. Cf also I.praef.96 ff.

De Correptione et Gratia (PL 44, cols. 915–46). Some similarities to a discussion of free will and grace at I.7.137–203, perhaps via an extract or quotation (untraced).

De Doctrina Christiana (ed. J. Martin, CCSL 32, Turnhout, 1962, pp. 1–167). A brief but close parallel (on herbs and medicine) at I.31.319–21.

Enarrationes in Psalmos (ed. E. Dekkers and J. Fraipont, 3 vols., CCSL 38–40, Turnhout, 1956). A faint parallel at II.40.80–85.

Enchiridion (ed. E. Evans, CCSL 46, Turnhout, 1969, pp. 23–114). Cf the parallel, on grace, at II.5.227–33.

De Genesi ad Litteram (ed. J. Zycha, CSEL 28.1, Vienna, 1894, pp. 3–435). Cf I.1.62–94.

In Iohannis Evangelium Tractatus CXXIV (ed. R. Willems, CCSL 36, Turnhout, 1954). Thirteen of the homilies show apparent use of the Tractates, and only in three cases are the relevant parts known to have been available in PD (I.12, II.13, partially, and II.35). Ælfric seems to have known the work independently and consulted it as a matter of course when commenting on John's Gospel. See homilies I.1, 4, 8, 12, 17, 25.138–48, II.3, 12, 13, 14, 15, 20, 22, 24, 35.

De Libero Arbitrio (ed. W. M. Green, CCSL 29, Turnhout, 1970, pp. 211–321). See I.1.170–6.

De Sermone Domini in Monte (ed. A. Mutzenbecher, CCSL 35, Turnhout, 1967). Used for I.3, I.19 and I.36 and for the comment on St Thomas in the *Excusatio Dictantis*. PD contains the relevant excerpts for I.3 and I.36 but not for I.19.

Sermones (1–50, in *Sermones de Vetere Testamento*, ed. C. Lambot, CCSL 41, Turnhout, 1961; the rest in PL 38–39). There are parallels, often very close, with some 36 of Augustine's sermons, of which only six are known to have been available in versions of PD. The material was frequently recycled in excerpts, in sermons by other, often anonymous, writers and in other works, and it is hard to be sure of the form in which Ælfric knew it. But it looks as if he had read a good range of Augustine's sermons outside Paul the Deacon's selection.

Sermo 5: II.14
Sermo 46: I.17 (perhaps via canons)
Sermo 56–59: I.19 (?)
Sermo 61: I.18
Sermo 71: I.33 (?)
Sermo 72: II.26
Sermo 76: II.24 (in PD)
Sermo 83: I.31 (?), but certainly used in Irvine 2.
Sermo 84: I.32
Sermo 90: I.35 (?)
Sermo 93: II.39 (in PD)
Sermo 103: II.29 (in PDM)
Sermo 104: II.29 (in PDM)
Sermo 105: I.18 (in PD)
Sermo 112: II.23
Sermo 115: II.28 (in PD)
Sermo 117: I.20
Sermo 118: I.20
Sermo 120: I.20
Sermo 186: I.2
Sermo 200: I.7
Sermo 202: I.7
Sermo 204: I.7
Sermo 206: II.7
Sermo 272: II.15
Sermo 279: I.27
Sermo 288: I.25
Sermo 350: II.19
Sermo 370: I.9 (excerpt in PD) and II.1
Sermo 382: I.3 and II.2 (perhaps from a Fleury homiliary)
Sermo 384: I.20

Sermones inediti (PL 46, cols. 817–940). Sermo 10 shows a parallel to II.19.

De Trinitate (ed. W. J. Mountain and F. Glorie, 2 vols., CCSL 50, 50A, Turnhout, 1968). Perhaps the work of Augustine's referred to at I.20.6–7, but no clear evidence of use.

Ps-Augustine

Sermones (PL 39). Many of the sermons in this section of PL 39 (*Sermones suppositi*) have since been reattributed and (mostly) re-edited, and are to be found here under the names of Caesarius, Pelagius, Quodvultdeus, Ildefonsus, etc. For the reattributions see *Clavis Patrum Latinorum*. Of the remainder, twelve may have been consulted by Ælfric, and only two of them are known to have been available in PD.

Sermo 72: II.24
Sermo 109: I.16 (?)
Sermo 195: I.13
Sermo 196: I.25
Sermo 197: I.25
Sermo 199: I.25
Sermo 204: I.27 (?, in PD)
Sermo 245: I.20
Sermo 246: I.20
Sermo 303: cf II.6.115
Sermo 310 (in the version ed. Cross 1990, from a Salisbury MS containing a form of PD): II.7

Bede (c. 673–735)

Commentarius in Epistolas Septem Catholicas (ed. D. Hurst, CCSL 121, Turnhout, 1983, pp. 181–342). The commentary on 1 Peter appears to have been used in II.40.

Commentarius in Genesim (ed. C. W. Jones, CCSL 118A, Turnhout, 1967). Probably used in I.1, and a possible source for the passage on the sabbath in the *Ps-Egbert Excerptiones* and the similar passage at II.12.273–311.

Commentarius in Lucam (ed. D. Hurst, CCSL 120, Turnhout, 1960, pp. 5–425). Parallels are noted below in 14 homilies, but in three cases (I.33, II.28 and 31) the relevant excerpts were in PD, and elsewhere the parallels are slight or the material is found in similar form in Smaragdus or Haymo. It is not after all entirely certain that Ælfric had direct access to the commentary (but see Pope, p. 167). See homilies I.2, 9, 11, 13, 14, 21, 33, 40, II.5.140–2, 6, 14, 16, 28, 31.

Commentarius in Marcum (ed. D. Hurst, CCSL 120, Turnhout, 1960, pp. 431–648). The passages used in II.24 and II.25 were available as excerpts in PD, and the material used in I.34 was also available in Smaragdus; there is a slight parallel in II.14; but II.23 seems to show direct use of the commentary.

Expositio Actuum Apostolorum (ed. M. Laistner, CCSL 121, Turnhout, 1983, pp. 3–99). Used for I.21 and possibly details in I.20, II.14 and II.24.

Historia Ecclesiastica Gentis Anglorum (ed. B. Colgrave and R. A. B. Mynors, Oxford, 1969). Cited as *historia anglorum* and used as source in II.9 (along with the OE translation, attributed by Ælfric to King Alfred) and II.21, and also used for details in II.10; cf also I.11.138–50; and possibly used for II.20.

Homiliae (ed. D. Hurst, CCSL 122, Turnhout 1955, pp. 1–378). 25 of Bede's 50 homilies are identified as sources below. PD used most of Bede's homilies, including all but one of those used for the Catholic Homilies; the exception (I.13) is a very doubtful source anyway.

Hom. I.3: I.13
Hom. I.4: I.13
Hom. I.6: I.2
Hom. I.7: I.2
Hom. I.9: I.4 and 37.245–9
Hom. I.10: I.5
Hom. I.11: I.6
Hom. I.12: II.3
Hom. I.13: I.27 (?).
Hom. I.14: II.4
Hom. I.18: I.9
Hom. I.20: I.26
Hom. I.21: II.32
Hom. II.2: I.12
Hom. II.3: I.14
Hom. II.5: II.15 faint and doubtful
Hom. II.7: I.15
Hom. II.9: I.21
Hom. II.16: I.22 (?)
Hom. II.17: I.22 (very doubtful)
Hom. II.18: II.24
Hom. II.19: I.25 faint but possible.
Hom. II.20: I.25 probable
Hom. II.21: II.27 and II.37 (possible detail; in PDM)
Hom. II.23: I.32
Hom. II.24: II.40

De Natura Rerum (ed. C. W. Jones, CCSL 123A, Turnhout, 1975, pp. 189–234). Used for some astronomical explanations at I.40.37–51.

De Temporum Ratione (ed. C. W. Jones in *Bedae Opera De Temporibus*, CCSL 123B, Turnhout, 1977, pp. 263–460). Used for several points about seasons and astronomy in I.6 and I.40.

Vita Cuthberti Prosa (ed. B. Colgrave in *Two Lives of Saint Cuthbert*, Cambridge, 1940, pp. 142–306), and *Vita Cuthberti Metrica* (ed. W. Jaager in *Bedas metrische Vita sancti Cuthberti*, Leipzig, 1935). Used extensively, and in combination with the anonymous life, in II.10.

Ps-Bede

In Matthaei Evangelium Expositio (PL 92, cols. 9–132). Probably not used by Ælfric, but does give a closer version of Bede's words at II.8.37–44, II.25.111–3.

Benedict of Nursia (c. 480–c. 550)

Regula (ed. R. Hanslik, CSEL 75, 2nd ed., Vienna, 1977). Not apparently used as a source, but obviously familiar to Ælfric and its influence on his wording can be seen at I.8.76–86; II.11.219–33; and II.19.125–6.

Caesarius of Arles (470–542)

Sermones (ed. G. Morin, 2 vols., CCSL 103–4, Turnhout, 1953). Often transmitted under the name of Augustine; PD included the two sermons most substantially used by Ælfric, but not apparently the others.

Sermo 25: cf. I.18.208–10.
Sermo 50 and 54: cf I.31.303–34 (parallels)
Sermo 179: II.40
Sermo 219: I.3 (included in PD as a work of St Augustine, and so cited by Ælfric).
Sermo 222: I.5 (in PD).

Candidus Fuldensis

De Passione Domini (PL 106, cols. 57–104). Candidus is a little-known figure from the early ninth century, and there is no good reason to think that Ælfric knew his work, except that it does provide parallels that are not in the other commentaries. See II.14.

John Cassian (c. 360–435)

Conlationes (ed. M. Petschenig, CSEL 13, Vienna, 1886). Required reading for Benedictine monks; used for II.12.

De Institutis Coenobiorum (ed. M. Petschenig, CSEL 17, Vienna, 1888, pp. 3–231). Perhaps a distant influence on I.27.210–47.

Cassiodorus (d. c. 580)

De Anima (ed. J. W. Halporn, CCSL 96, Turnhout, 1973, pp. 534–75). Cf I.1.106–10.

Ps-Chrysostom

Homily on the Decollation of John the Baptist (PL 95, cols. 1508–14). In PDM, used for I.32.

Opus Imperfectum (PG 56, cols. 834–8). Homily 37 in this series of homilies on Matthew's Gospel (ascribed to a fifth-century Arian) was included in PD and used for I.14.

Ps-Cyprian

De Duodecim Abusivis (ed. S. Hellman, Texte und Untersuchungen 4.1, Leipzig, 1909, pp. 1–62). Ælfric produced an OE adaptation of this Hiberno-Latin tract (printed by Morris, pp. 299–304). Probably used for II.19.

Eusebius Gallicanus

Collectio Homiliarum (ed. F. Glorie, 3 vols., CCSL 101–101B, Turnhout, 1970–71). Various homilies with different earlier attributions and associations were re-edited in this collection. Whether the shadowy figure of Eusebius to whom the seventh-century collection has been attributed was author or merely compiler is unclear. Of the three items apparently used by Ælfric, two (hom. 47 in II.40 and hom. 51 in II.38) were available in versions of PD and the other (hom. 4 in I.5) involves material which circulated in other forms too.

Fulgentius of Ruspe (468–533)

Sermones (ed. J. Fraipont, CCSL 91A, Turnhout, 1968, pp. 889–942).

Sermo 3: I.3
Sermo 4: I.7
(Both included in PD.)

Gregory the Great (c. 540–604)

Dialogues (*Dialogi*, ed. A. de Vogüé and P. Antin, 3 vols., Sources Chrétiennes 251, 260 and 265, Paris, 1978–80). Cited by name and title at II.21.115, as source for a short passage, and again at II.21.177, as authority for the efficacy of the mass; the sole source for II.11, on St Benedict; and possibly or probably used for details at I.33.51–3, I.35.122–32, and for a story at II.19.204–11.

Homiliae in Evangelia (PL 76). 33 of the 40 homilies are used by Ælfric here, several of them more than once (and homily 27 seems to have been used for no less than four of his own homilies). All were available in versions of PD (except possibly 31).

Hom. 1: I.40
Hom. 2: I.10
Hom. 5: I.38
Hom. 6: I.32
Hom. 7: I.25
Hom. 8: I.2
Hom. 9: II.38
Hom. 10: I.7 and I.15
Hom. 12: I.28, II.39
Hom. 14: I.17
Hom. 15: II.6
Hom. 16: I.11, II.7
Hom. 17: II.36, II.38
Hom. 18: II.13
Hom. 19: I.35, II.5
Hom. 20: I.25, II.3
Hom. 21: I.15, II.12
Hom. 22: II.15
Hom. 23: II.16
Hom. 24: II.16
Hom. 25: I.14
Hom. 26: I.16 and I.22
Hom. 27: I.35, I.36, II.19, II.35
Hom. 28: I.8, I.40 (?)
Hom. 29: I.3, I.21
Hom. 30: I.22, II.3, II.5, II.19
Hom. 31: II.26 (?)
Hom. 34: I.2, I.24, II.5
Hom. 35: II.37
Hom. 36: II.23
Hom. 38: I.17, I.35
Hom. 39: I.23, I.28
Hom. 40: I.23, II.37

Moralia siue Expositio in Iob (ed. M. Adriaen, 3 vols., CCSL 143–143B, Turnhout, 1979–85). Ælfric's homily on Job (II.30) shows familiarity with the *Moralia* but uses it little; there are parallels to the preface in I.31, and a possible influence at I.34.266–9 and I.40.157–65.

Regula Pastoralis (PL 77, cols. 13–128). A faint parallel at II.5.50–61 and II.36.131–7; the influence could have been from the Old English version (for which see below).

Gregory of Tours (c. 540–94)

Historia Francorum (ed. B. Krusch and W. Levison, MGH, Scriptores rerum Merovingicarum, 1.1, Berlin, 1937–51). No evidence of direct use; there is a passage in I.18 taken from Amalarius, and another in II.34 which Ælfric probably found as an excerpt along with other material on St Martin in his copy of CC.

Liber Miraculorum (ed. B. Krusch, MGH, Scriptores rerum Merovingicarum, 1.2, Berlin, 1969). The account of a miracle of St. Clement is used in I.37, but Ælfric probably found it as an excerpt in CC.

Haymo of Auxerre (d. c. 865)

Mentioned in the CH I preface as a source, presumably meaning his homilies.

Commentaria in Cantica Canticorum (PL 116, cols. 695–714). See I.34.259–78.

Commentarius in Apocalypsin: see Remigius of Auxerre

Expositio in Pauli Epistolas (PL 117, cols. 361–938). Some clear signs of use in II.40, and possible use in I.39 and II.12.273 ff.

Historiae Sacrae Epitome (PL 118, cols. 817–74). No certain evidence of use, but possible uses at I.20, I.21.234–44, I.22.102–8, I.30.199–206. Cf too I.5.162–6

Homiliae (PL 118). Haymo is cited by name in I.8 and I.34, and his homilies used as the main source for those two items. Otherwise Ælfric seems to have used Haymo's exegesis as a supplement to material drawn from the commentaries of Augustine, Gregory or Bede, in order to provide historical background information, or apposite Biblical quotations, or exposition of additional detail, or more pointed phrasing. Frequently Haymo was himself adapting and expanding the authors whom Ælfric was using, and it is not always easy to be sure whether Ælfric actually used Haymo or independently adapted them in the same way. But altogether 36 of the 153 homilies that occur in the collection printed by Migne are cited as possible sources below, several of them for more than one of Ælfric's homilies. Not all are actually by Haymo himself.

Homiliae de Tempore

Hom. 2: I.40
Hom. 11: I.4
Hom. 12: I.5
Hom. 13: I.9
Hom. 14: I.6, I.9
Hom. 15: I.5, I.7
Hom. 18: I.4, II.4
Hom. 19: I.8, I.35
Hom. 20: II.23
Hom. 21: II.5
Hom. 23: I.10
Hom. 28: I.11
Hom. 33: II.12
Hom. 35: II.8
Hom. 49: I.12
Hom. 56: II.13
Hom. 63: I.14
Hom. 64: II.14
Hom. 81: I.16
Hom. 83: I.17
Hom. 92: I.18
Hom. 95: I.21 (not Haymo)
Hom. 96: I.21
Hom. 108: II.3, II.13, II.24
Hom. 112: II.23
Hom. 114: I.24
Hom. 119: II.25
Hom. 120: II.26
Hom. 122: I.28
Hom. 123: II.28
Hom. 127: II.31
Hom. 135: I.35
Hom. 136: I.8

Homiliae de Sanctis

Hom. 1: I.38
Hom. 2: I.25
Hom. 7: I.34 = PL 95, cols. 1525–30
Hom. 8: I.36

Hericus of Auxerre (840–76)

Homiliae in Circulum Anni (ed. R. Quadri, 3 vols., CCCM 116–116B, Turnhout, 1992–4). Never mentioned by Ælfric and perhaps not known by name, but at least 39 of his homilies were included in the version of PD printed in PL 95, and a number of others show distinctive parallels with Ælfric. Like Ælfric, and indeed like the other Carolingians Haymo and Smaragdus, Hericus was engaged in adapting the work of his patristic predecessors, though he generally rewrites more fully than the other two, and the parallels are mainly a matter of details or turns of phrase in material which is otherwise to be found in other writers familiar to Ælfric.

Hom. I.8: CH I.2
Hom. I.15: CH I.6 (?)
Hom. I.28: CH I.11
Hom. I.32: CH I.11, II.13 (PDM)
Hom. II.23: CH I.26 (PDM)
Hom. II.30: CH II.28 (?,PDM)
Hom. II.37: CH I.33 (PDM 179)
Hom. II.46: CH I.13 and I.38 (PDM)

Ps-Hilary

Tractatus in Septem Epistolas (ed. R. E. McNally, CCSL 108B, Turnhout, 1973, pp. 53–124). Possibly Hiberno-Latin. Cited by name and quoted in a Latin note at I.21.148.

Hilduinus

Passio Sanctorum Dionysii, Rustici et Eleuterii Martyrum (printed in Mombritius 1910, I.394–409). Used for a passage on St Denis in I.37, and more fully for the account of the saint in LS 29. Included in CC.

Ildefonsus of Seville (c. 607–67)
Presumed author of Ps-Augustine Sermo 245 (PL 39, cols. 2196–8), which is included in PDM and may have been used for I.20 and II.1.

Iohannes Diaconus (interpolator of Pelagius on the epistles)
See under Pelagius.

Isidore of Seville (560–636)

De Ecclesiasticis Officiis (ed. C. M. Lawson, CCSL 113, Turnhout, 1989). The short section on the nativity of Christ was excerpted in PD and seems to have been used for Ælfric's two sermons for the occasion, I.2 and II.1.

Etymologiae (ed. W. M. Lindsay, Oxford, 1911). Slight parallels at I.2.52–62; and II.40.74–85.

De Ortu et Obitu Patrum (ed. C. Chaparro Gómez, Paris, 1985). Possible source for some details on apostles in I.26.

Quaestiones in Vetus Testamentum, PL 83, cols. 207–424. The work seems to provide the closest parallels for the interpretations of the Pentateuch in II.12, and for details in I.28 and II.15.

Ps-Isidore

Liber de Ortu et Obitu Patrum (PL 83, cols. 1275–94). Possible source for some details on apostles in I.4 and I.38.

Jerome (c. 345–420)
Cited as an authority in the CH I preface, and also several times in individual homilies (I.30.4 ff; II.18.3, 51; II.29.2, 124); but the references are in fact to pseudonymous works, those in I.30 and II.29 to the tract on the assumption of the Virgin by Paschasius Radbertus and those in II.18 to the *Historia Ecclesiastica* of Eusebius and Rufinus. If, as is suggested by the evidence below, Ælfric may not have known directly the Commentary on St Matthew's gospel, Jerome's prominence in the preface rests largely on pseudonymous works and perhaps Ælfric's awareness that his more immediate exegetical authorities were drawing on Jerome.

Adversus Iovinianum (PL 23, cols. 212–338). See CH I.27.141–50 (probably not a direct influence).

Chronicon (ed. R. Helm, in *Eusebius Werke*, vol. 7, GCS 47, Berlin, 1984). See CH I.40.32–7 (possible source for historical detail).

Commentarii in Evangelium Matthaei (ed. D. Hurst and M. Adriaen, CCSL 77, Turnhout, 1969). There are frequent parallels to Jerome's commentary in Ælfric's exegesis of Matthew, but Jerome was so heavily used by other sources known to Ælfric (Bede, Haymo, Smaragdus) that it is hard to be certain of his direct use of Jerome. Excerpts are hardly ever used in PD. Ælfric's attribution, at I.11.108–15, of a passage from the commentary to an untraced letter by Jerome suggests he may not have had direct access to it. See CH I.11, I.27, I.34, II.14, II.26, II.38.

For Jerome's translation of homilies attributed to Origen, see below under the latter.

Liber Interpretationis Hebraicorum Nominum (ed. P. de Lagarde, CCSL 72, Turnhout, 1959, pp. 59–161). Probably the ultimate source for much of Ælfric's exegesis of Biblical names, but the material may often have been transmitted through commentaries by others. See esp. I.2.65–75, I.13.117–24, I.14.90–7.

De Viris Inlustribus (ed. E. C. Richardson, Texte und Untersuchungen 14.1, Leipzig, 1896, pp. 1–56). Cf I.26.100–9 and 273–5.

Julian of Toledo (archbishop 680–90)

Prognosticon Futuri Saeculi (ed. J. Hillgarth, CCSL 115, Turnhout, 1976, pp. 11–126). Ælfric's main authority on matters of eschatology; his Latin abridgement and adaptation of this work is preserved in the Boulogne MS (edited by Gatch 1977), and both these *Excerpts* and the *Prognosticon* itself seem to have been drawn on for Pope 11. Julian's work is itself largely a digest, development and rearrangement of arguments and evidences used by earlier writers, and it is not always easy to tell whether Ælfric was using Julian himself or his sources, or indeed his own *Excerpts*. The Prognosticon is cited below as source for: I.5; I.15.109–15; I.16; I.21; I.27; I.40; II.35. There is good evidence for the use of the *Excerpts* in I.27 (see also Gatch 1966), but for the *Prognosticon* rather than the abridgement in I.16.

Martin of Braga (520–80)

De Correctione Rusticorum (ed. C. W. Barlow in *Martini Episcopi Bracarensis Opera Omnia*, New Haven, 1950, pp. 183–203). Probably a model for I.1, and used for details in I.6 (and a major source for Pope 21, *De Falsis Deis*).

Origen/Ps-Origen

Latin versions of two homilies attributed to Origen, on Matthew's Gospel (*Homiliae in Matthaeum*, PLS 4, Hom. 5 and 6, cols. 872–87) are used in I.8 and II.26. And a Latin version, apparently by Jerome, of one of Origen's homilies on Luke (ed. M. Rauer, in *Origenes Werke*, vol. 9, GCS 49, 2nd ed., Berlin, 1959) was used in I.9; all three texts were included in PD.

Paschasius Radbertus (d. c. 860)

De Assumptione Sanctae Mariae Virginis (ed. A. Ripberger, CCCM 56C, Turnhout, 1985, pp. 109–62). Presented as a work by Jerome, and so identified by Ælfric, but now thought to be a forgery by Paschasius. It was included for the occasion both in CC and in PD. The main source for I.30, and also used for points on the Virgin at I.9.169–80 and I.36.124–37, and for a point of doctrine at I.15.130–42.

De Corpore et Sanguine Domini (ed. B. Paulus, CCCM 16, Turnhout, 1969, pp. 1–131). Possibly the source for the two exempla in II.15.

Paulus Diaconus, of Monte Cassino (720–99?)

For the importance of his homiliary to Ælfric, see above. The preface probably influenced Ælfric's own preface to CH I as well.

Vita Gregorii (ed. H. Grisar, 'Die Gregorbiographie des Paulus Diakonus in ihrer ursprünglichen Gestalt, nach italienischen Handschriften', *Zeitschrift für katholische Theologie* 11 (1887), 158–73). The main source for Ælfric's account of Gregory the Great, in II.9, and perhaps also used for a detail in II.19. Available in CC.

Paulus Diaconus Neapolitanus

Miraculum Sanctae Mariae de Theophilo (ASS Feb. I.489–93). Available in CC, and briefly summarised in I.30.

Pelagius (4th-5thC)

Pelagius's Expositions of Thirteen Epistles of St Paul (ed. A. Souter, in Texts and Studies IX, 3 parts, Cambridge, 1922–31). Often attributed to Jerome in the Middle Ages, and so printed in PL 29. Apparently used for the exposition of the epistle in I.39; Ælfric may have known the version interpolated by one John the Deacon.

Petrus Chrysologus (400–450)

Collectio Sermonum (ed. A. Olivar, 3 vols., CCSL 24–24B, Turnhout, 1975–82). Sermo 152 was included in PD and used for I.5. For Sermo 91, see I.25.96–100.

Prosper of Aquitaine (390–463)

Epitoma Chronicon (ed. T. Mommsen, MGH, Auctores antiquissimi 9, Berlin, 1892, pp. 385–485). A faintly possible source for a historical detail in I.40.32–7.

Quodvultdeus (Bishop of Carthage, d. 454?)

Contra Iudaeos, Paganos et Arrianos (ed. R. Braun, CCSL 60, Turnhout, 1976, pp. 227–58). An excerpt, dealing with the prophecies of Christ in the Old Testament and elsewhere, appears in PD for the Annunciation, and in PDM for the Nativity period, and was probably used for II.1; cf also I.13.18–40.

Rabanus Maurus (d. 856)

The *Commentarius in Matthaeum* (PL 107, cols. 727–1156), the *Homiliae in Evangelia* (PL 110, cols.135–468) and the *Homiliae de Festis Praecipuis* (PL 110, cols. 9–134) draw on the same exegetical traditions as Ælfric and often show parallels, but there are no similarities of phrasing or distinctive details which might suggest that he knew these works; see esp. I.19, I.25 and II.25.

Ratramnus of Corbie (d. 868)

De Corpore et Sanguine Domini (ed. J. N. Bakhuizen van den Brink, Amsterdam, 1974). The main source for II.15.

Remigius of Auxerre (841–908)

Commentarius in Apocalypsin (PL 117, cols. 937–1220, but attributed to Haymo in PL). A possible source for a citation of Augustine used in Ælfric's excerpts from the *Prognosticon* of Julian of Toledo, and for the corresponding detail at I.40.142–3.

Rufinus of Aquileia (c. 345–410)

Historia Ecclesiastica (a free translation and continuation of the Greek text of Eusebius; ed. T. Mommsen, in *Eusebius Werke*, ed. E. Klostermann, vol. 2, 2 parts, GCS 9.1 and 9.2, Leipzig, 1903–8). Referred to as the *ecclesiastica historia* of Jerome (the usual medieval attribution) at II.18.3, and as the *cyrclic gereccednyss* at I.32.189 (though for an excerpt from Josephus). A major source for I.5, I.28, I.32, II.17 and II.18, and possibly used for details in I.21 and II.24.

Caelius Sedulius (fl. early fifth century)

Carmen Paschale (ed. J. Huemer, CSEL 10, Vienna, 1885, pp. 1–146). Not a direct source, but the passage quoted by Bede in his commentary on Luke (6.1533–44) influenced II.14.241–4, and perhaps encouraged Ælfric's use of a poetic style in this homily.

Smaragdus of Saint-Mihiel (fl. 809–19)

Collectiones in Evangelia et Epistolas (PL 102, cols. 13–552). Ælfric cites Smaragdus as a source in the preface to CH I and presumably had a copy of this collection of (mainly brief) expositions of the epistles and pericopes for the whole year. Since Smaragdus compiled his collection by simply extracting relevant comments from various patristic authorities, usually the ones that Ælfric also regularly used (and frequently the same as those included in Paul the Deacon's homiliary), it is hard to be sure of any particular instances where he might have been used.[39] For possible influences, see I.3, 7, 8, 9, 12, 14, 16, 27, 33, 34, 39, 40; II.4, 6, 8, 14, 15, 16, 26; but apart from I.7, I.27 and esp. II.8 it is a matter of occasional details which could have come from elsewhere, and Smaragdus is never the sole source. It remains a puzzle to me that Ælfric should cite Smaragdus so prominently in the preface, when Haymo, who is used much more extensively and is much less derivative, is cited as being used merely *aliquando* and others, such as Alcuin and Julian of Toledo, are not mentioned at all. Perhaps Smaragdus's status as author of a commentary on the Benedictine Rule and a treatise on the monastic life made him a key authority figure for a writer of the monastic movement to cite.

De Diadema Monachorum (PL 102, cols. 593–690). Cf I.6.171–7.

Sulpicius Severus (360–420)

The *Vita Sancti Martini*, the *Epistula ad Bassulam* and possibly also the *Dialogi* (all ed. K. Halm, CSEL 1, Vienna, 1866) were used for Ælfric's account of St Martin, II.34; they were included in CC.

Tacitus (55–c. 120)

Historiarum Libri (ed. E. Koestermann, Leipzig, 1969). See I.28.39–45.

Theodulf of Orleans (750–821)

The *Capitula* (in H. Sauer, ed., *Theodulfi Capitula in England*, Texte und Untersuchungen zur englischen Philologie, Bd. 8 (Münich, 1978)) were well known in England in Ælfric's time, and offer occasional parallels but there is no clear evidence of use.

The *De Ordine Baptismi* (PL 105, cols. 223–40) offers at least a parallel, perhaps a source, for II.3.

[39] See Hill 1992, who is more inclined to see the hand of Smaragdus in Ælfric's work than I am.

2. Anonymous Writings

(a) Hagiography

Acta Alexandri (ASS Maii I.374–5). In CC, and used for II.18.

Passio Andreae (ed. M. Bonnet, in Lipsius and Bonnet, II.1–37). In CC, and used for I.38.

Passio Bartholomaei (Mombritius 1910, I.140–44). In CC, and used for I.31. See also I.11.42–7.

Vita Basilii (Surius, I.4–19). In CC; an episode summarised in I.30.

Passio Clementis (ed. F. Diekamp in *Patres Apostolici,* ed. F. X. Funk and F. Diekamp, 2 vols., 3rd ed., Tübingen, 1901–13, II.51–81). In CC (Hereford MS) and used for I.37.

Vita Cuthberti (ed. and trans. B. Colgrave in *Two Lives of Saint Cuthbert,* Cambridge, 1940, pp. 60–138). Used, in addition to Bede's two lives, for II.10.

Vita Fursei (ASS Jan. II.36–41). In CC, and used for II.20.

Passio Iacobi Apostoli (Mombritius 1910, II.37–40). In CC (though not very close); used in II.27 and, for the list of prophecies of Christ, in II.1.

Passio Iohannis Apostoli (Mombritius 1910, II.55–61). In CC; used for I.4, and summarised in I.37.

Rescriptum Marcelli (ASS Maii III.9–10). An account of St Peter's conflict with Simon Magus, incorporated in the Acta of Saints Nereus and Achilles in CC; used for I.26.

Certamen Sancti Martyris Mercurii (Surius, VI.569–72). In CC and possibly used for I.30.

Passio Matthaei (Fabricius, II.636–68). In CC (but not close), and used for II.32.

Relatio de Dedicatione Ecclesiae Sancti Michaelis (PL 95, cols. 1522–5, and ASS Sept. VIII.61–2). In PDM and CC, and used for I.34.

Passio Sanctorum Apostolorum Petri et Pauli (ed. R. A. Lipsius, in Lipsius and Bonnet, I.119–77). Not in CC; used for I.26, and St Paul's account of his preaching used as basis for part of II.19.

Passio Philippi (Mombritius 1910, II.385). In CC, and used for II.17.

Passio Polochronii, Parmenii, Abdon et Sennen, Xysti, Felicissimi et Agapiti et Laurentii et aliorum Sanctorum (ed. H. Delehaye, 'Recherches sur le légendier romain', *Analecta Bollandiana* 51 (1933), 34–98). In CC, and used for I.29.

Passio Septem Dormientium (ed. M. Huber, 'Beitrag zur Visionsliteratur und Siebenschläferlegende des Mittelalters, I Teil: Text', *Beilage zum Jahresbericht des humanistischen Gymnasiums Metten* (1902–3), 39–78). In CC; summarised in II.27 and alluded to in I.16.

Passio Simonis et Iudae (Mombritius 1910, II.534–9). In CC (probably), and used for II.33.

Vitae Patrum (PL 73). Referred to as *vita patrum* at I.36.111, and its subject summarised; there is a detail at I.6.180–81, conceivably found in the *De Diadema Monachorum* of Smaragdus, and an episode is retold at II.15.159–67, but this was probably read in some eucharistic collection.

(b) Homilies

Homiliare Floriacense, Hom. 15 (PLS 4, cols. 1903–10). Used (in a form somewhat different from this printed copy) for II.2.

Homily on All Saints, beginning 'Legimus in ecclesiasticis historiis' (ed. J. E. Cross, in '*Legimus in ecclesiasticis historicis*: A Sermon for All Saints and its use in Old English Prose,' *Traditio* 33 (1977), 101–35; also printed as Homily 71 in the works of Bede, PL 94, cols. 452–5). In PDM, and used for I.36.

(c) Liturgical texts

Verses from the psalms are frequently incorporated, often without specific citation and without prompting from sources. A line from an Office for the Assumption (PL 78, col. 799) is used at I.30.165–7 (and also in II.29.134–7), and some words from a hymn for the Annunciation in I.13.106–8.

B. Old English texts

Ælfric rarely seems to use vernacular sources, but he clearly knew the Alfredian works well and mentions them in general in the preface; he specifies the translation of Bede in II.9 and of Gregory's *Dialogues* at II.21.176–80. The *Old English Bede* is used at II.9.53–80; there is a clear borrowing of a sentence from the *Pastoral Care* at II.28.106–9, and a parallel, perhaps a borrowing, from either the *Pastoral Care* or the *Old English Boethius* at II.23.186–94.

COMMENTARY

Ælfric's Catholic Homilies have been studied and discussed since the sixteenth century, for a variety of purposes from the history of the doctrines and practice of the church and the nature of Anglo-Saxon society and its ideas to the development of the English language and its literature, and one cannot hope to take proper account of all these aspects. The commentary deals primarily with the processes by which Ælfric created the homilies and the sources which he used to create them, together with occasional difficulties of meaning. I have followed the practice of previous editions of Old English homilies published by the Society (those by Pope, Scragg and Irvine) in printing source-passages in full, in recognition of their importance for scholarly work on the Old English language, the transmission of texts and the history of ideas. Despite the important work done by past scholars on the sources, notably Förster, Smetana, Cross and Zettel, the task of identifying influences, choosing between different possible sources or versions of those sources, and identifying the precise words and phrases which lie behind Ælfric's formulations has been long and complicated, and one cannot claim that the final answer has been given; in some cases I have been convinced that Ælfric was drawing on a source but have been unable to locate it so far.

Source-quotations are drawn from a wide variety of printed editions, ranging from the sixteenth century to the present, each with its own conventions in spelling, capitalisation, word-division and punctuation. I have attempted a degree of normalisation to avoid too much distracting variation, especially in the continual alternation between PL and CCSL, though it has been difficult to be consistent: in standardising spellings I use **i** rather than **j**, **v** rather than **u**, **ae** in preference to **e** or tailed **e**. Obvious small printing errors in older editions are silently corrected. Connecting words like *autem* or *inquit* are sometimes omitted at the beginning of passages.

For the Bible I have quoted from *Biblia sacra iuxta vulgatam versionem*, ed. R. Weber (4th edn, Stuttgart, 1994), adding punctuation and capitals, in all cases where Ælfric seems to be quoting directly from the Bible, except in a few instances where another version is closer. But where, as often, he seems to be translating the version quoted by one of the sources which he was using, which often differ quite considerably from the standard Vulgate form, I have reproduced the quotation in the form in which it appears in the sources.

The general pattern of Ælfric's development and revision of the text and its subsequent circulation is analysed in the textual introductions in the two previous volumes. The present commentary deals with individual points of authorial revision in CH I where appropriate; those in CH II are mostly covered in the textual notes to that volume (or, for the larger passages which were printed by Pope, in his edition), but some further points are noted here.

CATHOLIC HOMILIES I

PREFACE

The Latin part of the preface is addressed to Archbishop Sigeric and invites him to correct the text, but is evidently also addressed to a wider circle of readers and users (cf esp. 29–37); this was not, then, written for a preliminary version of the series to be approved by the archbishop in advance of 'publication', but for a version that was itself to be circulated widely as well as being sent to Sigeric. Evidently Sigeric's authority was not needed for its circulation, and the dedication to Sigeric was part of the general publication of the text (there is no hint in Ælfric's words that Sigeric might already have seen or even known of the project). The Old English part of the preface is presumably addressed to the Latin-less priests who might use the collection for preaching and to individual readers. The absence of any reference to being commissioned or prompted by others is particularly striking.

The implications of the preface for the origin, purpose and date of the collection are discussed above pp. xxii–xxx. The text is also printed in Wilcox 1994, pp. 107–10 (translation of the Latin part at 127–8) and there are detailed notes and discussion there.

The most obvious model for the preface, and indeed for the scheme of the work, is the one which introduces Ælfric's principal source-book for the homilies, the homiliary of Paul the Deacon. The preface, written in the voice at least of no less a figure than the emperor Charlemagne, records that he had been concerned by the many errors and deficiencies in the existing lections provided for the church, and their failure to signal the authorities on which they drew, and had asked Paul the Deacon to study the writings of the catholic fathers, and select the most suitable ones to form a new collection. He then goes on to say of Paul's work (PL 95, 1159):

> Qui nostrae celsitudini devote parere desiderans, tractatus atque sermones diversorum catholicorum Patrum perlegens, et optima quaeque decerpens, in duobus voluminibus, per totius anni circulum, congruentes cuique festivitati, distincte et absque vitiis, nobis obtulit lectiones. Quarum omnium textum nostra sagacitate perpendentes, nostra eadem volumina auctoritate constabilimus, vestraeque religioni in Christi ecclesiis tradimus ad legendum.

Ælfric seems to take his cue from Charlemagne or Paul in his emphasis on the need to replace erroneous books, his reliance on the orthodox fathers for his material, and the idea of collecting sound expositions from many sources and reducing them to a single collection in two volumes (though Paul's division is in fact between the two halves of the year).

Ælfric's preface as a whole is found only in MS K and is printed from there; but most of the Old English part, on Antichrist, is also found as an independent piece in three Ælfrician MSS, P, R and T, and as an apparently authorised addition to I.39 in the copy of CH I preserved in Q. Since all four manuscripts have an additional sentence in Ælfric's style at 119 and an adapted ending at that point to make it usable as an independent piece, and further revisions and additions occur in QRT at 74 and 106, the sequence seems to be: 1) the CH I preface; 2) adaptation as an independent extract, slightly revised, as in P; 3) the extract in RT, further revised; 4) incorporation in I.39 as in Q.[1] Wulfstan used the account of Antichrist as a source for his homilies IV and V, and evidently knew the text in more than one form: in homily IV lines 3–8 he follows the original wording of line 74 but in homily V line 66 he follows the revised wording of QRT.

Notes

3–4 Æthelwold was bishop of Winchester 963–84, and Sigeric archbishop of Canterbury 990–994 or 995. See Introduction, pp. xxxii–xxxv.

8–9 *Nec obscura posuimus uerba. sed simplicem anglicam.* Michael Lapidge plausibly sees Ælfric here indicating his opposition to the deliberately esoteric vocabulary which characterised so much Latin writing in England in this period.[2] There is, it is true, no evidence of the cultivation of hermeneutic diction in vernacular writing up to this time, but it is certainly evident shortly afterwards, in the work of Byrhtferth of Ramsey.

14–16 On Ælfric's citation of sources for the CH see above pp. xxxviii–xliv.

33–4 Instances of Biblical readings being treated at other times than the appointed occasion are I.13.160 ff, II.16a (cf 39–40) and16b (cf 102–4), 23b (acknowledged at 128–30) and 24a (cf 50–52); cf also the opening of I.7.

41 Wilcox emends *uilitati*, 'worthlessness', to *utilitati*, which he renders 'profit'. I do not know whether Clemoes noted this and preferred the MS reading, or simply overlooked it; the MS reading seems to me to make better sense in the context.

45–8 On Ælfric's use of the phrase 'in Ethelred's day' during the king's lifetime, see Sisam, *Studies*, pp. 170–1. Ælfeah was bishop of Winchester 984–1006. Æthelmær was the founder of Cerne and son of Æthelweard, ealdorman of the western provinces; the two are addressed in the preface to the Lives of Saints

[1] Clemoes (*CH I*, pp. 114–7) seems to suggest rather that R and T derived their extract from an expanded copy of I.39 like Q's, but it would be hard then to explain their use of the same selection as P.

[2] M. Lapidge, 'The hermeneutic style in tenth-century Anglo-Latin literature', *ASE* 4 (1975), 67–111, at 101.

collection. If Æthelmær was already a thegn in 987, and still active in 1013, he was presumably roughly co-eval with Ælfric. The two were evidently on close terms: Ælfric addresses him as *Æðelmer noster* in the LS preface (line 31), and Æthelmær was later to found the abbey at Eynsham, instal Ælfric as abbot and join the community himself.

49–50 On the implications of *awende* see Ann E. Nichols, '*Awendan*: a note on Ælfric's vocabulary', *JEGP* 63 (1964), 7–13.

50–56 On the many English books containing *gedwyld* and Ælfric's knowledge of Alfredian works, see Godden 1978. The former are perhaps to be identified especially with the 'false' stories and their associated doctrines which Ælfric mentions or hints at in CH I.30, II.20, II.39.184 ff, and the note *De Sancta Maria* (at *CH II*, p. 271), all of which survive in English versions from his time. In addition to the evidence for Ælfric's familiarity with the Alfredian translations of Gregory the Great's *Regula Pastoralis* and *Dialogues*, Boethius' *De Consolatione*, and Bede's *Historia Ecclesiastica* which I mentioned in the 1978 article, one should also note the apparent use of a passage from the *Anglo-Saxon Chronicle* in his Grammar, pointed out to me by Professor Ron Buckalew; and Aaron Kleist of Cambridge University has pointed out to me the further extensive use of the *Old English Boethius* in LS 17.222 ff, in addition to the use in LS 1 (which I have discussed further in Godden 1985a).

57 The end of the world and the coming of Antichrist. Ælfric reiterates the notion that this is the last period of the world at LS 13.294, and explores the question again in CH I.40, II.39 and in Pope 18. How close the end may be he does not say, perhaps deliberately. The perils that precede the end are evidently still in the future (lines 59–60); Antichrist is not yet born (lines 73–4; see below); and lines 106–8 seem to acknowledge that it is uncertain whether those now living will see his reign.

The origins of Antichrist are Biblical. He is mentioned by name, as one who denies Christ and is associated with the last age of the world, only in the epistles of John: 1 Jn 2.18 ff, 4.3, and 2 Jn 7. This is supplemented by 2 Thess 3–11, which suggests that he will represent himself as God and will work miracles, so that people follow him. The three and a half years of his reign are from Apoc 11.3. References to Antichrist were usually also seen in the synoptic Gospels, at Mt 24, Mc 13 and Lc 21, which speak of false Christs and prophets who will perform signs and wonders to lead astray the elect. Ælfric's account of Antichrist, here and again in Pope 18, reflects in general the tradition that had developed on this Biblical basis up to his time (for which see esp. Richard K. Emmerson, *Antichrist in the Middle Ages: a Study of Medieval Apocalypticism, Art and Literature* (Manchester, 1981)) but specific sources are hard to identify, and he seems at times not to share the orthodox views (see Pope, esp. p. 588). Pope tentatively suggests the influence of the detailed account by Adso, *De Ortu et Tempore Antichristi* (ed. D. Verhelst, CCCM 45, Turnhout, 1976), written just a few years before Ælfric, c. 954, but evidently known in England.

61–6 From Mt 24:

(21) Erit enim tunc tribulatio magna, qualis non fuit ab initio mundi. . . . (24) Surgent enim pseudochristi . . . (5) Multi enim venient in nomine meo, dicentes: Ego sum Christus; et multos seducent. . . . (24) et dabunt signa magna, et prodigia, ita ut in errorem inducantur (si fieri potest) etiam electi. (22) Et nisi breviati fuissent dies illi, non fieret salva omnis caro; sed propter electos breviabuntur dies illi.

68–9 perhaps alludes to Mt 10.22: *Et eritis odio omnibus propter nomen meum; qui autem perseveraverit in finem hic salvus erit.* (Used at CH II.19.268–70)

73–5 A crucial formulation on the nature of Antichrist, subsequently corrected by Ælfric. The original wording, matching Antichrist's dual nature to Christ's, seems to imply acceptance of a current but questioned view, that Antichrist would be the devil incarnate, as Christ was God incarnate, and would have a human mother but be fathered by the devil, just as Christ was born of a human mother and fathered by God. Cf Emmerson, *Antichrist*, pp. 81–2. The rewritten form, found in MSS QRT, affirms instead that Antichrist would be born in the normal fashion of human parents and presumably redefines his diabolic status as a matter of diabolic possession rather than something analogous to Christ's divinity. (Emmerson suggests (*Antichrist*, p. 151) that in making the change Ælfric was concerned only to clarify a view already expressed, if obliquely, in the First Series preface; it does seem to me that a change of view is involved.) Adso condemns the first view and supports the latter, and it is conceivable that Ælfric only read Adso's account after writing the preface. The careful distinction between *bið* in line 73 and *is* in line 74 is presumably meant to indicate a difference of tense: Christ is truly God and man, Antichrist will be human and devil (but is not yet born despite the imminence of the year 1000).

77–8 On the differing views of the nature of Antichrist's end and its relation to the end of the world, see Emmerson, *Antichrist*, pp. 101–7; Ælfric's reference to *grama* is unspecific as to whether it will be Christ himself or St Michael who destroys him.

79–84 On Antichrist only being able to heal those whom he has himself made sick or injured, cf I.31.9 ff on the devils and gods.

96–106 Ælfric makes the same point with reference to the devil apparently causing fire to appear from heaven in his account of Job, II.30.90 ff. Augustine, *De Civitate Dei*, XX.19 (noted by Emmerson, *Antichrist*, pp. 93–4), also cites Job as a parallel, but only to make the point that, like the fire caused by Satan which actually destroyed Job's livestock, the prodigies performed by Antichrist will be real rather than illusory. *Heofonas* at 98 is presumably written in error for gs. *heofenes* or *heofonan* (as in MSS QRT).

110–6 Ez 3.18–19:

> (18) Si dicente me ad impium morte morieris non adnuntiaveris ei neque locutus fueris ut avertatur a via sua impia et vivat, ipse impius in iniquitate sua morietur, sanguinem autem eius de manu tua requiram. (19) Si autem tu adnuntiaveris impio et ille non fuerit conversus ab impietate sua et via sua impia, ipse quidem in iniquitate sua morietur, tu autem animam tuam liberasti.

116–9 Is 58.1:

> Clama ne cesses quasi tuba, exalta vocem tuam et adnuntia populo meo scelera eorum et domui Iacob peccata eorum.

127–8 1 Cor 3.9: *Dei enim sumus adiutores.*

134 The Latin note about a contents list and Æthelweard's copy is written as if a continuation of the preface in the manuscript, beginning on the same line as *wile* (I presume that Clemoes consigned it to the apparatus to signal that it was not, in his view, in the original text of the preface, or not a proper part of it). It may perhaps be a note to Ælfric's scribes inadvertently copied with the preface and not intended for others, as Sisam suggested (Sisam, *Studies*, p. 161); but the similar comment in CH II is part of the general Old English preface to users and readers (lines 41–3), and both prefaces do address scribes or their supervisors, so that it seems quite likely that the first part of the note at least, up to *contineat*, was meant as part of the preface. Someone as close to Ælfric, and as important to him, as Æthelweard is likely to have been given a copy at the outset, rather than having to wait until after the general circulation signalled by the copy to Sigeric, and we know that he received copies of items in the LS collection before the collection was generally issued; since the note says that he 'would like to have' 44 homilies in his set, rather than that he has had them, the note is itself likely to date from the earliest state of the First Series. It is possible that Ælfric anticipated Æthelweard's copy being used as an exemplar for others, and needed to explain the existence of variant versions, given his emphasis on the precise number of homilies in each series and his sensitivity on the issue of other people's work being mixed with his own.

I ON THE ORIGIN OF THE CREATED WORLD

The opening sermon is not assigned to any occasion but is clearly conceived as a very basic introduction to Christian history and a preliminary to the more specific discussions in the subsequent sermons. Its focus is on the Old Testament rather than the New; the Old Testament material occupies the first 235 lines of the 296. The account of the creation and fall of the angels and the creation and fall of man is marked by some striking discussions of the issues raised: questions of free will, the origin and nature of the devil, the state of man before the fall, the origin of the soul. The account of the incarnation and redemption takes up only sixty lines and is in general a very straightforward account.

There are no obvious sources for this sermon. Virginia Day has placed it within a tradition of 'catechetical *narratio*' or outline of Christian cosmology and history for the simple and uneducated, going back to Augustine's *De Catechizandis Rudibus*.[1] She notes general resemblances of content and structure to Martin of Braga's *De Correctione Rusticorum* and the adaptation of it by Pirmin in his *Scarapsus*, and suggests probable influence from one or both, but notes that 'this agreement does not extend to the more detailed level of the words and phrases employed by Ælfric'.[2] Of the two, Martin seems a more likely influence, since his work was a source for two other Ælfric homilies, CH I.6 and Pope 21, and I know of no evidence that Ælfric knew or used Pirmin. After a brief preamble Martin discusses the creation and fall of the angels (§3), the creation, fall and expulsion of man (§4), the development of sin and the flood (§5), and the development of idolatry (§6); the last subject is then discussed in detail (§§7–12) before moving on to the life of Christ from incarnation to ascension (§13) and the last judgement (§14); the final sections deal with baptism, pagan and superstitious practices again, and general moral exhortation. Ælfric clearly knew this work well, and it seems likely enough that it functioned as a model for his own sermon, but his focus is rather different, with its emphasis primarily on the Old Testament and especially the creation and fall. His essential concern is fall and redemption. In the course of his discussion he takes up a number of points of doctrine, and there are parallels here with points made by Augustine, Cassiodorus, Bede, Alcuin and Haymo; a wide range of reading and some deliberation on difficult points of doctrine lie behind this apparently simple account.

Sources and Notes

The following texts are cited below:

1. Alcuin, *De Animae Ratione*, PL 101, cols. 639–50.
2. Alcuin, *Interrogationes et Responsiones in Genesim*, PL 100, cols. 516–66.
3. Augustine, *De Genesi ad Litteram*, ed. J. Zycha, CSEL 28.1 (Vienna, 1894), pp. 3–435.
4. Augustine, *In Iohannis Evangelium Tractatus CXXIV*, ed. R. Willems, CCSL 36 (Turnhout, 1954).

[1] See Day 1974. [2] Day 1974, p. 57.

5. Augustine, *De Libero Arbitrio*, ed. W. M. Green, CCSL 29 (Turnhout, 1970), pp. 211–321.
6. Bede, *Commentarius in Genesim*, ed. C. W. Jones, CCSL 118A (Turnhout, 1967).
7. Cassiodorus, *De Anima*, ed. J. W. Halporn, CCSL 96 (Turnhout, 1973), pp. 534–75.
8. Haymo of Auxerre, *Homiliae de Tempore*, PL 118, Hom. 32, cols. 211–7.
9. Martin of Braga, *De Correctione Rusticorum*, in *Martini Episcopi Bracarensis Opera Omnia*, ed. C. W. Barlow (New Haven, 1950), pp. 183–203.

1–21 Ælfric begins with the nature of God Himself. The passage has Biblical echoes but few precise quotations. With lines 8–9 cf *rex regum et Dominus dominantium*, used of God at 1 Tim 6.15 and Apoc 19.16. Lines 16–21 summarise Ælfric's characteristic views on the Trinity and creation.

22–61 The account of the creation and fall of the angels draws of course on Christian tradition rather than Scripture, though there is a Scriptural base. Lines 29–34 draw on Is 14.12–15:

> (12) Quomodo cecidisti de caelo lucifer qui mane oriebaris corruisti in terram qui vulnerabas gentes. (13) Qui dicebas in corde tuo in caelum conscendam super astra Dei exaltabo solium meum sedebo in monte testamenti in lateribus aquilonis. (14) Ascendam super altitudinem nubium ero similis Altissimo. (15) Verumtamen ad infernum detraheris in profundum laci.

In his *Hexameron* Ælfric places the creation of the angels on the first day of creation and the fall of the angels at or before the sixth day. On the question of the origin of the devil, lines 56–61, cf Augustine, *Tract.*, 42.10.33–6:

> Quaeritis autem fortasse, unde ipse diabolus? Inde utique unde et ceteri angeli. Sed ceteri angeli in [s]ua obedientia perstiterunt: ille inobediendo et superbiendo lapsus est angelus, et factus est diabolus.

Repeated by Haymo, Hom. 32, PL 118, 216D.

62–94 Ælfric moves directly on to the creation of man because, presumably, it follows causally and chronologically on the fall of the angels, though it comes after the rest of creation. The account follows Genesis 2. For 66–8 cf Gen 2.7:

> Formavit igitur Dominus Deus hominem de limo terrae et inspiravit in faciem eius spiraculum vitae et factus est homo in animam viventem.

For 68–73 cf Gen 2.15–17:

> (15) Tulit ergo Dominus Deus hominem et posuit eum in paradiso voluptatis ut operaretur et custodiret illum. (16) Praecepitque ei dicens ex omni ligno paradisi comede. (17) De ligno autem scientiae boni et mali ne comedas in quocumque enim die comederis ex eo morte morieris.

(Neither here nor in the *Hexameron* does Ælfric identify the tree, though he does indicate at 140–1 that the fruit conferred the knowledge of good and evil, or at least that Adam and Eve possessed that knowledge after eating it.) On the purpose of the tree, lines 74–83, cf Augustine, *De Genesi ad Litteram*, 8.6:

> Oportebat autem ut homo sub Domino Deo positus alicunde prohiberetur, ut ei promerendi Dominum suum virtus esset ipsa oboedientia.

Quoted by Bede in his *Commentarius in Genesim*, 1.1485–7. Augustine denies that the tree was itself evil. Bede goes on to discuss the issues of free will in more detail. For 83–6 cf Gen 2.19:

> Formatis igitur Dominus Deus de humo cunctis animantibus terrae et universis volatilibus caeli adduxit ea ad Adam ut videret quid vocaret ea omne enim quod vocavit Adam animae viventis ipsum est nomen eius.

(Ælfric's comment at 85–6 presumably refers to the Hebrew names of the animals, not the English ones.) For 86–8 cf Gen 2.18: *Dixit quoque Dominus Deus non est bonum esse hominem solum faciamus ei adiutorium similem sui.* For 88–93 cf Gen 2.21–3:

> (21) Inmisit ergo Dominus Deus soporem in Adam cumque obdormisset tulit unam de costis eius et replevit carnem pro ea. (22) Et aedificavit Dominus Deus costam quam tulerat de Adam in mulierem et adduxit eam ad Adam. (23) Dixitque Adam hoc nunc os ex ossibus meis et caro de carne mea haec vocabitur virago quoniam de viro sumpta est.

Her other name Eva is not in fact given until after the fall, at Gen 3.20: *Et vocavit Adam nomen uxoris suae Hava eo quod mater esset cunctorum viventium.*

95–124 turns to the rest of creation. For 95–100 cf Gen 2.1–3:

> (1) Igitur perfecti sunt caeli et terra et omnis ornatus eorum. (2) Conplevitque Deus die septimo opus suum quod fecerat et requievit die septimo ab universo opere quod patrarat (3) et benedixit diei septimo et sanctificavit illum quia in ipso cessaverat ab omni opere suo quod creavit Deus ut faceret.

For 101–2 cf Gen 1.3: *Dixitque Deus fiat lux et facta est lux.* For 102–3 cf Gen 1.6, 8: *Dixit quoque Deus fiat firmamentum . . . vocavitque Deus firmamentum caelum.* For 104–6 cf Gen 1.24–5:

> Dixit quoque Deus producat terra animam viventem . . . et fecit Deus bestias terrae iuxta species suas et iumenta et omne reptile terrae in genere suo.

For 106–10 cf Gen 1.20: *Dixit etiam Deus producant aquae reptile animae viventis et volatile super terram.* That animals do not have souls is a recurrent theme in Ælfric's writings (cf Godden 1985a, pp. 280–3). For the notion that the life of animals is based on blood rather than soul, cf Cassiodorus, *De Anima*, 3.1–2:

> Anima igitur hominis proprie dicitur, non etiam pecudum, quia illorum vita in sanguine noscitur constituta.

Lines 110–4 Bede, *Comm. Gen.*, 1.727–36 [drawing on Augustine, *Confessions*, XIII.xxii.15]:

> Cuius nobilitati creationis etiam hoc testimonium dat, quod non sicut in ceteris creaturis dixit Deus, 'fiat homo, et factus est homo,' vel 'producat

terra hominem, et produxit terra hominem'. Sed priusquam fieret, faciamus hominem dicitur, ut videlicet quia rationalis creatura condebatur quasi cum consilio facta videretur. Quasi per studium de terra plasmaretur et inspiratione conditoris in virtute spiritus vitalis erigeretur, ut scilicet non per iussionis vocem sed per dignitatem operationis existeret qui ad conditoris imaginem fiebat.

The subsequent lines seem to have prompted parts of Ælfric's discussion in his Preface to Genesis; see Crawford, pp. 76–80. I do not know which heretics Ælfric is referring to at 117–24. The last sentence, lines 122–4, implies that the belief in question referred to the origins of dangerous animals; cf the similar comments at I.6.175–82.

125–48 The fall of man. Ælfric's wording implies that the tempter is Satan himself; contrast his different view at I.13.70 ff. Lines 129–42 are based on Gen 3.1–8:

(1) Sed et serpens erat callidior cunctis animantibus terrae quae fecerat Dominus Deus qui dixit ad mulierem cur praecepit vobis Deus ut non comederetis de omni ligno paradisi. (2) Cui respondit mulier de fructu lignorum quae sunt in paradiso vescemur. (3) De fructu vero ligni quod est in medio paradisi praecepit nobis Deus ne comederemus et ne tangeremus illud ne forte moriamur. (4) Dixit autem serpens ad mulierem nequaquam morte moriemini. (5) Scit enim Deus quod in quocumque die comederitis ex eo aperientur oculi vestri et eritis sicut dii scientes bonum et malum. (6) Vidit igitur mulier quod bonum esset lignum ad vescendum et pulchrum oculis aspectuque delectabile et tulit de fructu illius et comedit deditque viro suo qui comedit. (7) Et aperti sunt oculi amborum cumque cognovissent esse se nudos consuerunt folia ficus et fecerunt sibi perizomata. (8) Et cum audissent vocem Domini Dei deambulantis in paradiso ad auram post meridiem abscondit se Adam et uxor eius a facie Domini Dei in medio ligni paradisi.

Both here (line 136) and at I.11.160 Ælfric has *englum gelice* for *sicut dii*. I can find no trace of such a variant reading in versions of the Bible or commentaries; *sicut angeli* seems to be cited only with reference to Mt 22.30 or Mc 12.25. Presumably it is his own paraphrase. Both Augustine and Bede accept the *dii* reading. On 136–8 cf Bede, *Comm. Gen.*, 1.1965–73:

Neque enim clausis oculis facti erant, et in paradiso delitiarum caeci palpantesque oberrabant . . . ad hoc ergo aperti sunt oculi primorum hominum ad quod antea non patebant, quamvis ad alia paterent.

For 142–8 cf Gen 3.17–21:

(17) Ad Adam vero dixit quia audisti vocem uxoris tuae et comedisti de ligno ex quo praeceperam tibi ne comederes maledicta terra in opere tuo in laboribus comedes eam cunctis diebus vitae tuae. (18) Spinas et tribulos germinabit tibi et comedes herbas terrae. (19) In sudore vultus tui vesceris pane donec revertaris in terram de qua sumptus es quia pulvis es et in

pulverem reverteris. . . . (21) Fecit quoque Dominus Deus Adam et uxori eius tunicas pellicias et induit eos.

149–66 The significance of the fall. For 149–50 cf Bede, *Comm. Gen.*, 1.2215–8:

Nam huiusmodi indumento dominus eos mortales iam factos fuisse insinuat. Pelles quippe, quae non nisi mortuis pecudibus subtrahuntur, mortis figuram continent.

Lines 161–6 This closely parallels a passage in the Latin sermon on the nativity which occurs in the Boulogne manuscript (Boulogne-sur-Mer, Bibliothèque Municipale MS 63; text from Leinbaugh 1980, lines 218–22):

Duabus vero dignitatibus a Creatore anima in sua natura glorificata est, id est, aeternitate et beatitudine. Sed cum libero arbitrio, maligno spiritu instigante, depravata est, beatitudinem perdidit, aeternitatem perdere non potuit.

As Leinbaugh shows, the source for this was Alcuin, *De Animae Ratione*, c. ix, PL 101, 643BC:

Sed dum libero arbitrio, spiritu instigante maligno, depravata est, partim mortalis ex immortali facta est, sed non tota. . . . Duabus vero dignitatibus a Creatore anima in sua natura glorificata est, id est, aeternitate et beatitudine. . . . Semiviva erit anima, si propter vitia et iniquitates, beatitudinem visionis et habitationis Dei perdiderit; ad quam autem creata est, aeternitatem perdere non potest.

Ælfric's source for the present passage was evidently the Boulogne text. If as I argued in 1985[3] this text was itself composed by Ælfric, we need to date it, or rather the adaptation and abridgement of Alcuin's *De Animae Ratione* which forms its second part, prior to his completion of CH I.

166–70 Cf Gen 5.4–5:

(4) Et facti sunt dies Adam postquam genuit Seth octingenti anni genuitque filios et filias (5) et factum est omne tempus quod vixit Adam anni nongenti triginta et mortuus est.

170–76 The various theories of the origin of the soul, including the traducianist theory to which Ælfric refers at 170–1, are discussed by Augustine in his *De Libero Arbitrio* (c. 21), and by Cassiodorus in his *De Anima* (c. 3). Perhaps it is this to which his 'sume men' alludes. Augustine himself professes his inability to reach a conclusion on the matter, though seeming to favour a version of the traducianist view. The creationist theory which Ælfric here asserts is the one developed by Jerome, and perhaps the orthodox one by this period. King Alfred seems to have favoured a third view, that the soul pre-exists the individual from the beginning of time (*Soliloquies*, 91.9–11). Cf further Godden 1985a, esp. pp. 283–5. This is a recurrent topic in Ælfric's writing, and its appearance in both his and Wulfstan of Winchester's lives of St Æthelwold suggests that it may have been a familiar talking point at Winchester.

[3] Godden 1985a. See further above p. xlvi.

177–202 The account of the flood draws on Gen 6.1–7.24, 9.8–17 and 9.28. That it was especially *forliger*, fornication, that caused God to send the flood is not Biblical. It is a view espoused by Alcuin in his *Interrogationes et Responsiones* (PL 100, 543) and thence by Ælfric in his version (*Interrogationes*, c. 67).

203–10 The account of Babel is from Gen 11.1–9 (though not the reference to the fear of God).

211–221 The growth of idolatry. There is no obvious Old Testament source for this, and it is not clear which Biblical period Ælfric is describing. Idolatry is the main theme of Martin of Braga's *De Correctione Rusticorum* and his account of its growth in Old Testament times, cc. 6–7, is probably an influence here; Ælfric follows it much more closely in his later piece *De Falsis Deis*, Pope 21.77–165. But despite his opening reference to the devil Ælfric places the initiative for idolatry on humans, who identify departed heroes and ents as gods and make statues of them for worship, whereas Martin says that the *daemones* assumed the names of criminals, such as Jove, in order to deceive people into worshipping them (cf Pope's notes, pp. 681 and 685).

222–35 The history of the Hebrews as God's chosen people. The progeny of Sem down to Abraham is listed at Gen 11.10–26 immediately after the Babel story. The idea that God cherished the Hebrews because he wished to be born of a woman from that people is a distinctive aspect of Ælfric's account.

236–50 The conception, birth and childhood of Christ. The denial that Christ worked miracles openly before he was thirty (lines 249–50) is perhaps a reference to the narratives of childhood miracles given in the apocryphal Gospels, though the term 'openlice' is teasing. Ælfric's repeated insistence that Christ did not reveal himself until he was thirty perhaps explains his failure to mention the episode with the doctors in the temple in any of his discussions of Christ's life.

251–64 Summarises Christ's ministry.

265–93 A rapid review of the conspiracy, passion, harrowing of hell, ascension and last judgement. For the striking detail that, after the harrowing of hell, Christ led the ransomed to their bodies and then arose with a *miclum werede* cf I.15.130 ff and notes. Ælfric does not here explain where the host of the redeemed then went; see note on I.15.165 ff.

2 THE NATIVITY OF CHRIST

This is the first of Ælfric's five homilies for the nativity (the others being CH II.1, LS 1, Belfour 9 and Pope 1; there is also a Latin version of LS 1). He chooses here to concentrate on the Gospel story of the birth of Christ and the visit of the shepherds, using Luke 2.1–20, which is actually a combination of two readings for the Christmas period, verses 1–14 and 15–20. In later homilies for the occasion he was to deal more with the theological issues and with the alternative text for the day, John 1.1 ff. He uses at least five identifiable sources in expounding the Gospel text and drawing out its significance. Chief among them are the two homilies on the Gospel text by Bede (Hom. I.6 and I.7). Ælfric is rarely close to Bede in wording, but that is frequently the case in his use of Bede's exegetical writing, and he also takes a decidedly different line from Bede on several points of interpretation, but much of the thought and information in Ælfric's piece does have parallels in Bede's two homilies, which were probably available to him in Paul the Deacon's homiliary. Also included in the homiliary was Gregory the Great's very brief sermon on the text from Luke (Hom. 8), which Ælfric follows closely for lines 151–74, a sermon by Augustine and an extract from Isidore's *De Ecclesiasticis Officiis* (I.26, *De Natale Domini*), from which he seems to have drawn a sentence or two of each.[1] But there remain a few points for which no precise sources have emerged, and the material from the sources is freely handled and reordered. Ælfric seems not to have used the homilies for the occasion by Smaragdus, who draws on Gregory and on Bede's commentary on Luke, or Haymo, who deals with the text from John, but there are some possible links with a homily for the occasion by Hericus.

In interpreting the text from Luke Ælfric shows little interest in the moral exegesis which he found in Bede, such as the long discussion of the phrase 'to men of good will' in the angel's greeting to the shepherds, or the extended use of the shepherds as models for all men (though this is touched on in his final sentence). Nor is he particularly interested in the purely historical explanations, such as the account of how the census originated or Bede's point that Christ chose to be born at a time of peace so that his disciples could evangelize in security, though he does add an historical explanation for Mary's marriage to Joseph. His primary concern is with showing how the literal events serve as a symbolic expression of the divine plan for redemption and drawing out the divine mysteries and purposes hidden in the narrative. Caesar Augustus, the governor Cyrinus and Bethlehem are all figures for Christ, while the census and tax-gathering and the empire of Augustus are spiritual symbols for God's extension of the empire of heaven by redeeming mankind. Ælfric emphasises the divine choice of time for the incarnation and the fulfilment of prophecy (lines 80–3, 220–9), as well as the divine reality and purpose hidden in the humbleness of the infant in the crib (lines 98–106), and touches on the union of divine and human in Christ (lines 176–98). A particular theme is the reunion of mankind with the angels, which prompted him to turn to Gregory as well as Bede.

[1] See Förster 1894, p. 13, for the use of Gregory, and Smetana 1959, pp. 182–3, for the other four sources, and their inclusion in versions of PD.

Sources and Notes

The following texts are cited below:

1. Augustine, *Sermones*, PL 38, Serm. 186, cols. 999–1000.
2. Bede, *Commentarius in Lucam*, ed. D. Hurst, CCSL 120 (Turnhout, 1960), pp. 5–425.
3. Bede, *Homiliae*, ed. D. Hurst, CCSL 122 (Turnhout, 1955), Hom. I.6 (pp. 37–45) and Hom. I.7 (pp. 46–51).
4. Gregory the Great, *Homiliae in Evangelia*, PL 76, Hom. 8, cols. 1103–5.
5. Hericus, *Homiliae in Circulum Anni*, ed. R. Quadri, CCCM 116 (Turnhout, 1992), Hom. I.8 (pp. 67–76).
6. Isidore, *De Ecclesiasticis Officiis*, ed. C. M. Lawson, CCSL 113 (Turnhout, 1989).
7. Isidore, *Etymologiae*, ed. W. M. Lindsay (Oxford, 1911).

8–41 A fairly close rendering of Lc 2.1–20:

(1) Factum est autem in diebus illis, exiit edictum a Caesare Augusto ut describeretur universus orbis. (2) Haec descriptio prima facta est praeside Syriae Cyrino. (3) Et ibant omnes ut profiterentur singuli in suam civitatem. (4) Ascendit autem et Ioseph a Galilaea de civitate Nazareth in Iudaeam civitatem David quae vocatur Bethleem, eo quod esset de domo et familia David, (5) ut profiteretur cum Maria desponsata sibi uxore praegnate. (6) Factum est autem cum essent ibi impleti sunt dies ut pareret. (7) Et peperit filium suum primogenitum et pannis eum involvit et reclinavit eum in praesepio, quia non erat eis locus in diversorio. (8) Et pastores erant in regione eadem vigilantes et custodientes vigilias noctis supra gregem suum. (9) Et ecce angelus Domini stetit iuxta illos et claritas Dei circumfulsit illos et timuerunt timore magno. (10) Et dixit illis angelus: nolite timere. Ecce enim evangelizo vobis gaudium magnum quod erit omni populo. (11) Quia natus est vobis hodie salvator qui est Christus Dominus in civitate David. (12) Et hoc vobis signum: invenietis infantem pannis involutum et positum in praesepio. (13) Et subito facta est cum angelo multitudo militiae caelestis laudantium Deum et dicentium: (14) gloria in altissimis Deo et in terra pax in hominibus bonae voluntatis. (15) Et factum est ut discesserunt ab eis angeli in caelum, pastores loquebantur ad invicem: transeamus usque Bethleem et videamus hoc verbum quod factum est, quod fecit Dominus et ostendit nobis. (16) Et venerunt festinantes et invenerunt Mariam et Ioseph et infantem positum in praesepio. (17) Videntes autem cognoverunt de verbo quod dictum erat illis de puero hoc. (18) Et omnes qui audierunt mirati sunt et de his quae dicta erant a pastoribus ad ipsos. (19) Maria autem conservabat omnia verba haec conferens in corde suo. (20) Et reversi sunt pastores glorificantes et laudantes Deum in omnibus quae audierant et viderant, sicut dictum est ad illos.

At line 10, *fram ðam ealdormenn* reflects the variant reading *a praesidio* (for *praeside*), and the variant *in excelsis*, familiar from the liturgy, is used in place of *in altissimis* at 29 and later. For the expansion of verse 3 at lines 11–12, explaining the nature of the census, cf Hericus, Hom. I.8, 75–8:

> Praecepto imperiali de singulis locis ad quae demigraverant, omnes revertebantur ad locum nativitatis, ut ibi profitentes tribum et familiam suam describerentur sub tributo in ordine parentum suorum.

Ælfric's substitution of the name Octavianus for Caesar Augustus at lines 9 and 53 is not prompted by any Biblical texts or expositions that I have found, but the same change is made by the translator of Orosius.[2] He may have been influenced by the fact that Caesar and Augustus were, or became, generic names for Roman emperors (a point made by Hericus, and cf too Professor Bately's note on the Orosius passage), and perhaps also by the point he was to make about the addition of the title Augustus at lines 54–5. The reference to the asses at line 19 presumably reflects traditional elaborations of the story (cf lines 211–2), though *heora* implies that this is not the ox and ass of the stable but Mary and Joseph's own animals, brought for the journey from Nazareth.

42–5 Some resemblance to the opening sentences of Isidore's brief account (Isidore, *De Ecclesiasticis Officiis*, I.26.3–5, 19–20):

> Christus pro redemptione mundi nasci corporaliter voluit, prodiens ex virginis utero, qui erat in patris imperio. . . . Ita idem deus et idem homo; in natura Dei aequalis patri, in natura hominis factus mortalis in nobis, pro nobis.

45–52 Probably based on scattered sentences in Bede's Hom. I.6:

> [34–6] Praemisit ergo tempora pacis et sic apparens in carne ipse auctor pacis et temporum conditor. [12–15] Quod enim maius in hac vita potuit esse pacis indicium, quam ab uno homine orbem describi universum atque unius census numismate concludi? [19–22] Hinc etenim scriptum est: 'Ipse est pax nostra qui fecit utraque unum' (Eph 2.14), id est qui de angelis et hominibus unam Dei domum pius mediator et reconciliator instituit.

52–62 The information that the emperor was Octavianus, who was renamed Augustus, meaning 'increasing his kingdom', because he had expanded the Roman empire to embrace the whole world, and the application of this to Christ expanding the heavenly kingdom to include mankind, thus more than making up for the loss of the fallen angels, is not in Bede's homily or any of the other sources that Ælfric is known to have used for this piece. A hint at the etymology and its significance occurs in Bede's commentary on Luke (*Comm. Luc.* 1.1049–51): *Qui vocabulum augusti perfectissime complens utpote suos et augescere desiderans et ipse augere sufficiens.* The point is borrowed by Smaragdus (*Collectiones*, PL 102, 23C). Closer on the historical aspect is Isidore in his *Etymologiae*, IX.3.16:

[2] OE Orosius, 59.2–3 and 130.26, and notes.

> Augustus ideo apud Romanos nomen imperii est, eo quod olim augerent rempublicam amplificando. Quod nomen primitus senatus Octavi[an]o Caesari tradidit, ut quia auxerat terras, ipso nomine et titulo consecraretur.

But there is no application to Christ here. Cf too Hericus, Hom. I.8, 15–18, 54–7:

> Augustus autem primus dictus est Octavianus imperator qui hic intellegitur et dictus est Augustus eo quod auxerit prae caeteris imperatoribus regibusque rem publicam, a quo et dicitur exisse edictum ut describeretur universus orbis. . . . Quod etiam census tunc exigebatur, non vacat a mysterio; Octavianus enim imperator, si dici fas est, significat ipsum dominum qui est rex regum et dominus dominantium.

Ælfric was perhaps drawing on the as yet unidentified source which gave him the etymology of Cyrinus (see below). The point that the number of those saved will eventually equal the number of angels left in heaven after the fall is also made by Ælfric at CH I.24.103–6, where he is drawing on Gregory the Great.

62–5 Closely renders Bede, Hom. I.6, 44–9:

> Sed et ipsa totius orbis descriptio, quae a terreno rege facta memoratur, caelestis opera regis manifeste designat, quia ad hoc nimirum apparuit in mundo ut de cunctis per orbem nationibus electos in unitatem fidei suae colligeret ac nomina eorum sicut ipse promisit in aeternum scriberet in caelo.

65–75 The etymology and interpretation of Cyrinus are not in Bede. Jerome's *Liber Interpretationes Hebraicorum Nominum* (CCSL 72, 64.9) gives the information that the name means inheritor, *haeres*, but is an unlikely source, since at the same place it glosses *Augusti* quite differently from Ælfric, as *solemniter stantis aut solemnitatem additam*. Alcuin offers the same etymology for Cyrinus as Ælfric but a different application, to St Peter not Christ (PL 101, 1174). Ambrose (PL 17, 608) and Bede in his commentary on Luke take Cyrinus as a figure for the teacher, which may have prompted Ælfric's reference to *lareowas* at 76, even though he rejects their interpretation of the name. The parallel between the city and the church is in Bede (Hom. I.6, 51–2): *Nostra civitas ecclesia sancta est*.

76–80 Bede (Hom. I.6, 102–5) refers to the prophecy of Bethlehem, but Ælfric seems rather to be following the wording given in Mt 2.6: *Et tu Bethlehem terra Iuda, nequaquam minima es in principibus Iuda: ex te enim exiet dux, qui regat populum meum Israel* (Mich 5.2). Bede goes on to suggest that Christ was born in a foreign city so that those who were involved in his birth might avoid his enemies, which perhaps inspired lines 79–80. Closer perhaps is Hericus, Hom. I.8, 92–8:

> Non vacat a mysterio quare dominus in Nazareth voluit concipi, et in Bethlehem nasci; nam quantum ad litteram pertinet, idcirco hoc actum est ut utraque civitas de adventu illius insignis haberetur; vel etiam ne facile inveniretur ab Herode si haberet diurnam continuamque mansionem in

Bethlehem, voluit concipi in Nazareth, et nasci in Bethlehem sub dubia mansione.

There is no obvious reason why the sentence at 79–80, added in a different hand in MS A, should have been overlooked by the scribe, and it may be an Ælfrician afterthought, taken from another manuscript.

80–85 Bede (Hom. I.6, 108–9) and Gregory (Hom. 8, PL 76, 1104A) both say that Bethlehem means house of bread (*domus panis*) and apply this to Christ, quoting Jn 6.41 in support: *Ego sum panis vivus qui de caelo descendi.* Ælfric adds the link with the eucharist and an echo of Jn 6.50: *Hic est panis de caelo descendens, ut si quis ex ipso manducaverit, non moriatur.*

88–92 Cf Bede, Hom. I.6, 143–53:

Primogenitum vocat dominum non quia credendum sit beatam Dei genetricem alios post eum filios peperisse . . . sed ob id eum recte primogenitum appellat, quia sicut Iohannes ait: 'Quotquot eum receperunt, dedit eis potestatem filios Dei fieri' (Jn 1.12). In quibus filiis, ipse iure primatum tenet, qui et ante quam nasceretur in carne Dei filius absque initio natus exstiterat . . . sicut ait apostolus: 'sit ipse primogenitus in multis fratribus' (Rom 8.29).

92–4 Bede, Hom. I.6, 167–70:

Ipse in adsumptione nostrae fragilitatis exiguis contegitur pannis, ut primam nobis stolam restituat, id est ad gratiam nos immortalitatis quam in primo parente accepimus miseratus reducat.

94–100 Combining Bede, Hom. I.6, 175–7:

Ille quem caelum et caeli caelorum non capiunt, parvi praesepis angustia continetur ut amplitudinem nobis supernarum sedium tribueret.

and 162–4:

Qui ad dexteram Dei patris sedet in caelo, loco egebat in diversorio ut nobis copiam felicium mansionum in domo patris sui donaret.

100–102 Perhaps prompted by Bede's citation (Hom. I.6, 158–9) of Ps 115.12: *Quid retribuam Domino pro omnibus quae retribuit mihi.*

102–11 The interpretation of the shepherds as teachers comes from Bede's second homily for the nativity (Hom. I.7, 17–18): *Significant autem mystice pastores isti gregum doctores quosque ac rectores fidelium animarum.* But the development of this to stress the *lareow*'s crucial role as mediator between God and his flock, so characteristic of Ælfric, seems to be his own.

111–15 Cf Bede, Hom. I.7, 6–11 (though the point is made at greater length in Hom. I.6):

Nusquam enim in tota veteris instrumenti serie repperimus angelos qui tam sedulo apparuere patribus cum luce apparuisse, sed hoc privilegium recte hodierno tempori servatum est, quando 'exortum est in tenebris lumen rectis corde misericors et miserator dominus' (Ps 111.4).

The psalm quotation is hidden in lines 114–5 (where the phrase *se mildheorta . . . drihten* evidently belongs with the preceding clause, though the punctuation suggests that the scribe was confused).

118–20 Cf perhaps Bede, Hom. I.6, 238–40: *Vere gaudium magnum, quia gaudium caeleste, gaudium aeternum*. But Bede goes on to gloss 'all people' as the Jews and the Gentiles, where Ælfric thinks of those in heaven, earth and hell.

120–7 Bede, Hom. I.6:

[248–60] Bene dixit, hodie natus est, non dixit, hac nocte. . . . Dominus Iesus dies est . . . nox praecessit antiquae caecitatis, dies autem adpropinquavit aeternae salutis. [264–6] Hoc nos signum nati in carne salvatoris semper animo retinere condecet, ut semper eius beneficiis gratias rependere bene vivendo discamus. . . . [270–3] Misericordias ergo domini in aeternum cantemus, qui, ut nos perpetuo beate vivamus, ipse abiectionis ac mortalitatis nostrae socius fieri non abnuit.

132–8 Bede, Hom. I.7, 11–17:

Verum ne parva unius angeli videretur auctoritas, postquam unus sacramentum novae nativitatis edocuit, statim multitudo caelestium agminum, quae gloriam Deo caneret pacemque simul hominibus praedicaret adfuit, aperte demonstrans quia per hanc nativitatem homines ad pacem unius fidei, spei et dilectionis, atque ad gloriam divinae laudationis essent convertendi.

141–62 Fairly closely based on the peroration to Gregory, Hom. 8, PL 76, 1104C-5B:

Prius quippe quam Redemptor noster nasceretur per carnem, discordiam cum angelis habuimus, a quorum claritate atque munditia per primae culpae meritum, per quotidiana delicta longe distabamus. Quia enim peccando extranei eramus a Deo, extraneos nos a suo consortio deputabant angeli cives Dei. . . . Quia enim coeli Rex terram nostrae carnis assumpsit, infirmitatem nostram illa iam angelica celsitudo non despicit. Ad pacem nostram angeli redeunt . . . et quos prius infirmos abiectosque despexerant, iam socios venerantur. Hinc est enim quod Loth et Iosue angelos adorant [*cf Gen 19.1 and Jos 5.15*], nec tamen adorare prohibentur; Ioannes vero in Apocalypsi sua adorare angelum voluit, sed tamen idem hunc angelus ne se debeat adorare compescuit, dicens: Vide ne feceris, conservus enim tuus sum et fratrum tuorum . . . [Adora Deum][3] (Apoc 22.9). Quid est quod ante Redemptoris adventum angeli ab hominibus adorantur, et tacent, postmodum vero adorari refugiunt, nisi quod naturam nostram, quam

[3] Quotation extended by Ælfric to include the last two words.

prius despexerant, postquam hanc super se assumptam conspiciunt, substratam sibi videre pertimescunt? Nec iam sub se velut infirmam contemnere ausi sunt, quam super se videlicet in coeli Rege venerantur. Nec habere dedignantur hominem socium, qui super se adorant hominem Deum. Curemus ergo, fratres charissimi, ne qua nos immunditia polluat, qui in aeterna praescientia et Dei cives, et angelis eius aequales sumus. . . . Dii etenim vocati sunt homines. Defende ergo tibi, o homo, contra vitia honorem Dei, quia propter te factus est Deus homo.

165–85 This theological excursus, building on the beginning of St John's Gospel, is suggested by Bede (Hom. I.7, 51–7):

'Et videamus, inquiunt, hoc verbum quod factum est.' Quam recta et pura fidei sanctae confessio. 'In principio erat verbum, et verbum erat apud Deum, et Deus erat verbum' (Jn 1.1). Hoc verbum natum ex patre non factum est, quia creatura Deus non est. In qua nativitate divina videri ab hominibus non potuit sed ut videri posset 'verbum caro factum est et habitavit in nobis' (Jn 1.14).

The formulation *word bið wisdomes geswutelung* (line 167) also occurs at CH I.25.140–1, in a similar context, but has no parallel in the sources for either passage. Isidore also argues, like Bede, that the word became flesh so that it could be seen by men, and provides a parallel for 174–5 (*De Ecclesiasticis Officiis*, I.26.16–18): *Ut autem videretur, 'verbum caro factum est', assumendo carnem, non mutatum in carne.* The analogy between the incarnation and the nature of man and the subsequent point about the relationship of divinity and humanity in Christ (lines 175–7, 180–81) seem to come from Augustine's Serm. 186, §1, PL 38, 999:

Caro ad verbum, ne ipsa periret, accessit ut quemadmodum homo est anima et caro, sic esset Christus Deus et homo. Idem Deus qui homo, et qui Deus idem homo: non confusione naturae, sed unitate personae.

The analogy with an egg (lines 181–5) seems to be Ælfric's own.

187–98 The discussion of Mary's marriage to Joseph and her virginity has no parallel in the sources. The first part is similar to a passage in Ælfric's Annunciation homily (CH I.13.79–102) but the sources for that homily only partly account for it.

199–202 From Bede, Hom. I.7, 93–7:

Visio Dei cognitio eius est et haec est sola beata hominis vita ipso dicente . . . 'Haec est autem vita aeterna ut cognoscant te verum et unum Deum et quem misisti Iesum Christum' (Jn 17.3).

204–17 The picture of Mary pondering the prophecies of the nativity is based on Bede, Hom. I.7:

[119–40] Maria, virginalis pudicitiae iura custodiens secreta christi quae noverat nemini divulgare volebat, sed ipsa haec quando vellet et quomodo vellet divulgare reverenter expectabat. . . . Legerat in propheta . . . 'Et tu Bethleem . . .' (Mich 5.2). . . . Videbat se in Bethleem peperisse dominatorem Israhel qui aeternus ex patre Deus ante saecula natus est; videbat se virginem concepisse et peperisse filium et vocasse nomen eius Iesum. Legerat in prophetis: 'Ecce virgo concipiet et pariet filium, et vocabitur nomen eius Emmanuhel' (Is 7.14). Legerat: 'Bos cognovit possessorem suum et asinus praesepe domini sui' (Is 1.3). Videbat dominum positum in praesepe quo bos et asinus solet nutriendus advenire. Meminerat sibi dictum ab angelo: 'Spiritus sanctus superveniet in te, et virtus altissimi obumbrabit tibi' (Lc 1.35). . . . [150] Noverat tunc venisse in carne dominum.

218–9 Bede mentions the memorial to the shepherds as part of the preceding discussion of prophecies fulfilled (Hom. I.7, 145–9):

Audiebat angelicas virtutes . . . apparuisse pastoribus in loco qui a conventu pecorum antiquitus turris gregis vocabatur, et est uno miliario ad orientem Bethleem ubi etiam nunc tria pastorum illorum monumenta in ecclesia monstrantur.

3 ST STEPHEN

The traditional readings for St Stephen's day were Matthew 23.34–9, 'I send you as sheep among wolves', and the account of Stephen's martyrdom from the Acts of the Apostles (Acts 6.8–10 and 7.54–60 seem to be the usual selection). Ælfric takes Acts as his text but gives a fuller account, covering the choosing of the seven deacons, the accusations against Stephen and a summary of his long speech at his trial, as well as the martyrdom itself. His discussion begins with close exegesis of the text (lines 60–98), examining the wording of Stephen's vision of God and its implications, the meaning of his name and his status, and the historical reasons why the witnesses against Stephen played a part in his stoning. Stephen's final prayer for forgiveness for his enemies then leads into a long discussion of true love and forgiveness, at first in terms of the relationship between Stephen and Paul and then in more general terms.

Ælfric drew on at least six sources for his discussion. The major source, providing more than half the material, was a Latin sermon for the occasion which came down to him as St Augustine's (and is so ascribed at line 60) but is now attributed to Caesarius of Arles. Ælfric followed this through from beginning to end, apart from the last thirty lines, with very little omitted and little rearrangement. At various points he interrupts Caesarius's argument to introduce further ideas and discussion. Some of this comes from a sermon for the occasion by Fulgentius. This offers no close exegesis but begins with a series of antitheses between Christ's nativity and Stephen's martyrdom, develops the theme of charity and ends with a contrast between Stephen and Paul. Ælfric draws on it for two rhetorical passages, lines 114–25 and 186–202. Other points come from a similar sermon for the occasion possibly by Augustine (Serm. 382) and from the exposition by Smaragdus, who gives a close commentary on the text from Acts. At two points where Ælfric makes comparisons with other Biblical texts, he seems to have drawn on his memory of sermons by Gregory and Augustine (on the Sermon on the Mount) which he was to use more extensively later when he tackled those other Biblical texts in subsequent homilies. One or two points may be entirely his own, but in this homily he is unusually close to his sources, in wording as well as material.[1]

The sermons by Caesarius and Fulgentius, as well as those by Augustine (Sermon on the Mount) and Gregory, were probably available in Ælfric's copy of Paul the Deacon's homiliary,[2] along with some sermons on the Gospel text and an Augustinian account of miracles associated with Stephen. He may have found the Augustinian sermon 382 in a collection of Augustinian material on Stephen; see below on II.2.

Ælfric's homily is not quite like any of the homilies for the occasion which were known to him, for all his reliance on them for wording and ideas: with his full account from Acts and his additional commentary material he is more directly engaged with the Biblical text than Caesarius or Fulgentius, yet more rhetorical and suasive than Smaragdus; he is not as fully hagiographical as Augustine's account of post-mortem miracles, but does emphasise the historical reality of the martyrdom and lends a degree of hagiographical colouring to the account with such phrases as *se eadiga Stephanus* and *þa ungeleaffullan Iudei*.

Sources and Notes

The following texts are cited below:

1. Augustine, *De Sermone Domini in Monte*, ed. A. Mutzenbecher, CCSL 35 (Turnhout, 1967).
2. Augustine(?), *Sermones*, PL 39, Serm. 382 [=Augustine, *Sermones dubii*], cols. 1684–6.
3. Caesarius of Arles, *Sermones*, ed. G. Morin, CCSL 104 (Turnhout, 1953), Serm. 219 (pp. 866–70) [cited by section and line numbers].
4. Fulgentius, *Sermones*, ed. J. Fraipont, CCSL 91A (Turnhout, 1968), Serm. 3 (pp. 904–9).
5. Gregory the Great, *Homiliae in Evangelia*, PL 76, Hom. 29, cols. 1213–19.
6. Smaragdus, *Collectiones in Evangelia et Epistolas*, PL 102, cols. 35–8.

[1] Cross (1963b, pp. 18–20) identified the use of Augustine's Serm. 382, Gregory and Smaragdus; Caesarius (as Ps-Augustine, Serm. 210) was noted by Förster (1894, pp. 34–5) and Fulgentius by Smetana (1959, pp. 183–4).

[2] See Smetana 1959, pp. 183 and 190, and Pope, p. 165.

1–29 Acts 6.5–15, 7.1:

(5) Et placuit sermo coram omni multitudine et elegerunt Stephanum virum plenum fide et Spiritu Sancto et Philippum et Prochorum et Nicanorem et Timonem et Parmenam et Nicolaum advenam Antiochenum. (6) Hos statuerunt ante conspectum apostolorum et orantes inposuerunt eis manus. (7) Et verbum Dei crescebat et multiplicabatur numerus discipulorum in Hierusalem valde; multa etiam turba sacerdotum oboediebat fidei. (8) Stephanus autem plenus gratia et fortitudine faciebat prodigia et signa magna in populo. (9) Surrexerunt autem quidam de synagoga quae appellatur Libertinorum et Cyrenensium et Alexandrinorum et eorum qui erant a Cilicia et Asia disputantes cum Stephano. (10) Et non poterant resistere sapientiae et Spiritui quo loquebatur. (11) Tunc submiserunt viros qui dicerent se audisse eum dicentem verba blasphemiae in Mosen et Deum. (12) Commoverunt itaque plebem et seniores et scribas et concurrentes rapuerunt eum et adduxerunt in concilium. (13) Et statuerunt testes falsos dicentes homo iste non cessat loqui verba adversus locum sanctum et legem. (14) 'Audivimus enim eum dicentem quoniam Iesus Nazarenus hic destruet locum istum et mutabit traditiones quas tradidit nobis Moses.' (15) Et intuentes eum omnes qui sedebant in concilio viderunt faciem eius tamquam faciem angeli. (7.1) Dixit autem princeps sacerdotum: Si haec ita se habent?

29–41 In suggesting that Stephen's speech to the Jewish elders, for all its hostility, was prompted by a charitable desire to convert them (not from Acts), Ælfric may have been influenced by a comment in the sermon of Fulgentius used later (Serm. 3, 66–70):

Ipsa sancta et indefessa caritas desiderabat orando acquirere quos nequivit monendo convertere. Neque enim, fratres, existimandus est Stephanus tunc inimicos dilexisse cum pro eis oraret et non dilexisse cum eorum incredulitatem arguendo corriperet.

Lines 31–41 summarise Stephen's long account of the history of the Jews at Acts 7.2–50.

41–59 Acts 7.51–59:

(51) 'Dura cervice et incircumcisi cordibus et auribus vos semper Spiritui Sancto resistitis sicut patres vestri et vos. (52) Quem prophetarum non sunt persecuti patres vestri et occiderunt eos qui praenuntiabant de adventu Iusti cuius vos nunc proditores et homicidae fuistis. (53) Qui accepistis legem in dispositionem angelorum et non custodistis.' (54) Audientes autem haec dissecabantur cordibus suis et stridebant dentibus in eum. (55) Cum autem esset plenus Spiritu Sancto intendens in caelum vidit gloriam Dei et Iesum stantem a dextris Dei et ait: ecce video caelos apertos et Filium hominis a dextris stantem Dei. (56) Exclamantes autem voce magna continuerunt aures suas et impetum fecerunt unianimiter in

eum. (57) Et eicientes eum extra civitatem lapidabant et testes deposuerunt vestimenta sua secus pedes adulescentis qui vocabatur Saulus. (58) Et lapidabant Stephanum invocantem et dicentem: Domine Iesu suscipe spiritum meum. (59) Positis autem genibus clamavit voce magna: Domine ne statuas illis hoc peccatum. Et cum hoc dixisset obdormivit.

61–74 In fact from Caesarius, Serm. 219, 1.5–20:
Considerate adtentius, fratres dilectissimi, cum beatus martyr dominum nostrum Iesum Christum ad dexteram dei Patris stare vidisset, cur se filium hominis videre testatus est, et non potius filium dei; cum utique plus delaturus honoris domino videretur, si se dei potius quam hominis filium videre dixisset. Sed certa ratio postulabat, ut hoc ita et ostenderetur in caelo, et praedicaretur in mundo: omne enim Iudaeorum scandalum in hoc erat, cur dominus noster Iesus Christus, qui secundum carnem erat filius hominis, esse etiam dei filius diceretur. Ideo ergo pulchre divina scriptura filium hominis ad dexteram dei patris stare memoravit, ut ad confundendam Iudaeorum incredulitatem ille martyri ostenderetur in caelo, qui a perfidis negabatur in mundo; et illi testimonium caelestis veritas daret, cui fidem terrena impietas derogaret.

The argument that Christ is properly called the son of man because only he is the child of a single human parent (lines 73–4) is a favourite point of Ælfric's, repeated at CH I.40.68–9, II.7.138 and 24.99; neither here nor in those cases is there anything like it in his sources.

74–81 Cf Gregory the Great's homily on the ascension, Hom. 29, PL 76, 1217C:
Sed scitis, fratres, quia sedere iudicantis est, stare vero pugnantis vel adiuvantis. Quia ergo Redemptor noster assumptus in coelum, et nunc omnia iudicat, et ad extremum iudex omnium venit, hunc post assumptionem Marcus sedere describit, quia post Ascensionis suae gloriam iudex in fine videbitur. Stephanus vero in labore certaminis positus stantem vidit, quem adiutorem habuit.

Gregory is here contrasting the Mark text with that from Acts, Ælfric is contrasting the Acts text with the creed, but Gregory is certainly the source for the similar passage in Ælfric's own Ascension homily, CH I.21.224–33. The two Old English passages seem to draw independently on the Latin, though with some wording in common.

81–91 Closely follows Caesarius, Serm. 219, 1.20–33:
Unde licet, iuxta psalmum qui lectus est, 'pretiosa sit in conspectu domini mors sanctorum eius' (Ps 115.15), si quid tamen distare inter martyres potest, praecipuus videtur esse prae omnibus, qui primus est. Nam cum sanctus Stephanus ab apostolis diaconus ordinatus sit, apostolos ipsos beata ac triumphali morte praecessit: ac sic, qui erat inferior ordine, primus factus est passione; et qui erat discipulus gradu, magister coepit esse martyrio. . . . Retribuere enim primus voluit Stephanus martyr domino,

quod cum omni humano genere accepit a domino: mortem enim, quam salvator dignatus est pro omnibus pati, hanc ille primus reddidit salvatori.

91–8 Probably from Smaragdus, *Collectiones*, PL 102:

[36A] Stephanus, *Στέφανος* Graece, Latine coronatus dicitur, qui pulcherrima ratione quod percepturus erat in re, quodam praesagio praeoccuparet in nomine: . . . [37D] Quare testes falsi primum lapidaverunt? Quia lex praeceperat ut quicunque testimonium diceret contra aliquem causae mortis, ipse primum lapidem mitteret in eum, quem primum ore occiderat suo (Deut 17.7).

100–7 Caesarius, Serm. 219, 1.36–46:

Videte magnam et ammirabilem caritatem. In persecutione positus erat, et pro persecutoribus subplicabat; atque in illa lapidum ruina, quando alius oblivisci poterat etiam carissimos suos, ille domino commendabat inimicos. Quid enim dicebat, cum lapidaretur? 'Domine, ne statuas illis hoc in peccatum.' Plus itaque tunc illorum dolebat peccata, quam sua vulnera; plus illorum impietatem, quam suam mortem. Et recte plus: . . . illorum impietatem mors sequebatur aeterna, huius autem mortem vita perpetua.

107–14 That Saul urged the Jews on to stone Stephen is rather more than the Bible says, Acts 7.59: *Saulus autem erat consentiens neci eius.* The subsequent comment perhaps derives from the discussion of charity in Augustine's Serm. 382, §4, PL 39, 1686:

Denique, fratres, ut noveritis quantum valuerit oratio sancti martyris Stephani, recurrite nobiscum ad illum adolescentem nomine Saulum: qui, cum sanctus Stephanus lapidaretur, omnium vestimenta servabat, et tanquam manibus omnium lapidabat. . . . [*Augustine imagines God addressing Saul on the road to Damascus:*] Olim quidem debui perdere te, sed Stephanus servus meus oravit pro te. . . . Nam si martyr Stephanus non sic orasset, Ecclesia Paulum hodie non haberet. Sed ideo de terra erectus est Paulus, quia in terra inclinatus exauditus est Stephanus.

Ælfric's surprising statement that Stephen prayed for Saul (lines 109–10) is presumably a literalisation of Augustine's imagined address.

114–25 The comparison with Saul is developed further using Fulgentius, Serm. 3, 120–34:

Et ecce nunc Paulus cum Stephano laetatur, cum Stephano Christi claritate perfruitur, cum Stephano exsultat, cum Stephano regnat. Quo enim praecessit Stephanus trucidatus lapidibus Pauli, illuc secutus est Paulus, adiutus orationibus Stephani. Quam vero vita, fratres mei, ubi non Paulus de Stephani occisione confunditur, sed Stephanus de Pauli consortio gratulatur, quoniam caritas in utroque laetatur. Caritas quippe in Stephano superavit saevitiam Iudaeorum, caritas in Paulo 'cooperuit multitudinem peccatorum' (1 Petr 4.8), caritas in utroque pariter regnum

> meruit possidere caelorum. Caritas est igitur omnium fons et origo bonorum, munimen egregium, via quae ducit ad caelum. In caritate qui ambulat, nec errare poterit, nec timere. Ipsa dirigit, ipsa protegit, ipsa perducit.

125–30 Probably from an earlier passage in Fulgentius, Serm. 3, 32–9:

> Usque adeo, enim, inter frementes permansit interritus et inter lapidum fuit cruciamenta securus, ut incredulitatem Iudaeorum fidenter argueret, et benignus pro lapidantibus exoraret . . . et occisus aulam caelestis regni vivus et coronatus intraret.

But for the image of hailstones cf the similar passage at Augustine, Serm. 382, §3, PL 39, 1685:

> Qui cum a Iudaeis saxorum grandine caederetur, non solum non comminabatur, sed insuper lapidatoribus suis veniam precabatur.

131–49 Closely follows Caesarius, Serm. 219, 2:

> [2.1–4] Imitemur ergo in aliquo, dilectissimi fratres, tanti magistri fidem, tam praeclari martyris caritatem; diligamus hoc animo in ecclesia fratres nostros, quo ille tunc dilexit inimicos. . . . [2.11–29] Recole quid tibi in evangelio veritas ipsa promiserit, et . . . quale tecum pactum inierit. 'Si enim, inquid, dimiseritis hominibus peccata eorum, dimittet et vobis pater vester caelestis peccata vestra; si autem non dimiseritis, nec pater vester dimittet debita vestra' (Mt 6.14–15). Videtis, fratres, quia cum dei gratia in potestate nostra positum est, qualiter a domino iudicemur. Si, inquid, dimiseritis, dimittetur vobis. . . . Nemo se circumveniat, nemo se seducat: qui vel unum hominem in hoc mundo odio habet, quicquid deo in operibus bonis obtulerit, totum perdit; quia non mentitur Paulus apostolus dicens: 'Si dedero omnes facultates meas in cibos pauperum, et si tradidero corpus meum ut ardeam, caritatem autem non habuero, nihil mihi prodest' (1 Cor 13.3). Quam rem etiam beatus Iohannes confirmat dicens: 'Omnis qui non diligit fratrem suum, manet in morte' et iterum: 'Qui fratrem suum odit, homicida est' (1 Jn 3.14–15).

149–60 Continuing with Caesarius, Serm. 219, 2.29–41:

> Hoc loco fratrem omnem hominem oportet intellegi: omnes enim in Christo fratres sumus. Nemo itaque sine caritate de virginitate praesumat; nemo de elemosinis, nemo de ieiuniis, nemo de orationibus confidat: qui quamdiu inimicitiam in corde tenuerit, neque istis neque aliis quibuslibet bonis operibus placare sibi deum poterit. Sed si vult habere propitium deum, non dedignetur audire consilium bonum; audiat non me, sed ipsum dominum suum: 'Si offeris, inquid, munus tuum ad altare, et ibi recordatus fueris, quia frater tuus habet aliquid adversum te, relinque ibi munus tuum ante altare, et vade, prius reconciliare fratri tuo; et tunc veniens offer munus tuum' (Mt 5.23–4).

160–6 Caesarius offers no commentary on his quotation from Matthew 5. Ælfric's brief explanation shows some general similarity to the sources he used (Augustine and Haymo) when expounding the text at greater length in a later homily, Pope 15, but no very close agreement; rather, the passage in Pope 15 (lines 203–20) seems to depend on this one. Ælfric's definition of *munus* or *lac* (lines 174–5) derives in part from Augustine's *prophetiam sive doctrinam sive orationem sive hymnum sive psalmum, et si quid tale aliud spiritalium donorum animo occurrit* (Augustine, *Sermone Domini*, 1.602–4), whereas the interpretation in Pope 15 is closer to Haymo. Probably the whole passage reflects Ælfric's memory of Augustine and was itself recollected when he came to write Pope 15.

167–72 From Caesarius, Serm. 219, 2.6–11:

> Sed dicit aliquis: non possum diligere inimicum meum, quem cotidie velud hostem patior crudelissimum. O quicumque ille es, adtendis quid tibi fecerit homo, et non consideras quid tu feceris deo; cum enim tu multo graviora in deum peccata commiseris, quare non dimittas homini parum, ut tibi deus dignetur dimittere multum?

172–80 From Caesarius, Serm. 219, 3.1–8:

> Sed dicit aliquis: grandis labor est, inimicos diligere, pro persecutoribus subplicare. Nec nos negamus, fratres: non parvus quidem labor est in hoc saeculo, sed grande erit praemium in futuro. Per amorem enim hominis inimici efficeris amicus dei; immo non solum amicus, sed etiam filius, sicut ipse dominus dicit: 'Diligite inimicos vestros, benefacite iis qui vos oderunt, ut sitis filii patris vestri qui in caelis est' (Mt 5.44–5).

180–85 More loosely based on the next passage in Caesarius, Serm. 219, 3.8–14:

> Si te aliquis potens homo et dives in hoc saeculo vellet adoptivum filium facere, quomodo servires, quas indignitates etiam servorum eius, quae servitia durissima et aliquotiens etiam turpissima sustineres, ut ad caducam et fragilem hereditatem illius pervenires? Quod ergo alius sustinet propter substantiam terrenam, tu sustine propter vitam aeternam.

Caesarius continues with this contrast to the end of his sermon, developing the theme of patience in hostility.

186–94 A reworking of Fulgentius, Serm. 3, 103–14:

> Christi ergo caritate compulsi, et bonos hortamur ut in bono permaneant et malos compellimus ut a malo discedant. . . . Si quis bonus est, imitetur perseverantiam caritatis in Stephano, qui autem malus est, sectetur exemplum conversionis in Paulo. Et qui bonus est, aequitatem usque in finem teneat. . . . Nec bonum hominem praesumptio iustitiae faciat neglegentem, nec malum iniquitatis consideratio faciat desperantem. . . . Bonus timeat ne cadat, malus conetur ut surgat.

195–202 Loosely based on some sentences from the beginning of Fulgentius, Serm. 3, 3–14:

Heri rex noster, trabea carnis indutus, de aula uteri virginalis egrediens visitare dignatus est mundum; hodie miles de tabernaculo corporis exiens, triumphator migravit ad caelum. . . . Ille descendit carne velatus, iste ascendit sanguine laureatus. . . . Gloria in excelsis Deo heri exultantes sancti angeli cantaverunt; hodie Stephanum laetantes in suum consortium susceperunt.

4 ST JOHN THE EVANGELIST

The Gospel reading for this occasion was John 21.21–3, a brief passage which raises the possibility that the evangelist will never meet death. Ælfric would have been familiar with various exegetical discussions, by Bede, Smaragdus and Haymo for instance, which took issue with this implication and argued that what Christ meant by the words 'If I wish him to remain until I come, what is it to you?' was that John would die a peaceful and natural death in contrast to the martyrdom of most of the other apostles. Ælfric makes no reference to the reading, however, but focuses entirely on the saint's life and death, beginning briefly with his role in the Gospels and then covering at length the story as told in the traditional legends: his persecution and exile under Domitian, his return to Ephesus and the miracles which he performed there, the writing of the fourth Gospel and his peaceful departure at the age of ninety-nine. Much of the text is taken up with the story of two rich young brothers who sell everything to follow first philosophy and then Christ but look back regretfully to their former wealth (lines 45–173); it provides an opportunity for an extensive and powerful speech from the apostle on the subject of riches and a vision of the after-life. In implicit response to the Gospel reading and subsequent controversy, Ælfric carefully records at the beginning only that John was 'taken up' to heaven, and in describing St John's mysterious end, a story which seems to have developed in response to the Gospel hint that he might not die, Ælfric says only that he gave his spirit to God and departed 'free of the pain of death', and that there was no trace of his body.

For the opening section Ælfric drew mainly on Bede's homily for the occasion, which is primarily an exposition of the Gospel reading but touches on the saint's life at several points. There is also some use of texts from Haymo's homiliary. But for the subsequent narrative his main source was the Ps-Mellitus Passion of St John (BHL 4320), which tells his story from the persecutions of Domitian to his death. This *Passio* survives in many different versions and it is not easy to be sure which one he used. BHL distinguishes between a short type which begins with the saint's exile to Pathmos and an interpolated type which starts at an earlier point, with a long account of the saint's trial and torment under Domitian. Ælfric was probably using the shorter type, since what few details he gives of the trial and torment (lines 21–5) seem to come from Bede rather than the *Passio*. His version resembled that printed by Fabricius (II.604) in identifying the two brothers who followed the philosopher with the two who repented of giving their wealth to the poor, but Fabricius lacks other details which were evidently in Ælfric's source. Zettel has shown that an unprinted version in a late derivative of the Cotton-Corpus legendary, a manuscript now at Hereford, contains many of the variant readings that Ælfric must have had in his source, and also has a section on the writing of the fourth Gospel which is very similar to his.[1] It seems likely that he found in his version of the legendary a copy of the *Passio* which resembled the Hereford version in many respects, though it had evidently experienced some contamination of its own.[2] He follows the substance of the *Passio* faithfully, condensing occasionally but omitting nothing material, and adding only the occasional explanatory comments, although the apostle's sermon on riches is reorganised with some care and eloquence. In expression his version is generally independent; the rather verbose style of the *Passio* is sharpened, and some pointed antitheses are created.

Sources and Notes

The following texts are cited below:

1. Anon., *Passio Iohannis Apostoli*, in Mombritius 1910, II.55–61. Relevant variant readings are cited (in square brackets) from the versions printed in Fabricius, II.604–23, and G. Heine, *Bibliotheca Anecdotorum* (Leipzig, 1848), pp. 108–17, and from Hereford, Cathedral Library, MS P.7.vi as cited in Zettel 1979.
2. Augustine, *In Iohannis Evangelium Tractatus CXXIV*, ed. R. Willems, CCSL 36 (Turnhout, 1954).
3. Bede, *Homiliae*, ed. D. Hurst, CCSL 122 (Turnhout, 1955), Hom. I.9 (pp. 60–67).
4. Haymo of Auxerre, *Homiliae de Tempore*, PL 118, Hom. 11 and 18, cols. 70–75 and 126–37.

1–20 Cf Bede, Hom. I.9, 55–69:

Diligebat autem eum Iesus . . . prae ceteris quos diligebat familiarius unum quem specialis praerogativa castitatis ampliori dilectione fecerat dignum. . . . Sed hunc prae omnibus diligit qui, virgo electus ab ipso, virgo in aevum permansit. Tradunt namque historiae quod eum de nuptiis volentem nubere vocaverit; et propterea quem a carnali voluptate retraxerat, potiori sui amoris dulcedine donavit. Denique huic moriturus in

[1] Zettel 1979, pp. 158–66, 238–41, 310–11; Zettel 1982, pp. 32–4. Zettel also demonstrated Ælfric's use of Bede's homily, Haymo's homily 18 and Augustine's Tractates on John.

[2] On the apparent attribution of the legend to St Jerome, see my discussion in Godden 1985b, pp. 90–92, and on some of the other points raised here, see my discussion in Godden 1996, pp. 266–9.

cruce matrem suam commendavit, ut virginem virgo servaret, et ipso post mortem ac resurrectionem caelos ascendente non deesset eius genetrici filius, cuius casta vita castis eius tueretur obsequiis.

For the tradition that St John's mother was the Virgin Mary's sister, much cited by Ælfric, see Pope, pp. 217–8. In developing the story that St John was the intended bridegroom at the wedding-feast at Cana (lines 8–15), touched on briefly by Bede here, Ælfric drew on Jn 2.1–11 and possibly the somewhat fuller treatment in Haymo's homily on the Gospel story (Hom. 18, PL 118, 136CD):

Iste sponsus, iuxta litteram, ut quidam tradunt, accipitur Ioannes apostolus; qui cum nuptias fecisset, viso miraculo Domini, relinquens nuptias, virgo eum secutus est, unde et dilectus Domini dicitur.

20–31 The first sentence follows the opening words of the Ps-Mellitus *Passio Iohannis*, Mombritius 1910, II.55.7–8: *Secundam post Neronem Caesarem persecutionem christianorum Domitianus exercuit*. The point is that Domitian was responsible for the next great persecution after Nero, not, as might appear from Ælfric's version, that he immediately followed Nero. The rest is from Bede, Hom. I.9, 125–34:

Et a Domitiano Caesare in ferventis olei dolium missus in ecclesiastica narratur historia, ex quo tamen divina se protegente gratia tam intactus exierit quam fuerat a corruptione concupiscientiae carnalis extraneus. Nec multo post ab eodem principe, propter insuperabilem evangelizandi constantiam, in Phatmos insulam exilio religatur, ubi humano licet destitutus solatio divinae tamen visionis et allocutionis meruit crebra consolatione relevari. Denique ibidem apocalipsin quam ei dominus de statu ecclesiae praesenti vel futuro revelavit manu sua conscripsit.

None of the accounts suggest that the exile was intended to starve the apostle to death (cf 37–8).

31–37 Mainly from the *Passio Iohannis*, Mombritius 1910, II.55.50–56.3:

Domitianus autem, eodem anno quo iussit sanctum Iohannem exilio damnari, a senatu romano interfectus est. Et . . . ex totius senatus consulto hoc definitum est, ut quidquid Domitianus fieri voluit cassaretur. Hinc factum est, ut sanctus Iohannes, qui voluntate Domitiani deportatus cum iniuria fuerat, cum honore ad Ephesum remearet. Occurrit autem illi omnis populus virorum ac mulierum, omnes exultantes et dicentes: 'Benedictus qui venit in nomine domini.'

The reference to Nerva's role in the apostle's return (lines 33–4) is from Bede, Hom. I.9, 227–9: *Sed dum ipse post occisionem Domitiani permittente pio principe Nerva rediret Ephesum* (or possibly from Haymo's adaptation, cited below under 174–93).

38–45 *Passio Iohannis*, Mombritius 1910, II.56.3–13:

Cum autem ingrederetur civitatem, Drusiana quae semper eum secuta fuerat . . . efferebatur. Tunc sanctus Iohannes videns flaentes pauperes et parentes ac viduas simul cum orphanis clamantes . . . iussit deponi feretrum . . . et voce clara ait: 'Dominus meus Iesus christus excitet te, Drusiana. Surge, et pedibus tuis revertere domum tuam, et para mihi refectionem [in domo tua].' Ad hanc vocem surrexit, et coepit ire sollicita de iussione apostoli ut videretur ipsi Drusianae quia non de morte sed de somno excitasset eam.

Ælfric's identification of Drusiana as a widow seems not to come from the *Vita*; but it may be a genuine tradition: Ps-Isidore's *Liber de Ortu et Obitu Patrum* refers to John's resurrection of a widow (PL 83, 1288C).

45–58 The substance is from the *Passio Iohannis*, Mombritius 1910, II.56.15–22:

Altera die Craton philosophus in foro proposuerat de contemptu mundi huiusmodi spectaculum, ut duo iuvenes fratres ditissimi quos fecerat distracto patrimonio suo gemmas emere singulas easdem in conspectu omnium frangerent populorum. Quas cum frangerent pueri contigit transitum habere apostolum et convocans ad se philosophum ait: 'Stultus est iste mundi contemptus qui hominum ore laudatur sed condemnatur divino iudicio. Sicut vana medicina est ex qua non curantur aegretudines corporum, ita vana doctrina est ex qua non vicia curantur animarum et morum.'

Ælfric ascribes the initiative to the brothers rather than the philosopher. More significantly, he offers an explanation of this form of contempt for the world that links it to the pursuit of wisdom and goes into some rather specific detail (lines 49–53). He gives a very similar explanation at CH I.27.142–50, apparently prompted by a brief comment in Smaragdus but evidently drawing on wider reading in Jerome, perhaps the *Adversus Iovinianum* (see the notes to I.27). The original reference in Jerome was probably to the philosopher Crates, perhaps to be identified with the Craton of the *Passio Iohannis*. But since Ælfric's version of the *Passio* evidently had the reading *Graton* and his source for I.27 read *Socrates* rather than *Crates*, the identification was not obvious. His interest in the practice of classical philosophers remains striking.

58–64 *Passio Iohannis*, Mombritius 1910, II.56.22–9:

'Magister itaque meus iuvenem cupientem ad vitam aeternam attingere his verbis instruxit, quibus diceret ut si vellet perfectus esse, venderet omnia sua et daret pauperibus quo facto thesaurum in caelis acquireret, et vitam quae finem non habet inveniret.'[*Cf Mt 19.16–21.*] Cui Craton dixit: '. . . Si vere est deus magister tuus et vult hoc fieri ut pauperibus errogetur census pretii harum duarum gemmarum, facias redintegrari, ut quod ego ad famam hominum, tu facias ad gloriam eius fieri.'

64–69 Loosely based on the *Passio Iohannis*, Mombritius 1910, II.56.29–37:

Tunc beatus Iohannes colligens fragmenta gemmarum in manu sua, elevavit oculos ad caelum et dixit: 'Domine Iesu christe, cui nihil impossibile est, qui fractum mundum per lignum crucis tuae in tuis

> fidelibus restaurasti . . . adesto nunc super istos lapides pretiosos . . . tu domine per manus angelorum tuorum modo recupera, ut preti[o] earum in misericordiae usus explet[o] facias credentes pervenire ad tuum imperium.

Ælfric's *tacen* (line 67) presumably reflects a variant reading *signum* for *lignum*.

70–76 Closely follows the *Passio Iohannis*, Mombritius 1910, II.56.39–44:

> Ita sunt sollidata fragmenta gemmarum, ut nec signum aliquod de eo quod fractae fuerant remaneret. Hic philosophus Craton simul cum iuvenibus et cum universis discipulis suis pedibus eius advolutus credidit et baptizatus est, coepitque fidem domini nostri Iesu Christi publice praedicare. Tunc vero illi duo fratres vaenundantes gemmas quas vendito patrimonio suo emerant, pauperibus tradiderunt, coepitque infinita turba credentium adhaerere apostolo.

The *Passio*, as represented by Mombritius and all other versions that I have seen, except that of Fabricius, here introduces a second pair of brothers, from Ephesus, who sell their patrimony and give the proceeds to the poor in imitation of the first two, and these are the subject of the following story, given in lines 77–173. Ælfric was presumably following a version which did not distinguish the two pairs. The names Atticus and Eugenius (cf 74) are first mentioned in the source in the passage corresponding to lines 139–45.

77–87 *Passio Iohannis*, Mombritius 1910, II.56.47–55:

> Contigit ut, intrantes urbem Pergamum, videre servos suos sericis indutos vestibus procedentes et in gloria saeculari fulgentes. Et hinc factum est ut, sagittis diaboli percussi, tristes efficerentur quod se in uno pallio viderent egentes, suos vero servos potentissimos atque fulgentes. Sed hos dolos diaboli intelligens apostolus ait: 'Video vos et animos vestros mutasse et vultus propter hoc, quod doctrinam domini mei secuti omnia quae habere potuistis pauperibus errogastis. . . . Deferte mihi virgas rectas in singulis fascibus.' Quod ubi fecissent, [invocato nomine domini] conversae sunt in aurum.

Ælfric apparently adds the explanation about Pergamum in 77–8, and the striking opposition of colours at 87.

88–95 *Passio Iohannis*, Mombritius 1910, II.56.55–57.4:

> Iterum dixit eis: 'Deferte mihi lapides minutos a littore maris'; quod cum fecissent, [invocata maiestate domini] conversi sunt in gemmas. Tunc dicit eis apostolus: 'Per septem dies ite per aurifices et gemmarios et dum probaveritis verum aurum et veras gemmas, nuntiate mihi.' Euntes autem ambo post septem dies reversi sunt ad apostolum dicentes: 'Domine omnium aurificum officinas circuivimus, et omnes dixerunt tam purum et optimum se nunquam vidisse aurum; sed et [gemmarii] eadem dixerunt, tam optimos lapides et pretiosos nunquam vidisse.

The redness of the gold (line 93) is again from Ælfric.

95–103 (The sentence ends at *forhogiað*.) *Passio Iohannis*, Mombritius 1910, II.57.4–12:

Dicit eis sanctus Iohannes: 'Ite et redimite vobis terras quas vendidistis, [quia celorum predia perdidistis]. Emite vobis sericas vestes ut pro tempore fulgeatis sicut rosa, quae dum odorem pariter et ruborem ostendit repente marcescit. . . . Estote floridi ut marcescatis. Estote divites temporaliter, ut in perpetuum mendicetis. Nunquid valet manus domini ut faciat servos suos divitiis affluentes et incomparabiliter splendentes. Sed certamen statuit animarum ut credant se aeternas habituros divitias qui pro eius amore omnes temporales opes habere noluerint.'

In the *Passio* St John now goes on to tell the story of the rich man and Lazarus (from Lc 16.19–31) and of various miracles performed by Christ and himself.

103–8 *Passio Iohannis*, Mombritius 1910, II.57.34–8:

Denique vos ipsi quando ad infirmos intrastis invocato nomine Christi salvati sunt. Fugastis daemonia et caecatis etiam lumina reddidistis. Ecce ablata est haec gratia a vobis, et facti estis miseri, qui eratis fortes et magni. Sed et cum tantus timor vester esset in daemoniis ut iussu vestro homines relinquerent, modo vos timetis daemonia.

109–21 From *Passio Iohannis*, Mombritius 1910, II.57.38–54, but this part of St John's long speech is radically rearranged by Ælfric:

[57.45–54] Nudos nos fuderunt in lucem partus mulierum egentes cibo amictu et poculo, nudos recipiet terra quos edidit. In commune possidemus caeli divitias. Splendor solis diviti et pauperi aequalis est; similiter lunae lumen et syderum. Aeris quoque temperies et pluviarum guttae, ecclesiae ianua, fontis sanctificatio, remissio peccatorum et participatio altaris, esca corporis et sanguinis sancti et chrismatis unctio et gratia largitoris, visitatio domini. . . . Sed miser et infelix homo qui vult plus habere aliquid quam sufficit, cum nec possit securus uti quod sufficit. [57.41–45] Nam cum sit unus venter et sint reposita tanta quae mille ventribus satis sunt; ut cum sit unum corpus et sunt tantae vestes quae mille hominum corporibus praebere valeant indumenta; utique quod uti non potest custoditur, omnino nescitur dicente spiritu sancto per prophetam: 'Sane conturbabitur omnis homo qui thesaurizat et ignorat cui congreget ea' (Ps 38.7). [57.38–41] Amator enim pecuniae servus est Mammonae. . . . Ipsi autem amatores mundi non possident divitias sed ipsi a divitiis possidentur.'

122–8 *Passio Iohannis*, Mombritius 1910, II.57.54–58.7, but much abridged and adapted:

Nascuntur enim ei calores febrium, rigores frigorum dolores varii in cunctis corporum membris. Et neque esca cibari potest neque poculo satiari, ut cognoscat aviditas non sibi pecunias pro futuras quae reposite custodibus sollicitudinem [diurnam et nocturnam] incutiunt. . . . Nam . . .

dum possessio colitur . . . dum solvunt fiscalia, dum aedificant promptuaria . . . dum minus potentes nudare contendunt . . . dum blandimento carnis assentiunt, dum ludere tabulis et spectaculis non perhorrescunt . . . subito exeunt de isto [saeculo] nudi [sola] secum peccata portantes, pro quibus poenas passuri sunt perpetuas.

129–44 *Passio Iohannis*, Mombritius 1910, II.58.7–20:
Haec dicente sancto Iohanne, ecce efferebatur iuvenis a matre vidua, qui triginta dies habebat quod uxorem acceperat. Venientes turbae quae exequias faciebant simul cum matre eius vidua, iactaverunt se ad pedes eius omnes pariter gemitum mugitumque mittentes, rogabantque ut in nomine dei sui sicut Drusianam sic et hunc iuvenem suscitaret. Tantus omnium extitit flaetus ut etiam ipse sanctus apostolus vix a flaetu et lachrymis se temperaret. Itaque prosternens se in oratione, diutissime flevit et exurgens ab oratione expandit manus suas ad caelum et tacitam precem diutissime fudit. Hoc cum fecisset tertio iussit solvi involutum corpus et ait: 'O iuvenis [Stactee] qui amore carnis tuae ductus cito animam misisti. O iuvenis qui nescisti creatorem tuum, nescisti salvatorem [hominum], nescisti amicum verum, et ideo hostem pessimum incurristi. Pro ignorantia tua lachrymas domino meo simul et preces fudi, ut exurgas a mortis vinculo resolutus. Et istis duobus Attico et Eugenio annuncies quantam gloriam amiserunt et quantam incurrerint poenam.'

144–56 *Passio Iohannis*, Mombritius 1910, II.58.20–31:
Tunc exurgens Stacteus adoravit apostolum et coepit increpare discipulos eius dicens: 'Vidi angelos vestros flaentes et satanae angelos in vestra deiectione gratulantes. Iam regnum paratum vobis et ex corruscantibus gemmis zetas instructas plenas gaudiis, plenas epulis . . . plenas lumine aeterno . . . quas amisistis incauti, et acquisistis loca tenebrarum plena draconibus, plena stridentibus flammis, plena cruciatibus et [incomparabilibus] tormentis, . . . in quibus die noctuque non cessat mugitus et hululatus et luctus. Iam nihil aliud vobis superest nisi ut rogetis apostolum domini ut sicut me resuscitavit ad vitam, ita quoque vos resuscitet ab interitu ad salutem et animas vestras, quae iam de libro vitae deletae sunt, [reducat ad domini gratiam].'

157–69 *Passio Iohannis*, Mombritius 1910, II.58.31–43:
Tunc qui resuscitatus fuerat prosternens se cum omni populo et Attico et Eugenio omnes pariter orabant apostolum ut intercederet pro his apud dominum; quibus sanctus apostolus hoc dedit in responsis ut per triginta dies poenitentiam offerrent in quo spatio hoc maxime precarentur ut virgae aureae ad suam naturam redirent; similiter et lapides ad suam vilitatem qua antea fuerant remearent. Factum est autem ut triginta dierum transacto spatio cum neque virgae mutarentur in lignum neque gemmae mutarentur in petras, venientes Atticus et Eugenius dixerunt apostolo: 'Semper

misericordiam docuisti . . . et praecepisti ut homo homini indulgeret. . . . Et si homo homini indulgere vult quanto magis deus ipse cum sit deus homini indulget et parcit. . . . qui oculis concupiscentibus mundum dereliquimus, oculis flentibus poeniteamus.'

169–73 *Passio Iohannis*, Mombritius 1910, II.58.44–55 (omitting St John's speech on God's joy over the penitent sinner):

Tunc beatus Iohannes . . . dixit: 'Ite et reportate virgas ad sylvam unde eas assumpsistis, quoniam ad suam sunt naturam reversae, et lapides [reportate ad litora maris], quoniam petrae effecti sunt ut fuerunt.' Quod cum fuisset impletum, receperunt gratiam quam amiserant ita ut etiam fugarent daemones sicut et prius, infirmos curarent, [et cecos illuminarent] et virtutes multas dominus per eos faceret.

174–93 For the opening words of this passage cf the next sentence in the *Passio Iohannis*, Mombritius 1910, II.58.55–7: *Cum autem omnis civitas Ephesiorum immo omnes provinciae Asiae Iohannem excollerent et praedicarent, accidit ut. . . .* But the rest of Ælfric's account of the writing of the fourth Gospel seems to come, directly or not, from Haymo's homily 11, for St John's day (PL 118, 75AB):

Postea vero, cum permittente Nerva piissimo rege, de exsilio reversus Ephesi moraretur, rogatus dicitur ab omnibus Asiae episcopis et presbyteris, quia iam in tribus evangelistarum libris de humanitate Salvatoris satis scriptum habebant, ut eis de divinitate sermonem faceret, atque ad memoriam futurorum scriptum relinqueret, maxime ad convincendam illorum haeresim, qui dicebat Christum ante Mariam non fuisse: quod primum se negavit facturum, sed illis in prece perseverantibus, non aliter acquievit, nisi omnes triduano ieiunio Dominum in commune precarentur. Quod cum fecissent, tanta gratia Spiritus sancti dicitur fuisse repletus, ut usque ad contemplandam patris et filii eiusdemque spiritus sancti divinitatem mente raperetur, et de aeternae vitae purissimo fonte potaret, quod nobis sitientibus propinaret. Unde et evangelii sui tale est exordium: 'In principio erat Verbum, et Verbum erat apud Deum, et Deus erat Verbum; [hoc erat in principio apud Deum. Omnia per ipsum facta sunt; et sine ipso factum est nihil[3]]' et sic per totum evangelii sui textum, pauca de humanis actibus interponens, sufficienter de divinitate Salvatoris scripta reliquit.

Most of this passage from Haymo appears as an interpolation in the Hereford MS of the *Passio*, immediately before the sentence beginning 'Cum autem omnis civitas' cited above, but without the closing words from 'et sic' onwards.[4] Possibly Ælfric had a version of the *Passio* with a similar, but longer, interpolation. Haymo is here rewriting Bede's homily I.9, and Bede is in turn

[3] Apparently extended by Ælfric.

[4] Noted by Zettel (1979), but without noting the derivation from Haymo.

rewriting Jerome's preface to his commentary on Matthew, but Haymo is the closest of the four versions. The reference to surpassing the angels and all creation at 183–4 perhaps draws ultimately on Augustine, *Tract.*, 1.5.7–9:

> Transcenderat omnes choros et legiones angelorum. Nisi enim transcenderet ista omnia quae creata sunt, non perveniret ad eum per quem facta sunt omnia.

194–203 *Passio Iohannis*, Mombritius 1910, II.58.57–59.6 (continuing the sentence cited above for 174–5):

> Accidit ut cultores idolorum excitarent seditionem. Ex quo factum est ut Iohannem traherent ad templum Dianae et urgerent eum ut ei faeditatem sacrifitiorum offerret. Tunc beatus Iohannes ait: 'Ducam vos omnes ad ecclesiam domini mei Iesu Christi et invocantes nomen Dianae vestrae facite cadere ecclesiam eius et consentiam vobis. Si autem hoc facere non potestis, ego invocabo nomen domini mei Iesu Christi, et faciam cadere templum hoc, et comminuam idolum vestrum; quod cum factum fuerit, iustum vobis videri debet ut relicta supersticione illius rei quae a deo victa est et confracta ad ipsum convertamini.'

Ælfric substitutes 'gods' for Diana throughout this episode.

203–11 *Passio Iohannis*, Mombritius 1910, II.59.6–16:

> Ad hanc vocem conticuit populus . . . pars maxima consensum praestitit. Quare beatus Iohannes blandis alloquiis orabat populum ut a templo longe se faceret . . . voce clara coram omnibus dixit: 'Ut sciat haec omnis turba quia idolum hoc Dianae daemonium est et non deus, corruat cum omnibus manufactis idolis quae coluntur in eo.' . . . Continuo . . . omnia simul cum templo suo idola corruerunt ut efficerentur sicut pulvis. . . . Conversi sunt eodem die ad duodecim millia gentium praeter parvulos et mulieres, et baptismatis sancti consecrati sunt virtute.

(Note that *deofulgyldum* at 206 is from *deofulgyld* 'pagan god or idol' rather than *deofulgylda* 'pagan worshipper or priest'.)

212–9 *Passio Iohannis*, Mombritius 1910, II.59.16–25:

> Aristodemus vero qui erat pontifex idolorum repletus spiritu nequissimo sedicionem excitavit. . . . Aristodemus ait: 'Si vis ut credam deo tuo, dabo tibi venenum bibere; quod cum biberis si non fueris mortuus, apparebit verum esse deum tuum.' Cui apostolus ait: 'Venenum si dederis mihi bibere; invocato nomine dei mei non poterit mihi nocere.' Cui Aristodemus: 'Prius est ut videas bibentes et statim morientes, ut vel sic possit cor tuum ab hoc poculo formidare.' Cui beatus Iohannes ait: 'Iam dixi tibi, tu paratus esto credere in dominum Iesum christum dum me videris post veneni poculum sanum.'

219–31 *Passio Iohannis*, Mombritius 1910, II.59.25–33, 42–9 (condensed and omitting St John's prayer):

Perrexit Aristodemus ad proconsulem et petiit ab eo duos viros qui pro suis sceleribus erant decollandi. Et statuens eos in medio foro coram omni populo in conspectu apostoli, fecit bibere venenum; qui mox ut biberunt spiritum exhallarunt. Tunc dicit Aristodemus: 'Audi me Iohannes . . . accipe et bibe. . . . Beatus Iohannes . . . accepit calicem et signaculum crucis faciens in eo . . . [os suum et] totum semetipsum armavit signo crucis et bibit totum quod erat in calice. . . . Contendentes populus per tres horas Iohannem habere vultum hillarem et nulla penitus signa palloris aut trepidationis habentem, clamare coeperunt: 'Unus deus verus est quem colit Iohannes.' Aristodemus . . . conversus ad Iohannem dixit: 'Est mihi adhuc dubietas. Si hos qui hoc veneno mortui sunt excitaveris, emundabitur ab omni dubietate mens mea.'

Ælfric then omits the arguments of St John, Aristodemus and the people.

231–43 *Passio Iohannis*, Mombritius 1910, II.60.4–9, 16–21:

Apostolus: 'Vade et mitte eam [= *tunicam*] super corpora defunctorum et dices ita: "Apostolus domini nostri Iesu christi misit me, ut in nomine eius exurgatis ut cognoscant omnes quia vita et mors famulantur domino meo Iesu christo."' At cum hoc fecisset Aristodemus et vidisset eos exurgere, adorans Iohannem festinavit et perrexit ad proconsulem, coepitque clamosa voce dicere. . . . [*The ensuing dialogue with the proconsul is summed up at 238–9.*] Tunc venientes simul prostraverunt se ad pedes apostoli indulgentiam flagitantes . . . praecepit eis unius hebdomados ieiunium agere, quo expleto baptizavit eos. Qui cum baptizati essent cum universa parentela sua et affinitate et famulis suis, fregerunt omnia simulacra et fabricaverunt basilicam in nomine sancti Iohannis in qua ipse sanctus Iohannes assumptus est hoc ordine.

244–53 *Passio Iohannis*, Mombritius 1910, II.60.21–8:

Cum esset annorum nonaginta et [novem] apparuit ei dominus Iesus Christus cum discipulis suis et dixit ei: 'Veni ad me, quia tempus est ut epuleris in convivio meo cum fratribus tuis.' Surgens autem Iohannes coepit ire, sed dominus dixit ei: 'Dominica resurrectionis meae die qui post quinque dies futurus est, ita venies ad me.' Et cum haec dixisset, caelo receptus est. Veniente itaque dominica convenit universa multitudo in ecclesiam . . . et a primo pullorum cantu agens mysteria dei omnem populum usque ad horam diei tertiam allocutus est.

Some versions have a speech here, ending: *Me enim Dominus iam de hoc mundo vocare dignatur* (cf 252–3, and the apparatus in Mombritius 1910, II.667).

253–60 As *Passio Iohannis*, Mombritius 1910, II.60.28–37, but condensed:

Post haec iuxta altare iussit foveam fieri quadratam et terram eius foras ecclesiam proiici, et descendens in eam expandit manus suas ad dominum dicens: 'Invitatus ad convivium tuum venio gratias agens, quia me dignatus es domine Iesu Christe ad tuas epulas invitare, sciens quod ex toto corde desiderabam te. . . . Quotiens te rogavi ut advenirem et dixisti: expecta ut populum liberes crediturum mihi. Et custodisti corpus meum ab omni pollutione et animam meam semper illuminasti et non dereliquisti me.'

260–70 As *Passio Iohannis*, Mombritius 1910, II.60.37–45, but evidently using a text with much variation from Mombritius's version:

Et posuisti in ore meo verbum veritatis . . . et scripsi ea opera quae audivi auribus meis ex ore tuo, [et conspexi oculis meis]. Et nunc domine commendo tibi filios tuos quos tibi ecclesia tua virgo vera mater per aquam et spiritum sanctum regeneravit. Suscipe me ut cum fratribus meis sim, cum quibus veniens invitasti me. Aperi mihi pulsanti ianuam vitae. Principes tenebrarum non occurrant mihi. . . . Tu es Christus filius dei vivi, [qui praecepto patris tui mundum salvasti, qui et Spiritum sanctum nobis destinare dignatus es. . . . Per eundum spiritum tibi gratiam referimus per infinita secula secularum].

271–82 As *Passio Iohannis*, Mombritius 1910, II.60.46–50:

Lux tanta apparuit super tumulum per unam fere horam, ut nullus eius sustineret aspectus [et statim emisit spiritum. Et collectus est ad patres suos in senectute bona, tam extraneus a dolore mortis, quam a corruptione carnis invenitur alienus]. Postea vero inventa est et fovea illa plena nihil aliud in se habens nisi mana quod usque hodie gignit locus ille. Et fiunt virtutes orationum eius et ab omnibus infirmitatibus et periculis liberantur omnes.

The passage in brackets is taken from the Hereford version of the *Passio*, but the part from *Et collectus* . . . also appears, with a few differences, in Haymo's homily (Hom. 11, PL 118, 73C), and in a form slightly closer to Ælfric, with *liber* for *extraneus*, in Bede's homily (Hom. I.9, 142–3). The interpolation in the *Passio* here shows some sensitivity on the question of the apostle's death. Ælfric adds the explanation of manna at 277–9, and the characteristic attribution of the miracles at the tomb to God's work and the apostle's intercession (lines 282–3).

5 INNOCENTS

Ælfric's text is from Matthew 2, covering the visit of the magi to the infant Christ and the ensuing massacre of the innocents by Herod, the latter's death and the return of the holy family to Nazareth. The visit of the magi, Matthew 2.1–12, forms the reading for Epiphany and is dealt with again in more detail in homily 7, but is included here as a necessary prelude to the reading for Innocents' Day, verses 13–23. The commentaries on Matthew 2 best known to Ælfric (Bede, Smaragdus, Haymo) developed a detailed allegorical and doctrinal interpretation, and he used some of this material in his subsequent Epiphany homily, but here he rigorously excludes such reading, apart from the one comment on Rachel (lines 117–22) and the point of doctrine touched on at 112–6. Instead he elaborates the historical aspect of the story: Herod's background, the summons to Rome which delayed his search for the Christ-child, his motives and those of Christ, his long drawn-out and painful death. At the heart of his discussion, however, comes a highly rhetorical celebration of the martyred innocents (lines 93–112). What seems particularly to have interested Ælfric and governed his selection of material is the contrast between the mundane view of the events, in which the tyrant Herod uses his power and cunning to protect himself from rivals, and the higher and longer-term perspective of the divine plan, in which Herod's murder of the innocents serves them better than any favours he could have done them, the flights to which his persecution drives the holy family serve only to fulfil ancient prophecies of the Messiah, and even his desperate murder of the Jewish elders to accompany him in death serves the cause of divine retribution.

Ælfric drew on at least seven sources for this homily, apart from the Bible: Haymo's homilies for Innocents and Epiphany; the *Historia Ecclesiastica* of Rufinus; Caesarius of Arles' Serm. 222; Serm. 152 of Petrus Chrysologus; Serm. 4 from the collection of Eusebius Gallicanus (or to be more precise, a passage which occurs in that sermon but also in at least two Ps-Augustinian sermons on the innocents[1]); and Bede's sermon on the innocents.[2] Haymo's homilies, supplemented by Rufinus and Eusebius Gallicanus, provided most of the historical information and explanation. The much more rhetorical passage on the martyrdom of the innocents and their mothers interweaves sentences from Caesarius, Chrysologus and Eusebius Gallicanus. And Bede's sermon provided the comment on Rachel and possibly a detail in the closing lines. The range of reading is unusually wide for a single homily, but the pieces by Caesarius, Chrysologus and Bede all occur in Paul the Deacon's homiliary for the occasion and both Haymo and Rufinus were authors well known to Ælfric.

Sources and Notes

The following texts are cited below:

1. Bede, *Homiliae*, ed. D. Hurst, CCSL 122 (Turnhout, 1955), Hom. I.10 (pp. 68–72).
2. Caesarius of Arles, *Sermones*, ed. G. Morin, CCSL 104 (Turnhout, 1953), Serm. 222 (pp. 877–81) [cited by section and line numbers].

[1] Serm. 218, PL 39, cols. 2149–50, at 2150, and the Sermo de SS Innocentibus, PLS 3, cols. 705–9, at 705–6. Since Ælfric's text shows no use of the surrounding material in any of these three sermons, he could have found the passage in any one of them or in some other context.

[2] See Förster 1894, pp. 44 and 53, Smetana 1959, pp. 184–5, and Smetana 1961, pp. 460–1, and Cross, who gives a full discussion of sources (Cross 1969, pp. 137–47); but note that Caesarius and Eusebius are cited by Smetana and Cross as Ps-Augustine, Serm. 220 and 218, respectively.

3. Eusebius Gallicanus, *Collectio Homiliarum*, ed. F. Glorie, CCSL 101 (Turnhout, 1970), Hom. 4 (pp. 45–53).
4. Haymo of Auxerre, *Homiliae de Tempore*, PL 118, Hom. 12 and 15, cols. 75–82 and 107–15.
5. Julian of Toledo, *Prognosticon Futuri Saeculi*, ed. J. Hillgarth, CCSL 115 (Turnhout, 1976), pp. 11–126.
6. Petrus Chrysologus, *Collectio Sermonum*, ed. A. Olivar, CCSL 24B (Turnhout, 1982), Serm. 152 (pp. 949–55).
7. Rufinus, *Historia Ecclesiastica*, ed. T. Mommsen, in *Eusebius Werke*, ed. E. Klostermann, vol. 2, 2 parts, GCS 9.1 and 9.2 (Leipzig, 1903–8).

1–39 A close rendering of Mt 2.1–15:

> (1) Cum ergo natus esset Iesus in Bethleem Iudaeae in diebus Herodis regis, ecce magi ab oriente venerunt Hierosolymam, (2) dicentes: ubi est qui natus est rex Iudaeorum? Vidimus enim stellam eius in oriente et venimus adorare eum. (3) Audiens autem Herodes rex turbatus est et omnis Hierosolyma cum illo. (4) Et congregans omnes principes sacerdotum et scribas populi sciscitabatur ab eis ubi Christus nasceretur. (5) At illi dixerunt ei in Bethleem Iudaeae; sic enim scriptum est per prophetam: (6) et tu Bethleem terra Iuda nequaquam minima es in principibus Iuda; ex te enim exiet dux qui reget populum meum Israhel. (7) Tunc Herodes clam vocatis magis diligenter didicit ab eis tempus stellae quae apparuit eis. (8) Et mittens illos in Bethleem dixit: ite et interrogate diligenter de puero et cum inveneritis renuntiate mihi ut et ego veniens adorem eum. (9) Qui cum audissent regem abierunt et ecce stella quam viderant in oriente antecedebat eos usque dum veniens staret supra ubi erat puer. (10) Videntes autem stellam gavisi sunt gaudio magno valde. (11) Et intrantes domum invenerunt puerum cum Maria matre eius et procidentes adoraverunt eum; et apertis thesauris suis obtulerunt ei munera aurum, tus et murram. (12) Et responso accepto in somnis ne redirent ad Herodem, per aliam viam reversi sunt in regionem suam. (13) Qui cum recessissent ecce angelus Domini apparuit in somnis Ioseph dicens: surge et accipe puerum et matrem eius et fuge in Aegyptum et esto ibi usque dum dicam tibi. Futurum est enim ut Herodes quaerat puerum ad perdendum eum. (14) Qui consurgens accepit puerum et matrem eius nocte et recessit in Aegyptum. (15) Et erat ibi usque ad obitum Herodis, ut adimpleretur quod dictum est a Domino per prophetam dicentem: ex Aegypto vocavi filium meum.

Ælfric adds the identification of Micheas at line 17, the detail *gesthuse* at 26 and the reference to God at 30.

40–45 Closely based on Haymo's sermon on the innocents (Hom. 12, PL 118, 78CD):

> Tradunt historiae Iosephi et Hegesippi, quod eo tempore quando natum regem Iudaeorum a magis audierat, accusantibus adversariis, vocatus ab

imperatore, Romam venit: et cum venisset ante Caesarem et universum senatum, ut erat callidus animo et prudens eloquio, potentissime et honestissime purgavit quaecunque sibi fuerant obiecta. Cumque aliter ab inimicis putaretur, maiori gloria ab imperatore est exaltatus, in tantum ut ei regium diadema tribueret, et regnandi potestatem in Iudaea confirmaret: et cum post duos annos in magna gloria in Iudaeam esset reversus. . . .

Haymo uses this episode to explain the Gospel report that Herod directed his attack on children of two years and less, not just the new-born.

46–53 Mt 2.16–18:

(16) Tunc Herodes, videns quoniam inlusus esset a magis, iratus est valde et mittens occidit omnes pueros qui erant in Bethleem et in omnibus finibus eius a bimatu et infra, secundum tempus quod exquisierat a magis. (17) Tunc adimpletum est quod dictum est per Hieremiam prophetam dicentem: (18) vox in Rama audita est ploratus et ululatus multus, Rachel plorans filios suos et noluit consolari quia non sunt.

Ælfric glosses *infra* as *to anre nihte*, no doubt at the prompting of Haymo (Hom. 12, PL 118, 78C): *Unde 'a bimatu et infra' pueros iussit occidere, hoc est, a puero duorum annorum, usque ad puerum unius noctis*. The rendering of *in rama* as *on heannysse* (line 52) perhaps comes from Haymo too (Hom. 12, PL 118, 79D), drawing in turn on Jerome's commentary on Matthew, but it appears also in the *OE Gospels* and the Rushworth gloss, and was presumably well established anyway.

54–62 Ælfric here draws out the implications of Haymo's historical details and the church calendar for the chronology of the story, presumably to explain why the massacre is commemorated before the visit of the Magi at Epiphany.

62–9 Based on Haymo's homily for Epiphany (Hom. 15, PL 118):

[107D-8A] Recte etiam in diebus Herodis nasci voluit, ut impleretur prophetia Iacob, dicentis: 'Non auferetur sceptrum de Iuda, nec dux de femoribus eius, donec veniat qui mittendus est, et ipse erit exspectatio gentium' (Gen 49.10). . . . [*Haymo then gives a detailed account of Herod's background, describing the fraudulent way in which he achieved power.*] [108D-9A] Quia enim deficientibus principibus ex Iuda, alienus et extraneus atque falsus regnum Iudaeorum arripuerat, instabat tempus quo verus Rex nasceretur, cuius tertia decima die nativitatis magi ab oriente venerunt Hierosolymam. . . . [111C] Herodes (ut diximus), qui fraudulenter et callide regnum obtinebat Iudaeorum, mox ut regem Iudaeorum audivit natum, metuens successorem, conturbatus est animo.

69–81 The references to Herod's motives are similar in phrasing to points in Haymo's two homilies:

[Hom. 15, PL 118, 112D-3A] Quod scilicet ideo fecit, ut si magi ad eum non redirent, quod postea contigit . . . [Hom. 12, PL 118, 78C] Putabat enim, quod si omnes pueri occiderentur, unus quem quaerebat evadere non posset, non aestimans, infelix, quia 'non est consilium, non est sapientia, non est prudentia contra Deum' (Prov 21.30). . . . [Hom.15, PL 118, 113A] In eadem calliditate qua Herodes fraudulenter regnum Iudaeorum arripuerat, etiam in Domini nece perseveravit, promittens se adorare, quem disponebat occidere.

81–6 From Eusebius Gallicanus, Serm. 4, 86–97:

Nihil ergo proficis ferocissimae impietatis audacia: potes martyres facere, Christum non potes invenire. . . . Non ad hoc venerat Christus: ut alienam invaderet gloriam, sed ut suam donaret; nec ut regnum terrestre praeriperet, sed ut caeleste conferret. . . . Non, inquam, ad hoc venerat: ut constitueretur super sceptra magnificus, sed ut crucifigeretur illusus.

But with some use too of Haymo's recasting of this (Hom. 15, PL 118, 111CD): *Non intelligens quia ille non venerat ut tolleret regnum terrenum, sed ut credentibus conferret aeternum.*

86–92 Cf Haymo, Hom. 12, PL 118, 76CD:

Fugit autem puer Iesus ante persecutionem Herodis, non quod mortem timeret, qui pro hominibus mori venerat, sed ut tempore congruo, non quam persecutor inferre volebat, sed quam ipse disposuerat, sustineret mortem. . . . Si enim tunc occideretur, quis eum Dominum cognosceret?

93–5 Cf the sermon on the innocents by Petrus Chrysologus, Serm. 152, 63–5: *Christus non despexit suos milites, sed pervexit, quibus dedit ante triumphare quam vivere.*

95–102 Closely based on a series of rhetorical paradoxes in Eusebius Gallicanus, Serm. 4, 75–86:

Quam beata aetas, quae necdum Christum potest eloqui, et iam pro Christo meretur interfici . . . quam feliciter nati, quibus in primo nascendi limine, aeterna vita obviam venit! . . . immaturi quidem videntur ad mortem, sed feliciter moriuntur ad vitam: . . . rapiuntur quidem a complexibus matrum, sed redduntur gremiis angelorum.

102–7 From Caesarius, Serm. 222:

[1.5–6] Ecce profanus hostis numquam beatis parvulis tantum prodesse potuisset obsequio, quantum profuit odio. . . . [2.9–12] Qui iure dicuntur martyrum flores, quos in medio frigore infidelitatis exortos velud primas erumpentes ecclesiae gemmas quaedam persecutionis pruina decoxit.

107–12 Petrus Chrysologus, Serm. 152, 73–80:

Beati ventres qui portaverunt tales. Beata ubera, quae se talibus infuderunt. . . . Nam diverso modo, dono uno, in lacrimis suis matres et sui filii suo sanguine baptizantur. In martyrio filiorum passae sunt matres, nam gladius filiorum pertransiens membra ad matrum corda pervenit. Et necesse est ut sint praemii consortes, quae fuerunt sociae passionis.

112–6 The references in the preceding passages to the infancy and immaturity of the innocents seem to have prompted this explanation, for which there is no parallel in the sources, that at the general resurrection all are resurrected at the same adult age and in full health and senses, whatever their condition at the time of death. It is a doctrine which Ælfric mentions several times in his writings, often without any parallel in his sources (cf e.g. CH I.16.126–35, Pope 11.305 ff). The ultimate source, as Cross notes, is probably Augustine's *De Civitate Dei*, XXII.16 (CCSL 48), drawing on Ephesians 4.18, but Ælfric probably knew the material best in the form of Julian of Toledo's *Prognosticon Futuri Saeculi*, which he excerpted and used as source for Pope 11 (*Prognosticon*, III.xx.20–23):

> Resurgent ergo omnes tam magni corpore, quam vel erant vel futuri erant aetate iuvenali; quamvis nihil oberit, etiamsi erit infantilis vel senilis corporis forma, ubi nec mentis nec ipsius corporis ulla remanebit infirmitas.

117–22 The sources refer to Rachel as mother of Benjamin rather than wife of Jacob, but otherwise Haymo and Bede (copied by Smaragdus) agree closely with Ælfric; Bede, Hom. I.10, 31–7 is slightly closer:

> Rachel . . . significat ecclesiam plorare quidem sanctorum de hoc saeculo ablationem, sed non ita velle consolari ut qui saeculum morte vicerunt, rursus ad saeculi certamina secum toleranda redeant, quia nimirum non sunt ultra revocandi in mundum, de cuius aerumnis semel evaserunt coronandi ad Christum.

123–30 From Rufinus, *Historia Ecclesiastica*, I.viii.3–6 (65.10–13, 65.23–67.3):

> Statim namque nec mora ultio in eum divina convertitur, quae non solum praesens inferret exitium, verum et quibus post interitum suppliciis esset excruciandus ostenderet. . . . Herodem porro amarior in dies morbus urgebat. . . . Lento namque igni extrinsecus in superficie corporis urebatur, intrinsecus vero vastum condebatur incendium. Aviditas inexplebilis semper inerat cibi, nec tamen satiare umquam rabidis incitata faucibus valebat.

130–41 Ælfric seems to combine phrasing from Rufinus, *Historia Ecclesiastica*, I.viii.7, and Haymo, Hom. 12, PL 118:

> [Haymo, 80D] Erat enim febris, acerrima suspiria, et anhelitus assidui, spasmus quoque totius corporis, ita ut vix respirare posset. Hydropis morbus corpus attenuaverat. . . . [Rufinus, 67.5–7] Umor liquidus et luridus erga pedes tumidos oberrabat, et ab inferioribus partibus pube tenus tumore distentus, sed et verenda ipsa putredine corrupta scatere vermibus. . . . [Haymo, 80D] Prurigo quoque totius corporis in tantum

intolerabilis erat. . . . [Rufinus, 67.7–8] Spiritus quoque incredibilis inflatio et tentigo obscaena. . . . [Haymo, 80D-81A] Inerat etiam et anhelitus fetidus, in tantum ut vix medicorum aliquis pro adhibendis medicaminibus ad eum accedere posset. Denique nonnullos medicorum in ipsa aegritudine positus dicitur occidere praecepisse, quasi qui eius saluti prodesse possent, nec vellent. . . . Insomnietatem talem sustinebat, ut dies noctesque pervigiles duceret. Quod si parum obdormisset, phantasma patiebatur, ut se obdormisse poeniteret.

141–8 From Haymo, Hom. 12, PL 118, 81AB:

Sed cum nimio amore praesentis vitae aestuaret, iussit se deferri trans Iordanem, ubi erant aquae calidae, quae etiam languentibus medicabiles dicebantur. . . . Visum etiam fuit medicis, ut in fomentum olei tepidi eum deponerent. Quod cum fuisset ingressus, ita totum corpus eius resolutum dicitur, ut etiam oculi in similitudinem morientium versarentur, intercluderetur vox, et sensus abesset. Et cum . . . sensum recepisset, iussit se deferri Iericho.

149–57 From Haymo, Hom. 12, PL 118, 81B:

Cumque iam de sua vita desperatus esset, omnes principes Iudaeorum ex singulis civitatibus et castellis ad se convocatos, in custodia retrudi iussit. Vocansque sororem suam Salomen, et virum eius nomine Alexandrum, dixit: 'Novi Iudaeos de mea morte gavisuros, sed honorabiles exsequias habere potero ex planctu lugentium, si vos meis volueritis parere praeceptis, ut mox cum ego spiritum exhalavero, omnes principes Iudaeorum, quos in custodia reclusi, interficiatis. Sicque fiat, ut qui de mea morte gaudere cupiunt, suorum civium interitum lugere cogantur.'

157–62 From Haymo, Hom. 12, PL 118, 81BC:

Et ne ab eorum sanguinis effusione manum retraherent, singulis quinquagenas argenti drachmas dari iussit. [*Rufinus specifies* militibus.] Cumque dolore ingenti angustiaretur, Antipatrum filium suum, quem quasi de nece paterna tractantem vinculis religaverat, iussit interficere.

It is Rufinus (*Historia Ecclesiastica*, I.viii.5) who specifies the earlier killing of two sons.

162–6 Apparently from Haymo, Hom. 12, PL 118, 81CD:

Iam vero tantis malis obsessus, et quia se vivere non posse cognoverat, mortem accelerare cupiebat. Unde quadam die cum resedisset, iussit sibi dari pomum, et ad eius purgationem gladium. Cumque super sinistram recubuisset, ictum ferientis in seipsum libravit, seque propria manu percussit, atque statim vitam finisset, nisi unus ex amicis qui vicinior astabat, Achiab nomine, manum cum gladio retraxisset. Talem igitur Herodes habuit finem, qui propter Salvatoris odium, multum sanguinem fuderat innoxium.

But Ælfric resembles Rufinus in implying that Herod's attempt at suicide succeeded. Ælfric's *acwehte* ('shook') at 164 may reflect the variant reading *vibravit* for *libravit* which occurs in Haymo's other version, in his *Historiae Sacrae Epitome* (PL 118, 821).[3]

167–78 A close rendering of Mt 2.19–23:

> (19) Defuncto autem Herode, ecce apparuit angelus Domini in somnis Ioseph in Aegypto (20) dicens: surge et accipe puerum et matrem eius et vade in terram Israhel. Defuncti sunt enim qui quaerebant animam pueri. (21) Qui surgens accepit puerum et matrem eius et venit in terram Israhel. (22) Audiens autem quod Archelaus regnaret in Iudaea pro Herode patre suo timuit illo ire et admonitus in somnis secessit in partes Galilaeae. (23) Et veniens habitavit in civitate quae vocatur Nazareth, ut adimpleretur quod dictum est per prophetas quoniam Nazareus vocabitur.

The explanatory comment at 174–6 is not apparently from the sources.

178–82 Probably from Haymo, Hom. 12, PL 118, 81D:

> Et quia non dixit, defunctus, sed defuncti, ex his angeli verbis intelligimus, multos principes Iudaeorum cum Herode in nece Domini consensisse: et ideo divina ultione actum est, ut multi ex his cum illo perirent, cum quo in nece Domini consenserant.

184–8 Referring to Apoc 14.1–5, the epistle for the day:

> (3) Et cantabant quasi canticum novum ante sedem . . . (4) hii sunt qui cum mulieribus non sunt coinquinati; virgines enim sunt hii qui sequuntur agnum. (5) . . . Sine macula sunt.

The palms are from Apoc 7.9 [cited by Bede, Hom. I.10, 127–8]: *Post haec vidi turbam magnam . . . amicti stolas albas et palmae in manibus eorum.*

6 CIRCUMCISION

The original name for the feast on 1 January was the octave of Christ's nativity, but for the Anglo-Saxons and for Ælfric's Carolingian authorities it was primarily a festival in commemoration of the circumcision and the naming of Christ. The Gospel text for the occasion in the Anglo-Saxon church was, as Ælfric notes, a very brief one, just Luke 2.21 on Christ's circumcision and naming. Haymo and Smaragdus both extend the text, at least in their homilies, by including the presentation in the temple, but this was the reading for the Purification on 2 February in Ælfric's time and he covers it in a later homily. Instead, he turns back to the account in Genesis 17 of the institution of the rite of circumcision, with Abraham and his household, and the renaming of

[3] So Cross 1969.

Abraham and Sarah, and uses this as the basis for most of the homily. In points of detail his exposition often parallels that in Bede's homily for the occasion and occasionally Haymo's, which resembles Bede's but seems to draw more on his commentary on Luke. Ælfric probably knew and used both homilies (the former appears in PD), and perhaps also the homily by Hericus which expands on Bede's, but he handles their material in a very free and selective manner and the agreement is seldom close.[1]

At line 129 Ælfric turns to a separate issue, the question of New Year's Day. Caesarius of Arles had devoted two of his sermons for the occasion to an attack on pagan celebrations of the beginning of the year, particularly masquerading, and there are two Augustinian sermons on pagan rites which are assigned to 1 January.[2] Such precedents may have influenced him, but his own target is the observation of auguries or prognostics, initially those associated with New Year's Day, but then also those linked to phases of the moon or days of the week, and other unrelated superstitions, before returning to the question of auguries to explain that certain types of reference to the phases of the moon are acceptable science rather than superstition. A probable influence here is the *De Correctione Rusticorum* of Martin of Braga, written c. 572, which was a major source for his later *De Falsis Deis* and a probable model for CH I.1.[3] The primary concern of the Latin text is with various contemporary practices of Spanish Christians, including prognostics and auguries, which the author identifies with paganism or idolatry, and which he places in the context of the long history of idolatry from Old Testament times. Among those practices are prognostics related to the first day of January (see below under 129 ff). It is presumably from Martin that Ælfric developed the idea that prognostication by January 1st was a pagan practice. But though Martin associated it with the ignorant and the peasantry, in England it was perhaps more the territory of the learned. The 1 January date is, as Ælfric says, a feature of calendars and computistical texts (in contrast to Anglo-Saxon popular tradition, which preferred Christmas as the start of the year), and the prognostics are a feature of monastic manuscripts and a Latinate tradition.[4] Presumably he uses the term heathen to repudiate practices which he viewed as superstitious if not diabolic, but which were current amongst the semi-learned. He was to take up the issue

[1] For the use of Bede and Haymo, see Förster 1894, p. 20 (and p. 30 for the use of Bede's works on time), Smetana 1959, p. 184, and Smetana 1961, p. 459.

[2] Caesarius of Arles, *Sermones*, ed., G. Morin, Serm.193 and 194, CCSL 104 (Turnhout, 1953); Augustine, *Sermones*, PL 38, Serm. 197 and 198.

[3] This and other parallels are discussed by Audrey Meaney, 'Ælfric and Idolatry', *Journal of Religious History* 13 (1984), 119–35, at 123–6.

[4] Cf H. Henel, 'Altenglischer Mönchsaberglaube', *Englische Studien* 69 (1934–5), 329–49. And see further Godden, 'New Year's Day in Late Anglo-Saxon England', *Notes and Queries* 237 (June 1992), 148–50, and R. Jayatilaka, 'The *Regula Sancti Benedicti* in Late Anglo-Saxon England: The Manuscripts and their Readers' (unpubl. D.Phil. thesis, Oxford Univ., 1996), pp. 320–31.

of auguries in more detail later, in his Lives of Saints collection (LS 17), though the target there seems more evidently a matter of popular superstition.[5]

Sources and Notes

The following texts are cited below:

1. Anon., *Vitae Patrum*, PL 73.
2. Bede, *Homiliae*, ed. D. Hurst, CCSL 122 (Turnhout, 1955), Hom. I.11 (pp. 73–9).
3. Bede, *De Temporibus*, ed. C. W. Jones in *Bedae Opera De Temporibus*, CCSL 123B (Turnhout, 1977), pp. 585–611.
4. Bede, *De Temporum Ratione*, ed. C. W. Jones in *Bedae Opera De Temporibus*, CCSL 123B (Turnhout, 1977), pp. 263–460.
5. Caesarius of Arles, *Sermones*, ed. G. Morin, CCSL 103 (Turnhout, 1953), Serm. 54 (pp. 235–40) [cited by section and line numbers].
6. Haymo of Auxerre, *Homiliae de Tempore*, PL 118, Hom. 14, cols. 90–107.
7. Hericus, *Homiliae in Circulum Anni*, ed. R. Quadri, CCCM 116 (Turnhout, 1992), Hom. I.15 (pp. 127–31).
8. Martin of Braga, *De Correctione Rusticorum*, in *Martini Episcopi Bracarensis Opera Omnia*, ed. C. W. Barlow (New Haven, 1950), pp. 183–203.
9. Smaragdus, *De Diadema Monachorum*, PL 102, cols. 593–690.

3–5 Cf the opening words of Bede's homily for the occasion (Hom. I.11, 1–3): Sanctam venerandamque praesentis festi memoriam paucis quidem verbis evangelista conprehendit, sed non pauca caelestis mysterii virtute gravidam reliquit.

5–11 Lc 2.21.

12–32 Haymo similarly begins his homily for the occasion by referring back to Abraham and the initiation of the rite of circumcision. Lines 14–32 follow Gen 17.1–23, with some omissions and rearrangement, and 21.4:

(17.1) Postquam vero nonaginta et novem annorum esse coeperat apparuit ei Dominus dixitque ad eum: ego Deus omnipotens, ambula coram me et esto perfectus; (2) ponamque foedus meum inter me et te et multiplicabo te vehementer nimis. . . . (4) Erisque pater multarum gentium. (6) . . . Regesque ex te egredientur, (7) et statuam pactum meum inter me et te et inter semen tuum post te in generationibus suis foedere sempiterno, ut sim Deus tuus et seminis tui post te. (3) Cecidit Abram pronus in faciem. (9) Dixit iterum Deus ad Abraham: et tu ergo custodies pactum meum et semen tuum post te in generationibus suis. (10) Hoc est pactum quod observabitis inter me et vos et semen tuum post te: circumcidetur ex vobis

[5] For the sources of LS 17, see Audrey Meaney, 'Ælfric's Use of his Sources in his Homily on Auguries', *English Studies* 66 (1985), 477–95.

omne masculinum; (11) et circumcidetis carnem praeputii vestri ut sit in signum foederis inter me et vos; (12) infans octo dierum circumcidetur in vobis omne masculinum in generationibus vestris, tam vernaculus quam empticius circumcidetur, et quicumque non fuerit de stirpe vestra. (14) Masculus cuius praeputii caro circumcisa non fuerit delebitur anima illa de populo suo, quia pactum meum irritum fecit. (5) Nec ultra vocabitur nomen tuum Abram sed appellaberis Abraham, quia patrem multarum gentium constitui te. (15) Dixit quoque Deus ad Abraham: Sarai uxorem tuam non vocabis Sarai sed Sarram (16) et benedicam ei et ex illa dabo tibi filium. (19) Et ait Deus ad Abraham: Sarra uxor tua pariet tibi filium vocabisque nomen eius Isaac et constituam pactum meum illi in foedus sempiternum et semini eius post eum. (22) Cumque finitus esset sermo loquentis cum eo ascendit Deus ab Abraham. (23) Tulit autem Abraham Ismahelem filium suum et omnes vernaculos domus suae universosque quos emerat cunctos mares ex omnibus viris domus suae et circumcidit carnem praeputii eorum statim in ipsa die sicut praeceperat ei Deus. (21.4) Et circumcidit eum octavo die sicut praeceperat ei Deus.

The rendering is very similar to that in his later translation of Genesis (Crawford, pp. 25–7). The contrast in Gen 17.12 between members of the kindred and foreign slaves is turned by Ælfric into a question of rank: *ægðer ge æðelboren ge ðeowtling*.

33–40 Probably based on Bede's homily (Hom. I.11):

[83–90] Abraham patriarcha qui primus circumcisionis sacramentum . . . accepit, eodem die suae suorumque circumcisionis etiam nominis amplificatione simul cum sua coniuge benedici promeruit, ut qui eatenus Abram, id est pater excelsus, dictus est deinde Abraham, id est pater multarum gentium, vocaretur, quia 'patrem multarum gentium constitui te.' . . . [95–100] 'Et Sarai, inquit, uxorem tuam non vocaveris sarai sed saram', id est non vocabis principem meam sed principem, videlicet aperte docens ut eam quae tantae fidei particeps et socia facta est non proprie principem suae domus sed absolute principem, id est omnium recte credentium feminarum vocaret et intellegeret esse parentem.

Haymo (Hom. 14, PL 118, 93AB), following Jerome, notes that the correct spelling is *Sara* not *Sarra*, but the latter is the spelling of the manuscripts here and in Ælfric's Genesis (Crawford), though MS A has *Sara* here at line 118.

40–48 For the ages (lines 40–41) cf Gen 17.17: *Putasne centenario nascetur filius et Sarra nonagenaria pariet*.

49–60 The details of the rite refer back to Gen 17, though the *scearpecged flint* of 52 seems to come from Exod 4.25 (*acutissimam petram*) or Jos 5.2 (*cultros lapideos*). The comparison of circumcision and baptism (lines 53–60) follows Bede (Hom. I.11, 41–8):

Idem salutiferae curationis auxilium circumcisio in lege contra originalis peccati vulnus agebat, quod nunc baptisma agere revelatae gratiae tempore consuevit, excepto quod regni caelestis ianuam necdum intrare poterant, donec adveniens benedictionem daret qui legem dedit, ut videri possit Deus deorum in Sion, tantum in sinu abrahae post mortem beata requie consolati supernae pacis ingressum spe felici expectabant.

With Ælfric's explanation about limbo, *buton tintregum þeah on hellewite* (line 58), cf CH II.5.151–2, *on hellicere clysunge . . . buton þinungum.*

61–65 From Bede, Hom. I.11, 48–53:

Qui enim nunc per evangelium suum terribiliter ac salubriter clamat, 'Nisi quis renatus fuerit ex aqua et spiritu, non potest introire in regnum dei' (Jn 3.5), ipse dudum per legem suam clamabat, 'Masculus cuius praeputii caro circumcisa non fuerit, peribit anima illa de populo suo, quia pactum meum irritum fecit' (Gen 17.14).

66–72 Bede and Haymo make similar points in explaining why Christ submitted to the old law; cf Bede, Hom. I.11, 28–34:

Factum sub lege filium suum misit Deus in mundum; non quia ipse legi quicquam debeat . . . sed ut eos qui sub lege positi . . . de servili conditione quae sub lege erat ereptos in adoptionem filiorum quae per gratiam est sua largitate reduceret.

and Haymo, Hom. 14, PL 118, 92A:

Nec putandum est quod aliqua necessitate Dominus circumcisionem susceperit . . . sed ideo circumcidi voluit, ut etiam suo tempore circumcisionem sanctam fuisse et bonam ostenderet. Et . . . noluit patribus esse dissimilis, qui non venerat legem solvere, sed adimplere (Mt 5.17).

72–8 Cf Hericus, Hom. I.15, 56–76:

Illud etiam quod in die suae circumcisionis nomen ut Ihesus vocaretur accepit, ab antiqua consuetudine aeque exordium sumpsit, quoniam sicut moderno tempore parvulis die quo baptizantur aptantur vocabula, ita et in Iudaeorum populo sublegales parvuli ipsa die suae circumcisionis propriis designabantur nominibus. . . . Interpretatur autem Ihesus salvator sive salutaris, exponente angelo quod ipse salvum faciet populum suum a peccatis eorum.

79–102 This rather apologetic and defensive discussion of the meaning of circumcision has no real parallel in the sources, though both Bede and Haymo interpret circumcision spiritually in a similar way. The prohibition of circumcision at 79–80 is repeated in Ælfric's translation of Genesis, at the end of c.17 (Crawford, p. 127). The interpretation of circumcision with specific reference to sexual appetite (*galnyss* 82, 87) seems logical enough, but differs from the more general application which Ælfric draws from Bede and Haymo at 102 ff. At 93–5 Ælfric quotes Ps 48.13: *Et homo cum in honore esset non intellexit; conparatus est iumentis insipientibus et similis factus est illis*. This leads into a discussion of man's separation from the beasts by virtue of his reason and his soul, a favourite theme with Ælfric (cf CH I.21.125–7, and *Interrogationes*, c. 33[6]) and one generally not prompted by his sources. The implication here is perhaps that sexual licence in particular destroys the distinction between rational man and the beasts; cf CH II 19.170–81.

102–6 A general similarity to Bede (Hom. I.11, 175–211) but rather closer to Haymo, though ignoring the wealth of Scriptural quotation which Haymo supplies in support of his interpretation; Haymo, Hom. 14, PL 118, 95C-97A:

> Hoc summopere considerandum est, quia cirçumcisio spiritualis non unius membri sed omnium membrorum vitia amputare docet. . . . Circumcidendi sunt oculi ab illicito visu. . . . Circumcidendae aures sunt, ne libenter audiant verba detractionis. . . . Circumcidenda est lingua a maledictionibus. . . . Circumcidamus manus ab effusione sanguinis. . . . Circumcidamus pedes, ne festinent ad effundendam sanguinem. . . . Circumcidere debemus . . . cor, ut abstineamus nos a malis et immundis cogitationibus.

106–10 Similar in thought to an earlier point by Bede, following the passage on the renaming of Abraham and Sarah quoted above as source for 32–40 (Hom. I.11, 111–21):

> . . . Gaudentes in se illud Isaiae vaticinium esse conpletum: 'Et servos suos vocabit nomine alio' (Is 65.15); hoc est nomine christiano quo nunc omnes servi Christi se delectantur insigniri. . . . 'Vocabitur tibi nomen novum quod os domini nominavit' (Is 62.2).

110–16 Cf Bede, Hom. I.11, 90–95:

> Quae fidelissima promissio tam late per orbem iam patet impleta, ut etiam nos ipsi, de gentibus ad fidei illius devotionem vocati, ipsum nos patrem spiritaliter habere gaudeamus, dicente etiam nobis apostolo: 'Si autem vos christi, ergo semen Abrahae estis secundum promissionem heredes' (Gal 3.29).

116–20 From Bede, Hom. I.11, 100–105:

> Vnde beatus apostolus Petrus credentes de gentibus feminas ad humilitatis, castitatis et modestiae virtutem provocans, eiusdem matris nostrae Sarae debita cum laude meminit: 'Sicut Sara, inquit, oboediebat Abrahae dominum eum vocans; cuius estis filiae bene facientes et non timentes ullam perturbationem' (1 Petr 3.6).

121–9 From Bede, Hom. I.11, apart from the parenthetic explanation at 125–6:

> [153–8] Octava autem aetas ipsa est dies resurrectionis sine ullo temporis fine beata quando . . . corpus iam incorruptibile laetificat animam. . . . [211–6] Petrinis quidem cultris circumcisionem fieri legimus; petra autem erat Christus [*cf 1 Cor 10.4*] cuius fide, spe et caritate non solum in

[6] And see further Godden 1985a, pp. 278–85. The passage is reworked as Pope 16.50 ff.

baptismate sed in omni prorsus actione devota purificantur corda bonorum. Quae et ipsa cotidiana nostra circumcisio, id est continua cordis mundatio. . . .

129–44 The rejection of 1 January as the start of the new year, and the argument for the spring equinox instead, closely parallels Martin of Braga, *De Correctione Rusticorum*, c.10:

> Similiter et ille error ignorantibus et rusticis subrepit, ut Kalendas Ianuarias putent anni esse initium, quod omnino falsissimum est. Nam, sicut scriptura sancta dicit, VIII Kal. Aprilis in ipso aequinoctio initium primi anni est factum. Nam sic legitur: 'et divisit deus inter lucem et tenebras'. . . . Et ideo falsum est ut Ianuariae Kalendae initium anni sint.

The intervening account of the different practices for the start of the year, lines 132–5, is probably from Bede, *De Temporibus,* c.9, or *De Temporum Ratione,* 36.44–6:

> Annum autem civilem, id est solarem, Hebraei ab aequinoctio verno, a solstitio Graeci, Aegyptii ab autumno, a bruma incipiunt Romani.

The point is repeated by Ælfric, along with lines 141–5, in his *De Temporibus Anni,* 4.18–21, where he follows Bede more precisely. The *gerim* and *gerimbec* (lines 136 and 140) perhaps represent not simply a calendar, though Anglo-Saxon calendars do all start with 1 January, but a collection of computistical tables and notes, including calendars, as Henel argues.[7]

145–6 Exod 12.2: *Mensis iste vobis principium mensuum; primus erit in mensibus anni.*

148–59 Probably based on c.6 of Bede's *De Temporum Ratione*, summed up as follows (6.78–81):

> Nunc admonere contenti xii kalendarum Aprilium die occursum aequinoctii, et ante triduum, hoc est xv kalendarum earundem, primum saeculi diem esse notandum.

The reference at 153–4 is to Gen 1.14:

> Dixit autem Deus: fiant luminaria in firmamento caeli ut dividant diem ac noctem, et sint in signa et tempora et dies et annos.

162–70 Auguries or prognostics of health or long life according to the day on which the New Year begins occur in a text from BL, MS Cotton Tiberius A.iii, a mid-eleventh century manuscript from Canterbury, and similar texts in two other manuscripts, BL, MS Cotton Vespasian D.xiv and Bodleian, MS Hatton 115.[8] Prognostications for journeys according to phases of the moon also appear in the

[7] H. Henel, *Studien zum altenglischen Computus*, Beiträge zur englischen Philologie 26 (Leipzig, 1934).

[8] Printed respectively by M. Förster, 'Beiträge zur mittelalterlichen Volkskunde II', *Archiv* 120 (1908), 296–305; Warner, p. 66; and T. O. Cockayne, *Leechdoms, Wortcunning and Starcraft of Early England*, Rolls Series 35, 3 vols. (London, 1864–6), III.162–4.

Tiberius manuscript.[9] Lists of days unsuitable for bloodletting (if that is indeed the meaning of *heora þing wanian* as Förster argued[10]) occur in the Vitellius Psalter manuscript from the New Minster at Winchester,[11] among others, and Förster also published a list of three unlucky Mondays for bloodletting.[12] Appropriate days for particular actions are mentioned occasionally in the medicinal texts. When Ælfric reverted to the question of lucky and unlucky days in LS 17 he reproduced the objections voiced in sermon 54 of Caesarius of Arles (Serm. 54, 1.19–21):

> Nullus ex vobis observet, qua die de domo exeat, qua die iterum revertatur; quia omnes dies deus fecit, sicut scriptura dicit.

But his argument here is a different one, objecting to the treatment of Monday as the first day of the week, and I know of no parallel for that.

171–7 The belief that some animals were improved by cursing is presumably related to the notion that the devil created some animals, which Ælfric alludes to at 175–7 and mentions more explicitly at I.1.117–24. The subsequent remarks both here (lines 177–82) and in I.1 imply that the belief in diabolic creation was offered, or at least understood, as an explanation for savage and dangerous animals. Lines 178–82 presumably reflect Ælfric's reading in the *Vitae Patrum*, and 180–81 seems to recall a particular episode, printed at PL 73, 1002D:

> Narravit quidam Patrum de aliquo abbate Paulo, qui erat in inferiores partes Aegypti, habitans iuxta Thebaidam. Hic ergo Paulus tenebat manibus eos, qui dicuntur cornutae, aspides et serpentes atque scorpiones, et scindebat eos per medium. Videntes autem haec fratres, satisfacientes ei, interrogabant eum, dicentes: Dic nobis quid operatus es, ut acciperes gratiam istam?

(This is quoted by Smaragdus, *De Diadema Monachorum*, PL 102, 682B, but without reference to the desert context.)

184–6 Col 3.17:

> Omne quodcumque facitis in verbo aut in opere omnia in nomine Domini Iesu gratias agentes Deo et Patri per ipsum.

189–91 Gal 4:

> (11) Timeo vos ne forte sine causa laboraverim in vobis. (10) Dies observatis et menses et tempora et annos.

191–95 Cf Bede, *De Temporum Ratione,* 28:

> [38–42, quoting Basil's *Hexameron*, 6.10–11] Opinor quod et animalibus creandis ceterisque omnibus quae terra producit non parva confertur ex

[9] BL, MS Cotton Tiberius A.iii, f. 152v; printed Cockayne, *Leechdoms,* III.176.

[10] M. Förster, 'Vom Fortleben antiker Sammellunare im Englischen und in anderen Volkssprachen', *Anglia* 67–8 (1944), 1–171, at 61.

[11] BL, MS Cotton Vitellius E.viii, printed and discussed by Henel, 'Altenglischer Mönchsaberglaube'.

[12] M. Förster, 'Die ae. Verzeichnisse von Glücks- und Unglückstagen', in *Studies in English Philology: A Miscellany in Honor of F. Klaeber*, ed. K. Malone and M. B. Ruud, (Minneapolis, 1929), pp. 258–77.

lunae mutatione formatio; modo enim laxiora eorum corpora videntur et vacua cum senescit, modo integra et repleta cum crescit. . . . [24–32, quoting Vegetius] A quinta decima luna usque ad vicesimam et secundam, arbores praecidantur, ex quibus vel liburnae texendae vel publica quaeque sunt opera facienda. His enim tantum octo diebus caesa materies immunis servatur a carie. . . . His namque mensibus, arescente humore, sicciora et ideo fortiora sint ligna.

Ælfric repeats the point in *De Temporibus Anni,* 8.13–14.

196–9 Cf Bede *De Temporum Ratione*, 29:

[1–2] Maxime autem prae omnibus admiranda tanta oceani cum lunae cursu societas. . . . [11–16] Sicut enim luna . . . iiii punctorum spatio quotidie tardius oriri, tardius occidere, quam pridie orta est vel occiderat solet; ita etiam maris aestus uterque . . . eiusdem pene temporis intervallo tardius quotidie venire tardius redire non desinit.

200–2 Cf Sap 11.21: *Omnia mensura et numero et pondere disposuisti.*

7 EPIPHANY

Ælfric's subject is the visit of the magi to the infant Christ, using the Gospel reading appointed for the occasion, Matthew 2.1–12. His approach is mainly figurative, interpreting the magi as representatives of the Gentiles or heathen who are called by the star to acknowledge Christ as God and to follow him. The magi's questions and offerings testify to the triple nature of Christ as man, king and God, while their journey enacts the Christian progress from the devil represented by Herod to divine grace represented by the star. In his characteristic contrast between the heathen races and the Jews, Ælfric develops the suggestions of patristic commentary on the text. A tradition handed down from Augustine compared the call to the Gentiles in the person of the magi with the call to the Jews in the person of the shepherds, identifying Christ as the cornerstone that linked the two peoples in peace and unity. A less sympathetic tradition initiated by St Gregory contrasted the faith and reverence shown by the magi, representing the heathen, with the obduracy shown by the Jews in Jerusalem, aware of the prophecies and informed of the birth of Christ but refusing to respond. Ælfric combines and reconciles the two traditions, drawing a distinction between the apostles and teachers (represented by the shepherds, allegorically understood), together with the prophets and other faithful Jews, who preached the true faith to the Gentiles, and the hard-hearted Jews represented by the bishops and scribes, who are called once again, as he emphasises, by the visit of the magi but choose to remain behind.

Nearly a third of the homily (lines 116–201) is taken up with a discussion of fate, free will, predestination and divine grace, prompted by the association of

Christ's birth with the appearance of a new star. Arguments against the belief in fate, operating through the configuration of the stars at birth, had been a standard feature of commentary on the story of the magi since at least Augustine's time, and Ælfric briefly rehearses the same examples of twins and the contrasting fates of princes and slaves born at the same time, but he then goes on, uniquely, to tackle the fatalism implied by the Christian theory of predestination (lines 137–201). The doctrines which Ælfric puts forward are Augustinian in the main, though no close parallels have yet been found, and his delicate distinctions between the good who are predestined to salvation through God's foreknowledge of their wills and nature, and the wicked who are not predestined but left to destruction (lines 161–76), testify to his grasp of the subtleties of Augustinian theory.[1] But his emphasis on free will and the importance of merit (lines 131–3, 140–58, 181–93) leads the argument in a rather un-Augustinian direction, perhaps prompted by the immediate need to counter fatalism; Ælfric was clearly aware of the similarity between predestination theory and the fatalistic beliefs he was trying to counter.

Ælfric knew a wide range of Latin homilies for Epiphany. Paul the Deacon's homiliary originally included seven homilies for the occasion, and a later version circulating in Anglo-Saxon England (Durham Cathedral, MS B.II.2) has eleven, most of them attributed to Maximus and Leo. Of these he used only Gregory the Great's homily on the Gospel text and possibly a little from another, by Fulgentius, but he also drew on Haymo, Smaragdus and, it appears, several homilies by Augustine, apart from whatever Augustinian writings might lie behind his discussion of predestination. The material in these eight source-texts often overlaps very closely, and Ælfric frequently combines points and phrasing from several parallel treatments, selecting freely, recasting and interweaving ideas.[2]

Sources and Notes

The following texts are cited below:

1. Augustine, *De Correptione et Gratia*, PL 44, cols. 915–46.
2. Augustine, *Sermones*, PL 38, Serm. 200, 202 and 204, cols. 1028–31, 1033–5 and 1037–9.
3. Fulgentius, *Sermones*, ed. J. Fraipont, CCSL 91A (Turnhout, 1968), Serm. 4 (pp. 911–17).
4. Gregory the Great, *Homiliae in Evangelia*, PL 76, Hom. 10, cols. 1110–14.
5. Haymo of Auxerre, *Homiliae de Tempore*, PL 118, Hom. 15, cols. 107–15.
6. Smaragdus, *Collectiones in Evangelia et Epistolas*, PL 102, cols. 70–75.

[1] See the excellent discussion by Grundy 1991, esp. pp. 115–47.

[2] The use of Gregory, Smaragdus and Augustine's Serm. 202 was demonstrated by Förster (1894, p. 11); and the use of Haymo and Fulgentius by Smetana (1959, p. 186 and 1961, p. 462).

1–8 A reference back to I.5, the homily for Innocents' Day nine days earlier.

9–36 A fairly close rendering of Mt 2.1–12, identical to that given above at I.5.8–32.

37–47 On the meaning of the feast cf Augustine, Serm. 202, §1, PL 38, 1033: *Epiphania quippe graece, latine manifestatio dici potest*. The three manifestations of Christ celebrated on this day are similarly noted by Amalarius in his *Liber Officialis*, IV.33 and in a sermon by Maximus included in PD (PL 57, 271), but neither resemble Ælfric in wording. The point is partially repeated at the beginning of CH II.3. Lines 40–43 refer to the account of the baptism at Mt 3.16–17, quoting *hic est filius meus dilectus, in quo mihi complacui*; but Ælfric's *gehyrað him* is a presumably mistaken recall of Mt 17.5 on the transfiguration: *Hic est filius meus dilectus, in quo mihi bene complacuit: ipsum audite* (cf CH II.14.12–13). Lines 43–5 refer to Jn 2.1–11, discussed in CH II.4.

47–51 Cf Augustine, Serm. 202, §1, PL 38, 1033:

> Manifestatus est quidem et die ipso nativitatis suae Dominus pastoribus ab angelo admonitis; quo etiam die per stellam et illis est longe in Oriente nuntiatus: sed isto die ab eis est adoratus.

52–5 From Gregory, Hom. 10, PL 76, 1110C:

> Iudaeis, tanquam ratione utentibus, rationale animal, id est angelus, praedicare debuit; gentiles vero, quia uti ratione nesciebant, ad cognoscendum Dominum non per vocem, sed per signa perducuntur.

and perhaps also Haymo (Hom. 15, PL 118, 109C): *Dignum fuit ut pastoribus qui Israelitae erant et Deum coeli cognoscebant, rationalis creatura, id est angelus appareret.*

55–70 Most of the commentaries identify the shepherds with the Jews but none specifically with the apostles and teachers. Ælfric is here repeating an identification made at I.2.102–4, drawn from Bede. The commentaries generally identify the *magi* with the Gentiles, and Augustine, Fulgentius and Haymo all quote Eph 2.14 on Christ as the corner-stone, joining the two peoples. Smetana suggests Fulgentius as the source, but Augustine's Serm. 202 seems the closest (Serm. 202, §1, PL 38, 1033):

> Israelitae pastores, Magi gentiles: illi prope, isti longe: utrique tamen ad angularem lapidem concurrerunt. 'Veniens quippe, sicut apostolus dicit, evangelizavit pacem nobis qui eramus longe, et pacem his qui prope. Ipse est enim pax nostra, qui fecit utraque unum, et duos condidit in se, in unum novum hominem, faciens pacem, et commutavit utrosque in uno corpore Deo, interficiens inimicitias in semetipso' (Eph 2.14–17 rearranged).

The psalm verse to which Ælfric refers at 59–61 is 117.22: *Lapidem quem reprobaverunt aedificantes, hic factus est in caput anguli*. Fulgentius's comment (Serm. 4, 39–41), *prope erant Iudaei qui Deum colebant, longe erant gentes quae idolis serviebant*, may have contributed; but the idea of geographical distance from Christ, suggested by Ælfric's *stowlice*, would perhaps have particular resonance for the Anglo-Saxons.

71–8 The astronomical issues seem to have exercised Haymo and Smaragdus as well as Ælfric. Haymo seems to argue that the star rose in the east but then travelled through the sky to Bethlehem, as a guide to the magi (Hom. 15, PL 118, 109D-10A):

> Sed forte interrogat aliquis utrum haec stella in coelo sidereo permaneret, sicut et caeterae, vel per aerem an per terram discurreret. Ad quod dicendum quia neque in coelo sidereo fixa erat, neque in terra, sed per aera discurrebat, ut dux et praevia magorum usque ad natum puerum esset.

(Cf too the passage cited at 105 ff.) Smaragdus dismisses such a view as contrary to Scripture, apparently arguing instead that the star was seen in the east but only acted as guide in Judaea (Smaragdus, *Collectiones*, PL 102, 73AB):

> Sed et de stella quae eis apparuit, quidam dicunt ab oriente usque ad vicinia Bethleem, ducem eis itineris exstitisse, quod nequaquam ita esse, ipsa Evangelii veritas inquisita demonstrat, sed potius in oriente tantum eos stellam vidisse, statimque intellexisse, quia haec ortum nati in Iudaea Regis signaret, ideo venerunt Iudaeam. Cumque testimoniis propheticis, in Bethleem illum natum cognovissent, mox illuc iter agentes, stellam quam in oriente viderant, ducem habere meruerunt. Quae non in summa coeli altitudine inter caeteras stellas, sed in vicinia terrae visa est illis.

(Smaragdus had earlier (*Collectiones*, PL 102, 72C) cited Jerome's argument that the star was not itself in the east but was seen from the east by the magi.) Ælfric's imaginative picture of the star as *angenga* between earth and sky, and his careful argument that the star was understood by the magi as signifying the birth of a king in Judaea, over which it moved, but did not act as a guide for them until they reached Judaea (cf 108–10), seems to reflect a reading of Smaragdus.

The comment on Herod's reaction (lines 75–9) seems to be from Gregory, quoted immediately afterwards by Smaragdus (*Collectiones*, PL 102, 73A); Gregory, Hom. 10, PL 76, 1110C: *Coeli rege nato, rex terrae turbatus est, quia nimirum terrena altitudo confunditur cum celsitudo coelestis aperitur.*

79–82 Cf Smaragdus, *Collectiones*, PL 102, 72D-3A:

> Constat quippe magos Christum hominem intellexisse, propter quod dicunt: 'Ubi est qui natus est?' et regem, quia dicunt: 'Rex Iudaeorum'; et dominum, quia dicunt: 'Venimus adorare eum.'

83–91 Perhaps combining ideas suggested by Augustine, Serm. 200, §3, PL 38, 1030:

> Iam vero quod eadem stella quae magos perduxit ad locum ubi erat cum matre virgine Deus infans, quae utique poterat eos et ad ipsam perducere civitatem, se tamen subtraxit, nec eis prorsus apparuit, donec de civitate, in

qua Christus nasceretur, iidem ipsi interrogarentur Iudaei, ut ipsi eam secundum divinae Scripturae testimonium nominarent.

and Haymo, Hom. 15, PL 118, 109AB:

Si cum ipsis ad adorandum pergerent, salvarentur; si autem pergere nollent, inexcusabiles essent. Sed ipsi locum nativitatis ex suis libris aliis ostenderunt, sed tanquam stulti et caeci in tenebris permanserunt.

and Smaragdus, *Collectiones*, PL 102, 73C: *Nam perrexerunt Magi et adoraverunt, remanserunt Iudaei, qui demonstraverunt.*

92–104 Mainly from Haymo, Hom. 15, PL 118, 110A:

Omnia enim elementa Creatorem suum in mundo venisse cognoverunt. Coelum cognovit, quia mox eo nato stellam novam misit; mare cognovit, quia sub plantis eius se calcabile praebuit; sol cognovit, quia in eius morte radios sui luminis abscondit; saxa et lapides cognoverunt, quia eo moriente scissae sunt; terra cognovit, quia eo resurgente contremuit. Sed quem irrationales creaturae cognoverunt, dura et stulta corda Iudaeorum adhuc non cognoscunt.

Haymo is here closely following Gregory, who has instead of the words *terra . . . contremuit* the sentence (Hom. 10, PL 76, 1111A): *Infernus agnovit, quia hos quos tenebat mortuos reddidit*. Ælfric includes both points. The parenthetic qualification (lines 102–4) that not all the Jews were obdurate (linking back to the earlier point about the cornerstone) has a parallel in Augustine, Serm. 204, §3, PL 38, 1038:

Illi cogitentur qui discipuli inde electi, et apostoli facti sunt. . . . Cogitentur etiam ex ipsis persecutoribus tot millia credentium, quando venit spiritus sanctus.

105–15 Mainly based on Haymo, Hom. 15, PL 118, 113BC:

Non casu contigit, sed nutu Dei actum est, ut stella quae magorum praevia fuerat, appropinquantes eos ad Herodem relinqueret, quatenus ipsi Iudaeis Christum natum nuntiarent, et ab eis locum nativitatis auctoritate Scripturae discerent. Sed cum ab Herode recessissent, 'ecce stella quam viderant in oriente, antecedebat eos sicut prius, usque dum veniens staret supra ubi erat puer.' Discimus ergo per hanc stellam gratiam Domini non incongrue figurari, et per Herodem diabolum. Ingredientibus ergo magis ad Herodem, stella eos reliquit: quia eos qui servitio diaboli se subdunt, divina gratia deserit. Sed si ab Herode egressi fuerint, si per poenitentiam iugum diaboli a cervicibus suis excutientes, Deum quaerere coeperint, iterum divina gratia eis apparebit, iterum eos illuminabit, iterum viam qua Dominus inveniatur, demonstrabit.

But Haymo's formulation (esp. *relinqueret*) assumes that the star had previously been guiding the magi. Ælfric's careful rephrasing with *ungesewen* (line 106) and *forluron* (line 112) probably reflects the different views of Jerome and Smaragdus; cf esp. Smaragdus, *Collectiones*, PL 102, 74A: *Ubi est Herodes, stella non videtur*.

116–33 Follows Gregory, Hom. 10, PL 76, 1111D-2B:

> Sed inter haec sciendum quod Priscillianistae haeretici nasci unumquemque hominem sub constitutionibus stellarum putant; et hoc in adiutorium sui erroris assumunt, quod nova stella exiit cum Dominus in carne apparuit, cuius fuisse fatum eamdem quae apparuit stellam putant. . . . Sed a fidelium cordibus absit ut aliquid esse fatum dicant. Vitam quippe hominum solus hanc conditor qui creavit administrat. Neque enim propter stellas homo, sed stellae propter hominem factae sunt. Et si stella fatum hominis dicitur, ipsis suis ministeriis subesse homo perhibetur. Certe cum Iacob, de utero egrediens, prioris fratris plantam teneret manu, prior perfecte nequaquam egredi potuit, nisi et subsequens inchoasset; et tamen cum uno tempore, eodemque momento utrumque mater fuderit, non una utriusque vitae qualitas fuit.

Ælfric adds the relevant quotation from Rom 9.12–13 at 131–3: *Quia maior serviet minori, sicut scriptum est: Iacob dilexi, Esau autem odio habui* (Ælfric was perhaps prompted by Haymo, Hom. 15, PL 118, 110C, who paraphrases Gregory here). He also adds the two references to merit, *geearnungum* (lines 131, 133); an insistence on the importance of merit all the more striking given that St Paul was using the example of Esau and Jacob to make the opposite point—*non ex operibus* (Rom 9.12).

133–6 Gregory refers to the practice of hereditary kingship among the kings of Persia and of the Franks; Haymo, paraphrasing, mentions the Franks only. Ælfric presumably saw no need to cite foreign models for a practice familiar to his audience. He seems to have followed Haymo (Hom. 15, PL 118, 110C) but very freely:

> Nam in Francia plurimarumque gentium regnis, reges ex origine succedere solent, et nullus ignorat quia sub eodem signo et eadem hora qua filius regis nascitur, multi ex servili conditione in eodem regno sub eodem sidere nascuntur, et tamen filius regis, cum adultus fuerit, regni dignitate sublimatur, cum illi qui cum eo nati sunt usque ad mortem in servitute permaneant.

137–201 Ælfric presents here one of his major discussions of free will, divine grace and predestination. There are some similarities with Augustine's *De Correptione et Gratia*, but little that suggests a direct debt. For the notion that God's preordination included the precise number of those who would be saved and damned, of mortals and of angels (lines 163–5), cf Augustine, *De Correptione*, §39, PL 44. With 156–7 cf Augustine, *De Correptione*, §28, PL 44, 933: *Unde etiamsi nullus liberaretur, iustum Dei iudicium nemo iuste reprehenderet.* (This is occasionally quoted in Carolingian treatises on predestination, but there is nothing to suggest that Ælfric knew them rather than Augustine directly. Even so, it seems likely that he knew it as a quotation or extract.) Lines 180–1 are perhaps from Eph 2.8 (so Grundy 1991, p. 136, rather than 1 Petr): *Gratia enim estis salvati per fidem, et hoc non ex vobis.* Lines 184–6 are from Jer 17.10: *Ego Dominus scrutans cor et probans renes; qui do unicuique iuxta viam suam, et iuxta fructum adinventionum suarum.* At 190–8 Ælfric seems to be implicitly answering an objection based on Exod 20.5, that the sins of the fathers are visited on their descendants. Lines 197–9 perhaps draw on Eph 1.4: *Sicut elegit nos in ipso ante mundi constitutionem.*

202–25 The material is all in Gregory, Fulgentius and Haymo, but Gregory seems the closest (Hom. 10, PL 76, 1112D-3A):

> Magi vero aurum, thus et myrrham deterunt. Aurum quippe regi congruit, thus vero in Dei sacrificium ponebatur, myrrha autem mortuorum corpora condiuntur. Eum ergo magi quem adorant etiam mysticis muneribus praedicant, auro regem, thure Deum, myrrha mortalem. Sunt vero nonnulli haeretici qui hunc Deum credunt, sed ubique regnare nequaquam credunt. Hi profecto ei thus offerunt, sed offerre etiam aurum nolunt. Et sunt nonnulli qui hunc regem existimant, sed Deum negant. Hi videlicet ei aurum offerunt, sed offerre thus nolunt. Et sunt nonnulli qui hunc et Deum et regem fatentur, sed assumpsisse carnem mortalem negant. Hi nimirum ei aurum et thus offerunt, sed offerre myrrham assumptae mortalitatis nolunt. Nos itaque nato Domino offeramus aurum, ut hunc ubique regnare fateamur; offeramus thus, ut credamus quod is qui in tempore apparuit Deus ante tempora exstitit; offeramus myrrham, ut eum quem credimus in sua divinitate impassibilem credamus etiam in nostra fuisse carne mortalem.

226–46 The tropological interpretation is also from Gregory, Hom. 10, PL 76, 1113A-C:

> Quamvis in auro, thure et myrrha intelligi et aliud potest. Auro namque sapientia designatur, Salomone attestante, qui ait: 'Thesaurus desiderabilis requiescit in ore sapientis' (Prov 21.20, *but in the Septuagint version according to PL*). Thure autem quod Deo incenditur virtus orationis exprimitur, Psalmista testante, qui dicit: 'Dirigatur oratio mea sicut incensum in conspectu tuo' (Ps 140.2). Per myrrham vero carnis nostrae mortificatio figuratur; unde sancta Ecclesia de suis operariis usque ad mortem pro Deo certantibus dicit: 'Manus meae distillaverunt myrrham' (Cant 5.5). Nato ergo Regi aurum offerimus, si in conspectu illius claritate supernae sapientiae resplendemus. Thus offerimus, si cogitationes carnis per sancta orationum studia in ara cordis incendimus, ut suave aliquid Deo per coeleste desiderium redolere valeamus. Myrrham offerimus, si carnis vitia per abstinentiam mortificamus. Per myrrham namque, ut diximus, agitur ne mortua caro putrefiat. Mortuam vero carnem putrescere, est hoc mortale corpus fluxui luxuriae deservire, sicut de quibusdam per prophetam dicitur: 'Computruerunt iumenta in stercore suo' (Joel 1.17). Iumenta quippe in stercore suo putrescere est carnales homines in fetore luxuriae

vitam finire. Myrrham ergo Deo offerimus, quando hoc mortale corpus a luxuriae putredine per condimentum continentiae custodimus.

247–58 Mainly from Gregory, Hom. 10, PL 76, 1113CD:

Magnum vero nobis aliquid magi innuunt, quod in regionem suam per aliam viam revertuntur. In eo namque quod admoniti faciunt, nobis profecto insinuant quid faciamus. Regio quippe nostra paradisus est, ad quam, Iesu cognito, redire per viam qua venimus prohibemur. A regione etenim nostra superbiendo, inobediendo, visibilia sequendo, cibum vetitum gustando, discessimus; sed ad eam necesse est, ut flendo, obediendo, visibilia contemnendo, atque appetitum carnis refrenando, redeamus.

Haymo's paraphrase of this has *humiliando* (Hom. 15, PL 118, 115A) instead of *flendo*, which may have prompted Ælfric's *eadmodnysse* (line 256).

258–61 From Gregory, Hom. 10, PL 76, 1111D (repeated by Haymo and Smaragdus):

Sicque fit ut Iesum, quem quaerit Herodes, invenire non possit. Cuius persona qui alii quam hypocritae designantur, qui dum ficte quaerunt, invenire Dominum nunquam merentur?

8 THIRD SUNDAY AFTER EPIPHANY

After the series of homilies on Christ's birth and infancy, interspersed with those on Stephen the first martyr and John the evangelist, Ælfric turns for the first time to the events of Christ's ministry. His focus, however, is firmly directed to the Gospel reading for the occasion, Matthew 8.1–13, which describes Christ's healing of a leper and a centurion's servant, and more general issues are not taken up. He treats the two miracles separately, translating and expounding the first in lines 1–86 and the second in lines 86–210, and following general patristic tradition in comparing the second with the similar story of the healing of the sub-king's son in John 4.46 ff. He was to return to this comparison in a later homily, Irvine 1, which deals more fully with the story from John 4. Though his interpretation begins with allegory, his main concern is with a literal reading, drawing out the exemplary aspects of Christ in his treatment of the leper and of the centurion in his appeal to Christ to heal his servant. Ælfric had read the expositions by Haymo and Smaragdus, and a Latin homily attributed (wrongly) to Origen which is given for the occasion in PD. His main source, as he says, was Haymo, homily 19, which provided a wealth of varied interpretations and Scriptural parallels and proofs. He used it very selectively, however, to focus on the issues of faith and divine power, accepting some of Haymo's allegorical reading of the leper but preferring a literal reading of the centurion. Both the leper and the centurion are for him representative of mankind, and he resists Haymo's repeated references to a contrast between Jews and Gentiles.

The rendering of what he uses from Haymo is very free, and he rearranges the order of his points quite radically. He seems to have also made occasional use of Smaragdus and Ps-Origen, and for the comparison with the story of the sub-king drew also on Augustine's Tractates on John and Gregory's Homily 28.[1] Some further touches of his own include a parallel between the Old Testament treatment of lepers and the Christian treatment of penitents (lines 76–86), the great number of those who will be saved (lines 156–9), the salvation of the rich (lines 170–76) and some aspects of hell (lines 186–94).

Sources and Notes

The following texts are cited below:

1. Ps-Ambrose, *Sermones*, PL 17, Serm. 24, cols. 651–4.
2. Augustine, *In Iohannis Evangelium Tractatus CXXIV*, ed. R. Willems, CCSL 36 (Turnhout, 1954).
3. Benedict of Nursia, *Regula*, ed. R. Hanslik, CSEL 75 (2nd ed., Vienna, 1977).
4. Gregory the Great, *Homiliae in Evangelia*, PL 76, Hom. 28, cols. 1210–13.
5. Haymo of Auxerre, *Homiliae de Tempore*, PL 118, Hom. 19, cols. 137–47.
6. Ps-Origen, *Homiliae in Matthaeum*, PLS 4, Hom. 6, cols. 878–87.
7. Smaragdus, *Collectiones in Evangelia et Epistolas*, PL 102, cols. 93–6.

5–14 A fairly close translation of Mt 8.1–4, but adding the explanatory phrases *and he wæs gehæled* (10–11) and *to godes temple* (12):

> (1) Cum autem descendisset de monte, secutae sunt eum turbae multae. (2) Et ecce leprosus veniens adorabat eum dicens: Domine si vis potes me mundare. (3) Et extendens manum tetigit eum Iesus dicens: volo mundare. Et confestim mundata est lepra eius. (4) Et ait illi Iesus: vide nemini dixeris, sed vade, ostende te sacerdoti et offer munus quod praecepit Moses in testimonium illis.

On the term *hreoflig* for *leprosus*, and Ælfric's subsequent description of the disease at 44–6, see the note in I.23.

15–24 Haymo, Hom. 19, PL 118:

> [137C] Spiritualiter montem, in quo Dominus sedit, coelum intelligere possumus. . . . Tunc autem de monte descendit, quando propter nos et propter nostram salutem in convalle plorationis veniens, humanitatem nostram assumpsit, ut qui invisibilis erat in suis, visibilis appareret in nostris: et quem non poteramus videre in sua altitudine, saltem cognosceremus in nostra infirmitate. [*Haymo goes on to interpret the disciples as the Jews and the crowds as the Gentiles.*] . . . [138A] Sequuntur autem turbae

[1] Förster (1894, p. 45) noted the debt to Haymo; Smetana (1959, p. 185) identified the use of Ps-Origen.

Dominum, quando eius vestigia humanitatis imitantur fideles. Sequi enim Dominum, imitari est.

29–39 Haymo, Hom. 19, PL 118:

[138B] Ubi cum magna appareat Domini potestas, non minor eius declaratur humilitas. . . . [138BC] Quaeritur quare Dominus leprosum tetigerit, cum lex praecipiat eum non tangere? Primum, ut humilitatis et compassionis exemplum nobis ostenderet, nec despiciendos proximos propter debilitates aliquas declararet. Deinde, ut non servum, sed Dominum legis se esse ostenderet. . . . [138B] Ille tangere non recusavit, qui eum mundare poterat sine tactu, ostendens quia eius tactus salus est credentibus. . . . [*earlier*] Non parvam fidem habuisse leprosus iste cognoscitur. . . . [138CD] Inter dicere autem Domini et facere, nulla est differentia: 'Dixit enim et facta sunt, mandavit et creata sunt' (Ps 32.9).

For *mid his worde* (line 33) cf Haymo's later *qui verbo leprosum curare poterat* (Hom. 19, PL 118, 139A).

40–4 Haymo, Hom. 19, PL 118, 138D-9A:

Allegorice autem leprosus iste genus designat humanum . . . quoniam veniens Dominus in carne, invenit genus humanum variis erroribus et iniquitatibus inquinatum. . . . leprosus ei occurrit: quia intellexit genus humanum . . . aliter mundationem animae se non posse accipere, nisi per eius fidem qui peccatum non fecit, nec inventus est dolus in ore eius.

44–9 For the physical details of leprosy, cf Lev 13.2 (the text already referred to at 30): *Homo in cuius carne et cute ortus fuerit diversus color sive pustula aut quasi lucens*. Ælfric's *springum* corresponds to *pustula*, his *geswelle* to *ortus*, and *mislice fagnyssum* to *diversus color* and *lucens*. For the clause *se inra man þæt is seo sawul* cf *Interrogationes*, 175–6.

49–53 Haymo, Hom. 19, PL 118:

[141A] Manus enim Domini in Scripturis aliquando maiestatis suae potentiam, aliquando Incarnationis mysterium significat. . . . [139A] Quasi enim leprosum tangendo curavit, quando per hoc, quod nostrae carnis similitudinem assumpsit, a peccatis animae nos liberavit. . . . [139B] 'Vere languores nostros ipse tulit, et dolores nostros ipse portavit' (Is 53.4).

54–60 Cf Haymo, Hom. 19, PL 118, 139C:

Nos nimirum in hoc facto instruit, quos frequenter inanis gloria tentat, ostendens etiam in bono opere iactantiam esse fugiendam.

Cf too CH II 28.50–58.

60–65 Summarising Lev 13 and 14, also quoted and discussed by Haymo but not in similar wording. Ælfric adds *and godes miht hine syððan gehælde*.

65–8 Cf Haymo, Hom. 19, PL 118:

[142B] In cuius ergo cute lepra apparuerit, id est, in cuius anima peccatum fuerit, veniat ad sacerdotem, locum leprae ostendens, id est, peccata sua humiliter ei confiteatur. . . . [141C] Ipsa peccata vice Domini sacerdotibus confiteri debemus, et ad eorum consilium poenitentiam agere.

68–75 Haymo, Hom. 19, PL 118, 141CD:

Forte etiam sunt nonnulli, qui sufficere sibi credunt, quod soli Deo compuncto corde peccata sua confiteantur, nec ea esse necesse sacerdotibus confiteri, tantummodo ut a malis suis operibus cessent. Quorum opinio si vera esset, nequaquam Dominus leprosos, quos per semetipsum mundaverat, ad sacerdotes misisset. Denique si peccata non essent sacerdotibus confitenda, et ad eorum iudicium excutienda, Paulum quem in via fuerat allocutus, nequaquam Ananiae sacerdoti destinaret, dicens: 'Vade in civitatem, et ibi dicetur tibi quid te oporteat facere' (Acts 9.7).

(At 72–3 most manuscripts begin the sentence with *For þære ylcan* . . . rather than *eac*, and that seems likely to be what Ælfric intended.)

76–86 Ælfric's interpretation of Leviticius 13–14 on the treatment of lepers, applying it to excommunication and the treatment of penitents, has very little resemblance to Haymo's discussion (though this does deal with penance), and even less to other commentaries on the text (Jerome, Isidore and Bede all apply it to various types of heresy). The Pauline quotation signalled at 82 seems to be 1 Cor 5.13: *Auferte malum ex vobis ipsis*. But the reference to the sick sheep suggests that Ælfric was recalling the way this verse is used in the provisions of the Rule of St Benedict for dealing with sinful and incorrigible monks (*Regula*, 28.6–8):

Quod si nec isto modo sanatus fuerit, tunc iam utatur abbas ferro abscisionis, ut ait apostolus: 'Auferte malum ex vobis', et iterum: 'Infidelis, si discedit, discedat' (1 Cor 7.15), ne una ovis morbida omnem gregem contagiet.

The cross-mark at 86, which also occurs in H but not in other MSS, may be a paragraph marker, indicating the transition to the second miracle, or a vestigial indication of a passage added by Ælfric in revision, presumably lines 76–86 (Eliason takes the former view of cross-signs in MS A, Clemoes the latter; see Eliason and Clemoes 1966, pp. 27 and 31–2).

86–103 A mostly close rendering of Mt 8.5–13:

(5) Cum autem introisset Capharnaum accessit ad eum centurio rogans eum (6) et dicens: Domine puer meus iacet in domo paralyticus et male torquetur. (7) Et ait illi Iesus: ego veniam et curabo eum. (8) Et respondens centurio ait: Domine non sum dignus ut intres sub tectum meum sed tantum dic verbo et sanabitur puer meus. (9) Nam et ego homo sum sub potestate habens sub me milites et dico huic vade et vadit et alio veni et venit, et servo meo fac hoc et facit. (10) Audiens autem Iesus

miratus est et sequentibus se dixit: Amen dico vobis non inveni tantam fidem in Israhel. (11) Dico autem vobis quod multi ab oriente et occidente venient et recumbent cum Abraham et Isaac et Iacob in regno caelorum. (12) Filii autem regni eicientur in tenebras exteriores ibi erit fletus et stridor dentium. (13) Et dixit Iesus centurioni: Vade et sicut credidisti fiat tibi; et sanatus est puer in hora illa.

For the curious rendering of *filii regni*, 'sons of the kingdom', as *ða rican bearn*, 'the rich children', see below. On the terminology for the centurion's servant and his soldiers (here *cniht* and *cempan* respectively, but *cnapa* and *cnihtæs* in Irvine 1), see Irvine, pp. 26–7.

104–16 Cf Ps-Origen (Hom. 6, §5, PLS 4, 882) for the opening: *Accessit vere, non dimidius, sed totus*. The rest seems to be from Haymo, Hom. 19, PL 118, 144AB:

In opere huius centurionis, tres imitabiles virtutes nobis ostenduntur, humilitas scilicet, fides et prudentia. Magnam enim habet humilitatem, qui . . . respondit: 'Domine, non sum dignus ut intres sub tectum meum.' Perfectam autem habuit fidem, quia, cum esset gentilis, solo verbo Dominum credidit posse puero reddere sanitatem, dicens: 'Tantum dic verbo, et sanabitur puer meus.' . . . Habuit etiam non parvam prudentiam, cum eum quem corporaliter ambulantem vidit, ubique per divinitatem esse praesentem intellexit. Nec caritas in eo defuisse credenda est, quia cum multi pro sua, suorumque filiorum ac carorum salute ad Dominum rogaturi accederent, ille pro servi tantum sanitate.

118–26 From Jn 4.46–53:

(46) Venit ergo iterum in Cana Galilaeae ubi fecit aquam vinum et erat quidam regulus cuius filius infirmabatur Capharnaum. (47) Hic cum audisset quia Iesus adveniret a Iudaea in Galilaeam abiit ad eum et rogabat eum ut descenderet et sanaret filium eius; incipiebat enim mori. . . . (50) Dicit ei Iesus: vade filius tuus vivit. Credidit homo sermoni quem dixit ei Iesus et ibat. (51) Iam autem eo descendente servi occurrerunt ei et nuntiaverunt dicentes quia filius eius viveret. (52) Interrogabat ergo horam ab eis in qua melius habuerit et dixerunt ei quia heri hora septima reliquit eum febris. (53) Cognovit ergo pater quia illa hora erat in qua dixit ei Iesus filius tuus vivit et credidit ipse et domus eius tota.

The passage is cited by Haymo and Ps-Origen, just as comparison with the present text, Mt 8.5–13, is made in commentaries on Jn 4.46 ff by Augustine (Tractates on John), Gregory (Homily 28), and Ælfric himself (Irvine 1).

127–38 Haymo, Hom. 19, PL 118, 143CD:

Quid est ergo quod Dominus ad filium reguli rogatus ire noluit, et ad servum centurionis etiam non rogatus ire paratus fuit? Quis enim ignorat maioris potestatis regulum quam centurionem? Nostra in hoc facto . . . superbia confunditur, qui in hominibus non naturam, sed potentiam consideramus. . . . Quos autem pauperes, contemnimus, negligimus et

> despicimus. At vero Filius Dei, qui de coelo venit in terram ut superbiam fugiendam, et humilitatem amandam, atque naturam hominis diligendam ostenderet, ad filium reguli rogatus ire noluit, et ad servum centurionis, etiam cum non rogaretur, ire paratus fuit. 'Excelsus enim Dominus humilia a prope respicit: alta autem, id est superba, a longe contemnit' (Ps 137.6).

For the clause at 134, *ac we sceolon godes anlicnysse on him wurþian*, cf Gregory's treatment (Hom. 28, PL 76, 1211C):

> Quid est hoc, nisi quod superbia nostra retunditur, qui in hominibus non naturam qua ad imaginem Dei facti sunt, sed honores et divitias veneramur?

But Ælfric may have had a version of the Haymo passage containing the relevant words from Gregory, *qua . . . facti sunt*, since they occur in the same passage when it is repeated in Haymo's homily 136 (PL 118, 727). For 135–6 cf also Augustine's comments (*Tract.*, 16.5.15–16): *Illi praesentiam promittebat, hunc verbo sanabat*. Ælfric perhaps underlines the subtle distinctions of rank referred to at 130–1 by using *cnapa, þeowa* and *cempan* for the followers of the centurion but designating the followers of the king (*servi*) as *þegnas*, the word he uses for the centurion himself at 142.

139–46 From Haymo, Hom. 19, PL 118, 144D-5A:

> Admirabatur Dominus fidem centurionis, quam cordi eius mirabiliter administrabat, non quod aliquid ei mirandum esset, qui cuncta operatur mirabiliter, sed ut eumdem nos mirari debere doceret. Cuius fidem Dominus admirans, pariter et collaudans: Sequentibus se dixit: Amen dico vobis, non inveni tantam fidem in Israel. Quod non de patriarchis et prophetis dicit . . . sed de Israel carnali, id est populo Iudaeorum, vel de illis qui praesentes erant . . . Quia non sic cito crediderunt, quomodo centurio.

147–9 Cf Ps-Origen, Hom. 6, §6, PLS 4, 886:

> Maria et Martha me nimium diligentes dicunt: 'Domine, si hic fuisses, non esset mortuus frater meus' (Jn 11.21), tanquam dubitantes quod ubique non velox sit adesse mea potentia.

149–54 Following Haymo (Hom. 19, PL 118, 144BC) but presenting as the centurion's actual words what Haymo had offered as only his implication:

> Ac si diceret: Si ego qui homo sum sub potestate principis, habeo sub me milites, et dico huic, Vade, et vadit: et alio, Veni, et venit: et servo meo, Fac hoc, et facit: quanto magis tu, cum sis Deus.

156–9 The expression of pleasure at the multitudes who will be saved has no parallel in the sources but is wholly characteristic of Ælfric who uses the verse in a similar way at CH I.35.277 ff and II.5.184–7. Haymo interprets the verse quite differently (Hom. 19, PL 118, 145C): *Recumbere . . . in regno coelorum est in fide patriarcharum gentes requiescere*.

159–65 Haymo, Hom. 19, PL 118:

[145AB] Per orientem et occidentem quatuor mundi partes designantur, a quibus ex omnibus gentibus erant in fide. . . . [*For east and west Haymo proposes first the Jews and the Gentiles, but then adds infancy and old age, 145C:*] Vel, ab oriente, qui ab ipsa infantia vel pueritia Deo servit: ab occidente, qui in senectute vel decrepita aetate ad Dei servitutem convertitur.

The additional passage by Ælfric found here in MSS N and Q (see App. B1 and *CH I*, p. 133) shows him emphasising the multitude who will be saved, as he did also in an addition at II.5.194. The image of a king's retinue is used in similar ways in the preface to LS (lines 59 ff), and at Pope 2.241 and 11.546 ff.

166–76 For the opening cf Haymo, Hom. 19, PL 118, 145C: *Terribilis autem de Iudaeis praedicitur sententia*. Haymo, like most commentators, interprets the *filii regni* as the Jews but his reason is their love for the earthly kingdom. Ælfric is perhaps following Smaragdus instead (*Collectiones*, PL 102, 96C): *Filios regni Iudaeos significat, in quos ante regnavit Deus*. But this applies to the Latin phrase, not to Ælfric's *ða rican bearn*, 'the rich children'. None of the commentaries or Biblical versions offer any parallel to this reading, which seems indeed more likely to have arisen within Old English, through the association of *rice* adjective and *rice* noun; the *Old English Gospels* have *þises rices bearn* and the Lindisfarne Gospels have *suna rices*, both properly rendering *filii regni*. But there are no relevant variants in Ælfric's text, and it is clear from the subsequent discussion that he was indeed thinking of the adjective *rice*, unaccountable though that is. The rest of the passage takes up the theme of the rich and, not surprisingly, has no equivalent in the sources which Ælfric was using. Caesarius of Arles cites as examples of the rich who were saved Abraham, Isaac, Jacob, Joseph and David from the Old Testament, and Zacheus and the two centurions from the New (Caesarius of Arles, *Sermones*, Serm. 49, §3, CCSL 103, pp. 223–4), but there is no evidence that Ælfric knew this sermon. The clause *fela ricra manna geðeoð Gode* recurs at I.13.203–4, but there too it has no parallel in the sources. The reference there to Lc 1.53 *divites dimisit inanes* and here to Zacheus confirms that by *rican* Ælfric meant 'rich' rather than 'powerful'; but see further the notes on I.13 and Godden 1990, esp. pp. 59 ff.

177–9 Haymo, Hom. 19, PL 118, 146A:

Sicut enim filii Dei vocantur, qui magis Deum quam mundum diligunt, sic filii regni dicuntur, qui in amore terreni regni radices cordis perseverabiliter plantaverunt.

180–94 For the beginning cf Haymo, Hom. 19, PL 118, 146AB:

In quo loco considerandum, quia, cum tenebrae semper sint interiores et non exteriores, in tenebras exteriores mittuntur post mortem, qui in tenebras interiores, id est in caecitate mentis, se concluserunt dum viverent. . . . Tenebrae interiores caecitas mentis dicuntur, exteriores vero poenae infernales.

Though Ælfric seems to propose blindness of body for the outer darkness (lines 181–2) his subsequent comments suggest he does in fact mean the darkness of hell. His explanation as to why hell is dark though it is fiery (lines 186–90) seems to be his own; the Biblical reference is to Mc 9.43: *Ubi vermis eorum non moritur, et ignis non extinguitur*. Lines 190–94 on the damned are not from Ælfric's main sources for this homily. The notion of the damned being grouped in hell according to their sin, with the formulae *homicidae cum homicidis* etc., seems to have been something of a Latin commonplace, occurring for instance in Ps-Ambrose, Serm. 24 (PL 17, 653), Ps-Augustine, *Sermo ad Fratres in Eremo* 67 (PL 40, 1354), Ps-Isidore, Serm. 3 (PL 83, 1224B), and two sermons by Haymo, Hom. 81 and 100 (PL 118, 491 and 559). None of these texts is on the same text or subject as Ælfric's, and none has quite the same list as his: the closest in general is the Ps-Ambrose, whose *falsi cum falsis, sacrilegi cum sacrilegis* is closest to Ælfric's *ða forsworenan mid forsworenum* and which has parallels in the preceding passage, including a reference to Mc 9.43 which is quoted by Ælfric; the Ps-Ambrose passage reads (Serm. 24, PL 17, 653A):

Illi sine fine cruciantur in inferno, ubi vermes eorum non morientur, et ignis eorum non exstinguetur, quia scriptum est: 'Potentes potenter tormenta patientur' (Sap 6.7). Ibi vitam tenebrosam et mansionem obscuram perpetuo habebunt: ibi miseri cum miseris, superbi cum superbis, homicidae cum homicidis, adulteri cum adulteris, iniqui cum iniquis, falsi cum falsis, sacrilegi cum sacrilegis, omnes simul cruciantur in inferno sine fine.

The phrase *nulla lux umquam nisi tenebrae* in the same text at 652A might just have influenced Ælfric's reference to the absence of light in hell. But Ps-Ambrose does not have a parallel to Ælfric's *gitseras mid gitserum*, whereas others have *avari cum avaris* or *rapaces cum rapacibus.* There are other examples with *avari* in PL (e.g. Gregory's *Dialogues* PL 77, 380), but there seem to be no examples in PL with both *homicidae* and *avari* before Ælfric's time (the Ps-Augustine *Sermones ad Fratres in Eremo* have been identified as thirteenth-century work by J. Bonnes in 'Un des plus grands prédicateurs du XIIe siècle', *RB* 56 (1945–6), 174–9).

194–9 Cf Haymo, Hom. 19, PL 118:

[146B] Oculi enim prae nimio fumo solent lacrymari, et dentes prae nimio frigore stridescere. . . . [146C] Si quis autem de resurrectione sui corporis dubitat, ipsam per hunc locum fieri intelligere valet. Oculi enim carnei sunt, et dentes ex ossibus.

Cf I.35.198 ff.

201–6 From Haymo, Hom. 19, PL 118, 146D:

Hic considerandum est quantum unumquemque propria fides adiuvet, quando tantum profuit aliena. Propter fidem enim centurionis, reddita est puero sanitas. Fides namque magna est virtus, et, ut ait Apostolus, 'sine qua impossibile est placere Deo' (Hebr 11.6). De qua etiam per Habacuc prophetam dicitur: 'Iustus autem meus ex fide vivit' (Hab 2.4).

At 204–5 MS A has *cniht* with *bedreda* added above in a different hand, while all other manuscripts have just *bedreda*. Presumably Ælfric originally wrote *cniht* and then added *bedreda* above the line in some other manuscript from which all others descend, either intending it as a replacement or, perhaps, intending an addition which was then misunderstood as a substitution by his scribe.

9 PURIFICATION

Ælfric's main subject is the presentation of Christ in the temple, Luke 2.22–40. The reading for the occasion was probably verses 22–32 only, which are paraphrased at the beginning of the homily,[1] but Ælfric eventually goes on to discuss the prophecies of Simeon and Anna (verses 33–40), which formed the reading for the Sunday after Christmas. As in the Circumcision homily, he begins by discussing the Old Testament rite of purification which was being followed by Mary and Joseph, giving much fuller detail than the Gospel passage itself provides, and developing both the literal and allegorical senses of the offerings (lines 4–13, 59–123). His interpretation of the Gospel passage itself (lines 13–58, 124–243) is mainly literal, avoiding the allegorical identification of Simeon with the *vetus homo* and Anna with the church suggested by some of his authorities. Despite the title, the homily is not primarily concerned with the Virgin herself, still less with her purification, barely alluding, for instance, to the lengthy argument of Bede that Mary needed no purification, though he does highlight her role in the events rather than Joseph's and emphasises her high status at the end. Instead he uses the Gospel text to explore a range of topics: purification, offerings to God, the dual nature of Christ, the devotion of Simeon, the exemplary role of Anna, the three orders of chastity, the status of Mary, the ceremonies of Candlemas.

Ælfric drew on at least six main sources for his interpretation of the Gospel: Bede's homily for the purification; his commentary on Luke; Haymo's homily 13, for the week after Christmas, and his homily 14, for the Circumcision; the Augustinian sermon 370 (possibly not entirely by Augustine himself); and two homilies attributed to Origen in the translation by Jerome, probably via an adaptation found in Paul the Deacon's homiliary. Smaragdus and Paschasius Radbertus also contribute some details.[2] As well as the Origen material, the Bede

[1] Lenker, p. 354.

[2] Förster (1894, p. 24) identified the use of Bede's homily and his commentary on Luke; Smetana (1959, p. 187 and 1961, p. 463) demonstrated the use of Haymo and Augustine. Mary Clayton (1983) gives an excellent detailed account of the homily and its use of sources, and identifies the use of Paschasius Radbertus.

homily and a version of the Augustine sermon were available in PD. Bede and Haymo provide most of the material, but Ælfric habitually reduces their verbose arguments to succinct statements; extreme cases are the reduction of Bede's argument that Mary did not need purification to the words *þis wæs geset be wifum* and Haymo's explanation about the reference to Joseph as Christ's father to the phrase *þæs cyldes fostorfæder*.

Given the prominence of Ælfric's discussion of the rite of purification, it is striking that at no point does he indicate whether any part of it still applies in his time (whereas he is careful to emphasise that the Old Testament practice of offerings (line 64) and circumcision (I.6.79–80) are no longer to be followed). In the western church the Christian rite of purification is not recorded until much later and Gregory the Great had supposedly told Augustine of Canterbury that the rules set down in Leviticus that a woman should not enter church after childbirth no longer applied literally (Bede, *Historia Ecclesiastica*, I.xxvii), though the rules against intercourse between husband and wife still did apply. The Ps-Theodore penitential, which seems to have been copied and presumably consulted in Ælfric's time (it appears in the Wulfstan manuscript, Cambridge, Corpus Christi College, MS 190), prescribes a penance for women entering a church before the due time after childbirth,[3] and both the Ps-Egbert Confessional and the Ps-Egbert Penitential prescribe abstinence from intercourse for forty days after childbirth (a point which Ælfric, following Bede, includes in his description of Old Testament practice, though it is not specifically mentioned in Leviticus). In the eastern church sources describe a ceremony of purification in which the priest meets the mother and child outside the church door, blesses the mother and carries the child to the altar. This seems strikingly similar to what Ælfric describes, quite without warrant from the Gospel or his other sources: Simeon goes to meet Mary, takes the child in his arms and carries him into the temple. One wonders whether Ælfric unconsciously visualised the scene in the light of a Christian ceremony derived from it which he had seen somewhere or heard about.[4]

Sources and notes

The following texts are cited below:

1. Anonymous homily adapted from Jerome's translation of two homilies by Origen on Luke's Gospel (ed. M. Rauer, *Origenes Werke*, vol. 9, GCS 49 (2nd ed., Berlin, 1959)), printed PL 95, cols. 1179–85.

[3] B. Thorpe, ed., *Ancient Laws and Institutes*, 2 vols. (London, 1840), II.71.

[4] A perhaps more convincing explanation for this feature has been independently suggested by Brad Bedingfield, who argues that it is one of a number of cases in which Ælfric's rendering of the Gospels has been influenced by his familiarity with liturgical ritual, in this case the ritual of Candlemas; see M. B. Bedingfield, 'Reinventing the Gospel: Ælfric and the Liturgy', *Medium Ævum* 68 (1999), 13–31, esp. 15–23.

2. Augustine, *Sermones*, PL 39, Serm. 370 [=*Sermones dubii*], cols. 1657–9.
3. Bede, *Commentarius in Lucam*, ed. D. Hurst, CCSL 120 (Turnhout, 1960), pp. 5–425.
4. Bede, *Homiliae*, ed. D. Hurst, CCSL 122 (Turnhout, 1955), Hom. I.18 (pp. 128–33).
5. Haymo of Auxerre, *Homiliae de Tempore*, PL 118, Hom. 13 and 14, cols. 83–90 and 90–107.
6. Paschasius Radbertus, *De Assumptione Sanctae Mariae Virginis*, ed. A. Ripberger, CCCM 56C (Turnhout, 1985), pp. 109–62.
7. Smaragdus, *Collectiones in Evangelia et Epistolas*, PL 102, cols. 64–8.

4–12 From Lev 12.2–6, but Ælfric is here following the summary given in Bede's homily I.18:

> [11–17] Praecepit namque lex ut mulier quae suscepto semine peperisset filium inmunda esset septem diebus, et in dei octavo circumcideret infantulum nomenque aptaret; deinde etiam alios triginta tres dies ab ingressu templi ac viri thoro abstineret donec quadragesimo nativitatis die filium cum hostiis ad templum domini deferret. . . . [20–25] Si autem feminam peperisset mulier, inmunda fieri iussa est quattuordecim diebus et sexaginta sex diebus aliis a templi ingressu suspendi donec octogesimo nativitatis die quae dies purgationis eius vocabatur illo se suamque sobolem hostiis sanctificatura veniret ac sic demum ad thorum viri libera redire deberet.

Bede goes on to explain at length that Mary, as a virgin, was not bound by the law on purification, and Ælfric alludes to this at 12–13. Though the title of the homily, and the Latin incipit, alludes to the idea of purification, Ælfric seems to have avoided the notion of uncleanness in his adaptation of Leviticus and Bede.

13–37 A free paraphrase of Lc 2.22–32, drawing out the doctrinal significance of the event:

> (22) Et postquam impleti sunt dies purgationis eius secundum legem Mosi, tulerunt illum in Hierusalem ut sisterent eum Domino, (23) sicut scriptum est in lege Domini . . . (25) Et ecce homo erat in Hierusalem cui nomen Symeon et homo iste iustus et timoratus expectans consolationem Israhel et Spiritus Sanctus erat in eo. (26) Et responsum acceperat ab Spiritu Sancto non visurum se mortem nisi prius videret Christum Domini. (27) Et venit in Spiritu in templum et cum inducerent puerum Iesum parentes eius ut facerent secundum consuetudinem legis pro eo, (28) et ipse accepit eum in ulnas suas et benedixit Deum et dixit: (29) Nunc dimittis servum tuum Domine secundum verbum tuum in pace, (30) quia viderunt oculi mei salutare tuum (31) quod parasti ante faciem omnium populorum; (32) lumen ad revelationem gentium et gloriam plebis tuae Israhel.

Mary becomes the subject in lines 13–14, where the Vulgate has plural forms implying Mary and Joseph. The expanded treatment of Simeon at 20–25 reflects the interpretation of his story given in the Augustinian passage which Ælfric follows more closely at 38–45, but the dramatisation of the meeting outside the temple at 29–34 seems to be his own.

38–47 From Augustine, Serm. 370, §3, PL 39, 1658:

> Intelligite, fratres, quantum desiderium habebant antiqui sancti videndi Christum. Sciebant illum esse venturum. . . . Et hoc illi concessum erat iam decrepito, quasi desideranti et suspiranti et dicenti quotidie in orationibus suis: Quando veniet? quando nascetur? quando videbo? Putas durabo? . . . Dicebat ista in orationibus suis, et pro desiderio suo accepit responsum, quod non gustaret mortem, nisi prius videret Christum Domini. Gestabat eum Maria mater eius infantem: vidit ille, et agnovit.

By *oðrum bocum* (lines 38) Ælfric perhaps means the Old Testament texts cited by Haymo in his reworking of this passage (Hom. 14, PL 118, 104B); *cristes bec* refers specifically to the Gospels.

47–55 Ælfric continues with Augustine, Serm. 370, §3, PL 39, 1658:

> Portabat a quo portabatur. Ipse enim est Christus sapientia Dei, attingens a fine usque ad finem fortiter, et disponens omnia suaviter (Sap 8.1). Quantus ibi erat, et quam magnus, quam parvus factus erat? Parvus factus, parvos quaerebat. Quid est, parvos quaerebat? Non superbos, non elatos; sed humiles et mites colligebat.

The rhetorical expansion on pride (lines 55–8) seems to be Ælfric's own.

59–64 Ælfric returns to a further prescription of the Old Law, again following Bede's homily (Hom. I.18, 17–20):

> Primogenitum autem omnis masculini sexus sanctum domino vocari atque ideo munda quaeque offerri Deo; inmunda autem mundis mutari vel occidi; et hominis primogenitum quinque siclis argenti debere redimi.

(Bede is here drawing on Exod 13.2 and Num 18.15–16.)

65–73 Bede's homily gives no explanation of this prescription, but his commentary on Luke provided Ælfric with an interpretation of the first part (*Comm. Luc.*, 1.1705–14):

> Illa omnia primogenita . . . nostrae fuerint devotionis indicium qui omnia bonae actionis initia, quae quasi corde gignimus, domini gratiae deputare, male autem gesta redimere debeamus dignos videlicet paenitentiae fructus pro singulis quinque corporis vel animae sensibus offerentes.

Haymo's recasting of this is similar but less close. But Bede's *pro singulis . . . sensibus* seems to mean 'on behalf of the five senses (which have sinned)' rather than Ælfric's notion of repenting *with* the five senses. For the prescription on animals Bede has nothing and Ælfric turns to Haymo, Hom. 14, PL 118, 100A:

> Si autem immundum aliquid parimus, id est, si peccatum in opere perpetramus, aut occidamus malum quod latebat, et radicitus evellamus.

. . . Aut certe mutuemus ea mundis, declinantes a malo, et facientes bonum.

75–80 Returning to Bede's homily for further prescriptions from the Old Law (Hom. I.18, 44–7):

Praecepit quippe dominus in lege ut qui possent agnum pro filio vel pro filia simul et turturem sive columbam offerrent; qui vero non sufficeret ad offerendum agnum duos iam turtures vel duos columbae pullos offerret.

That what was offered for Christ was the latter, the offering of the poor (lines 80–81), is indicated by the Gospel verses which Ælfric had omitted earlier, Lc 2.23–4:

(23) Quia omne masculinum adaperiens vulvam sanctum Domino vocabitur, (24) et ut darent hostiam secundum quod dictum est in lege Domini par turturum aut duos pullos columbarum.

The birds in question are the turtle-dove and some other kind of dove or pigeon, perhaps the wood-pigeon.

80–5 For the literal explanation Ælfric continues with Bede's homily (Hom. I.18, 43–4, 48–51):

Hostia haec pauperum erat. . . . Ergo dominus nostrae per omnia memor salutis non solum homo fieri cum Deus esset sed etiam cum dives esset pauper fieri dignatus est pro nobis ut nos sua paupertate simul et humanitate divitiarum et divinitatis suae donaret esse participes.

The phrase *dæl on his rice* (line 84) seems to reflect not the *divitiarum . . . participes* of this passage but the *heredes regni* of the similar passage in Bede's commentary on Luke (*Comm. Luc.*, 1.1742).

85–92 For the allegorical interpretation of the offerings Ælfric turns to Haymo, Hom. 14, PL 118:

[101CD] In hoc praecepto nos commonemur, ut si de grege operum nostrorum agnum innocentiae, vel principales virtutes . . . non inveniamus, offeramus saltem duos turtures, vel duos pullos columbarum, id est duo genera compunctionis, timoris videlicet et amoris. . . . [102AB] Cum enim quis mala opera sua ad memoriam revocans, poenas etiam inferni reminiscens, flere incipit . . . quasi turturem vel columbam pro peccato offert. Cum vero ex longa consuetudine flendi, animus securitatem acceperit, et coeperit flere, non timens ne ducatur ad poenam, sed quia tanto tempore differatur a regno . . . quasi turturem vel columbam in holocausto offert.

The same ideas are in Bede's homily, but expressed less succinctly. The interpretation depends on the point that the birds lament rather than sing, which is mentioned later in Ælfric's text (lines 117–20), and on the distinction between offering for sacrifice and offering for sin, which he ignores. By *onbryrdnes* (line 88) he seems to mean 'grieving' rather than 'stimulation'.

93–106 Ælfric here turns away from his sources and from close exegesis for a brief discussion of offerings to God. The passage was later reworked by Ælfric in a text printed as Pope 30.30–54 (see Clayton 1985b). The reference there is specifically to alms-giving.

107–17 Bede's homily mentions the offering of *columbae* and *turtures* by Abraham and 'in many ceremonies of the law'. Ælfric's explanation of the two kinds of birds is largely a recasting of points by Bede (Hom. I.18, 56–9):

> Columba ergo simplicitatem, turtur indicat castitatem, quia et columba simplicitatis, et castitatis amator est turtur, ita ut si coniugem casu perdiderit non alium ultra quaerere curet.

and Haymo, Hom. 14, PL 118, 102C:

> Per columbas, qui gregatim volant vel gemunt, activae vitae societas designatur. De qua scriptum est: 'Multitudinis credentium erat cor unum et anima una' (Acts 4.32). Et iterum: 'Ecce quam bonum et quam iucundum habitare fratres in unum!' (Ps 132.1).

Ælfric, however, holds back from Bede's equation of the two birds with public and private prayer or Haymo's with the active and contemplative lives, preferring to take the turtle-dove more literally as a model of chastity (presumably in widowhood). The reference to the *culfre* as *unscæððig* perhaps derives from a hint by Bede (Hom. I.18, 64) but Ælfric may have recalled Augustine's Tractates on John, which he used for his later homily on Epiphany (cf CH II.3.158 ff) and which develops more fully both this point and the association with the unity of the church.

117–23 From Bede, Hom. I.18, 65–71:

> Sed utraque avis memorata, quia gemitum pro cantu edere solet, sanctorum in hoc saeculo designat ploratum, de quo dominus memorat dicens: '. . . vos autem contristabimini, sed tristitia vestra vertetur in gaudium' (Jn 16.20). Et rursus: 'Beati lugentes quoniam ipsi consolabuntur' (Mt 5.5).

124–30 Ælfric now returns to Simeon; his comments show some resemblance to the Augustinian sermon used earlier (Serm. 370, §3, PL 39, 1658):

> Non exspectavit ut Christum audiret loquentem, quoniam agnovit infantem. . . . Agnovit Simeon infantem tacentem.

His further point, that the infant Christ could have spoken but preferred to wait until the natural age of human speech, has no parallel in the sources, though there is a somewhat similar reference to nature and the growth of wisdom in a comment by Smaragdus on the final verse of the Gospel text (*Collectiones*, PL 102, 68AB):

> Hoc hominum natura non recipit, ut ante duodecim annos sapientia compleatur, quomodo omnia in illo mirabilia fuerunt, ita pueritia mirabilis fuit, ut Dei sapientia compleretur.

(This comes from Jerome's version of Origen, but is not included in the shortened version of that text included in the PL 95 version of PD.)

132–7 Cf Haymo, Hom. 14, PL 118, 106CD:

> 'Quia viderunt oculi mei salutare tuum.' Salutare Dei Iesu est; nam ubicunque apud nos salvator sive salutaris legitur, in Hebraeo Iesus habetur. Quod vero subditur: 'Quod parasti ante faciem omnium populorum.' Manifestum est quia salutare Dei, id est Christum, omnes populi in carne videre non potuerunt, quia tantummodo in Iudaea per semetipsum praedicavit; sed ante faciem omnium populorum praeparatum dicitur, quod per praedicationem apostolorum ad notitiam pervenit omnium populorum.

Haymo goes on to say that Christ will appear to all men, just and unjust, at the last judgement, which is not Ælfric's point; but Bede refers to Christ being seen by all peoples with mind and faith (*Comm. Luc.*, 1.1887–8): *Omnibus postmodum gentibus populis et linguis mente ac fide conspiciendum.*

137–45 Ælfric's interpretation of Lc 2.32 is not at all like that of his sources, which mainly concentrate on the distinction between Jews and Gentiles (an issue somewhat masked in any case by Ælfric's rendering of *gentibus* as *þeoda*), but Haymo (Hom. 14, PL 118, 107A) does quote Jn 8.12 which Ælfric uses at 142–3: *Ego sum lux mundi qui sequitur me non ambulabit in tenebris sed habebit lucem vitae.*

146–50 Ælfric now moves on from the Gospel reading appointed for the day, quoting Lc 2.33–4 (and characteristically rendering *pater* as *fostorfæder*):

> (33) Et erat pater eius et mater mirantes super his quae dicebantur de illo.
> (34) Et benedixit illis Symeon et dixit ad Mariam matrem eius: ecce positus est hic in ruinam et resurrectionem multorum in Israhel et in signum cui contradicetur.

155–63 Cf Haymo's Hom. 13, PL 118:

> [84B] Post haec prophetat in ruinam et resurrectionem multorum venisse Dominum Salvatorem, ut intelligamus quia Christi nativitas, non credentibus ruina, et credentibus resurrectio facta est. Quod vero ait, 'Positus est hic in ruinam et resurrectionem multorum', spiritu prophetiae intellexit nonnullos ex Iudaeis credituros, multos autem in incredulitate permansuros. . . . [85AB] Sed si subtilius consideremus, inveniemus, quia non solum aliis in ruinam, et aliis in resurrectionem Salvator venit, sed etiam uni eidemque homini in ruinam pariter et resurrectionem apparet, in ruinam scilicet vitiorum, et resurrectionem virtutum. . . . superbiam calcare, et humilitatem didicerit amare, in ruinam pariter et resurrectionem illi Salvator venit. . . . carnis suae desideria calcare et castitatem didicerit amare, in ruinam et resurrectionem pariter ei Dominus venit. [*Haymo works his way through other vices.*] . . . [85C] nisi corruant vitia, virtutes in homine resurgere non possunt.

163–8 Ælfric's interpretation of the *signum* is close to Haymo's but closer still to Haymo's source, the adaptation of Jerome's translation of Origen printed in PL 95, 1183CD:

> Virgo mater est, signum est cui contradicitur. Marcionistae contradicunt huic signo. . . . Resurrexit a mortuis, et hoc signum est cui contradicitur. . . . Omnia quae de eo narrat historia, signum est cui contradicitur, non cui contradicant hi qui credunt in eum.

(The same material is in Hericus, Hom. I.16, 79 ff.) Neither Jerome nor Haymo mention the ascension.

169–80 The sword as metaphor for Mary's mental suffering at the passion is discussed by most of the commentators, but Haymo seems closest (Hom. 13, PL 118, 86BC):

> Nulla docet littera, nulla commemorat historia, beatam Mariam virginem materialis gladii percussione ab hac vita migrasse, quamvis et si hoc fieret, non anima invisibilis, sed caro corporali gladio posset transverberari. Unde in hoc loco, gladii nomine, duram tribulationem et immanissimum dolorem, quem de Domini passione toleravit, debemus intelligere. Licet enim Filium Dei non dubitaret, licet resurrecturum sine dubio crederet, nequaquam tamen putandum est, quod sine magno dolore potuerit videre crucifixum, quem de sua carne immaculata noverat natum.

For the argument that Mary's mental suffering raises her above the martyrs (lines 174–6, not in Haymo), cf the *De Assumptione* of Paschasius Radbertus which was Ælfric's source for CH I.30 (Paschasius, *De Assumptione*, 766–9):

> Beata vero Dei genitrix, quia in ea parte passa est, quae impassibilis habetur, ideo ut ita fatear, quia spiritaliter et atrocius passa est gladio passionis Christi, plus quam martyr fuit.

181–6 A paraphrase of Lc 2.36–8, adding the detail *and on clænnysse*:

> (36) Et erat Anna prophetissa filia Phanuhel de tribu Aser haec processerat in diebus multis et vixerat cum viro suo annis septem a virginitate sua. (37) Et haec vidua usque ad annos octoginta quattuor quae non discedebat de templo ieiuniis et obsecrationibus serviens nocte ac die. (38) Et haec ipsa hora superveniens confitebatur Domino et loquebatur de illo omnibus qui expectabant redemptionem Hierusalem.

186–97 The comments on Anna primarily come from Origen (PL 95, 1184C):

> Et iuste sancta mulier spiritum prophetandi meruit accipere, quia longa castitate longisque ieiuniis ad hoc culmen ascenderat. Videte, mulieres, testimonium Annae, et imitamini illud, si quando vobis evenerit ut perdatis viros. Considerate quid de ea scriptum sit: Septem annis vixit a virginitate sua cum viro suo, et reliqua.

and Haymo, Hom. 13, PL 118, 88BC:

> Habent et viduae exemplum viduitatis in Anna quod imitentur, ut discant, non circuire domos, nec deliciose vivere, non fabulis otiosis occupare

linguam, sed in ieiunio et oratione semper serviant Domino nocte ac die, ut in eorum numero computentur, de quibus ait Apostolus: '. . . vidua quae in deliciis est, vivens mortua est' (1 Tim 5.6).

198–220 Most of the commentaries on this Gospel text note the range of social classes represented in the incarnation, but none has anything at all similar to Ælfric's passage on virginity, widowhood and marriage. The nearest is Augustine's sermon 370, which cites Mary, Anna and Elizabeth as representatives of virgins, widows and married women, and then goes on to invoke Zacharias as representative of married men and sums up the witnesses as *virgo aut vidua aut coniugata, aut puer, aut continens, aut uxoratus* (Serm. 370, §4, PL 39, 1659). The association of the three classes with the thirtyfold, sixtyfold and hundredfold crop of Matthew 13 is made frequently by Ælfric, most fully in CH II.6.115–66, but also in CH II.4.297–305, Assmann 2.132–8, Assmann 3.367–82. For the possible sources see the commentary on II.6. The quotation at 215 is from 1 Cor 7.29: *Qui habent uxores tamquam non habentes sint*. For the association of lust with man's animal nature, cf CH I.6.91 ff.

221–4 From Lc 2.39–40:

> (39) Et ut perfecerunt omnia secundum legem Domini reversi sunt in Galilaeam in civitatem suam Nazareth. (40) Puer autem crescebat et confortabatur plenus sapientia et gratia Dei erat in illo.

224–32 Ælfric's comments on the last two verses owe something to Bede's commentary on Luke (*Comm. Luc.*, 1.2025–34):

> Notanda distinctio verborum quia dominus Iesus Christus in eo quod puer erat, id est habitum humanae fragilitatis induerat, crescere et confortari habebat; in eo vero quod etiam verbum Dei et Deus aeternus erat, nec confortari indigebat nec habebat augeri. Vnde rectissime plenus sapientia perhibetur et gratia, sapientia quidem 'quia in ipso habitat omnis plenitudo divinitatis corporaliter' (Col 2.9), gratia autem quia eidem mediatori Dei et hominum homini Iesu Christo magna gratia donatum est, ut ex quo homo fieri coepisset perfectus esset et Deus.

232–43 Apparently Ælfric's own expansion on the Trinity and Christ's dual nature.

244–9 The ceremonies of Candlemas are described in greater detail in the *Regularis Concordia* (pp. 30–31), and summarised from there in Ælfric's Letter to the Monks of Eynsham (Jones 1998, §25). That description does not quite tally with this one. There, the ceremony is clearly monastic and the monks go in procession to the church where the candles are waiting for them; the candles are then blessed and distributed to the monks, who process back with them to their own church. Here the ceremony is not explicitly just for monks and the reference to those who cannot sing (line 247) suggests the inclusion of the laity, who are indeed those presumably addressed by this homily. The participants here carry their candles (presumably provided by the laity themselves) to the church (presumably their own church) for blessing and then process to other churches or religious houses, perhaps joining with monks where appropriate. Possibly the extension beyond the monastic sphere involved a difference of practice. Though one might note that Ælfric writes as if this custom is not familiar to all those he addresses (*wite gehwa . . .*).

10 QUINQUAGESSIMA

Ælfric's text is Luke 18.31–43, on Christ's healing of a blind man on the road to Jericho, which is the standard reading for the occasion. He offers a primarily allegorical reading, though one operating at both typological and tropological levels: the blind man is mankind expelled from the light of paradise but restored to the light by Christ's coming; his responses are those of the individual Christian, appealing for divine illumination despite the attempts of his carnal thoughts to silence him. The final image, of the blind man now following Christ, leads Ælfric into a long discussion, occupying the last third of the homily (lines 145–204), on what it means to follow Christ and on Christ's own choice of poverty and hardship; the imminent Lenten season was perhaps in his mind here.

The main source seems to be Gregory's homily on the text, which was included in PD, though Ælfric seems also to have used Haymo's lengthy expansion of that homily. He no doubt knew the commentary by Smaragdus and Bede's account in his commentary on Luke as well, but both are heavily indebted to Gregory and offered him nothing new.[1] Haymo separates out the typological and tropological interpretations, treating one at a time, and fills them out, as was his fashion, with numerous Biblical citations and elaborations. Ælfric followed Gregory's line but occasionally found Haymo's rewording helpful. His treatment is often, though, quite independent, developing especially the treatment of the mind and soul and the images of the world as a prison and a place of exile, as well as the final excursus. The anonymous Old English homily on the same text, Blickling 2, also uses Gregory and at times develops the source in similar ways (cf esp. 38–50, 75–87 and 105–16); this may be no more than a mixture of coincidence and the influence of Haymo, but it does raise the possibility that there was a lost adaptation of Gregory's sermon used by both Anglo-Saxon authors.

[1] Förster (1894, p. 2) noted the use of Gregory homily 2; Smetana (1959, p. 187) noted its inclusion in PD, and (1961, p. 466) a detail possibly from Haymo.

Sources and notes

The following texts are cited below:

1. Alcuin, *De Animae Ratione*, PL 101, cols. 639–50.
2. *The Blickling Homilies*, ed. R. Morris, EETS os 58, 63 and 73 (1874–80, repr. 1990).
3. Gregory the Great, *Homiliae in Evangelia*, PL 76, Hom. 2, cols. 1081–6.
4. Haymo of Auxerre, *Homiliae de Tempore*, PL 118, Hom. 23, cols. 172–82.

2–22 A free paraphrase of Lc 18.31–43:

> (31) Assumpsit autem Iesus duodecim, et ait illis: Ecce ascendimus Hierosolyma, et consummabuntur omnia quae scripta sunt per prophetas de Filio hominis. (32) Tradetur enim gentibus, et illudetur, et flagellabitur, et conspuetur. (33) Et postquam flagellaverint, occident eum, et die tertia resurget. (34) Et ipsi nihil horum intellexerunt. Et erat verbum istud absconditum ab eis, et non intellegebant quae dicebantur. (35) Factum est autem, cum appropinquaret Hiericho, caecus quidam sedebat secus viam, mendicans. (36) Et cum audiret turbam praetereuntem, interrogabat quid hoc esset. (37) Dixerunt autem ei quod Iesus Nazarenus transiret. (38) Et clamavit, dicens: Iesu fili David, miserere mei. (39) Et qui praeibant increpabant eum, ut taceret. Ipse vero multo magis clamabat: Fili David, miserere mei. (40) Stans autem Iesus iussit illum adduci ad se. Et cum appropinquasset, interrogavit illum, (41) dicens: Quid tibi vis faciam? At ille dixit: Domine, ut videam. (42) Et Iesus dixit illi: Respice, fides tua te salvum fecit. (43) Et confestim vidit, et sequebatur illum, magnificans Deum. Et omnis plebs, ut vidit, dedit laudem Deo.

Significant differences are the shift from third person (the son of man) to first in verses 31–3; the curtailment of verse 34; the omission of *mendicans* in verse 35 (line 11), and the addition of *mid micelre onbryrdnysse* at line 22.

23–9 Ælfric follows Haymo on Christ's words to the disciples (Hom. 23, PL 118, 172CD):

> Praevidens Dominus ex sua passione animos discipulorum conturbandos, longe eis ante eamdem passionem praedicere voluit, ut tanto minus turbarentur tempore passionis. . . . Et quos contristabat denuntiata passio, laetificaret praedicta resurrectio.

Gregory, Hom. 2, PL 76, 1082A, is similar but less close.

30–8 Cf Gregory, Hom. 2, PL 76, 1082BC:

> Sed quia carnales adhuc discipuli nullo modo valebant capere verba mysterii, venitur ad miraculum. Ante eorum oculos caecus lumen recipit, ut qui coelestis mysterii verba non caperent, eos ad fidem coelestia facta solidarent. Sed miracula Domini et Salvatoris nostri sic accipienda sunt,

fratres charissimi, ut et in veritate credantur facta, et tamen per significationem nobis aliquid innuant. Opera quippe eius et per potentiam aliud ostendunt, et per mysterium aliud loquuntur.

The note that it is the *folc*'s faith (line 37) that is strengthened by miracles is characteristic of Ælfric's view on the subject; in context it is of course the disciples who are to be strengthened.

38–50 Gregory provides the starting-point for this passage (Hom. 2, PL 76, 1082C):

Caecus quippe est genus humanum, quod in parente primo a paradisi gaudiis expulsum, claritatem supernae lucis ignorans, damnationis suae tenebras patitur; sed tamen per Redemptoris sui praesentiam illuminatur, ut internae lucis gaudia iam per desiderium videat, atque in via vitae boni operis gressus ponat.

Ælfric develops the ideas by introducing the image of the dark prison (lines 41, 45, 50) to express mankind's exclusion from the light of paradise and his position after the redemption, granted the light of faith and the hope of heaven but still physically excluded from heaven. Blickling 2 also refers to a prison (*carcern*, Blickling 2, 19.24) but that is in a different context and seems in any case to be an error of translator or scribe.[2]

51–59 Ælfric's interpretation of Jericho as mortality and mutability draws on both Haymo, Hom. 23, PL 118, 176CD:

Interpretata autem Iericho in nostra lingua dicitur luna. Luna quippe quae menstruis horis crescit et decrescit, in Scripturis aliquando defectum nostrae mortalitatis insinuat, qui crescimus nascendo, decrescimus moriendo.

and Gregory, Hom. 2, PL 76, 1082D:

Dum igitur conditor noster appropinquat Iericho, caecus ad lumen redit, quia dum divinitas defectum nostrae carnis suscepit, humanum genus lumen, quod amiserat, recepit.

Note the slightly different interpretation of Jericho, as the world, at CH II.12.425 ff; the two ideas are combined in *De Temporibus Anni*, 1.35–6.

59–67 A succinct rendering of Gregory, Hom. 2, PL 76, 1083A:

Qui videlicet caecus recte et iuxta viam sedere et mendicans esse describitur; ipsa enim Veritas dicit: 'Ego sum via' (Jn 14.6) . Qui ergo aeternae lucis claritatem nescit, caecus est; sed si iam in Redemptorem credit, iuxta viam sedet; si autem iam credit, sed ut aeternam lucem recipiat rogare dissimulat, atque a precibus cessat, caecus quidem iuxta viam sedet, sed minime mendicat. Si vero et crediderit, et caecitatem cordis sui cognoverit, et ut lumen veritatis recipiat postulat, iuxta viam

[2] See R. Dawson, 'The Blickling Homilies: Some Emendations', *Notes and Queries* 214 (1969), 248–9.

> caecus sedet, et mendicat. Quisquis ergo caecitatis suae tenebras agnoscit, quisquis hoc, quod sibi deest, lumen aeternitatis intelligit, clamet medullis cordis, clamet et vocibus mentis, dicens: Iesu fili David, miserere mei.

Both expositors have here silently shifted from a typological reading, interpreting the blind man as mankind and Christ's coming as the redemption, to a tropological one, reading the blind man as the individual Christian coming to know Christ. The distinction here, made by both Gregory and Ælfric, between believing in Christ and knowing the eternal light, and the association of faith with the state of blindness rather than illumination, seem at odds with Ælfric's interpretation of faith as light at 47–50; but he makes a similar distinction between the basic faith of the blind man and the fuller belief of the illuminated man at Irvine 3.162–5. Gregory refers to the 'light of truth' but for Ælfric the light seems to be more an infusion of divine grace which purifies the will (cf 77–82).

68–75 Ælfric follows Gregory in interpreting the crowd as the hindering thoughts and sins (Hom. 2, PL 76, 1083B):

> Quid autem designant isti qui Iesum venientem praecedunt, nisi desideriorum carnalium turbas, tumultusque vitiorum, qui, priusquam Iesus ad cor nostrum veniat, tentationibus suis cogitationem nostram dissipant, et voces cordis in oratione perturbant? Saepe namque dum converti ad Dominum post perpetrata vitia volumus, dum contra haec eadem exorare vitia quae perpetravimus conamur, occurrunt cordi phantasmata peccatorum quae fecimus, mentis nostrae aciem reverberant, confundunt animum, et vocem nostrae deprecationis premunt.

75–87 The starting-point is again Gregory, Hom. 2, PL 76:

> [1083C] Sed quid ad haec illuminandus iste caecus fecit audiamus. Sequitur: 'Ipse vero multo magis clamabat: Fili David, miserere mei'. Ecce quem turba increpat ut taceat magis ac magis clamat, quia quanto graviori tumultu cogitationum carnalium premimur, tanto orationi insistere ardentius debemus. Contradicit turba, ne clamemus, quia peccatorum nostrorum phantasmata plerumque et in oratione patimur. . . . [1084A] Sed cum in oratione nostra vehementer insistimus, transeuntem Iesum menti figimus. . . . Stat Iesus ut lucem restituat, quia Deus in corde figitur, et lux amissa reparatur.

Ælfric however expands this account of the workings of the mind to give a central role to the devil as instigator of sinful thoughts (lines 77, 84–6). This is in fact a thoroughly Gregorian view, though not used by him on this occasion, and Ælfric draws on Gregory in developing this picture in the next homily, at CH I.11.138–53. (Cf too his short piece *De Cogitatione*.) Haymo also introduces devils in his recasting of the present passage by Gregory (Haymo, Hom. 23, PL 118, 181B):

> Quo enim acrius se aliquis sentit impugnari a malignorum spirituum tentatione, seu ab ipsa consuetudine peccandi, eo fortius debet pugnare in oratione.

Blickling 2 also mentions the devil (Blickling 2, 19.17). That the evil thoughts induced by the devil are not themselves harmful is a line which Ælfric returns to in I.11 and again in *De Cogitatione* and his pastoral letter for Wulfstan (Fehr II, §§ 96–8).

87–97 A close rendering of Gregory, Hom. 2, PL 76, 1084B:

> Transire namque humanitatis est, stare divinitatis. Per humanitatem quippe habuit nasci, crescere, mori, resurgere, de loco ad locum venire. . . . Per divinitatem vero ei semper stare est, quia ubique praesens, nec per motum venit, nec per motum recedit. Caecum igitur clamantem Dominus transiens audit, stans illuminat, quia per humanitatem suam vocibus nostrae caecitatis compatiendo misertus est, sed lumen nobis gratiae per divinitatis potentiam infudit.

98–104 From Gregory, Hom. 2, PL 76, 1084BC:

> Nunquid qui lumen reddere poterat quid vellet caecus ignorabat? Sed peti vult id quod et nos petere et se concedere praenoscit. Importune namque ad orationem nos admonet, et tamen dicit: 'Scit namque Pater vester coelestis, quid opus sit vobis, antequam petatis eum' (Mt 6.8) . Ad hoc ergo requirit ut petatur: ad hoc requirit, ut cor ad orationem excitet.

105–16 Ælfric's comments on the blind man's prayer for sight correspond fairly closely to Gregory, Hom. 2, PL 76, 1084CD:

> Ecce caecus a Domino non aurum, sed lucem quaerit. Parvipendit extra lucem aliquid quaerere, quia etsi habere caecus quodlibet potest, sine luce videre non potest quod habet. Imitemur ergo, fratres charissimi, eum quem et corpore audivimus et mente salvatum. Non falsas divitias, non terrena dona, non fugitivos honores a Domino, sed lucem quaeramus; nec lucem quae loco clauditur, quae tempore finitur, quae noctium interruptione variatur, quae a nobis communiter cum pecoribus cernitur, sed lucem quaeramus quam videre cum solis angelis possimus, quam nec initium inchoat, nec finis angustat. Ad quam profecto lucem via fides est. Unde recte et illuminando caeco protinus respondetur: 'Respice, fides tua te salvum fecit'.

The expansion of *aurum* to gold, silver and other worldly things (line 106) perhaps reflects Haymo's recasting (Hom. 23, PL 118, 179A): *Non aurum, non argentum, non terrenas divitias, non longiturnam vitam, non vindictam inimicorum, sed ineffabile lumen quaerere debemus*. Blickling 2 has a strikingly similar formulation: *Se blinda ne bæd goldes, ne seolfres, ne worldglenga, ah bæd his eagena leohtes* (Blickling 2, 21.5–6).

117–25 A paraphrase of Gregory's remarks on spiritual sight and the soul (Hom. 2, PL 76, 1084D-5A):

Sed ad haec cogitatio carnalis dicit: Quomodo possum lucem spiritalem quaerere, quam videre non possum? . . . Cui scilicet cogitationi est quod breviter quisque respondeat, quia et haec ipsa quae sentit, non per corpus, sed per animam cogitat. Et nemo suam animam videt, nec tamen dubitat se animam habere, quam non videt. Ex invisibili namque anima visibile regitur corpus. Si autem auferatur quod est invisibile, protinus corruit hoc quod visibile stare videbatur.

125–36 Ælfric now extends the discussion of the soul and body. Some of the points come ultimately from Alcuin's *De Animae Ratione,* PL 101, 643B:

Sicut corporis vita anima est, ita animae vita Deus est. Dum anima deserit corpus, moritur corpus, et mortuum recte dicitur, quia insensibile est. . . . Animae vero mors est, dum eam Deus deserit dono suae gratiae, ob magnitudinem scelerum, moritur meliore sui parte.

Alcuin goes on to emphasise that the soul cannot lose its *aeternitas*. The immediate source was perhaps the Latin adaptation of Alcuin's treatise preserved in the Boulogne manuscript (Boulogne-sur-Mer, Bibliothèque Municipale MS 63; text from Leinbaugh 1980, lines 212–6)[3]:

Anima namque corporis uita est, anime uero uita Deus est. Dum anima corpus deserit, moritur. Animae uero mors est dum eam Deus deserit dono suae gratiae, et ob magnitudinem scelerum moritur meliore sui parte, et erit semiviva.

Ælfric's English translation of that précis, incorporated in LS 1, elaborates and extends the last words in very much the same way as the present passage (LS 1.141–6):

Seo sawul soðlice is þæs lichoman lif . and þære sawle lif is god . Gif seo sawul forlæt þonne lichoman þonne swælt seo lichoma . and gif god forlæt þa sawle for ormættum synnum . þonne swælt heo on þam sælran dæle swa þæt heo bið forloren þam ecan life . and swa þeah næfre ne geendað on þam ecum wytum.

At the end (lines 134–7; a new sentence evidently begins with *hu* at 134) Ælfric returns to Gregory, Hom. 2, PL 76, 1085A: *Ex invisibili ergo substantia in hac vita visibili vivitur, et esse vita invisibilis dubitatur?.*

138–45 A summary rendering of Gregory on the blind man following Christ (Hom. 2, PL 76, 1085AB):

Videt et sequitur, qui bonum quod intelligit operatur. Videt autem, sed non sequitur, qui bonum quidem intelligit, sed bona operari contemnit. Si ergo, fratres charissimi, caecitatem iam nostrae peregrinationis agnoscimus

3 I am very grateful to Professor Leinbaugh for sending me the relevant passage from his unpublished edition, and allowing me to quote it. For the relationship, and date, of the Boulogne version and its OE translation, see above p. xlvi.

. . . Iesum quem mente cernimus opere sequamur. Aspiciamus qua graditur, et eius vestigia imitando teneamus. Iesum etenim sequitur qui imitatur. . . . Hinc rursus admonet, dicens: 'Si quis mihi ministrat, me sequatur' (Jn 12.26).

145–204 Gregory goes on to discuss at length Christ's choice of poverty and suffering. So too does Ælfric, but there is very little similarity of detail or expression, and he seems to abandon his sources from here to the end of the homily.

146–7 Mt 8.20: *Vulpes foveas habent, et volucres caeli tabernacula; filius autem hominis non habet ubi caput reclinet.*

150–56 Jn 6.15–19:

(15) Iesus ergo cum cognovisset quia venturi essent ut raperent eum et facerent eum regem, fugit iterum in montem ipse solus. (16) Ut autem sero factum est descenderunt discipuli eius ad mare. (17) Et cum ascendissent navem venerunt trans mare in Capharnaum et tenebrae iam factae erant et non venerat ad eos Iesus. (18) Mare autem vento magno flante exsurgebat. (19) Cum remigassent ergo quasi stadia viginti quinque aut triginta vident Iesum ambulantem super mare et proximum navi fieri et timuerunt.

With *drium fotum* (line 155) cf CH I.1.232 and 255.

156–60 The thought perhaps owes something to Gregory but not the series of antitheses (Hom. 2, PL 76, 1085C):

Prosperari in mundo noluit; opprobria irrisionesque toleravit; sputa, flagella, alapas, spineam coronam, crucemque sustinuit.

161–6 The concept of life as an exile is touched on incidentally by Gregory earlier in his homily (see above under lines 138–44); the point is somewhat similarly expanded in Blickling 2 (23.2–7), though in a different context. Lines 165–6 are Jac 4.4: *Quicumque ergo voluerit amicus esse saeculi huius, inimicus Dei constituitur.* The two sentences together seem to be expanded by Ælfric at Pope 11.139 ff.

167–97 The reference at 167–8 is to Mt 7.13–14:

(13) Intrate per angustam portam quia lata porta et spatiosa via quae ducit ad perditionem et multi sunt qui intrant per eam. (14) Quam angusta porta et arta via quae ducit ad vitam et pauci sunt qui inveniunt eam.

In turning to this image Ælfric is perhaps picking up the pericope's reference to the *weg* as well as developing the idea of a journey to one's true *eðel*. None of his sources use this text. Lines 192–3 are 1 Petr 2.21: *Christus passus est pro nobis, vobis relinquens exemplum ut sequamini vestigia eius.* Haymo also cites it (Hom. 23, PL 118, 179D), but his comments are unlike Ælfric's.

200–4 Gregory also ends by returning to the end of the Gospel text (Hom. 2, PL 76, 1086A):

> Sicque fit ut non solum vita nostra in Deum proficiat, sed haec ipsa nostra conversatio ad laudem Dei et alios accendat.

11 FIRST SUNDAY IN LENT

Ælfric's subject is the devil's temptation of Christ in the wilderness, as described in Matthew 4.1–11, the standard reading for the occasion. Both Matthew and Luke present this as the final preparation for Christ's mission, immediately following his baptism and preceding his journeying and teaching, and some of the commentators discuss this aspect, but Ælfric says nothing of the context. The story has for him two main significances: it is a crucial (and perhaps potentially dangerous—cf lines 3–7) representation of the relations between God and the devil, with implications for the nature of Christ and the relation between man and the devil; and it initiates and explains the tradition of the Lenten fast. Ælfric's exposition keeps fairly close to the literal sense of the Gospel but takes up a series of important aspects: Christ's patience and humility in concealing his divine power; the nature of temptation and testing, of Christ and of man; the three temptations offered to Adam and Christ; and the significance of the forty-day fast. He sees the temptation of Christ as a parallel to the redemption itself, involving a similar defeat of the devil and a similar concealment of divinity in humanity. Ælfric shows little interest in the kind of allegorical interpretation suggested by Haymo, which applies the text to the temptation of man, but does several times draw out the analogical implications for man, especially on the nature of temptation and the roles of angels and devils.

Sources present a complicated question. There is material from Gregory the Great's homily on the Gospel text, and from Haymo's reworking of it, as well as points in common with Jerome's commentary on Matthew, Bede's commentary on the parallel text in Luke and homilies by Hericus of Auxerre, all of which may easily have been consulted by Ælfric.[1] However, some of Ælfric's points and details of expression, even in material drawn ultimately from these Latin commentaries, find a closer parallel in an anonymous Old English homily on the same text, Irvine 5, which survives only in one twelfth-century manuscript.[2] There are no close verbal parallels and it is probably not a matter of one Old English text influencing the other, but of both drawing on

[1] Förster (1894, pp. 11–12 and 43–5) suggested Gregory's homily, and the commentaries of Jerome, Bede and Smaragdus; Smetana (1959, pp. 187–8) noted that the Gregory homily was in PD for the occasion, and (Smetana 1961, p. 462) suggested Haymo's homily as a source for one detail.

[2] See the detailed discussion by Irvine, pp. 116–22.

the same Latin source-material, which itself presumably derived from Gregory, Haymo and Hericus, if not others, but was already adapted in some way. The same source was evidently used by another Old English homily, Blickling 3, as well, though the latter provides no parallels to Ælfric closer than those cited from the Latin commentaries or Irvine 5. The material common to Ælfric's homily and Irvine 5 occurs in different orders in the three vernacular homilies; Susan Irvine plausibly suggests that we should be thinking of a collection of several Latin texts or excerpts on the Gospel text rather than a single lost adaptation. Despite the use of the same source-material in part, Ælfric produces a quite different homily from the other two vernacular texts, much more concerned with the theological issues rather than the moral applications and frequently developing concerns of his own not found in any of the analogous texts.

Sources and Notes

The following texts are cited below (though because of the problems noted above, it is hard to be confident which of them was definitely used, even indirectly):

1. Gregory the Great, *Homiliae in Evangelia*, PL 76, Hom. 16, cols. 1134–8.
2. Haymo of Auxerre, *Homiliae de Tempore*, PL 118, Hom. 28, cols. 190–203.
3. Hericus, *Homiliae in Circulum Anni*, ed. R. Quadri, CCCM 116 (Turnhout, 1992), Hom. I.28 (pp. 228–40) and Hom. I.32 (pp. 270–81).
4. Jerome, *Commentarii in Evangelium Matthaei*, ed. D. Hurst and M. Adriaen, CCSL 77 (Turnhout, 1969).
5. *Old English Homilies from MS Bodley 343*, ed. S. Irvine, EETS os 302 (1993).

3–7 It is not clear why Ælfric stresses the complexity of this Gospel text rather than any other. Possibly he feared that wrong inferences could be drawn about the nature of Christ or the relation between God and the devil.

8–26 Mt 4.1–11:

(1) Tunc Iesus ductus est in desertum ab Spiritu ut temptaretur a diabolo. (2) Et cum ieiunasset quadraginta diebus et quadraginta noctibus postea esuriit. (3) Et accedens temptator dixit ei: si Filius Dei es dic ut lapides isti panes fiant. (4) Qui respondens dixit: scriptum est non in pane solo vivet homo sed in omni verbo quod procedit de ore Dei. (5) Tunc adsumit eum diabolus in sanctam civitatem et statuit eum supra pinnaculum templi. (6) Et dixit ei: si Filius Dei es mitte te deorsum; scriptum est enim quia angelis suis mandabit de te et in manibus tollent te, ne forte offendas ad lapidem pedem tuum. (7) Ait illi Iesus rursum: scriptum est non temptabis Dominum Deum tuum. (8) Iterum adsumit eum diabolus in montem excelsum valde et ostendit ei omnia regna mundi et gloriam eorum. (9) Et

> dixit illi: haec tibi omnia dabo si cadens adoraveris me. (10) Tunc dicit ei Iesus: vade Satanas; scriptum est: Dominum Deum tuum adorabis et illi soli servies. (11) Tunc reliquit eum diabolus et ecce angeli accesserunt et ministrabant ei.

In rendering *ab spiritu* as *fram ðam halgan gaste* (rather than 'by the devil') Ælfric silently incorporates an interpretation argued at length by Gregory (Hom. 16, PL 76, 1135B) and others. The clause *swa þæt . . . fyrste* (lines 10–11) is imported from the parallel text Lc 4.2: *Et nihil manducavit in diebus illis et consummatis illis esuriit*, perhaps because of its importance to the exposition. Ælfric's *is beboden* and *þæt hi* (line 17) probably reflect the common variants *mandavit* for *mandabit* and *ut* for *et* in verse 6 (both variants are followed in the *OE Gospels*). In verse 10 he follows the variant reading *vade retro* for *vade* (see below on 108 ff).

Ælfric's distinction between *costnian* (v.1) and *fandian* (v.7) is clearly an important one in his philosophy. The Vulgate uses *tentare* (*temptare*) at both points, and *tentare* and *tentationes* are the terms used by the Latin commentaries throughout for the devil's temptations. The Old English versions of the Gospel all use *costnian/costian* for both verses, and *costnian* and *costnung* are the regular terms used by the other two Old English homilies on this text. Ælfric explains his distinction between the two words in CH I.19 and in his *Interrogationes*: *fandian* can be predicated of both God and the devil, and is a neutral term, meaning to try or test what a man really is; *costnian* is predicated of the devil, and means to tempt or induce someone to sin (though it seems also to have a wider range, covering malicious attacks and tribulations of all kinds). The two words can both be used of the devil's temptation of Christ, because he is attempting both to induce him to sin (or perhaps to destroy him) and to discover what sort of being he is, as Ælfric goes on to explain. But *fandian* is used at verse 7 because Ælfric interprets 'Tempt not the Lord your God' not as a rebuke to the devil for inciting Christ to do wrong but as Christ's statement that he himself (and men too) should not try or test God by demanding a sign of divine power. To *fandian* men is not itself wrong, since *fandung* is beneficial and necessary to salvation, Ælfric argues (line 71 ff).

27–36 Cf Gregory, Hom. 16, PL 76, 1135BC:

> Vere et absque ulla quaestione convenienter accipitur ut a sancto Spiritu in desertum ductus credatur, ut illuc eum suus Spiritus duceret, ubi nunc ad tentandum malignus spiritus inveniret. . . . Qui tamen non esse incredibilia ista cognoscimus, si in illo et alia facta pensamus. . . . Iustum quippe erat ut sic tentationes nostras suis tentationibus vinceret, sicut mortem nostram venerat sua morte superare. . . . [*earlier*] Quid ergo mirum si se ab illo permisit in montem duci, qui se pertulit etiam a membris illius crucifigi? . . . [*earlier*] Certe iniquorum omnium caput diabolus est, et huius capitis membra sunt omnes iniqui. . . . Non est ergo indignum Redemptori nostro quod tentari voluit, qui venerat occidi.

For 28–30 cf too Irvine 5.26–9:

> . . . Na for þam þæt þe deofel hæfde æniȝ fare to ure Hælende oðer his mæð wære þæt he him ahwær on neawste come, ȝif he hit for ure lufe ne ȝeðafede.

37–42 The devil's doubts about Christ are discussed by Jerome and Haymo, and were no doubt familiar to Ælfric from Gregory's *Moralia*, II.xxiv (CCSL 143)[3], but none is close in detail. The central idea is succinctly put by Jerome (*Comm. Matth.*, 1.342–5):

> In omnibus temptationibus hoc agit diabolus ut intellegat si Filius Dei sit. Sed Dominus sic responsionem temperat ut eum relinquat ambiguum.

The two sentences are repeated in Bede's commentary on Luke (*Comm. Luc.*, 1.3072–5). Haymo, by contrast, insists that the devil did recognize Christ as God. In citing Christ's sinlessness rather than his power or miracles as evidence of his divinity Ælfric resembles a passage which appears in Hericus, Hom. I.28, 112–8:

> Ecce avaritiae radix in eo nulla est, nescit eius lingua mendacium, oculi eius concupiscentiam non admittunt, nulla aurium voluptate mollitur, luxuries certe per quam michi humanum genus subieci in eo nulla consurgit, nulla pectus eius tangit libido, nichil in eo reperio quod me delectet, omnes meos conatus evacuat; ad ultimum ecce esurit ut homo, cum esurire Deum ratio nulla persuadeat.

(The passage also appears in a sermon printed among the works of Maximus, PL 57, 304.) Cf too Irvine 5.56–7: *And þæt on him næs nare synne wem.*

42–7 Haymo's comments on Christ's fast and hunger are slightly similar (Hom. 28, PL 118, 196B):

> Quem enim quadraginta diebus et noctibus ieiunantem videbat, fortasse tentare non auderet, nisi eum esurientem iterum cerneret. Et quem post ieiunium esurientem vidit, quasi hominem tentare praesumpsit. Unde et subditur: 'Et accedens tentator, dixit ei: Si Filius Dei es, dic ut lapides isti panes fiant.'

But cf also a passage in the *Passio Bartholomaei* which Ælfric used as source for I.31 (the apostle is speaking to the Indian king); *Passio Bartholomaei*, Mombritius 1910, I.142.16–24:

> Ita raperet haec filium hominis et virginis et poneret eum inter feras in deserto, et per quadraginta dies non dixit ei manduca quia non vidit eum esurientem. Hoc enim statuerat ipse diabolus in corde suo ut si per quadraginta dies transactos non esuriret pro certo nosset quia deus verus est. . . . Hoc autem Sathanas ubi vidit post quadraginta dies deum esurire quasi securus effectus quod deus non esset, dixit ei: 'Quare esuris? Dic ut lapides isti panes fiant et manduca.'

[3] See Gabrielson 1912.

47–50 Ælfric's comments on Christ's power have no equivalent in the Latin texts but have a slight parallel in Irvine 5.65–71:

> Næs Criste nan earfoðnesse þæt he þa stanes mid his worde to lafes wrohte; for ȝif he hit icwæde, hit wære sone iworden . . . swa he alle sceafte iscop and iwrohtæ.

The Old English homily seems here to be following Hericus, Hom. I.28, 147 ff.

52–7 Cf Hericus, Hom. I.28, 173–6:

> Integer homo duabus consistit substantiis, anima videlicet et corpore; sicut enim corpus si non terreno pane alatur tabescit ac deficit, sic nisi anima verbi Dei alimonia fuerit saginata a status sui rectitudine deperit.

And Irvine 5.76–80:

> Hwæt we witen þæt monnes lichame sceal bi mete libban þa hwile þe he on þisse life bið; swa sceal eac þeo sawle libbæn bi Godes wordes, þæt is þæt heo sceal Godes lare ȝeorne lystæn, and his bode æfre healden ȝyf heo sceal þæt ece lif habben.

Cf also the Haymo and Ps-Bede cited by Irvine.

62–75 The devil's mis-citation of Psalm 91.11 is discussed by Haymo (Hom. 28, PL 118, 198A):

> Ex quo loco cognoscimus quia diabolus male Scripturas interpretatur. Hoc enim non de persona Domini scriptum est, sed in persona iusti viri canitur, qui adiutorio indiget angelorum, ne offendat ad lapidem.

And Hericus, Hom. I.28, 242–7:

> Diabolus scripturas sanctas quidem bene intellegit sed eas falso semper interpretatur, unde et hoc testimonium falsa interpretatione ad Christum retulit, cum hoc psalmista non de Christo sed de quolibet electorum dixerit; unicuique enim fidelium angelus ad custodiam ex tempore baptismatis delegatur. . . .

Haymo is perhaps more likely, since he goes on to relate the rest of the psalm verse to the assaults of the devil, which may have prompted Ælfric's independent development. Irvine 5 is again very close (5.100–3):

> On þesne ænne godspel we rædæþ þæt deofel ongan haliȝe bec to reccan, ah he þa sone þone forme cwide leah, swa him ealc lyȝe and elc leasunge bilimpð.

Ælfric develops the idea of guardian angels, introduced here by Haymo and Hericus, more fully in CH I.34, using the same verse from Psalm 91. Here, he turns instead to the nature of diabolic temptation and the value of trial, silently answering the question of how the concept of a guardian angel is reconciled with the role of the devil and the possibility of succumbing to temptation; that is, he is arguing that the temptations of the devil are part of the system for testing mankind that God and his angels permit for the good of man. Similar ideas are developed in CH I.19, but there too Ælfric is mainly expanding freely on his sources. Cf, too, Ælfric's *Interrogationes*, where he again introduces these ideas in expanding his source.

76–85 That this was a temptation to vainglory is noted by Gregory in discussing the nature of the three temptations and their connections with Adam's temptation (Hom. 16, PL 76, 1136B): *Per vanam gloriam tentat cum dicit: Si Filius Dei es, mitte te deorsum.* For the explanation of tempting the Lord, cf Bede, *Comm. Luc.*, 1.3092–5:

> Non temptabis dominum Deum tuum. Suggerebatur enim tanquam homini ut signo aliquo exploraret ipse quantus esset, id est quam multum apud Deum posset.

Cf too Hericus, Hom. I.28, 254–55: *Deum temptat, qui iactantiae suae vitio superfluam et inutilem vult ostendere virtutem.* The rhetoric of Ælfric's phrasing at 78–9, 'he who bent the high arch of heaven' is particularly striking. Despite the point after *awyrdnysse*, the sense of 77–8 appears to be something like 'he could easily have fallen down without injury to his limbs'.

89–107 This extensive discussion of the devil's claim to be ruler of the world is largely Ælfric's own. His discussion of the devil's presumption perhaps takes a hint from Jerome, *Comm. Matth.*, 1.373–6:

> Arrogans et superbus etiam hoc de iactantia loquitur, non quod in toto mundo habeat potestatem ut possit omnia regna dare diabolus, cum sciamus plerosque sanctos viros a Deo reges factos.

Cf too Haymo, who also quotes Ps 23.1 (cf Ælfric's lines 96–8), Hom. 28, PL 118, 203B:

> Fefellit diabolus, et hoc per arrogantiam dixit, non per potentiam. Absit hoc ad intelligendum ut eius sit universus mundus. Neque enim potest fore ut sit, sed illius est qui cuncta ex nihilo creavit. Cuius namque sit Propheta declarat, dicens: 'Domini est terra et plenitudo eius, orbis terrarum et universi qui habitant in eo' (Ps 23.1).

But Ælfric goes on, independently, to explain in what way the devil can actually be said to be ruler of the world, quoting Jn 12.31: *Nunc princeps huius mundi eicietur foras.* He interjects a similar point, with the parallel quotation from Jn 14.30, in *Interrogationes*, 273 ff.

108–115 None of the commentaries have anything resembling this, and the Latin note which Ælfric seems to have added in support proves a veritable mare's nest.[4] For the etymology of Satan's name, which Ælfric gives as *niðerhreosende* in the Old English text and *deorsum ruens* in his Latin note, Jerome gives rather *deorsum fluens* (in his *Liber Interpretationis Hebraicorum Nominum*, CCSL 72, 80.16, and in his commentary on the epistle to the Ephesians, PL 26, 544), as does Isidore (*Etymologiae* VIII.11.18). The same

[4] Cf Förster 1894, pp. 44–6; and see also Joyce Hill, 'Ælfric's Use of Etymologies', *ASE* 17 (1988), 35–44, at 37–8.

etymology is given by Haymo at an earlier point in his homily (Hom. 28, PL 118, 198A):

> Non enim quos decipit sursum ascendere monet, sed deorsum ruere suadet. Unde pulchre Symmachus diaboli nomen deorsum fluens interpretatus est, ut quod ait in voluntate, hoc etiam sonaret in nomine.

The alternative form *deorsum ruens* seems very rare, but it is given by Hericus in his homily I.32, 217 (a text which Ælfric appears to have used as a source for CH II.13): *Diabolus enim interpretatur deorsum ruens.* Presumably both interpretations were current, at least in Carolingian texts, and Ælfric may of course have seen it as a variant reading in copies of Jerome or Haymo.

The Latin note is puzzling. *Vade* is the standard Vulgate reading for Christ's reply to Satan, but the variant reading *Vade retro*[5] is very common in Anglo-Saxon England, followed not only by Ælfric but also by the *OE Gospels*, Blickling 3, Irvine 5, the Rushworth Gospels and the poem *Christ and Satan*. The contrast between Christ's words to the devil here and his words to St Peter at Mt 16.23, *Vade retro me*, to which Ælfric refers in his note, apparently attributing the point to Jerome, is indeed drawn by Jerome in his Commentary on Matthew (*Comm. Matth.*, 1.378–85):

> 'Tunc dixit ei Iesus: vade satanas; scriptum est: Dominum Deum tuum adorabis et illi soli servies.' . . . Petro enim dicitur: 'Vade retro me satana', id est sequere me qui contrarius es voluntati meae; hic vero audit: 'Vade satanas', et non ei dicitur retro, ut subaudiatur: vade in ignem aeternum qui praeparatus est tibi et angelis tuis.

This is not quite what Ælfric records, but one manuscript has *Vade retro satanas* for *Vade satanas*, and *retro me* for *retro*, and this is presumably what Ælfric saw;[6] admittedly this is a commentary not a letter, but no parallel in an epistle by Jerome has yet surfaced. Haymo, recasting this passage in his homily, gives only *vade* and Smaragdus insists that Christ did not say *retro*. It is certainly striking that Ælfric should cite Jerome's authority in support of a Biblical reading and an interpretation of Satan's name when in neither case did he actually agree with Jerome. Ælfric may have had his attention drawn to the problem of the reading by Hericus, who quotes and interprets the *Vade satanas* reading and then adds (Hom. I.28, 302–4):

> Si autem secundum nonnulla exemplaria quis legere voluerit: 'Vade retro, Satanas', potest ita sentire quod 'retro' ad anteriora tempora respiciat.

But Ælfric's reference to older and more correct exemplars suggests he had done his own research into the matter, and preferred *Vade retro* against whatever other authorities he had seen. The argument from the interpretation of Satan's name seems to be his own.

[5] It is reported from several manuscripts by Wordsworth and White.

[6] Jerome, *Comm. Matth.*, repeats the point at 3.152 and again the manuscripts show a variety of variant readings apparently attempting to bring it into line with the *Vade retro* variant.

116–26 The passage on praying to none but God has no parallel in the Latin commentaries, but Irvine 5.143–9 is clearly summarising the same material on not praying to angels and saints:

> Crist cwæð þæt mon sceal to Gode Almihtiȝ ane biddan and him ane þeowian. Soðlice ne sceole we us biddæn naþor ne to englum ne to oþre haliȝe monnum, buton to ure Drihtne ane þe þe is soð God. Ac we sceolen þeah ælcne Godes halȝe biddæn to fultume and to þingunge, and þeahhwæþre to nan oðre us ne biddan, buton to þam ane þe is soð God.

The notion that Christians ask saints for intercession but do not actually pray to them perhaps relates to Ælfric's care to establish that saints do not themselves perform miracles but intercede with God to do so.[7] The exchange between St John and the angel cited at 123–6 is a somewhat adapted version of Apoc 22.8–9:

> (8) Cecidi ut adorarem ante pedes angeli . . . (9) et dixit mihi: Vide ne feceris; conservus enim tuus sum, et fratrum tuorum prophetarum . . .; Deum adora.

Ælfric had used it, in a slightly different context, at I.2.149–52, and may have introduced it here independently of any source.

127–31 Ælfric now turns to a point made by Gregory on the dual nature of Christ (Hom. 16, PL 76, 1136D):

> Et homo est quem diabolus tentat, et idem ipse Deus est cui ab angelis ministratur. . . . Nisi hunc diabolus hominem cerneret, non tentaret. . . . Nisi super omnia Deus existeret, ei nullo modo angeli ministrarent.

Irvine 5 uses the same material (lines 151–5).

131–7 Cf Gregory, Hom. 16, PL 76, 1136C, on Christ's patience:

> Qui eo verbo quod erat tentatorem suum mergere in abyssum poterat, virtutem suae potentiae non ostendit, sola divinae Scripturae praecepta dedit, quatenus suae nobis patientiae praeberet exemplum, ut quoties a pravis hominibus aliquid patimur, ad doctrinam excitemur potius quam ad vindictam. Pensate quanta est patientia Dei.

Christ's humility is not mentioned by Gregory, but is noted by Bede in a similar context (*Comm. Luc.*, 1.3004–6, taken from Jerome, *Comm. Matth.*, 1.325–6):

> Ideo sic respondit Dominus quia propositum ei erat humilitate diabolum vincere non potentia.

138–50 Gregory considers in what way Christ could be said to be tempted (Hom. 16, PL 76, 1135CD):

> Sed sciendum nobis est quia tribus modis tentatio agitur, suggestione, delectatione et consensu. Et nos cum tentamur, plerumque in delectationem, aut etiam in consensum labimur, quia de carnis peccato propagati, in

[7] Cf, e.g. CH I.4.280–3, and Theodor Wolpers, *Die englische Heiligenlegende des Mittelalters* (Tübingen, 1964).

> nobisipsis etiam gerimus unde certamina toleremus. Deus vero qui, in utero Virginis incarnatus, in mundum sine peccato venerat, nihil contradictionis in semetipso tolerabat. Tentari ergo per suggestionem potuit, sed eius mentem peccati delectatio non momordit. Atque ideo omnis diabolica illa tentatio foris non intus fuit.

Ælfric develops this to say something more about the moral aspect of human temptation, making the point (a familiar one in his work[8]) that the suggestion to sin comes from the devil but taking pleasure and acceptance of it come from within, through man's sinful nature. He perhaps recalled the fuller elaboration of this theory of temptation in Gregory's answer to Augustine of Canterbury in Bede's *Historia Ecclesiastica*, I.xxvii.

150–3 Cf the passage cited from Jerome above under 37–42.

154–76 Ælfric now follows Gregory very closely on the three temptations offered to Adam and Christ (Hom. 16, PL 76, 1136AB):

> Antiquus hostis contra primum hominem parentem nostrum in tribus se tentationibus erexit, quia hunc videlicet gula, vana gloria et avaritia tentavit; sed tentando superavit, quia sibi eum per consensum subdidit. Ex gula quippe tentavit cum cibum ligni vetitum ostendit, atque ad comedendum suasit. Ex vana autem gloria tentavit cum diceret: 'Eritis sicut dii' (Gen 3.5). Et ex provectu avaritiae tentavit cum diceret: 'Scientes bonum et malum.' Avaritia enim non solum pecuniae est, sed etiam altitudinis. [*Haymo's rephrasing,* sed etiam in ambitione honoris *(Hom. 28, PL 118, 200BC), is perhaps closer.*] Recte enim avaritia dicitur cum supra modum sublimitas ambitur. . . . Sed quibus modis primum hominem stravit, eisdem modis secundo homini tentato succubuit. Per gulam quippe tentat cum dicit: 'Dic ut lapides isti panes fiant.' Per vanam gloriam tentat cum dicit: 'Si Filius Dei es, mitte te deorsum.' Per sublimitatis avaritiam tentat cum regna omnia mundi ostendit, dicens: 'Haec omnia tibi dabo, si procidens adoraveris me.' Sed eisdem modis a secundo homine vincitur, quibus primum hominem se vicisse gloriabatur, ut a nostris cordibus ipso aditu captus exeat, quo nos aditu intromissus tenebat.

Ælfric silently renders *sicut dii* (from Gen 3.5) as *swa swa englas*; cf the *englum gelice* of CH I.1.136 and his version of Genesis.

177–86 The parallel between Christ's fast and those of Moses and Elijah, as well as the contemporary Lenten fast, is briefly drawn by Gregory (Hom. 16, PL 76, 1137A):

> Moyses enim ut legem acciperet secundo diebus quadraginta ieiunavit (Exod 34.28). Elias in deserto quadraginta diebus abstinuit (3 Reg 19.8). Ipse auctor hominum ad homines veniens, in quadraginta diebus nullum

[8] See above on I.10.75 ff.

> omnino cibum sumpsit (Mt 4.2). Nos quoque in quantum possumus, annuo Quadragesimae tempore carnem nostram per abstinentiam affligere conemur.

The same comparison, though in wording less close, is made by Jerome, Haymo, Irvine 5 and Blickling 3, but Ælfric's insistence that the forty-day fast without any food was made possible only by divine power, for Moses and Elijah as much as for Christ, is distinctive; there is perhaps a hint of the same idea in Haymo's *quasi Deus ieiunavit, quasi homo esuriit* (Hom. 28, PL 118, 196C), and possibly the vestige of a similar point about Elijah in Irvine 5.41–4.

187–99 Gregory (followed by Haymo) gives two other numerological explanations for the forty days of Lent and then this argument about tithing (Hom. 16, PL 76, 1137BC):

> A praesenti etenim die usque ad Paschalis solemnitatis gaudia sex hebdomadae veniunt, quarum videlicet dies quadraginta duo fiunt. Ex quibus dum sex dies Dominici ab abstinentia subtrahuntur, non plus in abstinentia quam triginta et sex dies remanent. Dum vero per trecentos et sexaginta quinque dies annus ducitur, nos autem per triginta et sex dies affligimur, quasi anni nostri decimas Deo damus, ut qui nobismetipsis per acceptum annum viximus, auctori nostro nos in eius decimis per abstinentiam mortificemus. Unde, fratres carissimi, sicut offerre in lege iubemini decimas rerum (Lev 27.30 ff), ita ei offerre contendite et decimas dierum.

Ælfric's wording is fairly close to this, but his different ordering of the argument is paralleled by Irvine 5 and Blickling 3.

199–205 The Biblical text referred to at 200 is 2 Corinthians 6.3–7 (part of the epistle for the day), but Ælfric seems to be following Haymo's rendering and commentary (Hom. 28, PL 118, 195AB):

> Quapropter secundum Apostolum, qui ait: '. . . dignum est ut in his diebus exhibeamus nosmetipsos sicut Dei ministros, in multa patientia, in ieiuniis, in vigiliis, in castitate, in caritate non ficta.' Quantum autem pacis concordiam Dominus in nobis diligat, ipse manifestat in Evangelio, cum clamat: 'Si offers munus . . .' (Mt 5.23).

Irvine 5 uses the same material (lines 162–72). Ælfric's point about sexual abstinence in Lent is not in the sources or analogues, but seems a favourite comment of his, recurring in a penitential admonition for Lent (Thorpe, II.602) and added by him when revising CH II.7 (at 28). Cf, too, Augustine, Serm. 210, c.7 (PL 38, 1052) for this point.

205–13 A series of points on fasting drawn from Haymo, Hom. 28, PL 118:

> [195BC] Dominus . . . dixisset per Prophetam: 'Hoc est ieiunium quod elegi: frange esurienti panem tuum, et egenos vagosque induc in domum tuam: cum videris nudum, operi eum, et carnem tuam ne despexeris' (Is 58.7). . . . [195A] Sibi enim et non Deo ieiunat, qui hoc quod corpori

> subtrahit per abstinentiam, non pauperibus erogat, sed sibi in posterum reservat. . . . [194D] Dignum est, ut quod corpori nostro subtrahimus per abstinentiam, pauperibus erogemus per misericordiam. Illud ergo ieiunium Deus non approbat, quod eleemosyna non ornat.

214–7 From Lc 6.25: *Vae vobis, qui ridetis nunc, quia lugebitis et flebitis*, and Mt 5.5: *Beati qui lugent, quoniam ipsi consolabuntur.*

218–27 Cf Haymo, Hom. 28, PL 118:

> [194A] Dignum est ut qui per totum annum nobis viximus saltem istis diebus sacris Deo vivamus. . . . [201A] [Diabolus] tentat per vanam gloriam, ut in eo quod ieiunamus, vel largiores eleemosynas tribuimus, laudem hominum magis quam Dei quaeramus.

Underlying 223–5 is probably Mt 5.16: *Sic luceat lux vestra coram hominibus, ut videant opera vestra bona, et glorificent patrem vestrum, qui in caelis est.* At 225–7 is a favourite saying of Ælfric's, frequently treated as a Scriptural quotation though it is not one (cf CH I.18.203–4; 27.208–9; and esp. II.7.110–12 and commentary).

12 MID-LENT SUNDAY

The Gospel text for the occasion, John 6.1–14, describes the feeding of the five thousand with five loaves and two fishes. Ælfric focuses on a strictly allegorical interpretation, relating to the history of redemption: the five thousand are the Jewish people, the five loaves the Pentateuch, the two fishes are the psalms and prophets, and the miracle by which Christ breaks and distributes the food to make enough for all stands for his revelation to mankind of the spiritual truths hidden within the Old Testament. He justifies and explains his approach by a discussion of the miraculous: miracles are in fact less significant as signs of God's power than his daily work of governing and feeding the world, and to do no more than marvel at them is to be like an illiterate praising the visual appearance of writing; one must learn also to read them for their spiritual meaning. In this case the spiritual sense is, neatly, Christ's own revelation of such meaning in the Old Testament.

Ælfric's primary source was Augustine's 24th Tractate on St John's Gospel, which begins with a discussion of the theory of miracles and then briefly sketches the allegorical interpretation of this text. Bede expanded this discussion in his homily for the occasion (Hom. II.2), covering details not dealt with by Augustine and developing the moral or tropological application of the text, relating the sea to the Christian's life in this world, the hill to the higher levels of Christian teaching for perfection, the five thousand to the disciplining of the five senses. Haymo in turn expanded Bede's homily, developing the moral application further. Ælfric used all three texts, as well as Alcuin's adaptation of the Tractates (or perhaps the extract from it by Smaragdus),[1] but took Augustine as his model, adapting his discussion of miracles and following him in pursuing a primarily typological interpretation. He uses nearly all of Augustine's ideas, and differs from him in interpretation in only two points. However, his wording often owes debts to Bede or Haymo, and he sometimes goes to them for details not covered by Augustine, though rejecting some of their tropological readings. The focus of the homily on the issue of reading and interpreting the Old Testament was perhaps sharper in its original form, before Ælfric deleted his account of Moses and the exodus (see *CH I*, p. 65); part of his initial intention may have been to explain the place in Christian doctrine of the readings from the Pentateuch which formed part of the liturgy for Lent, an intention subsequently overtaken by the decision to give a much fuller account in the Second Series homily for Mid-Lent Sunday. On the interpretation of miracles Ælfric is somewhat more forthright than Augustine, omitting all his references to the value of ordinary wonder and reshaping his second section to suggest that reading miracles literally, without attention to their spiritual meaning, is itself a kind of illiteracy. The tone is picked up in the final sentences, where Ælfric contrasts the *folc* who were amazed at the miracle but did not recognize Christ as God, and those in the present who comprehend the miracle and the true nature of Christ.

Sources and Notes

The following texts are cited below:

1. Alcuin, *Commentaria in S. Ioannis Evangelium*, PL 100, cols. 737–1008.
2. Augustine, *In Iohannis Evangelium Tractatus CXXIV*, ed. R. Willems, CCSL 36 (Turnhout, 1954).
3. Bede, *Homiliae*, ed. D. Hurst, CCSL 122 (Turnhout, 1955), Hom. II.2 (pp. 193–9).
4. Haymo of Auxerre, *Homiliae de Tempore*, PL 118, Hom. 49, cols. 284–94.
5. Smaragdus, *Collectiones in Evangelia et Epistolas*, PL 102, cols. 151–55.

1–25 A fairly close rendering of Jn 6.1–14:

> (1) Post haec abiit Iesus trans mare Galilaeae quod est Tiberiadis (2) et sequebatur eum multitudo magna quia videbant signa quae faciebat super his qui infirmabantur. (3) Subiit ergo in montem Iesus et ibi sedebat cum discipulis suis. (4) Erat autem proximum pascha dies festus Iudaeorum. (5) Cum sublevasset ergo oculos Iesus et vidisset quia multitudo maxima venit ad eum, dicit ad Philippum: unde ememus panes ut manducent hii. (6)

[1] Förster 1894, p. 19, suggested Ælfric's use of Bede's homily and also his commentary on John; Smetana 1959, p. 188, noted the inclusion of Bede's homily in PD for this occasion, and suggested also the use of what he calls a 'homily by Augustine' given in PD for the fifth Sunday after Christmas (in PL 95 it is under the 26th Sunday after Pentecost), but as his references indicate this is in fact Augustine's Tractate 24.

> Hoc autem dicebat temptans eum; ipse enim sciebat quid esset facturus. (7) Respondit ei Philippus: ducentorum denariorum panes non sufficiunt eis ut unusquisque modicum quid accipiat. (8) Dicit ei unus ex discipulis eius Andreas frater Simonis Petri: (9) est puer unus hic qui habet quinque panes hordiacios et duos pisces sed haec quid sunt inter tantos? (10) Dixit ergo Iesus: facite homines discumbere. Erat autem faenum multum in loco. Discubuerunt ergo viri numero quasi quinque milia. (11) Accepit ergo panes Iesus et cum gratias egisset distribuit discumbentibus; similiter et ex piscibus quantum volebant. (12) Ut autem impleti sunt dixit discipulis suis: colligite quae superaverunt fragmenta ne pereant. (13) Collegerunt ergo et impleverunt duodecim cofinos fragmentorum ex quinque panibus hordiaciis quae superfuerunt his qui manducaverunt. (14) Illi ergo homines cum vidissent quod fecerat signum dicebant quia hic est vere propheta qui venturus est in mundum.

Ælfric's rendering of *unde* (v.5) as *mid hwam* (line 10) combines with the next verse to suggest poverty rather than the distance from towns as the difficulty; but *hwanon* is used at 44. *To fandunga* (line 11) reflects Ælfric's usual distinction between *fandian* and *costnian* for Latin *tentare* (see above, I.11.8 ff, and I.19; the *OE Gospels* have *fandigende* for this verse, Lindisfarne and Rushworth have *gecostian*). His description of the grass as 'pleasant to sit on' (line 17) has no parallel in any Biblical version, although Haymo does describe the grass in curiously similar terms in his commentary (Hom. 49, PL 118, 290CD):

> Fenum herba est pratorum, quae, dum viridis est, et visu est delectabilis, et sessioni atque deambulationi suavis.

Ælfric's *bletsode and tobræc* for *cum gratias egisset* is probably influenced by the other Gospel accounts of the miracle (Mt 14.19, Mc 6.41, Lc 9.16; cf below on lines 84–91).

26–38 Augustine has no comment on the sea, and reads the mountain as the heights of learning rather than heaven. Bede relates the sea to the turbulence of the world in which the wicked (the fish) take delight, neglecting heaven. Haymo, developing Bede, comes closer to Ælfric in his use of the sea as an image of the world's mutability over which Christ passes, but he seems still to be thinking of the sea's turbulence and the peaks and troughs of the waves (Hom. 49, PL 118, 284D):

> Spiritualiter, hoc mare navigerum praesens significat seculum, quod, concussum, quietum permanere non potest. . . . Sicut enim mare quietum et tranquillum stare non valet, sic mundus conturbationibus et tumultuationibus commovetur; nunc prosperitatibus elevatur, nunc adversitatibus deiicitur, crescit nascendo, decrescit moriendo. Hoc ergo mare Dominus pertransiit, quando, calcatis mundi fluctibus, iter vitae coelestis nobis ostendit.

Ælfric instead thinks of the contrasting moods of the sea, now calm, now stormy, which match the varying world, sometimes pleasant, sometimes troubled. As for the mountain, Bede, followed by Haymo, interprets it as the higher learning and perfection which Christ imparts only to his disciples, and both discuss at some length the different levels of Christian ideals; but Haymo also interprets Christ's journey, somewhat like Ælfric, as his passage over the sea of life to the mountain of heaven (Hom. 49, PL 118, 285BC):

> Mons in quem Dominus, transnavigato mari, subiit, coelum significat, in quod postquam per triumphum sanctae crucis, frementis mundi fluctibus calcatis, victor ascendit. Quod autem ibi cum discipulis sedebat, ostendit quia, ubi praecessit caput, secutura erant et membra.

39–44 Ælfric's delicate balance of the human impulse to faith and the divine assistance to understanding is developed from Bede, Hom. II.2, 94–8:

> Quod sublevasse oculos Iesus, et venientem ad se multitudinem vidisse perhibetur, divinae pietatis indicium est, quia videlicet cunctis ad se venire quaerentibus gratia misericordiae caelestis occurrere consuevit. Et ne quaerendo errare possint, lucem sui Spiritus aperire currentibus solitus est.

44–6 Ælfric concisely summarises Augustine's conclusions on Christ's reasons for questioning Philip (*Tract.*, 24.3.24–6):

> Quod interrogabat sciebat, quid enim esset facturus ipse noverat; et hoc nescire Philippum sciebat similiter. Quare itaque interrogabat, nisi quia illius ignorantiam demonstrabat?

49–54 From Augustine (*Tract.*, 24.3.4–11) on Christ's goodness and power:

> Turbas vidit, esurientes agnovit, misericorditer pavit; non solum pro bonitate, verum etiam pro potestate. Quid enim sola prodesset bonitas, ubi non erat panis, unde turba esuriens pasceretur? Nisi bonitati adesset potestas, ieiuna illa turba et esuriens remaneret. Denique et discipuli qui erant cum Domino in fame, et ipsi turbas volebant pascere, ut non remanerent inanes, sed unde pascerent non habebant.

54–63 Ælfric now turns back to Augustine's opening discussion of the nature of God's miracles and freely recasts it (*Tract.*, 24.1.1–21):

> Miracula quae fecit Dominus noster Iesus Christus, sunt quidem divina opera, et ad intellegendum Deum de visibilibus admonent humanam mentem. . . . Miracula eius quibus totum mundum regit universamque creaturam administrat, assiduitate viluerunt. . . . Maius enim miraculum est gubernatio totius mundi, quam saturatio quinque millium hominum de quinque panibus; et tamen haec nemo miratur: illud mirantur homines non quia maius est, sed quia rarum est. Quis enim et nunc pascit universum mundum, nisi ille qui de paucis granis segetes creat? Fecit ergo quomodo Deus. Unde enim multiplicat de paucis granis segetes, inde in manibus suis multiplicavit quinque panes. Potestas enim erat in

manibus Christi: panes autem illi quinque, quasi semina erant, non quidem terrae mandata, sed ab eo qui terram fecit multiplicata.

Augustine also emphasises the value and importance of miracles for stirring the senses to wonder and thence to faith, but Ælfric does not choose to follow him in this.

64–73 A recasting of Augustine's next paragraph, on the art of reading miracles (*Tract.*, 24):

[2.5–25] Hoc ergo miraculum, sicut audivimus quam magnum sit, quaeramus etiam quam profundum sit. . . . Si litteras pulchras alicubi inspiceremus, non nobis sufficeret laudare scriptoris articulum, quoniam eas pariles, aequales decorasque fecit, nisi etiam legeremus quid nobis per illas indicaverit. . . . Aliter enim videtur pictura, aliter videntur litterae. Picturam cum videris, hoc est totum vidisse, laudasse: litteras cum videris, non hoc est totum; quoniam commoneris et legere. . . . Tu ergo vides et laudas: ille videt, laudat, legit et intellegit. . . . [2.1–2] Nec tamen sufficit haec intueri in miraculis Christi. Interrogemus ipsa miracula, quid nobis loquantur de Christo.

74–84 Ælfric now returns to the allegorical interpretation of the bread and the boy; Augustine (*Tract.*, 24.5.1–2, 9–12) is the closest here:

Quinque panes intelleguntur quinque libri Moysi. . . . Si quaeramus quis fuerit puer iste, forte populus Israel erat; sensu puerili portabat, nec manducabat. Illa enim quae portabat, clausa onerabant, aperta pascebant.

The brief account of Moses and the ten commandments which once followed here at line 79 (see App. A1) was apparently directed at those who did not know who Moses was. It suggests a remarkably lower standard of understanding in the audience which Ælfric imagined than in those for whom Bede and Haymo, and still more Augustine, were writing. Exodus was read in the monastic and clerical office during Lent, and is covered not only in this homily but in two other Lenten homilies, CH II.12 and 13; but Ælfric was presumably not addressing monks or clerics in this passage.

84–91 Despite the manuscript punctuation, a new sentence evidently begins with *he tobræc* at 84. Ælfric's Latin note (see app. crit. for 84), explaining that the other evangelists' accounts of this miracle specify that Christ broke the loaves and gave them to the disciples to distribute, is reproduced verbatim from Bede's homily (II.2, 132–4). Cf the similar notes on Biblical readings at CH I.11.110 and II.30.19. He incorporates this detail into his version of the Gospel text (see above line 19) and draws on it in his interpretation. Presumably he added the explanatory note for learned readers, at some stage after deleting the passage on Moses above. His interpretation of the Gospel passage shows some relation to Bede's (Hom. II.2, 112–5, 131–2):

Quinque autem panes, quibus multitudinem populi saturavit, quinque sunt libri Moysi, quibus spirituali intellectu patefactis, et abundantiore iam sensu multiplicatis, auditorum fidelium quotidie corda reficit. . . . Et haec per apostolos suos apostolorumque successores cunctis nationibus ministrando porrexit.

and Augustine's (*Tract.*, 24.5.22–5):

Et frangi iussit panes: frangendo multiplicati sunt. Nihil verius. Quinque enim illi libri Moysi, quam multos libros, cum exponuntur, tamquam frangendo, id est disserendo, fecerunt?

91–6 Augustine, Bede and Haymo all explain the barley loaves similarly, but Augustine seems closest to Ælfric (*Tract.*, 24.5.3–8):

Nostis autem hordeum ita creatum, ut ad medullam eius vix perveniatur: vestitur enim eadem medulla tegmine paleae, et ipsa palea tenax et inhaerens, ut cum labore exuatur. Talis est littera Veteris Testamenti, vestita tegminibus carnalium sacramentorum: sed si ad eius medullam perveniatur, pascit et satiat.

96–101 Bede and Haymo both relate the five thousand to the five senses; Ælfric instead follows Augustine on this point and also on Philip (*Tract.*, 24):

[6.3–4] Cur enim quinque millia erant, nisi quia sub lege erant, quae lex quinque libris Moysi explicatur? . . . [5.30–2] Quia ergo ignorantia populi erat in lege, propterea illa Domini tentatio ignorantiam discipuli demonstrabat.

102–6 Augustine interprets the two fishes as the two personae of Christ, as priest and as king; Ælfric follows Bede in equating the fishes with the psalms and prophets (Hom. II.2, 118–22):

Duo autem pisces quos addit, psalmistarum non inconvenienter et prophetarum scripta significant, quorum unum canendo, alterum colloquendo suis auditoribus futura Christi et ecclesiae sacramenta narrabant.

The idea of *syfling* or savour is not in Augustine, Bede or Haymo, but it does appear in Alcuin's commentary on John (PL 100, 821D), where he is recasting Bede's explanation (and referring obliquely to Augustine's):

Sunt qui putant duos pisces qui saporem suavem pani dabant, duas illas personas significare.

Precisely the same words appear in the exposition for this occasion by Smaragdus (*Collectiones*, PL 102, 153B), and this may have been Ælfric's immediate source.

106–11 Ælfric probably follows Bede on the interpretation of the grass (Hom. II.2, 142–7):

Faenum in quo discumbens turba reficitur, concupiscentia carnalis intellegitur, quam calcare ac premere debet omnis, qui spiritualibus alimentis satiari desiderat. 'Omnis enim caro faenum, et omnis gloria eius tanquam flos faeni' (Is 40.6). Discumbat ergo super faenum ut florem faeni conterat, id est, castiget corpus suum, et servituti subiciat, voluptates carnis edomet.

Augustine takes it in the opposite sense, that the people (i.e. the Jews) were carnally minded and rested in carnal things.

112–7 A similar explanation of *viri* comes in Bede, but Ælfric seems to follow Haymo (Hom. 49, PL 118, 291BC):

> Cum ergo in hoc convivio Domini tantummodo viri fuisse dicuntur, mystice monemur ut, si quam suavis sit Dominus gustare desideramus, viri simus, id est fortes contra diaboli tentationes, Apostolo monente: '[Vigilate, state in fide,[2]] viriliter agite, et confortamini, omnia vestra in caritate fiant (1 Cor 16.13–14).' . . . Nec ab hac refectione Dominica femina ieiuna remanebit, si sexu femineo viriliter tentamenta diaboli compresserit.

117–20 As Bede, Hom. II.2, 150–2, 155–7:

> Quinque millia viri qui manducaverunt, perfectionem eorum qui verbo vitae reficiuntur, insinuant. . . . Millenarius autem numerus, ultra quem nulla nostra computatio succrescit, plenitudinem rerum de quibus agitur indicare consuevit.

Bede and Haymo go on to equate the five with the five senses.

121–6 Augustine and Bede have the same interpretation of the fragments of food that remain, but Haymo's wording is rather closer (Hom. 49, PL 118, 293AB):

> Possumus et per fragmenta quae remanserunt, obscuriores quasque sententias eiusdem Scripturae intelligere. Quod ergo plebeia multitudo[3] non capit, Dominus apostolis ut colligerent praecepit: quia obscuriores sententias, quas simplex multitudo capere non potest, magistri Ecclesiae, episcopi scilicet et sacerdotes, in propriis pectoribus debent recondere, ut tempore necessitatis non solum ad eam docendam, sed ad defendendam idonei inveniantur.

Ælfric's reference to both testaments (line 126), somewhat at odds with the previous interpretation of the five loaves, is paralleled in Bede's subsequent discussion.

126–9 Cf Haymo, Hom. 49, PL 118, 293D: *Per duodecim cophinos, duodecim apostoli congrua ratione figurantur.*

130–5 For Ælfric's discussion of Christ as prophet there are hints in Augustine (*Tract.*, 24.7.5–7), *Erat autem ille Dominus prophetarum, impletor prophetarum, sanctificator prophetarum, sed et propheta*, and in Bede (Hom. II.2, 203–5), *Recte quidem dicebant, 'Quia hic est vere propheta', dominum prophetam magnum magnae salutis praeconem iam mundo futurum.* Cf the very similar passage at CH I.33.68–75 and the notes on it.

135–40 Ælfric's contrast between the folk who marvel and those in the present who believe without seeing miracles follows Augustine (*Tract.*, 24.6.16–23):

[2] Ælfric starts the quotation earlier than Haymo.
[3] Bede has *sensus vulgi*.

> Qui tunc viderunt, admirati sunt; nos autem non miramur cum audimus. Factum est enim ut illi viderent, scriptum est autem ut nos audiremus. Quod in illis oculi valuerunt, hoc in nobis fides. Cernimus quippe animo, quod oculis non potuimus: et praelati sumus illis, quoniam de nobis dictum est, 'Beati qui non vident, et credunt' (Jn 20.29). Addo autem quia forte et intelleximus quod illa turba non intellexit.

141–8 The conclusion perhaps expands on Bede's, Hom. II.2, 207–13:

> Sed necdum plena fide proficiebant, qui hunc etiam Dominum dicere nesciebant. Ergo illi videntes signum quod fecerat Iesus, dixerant: 'Quia hic est vere propheta qui venturus est in mundum.' Nos certiori cognitione veritatis et fidei videntes mundum, quem fecit Iesus, et signa quibus illum replevit, dicamus: Quia hic est vere mediator Dei et hominum.

Cf too Haymo, Hom. 49, PL 118, 294A:

> Videntes enim tale tantumque miraculum, debuerant dicere Quod hic est vere Filius Dei, qui venit in mundum. Sed, quia homines erant, et humana sapiebant, Filium Dei tacentes, prophetam confitentur.

ne cuðe þæra goda þæt hi cwædon (line 144) presumably means something like 'did not know the blessings of being able to say', but there is no other instance of *cunnan* taking a genitive in the CH.

13 ANNUNCIATION

Ælfric's text is the account of the annunciation in Luke 1.26–38, the appointed reading for the occasion, which he translates and expounds in detail (lines 42–159) before going on to narrate and briefly discuss the visitation to the Virgin's cousin Elizabeth, from Luke 1.39–55. The story of the annunciation was originally one of the readings for the week before Christmas, but by Ælfric's time it had become established on its own feast-day, 25 March, to which he refers at 152 ff. The visitation narrative was not part of the reading for the Annunciation but remained as a lection for the pre-Christmas period and for the Vigil of the Assumption. The CH collection does not cover these occasions, and the opportunity to discuss so central a feature of the liturgy as the Magnificat (cf lines 183–5) as well as the narrative interest of the episode presumably prompted Ælfric to include the visitation story briefly here.[1]

In his introduction (lines 1–40) Ælfric places the annunciation in the context of the history of fall and redemption, and the divine plan for mankind. In his commentary he draws out the Christological implications of the text concerning the dual nature of Christ and the role of the Trinity in his birth, rather than the moral implications for man or the representation of the Virgin. The latter's

[1] I rely heavily here on the detailed discussion of this homily by Mary Clayton in her D.Phil. thesis (Clayton 1983), pp. 330–41; see also Clayton 1990, pp. 230–2.

humility and prior dedication to virginity are noted, but there is no suggestion here that she is free from the taint of sin before the annunciation. Despite its title, this is for Ælfric more a feast-day of Christ than of the Virgin Mary. The moral teaching prominent in Ælfric's sources for this text plays little part until he turns to the Magnificat, where his discussion seems primarily concerned to discount any naive suppositions that the hymn is a genuine attack on the rich and powerful; it is only the arrogant, he says, who are cast down, and many of the rich will be saved.

Ælfric's main sources are two homilies by Bede, I.3 and I.4, on the annunciation and visitation, both given for the pre-Christmas period in PD.[2] The homiliary also gives, under the annunciation in late versions, a long extract from the *Contra Iudaeos, Paganos et Arrianos* of Quodvultdeus, on the prophecies of Christ's birth, and this may have influenced Ælfric's approach, as it certainly contributed to the approach and content of his later homily on the prophecies of Christ, II.1. There are also some striking parallels to a Ps-Augustine homily for the annunciation (Serm. 195),[3] as well as some etymological material from Jerome. As is usual when his source is Bede, Ælfric selects and paraphrases very freely, and occasionally disagrees sharply (see lines 70–72).

Sources and Notes

The following texts are cited below:

1. Alcuin, *Interrogationes et Responsiones in Genesim*, PL 100, cols. 516–66.
2. Ps-Augustine, *Sermones*, PL 39, Serm. 195 [= Augustine, *Sermones suppositi*], cols. 2107–10.
3. Bede, *Homiliae*, ed. D. Hurst, CCSL 122 (Turnhout, 1955), Hom. I.3 (pp. 14–20) and Hom. I.4 (pp. 21–31).
4. Jerome, *Liber Interpretationis Hebraicorum Nominum*, ed. P. de Lagarde, CCSL 72 (Turnhout, 1959), pp. 59–161.
5. Quodvultdeus, *Contra Iudaeos, Paganos et Arrianos*, ed. R. Braun, CCSL 60 (Turnhout, 1976), pp. 227–58.

4–17 A brief summary of doctrine on the fall and redemption of mankind, showing Ælfric's characteristic emphases and very similar in ideas, rhetoric and diction to that in CH I.1; it draws on a tradition of catechetical *narratio*[4] rather than any particular source. The distinction between unredeemed devil and

[2] Identified by Förster (1894, p. 20); Smetana (1959, p. 188) pointed to their inclusion in PD.

[3] Glorieux (1952, p. 26) notes an attribution to Ambrosius Autpertus; but since it is not included or mentioned in the more recent edition of the latter's works (*Ambrosii Autperti Opera*, ed. R. Weber, 3 vols., CCCM 27–27B (Turnhout, 1975–9)), nor mentioned in the *Clavis Patrum Latinorum*, I have left it as Ps-Augustine.

[4] See Day 1974, esp. p. 59 and n.3.

redeemed man (lines 12–17), however, may be influenced by Alcuin's *Interrogationes et Responsiones* (PL 100, 517CD):

> Cur summi angeli peccatum insanabile fuit, et hominis sanabile? Angelus sui sceleris inventor fuit, homo vero alterius fraude seductus fuit.

Ælfric included this point in his own version of the *Interrogationes* (lines 29–32). Ælfric's only other use of *ofermettu* (line 7) is similarly with reference to Lucifer at CH I.1.45. On the implications of God pondering how to redeem mankind (lines 11–12) see Grundy 1992.

18–40 Ælfric's discussion of the prophecies of the incarnation may have been prompted by the sermon of Quodvultdeus on the prophecies of Christ, but there are no close parallels. Lines 25–7 are from Is 7.14: *Ecce virgo concipiet et pariet filium et vocabitis nomen eius Emmanuhel.* It appears in Quodvultdeus but was in any case universally familiar from the liturgy and from Mt 1.23. The prophecy from Ezekiel 44.2 at 27–30 is surprisingly absent from texts likely to have been known by Ælfric, but does appear in an unattributed homily for the annunciation, in a form closer to Ælfric's wording than the Vulgate text is and with similar comments (Ps-Augustine, Serm. 195, §1, PL 39, 2107):

> 'Vidi portam in domo Domini clausam: et dixit ad me angelus, Porta haec quam vides, non aperietur, et homo non transiet per eam; quoniam Dominus solus intrabit, et egredietur per eam, et clausa erit in aeternum.' . . . Quid est porta in domo Domini clausa, nisi quod Maria Virgo semper erit intacta? Et quid est, Homo non transiet per eam; nisi, Ioseph non cognoscet eam? Et quid est, Dominus solus intrabit et egredietur per eam; nisi, Spiritus sanctus impraegnabit eam, et Angelorum Dominus nascetur per eam? Et quid est, Clausa erit in aeternum, nisi quia erit Maria virgo ante partum, virgo in partu, virgo post partum?

(The Vulgate has no equivalent to *et egredietur per eam.*) Lines 38–40 are from Gal 4.4–5:

> (4) At ubi venit plenitudo temporis misit Deus Filium suum factum ex muliere factum sub lege, (5) ut eos qui sub lege erant redimeret ut adoptionem filiorum reciperemus.

This can hardly be intended as a prophecy, but perhaps the rendering of *plenitudo temporis* as 'the fulfilment of those times' is designed to make the Pauline quotation underline the link between Old Testament prophecy and New Testament event.

The A reading at 23–4, 'one of those prophecies is [by] Isaiah', is awkward and the QRT variant *witegena* 'prophets' could be authorial; but the independent correction in MS H shows that others were aware of the awkwardness.

41–64 A generally close rendering of the pericope, Lc 1.26–38:

> (26) In mense autem sexto missus est angelus Gabrihel a Deo in civitatem Galilaeae cui nomen Nazareth (27) ad virginem desponsatam viro cui nomen erat Ioseph de domo David; et nomen virginis Maria. (28) Et

> ingressus angelus ad eam dixit: have gratia plena Dominus tecum; benedicta tu in mulieribus. (29) Quae cum vidisset [*var.* audisset] turbata est in sermone eius et cogitabat qualis esset ista salutatio. (30) Et ait angelus ei: ne timeas Maria, invenisti enim gratiam apud Deum. (31) Ecce concipies in utero et paries filium et vocabis nomen eius Iesum. (32) Hic erit magnus et Filius Altissimi vocabitur et dabit illi Dominus Deus sedem David patris eius. (33) Et regnabit in domo Iacob in aeternum et regni eius non erit finis. (34) Dixit autem Maria ad angelum: quomodo fiet istud quoniam virum non cognosco. (35) Et respondens angelus dixit ei: Spiritus Sanctus superveniet in te et virtus Altissimi obumbrabit tibi ideoque et quod nascetur sanctum vocabitur Filius Dei. (36) Et ecce Elisabeth cognata tua et ipsa concepit filium in senecta sua et hic mensis est sextus illi quae vocatur sterilis. (37) Quia non erit inpossibile apud Deum omne verbum. (38) Dixit autem Maria [*var.* ad angelum]: ecce ancilla Domini; fiat mihi secundum verbum tuum; et discessit ab illa angelus.

Ælfric's rephrasing of verse 27, so that 'of the house of David' applies to Mary not Joseph (lines 44–5), silently incorporates the argument of Bede's commentary (Hom. I.3, 30–1): *Quod dicitur de domo Dauid non tantum ad Ioseph sed etiam pertinet ad Mariam.* His use of *wifmannum* (line 49) to render *mulieribus* (v.28), where all other Old English versions of the Gospels have *wifum*, reflects a careful distinction evident also at CH II.1.38 and below, lines 75–6.

65–73 Generally close to Bede on the relation between the fall and the incarnation (Hom. I.3, 1–5, 10–17):

> Exordium nostrae redemptionis, fratres carissimi, hodierna nobis sancti evangelii lectio commendat . . . per quem nos abiecta vetustate noxia renovari atque inter filios Dei conputari possimus. . . . Aptum profecto humanae restaurationis principium ut angelus a Deo mitteretur ad virginem partu consecrandam divino, quia prima perditionis humanae fuit causa cum serpens a diabolo mittebatur ad mulierem spiritu superbiae decipiendam; immo ipse in serpente diabolus veniebat qui genus humanum deceptis parentibus primis inmortalitatis gloria nudaret. Quia ergo mors intravit per feminam apte redit et vita per feminam.

Where Bede, however, says that the serpent was sent by the devil, 'or rather the devil was in the serpent', Ælfric says firmly that the devil sent another devil in the shape of a serpent. That the temptation in Eden was not the work of Satan but another devil is an idea not found in any of Ælfric's known sources, but it is present in the poem *Genesis B* and implied in the poem *Juliana* (line 261). The latter reference is pointed out by J.R. Evans in the course of a discussion of the idea;[5] he notes some Biblical verses which might have given currency to the notion, and an early patristic criticism of it, but finds no more immediate source.

[5] J. R. Evans, '*Genesis B* and its background', *Review of English Studies* 14 (1963), 1–16, 113–23, at 6.

Ælfric's other references to the fall (e.g. in CH I.1) imply that the tempter was Satan. The distinction enables him here to set up a rather neater correlation than Bede achieved, between God sending his angel to redeem mankind and Satan sending his devil to subvert mankind.

73–8 Adapted from Bede's discussion of Gabriel's name (Hom. I.3, 23–8):

> Gabrihel namque fortitudo Dei dicitur. Et merito tali nomine praefulget qui nascituro in carne Deo testimonium perhibet. De quo propheta in psalmo: 'Dominus, inquit, fortis et potens dominus potens in proelio' (Ps 23.8). Illo nimirum proelio quo potestates aerias debellare et ab earum tyrannide mundum veniebat eripere.

Bede is here drawing on Gregory, PL 76, 1250–1.

79–87 Bede notes that there were a variety of reasons for Mary's marriage to Joseph, of which the most important, he says, was the risk of condemnation for fornication (Hom. I.3, 38–42). Ælfric paraphrases freely, specifying the punishment in a way similar to Bede, *Comm. Luc.*, 1.462 [repeated by Haymo, Hom. 4, PL 118, 32C]: *Ne velut adultera lapidaretur a Iudaeis.*

87–102 Ælfric's discussion of Joseph's reaction (lines 87–92) draws on Mt 1.19–20:

> (19) Ioseph autem vir eius cum esset iustus et nollet eam traducere voluit occulte dimittere eam. (20) Haec autem eo cogitante ecce angelus Domini in somnis apparuit ei dicens: Ioseph fili David noli timere; accipere Mariam coniugem tuam quod enim in ea natum est de Spiritu Sancto est.

But the Bible says nothing of his grief or reluctance to approach Mary. There is perhaps some influence ultimately from the Ps-Matthew Gospel's account,[6] but this detail had no doubt become part of general tradition (it appears for instance in the poem *Christ I*). Ps-Augustine, Serm. 195 has a graphic account, as if in Joseph's own words, of his anxieties and grief (PL 39, 2108–9). The firm denial that either Joseph or the Holy Spirit was Christ's father (lines 87, 93–8) is not from the sources. Lines 98–102 return to Bede's reasons for the marriage, though with greater emphasis on Joseph's care for the Christ-child (Hom. I.3, 42–50):

> Deinde ut in his etiam quae domestica cura naturaliter exigebat puerpera solatio sustentaretur virili. Oportebat ergo beatam Mariam habere virum qui et testis integritatis eius certissimus et nati ex ea domini ac salvatoris nostri esset nutritius fidissimus . . . aliaque illi perplura quae adsumptae humanitatis fragilitas poscebat necessaria ministraret.

103–6 From Bede, Hom. I.3, 64–6:

> Vere gratia erat plena cui ipsum per quem gratia et veritas facta est Iesum Christum generare donatum est.

[6] *Evangelia Apocrypha*, ed. C. Tischendorf (2nd ed., Leipzig, 1876), pp. 51–111, esp. c.6.

106–8 Not from Bede but perhaps, as Mary Clayton suggested,[7] from a hymn *Quem terra pontus* (Gneuss 1968, p. 347), used for the annunciation in Ælfric's time:

> Est beata mater munere, quia clausus est supernus artifex sub arca ventris cuiusque est continens mundum suo pugillo.

108–10 Close to Bede, Hom. I.3, 69–72:

> Vere benedicta in mulieribus quae sine exemplo muliebris conditionis cum decore virginitatis gavisa est honore parentis, quodque virginem matrem decebat Deum filium procreavit.

112–7 From Bede, Hom. I.3:

> [86–7] Agnosce verum hunc hominem veram de carne virginis adsumpsisse substantiam carnis. . . . [83–4] nam manifestissime dominum Iesum, id est salvatorem nostrum. . . . [88–90] Confitere eundem etiam Deum verum de Deo vero et aeterno patri filium semper esse coaeternum.

117–24 Bede explains verses 32–3 by identifying the people of David with the Jews and the house of Jacob with the other believing races, all of whom will form Christ's spiritual kingdom. Cf esp. Hom. I.3, 101–3:

> Populum quem David temporali imperio rexit, ipse gratia spiritali ad aeternum proveheret regnum.

Ælfric succinctly summarises this argument but then goes on to justify it by invoking the etymologies of Jacob and Israel. These derive ultimately from Jerome's *Liber Interpretationis Hebraicorum Nominum*, where *Iacob* is given as *subplantator vel subplantans* (CCSL 72, 61.27) and *Israhel* as *videre deum sive vir aut mens videns deum* (CCSL 72, 13.21). Ælfric's *forscrencend* for *Iacob* is translated 'witherer' by Thorpe and 'supplanter' in BT. It is presumably a direct translation of *subplantans*, and both *supplantare* and *screncan* can mean 'to trip up'. Etymology and context suggest that *forscrencend* means 'one who casts down', or perhaps 'one who uproots'. The etymology of 'Israhel' is also given in Bede's homily I.4, which Ælfric uses later.

125–8 Ælfric incorporates into Mary's reply Bede's suggested expansion of it, as if her appeal to virginity was actually spoken (Hom. I.3, 129–31):

> Quomodo, inquit, fieri potest ut concipiam pariamque filium, quae in castimonia virginitatis vitam consummare disposui.

132–5 Summarises Bede's argument at 151–5, making it clear, as in Bede, that the Virgin became sinless at the annunciation, rather than being born without sin (Hom. I.3, 151–5):

> Obumbravit autem beatae Dei genetrici virtus altissimi quia spiritus sanctus cor illius cum implevit ab omni aestu concupiscentiae carnalis

[7] Clayton 1990, pp. 230–1.

temperavit emundavit a desideriis temporalibus ac donis caelestibus mentem simul illius consecravit et corpus.

136–41 Adapted from Bede, Hom. I.3, 160–6:

Omnes quippe homines in iniquitatibus concipimur et in delictis nascimur. . . . Solus vero redemptor noster pro nobis incarnari dignatus est mox sanctus natus est quia sine iniquitate conceptus est; filius Dei natus est quia operante spiritu sancto de virgine conceptus est.

Ælfric correctly identifies the first sentence as a virtual quotation from the Psalms (50.7: *Ecce enim in iniquitatibus conceptus sum et in peccatis concepit me mater mea*) and develops the Christological point at 138–41.

143–8 Developed from Bede's comment on Mary's humility (Hom. I.3, 219–20): *Magnam humilitatis constantiam tenet quae se ancillam sui conditoris dum mater eligitur appellat*. The title 'queen of all the world', supplied by Ælfric here, is also used in his assumption homily (lines 43–4), where it translates the *regina mundi* of Paschasius. Lines 146–8 are from Sir 3.20: *quanto magnus es, humilia te in omnibus, et coram Deo invenies gratiam*. Hericus quotes it in a similar context (Hom. I.5, 212–14, CCCM 116):

Satis ammiranda humilitas: mater eligitur, et ancillam se vocat; implevit illud: Quanto magnus es, humilia te in omnibus, et impletum est illud: Omnis qui se humiliat exaltabitur.

148–52 Adapted from Bede, though Ælfric's notion of Christ taking flesh from Mary is subtly different from Bede's (Hom. I.3, 229–31):

Fiat ut in meo utero filius Dei humanae substantiae habitum induat atque ad redemptionem mundi tamquam sponsus suo procedat de thalamo.

152–9 Ælfric now summarises the doctrine of annunciation and incarnation before turning to the visitation. Lines 155–6 perhaps hint at the theory that the moment of conception was the moment of Mary's belief in the angel's message.

160–9 Ælfric's account of Elizabeth and Zacharias summarises Luke 1.5–20; the full text of the Gospel passage is given in CH I.25.

169–82 An almost verbatim rendering of Lc 1.40–45:

(40) Et intravit in domum Zacchariae et salutavit Elisabeth (41) et factum est ut audivit salutationem Mariae Elisabeth exultavit infans in utero eius et repleta est Spiritu Sancto Elisabeth (42) et exclamavit voce magna et dixit: benedicta tu inter mulieres et benedictus fructus ventris tui; (43) et unde hoc mihi ut veniat mater Domini mei ad me? (44) Ecce enim ut facta est vox salutationis tuae in auribus meis exultavit in gaudio infans in utero meo. (45) Et beata quae credidit quoniam perficientur ea quae dicta sunt ei a Domino.

Ælfric's expansion of verse 44 with the words 'and hoppode ongean his drihtne þe ðu berst on ðinum innoðe' presumably reflects his recognition that *exulto* means 'to leap' as well as 'to rejoice'. The OE Gospel versions all have words for 'rejoice' and there is nothing in Bede's commentary to point specifically to the physical sense (indeed, the non-physical sense is suggested by the comment of Bede used for Ælfric's next sentence). The sermon by Quodvultdeus similarly makes the physical sense clear (*Contra Iudaeos*, 14.25): *Ioannes . . . motu salu[t]avit, quem voce non poterat*. Ælfric's further comment on this, at 178–9, seems to reflect both the words of Quodvultdeus and the comment in Bede's visitation homily, I.4, 49–50: *Et quia lingua necdum valuit, animo exultante salutavit*.

183–93 Bede similarly refers to the daily singing of the Magnificat. The text is from Lc 1.46–55, though Ælfric omits verse 49:

> (46) Magnificat anima mea Dominum (47) et exultavit spiritus meus in Deo salutari meo (48) quia respexit humilitatem ancillae suae; ecce enim ex hoc beatam me dicent omnes generationes; (49) quia fecit mihi magna qui potens est et sanctum nomen eius; (50) et misericordia eius in progenies et progenies timentibus eum. (51) Fecit potentiam in brachio suo, dispersit superbos mente cordis sui; (52) deposuit potentes de sede et exaltavit humiles; (53) esurientes implevit bonis et divites dimisit inanes. (54) Suscepit Israhel puerum suum memorari misericordiae (55) sicut locutus est ad patres nostros Abraham et semini eius in saecula.

Ælfric's version surprisingly obscures the threefold distinction of *superbi*, *potentes* and *divites* in verses 51–3 by rendering the latter two both as *rican*.[8] The Lindisfarne and Rushworth Gospels keep the three terms distinct, using *maehtigo* and *weligo* for *potentes* and *divites*, but the prose version of the Gospels creates a different confusion by rendering *superbi, potentes* and *divites* as *ofermodan, rican* and *ofermode* respectively. Though Ælfric does occasionally use *rice* to cover powerful as well as rich, his rendering here may have been influenced by his exegetical concern to identify the powerful and rich who are cast down and rejected as only those who can be identified with the *superbi*.

195–9 The commentary is closely based on Bede, Hom. I.4:

> [244–6] Eosdem potentes appellat quos ante dixerat superbos. Qui ideo nimirum superbi vocantur quia super mensuram se suae conditionis extollunt. . . . [252–4] Deposuit ergo potentes de sede et exaltavit humiles quia 'omnis qui se exaltat humiliabitur et qui se humiliat exaltabitur' (Lc 14.11).

199–201 Not from Bede, though his interpretation is similar, but an expansion of Mt 5.6: *Beati qui esuriunt et sitiunt iustitiam, quoniam ipsi saturabuntur*. The expansion as *gefyllede mid rihtwisnysse* is justified by the fuller discussion of this beatitude at CH I.36.211 ff.

[8] See further Godden 1990 on the association of wealth and power and the development of the word *rice*, esp. p. 42.

202–9 The opening and closing lines, on the damnation of the rich and proud, draw on Bede, Hom. I.4:

> [265–7] At quicumque caelestibus divitiis terrenas praeponere gaudent hi nimirum tempore ultimae discretionis inanes totius beatitudinis dimittuntur a domino. . . . [271–2] qui de terrenis divitiis gloriantes superbiunt.

The intervening lines, emphasising how many rich are saved (lines 203–7), are Ælfric's own qualification of the critique, similar to the passage at CH I.8.170 ff, using Prov 13.8: *Redemptio animae viri divitiae suae*.[9]

209–12 From Bede, Hom. I.4:

> [284–5] Quo nomine omnis redemptorum hominum coetus designatur. . . . [290–1] Et bene addidit, 'puerum suum', videlicet humilem obedientemque significans.

212–19 From Bede, Hom. I.4:

> [309–15] 'Atque in te benedicentur universae cognationes terrae' (Gen 12.3). . . . Semen autem Abrahae non illos tantum dicit electos qui ex Abrahae progenie sunt corporaliter editi verum etiam nos qui de gentibus ad Christum congregati illis fidei societate patribus copulamur. . . . [321–2] Hinc etenim ait apostolus: 'Si autem vos Christi, ergo Abrahae semen estis secundum promissionem heredes' (Gal 3.29).

Cf too Bede's commentary on Luke (*Comm. Luc.*, 1.782): *Semen Abrahae non carnale sed spiritale significat.* (Repeated by Haymo, Hom. 5, PL 118, 39A.)

219–21 From Bede, Hom. I.4, 322–5:

> Recte autem in conclusione subiungitur, in saecula, quia nimirum praefata promissio supernae hereditatis nullo umquam fine claudetur.

14 PALM SUNDAY

The main Gospel reading for Palm Sunday, as Ælfric points out (lines 2, 179–81), was the narrative of Christ's passion, usually Matthew 26.2–27.66, with the accounts from the other Gospels being read during the subsequent days. He leaves this for discussion in the Second Series and takes as his subject here Christ's entry into Jerusalem, the event commemorated in the liturgy and ceremonies of Palm Sunday. In this he in part follows the practice of both Paul the Deacon and Haymo, whose homiliaries give homilies on both the entry and the passion for Palm Sunday. The entry is described in all four Gospels but with much variation in detail, often quite substantial, and Ælfric draws on all four to produce a coherent version of his own. (According to the *Regularis Concordia* and Ælfric's own Letter to the Monks of Eynsham, the account in

[9] See further Godden 1990.

John 12.9–13 was read as part of the Palm Sunday procession with palms; but the version in Matthew 21.1–9 is the one used in PD and Haymo, and in Bede's homily for the occasion, while it is the Luke account which is signalled in the *OE Gospels* (p. 143) for this occasion.)

Ælfric's exposition is a fairly complex one, working at several levels of interpretation. He interprets the narrative historically, as an allegory of mankind's redemption, with the ass and the foal standing, like the people who welcome Christ, for the Jews and the Gentiles. But he also uses the moral or tropological level, with the animals and the people representing man in his moral state, choosing to bear Christ or the devil, and casting his good works or life as garments before Christ. The anagogical level finds a place in the concluding interpretation of the Palm Sunday procession. One of Ælfric's main concerns seems to be the question of choice and free will: both the argument that God permitted, but did not compel, the devil and the Jewish leaders to kill him, and the careful argument that man chooses of his own free will to be bound by the devil but needs both divine grace and free will to come to Christ.

Ælfric was evidently familiar with a wide range of expositions of the Gospel narratives and redemption theory. A major source is Bede's homily on Matthew 21.1–9, given for the occasion in PD, but there is also extensive use of a homily going under the name of St John Chrysostom, which appears in PD for the first Sunday in Advent (since this uses the same pericope as Palm Sunday).[1] Haymo's homily for the occasion draws heavily on Bede's homily and commentaries and apparently on Ps-Chrysostom, but was probably used by Ælfric in addition to the others. Other details could have come from Bede's commentaries on Luke and Mark or from the exposition of Smaragdus, while Gregory the Great supplied the striking image of the fishhook snaring the devil.[2]

Sources and Notes

The following texts are cited below:

1. Augustine, *In Iohannis Evangelium Tractatus CXXIV*, ed. R. Willems, CCSL 36 (Turnhout, 1954).
2. Bede, *Commentarius in Lucam*, ed. D. Hurst, CCSL 120 (Turnhout, 1960), pp. 5–425.
3. Bede, *Homiliae*, ed. D. Hurst, CCSL 122 (Turnhout, 1955), Hom. II.3 (pp. 200–6).
4. Ps-Chrysostom, *Opus Imperfectum*, PG 56, Hom. 37, cols. 834–8.
5. Gregory the Great, *Homiliae in Evangelia*, PL 76, Hom. 25, cols. 1188–96.
6. Haymo of Auxerre, *Homiliae de Tempore*, PL 118, Hom. 63, cols. 353–8.

[1] It is taken from the *Opus Imperfectum*, a commentary on Matthew's Gospel now attributed to an anonymous fifth-century Arian.

[2] Förster (1894, pp. 21–2) identified Bede's homily; Smetana (1959, pp. 188–9) noted its inclusion in PD and (Smetana 1961, pp. 459–60) suggested the use of Haymo.

7. Jerome, *Commentarii in Evangelium Matthaei*, ed. D. Hurst and M. Adriaen, CCSL 77 (Turnhout, 1969).
8. Smaragdus, *Collectiones in Evangelia et Epistolas*, PL 102, cols. 513–15.

6–25 The account of the entry into Jerusalem, mainly close translation but partly paraphrase, combines material from Matthew, Luke and John. Lines 6–11 are mainly from Mt 21.1–3:

> (1) Et cum adpropinquassent Hierosolymis et venissent Bethfage ad montem Oliveti tunc Iesus misit duos discipulos (2) dicens eis: ite in castellum quod contra vos est et statim invenietis asinam alligatam et pullum cum ea; solvite et adducite mihi; (3) et si quis vobis aliquid dixerit dicite quia Dominus his opus habet et confestim dimittet eos.

Castellum in verse 2 is rendered *castel* or *cæstra* in the Old English versions of the Gospels, and *wic* in Blickling 6, but Ælfric renders it *byrig* (line 8), perhaps identifying it with Jerusalem itself; if so, he may have been following a tradition reflected in Haymo's homily (Hom. 63, PL 118, 354), which explains *castellum* as a contemptuous term for Jerusalem. (Note, though, CH II.16.4, where the *castellum* Emmaus, five miles from Jerusalem, is also called *byrig*.) In verse 2, Ælfric's use of masculine forms (line 9; cf too 42) for the she-ass of the Gospel is baffling; the Old English versions of the Gospels all follow the Latin gender. In verse 3, his *sent hi eft agean* perhaps reflects the Old Latin reading *remittet*, used by Ps-Chrysostom (see below on lines 80–87), rather than Vulgate *dimittet*.

For lines 11–16 Ælfric turns to Luke 19.30–35, which gives the exchange with the owners and indicates that it is the colt or foal that Christ rides on (Luke does not in fact have the ass but Ælfric adds it for consistency with Matthew's account):

> (32) Abierunt autem qui missi erant et invenerunt sicut dixit illis stantem pullum; (33) solventibus autem illis pullum dixerunt domini eius ad illos: quid solvitis pullum? (34) At illi dixerunt quia Dominus eum necessarium habet. (35) Et duxerunt illum ad Iesum et iactantes vestimenta sua supra pullum inposuerunt Iesum. [*Cf Mc 11.7* et sedit super eo.] . . . (30) pullum asinae alligatum cui nemo umquam hominum sedit.

His singular *hlaford* (13) for the Gospel's *domini* (v.33) is odd. The prophecy at 16–18 is taken from Mt 21.4–5:

> (4) Hoc autem factum est ut impleretur quod dictum est per prophetam dicentem: (5) dicite filiae Sion: ecce rex tuus venit tibi mansuetus et sedens super asinam et pullum filium subiugalis.

It is not in fact from Isaiah as Ælfric says but a version of Zechariah 9.9. Jerome and Haymo both identify it correctly; the same quotation lies behind CH II.1.143–5, and Ælfric there attributes it to Ezekiel, following his source. The reception by the people of Jerusalem (lines 18–23) combines Matthew and John:

> (Jn 12.12) In crastinum autem turba multa quae venerat ad diem festum cum audissent quia venit Iesus Hierosolyma (13) acceperunt ramos palmarum et processerunt obviam ei, et clamabant: osanna benedictus qui venit in nomine Domini rex Israhel. . . . (Mt 21.8) Plurima autem

turba straverunt vestimenta sua in via; alii autem caedebant ramos de arboribus et sternebant in via. (9) Turbae autem quae praecedebant et quae sequebantur clamabant dicentes: osanna Filio David, benedictus qui venturus est in nomine Domini, osanna in altissimis.

The exclamations ascribed to the people manage to combine both Matthew and John as above and also Lc 19.38:

Benedictus qui venit rex in nomine domine; pax in caelo et gloria in excelsis.

The commentators offer various interpretations of the Hebrew word *osanna*. Augustine says it is a meaningless interjection expressing emotion (*Tract.*, 51.2.9). Jerome argues that it means *salvum fac*, 'make whole', but renders it *salus* (*Comm. Matth.*, 3.1248 ff). Ps-Chrysostom notes several possibilities (Hom. 37, PG 56, 838): *Quidem interpretantur gloriam, alii redemptionem, alii Salvifica, sive Salvum fac*. Bede (Hom. II.3, 167) suggests *salus* or *salvifica*. Smaragdus says *salvator* (*Collectiones*, PL 102, 515C). Haymo gives a learned philological discussion but ends with *salus* as one alternative (Hom. 63, PL 118, 358A). Ælfric's *sy hælu davides bearne* follows Bede's and Haymo's suggested *salus filio David* (Bede, Hom. II.3, 142–3).

26–34 Cf Jn 12.9–11:

(9) Cognovit ergo turba multa ex Iudaeis quia illic est et venerunt non propter Iesum tantum sed ut Lazarum viderent quem suscitavit a mortuis.
(10) Cogitaverunt autem principes sacerdotum ut et Lazarum interficerent
(11) quia multi propter illum abibant ex Iudaeis et credebant in Iesum.

Ælfric turns this into a striking, and unexpected, picture of both believing and unbelieving Jews coming to meet Christ as he approaches the city.

34–41 Bede first identifies the two disciples as teachers sent to the Jews and the Gentiles, but then offers the alternative followed by Ælfric (Hom. II.3, 58–61):

Vel certe duos misit ut eosdem praedicatores doctrina simul et operatione perfectos esse moneret ne vel erroris verba indocti veritati miscerent vel ea quae recte docuissent perverse vivendo negarent.

42–5 Cf Bede, Hom. II.3, 36–8, for the interpretation:

Asina et pullus quibus sedens Hierosolimam venit utriusque populi Iudaei videlicet et gentilis simplicia corda designant.

Ælfric's comment on *hæðen* makes explicit a point already assumed in earlier homilies, e.g. I.7.52 ff.

45–7 Cf Bede, Hom. II.3, 64–5: *Uterque populus funibus peccatorum erat circumplexus*, and Prov 5.22: *Funibus peccatorum suorum constringitur* (not cited by Bede or other sources, but presumably Ælfric recognized the allusion in Bede).

47–53 Expanding from a hint in Ps-Chrysostom (Hom. 37, PG 56, 835):

'Solvite', inquit. Quomodo? Per doctrinam vestram, per miracula vestra: quia omnes Iudaei et gentes per apostolos sunt liberati. 'Adducite mihi'. Per ministerium, id est, ad gloriam corrigite illos.

Ælfric's *fulluht* focuses on the specific moment of conversion.

54–9 For the nature of the ass and its symbolism Bede offers nothing and Ælfric turned again to Ps-Chrysostom (Hom. 37, PG 56, 834–5):

> Est enim animal hoc immundum, et prae caeteris pene iumentis magis irrationabile et stultum, et infirmum, et ignobile, et oneriferum magis; sic fuerunt et homines ante Christi adventum idololatrae, passionibus diversis immundi et irrationabiles, verbi ratione carentes, quantum ad Deum stulti. Quid autem stultius quam factorem contemnere, quam facturam et opus manuum suarum adorare, quasi factorem? . . . Et quicumque daemonum vel philosophorum cuiusque erroris vel dogmatis alicuius sarcinam eis voluisset imponere, sufferebant.

The references to idolatry and devil-worship seem to point to the Gentiles rather than the Jews who are nevertheless identified with the ass at 61.

59–60 Ps-Chrysostom, Hom. 37, PG 56, 835:

> At ubi Christus super eos ascendit, et induxit in templum, lavati per baptismum, facti sunt de immundis animalibus homines sancti. Percepta enim verbi ratione, sapientia Dei facti sunt rationabiles et prudentes.

61–8 The distinction between ass and foal comes from Haymo, drawing on Bede's commentary on Luke (Haymo, Hom. 63, PL 118, 354D):

> Asina enim, quae oneribus ferendis assueta est, populum Iudaeorum significat, qui longo tempore sarcinam legis traxerat. Pullus ergo, qui lascivus et liber est, significat gentilium plebem, quae ante adventum Domini sine legis doctrina et prophetarum quasi libera et vaga incessit.

Ælfric then expands on this, quoting Mt 28.19–20:

> (19) Euntes ergo docete omnes gentes, baptizantes eos in nomine Patris et Filii et Spiritus Sancti, (20) docentes eos servare omnia quaecumque mandavi vobis.

69–74 Ælfric is here using Luke's account, and Bede's commentary on Luke probably inspired his interpretation of the ass's owner (*Comm. Luc.*, 5.1915–22):

> Qui solvendo pullo contradixerant audito domini nomine quiescunt, quia magistri errorum qui venientibus ad salutem gentium doctoribus obsistebant eatenus suas tenebras defendere, donec miraculis attestantibus veri possessoris ac domini virtus emicuit; at postquam fidei dominicae potestas apparuit, cedentibus passim adversariorum querellis liber credentium coetus qui Deum corde portet adducitur.

Smaragdus reproduces this passage, *Collectiones*, PL 102, 514D-5A. It was Haymo, however, who suggested equating the owners with kings and rulers rather than heretics (Hom. 63, PL 118, 355B): *Mox enim ut sancti apostoli, accepto divinitus praecepto, mundo praedicaverunt, statim reges gentium et principes eis obsistere coeperunt*, and it is apparently Ælfric's own contribution to the interpretation to suggest that the rulers themselves are converted by miracles and follow Christ.

74–7 Cf Ps-Chrysostom, Hom. 37, PG 56, 836:

> Ne dicatis, Dominus tuus; neque Dominus noster; neque Dominus iumentorum: ut intelligant, omnes, quia ego solus Dominus, non solum animalium . . . sed omnium hominum.

77–85 Ælfric's distinction between the divine grace which calls man and the free will on which he must partially rely thereafter, along with God's grace, draws freely on Ps-Chrysostom (Hom. 37, PG 56, 836):

> Nam quod vocati sumus, Dei est, quod autem digne post vocationem vivimus, nostrum pariter est et Dei. Hoc est quod ait, 'Iterum remittet eos', non ad diabolum, qui prius tenebat eos, sed in arbitrio suo, adiuvante gratiae scilicet dono.

Lines 80–1 owe something to the source-passage for 112–23.

86–90 The contrast between the humble ass and the proud steed comes from Haymo, Hom. 63, PL 118, 354CD:

> Humilitas magna Salvatoris commendatur, qui Ierusalem tendens, non equo superbo neque phalerato invehi voluit, sed potius asinam et pullum eius, vilia scilicet animalia, ad sedendum quaesivit.

Cf too Ps-Chrysostom (Hom. 37, PG 56, 837), Haymo's apparent source:

> Non sedet in curru aureo, pretiosa purpura fulgens; nec ascendit super fervidum equum.

89–90 is from Mt 11.29: *Discite a me quia mitis sum et humilis corde et invenietis requiem animabus vestris.* It is used later by Haymo (Hom. 63, PL 118, 356B) and by Bede (Hom. II.3, 95).

90–7 The first sentence seems to mean: 'This (i.e. riding on the ass) and all the other things that Christ did were prophesied of him before he was born.' Ælfric is evidently thinking of the verse from Zechariah quoted at Matthew 21.5 (lines 16–18 of the Old English), since the second sentence goes on to interpret that verse, but the connection is obscure, especially since Jerusalem is not in fact mentioned in the Matthew quotation; Ælfric was perhaps thinking of the full text of Zechariah 9.9, which does mention Jerusalem. His interpretation of the daughters of Sion as the church and Jerusalem as the heavenly city comes from Bede, Hom. II.3, 90–91:

> Filia Sion ecclesia est fidelium, pertinens ad supernam Hierusalem.

Haymo, following Jerome and Augustine, simply identifies Sion with Jerusalem. But the etymological explanations are Ælfric's own contribution. Jerusalem as *visio pacis* is a commonplace; Sion as *sceawung-stow* perhaps draws on Jerome's *Liber Interpretationis Hebraicorum Nominum* (CCSL 72, 39.25): *Sion specula vel speculator sive scopulus.* Thorpe translates *sceawung-stow* 'a place of contemplation', but it occurs as a gloss for *specula* 'a watchtower or lookout' and Ælfric's point is perhaps rather that Sion or the earthly church is the vantage-point or 'place of looking' for looking towards the heavenly Jerusalem, which is itself the *visio pacis*, the object of sight.

98–110 The initial equation of the garments laid on the ass with righteousness is developed from Bede's Hom. II.3, 109–18:

> Vestimenta discipulorum opera sunt iustitiae psalmista teste qui ait: 'Sacerdotes tui induantur iustitia' (Ps 131.9). . . . Non enim nudam dominus asinam non nudum voluit ascendere pullum quia sive Iudaeus quis seu gentilis nisi sanctorum fuerit dictis ornatus et actis non potest dominum habere rectorem.

Ælfric then extends the idea of bearing God, using St Paul: *Empti enim estis pretio magno; glorificate et portate Deum in corpore vestro* (1 Cor 6.20), and *Nescitis quia templum Dei estis et Spiritus Dei habitat in vobis. Si quis autem templum Dei violaverit, disperdit illum Deus* (1 Cor 3.16–17).

111–21 Ælfric's parable on kingship, applied to the idea of man as an ass carrying the devil, closely follows an earlier passage in Ps-Chrysostom, commenting on the image of untying the ass (Hom. 37, PG 56, 835):

> Sicut enim videmus in istis mundialibus regnis, quomodo in primis quidem nemo potest facere seipsum regem, sed populus creat sibi regem quem elegerit; cum rex ille fuerit factus et confirmatus in regno, iam habet potestatem in hominibus, et non potest populus iugum eius de cervice sua repellere. [*Ps-Chrysostom goes on to say that it is not in the people's power to drive a king, once made, from power.*] . . . Sic et homo, priusquam peccet, liberum habet arbitrium, utrum velit sub regno esse diaboli; cum autem peccando se tradiderit sub regno ipsius, iam non potest de potestate eius exire: . . . nemo potest eos de potestate diaboli eripere, nisi solus Deus.

The subsequent lines in Ælfric, 118–21, draw on the immediately preceding lines in Ps-Chrysostom (Hom. 37, PG 56, 835):

> Si semel peccantes obligaverimus nos operibus eius, iam nostra virtute evadere non possumus. . . . Et nisi Deus valida manu misericordiae suae solverit eum, usque ad mortem in peccatorum suorum vinculis permanebit. Ergo nostra quidem voluntate et negligentia alligamur, sed per Dei misericordiam absolvimur.

The passage has acquired some independent fame amongst historians, ever since Felix Liebermann drew attention to it in 1919 as apparent evidence for Anglo-Saxon views on the sacred nature of kingship.[3] Given the analogy between the king and the devil and the fact that he is following Ps-Chrysostom, one should perhaps understand Ælfric to be referring to the practical realities of royal power in general rather than the sacramental quality of English kingship. Part of the passage is quoted by Atto of Vercelli in the tenth century, and Atto has *populus eligit sibi regem quem vult* instead of *populus creat sibi regem quem elegerit*

[3] F. Liebermann, 'Ein staatsrechtlicher Satz Ælfrics aus lateinischer quelle', *Archiv* 139 (1919), 84–5. For the subsequent discussion, see my note, 'Ælfric and Anglo-Saxon kingship', *English Historical Review* 102 (1987), 911–5.

near the beginning of the passage[4]; this is marginally closer to Ælfric's reading, and it may be what his copy of the Ps-Chrysostom homily (in PD) had at this point too.

122–46 Ælfric takes his cue from Bede's homily in interpreting those who cast garments under the ass's feet as the martyrs (Hom. II.3, 120–26):

> Plurima haec turba innumerabilem martyrum designat exercitum, qui corpora sua animarum videlicet tegumenta pro domino dabant, quo sequentibus electis planiorem recte vivendi callem facerent ne qui videlicet dubitarent ibi pedem bonae actionis ponere in pace ubi non paucos viderent in bello praecessisse martyrii.

In developing the point, he characteristically invokes the theme of the varieties of death and punishment. Cf the fuller discussion at CH I.36.71 ff., and Cross 1972, pp. 22–3.

133–7 A succinct summary of Bede (Hom. II.3, 128–34):

> Rami arborum dicta sunt patrum praecedentium. Et quisquis in exemplum recte credendi sive operandi quid prophetae quid apostoli quid ceteri sancti dixerunt seu fecerunt pandit ramos profecto de arboribus caedit, quibus iter asini dominum portantis conplanet, quia sententias de sanctorum libris excerpit per quas simplicium Christi corda ne in via veritatis errent aedificet.

Gedæfton (line 134) perhaps means 'made level' here, with a notion of filling holes in the road, since Bede has *complanet* and Ælfric had earlier described the garments as 'bridging' Christ's way (line 21).

137–48 The interpretation is again mainly from Bede (Hom. II.3, 136–42):

> Una eademque confessionis et laudationis voce dominum qui praecedunt et qui sequuntur exaltant, quia nimirum una fides est eorum qui ante incarnationem dominicam et qui postea fuere probati . . . Petro adtestante qui ait: 'Sed per gratiam domini Iesu credimus salvari quemadmodum et illi' (Acts 15.11).

But the specific identifications seem to come from Haymo (Hom. 63, PL 118, 357D):

> Eadem enim fides quae fuit in patriarchis et prophetis ante adventum Salvatoris, eadem est in omnibus gentibus post resurrectionem illius.

None of the other commentators bothers to explain the term 'son of David'. Ælfric here repeats a point made at CH I.13.44–5.

148–51 The interpretation is from Haymo, recasting Bede's Hom. II.3, 150–3 (Haymo, Hom. 63, PL 118, 358A):

[4] PL 134, 99C. Atto was suggested as a source for Ælfric by Karl Jost, 'The legal maxim in Ælfric's homilies', *English Studies* 36 (1955), 204–5.

Intelligitur, quia Filius a Patre venit in mundum. Quia quidquid secundum carnem in hoc mundo egit, totum ad gloriam et nomen Patris sui retulit.

The text is not quite as cited earlier at 23–4, or indeed as any of the Gospels.

151–6 The text is from Matthew 21.9, *osanna in excelsis* (not in fact included in the initial version of the Gospel passage cited at 23–4), and the commentary draws on Bede (Hom. II.3, 167–73):

Osanna . . . in altissimis perspicue docet adventum domini in carne, non solum humani generis in terra sed et angelorum in caelis esse salutem, quia dum nos redempti ad superna reducimur eorum profecto numerus qui satana cadente erat minoratus impletur. Hinc etenim Paulus ait: 'Instaurari omnia in Christo quae in caelis et quae in terra sunt in ipso' (Eph 1.10).

Ælfric's *geeacniað* (line 154) for *impletur* carefully avoids Bede's implication that the number of saved matches the number of fallen angels (his own view was that it would equal the number of angels who remained, cf CH I.1.58–62). For *tocyme and his ðrowung* cf Haymo's adaptation of Bede, *incarnatio et passio*.

157–61 Probably a summary of Lc 19.47–8:

(47) Et erat docens quotidie in templo. Principes autem sacerdotum, et scribae, et principes plebis quaerebant illum perdere. (48) Et non inveniebant quid facerent illi. Omnis enim populus suspensus erat, audiens illum.

But Ælfric's reference to miracles is rather loose; the Gospels record much teaching by Christ in the subsequent days, but only the single miracle of the fig-tree (Mt 21.18–20).

161–79 Ælfric now moves away from his sources into a general explanation of the divine scheme of redemption, countering the Gospels' emphasis on the high-priests' responsibility. Bede's homily and Ps-Chrysostom both begin by stressing Christ's volition but there is little similarity otherwise. Lines 161–71 closely parallel the earlier discussion in CH I.1.265–76, but there is no other extant text to which Ælfric's comment 'we have often said' (line 167) might refer; possibly he is referring to his own preaching rather than written texts. The image of the fish, representing the devil, snatching at the hook presumably comes from Gregory the Great's homily for Easter Day (Hom. 25, PL 76, 1194CD):

In hamo autem esca ostenditur, aculeus occultatur. Hunc [= *the devil*] ergo pater omnipotens hamo coepit, quia ad mortem illius unigenitum filium incarnatum misit, in quo et caro passibilis videri posset, et divinitas impassibilis videri non posset. Cumque in eo serpens iste per manus persequentium escam corporis momordit, divinitatis illum aculeus perforavit.

(The same points are also in the *Moralia siue Expositio in Iob*, II.xxv.8; the wording is not close.)

181–92 A summary of the rest of the passion narrative, which was to be read during the rest of Passion week but not, presumably, to be translated or discussed for the laity, since there was no further preaching occasion until Easter Day. Ælfric's insistence on the non-Biblical detail of the four nails (line 183), linked to the spear-wound, suggests the possibility of an early reference to the motif of the five wounds of Christ; cf, too, CH II.14.241–2 and notes. In asserting that the body was in the tomb from Friday evening through to Sunday and that Christ's divinity was in hell during that period, Ælfric is presumably taking a stand against the tradition that Christ led those harrowed from hell, and the good thief, to paradise at this time, and himself went to heaven.[5]

195–209 Ælfric's account of the Palm Sunday ceremonies parallels that in the *Regularis Concordia* (pp. 34–6), which he subsequently paraphrased in his own letter to the monks of Eynsham (Jones 1998, §32), but appropriately deals with the role of the laity, whereas those texts concentrate on the monastic role. (Cf too Ælfric's second Old English letter for Wulfstan, Fehr III, §181.) The ceremonies are also briefly described by Alcuin (PL 101, 1200–02) and Amalarius (*Liber Officialis*, I.10, pp. 58–9); the latter is cited in Ælfric's Eynsham Letter. None of these other accounts offers an interpretation of the ceremony, such as Ælfric gives here (lines 199–209), except to make the point that it commemorates the entry into Jerusalem. The symbolic drama by which the laity offering their palm-leaves to the priest represent the Christians offering their tokens of spiritual victory to God as they enter heaven shows the same kind of sensibility to the liturgy as the famous *Quem quaeritis* ceremony of Easter Day recorded in the *Regularis Concordia*, but it is not mentioned in that text. The palms are similarly associated with victory in Augustine's discussion of the entry (*Tract.*, 51.2.7) and the point is repeated in Ælfric's Eynsham Letter. He presumably envisaged the ceremony taking place in the church after the sermon.

215–19 The resurrection of the body is a favourite theme with Ælfric; cf esp. I.16.111 ff and his excerpts from the *Prognosticon* (*Excerpts*, p. 141). Lines 218–9 allude to Mt 13.43: *Tunc iusti fulgebunt sicut sol in regno Patris eorum*, similarly quoted in association with this topic at Pope 11.569–71.

220 app. crit. '*Circlice þeawas . . . swigdagum*' The same note, undoubtedly by Ælfric (see *CH I*, p. 69), occurs also at the end of CH II.14. See the study by Joyce Hill, 'Ælfric's silent days', *Leeds Studies in English* 16 (1985), 118–25. As she shows, though there is reference to the observance of silence in the three days before Easter, called *swigdagas* or *swigeniht*, in the *Regularis Concordia* and Ælfric's letters, this seems to have been a primarily monastic practice and there is no other reference to the omission of preaching in Anglo-Saxon England; texts seem to have been provided for these days both in the Latin homiliaries used by Ælfric and in the vernacular homiliaries, and the disagreements of contempor-

[5] See, for instance, the Old English version of the Gospel of Nicodemus in Cross 1996, p. 233.

aries with Ælfric on this issue are evident from the comments in the manuscripts. Hill suggests that the extension of monastic liturgical silence to preaching was either a Winchester phenomenon or an initiative of Ælfric himself.

15 EASTER DAY

The appointed reading for Easter Day was the brief account in Mark 16.1–7, covering the visit of the three Marys to Christ's tomb and the angel's report of his resurrection. Ælfric gives the incipit from this reading at the beginning, but in fact provides a much fuller narrative of the events surrounding the resurrection, drawing on the accounts in all four Gospels and adding material on the setting and bribing of the guards and Christ's other appearances to the disciples, and his ascension. A concern to dispel doubts about the reality of Christ's resurrection possibly influenced his choice of details to include, such as the Jews sealing and guarding the tomb, the angel rolling away the stone from the tomb, the empty clothes, the evidence of the guards and their agreement to tell a false story. As in the previous homily, the task of reconciling or selecting from the variant and apparently contradictory accounts of the Gospels could not have been easy, and sometimes different details are used in the subsequent commentary. The commentary itself (lines 75–200) focuses mainly on the literal and doctrinal implications of the resurrection and the events at the tomb, both for Christ's resurrection and for that of mankind, but with some use of allegorical readings.

The commentary derives mainly, as Ælfric says, from Gregory the Great, specifically from his homily on Mark 16.1–7, which appears for this occasion in Paul the Deacon's homiliary, but there are also points which seem to derive from Bede's Homily on Matthew 28 (included for the Vigil of Easter in PD), from Paschasius Radbertus and Julian of Toledo. The homilies on Mark 16 included in the homiliaries of Haymo and Smaragdus draw heavily on Gregory and were probably not used by Ælfric.[1]

Sources and Notes

The following texts are cited below:

1. Bede, *Homiliae*, ed. D. Hurst, CCSL 122 (Turnhout, 1955), Hom. II.7 (pp. 225–32).
2. Gregory the Great, *Homiliae in Evangelia*, PL 76, Hom. 21, cols. 1169–74.
3. Haymo of Auxerre, *Homiliae de Tempore*, PL 118, Hom. 70, cols. 445–55.

[1] Förster (1894, pp. 3–4) noted the use of Gregory's homilies 21 and 10 (see below on lines 171–82), and Smetana (1959, p. 189) noted that both were included in PD.

4. Julian of Toledo, *Prognosticon Futuri Saeculi*, ed. J. Hillgarth, CCSL 115 (Turnhout, 1976), pp. 11–126.
5. Paschasius Radbertus, *De Assumptione Sanctae Mariae Virginis*, ed. A. Ripberger, CCCM 56C (Turnhout, 1985), pp. 109–62.

6–14 The setting of the guards is from Mt 27.62–6:

> (62) Altera autem die quae est post parasceven convenerunt principes sacerdotum et Pharisaei ad Pilatum (63) dicentes: domine recordati sumus quia seductor ille dixit adhuc vivens post tres dies resurgam; (64) iube ergo custodiri sepulchrum usque in diem tertium ne forte veniant discipuli eius et furentur eum et dicant plebi surrexit a mortuis et erit novissimus error peior priore. (65) Ait illis Pilatus: habetis custodiam, ite custodite sicut scitis. (66) Illi autem abeuntes munierunt sepulchrum signantes lapidem cum custodibus.

15–36 The movements and identities of the women involved in the resurrection story are the subject of detailed discussion in the commentaries, as they attempt to reconcile the disparate accounts of the four Gospels, but Ælfric succeeds in differing from all of them.[2] He follows Luke 23.55–6 in recording that the women watched the burial and then returned to the city:

> (55) Subsecutae autem mulieres quae cum ipso venerant de Galilaea viderunt monumentum et quemadmodum positum erat corpus eius, (56) et revertentes paraverunt aromata et unguenta et sabbato quidem siluerunt secundum mandatum.

Luke does not identify the women, but Mark (15.47) reports that the burial was watched by Maria Magdalene and Maria Ioseph (who was traditionally understood to be the Mary who was the mother of Joseph and of James 'the brother of the Lord', and the sister of the Virgin Mary; see Pope, p. 217, and also notes on CH I.4, II.17 and II.27), while Matthew (27.61) describes Maria Magdalene and *altera Maria* sitting by the tomb immediately after the burial. Ælfric is alone in specifying the Virgin Mary's presence at the burial and I can find no parallel or support in commentary or apocrypha. Possibly it is his own interpretation of *Maria Ioseph*, possibly a tradition that had developed as part of the cult of the Virgin, helped by Matthew's reference (27.61) to Maria Magdalene and *altera Maria* sitting by the tomb immediately after the burial. Ælfric then names Mary Magdalene and Mary mother of James as those who bought the ointments for the body, and possibly as those who then went to the tomb on Easter Day, though his phrase *ða wimmen* (line 19) might refer more generally. Matthew records two women visiting the tomb, Mary Magdalene and an otherwise unnamed *altera Maria*; Mark specifies three buying ointments and then visiting the tomb, Mary Magdalene, Maria Jacobi and Salome; Luke refers to them only as *mulieres* but later names three of them as Mary Magdalene, Iohanna and

[2] See now the excellent discussion in M. B. Bedingfield, 'Reinventing the Gospel: Ælfric and the Liturgy', *Medium Ævum* 68 (1999), 13–31.

Maria Iacobi, implying there were others; John reports only the visit to the tomb of Mary Magdalene. If, as seems likely, Ælfric knew the tradition that Salome, or Mary Salome, was the mother of James and John (cf Pope, pp. 217–20), it is conceivable that he took the *Maria Iacobi* and Salome of Mark's account to be one person, helped by Matthew's reference to only two visiting the tomb. But if he really meant to imply that only two women went to the tomb, it is in remarkable contrast to the famous *Quem quaeritis* drama described in the *Regularis Concordia*,[3] which has three brethren representing the women at the tomb; Ælfric must have seen this ritual many times in his youth, and one might have expected the number three to figure in his own narrative. The Old English versions of the Gospels show no sign of a variant tradition.

Ælfric ignores the commentators' lengthy attempts to reconcile the time-references of Matthew with the other Gospels, and his explanation of the function of anointing (line 18) is his own (though cf Jn 19.40 for the reference to Jewish custom: *Acceperunt ergo corpus Iesu, et ligaverunt illud linteis cum aromatibus, sicut mos est Iudaeis sepelire*; cf too CH I.7.206).
The details of the approach to the tomb draw mainly on Mc 16.1–4:

> (1) Et cum transisset sabbatum Maria Magdalene et Maria Iacobi et Salome emerunt aromata ut venientes unguerent eum. (2) Et valde mane una sabbatorum veniunt ad monumentum orto iam sole, (3) et dicebant ad invicem: quis revolvet nobis lapidem ab ostio monumenti. (4) . . . Erat quippe magnus valde.

Mark then describes the women entering the tomb (the stone is already away) and finding a young man inside, but no body. Ælfric preferred Matthew's version (28.2–8) of what they saw, perhaps because it gives better evidence for the resurrection:

> (2) Et ecce terraemotus factus est magnus. Angelus enim Domini descendit de caelo et accedens revolvit lapidem et sedebat super eum. (3) Erat autem aspectus eius sicut fulgur et vestimentum eius sicut nix. (4) Prae timore autem eius exterriti sunt custodes et facti sunt velut mortui. (5) Respondens autem angelus dixit mulieribus: nolite timere vos; scio enim quod Iesum qui crucifixus est quaeritis. (6) Non est hic. Surrexit enim sicut dixit. Venite videte locum ubi positus erat Dominus. (7) Et cito euntes dicite discipulis eius quia surrexit et ecce praecedit vos in Galilaeam. Ibi eum videbitis ecce praedixi vobis [*Ælfric follows the* sicut dixit vobis *of some manuscripts of Matthew or of Mark.*] (8) Et exierunt cito de monumento cum timore et magno gaudio currentes nuntiare discipulis eius.

Ælfric's words 'tell them to meet him there' (lines 32–3) are an expansion of the angel's speech perhaps influenced by Christ's own words later, at Mt 28.10 (see below). The detail of the empty shroud in the tomb (lines 34–5) is not from

[3] *Regularis Concordia*, pp. 49–50.

Matthew but comes from the subsequent visit of Peter as described in Lc 24.12 or Jn 20.6–7; cf further lines 46–7 and 111–5.

37–47 Continuing with Matthew's account, 28.9–15:

(9) Et ecce Iesus occurrit illis dicens havete. Illae autem accesserunt et tenuerunt pedes eius et adoraverunt eum. (10) Tunc ait illis Iesus: nolite timere ite nuntiate fratribus meis ut eant in Galilaeam ibi me videbunt. (11) Quae cum abissent ecce quidam de custodibus venerunt in civitatem et nuntiaverunt principibus sacerdotum omnia quae facta fuerant. (12) Et congregati cum senioribus consilio accepto pecuniam copiosam dederunt militibus (13) dicentes dicite quia discipuli eius nocte venerunt et furati sunt eum nobis dormientibus; (14) et si hoc auditum fuerit a praeside nos suadebimus ei et securos vos faciemus. (15) At illi accepta pecunia fecerunt sicut erant docti et divulgatum est verbum istud apud Iudaeos usque in hodiernum diem.

The final words of verse 15 would seem to mean that the false story told by the bribed guards was spread amongst the Jews and continued current up to the time of writing. Ælfric turns it into a statement that the fact that the guards had been bribed and that Christ had in fact risen from the dead was widely publicised throughout Judaea; I have found no parallel to this way of reading it. The same anxiety to counter the Jewish leaders' story is evident in his interjected reference to the empty shroud (lines 46–7), for which there is again no parallel, and the suggestion that the guards testified to Christ's resurrection (lines 40–41). There is much dramatic emphasis on the empty shroud in the liturgical Easter play described in the *Regularis Concordia*.

47–70 Ælfric alludes to the further appearances described at Lc 24.12 (St Peter) and 13–35 (the road to Emmaus) and then (lines 49–66) translates closely the appearance to the assembled disciples from Lc 24.36–47:

(36) Dum haec autem loquuntur, Iesus stetit in medio eorum et dicit eis: pax vobis; ego sum, nolite timere. (37) Conturbati vero et conterriti, existimabant se spiritum videre. (38) Et dixit eis: quid turbati estis et cogitationes ascendunt in corda vestra? (39) Videte manus meas et pedes, quia ipse ego sum; palpate et videte quia spiritus carnem et ossa non habet, sicut me videtis habere. (40) Et cum hoc dixisset ostendit eis manus et pedes. (41) Adhuc autem illis non credentibus et mirantibus prae gaudio dixit: habetis hic aliquid quod manducetur. (42) At illi obtulerunt ei partem piscis assi et favum mellis (43) et cum manducasset coram eis sumens reliquias dedit eis (44) et dixit ad eos: haec sunt verba quae locutus sum ad vos cum adhuc essem vobiscum, quoniam necesse est impleri omnia quae scripta sunt in lege Mosi et prophetis et psalmis de me. (45) Tunc aperuit illis sensum ut intellegerent scripturas (46) et dixit eis: quoniam sic scriptum est et sic oportebat Christum pati et resurgere a

> mortuis die tertia, (47) et praedicari in nomine eius paenitentiam et remissionem peccatorum in omnes gentes.

His addition of the wound in the side at 56 (perhaps influenced by Jn 20.20 *ostendit eis manus et latus*) shows a concern with the number of the wounds already seen at CH I.14.183. Luke passes straight on to the ascension at this point, as if it happened on Easter Day; Ælfric (lines 67–70) follows Mt 28.16–20 or Jn 20–21 in mentioning further appearances, and takes the date of the ascension from Acts 1.3

75–84 Ælfric now moves to Gregory's homily on the Mark version of the resurrection. He ignores Gregory's first paragraph, on time-references in the Gospels, and then follows closely his interpretation of the visit to the tomb (Hom. 21, PL 76, 1170CD):

> Audistis, fratres carissimi, quod sanctae mulieres quae Dominum fuerant secutae cum aromatibus ad monumentum venerunt, et ei, quem viventem dilexerant, etiam mortuo, studio humanitatis obsequuntur. Sed res gesta aliquid in sancta ecclesia signat gerendum. . . . Et nos ergo in eum qui est mortuus credentes, si, odore virtutum referti, cum opinione bonorum operum Dominum quaerimus, ad monumentum profecto illius cum aromatibus venimus. Illae autem mulieres angelos vident, quae cum aromatibus venerunt, quia videlicet illae mentes supernos cives aspiciunt, quae cum virtutum odoribus ad Dominum per sancta desideria proficiscuntur.

85–9 Gregory has nothing on the angel rolling away the stone, since this detail is from Matthew's Gospel. The comment comes from Bede's Easter homily, II.7, 91–6:

> Revolvit autem lapidem non ut egressuro domino ianuam pandat sed ut egressus eius iam facti hominibus praestet indicium. Qui enim mortalis adhuc clauso virginis utero potuit nascendo mundum ingredi ipse absque ulla dubietate iam factus inmortalis clauso licet sepulchro potuit resurgendo exire de mundo.

The Old English passage was perhaps an authorial afterthought, since it was added on a supplementary slip in MS A and derives from a different Latin source; but since both this and the following passage begin with the same phrase, it could alternatively have been omitted in error by the scribe.

89–100 That the angel was sitting on the right and wearing shining garments comes from Mark 16 and is not mentioned in the initial rendering of the Gospel above; Ælfric follows Gregory for the interpretation (Hom. 21, PL 76, 1170D–1A):

> Notandum vero nobis est quidnam sit quod in dextris sedere angelus cernitur. Quid namque per sinistram nisi vita praesens, quid vero per dextram nisi perpetua vita designatur? . . . Quia ergo Redemptor noster iam praesentis vitae corruptionem transierat, recte angelus qui nuntiare

perennem eius vitam venerat in dextera sedebat. Qui stola candida coopertus apparuit, quia festivitatis nostrae gaudia nuntiavit. . . . Nostrae dicamus, an suae? Sed ut fateamur verius, et suae dicamus et nostrae. Illa quippe Redemptoris nostri resurrectio et nostra festivitas fuit, quia nos ad immortalitatem reduxit; et angelorum festivitas exstitit, quia nos revocando ad coelestia eorum numerum implevit.

101–9 From Gregory, who draws in part on the Matthew account (Hom. 21, PL 76, 1171B):

> Nolite expavescere. Ac si aperte dicat: Paveant illi qui non amant adventum supernorum civium; pertimescant qui, carnalibus desideriis pressi, ad eorum se societatem pertingere posse desperant. Vos autem cur pertimescitis, quae vestros concives videtis? Unde et Matthaeus angelum apparuisse describens, ait: 'Erat aspectus eius sicut fulgur, et vestimenta eius sicut nix' (Mt 28.3). In fulgure etenim terror timoris est, in nive autem blandimentum candoris. Quia vero omnipotens Deus et terribilis peccatoribus, et blandus est iustis, recte testis resurrectionis eius angelus et in fulgure vultus, et in candore habitus demonstratur, ut de ipsa sua specie et terreret reprobos, et mulceret pios.

109–15 Cf Gregory, Hom. 21, PL 76, 1171D: *Non est hic dicitur per praesentiam carnis, qui tamen nusquam deerit per praesentiam maiestatis*. But Gregory has no comment on the empty clothing, since it is only mentioned in Luke and John; I have found no parallel for Ælfric's comment. The question whether the elect are clothed, and if so whether with material or spiritual garments, is discussed and similarly resolved in the *Prognosticon* of Julian of Toledo (III.xxvi). Ælfric briefly summarises the point in his excerpts from the *Prognosticon* (*Excerpts*, 284–5): *Etsi indumenta fuerint, spiritalium corporum spiritalia erunt*. He repeats the point made here at Pope 11.339–42.

116–20 The interpretation of Galilee is from Gregory, Hom. 21, PL 76, 1172AB:

> Bene autem de Redemptore nostro dicitur: 'Praecedet vos in Galilaeam, ibi eum videbitis, sicut dixit vobis.' Galilaea namque transmigratio facta interpretatur. Iam quippe Redemptor noster a passione ad resurrectionem, a morte ad vitam, a poena ad gloriam, a corruptione ad incorruptionem transmigraverat. Et prius post resurrectionem in Galilaea a discipulis videtur, quia resurrectionis eius gloriam post laeti videbimus, si modo a vitiis ad virtutum celsitudinem transmigramus.

120–9 From Gregory, Hom. 21, PL 76, 1172BC:

> Duae etenim vitae erant, quarum unam novimus, alteram nesciebamus. Una quippe mortalis est, altera immortalis . . . . Sed venit Mediator Dei et hominum homo Christus Iesus, suscepit unam, et ostendit alteram. Unam pertulit moriendo, et ostendit alteram resurgendo. Si ergo nobis mortalem

> vitam scientibus resurrectionem promitteret carnis, et tamen hanc visibiliter non exhiberet, quis eius promissionibus crederet? Factus itaque homo apparuit in carne, mori dignatus est ex voluntate, resurrexit ex potestate, et ostendit exemplo quod nobis promisit in praemio.

130–42 Gregory similarly invokes Mt 27.52 as evidence of a general resurrection (Hom. 21, PL 76, 1172CD):

> Sed fortasse aliquis dicat: Iure ille surrexit qui, cum Deus esset, teneri a morte non potuit. . . . Solus in illo tempore mortuus est, et tamen solus minime resurrexit. Nam scriptum est: 'Multa corpora sanctorum qui dormierant surrexerunt'. Ablata ergo sunt omnia argumenta perfidiae. Ne quis enim dicat: Sperare de se non debet homo quod in carne sua exhibuit Deus homo, ecce cum Deo homines resurrexisse cognoscimus, et quos puros homines fuisse non dubitamus.

But Ælfric characteristically extends the discussion of the bodily resurrection, invoking further learned authority against any theory that the dead who rose at the crucifixion might have returned to their graves afterwards and thus not be evidence for a general resurrection (lines 135–9). He makes the same point in his homily on the assumption of the Virgin (CH I.30.76–80), and is evidently drawing on his source for that homily, the tract by Paschasius Radbertus on the assumption which masqueraded as a letter by Jerome (Paschasius, *De Assumptione*, 83–6):

> De quibus profecto nonnulli doctorum senserunt, etiam et in suis reliquerunt scriptis, quod iam in illis perpetua sit completa resurrectio. Fatentur enim, quod veri testes non essent, nisi et vera esset eorum resurrectio.

The *Old English Martyrology* similarly cites the rising of the dead men at the crucifixion as a case of resurrection in body and soul and evidence for a universal resurrection in both forms, in its discussion of the crucifixion under 25 March (OE Martyrology, II.44).

143–57 From Gregory, Hom. 21, PL 76, 1173AB:

> Ecce vero ad memoriam redit quod crucifixo Dei filio Iudaei insultantes dicebant: 'Si rex Israel est, descendat de cruce, et credimus ei' (Mt 27.42). Qui si de cruce tunc descenderet, nimirum insultantibus cedens, virtutem nobis patientiae non demonstraret. Sed exspectavit paululum, toleravit opprobria, irrisiones sustinuit, servavit patientiam, distulit admirationem; et qui de cruce descendere noluit, de sepulcro surrexit. Plus igitur fuit de sepulcro surgere quam de cruce descendere. Plus fuit mortem resurgendo destruere quam vitam descendendo servare. Sed cum Iudaei hunc ad insultationes suas de cruce descendere minime cernerent, cum morientem viderent, eum se vicisse crediderunt, nomen illius se quasi exstinxisse gavisi sunt. Sed ecce de morte nomen eius per mundum crevit, . . . et

> quem gaudebat occisum, dolet mortuum, quia hunc ad suam gloriam cognoscit pervenisse per poenam.

Ælfric's rendering of the final sentence (lines 156–7) suggests that he had a different reading in his source here (but the 1516 version of PD reads as PL here).

158–70 The analogy with Samson and the gates of Gaza is from Gregory (Hom. 21, PL 76, 1173BC):

> Quod bene in libro Iudicum Samson illius facta significant (Jud 16.1–3), qui cum Gazam civitatem Philisthinorum fuisset ingressus, Philisthaei, ingressum eius protinus cognoscentes, civitatem repente obsidionibus circumdederunt, custodes deputaverunt, et Samson fortissimum se iam comprehendisse gavisi sunt. . . . Media nocte portas civitatis abstulit, et montis verticem ascendit. Quem, fratres carissimi, hoc in facto, quem nisi Redemptorem nostrum Samson ille significat? Quid Gaza civitas nisi infernum designat? Quid per Philisthaeos nisi Iudaeorum perfidia demonstratur? . . . Samson vero media nocte non solum exiit, sed etiam portas tulit, quia videlicet Redemptor noster ante lucem resurgens, non solum liber de inferno exiit, sed et ipsa etiam inferni claustra destruxit. Portas tulit, et montis verticem subiit, quia resurgendo claustra inferni abstulit, et ascendendo coelorum regna penetravit.

Ælfric adds a reference to Adam and Eve and the other souls rescued from hell (lines 167–8), who are not mentioned by Gregory. Haymo, recasting Gregory, also introduces a reference to the souls of the righteous being freed (Haymo, Hom. 70, PL 118, 451A):

> Non solum liber exiit, sed etiam portas tulit: quia non solum ipse ab inferis liber exiit, sed etiam omnes animas iustorum de inferno liberavit, et ad montana, id est, ad coelestia revocavit.

Neither touches on the difficult question of the location of those rescued souls after the resurrection; the Gospel of Nicodemus describes them being led to paradise by the archangel Michael (cf above, note to I.14.181 ff). The comment at 168–9, *þa . . . witum*, was perhaps an authorial afterthought, since it is added in another hand in MS A and is not from Gregory. That Christ left the evil behind in hell perhaps needed emphasising in the light of a sustained heterodox tradition that he rescued all its inhabitants; cf esp. the firm comment in an anonymous Old English homily on the harrowing in Bodleian, MS Junius 121:

> Ne wene nu æfre ænig mann þæt Drihten Crist ealle þa of helle gelædde þe he ðær gemette; ac þa ane ða þe heora lif her on worulde rihtlice leofedon, þa he ðanon gelædde[4].

[4] Anna Maria Luiselli Fadda, ed., in '*De descensu Christi ad inferos*: una inedita omelia anglosassone', *Studi Medievali* 13 (1972), 989–1011, lines 177–9. I owe the reference, and also much useful information about the issue, to Daniel Anlezark, 'The Old Testament Patriarchs in Anglo-Saxon England: Abraham and Noah' (unpubl. D.Phil. thesis, Oxford Univ., 1997), esp. p. 205.

171–82 Either the reference to hell giving up its captives in the preceding lines, or Gregory's mention of the lack of faith of the Jews, may have prompted Ælfric here to introduce the topos of all creation except the Jews acknowledging Christ. The ultimate source is another homily by Gregory (PL 76, 1111A), but the similarity of wording and details shows that Ælfric is here relying on his own earlier rendering of the topos (CH I.7.92–104), for which he had used both Gregory and Haymo's adaptation.

183–93 A general statement of trinitarian doctrine and the redemption, which probably had no direct source.

16 FIRST SUNDAY AFTER EASTER

Ælfric follows the prescribed reading for the occasion, John 20.19–31, on Christ's appearance to the apostles after the resurrection and his reappearance a week later to assuage the doubts of Thomas. His commentary deals mainly with the literal level, focusing on the problem of Christ's corporeality and spirituality, the value of the disciples' doubts and fears and the institution of apostolic and episcopal powers of absolution. The Gospel's emphasis on the physical corporeality of the risen Christ prompted Gregory the Great, Ælfric's main source, into a concluding discussion of the bodily resurrection of mankind. Ælfric follows him in this but substantially extends the discussion (lines 111–42), adding a series of points on the age, stature and condition of the resurrected at the last judgement, drawn mainly from one of his favourite sources, the *Prognosticon Futuri Saeculi* of Julian of Toledo. At a later date, but possibly after becoming abbot of Eynsham in 1005, he added a further substantial section on the resurrection of the body (printed as Appendix B2; see *CH I*, pp. 133, 161–2 and below), offering a series of analogies, including the seasons, silkworms, the phoenix and the Seven Sleepers of Ephesus. It was perhaps a subject that posed problems for Ælfric's contemporaries and demanded serious discussion: it is noticeable that whereas Augustine and Gregory (Julian of Toledo's main authorities on the subject) concern themselves with extreme, even absurd, cases, of men with two heads or three legs, or a man eaten by a wolf, which was in turn eaten by a lion, Ælfric concentrates on the serious and more practical question whether the ordinary deficiencies and differences of the earthly body will remain in the after-life.

Gregory's homily on the Gospel text was Ælfric's main source for the commentary and is indeed the only item given for the occasion in PD. He follows his interpretation fairly closely but is often influenced as well by Haymo's expansion and revision of Gregory, and may also have used Smaragdus briefly.[1]

[1] Förster (1894, p. 5) identified the homily by Gregory as source, and Smetana (1959, p. 189) noted its inclusion in PD. Gatch (1966) identified the use of Julian of Toledo for the additional material on resurrection.

The later addition shows the possible influence of Ambrose's *Hexameron* and Ps-Augustine sermon 109.

Sources and Notes

The following texts are cited below:

1. Ælfric's *Excerpts* from the *Prognosticon Futuri Saeculi* of Julian of Toledo, ed. Gatch 1977, pp. 129–46.
2. Alcuin, *Commentaria in S. Ioannis Evangelium*, PL 100, cols. 737–1008.
3. Ambrose, *Hexameron*, ed. K. Schenkl, CSEL 32.1 (Vienna, 1897), pp. 3–261.
4. Ps-Augustine, *Sermones*, PL 39, Serm. 109 [=Augustine, *Sermones suppositi*], cols. 1961–2.
5. Basil of Cappadocia, *Homiliae in Hexaemeron*, PG 29, cols. 3–208.
6. Gregory the Great, *Homiliae in Evangelia*, PL 76, Hom. 26, cols. 1197–1204.
7. Gregory the Great, *Homiliae in Ezechielem*, ed. M. Adriaen, CCSL 142 (Turnhout, 1971).
8. Haymo of Auxerre, *Homiliae de Tempore*, PL 118, Hom. 81, cols. 489–98.
9. Julian of Toledo, *Prognosticon Futuri Saeculi*, ed. J. Hillgarth, CCSL 115 (Turnhout, 1976), pp. 11–126.
10. Smaragdus, *Collectiones in Evangelia et Epistolas*, PL 102, cols. 279–84.

2–26 A fairly close rendering of Jn 20.19–31:

> (19) Cum esset ergo sero die illo una sabbatorum, et fores essent clausae, ubi erant discipuli propter metum Iudaeorum, venit Iesus, et stetit in medio, et dicit eis: Pax vobis. (20) Et hoc cum dixisset, ostendit eis manus et latus. Gavisi sunt ergo discipuli viso Domino. (21) Dixit ergo eis iterum: Pax vobis. Sicut misit me Pater, et ego mitto vos. (22) Hoc cum dixisset, insuflavit, et dicit eis: Accipite Spiritum Sanctum: (23) quorum remiseritis peccata, remittuntur eis, quorum retinueritis detenta sunt. (24) Thomas autem unus ex duodecim, qui dicitur Didymus, non erat cum eis quando venit Iesus. (25) Dixerunt ergo ei alii discipuli: Vidimus Dominum. Ille autem dixit eis: Nisi videro in manibus eius figuram clavorum, et mittam digitum meum in locum clavorum, et mittam manum meam in latus eius, non credam. (26) Et post dies octo iterum erant discipuli eius intus et Thomas cum eis. Venit Iesus ianuis clausis, et stetit in medio, et dixit: Pax vobis. (27) Deinde dicit Thomae: Infer digitum tuum huc, et vide manus meas; et adfer manum tuam, et mitte in latus meum; et noli esse incredulus, sed fidelis. (28) Respondit Thomas, et dixit ei: Dominus meus, et Deus meus. (29) Dicit ei Iesus: Quia vidisti me, Thoma, credidisti: beati qui non viderunt, et crediderunt. (30) Multa quidem et alia signa fecit Iesus in conspectu discipulorum suorum, quae non sunt

scripta in libro hoc. (31) Haec autem scripta sunt, ut credatis quia Iesus est Christus Filius Dei, et ut credentes vitam aeternam habeatis in nomine eius.

The dating clause in verse 19 is usually understood as meaning 'late in that day, the first of the sabbaths', i.e. Sunday, which in context means Easter Day, and Haymo says this very emphatically (Hom. 81, PL 118, 489D-9A):

Quod autem ait 'una sabbatorum,' ipsam diem Dominicae resurrectionis intelligere debemus, quam, ob honorem et reverentiam eiusdem resurrectionis, Dominicam nominamus.

Ælfric's phrase *on anum restendæge* is curiously vague, though in some respects a very literal rendering, and all the more puzzling since the dating should in any case have been clear, because the passage goes on to assign the main event, the appearance to Thomas, to a week later and the reading, like the homily, is assigned to the first Sunday after Easter. The *OE Gospels* have a similar odd and over-literal rendering: *Ða hit wæs æuen on anon þæra restedaga* (*OE Gospels*, p. 200). Two of the manuscripts note opposite this, correctly enough, that it is the reading for the Sunday after Easter, but perhaps there was confusion about which of the two appearances were assigned to that day. Ælfric adds the reference to the wounds in the feet (line 15; cf the similar additions at I.14.183 and I.15.56). His reading *gelyfað* (line 22) for Vulgate *crediderunt* (v.29) possibly comes from a Bible with the Old Latin reading *credent*; he repeats it at 104 though Gregory has the past tense, and follows Augustine in the present tense at CH I.12.140.

27–33 From the opening section of Gregory, Hom. 26 (PL 76, 1197CD):

Prima lectionis huius evangelicae quaestio animum pulsat, quomodo post resurrectionem corpus dominicum verum fuit, quod clausis ianuis ad discipulos ingredi potuit. . . . Illud enim corpus Domini intravit ad discipulos ianuis clausis, quod videlicet ad humanos oculos per nativitatem suam clauso exiit utero Virginis. Quid ergo mirum si clausis ianuis post resurrectionem suam in aeternum iam victurus intravit, qui moriturus veniens non aperto utero Virginis exivit?

But influenced too by part of Haymo's rewording of this (Hom. 81, PL 118, 490BC):

Quid ergo est mirum si incorruptibilia et immortalia membra ad discipulos ianuis clausis introduxit, qui mortale et corruptibile corpus ex utero Virginis clauso eduxit?

34–7 Ælfric adds the parallel from Acts 5.17–23:

(17) Exsurgens autem princeps sacerdotum . . . (18) et iniecerunt manus in apostolos et posuerunt illos in custodia publica. (19) Angelus autem Domini per noctem aperiens ianuas carceris et educens eos. . . . (22) Cum venissent autem ministri et aperto carcere non invenissent illos reversi nuntiaverunt, (23) dicentes carcerem quidem invenimus clausum

cum omni diligentia et custodes stantes ad ianuas aperientes autem neminem intus invenimus.

38–43 From Gregory, Hom. 26, PL 76, 1197D-8A:

Palpandam carnem praebuit, quam clausis ianuis introduxit. Qua in re duo mira . . . ostendit, dum post resurrectionem suam corpus suum et incorruptibile et tamen palpabile demonstravit. . . . Et incorruptibilem se ergo, et palpabilem demonstravit, ut profecto esse post resurrectionem ostenderet corpus suum et eiusdem naturae, et alterius gloriae.

44–6 Gregory has no comment on *pax vobis*, but a similar point to Ælfric's is made in Alcuin's commentary on John (*Comm. Ioan.*, PL 100, 992D), and is repeated verbatim in the homily for this occasion given in the homiliary of Smaragdus (*Collectiones*, PL 102, 280D):

Pacem offerebat, qui propter pacem venit, et quibus ante dixit: 'Pacem meam relinquo vobis, pacem meam do vobis', modo dicit: 'Pax vobis'. Quam pacem nascente Christo angeli praedicaverunt mundo.

47–53 A paraphrase of Gregory, Hom. 26, PL 76, 1198B:

Pater filium misit, qui hunc pro redemptione generis humani incarnari constituit. Quem videlicet in mundum venire ad passionem voluit, sed tamen amavit filium quem ad passionem misit. Electos vero apostolos Dominus non ad mundi gaudia, sed, sicut ipse missus est, ad passiones in mundum mittit. Quia ergo et filius amatur a patre, et tamen ad passionem mittitur, ita et discipuli a Domino amantur, qui tamen ad passionem mittuntur in mundum.

Perhaps influenced by Haymo's recasting of this (Hom. 81, PL 118, 492AB):

Misit filius apostolos, quando ad eamdem incarnationem *praedicandam in universum orbem eos direxit*. Vel sicut misit Deus pater filium suum ad diversa opprobria et passiones sufferendas, sic et filius apostolos non ad *honorem et* gloriam huius saeculi accipiendam, sed ad angustias, et iniurias, et opprobria, et varias persecutiones sustinendas.

(The relevant phrases are italicized.)

54–65 From Gregory, Hom. 26, PL 76, 1198C-99A:

Quaerendum nobis est quid est quod Spiritum sanctum Dominus noster et semel dedit in terra consistens, et semel coelo praesidens? . . . In terra datur Spiritus, ut diligatur proximus; e coelo datur Spiritus, ut diligatur Deus. Sicut ergo una est caritas, et duo praecepta, ita unus Spiritus, et duo data. Prius a consistente Domino in terra, postmodum e coelo, quia in proximi amore discitur qualiter perveniri debeat ad amorem Dei. Unde et idem Ioannes dicit: 'Qui non diligit fratrem suum quem videt, Deum quem non videt quomodo potest diligere' (1 Jn 4.20)?

Ælfric repeats the passage almost verbatim in CH I.22.214–27.

65–72 Gregory provides no more than a vague parallel (Hom. 26, PL 76, 1199C):

Sciendum vero est quod hi qui prius Spiritum sanctum habuerunt, ut et ipsi innocenter viverent, et in praedicatione quibusdam prodessent, idcirco hunc post resurrectionem Domini patenter acceperunt, ut prodesse non paucis, sed pluribus possent.

But cf an earlier point in Haymo (Hom. 81, PL 118, 489BCD):

Fragiles namque et infirmi, necdum gratia spiritus sancti plenitur fuerant corroborati . . . Sed qui prius propter metum Iudaeorum in conclavi residebant, postquam Spiritum sanctum visibiliter acceperunt, tanta constantia sunt confirmati, ut absque ulla trepidatione ante principes et sacerdotes Dominum confiterentur. . . . [*of Peter:*] Qui enim prius ad vocem ancillae Dominum et magistrum suum negaverat, postea ante tremendos principes, et metuendas potestates, libera voce eum confessus est.

73–8 Based on Gregory, Hom. 26, PL 76, 1200AB:

Horum profecto nunc in ecclesia episcopi locum tenent. . . . [*Ælfric passes over Gregory's reference to bishops whose ways of life undermine their role as judges of others.*] Ac saepe agitur, ut vel damnet immeritos, vel alios ipse ligatus solvat. Saepe in solvendis ac ligandis subditis suae voluntatis motus, non autem causarum merita sequitur. Unde fit, ut ipsa hac ligandi et solvendi potestate se privet, qui hanc pro suis voluntatibus, et non pro subiectorum moribus exercet.

Haymo, recasting this passage (Hom. 81, PL 118, 493D), ascribes the power to bishops and priests but Ælfric follows Gregory in limiting the power to release penitent sinners from punishment to bishops.

78–92 From Gregory, Hom. 26, PL 76, 1200B–1B:

Videndum est quae culpa praecessit, aut quae sit poenitentia secuta post culpam, ut quos omnipotens Deus per compunctionis gratiam visitat, illos pastoris sententia absolvat. . . . Quod bene quatriduani mortui resuscitatio illa significat, quae videlicet demonstrat quia prius mortuum Dominus vocavit et vivificavit, dicens: 'Lazare, veni foras' (Jn 11.43); et postmodum is qui vivens egressus fuerat a discipulis est solutus, sicut scriptum est: Cumque egressus esset qui fuerat ligatus institis, tunc dixit discipulis: 'Solvite eum, et sinite abire' (Jn 11.44). Ecce illum discipuli iam viventem solvunt, quem magister resuscitaverat mortuum. . . . Ex qua consideratione intuendum est quod illos nos debemus per pastoralem auctoritatem solvere quos auctorem nostrum cognoscimus per suscitantem gratiam vivificare. . . . Omnis quippe peccator dum culpam suam intra conscientiam abscondit, introrsum latet, in suis penetralibus occultatur. Sed mortuus venit foras, cum peccator nequitias suas sponte confitetur. Lazaro ergo dicitur 'Veni foras'. . . . Venientem vero foras solvant discipuli, ut

> pastores ecclesiae ei poenam debeant amovere, quam meruit qui non erubuit confiteri quod fecit. . . . Is autem qui sub manu pastoris est, ligari timeat vel iniuste; nec pastoris sui iudicium temere reprehendat, ne etsi iniuste ligatus est, ex ipsa tumidae reprehensionis superbia culpa quae non erat fiat.

Gregory does not specify whether the releasing of the sinner is from temporal, purgatorial or eternal punishment; Ælfric defines it as eternal (line 89).

93–8 From Gregory, Hom. 26, PL 76, 1201C:

> Non hoc casu, sed divina dispensatione gestum est. . . . Plus enim nobis Thomae infidelitas ad fidem quam fides credentium discipulorum profuit, quia dum ille ad fidem palpando reducitur, nostra mens, omni dubitatione postposita, in fide solidatur.

98–100 Haymo reports that the pagans ask why Christ could not appear without his wounds if he was truly God and offers a series of reasons why Christ retained the signs of his wounds; Ælfric summarises the first (Hom. 81, PL 118, 496C):

> Maius est enim carnem a mortuis resuscitare, quam vulnera clavorum in carne sanare. Qui ergo quod minus est fecit, et quod maius est facere poterat, nisi varias ob causas ipsa vulnera in corpore suo servare voluisset. Primum, ut fidem apostolorum ad credendum invitaret vel reformaret.

101–2 Cf Gregory, Hom. 26, PL 76, 1202A:

> Videndo ergo credidit, qui considerando verum hominem, hunc Deum, quem videre non poterat, exclamavit.

102–10 From Gregory, Hom. 26, PL 76, 1202AB:

> Laetificat valde quod sequitur: 'Beati qui non viderunt, et crediderunt.' In qua nimirum sententia nos specialiter signati sumus, qui eum quem carne non vidimus mente retinemus. . . . Ille etenim vere credit, qui exercet operando quod credit. Quo contra de his qui fidem nomine tenus retinent Paulus dicit: 'Confitentur se nosse Deum, factis autem negant' (Tit 1.16). Hinc Iacobus ait: 'Fides sine operibus mortua est' (Jac 2.26).

Ælfric silently changes the tense of Christ's *crediderunt* (cf above line 22 and note); Haymo notes the use of past tense, but argues that it has future signification (Hom. 81, PL 118, 497D).

111–25 Gregory's next two sections are exhortations to think on the last judgement; Ælfric moves directly to the discussion of resurrection with which Gregory concludes (Hom. 26, PL 76, 1203C–4B):

> Sed quia sunt nonnulli qui de resurrectione carnis incerti sunt . . . pauca nobis de ipsa resurrectionis fide loquenda sunt. Multi etenim de resurrectione dubitant, sicut et nos aliquando fuimus, qui dum carnem in putredinem ossaque in pulverem redigi per sepulcra conspiciunt, reparari ex pulvere carnem et ossa diffidunt, sicque apud se quasi ratiocinantes dicunt: Quando ex pulvere homo reducitur? quando agitur ut cinis animetur? Quibus breviter

> respondemus quia longe minus est Deo reparare quod fuit quam creasse quod non fuit. Aut quid mirum si hominem ex pulvere reficit, qui simul omnia ex nihilo creavit? Mirabilius namque est coelum et terram ex nullis existentibus condidisse, quam ipsum hominem ex terra reparare. . . . Nam ecce in uno grano parvissimi seminis latet tota quae nascitura est arboris moles. . . . Consideremus nunc ubi in illo parvo grano seminis latet fortitudo ligni, asperitas corticis, saporis odorisque magnitudo, ubertas fructuum, viriditas foliorum. . . . Quid igitur mirum, si ossa, nervos, carnem, capillosque reducat ex pulvere, qui lignum, fructus, folia, in magna mole arboris ex parvo quotidie semine restaurat?

Ælfric adds at the end the reference to Lc 21.18: *Et capillus de capite vestro non peribit.*

126–42 Ælfric now develops the topic of bodily resurrection independently of Gregory, drawing on Julian of Toledo's *Prognosticon Futuri Saeculi*. Most of this material appears in Ælfric's *Excerpts* from the *Prognosticon*, but he includes in this homily several details from the *Prognosticon* which do not appear in the *Excerpts*; indeed there is no firm evidence that he used the *Excerpts* at all as a source for this passage.[2] He later covered the same ground in Pope 11.305–31, where he seems to have used the *Prognosticon* again, with some influence from his treatment of the general resurrection here and in the *Excerpts*. Lines 126–30 are from *Prognosticon*, III.xx.7–21:

> Restat ergo, ut suam recipiat quisque mensuram, quam vel habuit in iuventute, etiamsi senex est mortuus, vel fuerat habiturus, si est ante defunctus, atque illud, quod commemoravit apostolus de 'mensura aetatis plenitudinis Christi' (Eph 4.13), sic accipiamus dictum, ut nec infra nec ultra iuvenalem formam resurgant corpora mortuorum; sed in eius aetate et robore, usque ad quam Christum hic pervenisse cognovimus (circa triginta quippe annos . . .). . . . Resurgent omnes tam magni corpore, quam vel erant vel futuri erant aetate iuvenali.

The *Excerpts* omit the reference to dying in old age and to Christ's age, though both are preserved here. The main points are repeated at Pope 11.305–11. For 130–3 cf *Prognosticon*, III.xxii.3–6:

> Resurgent omnium sanctorum corpora, omni felicitate et gloria immortalitatis conspicua, sicut sine ulla corruptione, difficultate, vel onere, ita sine ulla deformitate: in quibus, ut ait sanctus Augustinus, tanta facilitas quanta felicitas erit.

Ælfric's elaboration of this is influenced by *Prognosticon*, III.xxviii; the same points are made later in Pope 11.320–5. For 133–5 [= Pope 11.326–31] cf *Prognosticon*, III.xxiii.8–9:

> Ubi erit dentium stridor, aeternus et incessabilis fletus, inaniter quaeritur corporum decus.

[2] Gatch 1966 takes a contrary view.

Lines 136–8 are from Lc 20.35–6:

> (35) Illi vero qui digni habebuntur saeculo illo, et resurrectione ex mortuis, neque nubent, neque ducent uxores; (36) neque enim ultra mori poterunt; aequales enim angelis sunt.

Prognosticon, III.xxiv (followed by *Excerpts*, 251–6 and Pope 11.312–9) quotes the parallel verse from Mt 22.30 at this point. The absence of sin and pain in heaven (lines 138–40) has no obvious parallel in the *Prognosticon*, and is perhaps just a commonplace, but cf III.xxiv.27 *cor nullatenus inflectat ad vitium* and III.xxvi.40–1 *nulla doloris aut laboris erit adversitas*. The notion that in heaven one will be able to recognise both familiar faces and strange ones (line 140) comes originally from Gregory's *Dialogues* (IV.34) but is quoted at a much earlier point in the *Prognosticon*, II.xxiv.34–7:

> Fit autem in electis quiddam mirabilius; quia non solum eos agnoscunt quos in hoc mundo noverunt, sed velut visos ac cognitos recognoscunt bonos quos nunquam viderant.

Appendix B2

1–8 Ælfric extends the discussion of resurrection with a series of analogies which had nearly all been used before, but the selection seems to be his own. The first, the regrowth of plants and trees after the 'death' of winter, which appropriately follows Gregory's own tree-analogy, seems to be a commonplace (cf the Old English poem *The Phoenix*, lines 243 ff, and the notes in Cook's edition[3]). A close parallel for lines 1–5 which Ælfric might have known is in Ps-Augustine, Serm. 109, §4 (PL 39, 1962):

> Videmus certe hiemis adventu arbores spoliari pomis, nudari foliis; sed eas rursus verno tempore speciem resurrectionis exprimere: quae primo quidem incipiunt turgere in gemmis, tum ornari in floribus, vestiri in foliis, et postmodum pomis gravari.

The sermon similarly offers this as an analogy to man's resurrection. Cf too Gregory, *In Ezechielem*, 2.8.220. I have not found the hibernation of animals and insects as an analogy elsewhere. Cf too Ælfric's LS 12.31–2.

8–24 The silkworm is cited as an analogy for resurrection in the *Hexaemeron* of St Basil (PG 29, 185–6) and that of St Ambrose (*Hexameron*, 5.23.77).[4] The fifth-century Latin translation of Basil's work could have been known to Ælfric and is a probable source for passages in his own *Hexameron*, but the account of the silkworm is not at all like his; it is the series of mutations that Basil emphasises, not the apparent death. Ambrose cites the silkworm and the phoenix as analogies in the same chapter, but the details of the former are again not close. No adequately close parallels to Ælfric's account have so far appeared, and it

[3] A. S. Cook, *The Old English Elene, Phoenix, and Physiologus* (New Haven, 1919).

[4] See J. Kantrowitz, '*The Anglo-Saxon Phoenix* and Tradition', *Philological Quarterly* 43 (1964), 1–13.

may be, as Pope suggested,[5] that he was drawing on personal observation of silkworms on a visit to Italy (cf lines 15–16).

25–34 The phoenix was frequently cited as an analogy for resurrection[6] and Ælfric had already cited the main details and drawn the parallel in a passing comment in his Grammar (p. 70). The account which he gives here is very close in details to that given by Ambrose in his *Hexameron* (5.23.79–80):

> [79] Phoenix quoque avis in locis Arabiae perhibetur degere atque eam usque ad annos quingentos longaevam aetatem producere. Quae cum sibi finem vitae adesse adverterit, facit sibi thecam de ture et murra et ceteris odoribus, in quam impleto vitae suae tempore intrat et moritur. De cuius umore carnis vermis exsurgit paulatimque adolescit ac processu statuti temporis induit alarum remigia atque in superioris avis speciem formamque reparatur. Doceat igitur haec avis vel exemplo sui resurrectionem credere. . . . .Sit igitur exemplo nobis quia auctor et creator avium sanctos suos in perpetuum perire non patitur, qui avem unicam perire non passus resurgentem eam sui semine voluit propagari. . . . [80] Fac et tu, homo, tibi thecam . . . Theca ergo tua est fides; imple eam bonis virtutum tuarum odoribus.

With the last two sentences cf lines 44–5, though Ambrose is not referring to heavenly dwellings.

34–43 Ælfric had already told the story of the Seven Sleepers in CH II.27, and his source there presents the miracle as the resolution of a controversy over the question of bodily resurrection, though Ælfric himself makes only brief reference to this in II.27.

44–52 Apparently Ælfric's own development of the image in Jn 14.2: *In domo Patris mei mansiones multae sunt*. The topos of building a home in heaven during one's life is explored in Book IV of Gregory's *Dialogues*, and some of the material from there is used in CH II.21.112–30. The personal reference (lines 48–50) is rare in his writings, and the mention of frequent travelling presumably dates it after his election as abbot of Eynsham. It is not clear what he means by *to hirede geridan* (lines 50–1): Gatch translates 'ride to a monastery',[7] which is certainly possible, though the absence of any explanatory modifier is odd since this cannot presumably be Ælfric's own house that lies at the end of a long journey; *hired* could also mean the king's court and refer to journeys to meetings of the king's advisers.[8]

[5] As reported by Gatch 1977, p. 229, n.9.

[6] See Cook, *Old English Elene* and Kantrowitz, '*Anglo-Saxon Phoenix*'.

[7] Gatch 1977, p. 230, n.15.

[8] Gatch (1977, p. 230, n. 16) notes some distant parallels to this passage.

17 SECOND SUNDAY AFTER EASTER

Ælfric uses the Gospel reading for the occasion, John 10.11–16 on the good shepherd and the hireling, as the basis for a brief homily on bishops and clergy, discussing the role of the good pastor and contrasting this with the negligence of the mercenary cleric. It is easily the shortest of the First Series homilies, a mere 89 lines, in its original form, perhaps reflecting a reluctance to discuss the shortcomings of the clergy at greater length, or a doubt of its importance to do so at the time of writing. But in the course of his exposition Ælfric introduced some appropriate verses from Ezekiel 34, which use the same pastoral imagery to criticise the false teachers who neglect their flocks, and this became the germ of a substantial expansion of the homily some years later (See *CH I*, pp. 69, 133). In this expanded form the brief quotation from Ezekiel (lines 59–73) is deleted and the concluding sentence replaced by a long additional passage, running to 253 lines, in rhythmical prose, presenting the full text of Ezekiel 34.1–16 and a lengthy exposition which details the failings and dangers of a negligent clergy and the corrupt state of the nation, particularly its leading advisers. Clemoes (*CH I*, pp. 61–2) tentatively dated this revision to the period 1002–5, but, like the passage added to the previous homily, this one seems to reflect the additional experience that becoming an abbot brought to Ælfric in 1005. The shift in tone and treatment perhaps owes something to the change in Ælfric's own status, no longer a young monk and priest but a writer with an established reputation and authority, and possibly by now an abbot with larger responsibilities, but the degree of contemporary reference suggests that he was provoked by what he saw as an alarming decline in the English scene. Where the original homily had dealt mainly in generalities the expanded version speaks urgently of the specific troubles of the present time, in the last days of the world. There seems a note of desperation in the comment that God's mercy may provide the teachers that the people need, if we contrast the more confident statement in the preface to the Grammar that sound study in youth will produce the teachers. There is much that resembles Wulfstan's preaching in this late addition to the homily, but the complaint of the worldliness of rulers and teachers has a precedent in Ælfric's own work, in LS 12.128 ff.

For the original homily Ælfric drew on the homily by Gregory the Great assigned to this occasion in PD, and Haymo's recasting and expansion of it,[1] as well as Augustine's Tractates on John, sometimes combining ideas from different sources within a single sentence. The treatment is very free, with little close translation, and concentrates on the moral interpretation, contrasting the good teacher motivated by true love for his flock and willing if need be to give his life for them, with the neglectful cleric concerned only with the wealth and status which his office gives him, rather than the allegorical level, applied to

[1] Noted by Smetana (1959, p. 189 and 1961, pp. 462–3).

Christ, which had exercised the Latin commentators. For the later section his usual sources provided no help, with none of the homiliaries giving an exposition of Ezekiel 34. Neither Gregory's homilies on Ezekiel nor Jerome's commentary provide any significant parallel. There are, however, many parallels with a sermon of St Augustine on Ezekiel 34.1–16 (sermon 46). This is a very long piece directed, as the editor points out, primarily at the Donatist sect, whom Augustine represents as pastors who neglect the wandering sheep. If this was his source, Ælfric has been very selective and seldom translated as closely as had been his practice earlier with Augustine, but there are sufficient parallels to indicate a debt, direct or indirect. Ælfric may have found the sermon as part of the canons of the 817 Council of Aachen[2]: this is an abridged version but it includes all the material that Ælfric used, and its presence as one of a series of patristic excerpts on the duties of bishops and clergy reflects Ælfric's interest in using it. The canons of this Council are cited in the *Regularis Concordia* (p. 62), and in any case Ælfric's familiarity with canonical literature is well established. But if that was his source, it is all the more striking that even in the expanded version, with its extensive critique of the clergy and its briefer one of the *witan*, he still evidently thinks of himself as speaking to the ordinary laity (cf for instance lines 1–8 of the addition).

Sources and Notes

The following texts are cited below:

1. Alcuin, *De Virtutibus et Vitiis*, PL 101, cols. 613–38.
2. Augustine, *In Iohannis Evangelium Tractatus CXXIV*, ed. R. Willems, CCSL 36 (Turnhout, 1954).
3. Augustine, *Sermones*, ed. C. Lambot, CCSL 41 (Turnhout, 1961), Serm. 46 (pp. 527–70).
4. Gregory the Great, *Homiliae in Evangelia*, PL 76, Hom. 14, cols. 1127–30.
5. Haymo of Auxerre, *Homiliae de Tempore*, PL 118, Hom. 83, cols. 499–506.
6. Wulfstan, *Institutes of Polity*, ed. K. Jost, *Die 'Institutes of Polity, Civil and Ecclesiastical'* (Berne, 1959).

2–12 A fairly close rendering of Jn 10.11–16:

(11) Ego sum pastor bonus; bonus pastor animam suam dat pro ovibus. (12) Mercenarius, et qui non est pastor, cuius non sunt oves propriae, videt lupum venientem et dimittit oves, et fugit; et lupus rapit et dispergit oves. (13) Mercenarius autem fugit quia mercenarius est et non pertinet ad eum de ovibus. (14) Ego sum pastor bonus et cognosco meas et cognoscunt me meae. (15) Sicut novit me Pater et ego agnosco Patrem et animam meam pono pro ovibus. (16) Et alias oves habeo quae non sunt ex hoc ovili

[2] See *Concilia Aevi Karolini I*, ed. A. Werminghoff, MGH, Legum Sectio III, Concilia II (Hanover, 1906), pp. 330–6.

et illas oportet me adducere et vocem meam audient et fiet unum ovile, unus pastor.

13–18 Gregory begins in a similar fashion (Hom. 14, PL 76, 1127C):

Ecce enim is qui non ex accidenti dono, sed essentialiter bonus est, dicit: Ego sum pastor bonus.

But Haymo's rendering of this, though much later in his discussion, seems rather closer to Ælfric (Hom. 83, PL 118, 501CD):

Aliud est bonum essentialiter, sicut Domino; et aliud nuncupative, sicut discipulis; aliud per naturam, et aliud per gratiam. Illi vere ut boni essent a Domino acceperunt, ipse autem a nemine, nisi a seipso, ut bonus esset, accepit.

The basic interpretation, lines 16–17, is perhaps too obvious to need a source. For 17–18 cf Gregory (Hom. 14, PL 76, 1127C): *Fecit quod monuit, ostendit quod iussit*.

18–22 Haymo has something similar (Hom. 83, PL 118, 501C), but Ælfric's source, and Haymo's, seems to be Augustine's *Tract.*, 46.7.5–9:

Numquid talis erat apostolus Paulus? Absit. Numquid talis Petrus? Absit. Numquid tales ceteri apostoli, excepto Iuda filio perditionis? Absit. . . . Iam dixi, pastores, quia membra pastoris. Illo capite gaudebant, sub illo capite concordabant.

23–36 Gregory and Haymo interpret the wolf initially as an earthly robber and oppressor (see below under 55–60), but subsequently add the identification with the devil, as in Ælfric, and this is also Augustine's interpretation (*Tract.*, 46.7.1); cf Gregory, Hom. 14, PL 76, 1128C: *Est alius lupus . . . malignus spiritus*; and Haymo, Hom. 83, PL 118, 503B: *Est et alius lupus invisibilis, qui . . . animas peccantium lacerat*. Ælfric then develops his own application of the passage to the bishop and *lareow* (where the Latin commentaries retain the simple term *pastor* without further explanation) and their primary duties of instruction and prayer, before giving a brief mention to the duties of almsgiving and self-sacrifice which are all that Gregory discusses (Hom. 14, PL 76, 1127CD):

Primum nobis est exteriora nostra misericorditer ovibus eius impendere; postremum vero, si necesse sit, etiam mortem nostram pro eisdem ovibus ministrare.

(Cf 34–6). There are similar discussions of the duties of the clergy at CH I.2.104–15 and II.19.100–27, and Wulfstan uses the same Gospel imagery in prescribing the duties of bishops and priests in his *Institutes of Polity* (Jost, I.47–54 and II.106–14), and in the Laws of Cnut. As in II.19 Ælfric is at pains to counter an implied charge that the sins of the people must necessarily be laid at the door of the clergy. With his discussion of the strong and the weak at 30–2 (prompted perhaps more by Ezekiel 34.16 than by the Gospel text) cf CH II.24.174–88.

37–43 A paraphrase of Gregory, Hom. 14, PL 76, 1128AB:

Non pastor, sed mercenarius vocatur, qui non pro amore intimo oves dominicas, sed ad temporales mercedes pascit. Mercenarius quippe est qui locum quidem pastoris tenet, sed lucra animarum non quaerit; terrenis commodis inhiat, honore praelationis gaudet, temporalibus lucris pascitur, impensa sibi ab hominibus reverentia laetatur. Istae sunt etenim mercedes mercenarii, ut pro eo ipso quod in regimine laborat, hic quod quaerit inveniat, et ab haereditate gregis in posterum alienus existat. Utrum vero pastor sit, an mercenarius, cognosci veraciter non potest, si occasio necessitatis deest. . . . Sed lupus veniens indicat quo quisque animo super gregis custodiam stabat.

43–9 Closely based on Gregory, Hom. 14, PL 76, 1128CD:

Lupus rapit et dispergit oves cum alium ad luxuriam pertrahit, alium ad avaritiam accendit, alium in superbiam erigit, alium per iracundiam dividit, hunc invidia stimulat, illum in fallacia supplantat. . . . Sed contra haec mercenarius nullo zelo accenditur, nullo fervore dilectionis excitatur: quia dum sola exteriora commoda requirit, interiora gregis damna negligenter patitur.

(Despite the manuscript punctuation, the sentence continues through *þonne* = 'when', at 44.)

49–54 Cf Haymo, Hom. 83, PL 118, 504A:

Ille recedit, etsi non corpore, tamen mente.

And Gregory, Hom. 14, PL 76:

[1128B] Fugit, quia iniustitiam vidit, et tacuit. . . . [1129A] Sola enim causa est ut mercenarius fugiat quia mercenarius est. Ac si aperte diceretur: Stare in periculo ovium non potest qui in eo quod ovibus praeest non oves diligit, sed lucrum terrenum quaerit.

55–9 For the interpretation of the wolf as the *rica* Ælfric develops points from Gregory, Hom. 14, PL 76:

[1128B] Lupus etenim super oves venit cum quilibet iniustus et raptor, fideles quosque atque humiles opprimit. Sed is qui pastor esse videbatur et non erat, relinquit oves et fugit, quia dum sibi ab eo periculum metuit, resistere eius iniustitiae non praesumit. . . . [1129A] Dum enim honorem amplectitur, dum temporalibus commodis laetatur, opponere se contra periculum trepidat, ne hoc quod diligit amittat.

In referring to Gregory's robber as a *rica*, a man of power and wealth, Ælfric is presumably thinking of the pastor's reluctance to offend a secular lord.

59–68 Ælfric turns to Ez 34.5–16 for support, summarising in part:

(7) Propterea pastores audite verbum Domini: (5) et dispersae sunt oves meae eo quod non esset pastor; et factae sunt in devorationem omnium bestiarum agri et dispersae sunt. (8) Neque enim quaesierunt pastores

gregem meum sed pascebant pastores semet ipsos, et greges meos non pascebant. . . . (10) Haec dicit Dominus Deus: ecce ego ipse super pastores requiram gregem meum de manu eorum et cessare eos faciam . . . et liberabo gregem meum de ore eorum . . . (13) et congregabo eas de terris . . . (14) In pascuis uberrimis pascam eas. . . . (16) Quod perierat requiram et quod abiectum erat reducam et quod confractum fuerat alligabo et quod infirmum erat consolidabo et quod pingue et forte custodiam et pascam illas in iudicio.

Gregory briefly cites a different Ezekiel text at this point in the commentary, and Haymo cites verses from Ezekiel 34 at various points in his homily, among many other Biblical quotations. Ezekiel 34.11–16 was a reading prescribed for Monday in the first week of Lent, but has an obvious relevance to the Gospel reading for this occasion too. Ezekiel 34 is similarly cited as a warning to negligent clergy in St Boniface's letter to Archbishop Cuthbert (PL 89, 766), and thence by Wulfstan in his homily XVI, and in *De Duodecim Abusivis* (56.10–13), which Ælfric knew and in part translated.

70–3 Perhaps an allusion to Mt 23.3 [paraphrased by Augustine, *Tract.*, 46.6.6–7]:

Omnia ergo quaecumque dixerint vobis, servate, et facite; secundum opera vero eorum, nolite facere.

73–7 Cf Gregory, Hom. 14, PL 76, 1129A:

'Et cognosco oves meas', hoc est diligo, 'et cognoscunt me meae.' Ac si patenter dicat: Diligentes obsequuntur. Qui enim veritatem non diligit, adhuc minime cognovit.

Haymo, Hom. 83, PL 118, 504C:

'Cognosco meas', id est diligo eas. 'Et cognoscunt me meae,' id est diligentes me voci meae obediunt.

and Gregory again (Hom. 14, PL 76, 1129B):

Videte si oves eius estis, videte si eum cognoscitis, videte si lumen veritatis scitis. Scitis autem dico, non per fidem, sed per amorem.

79–81 Cf Augustine, *Tract.*, 47.3.2–3: *Ipse agnoscit patrem per se, nos per illum*; and Gregory, Hom. 14, PL 76, 1129B:

Ac si aperte dicat: In hoc constat quia et ego agnosco patrem, et cognoscor a patre, quia animam meam pono pro ovibus meis; id est, ea caritate qua pro ovibus morior quantum patrem diligam ostendo.

84–7 Generally similar explanations of the verse appear in Gregory, Haymo and Augustine, but with no close parallel; cf perhaps Gregory, Hom. 14, PL 76, 1129C:

Quia vero non solum Iudaeam, sed etiam gentilitatem redimere venerat, adiungit. . . . Quasi enim ex duobus gregibus unum ovile efficit, quia Iudaicum et gentilem populum in sua fide coniungit, Paulo attestante. . . . Dum enim ad aeternam vitam ex utraque natione simplices eligit, ad ovile proprium oves deducit.

Appendix B3

8–30 From Ez 34.2–16:

(2) Haec dicit Dominus Deus: vae pastoribus Israhel qui pascebant semet ipsos. Nonne greges pascuntur a pastoribus? (3) Lac comedebatis et lanis operiebamini et quod crassum erat occidebatis; gregem autem meum non pascebatis. (4) Quod infirmum fuit non consolidastis et quod aegrotum non sanastis; quod fractum est non alligastis et quod abiectum est non reduxistis; quod perierat non quaesistis sed cum austeritate imperabatis eis et cum potentia. (5) Et dispersae sunt oves meae eo quod non esset pastor; et factae sunt in devorationem omnium bestiarum agri et dispersae sunt. (6) Erraverunt greges mei in cunctis montibus et in universo colle excelso; et super omnem faciem terrae dispersi sunt greges mei et non erat qui requireret non erat inquam qui requireret. . . . (9) Propterea pastores audite verbum Domini. (10) Haec dicit Dominus Deus: ecce ego ipse super pastores requiram gregem meum de manu eorum et cessare eos faciam ut ultra non pascant gregem, nec pascant amplius pastores semet ipsos; et liberabo gregem meum de ore eorum et non erunt ultra eis in escam. (11) Quia haec dicit Dominus Deus: ecce ego ipse requiram oves meas et visitabo eas. (12) Sicut visitat pastor gregem suum in die quando fuerit in medio ovium suarum dissipatarum sic visitabo oves meas et liberabo eas de omnibus locis quo dispersae fuerant in die nubis et caliginis. (13) Et educam eas de populis et congregabo eas de terris et inducam eas in terram suam et pascam eas in montibus Israhel, in rivis et in cunctis sedibus terrae, (14) in pascuis uberrimis pascam eas et in montibus excelsis Israhel erunt pascuae eorum; ibi requiescent in herbis virentibus. . . . (16) Quod perierat requiram et quod abiectum erat reducam et quod confractum fuerat alligabo et quod infirmum erat consolidabo et quod pingue et forte custodiam; et pascam illas in iudicio.

31–46 In part a resumé of the arguments of the original homily. Lines 39–41 are from Phil 2.21, also cited in this context by Augustine, Serm. 46, 20–21:

Qui sunt qui se ipsos pascunt? De quibus apostolus dicit: 'Omnes enim sua quaerunt, non quae Iesu Christi'.

Lines 41–6 perhaps draw in part on Augustine, Serm. 46, 47–50:

Videte quemadmodum vos securos fecerit deus, qualescumque sint qui vobis praesunt. . . . Deus non deserit oves suas.

Ælfric adds the quotation from Is 49.15:

Numquid oblivisci potest mulier infantem suum ut non misereatur filio uteri sui? Et si illa oblita fuerit ego tamen non obliviscar tui.

47–57 A careful and important argument that, despite the apparent implications of the text from Ezekiel, the pastors have the right to live off their flocks. Augustine has something of the same concern (Serm. 46, 65–71):

> Invenimus ergo esse lac gregis quidquid a plebe dei tribuitur praepositis ad sustentandum victum temporalem. . . . Apostolus . . . dixit . . . dominum disposuisse ut qui evangelium annuntiant de evangelio vivant.

Augustine is referring to 1 Cor 9.14; Ælfric to Lc 10.7: *Dignus est enim operarius mercede sua*. (One might expect *medes* rather than *metes* at 50, but all manuscripts seem to have the latter.) The argument that this is not selling the word, lines 50–3, draws on Augustine, Serm. 46, 111–15:

> Non tamquam venale sit evangelium, ut illud sit pretium eius quod sumunt qui annuntiant unde vivant. Si enim sic vendunt, magnam rem vili vendunt. Accipiant sustentationem necessitatis a populo, mercedem dispensationis a domino.

However, Ælfric's reference to the people's offering as *mede* runs quite counter to Augustine's subsequent remarks; he is perhaps recalling his similar discussion of the twofold meed at CH II.36.104–30, where he was drawing on Gregory.

62–82 The strong attack on the ill-living cleric draws in part on Augustine, Serm. 46:

> [182–3] 'Quomodo, inquis, occidunt?' Male vivendo, malum exemplum praebendo. . . . [186–90] Attendendo ovis etiam fortis plerumque praepositum suum male viventem . . . incipit dicere in corde suo: 'Si praepositus meus sic vivit, ego qui sum qui non faciam quod ille facit?' Occidit ovem fortem. . . . . [175–80] Sanae atque crassae oves perpaucae sunt, id est, solidae in cibo veritatis. . . . Sed mali illi pastores non parcunt talibus. Parum est quod illas languentes et infirmas et errantes et perditas non curant. Etiam istas fortes et pingues necant, quantum in ipsis est. . . . [140–44, *on the mercenary*] Diceret apud seipsum: 'Quid ad me pertinet? Quis quod velit agat; victus meus salvus est, honor meus salvus est: et lac et lana, satis est mihi; eat quisque qua potest.'

The point at 79–82 is essentially one that Ælfric had already made in the original homily (lines 70–73), but Augustine does cite the underlying verse, Matthew 23.3, at this point (lines 195–6).

83–105 Ælfric's account of the role of the good cleric is perhaps adapted in part from Augustine's description of himself as the good pastor, determinedly rescuing his flock from the Donatists (Serm. 46, 356–66):

> Revocabo errantem, requiram perditam. Velis nolis id agam. Et si me inquirentem lanient vepres silvarum, per omnia angusta me coartabo; omnes sepes excutiam; quantum mihi virium terrens dominus donat, omnia peragrabo. . . . Timeo ne negligens te, etiam quod forte est occidam. . . . Si neglexero errantem atque pereuntem, et eum qui fortis est delectabit errare et perire.

Is there, however, a reference to a more specific, contemporary problem when Ælfric talks of the good clergy being criticised and threatened for what they preach (lines 86–9)? The interpretation of the imagery of Ezekiel verse 16 is only implicit here. Lines 93–7 are the converse of Augustine's account of the negligent pastor (Serm. 46, 216–9):

> Pastor neglegens . . . non illi dicit: 'Fili accedens ad servitutem dei, sta in iustitia et timore, et praepara animam tuam ad temptationem' (Sir 2.1).

Lines 97–100 are from Ps 33.20 (not cited by Augustine). Lines 100–3 are from 2 Tim 3.12 [quoted at this point by Augustine, Serm. 46, 239–40]:

> Et omnes qui pie volunt vivere in Christo Iesu, persecutionem patientur.

106–22 Cf Augustine, Serm. 46, 253–61:

> 'Flagellat omnem filium quem recipit' (Hebrews 12.6). Et tu dicis: Forte exceptus eris? Si exceptus a passione flagellorum, exceptus a numero filiorum. . . . Unicus ille de patris substantia natus, aequalis patri in forma dei . . . non habebat ubi flagellaretur. . . . Qui ergo flagellat unicum sine peccato, relinquit cum peccato adoptatum?

The argument that the good pastor warns his flock of the tribulations to come reflects the general tenor of Augustine's argument, §§10–14, without being verbally close. Ælfric's train of thought is difficult to follow, but he seems to be arguing that each man must suffer tribulation for his sins, either in this life (Augustine's point) or the next, but that this will not necessarily purge his sins (lines 120–2). Cf LS 19.155 ff.

123–44 Both the idea of tribulation and the importance of summoning people to repentance bring in the theme of the end of the world. In turning to the particular tribulations of the end of the world, Ælfric reflects the concerns already seen in the preface to CH I, rather than Augustine, but his wording may have been influenced by a much earlier passage in the latter's sermon (Augustine, Serm. 46, 35–41):

> Veniet enim dies, quo cuncta adducantur in iudicium. Et ille dies, si saeculo longe est, unicuique homini vitae suae ultimus prope est. Tamen utrumque latere Deus voluit, et quando veniat finis saeculi, et quando sit in unoquoque homine huius vitae finis. Vis non timere diem occultum? Dum venerit, inveniat te paratum.

Lines 127–31 allude to Mc 13.32: *De die autem illo vel hora nemo scit, neque angeli in caelo, neque Filius, nisi Pater*. For 139 ff Augustine (Serm. 46, 398 ff) makes the same, perhaps obvious, equation of mountains and pride but otherwise offers no parallels.

145–56 Ælfric's own lament over the avarice of his times, not exclusively, it seems, among the clergy. Lines 146–8 are from 1 Timothy 6.10. That to possess wealth is in itself good (line 153), striking though the comment is for a monk, is wholly characteristic of Ælfric (see Godden 1990).

157–84 The first part is from 2 Tim 3.1–5:

> (1) Hoc autem scito quod in novissimis diebus instabunt tempora periculosa; (2) et erunt homines se ipsos amantes, cupidi, elati, superbi,

> blasphemi, parentibus inoboedientes, ingrati, scelesti, (3) sine affectione, sine pace, criminatores, incontinentes, inmites, sine benignitate, (4) proditores, protervi, tumidi, voluptatium amatores magis quam Dei, (5) habentes speciem quidem pietatis, virtutem autem eius abnegantes.

What follows (lines 167–78) seems to be particularly directed against treachery among the governing class, the *witan*. One might compare Ælfric's reference to the breaking of promises in the face of the Vikings (On the Old and New Testament, 797–802, Crawford, p. 49), and indeed the complaints in the contemporary annals of the *Anglo-Saxon Chronicle*. Lines 179–81 are from 1 Corinthians 3.19.

184–208 Ælfric now returns to the text from Ezekiel. For the interpretation of the mist, 200–8, cf Augustine, Serm. 46:

> [626–7] Pastor non deserit eas. Inquirit eas, penetrat nebulam oculis acutissimis, non impeditur caligine nubium. . . . [623–4] Pluvia et nebula, error saeculi huius; caligo magna surgens de cupiditatibus hominum.

209–34 The interpretation of the final verse takes Ælfric into questions of grace and merit. He perhaps draws in part on Augustine, Serm. 46, 677–82:

> De quo desperaverimus subito convertitur et fit optimus. De quo multum praesumpserimus subito deficit et fit pessimus. . . . Quid sit hodie quisque homo, vix novit ipse homo. Tamen utcumque ipse quid hodie. Quid autem cras nec ipse.

But Ælfric's wording suggests a recall of his earlier discussion of changing moral fortunes, CH I.35.211 ff, where he was drawing on Gregory. The contrast between Judas and Paul is drawn in similar terms by Alcuin, *De Virtutibus et Vitiis* (PL 101, 632C):

> Sunt enim qui bene incipiunt, et male finiunt conversationem suam; sicut Iudas primo apostolus, et postea proditor Domini, et facti sui conscius laqueo se suspendit. Saulus [*var.* Paulus] male coepit, sed bene finivit: primo persecutor, postea praedicator.

239–45 Cf Augustine, Serm. 46:

> [756–9] Si sunt bonae oves, sunt et boni pastores, nam de bonis ovibus fiunt boni pastores. Sed omnes boni pastores in uno sunt, unum sunt. Illi pascant, Christus pascit. . . . [781–3] Sint ergo omnes in pastore uno, et dicant vocem pastoris unam, quam audiant oves, et sequantur pastorem suum.

With 245–8 cf the list of capital sins at CH II.40.279–82.

18 IN LETANIA MAIORE (ROGATIONTIDE)

The Greater Litany was originally the Roman fast of 25 April, but by Ælfric's time the term had come to be used for the originally Gallican observance of Rogationtide, the three days of fasting, prayer and procession, formerly known as the Letania Minor, which immediately preceded Ascension Day.[1] The abundance of Old English sermons for the period shows that it was a major occasion for preaching to the laity, and Ælfric provides homilies for all three days in both Series. In this first homily he gives an account of the Rogationtide fast and its origins (lines 1–43), before turning to a close, mainly allegorical, exposition of the pericope, Luke 11.5–13, which deals with the topic of prayer. The final verse of Luke then leads him into a long discussion of the relation between goods and goodness and the duties of the rich to the poor (lines 174–233), linking the idea of prayer to God with the prayers of the poor to the rich.

Ælfric would probably have found an exposition of the Luke text by Bede in his copy of Paul the Deacon's homiliary,[2] and also knew the interpretations of Smaragdus and Haymo, but only the last of these seems to have influenced him at all. He seems rather to have drawn on an Augustinian sermon on the Luke passage, Serm. 105, though if this was his source he has handled it very freely and selectively. For the final section he evidently turned to another Augustinian sermon, Serm. 61, which deals mainly with the second part of the Gospel passage (or, as the PL edition suggests, with the parallel version of Matthew 7.7–11) but also touches on the first part and has much to say about charity and almsgiving.[3]

Sources and Notes

The following texts are cited below:

1. Amalarius, *Liber Officialis*, ed. J. Hanssens in *Amalarii Episcopi Opera Liturgica Omnia*, Studi e Testi 139 (Vatican City, 1948).
2. Augustine, *Quaestiones Evangeliorum*, ed. A. Mutzenbecher, CCSL 44B (Turnhout, 1980).
3. Augustine, *Sermones*, PL 38, Serm. 61 and 105, cols. 409–14 and 618–25.
4. Caesarius of Arles, *Sermones*, ed. G. Morin, CCSL 103 (Turnhout, 1953), Serm. 25 (pp. 111–4) [cited by section and line numbers].

[1] See Bazire and Cross, pp. xv-xvii.

[2] The Bede exposition (a composite of his commentary on Luke and his homily) appears in the original homiliary under the Greater Litany of April and in the late version printed in PL 95 under In Letania Minore.

[3] For the identification of Amalarius (for the opening discussion of the occasion) and Augustine, Serm. 105 as sources, see Förster (1894, pp. 32–3, 48–9), and for Augustine, Serm. 61 and Haymo see Smetana (1959, p. 189 and 1961, p. 466), who also points out that Augustine, Serm. 105 was in one version of PD.

5. Haymo of Auxerre, *Homiliae de Tempore*, PL 118, Hom. 90 and 92, cols. 527–8 and 530–4.
6. Hericus, *Homiliae in Circulum Anni*, ed. R. Quadri, CCCM 116B (Turnhout, 1994), Hom. II.12 (pp. 97–103).

2–5 Most homilies for the occasion, Latin and English, emphasise penitence and almsgiving as the particular concerns of Rogationtide; in specifying prayer Ælfric reflects the traditional name for the three-day fast and the implications of the pericope, as well as some Carolingian discussion (see below). His statement of the objects of prayer at this time shows a striking and curious similarity to the account which the *Old English Martyrology* gives for an earlier occasion in the church year, the one traditionally known as Letania Maior on 25 April (OE Martyrology, II.63.12–16):

> On ðæm dæge eall Godes folc mid eaðmodlice relicgonge sceal God biddan þæt he him forgefe ðone gear siblice tid, ond smyltelico gewidra, ond genihtsume wæstmas, ond heora lichoman trymnysse.

Ælfric nowhere mentions this earlier occasion, and it may be that as the name Letania Maior shifted from the Roman rite of 25 April to the originally Gallican rite of the three days before Ascension Day so some of the traditional functions of the Roman observance shifted to Rogationtide. There are however precedents in other texts for some of these elements. That Rogationtide is a proper time to pray for fruitful harvests is a tradition mentioned by Haymo in a brief homily for the occasion (Hom. 90, PL 118, 528D: *Pro frugum ubertate*), and both Amalarius (*Liber Officialis*, I.37) and the Ps-Alcuinian *Liber de Divinis Officiis* (PL 101, 1225) mention praying for the material necessities of life. The Ps-Alcuin text suggests as explanation that Rogationtide falls at the season of natural growth, and there is some evidence that the Christian rite may have replaced a pre-Christian fertility festival.[4] Praying for peace is mentioned by Haymo (Hom. 90, PL 118), and Amalarius (*Liber Officialis*, I.37.10–12) says that the period is particularly a time for praying for God's protection against warfare, since spring is the season when hostile armies advance. Forgiveness of sins (lines 4–5) is more commonly a concern of Lenten fasts, though it is clearly associated with the supposed origins of Rogationtide.

5–11 As Förster pointed out, Ælfric probably took his account of the origin of Rogationtide in fifth-century Vienne from the *Liber Officialis* of Amalarius (I.37.18–32):

> A quo primo initium praesens ieiunium sumeret, Gregorius Turonensis manifestat in Gestis Francorum, ita dicens: In his temporibus fuit in Vienna urbe terrae motus maximus, ubi multae ecclesiae et domus multorum concussae fuerunt et subversae: ubi bestiae multae oberrantes, lupi, ursi ac cervi[5] ingressi per portam civitatis, devorantes plurimos, per totum

[4] Bazire and Cross, pp. xxi-ii.
[5] There is a variant *acerbi* for *ac cervi*, which is no doubt what Ælfric's version had.

> annum hoc faciebant. Nam veniente sollempnitate sancti Paschae, sanctus Mamertus, qui in ea urbe erat episcopus, dum missarum sacrificia ipsa vigilia caelebraret, palatium quoque regale quod in ea civitate erat, divino igne succensum est. Cumque haec agerentur appropinquante Ascensione Domini, indixit ieiunium vir sanctus Dei triduanum in populo cum gemitu et contritione. Et paulo post: Tunc cessavit ipsa tribulatio et subversio. Deinceps omnes ecclesiae Dei et sacerdotes hoc exemplum imitantes usque ad praesens, ipsas triduanas laetanias ubique celebre colunt.

If so, he was presumably unaware that Amalarius subsequently corrected this view, noting (*Liber Officialis*, IV.24) that he had since come across evidence that Gregory the Great had instituted the fast in Rome and quoting at length the sermon by Gregory which Ælfric himself also quotes, in CH II.9.111–55.

12–41 Amalarius says nothing of the people of Vienne following the precedent of Nineveh, and nor does his source Gregory of Tours. Haymo (Hom. 90, PL 118, 527) sees the fast as having its origins in the Gospels and apostolic practice. Gregory the Great does mention the Ninevites as a precedent for the time of fasting and prayer which he ordained in Rome at a time of plague (cf CH II.9.137), and the reference is quoted by Amalarius at IV.25, but not as a precedent for Vienne or indeed the three-day fast. There is though a parallel in an Old English homily, Vercelli 19, which mentions in turn both Vienne and Nineveh as the origin of the Rogationtide fast (Vercelli Homilies, pp. 321–5); it is apparently combining material from two different sources in the Pembroke 25 homiliary here (see Vercelli Homilies, apparatus), but one of those sources (Hom. 40; see Cross 1987, pp. 111–8) does specify both precedents and indeed quotes Mamertus himself citing Nineveh as a precedent when instituting the fast at Vienne (Cross 1987, Hom.40, line 45). Presumably by Ælfric's time it had become a common tradition that Vienne was imitating Nineveh.

Ælfric's account of Jonah and the Ninevites summarises the Book of Jonah, with a few variations:[6]

> (1.1) Et factum est verbum Domini ad Ionam filium Amathi dicens: (2) surge vade in Nineven civitatem grandem et praedica in ea quia ascendit malitia eius coram me. (3) Et surrexit Iona ut fugeret in Tharsis a facie Domini et descendit Ioppen et invenit navem euntem in Tharsis et dedit naulum eius et descendit in eam ut iret cum eis in Tharsis a facie Domini. (4) Dominus autem misit ventum magnum in mari et facta est tempestas magna in mari et navis periclitabatur conteri; (5) et timuerunt nautae et clamaverunt viri ad deum suum et miserunt vasa quae erant in navi in mare ut adleviaretur ab eis et Iona descendit ad interiora navis et dormiebat sopore gravi. . . . (7) Et dixit vir ad collegam suum: venite et mittamus sortes et sciamus quare hoc malum sit nobis et miserunt sortes et

[6] Paul E. Szarmach ('Three versions of the Jonah story', *ASE* 1 (1972), 183–92) discusses some of the variations and the narrative style.

cecidit sors super Ionam; (8) et dixerunt ad eum: indica nobis cuius causa malum istud sit nobis quod est opus tuum, quae terra tua et quo vel ex quo populo es tu. (9) Et dixit ad eos: Hebraeus ego sum et Dominum Deum caeli ego timeo qui fecit mare et aridam. (10) Et timuerunt viri timore magno et dixerunt ad eum: quid hoc fecisti? Cognoverunt enim viri quod a facie Domini fugeret quia indicaverat eis. (11) Et dixerunt ad eum: quid faciemus tibi et cessabit mare a nobis quia mare ibat et intumescebat. (12) Et dixit ad eos: tollite me et mittite in mare et cessabit mare a vobis; scio enim ego quoniam propter me tempestas grandis haec super vos . . . (15) Et tulerunt Ionam et miserunt in mare et stetit mare a fervore suo. (16) Et timuerunt viri timore magno Dominum et immolaverunt hostias Domino et voverunt vota. . . . (2.1) Et praeparavit Dominus piscem grandem ut degluttiret Ionam et erat Iona in ventre piscis tribus diebus et tribus noctibus. . . . (11) et dixit Dominus pisci et evomuit Ionam in aridam.

(3.1) Et factum est verbum Domini ad Ionam secundo dicens: (2) surge vade ad Nineven civitatem magnam et praedica in ea praedicationem quam ego loquor ad te. (3) Et surrexit Iona . . . (4) et clamavit et dixit adhuc quadraginta dies et Nineve subvertetur. . . . (6) Et pervenit verbum ad regem Nineve et surrexit de solio suo et abiecit vestimentum suum a se et indutus est sacco et sedit in cinere. (7) Et clamavit . . . dicens homines et iumenta et boves et pecora non gustent quicquam nec pascantur et aquam non bibant; (8) et operiantur saccis homines et iumenta et clament ad Dominum in fortitudine et convertatur vir a via sua mala et ab iniquitate quae est in manibus eorum. . . .(10) Et vidit Deus opera eorum quia conversi sunt a via sua mala et misertus est Deus super malitiam quam locutus fuerat ut faceret eis et non fecit.

The drama of God changing his mind, which is developed in the subsequent verses in the Bible, disappears with Ælfric's qualification that God would destroy the city 'if they would not turn to him' (line 32). The sailors become followers of God rather than their own gods. The king is presented, in medieval fashion, with ashes on his head rather than sitting on ashes. The detail of suckling children (line 35) fasting as well as men and animals follows a tradition recorded in homilies such as Caesarius, Serm. 143, and a Ps-Chrysostom piece (PLS 4, 849).[7] The same homilies transmit the pre-Vulgate text of Jonah 3.4, which gives the duration of the fast and penitence as three days rather than forty.

40–42 The practice of processing with relics at Rogationtide is well evidenced in England from Bede's time onwards; see Bazire and Cross, pp. xviff.

44–60 Lc 11.5–13:

(5) Et ait ad illos: quis vestrum habebit amicum et ibit ad illum media nocte et dicit illi amice: commoda mihi tres panes (6) quoniam amicus

[7] The references are from Bazire and Cross, p. 59.

> meus venit de via ad me et non habeo quod ponam ante illum. (7) Et ille de intus respondens dicat: noli mihi molestus esse, iam ostium clausum est et pueri mei mecum sunt in cubili; non possum surgere et dare tibi. (8) Dico vobis et si non dabit illi surgens eo quod amicus eius sit, propter inprobitatem tamen eius surget et dabit illi quotquot habet necessarios. (9) Et ego vobis dico: petite et dabitur vobis; quaerite et invenietis; pulsate et aperietur vobis. (10) Omnis enim qui petit accipit et qui quaerit invenit et pulsanti aperietur. (11) Quis autem ex vobis patrem petet panem, numquid lapidem dabit illi? aut piscem, numquid pro pisce serpentem dabit illi? (12) aut si petierit ovum numquid porriget illi scorpionem? (13) Si ergo vos cum sitis mali nostis bona data dare filiis vestris, quanto magis Pater vester de caelo dabit spiritum bonum petentibus se?

Ælfric's very free rendering owes more to the paraphrase which Augustine offers in his sermon 61, §6 than to the Bible (PL 38, 411):

> Venit, inquit, ad amicum suum, cui hospes venerat; et coepit pulsare, et dicere: Hospes mihi venit, commoda mihi tres panes. Respondit ille: Iam requiesco, et mecum servi mei requiescunt. Ille non cessat, astat, instat, pulsat; et tanquam amicus ab amico mendicat. Et quid ait, Dico vobis, quia surgit, et non propter amicitiam eius, sed propter improbitatem dat illi quantos voluerit.

Note his 'sum cuma' (line 47) for Vulgate *amicus meus*, his reference to the continued knocking and calling at 51, and his *for freondscype* (line 52), reflecting the Old Latin reading *ob amicitiam* used by Augustine. The *pueri* of verse 7 are understood as servants by most commentators (cf Augustine's rendering *servi*) and, probably, by the Old English Gospel versions, which all render them as *cnihtas*; Ælfric's interpretation of them as the householder's children may be influenced by Haymo (Hom. 92, PL 118, 532A), who describes the *pueri* as 'puri et innocentes'. The *OE Gospels* give only a gloss for *scorpio* ('þæt is an wyrmcynn') but Ælfric's term *þrowend* is known to other Old English writers (see BT).

61–71 Ælfric seems initially to draw on Augustine's Serm. 105 for his exposition, conflating two separate points (PL 38, 619–20):

> [§3] Saeculi huius ignorantia valida est, hoc est, nox media. . . . [§4] Cum autem perveneris ad tres panes, hoc est, ad cibum et intelligentiam Trinitatis, habes et unde vivas, et unde pascas.

Augustine explains the man who comes from a journey as one who seeks Christian teaching; his host is the Christian unable, in the night of ignorance, to furnish it, who therefore turns for teaching to his friend, who is Christ. In his *Quaestiones Evangeliorum*, however, Augustine identifies the traveller as the appetite of man, turning at first to his own self for knowledge (*Quaestiones*, II.21). Bede, perhaps developing this interpretation, renders the traveller as the *animus* or mind (*Comm. Luc.*, 3.2437), and is followed by Haymo and Smaragdus. Ælfric does not elaborate on the visitor and the host but seems to assumes something like the first interpretation, though he somewhat confuses the issue by referring to both as visitors, *cuman* (cf 70), perhaps in anticipation of the next point.

71–7 Cf Augustine, Serm. 105, §2, PL 38, 619:

> Venit tibi amicus de via, id est, de vita huius saeculi, in qua omnes velut peregrini transeunt, nec ullus quasi possessor manet; sed omni homini dicitur: 'Refectus es, transi; age iter, da venturo locum'.

(PL suggests Sirach 29.33 as the source for the latter, but it does not seem to be from the Bible.)

78–87 Augustine imagines the Christian (that is, the host) turning to the prophets and apostles for knowledge and finally turning to Christ himself, with whom those other authorities now rest in heaven (Serm. 105, §3, PL 38, 619):

> Iam enim requiescit familia ista cum Domino suo. . . . Ergo ad ipsum Dominum, ad ipsum cum quo familia requiescit, pulsa orando, pete, insta. . . . Dare vult: tu pulsans nondum accepisti; pulsa, dare vult. Et quod dare vult, differt, ut amplius desideres dilatum, ne vilescat cito datum.

Cf Ælfric's lines 84–7. In interpreting the *pueri* not as those who formerly preached in the world but as apostles, martyrs and all saints Ælfric is possibly influenced by Haymo (Hom. 92, PL 118, 532), who interprets them as the apostles and their successors.

87–96 The Biblical idea that the friend will respond not out of friendship but because of his visitor's importunity is not dealt with in Augustine's Serm. 105, but in his *Quaestiones Evangeliorum* (II.21) he explains it as a comparison of lesser with greater; if even a man will give, though reluctant, how much more will God give, who urges men to importune him and wishes to give. He is followed by Bede and Haymo. Ælfric's rather different discussion is perhaps suggesting that man has no claims on God as a friend but depends on his free act of grace, which is to be invoked by incessant prayer.

99–104 The equation of fish, egg and bread with the faith, hope and charity of 1 Cor 13.13 is made by Augustine in Serm. 105 (PL 38, 620) and followed by Bede and Haymo, but Ælfric's wording is not very similar.

104–9 Augustine and Bede make the point that the fish, like faith, survives the battering of the sea, but it is Haymo who offers the curious piece of natural history that the fish thrives on it (Hom. 92, PL 118, 533CD):

> Per piscem fides intelligitur, quia sicut piscis quo amplius fluctibus tunditur, eo magis crescit, sic fides quo amplius persecutiones patitur, eo magis proficit.

109–13 Perhaps an expansion of Augustine, Serm. 105, §7, PL 38, 621:

> Restat spes, quae, quantum mihi videtur, ovo comparatur. Spes enim nondum pervenit ad rem: et ovum est aliquid, sed nondum est pullus. Quadrupedes ergo filios pariunt, aves autem spem filiorum.

113–21 Cf Haymo (Hom. 92, PL 118, 533A) for the initial point:

Panis in hoc loco caritatem significat. Et pulchre, quia sicut panis principalis est in victualibus hominum, sic caritas inter caeteras virtutes principatum tenet.

122–4 Possibly an expansion of Augustine, Serm. 105, §6, PL 38, 620–1:

Opposuit autem Dominus serpentem pisci, diabolum fidei. . . . Diabolus ergo non corrumpat fidem, non devoret piscem.

Cf also Hericus, Hom. II.12, 111–2:

Huic contrarius est serpens, per quem primus homo fuit deceptus.

124–31 Cf Augustine, Serm. 105, §7, PL 38, 621:

Quae enim videntur, temporalia sunt. 'Non respicientes, inquit, quae videntur, sed quae non videntur. Quae enim videntur, temporalia sunt; quae autem non videntur, aeterna' (2 Cor 4.18). In illa ergo quae non videntur, extende spem: exspecta, sustine. Noli retro respicere. Ovo tuo scorpium time. Vide quia de cauda percutit, quam retro habet. . . . Quanta tibi loquitur mundus . . . ut retro respicias: id est, ut in rebus praesentibus . . . spem tuam ponas; et ab eo quod promisit Christus et nondum dedit, sed quia fidelis est dabit, avertas animum tuum.

131–6 Augustine, Serm. 105, §8, PL 38, 622:

Ego si habeo spem, si teneo spem, ovum meum non est ab scorpione percussum. 'Benedicam Dominum in omni tempore; semper laus eius in ore meo' (Ps 33.2).

Augustine argues that God promised eternal things, not to preserve the temporal; he is thinking of universal disaster (*ecce pereunt omnia cristianis temporibis*) not personal misfortune like Ælfric.

137–9 Cf Augustine, Serm. 105, §6 (PL 38, 620), *Propterea pani lapidem opposuit, quia duritia contraria est caritati*, or Haymo, Hom. 92 (PL 118, 533C), *Huic contrarius est lapis, id est duritia cordis et immisericordia.*

142–5 Cf Augustine, Serm. 61, §2, PL 38, 409–10:

Bona ergo secundum tempus, bona temporalia, corporalia, carnalia novimus dare filiis nostris, etiam dum simus mali. Bona enim sunt et ista, quis dubitet? Piscis, ovum, panis, pomum, frumentum, lux ista, aer iste quem ducimus, bona sunt haec.

145–50 Perhaps based on Haymo, Hom. 92, PL 118, 534A:

Non enim [Deus] pro pane lapidem donat, quia caritatem amanti durum et immisericordem animum non tribuit. Nec pro pisce serpentem donat, quia fidem quaerenti nequaquam ad infidelitatem cogit. Sed neque pro ovo porrigit scorpionem, quia qui in se habet spem, in desperationem cadere non compellit.

150–2 Augustine has no discussion of this part of verse 13 and Bede and Haymo both interpret the reference to *spiritum bonum* as meaning that all God's gifts come from the Spirit. But Haymo's further point is perhaps relevant to Ælfric's identification of spirit with good will (Hom. 92, PL 118, 534B):

> Pater de coelo dabit Spiritum bonum petentibus se, ut scilicet, eius Spiritu illuminati, non solum fidem, spem et caritatem petere discant, sed etiam accipere mereantur.

153–8 For the interpretation of the difficult phrase 'you who are evil' Ælfric turns to Augustine's Serm. 61, on the parallel text Mt 7.7–11 (Serm. 61, §1, PL 38, 409):

> Mali sumus, et bonum Patrem habemus. . . . Audivimus nomen nostrum. . . . Et quos dixit malos, videte qualem Patrem illis ostendit. . . . Quorum Pater? Certe malorum. Et qualis Pater? 'Nemo bonus, nisi solus Deus' (Lc 18.19).

158–64 An adaptation of Augustine, Serm. 61, §2, PL 38, 409:

> Facit de malo bonum, qui semper est bonus. 'Sana me, Domine', inquit, 'et sanabor; salvum me fac, et salvus ero' (Jer 17.14) . . . Nos boni conditi sumus a bono: 'fecit enim Deus hominem rectum' (Eccl 7.30); arbitrio autem nostro facti sumus mali.

165–72 Augustine, Serm. 61, §3, PL 38, 410:

> Non facit hominem bonum, nisi ille qui semper est bonus. Ergo ut sis bonus, Deum invoca. . . . Aurum est, argentum est; bonum est, non quod te faciat bonum, sed unde facias bonum. . . . 'Dispersit, dedit pauperibus; iustitia eius manet in saeculum saeculi (Ps 111.9). . . . Minuitur pecunia, augetur iustitia. Illud minuitur quod eras dimissurus, illud minuitur quod eras relicturus; illud augetur quod in aeternum es possessurus.

172–4 Augustine, Serm. 61, §4, PL 38, 410:

> Laudas mercatorem, qui vendit plumbum, et acquirit aurum; et non laudas mercatorem qui erogat pecuniam, et acquirit iustitiam?.

174–9 Cf Augustine, Serm. 61, §12, PL 38, 414, addressing the rich man:

> Sed non solum te fecit, sed et pauperem tecum. Dedit vobis unam viam istam vitam; invenistis vos comites, unam viam ambulatis: ille nihil portat, tu nimium oneratus es: ille nihil secum portat, tu tecum plus portas quam opus est. Oneratus es: da illi de eo quod habes; et illum pascis, et onus minuis.

179–87 Augustine, Serm. 61, §8, PL 38, 411:

> Mendici Dei sumus: ut agnoscat ille mendicos suos, agnoscamus et nos nostros. Sed et ibi etiam cogitemus, quando petitur a nobis, qui petunt, a quibus petunt, quid petunt. Qui petunt? Homines. A quibus petunt? Ab hominibus. Qui petunt? Mortales. A quibus petunt? A mortalibus. Qui

petunt? Fragiles. A quibus petunt? A fragilibus. Qui petunt? Miseri. A quibus petunt? A miseris. Excepta substantia facultatum tales sunt qui petunt, quales sunt a quibus petunt. Quam frontem habes petendo ad Dominum tuum, qui non agnoscis parem tuum? Non sum, inquit, talis: absit a me, ut talis sim. Inflatus obsericatus ista loquitur de pannoso.

187–93 Augustine, Serm. 61, §9, PL 38, 412:

Apostolum audi: 'Nihil intulimus in hunc mundum . . . sed nec auferre aliquid possumus' (1 Tim 6.7). . . . Pariant simul mulier dives et mulier pauper: non attendant quod pariunt, discedant paululum, redeant et agnoscant. . . . Certe quando aliquo casu vetera sepulcra franguntur, ossa divitis agnoscantur.

193–204 Augustine, Serm. 61, §§10–11, PL 38, 412–3:

'Qui volunt divites fieri, incidunt in tentationem et desideria multa et noxia, quae mergunt hominem in interitum et perditionem. Radix est enim omnium malorum avaritia: quam quidam sequentes, a fide pererraverunt.' (1 Tim 6.9–10). . . . Aliud est, esse divitem; aliud, velle fieri divitem. Dives est, qui a divitibus natus est: non quia voluit, dives est, sed quia multi haereditates dimiserunt. . . . Hic cupiditas accusatur . . . non divitiae . . . Nam qui . . . non ardent cupiditatibus . . . sed divites sunt, audiant Apostolum. Hodie lectum est, 'Praecipe divitibus huius mundi . . . non superbe sapere . . . neque sperare in incerto divitiarum. . . . Divites sint in operibus bonis, facile tribuant, . . . communicent, thesaurizent sibi fundamentum bonum in futurum' (1 Tim 6.17–19).

But Ælfric characteristically expands the Biblical quotation with one of his favourite sayings, on the hundredfold reward; cf CH I.11.225–7 and note.

205–12 The final passage is Augustinian in style but not from Augustine's Serm. 61 or 105. With 208–10 cf Caesarius, Serm. 25, 2.11–15:

Plus est quod pro paupere recipis, quam id quod pauperi largiris. .. Das pauperi nummum, et a Christo recipis regnum: das bucellam, et a Christo recipis vitam aeternam.

211–2 is Mt 25.40: *Amen dico vobis, quamdiu fecistis uni ex his fratribus meis minimis, mihi fecistis.*

19 TUESDAY IN ROGATIONTIDE: ON THE LORD'S PRAYER

Ælfric's choice of the Lord's Prayer as his theme for the occasion has no parallel in any of the homiliaries which he is known to have used, and there is no evidence of its use as a pericope, but it is used as the theme for a homily *In Litaniis* in the shorter homiliary of Rabanus Maurus (Hom. 20, PL 110, 41), which suggests that there may have been an established link with Rogationtide. Prayer in general is a major concern of the period, and one common reading for the occasion, Luke 11.5 ff, immediately follows the Lucan version of the Lord's Prayer. As Ælfric remarks in the next homily, the Lord's Prayer was one of the two texts which every Christian should know. His opening sentences appear to be addressed to those of very little knowledge, but his discussion of the prayer itself shows no signs of being designed for the most basic understanding. He provides a close, detailed exegesis of the prayer, employing multiple interpretations and carefully discounting some of the more superficial implications (e.g. that God is physically located in heaven alone, or that he leads men into temptation). The underlying motive seems to be to reinterpret what is superficially an unsophisticated, rather unspiritual prayer in order to make it fit with a much more sophisticated, primarily Augustinian, theology. The opening and closing sections draw out the general implications of the prayer to stress ideas of community and the equality of all ranks before God. Possibly this was felt to be an appropriate theme for Rogationtide when the whole populace might be present; cf the fuller discussion of the duties of society in the Second Series Rogationtide homily, II.19.

Ælfric's usual sources provide no help for this homily. PD has only the Bede commentary on Luke 11.5 ff for the occasion, while Smaragdus has commentaries on James 5 and Luke 11.5 ff and Haymo has homilies on Luke 11.5 ff and Matthew 7. Förster suggested that Ælfric was drawing on Augustine's sermons *ad competentes*, numbers 55–9, as well as material traditionally used in teaching in the monastic schools.[1] The sermons do contain similar material, but the same points are made more fully in Augustine's commentary on the Sermon on the Mount, which includes some passages very close to Ælfric. Virtually all Ælfric's other material from the Sermon on the Mount commentary could well have come to him from extracts in PD's homiliary, but this part does not seem to occur there. Occasional similarities of phrasing in the sermons, especially 59, suggest that Ælfric may have known those too, but the debt could be indirect. The brief homily on the Lord's Prayer provided for Rogationtide by Rabanus Maurus draws mainly on Augustine and there is no good evidence that Ælfric knew it (he is not otherwise known to have used Rabanus, or indeed to have known his work). There remains much however for which no source is yet in evidence.

Sources and Notes

The following texts are cited below:

1. Augustine, *De Sermone Domini in Monte*, ed. A. Mutzenbecher, CCSL 35 (Turnhout, 1967).
2. Augustine, *Sermones*, PL 38, Serm. 56 to 59 (*ad competentes*), cols. 377–402.

[1] Förster 1894, p. 33.

3. Rabanus Maurus, *Homiliae de Festis Praecipuis*, PL 110, Hom. 20, cols. 39–42.

7–16 The detail of the disciples asking Christ how to pray comes from Lc 11.1:

Et factum est cum esset in loco quodam orans ut cessavit dixit unus ex discipulis eius ad eum: Domine doce nos orare sicut et Iohannes docuit discipulos suos.

But the prayer itself follows not Luke but the version of Mt 6.9–13:

(9) Sic ergo vos orabitis: Pater noster qui in caelis es, sanctificetur nomen tuum; (10) veniat regnum tuum; fiat voluntas tua sicut in caelo et in terra; (11) panem nostrum supersubstantialem da nobis hodie, (12) et dimitte nobis debita nostra sicut et nos dimisimus debitoribus nostris; (13) et ne inducas nos in temptationem, sed libera nos a malo.

(*Sy hit swa* renders *Amen*.) This version is also quoted piecemeal but verbatim in the course of the commentary. In verse 11 Ælfric uses the variant reading *cotidianum* rather than *supersubstantialem* (line 106).

18–52 A general commentary on the implications of the phrase 'pater noster'. With 18–40 Augustine offers vague parallels but no more (Serm. 57, §2, PL 38, 387 is perhaps the nearest, but cf too his *Sermone Domini*, 2.333 ff); his central proposition here is at odds with Ælfric's, for he argues that all are God's children through grace and redemption and not through creation or according to the degree of their merit (*non est meritorum nostrorum sed gratiae dei*, *Sermone Domini*, 2.335). Ælfric's argument, that men are children of God through creation and redemption and remain so, or become children of the devil, through imitation and obedience, resembles the discussion at CH II.13.50–74, where he is developing suggestions in Augustine's Tractates on John 42. In his repeated insistence, in both texts, that sinners are children of the devil by their imitation and not by nature Ælfric is perhaps combating heterodox views of his own time. Lines 38–40 are Mt 12.50:

Quicumque fecerit voluntatem Patris mei qui in coelis est, ipse meus frater, et soror, et mater est.

For 40–52 there is a possible hint in Augustine, Serm. 59, §2 (PL 38, 400):

Sub isto patre fratres sunt dominus et servus, . . . imperator et miles, . . . dives et pauper. Omnes Christiani fidelos diversos in terra habent patres, alii nobiles, alii ignobiles: unum vero patrem invocant, qui est in coelis.

Ælfric takes the egalitarian argument considerably further.

53–64 The argument that *on heofenum* does not imply physical location resembles in general the discussion in Augustine, *Sermone Domini*, 2: cf esp 365–6: *Non enim spatio locorum continetur deus*. Line 55 quotes Jer 23.24: *Caelum et terram ego impleo ait Dominus*; and 56–7 is Mt 5.34–5 [quoting Is 66.1]:

(34) Autem dico vobis non iurare omnino neque per caelum quia thronus Dei est (35) neque per terram quia scabillum est pedum eius.

(Cited by Augustine, *Sermone Domini*, 2.690–93.) In arguing that facing east in prayer does not imply God's location either (lines 57–64) Ælfric is more closely matching Augustine, *Sermone Domini*, 2.382–9:

> Cum ad orationem stamus, ad orientem convertimur, unde caelum surgit; non tamquam ibi habitet deus, quasi ceteras mundi partes deseruerit qui ubique praesens est non locorum spatiis sed maiestatis potentia, sed ut admoneatur animus ad naturam excellentiorem se convertere, id est ad deum, cum ipsum corpus eius, quod terrenum est, ad corpus excellentius, id est ad corpus caeleste, convertitur.

64–70 The allegorical reading of the same verse is based on Augustine, *Sermone Domini*, 2.373–81:

> Sed quemadmodum terra appellatus est peccator, cum ei dictum est: 'Terra es et in terram ibis', sic caelum iustus e contrario dici potest. Iustis enim dicitur: 'Templum enim dei sanctum est, quod estis vos'. Quapropter si in templo suo habitat deus, et sancti templum eius sunt, recte dicitur qui es in caelis: qui es in sanctis. Et accommodatissima ista similitudo est, ut spiritaliter tantum interesse videatur inter iustos et peccatores, quantum corporaliter inter caelum et terram.

As at CH I.14.109–10, Ælfric introduces the idea of the sinner as the devil's temple (lines 67–8) to complement the Pauline concept of the temple of God.

73–9 The comment on the first petition shows some similarity to Augustine, *Sermone Domini*, 2.411–5:

> Quod non sic petitur, quasi non sit sanctum nomen dei, sed ut sanctum habeatur ab hominibus, id est ita illis innotescat deus, ut non existiment aliquid sanctius quod magis offendere timeant.

80–94 Ælfric interprets the kingdom of the second petition with reference first to the spiritual kingdom on earth, then to the heavenly kingdom, and finally to the community of the elect. Augustine, in *Sermone Domini* and his sermons, concentrates on the heavenly kingdom and the last judgement, but with lines 81 and 87 cf Serm. 57, §5, PL 38, 388:

> Habet quidem regnum Deus sempiternum . . . regnum ipsius nos erimus, si in illum credentes in eo profecerimus.

Lines 85–6 quote Mt 25.34 [also cited in Augustine, Serm. 57 and 58]: *Venite benedicti Patris mei, possidete paratum vobis regnum a constitutione mundi*; lines 89–90 are from 1 Cor 15.24; and 94 alludes to Mt 22.30, *In resurrectione . . . erunt sicut angeli Dei in caelo* [cited in Augustine, *Sermone Domini*, 2.445].

95–105 Ælfric offers two interpretations of the third petition, a literal one referring to angels and men and an allegorical one relating to soul and body; both are in Augustine, *Sermone Domini*, 2:

> [449–63] Id est, sicut est in angelis, qui sunt in caelis, voluntas tua, ut omnimodo tibi adhaereant teque perfruantur . . . ita fiat in sanctis tuis, qui in terra sunt, et de terra quod ad corpus attinet facti sunt. . . . Item fiat

voluntas tua recte intellegitur: oboediatur praeceptis tuis . . . sicut ab angelis ita ab hominibus. . . . [484–94] Ille non absurdus . . . intellectus est, ut caelum et terram accipiamus spiritum et carnem . . . id est, ut quemadmodum spiritus non resistit deo sequens et faciens voluntatem eius, ita et corpus non resistat spiritui vel animae.

106–26 The three interpretations (physical food, spiritual food and the eucharist) are similarly offered by Augustine, though as alternatives, of which he strongly favours the second; cf *Sermone Domini*, 2.516–20:

Panis cotidianus aut pro his omnibus dictus est quae huius vitae necessitatem sustentant . . . aut pro sacramento corporis Christi, quod cotidie accipimus; aut pro spiritali cibo.

On 113 ff cf Augustine, Serm. 58, §5, PL 38, 395: *Quomodo illum panem ventres, sic istum esuriunt mentes*. But this is a commonplace. *Bealu* (line 122) is a mainly poetic word not otherwise used in the Catholic Homilies; there are instances in the Lives of Saints, though not in the sense 'destruction' required here.

127–45 The discussion of forgiveness has only a general parallel in Augustine. Lines 135–9 are Mc 11.25–6:

(25) Et cum stabitis ad orandum, dimittite si quid habetis adversus aliquem: ut et Pater vester, qui in caelis est, dimittat vobis peccata vestra. (26) Quod si vos non dimiseritis: nec Pater vester, qui in caelis est, dimittet vobis peccata vestra.

140–2 paraphrase and partially interpret Mt 5.25–6:

(25) Ne forte tradat te adversarius iudici, et iudex tradat te ministro; et in carcerem mittaris. (26) Amen dico tibi, non exies inde, donec reddas novissimum quadrantem.

Ælfric's concern with distinguishing proper reproval from improper reproach (lines 142–5) is evident also at CH II.36.62–5 and 40.264, but perhaps takes a hint from Augustine, Serm. 56, §17, PL 38, 385:

Odium dimittas ex corde, non disciplinam. Quid si ille qui petit veniam, castigandus est a me? Fac quod vis: puto enim quod filium tuum diligis et quando caedis.

146–77 Ælfric's paraphrase of the sixth petition as *ne geþafa þu god þæt we beon gelædde on costnunge*, in contrast to the literal translation at the beginning of the homily (line 16), corresponds to a point made by Augustine, *Sermone Domini*, 2.640: *Multi in precando ita dicunt: Ne nos patiaris induci in temptationem*; but it was no doubt common, as Augustine says. Augustine draws a distinction between being tempted and being led into temptation (that is, succumbing). Ælfric uses this briefly (lines 149–51) but concentrates on his own distinction between *costnung* and *fandung*, assailing and testing, and the justification for the latter. There is a hint of such a distinction in Serm. 57, §9 (PL 38, 390), *Est alia tentatio, quae appellatur probatio*, but it seems to be a familiar idea to Ælfric, also used extensively in CH I.11 and in his adaptation of Alcuin's *Interrogationes et*

Responsiones. With 149–51 cf Augustine, *Sermone Domini*, 2.671–2: *Non ergo hic oratur ut non temptemur, sed ut non inferamur in temptationem*. The contrast between the good and the evil under temptation, and the image of the damaged ship, seem to be Ælfric's own.

178–85 There is nothing similar on the seventh petition in Augustine, who relates it closely to his interpretation of the preceding clause, so that evil is understood as succumbing to temptation. Rabanus Maurus (Hom. 20, PL 110, 41D) is similar:

> Sed libera nos a malo, hoc est ab omni peccato, sive etiam ab auctore peccati, hoc est, diabolo, ne ille nos suis tentationibus seducat atque decipiat.

186–94 Augustine makes a very similar point about the first three petitions (*Sermone Domini*, 2.785–95):

> Trium primarum petitionum impetrationes, quamquam in hac vita quae isto saeculo agitur, exordium capiant—nam et sanctificatio nominis dei ab ipso humilitatis domini adventu agi coepit; et adventus regni eius, quo in claritate venturus est, non iam finito saeculo sed in fine saeculi manifestabitur; et perfectio voluntatis eius sicut in caelo et in terra . . . ipsa perfectione nostrae beatitudinis et ideo saeculi terminatione complebitur, tamen omnia tria in aeternum manebunt.

194–212 The general points about the other four petitions are to be found in Augustine, but Ælfric is much fuller (*Sermone Domini*, 2):

> [800–5] Reliqua quattuor quae petimus ad temporalem istam vitam pertinere mihi videntur. . . . Hoc ipso quod dictus est cotidianus panis—sive spiritalis significetur sive in sacramento aut in victu iste visibilis—ad hoc tempus pertinet, quod appellavit hodie. . . . [819–25] Et peccata nobis nunc dimittuntur et nunc dimittimus, quae harum quattuor reliquarum secunda petitio est; tunc autem nulla erit venia peccatorum, quia nulla peccata. Et temptationes temporalem istam vitam infestant; non autem erunt. . . . Et malum, a quo liberari optamus, et ipsa liberatio a malo ad hanc utique vitam pertinet.

For 201–3 there is a parallel of sorts in Augustine, Serm. 59, §6, PL 38, 401:

> Cum autem vita ista transierit, nec panem illum quaeremus quem quaerit fames, nec sacramentum altaris habemus accipere, quia ibi erimus cum Christo, cuius corpus accipimus; nec verba nobis ista dici habent . . . nec codex legendus est, quando ipsum videbimus, quod est Verbum Dei . . . quo sapientes fiunt angeli.

213–43 The final discussion of the unity and interdependence of the whole community, who join together in the same prayer which covers all their needs, owes nothing to Augustine.

20 WEDNESDAY IN ROGATIONTIDE: ON THE CATHOLIC FAITH

While the Lord's Prayer was an appropriate subject for Rogationtide exposition, because of the occasion's concern with prayer, and may have become traditional, there seems to be no evidence of any conventional association of the creed with this period in the year. In earlier times it was common to expound the creed in the period before Easter, when catechumens were being prepared for baptism. But the association of the Lord's Prayer and the creed as the two items fundamental to Christian understanding in Ælfric's time (cf lines 1–3 and Wulfstan's homily VII) may have been enough to prompt his choice of subject here. In a kind of appendix which appears at the end of MS K's copy of the Catholic Homilies Ælfric has provided Old English texts of two creeds: the first, which he calls the *læsse creda*, is a version of what is traditionally known as the apostles' creed; the second, which he calls the *mæsse creda*, is a translation of what has usually been known as the Nicene creed, though modern scholarship now doubts any connection with the Council of Nicaea. In the homily he does not say which creed he is concerned with, but what he in fact offers is a verse-by-verse exposition mingling elements freely from both the Nicene creed and the so-called Athanasian creed (a profession of probably fourth or fifth century Gallic origin which circulated only in the West). As Ælfric suggests in his opening lines, his primary concern is with the nature of God and especially the doctrine of the Trinity, so that he parts company with the creeds after a brief reference to the incarnation (lines 147–8) and does not discuss any of the further verses apart from the reference to the Holy Spirit. Thus lines 7–29 quote and expound the first verse of the Nicene creed; lines 30–139 provide a discussion of the Trinity based on verses from the Athanasian creed; lines 139–57 consider the trinitarian aspects of the incarnation; lines 158–89 are on the glory of God; lines 190–212 consider the parallel between the Trinity and man's soul; lines 213–34 describe heresies concerning the Trinity; lines 235–45 consider redemption theory with reference to the Trinity; lines 246–56 affirm the confirmation of the Christian faith by miracles; and the final passage, lines 257–77, briefly mentions three points of doctrine, double baptism, the origin of the human soul and the fate of the soul. No other Anglo-Saxon homily provides any sort of parallel for this detailed discussion of trinitarian doctrine, indeed it is impossible to find any precedent, at least in homilies and sermons, without going back to the period of St Augustine when it was still a subject of fierce debate with the Arians. The first of the sermons attributed to St Boniface, which briefly discusses each article of the creed in turn (PL 89, 843–5), is probably characteristic of the usual pattern. A few passing remarks by Ælfric suggest that he may have been facing doubts and misconceptions in his own time. Some of the material is repeated in the Admonition in Lent which occurs at the end of the Catholic Homilies in MS K (printed Thorpe, II.602–8), and in LS 1.

Like the previous homily, this one handles patristic concepts freely without showing a sustained debt to any particular source. None of the homiliaries used by Ælfric has anything at all on the subject for the Greater Litany. Lines 6–7, 'as the wise Augustine expounded concerning the Holy Trinity', might be taken, as Förster argued, as evidence of Ælfric's use of Augustine's *De Trinitate*.[1] Not surprisingly, that lengthy treatise does furnish a number of parallels, but there seems to be nothing either sustained or particularly close in wording, and it lacks much of the imagery used by Ælfric. There is no other evidence of Ælfric's use of the treatise in the Catholic Homilies, and Pope finds only one brief possible borrowing from it in the homilies which he has edited. As Cross (1963b) has demonstrated, Ælfric may well be referring to sermons by Augustine, or ascribed to him, which discuss the doctrine of the Trinity. Cross found close parallels to particular passages in sermons 117, 118 and 120 and the Ps-Augustine sermon 245. There are further parallels, possibly sources, in sermon 384 (doubtfully Augustine's) and Ps-Augustine sermon 246 (now attributed to Pelagius), and in Alcuin's *De Animae Ratione*, a treatise drawing heavily on Augustine which Ælfric excerpted in Latin and drew on as a source for LS 1. For the account of the heretics Arius and Sabellus, Cross suggests as source Haymo's *Historiae Sacrae Epitome* rather than the *Ecclesiastical History* of Rufinus suggested by Förster; it is certainly closer, but if it was Ælfric's source he was relying on memory. Indeed the whole homily looks like the effect of much teaching and discussion, and personal deliberation, with patristic and Carolingian texts left some distance behind. The sun and fire imagery which recurs repeatedly, for the relationship of Father and Son (lines 62–7), for the relationship of Father, Son and Holy Spirit (lines 100–9), for the different operations of the three (lines 150–7), and for the omnipresence of God (lines 176–89), seems to go back ultimately to five different Latin sermons. Other sources and influences are still to be found. Ps-Augustine sermon 245 (now attributed to Ildefonsus of Seville) appears in Paul the Deacon's homiliary for the Christmas period, but for the others Ælfric had to look outside the usual homiliaries; possibly he was drawing here on material collected earlier at Winchester.

Sources and Notes

The following texts are cited below:

1. Alcuin, *De Animae Ratione*, PL 101, cols. 639–50.
2. Alcuin, *Interrogationes et Responsiones in Genesim*, PL 100, cols. 516–66.
3. Augustine, *Sermones*, PL 38, Serm. 117, 118 and 120, cols. 661–71, 671–3 and 676–8.
4. Augustine, *Sermones*, PL 39, Serm. 384 [=Augustine, *Sermones dubii*], cols. 1689–90.

[1] Förster 1894, pp. 37–8.

5. Augustine, *De Trinitate*, ed. W. J. Mountain and F. Glorie, 2 vols., CCSL 50, 50A (Turnhout,1968).
6. Ps-Augustine, *Sermones*, PL 39, Serm. 245 and 246 [= Augustine, *Sermones suppositìti*], cols. 2196–8 and 2198–200 (Serm. 245, now attributed to Ildefonsus of Seville; Serm. 246, now viewed as part of the *De Fide Trinitatis* of Pelagius).
7. *Excerptiones Ps-Egberti*, printed in B. Thorpe, ed., *Ancient Laws and Institutes*, 2 vols. (London, 1840), II.97–127.
8. Haymo of Auxerre, *Historiae Sacrae Epitome*, PL 118, cols. 817–74.
9. Nicene Creed and Athanasian Creed: *Kompendium der Glaubensbekenntnisse und kirchlichen Lehrentscheidungen*, ed. H. Denzinger and others (Freiburg, 1991), nos. 150 (pp. 83–5) and 75–6 (pp. 50–52).
10. Rufinus, *Historia Ecclesiastica*, ed. T. Mommsen, in *Eusebius Werke*, ed. E. Klostermann, vol. 2, 2 parts, GCS 9.1 and 9.2 (Leipzig, 1903–8).

7–16 Lines 7–8 are from the Nicene creed, v.1:

> Credo in unum Deum, Patrem omnipotentem, factorem caeli et terrae, visibilium omnium et invisibilium.

The discussion of the orders of creation shows some resemblance to Ælfric's rendering of Book V met. 5 of Boethius, *De Consolatione Philosophiae*, in LS 1 and its adaptations, particularly in the later versions (see Godden 1985a, pp. 296–8). That animals were created without souls (line 14) is a characteristic insistence of Ælfric (see Godden 1985a). With 13–14 cf also the passage 'De Sabbato' in the *Excerptiones Ps-Egberti* (c. 36, cited and discussed Godden 1985a):

> Homines creat in animabus et corporibus, et animalia et bestias sine animabus.

The significance of man's erectness is also mentioned in Augustine's *De Trinitate*, XII.i.

30–8 Cf Athanasian creed, vv.5–6, 13–14:

> Alia est enim persona patris, alia filii, alia spiritus sancti, sed patris et filii et spiritus sancti una est divinitas, aequalis gloria, coaeterna maiestas. . . . Similiter omnipotens pater, omnipotens filius, omnipotens spiritus sanctus: et tamen non tres omnipotentes sed unus omnipotens.

39–50 For 45–6 cf Athanasian creed, v.21: *Pater a nullo est factus nec creatus nec genitus.*

51–72 For 55–6 cf Athanasian creed, v.22: *Filius a patre solo est, non factus nec creatus, sed genitus.* For 57–72 see Augustine, Serm. 118, §2 (PL 38, 673):

> Sed homo quando generat filium, maior est qui generat, et minor qui generatur. . . . Sed quare, nisi quia cum ille crescit, ille senescit? . . . Non invenis in hominibus nisi minores filios maiores patres; non invenis coaevos. . . . Sed ecce do tibi unde intelligas. Ignis generat splendorem coaevum. . . . Generat enim ignis splendorem, sed nunquam sine

splendore. Cum ergo videas splendorem igni esse coaevum, permitte Deum generare coaeternum. Qui intelligit, gaudeat: qui autem non intelligit, credat. Quoniam verbum Prophetae evacuari non potest: 'Nisi credideritis, non intelligetis' (*a version of* Is 7.9).

But 63–4 seems to come from the similar discussion in the preceding homily, Serm. 117, §11 (PL 38, 667): *Splendor ille de igne existit, non ignis de splendore.*

77–8 Sap 1.7: *Quoniam spiritus Domini replevit orbem terrarum; et hoc quod continet omnia, scientiam habet vocis.*

79–80 Athanasian creed, v.23:

Spiritus Sanctus a patre et filio non factus nec creatus nec genitus, sed procedens.

84–6 Jn 15.26:

Cum autem venerit paracletus, quem ego mittam vobis a Patre, Spiritum veritatis, qui a Patre procedit, ille testimonium perhibebit de me.

86–8 Nicene creed, v.5:

Et in spiritum sanctum, dominum et vivificantem, qui ex Patre Filioque procedit.

100–11 The passage seems to have been an authorial afterthought, added after the first draft (it was added on a loose slip, now lost, in MS A but appears in all other manuscripts). It is repeated at Thorpe, II.606 and recycled in LS 1.71–9. Analogies with sun and fire for God are common, but the only relevant text I have found which draws an analogy between the Trinity and the threefold nature of the sun is Augustine, Serm. 384, §2 (PL 39, 1689–90):

Quomodo divinitas a semetipsa discernitur cum lucis splendor aut solis calor nullatenus separetur? Ecce enim sicut videmus in sole tria sunt, et separari omnino non possunt. Quae autem tria sunt videamus: cursus, splendor et calor. Videmus enim solem in coelo currentem, fulgentem, calentem. Divide ergo si potes ariane solem, et tum demum divide Trinitatem.

The similarity is slight and may be coincidental; the third element, *cursus*, meaning the sun's course or journey, is not at all the same as Ælfric's *trendel* or orb. But the Latin sermon does go on to quote, like Ælfric (lines 106–7), Hebr 1.3: *Qui cum sit splendor gloriae, et figura substantiae eius.* Alternatively, Ælfric may have simply extrapolated from the following passage in Ps-Augustine, Serm. 246, which provides a close parallel for 104–6 in comparing the relationship of Father and Son to the sun and its brightness (Serm. 246, §4, PL 39, 2199):

Sicut splendor ex sole natus replet orbem terrarum; et tamen a genitore suo non abscinditur aliquando, nec recedit: ita filius ex patre genitus ubique dum sit, in patre semper permanet.

Line 109 is from Ps 18.7: *Nec est qui se abscondat a calore eius.*

111–12 Cf Augustine, *De Trinitate*, VI.viii.3: *Nullo modo triplex dicendus est.*

112–13 Athanasian creed, vv.15–16:

Ita deus pater, deus filius, deus spiritus sanctus: et tamen non tres dii sed unus deus.

121–8 Cf Athanasian creed, v.25–26:

Et in hac trinitate nihil prius aut posterius, nihil maius aut minus, sed totae tres personae coaeternae sibi sunt et coaequales.

132–3 Cf Augustine, *De Trinitate*, I.viii.128–29:

Nec inde separatur utriusque spiritus, id est patris et filii spiritus, qui spiritus sanctus proprie dicitur.

143–5 Nicene creed, v.4: *Incarnatus est de spiritu sancto ex Maria virgine.*

150–7 Cf Ps-Augustine, Serm. 245, §2, PL 39, 2196–7:

In sole calor et splendor in uno radio sunt: sed calor exsiccat, splendor illuminat; aliud suscipit calor, aliud splendor. Et licet calor et splendor ab invicem non queant separari, suscipit splendor illuminationem, non fervorem; suscipit calor fervorem, non illuminationem. . . . Sic et filius suscepit carnem; et non deseruit patrem, nec se divisit a patre. . . . Sic nec pater nec spiritus sanctus susceperunt carnem; et tamen cum filio pariter operantur.

The Old English passage reflects a succession of developments in the text of this homily. Clemoes (Eliason and Clemoes 1966, pp. 31–2) argues that the cross-sign seen here in MS A at 150 and again at 190, 213 and 260 marks passages added by Ælfric in the course of revision, prior to the writing of A. After A was written, and after the passage at 100–11 was added, a back-reference to that passage was added in A at 150, in another hand but evidently authorial in origin. The additional sentence in rhythmical prose at 157, occurring in MSS NUV, is a much later authorial revision, apparently acknowledging the difficulties of the arguments.

158–75 Cf Augustine, Serm. 117, §5, PL 38, 663–4:

De Deo loquimur, quid mirum si non comprehendis? Si enim comprehendis non est Deus. . . . Sed corpus oculo comprehendere te putas? Omnino non potes. Quidquid enim aspicis, non totum aspicis. Cuius hominis faciem vides, dorsum non vides eo tempore quo faciem vides: et quando dorsum vides, eo tempore faciem non vides. . . . Tractas quod vides, versas huc atque illuc, vel ipse circuis ut totum videas. Uno ergo aspectu totum videre non potes.

There are perhaps also allusions in lines 160–4 to Sap 11.21:

Omnia mensura et numero et pondere disposuisti.

and Is 40.12:

Quis mensus est pugillo aquas et caelos palmo ponderavit, quis adpendit tribus digitis molem terrae, et libravit in pondere montes et colles in statera.

177–85 There is a faint and rather uncompelling parallel in Augustine Serm. 120, §2, PL 38, 676:

> Ecce lux ista de coelo, quae solis nomine appellatur, cum processerit, illustrat terras, explicat diem, facit formas, coloresque discernit. . . . Si tam pulcher est sol; solis factore quid pulchrius? Et tamen videte, fratres: ecce diffundit radios suos per universam terram; patentia penetrat, clausa resistunt: lucem suam mittit per fenestras, numquid et per parietem? Verbo Dei totum patet, Verbum Dei nihil latet.

In specifying Jerusalem and Rome (line 180) Ælfric may have been recalling a sentence (on a different topic) in Alcuin's *De Animae Ratione* (PL 101, 642D): *Dum de Ierusalem cogito, non eo momento de Roma possum cogitare.*

186–89 A favourite topos for Ælfric; cf, e.g. CH II.32.40–45, where this passage is virtually repeated.

190–212 Gen 1.26, *Faciamus hominem ad imaginem et similitudinem nostram*, is frequently cited in support of trinitarian doctrine, but not with reference to the threefold nature of man's soul. The ultimate source here is probably Augustine's *De Trinitate*, X.xi.18, but Ælfric is expanding on Alcuin's development of it in *De Animae Ratione* (PL 101, 641C):

> Habet anima in sua natura . . . imaginem sanctae Trinitatis in eo quod intelligentiam voluntatem et memoriam habet. Una est enim anima, quae mens dicitur, una vita et una substantia, quae haec tria habet in se.

His wording, esp. at 195–7, 200–2, is very close to the Old English version he gives of this in LS 1.112–5 (which is based on the Latin adaptation of Alcuin found in the Boulogne sermon):

> Seo sawul hæfð swa swa we ær cwædon on hire gecynde . þære halgan þrynnysse anlicnysse . on þan þe heo hæfð gemynd . and andgit . and wyllan. An sawul is . and an lif . and an edwist . þe þas ðreo þing hæfð on hire. . . .

The following comment, at 202–3, exactly parallels LS 1.122: *þær þær þæt gemynd bið . þær bið þæt andgyt and se wylla.* This has no close equivalent in Alcuin, and Leinbaugh (1994, pp. 207–8) argues that it represents Ælfric's attempt to avoid a clause which had become meaningless through the corruption of Alcuin's *memini me* to *minime* in the Boulogne adaptation of Alcuin's text. The corruption is in fact to be found in at least one manuscript of Alcuin,[2] so is clearly inherited rather than being original to the adaptation, but the argument remains otherwise plausible. If it is right, we must presumably assume that Ælfric recalled the way he had paraphrased the Boulogne version (or his copy of Alcuin) here when translating it somewhat later.[3] The rhetorical question and

[2] See the critical edition by Joseph Curry, 'Alcuin, *De Ratione Animae*: a text with introduction, critical apparatus, and translation', unpubl. Ph.D. dissertation, Cornell Univ., 1966.

[3] LS 1 must be later than CH I at least, since its opening sentence refers back to CH I.2

answer at 193–5 probably owes something to Alcuin's *Interrogationes et Responsiones* (PL 100, 520B), *In quo est homo conditoris sui imago? in interiori homine,* rendered in Ælfric's version (*Interrogationes*, 174–7):

On hwam is se mann his scyppendes anlicnyss? On þam inran men þæt is on þære sawle, seo hæfð on hire þreo þing on annysse æfre wyrcende, þæt is on gemynd and andgit and willa.

213–31 The story of Arius shows some resemblance to that in Haymo's *Epitome*, IX.i-vi, PL 118, 863A-7A:

[c.1] Etenim Arius quidam . . . prava quaedam dogmatizat, et ab illa aeterna . . . Dei patris substantia vel natura filium conatur abscindere. . . . [c.6] Credens ergo imperator, suscipi eum ab Alexandro, Constantinopolitano episcopo, in communionem iubet. Quo renuente adhuc propter infamiam, et suspicionem haeresis devitante, iubet Constantinopolim synodum congregari. Ante vero unum concilii diem constitutum, prosternens se Alexander sub altare, tota nocte clamat ad Dominum, dicens: 'Iudica, Domine, inter Eusebii mina et Arii iuramentum'. Quo valde supplicante, praesumptionem Arii et iuramentum mendax mox vindicta Dei persequitur. Etenim, cum in crastinum matutinum ad ecclesiam properaret . . . humanae necessitatis causa ad secessum declinat; ibique cum sederet, intestina eius atque omnia viscera in secessum cuniculorum defluxere.

However lines 217–9 on Alexander's formulation have no parallel at all in Haymo, or in his source Rufinus (*Historia Ecclesiastica*, X). In the chronology of the story they occupy the position of the Nicene Synod and its decrees, which could be said to include the statement ascribed to Alexander, though neither his name nor his precise wording are to be found in Haymo or Rufinus. For the epigrammatic comment at 227–8 Cross cites Bede's commentary on Acts: *Sicut sensu inanes vixerant sic quoque ventre vacui perirent* (*Expositio Actuum Apostolorum*, 1.208–9 (CCSL 121, pp. 3–99); see Pope, p. 394 and note 3).

231–4 Perhaps also from Haymo, *Epitome*, IX.x, PL 118, 868D-9A:

Ideoque propter Sabelli haeresim, confundentis personas, et dicentis quia idem Deus, quando vult pater est, quando vult, filius est, quando vult, spiritus sanctus. . . .

235–45 In his summary account of the redemption Ælfric is perhaps silently countering possible arguments that Christ's suffering and death prove him to be less than God.

and the remark at 82–3 seems to refer back to CH I.20 and other homilies; and it has occasional flashes of alliterative prose. But it is mainly in plain prose and could belong to the period when Ælfric was working on CH II; there is no obvious place for it in CH II and given its rather esoteric subject, not evidently suitable for preaching to the laity, he may have decided to leave it for inclusion in the LS set.

246–56 Cf the very similar argument that miracles prove the Christian position to be true and the Jewish one false at the end of Ælfric's Life of St Edmund (LS 32.264 ff). It is difficult to believe that Judaism was any kind of threat in late Anglo-Saxon England; perhaps he is simply using it as an example of disbelief in the Trinity, with implicit reference to contemporary heretics and perhaps also to those of pagan persuasion.

257–60 The discussion of double baptism was presumably prompted by verse 5 of the Nicene creed: *Confiteor unum baptisma in remissionem peccatorum.* If Ælfric's mind was still running on the heresies that affected the early Christian church he may have been thinking of such sects as the Donatists, but his phrasing suggests he is thinking of current unorthodoxies. He mentions the issue again in CH II.3.224–7 and in the opening words of the Admonition in Lent (Thorpe, II.602); perhaps it was a problem associated with Vikings or descendants of Vikings in contemporary England.

260–76 On Ælfric's repeated rejection of the theory of the soul's pre-existence see Godden 1985a, pp. 283–5. His mind is perhaps here reverting to the exposition of Genesis 1.26, touched on at 190 ff. The theory that the soul is formed from the divine essence is similarly rejected at LS 1.84–8, drawing on Alcuin's *De Animae Ratione*. The final remarks on the fate of the soul are perhaps prompted by the closing verses of the Athanasian creed.

21 ASCENSION DAY

The New Testament provides several accounts of the ascension and Christ's last words to the disciples, and Ælfric takes first the fullest, Acts 1.3–15, which is the epistle for the day, paraphrasing it with supplementary details from the account in Luke 24.50–53 and then expounding it (lines 1–95). He then turns to the alternative account in Mark 16.14–20, the Gospel reading for the day, and expounds this in turn for the rest of the homily (lines 96–248). His concern is primarily with the literal sense of the two texts and the doctrinal and moral problems raised by various details: Christ's eating and drinking after the resurrection, the clouds at his ascension, the garments of the angels, the reference to man as 'all creation', the miracles which Christ says his followers will work, the difference between Christ's ascension and that of Enoch and Elijah, the reference to Christ sitting beside the Father in heaven. It is, characteristically, the problems of the relation of body and spirit that most interest him.

The homily draws on at least eight different sources.[1] For the exposition of

[1] Förster (1894, pp. 7–8) noted the debt to Gregory and to Bede on Acts; Smetana (1959, p. 190), noted that the Gregory homily was included in PD; Cross (1968), in a very thorough study, identified the use of the two further texts by Bede, Haymo's homily 96, Rufinus and Ps-Hilary, and analysed Ælfric's use of them in some detail.

Acts 1.3–15 Ælfric uses not only Bede's commentary on Acts but also his homily on Christ's appearance to the disciples at Luke 24.36–47 (Hom. II.9, for the period after Easter) and the discussion of the same episode in his commentary on Luke. For the second part, lines 95–248, he turns mainly, as he says, to Gregory the Great's homily, which appears for the occasion in Paul the Deacon's homiliary (the only other item included being a general sermon by Leo which Ælfric did not use). The homily for the occasion by Haymo, on Mark 16, draws mainly on Gregory but was probably also used by Ælfric. Further in the background are three other sources. For his brief comment on a verse from the Epistle of St James at 148–51, Ælfric himself added a note pointing to the source: an anonymous exposition of the epistles, attributed to St Hilary but possibly of Irish origin. How he came to know this rare text is a mystery, but the remaining sources are texts very familiar to him, Julian of Toledo's *Prognosticon*, which may have influenced a point of eschatology at 93–4, and Haymo's historical *Epitome*.

Sources and Notes

The following texts are cited below:

1. Ælfric's *Excerpts* from the *Prognosticon Futuri Saeculi* of Julian of Toledo, ed. Gatch 1977, pp. 129–46.
2. Bede, *Commentarius in Lucam*, ed. D. Hurst, CCSL 120 (Turnhout, 1960), pp. 5–425.
3. Bede, *Expositio Actuum Apostolorum*, ed. M. Laistner, CCSL 121 (Turnhout, 1983), pp. 3–99.
4. Bede, *Homiliae*, ed. D. Hurst, CCSL 122 (Turnhout, 1955), Hom. II.9 (pp. 239–45).
5. Gregory the Great, *Homiliae in Evangelia*, PL 76, Hom. 29, cols. 1213–19.
6. Haymo of Auxerre, *Historiae Sacrae Epitome*, PL 118, cols. 817–74.
7. Haymo of Auxerre, *Homiliae de Tempore*, PL 118, Hom. 96, cols. 542–9.
8. Ps-Hilary, *Tractatus in Septem Epistolas*, ed. R. E. McNally, CCSL 108B (Turnhout, 1973), pp. 53–124.
9. Isidore, *Sententiae*, PL 83, cols. 537–738.
10. Julian of Toledo, *Prognosticon Futuri Saeculi*, ed. J. Hillgarth, CCSL 115 (Turnhout, 1976), pp. 11–126.
11. Rufinus, *Historia Ecclesiastica*, ed. T. Mommsen, in *Eusebius Werke*, ed. E. Klostermann, vol. 2, 2 parts, GCS 9.1 and 9.2 (Leipzig, 1903–8).

1–33 Acts 1.3–15:

> (3) Quibus [= *the apostles*] et praebuit se ipsum vivum post passionem suam in multis argumentis, per dies quadraginta apparens eis, et loquens de regno Dei. (4) Et convescens, praecepit eis ab Hierosolymis ne discederent, sed expectarent promissionem Patris, quam audistis inquit

> per os meum: (5) quia Iohannes quidem baptizavit aqua, vos autem baptizabimini Spiritu Sancto non post multos hos dies. (6) Igitur qui convenerant, interrogabant eum, dicentes: Domine, si in tempore hoc restitues regnum Israhel? (7) Dixit autem eis: Non est vestrum nosse tempora vel momenta, quae Pater posuit in sua potestate: (8) sed accipietis virtutem supervenientis Spiritus Sancti in vos, et eritis mihi testes in Hierusalem, et in omni Iudaea, et Samaria, et usque ad ultimum terrae. (9) Et cum haec dixisset, videntibus illis, elevatus est: et nubes suscepit eum ab oculis eorum. (10) Cumque intuerentur in caelum euntem illum, ecce duo viri astiterunt iuxta illos in vestibus albis, (11) qui et dixerunt: Viri Galilaei, quid statis aspicientes in caelum? hic Iesus, qui assumptus est a vobis in caelum, sic veniet quemadmodum vidistis eum euntem in caelum. (12) Tunc reversi sunt Hierosolymam a monte qui vocatur Oliveti, qui est iuxta Hierusalem, sabbati habens iter. (13) Et cum introissent in coenaculum, ascenderunt ubi manebant Petrus, et Iohannes, Iacobus, et Andreas, Philippus, et Thomas, Bartholomaeus, et Matthaeus, Iacobus Alphaei, et Simon Zelotes, et Iudas Iacobi. (14) Hii omnes erant perseverantes unianimiter in oratione cum mulieribus, et Maria matre Iesu, et fratribus eius. (15) . . . erat autem turba hominum simul, fere centum viginti.

The journey to Olivet and blessing at 16–18, the great joy of 25, and further details at 26–7, are taken from the parallel account of Lc 24.50–53:

> (50) Eduxit autem eos foras in Bethaniam, et elevatis manibus suis benedixit eis. (51) Et factum est, dum benediceret illis, recessit ab eis, et ferebatur in caelum. (52) Et ipsi adorantes regressi sunt in Hierusalem cum gaudio magno: (53) et erant semper in templo, laudantes et benedicentes Deum.

The translation is mostly fairly close, but Ælfric has added a few details (cf esp. *se æðela cyning* 28). The phrase *in multis argumentis* (v.3) is taken by most translators to mean 'proofs' but Ælfric clearly understands it as 'reproofs' (*on manegum þrafungum* 4–5).

34–8 The reference to Christ reproaching the disciples after the resurrection presumably alludes to Mc 16.14 (translated and discussed later in the homily) and to the *þrafungum* of line 5.

38–47 For the first two sentences cf Bede's commentary on Luke 24.41 (*Comm. Luc.*, 6.2297–304):

> Ad insinuandam resurrectionis suae veritatem non solum tangi a discipulis sed etiam convesci cum illis dignatur, non quidem quasi post resurrectionem cibo indigens nec quasi nos in resurrectione quam expectamus cibis egere significans, sed ut eo modo naturam corporis resurgentis astrueret ne illud non corpus sed spiritum esse arbitrarentur et sibi non solide sed imaginaliter apparere. Manducavit potestate non necessitate.

(Smaragdus repeats this passage verbatim in *Collectiones*, PL 102, 239CD.) The rest follows Bede's homily on the same passage from Luke (Hom. II.9, 177–84):

> Sed quomodo in ignem missa aqua, ita mox comesti spiritali eius sint virtute assumpti. Sed et nostra post resurrectionem corpora caelesti gloria praedita credendum est, ad quicquid voluerint agendum esse potentia, ad veniendum ubicumque libuerit esse promptissima; sed quia nulla tunc manducandi necessitas vel utilitas aliunde possit inferri nullatenus immortale saeculum cibis mortalibus esse fruiturum.

The lack of need for food and drink in heaven is also noted in Ælfric's *Excerpts* from Julian of Toledo's *Prognosticon*, lines 404–5, *et non egemus [for agemus?] sustentari cibis aut poculis, quia non erit ibi esuries aut sitis*, but the point does not apparently come from the *Prognosticon* itself. Cf too the later discussion of Christ's eating and drinking after the resurrection at Pope 7.127–61, again without specific source. The emphasis on Christ's eating and drinking after his resurrection, both here and at II.16.99, gains significance from Ælfric's damning reference to an opposing view, perhaps a contemporary Anglo-Saxon heresy, at Pope 5.230–32.

48–50 Cf Jn 14.26:

> Paracletus autem Spiritus Sanctus, quem mittet Pater in nomine meo, ille vos docebit omnia, et suggeret vobis omnia quaecumque dixero vobis.

50–54 Based on Acts 2. The idea that the apostles were emboldened to preach by the coming of the Holy Spirit (*bodedon unforhtlice* 53–4) is dealt with more fully at CH I.16.65–72, possibly suggested by a passage in Gregory the Great's Pentecost homily.

57–61 Mt 24.36: *De die autem illa et hora nemo scit, neque angeli caelorum nisi Pater solus*. On the signs of imminent ending cf CH I.40.

62–7 Nothing similar in Bede. Ælfric is perhaps seeking to explain away the possible implication of Christ's *on eallum middanearde oð þam endenextan lande* (lines 15–16) that the apostles themselves journeyed to all regions of the world.

68–73 Bede, in his commentary on Acts 1.9, similarly comments on the clouds receiving Christ (*Expos. Act.*, 1.88–91):

> Ubique creatura suo creatori praestat obsequium. Astra indicant nascentem, patientem obnubunt, recipiunt nubes ascendentem, redeuntem ad iudicium comitabuntur.

Ælfric's careful denial of the implications of Acts 1.9 that the clouds carried Christ owes nothing to Bede; he is perhaps thinking of the argument that is to follow at 195–211.

73–81 Both Bede (*Expos. Act.*, 1.10) and Gregory (Hom. 29, PL 76, 1218) seem to have contributed to Ælfric's point about the angels' white garments:

[Bede, *Expos. Act.*, 1.92–6] Albae vestes exaltationi magis congruunt quam humiliationi. Et ideo domino ascendente in albis vestibus angeli apparent, qui nato domino in albis vestibus apparere non dicuntur, quia qui in nativitate sua apparuit deus humilis in ascensione sua ostensus est homo sublimis.

[Gregory, Hom. 29, PL 76, 1218AB] In albis vestibus gaudium et solemnitas mentis ostenditur. . . . Quia nascente Domino videbatur divinitas humiliata, ascendente vero Domino, est humanitas exaltata.

81–6 Gregory, Hom. 29, PL 76, 1218B:

Deletum est hodierna die chirographum damnationis nostrae, mutata est sententia corruptionis nostrae. Illa enim natura cui dictum est: 'Terra es, et in terram ibis' (Gen 3.19), hodie in coelum ivit.

Gregory gives the Biblical quotation in the Old Latin form (see *Vetus Latina: Die Reste der altlateinischen Bibel,* vol. 2, *Genesis*, ed. B. Fischer (Freiburg, 1951–54)). Ælfric translates this but follows it with a version of the Vulgate reading *pulvis es et in pulverem reverteris*. The first part is perhaps meant to stand for the preceding clause in Gen 3.19, *revertaris in terram de qua sumptus es*. He gives similar wording at CH I.1.146–7.

86–93 The explanation that Christ will come to the last judgement in human form, and that the damned will not be allowed to see him in his glory, appears similarly in Bede on Acts 1.11 (*Expos. Act.*, 1.103–8):

Id est, in eadem forma carnis et substantia veniet iudicaturus in qua venerat iudicandus. Cui profecto immortali[ta]tem dedit naturam non abstulit. Cuius aeterna gloria divinaque quondam in monte tribus discipulis apparuit, peracto iudicio ab omnibus sanctis videbitur, quando tolletur impius ne videat gloriam dei.

As Cross points out, the final clause is rightly identified by Ælfric as a Biblical quotation, Isaiah 26.10, but in the Old Latin form. The same quotation appears in Ælfric's *Excerpts* from Julian of Toledo's *Prognosticon Futuri Saeculi*, where a similar argument is made, adding the point that the damned will see Christ in his terrible aspect (*Excerpts*, 262–6):

Ideo reprobi terribilem illum conspicient . . . Humanitatem namque eius et iusti et iniusti visuri sunt; divinitatem vero eius non videbunt nisi soli iusti, sicut Isaias dicit: 'Tollatur impius, ne videat magestatem Domini'.

His source for this is Julian of Toledo, *Prognosticon*, III.vii-viii:

Redemptor humani generis cum apparuerit, et mitis iustis et terribilis erit iniustis. Quem enim mansuetum aspicient electi, hunc eundem pavendum atque terribilem conspicient reprobi. . . . Divinitatem eius iniusti non videbunt, quae iustis tantum visura promittitur. Nam quod ab iniustis tunc divinitas eius non videatur, testatur Isaias, qui dicit: 'Tollatur impius, ne

> videat maiestatem Domini'. Ex quo apertissime patet quod reprobi tunc humanitatem utique Christi, in qua iudicatus est, videbunt ut doleant.

The last part, from *reprobi*, comes in turn from Isidore, *Sententiae*, I.xxvii.8 (PL 83, 596B). The argument that Christ appears in human form so that his killers and adversaries will recognise him and the justice of their punishment (lines 88–91) does not occur in Bede on Acts but does appear in Bede's Homily II.9 with reference to Christ's appearance earlier to the disciples (Hom. II.9, 132–7):

> Ad extremum, ut etiam reprobi in iudicio signa eiusdem passionis aspiciant . . . ac se iustissime damnandos intellegant non solum hi qui ei impias intulere manus sed et illi qui vel suscepta eius mysteria pro nihili contemnunt.

94–108 Mc 16.14–20:

> (14) Novissime recumbentibus illis undecim apparuit: et exprobravit incredulitatem eorum et duritiam cordis: quia eis, qui viderant eum resurrexisse, non crediderunt. (15) Et dixit eis: Euntes in mundum universum praedicate Evangelium omni creaturae. (16) Qui crediderit, et baptizatus fuerit, salvus erit: qui vero non crediderit, condemnabitur. (17) Signa autem eos qui crediderint, haec sequentur: In nomine meo daemonia eiicient: linguis loquentur novis: (18) serpentes tollent: et si mortiferum quid biberint, non eis nocebit: super aegros manus imponent, et bene habebunt. (19) Et Dominus quidem Iesus postquam locutus est eis, assumptus est in caelum, et sedet a dextris Dei. (20) Illi autem profecti praedicaverunt ubique, Domino cooperante, et sermonem confirmante, sequentibus signis.

110–7 Gregory, Hom. 29, PL 76, 1213C–4A:

> Quod resurrectionem dominicam discipuli tarde crediderunt, non tam illorum infirmitas quam nostra . . . futura firmitas fuit. . . . Minus mihi Maria Magdalene praestitit, quae citius credidit quam Thomas qui diu dubitavit. Ille etenim dubitando vulnerum cicatrices tetigit, et de nostro pectore dubietatis vulnus amputavit . . . Dominus tunc discipulos increpavit, cum eos corporaliter reliquit, ut verba quae recedens diceret in corde audientium arctius impressa remanerent.

119–22 Cf the expansion of this brief comment on *godspel* at Pope 8.1–25.

122–35 Gregory, Hom. 29, PL 76, 1214ABC:

> Omnis creaturae nomine signatur homo. Sunt namque lapides, sed nec vivunt, nec sentiunt. Sunt herbae et arbusta; vivunt quidem, sed non sentiunt. Vivunt dico, non per animam sed per viriditatem . . . Bruta vero animalia sunt, vivunt, sentiunt, sed non discernunt. Angeli etenim sunt, vivunt, sentiunt, et discernunt. Omnis autem creaturae aliquid habet homo. Habet namque commune esse cum lapidibus, vivere cum arboribus, sentire cum animalibus, intelligere cum angelis. Si ergo commune habet

> aliquid cum omni creatura homo, iuxta aliquid omnis creatura est homo. Omni ergo creaturae praedicatur Evangelium, cum soli homini praedicatur, quia ille videlicet docetur, propter quem in terra cuncta creata sunt, et a quo omnia per quamdam similitudinem aliena non sunt.

On Ælfric's characteristic reminder (lines 126–7) that animals do not have souls see Godden 1985a, pp. 280–83.

136–9 Gregory, Hom. 29, PL 76, 1214D-5A:

> Vera fides est, quae in hoc quod verbis dicit, moribus non contradicit. . . . Hinc Iohannes ait: 'Qui dicit se nosse Deum, et mandata eius non custodit, mendax est' (1 Jn 2.4).

139–51 Ælfric develops the point about faith without works with three verses from Jac 2:

> (17) Sic et fides, si non habeat opera, mortua est in semetipsa. . . . (14) Quid proderit . . . si fidem quis dicat se habere, opera autem non habeat? . . . (19) et daemones credunt, et contremescunt.

The last of these evidently needed explanation, and he cites in support a version of Lc 4.34:

> Sine, quid nobis, et tibi Iesu Nazarene? venisti perdere nos? scio te quis sis, Sanctus Dei.

He was perhaps recalling Augustine here: Augustine cites this verse, with the reading *Filius Dei* for *Sanctus Dei*, in association with James 2.19 in sermons 53, 168 and 183 (PL 38, 369, 912, 993).[2] The further elaboration of the argument at 146–8 derives from the Latin text which Ælfric added in a marginal note incorporated in MS K; as Cross shows, the Latin is found in the Ps-Hilary commentary on the Epistle of James (CCSL 108B, 65.445–8).

155–62 Gregory, Hom. 29, PL 76, 1215BC:

> Haec necessaria in exordio ecclesiae fuerunt. Ut enim fides cresceret, miraculis fuerat nutrienda, quia et nos cum arbusta plantamus, tandiu eis aquam infundimus, quo usque ea in terra iam convaluisse videamus; et si semel radicem fixerint, in rigando cessamus.

Haymo paraphrases this but, like Ælfric, takes the point a little further and states firmly that external miracles have ceased (Hom. 96, PL 118, 546A):

> Postquam in fide firmiter radicata est, exteriora miracula cessaverunt.

On this passage and Ælfric's attitude to miracles, see further Godden 1985b, pp. 83–100.

163–81 Gregory, Hom. 29, PL 76, 1215C-6A:

> Sancta ecclesia quotidie spiritaliter facit quod tunc per apostolos corporaliter faciebat. Nam sacerdotes eius cum per exorcismi gratiam manum credentibus imponunt, et habitare malignos spiritus in eorum mente contradicunt, quid aliud faciunt, nisi daemonia eiiciunt? Et fideles

[2] Cross 1968, p. 75.

quique qui iam vitae veteris saecularia verba derelinquunt, sancta autem mysteria insonant, conditoris sui laudes et potentiam, quantum praevalent, narrant, quid aliud faciunt, nisi novis linguis loquuntur? qui dum bonis suis exhortationibus malitiam de alienis cordibus auferunt, serpentes tollunt. Et dum pestiferas suasiones audiunt, sed tamen ad operationem pravam minime pertrahuntur, mortiferum quidem est quod bibunt, sed non eis nocebit. Qui quoties proximos suos in bono opere infirmari conspiciunt, dum eis tota virtute concurrunt, et exemplo suae operationis illorum vitam roborant, qui in propria actione titubant; quid aliud faciunt, nisi super aegros manus imponunt, ut bene habeant? Quae nimirum miracula tanto maiora sunt, quanto spiritalia; tanto maiora sunt, quanto per haec non corpora, sed animae suscitantur. . . . Illa habere et mali possunt, istis autem perfrui nisi boni non possunt.

Haymo again paraphrases this and at times is slightly closer to Ælfric (Haymo, Hom. 96, PL 118):

[546A] Linguis loquuntur novis, cum hi qui erant consueti mendaciis, periuriis, detractionibus, maledictionibus, ad Deum laudandum et benedicendum convertuntur. [546C] Et tanto meliora, quanto per haec non corpora sanantur cito moritura, sed animae in aeternum victurae.

But both Haymo and Gregory relate the casting out of devils to exorcism where Ælfric relates it to baptism.

181–7 The example of Judas is Ælfric's own, but Gregory (Hom. 29, PL 76, 1216B) similarly proceeds to quote Mt 7.22–3:

(22) Multi dicent mihi in illa die: Domine, Domine, nonne in nomine tuo prophetavimus, et in nomine tuo daemonia eiecimus, et in nomine tuo virtutes multas fecimus? (23) Et tunc confitebor illis: Quia numquam novi vos: discedite a me, qui operamini iniquitatem.

187–93 Gregory, Hom. 29, PL 76, 1216B:

Nolite ergo, fratres carissimi, amare signa quae possunt cum reprobis haberi communia; sed haec quae modo diximus caritatis atque pietatis miracula amate, quae tanto securiora sunt, quanto et occulta, et de quibus apud Dominum eo maior sit retributio, quo apud homines minor est gloria.

195–208 Gregory, Hom. 29, PL 76, 1216BCD:

In veteri testamento cognovimus, quod Elias sit raptus in coelum. Sed aliud est coelum aereum, aliud aethereum . . . In coelum aereum Elias sublevatus est, ut in secretam quamdam terrae regionem repente duceretur, ubi in magna iam carnis et spiritus quiete viveret, quousque ad finem mundi redeat, et mortis debitum solvat. Ille mortem distulit, non evasit. Redemptor autem noster quia non distulit, superavit, eamque resurgendo consumpsit, et resurrectionis suae gloriam ascendendo declaravit. Notandum quoque est quod Elias in curru legitur ascendisse, ut videlicet aperte demonstraretur quia homo purus adiutorio indigebat alieno. Per angelos quippe facta illa et ostensa sunt adiumenta, quia nec in coelum quidem aereum per se ascendere poterat, quem naturae suae infirmitas gravabat. Redemptor autem noster non curru non angelis sublevatus legitur, quia is qui fecerat omnia nimirum super omnia sua virtute ferebatur.

Haymo, like Ælfric, rearranges Gregory's discussion so as to consider Enoch (mentioned later by Gregory) alongside Elijah from the beginning, but his wording is nowhere closer.

208–11 Gregory, Hom. 29, PL 76, 1217AB:

Enoch translatus, Elias vero ad coelum subvectus esse memoratur, ut veniret postmodum qui nec translatus, nec subvectus, coelum aethereum sua virtute penetraret.

212–23 Gregory, Hom. 29, PL 76, 1217BC:

Pensate ergo quomodo per incrementa creverit munditia sanctitatis, quod et per translatos famulos et per ascendentis Domini personam patenter ostenditur. Translatus namque est Enoch et per coitum genitus, et per coitum generans. Raptus est Elias per coitum genitus, sed non iam per coitum generans [*cf earlier* Elias vero neque uxorem neque filios legitur habuisse]. Assumptus vero est Dominus neque per coitum generans neque per coitum generatus.

Ælfric develops the reference to Christ's chastity further, quoting Lc 14.26: *Si quis venit ad me, et non odit patrem suum, et matrem, et uxorem . . . non potest meus esse discipulus.*

224–33 Gregory, Hom. 29, PL 76, 1217CD:

Considerandum vero nobis est quid est quod Marcus ait: Sedet a dextris Dei; et Stephanus dicit: Video coelos apertos, et filium hominis stantem a dextris Dei (Acts 7.55). . . . Sed scitis quia sedere iudicantis est, stare vero pugnantis vel adiuvantis. Quia ergo Redemptor noster assumptus in coelum, et nunc omnia iudicat, et ad extremum iudex omnium venit, hunc post assumptionem Marcus sedere describit. . . . Stephanus vero in labore certaminis positus stantem vidit, quem adiutorem habuit, quia ut iste in terra persecutorum infidelitatem vinceret, pro illo de coelo illius gratia pugnavit.

Ælfric also uses this passage in his homily on St Stephen, I.3.74–81.

234–44 Gregory does not discuss the last verse of the pericope. As Cross suggests, the ultimate source for Ælfric's account of where the apostles preached is probably Rufinus, *Historia Ecclesiastica*, III.i, but he may have been recalling the summary account in Haymo's *Epitome*, III.ii (PL 118, 831A):

Thomas sortitur Parthos, Matthaeus Æthiopiam, Bartholomaeus Indiam citeriorem, Ioannes Asiam, Andreas Scythiam, Petrus Pontum, Galatiam, Bithyniam, Cappadociam, Paulus ab Hierosolymis usque ad Illyricum

Evangelio Christi cunctos replevit, alii vero vel per haec, vel per alia loca, secundum quod spiritus sanctus voluit, dimittuntur.

For Peter he may have summarised the regions here listed as Judaea or recalled Judaea from the list given by Gregory in his Hom. 17 (PL 76, 1148), used as source for CH II.38.182–6. In both the latter texts Andrew's province is given as Achaia rather than Scythia (note the presumably non-authorial changes in MSS CDE and K here), while Thomas, not mentioned by Ælfric here, is said in CH II.38 and in LS 36 to have preached in India, which is here assigned to Bartholomew (but Ælfric carefully distinguishes the three nations called India at the beginning of CH I.31 on Bartholomew). Ælfric ends by quoting Jn 15.5 *sine me nihil potestis facere* and Mt 28.20 *et ecce ego vobiscum sum omnibus diebus, usque ad consummationem saeculi.*

22 PENTECOST

Ælfric takes as his subject the events of Pentecost rather than the Gospel passage appointed for the occasion, John 14.23–31. He begins with an account of the origin of the festival and the parallels between the giving of the law to Moses, commemorated by the Hebrew Pentecost, and the giving of the Holy Spirit to the apostles and thence to all Christians, commemorated by the Christian festival. He then proceeds to narrate the story from Acts, covering not only the coming of the Spirit in tongues of fire, Acts 2.1–11, which forms the epistle for the day, but also the subsequent preaching and healing by the apostles and the establishment of the first Christian community. In his selection of material and subsequent commentary on it he seems particularly concerned with the models for subsequent Christian practices—episcopal confirmation, the monastic life of poverty and obedience—but also with the ways in which the story of Pentecost relates to the Old Testament (Babel, the law of Moses, various prophecies) and to the Gospels (the earlier manifestations of the Holy Spirit). In contrasting the Holy Spirit's appearance here in fire with his appearance as a dove at Christ's baptism, he carefully applies the distinction first to Christ himself (lines 128–44), then to the apostles and subsequent teachers (lines 145–55) and then to Christians in general (lines 156–72), before moving on to discuss more generally the work of the Spirit (lines 173–213) and the differences between the coming of the Spirit at Pentecost and its earlier bestowal on the apostles by Christ (lines 214–27).

Ælfric's main source was Gregory's homily 30, included in Paul the Deacon's homiliary for the occasion, which provided much of the material for lines 109–227. This is ostensibly on the Gospel text, John 14.23 ff, but deals very extensively with the details of the Holy Spirit's appearance to the apostles and the contrasts with the earlier references to the Spirit. Ælfric selects very freely, reducing Gregory's rather repetitive discussion to a much shorter, more precise account. For the discussion of the festival there are similarities with Bede's Pentecost homily, but no certain borrowings, and possibly some slight debt to Amalarius. Haymo's historical *Epitome* may have furnished some details.[1] It seems likely that Ælfric was also drawing, perhaps from memory, on a commentary on Acts (particularly for 233–55), but there are no evident parallels with either Bede's commentary or the homily on Acts 2.1–11 included in the homiliary of Smaragdus.

Sources and Notes

The following texts are cited below:

1. Amalarius, *Liber Officialis*, ed. J. Hanssens in *Amalarii Episcopi Opera Liturgica Omnia*, Studi e Testi 139 (Vatican City, 1948).
2. Bede, *Homiliae*, ed. D. Hurst, CCSL 122 (Turnhout, 1955), Hom. II.16 (pp. 290–300) and Hom. II.17 (pp. 301–10).
3. Gregory the Great, *Homiliae in Evangelia*, PL 76, Hom. 26 and 30, cols. 1197–1204 and 1219–27.
4. Haymo of Auxerre, *Historiae Sacrae Epitome*, PL 118, cols. 817–74.
5. *The Old English Martyrology*, ed. G. Kotzor, *Das altenglische Martyrologium*, 2 vols., Bayerische Akademie der Wissenschaften, philos.-hist. Klasse ns 88.1–2 (Münich, 1981).

1–3 Cf Amalarius, *Liber Officialis*, I.36:

> Tempus Pentecostes inchoatur a prima die resurrectionis, et currit usque ad diem quinquagesimam post Pascha.

3–38 The origins of Pentecost. According to Exodus, after giving the law to Moses God ordained a festival of the first fruits of the harvest. Its date is not specified, but in Jewish tradition it soon came to be fixed on the day of the giving of the law, calculated as the fiftieth day after the passover, and known therefore as Pentecost. The doctrine that this feast was established in memory of the giving of the law to Moses only became an accepted view of Judaism at a much later stage, in the second century AD. Augustine, in his letter to Januarius (*Epistula* 55, CSEL 34, pp. 202–19), draws on this tradition, explaining the numerical calculations and making comparisons between the giving of the law which is celebrated by the Jewish Pentecost and the coming of the Holy Spirit which is commemorated by the Christian Pentecost. This became the accepted account of Pentecost, appearing, for instance, in Isidore's *De Ecclesiasticis Officiis*. A brief reference to this tradition appears in the *Old English Martyrology* under

[1] Förster (1894, pp. 8, 20, 38, 49) suggested Gregory, Bede and Amalarius as sources (as well as the possible sources for the nature of the dove noted at 130–2). Smetana (1959, p. 90) pointed to the inclusion of Gregory 30 and Bede's homily in PD.

15 May. It is not clear whether Ælfric was relying on a particular formulation of this tradition. Förster argues that he was drawing on Bede's Pentecost homily (Hom. II.17, 201–10), which similarly summarises the Exodus with the precise chronology, and draws parallels between the lamb of the passover and Christ, between the granting of the law when God descended on Mount Sinai and the granting of grace with the descent of the Holy Spirit, and between the observation of the Mosaic law and the preaching of the Gospel. But the wording is not close, and where Bede says firmly that God established the festival of Pentecost in memory of the giving of the law, Ælfric is careful to attribute only the festival of Easter to God's own ordinance. His account of the events is also fuller, using Exodus 12–14 and 19–22. That the Hebrews made the sign of the cross in blood on their doorposts and lintels (line 7) is an idea repeated by Ælfric in CH II.3.82 and II.15.12, where he further identifies it as the Greek letter τ or TAU. But there is no reference to the shape of the mark in Exodus or in the commentaries which Ælfric normally used. On 27–9, cf Amalarius, *Liber Officialis* (quoted above for lines 1–3). The traditional division of the three ages of the world (see, for instance, V. F. Hopper, *Medieval Number Symbolism* (New York, 1938), p. 83), discussed at 33–8, recurs in Ælfric's preface to Genesis.

39–56 A free rendering of the epistle for the day, Acts 2.1–11:

> (1) Et cum complerentur dies Pentecostes, erant omnes pariter in eodem loco; (2) et factus est repente de caelo sonus, tanquam advenientis spiritus vehementis, et replevit totam domum ubi erant sedentes. (3) Et apparuerunt illis dispertitae linguae tanquam ignis, seditque supra singulos eorum: (4) et repleti sunt omnes Spiritu Sancto, et coeperunt loqui variis linguis, prout Spiritus Sanctus dabat eloqui illis. (5) Erant autem in Hierusalem habitantes Iudaei, viri religiosi ex omni natione, quae sub caelo est. (6) Facta autem hac voce, convenit multitudo, et mente confusa est, quoniam audiebat unusquisque lingua sua illos loquentes. (7) Stupebant autem omnes, et mirabantur, dicentes: Nonne ecce omnes isti, qui loquuntur, Galilaei sunt, (8) et quomodo nos audivimus unusquisque linguam nostram, in qua nati sumus? . . . (11) . . . Audivimus eos loquentes nostris linguis magnalia Dei.

56–74 Ælfric continues the story further, paraphrasing and abridging Acts 2.12–45:

> (12) Quidnam vult hoc esse? (13) Alii autem irridentes dicebant: Quia musto pleni sunt isti. (14) Stans autem Petrus . . . (15) Non enim . . . hi ebrii sunt, cum sit hora diei tertia: (16) sed hoc est quod dictum est per prophetam Ioel: (17) . . .'Effundam de Spiritu meo super omnem carnem: Et prophetabunt filii vestri, et filiae vestrae . . . (19) Et dabo prodigia in caelo sursum, Et signa in terra deorsum' (Joel 2.28–30). (32) Hunc Iesum resuscitavit Deus, cuius omnes nos testes sumus. (33) Dextera igitur Dei

exaltatus . . . (34) . . . dixit autem ipse [David]: 'Dixit Dominus Domino meo: Sede a dextris meis. (35) Donec ponam inimicos tuos scabellum pedum tuorum (Ps 109.1). . . . (37) His autem auditis, compuncti sunt corde, et dixerunt ad Petrum, et ad reliquos apostolos: Quid faciemus, viri fratres? (38) Petrus vero ad illos: Poenitentiam inquit agite, et baptizetur unusquisque vestrum in nomine Iesu Christi in remissionem peccatorum vestrorum: et accipietis donum Spiritus Sancti. . . . (41) Qui ergo receperunt sermonem eius, baptizati sunt: et appositae sunt in die illa animae circiter tria millia. . . . (44) Omnes etiam qui credebant, erant pariter, et habebant omnia communia. (45) Possessiones et substantias vendebant, et dividebant illa omnibus, prout cuique opus erat.

74–80 Acts 4.4, 32–5:

(4) Multi eorum, qui audierant verbum, crediderunt: et factus est numerus virorum quinque millia. . . . (32) Multitudinis autem credentium erat cor unum, et anima una: nec quisquam eorum quae possidebat, aliquid suum esse dicebat, sed erant illis omnia communia. . . . (34) Neque enim quisquam egens erat inter illos. Quotquot enim possessores agrorum aut domorum erant, vendentes afferebant pretia eorum quae vendebant, (35) et ponebant ante pedes Apostolorum. Dividebatur autem singulis prout cuique opus erat.

81–7 Acts 5 and 8:

(5.12) Per manus autem apostolorum fiebant signa et prodigia multa in plebe. . . .(15) ita ut in plateas eiicerent infirmos, et ponerent in lectulis ac grabatis, ut, veniente Petro, saltem umbra illius obumbraret quemquam illorum, et liberarentur ab infirmitatibus suis. (16) Concurrebat autem et multitudo vicinarum civitatum Hierusalem, afferentes aegros, et vexatos a spiritibus immundis: qui curabantur omnes. . . . (8.17) Tunc imponebant manus super illos, et accipiebant Spiritum Sanctum.

The last verse refers in Acts 8 specifically to the inhabitants of Samaria, but Ælfric places it much earlier and applies it to the faithful in general, in accordance with the traditional Christian emphasis on this verse as the basis for the rite of episcopal confirmation, bestowing the Holy Spirit, quite distinct from baptism. Cf 250–5 below. A similar point is made in the *Old English Martyrology* in the entry for Pentecost (OE Martyrology, II.105.6–8):

Ðæm gaste æghwelc gefullwad man nu onfehð þurh biscopa handa onsetenesse.

88–101 Acts 5.1–11, rather freely and dramatically rendered:

(1) Vir autem quidam nomine Ananias, cum Saphira uxore sua vendidit agrum, (2) et fraudavit de pretio agri, conscia uxore sua: et afferens partem quamdam, ad pedes apostolorum posuit. (3) Dixit autem Petrus: Anania, cur tentavit Satanas cor tuum, mentiri te Spiritui Sancto, et fraudare de pretio agri? (4) . . .Quare posuisti in corde tuo hanc rem? Non es mentitus

hominibus, sed Deo. (5) Audiens autem Ananias haec verba, cecidit et expiravit. . . .(6) Surgentes autem iuvenes amoverunt eum, et efferentes sepelierunt. (7) Factum est autem quasi horarum trium spatium, et uxor ipsius, nesciens quod factum fuerat, introivit. (8) Dixit autem ei Petrus: Dic mihi mulier, si tanti agrum vendidistis? At illa dixit: Etiam tanti. (9) Petrus autem ad eam: Quid utique convenit vobis tentare Spiritum Domini? . . . (10) Confestim cecidit ante pedes eius, et expiravit. Intrantes autem iuvenes invenerunt illam mortuam: et extulerunt, et sepelierunt ad virum suum. (11) Et factus est timor magnus in universa ecclesia, et in omnes qui audierunt haec.

Ælfric identifies Annanias as a *þegn*, perhaps because of his evident wealth.

102–8 The authority of James in Jerusalem is implied by Acts 15.13 and 21.18, but the details of his position, and his successor Simeon, are not given. Ælfric may have been drawing on Haymo's *Epitome* (PL 118), where the details occur in I.ii, II.xxvi and III.x (though the form of the name is 'Simon' not 'Symeon'). Neither Bede nor Gregory make the point that the communal organisation of the disciples and their obedience to one leader was the model for monasticism.

110–29 The germ of the contrast between Babel and Pentecost is from Gregory, Hom. 30 (PL 76, 1222C):

Qui vero contra Deum turrim aedificare conati sunt communionem unius linguae perdiderunt, in his autem qui Deum humiliter metuebant linguae omnes unitae sunt. Hic ergo humilitas virtutem meruit, illic superbia confusionem.

Ælfric expands the point by paraphrasing the account in Genesis 11. The identification of the builders of Babel as giants or *entas* is to be found also in his homily on the false gods, Pope 21.72–6, but without prompting from his main source there either. It is part of his more general identification of ents as the giants of the old days who were mistakenly honoured as gods; cf CH I.1.214 ff. There is a similar parallel between Babel and Pentecost in the St Matthew homily, CH II.32.92–105. In specifying Hebrews, Greeks, Romans and Egyptians as examples of nations who heard the apostles preaching in their own language Ælfric oddly differs from Acts, which does not mention the Greeks in its long list; possibly he is extrapolating from the reference to Cretans, possibly drawing on knowledge that Greek was used in the regions of Asia Minor and the Middle East specified in Acts.

128–30 Gregory, Hom. 30, PL 76, 1222D:

Sed quaerendum nobis est cur sanctus Spiritus . . . super unigenitum filium apparuit in columbae specie, et super discipulos in igne.

130–2 Förster suggested that the books to which Ælfric refers for the nature of the dove are texts of the bestiary or Physiologus tradition, or alternatively Augustine's Tractates on John 6; see CH II.3.179–91 and note.

132–40 Closely based on Gregory, Hom. 30, PL 76, 1224B:

Unigenitus Dei Filius iudex est generis humani. Sed quis eius iustitiam ferret, si priusquam nos per mansuetudinem colligeret culpas nostras per zelum rectitudinis examinare voluisset? . . . . Noluit peccatores ferire, sed colligere. Prius voluit mansuete corripere, ut haberet quos postmodum in iudicio salvaret. In columba ergo super eum apparere debuit Spiritus, qui non veniebat ut peccata iam per zelum percuteret, sed adhuc per mansuetudinem toleraret.

Ælfric refers more explicitly to Jn 12.47: *Non enim veni ut iudicem mundum, sed ut salvificem mundum.*

140–4 Ælfric now expands the analogy, relating the dove to Christ's gentleness during his life on earth. Lines 140–1 probably draw on Mt 12.19: *Non contendet, neque clamabit, neque audiet aliquis in plateis vocem eius.*

145–52 From Gregory, Hom. 30, PL 76, 1223B:

Vel certe in linguis igneis apparuit Spiritus, quia omnes quos repleverit ardentes pariter et loquentes facit. Linguas igneas doctores habent quia dum Deum amandum praedicant, corda audientium inflammant. Nam et otiosus est sermo docentis, si praebere non valet incendium amoris.

The phrasing of 148–50 is influenced by an earlier passage used for 166–72 (see below). Cf too for 150–2, *Quia nisi idem spiritus cordi adsit audientis, otiosus est sermo doctoris* (Gregory, Hom. 30, PL 76, 1222A).

152–5 No specific parallel in Gregory.

156–65 From Gregory, Hom. 30, PL 76, 1223D-1224B:

In columba vero Spiritus sanctus et in igne monstratus est, quia omnes quos repleverit, simplices et ardentes facit, simplices puritate, ardentes aemulatione. Neque enim placere Deo potest aut simplicitas sine zelo, aut zelus sine simplicitate. . . . Hinc de beato Iob dicitur: 'Erat vir simplex et rectus' (Job 1.1). Quae est autem rectitudo sine simplicitate aut quae simplicitas sine rectitudine? Quia ergo et rectitudinem docet iste Spiritus et simplicitatem, et in igne monstrari debuit et in columba, quatenus omne cor quod eius gratia tangitur, et mansuetudinis lenitate tranquillum, et zelo iustitiae accensum fiat.

166–72 Gregory, Hom. 30, PL 76, 1222D-3A:

Incorporeus, ineffabilis, atque invisibilis ignis est Deus, attestante Paulo: 'Deus noster ignis consumens est' (Hebr 12.29). . . . De hoc igne Veritas dicit: 'Ignem veni mittere in terram, et quid volo, nisi ut ardeat' (Lc 12.49)? . . . Ignem Dominus in terram mittit cum afflatu sancti Spiritus corda carnalium incendit. Et terra ardet cum cor carnale in suis pravis voluptatibus frigidum, relinquit concupiscentias praesentis saeculi, et incenditur ad amorem Dei.

173–5 The warning that the Holy Spirit is not in its own nature embodied in the dove or the fire is probably Ælfric's own comment.

175–9 Gregory, Hom. 30, PL 76, 1221CD:

> Graeca locutione paraclitus Latina advocatus dicitur, vel consolator. . . . Consolator . . . Spiritus vocatur, quia de peccati perpetratione moerentibus, dum spem veniae praeparat, ab afflictione tristitiae mentem levat.

179–83 1 Cor 12.8–10 [also quoted by Gregory, Hom. 30, PL 76, 1224–5]:

> (8) Alii quidem per Spiritum datur sermo sapientiae: alii autem sermo scientiae secundum eundem Spiritum: (9) alteri fides in eodem Spiritu: alii gratia sanitatum in uno Spiritu: (10) alii operatio virtutum, alii prophetia, alii discretio spirituum, alii genera linguarum, alii interpretatio sermonum.

183–92 From Gregory, Hom. 30, PL 76, 1225C-6A:

> Ecce, apertis eisdem oculis fidei, David, Amos, Danielem, Petrum, Paulum, Mattheum intueor, et sanctus iste spiritus qualis sit artifex considerare volo. . . . Implet citharoedum puerum, et psalmistam facit. Implet pastorem armentarium sycomoros vellicantem, et prophetam facit. . . . Implet piscatorem, et praedicatorem facit. Implet persecutorem, et doctorem gentium facit. Implet publicanum, et evangelistam facit. O qualis est artifex iste spiritus. Nulla ad discendum mora agitur in omne quod voluerit. . . . Nam humanum animum subito ut illustrat immutat.

192–5 Gregory, Hom. 30, PL 76, 1226AB (continuing the argument of the passage above):

> Certe qui in uno conclavi pro Iudaeorum metu residebant, nativitatis suae singuli linguam noverant, et tamen nec ea ipsa lingua quam noverant aperte Christum loqui praesumebant. Venit spiritus, et . . . coeperunt in aliena Christum eloqui, qui de illo prius et in sua lingua loqui metuebant. Inflammatum etenim cor despexit tormenta corporis, quae ante metuebat.

196–210 From Gregory, Hom. 30, PL 76, 1226B:

> Pensate . . . post incarnationem unigeniti filii Dei qualis sit hodierna solemnitas de adventu spiritus sancti. . . . . In illa Deus in se permanens suscepit hominem, in ista vero homines venientem desuper susceperunt Deum. In illa Deus naturaliter factus est homo, in ista homines facti sunt per adoptionem dii.

Ælfric adds in support of the last point the quotation from Ps 81.6, *Ego dixi: Dii estis, et filii Excelsi omnes*; Christ quotes this verse at John 10.34 in a way which distinguishes him from the *Ego*, but Ælfric treats it as Christ's own words. He then adds his own qualification, that men are only gods or sons of God by grace, not by nature like the Trinity.

210–13 The first sentence is repeated at CH II.3.181–2.

214–27 From Gregory, Hom. 30, PL 76, 1227B:

In terra datur ut diligatur proximus, e caelo vero ut diligatur Deus. Sed cur prius in terra, postmodum e caelo, nisi quod patenter datur intelligi qui, iuxta Iohannis vocem: 'Qui fratrem suum non diligit quem videt, Deum quem non videt, quomodo potest diligere?' (1 Jn 4.20). Diligamus ergo proximum, amemus eum qui iuxta nos est, ut pervenire valeamus ad amorem illius qui super nos est.

Gregory refers the reader to his homily 26, which may also have influenced this passage (Hom. 26, PL 76, 1198D-9A):

Cur prius in terra discipulis datur, postmodum de caelo mittitur, nisi quod duo sunt praecepta caritatis, dilectio videlicet Dei, et dilectio proximi. . . . Sicut una est caritas, et duo praecepta, ita unus Spiritus, et duo data.

Cf the very similar passage at CH I.16.54–65.

228–33 Bede similarly draws a parallel between the seven days of hymns for Pentecost and the seven gifts of the Holy Spirit (Hom. II.16, 317–9):

Quia spiritus sancti septiformis est gratia iure sollemnitas adventus eius per septem dies laude hymnorum debita simul et missarum celebratione colitur.

The point is repeated by Amalarius, *Liber Officialis*, I.39. The list comes ultimately from Is 11.2–3:

(2) Et requiescet super eum spiritus Domini: spiritus sapientiae et intellectus, spiritus consilii et fortitudinis, spiritus scientiae et pietatis; (3) et replebit eum spiritus timoris Domini.

233–56 Ælfric completes the homily with a brief discussion of three details in the subsequent verses of Acts, beyond the part appointed as epistle for the day and commented on by Gregory: the 3000 who were converted, interpreted as a reference to the Trinity; the community of possessions amongst the disciples; and the institution of episcopal confirmation. There are no parallels for any of this in Gregory or Bede's commentary on Acts. Line 247 refers to Col 3.5: *Avaritiam, quae est simulacrorum servitus.*

23 SECOND SUNDAY AFTER PENTECOST

In Paul the Deacon's original homiliary the text for the second Sunday was the parable of the feast from Luke 14.16 ff, but Christ's story of the rich man and Lazarus, Luke 16.19–31, is the one which figures for this occasion in later versions of that homiliary[1] and in the collections of Haymo and Smaragdus, and is so marked in the *Old English Gospels*. It is this story which Ælfric takes as his text. The account was traditionally interpreted both literally and as an allegory

[1] Smetana 1959, p. 190.

in which the rich man stands for the Jews and Lazarus for the Gentiles (so in Gregory, Haymo and Smaragdus) but Ælfric restricts his attention firmly to the literal level.

His main concern is with the relations of rich and poor and the treatment of the needy and despised, a theme which is illustrated by the additional exemplum of the monk and the leper. But one of the major points of interest raised by the story is the eschatological aspect, since it appears to give Christ's own account of the after-life, though the implications are full of problems around which Ælfric treads very carefully. In the view of modern commentators at least, when the parable reports that Lazarus died and was carried by angels to Abraham's bosom, the intended reference was to some Jewish concept of a place of rest for the blessed.[2] But in patristic thought the patriarchs could not attain heaven until after the redemption and remained till then in some limbo adjacent to hell, or indeed in hell. Julian of Toledo, in a passage familiar to Ælfric, affirmed that the events of the story took place before the coming of Christ to hell and hence before the patriarchs were removed from there.[3] Yet this causes problems later in the parable where Abraham speaks of the vast gulf separating his dwelling from hell and implies a system of rewards and punishments which makes the two places resemble heaven and hell. Gregory the Great, Ælfric's main authority, avoided the difficulty by simply treating Abraham's dwelling as if it were heaven and interpreting his words with reference to the blessed in heaven and the damned in hell (see below). Julian of Toledo (*Prognosticon*, II.xxxii) recognised the difficulty but resolved it by remarking that, though the story applies to limbo and hell proper, it was nevertheless worth asking whether the rich man would still have been able to see the patriarchs after their removal to heaven, and then quoted Gregory's discussion of the answer. Ælfric, in his abridgement and adaptation of Julian's *Prognosticon*, excerpted Gregory's remarks from this chapter[4] and although he did not refer to the Lazarus story at that point or incorporate Julian's initial explanation, he was clearly aware of the problem. In his initial translation of the Gospel passage he paraphrases 'Abraham's bosom' as 'a resting-place with Abraham' and again 'Abraham's dwelling', *abrahames wunung*. Elsewhere in his work the latter phrase is used explicitly of the limbo of the patriarchs, which is firmly located in hell (cf CH I.6.57–8 and II.5.152–3), though Ælfric insists that the souls there do not suffer torment. The limbo of hell is probably what he means here too, and the rest of the homily is certainly consonant with that view, but he does not in fact make the identification explicit at any point, indeed seems to be carefully employing phrases which avoid the issue, and follows Gregory in generalising from the story to describe the state of the blessed and the damned in the present. Like Julian of Toledo he clearly found Gregory's

[2] Cf, for instance, Lazarus, in the *New Catholic Encyclopedia*, 15 vols. (Washington, DC, 1967).

[3] Julian of Toledo, *Prognosticon Futuri Saeculi*, ed. J. Hillgarth, CCSL 115 (Turnhout, 1976), II.xxxii.

[4] Ælfric's *Excerpts*, p. 139.

discussion interesting and valuable and wished to use it while avoiding any misidentification of the scene with heaven. He perhaps interpreted the Lazarus story as an analogy rather than an event. Although many took the story as history he introduces it as *bigspell*, a parable.

As Ælfric notes, his source is a homily by Gregory, the fortieth in the collection of homilies on the Gospels.[5] This was not in the original version of Paul the Deacon's homiliary but appears as the only item for the occasion in the later version of PL 95. Recastings of Gregory's homily appear in the collections of Haymo and Smaragdus and in Bede's commentary on Luke, but there is no sign that Ælfric used any of them, though he would probably have known all three. Gregory begins with a brief explanation of the difference between allegorical and historical interpretation and then gives a long allegorical reading of the story before turning to the literal level. Ælfric ignores the allegorical reading apart from one small detail (line 61) but follows Gregory closely on the literal interpretation with no significant additions apart from two Biblical quotations. His version is briefer, but more from expressing pithily what Gregory elaborates and reiterates than from any substantial omission. Gregory closes with an exemplum of the nun Romula. Ælfric substitutes the exemplum from the preceding homily by Gregory, perhaps because its account of Christ appearing as a leper is so well suited as a complement to his presentation of Lazarus. He could have found the homily, together with the exemplum, in the later version of PD, for the 11th Sunday after Pentecost. But he was to use the story of Romula for a later homily, II.37.

Sources and Notes

The following texts are cited below:

1. Gregory the Great, *Homiliae in Evangelia*, PL 76, Hom. 39 and 40, cols. 1293–1301 and 1301–1312.

3–28 A free rendering of Lc 16.19–31:

(19) Homo quidam erat dives, qui induebatur purpura et bysso, et epulabatur quotidie splendide. (20) Et erat quidam mendicus, nomine Lazarus, qui iacebat ad ianuam eius, ulceribus plenus, (21) cupiens saturari de micis quae cadebant de mensa divitis, et nemo illi dabat: sed et canes veniebant, et lingebant ulcera eius. (22) Factum est autem ut moreretur mendicus, et portaretur ab angelis in sinum Abrahae. Mortuus est autem et dives, et sepultus est in inferno. (23) Elevans autem oculos suos, cum esset in tormentis, vidit Abraham a longe, et Lazarum in sinu eius: (24) et ipse clamans dixit: Pater Abraham, miserere mei, et mitte Lazarum ut intinguat extremum digiti sui in aquam, ut refrigeret linguam meam, quia crucior in hac flamma. (25) Et dixit illi Abraham: Fili, recordare quia recepisti bona

[5] Identified by Förster (1894, pp. 3–4).

in vita tua, et Lazarus similiter mala: nunc autem hic consolatur, tu vero cruciaris: (26) et in his omnibus inter nos et vos chaos magnum firmatum est ut hi qui volunt hinc transire ad vos, non possint, neque inde huc transmeare. (27) Et ait: Rogo ergo te, pater, ut mittas eum in domum patris mei: (28) habeo enim quinque fratres, ut testetur illis, ne et ipsi veniant in hunc locum tormentorum. (29) Et ait illi Abraham: Habent Moysen et prophetas: audiant illos. (30) At ille dixit: Non, pater Abraham: sed si quis ex mortuis ierit ad eos, poenitentiam agent. (31) Ait autem illi: Si Moysen et prophetas non audiunt, neque si quis ex mortuis resurrexerit, credent.

The rendering silently incorporates some points of interpretation and tradition, paraphrasing the references to Lazarus's death to fit Christian doctrine and identifying Lazarus as a leper (*licþrowere*), a medieval tradition which has no Biblical or early foundation.[6] The one difficulty with Ælfric's rendering of the Gospel passage is in verse 7 where the crumbs which fall from the table of the rich man become 'the crumbs which were carried out (or removed) with the *beodum*' (line 8). The latter word generally means 'table' in Old English though there is some slight evidence for 'dish'. Possibly Ælfric is thinking of trestle tables which are removed along with the remnants of food at the end of the meal. The phrase is translated literally at CH II.3.266 and II.8.18 but in those cases there is not the same logistical problem of explaining how the crumbs might reach the beggar.

29–34 From Gregory, Hom. 40, PL 76, 1304D-5A:

Dives iste non abstulisse aliena reprehenditur, sed propria non dedisse. Nec dicitur quia vi quempiam oppressit, sed quia in acceptis rebus se extulit. Hinc ergo summopere colligendum est qua poena multandus sit qui aliena diripit, si inferni damnatione percutitur qui propria non largitur.

34–6 Gregory, Hom. 40, PL 76, 1305A:

Hoc quoque fuit quod hunc inferno tradidit, quia in sua felicitate timidus non fuit, quia accepta dona ad usum arrogantiae inflexit . . . quia peccata sua redimere etiam cum sibi abundaret pretium noluit.

36–41 Gregory, Hom. 40, PL 76, 1305AB:

Et sunt nonnulli qui cultum subtilium pretiosarumque vestium non putant esse peccatum. Quod si culpa non esset, nequaquam sermo Dei vigilanter exprimeret quod dives qui torquetur apud inferos bysso et purpura indutus fuisset. Nemo quippe vestimenta praecipua nisi ad inanem gloriam quaerit, videlicet, ut honorabilior caeteris esse videatur.

41–3 Gregory, Hom. 40, PL 76, 1305B:

Si abiectio vilis indumenti virtus non esset, evangelista vigilanter de Iohanne non diceret: 'Erat indutus pilis camelorum' (Mt 3.4).

[6] See the additional note below.

That Christ praised John the Baptist for the roughness of his clothing is, however, rather more than Gregory or the Gospels warrant.

44–9 Gregory, Hom. 40, PL 76, 1305BC:

> Ecce dicitur: 'Homo quidam erat dives'; et protinus subinfertur; 'Et erat quidam mendicus nomine Lazarus'. Certe in populo plus solent nomina divitum quam pauperum sciri. . . . Ac si aperte dicat: 'Pauperem humilem scio, superbum divitem nescio. Illum cognitum per approbationem habeo, hunc per iudicium reprobationis ignoro.'

49–52 Gregory, Hom. 40, PL 76, 1305D-6A:

> Habuisset fortasse aliquam excusationem dives, si Lazarus pauper et ulcerosus ante eius ianuam non iacuisset. . . . Rursum si longe esset dives ab oculis ulcerosi pauperis, minorem tolerasset in animo tentationem pauper.

52–4 Gregory, Hom. 40, PL 76, 1306A:

> Quantas hunc egenum et vulneribus obsessum tentationes creditis in sua cogitatione tolerasse, cum ipse egeret pane, et non haberet etiam salutem, atque ante se divitem cerneret salutem et delicias habere cum voluptate; se dolore et frigore affici, illum gaudere conspiceret, bysso et purpura vestiri?

55–9 Gregory, Hom. 40, PL 76, 1306B:

> Certe poterat ad poenam sufficere paupertas, etiamsi sanus fuisset; et rursum suffecisset aegritudo, etiamsi subsidium adesset. Sed ut probaretur amplius pauper, simul hunc et paupertas et aegritudo tabefecit.

The general notion that the rich man is brought low by his indulgence and lack of compassion is reiterated by Gregory but there is nothing close to Ælfric's wording, or to his stress on the rich man's arrogance.

61 Gregory at this point refers to the dogs licking Lazarus's sores only as evidence for his statement that no-one visited the beggar, but in his earlier allegorical interpretation he does state that the licking cures wounds: *Canum lingua vulnus dum lingit, curat* (Hom. 40, PL 76, 1302D). His interest is only in the basis this offers for allegory, but Ælfric, who has not the same concern, was perhaps wishing to suggest that the dogs were agents of divine mercy, or at least, in their natural affection, a sharp contrast to human cruelty.

64–8 Gregory, Hom. 40, PL 76, 1306CD:

> Dives eum cui in hac vita misereri noluit in suo iam supplicio positus patronum quaerit. . . . Dives iste qui vulnerato pauperi mensae suae vel minima dare noluit, in inferno positus, usque ad minima quaerenda pervenit.

68–71 Gregory, Hom. 40, PL 76, 1307AB:

> Quia abundare in conviviis loquacitas solet . . . is qui convivando magis de loquacitate peccaverat, per retributionis iustitiam in lingua atrocius ardebat.

73–80 Gregory, Hom. 40, PL 76, 1307BC:

> Ista sententia pavore potius indiget, quam expositione. . . . Indicatur et dives iste boni aliquid habuisse, ex quo in hac vita bona reciperet. Rursumque . . . monstratur Lazarus habuisse malum aliquod quod purgaretur. Sed mala Lazari purgavit ignis inopiae, et bona divitis remuneravit felicitas transeuntis vitae. Illum paupertas afflixit et tersit, istum abundantia remuneravit et repulit.

Gregory demonstrates that the rich man must have done some good in his life and Lazarus some evil, but both received their respective reward and punishment in this life. Ælfric is more doubtful, expressing the good and evil only as hypotheses and dismissing even the hypothetical sins of Lazarus as little ones, perhaps in order to preserve his own eschatology with its purgatorial element (cf CH II.40).

81–4 Gregory, Hom. 40, PL 76, 1307D-8A:

> Et cum quoslibet pauperes nonnulla reprehensibilia perpetrare conspicitis, nolite despicere . . . quia fortasse quod superfluitas tenuissimae pravitatis inquinat, caminus paupertatis purgat. De vobis omnimodo pertimescite, quia nonnulla etiam male acta prospera vita secuta est.

84–9 As Gregory points out, the difficult part of this passage is Abraham's statement, according to the Vulgate, that those who wish to cannot pass 'from us to you', and he spends some time determining who might wish to make that journey, and why, and what it is that prevents them (essentially, the blessed feel the impulse to show mercy to the damned but it is overwhelmed by their sense of the justice of God). Ælfric avoids the issue by rendering Abraham's words as a hypothesis, 'even if anyone wished to go from us to you, he could not do it'. He nevertheless draws on Gregory's wording, though the emphasis is different (Hom. 40, PL 76, 1308AB):

> Quia hi qui in inferno sunt ad beatorum sortem transire cupiant dubium non est. . . . Nec iniusti ad beatorum sortem transeunt, quia damnatione perpetua constringuntur; nec iusti transire ad reprobos possunt quia, erecti iam per iustitiam iudicii, eis nullo modo ex aliqua compassione miserentur. . . . [*earlier*] quia tantum illos tunc a se videbunt extraneos, quantum ab eo quem diligunt auctore suo conspiciunt esse repulsos.

Gregory's repeated phrase *ad beatorum sortem* seems to place the scene firmly in heaven, where Ælfric's language allows the possibility of limbo.

94–8 Gregory, Hom. 40, PL 76, 1308C:

> Sed postquam ardenti diviti de se spes tollitur, eius animus ad propinquos quos reliquerat recurrit, quia reproborum mentem poena sua quandoque inutiliter erudit ad caritatem, ut iam tunc etiam suos spiritaliter diligant quos* hic, dum peccata diligerent, nec secum amabant. [**From variants in PL 76*]

The sense of 96–8 seems to be: 'as if they then love their kindred, having loved neither their kin nor themselves while they were alive.' The final comment, line 98, seems to be Ælfric's own explanation of this point.

98–108 Gregory, Hom. 40, PL 76, 1308C-9A:

Cognoscit Lazarum quem despexit, fratrum quoque suorum meminit quos reliquit. Perfecta quippe ei ultio de paupere non esset, si hunc in retributione non recognosceret. Et perfecta poena in igne non esset, si non hoc quod ipse patitur etiam in suis timeret. Ut ergo peccatores in supplicio amplius puniantur, et eorum vident gloriam quos contempserunt. . . . Iusti vero in tormentis semper intuentur iniustos, ut hinc eorum gaudium crescat, quia malum conspiciunt quod misericorditer evaserunt.

Ælfric's *nu hwiltidum* (line 104) again reflects his concern with eschatological precision, marking the shift in time from the situation at the time of the story, when Lazarus was presumably in limbo, to that of present time when the contrast is between hell and heaven.

108–14 Gregory, Hom. 40, PL 76, 1309AB:

Nec illam tantae beatitudinis claritatem apud iustorum animum fuscat spectata poena reproborum, quia ubi iam compassio miseriae non erit, minuere procul dubio beatorum laetitiam non valebit. Quid mirum si dum iusti iniustorum tormenta conspiciunt, hoc eis veniat in obsequium gaudiorum, quando et in pictura niger color substernitur, ut albus vel rubeus clarior videatur? . . . Qui Creatoris sui claritatem vident, nihil in creatura agitur quod videre non possint.

The notion of the just being frightened by the sight of hell is Ælfric's addition.

120–2 Gregory, Hom. 40, PL 76, 1309C:

Hi qui viliora legis praecepta implere negligunt, Salvatoris nostri mandatis altioribus obedire quando convalescunt?

123–31 Gregory, Hom. 40, PL 76, 1309D-10A:

Sed vos, fratres, et requiem Lazari, et poenam divitis cognoscentes, solerter agite, culparum vestrarum intercessores quaerite atque advocatos vobis in die iudicii pauperes procurate. Multos nunc Lazaros habetis; ante ianuas vestras iacent, atque his indigent, quae vobis iam satiatis quotidie de mensa cadunt. . . . Ecce importune se pauperes offerunt, rogant nos, qui tunc pro nobis intercessores venient. Certe nos omnino rogare debuimus, sed tamen rogamur. Videte si negare debemus quod petimur, quando patroni sunt qui petunt.

In the first sentence Gregory is perhaps alluding to Christ's words earlier in Luke 16, at verse 9, and Ælfric quotes the verse itself (Lc 16.9):

Et ego vobis dico: facite vobis amicos de mammona iniquitatis: ut, cum defeceritis, recipiant vos in aeterna tabernacula.

132–4 Ælfric adds the quotation from Mt 25.35–6, leading suitably into the following exemplum (which ends with a later verse from the same passage):

(35) Esurivi enim, et dedistis mihi manducare: sitivi, et dedistis mihi bibere: . . . (36) nudus, et cooperuistis me.

135–54 Gregory, Hom. 39, PL 76, 1300BCD:

> In . . . terra Lycaoniae . . . quidam, Martyrius nomine, vitae valde venerabilis monachus fuit, qui ex suo monasterio visitationis gratia ad aliud monasterium tendebat, cui spiritualis pater praeerat. Pergens itaque, leprosum quemdam, quem densis vulneribus elephantinus morbus per membra foedaverat, invenit in via, volentem ad suum hospitium redire, sed prae lassitudine non valentem. . . . Vir autem Dei eiusdem leprosi lassitudinem misertus, pallium quo vestiebatur in terram protinus proiecit et expandit, ac desuper leprosum posuit, eumque suo pallio undique constrictum super humerum levavit, secumque revertens detulit. Cumque iam monasterii foribus propiaret, spiritualis pater eiusdem monasterii magnis vocibus clamare coepit: 'Currite, ianuas monasterii citius aperite, quia frater Martyrius venit Dominum portans'. Statim vero ut Martyrius ad monasterii aditum pervenit, is qui leprosus esse putabatur, de collo eius exsiliens, et in ea specie apparens qua recognosci ab hominibus solet Redemptor humani generis . . . ad coelum Martyrio aspiciente rediit, eique ascendens dixit: 'Martyri, tu me non erubuisti super terram, ego te non erubescam super coelos'. Qui sanctus vir mox ut est monasterium ingressus, ei pater monasterii dixit:'Frater Martyri, ubi est quem portabas?' Cui ille respondit, dicens: 'Ego si scivissem quis esset, pedes illius tenuissem.' Tunc idem Martyrius narrabat quia cum eum portasset, pondus eius minime sensisset. Nec mirum quomodo enim pondus sentire poterat, qui portantem portabat?

Ælfric seems to place the climax at Martyrius's own monastery whereas Gregory places it at the other monastery which he was visiting; Ælfric also makes a point of remarking that the monk's journey is at the behest of his abbot. The phrase *yrnað earma* is hard to explain or justify; the abbot is calling to his monks and one would expect a plural form, even if it were appropriate to call them 'wretches'. It looks suspiciously like a scribal corruption of the *yrnað yrnað* of later versions, possibly through an interlinear addition of the second *yrnað*; but if so it has evidently escaped Ælfric's notice and survived through to the archetypes of MSS DEF and H.

155–65 Gregory, Hom. 39, PL 76, 1301AB:

> Ecce autem Redemptori . . . ad aedificationem nostram minime sufficit quod in extremo iudicio dicturum se esse perhibuit: 'Quamdiu fecistis uni de his fratribus meis minimis, mihi fecistis' (Mt 25.40), nisi et ante iudicium hoc in se ostenderet quod dixisset. . . . Quid in humana carne sublimius carne Christi, quae est super angelos exaltata? Et quid in humana carne abiectius carne leprosi, quae tumescentibus vulneribus scinditur, et exhalantibus fetoribus impletur? Sed ecce in specie leprosi apparuit; et is qui est reverendus super omnia, videri despectus infra omnia dedignatus non est. Cur hoc, nisi ut sensu nos tardiores admoneret, quatenus quisquis ei qui in coelo est festinat assistere, humiliari in terra et compati etiam abiectis et despicabilibus fratribus non recuset?

Additional note: Lazarus and leprosy

In I.23 the phrase *ulceribus plenus* (Lc 16.20) describing Lazarus is rendered *se wæs licþrowere* (line 7). The latter word is glossed 'leper' in the dictionaries, and seems to translate *leprosus* wherever else it occurs in Ælfric, and indeed in Old English. (That is also the meaning of the cognate Icelandic term *likþra*.) Yet the Bible does not use the word *leprosus* of Lazarus, nor do the Latin commentaries which Ælfric is likely to have known (Gregory, Bede, Smaragdus, Haymo), and there is no suggestion of leprosy at this point in the various Old English Gospels or in the other Old English works which refer to the story (Alfred's *Pastoral Care* and *Soliloquies*, Wærferth's version of Gregory's *Dialogues*). On the other hand, there is a widely current later medieval tradition associating Lazarus with leprosy: in Middle English, French and Italian the term *lazar* or its equivalents is used for lepers, there is a Mass of St Lazarus for the separation of lepers, and leper hospitals are dedicated to St Lazarus.[7] Where did Ælfric learn of the association, and what precisely did he mean by the term *licþrowere*?

It is generally agreed that the Vulgate Bible's terms *lepra* and *leprosus* do not refer to what is now called leprosy. They render Greek *lepra* which seems to denote other kinds of skin disease and is used in the Septuagint to translate a Hebrew word referring to any of a variety of skin ailments considered to be ritually unclean; *lepra* probably has the same meaning in the New Testament. Early Greek writers distinguished between *lepra* and another disease called *elephantiasis*, and modern commentators often identify the latter with what is now called leprosy. It would appear that in the transmission of medical theory from the Greeks through the Arabs to the Latin world the distinction was lost and the term *lepra* came to include, and eventually to be used exclusively for, the specific disease which is now called leprosy. How far those identified as lepers in the Middle Ages were suffering from leprosy in the modern sense remains very uncertain, and is likely to have varied in time and place. Equally uncertain is how far the treatment of lepers, for good or ill, was prompted by their medical condition and evidence of contagion and how far it was a response to the Biblical presentation of the disease as ritually unclean and a punishment from God.

Provision for dealing with lepers first appears in England soon after the Conquest and becomes widespread, until the incidence of the disease, or those thought to have it, declined at the end of the Middle Ages. Evidence for lepers, real or supposed, in Anglo-Saxon England rests almost entirely on the existence of native terminology. Ælfric's language is careful and precise, as one would expect. As has already been noted, apart from this one instance with Lazarus he uses the noun *licþrowere* exclusively as an equivalent to *leprosus*, occurring in the Bible and in Latin saints' legends and homilies. His other term is the adjective *hreoflig* which he also uses very strictly as an equivalent to *leprosus*. More doubtful is the Latin

[7] I owe this and much else on medieval leprosy to two useful studies: Peter Richards, *The Medieval Leper and his Northern Heirs* (Cambridge, 1927); and S. N. Brody, *The Disease of the Soul: Leprosy in Medieval Literature* (Ithaca, NY, 1974).

term *elephantinus morbus*. This is used by one of Ælfric's main authorities, Gregory the Great, as an equivalent to *leprosus*, but on the only two occasions in the Catholic Homilies where Ælfric uses the term[8] he does not connect it with leprosy or employ the terms *licþrowere* and *hreoflig*, and he uses the phrase as if it represents a specific disease not familiar to his audience. When paraphrasing the exemplum from Gregory above, in which *elephantinus morbus* and *leprosus* are used interchangeably, Ælfric uses *hreoflig* but not the Latin term. There is perhaps a hint in his usage that he had no experience of *elephantinus morbus* except from occasional references in books, whereas the ailment for which he used the terms *leprosus*, *licþrowere* and *hreoflig* was familiar to him, though he gives no examples of the latter in England and the familiarity may also have been from reading, especially the Bible. Ælfric gives a detailed description of the disease afflicting the *leprosus* or *hreoflic* man in CH I.8.44–6; this may derive entirely from Leviticus, but is written as if from familiar knowledge. (The limitation of the symptoms to the skin suggests that it may not have been leprosy in the modern sense, but the evidence is unclear.) Other Anglo-Saxon writers use the terminology somewhat differently. The apparent distinction between *elephantinus morbus* and *hreoflic* is not observed by Wærferth, who paraphrases Gregory's *elephantinus morbus* with *mid þære hreofan adle*,[9] and the terms *hreofl* and *hreoflic* seem often to have a wider reference, translating *scabies*, for instance, in the *Old English Bede*.[10]

It would appear, then, that Ælfric used the term *licþrowere* and related words with some care and precision and is unlikely to have used it of Lazarus without good reason. Leviticus might have encouraged him to associate the word *ulcer* with the *leprosus*, but he does not make the connection with Job, who has *ulceri* (the word does not appear in the New Testament except in the description of Lazarus). Given the strength of the later association, it remains likely that he knew of an existing tradition which identified Lazarus as a leper. So far, however, I have found no other evidence of that tradition which can be dated as early as Ælfric, and no convincing explanation as to how it arose. The association seems also to have covered Lazarus the brother of Mary and Martha, who is sometimes identified with Lazarus the beggar, but there seems to be no early tradition that the disease of which he died was leprosy, and Ælfric shows no sign of confusing the two figures.

24 FOURTH SUNDAY AFTER PENTECOST

The text which Ælfric presents for the occasion is the parable of the lost sheep, Luke 15.1–7, but this occupies only a small part of the homily. After a relatively brief allegorical commentary, interpreting the lost sheep as man and the others as the angels (lines 16–75), he turns to the next parable in Luke, on the lost coin

[8] CH II.11.395 and 32.211. [9] Hecht, p. 157. [10] OE Bede, 388.17.

(verses 8–10), and uses this as the basis for a very full account of the nine orders of angels which occupies the rest of the homily (lines 76–210). His source, the homily on the Gospel text by Gregory the Great, is the first extensive piece of angelology in the West, closely following on the Greek discussion by Ps-Dionysius. Ælfric's piece is in turn the first extensive discussion of the angelic orders in English.

The difficulty of the subject is evident both in Gregory's account and Ælfric's. The Biblical references to the identity and functions of heavenly spirits reflect the unsystematic thoughts of different writers at different times and they do not easily bear the systematic distinctions which Gregory sought to impose on them. He seems to be feeling his way in the argument, synthesising disparate material, noting difficulties and contradictions in the evidence and trying to reconcile them. There are also difficulties in the very principle of distinguishing nine levels of perfection among so perfect a body, difficulties that are doubled when he tries to apply the same distinctions to the elect among mankind. Ælfric has the advantage of coming after Gregory and being able to accept his arguments as established fact, and does not feel the same need to confront possible objections. He omits some of the Biblical citations which caused problems and rearranges the arguments so as to present a clear and logical pattern where Gregory tends to offer the dialectic of debate, but he does not evade the main difficulties of Gregory's account. The difficulties of distinguishing the nine orders and explaining how some can be lower than others while still perfect and possessed of all the qualities which higher orders have are fully faced. The result is often clearer than the Latin text, but still taxing. The primary concern of both writers is to reconstruct the cosmic hierarchies, but Ælfric like Gregory makes an equation between angelic virtues and human ones and there is perhaps also an implicit moral in the presentation of hierarchy. Gregory himself used the angelic orders as an analogy for political structures (*Epistula* 5.54, CCSL 140), and there is perhaps some political or ecclesiastical significance for Ælfric too in the picture of a hierarchical system in which some are higher than others but all are good and none need envy others. At the same time, his repeated reference to the fallen angels (lines 79–82, 84–5, 86–9 and 106–8) and the fact that a place was created for man by the fall of the tenth order of angels, a point entirely absent from Gregory, adds a further dimension of salvation-history.

Gregory's homily 34, on Luke 15.1–10, is the one item provided for this occasion in Paul the Deacon's homiliary and was almost Ælfric's sole source.[1] Of other discussions known to him, Smaragdus's homily on the same text and Bede's commentary on Luke merely reproduce Gregory but Haymo's homily paraphrases and recasts the latter more freely and at a few points his wording does seem closer to Ælfric, though it may be a coincidence. All three homilies treat verses 1–10 as the text for the occasion, and this seems also to have been the liturgical practice in

[1] See Förster 1894, p. 4, and Smetana 1959, p. 190.

England,[2] whereas Ælfric rather firmly presents the reading as verses 1–7, with the remaining three verses as an addendum. Ælfric renders Gregory's wording fairly closely and follows the outlines of his structure, though omitting the final exemplum and a fair amount of repetition and Biblical illustration.

Sources and Notes

The following texts are cited below:
1. Gregory the Great, *Homiliae in Evangelia*, PL 76, Hom. 34, cols. 1246–59.
2. Haymo of Auxerre, *Homiliae de Tempore*, PL 118, Hom. 114, cols. 609–15.

2–15 A fairly free rendering of Lc 15.1–7:

(1) Erant autem appropinquantes ei publicani, et peccatores ut audirent illum. (2) Et murmurabant Pharisaei, et scribae, dicentes: Quia hic peccatores recipit, et manducat cum illis. (3) Et ait ad illos parabolam istam dicens: (4) Quis ex vobis homo, qui habet centum oves; et si perdiderit unam ex illis, nonne dimittit nonaginta novem in deserto, et vadit ad illam quae perierat, donec inveniat eam? (5) Et cum invenerit eam, imponit in humeros suos gaudens: (6) et veniens domum convocat amicos et vicinos, dicens illis: Congratulamini mihi, quia inveni ovem meam, quae perierat? (7) Dico vobis quod ita gaudium erit in caelo super uno peccatore poenitentiam agente, quam super nonaginta novem iustis, qui non indigent poenitentia.

On the rendering of *publicani* as *gerefan* see the note on CH II 28.6–7; the *OE Gospels* have *manfulle*, 'sinful', and the Lindisfarne and Rushworth Gospels *bærsynnigo*, 'openly sinful'.

16–20 Gregory, Hom. 34, PL 76, 1246CD:

Audistis in lectione evangelica, fratres mei, quia peccatores et publicani accesserunt ad redemptorem nostrum; et non solum ad colloquendum, sed etiam ad convescendum recepti sunt. Quod videntes Pharisaei, dedignati sunt. Ex qua re colligite quia vera iustitia compassionem habet, falsa iustitia dedignationem.

20–3 Gregory, Hom. 34, PL 76, 1247B:

Sed quia aegri erant ita ut aegros se esse nescirent, quatenus quod erant agnoscerent, coelestis eos medicus blandis fomentis curat, benignum paradigma obiicit, et in eorum corde vulneris tumorem premit.

25–30 Gregory, Hom. 34, PL 76, 1247BC:

Quia centenarius perfectus est numerus, ipse centum oves habuit cum angelorum substantiam et hominum creavit. Sed una ovis tunc periit quando peccando homo pascua vitae dereliquit. Dimisit autem nonaginta

[2] See Lenker, p. 327.

novem oves in deserto, quia illos summos angelorum choros reliquit in coelo. . . . In deserto nonaginta novem oves remanserant, quando in terra Dominus unam quaerebat.

30–40 Gregory, Hom. 34, PL 76, 1247D-8A:

Ovem in humeris suis imposuit, quia humanam naturam suscipiens peccata nostra ipse portavit. . . . Inventa ove ad domum redit, quia Pastor noster, reparato homine, ad regnum coeleste rediit. Ibi amicos et vicinos invenit, illos videlicet angelorum choros qui amici eius sunt, quia voluntatem eius continue in sua stabilitate custodiunt. Vicini quoque eius sunt, quia claritate visionis illius sua assiduitate perfruuntur.

41–5 Gregory, Hom. 34, PL 76, 1248A:

Et notandum quod non dicit Congratulamini inventae ovi, sed Mihi, quia videlicet eius gaudium est vita nostra, et cum nos ad coelum reducimur, solemnitatem laetitiae eius implemus.

For *eius—nostra* Haymo (Hom. 114, PL 118, 612B) has *nostra salus illius est gaudium*, which is slightly closer to Ælfric's *ure alysednyss is his blis*.

48–59 Gregory, Hom. 34, PL 76, 1248A-D:

[§4] Considerandum nobis est, fratres mei, cur Dominus plus de conversis peccatoribus quam de stantibus iustis in coelo gaudium esse fateatur, nisi hoc quod ipsi per quotidianum visionis experimentum novimus, quia plerumque . . . pigri remanent ad exercenda bona praecipua, quia valde sibi securi sunt quod nulla commiserint mala graviora. At contra nonnunquam hi qui se aliqua illicita egisse meminerunt, ex ipso suo dolore compuncti, . . . [§5] Cuncta licita respuunt, . . . contemnunt visibilia, invisibilibus accenduntur, lamentis gaudent, in cunctis semetipsos humiliant; . . . [§4] et quia se errasse a Deo considerant, damna praecedentia lucris sequentibus recompensant.

The phrases in §5 actually describe the righteous penitents whom Ælfric turns to in lines 68–72, rather than the former sinners.

59–63 Not in Gregory (or Haymo or Smaragdus).

63–8 Gregory, Hom. 34, PL 76, 1248C:

Maius ergo de peccatore converso quam de stante iusto gaudium fit in coelo, quia et dux in praelio plus eum militem diligit, qui, post fugam reversus, hostem fortiter premit, quam illum qui nunquam terga praebuit, et nunquam aliquid fortiter gessit. Sic agricola illam amplius terram amat quae post spinas uberes fruges profert, quam eam quae nunquam spinas habuit et nunquam fertilem messem producit.

68–75 Gregory, Hom. 34, PL 76, 1248CD:

Sed inter haec sciendum est quia sunt plerique iusti, in quorum vita tantum est gaudium, ut eis quaelibet peccatorum poenitentia praeponi nullatenus possit. Nam multi et nullorum sibi malorum sunt conscii, et tamen in tanti ardoris afflictione se exerunt, ac si peccatis omnibus coangustentur. . . . Quid itaque istos dixerim, nisi et iustos et poenitentes. . . . Hinc ergo colligendum est quantum Deo gaudium faciat quando humiliter plangit iustus, si facit in coelo gaudium quando hoc quod male gessit et per poenitentiam damnat iniustus.

76–7 Referring to Lc 15.8–10:

(8) Aut quae mulier habens dragmas decem si perdiderit dragmam unam nonne accendit lucernam et everrit domum et quaerit diligenter donec inveniat? (9) Et cum invenerit convocat amicas et vicinas dicens congratulamini mihi quia inveni dragmam quam perdideram. (10) Ita dico vobis gaudium erit coram angelis Dei super uno peccatore poenitentiam agente.

Gregory continues with a commentary on these verses, which had formed part of his original text, and discusses the interpretation of the woman and the lamp in §6. Ælfric briefly summarises the three verses and turns directly to the interpretation of the ten coins. The *OE Gospels* agree in rendering drachmas as *scyllingas*, where the Lindisfarne and Rushworth Gospels use *sceattas*.

77–84 Gregory, Hom. 34, PL 76, 1249CD:

Decem vero drachmas habuit mulier, quia novem sunt ordines angelorum. Sed ut compleretur electorum numerus, homo decimus est creatus. . . . Novem vero angelorum ordines diximus, quia videlicet esse, testante sacro eloquio, scimus angelos, archangelos, virtutes, potestates, principatus, dominationes, thronos, cherubim, atque seraphim.

Ælfric adds two extensive references to the fallen angels who had originally formed the tenth order, lines 78–81 and 83–4. Perhaps coincidentally, Haymo adds a similar reference in expanding Gregory's second sentence (Haymo, Hom. 114, PL 118, 613D):

Decimus enim per superbiam cecidit. Sed ut electorum numerus compleretur, ad illius restaurationem homo decimus creatus est.

The notion that mankind was created to fill the gap left by the fallen angels does not appear in Gregory's homily, perhaps because it suggests a different (and Augustinian: cf *De Civitate Dei*, XXII.1) theory that the number of mankind to be saved would match the number of angels who fell rather than those who remained. Gregory now goes on to cite the Biblical evidence for these nine orders.

85 Gregory, Hom. 34, PL 76, 1250C:

Graeca etenim lingua angeli nuntii, archangeli vero summi nuntii, vocantur.

Gregory explains with illustrations that the name 'angel' thus refers to a function rather than the nature of angels. In §9 he considers the names and functions of three individual angels, Michael, Gabriel and Raphael.

86–9 Gregory, Hom. 34, PL 76, 1251CD:

Virtutes etenim vocantur illi nimirum spiritus, per quos signa et miracula frequentius fiunt. Potestates etiam vocantur hi qui hoc potentius caeteris in suo ordine perceperunt, ut eorum ditioni virtutes adversae subiectae sint, quorum potestate refrenantur, ne corda hominum tantum tentare praevaleant quantum volunt.

Virtutes adversae, 'adverse strengths' is a curiously oblique term but Gregory presumably is alluding to the fallen angels, as Ælfric concludes.

89–93 Gregory, Hom. 34, PL 76, 1251D-2A:

Principatus etiam vocantur qui ipsis quoque bonis angelorum spiritibus praesunt, qui subiectis aliis dum quaeque sunt agenda disponunt, eis ad explenda divina ministeria principantur. . . . Ea ergo angelorum agmina, quae mira potentia praeeminent, pro eo quod eis caetera ad obediendum subiecta sunt, dominationes vocantur.

92–5 Gregory, Hom. 34, PL 76, 1252A:

Throni Dei dicti sunt hi qui tanta divinitatis gratia replentur, ut in eis Dominus [*earlier* Deus omnipotens] sedeat, et per eos sua iudicia decernat.

95–102 Gregory, Hom. 34, PL 76, 1252AB:

Cherubim quoque plenitudo scientiae dicitur. Et sublimiora illa agmina idcirco cherubim vocata sunt, quia tanto perfectiori scientia plena sunt, quanto claritatem Dei vicinius contemplantur; ut, secundum creaturae modum, eo plene omnia sciant, quo visione conditoris sui per meritum dignitatis appropinquant. . . . Seraphim namque ardentes vel incendentes vocantur. Quae, quia ita Deo coniuncta sunt ut inter haec et Deum nulli alii spiritus intersint, tanto magis ardent, quanto hunc vicinius vident. Quorum profecto flamma amor est.

103–9 Gregory, Hom. 34, PL 76, 1252BC:

Superna illa civitas ex angelis et hominibus constat, ad quam tantum credimus humanum genus ascendere, quantos illic contigit electos angelos remansisse. . . . Distincte namque conversationes hominum singulorum agminum ordinibus congruunt, et in eorum sortem per conversationis similitudinem deputantur.

109–15 Gregory, Hom. 34, PL 76, 1252CD:

Sunt plerique qui parva capiunt, sed tamen haec eadem parva pie annuntiare fratribus non desistunt. Isti itaque in angelorum numerum currunt. Et sunt nonnulli qui, divinae largitatis munere refecti, secretorum coelestium summa et capere praevalent, et nuntiare. Quo ergo isti nisi inter archangelorum numerum deputantur?

Ælfric makes a similar distinction between different levels of understanding and teaching at CH II.38.54 ff.

115–20 Gregory, Hom. 34, PL 76, 1252D-3A:

Et sunt alii qui mira faciunt, signa valenter operantur. Quo ergo isti nisi ad supernarum virtutum sortem et numerum congruunt? Et sunt nonnulli qui etiam de obsessis corporibus malignos spiritus fugant, eosque virtute orationis . . . eiiciunt. Quo itaque isti meritum suum nisi inter potestatum coelestium numerum sortiuntur?

122–32 Gregory, Hom. 34, PL 76, 1253A:

Et sunt nonnulli qui acceptis virtutibus etiam electorum hominum merita transcendunt. . . . Quo ergo isti sortem suam nisi inter principatuum numeros acceperunt? Et sunt nonnulli qui sic in semetipsis cunctis vitiis omnibusque desideriis dominantur, ut ipso iure munditiae dii inter homines vocentur; unde et ad Moysen dicitur: 'Ecce constitui te deum Pharaonis' (Exod 7.1). Quo ergo [etsi, quorum comparatione caeteri homines, ut ita dicam, servi sunt,*] nisi inter numeros dominationum currunt? [**Variant from PL 76*]

132–9 Gregory, Hom. 34, PL 76, 1253AB:

Et sunt nonnulli qui, dum sibimetipsis vigilanti cura dominantur . . . Quorum profecto mentibus dum divina contemplatio praesto est, in his velut in throno suo Dominus praesidens, aliorum facta examinat, et cuncta mirabiliter de sua sede dispensat. Quid ergo isti nisi throni sui conditoris sunt. . . . Et sunt nonnulli qui tanta Dei ac proximi dilectione pleni sunt, ut cherubim iure nominentur. Quia enim, ut praefati sumus, cherubim plenitudo scientiae dicitur, et Paulo dicente didicimus quia 'plenitudo legis est caritas' (Rom 13.10). . . .

In 138–9 there is perhaps an echo of Mt 22.37–40 (cf the wording at CH II.19.7).

140–6 Gregory, Hom. 34, PL 76, 1253C:

Et sunt nonnulli qui supernae contemplationis facibus accensi in solo conditoris sui desiderio anhelant . . . terrena quaeque abiiciunt, cuncta temporalia mente transcendunt, amant et ardent, atque . . . loquendo et alios accendunt et quos verbo tangunt, ardere protinus in Dei amore faciunt. . . . Qui ergo ita ad amorem sui conditoris inflammati sunt quo nisi inter seraphim numerum sortem suae vocationis acceperunt?

147–56 Gregory, Hom. 34, PL 76, 1254AB:

Videte si in numero horum agminum quae breviter tangendo perstrinximus, sortem vestrae vocationis invenitis. Vae autem animae quae in se de his bonis quae enumeravimus minime aliquid recognoscit, eique adhuc vae deterius imminet, si et privatam se donis intelligit, et nequaquam gemit. . . . Qui in se donorum gratiam minime recognoscit gemat. Qui vero in se minora cognoscit, aliis maiora non invideat, quia et supernae illae distinctiones beatorum spirituum ita sunt conditae, ut aliae aliis sint praelatae.

The arguments are not very close here. Gregory seems to be taking the notion of these virtues as a gift of grace very strictly, almost as a fixed destiny, and can only call on those who are deprived of them to weep; Ælfric prefers to envisage the possibility of desiring God to change their lot. Similarly, Gregory presents the hierarchies of the elect as part of a system parallel to the hierarchies of angels, while Ælfric suggests that God awards different degrees of virtue according to the degrees of zeal (*gecnyrdnyssum*).

157–64 Gregory, Hom. 34, PL 76, 1254C:

Per Danielem dicitur: 'Millia millium ministrabant ei, et decies millies centena millia assistebant ei' (Dan 7.10). Aliud namque est ministrare, aliud assistere, quia hi administrant Deo, qui et ad nos nuntiando exeunt; assistunt vero qui sic contemplatione intima perfruuntur, ut ad explenda foras opera minime mittantur.

Gregory invokes the quotation from Daniel to support his distinction (based on Dionysius the Areopagite) between the lesser orders of angels who leave God's presence to take his messages to man or fulfil his commands on earth (who thus number a thousand thousand, or one million) and the higher orders who never leave his presence (who form the ten thousand times a hundred thousand, or one thousand million). Ælfric is perhaps more interested in the sheer multitude of heavenly spirits.

164–9 Gregory, Hom. 34, PL 76, 1255AB:

Cum ad nos veniunt, sic exterius implent ministerium, ut tamen nunquam desint interius per contemplationem. Et mittuntur igitur, et assistunt, quia etsi circumscriptus est angelicus spiritus, summus tamen spiritus ipse, qui Deus est, circumscriptus non est. Angeli itaque et missi, et ante ipsum sunt, quia quolibet missi veniant, intra ipsum currunt.

169–83 Based on Gregory §14 (Hom. 34, PL 76, 1255BC) but much rearranged:

[*Ælfric* 173–4] Tamen per Psalmistam dicitur: 'Qui sedes super cherubim, apparere' (Ps 79.2). . . . [169–72] Specialia quaedam singulorum sunt, ut tamen sint communia omnium; et quod in se ex parte quisque habet, hoc in alio ordine totum possidet. [182–3] Sed idcirco uno eodemque vocabulo communiter non censentur, ut ille ordo vocari privato uniuscuiusque rei nomine debeat, qui hanc in munere plenius accepit. [178–82] Seraphim namque incendium diximus, et tamen amore conditoris simul omnes ardent. Cherubim vero plenitudinem scientiae, et tamen quis ibi aliquid nesciat ubi ipsum omnes simul fontem scientiae Deum vident? [175–7] Throni quoque illa agmina quibus conditor praesidet vocantur, sed beatus esse quis potest, nisi Creator suus eius menti praesideat?

A difficult passage. As in the rest of this discussion, Gregory organises the material as a dialectic, posing objections to his arguments, countering them and producing a new synthesis, while Ælfric orders the material to present the full complexity in all possible clarity and logical order.

184–92 The opening words owe something to the beginning of the next passage in Gregory (Hom. 34, PL 76, 1255D-6A):

> Taceamus interim de secretis coeli [*earlier* coelestium civium secreta], sed ante conditoris oculos manu poenitentiae tergamus maculas pulveris nostri.

But the rest does not derive from him. The quotation is from Jn 14.2: *In domo patris mei mansiones multae sunt*. The sentiments are entirely Ælfric's: a similar and equally independent emphasis on the multitude who are to be saved appears in CH I.35.274 ff and II.5.183 ff. His reference to the multitude of angels at 157 is perhaps relevant, since as he has earlier stated, an equal number of humans will be saved.

193–7 Gregory, Hom. 34, PL 76, 1256A:

> Ecce ipsa divina misericordia pollicetur, dicens: 'Gaudium erit in coelo super uno peccatore poenitentiam agente'; et tamen per prophetam Dominus dicit: 'Quia quacunque die iustus peccaverit, omnes iustitiae eius in oblivione erunt coram me' (Ez 33.12–13).

Ælfric's version perhaps shows familiarity with the rest of verses 12–13, and he goes on to paraphrase verses 14 and 16 of Ezechiel, which are not cited by Gregory (Ez 33.14, 16):

> (14) Si autem dixero impio: Morte morieris, et egerit poenitentiam a peccato suo, feceritque iudicium et iustitiam . . . (16) omnia peccata eius, quae peccavit, non imputabuntur ei.

A similar quotation is used at this point by Haymo, in place of the one used by Gregory about the just (Haymo, Hom. 114, PL 118, 615B):

> In quacunque die peccator conversus fuerit, et ingemuerit, peccata illius oblivioni tradentur.

197–210 Gregory continues in §§15–17 to discuss sin and repentance, and gives as an illustration in §18 the story of a repentant sinner who becomes an exemplary monk, but none of this seems particularly close to Ælfric's final section. His 207–8 is perhaps suggested by Gregory's conclusion (Hom. 34, PL 76, 1258D-9A):

> Praebet apud Deum homini fiduciam Deus homo. Est nobis spes magna poenitentibus, quia advocatus noster factus est iudex noster.

Lines 205–7 quote Jn 5.14: *Ecce sanus factus es; iam noli peccare, ne deterius tibi aliquid contingat* (part of the Gospel passage which Ælfric discusses in detail in Pope 2). Lines 203–4, that true repentance involves not sinning again, are the burden of much of Gregory's §15; cf, e.g. *Poenitentiam quippe agere est et perpetrata mala plangere, et plangenda non perpetrare* (Hom. 34, PL 76, 1256B). Several of the points, including the paraphrase of Ezekiel above, recur in Ælfric's piece on penitence in Lent, printed Thorpe, II.602 ff.

25 NATIVITY OF ST JOHN THE BAPTIST

John the Baptist had, as Ælfric points out, a unique status in the early church, the greatest of men born of women according to Christ's own words and the only figure, apart from Christ himself and the Virgin Mary, to have his day of birth marked by the church as well as the date of his death. The homily describes his life and preaching and attempts to explain that special status and the significance of John's role. It begins with a narrative of his birth and life (lines 1–49) freely based on the Bible. The usual text for the occasion seems to have been Luke 1.57–68, the verses covering the actual birth of John, but Ælfric extends back to incorporate the events of his miraculous conception, Luke 1.5–17 (the reading for the Vigil of the feast), and forward to cover John's baptising and preaching, based on Luke 3.1–4 and details in the other Gospels. He then explains the nature of John's baptism (lines 49–56) and the reason for celebrating the nativity of Christ, John and the Virgin (lines 56–88) before commenting on various aspects of the Biblical account of John's birth (lines 88–134). After a brief digression on the figurative names for Christ (lines 135–48) he turns to the theme of ascetism, presenting John as the founder of the ascetic life and applying Matthew 11.12 allegorically to the virtues of abstinence (lines 149–84). Finally he returns to the account of John's preaching at Luke 3.5–6 and offers an allegorical exegesis. The homily ranges over a variety of topics but the underlying theme is perhaps the high status of John the Baptist and especially his role as representative and indeed inaugurator of the ascetic life.

The question of sources is unusually complex. Paul the Deacon's homiliary provided two homilies by Bede, II.19 and 20, the former on Luke 1.5–17 and the latter on Luke 1.57–68, and a more general sermon by Augustine, Serm. 292. Ælfric would also have known the exegetical homilies for the occasion included by Haymo and Smaragdus, both on Luke 1.57–68, and there are a number of other general sermons by Augustine (nos. 287–93) or attributed to him (Ps-Augustine, nos. 196–200) which are similar in general approach to Ælfric and may have been known to him. Förster suggested as sources the two Bede homilies and Gregory's homily 20 on John's preaching (based on Luke 3.1–11), and Smetana added Ps-Augustine 196 and Haymo's homily.[1] There are indeed fairly extensive parallels with both Ps-Augustine 196 and Gregory 20 (which appears in PD for the period before Christmas), as well as looser but quite extended similarities to Bede II.20 and slighter parallels to passages in Haymo and the other text by Bede and in several of the Augustinian and Ps-Augustinian sermons. But there is much for which no parallels can be found and the connections are seldom of the close and extensive kind that normally appears between Ælfric's work and his sources, and this may well be a case where he was

[1] Förster 1894, pp. 9 and 21; Smetana 1959, pp. 190–1; Smetana 1961, pp. 465–6.

using another Latin text, yet to be found, which had already combined many of these sources.

Sources and Notes

The following texts are cited below:

1. Augustine, *In Iohannis Evangelium Tractatus CXXIV*, ed. R. Willems, CCSL 36 (Turnhout, 1954).
2. Augustine, *Sermones*, PL 38, Serm. 288, cols. 1302–8.
3. Ps-Augustine, *Sermones*, PL 39, Serm.196, 197 and 199 [= Augustine, *Sermones suppositi*], cols. 2110–3, 2113–5 and 2117–8.
4. Bede, *Homiliae*, ed. D. Hurst, CCSL 122 (Turnhout, 1955), Hom. II.19 (pp. 318–27) and Hom. II.20 (pp. 328–34).
5. Gregory the Great, *Homiliae in Evangelia*, PL 76, Hom. 7 and 20, cols. 1099–1103 and 1159–70.
6. Haymo of Auxerre, *Homiliae de Sanctis*, PL 118, Hom. 2, cols. 755–9.
7. *The Old English Martyrology*, ed. G. Kotzor, *Das altenglische Martyrologium*, 2 vols., Bayerische Akademie der Wissenschaften, philos.-hist. Klasse ns 88.1–2 (Münich, 1981).
8. Paschasius Radbertus, *De Partu Virginis*, ed. E. A. Matter, CCCM 56C (Turnhout, 1985), pp. 47–89.
9. Rabanus Maurus, *Homiliae in Evangelia*, PL 110, Hom. 102, cols. 337–9.

3–27 A rendering of Lc 1.5–24, close in parts but freely paraphrasing some verses, especially 8–11 and 21–3:

> [For 3–7:] (5) Fuit in diebus Herodis, regis Iudaeae, sacerdos quidam nomine Zacharias de vice Abia, et uxor illius de filiabus Aaron, et nomen eius Elisabeth. (6) Erant autem iusti ambo ante Deum, incedentes in omnibus mandatis et iustificationibus Domini sine querela, (7) et non erat illis filius, eo quod esset Elisabeth sterilis, et ambo processissent in diebus suis.
>
> [8–20:] (8) Factum est autem . . .(9) . . . ingressus in templum Domini: . . .(11) Apparuit autem illi angelus Domini . . . (13) Ait autem ad illum angelus: Ne timeas Zacharia, quoniam exaudita est deprecatio tua: et uxor tua Elisabeth pariet tibi filium, et vocabis nomen eius Iohannem: (14) et erit gaudium tibi, et exsultatio, et multi in nativitate eius gaudebunt: (15) erit enim magnus coram Domino: et vinum et siceram non bibet, et Spiritu Sancto replebitur adhuc ex utero matris suae: (16) et multos filiorum Israhel convertet ad Dominum Deum ipsorum: (17) et ipse praecedet ante illum in spiritu et virtute Eliae: ut convertat corda patrum in filios, et incredulos ad prudentiam iustorum, parare Domino plebem perfectam.

> [21–27:] (18) Et dixit Zacharias ad angelum: Unde hoc sciam? ego enim sum senex, et uxor mea processit in diebus suis. (19) Et respondens angelus dixit ei: Ego sum Gabriel, qui asto ante Deum: et missus sum loqui ad te, et haec tibi evangelizare. (20) Et ecce eris tacens, et non poteris loqui usque in diem quo haec fiant, pro eo quod non credidisti verbis meis, quae implebuntur in tempore suo. . . . (22) Egressus autem non poterat loqui ad illos . . . et permansit mutus. (23) Et factum est, ut . . . abiit in domum suam: (24) post hos autem dies concepit Elisabeth uxor eius. . . .

The Biblical account gives prominence to Zacharias's role as priest and carefully sets the scene in the temple, with the people expectantly waiting outside while he enters the inner sanctum and converses with the angel. Bede's exegesis also makes much of his priestly office and functions. But Ælfric carefully excludes all reference to his priesthood (unless there is a hint in the phrase *godes þegn*, 4), saying only that Zacharias went to the temple to pray, and presumably for the same reason omits reference to the waiting people. His phrase *æfter feawum dagum* at 26 carefully but silently alludes to the period during which Zacharias was completing his period of duty as priest. Ælfric's briefer discussion of the birth of John in CH I.13 is similarly free of allusion to the priestly office of Zacharias. Possibly he was reluctant to remind his listeners of a further precedent for the marriage of priests, a controversial subject in his time (he discusses and discounts the case of St Peter in his preface to Genesis and his pastoral letters).

The one other point worth noting in this paraphrase is the rendering of *sicera* as 'those liquids by which men become drunk' (line 15). The various Old English translations and glosses of the Gospels all give *beor*. Ælfric was presumably familiar with a tradition recorded by Rabanus Maurus (Hom. 102, PL 110, 339B):

> Sicera interpretatur ebrietas, quo vocabulo Hebraei omne quod inebriare potest poculum . . . significant.

27–40 A translation and paraphrase of Lc 1.57–68 (thus omitting the annunciation and salutation, verses 26–56, dealt with in CH I.13):

> [For 27–34:] (57) Elisabeth autem impletum est tempus pariendi, et peperit filium. (58) Et audierunt vicini et cognati eius quia magnificavit Dominus misericordiam suam cum illa, et congratulabantur ei. (59) Et factum est in die octavo, venerunt circumcidere puerum, et vocabant eum nomine patris sui Zachariam. (60) Et respondens mater eius, dixit: Nequaquam, sed vocabitur Iohannes. (61) Et dixerunt ad illam: Quia nemo est in cognatione tua, qui vocetur hoc nomine. (62) Innuebant autem patri eius, quem vellet vocari eum. (63) Et postulans pugillarem scripsit, dicens: Iohannes est nomen eius. . . . (64) Apertum est autem illico os eius, et lingua eius, et loquebatur benedicens Deum.
>
> [For 34–39:] (65) Et factus est timor super omnes vicinos eorum: et super omnia montana Iudaeae divulgabantur omnia verba haec: (66) et posuerunt

> omnes qui audierant in corde suo, dicentes: Quis, putas, puer iste erit? Etenim manus Domini erat cum illo. (67) Et Zacharias pater eius repletus est Spiritu Sancto: et prophetavit, dicens: (68) Benedictus Dominus Deus Israhel, quia visitavit, et fecit redemptionem plebis suae.

Ælfric omits the rest of Zacharias's hymn (vv. 69–79).

41–49 The account of John's subsequent life is pieced together from various Biblical details. Lines 41–3 expand Lc 1.80:

> Puer autem crescebat, et confortabatur spiritu: et erat in desertis usque in diem ostensionis suae ad Israhel.

The notion that John fled the proximity of people and worldly sins is perhaps a natural expansion of the Biblical statement that he dwelt in the desert, but the point is made by Bede in the source-passage for lines 108–10 below. The clothing of camel's hair comes from Mt 3.4 (= Mc 1.6): *Iohannes habebat vestimentum de pilis camelorum*. The drink (lines 44–5) comes from Lc 1.15, already paraphrased above. The food comes from Mt 3.4 (= Mc 1. 6): *Locustae et mel silvestre*. The *OE Gospels* render *locustae* as *gærstapan*, 'grasshoppers', presumably as the nearest native equivalent to the locust. Ælfric's *ofet* reflects the alternative interpretation of *locustae* as the locust-bean. (Cf further Cross 1975.) The final sentence, lines 46–9, is based on Lc 3.1–4:

> (1) Anno autem quintodecimo imperii Tiberii Caesaris . . . (2) . . . factum est verbum Domini super Iohannem, Zachariae filium in deserto. (3) Et venit in omnem regionem Iordanis, praedicans baptismum poenitentiae in remissionem peccatorum, (4) sicut scriptum est in libro sermonum Isaiae prophetae.

50–56 The careful distinction between John's baptism and Christ's probably comes from Gregory, Hom. 20, PL 76, 1160D-61A:

> Cunctis legentibus liquet quia Iohannes . . . baptismum suum in remissionem peccatorum dare non potuit. . . . sicut incarnatum verbum patris praecurrebat verbo praedicationis, ita baptismum poenitentiae, quo peccata solvuntur, praecurreret suo baptismate, quo peccata solvi non possunt.

The point is developed more fully in CH II.3.

57–66 The point that John's birth is to be celebrated because of the miracles which accompanied it is expressed in the opening lines of Bede's homily II.20, and the account of the miracles is similar (Hom. II.20, 1– 8):

> Praecursoris domini nativitas . . . multa miraculorum sublimitate refulget. . . . Senes ac diu infecundi parentes dono nobilissimae prolis exultant, ipsi patri quem incredulitas mutum reddiderat ad salutandum novae praeconem gratiae os et lingua reseratur.

Ælfric adds references to the visitation.

67–79 Bede goes on to say that it is right therefore that, whereas other saints have their death-day celebrated, John alone, apart from Christ, has his birthday marked by the church. This is indeed a commonplace of homilies on John, appearing in several Augustinian and Ps-Augustinian sermons. Ælfric properly extends the idea to include the Virgin Mary, whose nativity had been celebrated in Rome and in England since the seventh century. Yet parallels for this extension are hard to find. The Blickling homilist anachronistically repeats the formulation of Augustine. The only reference to the three nativities which Mary Clayton was able to find prior to Ælfric[2] is in Paschasius Radbertus, *De Partu Virginis* (1.195–6): *Nullius igitur nativitas celebratur in mundo, nisi Christi et eius atque beati Ioannis*; but there is no evidence that Ælfric knew this work and the wording and argument are not similar. Ælfric may have independently extended the formulation which he found in his Latin sources. Of these, the closest in detail is Ps-Augustine, Serm. 196, §1 (PL 39, 2111):

> Post illum sacrosanctum Domini natalem diem, nullius hominis nativitatem legimus celebrari, nisi solius beati Iohannis Baptistae. In aliis sanctis et electis Dei novimus illum diem coli, quo illos post consummationem laborum, et devictum trumphatumque mundum in perpetuas aeternitates praesens haec vita parturiit.

But Ælfric would seem to have considerably developed the argument, contrasting the day of birth into the troubled world with the day of death.

79–88 While the notion of the three nativities has a justification as liturgical fact, Ælfric faced some difficulties in adapting the explanations offered by earlier writers for John to cover Mary as well. To extend to Mary the argument that John's nativity was celebrated because his birth was of special significance and marked by miracles was implicitly to accept the apocryphal narratives of the Virgin's birth, something Ælfric was reluctant to do (cf his note *De Sancta Maria* on the nativity (*CH II*, p. 271), and Clayton 1990, pp. 246–7). Radbertus, indeed, argues from the existence of the festival of the Virgin's birth that she must, like Christ and John, have been born without sin. Ælfric avoids the problem by arguing instead that the liturgical celebration is a sign of the special status of the Baptist and Mary, next to Christ himself: John is the greatest of men born of women, his status shown by the miracles accompanying his birth and the austerity of his life, while Mary, too, is like no other human (line 85). The role of John as bridge between the Old Law and the New, lines 80–1, is a point frequently made; a possible source is Bede, Hom. II.19, 5–9 [though this merely paraphrases Augustine, Serm. 293, PL 38, 1328]:

> Horum ultimus et quasi limes quidam legis et evangelii figurae et veritatis Iohannes apparuit, domino attestante qui ait: 'Lex et prophetae usque ad Iohannem, ex eo regnum Dei evangelizatur' (Lc 16.16).

[2] Clayton 1983, p. 374.

For 85, Bede, Hom. II.20 (20–23) similarly quotes Lc 1.14 *et erit gaudium tibi et exultatio et multi in nativitate eius gaudebunt* in support of the festival, but there is no close similarity otherwise.

89–94 A similar point is made by Haymo, Hom. 2, PL 118, 756D-7A:

> Haec enim a marito non didicerat, quippe qui ex eo, quod sibi filium nasci non crediderat, mutus permanebat: sed quia ille ab angelo, ista didicerat a spiritu sancto.

94–6 The etymologies are similarly used by Bede, Hom. II.20, 109–116:

> Iohannes interpretatur Dei gratia sive in quo est gratia. Quo nomine et totam evangelicae dispensationis gratiam quam praedicabat et ipsum specialiter dominum per quem eadem gratia mundo donata est. . . . Unde bene Zacharias memoria domini interpretatur. . . .

96–100 The image of John as a messenger, from Mt 11.10, appears in many of the Latin sermons, but the image of the day-star is rare; a possible source is the Ps-Augustine sermon 199, §2 (PL 39, 2117):

> Surgat novus lucifer, quia iubar iam veri solis erumpit. Det vocem praeco, quia adest iudex; clamet tuba, quia venit rex.

(The sermon is also found among the works of Petrus Chrysologus, *Collectio Sermonum*, Serm. 91, CCSL 24, p. 566.) The same image is used in the *Old English Martyrology* (OE Martyrology, II.131) and Cross (1975) suggests Ps-Augustine, Serm. 199 as a possible source. The parallel with the Old Law and the New could be an expansion of the point made at 80–82, though similar wording is used in Ps-Augustine, Serm. 196, §3 (PL 39, 2111):

> Praemittitur ante Iesum Christum Iohannes, quasi testamentum vetus ante novum. . . . Praemittitur ergo lucerna ante solem, servus ante Dominum, amicus ante sponsum, praeco ante iudicem, vox ante verbum.

Precisely the same contrast between shadow and truth is made by Ælfric at CH II.4.65–6, prompted there by Bede.

101–8 Similar points contrasting John and Christ are made by Ps-Augustine, Serm. 197, §1 (PL 39, 2113–4), though organised differently:

> Illum enim sterilis peperit; istum virgo concepit. . . . Hominem concepit Elisabeth, et hominem Maria; sed Elisabeth solum hominem, Maria Deum et hominem. . . . Magnus igitur Iohannes, cuius magnitudini etiam Salvator testimonium perhibet, dicens: 'Non surrexit inter natos mulierum maior Iohanne Baptista' (Mt 11.11). . . . Iohannes enim natus mulieris, Christus autem virginis natus est.

The contrast between the times of year at which they were born perhaps derives from the sources for 118 ff.

108–14 Probably from Bede, Hom. II.20, 32–41:

> Iste peccatorum consortia declinans ab omni quod inebriare potest abstinebat, ille inter peccatores conversatus peccati omnis immunis

permansit. . . . Iste multos filiorum Israhel ad dominum suo tempore praedicando convertit, ille multos cotidie de universis per orbem nationibus ad suam fidem et caritatem interius illustrando convertere non desistit.

115–18 The commentary on the parallel with Elijah is to be found in Gregory's homily 7 (PL 76, 1100A):

Sicut Elias secundum Domini adventum praeveniet, ita Iohannes praevenit primum.

The comment recurs, slightly expanded, in Bede's homily II.19, 297–300.

118–34 Similar points are made by Bede, Hom. II.20, 61–71, but in a different order and more briefly:

Nec vacat a mysterio quod Iohannis nativitas cum dies decrescere domini autem cum dies crescere inchoat facta memoratur. Huius etenim secretum distantiae revelat ipse Iohannes qui cum prae magnitudine virtutum Christus crederetur a turbis, dominus autem prae infirmitate carnis a quibusdam non Christus sed esse propheta putaretur, 'Illum oportet', inquit, 'crescere me autem minui' (Jn 3.30). Crevit quippe dominus quia per totum orbem fidelibus quod Christus esset qui propheta credebatur innotuit. Decrevit ac minoratus est Iohannes quia qui Christus aestimabatur quod non Christus ipse sed praeco Christi esset apparuit.

135–8 The general point, that John was the last and greatest of the prophets because where others only prophesied Christ's coming John pointed to his presence, is common; Ps-Augustine, Serm. 196, §5 (PL 39, 2112) is close:

Hanc itaque gloriam beatus Iohannes Baptista non de longinquo, sicut reliqui prophetae; sed vicinus et proximus antecessit. Illi adventum regis ante multa tempora praedicaverunt, alii dixerunt, Quandoque venturus est; alii, Ecce cito venit: iste autem quem venturum praedixit, venisse monstravit.

The specific detail of pointing with the finger and the quotation from John 1 appears in Augustine, Serm. 288, §1 (PL 38, 1302):

Iam in terra praesentem mente discernens, digito ostendens . . . 'Ecce Agnus Dei, ecce qui tollit peccatum mundi'.

But the detail seems to have been common, appearing in the liturgy for the day and in the source for Ælfric's All Saints homily.

138–48 The discussion of the various names for Christ, prompted by John's reference to him as Lamb of God, is essentially a digression and has no parallel in the Latin sermons on John the Baptist (the discussions of voice and word, e.g. Ps-Augustine, Serm. 196, §4, seem unrelated). A possible influence is Augustine's Tractates on John, 13.5 and 46.3, where reference is made to Christ being called lion, lamb and word. Ælfric draws on Jn 1.1 for 142–3 and Apoc 5.5 for 146.

149–60 The quotation, lines 152–3, is from Mt 11.12:

> A diebus autem Iohannis Baptistae usque nunc, regnum caelorum vim patitur, et violenti rapiunt illud.

The verse is quoted in Ps-Augustine, Serm. 196, §6 (PL 39, 2112), with the same omission of *usque nunc* for the sake of the interpretation, and the subsequent commentary is close to Ælfric, but there is nothing to parallel his contrast between the ease of the Old Law and the rigour of the New or his analogy with contemporary politics, at 156–8. The notion that John the Baptist initiated the ascetic life (lines 149–51) is also without parallel in the sources, and seems a somewhat surprising point given the explicit parallels drawn with Elijah. For the interpretation of *Godes rice* as the church on earth, one might compare CH I.35 and II.5.37–8. Ælfric quotes and briefly interprets Mt 11.12 in a similar way in his pastoral letters, Fehr 2, §15 and II, §§ 20–22.

161–9 Cf Ps-Augustine, Serm. 196, §6, PL 39, 2112:

> Non, inquam, sine violentia fieri potest ut unusquisque iracundiam patientia, superbiam humilitate commutet; amore paupertatis, divitiarum ac sufficientiae affluentiam superet; vinolentiam sobrietate, luxuriam castitate condemnet; et homo subito in virum transformetur perfectum, et quodam modo alter reddatur ex altero; ac sic a talibus per violentiam regnum coeleste diripitur.

If this was Ælfric's source, his substitution of generosity for love of poverty suggests a concern with adapting the argument to a non-monastic audience.

170–77 Cf Ps-Augustine, Serm. 196, §7, PL 39, 2112–13:

> Duo autem sunt abstinentiae et crucis genera, unum corporale, aliud spirituale. Unum a potu atque epulis temperare, appetitum gulae a delectationibus et mollissimis suavitatibus coercere . . . sensum viriliter revocare, ac violenter abstrahere. Alterum abstinentiae et crucis genus est pretiosius atque sublimius, motus animi regere, et perturbationes illius modestiae tranquillitate placare, irae ac superbiae impetus quasi feram bestiam refrenare, litigare quotidie contra vitia sua, increpare se quadam censoria austeritate virtutis, et rixam quodam modo cum homine interiore conserere.

If this is indeed Ælfric's source, his *wærlice* (line 172) is presumably for *werlice* = 'bravely, in manly fashion', corresponding to *viriliter*, rather than *wærlice* 'warily'. This is in fact the reading of the two best manuscripts after A, viz. K and Q, and also of S, and K actually has *viriliter* above the word in the main hand, as if the scribe or a reviser of his exemplar (Ælfric himself perhaps) has seen the problem and marked the word accordingly. The other six manuscripts all have *wærlice* however, so the spelling was clearly not just an aberration of the scribe of MS A. In adapting Ps-Augustine, Ælfric has extended the image of anger and pride like a wild beast to all eight capital sins.

177–82 Ps-Augustine, Serm. 196, §7, PL 39, 2113:

Pretiosa haec in conspectu Dei et gloriosa crux, cogitationes malas in potestatem redigere, voluntates proprias abnegare . . . et regentis imperio subiugare; a sermone atque opere quo anima laeditur, tanquam a cibis noxiis abstinere. . . . Haec qui facit, perrupto passionis muro violenter ad coelorum regna conscendit.

182–4 Ps-Augustine, Serm. 196, §8, PL 39, 2113:

Adhuc et alio ordine regnum coelorum vim patitur, quando illud homines acquirunt quod angeli perdiderunt, quando illuc adoptati humiles ascendunt, unde superbi incolae ceciderunt.

185–9 Ælfric now returns to Luke 3, quoting the prophecy from Is 40.3 given in verses 4–5 and alluded to at lines 48–9 (Lc 3.4–5):

(4) Vox clamantis in deserto: parate viam Domini: rectas facite semitas eius: (5) omnis vallis implebitur: et omnis mons et collis humiliabitur: et erunt prava in directa, et aspera in vias planas.

189–97 Cf Gregory, Hom. 20, PL 76, 1161B:

Ideo vox a propheta vocatus est, quia verbum praeibat.

and Gregory, Hom. 7, PL 76, 1100B:

Prius vox sonat, ut verbum postmodum possit audiri. Iohannes ergo vocem se esse asserit, quia Verbum praecedit.

The explanation of word as the revelation of wisdom also appears in CH I.2.179, but there is no parallel in Ælfric's sources.

197–206 Gregory, Hom. 20, PL 76, 1161B:

Omnis qui fidem rectam et bona opera praedicat, quid aliud quam venienti Domino ad corda audientium viam parat? ut haec vis gratiae penetret, ut lumen veritatis illustret, ut rectas Deo semitas faciat dum mundas in animo cogitationes per sermonem bonae praedicationis format.

Ælfric expands the point, citing Jn 14.23:

Si quis diligit me, sermonem meum servabit, et Pater meus diliget eum, et ad eum veniemus, et mansionem apud eum faciemus.

206–9 Gregory, Hom. 20, PL 76, 1161BC:

Quid hoc loco vallium nomine nisi humiles, quid montium et collium nisi superbi homines designantur? In adventu ergo Redemptoris valles impletae, montes vero et colles humiliati sunt, qui iuxta eius vocem: 'Omnis qui se exaltat humiliabitur, et omnis qui se humiliat exaltabitur' (Lc 14.11 = Lc 18.14).

209–13 Cf Gregory, Hom. 20, PL 76, 1161C:

A montibus namque aqua dilabitur; quia superbas mentes veritatis doctrina deserit. Sed fontes in convallibus surgunt, quia mentes humilium verbum praedicationis accipiunt.

Ælfric's Biblical quotation from 'the prophet' is not easily identifiable; Cook (1898, p. 120) tentatively suggests Is 57.15: *Habitans . . . cum contrito et humili spiritu*.

213–17 Gregory, Hom. 20, PL 76, 1162D-3A:

> Prava directa fiunt cum malorum corda per iniustitiam detorta ad iustitiae regulam diriguntur. Et aspera in vias planas immutantur cum immites atque iracundae mentes per infusionem supernae gratiae ad lenitatem mansuetudinis redeunt.

Ælfric's imagery is difficult here. He introduces the curious image of the 'hooks' of unrighteousness which make men's hearts crooked, and then takes 'regula' not in its usual abstract sense but in the concrete sense of a ruler or straight edge (of the sort used in ruling margins, presumably).

218–26 Gregory continues with a detailed commentary on the rest of John's preaching, along the lines which Ælfric describes but is reluctant to follow, and then gives an interpretation of Matthew 11.12 quite different from the one which Ælfric offers at 149–84. Gregory does not refer to John's preaching to the inhabitants of hell, a feature which Ælfric presumably drew from the Gospel of Nicodemus tradition (see, for instance, the text in Cross 1996, p. 204).

26 ST PETER AND ST PAUL

For this occasion Ælfric provides the first of his two-part homilies, combining exposition of the Gospel text for the day with hagiographical narrative; subsequent examples are the homilies on St Paul, St Michael and St Andrew in the First Series and St Peter and St Matthew in the Second (the All Saints homily in the First Series has a similar pattern too). The form possibly originated with Ælfric: hagiographical narrative is uncommon generally in earlier homiliaries, and where it does occur (as occasionally in the St Père de Chartres collection, Rabanus Maurus and Blickling[1]) tends to be used alone.

The Gospel text is Matthew 16.13–19, where St Peter gives his great confession of faith in Christ as the son of the living God and Christ names him the rock on which he will build his church, giving him power of binding and unloosing. Ælfric's main source for his commentary, as he says, is Bede, whose homily on the text (Hom. I.20) is included in Paul the Deacon's homiliary for this occasion,[2] but he probably also used the homily by Hericus which is included under the same heading in late versions of the homiliary (it is in PL 95, cols. 1477–83); Hericus follows Bede closely but includes additional points that are occasionally closer to Ælfric. There are no signs that he used the

[1] See Clayton (1985a), who points out that in the monastic life homilies and narratives belonged to different parts of the daily round.

[2] Identified by Förster (1894, p. 21); cf Smetana 1959, p. 191.

homilies by Smaragdus and Haymo, both closely based on Bede's. Ælfric follows Bede in presenting Peter primarily as a representative figure, exemplifying true faith and receiving the keys of the kingdom on behalf of the whole church, but he does stress the apostle's continuing control over the gates of heaven (lines 79–81) and the continuing role of apostolic intercession (lines 88–90), and adds comments on a characteristic concern of his, the false gods (lines 42–5).

Hagiographical accounts of the passion of St Peter and St Paul exist in great profusion, and it is not easy to identify quite which version Ælfric used. The collection of saints' lives which he generally employed, the Cotton-Corpus legendary, has a narrative which begins with the details of St Peter's calling and his apostleship in the Gospels and Acts of the Apostles, then describes his missionary experiences and finally his conflict with Simon Magus in Rome and his martyrdom under Nero. But Ælfric could not accept this account as an authoritative one, for it reflects a tradition according to which St Peter and St Paul were not martyred on the same occasion; St Paul is entirely omitted from the story, and his sufferings and martyrdom are covered separately in the next item in the collection. Ælfric inherited an ecclesiastical tradition that the two apostles suffered together and were martyred on the same day, a point on which he twice insists in Latin notes appearing in MS K (see lines 156 and 275), as well as in the comment in English at 273–4.[3] Much of the material in the Cotton-Corpus narrative would even so have been adequate, but Ælfric rejected the whole account and turned elsewhere for material that is in many respects similar. He begins with just two sentences on St Peter's experiences before the events preceding his martyrdom, probably drawing on historical sources. The detailed account of Peter's conflict with Simon Magus comes from a letter purporting to be by one Marcellus, a former disciple of Simon Magus, incorporated in a legend of SS Nereus and Achilles which appears in the Cotton-Corpus legendary under their feast. Ælfric adapts this to third person narrative but otherwise follows it fairly closely (lines 108–55). The story from the entry of Paul to the martyrdom itself (lines 155–293) comes from a *Passio Petri et Pauli*[4] which begins with Paul's arrival in Rome to join Peter and covers the apostles' conflict with Simon Magus and their martyrdom. The author used the legend as a vehicle for discussion of doctrinal issues, particularly the problems raised by the extension of Christianity from Jews to Gentiles, and Ælfric omits virtually all of this discussion, but follows the narrative details fairly closely. Whether Ælfric himself combined the two sources or found them already fused is unclear, though no such combination of the Latin texts appears to have survived. If he was responsible for searching out and adding the additional material on Simon Magus from the letter of Marcellus, this shows an interest in the problems posed

[3] There is an excellent discussion by Zettel (1979, pp. 94–7 and 177–8), who suggests that it was the presence of the opposing tradition in the legendary which prompted these Latin notes.

[4] Both of these sources were identified by Förster (1892, p. 10).

by black magic and demonic powers which is evident too in the selection of material from the two sources, and this is a concern seen elsewhere in Ælfric's writing: the comments on Antichrist in the First Series preface, the digression on the powers of the devil and Antichrist in II.30 on Job, the remarks on the Egyptian conjurors in Pope 1.258, and the piece on Saul and the Witch of Endor in Pope 29. Ælfric presents Simon as part devil himself and therefore able to command devils to help him, much like Antichrist himself.[5]

The copy of this homily in MS C shows some striking alterations and additions to the text, but these appear to have nothing to do with Ælfric; for the sprinkling of small agreements with MS A which mark C's text as originating in the first or *α* phase of Ælfric's text, see *CH I*, p. 100.

Sources and Notes

The following texts are cited below:

1. Anon., *Rescriptum Marcelli*, ASS Maii III.9–10.
2. Anon., *Passio Sanctorum Apostolorum Petri et Pauli*, ed. R. A. Lipsius, in Lipsius and Bonnet, I.119–77. [Variant readings are incorporated from the apparatus where relevant.]
3. Bede, *Homiliae*, ed. D. Hurst, CCSL 122 (Turnhout, 1955), Hom. I.20 (pp. 141–7).
4. Hericus, *Homiliae in Circulum Anni*, ed. R. Quadri, CCCM 116B (Turnhout, 1994), Hom. II.23 (pp. 209–19).
5. Isidore, *De Ortu et Obitu Patrum*, ed. C. Chaparro Gómez (Paris, 1985).
6. Jerome, *De Viris Inlustribus*, ed. E. C. Richardson, Texte und Untersuchungen 14.1 (Leipzig, 1896), pp. 1–56.

3–16 Mt 16.13–19:

> Venit autem Iesus in partes Caesareae Philippi: et interrogabat discipulos suos, dicens: Quem dicunt homines esse filium hominis? (14) At illi dixerunt: Alii Iohannem Baptistam, alii autem Eliam, alii vero Hieremiam, aut unum ex prophetis. (15) Dicit illis Iesus: Vos autem quem me esse dicitis? (16) Respondens Simon Petrus dixit: Tu es Christus, filius Dei vivi. (17) Respondens autem Iesus, dixit ei: Beatus es, Simon Bar Iona: quia caro et sanguis non revelavit tibi, sed Pater meus, qui in caelis est. (18) Et ego dico tibi, quia tu es Petrus, et super hanc petram aedificabo ecclesiam meam, et portae inferi non praevalebunt adversum eam. (19) Et tibi dabo claves regni caelorum. Et quodcumque ligaveris super terram, erit ligatum et in caelis: et quodcumque solveris super terram, erit solutum et in caelis.

Ælfric silently translates Bar Jona as *culfran bearn*, 'son of the dove', and Petrus as *stænen*, 'of stone', incorporating the etymological explanations of the commentaries rather than giving the proper names of the Biblical text.

[5] See further Godden 1996, pp. 269–71.

17–22 Bede does indeed say that Philip the tetrarch built Caesarea Philippi: *Philippus . . . erat tetrarcha . . . statuens civitatem* (Hom. I.20,14–16) but he does not explain the name further. The details are in Hericus (Hom. II.23, 9–14):

> Philippus . . . in honorem Tiberii Caesaris civitatem statuit . . . quam Caesaream Philippi in memoriam sui nominis, pariterque in honorem Tiberii Caesaris appellari constituit.

Much the same words appear as an addition to Bede's comment in some manuscripts of the latter's homily, and it is possible that Ælfric saw them in his copy of Bede.

22–6 Based on two sentences of Bede's homily (Hom. I.20, 20–30):

> Non autem quasi nesciens sententiam de se vel discipulorum vel extraneorum inquirit sed ideo discipulos quid de se sentiant interrogat ut confessionem rectae fidei illorum digna mercede remuneret. . . . Ideo quid alii de se sentiant inquirit ut expositis primo sententiis errantium discipuli probarentur veritatem suae confessionis non de opinione vulgata sed de ipso percepisse dominicae revelationis archano.

Ælfric's *woruldmenn* (line 23) for *homines* reflects Bede's subsequent explanation that *homines* means those who are unaware of Christ's divinity, in contrast to the apostles.

28–33 Cf Bede, Hom. I.20, 43–6:

> Quasi ab hominum generalitate illos sequestrans et deos ac Dei filios per adoptionem iam factos insinuans iuxta illud psalmistae: 'Ego dixi dii estis et filii excelsi omnes' (Ps 81.6).

Ælfric uses the same Psalm verse at CH I.22.200–1, and there too, though at greater length, feels the need to add a comment to explain this troubling idea.

34–45 Cf Bede, Hom. I.20, 48–53:

> Deum vivum appellat ad distinctionem falsorum deorum quos vario delusa errore gentilitas vel de mortuis sibi hominibus instituit vel maiori dementia de insensibili materia quos adoraret creavit de qualibus canitur in psalmo: 'Simulacra gentium argentum et aurum opera manuum hominum. Os habent et non loquentur; [*Ælfric continues the quotation:* oculos habent, et non videbunt. Aures habent, et non audient; nares habent, et non odorabunt. Manus habent, et non palpabunt, pedes habent, et non ambulabunt; non clamabunt in gutture suo' (Ps 113.12–15)].

Ælfric continues further on the nature of the false gods and of the true God. This is a repeated theme in Ælfric's writing, with similar discussions in CH I.1 and a full account in Pope 21. In all three passages he identifies the gods with the *entas*; see the note to Pope 21.101–3 where Isidore is suggested as an influence.

46–50 A characteristic Ælfrician interjection on the Trinity.

52–5 Cf Bede, Hom. I.20, 78–86:

> Bar Iona Syriace, Latine dicitur filius columbae. Filius autem columbae recte vocatur apostolus Petrus, quia videlicet columba multum simplex est animal et ipse prudenti ac pia simplicitate dominum sequebatur . . . vel certe quia sanctus spiritus super dominum in columbae specie descendit, recte filius columbae nuncupatur qui spiritali gratia plenus exstitisse monstratur.

56–9 Neither Bede nor Hericus (nor any other commentator so far found) suggests anything resembling Ælfric's identification of flesh and blood with kindred, though it seems straightforward enough (Bede interprets them as 'men inflated with the wisdom of the flesh', Hom. I.20, 113–5). In his further comment Ælfric subsumes Bede's preceding explanation that the Father and the Spirit act as one.

60–73 See Bede, Hom. I.20, 122–34 for the first part:

> Petrus qui Simon ante ea dicebatur ob fortitudinem fidei et confessionis suae constantiam a domino Petri nomen accepit, quia videlicet illi firma ac tenaci mente adhaesit de quo scriptum est: 'Petra autem erat Christus' (1 Cor 10.4). Et super hanc petram, id est super dominum salvatorem . . . aedificatur ecclesia . . . apostolo adtestante qui ait 'Fundamentum enim aliud nemo potest ponere praeter id quod positum est, quod est Christus Iesus' (1 Cor 3.11).

Bede implies here that it was at this moment that Christ gave Simon the name Peter, but Hericus points out that this is unlikely since Simon is surnamed Peter from the time of his calling (Hom. II.23, 228 ff). Ælfric is perhaps influenced by Hericus, for he silently renders Petrus here as *stænen* as if it were a common noun and makes no reference to the name Petrus or the act of naming. If so, he implies a different view in his homily on St Andrew (I.38.156–61), where he says that Peter was called Simon before his conversion but Christ called him Peter because of his confession of faith when he said 'you are the son of the living God', implying that this was the moment of naming (though he gives a quite different etymology or meaning to the name Petrus, *oncnawende* or 'acknowledging', using the Hebrew rather than the Latin interpretation). The Second Series homily on St Peter similarly sees this as the moment of naming, but renders Christ's words *Petrus, þæt is stænen* (CH II.24.146 ff). Ælfric follows Bede in interpreting the rock as Christ, but agrees with Hericus in offering an alternative definition, as faith (Hom. II.23, 251–3):

> Sive 'super hanc petram', hoc est, super hanc fidem qua me filium Dei vivi confessus es, 'aedificabo ecclesiam meam'.

Thorpe reads *Se þe ne bytlað* . . . at 70–71 but there is no *ne* in any of the manuscripts and the text is I think right as it stands; the sense seems to be 'he who builds away from that foundation'.

72–8 Bede, Hom. I.20, 135–7, 144–8:

> Portae inferi doctrinae sunt nequam quae seducendo imprudentes ad inferos trahunt. [*For* leahtras *cf Hericus:* portas inferi vitia atque peccata

vocat] . . . Multae itaque sunt portae inferi sed harum nulla ecclesiae quae super petram fundata est praevalet, quia qui fidem Christi intimo cordis amore perceperit omne quicquid exterius periculi temptantis ingruerit facillime contemnit.

78–81 The reference to literal keys is from Hericus, who is otherwise following Bede here (Hericus, Hom. II.23, 282–6):

Claves regni caelorum non debemus pueriliter opinari cuiuscumque esse materiae, ut puta argenti vel auri, sed per claves ipsa discernendi scientia potentiaque signatur, qua dignos sciret in regnum recipere, indignos vero a beatitudine illius supernae felicitatis excludere.

In recasting this Ælfric seems to ascribe to St Peter a personal and continuing power over entry into heaven, though the point is then qualified by his subsequent discussion.

83–7 Bede, Hom. I.20, 165–71:

Quae solvendi ac ligandi potestas quamvis soli Petro data videatur a domino, absque ulla tamen dubietate noscendum est quia et ceteris apostolis datur ipso teste qui post passionis resurrectionisque suae triumphum apparens eis insufflavit et dixit omnibus: 'Accipite spiritum sanctum. Quorum remiseritis peccata remittuntur eis et quorum retinueritis retenta sunt' (Jn 20.22–3).

88–92 Cf Bede, Hom. I.20, 171–5:

Necnon etiam nunc in episcopis ac presbyteris omni ecclesiae officium idem committitur, ut videlicet agnitis peccantium causis quoscumque humiles ac vere paenitentes aspexerit hos iam a timore perpetuae mortis miserans absolvat.

In adapting this Ælfric reverses the two points and introduces the notion of a continuing role of absolution for the apostles, whereas it is only with reference to the absolution offered by the clergy that Bede (and Hericus) refer to present time and the need for penitence. His final clause of qualification, *gif he—healdað*, was perhaps prompted by the long attack on the abuse of clerical powers of absolution and damnation which Hericus develops at this point.

92–6 Bede, Hom. I.20, 185–91:

Sed ideo beatus Petrus qui Christum vera fide confessus est . . . specialiter claves regni caelorum . . . accepit, ut omnes per orbem credentes intellegant quia quicumque ab unitate fidei vel societatis illius quolibet modo semet ipsos segregant tales nec vinculis peccatorum absolvi nec ianuam possint regni caelestis ingredi.

98–100 Ælfric is perhaps referring to the Blickling version of the legend of SS Peter and Paul, though if so he is exaggerating somewhat to say that the legend is 'fully' narrated there (see Godden 1996, pp. 284–5).

100–109 The places where Peter preached are those cited in 1 Peter 1.1, with the addition of Italy, which is evident enough from the legend itself but is similarly added to the list by Isidore, *De Ortu et Obitu Patrum* (67.3). The figure of 25 years for Peter's time in Rome could have been taken from Isidore too, or from Jerome, *De Viris Inlustribus*, c. 1 (6.27–8): *Romam pergit ibique viginti quinque annis cathedram sacerdotalem tenuit*. The ten years between the death of Christ and Peter's arrival in Rome is not specified by either, but is deducible from the date Isidore gives for the martyrdom (see below, lines 273–5). The fact that Simon Magus was Peter's opponent throughout his journeying could perhaps have been drawn from the fuller version of the legend which Ælfric knew but rejected, and so could Simon's claim to be the son of God, though that is also mentioned later in the version used by Ælfric.

110–13 Ælfric now takes up the story from the Letter of Marcellus (*Rescriptum*, ASS Maii III.9–10, c.12):

> Subito in loco, in quo Petrum Simon arguebat, transibat vidua cum ingenti populo clamosisque vocibus et luctu, efferens unicum filium suum. Tunc ait Petrus ad populum, qui credebat Simoni: 'Accedite ad feretrum, et deponite illum qui mortuus ducitur: et qui eum suscitaverit huius vera fides esse credatur.'

113–7 *Rescriptum*, ASS Maii III.9–10, c.12:

> Quod cum fecisset populus, dixit Simon: 'Modo, si eum suscitavero, interficietis Petrum?' Responditque omnis turba: 'Vivum eum incendemus'. Tunc Simon invocatis omnibus daemoniis, ministerio eorum coepit agere, ut moveretur corpus. Quod populi videntes coeperunt clamare in laudem Simonis et in perniciem Petri.

117–22 *Rescriptum*, ASS Maii III.9–10, c.12:

> Tunc Petrus, vix impetrato silentio, ait ad populum: 'Si vivit, loquatur, ambulet, accipiat cibum, revertatur ad domum suam. Quod si hoc non fecerit a Simone, sciatis vos falli.' Ad haec populus una voce clamabat dicens: 'Si hoc non fecerit Simon, poenam quam Petro posuit ipse patiatur'. Simon vero fingens se iratum, fugam petebat. Populus vero tenuit eum cum ingenti exprobratione, et custodiebat eum.

123–8 *Rescriptum*, ASS Maii III.9–10, c.12:

> Tunc Petrus, expandens manus suas ad coelum, dixit: 'Domine Iesu Christe, qui nobis discipulis tuis dixisti: "Ite in nomine meo et daemonia eiicite, infirmos curate, et mortuos suscitate" (Mt 10.8), excita puerum istum: ut omnis haec turba cognoscat, quia tu es Deus, et non est alius praeter te, qui cum patre et spiritu sancto vivis et regnas in secula seculorum, Amen.'

128–33 *Rescriptum*, ASS Maii III.9–10, c.12:

> Exsurgens autem puer adorabat Petrum, dicens: 'Vidi Dominum Iesum Christum, iubentem angelis et dicentem: "Ad petitionem amici mei Petri,

restituatur orphanus viduae matri suae"'. Tunc omnis populus una voce clamabat: 'Unus est quem praedicat Petrus'. Simon vero transfiguravit se in caput caninum et coepit fugere. Populus autem tenuit eum et dum vellent eum in ignem mittere, misit se Petrus in medium, et liberavit eum dicens: 'Magister noster hoc nos docuit, ut pro malis bona reddamus'.

135–9 *Rescriptum*, ASS Maii III.9–10, c.13:

Cum ergo evasisset Simon . . . canem immanem, quem vix catena ferrea vinctum tenebat, hunc ligavit in ingressu dicens: 'Videamus si Petrus . . . poterit ingredi.' Sed post unam horam venit Petrus, et facto signo crucis solvit canem, et dixit ei: 'Vade obloquere Simoni: "Desine ministerio daemonum decipere populum, pro quo Christus suum sanguinem fudit"'.

139–44 *Rescriptum*, ASS Maii III.9–10, c.13:

Canis autem . . . solum Simonem persequebatur: quem cum misisset subtus se, cucurrit Petrus clamans et dicens: 'Praecipio tibi in nomine Domini nostri Iesu Christi, ut non figas morsum in aliquam partem eius corporis'. Canis autem nullum eius contingere potuit membrum, sed vestimenta ita morsibus attrectavit, ut nulla pars eius corporis tecta remaneret. Populus autem omnis, et praecipue pueri, simul cum cane post eum tamdiu cucurrerunt, quamdiu illum cum ululatu quasi lupum extra muros civitatis eiicerent.

144–57 *Rescriptum*, ASS Maii III.9–10, c.14:

Post haec autem, opprobrium huius pudoris non ferens, per annum unum nusquam comparuit. Postea vero invenit, qui eum Neroni Caesari insinuaret: sicque factum est, ut homo malignus malignum, imo peiorem se suis amicitiis copularet. Post haec etiam apparuit Dominus apostolo Petro, per visionem dicens: 'Simon et Nero, pleni daemonibus, adversus te cogitant; noli timere, quia tecum ego sum, et dabo tibi servi mei apostoli Pauli solatium, qui cras Romam ingredietur: cum quo post septem menses simul habebitis contra Simonem bellum, et postquam eieceritis et viceritis eum, et deposueritis eum in infernum, simul ad me venietis ambo victores.' Quod et factum est. Nam altera die venit Paulus.

For the Latin note at 156 in MSS KLf^k, almost certainly by Ælfric, see below, under 273–5.

158–60 With the arrival of Paul Ælfric now turns to the *Passio Petri et Pauli*, Lipsius, c.3:

Audiens haec Petrus gaudio gavisus est magno et statim exsurgens perrexit ad eum. Videntes autem se prae gaudio fleverunt. . . .

Chapters 4–9 cover the apostles' preaching and resolution of disputes between Jews and Gentiles.

160–4 *Passio Petri et Pauli*, Lipsius, c.10:

Innumerabiles enim populi dum converterentur ad dominum per praedicationem Petri, contigit etiam uxorem Neronis Liviam et Agrippae praefecti coniugem nomine Agrippinam ita converti, ut a latere se suorum maritorum auferrent. Per Pauli vero praedicationem multi deserentes militiam adhaerebant deo, ita ut etiam ex cubiculo regis venirent ad eum, et facti Christiani nollent reverti ad militiam neque ad palatium.

165–70 *Passio Petri et Pauli*, Lipsius, cc. 11–12:

[Simon] faciebat serpentem aereum movere se, et lapideas statuas et aereas ridere et movere, se ipsum autem currere et subito in aere videri. Contra haec Petrus infirmos curabat verbo, caecos videre faciebat orando, daemonia iussu fugabat, interea et ipsos mortuos suscitabat. Dicebat autem ad populum, ut ab eius seductione non solum fugerent, sed etiam detegerent eum, ne viderentur diabolo consentire.

171–7 *Passio Petri et Pauli*, Lipsius, cc. 13–14:

Qui sermo usque ad Neronem Caesarem venit; et Simonem magum ut ad se ingrederetur praecepit. Qui ingressus coepit stare ante illum et subito mutare effigies, ita ut fieret subito puer et posthaec senior, altera vero hora adolescentior. Mutabatur sexu, aetate. . . . Quod cum videret Nero, vere hunc esse dei filium aestimabat. Petrus vero apostolus dicebat hunc furem esse, mendacem, magum, turpem, sceleratum, apostaticum, et in omnibus quae sunt dei praecepta adversarium veritatis.

Ælfric here omits a long debate in which Peter and Paul inform the emperor about Christ and his teachings, before completing Peter's attack on Simon with a detail from chapter 22: *In isto autem Simone sunt duae substantiae, hominis et diaboli.*

177–82 *Passio Petri et Pauli*, Lipsius, c. 23:

Simon dixit: 'Miror te, bone imperator, hunc te alicuius momenti existimare, hominem inperitum, piscatorem, mendacissimum . . . Sed ne diutius hunc patiar inimicum, modo praecipiam angelis meis, ut veniant et vindicent me de isto'. Petrus dixit: 'Non timeo angelos tuos, illi autem me poterunt timere in virtute et confidentia Iesu Christi domini mei'.

182–9 *Passio Petri et Pauli*, Lipsius, c. 24:

Nero dixit: 'Non times, Petre, Simonem qui divinitatem suam rebus adfirmat?' Petrus dixit: '. . . [*var.* Si ergo divinitas est in isto] dicat nunc mihi quid cogito vel quid facio.' . . . Nero dixit: 'Accede huc, et dic mihi quid cogitas'. Petrus dixit: 'Iube mihi adferri panem ordeaceum et occulte dari'. Cumque hoc iussum fuisset occulte adferri et dari Petro, [*var.* accepto pane fregit et abscondit sub manica sua et] Petrus dixit: 'Dicat nunc Simon, quid cogitatum, quid dictum, quidve sit factum'.

189–95 *Passio Petri et Pauli*, Lipsius, c. 27:

Tunc Simon indignatus quod dicere non posset secretum apostoli, exclamavit dicens: 'Procedant canes magni et devorent eum in conspectu

Caesaris'. Et subito apparuerunt canes mirae magnitudinis et impetum fecerunt in Petrum. Petrus vero extendens manus in orationem, ostendit canibus eum quem benedixerat panem; quem ut viderunt canes subito nusquam conparuerunt. Tunc Petrus dixit ad Neronem: '. . . Qui angelos promiserat contra me esse venturos, canes exhibuit, ut se ostenderet non divinos angelos sed caninos habere'.

195–8 *Passio Petri et Pauli*, Lipsius, c. 28:

Tunc Nero ad Simonem dixit: 'Quid est, Simon? Puto victi sumus.' Simon dixit: '. . . Cogitationes hominum nemo novit nisi unus deus'. Et Petrus ad Simonem dixit: 'Certe deum te esse mentiris. Quare ergo non manifestas cogitationes singulorum?'

199–203 *Passio Petri et Pauli*, Lipsius, cc. 33–4:

Nero . . . conversus ad Paulum ait: 'Tu Paule, quare nihil loqueris? Aut quis te docuit aut quem magistrum habuisti, aut qualiter in civitatibus docuisti . . .'. Paulus respondit: 'Putas me contra hominem perfidum et desperatum magum maleficum, qui animam suam morti destinavit, cuius interitus et perditio cito adveniet, debere loqui? . . . Huius tu verba si volueris audire vel fovere eum, perdes animam tuam et imperium tuum.'

203–11 *Passio Petri et Pauli*, Lipsius, cc. 36–7, 44:

[c.36] De doctrina autem magistri mei, de qua me interrogasti, non eam capiunt, nisi qui fidem mundi pectoris adhibuerint. [*Supplied from* c.44] Qui Petrum praesens docuit, ipse me per revelationem instruxit. [c.36–7] Nam quaecumque sunt pacis et caritatis, ea docui: per circuitum ab Hierusalem usque Illiricum replevi verbum pacis. Docui, ut homines se invicem diligant. Docui ut invicem se honore praeveniant. Docui sublimes et divites non se extollere et sperare in incerto divitiarum, sed in deo ponere spem suam. Docui mediocres victu et vestimento contentos esse. Docui pauperes in sua egestate gaudere.

211–17 *Passio Petri et Pauli*, Lipsius, c. 37:

Docui patres docere filios suos disciplinam timoris dei. Docui filios obtemperare parentibus et monitis salutaribus. . . . Docui uxores diligere viros suos et timere eos quasi dominos. Docui viros fidem servare coniugibus, sicut illi sibi servare pudorem omnimodis volunt. Quod enim punit maritus in uxore adultera, hoc punit in marito adultero ipse pater et conditor rerum deus.

217–21 *Passio Petri et Pauli*, Lipsius, c. 37:

Docui dominos ut mitius cum servis suis agant. Docui servos ut fideliter et quasi deo ita serviant dominis suis. Docui ecclesias credentium unum et omnipotentem invisibilem et inconprehensibilem colere deum.

For 218–9, not apparently from the *Passio*, cf CH I.19.41–2.

222–5 *Passio Petri et Pauli*, Lipsius, c. 38:

Haec autem mihi doctrina non ab hominibus neque per hominem aliquem data est, sed per Iesum Christum et patrem gloriae, qui mihi de caelo locutus est. Et dum me mitteret ad praedicationem dominus meus Iesus Christus, dixit mihi: 'Vade et ego ero in te spiritus vitae omnibus credentibus in me; et omnia quaecumque dixeris aut feceris ego iustificabo'.

226–8 *Passio Petri et Pauli*, Lipsius, cc. 39–40:

Nero his auditis obstupuit. . . . Simon dixit: 'Bone imperator, intellege conspirationem horum duorum adversum me. Ego enim sum veritas et isti adversum me sapiunt.'

228–33 *Passio Petri et Pauli*, Lipsius, c. 50:

Simon dixit: 'Iube turrim excelsam fieri ex lignis et trabibus magnis, ut ascendam in illam; et cum in illam ascendero, [*var.* imperabo angelis meis ut descendant ad me de caelo et tollant me in caelum ad patrem] angeli mei ad me in aera venient: non enim in terra inter peccatores ad me venire possunt.' Nero dixit: 'Volo videre, si imples quod dicis'.

233–9 *Passio Petri et Pauli*, Lipsius, cc. 51, 54, 52:

[c.51] Tunc Nero praecepit in campo Martio turrim excelsam fieri et praecepit ut omnes populi et omnes dignitates ad istud spectaculum convenirent. . . . [c.54] Tunc ascendit Simon in turrim coram omnibus, et extensis manibus coronatus lauro coepit volare. [c.52] Et conversus Paulus ad Petrum dixit: 'Meum est genibus positis deum exorare, tuum est impetrare si quid videris eum conari, quoniam tu prior electus es a domino.'

239–44 *Passio Petri et Pauli*, Lipsius, c. 56:

Et aspiciens contra Simonem Petrus dixit: 'Adiuro vos, angeli Satanae . . . per deum creatorem omnium et per Iesum Christum . . . ut eum ex hac hora iam non feratis, sed dimittatis illum. Et continuo dimissus cecidit . . . et in quattuor partes fractus quattuor silices adunavit, qui sunt ad testimonium victoriae apostolicae usque in hodiernum diem.

244–9 Apparently Ælfric's own interjection, emphasising that it was only with the permission of the apostles that Simon was able to fly; for similar points about the limitations on diabolic powers, cf CH I.praef.96–106 and II.30.90 ff.

250–5 *Passio Petri et Pauli*, Lipsius, cc. 57–8:

Tunc Nero teneri fecit Petrum et Paulum in vinculis; corpus autem Simonis iussit diligenter tribus diebus custodiri, putans eum resurgere tertia die. Cui Petrus dixit: 'Hic iam non resurget, quoniam vere mortuus est et in aeterna poena dampnatus.' . . . Tunc Nero dixit ad praefectum suum Agrippam: 'Homines irreligiosos necesse est male perdere'. . . . Agrippa praefectus dixit: 'Ut mihi videtur, iustum est Paulo irreligioso caput amputari: Petrum autem eo quod insuper homicidium perpetraverit, iube eum in cruce levari'.

256–63 *Passio Petri et Pauli*, Lipsius, cc. 59–60:

Paulus decollatus est in via Ostiensi. Petrus autem dum venisset ad crucem ait: 'Quoniam dominus meus Iesus Christus de caelo ad terram descendens recta cruce sublimatus est, me autem quem de terra ad caelum evocare dignatur, crux mea caput meum in terra debet ostendere, et pedes ad caelum dirigere: ergo quia non sum dignus ita esse in cruce sicut dominus meus, girate crucem meam.' At illi verterunt crucem et pedes eius sursum fixerunt, manus vero deorsum.

264–6 *Passio Petri et Pauli*, Lipsius, c. 61:

Convenit autem innumerabilis multitudo maledicentes Caesarem Neronem, ita furore pleni ut vellent ipsum Caesarem incendere. Petrus autem prohibebat eos dicens: 'Ante paucos dies rogatus a fratribus abscedebam, et occurrit mihi dominus meus Iesus Christus, et . . . dixit mihi: "Sequere me, quia vado Romam iterum crucifigi."

267–72 *Passio Petri et Pauli*, Lipsius, c. 62:

Et ideo, filioli, nolite impedire iter meum. Iam pedes mei viam caelestem ambulant. Nolite tristari, sed congaudete mecum, quia hodie laborum meorum fructum consequor.' Et cum haec dixisset, ait: 'Gratias tibi ago, bone pastor, quia oves quas mihi credidisti compatiuntur mihi. . . . Commendo tibi oves quas mihi credidisti, ut non sentiant se sine me esse, qui te habent per quem ego gregem hunc regere potui.' Et haec dicens emisit spiritum.

273–5 The thirty-sixth year after the passion is the date given by Isidore (*De Ortu et Obitu Patrum*, 67.5). In citing Jerome (Latin note in MSS KL at 275) as authority for the fact that the two apostles were martyred on the same day, Ælfric is presumably referring to the *De Viris Inlustribus*, c.5 (10.21–3):

Hic ergo quarto decimo Neronis anno, eodem die quo Petrus Romae, pro Christo capite truncatur, sepultusque est in via Ostiensi, anno post passionem Domini tricesimo septimo.

The same text notes earlier that Paul had been taken as captive to Rome but subsequently released; cf the Latin note at 156 in MSS KLf[k].

275–82 *Passio Petri et Pauli*, Lipsius, cc. 63–4:

Statim ibi apparuerunt viri sancti, quos umquam nemo viderat ante nec postea videre potuerunt. Isti dicebant se propter ipsum de Hierosolymis advenisse, et ipsi . . . abstulerunt corpus eius occulte et posuerunt . . . in locum qui appellatur Vaticanus. Ipsi . . . dixerunt ad omnem populum: 'Gaudete et exultate, quia patronos magnos meruistis habere et amicos domini Iesu Christi. Sciatis autem hunc Neronem regem pessimum post necem apostolorum regnum tenere non posse.'

282–7 *Passio Petri et Pauli*, Lipsius, c. 65:

> Accidit autem post haec ut odium exercitus sui et odium populi Romani incurreret; ita statuerunt ut publice cathomis tamdiu caederetur, quousque ut erat meritus expiraret. Quod cum pervenisset ad eum consilium, inruit in eum tremor et metus intolerabilis, et ita fugit ut ulterius non apparuerit. Extiterunt autem qui dicerent, in silvis dum erraret fugiens frigore nimio et fame diriguisse et a lupis esse devoratum.

The phrase *on þam holte* at 286, occurring in all manuscripts except A and corresponding to the Latin *in silviis*, is presumably either an authorial addition made subsequent to the earliest version represented by A or an accidental omission by the scribe of A. In favour of the former explanation is the fact that *holt* otherwise occurs in the Catholic Homilies only in two alliterative homilies from the Second Series and is more likely to be a later usage.

287–95 *Passio Petri et Pauli*, Lipsius, c. 66:

> Sanctorum autem apostolorum dum a Graecis corpora tollerentur ad Orientem ferenda, extitit terrae motus nimius. Et occurrit populus Romanus et comprehenderunt eos in loco, qui dicitur Catacumba via Appia miliario tertio; et ibi custodita sunt corpora anno uno et mensibus septem, quousque fabricarentur loca in quibus fuerunt posita corpora eorum. Et illic revocata sunt cum gloria hymnorum et posita sancti Petri in Vaticano Naumachiae et sancti Pauli in via Ostiensi miliario secundo; ubi praestantur beneficia orationum in saecula saeculorum. Amen.

27 ST PAUL

Both here and in the previous homily Ælfric is at pains to stress that St Peter and St Paul were martyred on the same day, and their passions are jointly celebrated on that day. Even so, St Paul's importance gave him a commemorative feast-day of his own on the following day, though paradoxically with a pericope that applies more directly to Peter than to Paul. Having recounted the martyrdom of Paul in the previous homily (and having no use for the narrative of Paul's separate martyrdom which the Cotton-Corpus legendary contained), Ælfric begins with a narrative centring on Paul's conversion. The account of this in Acts 9.1–19 is the epistle for the day but Ælfric goes beyond this reading, sketching Paul's background and briefly narrating his later experiences. The account is distinctly hagiographic in content and tone: Ælfric resolutely defends Paul from criticism, even before his conversion, selects and reshapes the material to present Paul as a dominant and saintly figure and to shield the other disciples from criticism, and uses epithets characteristic of his own saints' lives—*godes cempa, wælhreow ehtere, þam gecorenan cempan*. He then turns to the pericope for the occasion, Matthew 19.27–9, where Christ promises the apostles that as a reward for forsaking all to follow him they will be judges at the last judgement. Ælfric applies the text to the monastic life in particular, and ends with a strong critique of the various failures of that ideal, but he is at pains to leave a place for other, if lesser, kinds of achievement (lines 181–5, 205–9).

The sources of this two-part homily are peculiarly elusive. The homiliary of Smaragdus provides homilies on both the epistle and the Gospel pericope, and Förster suggested that these were Ælfric's sources, together with Augustine's sermon 279 for the first part and a homily by Bede (Hom. I.13) for the second.[1] Smetana expressed reservations about the use of Smaragdus and Bede and suggested that for the first part Ælfric combined the Augustine sermon with material from a Ps-Augustinian sermon (Serm. 204, PL 39, 2124–5), both of them appearing in late versions of Paul the Deacon's homiliary; he also noted that the homily by Smaragdus on the Gospel was based on a homily by Jerome which also appears in PD.[2] A further source was indicated by Gatch, who argued that Ælfric used Julian of Toledo's *Prognosticon*, and his own epitome of it, for a passage on the last judgement.[3] For the first part, the situation remains perplexing: there are details in common with Smaragdus, others with Augustine and others with the Ps-Augustine homily, but there remains much unaccounted for, and the whole tone and organisation of this part suggests the use of a source quite different in kind from these three, one concerned more with Paul's life rather than the Acts text of his conversion. For the second part, the sources so far suggested overlap considerably: Smaragdus draws on both Jerome and Bede, and the *Prognosticon* material is very similar to parts of Bede. If the standard editions are a reliable guide, Ælfric would appear to have drawn material from Smaragdus, Bede and Julian. Jerome has nothing in common with Ælfric that is not also in Smaragdus, but the homily for this occasion which appears in the 1516 edition of PD, though ascribed to Jerome, seems in fact to be closer to Smaragdus and the two texts may have become conflated by Ælfric's time. For the eschatological material Julian seems closer than Bede, but the latter is elsewhere closer than Smaragdus. But here too there is much that has not been traced and there may still be another source to be found.

Sources and Notes

The following texts are cited below:

1. Ælfric's *Excerpts* from the *Prognosticon Futuri Saeculi* of Julian of Toledo, ed. Gatch 1977, pp. 129–46.
2. Augustine, *Sermones*, PL 38, Serm. 279, cols. 1275–80.
3. Ps-Augustine, *Sermones*, PL 39, Serm. 204 [= Augustine, *Sermones suppositii*], cols. 2124–5.

[1] Förster 1894, pp. 24, 42–3. [2] Smetana 1959, pp. 191–2. [3] Gatch 1966.

4. Bede, *Homiliae*, ed. D. Hurst, CCSL 122 (Turnhout, 1955), Hom. I.13 (pp. 88–94).
5. John Cassian, *De Institutis Coenobiorum*, ed. M. Petschenig, CSEL 17 (Vienna, 1888), pp. 3–231.
6. Jerome, *Adversus Iovinianum*, PL 23, cols. 211–338.
7. Jerome, *Commentarii in Evangelium Matthaei*, ed. D. Hurst and M. Adriaen, CCSL 77 (Turnhout, 1969).
8. Julian of Toledo, *Prognosticon Futuri Saeculi*, ed. J. Hillgarth, CCSL 115 (Turnhout, 1976), pp. 11–126.
9. Smaragdus, *Collectiones in Evangelia et Epistolas*, PL 102, cols. 395–99.

7–13 A summary of Paul's life before his conversion, drawing on Acts:

(22.3) Ego sum vir Iudaeus . . . secus pedes Gamaliel, eruditus iuxta veritatem paternae legis, aemulator legis. . . . (7.59) Saulus autem erat consentiens neci eius. . . . (8.3) Saulus autem devastabat Ecclesiam per domos intrans, et trahens viros ac mulieres tradebat in custodiam.

Ælfric's attempt to defend Saul, explaining that he persecuted Christians out of ignorance and noting that there is no evidence that he personally killed anyone with his own hands, is without parallel in his sources; Augustine, indeed, stresses Saul's vindictiveness, arguing that he held the coats of those stoning Stephen in order to help them all in their efforts, and thus to contribute more to the death of the martyr than any other individual. (It is most curious that Ælfric freely interchanges the names Saulus and Paulus without explaining that they refer to the same person; he seems to take for granted the audience's total familiarity with the name change.)

14–25 A fairly close paraphrase of Acts 9.1–9:

(1) Saulus autem adhuc spirans minarum, et caedis in discipulos Domini, accessit ad principem sacerdotum, (2) et petiit ab eo epistolas in Damascum ad synagogas: ut si quos invenisset huius viae viros ac mulieres, vinctos perduceret in Hierusalem. (3) Et cum iter faceret, contigit ut appropinquaret Damasco: et subito circumfulsit eum lux de caelo. (4) Et cadens in terram audivit vocem dicentem sibi: 'Saule, Saule, quid me persequeris? '(5) Qui dixit: 'Quis es Domine?' Et ille: 'Ego sum Iesus, quem tu persequeris; durum est tibi contra stimulum calcitrare.' (6) Et tremens ac stupens dixit: 'Domine, quid me vis facere.' (7) Et Dominus ad eum: 'Surge et ingredere civitatem, et ibi dicetur tibi quid te oporteat facere.' . . . (8) Surrexit autem Saulus de terra, apertisque oculis nihil videbat. Ad manus autem illum trahentes, introduxerunt Damascum. (9) Et erat ibi tribus diebus non videns, et non manducavit, neque bibit.

25–38 An adaptation of Acts 9.10–18:

(10) Erat autem quidam discipulus Damasci, nomine Ananias: et dixit ad illum in visu Dominus: 'Anania . . . (11) Surge, et . . . quaere . . . Saulum

nomine Tarsensem: ecce enim orat.' . . . (13) Respondit autem Ananias: 'Domine, audivi a multis de viro hoc, quanta mala fecerit sanctis tuis in Hierusalem: (14) et hic habet potestatem a principibus sacerdotum alligandi omnes qui invocant nomen tuum.' (15) Dixit autem ad eum Dominus: 'Vade, quoniam vas electionis est mihi iste, ut portet nomen meum coram gentibus, et regibus, et filiis Israhel. (16) Ego enim ostendam illi quanta oporteat eum pro nomine meo pati.' (17) Et abiit Ananias, et introivit in domum: et imponens ei manus, dixit: 'Saule frater, Dominus misit me Iesus, qui apparuit tibi in via qua veniebas, ut videas, et implearis Spiritu Sancto.' (18) Et confestim ceciderunt ab oculis eius, tanquam squamae, et visum recepit: et surgens baptizatus est.

38–50 Based on Acts 9.19–27 but omitting references to the disciples' suspicion of Paul:

(19) Fuit autem cum discipulis qui erant Damasci, per dies aliquot. (20) Et continuo in synagogis praedicabat Iesum, quoniam hic est Filius Dei. (21) Stupebant autem omnes qui audiebant, et dicebant: 'Nonne hic est qui expugnabat in Hierusalem eos qui invocabant nomen istud . . .?' (22) Saulus autem multo magis convalescebat, et confundebat Iudaeos, qui habitabant Damasci, affirmans quoniam hic est Christus. (23) Cum autem implerentur dies multi, consilium fecerunt in unum Iudaei, ut eum interficerent. (24) Notae autem factae sunt Saulo insidiae eorum. Custodiebant autem et portas die ac nocte, ut eum interficerent. (25) Accipientes autem eum discipuli nocte, per murum dimiserunt eum, submittentes in sporta. (26) Cum venisset in Hierusalem, tentabat se iungere discipulis, et omnes timebant eum. . . . (27) Barnabas autem . . . narravit illis quomodo in via vidisset Dominum, et quia locutus est ei.

51–64 This account of Paul's missionary career and writing of the epistles is ultimately based on Acts but there are few close parallels. The first part refers to Acts 13.2–3:

(2) Dixit illis Spiritus Sanctus: 'Segregate mihi Saulum et Barnabam in opus ad quod assumpsi eos'. (3) Tunc . . . dimiserunt illos.

The parting of Paul from Barnabas is at Acts 15.39 but Ælfric gives no hint of the dissension indicated there. The specific durations given in 59–60 do not tally closely with anything in Acts.

65–80 Ælfric's resolute defence of Saul, as one who misguidedly but honestly sought to defend the old law against what he saw as a threat to it, has no parallel in his sources, though it is difficult to believe that he was not prompted by some so far untraced text. Even so, he has chosen not to follow the line of Augustine, who sees Saul/Paul as the great model of conversion and divine mercy and hence accentuates his original savagery. Lines 76–80 expand and gloss God's words to Saul but present them still in God's voice, without indicating that they are a departure from the Biblical account; *werast* could in context mean either 'defend' or 'resist'. On 78–9 cf perhaps Augustine, Serm. 382, §4, PL 39, 1686: *Durum est tibi contra stimulum calcitrare: quia non stimulum, sed pedes quibus calcitras, vulnerabis.*

80–83 Cf Smaragdus, *Collectiones*, PL 102, 396D:

Non dixit 'quid persequeris membra mea' sed 'quid me persequeris?', quia ipse in corpore suo, quod est ecclesia, adhuc patitur iniquos.

and Ps-Augustine, Serm. 204, §2, PL 39, 2124:

Caput de coelo clamat pro membris.

or possibly, from a variant text of Augustine's Serm. 279 which appears in a late version of PD (the Basle edition of 1516, *Sanctorale*, f.5): *Ille caput et nos membra. Quicquid membra patiuntur caput pro membris clamat.* The quotation at 82–3 is Zach 2.8: *Qui enim tetigerit vos, tangit pupillam oculi mei.*

83–7 Cf Ps-Augustine, Serm. 204, §3, PL 39, 2124:

Ideo prosternitur superbia, ut erigatur sanctitas.

and Augustine, Serm. 279, §1, PL 38, 1276:

Ut interiore luce fulgeret cor eius, exterior ad tempus erepta est.

87–9 Cf Smaragdus, *Collectiones*, PL 102, 397A:

Quia dominum non crediderat tertia die mortem resurgendo vicisse, sua iam instruitur exemplo, qui tenebras triduanas, luce reversa, mutaret.

90–94 Cf Augustine (Serm. 279, §2, PL 38, 1276): *Ananias interpretatur ovis* and Ps-Augustine, Serm. 204, §3, PL 39, 2124:

Venit ergo Ananias, baptizavit Saulum et fecit Paulum. Baptizavit lupum et fecit agnum: et coepimus habere praedicatorem, quem habuimus persecutorem.

94–99 Another defence of Saul, for taking flight from his enemies, and again there is nothing in Ælfric's known sources. The argument is similar to that applied to Christ at CH II.13.231–6.

99–109 Cf Ps-Augustine, Serm. 204, §3, PL 39, 2124:

Patitur Paulus quod fecerat Saulus. Saulus lapidavit; Paulus lapidatus est. Saulus Christianos virgis affecit; Paulus pro Christo quinquies quadragenas una minus accepit. Saulus persecutus est ecclesiam Dei; Paulus submissus est in sporta.

But Ælfric's version incorporates further details from the account of Paul's missions in Acts.

109–22 Ælfric concludes with an account of Paul's evangelism, not covered in his sources. The reference to his vision of heaven comes from 2 Cor 12.2, 4:

(2) Scio hominem . . . raptum huiusmodi usque ad tertium coelum . . . (4) et audivit arcana verba, quae non licet homini loqui.

The notion that Paul worked at his trade of tent-making to support himself and his companions, refusing to be dependent on others, presumably derives from Acts 18.3:

> Et quia eiusdem erat artis, manebat apud eos, et operabatur, erant autem scenofactoriae artis.

and Acts 20.33–4:

> (33) Argentum et aurum aut vestem nullius concupivi, (34) sicut ipsi scitis: quoniam ad ea quae mihi opus erant, et his qui mecum sunt, ministraverunt manus istae.

122–33 Ælfric now turns to the Gospel passage for the day, Mt 19.27–9, which is concerned explicitly with St Peter but is neatly linked to St Paul by his transitional sentence:

> (27) Tunc respondens Petrus, dixit ei: 'Ecce nos reliquimus omnia, et secuti sumus te: quid ergo erit nobis?' (28) Iesus autem dixit illis: 'Amen dico vobis, quod vos, qui secuti estis me, in regeneratione cum sederit filius hominis in sede maiestatis suae, sedebitis et vos super sedes duodecim, iudicantes duodecim tribus Israhel. (29) Et omnis qui reliquerit domum, vel fratres, aut sorores, aut patrem, aut matrem, aut uxorem, aut filios, aut agros propter nomen meum, centuplum accipiet, et vitam aeternam possidebit.'

134–41 Smaragdus, *Collectiones*, PL 102, 397C:

> Grandis fiducia! Petrus piscator erat, dives non fuerat, cibos manu et arte quaerebat, et tamen loquitur confidenter, 'reliquimus omnia'. Omnia enim relinquit, qui voluntatem habendi deserit.

(The first sentence is in Jerome, *Comm. Matth.*, 3.193.) Ælfric develops the point in lines 138–41.

141–50 The basic idea is in Smaragdus, *Collectiones*, PL 102, 397D:

> Non dixit 'qui reliquistis omnia', hoc enim et Socrates fecit philosophus, et multi alii divitias contempserunt, sed 'qui secuti estis me'.

The point comes verbatim from Jerome's commentary on Matthew (*Comm. Matth.*, 3.922–4). The modern editors of this commentary in fact print *Crates*, though none of the manuscripts used seem to give that reading: one has *grates*, and the rest apparently *socrates* or *sogrates*. Crates is no doubt what Jerome wrote, since he mentions him in several of his works as a rich man who abandoned his wealth to pursue philosophy, but Ælfric evidently saw a version with the name Socrates. Neither Smaragdus nor Jerome at this point give the further details which Ælfric provides, but Jerome's *Adversus Iovinianum*, II.c.9 (PL 23, 298C) gives the main points:

> Et Crates ille Thebanus, proiecto in mari non parvo auri pondere, 'Abite' inquit 'pessum malae cupiditates: ego vos mergam, ne ipse mergar a vobis.'

Jerome's comments on Plato, Diogenes and the Stoics in the rest of the chapter could have sufficiently prompted Ælfric's general points about ancient philosophers. For Ælfric to make the connection, however, he would need to have seen a copy of this text in which the name Crates had been corrupted to Socrates, and there is no other evidence that he knew this work. He had clearly seen something like this story however; it is alluded to again in CH I.4.49–53 (see the note on these lines, above). On the golden *wecg*, see also CH I.34.165.

151–2 Cf Smaragdus, *Collectiones*, PL 102, 397CD [= Jerome, *Comm. Matth.*, 3.195]:

> 'Secuti sumus te', fecimus quod iussisti, quid igitur dabis praemii?

155–62 That *regeneratio* in this context means the general resurrection is explained by Smaragdus and Jerome, and the wording used by Smaragdus perhaps influenced Ælfric (Smaragdus, *Collectiones*, PL 102, 398B):

> Quod autem ait, in regeneratione, procul dubio mortuorum resurrectionem nomine voluit regenerationis intelligi, sic enim caro nostra regenerabitur per incorruptionem, quemadmodum est anima nostra regenerata per fidem.

But neither draws the distinction Ælfric makes with the two earlier births, the physical birth of man and the rebirth of baptism.

164–75 Cf Smaragdus, *Collectiones*, PL 102, 398B:

> Non enim quia dictum est, iudicantes duodecim tribus Israel, tribus Levi, quae tertia decima est, ab eis iudicanda non erit, aut solum illum populum, non cum eo gentes caeteras iudicabunt.

Smaragdus is adapting Bede (Hom. I.13, 30–31) but is closer than Bede. He gives some abstruse arguments for the symbolism of the number twelve, quite different from Ælfric's in lines 170–71.

176–7 Cf Bede, Hom. I.13, 35–8:

> Sciendum namque est omnes qui ad exemplum apostolorum sua reliquerunt omnia et secuti sunt Christum, iudices cum eo venturos, sicut etiam omne mortalium genus esse iudicandum.

177–92 The ideas are in Bede, but Ælfric's particular formulation seems to derive instead from Julian of Toledo's *Prognosticon*, incorporating some details from his own précis of that work (see Gatch 1966):

> [*Prognosticon*, III.xxxiii.4–6:] Duae sunt enim differentiae vel ordines hominum in iudicio collectorum, hoc est electorum et reproborum, qui tamen in quattuor dividuntur. [*Excerpts*, 307–16:] Igitur perfectorum sanctorum primus ordo erit, qui cum Domino iudicat, et non iudicatur, sed regnat. Alius quoque est ordo electorum quibus dicitur, 'Esurivi et dedistis mihi manducare' (Mt 25.35). Hi iudicantur et regnant. Item reproborum ordines duo sunt. Unus eorum, qui Dei cognitionem habuerunt, sed fidem dignis operibus non exercuerunt, isti iudicabuntur et peribunt, quibus dicetur a Domino: 'Esurivi et non dedistis mihi manducare; ite, maledicti, in ignem aeternum' (Mt 25.41–2). Alter

quoque ordo reproborum est paganorum videlicet, qui Dei cognitionem non habuerunt, qui sine lege peccaverunt, et sine lege peribunt.

The treatment of the heathen is striking. The last two clauses of this Latin passage, not found in Julian, paraphrase St Paul (Rom 2.12: *Quicumque enim sine lege peccaverunt, sine lege peribunt*) and Ælfric gives here, in the Old English passage, a more precise and attributed quotation, presumably invoked to make the point that the heathen are not judged but nevertheless perish. He has also rearranged the last part, so that God's curse to the damned, dismissing them to eternal torment with the devils, now apparently applies to the heathen who did not know God as well as to the sinners who did. Bede (Hom. I.13, 67–74) is equally emphatic that the fourth group are consigned to the same fate as the sinners, but he defines them as those who refused to accept the faith of Christ or apostasised from it, whereas Julian, followed by Ælfric, defines them very clearly as those who had no knowledge of God.

193–209 Ælfric now applies the text particularly to the monastic life. This is perhaps implicit in Bede's sermon, which turns at this point to the praise of Benedict Biscop, the subject of his text and one of the great founders of English monasticism, and there is possibly a starting point for this passage in Bede's argument that those who share in the spiritual life find an affection superior to that of parents and siblings, but the parallel is not close, and Ælfric develops the point much further.

210–47 Ælfric concludes with a discussion of the failures of the monastic ideal, in contrast to the ideal suggested by the apostolic life and the Gospel text. His use of Judas, Annanias and Sapphira, and Giezi as exemplars suggests a recall of Cassian, who uses the same three to represent the three kinds of avarice found amongst monks and hermits (*De Institutis Coenobiorum*, VII.14 (138.9))[4]; the reference to Giezi is similar: *Nam Giezi ea quae ne ante quidem possederat, volens acquirere*. . . . The story of Annanias and Sapphira, referred to at 217–23, is from Acts 5.1–11. The story of Elisha's servant Giezi, given at 228–47, is from 4 Reg 5:

(1) Naaman princeps militiae regis Syriae, erat vir magnus apud dominum suum . . . erat vir fortis et dives, sed leprosus. . . . (9) Venit ergo Naaman . . . et stetit ad ostium domus Elisei . . . (14) et restituta est caro eius. . . . (15) Reversus ad virum Dei . . . et ait: '. . .Obsecro ut accipias benedictionem a servo tuo.' (16) At ille respondit: 'Vivit Dominus, ante quem sto, quia non accipiam.' . . . (19) Abiit ergo ab eo. (20) Dixitque Giezi puer viri Dei: 'Pepercit dominus meus Naaman Syro isti, ut non acciperet ab eo quae attulit: vivit Dominus, quia curram post eum, et accipiam ab eo aliquid.' (21) Et secutus est Giezi post tergum Naaman . . . (22) et ait . . . 'Dominus meus misit me

[4] The passage is repeated by Rabanus Maurus, PL 112, 1375.

ad te dicens: Modo venerunt ad me duo adolescentes de monte Ephraim, ex filiis prophetarum: da eis talentum argenti, et vestes mutatorias duplices.' (23) Dixitque Naaman: 'Melius est ut accipias duo talenta.' Et coegit eum, ligavitque duo talenta argenti in duobus saccis, et duplicia vestimenta. . . . (24) Cumque venisset iam vesperi, tulit de manu eorum, et reposuit in domo. . . . (25) Ipse autem ingressus, stetit coram domino suo. Et dixit Eliseus: 'Unde venis Giezi? Qui respondit: 'Non ivit servus tuus quoquam.' (26) At ille ait: 'Nonne cor meum in praesenti erat, quando reversus est homo de curru suo in occursum tui? Nunc igitur accepisti argentum, et accepisti vestes. . . . (27) Sed et lepra Naaman adhaerebit tibi, et semini tuo, usque in sempiternum.' Et egressus est ab eo leprosus quasi nix.

The word *earfoþhylde* at 224 seems to be a unique occurrence, and there is no apparent source for this part. It is presumably the opposite of *eaþhylde* which occurs several times in Ælfric and elsewhere in the sense '(easily) contented, satisfied'; Thorpe's rendering 'discontented' seems right, with an implication of tolerating situations with difficulty, or perhaps tolerating hardships with difficulty.

28 ELEVENTH SUNDAY AFTER PENTECOST

The text for the day is Luke 19.41–7, which describes Christ weeping over the fate of Jerusalem and then driving the traders from the temple. Ælfric devotes the first half of his exposition to the literal implications and background of the two episodes, then analyses the allegorical meaning and finishes with a moral exemplum of a death-bed scene. He begins by narrating the siege of Jerusalem, which he presents as an exemplary story, modelled perhaps on Old Testament episodes such as the destruction of Sodom and Gomorrah. God is initially patient with the sinful and disbelieving Jews, giving them time and sufficient warning to repent, but at length takes vengeance on them by sending Vespasian and Titus against the city. Ælfric then briefly explains the application of verses 41–4 to the fall of the city before turning to the expulsion from the temple, which he sees as a presage of the fall of Jerusalem itself. Using additional details from the Gospels of Matthew and John, he explains the function of the traders in the temple and relates this to the avarice of the Jewish priests and bishops. Then he turns (line 105) to the allegorical level, explaining first Jerusalem and then the temple as metaphors for the human soul encompassed by devils and invaded by sin, and going on to relate the traders in the temple to the deficiencies of teachers and clergy in the Christian church (lines 163–93).

Ælfric refers three times in the course of the homily to Gregory as his source. As Förster showed, the references are to Gregory's homily 39, the main source for his exposition, and homily 12, which furnishes the final exemplum.[1] Homily 39 shows the same pattern as Ælfric's text, with first a literal exposition and then an allegorical interpretation, though the main emphasis is on the latter, and there are also many parallels of detail. There is also much that is not in Gregory, however, especially in the explanations of the literal meaning. Further details may have been supplied by Haymo's homily for the same occasion (Homily 122[2]), which is based on Gregory's but directs itself much more to the literal interpretation and similarly gives a detailed account of the siege. There are a number of parallels in the exposition, though the match is never as close as with Gregory. Most of the detail on the siege appears to come, however, not from Haymo but from Rufinus's Latin version of Eusebius's *Ecclesiastical History*, as Förster suggested.[3] The Bede commentaries on Matthew and John, suggested by Förster as sources for the parts where Ælfric draws on those Gospels rather than Luke, are not in fact by Bede and it is unclear whether Ælfric knew them; there are in any case no convincing parallels. Gregory's homily 39 ends with an exemplum, the story of a monk Martyrius who carries a helpless leper to shelter, only to discover that it is Christ in disguise. Ælfric uses this story in an earlier homily where it neatly parallels his main discussion of Lazarus, and here he uses instead another exemplum of Gregory's, drawn from his homily 12. The relevance is not immediately obvious, but the account of the devils appearing at the rich man's death-bed does illustrate Ælfric's earlier interpretation of verse 43, 'your enemies will surround you', and there is perhaps also a link with the preceding verse, 'if you knew [what was to come] you would weep too', referring to the rich man's attempt at belated repentance.

The two homilies by Gregory were probably both available to Ælfric in Paul the Deacon's homiliary,[4] and the homiliary of Haymo and *Ecclesiastical History* of Rufinus were both well known to him, but if these were his sources for this homily the material has been very freely selected and reshaped, and there remain a number of details on which Ælfric differs from them.

Sources and Notes

The following texts are cited below:

1. Gregory the Great, *Homiliae in Evangelia*, PL 76, Hom. 12 and 39, cols. 1118–23 and 1293–1301.
2. Haymo of Auxerre, *Homiliae de Tempore*, PL 118, Hom. 122, cols. 653–661.
3. Rufinus, *Historia Ecclesiastica*, ed. T. Mommsen, in *Eusebius Werke*, ed. E. Klostermann, vol. 2, 2 parts, GCS 9.1 and 9.2 (Leipzig, 1903–8).

[1] Förster 1894, pp. 11–12.
[2] Identified by Smetana (1961, p. 461).
[3] Förster 1894, p. 54.
[4] Smetana 1959, p. 192.

3–16 A free rendering of Lc 19.41–47:

(41) Et ut appropinquavit, videns civitatem flevit super illam, dicens: (42) Quia si cognovisses et tu, et quidem in hac die tua, quae ad pacem tibi, nunc autem abscondita sunt ab oculis tuis. (43) Quia venient dies in te: et circumdabunt te inimici tui vallo, et circumdabunt te: et coangustabunt te undique: (44) et ad terram prosternent te, et filios tuos, qui in te sunt, et non relinquent in te lapidem super lapidem: eo quod non cognoveris tempus visitationis tuae. (45) Et ingressus in templum, coepit eiicere vendentes in illo, et ementes, (46) dicens illis; Scriptum est: 'Quia domus mea domus orationis est.' Vos autem fecistis illam speluncam latronum. (47) Et erat docens quotidie in templo.

Ælfric silently interpolates after verse 46 a detail from the parallel account in Mt 21.14: *Et accesserunt ad eum caeci, et claudi in templo: et sanavit eos.* The detail recurs at 96–7 but plays no part in the commentary. The difficult verse 42 is translated literally in the *OE Gospels*, leaving the obscurities unexplained. The interpretation of it implied by Ælfric's paraphrase is the one assumed by his authorities, though they are not explicit about it.

17–20 Though Ælfric cites Gregory as source for this point, the latter says only that Christ's words refer to the destruction of Jerusalem by Titus and Vespasian (Hom. 39, PL 76, 1294A):

Quod flente Domino illa Ierosolymorum subversio describatur, quae a Vespasiano et Tito Romanis principibus facta est.

That the destruction was in vengeance for the killing of Christ is a point made in passing by Haymo (Hom. 122, PL 118, 654B) and also by Rufinus (*Historia Ecclesiastica*, III.vii.7).

20–23 There is some resemblance to Haymo, Hom. 122, PL 118:

[653D] Flevit, non pulchritudinem domorum, non altitudinem turrium, non aedificia murorum, sed metaphorice homines. . . . [653C] Humanae naturae indicium est, cum periturae civitati usque ad fletum compatitur.

But Ælfric's notion of a paternal pity shown by Christ is very different from Haymo's distinction between the divine nature of Christ which foresaw the city's fate and the human nature which pitied it.

23–5 Cf Rufinus, *Historia Ecclesiastica*, III.vii.8–9:

Quadraginta post admissum piaculum continuis protracta annis impiorum poena differtur . . . si forte possent commissi paenitudinem gerere. . . . Ostendebat eis deus per suam patientiam, quod ipsorum quaereret paenitentiam.

25–34 Cf Rufinus, *Historia Ecclesiastica*, III.v.2–3:

Verum post ascensionem domini et salvatoris nostri Iudaei vel in ipsum commissi piaculi vel persecutionis in apostolos et necis in Stefanum, sed et obtruncationis in apostolum Iacobum et in Iacobum nihilominus fratrem domini, qui appellabatur Iustus . . . omnibus malis poenas divinitus reposcebantur. . . . Ecclesia vero, quae in Hierusolymis fuerat congregata, responso a deo accepto emigrare iubetur et transire ad oppidum quoddam Pellam nomine trans Iordanen, quo ablatis ex urbe sanctis et iustis viris vindictae caelesti fieret locus.

The story of the church under James and the events in Jerusalem after his death is given in more detail in CH II.17.

37–9 Rufinus reports at III.v.1 that Vespasian entrusted the completion of the war against the Jews to his son Titus once he himself had been elected emperor by the troops (69 AD). The comment on Vespasian is conceivably an allusion to the oracle mentioned by Rufinus (*Historia Ecclesiastica*, III.viii.10), which prophesied the advent of a man 'qui totius orbis potiretur imperio'. Josephus applied this to Vespasian, but Rufinus applies it rather to Christ.

39–45 Cf Rufinus, *Historia Ecclesiastica*,:

[III.v.5–7] Ex omni Iudaea populi in die sollemni paschae Hierusolyma . . . convenerant, quos tricies centena milia hominum dicit fuisse . . . ut qui in diebus paschae salvatorem suum et salutarem Christum domini cruentis manibus et sacrilegis vocibus violaverant, in ipsis diebus velut in unum carcerem omnis multitudo conclusa feralis poenae exitium, quod merebatur, exciperet. Praeteribo quae in eos vel gladii caede vel aliis belli machinis conlata sunt, explicare; ea tantummodo, quae dirae famis exitio pertulerunt . . . proferam. [III.vi.12] Sepelire autem cadavera proximorum nec defunctorum multitudo nec virium debilitas permittebat, simul et pro suae unusquisque vitae incerto. Denique aliquanti supra eos quos sepeliebant animas emisere. . . . [III.vi.15] Ut vero omnem sumptum coepit vincere multitudo morientium, de muro cadavera praecipitabant.

But Ælfric's figure of 600,000 besieged in the city is quite different from Rufinus's figure of three million. Later Rufinus gives the number of dead in Jerusalem by the end of the siege as 1,100,000, with more than 90,000 taken prisoner. Haymo (Hom. 122, PL 118, 657C) gives the same number of dead and 100,000 captive. The *Anglo-Saxon Chronicle*, s.a. 71 gives 111,000 for the number of dead and the *Old English Orosius*, VI.vii has 1,100,000 (OE Orosius, 138.15). 600,000 is given as the number of dead by a number of authorities, including Ambrose, Jerome and Orosius, but the only parallel for Ælfric's figure of those besieged that I have found is, curiously, in Tacitus (*Historiarum Libri*, ed. E. Koestermann (Leipzig, 1969), V.13.3): *Multitudinem obsessorum omnis aetatis virile ac muliebre secus, sexcenta milia fuisse accepimus*. Ælfric's Latin note (preserved in MS K), *in cronica sic habetur*, shows that he was well aware that it was an area of dispute, but it is not clear which chronicle he was citing as his authority.

45–9 Cf Rufinus, *Historia Ecclesiastica*:

[III.vi.6] Verum ne ipsos quidem infelices et perexiguos sumentes latebant cibos, sed continuo aderat praedonum quis et statim . . . inruebant atque ab ipsis . . . faucibus exprimentes, si quid forte insumptum iam fuerat, revocabant. . . . [III.vi.19] Ad ultimum ne loris quidem vel cingulis aut ipsis etiam calciamentis abstinuerunt. . . . Nonnulli et faeni veteris festucas edebant.

52–5 Cf Haymo, Hom. 122, PL 118, 656A:

Ingressus est Titus cum Romano exercitu, alios gladio trucidavit, alios igne combussit, iuvenes quoque in captivitatem destinavit. Ipsam vero urbem a fundamentis ita destruxit, ut iuxta Domini vocem, non relinqueretur in ea lapis super lapidem.

55–8 Rufinus, *Historia Ecclesiastica*, III.vii.2:

Si qui vero intra septimum et decimum aetatis reperti sunt annum, per diversas provincias in servitutem distrahi iussi sunt, quorum numerus usque ad nonaginta milia perductus est.

58–9 The later rebuilding of Jerusalem on a different site, not mentioned by Rufinus or Haymo, is mentioned by Gregory, Hom. 39, PL 76, 1294B:

Ipsa iam eiusdem civitatis transmigratio testatur, quia dum nunc in eo loco constructa est, ubi extra portam fuerat Dominus crucifixus, prior illa Ierusalem, ut dicitur, funditus est eversa.

The anonymous translator of Orosius, VI.vii interpolates a reference to the same point, stating that Vespasian forbade the rebuilding of the city in the same place (OE Orosius, 138.14–15). None of these texts refers to the Saracens however.

60–2 Cf Haymo, Hom. 122, PL 118, 656BC:

Ex qua causa ruina praedictae civitati contigerit, Dominus manifestat, cum adiungit: 'Eo quod non cognoveris tempus visitationis tuae'.

62–6 Gregory, Hom. 39, PL 76, 1294BC:

Creator quippe omnium per incarnationis suae mysterium hanc visitare dignatus est, sed ipsa timoris et amoris illius recordata non est. Unde etiam per prophetiam in increpatione cordis humani aves coeli ad testimonium deducuntur, dum dicitur: 'Milvus in coelo cognovit tempus suum; turtur et hirundo et ciconia custodierunt tempus adventus sui, populus autem meus non cognovit iudicium Domini' (Jer 8.7).

Ælfric's 'storc and swalewe' correspond to *ciconia* and *hirundo* (see his Grammar, pp. 25 and 37). The *milvus* or kite (OE *cyta*) and *turtur* or dove (OE *culfre*) were both known to him and it is not clear why only the other two are cited (unless it is that he understood the verse as referring to summer migration and the kite and dove were not for him migratory birds, though the turtle-dove is currently).

69–74 Gregory, Hom. 39, PL 76, 1294CD:

Cum carnis se voluptatibus daret, et ventura mala non prospiceret, in die sua quae ad pacem esse ei poterant habebat. . . . Si cordis eius oculis mala quae imminerent abscondita non essent, laeta in praesentibus prosperis non fuisset.

76–84 There are some points of similarity with Haymo, Hom. 122, PL 118, 657D:

> Ostendit quia maxime ruina templi ex culpa sacerdotum venit. . . .Ad hoc in templo residebant, ut eos qui munera dabant, vanis favoribus extollerent; et qui dare nolebant, variis modis affligerent.

The scourge of ropes comes from the similar episode in Jn 2.15, *flagellum de funiculis*. Ælfric's understanding of the situation is, though, apparently different from Haymo's. The latter writes of priests who took gifts (*munera*) from the people who came to the temple in exchange for empty favours, and also encouraged the buying and selling of goods in the temple precincts, for religious offerings (*hostias*) but also for other purposes (with the implication, presumably, that the priests received a proportion of the profits). Ælfric uses the same word, *lac*, for the gifts received by the priests and for the religious offerings made by the people (lines 83–4, 92). His implication is perhaps that the priests themselves received the offerings made by the people (an idea illustrated at length in *De Falsis Deis*, Pope 21.370–431) and therefore facilitated the making of offerings by allowing traders to sell on the premises. Augustine and Bede, commenting on the similar episode in John's Gospel, take an altogether less hostile line, suggesting that buying and selling in the temple was in itself just and acceptable, and that Christ's action symbolised his opposition to more reprehensible acts.

87–9 From Jn 2.14: *Et invenit in templo vendentes boves, et oves, et columbas, et nummularios sedentes*. Gregory (Hom. 39, PL 76, 1295A) refers to Mark 11 for the doves; Haymo (Hom. 122, PL 118, 657–8) refers to the sheep, oxen and doves of John 2 but not the money-changers.

89–94 Cf Haymo, Hom. 122, PL 118, 657D:

> Avaritiae quoque suae consulentes, quoddam ingeniosum invenerant, et filiis Israel de longinquo venientibus persuadebant, ne secum hostias deferrent, ut ab illis carius emerent, quod in templo Dei offerrent.

For Ælfric's explanation of the allegorical meaning of sacrificial offerings, cf Isidore, *In Leviticum*, c.1 (*Quaestiones in Vetus Testamentum*, PL 83, 321B), a source used for similar points in CH II.12.344 ff:

> Sequens Leviticus liber hostiarum diversitates exsequitur, quarum typus imaginem passionis Christi praeferebat.

97–105 The essence of the argument is in Gregory, Hom. 39, PL 76, 1295B:

> Quia Redemptor noster praedicationis verba nec indignis et ingratis subtrahit, postquam disciplinae vigorem eiiciendo perversos tenuit, donum mox gratiae ostendit.

The allusion at 98–9 is to Mt 5.45:

> Ut sitis filii Patris vestri, qui in caelis est: qui solem suum oriri facit super bonos et malos: et pluit super iustos et iniustos.

105–11 Gregory, Hom. 39, PL 76, 1295BC:

Debemus ex rebus exterioribus introrsus aliquam similitudinem trahere, atque ex eversis aedificiis parietum morum ruinam timere. . . . Hoc quotidie Redemptor noster per electos suos agere nullatenus cessat, cum quosdam ex bona vita ad mores reprobos pervenisse considerat. Plangit enim eos qui nesciunt cur plangantur, quia, iuxta Salomonis verba: 'Laetantur cum male fecerint, et exsultant in rebus pessimis' (Prov 2.14).

114–23 Gregory, Hom. 39, PL 76, 1295D-6A:

Suam hic diem habet anima perversa, quae transitorio gaudet in tempore. Cui ea quae adsunt ad pacem sunt, quia dum ex rebus temporalibus laetatur, dum honoribus extollitur, dum in carnis voluptate resolvitur, dum nulla venturae poenae formidine terretur, pacem habet in die sua . . . abscondit sibi mala sequentia, quia praevidere futura refugit, quae praesentem laetitiam perturbant; dumque in praesentis vitae oblectationibus se deserit, quid aliud quam clausis oculis ad ignem vadit?

123–30 Gregory, Hom. 39, PL 76, 1295D-6B:

Ibi affligenda est, ubi iusti laetabuntur; et cuncta quae modo ei ad pacem sunt, tunc in amaritudinem rixae vertentur, quia rixari secum incipiet cur damnationem quam patitur non expavit, cur a prospiciendis malis sequentibus oculos mentis clausit. . . . Hinc namque scriptum est: 'Beatus homo qui semper est pavidus: qui vero mentis est durae, corruet in malum' (Prov 28.14).

130–2 Sir 7.40 (not cited by Gregory or Haymo):

In omnibus operibus tuis memorare novissima tua, et in aeternum non peccabis.

135–8 Gregory, Hom. 39, PL 76, 1296BC:

Qui unquam sunt humanae animae maiores inimici, quam maligni spiritus, qui hanc a corpore exeuntem obsident . . . hanc ad societatem suae damnationis trahentes coarctant.

138–43 Gregory, Hom. 39, PL 76, 1296C:

Maligni spiritus undique animam angustant, quando ei non solum operis, verum etiam locutionis atque insuper cogitationis iniquitates replicant. . . . [*earlier*] ut in ipsa iam extremitate vitae deprehensa, et a quibus hostibus circumclusa sit videat, et tamen evadendi aditum invenire non possit.

143–50 Gregory, Hom. 39, PL 76, 1296D:

Tunc anima per cognitionem reatus sui ad terram consternitur, cum caro quam vitam suam credidit redire ad pulverem urgetur. Tunc in mortem filii illius cadunt, cum cogitationes illicitae quae modo ex illa prodeunt, in extrema vitae ultione dissipantur, sicut scriptum est: '[Nolite confidere in principibus, in filiis hominum, in quibus non est salus. Exibit spiritus eius, et revertetur in terram suam;] in illa die peribunt omnes cogitationes eorum.' (Ps 145.2–4, *but Gregory quotes only the last part of verse 4.*)

151–6 Gregory, Hom. 39, PL 76, 1297A:

Perversa mens cum perversae cogitationi adhuc perversiorem adiicit, quid aliud quam lapidem super lapidem ponit? Sed in destructa civitate super lapidem lapis non relinquitur, quia cum ad ultionem suam anima ducitur, omnis ab illa cogitationum suarum constructio dissipatur.

156–61 Gregory, Hom. 39, PL 76, 1297A:

Pravam quamque animam omnipotens Deus multis modis visitare consuevit. Nam assidue hanc visitat praecepto, aliquando autem flagello, aliquando vero miraculo. . . . Sed quia visitationis suae tempus minime cognoscit, illis in extremo vitae inimicis traditur, cum quibus in aeterno iudicio damnationis perpetuae societate colligatur.

161–2 Cf Haymo, Hom. 122, PL 118, 659AB:

et ipsos habet exactores in poena, quos habuit persuasores in culpa.

164–5 Cf Gregory, Hom. 39, PL 76, 1297C:

Et saepe nonnulli religionis habitum sumunt, et dum sacrorum ordinum locum percipiunt, sanctae religionis officium in commercium terrenae negotiationis trahunt.

166–9 Cf Haymo, Hom. 122, PL 118, 660AB (though the resemblance is not close):

Per bovem praedicatores significantur. . . . Quicunque ergo verbum Dei ideo in ecclesia praedicat, ut solummodo humanam gloriam aut temporale praemium accipiat, quasi bovem venalem in templo minat.

169–72 Cf Haymo, Hom. 122, PL 118, 660B:

Et qui Deo sanctitatem [ut] ab hominibus laudetur ostendit, quasi ovem venalem in templo inducit. De quibus Dominus dicit . . .: 'Amen dico vobis, receperunt mercedem suam' (Mt 6.2).

172–5 Haymo, Hom. 122, PL 118, 660BC:

Per columbam vero spiritus sancti gratia figuratur . . . Igitur qui gradum ecclesiasticum, aut manus impositionem, per quam spiritum sanctum credimus dari, ideo tribuit, ut temporale lucrum acquirat, quasi columbam venalem in templo portat, id est in ecclesia, non considerans illud quod Dominus ait: 'Gratis accepistis, gratis date' (Mt 10.8).

175–9 Neither Haymo nor Gregory mention the money-changers.

180–4 Cf Gregory, Hom. 39, PL 76, 1297D-8A:

Dum nonnunquam perversi homines locum religionis tenent, ibi malitiae suae gladiis occidunt, ubi vivificare proximos orationis suae intercessione debuerunt.

184–6 Gregory, Hom. 39, PL 76, 1298A:

Templum quoque et domus Dei est ipsa mens atque conscientia fidelium.

and 1 Cor 3.17: *Templum enim Dei sanctum est, quod estis vos.*

186–8 Gregory, Hom. 39, PL 76, 1298A:

Mens fidelium iam non domus orationis, sed spelunca latronum est, quando, relicta innocentia et simplicitate sanctitatis, . . . [*earlier*] in laesione proximi perversas cogitationes profert.

189–93 Gregory, Hom. 39, PL 76, 1298B:

Cum mentem fidelium ad cavenda mala subtiliter erudit, quotidie Veritas in templo docet.

(191–3 seems a curious little corrective to Gregory.)

194–225 The story is from Gregory, Hom. 12, PL 76, 1122B-23A:

Rem, fratres carissimi, refero, quam si intente audire vult caritas vestra, ex consideratione illius vehementer instruetur. Quidam vir nobilis in Valeria provincia nomine Chrysaorius fuit . . . : vir valde idoneus, sed tantum plenus vitiis, quantum rebus; superbia tumidus, carnis suae voluptatibus subditus, in acquirendis rebus avaritiae facibus accensus. Sed cum tot malis Dominus finem ponere decrevisset . . . corporis languore percussus est. Qui ad extremum veniens, eadem hora qua iam de corpore erat exiturus, apertis oculis vidit tetros et nigerrimos spiritus coram se assistere, et vehementer imminere, ut ad inferni claustra se raperent. Coepit tremere, pallescere, sudare, et magnis vocibus inducias petere, filiumque suum nomine Maximum, quem ipse iam monachus monachum vidi, nimiis et turbatis clamoribus vocare, dicens: 'Maxime curre, nunquam tibi aliquid mali feci, in fidem tuam me suscipe. Turbatus mox Maximus adfuit. . . . Pavore tetrae eorum imaginis huc illucque vertebatur in lectulo, iacebat in sinistro latere, aspectum eorum ferre non poterat; vertebatur ad parietem, ibi aderant. Cumque constrictus nimis relaxari se iam posse desperaret, coepit magnis vocibus clamare, dicens: 'Inducias vel usque mane, inducias vel usque mane.' Sed cum haec clamaret in ipsis suis vocibus de habitaculo suae carnis evulsus est. De quo nimirum constat quia pro nobis ista, non pro se, viderit, ut eius visio nobis proficiat, quos adhuc divina patientia longanimiter exspectat. Nam illi tetros spiritus ante mortem vidisse, et inducias petiisse, quid profuit, qui easdem inducias quas petiit, non accepit? Nos ergo, fratres carissimi, nunc sollicite ista cogitemus, ne nobis in vacuum tempora pereant, et tunc quaeramus ad bene agendum vivere, cum iam compellimur de corpore exire.

29 ST LAURENCE

Laurence was probably a historical figure of the third century, a deacon martyred in Rome, but the legend which developed about him in the fourth and fifth centuries has little connection with historical reality, reflecting more the concerns of the later period.[1] His cult was prominent in early medieval Europe, and strikingly so in England, where his feast-day had the same prominence in monastic calendars as the apostles Peter and Paul[2] and was one of the select few saints' days apart from the apostles' which were celebrated by the laity as well as the monks. Relics of the saint were sent to King Oswiu of Northumbria in the seventh century, and the eighth-century church at Bradford-on-Avon was dedicated to him.[3] It is difficult to determine quite what caused the extraordinary growth of his cult, giving greater status to the humble deacon than to the pope, Sixtus II, whom he served and who was martyred three days before him. It may have been the exemplary function of this story of an archdeacon defending the church's treasure from the secular powers and converting it into spiritual wealth; or the accidents that his tomb in Rome lay on a popular pilgrim route and he found a place in the Roman liturgy; or the dramatic appeal of the vivid account of his torments, with his witty final words to the emperor (though the torments themselves seem to have been borrowed from the legend of St Vincent, who never achieved similar prominence). His story seems originally to have been part of an account which also covered Pope Sixtus but it was later absorbed into a much longer narrative, known in the manuscripts as the *Passio Polochronii, Parmenii, Abdon et Sennen, Xysti, Felicissimi et Agapiti et Laurentii et aliorum sanctorum* and more recently as the Roman legendary. This begins in Persia with the persecution of Abdon and Sennes (whose story was later told by Ælfric in LS 24) and other Christians by Decius and his prefect Valerian, then moves to Rome where the persecutions continue, leading to the martyrdom of Sixtus and his deacons, Laurence, Romanus, Hippolitus and his household, Decius's daughter and many of his soldiers. Historically these figures belong to different periods and their connection, as Delehaye shows, is rather that their feast-days formed a sequence within the church-year, but in the legend their stories are loosely linked in chronological sequence.

Ælfric's use of this legend was demonstrated by Förster,[4] who cited the sixteenth-century edition by Surius. Zettel has since shown that the critical edition by Delehaye provides a text rather closer to Ælfric, and that a version similar to Ælfric's was available to him in the Cotton-Corpus legendary.[5] Ælfric

[1] See H. Delehaye, 'Recherches sur le légendier romain', *Analecta Bollandiana* 51 (1933), 34–98.
[2] See Zettel 1979, p. 76.
[3] D. H. Farmer, *The Oxford Dictionary of Saints* (4th ed., Oxford, 1997), p. 296.
[4] Förster 1892, p. 26.
[5] Zettel 1979, pp. 178–9.

breaks into the long narrative at the point where the final persecution of Sixtus begins, and continues beyond the death of Laurence to the martyrdom of Yppolitus and his household, who had been converted by Laurence, and to the death of Decius and Valerian and the conversion of Decius's family and soldiers, thus ending on a note of victory rather than proceeding to the further persecutions with which the legend itself ends. He follows his source closely, adding scarcely any comments of his own but abridging some of the repetitive dialogues between martyrs and persecutors and omitting a few peripheral incidents. The style of the Latin text is rather crude, however, with very flat and repetitive diction, and Ælfric produces a much more varied and colourful language of the kind which becomes characteristic of his hagiographical writing.[6]

Sources and Notes

The following texts are cited below:

1. Anon., *Passio Polochronii, Parmenii, Abdon et Sennen, Xysti, Felicissimi et Agapiti et Laurentii et aliorum Sanctorum*, ed. H. Delehaye, 'Recherches sur le légendier romain', *Analecta Bollandiana* 51 (1933), 34–98 (text, pp. 72–98). Source passages are cited from Delehaye. Variant readings from Delehaye's critical apparatus or from the older edition printed by Surius, IV.581–91, are cited where these are closer to Ælfric's version.

3–11 *Passio*, c. 11:

> Eodem tempore Decius Caesar et Valerianus praefectus iusserunt sibi Xystum episcopum cum clero suo praesentari noctu intra civitatem in Tellure. Xystus igitur . . . dixit ad clerum suum: 'Fratres . . . nolite pavescere; omnes sancti quanta passi sunt tormenta ut securi perpetuam obtinerent vitae aeternae palmam. . . . Venite, nemo metuat terrores.' Responderunt Felicissimus et Agapitus diacones et dixerunt: 'Et nos sine patre nostro quo ibimus?'

Decius reigned 249–51AD and was responsible for the first systematic persecution of Christians. Valerian may be based on the emperor Valerian who reigned from 253–60AD and also persecuted Christians. Sixtus may be based on Pope Sixtus II, 257–8AD. Here and elsewhere in this homily Ælfric uses *preost* to designate clerics in general, including here the members of the pope's household, not just those in priest's orders.

11–18 *Passio*, c. 12:

> Et praesentatus est noctu Decio et Valeriano cum duobus diaconibus. . . . Decius dixit: 'Ergo sacrifica diis immortalibus, et esto princeps sacerdotum.'

[6] There is an excellent account of the cult and versions of the legend in Whatley (*Acta*, forthcoming), and a brief but informative discussion of the style and treatment in Hugh Magennis, 'Contrasting features in the non-Ælfrician Lives in the Old English *Lives of Saints*', *Anglia* 104 (1986), 316–48.

Beatus Xystus episcopus respondit: 'Ego semper sacrificavi et sacrifico Deo patri omnipotenti, et domino Iesu Christo, filio eius et spiritui sancto hostiam puram et immaculatam.' Decius dixit: '. . . Consule et tu tibi vel clero tuo. . . . Sacrifica; nam si non feceris, tu eris exemplum omnium.'

18–26 *Passio*, c. 12:

Xystus episcopus respondit: 'Iam semel tibi dixi: sacrificium semper offero Deo et domino Iesu Christo filio eius.' Decius dixit ad milites: 'Ducite eum ad templum Martis, [ut *Surius*] sacrificet deo Marti. Quod si noluerit, recludite eum in privata Mamertini.' Et duxerunt eum ad templum Martis, et coarctabant eum sacrificiis coinquinari. . . . Et contempto praecepto Decii, duxerunt eum in custodiam privatam cum duobus diaconibus Felicissimo et Agapito.

27–33 *Passio*, c. 13:

Cumque audisset beatus Laurentius archidiaconus beatum Xystum episcopum iterum in custodiam reduci, his verbis appellare coepit: 'Quo progrederis sine filio, pater? quo, sacerdos sancte, sine diacono properas. Tu nunquam sacrificasti sine ministro nec offerre consueveras. Quid in me displicuit, pater? . . . et tu, pater, ostende in filio virtutem tuam; et offer, quem erudisti, ut securus iudicii tui, comitatu nobili pervenias ad coronam.'

The point in the Latin seems to be that Laurence wishes to be martyred before, or with, Sixtus, so as to provide a noble retinue when the latter comes to heaven. Ælfric lacks this idea and seems to be rendering *securius (orsorglicor)* rather than *securus*.

35–41 *Passio*, c. 13:

Tunc Xystus episcopus dixit: 'Non ego te, fili, desero, neque derelinquo, sed maiora tibi debentur certamina. Nos quasi senes levioris pugnae cursum recipimus; te quasi iuvenem gloriosior de tyranno triumphus expectat. Post venies; flere desiste; post triduum sequeris sacerdotem levita. . . . Accipe facultates ecclesiae vel thesauros, et divide quibus tibi videtur.'

If *maran* at 36 in MSS A and E is not just an error for n.s. *mara* (as in other manuscripts), *gerist* is here impersonal and *maran campdom* an accusative.

42–7 *Passio*, c. 14:

Beatus Laurentius coepit per regiones [*but Ælfric may have been following the variant* peregrinos,[7] *cf his* ælþeodigum 43] curiose quaerere, ubicunque sancti clerici vel pauperes essent absconsi; et portans thesauros, prout cuique opus erat, ministrabat. Venit autem in Caelium montem, ubi erat quaedam vidua, . . . quae habebat in domo sua multos christianos et presbyteros et clericos absconsos. . . . Tunc veniens invenit multitudinem

[7] So J. E. Cross, 'The *Passio S. Laurentii et Aliorum*: Latin Manuscripts and the *Old English Martyrology*', *Mediaeval Studies* 45 (1983), 200–13, at 208.

christianorum in domo Cyriacae viduae et coepit pedes omnium christianorum lavare. Et . . . venit Cyriace ad pedes beati Laurentii, dicens ei: 'Per Christum te coniuro, ut manus tuas ponas super caput meum, quia multas infirmitates patior capitis.' Tunc beatus Laurentius . . . posuit manum super caput Cyriacae viduae . . . et salva facta est.

47–9 *Passio*, c. 15:

Et invenit . . . hominem nomine Crescentionem caecum, qui eum cum lacrimis coepit rogare. . . . Tunc beatus Laurentius . . . facto signo Christi in oculis eius, ipsa hora aperti sunt, et vidit lumen.

49–51 A summary reference to the details of the *Passio*, cc. 15–16.

52–8 *Passio*, c. 17:

Et eadem hora exiens inde, ecce beatus Xystus ducebatur ad Tellurem, ut audiretur, et cum eo duo diacones Felicissimus et Agapitus. Et sedit Decius et Valerianus. Dixit autem Decius ad beatum Xystum episcopum iracundia plenus: 'Nos quidem consulimus senectuti tuae; [audi praecepta nostra et sacrifica *MS C and Surius*].' . . . Respondit beatus Xystus: 'Miser, tu tibi consule . . . sed age poenitentiam de sanguine sanctorum, quem effudisti.'

58–68 *Passio*, c. 17:

Decius, furore plenus, dixit ad Valerianum: 'Si iste extinctus non fuerit, non erit clarus timor.' Valerianus respondit: 'Capite puniatur. . . . Ducantur ad templum Martis iterum [ut *Surius*] sacrificent. Quod si noluerint sacrificare, in eodem loco capite truncentur.' Et ducti foras muros portae Appiae, coepit beatus Xystus dicere: 'Ecce idola vana muta et surda et lapidea, quibus miseri inclinantur, ut perdant vitam aeternam.' Et dixit ad templum Martis: 'Destruat te Christus, filius Dei vivi.' Et cum hoc dixisset beatus Xystus . . . subito cecidit aliqua pars templi et comminuta est.

68–74 *Passio*, c. 18:

Tunc beatus Laurentius coepit clamare: 'Noli me derelinquere, pater sancte, quia iam thesauros expendi, quos tradidisti mihi.' Tunc milites tenuerunt beatum Laurentium archidiaconum, audientes de thesauris; sanctum vero Xystum episcopum et Felicissimum et Agapitum diacones duxerunt in clivum Martis ante templum et ibidem decollatus est cum duobus diaconibus . . . octavo idus augustas.

75–82 *Passio*, c. 19:

Decius fecit sibi beatum Laurentium praesentari. Quem ita aggreditur Decius Caesar dicens: 'Ubi sunt thesauri ecclesiae, quos apud te cognovimus esse reconditos?' Beatus Laurentius non respondit ei verbum. Eodem die Decius Caesar tradidit eum Valeriano praefecto dicens: 'Quaere thesauros ecclesiae diligenter et sacrificet. . . .' Tunc Valerianus dedit eum cuidam vicario, nomine Yppolito, qui reclusit eum cum multis.

82–8 *Passio*, c. 20:

Erat autem ibi homo in custodia multo tempore, gentilis, qui plorando amissis oculis caecus factus fuerat. Dixit ad eum beatus Laurentius: 'Crede in dominum Iesum Christum, filium Dei vivi, et baptizare et illuminabit te.' Respondit Lucillus, et dixit: 'Ego semper desideravi baptizari in nomine domini nostri Iesu Christi.' Beatus Laurentius dixit: 'Si ex toto corde credis?' Respondit Lucillus cum fletu dicens: 'Ego credo in dominum Iesum Christum et idola vana respuo.' Yppolitus patienter auscultabat verba eorum.

89–95 *Passio*, c. 20:

Laurentius catecizavit eum et accepta aqua . . . [*here a passage of dialogue about belief in the Trinity is summed up in a phrase by Ælfric, 89–90*] . . . continuo baptizavit eum. . . . Tunc aperti sunt oculi eius et coepit clamare dicens: 'Benedictus dominus Iesus Christus, Deus aeternus, qui me illuminavit per beatum Laurentium quia semper caecus fui et modo video.' Tunc audientes multi caeci veniebant ad beatum Laurentium cum lacrimis. Et beatus Laurentius . . . ponebat manus super oculos caecorum et illuminabantur.

The man's claim to have always been blind contradicts the initial account of him, and is changed by Ælfric.

96–106 *Passio*, c. 21:

Videns autem Yppolitus dixit ad beatum Laurentium: 'Ostende mihi thesauros ecclesiae.' Dicit ei beatus Laurentius; 'O Yppolite, si credas in Deum patrem omnipotentem et in filium eius dominum Iesum Christum, et thesauros tibi ostendo et vitam aeternam promitto.' Dicit ei Yppolitus: 'Si dictis facta compenses, faciam quae hortaris.' . . . [Et accepta aqua benedixit et baptizavit eum *MS C and Surius*]. Et extractus de aqua coepit dicere Yppolitus: 'Vidi animas innocentium laetas gaudere.' Et dixit ad beatum Laurentium cum lacrimis: 'Adiuro te, per dominum Iesum Christum, ut omnis domus mea baptizetur.' Et baptizati sunt promiscui sexus in domo Yppoliti numero decem et novem cum gloria.

107–14 *Passio*, cc. 21–2:

[c.21] Tunc mandavit Valerianus ad Yppolitum: 'Adduc ad palatium Laurentium.' Dixit autem Yppolitus ad beatum Laurentium: 'Valerianus ex praecepto Decii misit ut te ad eum perducam.' Beatus Laurentius dixit: 'Ambulemus, quoniam et mihi et tibi gloria paratur.' Et cum venissent ambo simul ante conspectum Valeriani, Valerianus dixit ad beatum Laurentium: 'Iam depone pertinaciam [et da thesauros *MSS BC*, profer thesauros *Surius*].' . . . [*Laurence asks for three days' grace and collects a large number of the poor and infirm and presents them to Decius, saying:* c.22] 'Ecce isti sunt thesauri aeterni, qui numquam minuuntur et semper crescunt.'

114–24 *Passio*, c. 22:

Valerianus praefectus dixit praesente Decio Caesare: 'Quid variaris per multa? Sacrifica diis et obliviscere artem magicam in qua confidis.' Beatus Laurentius dixit: 'Quare vos coartat diabolus ut christianis dicatis: "Sacrificate demoniis"? Si iustum est ut demonibus magis inclinemur quam domino creatori visibilium et invisibilium, vos ipsi iudicate, quis debet adorari, qui factus est an qui fecit.' Decius Caesar dixit: 'Quis factus est vel quis fecit?' Beatus Laurentius dixit: 'Deus, pater domini nostri Iesu Christi, creator est omnis creaturae. . . . Et tu dicis: "sacrifica lapidibus et adora facturas surdas et mutas."'

125–34 *Passio*, c. 23:

Decius Caesar iratus iussit eum in conspectu suo exspoliari et cedi cum scorpionibus, ipso Decio clamante: 'Deos blasphemare noli.' Beatus Laurentius inter ipsa tormenta dicebat: 'Ego quidem gratias ago Deo meo, qui me dignatus est coniungere inter servos suos. Tu, miser, torqueris in insania tua et in furore tuo.' Decius Caesar dixit: 'Levate eum a terra et date ante conspectum eius omne genus tormentorum.' Et allatae sunt lamminae ferreae et lecti et plumbatae et cardi. Et dixit ei Decius Caesar: 'Sacrifica diis; nam omne genus hoc tormentorum in corpore tuo vectabitur.'

The technical terms for the instruments of torture, here and subsequently, are taxing. *Lamminae ferrae* are (red-hot) iron plates, rendered *clutas* by Ælfric. *Plumbatae* are thongs with leaden balls attached, presumably rendered *leadene swipan*. *Cardi*, literally 'thistles', appear to be instruments similar to the combs used in preparing cloth (C. Du Cange, *Glossarium Mediae et Infimae Latinitatis*, 10 vols. (Paris, 1883–87), II); this may correspond to Ælfric's *isene clawan* (line 131), but the same word is rendered *gepiledum swipum*, 'spiked scourges or whips' at 245 (cf 132), a phrase which is also used for *scorpionibus* at 164; the similar list later in the *Passio*, c. 27, includes *ungues*, which might stand for *ungulas*, instruments of torture presumably shaped like a claw or hook, and *fustes*, cudgels or knobbed sticks.

134–42 *Passio*, cc. 23–4:

[c.23] Beatus Laurentius dixit: 'Infelix, has epulas ego semper desideravi; nam tormenta ista aeterna sunt tibi, nobis autem ad gloriam.' Decius Caesar dixit: 'Ergo si gloria est vobis, dic nobis ubi sunt profani similes tui absconsi . . . [c.24] ut mundetur civitas; et tu ipse sacrifica diis et noli confidere in thesauris quos absconditos habes.' Beatus Laurentius dixit: 'Vere et confido et securus sum de thesauris meis.' Decius Caesar dixit: 'An putas te de thesauris liberari aut redimi a tormentis?' . . . Decius, iracundia plenus, iussit eum nudum fustibus caedi.

142–57 *Passio*, c. 24:

Beatus Laurentius, cum caederetur clamabat dicens ad Decium: 'Ecce, miser, vel modo cognosce quia triumpho de thesauris Christi et non sentio tormenta tua.' Decius Caesar dixit: 'Fustibus augete, et date ad latera eius lamminas ferreas ardentes.' Beatus Laurentius dixit in illa hora: 'Domine Iesu Christe, Deus de Deo, miserere mihi servo tuo, quia accusatus non negavi, interrogatus te dominum confessus sum.' Decius Caesar iussit eum levari a terra et dicit ei: 'Video in te artem magicam; scio quia tormenta per artem magicam deludis; tamen me non deludis; testor deos deasque quia aut sacrificabis aut diversis poenis te interficiam.' Beatus Laurentius dixit: 'Ego in nomine domini nostri Iesu Christi non pavesco tormenta tua quae ad tempus sunt; fac quod facis; noli cessare.' Decius, nimio furore arreptus, iussit ut cum plumbatis diutissime caederetur.

157–68 *Passio*, c. 25:

Beatus Laurentius dixit: 'Domine Iesu Christe, qui pro nostra salute dignatus es formam servi accipere, ut nos a servitute daemonum liberares, accipe spiritum meum.' Eadem hora audita est vox . . . : 'Adhuc multa certamina tibi debentur.' Tunc Decius, furore plenus, dicebat voce clara: 'Viri Romani et coetus reipublicae, audistis consolationes daemonum in sacrilegum, qui nec deos nec principes nostros pavescit, nec tormenta metuit exquisita. . . . Extendite eum, et scorpionibus cedentes affligite.' Beatus Laurentius prostratus in catasta, subridens et gratias agens dicebat: 'Benedictus es, domine Deus, pater domini nostri Iesu Christi, qui nobis donasti misericordiam quam meriti non sumus. Sed tu domine, propter tuam pietatem, da nobis gratiam ut cognoscant omnes circum astantes, quia tu consolaris servos tuos.'

169–82 *Passio*, c. 26:

Eadem hora unus de militibus, nomine Romanus, credidit domino Iesu Christo per verba beati Laurentii et coepit dicere ad beatum Laurentium: 'Video in te hominem pulcherrimum stantem cum linteo et extergentem membra tua. De qua re adiuro te per Christum, . . . ne me derelinquas.' Tunc Decius, furore plenus et dolo, dixit ad Valerianum: 'Victi sumus per artem magicam.' Et iussit solvi eum de catasta et levari. . . . Tunc Decius . . . iussit ut Yppolito redderetur ibi tantum in palatio. Veniens autem Romanus et afferens aquam, misit se ad pedes beati Laurentii et rogabat eum cum lacrimis ut baptizaretur. Et accepta aqua, benedixit et baptizavit eum. Audiens Decius hoc factum dixit: 'Exhibete eum cum fustibus.' Et adductus ante conspectum Decii Caesaris, non interrogatus coepit clamare voce magna dicens: 'Christianus sum.' Et iussit eum Decius Caesar in ipsa hora capitis subire sententiam.

183–91 *Passio*, c. 27:

Eadem nocte Decius Caesar . . . pergit noctu ad thermas iuxta palatium Salustii et iussit sibi beatum Laurentium offerri. Tunc Yppolitus coepit tristis esse et plorare. Cui beatus Laurentius ita dixit: 'Noli flere, sed magis gaude et tace, quia vado ad gloriam Dei.' Dicit ei Yppolytus: 'Quare et ego non vocifero quia christianus sum et tecum incumbo?' Beatus Laurentius dixit ei: '. . . Et postmodum cum clamavero, audi et veni.' Et cum haec dixisset, iussit Decius Caesar omne genus tormentorum ante tribunal suum parari. . . . Adducitur noctu ante Decium Caesarem et Valerianum praefectum beatus Laurentius.

191–204 *Passio*, c. 27:

Cui ita dixit Decius: 'Depone perfidiam artis magicae et dic nobis generositatem tuam.' Beatus Laurentius dixit: 'Quantum ad genus, Hyspanus, eruditus vel nutritus Romanus et a cunabulis christianus eruditus omnem legem sanctam et divinam.' Decius Caesar dixit: 'Vere divinam, quia nec deos times, nec tormenta pavescis.' Beatus Laurentius dixit: 'In nomine domini nostri Iesu Christi tormenta tua non pavesco nec metuo.' Decius Caesar dixit: 'Sacrifica diis. Nam nox ista in te expendetur cum suppliciis.' Beatus Laurentius dixit: 'Mea nox obscurum non habet, sed omnia in luce clarescunt.' Tunc iussit ut os eius cum lapidibus tunderetur; ille autem ridens confortabatur et dicebat: 'Gratias tibi ago, domine Deus, quia tu es Deus omnium rerum.'

205–12 *Passio*, c. 28:

Decius Caesar dixit: 'Date lectum ferreum, ut requiescat Laurentius contumax.' . . . Et allatus est beatus Laurentius et expoliatus vestimentis suis in conspectu Decii et Valeriani et extensus in craticula ferrea. Et allati sunt batuli cum prunis et miserunt sub craticulam ferream et cum furcis ferreis coartari fecit beatum Laurentium; et dixit Decius Caesar: 'Sacrifica diis.' Respondit beatus Laurentius: 'Ego me obtuli sacrificium Deo in odorem suavitatis, quia sacrificium Deo est spiritus contribulatus.'

212–22 *Passio*, c. 28:

Carnifices tamen urguentes ministrabant carbones mittentes sub cratem ferream et desuper comprimentes cum furcis ferreis. Beatus Laurentius dixit: . . . . 'Infelices, non cognoscitis quia carbones vestri non ardorem sed refrigerium mihi praestant?' . . . Ille autem vultu [pulcherrimo *MSS BC*] dicebat: 'Gratias ago tibi, domine Iesu Christe, qui me confortare dignatus es.' Et elevans oculos suos contra Decium, sic dixit beatus Laurentius: 'Ecce, miser, assasti tibi partem unam; regira aliam et manduca.' Tunc gratias agens Deo cum gloria dixit: 'Gratias tibi ago, domine Iesu Christe, quia merui ianuas tuas ingredi.' Et statim emisit spiritum.

Ælfric concludes the account of Laurence with a characteristic interjection of assurance that the saint passed to heaven and remains there still.

223–29 *Passio*, c. 29:

Eadem nocte Decius una cum Valeriano ambulavit exinde in palatium Tyberianum, relicto corpore super craticulam. Mane autem primo adhuc crepusculo, rapuit corpus eius Yppolitus. . . . Iam hora vespertina sepelierunt eum in crypta in via Tyburtina, in praedio Cyriacae viduae . . . quarto idus augustas, et ieiunaverunt agentes vigilias noctis triduo cum multitudine christianorum; et non cessabant mugitum lacrimarum dantes. Beatus autem Iustinus presbyter optulit sacrificium laudis et participati sunt omnes.

229–38 *Passio*, c. 30:

Regressus itaque Yppolitus post diem tertium venit in domum suam et dedit pacem omnibus, etiam servis suis et ancillis; et communicavit de sacrificio. . . . Et . . . venerunt milites et tenuerunt eum et perduxerunt ad Decium Caesarem. Quem videns, Decius Caesar subridens dixit eis: 'Numquid et tu magus effectus es, quia corpus Laurentii abstulisse dicaris?' Respondit Yppolitus: 'Hoc feci non quasi magus, sed quasi christianus.' Quo audito, Decius Caesar, furore arreptus, iussit ut cum lapidibus os eius tunderetur et expoliavit eum veste. . . . Decius Caesar dixit: 'Numquid tu non es cultor deorum? quomodo tam insipiens factus es ut vel nuditatem tuam non erubescas?'

238–47 *Passio*, c. 30:

Yppolitus dixit: 'Ego sapiens et christianus factus sum, quia ignorans feci quod tu credis.' Decius Caesar dixit: 'Sacrifica et vive, aut peries per tormenta, sicut Laurentius.' Yppolitus dixit: 'Exemplum merear beati Laurentii martyris fieri. . . .' Decius Caesar dixit: 'Extendite eum et fustibus caedite'. Et cum diu caederetur dixit: 'Gratias ago Deo meo.' Decius dixit: 'Deridet Yppolitus fustes; cum cardis caedite eum.' Et caedentes defecerunt. Yppolitus autem clamabat voce magna dicens: 'Christianus sum.'

247–64 *Passio*, c. 31:

Decius Caesar, iracundia plenus, dixit ad Valerianum praefectum: 'Accipe omnes facultates eius et interfice eum crudeli examinatione.' Eodem die, Valerianus praefectus, exquisita omni facultate eius, invenit in domo Yppoliti omnem familiam christianam. . . . Valerianus praefectus dixit ad eos . . . : 'Considerate aetates vestras, ne simul pereatis cum Yppolito domino vestro.' Respondit Concordia [*the nurse of Yppolitus*]: 'Nos cum domino nostro desideramus pudice mori quam impudice vivere.' . . . Et iratus iussit eum duci foras muros portae Tyburtinae cum familia sua. Tunc Yppolitus coepit omnes confortare dicens: 'Fratres, nolite metuere, quia ego et vos unum dominum habemus.' Iussit vero Valerianus in conspectu Yppoliti, ut omnis familia eius capite truncarentur. Et decollati sunt promiscui sexus numero decem et novem cum gloria. Beati vero Yppoliti pedes iussit ligari ad colla equorum indomitorum et sic per cardetum et tribulos trahi; qui dum traheretur emisit spiritum . . . idibus augusti.

264–5 *Passio*, c. 32:

Eadem nocte veniens Iustinus presbyter collegit corpora et sepelivit in eodem loco.

The rest of this chapter deals with the recovery of the body of Concordia, whom Ælfric does not treat individually.

266–78 *Passio*, c. 33:

Iussit Decius Caesar editionem munerum in amphitheatro parari, sedente eo in carruca aurea una cum Valeriano praefecto. Cum iam descenderet de carruca et ad amphitheatrum introiret et multos martyres ad crudele munus exhiberet, clamabat Decius Caesar arreptus a daemonio: 'O Yppolite, tamquam vinctum catenis asperis et captivum me ducis.' Valerianus autem clamabat: 'O Laurenti, igneis catenis me trahis.' Et eadem hora expiravit Valerianus praesente Decio. Decius rediens in palatium triduo non cessavit a daemonio agi, qui et ipse clamabat omni die vel nocte: 'Adiuro te, Laurenti, modicum cessa a tormentis.' Et factus est luctus magnus in palatio. Tunc uxor eius . . . iussit omnes sanctos, qui clausi erant, dimitti. Eadem hora mortuus est Decius.

The *Passio* locates this scene in the amphitheatre at an *editio munera* (a giving of gifts or a display of entertainments) and Decius displays the martyrs as a kind of cruel show, similar to the earlier occasion when Abdon and Sennes are exposed to wild beasts in the amphitheatre. (In the Surius version it is more explicitly a slaughter of martyrs that is exhibited.) Ælfric locates it at a place of heathen worship and has Decius and Valerianus trying to compel the Christians to make offerings to the gods. There is nothing in the various texts of the *Passio* to explain this difference. Ælfric may have had a corrupt text, or may have interpreted *munera* as offerings, given the double meaning of the equivalent Old English word, *lac*.

279–87 *Passio*, c. 33:

Uxor autem eius Triphonia venit ad beatum Iustinum et misit se cum lacrymis ad pedes eius, simul et filia Decii Cyrilla, ut baptizarentur. Quas cum gaudio suscepit beatus Iustinus presbyter, et indixit eis ieiunium septem diebus. Et completis diebus septem, baptizavit eas. . . . Audito autem milites quod Triphonia uxor Decii christiana fuisset facta et filia eius Cyrilla, venerunt cum uxoribus suis numero quadraginta sex ad beatum Iustinum presbyterum et miserunt se ad pedes eius, rogantes et postulantes, ut baptismum perciperent.

287–91 *Passio*, c. 34:

Tunc beatus Iustinus presbyter collegit omnem clerum et exquisivit quem in locum beati martyris Xysti episcopi ordinaret. Et ordinaverunt venerabilem virum nomine Dionisium, quem ordinavit Maximus Hostiensis episcopus.

30 ASSUMPTION OF THE VIRGIN

The feast of the assumption had been observed in England since at least the eighth century, but the nature of the event being celebrated remained an uncertain question.[1] By Ælfric's time the practice had developed of celebrating the occasion with readings from the apocryphal legend, recounting in detail the Virgin's death and assumption into heaven, and English versions of the legend survive in the Blickling homilies and in Cambridge, Corpus Christi College MS 41, but Ælfric himself is scathing about this legend, both here and more particularly in his Second Series homily for the occasion (CH II.29.119–33). What he offers instead is a very cautious account of what is known for certain or can be surmised with confidence, drawing on an apparently reliable authority, Jerome. He begins with a chronological summary of Mary's life from the annunciation to her death, using New Testament evidence (lines 28–64). He notes the evidence of the empty tomb but emphasises that there is no reliable account of her end (lines 65–73) and then proceeds with a series of arguments and analogies indicating the probability that her body was resurrected and assumed into heaven, or at least that her soul was assumed into heaven with the glory of one who is greater than all other saints: Christ's own bodily resurrection (lines 73–6); the resurrection of others at the time of the crucifixion (lines 76–80); the death-bed scenes of other saints (lines 85–101); the instructions Christ himself gave to honour parents (lines 101–9); the symbolic account in the Song of Songs and the liturgy (lines 113–52); the heavenly rewards for merits (lines 153–8). He ends this sequence with an exhortation to celebrate the Virgin's day (lines 159–84) and then emphasises the idea of intercession by two stories of the Virgin's intervention taken from saints' lives: first a brief account of Theophilus who sold his soul to the devil, and then a long episode from the Life of St Basil in which the Virgin saves the saint and his people from destruction by the apostate Julian by arranging the emperor's assassination by the spirit of a departed soldier-saint. As Mary Clayton points out, in making the beginnings of a collection of miracles of the Virgin, Ælfric was inititating what became a major phenomenon of the later Middle Ages.

Ælfric's source for the main discussion is a letter purporting to be by Jerome but now agreed to be a forgery, probably by Paschasius Radbertus; it appears in both Paul the Deacon's homiliary and the Cotton-Corpus legendary.[2] It is a rambling, somewhat unorganised address to a community of religious women and involved Ælfric in an intensive effort of selection and reorganisation so as to produce a chronological and logical order. The mixture of freedom in handling the structure and often close rendering of detail suggests that he may have made

[1] See Clayton 1990, esp. pp. 25–51 on the feasts and pp. 232–44 on the homilies.

[2] The source was identified by Förster (1892, p. 28) and there is an excellent and detailed discussion of Ælfric's handling of it in Clayton 1990, to which this account is heavily indebted. For CC see Zettel 1979.

a Latin précis as a medium, as he did with other works such as Julian of Toledo's *Prognosticon* and Alcuin's *De Animae Ratione*. He uses much of sections 1–24, 35–52 and 88–97, though in a very different order; what he omits is mainly material on the theology of the Trinity and the incarnation, and direct address to the community of virgins for whom the text is purportedly written. He accepts the basic argument of Paschasius but is both more dismissive of the apocryphal legend and slightly more confident about the bodily resurrection. Paschasius draws heavily at points on the liturgy for the feast of the assumption, and Ælfric naturally recognised the source and was able to draw independently on it for further material. For the account of Theophilus he probably drew on a *Miraculum Sanctae Mariae de Theophilo* which was included in the Cotton-Corpus legendary, and for the second episode a *Vita Basilii* which also appears in the legendary, as well as, possibly, a *Certamen Sancti Martyris Mercurii* or some brief notice of that saint.[3]

Sources and Notes

The following texts are cited below:

1. Anon., *Vita Basilii*, in Surius, I.4–19.
2. Anon., *Certamen Sancti Martyris Mercurii*, in Surius, VI.569–72.
3. Paschasius Radbertus, *De Assumptione Sanctae Mariae Virginis*, ed. A. Ripberger, CCCM 56C (Turnhout, 1985), pp. 109–62.
4. Paulus Diaconus Neapolitanus, *Miraculum Sanctae Mariae de Theophilo*, ASS Feb. I.489–93.

4–16 The ascription to Jerome is standard in manuscripts of the letter, including Paul the Deacon's homiliary. The genuine letters of Jerome were apparently well known in England, particularly those addressed to Paula and Eustochium (Ogilvy 1967, pp. 173–4), but Ælfric shows no direct knowledge of them in his writings; the information about them that his introductory comments reveal could indeed have been derived from the opening paragraphs of Paschasius's letter.

20–27 Paschasius, *De Assumptione*, §§1 and 7:

> [§1] Cogitis me, o Paula et Eustochium . . . sermonem faciam de assumptione beatae et gloriosae semper virginis Mariae . . . [§7] ut habeat sanctum collegium vestrum in die tantae sollemnitatis munus latini sermonis . . . qualiter favente Deo per singulos annos tota haec dies expendatur in laudem et cum gaudio celebretur, ne forte si venerit vestris in manibus illud apocryphum de transitu eiusdem virginis, dubia pro certis recipiatis.

[3] See Förster 1892, p. 28; L. H. Loomis, 'The Saint Mercurius Legend in Medieval England and in Norse saga', in *Philologica: The Malone Anniversary Studies*, ed. T. A. Kirby and H. B. Woolf (Baltimore, 1949), pp. 132–43; Zettel 1979; and Clayton 1990.

28–32 Paschasius, *De Assumptione*, §§3 and 6:

[§3] Porro ab exordio sancti evangelii Gabrielem archangelum colloquentem Mariae audistis, et deinceps reliqua omnia plenius legistis. . . . [§6] Omnia salvatoris gesta et beatae Mariae obsequia necnon actus vitae ex evangelio didicistis.

32–52 Paschasius, *De Assumptione*, §§16–17:

[§16] Iohannes . . . qui sibi commissam 'accepit in suam' quasi matrem filius, cui benignus magister de cruce: 'Mulier', inquit, 'ecce filius tuus', ad discipulum autem: 'Ecce mater tua' (Jn 19.26–7) ut virgo virgini cohaereret et deserviret officiosissime cura adoptionis. Non enim pudicissima virginitas alicui discipulorum rectius quam virgini commendatur, ut esset ad invicem grata societas . . . et venustus conversandi. . . . Una virtus virginitatis in ambobus, sed altera proportio in Maria. Altera quidem quia fecundior, sed ipsa. . . . Idcirco et fecunditas in illa tota deifica est et virginitas, alioquin nusquam secundum naturam nascendi virginitas, ubi fecunditas praedicatur, neque fecunditas, ubi virginitas integra conservatur. [§17] Ideoque totum superexcellit de illa quae dicuntur, quia sunt divina atque ineffabilia.

Ælfric's phrasing shows the influence of Jn 19.26–7:

(26) Cum vidisset ergo Iesus matrem, et discipulum stantem, quem diligebat . . . (27) Et ex illa hora accepit eam discipulus in sua.

For the notion that Christ loved John specially because of his virginity (lines 38–9) cf CH I.4.4–7, based on Bede. The Latin note in MS A at 41, explaining that virginity can be attributed to men as well as women, is presumably Ælfric's; cf the similar point in the text at CH I.9.204–5.

52–60 Paschasius, *De Assumptione*, §§15 and 16:

[§15] Non quod eximius ille sanctorum chorus apostolorum deseruerit eam, inter quos post resurrectionem intrans et exiens familiarius . . . [§16] omnes venerati sunt discipuli eique famulabantur officio dilectionis . . .[§15] contulit de Christi incarnatione, tanto siquidem verius, quanto ab initio plenius per spiritum sanctum cuncta didicerat et perspexerat oculis universa, licet et apostoli per eundem spiritum sanctum omnia cognoverint et in omnem edocti pervenerint veritatem.

60–4 Details from Paschasius, *De Assumptione*, §§14, 20, 38 and 39:

[§14] Quam sane angelus Gabriel acsi caelestis paranimphus intactam custodivit . . . [§20] cum quibus [= *the apostles*] virgo vacat in schola virtutum et meditatur in lege mandatorum Dei . . . [§39] haec est dies in qua usque ad throni celsitudinem intemerata mater et virgo processit . . . [§38] 'haec est dies praeclara, in qua meruit exaltari super choros angelorum' [*from the Office for the Assumption*].

65–76 Paschasius, *De Assumptione*, §§7–9:

[§7] Nihil aliud experiri potest pro certo, nisi quod hodierna die gloriosa migravit a corpore. [§8] Monstratur sepulcrum eius cernentibus nobis usque ad praesens in vallis Iosaphat medio, quae vallis est inter montem Sion et montem Oliveti posita . . . ubi in eius honore fabricata est ecclesia miro lapideo tabulatu . . . sed nunc vacuum esse cernentibus ostenditur. . . . [§9] Quomodo vel quo tempore . . . sanctissimum corpus eius inde ablatum fuerit vel ubi transpositum, utrum vere surrexerit, nescitur, quamvis nonnulli astruere velint eam iam resuscitatam et beata cum Christo inmortalitate in caelestibus vestiri.

Ælfric strengthens the case for the assumption, writing *gehwylce lareowas*, (either 'all' or 'many' scholars), for Paschasius's *nonnulli*, and drawing the parallel with Christ's own resurrection. He now passes over Paschasius, *De Assumptione*, §10, which expresses parallel doubts about the bodily resurrection of St John the Evangelist, a point which Ælfric had presented without qualification in CH I.4 (cf Clayton 1990, p. 237).

76–80 Paschasius, *De Assumptione*, §11:

Sicuti et de his, quos cum Domino . . . resurrexisse credimus . . . de quibus profecto nonnulli doctorum senserunt, etiam et in suis reliquerunt scriptis, quod iam in illis perpetua sit completa resurrectio. Fatentur enim, quod veri testes non essent, nisi et vera esset eorum resurrectio.

80–4 Paschasius, *De Assumptione*, §12:

Quod, quia Deo nihil est impossibile, nec nos de beata Maria factum abnuimus, quamquam propter cautelam, salva fide, pio magis desiderio opinari oporteat quam inconsulte definire, quod sine periculo nescitur.

85–9 Paschasius, *De Assumptione*, §49:

Legimus quam saepe ad funera et ad sepulturas quorumlibet sanctorum angelos advenisse . . . necnon et animas electorum usque ad caelos cum hymnis et laudibus detulisse, ubi et utriusque sexus chori commemorantur, frequenter auditi laudes cecinisse, interea, et quod perspicacius est, multo nonnumquam lumine eosdem resplenduisse, insuper et adhuc viventes in carne ibidem miri odoris fragrantiam diutius persensisse.

89–97 Paschasius, *De Assumptione*, §50:

Quodsi . . . salvator noster Christus ob merita suorum amplius comprobanda talia et tanta dignatus est exhibere per suos caeli ministros circa defunctos, quanto magis credendum hodierna die militiam caelorum cum suis agminibus festive obviam advenisse genetrici Dei eamque ingenti lumine circumfulsisse et usque ad thronum olim sibi etiam ante mundi constitutionem paratum cum laudibus et canticis spiritalibus perduxisse?

98–107 Paschasius, *De Assumptione*, §§51–2:

[§51] Nulli dubium omnem illam caelestem Hierusalem tunc exultasse ineffabili laetitia. . . . Creditur enim, quod salvator omnium ipse, quantum datur intellegi, per se totus festivus occurrit, et cum gaudio eam secum in throno collocavit. [§52] Alias autem quomodo implevisse creditur quod in lege ipse praecepit: 'Honora', inquit, 'patrem tuum et matrem tuam' (Mt 15.4)? Porro quod patrem honoraverit, ipse sibi testis est, cum ad Iudaeos ait: 'Ego . . . honorifico patrem meum, et vos inhonorastis me' (Jn 8.49). De matre vero evangelista: 'Cum redirent, veniens', ait, 'Nazareth, erat subditus illis' (Lc 2.43, 51).

110–3 Paschasius, *De Assumptione*, §§45, 51:

[§45] Quae profecto festivitas, sicuti et virgo incomparabilis est ceteris virginibus, ita et incomparabilis est omnium sanctorum festivitatibus et admiranda etiam virtutibus angelicis. . . . [§51] Festivitas haec, quae nobis hodie revolvitur annua, illis omnibus facta est continua.

113–23 Paschasius, *De Assumptione*, §47:

De qua rursus idem spiritus sanctus in eisdem canticis: 'Quae est ista quae ascendit', inquit, 'quasi aurora consurgens, pulchra ut luna, electa ut sol, terribilis ut castrorum acies ordinata' (Cant 6.9). Admiratur autem spiritus sanctus, quia omnes de ascensu huius virginis admirantes facit. . . . 'Pulchra ut luna', immo pulchrior quam luna, quia iam sine defectu sui coruscat caelestibus illustrata fulgoribus. 'Electa ut sol' fulgore virtutum, quia ipse eam elegit sol iustitiae, ut nasceretur ex ea. . . . [*earlier*] Siquidem terribilis suis facta virtutibus, ut castrorum acies admodum ordinata, hinc inde sanctorum angelorum fulta praesidiis.

124–35 Paschasius, *De Assumptione*, §§88–90:

[§88] De huius nimirum ad caelos ascensione multo admirantis intuitu, secretorum contemplator caelestium in canticis, 'Vidi', inquit, 'speciosam ascendentem quasi columbam desuper rivos aquarum . . . cuius odor inaestimabilis erat nimis . . . [§89] quam circumdabant flores rosarum et lilia convallium', eo quod omnes animae martyrio rubricatae eam aeternae dilectionis complectuntur amplexibus, et virginitatis splendore candidatae acsi lilia in valle humilitatis enutritae circumdant eam venerationis gratia obsequentes. [§90] Recte igitur, quoniam beata Dei genetrix et martyr et virgo fuit. . . . [§88] Et vere speciosa quasi columba, quia illius speciem columbae ac simplicitatem praemonstrabat, quae super Dominum venit, et docuit Iohannem.

The words quoted are not in fact from the Bible but from the Office for the Assumption (PL 78, 798A; see A. Ripberger, CCCM, 56C, p. 149).

135–45 Paschasius, *De Assumptione*, §90:

Alii sancti, etsi passi sunt pro Christo in carne, tamen in anima, quia immortalis est, pati non potuerunt. Beata vero Dei genitrix, quia in ea parte passa est, quae impassibilis habetur, ideo ut ita fatear, quia spiritaliter et atrocius passa est gladio passionis Christi, plus quam martyr fuit. Unde constat, qui plus omnibus dilexit, propterea et plus doluit, intantum ut animum eius totam pertransiret et possideret vis doloris.

Cf the similar discussion at CH I.9.170 ff.

146–58 Paschasius, *De Assumptione*, §§92, 97, 96:

> [§92] Nihil virtutis est, nihil speciositatis, nihil candoris gloriae, quod ex ea non resplendeat. Et ideo bene circumdant eam flores rosarum et lilia convallium, ut virtutes virtutibus fulciantur, et formositas decore castitatis augeatur. . . . [*§§92–6 give the general sense of lines 149–52*] . . . [§97] Quodsi 'in domo patris mansiones multae sunt' (Jn 14.2), credimus splendidiorem matri hodie filium praestitisse. . . . [§96] Beata igitur . . . supernorum civium societas, et admirabilis caritatis eorum unanimitas, ubi nemo angelorum . . . alicuius sanctorum invidet gloriam sed totum in altero unusquisque possidet . . . ubi . . . meritorum qualitas sola discernitur.

Ælfric's extension of the idea of the elect in heaven being ordered according to merit but showing no envy of those higher placed bears some resemblance to his expansion of Julian of Toledo's *Prognosticon* (*Excerpts*, 395–400) and is clearly a particular interest for him.

159–65 Paschasius, *De Assumptione*, §23:

> 'Hodie namque gloriosa semper virgo caelos ascendit'; rogo 'gaudete, quia' . . . ineffabiliter sublimata 'cum Christo regnat in aeternum'. Regina mundi hodie de terris et de praesenti saeculo nequam eripitur. Iterum dico: gaudete, quia secura . . . ad caeli iam pervenit palatium. Exultate, inquam, ac gaudete, et laetetur omnis orbis, quia hodie nobis omnibus eius intervenientibus meritis salus aucta est.

The quotations are from the Office for the Assumption (PL 78, 799).

165–7 Cf the Office for the Assumption (PL 78, 799D):

> Paradisi porta per Evam cunctis clausa est, et per Mariam virginem iterum patefacta est, alleluia.

167–72 Paschasius, *De Assumptione*, §24:

> Si Deum ore prophetico in sanctis suis laudare iubemur (Ps 150.1), multo magis eum in hac celebritate beatae virginis matris eius oportet cum hymnis et canticis diligentius extollere. . . . Nulli dubium quin totum ad gloriam laudis eius pertineat, quicquid digne genetrici suae impensum fuerit ac sollemniter.

Ælfric interpolates an echo of Ps 67.36: *Mirabilis Deus in sanctis suis.*

173–84 Paschasius, *De Assumptione*, §§35–6:

> [§35] Propterea quia iter salutis nostrae in laudibus est salvatoris, hortor vos et commoneo in hac sacra sollemnitate genetricis Dei Mariae, nolite cessare a laudibus. Quod si virgo es, gaude quia meruisti esse et tu, quod laudas; tantum cura, ut sis quae digne laudare possis. Quod si continens et casta, venerare et lauda, quia non aliunde constat, ut possis esse casta, quam ex gratia Christi, quae fuit plenissime in Maria, quam laudas. Quod si coniugata, certe aut peccatrix, nihilominus confitere et lauda, quoniam

inde misericordia omnibus profluxit et gratia, ut laudent. [§36] Et quamvis 'non sit speciosa laus in ore peccatoris' (Sir 15.9), noli cessare, quia inde tibi promittitur venia.

190–98 A full version of the Theophilus story, entitled *Miraculum S. Mariae de Theophilo* (as printed in ASS), appears in CC, and Ælfric may have read it there, but his account is too summary to reveal any particular debts of detail or wording. In the full story the Virgin at first refuses to help, and does not appear quite the merciful and indulgent figure that she appears in Ælfric's version and in post-Conquest tradition.

199–206 Ælfric now turns to the miracle surrounding the death of Julian the Apostate, taken from the *Vita Basilii*. He begins with a few details from the early part of the story (*Vita Basilii*, Surius, I.5–8):

> [I.5] Condiscipulos habuit Gregorium Magnum . . . itemque Iulianum. . . .[I.7] venit in Cappadocum regionem . . . [I.8] Basilium elegerunt episcopum.

Ælfric refers to 'the city which is called Cappadocia' but that is the name of the region, and the city is called Caesarea in the *Vita*; in LS 3 he correctly uses Cappadocia as the name for the region but does not give a name to the city. The details of Julian's history, as cleric and then emperor and persecutor, are not given in the *Vita*. Ælfric could have learnt them from Haymo's *Historiae Sacrae Epitome*, where Julian is said to have been a *clericus* at first and afterwards become a pagan and persecutor of Christians (PL 118, 868–70), but they were perhaps a matter of common knowledge.

206–13 *Vita Basilii*, Surius, I.9:

> Ea tempestate Iulianus impius Imperator bellum in Persas suscipiens, venit in partes Caesareae Cappadocum, obviamque illi processit Basilius. . . . Quem ut vidit Iulianus, ait: 'In philosophia ego te excello, Basili.' Cui Basilius 'Utinam', inquit, 'philosophus esses', simul offerens illi pro benedictione tres panes hordeaceos, quos quidem Imperator voluit a satellitibus suis accipi, sed illi foenum reddi cum his verbis: 'Hordeum ab illo nobis datum, pabulum est iumentorum; recipiat igitur et ipse foenum.'

Thorpe (I.449) translates Ælfric's version of Basil's answer, 'God forgeafe þæt ðu uðwitegunge beeodest', as 'God has granted to you to cultivate philosophy', but as the subjunctive *forgeafe* and the Latin text indicate, the meaning is rather 'Would to God that you practised philosophy (rather than merely knowing it)'.

213–20 *Vita Basilii*, Surius, I.9:

> At Basilius illud suscipiens, ait: 'Nos quidem, O Imperator, ea tibi obtulimus, quibus ipsi vescimur; tu vero ea nobis restituis, unde bruta victitant animantia, ultro quidem nos irridens, sed non sponte nobis hoc foenum in cibum conferens. Iis Iulianus auditis, furore percitus, inquit: . . .

'Postquam edomitis Persis huc rediero, evertam urbem hanc, eamque sic aratro proscindam, ut farris potius quam hominum ferax sit. Nec enim me clam est, ut te suasore populus ad eam proruperit audaciam et temeritatem, ut quam ego collocaram deae a me adoratae statuam, ille non ferens incantationem, penitus dissiparet et confringeret.'

220–26 *Vita Basilii*, Surius, I.9:

His dictis, iter ad Persas intendit. Porro Basilius reversus in urbem, convocata omni multitudine, exposuit eis quae Imperator dixisset, atque huiusmodi sane optimum eis proposuit consilium, dicens: 'Fratres mei, argentum ducentes pro nihilo, saluti vestrae consulite, ut si tyrannus supervixerit, muneribus eum placemus.' At illi suas repetentes domos, singuli quae habebant, ad eum suis manibus alacriter apportabant, puta auri, argenti, et lapidum preciosorum immensam copiam.

227–37 *Vita Basilii*, Surius, I.9:

Mox vero praecepit clero et populo omni civitatis, ut . . . ascenderent in montem Didymi, in quo honoratur et colitur Dei genitricis venerabile templum, ubi triduanum exigentes ieiunium, petierunt a Deo dissipari impii Iuliani propositum. . . . Basilius in visione multitudinem vidit caelestis exercitus hinc inde in monte, et in medio residentem quandam in throno praeclaro in habitu muliebri, dicentemque viris eximiis, qui proxime illi adstabant: 'Vocate ad me Mercurium, ut eat ad interficiendum Iulianum, superbe blasphemantem Deum et filium meum.'

Basil's instruction that the people should offer their *lac* or gifts in the temple does not appear in the source. Ælfric adds the specific reference to the Virgin's intercession (lines 230–1).

237–42 *Vita Basilii*, Surius, I.9–10:

Sanctus autem cum suis armis adveniens, ea iubente velociter abscessit, . . . Stupens igitur magnus Basilius ad visionem, . . . accessit . . . ad sancti martyris Mercurii martyrium, ubi is conditus erat, et eius arma asservabantur; cum ea non inveniret, accersiit custodem, perquisivitque ex eo, ubinam essent. Illo cum sacramento asseverante, hora vespertina quo solerent loco ea fuisse, citra haesitationem ullam . . . Basilius . . . recurrit ad montem . . . atque . . . narravit eis divinitus sibi factam revelationem, de tyranno ea nocte perempto.

Ælfric perhaps adds the detail that the arms were placed at the martyr's head from his own imagination or experience.

242–52 *Vita Basilii*, Surius, I.10:

Rediit ad civitatem, adiensque sancti Mercurii martyrium, invenit lanceam eius cruore madidam. . . . [*A separate incident intervenes here.*] Populis . . . totos septem dies in ecclesia congregatis, ecce Libanius Iuliani quaestor fuga elapsus venit Caesaream . . . annuncians impium Iuliani tyranni

> obitum his verbis: 'Cum esset ad Euphratem fluvium et transacta nocte septima militum excubiae eum custodirent, quidam ignotus miles cum armis advenit, et lanceam valide vibrans, terribili impetu eum confodit, moxque abcedens nusquam comparuit; at miserrimus ille horrendum in modum dire vociferans, blasphemansque expiravit.' . . . Advolutusque genibus sancti pontificis, dari sibi poscebat Christi signaculum.

Ælfric perhaps saw a version with an interval of three days rather than seven, though in LS 3 he gives it as 'about seven days'. The final sentence (lines 251–2) is Ælfric's own comment on the Virgin's intercession.

252–7 *Vita Basilii*, Surius, I.10:

> Postero die voluit magnus Basilius, ut singuli suas pecunias reciperent, at illi omnes una voce dixerunt: 'Si mortali Imperatori eas elargiri voluimus, ne vastaret urbem nostram, multo magis immortali Imperatori Christo eas offerri convenit, qui ab hoc excidio nos servavit.' . . . Ille vero . . . tertiam partem etiam invitis restituit; de reliquo ornavit omne presbyterium cum ciborio, altare quoque auro puro et gemmis preciosis.

258–64 The *Vita Basilii* does not give any details of the life and death of Mercurius and although what Ælfric says here could have been guessed from the *Vita* the confident statement that he was a layman suggests a knowledge of the legend, which is printed in Surius, VI.569–72. This describes the martyr's career as a soldier and then his martyrdom in Cappadocia, though it does not mention the location of his body or his weapons, and says nothing of the miracle described here. Ælfric's comment perhaps reflects an anxiety to explain how a layman came to be buried in a church with his weapons. The further distinction, that Mercurius used a physical weapon but acted himself only in the spirit, is possibly intended to dispose of any superstitious conclusions about the fate of the body after death.

271–2 The analogy between the soul and body of man and the two natures of Christ is also made at CH I.2.175–7, where Ælfric was possibly drawing on Augustine, Serm.186 (PL 38, 999).

31 ST BARTHOLOMEW

The Gospel text for St Bartholomew's day is Luke 22.24 ff, describing the disciples competing among themselves for supremacy, and Ælfric's copy of Paul the Deacon's homiliary probably included Bede's homily on this text for the occasion. Ælfric chose however to concentrate on the legend of the saint's death and its implications for his own time. The story of Bartholomew's evangelism and martyrdom in farthest India was well known in Anglo-Saxon England, mentioned in the *Fates of the Apostles*, the *Menologium* and the *Old English*

Martyrology. Ælfric follows the story closely, omitting only a digressive passage on the virginity of Mary. A particular concern of the anonymous author of the legend is the claims of the false gods, or the devils who inhabit their effigies, to be able to heal the sick, and it is this issue which Ælfric takes up in a long independent discussion at the end (lines 244–334). He compares the reliance of the Indians of the legend on devils with his contemporaries' use of charms and superstitious practices,[1] but he also deals at length with the larger question of why God allows illness to afflict mankind.

Förster showed that Ælfric used as his main source a version of the legend like that printed by Mombritius.[2] Patrick Zettel pointed out that a version was included in the Cotton-Corpus legendary, and that the extant manuscripts occasionally have variant readings (also recorded in the apparatus to the 1910 edition of the Mombritius collection) which are closer to Ælfric.[3] Passages below are printed from Mombritius but with relevant variants from the apparatus, from the similar versions printed by Lipsius and Bonnet (1891) and Fabricius (1719) and from the Cotton-Corpus manuscripts as reported by Zettel. For the discussion of the moral aspects of illness and healing and the problems of idolatrous practices, there are no definite sources, though there are partial parallels to a passage in Augustine's *De Doctrina Christiana* and his Serm. 83 and to Gregory the Great's preface to his *Moralia siue Expositio in Iob*, and to proscriptions against idolatrous practices in Caesarius and the Ps-Egbert Penitential.[4]

Sources and Notes

The following texts are cited below:

1. Anon., *Passio Bartholomaei*, ed. M. Bonnet, in Lipsius and Bonnet, II.128–50.
2. Anon., *Passio Bartholomaei*, in Fabricius, II.669–87.
3. Anon., *Passio Bartholomaei*, in Mombritius 1910, I.140–44 [variants are printed in italics].
4. Augustine, *De Doctrina Christiana*, ed. J. Martin, CCSL 32 (Turnhout, 1962), pp. 1–167.
5. Augustine, *Sermones*, PL 38, Serm. 83, cols. 514–9.
6. Caesarius of Arles, *Sermones*, ed. G. Morin, CCSL 103 (Turnhout, 1953), Serm. 5 (pp. 25–29) and Serm. 50 (pp. 224–7) [cited by section and line numbers].
7. Gregory the Great, *Moralia siue Expositio in Iob*, ed. M. Adriaen, 3 vols., CCSL 143–143B (Turnhout 1979–85).

[1] See especially the valuable discussion by Audrey Meaney, 'Ælfric and Idolatry', *Journal of Religious History* 13 (1984), 119–35.

[2] Förster 1892, p. 21.

[3] Zettel 1979, pp. 181–2.

[4] Most of these parallels are pointed out by Audrey Meaney.

1 The date of the feast given here, *viii kalendas Septembris* or 25 August, is the one usual before 1100, when the present date of 24 August began to become standard; see B. Colgrave, *Felix's Life of St Guthlac* (Cambridge, 1956), p. 182.

4–9 *Passio Bartholomaei*, Mombritius 1910, I.140.33–7:

> Indiae tres esse ab historiographis asseruntur: prima est India quae ad aethiopiam mittit, secunda quae ad Medos, tertia quae finem facit; nam et in uno latere habet regionem tenebrarum, et ex alio latere mare oceanum. In hac ergo India ingressus Bartolamaeus apostolus; ingressus est templum in quo erat idolum Astaroth et quasi peregrinus ibi manere coepit.

It is unclear what Ælfric would have understood by the region of darkness; in his *De Temporibus Anni* he gives an accurate account of a spherical earth all parts of which receive the sun's light in turn, and mentions India as a region close to the equator.

9–17 *Passio Bartholomaei*, Mombritius 1910, I.140.37–43:

> In hoc idolo talis daemon erat qui diceret se curare languentes sed hos sine dubio quos ipse laedebat. . . . Facit eis dolores, infirmitates, dampna, pericula et dat responsa ut sacrificent ei ut quasi sanentur ab eo. Hoc videtur stultis quod sanet eos. Illi autem non sanando subveniunt sed a laesione cessando, et dum desinunt laedere, curasse creduntur.

18–25 *Passio Bartholomaei*, Mombritius 1910, I.140.43–50:

> Unde factum est ut sancto Bartolamaeo ibi manente, nulla responsa daret Astaroth et nulli poterat ex eis quos laeserat subvenire. Cumque iam plenum esset languentibus templum et quottidie sacrificantibus nullum daret Astaroth responsum, infirmi ex longinquis regionibus adducti iacebant. Sed cum in ipso templo nullum posset daemon dare responsum et neque sacrificando neque se ipsos more suo laniando *proficerent* [*var. Momb. app., Fab., Bonnet*], perrexerunt in aliam civitatem ubi alius daemon colebatur cui nomen erat Berith et illic sacrificantes coeperunt quaerere quare deus eorum Astaroth non eis daret responsa.

25–33 *Passio Bartholomaei*, Mombritius 1910, I.140.50–141.2:

> Respondens autem Berith daemon dixit: 'Deus vester sic captivus et religatus cathenis igneis strictus tenetur ut neque spirare neque loqui *audeat* [*var. CC*] ex illa hora qua illuc apostolus Bartolamaeus ingressus est'. Dicunt ei illi: 'Et quis est ille Bartolamaeus?' Respondit daemon: 'Amicus est dei omnipotentis et ideo venit huc in istam provinciam ut omnia numina quae colunt Indi evacuet'. Dixerunt autem cultores ydoli: 'Dic nobis signa eius ut possimus invenire eum'.

33–40 *Passio Bartholomaei*, Mombritius 1910, I.141.3–11:

> Respondens daemon dicit: 'Capillo nigro capitis et crispo; caro eius candida; oculi grandes; nares aequales et directae; aures cohoperte crine capitis; barba prolyxa habens paucos canos; statura aequalis . . . vestitur

colobio albo. . . . Viginti sex anni sunt et nunquam sordidantur vestimenta eius et nunquam veterascunt; similiter et sandalia eius stramentis latis per viginti sex annos nunquam veterascunt. Centies flexis genibus per diem, centies per noctem orat dominum. Vox eius quasi tuba vehemens est. Ambulant cum eo angeli domini qui non permittunt eum fatigari nec exurire.'

40–47 *Passio Bartholomaei*, Mombritius 1910, I.141.11–18:
'Semper eodem vultu, eodem animo perseverat. Omni hora hilaris est et laetus permanet. Omnia providet, omnia novit, omnem linguam omnium gentium et loquitur et intelligit. Ecce et hoc quod vos interrogatis et ego do vobis responsum de eo, iam novit ille. Angeli enim domini famulantur ei et ipsi nuntiant ei. Et cum coeperitis eum quaerere si vult ostendet se vobis, si non vult non poteritis eum videre. Rogo autem vos ut dum eum inveneritis rogetis eum ne huc veniat ne hoc mihi faciant angeli qui cum eo sunt quod fecerunt collegae meo Astaroth.' Et haec dicens daemon conticuit.

48–55 *Passio Bartholomaei*, Mombritius 1910, I.141.18–23:
Revertentes autem coeperunt circuire omnium peregrinorum vultus et habitus et per duos dies non invenerunt. Factum est ut quidam plenus daemonio clamaret et diceret: 'Apostole dei Bartolamaee, incendunt me orationes tuae.' Tunc apostolus dixit ei: 'Obmutesce et exi ab eo'. Et statim liberatus est homo qui per multos annos fuerat fatigatus ab eo.

55–60 *Passio Bartholomaei*, Mombritius 1910, I.141.23–6:
Polymius autem rex civitatis eiusdem cum haberet filiam lunaticam, nuntiatum est ei de hoc daemonioso et misit et rogavit apostolum dicens: 'Filia mea male a daemonio vexatur. Peto ut sicut liberasti Pseustium qui per multos annos passus est, ita et filiam meam libera.'

60–67 *Passio Bartholomaei*, Mombritius 1910, I.141.26–33:
Ubi vidit eam apostolus cathenis strictam, quia morsu omnes attrectabat et quos poterat tenere scindebat et caedebat, et nullus erat ausus accedere ad eam, iussit eam solvi. Dicunt ei ministri: 'Et quis est ausus manum mittere ad eam?' Dicit eis apostolus: 'Iam ego vinctum teneo inimicum qui cum ipsa erat et vos adhuc timetis eam? Ite et solvite eam et levate eam et reficite; et crastina die mane adducite eam ipsam ad me.' Euntes autem fecerunt sicut iussit apostolus et ulterius non potuit daemon vexare eam.

68–73 *Passio Bartholomaei*, Mombritius 1910, I.141.33–37:
Tunc rex oneravit camelos auro et argento, gemmis et vestibus et coepit quaerere apostolum, et penitus non inveniebat eum, et reportata sunt omnia ad palatium eius. Factum est autem cum transisset nox et aurora futuri diei inciperet, apparuit Bartolamaeus apostolus cum solo rege *hostio*

clauso [*var. Momb., Fab., Bonnet*] in cubiculo, et dixit ei: 'Ut quid me quaesisti tota die cum auro et argento, gemmis et vestibus?'

73–80 *Passio Bartholomaei*, Mombritius 1910, I.141.37–44:

Ista munera his sunt necessaria qui terrena quaerunt. Ego autem nihil terrenum nihilque carnale desidero. Unde scire te volo quia filius dei dignatus est per uterum virginis nasci cum homine . . . qui fecit caelum et terram, mare et omnia quaę in eis sunt. Hic simul cum homine natus in partu virginis coepit habere initium nascendo cum homine qui nunquam habuit initium, sed ipse semper initium fuit et omnibus initium dedit, sive invisibilibus sive visibilibus creaturis.

80–87 *Passio Bartholomaei*, Mombritius 1910, I.141.45–56:

'Haec autem virgo cum execraret omnem virum, et ipsa servandae virginitatis votum prima deo omnipotenti vovisset. . . . Huic . . . Gabriel angelus apparuit . . . ait ad illam angelus: "Noli timere maria quia concipies . . . vocabitur filius dei".'

The Latin text then devotes some forty lines to a discussion of the annunciation, the virgin birth and the temptation in the wilderness (but not the redemption itself, to which Ælfric refers in his summary reference, lines 83–7).

87–94 *Passio Bartholomaei*, Mombritius 1910, I.142.37–43:

'Homo Christus Iesus qui vicit misit nos in omnes provincias ut expellamus ministros diaboli qui per templa in statuis habitant ut homines qui eos colunt de potestate eius qui victus est auferamus. Ideo aurum et argentum non accipimus sed contemnimus, sicut ipse salvator noster contempsit, quia ibi esse cupimus divites ubi solum eius regnat imperium, ubi nec langor nec morbus nec tristitia nec mors locum aliquem habere noscuntur, ubi felicitas perpetua et beatitudo perhennis est, et gaudium sine fine et sunt deliciae sempiternae.'

94–102 *Passio Bartholomaei*, Mombritius 1910, I.142.43–50:

'Inde est ex quo ego templum vestrum ingressus sum daemonem qui in ydolo dabat responsa ab angelis eius qui misit me religatum obtineo; quem si baptizatus fueris et permiseris te illuminari, faciam te videre et cognoscere quanto malo caruisti. Nam omnes illos qui iacebant in templo aegrotantes audi qua arte videbatur curare eos. Diabolus qui primum hominem vicit, ut saepe iam dixi, per ipsam victoriam pessimam *potestatem* [*var. Fab., Bonnet*] habere videtur in aliis maiorem, in aliis minorem; minorem in his qui minus peccant, maiorem in his qui plus peccant.'

102–110 *Passio Bartholomaei*, Mombritius 1910, I.142.50–56:

'Ipse ergo diabolus facit arte sua homines aegrotare et suadet eos credere idolis, et postquam in animas eorum potestatem obtinuerit, cessat tunc laedere eos, cum dixerint lapidi aut metallo cuique: "Deus meus es tu".

Sed quia ipse daemon qui in ipsa statua erat a me vinctus tenetur, sacrificantibus et adorantibus se nullum potest dare responsum. Sed si vis probare ita esse, iubeo illi ut ingrediatur statuam suam et faciam eum confiteri hoc ipsum, quod sit religatus et responsa dare non possit.'

111–19 *Passio Bartholomaei*, Mombritius 1910, I.142.56–143.3:

Dixit ei rex: 'Crastina prima diei hora parati erunt pontifices sacrificare et ego illuc superveniam ut videam hoc factum mirabile'. Factum est autem altero die prima hora diei sacrificantibus eis coepit clamare daemon 'Cessate miseri, cessate sacrificare mihi ne peiora patiamini quam ego qui cathenis igneis religatus sum ab angelis Iesu Christi quem Iudei crucifixerunt, putantes eum posse teneri a morte.'

Ælfric suppresses the specific reference to *pontifices* here and again at lines 202 and 206.

119–23 *Passio Bartholomaei*, Mombritius 1910, I.143.3–8:

'Ille autem ipsam mortem quae regina nostra est captivavit et ipsum principem nostrum maritum mortis vinculis ignitis vinxit, et tertia die victor mortis et diaboli resurrexit. Et dedit signum crucis sue apostolis suis et misit eos per universas partes mundi; ex quibus unus hic est qui me vinctum tenet. Peto vos ut rogetis eum pro me ut dimittat me ire in aliam provinciam.'

124–8 *Passio Bartholomaei*, Mombritius 1910, I.143.8–12:

Tunc beatus Bartholamaeus ait: 'Confitere immundissime daemon istos omnes qui hic aegritudines varias patiuntur? Quis est qui eos laesit?' Respondit daemon: 'Princeps noster diabolus qui modo sic religatus est, ipse nos mittit ad homines ut laedamus primo quidem carnem eorum, quoniam in animas hominum non possumus habere potestatem nisi sacrificaverint.'

128–37 *Passio Bartholomaei*, Mombritius 1910, I.143.12–18:

'At ubi pro salute sui corporis nobis sacrificaverint, cessamus nocere eos quia iam in animabus eorum potestatem habere incipimus. Iam ergo per hoc quod ab eorum laesione cessamus, videmur curare eos; et colimur quasi dei, cum pro certo simus daemones ministri eius quem in cruce positus Iesus filius virginis religavit. A die autem qua discipulus eius huc venit apostolus Bartholamaeus, ardentibus cathenis strictus consumor, et ideo loquor quia iussit mihi. Nam ausus non essem loqui eo presente nec ipse princeps noster.'

138–45 *Passio Bartholomaei*, Mombritius 1910, I.143.18–23:

Dicit ei apostolus: 'Quare non salvas homines omnes qui ad te convenerunt?' Dicit ei daemon: 'Nos quando corpora laedimus nisi animam laeserimus corpora in sua laesione perdurant.' Dicit ei apostolus: 'Et quomodo animas laeditis?' Respondit daemon; 'Cum crediderint nos esse deos et sacrificaverint nobis, tollit se deus ab eis qui sacrificant et nos vulnera corporum non tollimus sed migramus ad animam.'

145–53 *Passio Bartholomaei*, Mombritius 1910, I.143.23–28:

Tunc dicit apostolus ad plebem: 'Ecce fratres carissimi quem *deum putabatis, ecce quem* [*var. Momb., Fab., Bonnet*] putabatis curare vos. Audite nunc verum deum creatorem nostrum qui in caelis habitat. Non in vanis lapidibus credite, et si vultis ut orem pro vobis et omnes hi sanitatem recipiant, deponite idolum hoc et confringite; et cum hoc feceritis templum hoc in christi nomine consecrabo et vos in isto templo christi baptismate renovabo'.

153–9 *Passio Bartholomaei*, Mombritius 1910, I.143.28–33:

Tunc iussu regis omnes populi miserunt funes et *trocleas* [*var. Momb., Fab., Bonnet*] in collo eius et simulacrum non poterant evertere. Tunc apostolus dixit eis: 'Solvite omnia vincula eius.' Cumque exsolvissent omnia, dixit ad daemonem qui in eo erat: 'Si vis ut non te faciam in abyssum mitti, exi de isto simulacro et confringe illud et vade in terram desertam ubi nec avis volat nec arator arat nec vox hominum resonat.'

159–63 *Passio Bartholomaei*, Mombritius 1910, I.143.33–7:

At ille statim egressus comminuit omnia genera idolorum, sed et minora ubicunque pro ornamento templi sigilla . . . posita minutavit, ita ut picturam omnem deleret. Tunc omnes una voce clamare coeperunt: 'Unus dominus omnipotens quem praedicat sanctus Bartholamaeus.'

163–76 *Passio Bartholomaei*, Mombritius 1910, I.143.37–50:

Tunc apostolus elevans manus suas ad caelum dixit: 'Deus Abraham, deus Ysaac, deus Iacob, qui ad redemptionem nostram unigenitum tuum filium deum et dominum nostrum direxisti, ut nos omnes qui eramus servi peccati suo sanguine redimeret et tibi filios faceret . . . unus pater ingenitus, unus filius unigenitus, unus spiritus sanctus qui ex patre procedit. . . . Qui in suo nomine dedit nobis hanc potestatem ut infirmos salvaremus, caecos illuminaremus, leprosos mundaremus, paraliticos absolveremus, demones effugaremus, mortuos suscitaremus et dixit nobis: "Amen dico vobis, quecunque in nomine meo petieritis a patre meo dabitur vobis": peto ergo ut in eius nomine ut omnis haec multitudo sanetur, ut cognoscant omnes quia tu es deus unus in caelo et in terra et in mari, qui salutem recuperas per ipsum deum nostrum Iesum Christum, qui tecum et cum spiritu sancto vivit et regnat in saecula saeculorum'.

Ælfric adjusts the apostle's statement of belief to fit the view which had become standard in the Western church, that the Holy Spirit proceeded from both the Father and the Son, adding the phrase *and of þinum bearne* (line 168) in echo of the *filioque* of the Western version of the creed. See ODCC under 'Double Procession' and 'Filioque' for a succinct account of the issue.

177–86 *Passio Bartholomaei*, Mombritius 1910, I.143.50–58:

> Cumque omnes respondissent amen, cuncti qui ab infirmitate detinebantur pristinae sunt restituti illico sanitati. Apparuitque angelus domini splendidus sicut sol, habens alas, et per quattuor angulos templi circumvolans digito suo in quadratis saxis exculpsit signum crucis, et dixit: 'Haec dicit dominus qui misit me: "Sicut vos omnes ab infirmitate vestra mundavi, ita mundavi templum hoc ab omni sorde et habitatorem eius *quem* [*var. Fab., Bonnet*] iussit apostolus ire in desertum locum." Sed prius ostendam vobis quem deum collebatis, quem videntes nolite', inquit, 'expavescere, sed quale signum sculpsi in his saxis tale vos digito vestro facite in frontibus vestris; et omnia mala fugient a vobis.'

186–91 *Passio Bartholomaei*, Mombritius 1910, I.144.1–5:

> Tunc angelus domini ostendit eis ingentem egyptium nigriorem fuligine, habentem faciem acutam cum barba prolixa, crines usque ad pedes, oculos igneos sicut ferrum ignitum, scintillas emicantem ex ore eius et ex naribus egrediebatur flamma sulphurea, pinarumque habens alas septem spineas, et erat vinctus a tergo manus habens ignitis cathenis strictas.

Ælfric would probably not confuse Egyptians with Ethiopians but was sufficiently familiar with the latter as a term for devils to substitute it here. The *Old English Martyrology*, which uses the same legend, similarly has *Sigelhearwan* (OE Martyrology, II.186–7).

192–7 *Passio Bartholomaei*, Mombritius 1910, I.144.5–9:

> Et dixit ei angelus domini: 'Quoniam audisti vocem apostoli, omnia pollutionem genera de isto templo mundasti secundum promissum apostoli solvam te, ut vadas ubi nulla conversatio hominum est vel esse potest, et ibi sis usque ad diem iudicii.' Et cum exolvisset eum, ille ululatum teterrimum dirae vocis emittens evolavit et nusquam comparuit.

197–205 *Passio Bartholomaei*, Mombritius 1910, I.144.9–16:

> Angelus autem domini cunctis videntibus evolavit ad caelum. Tunc rex una cum uxore sua et duobus filiis et cum exercitu suo et cum omni populo . . . credens baptizatus est; et deposito diademate capitis et purpura coepit apostolum non deserere. Interea colligentes se universorum templorum pontifices abierunt ad *Astrigem* [*var. Momb., Bonnet*] regem fratrem eius maiorem et dixerunt ei: 'Frater tuus discipulus est factus hominis magi qui templa nostra sibi vindicat et deos nostros confregit.'

Ælfric's comment that Astriges was king 'in another province' (lines 203–4) is presumably an attempt to explain why both brothers were kings, a subject on which he seems curiously sensitive (cf his preface to LS on two emperors).

205–11 *Passio Bartholomaei*, Mombritius 1910, I.144.17–21:

> Tunc rex Astriges indignatus misit mille viros armatos cum pontificibus ut ubicunque invenirent apostolum vinctum illum perducerent ad eum. Quod

cum fecissent, dixit ad eum Astriges rex: 'Tu es qui evertisti fratrem meum?' Cui apostolus dixit: 'Ego non everti eum sed converti.' Dicit ei rex: 'Tu es qui deos nostros fecisti comminui?'

211–16 *Passio Bartholomaei*, Mombritius 1910, I.144.21–6:
Dicit ei apostlus: 'Ego dedi potestatem daemonibus qui in eis erant ut conquassarent idola vana in quibus *degebant ut omnes homines* [*var. Momb., Fab., Bonnet*] relicto errore crederent omnipotenti domino qui in caelis habitat.' Dicit ei rex: 'Sicut tu fecisti fratrem meum ut relinqueret deum suum et deo tuo crederet, ita te ego faciam derelinquere deum tuum et deo meo credere et illi sacrificare.'

216–23 *Passio Bartholomaei*, Mombritius 1910, I.144.26–31:
Dixit ei apostolus: 'Ego deum quem collebat frater tuus religatum et vinctum ostendi, et ipsum frangere feci symulacrum suum. Si poteris tu hoc facere deo meo, poteris me ad sacrificium provocare. Sin autem tu nihil poteris deo meo facere, ego omnes deos tuos comminuam et tu crede domino meo'. Haec cum diceret, nuntiatum est regi quia deus eius Baldach cecidisset et minutum abisset.

223–34 *Passio Bartholomaei*, Mombritius 1910, I.144.31–7:
Tunc rex excidit purpuream vestem qua indutus erat et fecit fustibus caedi sanctum apostolum Bartholamaeum; cesum autem iussit eum decollari. Venientes autem innumerabiles populi duodecim civitatum qui per eum crediderunt una cum rege, abstulerunt cum hymnis et cum omni gloria *corpus eius et construxerunt ibi basilicam mirae magnitudinis et in ea posuerunt corpus eius* [*var. Momb., Bonnet*]. Factum est autem trigesimo die depositionis eius arreptus a daemonio rex Astriges venit ad tumulum eius et omnes pontifices pleni daemonibus, ubi confitentes apostolatum eius sic sunt mortui.

234–43 *Passio Bartholomaei*, Mombritius 1910, I.144.37–43:
Factus est autem timor et tremor super omnes incredulos et crediderunt universi et baptizati sunt a praesbiteris quos ordinaverat beatus apostolus Bartolamaeus. Factum est autem per revelationem universo populo et omni clero ammonente ut *ab apostolo* [*var. Momb., Fab., Bonnet*] ordinaretur rex episcopus. Et coepit in nomine domini Iesu Christi signa facere. Fuit autem in episcopatu annis viginti et perfectis omnibus atque bene compositis et bene stabilitis, migravit ad deum cui est honor et potestas et gloria in saecula saeculorum amen.

247–8 Mt 10.29: *Nonne duo passeres asse veneunt: et unus ex illis non cadet super terram sine Patre vestro?*

250 Apoc 3.19: *Ego quos amo, arguo et castigo.*

250–4 Cf Gregory, *Moralia*, Praefatio.V.12: *Percussionum quippe diversa sunt genera*. The kinds which Gregory then goes on to list are partly similar to Ælfric's: to punish sinners who are to be damned, to correct sinners, to dissuade from future sin, to show God's power.

255–9 On Herod's disease, see CH I.5.123 ff.

267–74 Cf Augustine, Serm. 83, §8, PL 38, 518:

> Quid enim tam pium quam medicus ferens ferramentum? Plorat secandus, et secatur: plorat urendus, et uritur. Non est illa crudelitas; absit ut saevitia medici dicatur. Saevit in vulnus, ut homo sanetur: quia si vulnus palpetur, homo perditur.

Ælfric used this source for a later homily, Irvine 2, but his concern there (lines 203–7), like Augustine's, is with the chastising role of the teacher rather than that of God. Caesarius (Serm. 5.5) uses the same image, but again for the preacher.

277–8 Mc 2.5, 11:

> (5) Cum autem vidisset Iesus fidem illorum, ait paralytico: Fili, dimittuntur tibi peccata tua. . . . (11) Surge, tolle grabatum tuum, et vade in domum tuam.

279–87 The details of Job are from the Book of Job 1, 2, 42 (though the Bible does not actually say that God healed him). For the worms of 283 cf CH II.30.194 and perhaps Job 17.14 or 30.17; for 283–6 cf Job 1.21–2. The notion that God was testing Job is the theme of Gregory's *Moralia* but Ælfric himself offers a different understanding in his later homily on Job, CH II.30.

288–95 Cf Jn 9.1–3, 6:

> (1) Et praeteriens Iesus vidit hominem caecum a nativitate: (2) et interrogaverunt eum discipuli eius: Rabbi, quis peccavit hic, aut parentes eius, ut caecus nasceretur? (3) Respondit Iesus: Neque hic peccavit, neque parentes eius; sed ut manifestentur opera Dei in illo. . . . (6) Haec cum dixisset, expuit in terram, et fecit lutum ex sputo, et linivit lutum super oculos eius.

The Gospel text is expounded at length in a later homily by Ælfric, Irvine 3.

296–302 2 Cor 12.7–9:

> (7) Et ne magnitudo revelationum extollat me, datus est mihi stimulus carnis meae angelus Satanae, qui me colaphizet. (8) Propter quod ter Dominum rogavi ut discederet a me; (9) et dixit mihi: 'Sufficit tibi gratia mea; nam virtus in infirmitate perficitur.' Libenter igitur gloriabor in infirmitatibus meis, ut inhabitet in me virtus Christi.

303–34 Four times in this final passage Ælfric touches on the association between healing and idolatry: seeking healing from illicit activities, accursed charms and witchcraft (lines 304 ff); seeking healing from a stone or tree or place other than a church (lines 312 ff); attaching a medicinal plant or herb to the body, except to the wound itself (lines 319 ff); and enchanting a herb with a charm (lines 323 ff). There are some similarities of treatment in Caesarius, Serm. 50 (1.14–19) and Serm. 54, and the latter was a source for Ælfric's fuller treatment in his later sermon *De Auguriis* (LS 17). For the identification of such superstitious practices with heathen worship, cf also CH I.6.129 ff, esp. 186–8. The Ps-Egbert Penitential, II.22 condemns offerings to wells, stones, trees or any object except a church, but does not relate this to ill-health; and at II.23 proscribes *wyrta gaderunga mid nanum galdre butan mid pater noster and mid credo.* The anonymous homily Assmann 11 also mentions seeking out a well, stone or tree as an example of heathen practice (lines 123–5), in a context that perhaps suggests cures for disease.

317–8 Is 38.21:

Et iussit Isaias ut tollerent massam de ficis, et cataplasmarent super vulnus, et sanaretur.

319–21 Cf Augustine, *De Doctrina Christiana*, II.29.9–13:

Aliud est enim dicere 'tritam istam herbam si biberis, venter non dolebit', et aliud est dicere 'istam herbam collo si suspenderis, venter non dolebit'. Ibi enim probatur contemperatio salubris, hic significatio superstitiosa damnatur.

32 DECOLLATION OF JOHN THE BAPTIST

Ælfric had already described the birth and early life of John the Baptist in I.25, for the feast of the nativity, and turns now to the story of his death at the hands of Herod. The reading for the occasion in Paul the Deacon's homiliary is Matthew 14.1–12 but the parallel account of the events in Mark 6.17–29 is the one marked for this day in the *OE Gospels* and used in later times, and it is the one chosen here by Ælfric. The homily interweaves a historical account of the events and background with a moral commentary on the death of John and its implications. It begins with the historical background of Herod's reign and the reasons for John's arrest (lines 33–61), continues with the story from Luke 7 of how John while in prison sent disciples to question Christ (lines 61–80), and then turns to the reading from Mark and the moral issues involved (lines 81–150). Ælfric then continues the historical account, with details of John's burial and the fate of his body (lines 150–62), before drawing out some more general implications of the story—the problem of his unjust fate (lines 162–71) and the cruelty of women (lines 172–88). He touches once more on the historical background, to give the subsequent fate of Herod, and concludes with a brief sermon on the toilsome nature of this life in comparison to the next.

The sources are numerous. His main source was Bede's homily for the occasion, on the text from Matthew 14. This provided much of the moral commentary on the reading and a fair amount of historical detail, but Ælfric supplemented the latter with material from the *Ecclesiastical History* of Rufinus. For commentary on Luke 7 he drew on a homily by Gregory the Great, and for the passage on dangerous women used a homily associated with St John Chrysostom (an extraordinarily fierce anti-feminist sermon, only partially redeemed by its concluding section on virtuous women in the Bible). Both this and the Bede homily are included in Paul the Deacon's homiliary for the same occasion, while the Gregory homily appears in PD for the third Sunday in Advent. For the final section Ælfric says he used a sermon by St Augustine, apparently a version of Serm. 84.[1]

Sources and Notes

The following texts are cited below:

1. Augustine, *Sermones*, PL 38, Serm. 84, cols. 519–20.
2. Bede, *Homiliae*, ed. D. Hurst, CCSL 122 (Turnhout, 1955), Hom. II.23 (pp. 349–57).
3. Ps-Chrysostom, Homily on the Decollation of John the Baptist [= Hom. 50], PL 95, cols. 1508–14.
4. Gregory the Great, *Homiliae in Evangelia*, PL 76, Hom. 6, cols. 1095–9.
5. Rufinus, *Historia Ecclesiastica*, ed. T. Mommsen, in *Eusebius Werke*, ed. E. Klostermann, vol. 2, 2 parts, GCS 9.1 and 9.2 (Leipzig, 1903–8).

5–28 A free rendering of Mc 6.17–29:

(17) Ipse enim Herodes misit, ac tenuit Iohannem, et vinxit eum in carcere propter Herodiadem uxorem Philippi fratris sui, quia duxerat eam. (18) Dicebat enim Iohannes Herodi: 'Non licet tibi habere uxorem fratris tui'. (19) Herodias autem insidiabatur illi; et volebat occidere eum, nec poterat. (20) Herodes enim metuebat Iohannem, sciens eum virum iustum et sanctum; et custodiebat eum, et audito eo multa faciebat, et libenter eum audiebat. (21) Et cum dies opportunus accidisset, Herodes natalis sui coenam fecit principibus, et tribunis, et primis Galilaeae; (22) cumque introisset filia ipsius Herodiadis, et saltasset, et placuisset Herodi, simulque recumbentibus; rex ait puellae: 'Pete a me quod vis, et dabo tibi'; (23) et iuravit illi: 'Quia quidquid petieris dabo tibi, licet dimidium regni mei'. (24) Quae cum exisset, dixit matri suae: 'Quid petam?' At illa dixit: 'Caput Iohannis Baptistae'. (25) Cumque introisset statim cum festinatione ad regem, petivit dicens: 'Volo ut protinus des mihi in disco caput Iohannis Baptistae'. (26) Et contristatus est rex; propter iusiurandum, et propter

[1] Förster (1894, pp. 23, 52–3) noted the use of Bede's homily and Rufinus; Smetana (1959 pp. 192–3) identified Gregory and Ps-Chrysostom as sources, and noted their presence, along with Bede, in PD.

simul discumbentes, noluit eam contristare; (27) sed misso spiculatore praecepit afferri caput eius in disco. Et decollavit eum in carcere, (28) et attulit caput eius in disco; et dedit illud puellae, et puella dedit matri suae. (29) Quo audito, discipuli eius venerunt, et tulerunt corpus eius; et posuerunt illud in monumento.

The Biblical account describes the dancing girl (anonymous in the Bible, but named Salome by Josephus) as the daughter of Herodias, presumably by Philip, but Ælfric firmly identifies her as Herod's own daughter (lines 14–16, 27); none of his possible sources discusses the question. The *OE Gospels* and Rushworth Gospels represent Herodias as the widow or 'laf' of Philip, presumably understanding 'duxerunt' as 'married', but Ælfric's rendering reflects the background story given later at 48–54, so that the issue becomes not simply a matter of marrying a brother's widow. Historically Philip the tetrarch was still alive at the time of John the Baptist's death.

29–32 Mt 11.11: *Non surrexit inter natos mulierum maior Iohanne Baptista*. Lines 31–2 perhaps refer back to Ælfric's earlier discussion, in I.25.

33–9 Bede, Hom. II.23, 48–51:

Herodes iste, qui et Iohannem decollavit et in passione redemptoris nostri Pilato assensum praebuit, filius est Herodis illius sub quo dominus natus est.

There is nothing in the sources to prompt the comment on naming practices at 36–9 and it may be Ælfric's speculation, reflecting on the difference from Anglo-Saxon practice (though the implication of the historical account which Ælfric and others give is that the second Herod was not in fact the *yrfenuma* or heir of the first). Supporting evidence would have been the proposal to name John the Baptist Zacharias after his father (see CH I.25.27–9). At CH II.27.147 (see note) he refers to a third Herod, whom he identifies as the grandson of the first.

39–42 Herod's killing of his three sons comes from Rufinus, *Historia Ecclesiastica*, I.viii.15, and has already been noted by Ælfric at I.5.159–62, along with Herod's miserable end. That there were five sons remaining is presumably deduced from the subsequent account of the kingdom, taken from Bede and Rufinus (below).

43–54 Bede, Hom. II.23, 51–63:

Qui cum post nativitate[m] dominicam pauco tempore regnaret, sicut evangelica testatur historia, Archelaus eius filius successit in regnum; qui cum vix decem annis potiretur, accusantibus insolentiam eius Iudaeis pulsus est regno ab Augusto, ac perpetuo damnatus exilio. Deinde Augustus ut regni Iudaici minueret potentiam, divisa in quattuor partes provincia quattuor fratres Archelai eidem regendae praefecit, qui singuli a principatu quartae partis Graeco sermone tetrarchae vocati sunt. E quibus Philippus Herodiam filiam Arethae regis Arabum accepit uxorem, quam idem Aretha postmodum ablatam ab eo dedit Herodi, eo quod ipse maioris potestatis esset et famae, factumque est adulterium publicum.

Bede is drawing here on the *Historia Ecclesiastica* of Rufinus, and Ælfric seems to have gone back to Rufinus too for some details (*Historia Ecclesiastica*, I.xi.1):

. . . Et suis ab Herode incestis nuptiis sociatae, propria et legitima uxore depulsa.

Rufinus, however, reports that Herod seized Herodias from Philip and that her father Areta waged war on him in revenge; Ælfric follows Bede's version, that it was Areta himself who took his daughter from Philip and gave her to Herod.

57–61 Rufinus, *Historia Ecclesiastica*, I.xi.6:

Quae cum ab eo per praecepta huiuscemodi docerentur atque ad audiendum eum perplurima multitudo concurreret, veritus Herodes, ne forte doctrinae eius persuasione populi a suo rege desciscerent . . . melius credidit, priusquam novi aliquid fieret, anticipare hominem nece, quam postmodum turbatis rebus seram paenitudinem gerere. Ex sola igitur suspicione Herodis, vinctus in castellum Macherunta abducitur Iohannes ibique obtruncatur.

Ælfric's Latin note at 57 (in MS K), citing Rufinus, must refer to what follows it, since the preceding sentence is essentially from the Gospels.

61–7 Ælfric now inserts at the appropriate chronological point the story from Mt 11.2–3 (= Lc 7.19) of John sending disciples from prison to question Christ:

(2) Iohannes autem cum audisset in vinculis opera Christi, mittens duos de discipulis suis, (3) ait illi: 'Tu es, qui venturus es, an alium exspectamus?'.

There is a long history of patristic commentary on this episode, explaining that John could not really have been in doubt whether Christ was the Messiah. Ælfric follows the explanation of Gregory the Great, as indeed his note in MS K points out (Hom. 6, PL 76, 1096A):

Ac si aperte dicat: 'Sicut pro hominibus nasci dignatus es, an etiam pro hominibus mori digneris insinua, ut qui nativitatis tuae praecursor exstiti, mortis etiam praecursor fiam, et venturum inferno te nuntiem, quem iam venisse mundo nuntiavi'.

68–74 Lc 7.21–3:

(21) In ipsa autem hora multos curavit a languoribus, et plagis, et spiritibus malis, et caecis multis donavit visum. (22) Et respondens, dixit illis: 'Euntes renuntiate Iohanni quae audistis et vidistis; quia caeci vident, claudi ambulant, leprosi mundantur, surdi audiunt, mortui resurgunt, pauperes evangelizantur; (23) et beatus est quicumque non fuerit scandalizatus in me'.

Ælfric cites Luke because the first of these verses is lacking from the parallel account in Matthew. For *pauperes evangelizantur* (v.22), 'the poor are preached to', Ælfric has *þearfan bodiað godspel*, 'the poor preach the Gospel'. No relevant variant readings are recorded in editions of the Vulgate, or the Old Latin text, and there is no other evidence that *evangelizantur* could be read as an active verb. Yet while Bede in his commentary on Luke takes the verb as passive, both Smaragdus (*Collectiones*, PL 102, 522) and Haymo (PL 118, 28) expound the Vulgate phrase as if it has active meaning, and all versions of the Gospels in Old English render it as an active construction, like Ælfric. There was presumably an unwritten tradition about the interpretation of the phrase, stemming in part from the grammatical difficulty, that *evangelizare* generally takes the message as its object while the recipients are usually the indirect object.

If the whole passage 68–78, added in another hand in MS A and partly recasting the beginning of the next sentence, is indeed an addition to the text by the author (see *CH I*, p. 127, n.8), Ælfric must originally have intended to pass over in silence the cryptic words (*diglum wordum*) of Christ's reply.

75–80 Cf Gregory, Hom. 6, PL 76, 1096BC:

> Ac si patenter dicat: 'Mira quidem facio, sed abiecta perpeti non dedignor. Quia ergo moriendo te subsequor, cavendum valde est hominibus, ne in me mortem despiciant, qui signa venerantur'.

82–3 Only Ælfric cites the celebration of birthdays as a custom of the past.

87–95 Bede, Hom. II.23, 89–97:

> Tria pariter impiorum scelera audimus: celebrationem natalis infaustam, saltationem puellae lascivam, iuramentum regis temerarium, quibus singulis oportet nos ne talia geramus instrui. Non enim festis diem nostri natalis in memoriam revocare, non ullum tempus illecebris indulgere carnalibus, sed diem potius exitus nostri debemus lacrimis et precibus et crebris praevenire ieiuniis. Hinc etenim vir sapiens ammonet dicens: 'In omnibus operibus tuis memorare novissima tua et in aeternum non peccabis' (Sir 7.40).

95–101 Bede, Hom. II.23, 97–103:

> Sed nec membra nostra quae iam domino consecrata sunt lusibus atque ineptis dare motibus decet. Dicit namque apostolus: 'Nescitis quoniam corpora vestra membra Christi sunt? . . .' (1 Cor 6.15). Unde et alibi obsecrat per misericordiam Dei ut exhibeamus corpora nostra hostiam viventem sanctam Deo placentem (Rom 12.1).

102–110 Bede, Hom. II.23, 103–5:

> Quantum vero temeritatem iurandi vitare debeamus et ipse in evangelio dominus et Iacobus in epistola sua docet.

Bede goes on to quote James 5.12, but Ælfric quotes instead Mt 5.34–7 (presumably alluded to by Bede here):

> (34) Ego autem dico vobis, non iurare omnino, neque per caelum, quia thronus Dei est; (35) neque per terram, quia scabellum est pedum eius; . . . (36) neque per caput tuum iuraveris, quia non potes unum capillum album

facere, aut nigrum. (37) Sit autem sermo vester, est, est; non, non; quod autem his abundantius est, a malo est.

Ælfric then adds the supporting example of Jn 4.21, *crede mihi*.

110–7 Bede, Hom. II.23, 110–20:

Ac si aliquid forte incautius nos iurasse contigerit, quod observatum scilicet peiorem vergat in exitum, libere illud consilio salubriore mutandum noverimus, ac magis instante necessitate peierandum nobis quam pro vitando periurio in aliud crimen gravius esse divertendum. Et denique iuravit David per dominum occidere Nabal, virum stultum et impium, atque omnia quae ad illum pertinerent demoliri, sed ad primam intercessionem Abigail feminae prudentis mox remisit minas, revocavit ensem in vaginam, neque aliquid culpae se tali peiurio contraxisse doluit (1 Sam 25).

The succession of alterations in MS A at line 116 seems simply to reflect attempts to restore some text accidentally omitted through the repetition of *herode(s)*.

118–28 Bede, Hom. II.23, 120–32:

Iuravit Herodes dare saltatrici quodcumque postulasset ab eo, et ne peiurus diceretur a convivis ipsum convivium sanguine polluit, dum prophetae mortem saltationis fecit praemium. Non solum autem in iurando sed in omni quod agimus haec est moderatio solertius observanda ut, si talem forte lapsum versuti hostis inciderimus insidiis, ex quo sine aliquo peccati contagio surgere non possimus, illum potius evadendi aditum petamus, in quo minus periculi nos perpessuros esse cernamus, iuxta exempla eorum qui hostilibus clausi muris dum evadere desiderant, sed portarum omnium accessum sibi interdictum considerant, ibi necesse est desiliendum locum eligant ubi muro existente breviore minimum periculi cadentes incurrant.

128–32 Bede, Hom. II.23, 76–80:

Qui quoniam noluit cohibere luxuriam ad homicidae reatum prolapsus est, minusque illi peccatum maioris erat causa peccati, cui districto Dei iudicio contigit ut propter appetitum adulterae quam detestandam sciebat sanguinem funderet prophetae quem Deo acceptum esse cognoverat.

132–40 Bede, Hom. II.23, 80–86:

Haec namque est illa divini dispensatio examinis de qua dicitur: 'Qui nocet noceat adhuc et qui in sordibus est sordescat adhuc' (Apoc 22.11). At contra quod sequitur, 'et sanctus sanctificetur adhuc', ad beati Iohannis personam convenienter aptatur qui sanctus exsistens sanctificabatur adhuc dum per officium evangelizandi ad martyrii palmam pervenit.

141–5 Bede, Hom. II.23, 145–52:

Herodes caput Iohannis petitus tristitiam quidem praetendebat in vultu. . . . Verum si diligentius cor nefandum inspicimus, laetabatur occulte quod ea petebatur quae et antea facere, si excusabiliter posset, disponebat. Qui si caput Herodiadis peteretur, nulli dubium quin illud dare veraciter tristis abnueret.

145–50 Bede, Hom. II.23, 176–82:

Non est dictum a persecutore ut Christum negaret sed ut veritatem reticeret; et tamen pro Christo occubuit. Quia enim Christus ipse ait 'Ego sum veritas' (Jn 14.6), ideo utique pro Christo quia pro veritate sanguinem fudit, et cui nascituro, praedicaturo, baptizaturo prius nascendo, praedicando ac baptizando testimonium perhibebat, hunc etiam passurum prior ipse patiendo signavit.

150–4 Cf Bede, Hom. II.23, 224–8:

Ut in ecclesiasticis invenimus historiis, corpus eius in civitate Samariae quae nunc Sabaste vocatur, caput autem in Hierosolimis humatum est; decollatus vero est in castello quodam Arabiae quod Macheronta nominant.

The information comes from Rufinus.

153–6 The curious story of the head of John the Baptist blowing Herodias all over the world is, not surprisingly, absent from Bede and Rufinus, but it is not to be found either in the standard legend of the Invention of the head (printed Mombritius 1910, II.46–51 and PL 67, 417–23) or, for instance, the *Old English Martyrology*, or indeed in any of the standard collections of apocrypha and saints' legends, and it is difficult to guess where Ælfric came across it. (It does appear in the account of St John in the South English Legendary,[2] and Whatley, *Acta*, notes its inclusion in the thirteenth-century *Legenda Aurea*.) Nor could he have discovered from any of the likely sources the evidence he cites in opposition, that Herodias lived on after the Baptist's death. Possibly Ælfric had seen a passage rejecting the legend and citing the reasons he gives, without actually meeting the legend itself. A number of early chronicles give an account of the exile of Herod and Herodias which might just have prompted Ælfric's reference to her living out her life until the end (line 156).

156–62 Bede, Hom. II.23, 228–38:

In quibus historiis hoc quoque reperimus, quod caput eius sanctissimum longo post decollationem tempore ab ipso revelatum sit duobus monchis orientalibus, qui orationis gratia venerant Hierosolimam atque inde in Emissam [*var.* Edissam] Foenicis civitatem perlatum debito fidelium sit honore frequentatum. At vero ossa eius tempore procedente de Samaria Hierosolimam translata ac mox Alexandriam missa nunc ibidem in ecclesia quae nominis ipsius est honore consecrata servantur. Quod divina providentia constat actum, ut scilicet per plura loca deportatis beati martyris reliquiis, plura virtutum signa fierent.

[2] *The South English Legendary*, ed. C. D'Evelyn and A. J. Mill, 3 vols., EETS os 235, 236 and 244 (1956–9), I.243.

The material is not in Rufinus but presumably reached Bede from hagiographical texts, such as the narrative of the Invention of the head mentioned in the previous note. Ælfric's attribution of the miracles to the head in particular, rather than the relics in general, as in Bede, perhaps reflects familiarity with that particular legend, though it is not in the Cotton-Corpus legendary.

162–71 Bede, Hom. II.23, 240–50, 272–81:

> [240–50] Considerandum est . . . quomodo omnipotens Deus electos dilectosque suos famulos, quos ad vitam regnumque praedestinavit aeternum, in tantum in hac vita pravorum patitur persecutione conteri, tot ac tantis poenarum mortiumque generibus consumi . . . quia 'quem diligit dominus castigat, flagellat autem omnem filium quem recipit' (Hebr 12.6). . . . [272–4] Sed non erat grave, immo leve ac desiderabile erat talibus tormenta pro veritate temporalia perpeti quae perpetuis noverant remuneranda gaudiis. . . . [280–81] 'Non sunt condignae passiones huius temporis ad superventuram gloriam quae revelabitur in nobis' (Rom 8.18).

172–6 Ælfric now reaches the end of Bede's homily. His next phrase *Nu cweð se trahtnere* invites us to suppose that he is still following the same source, but in fact the material comes, as Smetana showed, from a Ps-Chrysostom sermon on the Decollation included in Paul the Deacon's homiliary (Hom. 50, PL 95, 1509B):

> Nulla ergo in hoc mundo bestia similis est mulieri malae. Quid inter quadrupedia animalia leone saevius? Sed nihil ad haec. Aut in serpentibus quid dracone atrocius? Nec hoc quidem iuxta mulierem malam et litigiosam conferri potest. Nam et leo et draco in malo inferiores sunt. Attestatur huic sermoni meo sapientissimus Salomon, dicens: 'Cohabitare leoni et draconi melius est, quam cum muliere mala et litigiosa' (Sirach 25.23, *though the Vulgate reads* nequa *rather than* litigiosa).

177–88 Ps-Chrysostom, Hom. 50, PL 95:

> [1509C] Dracones et aspides et cornutae bestiae Iohannem Baptistam in deserto viventem subdita feritate tremuerunt. Herodias vero eidem caput abscidit, et tanti viri mortem in pretium saltationis accepit. . . . [*earlier*, 1509BC] Danielem leones in lacu reveriti sunt, iustum vero illum Naboth Iezabel interfecit. Cetus Ionam in ventre custodivit. Dalila autem Samsonem circumventum illecebris virum suum, novacula raso capite deformatum, alienigenis tradidit.

189–95 The *cyrclice gerecednys* is strictly the *Historia Ecclesiastica* of Rufinus rather than the *History of the Jews* by Josephus whom Rufinus quotes on the war between Areta and Herod (*Historia Ecclesiastica*, I.xi.2–3):

> In quo bello exercitum refert Herodis extinctum, haec autem omnia ei accidisse propter piaculum, quod in necem Iohannis ammisit. Idem quoque Ioseppus . . . Iohannem fuisse . . . ab Herode propter Herodiadem

capite caesum refert, propter quam etiam regno eum esse depulsum atque in exilium Viennam Galliae urbem trusum.

195–229 The sermon of Augustine which Ælfric says he is following would seem to be a version of Serm. 84, on Matthew 19.17 (PL 38, 519–20). It does not seem to appear in PD at all, and it looks as if Ælfric saw a different version from that printed in PL.[3] With 196–204 cf Augustine, Serm. 84, §1, PL 38, 519:

> Considerate, fratres, quantum amanda sit vita, ubi nunquam finias vitam. Amas ergo istam vitam, ubi tantum laboras, curris, satagis, anhelas; et vix enumerantur quae necessaria sunt in misera vita; seminare, arare, novellare, navigare, molere, coquere, texere: et post haec omnia finire habes vitam. Ecce quae pateris in misera ista quam diligis vita: et putas te semper victurum, et nunquam moriturum? Templa, saxa, marmora, ferro plumboque consolidata, tamen cadunt: et homo nunquam se putat moriturum? Discite ergo, fratres, quaerere aeternam vitam, ubi ista non tolerabitis, sed in aeternum cum Deo regnabitis.

Augustine has nothing similar to the lines on the privations and mutability of life, 205–11. With 211–3 cf Augustine, Serm. 84, §2, PL 38, 520:

> Et cum crescunt pueri, quasi accedunt illis dies; et nesciunt quia minuuntur: et ipsa est falsa computatio. Crescentibus enim decedunt dies potius, quam accedunt.

213–5 resembles the preceding passage in Augustine, Serm. 84, §2, PL 38, 519–20:

> Non sunt ergo dies mali quos agimus in corruptela huius carnis, in tanta vel sub tanta sarcina corruptibilis corporis, inter tantas tentationes, inter tantas difficultates, ubi falsa voluptas, nulla securitas gaudii, timor torquens, cupiditas avida, tristitia arida? Ecce quam malos dies: et nemo vult finire ipsos malos dies, multumque hinc rogant homines Deum, ut diu vivant. Quid est autem diu vivere, nisi diu torqueri? Quid est aliud diu vivere, quam malos dies malis diebus addere?

With the reference to the eighty-year span of life at 216–7 cf the subsequent lines in Serm. 84, §2, PL 38, 520: *Constitue alicui homini nato, verbi gratia, octoginta annos: quidquid vivit, de summa minuit.* The next two lines in Augustine mock the practice of celebrating birthdays (a passage which might have made it an appropriate sermon to use on the subject of Salome's dancing and the death of John the Baptist), and there then follows the passage which Ælfric uses at 218–227 (Serm. 84, §2, PL 38, 520):

> Mali ergo sunt dies: et eo peiores, quia diliguntur. Sic blanditur hic mundus, ut nemo velit finire aerumnosam vitam. Vera enim vita vel beata

[3] The more recent critical edition of this sermon, by R. Demeulenaere, 'Le sermon 84 de saint Augustin sur l'invitation de Jésus au jeune homme riche', in *Aevum inter utrumque: Mélanges offerts à Gabriel Sanders*, ed. M. Van Uytfanghe and R. Demeulenaere, Instrumenta Patristica 23 (Steenbruge, 1991), pp. 67–73 (text, pp. 71–3), has no relevant differences of substance, but the editor does suggest that the extant text is a fragment.

> haec est, cum resurgemus et cum Christo regnabimus. Nam et impii resurrecturi sunt, sed in ignem ituri. Vita itaque non est, nisi beata. Et vita beata esse non potest, nisi aeterna, ubi sunt dies boni; nec multi, sed unus. Ex consuetudine huius vitae appellati sunt dies. Dies ille nescit ortum, nescit occasum. Illi diei non succedit crastinus; quia non praecedit eum hesternus. Hunc diem, vel hos dies, et hanc vitam, et veram vitam in promissis habemus. Alicuius ergo operis merces est. Si enim mercedem amamus, in opere non deficiamus: et in aeternum cum Christo regnabimus.

What Ælfric firmly represents as a quotation from a prophet, however (lines 218–9), appears in Augustine as his own words, though referring back to his earlier quotation from St Paul (Serm. 84, §2, PL 38, 519): *De his autem diebus quos agimus, ait apostolus, 'Redimentes tempus, quoniam dies mali sunt'* (Eph 5.16). There seems to be no parallel in the Old Testament, except a partial one at Prov 15.15: *Omnes dies pauperis, mali.*

33 SEVENTEENTH SUNDAY AFTER PENTECOST

Ælfric begins with an exposition of the Gospel for the day, Luke 7.11–16, on the resurrection of the widow's son of Naim, which he interprets allegorically as a recovery from sin (lines 1–74). He then extends the discussion by drawing a comparison with the other two resurrection-miracles described in the Gospels—the daughter of Jairus, and Lazarus, the brother of Martha and Mary—interpreting them as three stages of sin (lines 74–123). Finally he discusses the general question of penitence and especially the sin against the Holy Ghost, the one sin from which there is no recovery (lines 123–58).

The sources present a problem. Ælfric begins his exposition by citing Bede as his authority, and as Smetana has pointed out,[1] the exposition of Luke 7 has much in common with Bede's commentary on Luke (*Comm. Luc.*, 2.2266–2332), while the account of the three resurrections is similar to a later section of the same commentary (*Comm. Luc.*, 3.1055–89). The two relevant sections were both excerpted as homilies in the original version of Paul the Deacon's homiliary (though for two different occasions). Yet paradoxically the particular detail for which he cites Bede, the interpretation of Naim, is not to be found in Bede's commentary, and there are also many differences of detail which make Bede not wholly convincing, at least as sole source. A much closer parallel in some respects is the homily for the occasion which appears in late versions of Paul the Deacon's homiliary, ascribed in the early printed editions to Ambrose but probably written by Hericus of Auxerre.[2] Like Ælfric, Hericus devotes the first part of his homily to an exposition of Luke 7.11–16 and then turns to the theme

[1] Smetana 1959, pp. 193–4. Förster (1894, p. 25) had earlier suggested Bede's commentary on Luke and his commentary on Mark.

[2] See Barré, p. 177.

of the three resurrections. He has much of Bede's material, but he also has the interpretation of Naim and two other parallels to Ælfric where Bede has nothing. On the other hand, he does not include all the Bede material used by Ælfric, and Bede's wording is sometimes slightly closer. One should perhaps conclude that Ælfric used both Bede and Hericus.[3]

Nothing in either Bede or Hericus prompts Ælfric's discussion of the sin against the Holy Spirit, though it obviously relates to the general issue of repentance and the possibility of spiritual resurrection from the death that is sin. Pope suggested Augustine's Serm. 71 as a source, possibly indirect, and Ælfric's views certainly reflect the general argument of this very long sermon, but there is seldom a close parallel.

The whole subject of this homily was revisited by Ælfric in a later homily, Pope 6. This has as its main subject the raising of Lazarus, but once again Ælfric introduced a discussion of the three resurrections, and in later revision added a passage on the sin against the Holy Ghost (see Pope's introduction). He seems to have been in large part rewriting the earlier material, though also drawing on his original sources again.

Sources and Notes

The following texts are cited below:

1. Augustine, Serm. 71, ed. P. Verbraken, 'Le sermon LXXI de saint Augustin sur le blasphème contre le Saint-Esprit' *RB* 75 (1965), 54–108 (text, pp. 65–108) [also in PL 38, cols. 444–68].
2. Bede, *Commentarius in Lucam*, ed. D. Hurst, CCSL 120 (Turnhout, 1960), pp. 5–425.
3. Hericus, *Homiliae in Circulum Anni*, ed. R. Quadri, CCCM 116B (Turnhout, 1994), Hom. II.37 (pp. 350–60) [also printed as Hom. 179 in the version of Paul the Deacon's homiliary printed by Migne, PL 95, cols. 1415–22].

4–15 A free paraphrase of Lc 7.11–16:

(11) Et factum est: deinceps ibat in civitatem quae vocatur Naim: et ibant cum eo discipuli eius et turba copiosa. (12) Cum autem appropinquaret

[3] For a different interpretation, though one which I find hard to accept, see Hill 1992, pp. 211–4. She argues that for the exposition of the pericope itself Ælfric used Smaragdus's abridged version of Bede alongside Bede himself and that 'on the basis of a detailed comparative analysis, I see no grounds for supposing that Ælfric used [Hericus]' (p. 212, n. 31). But the details supposedly dependent on Smaragdus amount to little more than the etymology of Naim, which is also in Hericus,whereas if one takes the homily as a whole into account, it seems to me impossible to ignore the important parallels with Hericus at 68 ff and 76 ff and the overall agreement in structure, for which neither Bede nor Smaragdus provides a parallel. Pope's rejection of Hericus as a source for his homily 6, cited Hill 1992, p. 215, n.45, refers to a quite different piece and does not relate to this issue, and the etymology of Naim is by no means clearly attributed to Jerome in Hericus (cited by Hill as 'a compelling reason' for rejecting Hericus as a source).

portae civitatis, ecce defunctus efferebatur filius unicus matris suae; et haec vidua erat; et turba civitatis multa cum illa. (13) Quam cum vidisset Dominus, misericordia motus super eam, dixit illi: Noli flere. (14) Et accessit, et tetigit loculum. Hi autem qui portabant, steterunt. Et ait: Adolescens, tibi dico, surge. (15) Et resedit qui erat mortuus, et coepit loqui. Et dedit illum matri suae. (16) Accepit autem omnes timor, et magnificabant Deum, dicentes: Quia propheta magnus surrexit in nobis, et quia Deus visitavit plebem suam.

Ælfric adds the details of the widow's grief (lines 7–8) and Christ's comforting of her (line 12).

16–19 The etymology is not in Bede but is in the homily for this occasion by Hericus (Hom. II.37, 15–16): *Interpretatur Naim fluctus vel commotio*. The same words appear in Smaragdus (*Collectiones*, PL 102, 464D). The rest could be from Bede, *Comm. Luc.*, 2.2266–71:

Defunctus hic, qui extra portam civitatis multis est intuentibus elatus, significat hominem letali criminum funere soporatum eandemque insuper animae mortem, non cordis adhuc cubili tegentem sed ad multorum notitiam per locutionis operisve indicium quasi per suae civitatis ostia propalantem.

The same points, probably based on Bede, are made by Hericus (Hom. II.37, 44–52).

19–23 Cf Bede, *Comm. Luc.*, 2.2271–4 [= Hericus, Hom. II.37, 93–100]:

Qui bene filius unicus matri suae fuisse perhibetur quia licet e multis collecta personis una sit perfecta et immaculata virgo mater ecclesia, singuli quique tamen fidelium universalis se ecclesiae filios rectissime fatentur.

23–7 Cf Bede, *Comm. Luc.*, 2.2274–8 [or Hericus, Hom. II.37, 100–4]:

Electus quilibet quando ad fidem imbuitur filius est, quando alios imbuit mater. An non materno erga parvulos agebat affectu qui ait: 'Filioli mei quos iterum parturio, donec formetur Christus in vobis'? (Gal 4.19).

28–35 Cf Bede, *Comm. Luc.*, 2.2278–86:

Portam civitatis . . . puto aliquem de sensibus esse corporeis. Qui enim seminat inter fratres discordias, qui iniquitatem in excelsum loquitur, per oris portam extrahitur mortuus. 'Qui viderit mulierem ad concupiscendum eam' (Mt 5.28) per oculorum portam suae mortis indicia profert. Qui fabulis otiosis, obscenisve carminibus, vel detractionibus aurem libenter aperit, hanc animae suae portam mortis efficit; ceterosque qui non servat sensus mortis sibi ipse reddit aditus.

36–8 Cf Bede, *Comm. Luc.*, 2.2302–6:

Pulchre evangelista dominum prius misericordia motum esse super matrem ac sic filium suscitare testatur, ut in uno nobis exemplum imitandae pietatis ostenderet, in altero fidem mirandae potestatis adstrueret.

39–51 Cf Bede, *Comm. Luc.*, 2.2308–17:

Loculus, in quo mortuus effertur, male secura desperati peccatoris conscientia est. Qui vero sepeliendum portant . . . lenocinia blandientium sunt venenata sociorum, quae peccata nimirum dum favoribus tollunt accumulant, peccantesque contemptu quasi aggere terrae obruunt, de quibus alibi dicitur: 'Dimitte mortuos sepelire mortuos suos' (Mt 8.22). Mortuos quippe mortui sepeliunt, cum peccatores quique sui similes alios nocivo favore demulcent, congestaque pessimae adulationis mole . . . opprimunt.

Ælfric's additional quotation at 43–4 is from Ps 9.24 (see Cook 1898, p. 110), despite the attribution to a prophet: *Quoniam laudatur peccator in desideriis animae suae, et iniquus benedicitur*. It does not appear in Bede or in the homilies on this text by Hericus, Smaragdus and Haymo.

51–3 The quotation is not used in the Latin commentaries. Cook (1898, p. 117) rather tentatively identified it as Prov 29.5: *Homo qui blandis fictisque sermonibus loquitur amico suo, rete expandit gressibus eius*. A much closer parallel is a phrase in Gregory the Great's *Dialogues*, I.4.127–8: *Lingua adulantium auditoris sui animam amplectendo necans*. It is not identified as a Biblical quotation by Gregory or his editors, but Ælfric only says that it is to be found 'in another place'. He had possibly met it somewhere else as a quotation and did not himself know its origin, though he did know the *Dialogues* well.

54–8 Cf Bede, *Comm. Luc.*, 2.2318–22:

Superni formidine iudicii attacta conscientia, et carnalium saepe affluentiam voluptatum et iniuste laudantium turbam coercens, . . . vocanti ad vitam festina respondet salvatori.

60–1 Cf Bede, *Comm. Luc.*, 2.2324–5:

Residet qui erat mortuus cum interna compunctione reviviscit peccator.

But the next sentence, 61–2, is quite unlike Bede's comment. Hericus is scarcely closer.

62–4 Cf Bede, *Comm. Luc.*, 2.2327–8: *Redditur matri cum per sacerdotalis decreta iudicii communioni sociatur ecclesiae*.

64–7 Cf Bede, *Comm. Luc.*, 2.2330–32: *Quanto desperatior animae mors ad vitam revocatur, tanto plures eodem corriguntur exemplo*.

68–75 Bede has nothing at all similar, but cf Hericus (PL 95, 1421A = Hom. II.37, 248–55):

In hoc nequaquam errabant, quod eum prophetam esse dicebant. Ipse enim verus erat propheta, quia quae ventura erant, verissima assertione praedicebat. . . . Propheta ergo erat, cum dominus esset prophetarum, sicut rex regum, et dominus dominantium.

Ælfric's discussion closely parallels his comments on a similar Biblical verse at CH I.12.130–5, where he expands on a brief remark by Augustine. His concern with the issue, and treatment of it, perhaps reflects an anxiety about views that Christ was no more than a prophet.

77–81 Hericus, like Ælfric, turns at this point to the topic of the three deaths, and his introductory comments are similar (Hom. II.37, 289–98):

Interea collatis quatuor evangelistarum narrationibus, tres mortuos invenimus a Domino suscitatos, quamvis plures eum resuscitasse dubium non sit, licet scriptum non legatur. Multi ergo, dicit beatus Augustinus, sine dubio sunt corporaliter a Domino suscitati, sed non frustra tres commemorati, filia scilicet archisynagogi adhuc intra domum mortua iacens, et iuvenis iste extra portam civitatis delatus, et Lazarus quatriduanus iam fetens. Qui tres mortui significant tria genera hominum peccatorum, quos hodieque in sancta ecclesia a morte animae suscitat Christus.

The Augustine text referred to is probably Serm. 98.

81–2 The summary is deducible from the subsequent arguments of Hericus and Bede (*Comm. Luc.* 3) but does not appear in either.

82–6 A summary of the story from Lc 8:

(41) Et ecce venit vir, cui nomen Iairus, et ipse princeps synagogae erat; et cecidit ad pedes Iesu, rogans eum ut intraret in domum eius, (42) quia unica filia . . . moriebatur. . . . (49) Venit quidam ad principem synagogae, dicens ei: Quia mortua est filia tua, noli vexare illum. . . . (51) Et cum venisset domum . . . (54) Ipse autem tenens manum eius clamavit, dicens: Puella, surge. (55) . . . Et surrexit continuo. Et iussit illi dari manducare.

87–92 Cf Bede, *Comm. Luc.*, 3.1055–59:

Nonnulli consensum malae delectationi praebendo, latente tantum cogitatione, peccati sibi mortem consciscunt. Sed tales vivificare significans, salvator suscitavit filiam archisinagogi nondum foras elatam sed in domo mortuam, quasi vitium secreto in corde tegentem.

Hericus, Hom. II.37, 299–304 is very similar. Both seem to be drawing on Augustine, Serm. 98 (PL 38, 592–5).

92–7 Cf Bede, *Comm. Luc.*, 3.1059–65:

Alii non solum noxiae delectationi consentiendo, sed et ipsum malum quo delectantur agendo mortuum suum quasi extra portas efferunt. Et hos, se si paeniteant, resuscitare demonstrans suscitavit iuvenem filium viduae extra portas civitatis elatum et reddidit matri suae, quia resipiscentem a peccati tenebris animam unitati restituit ecclesiae.

Hericus, Hom. II.37, 304–10 is similar.

98–105 Cf Bede, *Comm. Luc.*, 3.1065–72:

Quidam vero non solum cogitando vel faciendo illicita, sed et ipsa peccandi consuetudine se quasi sepeliendo corrumpunt. Verum nec ad hos erigendos minor fit virtus et gratia salvatoris, si tamen adsint cogitationes sollicitae. . . . Nam ad hoc intimandum resuscitavit Lazarum 'quattuor dies iam in monumento habentem' (Jn 11.17).

Cf Hericus, Hom. II.37, 310–16.

105–12 Cf Bede, *Comm. Luc.*, 3.1073–8:

Notandum autem quod quanto gravior animae mors ingruerit, tanto acrior necesse est ut resurgere mereatur paenitentis fervor insistat. Quod occulte volens ostendere, dominus iacentem in conclavi mortuam modesta levique voce resuscitat, dicens, 'Puella surge', quam et ob facilitatem resuscitandi iam mortuam fuisse negaverat.

Cf Hericus, Hom. II.37, 316–20.

112–3 Cf Bede, *Comm. Luc.*, 3.1079–80:

Delatum foras iuvenem pluribus ut reviviscere debeat dictis corroborat cum ait: 'Iuvenis tibi dico surge'.

Cf Hericus, Hom. II.37, 324–5.

113–6 Cf Bede, *Comm. Luc.*, 3.1086–7:

Publica noxa publico eget remedio, levia autem peccata leviori et secreta queunt paenitentia deleri.

117–21 For the first part cf Bede, *Comm. Luc.*, 3.1080–4:

Quatriduanus vero mortuus ut longa prementis sepulchri claustra deponere posset, fremuit spiritu Iesus turbavit se ipsum, lacrimas fudit, rursum fremuit ac magna voce clamavit: 'Lazare veni foras' (Jn 11.43).

Cf Hericus, Hom. II.37, 326–8.

121–8 Ælfric now moves on to the difficult question of the sin against the Holy Ghost, leaving behind Bede and Hericus. Lines 124–8 are from Mt 12.31–2:

(31) Omne peccatum et blasphemia remittetur hominibus, Spiritus autem blasphemia non remittetur. (32) Et quicumque dixerit verbum contra Filium hominis, remittetur ei; qui autem dixerit contra Spiritum Sanctum, non remittetur ei, neque in hoc saeculo, neque in futuro.

129–60 A characteristic excursus on the Trinity for which Ælfric seldom needed sources, but with 129–36 cf Augustine, Serm. 71, in Verbraken, 365–9:

Nostis . . . deum patrem non spiritus sancti patrem esse, sed filii; et deum filium non spiritus sancti filium esse, sed patris; deum autem spiritum sanctum non solius patris aut solius filii esse spiritum, sed patris et filii.

34 DEDICATION OF THE CHURCH OF ST MICHAEL

The cult of the archangel Michael as a Christian saint seems to have originated in Phrygia, perhaps under the influence of Hebrew apocrypha, and spread thence to Greece and the West by the fourth century. His place in the calendar has been subject to much variation. It would appear that a feast-day for the dedication of the church of St Michael was established on 29 September in the Roman calendar from the fifth century, in commemoration of the dedication of a church in Rome, and that a further feast on 8 May was initiated later, commemorating either an appearance of St Michael on Mount Gargano in southeastern Italy, ascribed to the late fifth century or the early sixth, or a victory of the Lombards over the Neapolitans in 663; but the spread of the former festival in Western usage seems to have led to an association of 29 September with other events.[1] The *Old English Martyrology* summarises the Mount Garganus story under 8 May but gives for 29 September the dedication of a church to St Michael in the city of Tracla in Eraclea, to commemorate St Michael's help in the defence of the city.[2] Ælfric gives yet another version of events, affirming that the festival on 29 September was established in commemoration of the appearance of St Michael at Mount Garganus on that day, and proceeding to tell the story of that appearance and the archangel's help for the people of Sepontinus in defeating the Neapolitans. In this he was following the pattern of some early calendars and, probably, of his sources: the legend of the apparition on Mount Garganus appears for this occasion both in expanded versions of Paul the Deacon's homiliary and in the Cotton-Corpus legendary.[3] The Blickling Homilies also provide a version of the Garganus legend, apparently for the 29 September date.

For the first part, then, Ælfric follows closely the traditional legend of the discovery of the church on Mount Garganus. He may well have found the Latin text both in his homiliary and in his legendary; as usual with hagiographic sources, texts vary considerably in points of detail and although the version printed in the PL 95 text of PD is quite close other versions occasionally have closer variants.[4] After giving his version of the Garganus legend, Ælfric turns to the Gospel passage for the day, Matthew 18.1–10 (this seems to have been the standard reading, so assigned in the Latin homiliaries as well as in the *OE Gospels*). For his exposition of the Gospel he says that he draws on Haymo, and the homily for this occasion which appears in both Haymo's homiliary and in

[1] See R. Grant, ed., *Three Homilies from Cambridge, Corpus Christi College 41* (Ottawa, 1982), pp. 42–55; Whatley, *Acta* (forthcoming); ODCC under 'Michael the Archangel'.

[2] OE Martyrology, II.223–4.

[3] See Smetana 1959, p. 194 and Zettel 1979, p. 144. The source was identified by Förster 1892, pp. 28–9.

[4] Cf esp. Zettel 1979, pp. 144, 182–4.

PL 95 is indeed very close (as pointed out by Förster and confirmed by Smetana)[5]. Yet at a number of places Ælfric appears to be rather closer to earlier authorities, such as Jerome and Bede. In each case where such a parallel can be traced the material also appears in the homily by Smaragdus, and it may simply be that Ælfric interwove material from Haymo and Smaragdus. But the absence of parallels for other details, especially the concluding discussion of angels, suggests that he may have been using an expanded version of Haymo's homily.

Sources and Notes

The following texts are cited below:

1. Anon., *Relatio de Dedicatione Ecclesiae Sancti Michaelis*, PL 95, cols. 1522–5 (BHL 5948). Also known as the *Apparitio Sancti Michaelis*, and printed in: G. Waitz, ed., MGH, Scriptores rerum Langobardicarum (Hanover, 1878), pp. 541–43; Mombritius 1910, I.389–91; ASS Sept. VIII.61–2. Passages below are based on the PL 95 version but incorporating variants from other versions (printed in italics) where these are closer to Ælfric's text.
2. Haymo of Auxerre, *Homilia in Festo Sancti Michaelis*, PL 95, cols. 1525–30 [= Haymo, *Homiliae de Sanctis*, PL 118, Hom. 7, cols. 770–6].
3. Smaragdus, *Collectiones in Evangelia et Epistolas*, PL 102, cols. 477–80.

4–8 *Relatio de Dedicatione*, PL 95, 1522BC:

> Memoriam beati Michaelis archangeli toto orbe venerandam, ipsius et opere condita, et consecrata nomine demonstrat ecclesia. . . . Est locus in *Campaniae* finibus, ubi inter sinum Adriaticum et montem Garganum civitas Sepontus posita est. Qui mons civitatis a moenibus ad duodecim millia *passuum* erectus.

Ælfric's rather abrupt and unusual opening, not mentioning the festival but stating that this distant site is known to many, is unprompted by anything in his source; perhaps he knew Anglo-Saxons who had visited the place or at least reported its fame in Italy.

8–18 *Relatio de Dedicatione*, PL 95, 1522CD:

> Erat in ea civitate vir praedives quidam Garganus nomine, qui ex eventu suo monti vocabulum indidit. Huius dum pecora, quorum infinita multitudine pollebat, passim per devexi montis latera pascerentur, contigit taurum armenti communis gregis consortia spernentem, per montem singularem incedere solitum. . . . Quem dominus collecta multitudine servorum per devia quaeque requirens, invenit tandem in vertice eiusdem montis pro foribus cuiusdam assistere speluncae. Itaque ira permotus, cur

[5] Förster 1894, pp. 45–6, and Smetana 1959, p. 194.

solivagus incederet, arrepto arcu appetiit illum sagitta toxicata. Quae veluti venti flamine retorta, eum a quo iacta est, mox reversa percussit.

19–33 *Relatio de Dedicatione*, PL 95, 1522D-3A:

Turbati cives et stupefacti qualiter res fuerit effecta, non enim accedere propius audebant, consulunt episcopum, quid facto opus sit. Qui indicto ieiunio triduano, a Deo monuit esse quaerendum. Quo peracto sanctus Domini archangelus episcopum per visionem alloquitur, dicens: 'Iam bene fecisti, quod homines latebat, a Deo quaerendo mysterium, causam videlicet hominis suo telo percussi. Sciatis hoc mea gestum voluntate. Ego enim sum Michael archangelus, qui in conspectu Domini semper assisto, locumque hunc in terris incolere, tutumque servare instituens, hoc volui indicio probare, omnium quae ibi geruntur, ipsius quoque loci me esse inspectorem atque custodem.'

34–9 *Relatio de Dedicatione*, PL 95, 1523A:

Hac revelatione comperta, consuetudinem fecerunt cives hic Dominum precibus per sanctum deposcere Michaelem. Duas ianuas ibi cernentes, quarum australis, quae et maior erat, aliquot gradibus in occasum vergentibus, adiri poterat, sed nec ultra cryptam intrare ausi, prae foribus quotidie orationi vacabant.

39–46 *Relatio de Dedicatione*, PL 95, 1523AB:

Inter haec Neapolitani paganis adhuc ritibus aberrantes, Sepontinos et Beneventanos . . . bello lacessere tentant. Qui antistitis sui monitis edocti, tridui petunt inducias, ut triduano ieiunio liceret quasi fidele patrocinium sancti Michaelis implorare et praesidium. Quo tempore, pagani ludis scenicis falsorum invitant auxilia deorum.

47–52 *Relatio de Dedicatione*, PL 95, 1523B:

Ecce nocte ipsa quae belli antecedebat diem, adest in visione sanctus Michael antistiti, preces dixit exauditas, victoriam spopondit adfuturam, et quarta diei hora bello praemonet hostibus occurrendum. Laeti ergo facti, et de angelica certi victoria, Domini coacti spiritu obviant Christiani paganis.

52–63 *Relatio de Dedicatione*, PL 95, 1523BC:

Atque in primo belli apparatu Garganus immenso tremore concutitur, fulgura crebra volant, et caligo tenebrosa totum montis cacumen obduxit. . . . Fugiunt pagani, partim ferro hostium, partim igniferis impulsi sagittis, ad Neapolim usque sequentibus, atque . . . moenia tandem suae urbis moribundi subintrant. Qui evasere periculum, comperto quod angelus Dei in adiutorium venerit Christianis, nam et sexcentos ferme suorum fulmine videbant interemptos, Regi regum Christo continuo colla submittentes, armis induuntur fidei.

63–70 *Relatio de Dedicatione*, PL 95, 1523CD:

Cumque domum reversi victores, vota Domino gratiarum ad templum referrent archangeli, vident mane iuxta ianuam septentrionalem . . . quasi hominis vestigia marmori arctius impressa, agnoscunt beatum Michaelem hoc presentiae suae signum voluisse monstrare. Ubi postea culmen appositum et altare impositum, ipsa ecclesia ob signa vestigiorum Appodonia est vocata.

71–75 *Relatio de Dedicatione*, PL 95, 1523D:

Multa dubitatio inter Sepontinum et Beneventanum quid de loco agerent, utrum intrare *vel* dedicare ibi debeant ecclesiam. Unde collatione facta, ad *orientem* loci illius beati Petri apostolorum principis nomine condunt ecclesiam et dedicant. In qua etiam beatae semper virginis Mariae, sanctique Baptistae Ioannis altaria statuunt.

75–84 *Relatio de Dedicatione*, PL 95, 1523D-4A:

Tandem antistites salubri reperto consilio Romanum episcopum quid de his agendum sit per nuntios sciscitantur. . . . Taliaque mandata remittit: 'Si hominis est illam dedicare basilicam, hoc maxime die quo victoria data est fieri oportet. Sin autem alias sancto provisori loci placuerit, eodem praecipue die illius in hoc voluntas est requirenda. Hoc ergo tempore imminente, agamus ambo triduanum cum civibus nostris ieiunium, sanctam Trinitatem rogantes, ut munera quae summo suae sedis ministro conferre dignatus est, ad certum usque finem perducat.'

84–91 *Relatio de Dedicatione*, PL 95, 1524AB:

Nocte vero constituti ieiunii suprema, angelus Domini Michael episcopo Sepontino per visionem apparens: 'Non est', inquit, 'vobis opus hanc quam aedificavi dedicare ecclesiam. Ipse enim qui condidi, etiam dedicavi. Vos tantum intrate, et me assistente patrono, precibus locum frequentate. Et te quidem ibi cras missam celebrante, populus iuxta morem communicet. Meum autem erit ostendere quomodo per memet locum sacraverim ipsum.'

92–7 *Relatio de Dedicatione*, PL 95, 1524B:

Illi adveniunt mane cum oblationibus, et magna instantia precum intrant regiam australem, et ecce longa porticus in aquilonem porrecta, atque illam attingens posterulam extra quam vestigia marmori diximus impressa. Sed priusquam huc pervenias, apparet ad orientem basilica praegrandis, qua per gradus ascenditur.

97–105 *Relatio de Dedicatione*, PL 95, 1524BC:

Haec cum ipsa porticu sua quingentos fere homines capere videbatur, altare venerandum, rubroque contectum palliolo, prope medium parietis meridiem ostendens. Erat ipsa domus angulosa, non in more operis humani parietibus erectis, sed instar speluncae praeruptis et saepius eminentibus asperata scopulis, culmine quoque diversae altitudinis, quod hic vertice tangi, alibi manu vix possit attingi, credo docente archangelo, Deum non ornatum lapidum, sed cordis quaerere et diligere puritatem.

105–12 *Relatio de Dedicatione*, PL 95, 1524C:
Vertex vero montis extrinsecus partim cornea sylva tegitur, partim virenti planitie dilatatur. Missarum itaque celebratione completa, magno attoniti gaudio quique redierunt in sua. Episcopus autem delegato ministrorum, cantorum, sacerdotumque officio, et mansione constructa, omnem ibidem quotidie psalmorum, hymnorum, missarumque cursum congruo praecepit ordine celebrari.

112–20 *Relatio de Dedicatione*, PL 95, 1524CD:
Nullus autem huc nocturno est tempore ausus ingredi, sed aurora transacta matutinos ibi decantavit hymnos. Ex ipso autem saxo quo sacra tegitur aedes, ad aquilonem altaris, dulcis et nimium lucida guttatim aqua dilabitur, quam incolae *loci illius* stillam vocant. Ob hoc et vitreum vas eiusdem receptui praeparatum argentea pendet catena suspensum, morisque est populo communicato singulos ad vasculum ascendere per gradus, donumque coelestis degustare liquoris.

120–32 *Relatio de Dedicatione*, PL 95, 1524D-5A:
Nam et gustu suavis et tactu salubris; denique nonnulli per longas febrium flammas hac hausta stilla, celeri confestim refrigerio potiuntur salutis. Innumeris quoque et aliis modis ibi crebro sanantur aegroti, et multa quae angelicae tantum congruunt potestati, geri illic miracula comprobantur, maxime tamen eiusdem die natalis, cum et de provinciis circumpositis plus solito conflua turba recurrit, et angelicae virtutis maior quodammodo creditur adesse frequentia, ut quod spiritualiter dixit apostolus, etiam corporaliter agi videatur: 'Quia angeli sunt administratorii spiritus in ministerium missi, propter eos qui haereditatem capiunt salutis, in Christo Iesu Domino nostro' (Hebr 1.14).

136–54 A close rendering of Mt 18.1–10:
(1) In illa hora accesserunt discipuli ad Iesum, dicentes: Quis, putas, maior est in regno caelorum? (2) Et advocans Iesus parvulum, statuit eum in medio eorum, (3) Et dixit: Amen, dico vobis, nisi conversi fueritis, et efficiamini sicut parvuli, non intrabitis in regnum caelorum. (4) Quicumque ergo humiliaverit se sicut parvulus iste, hic est maior in regno caelorum. (5) Et qui susceperit unum parvulum talem in nomine meo, me suscipit; (6) qui autem scandalizaverit unum de pusillis istis, qui in me credunt, expedit ei ut suspendatur mola asinaria in collo eius, et demergatur in profundum maris. (7) Vae mundo a scandalis! Necesse est enim ut veniant scandala; verumtamen vae homini illi, per quem scandalum venit. (8) Si autem manus tua, vel pes tuus scandalizat te, abscide eum, et proiice abs te; bonum tibi est ad vitam ingredi debilem, vel

> claudum, quam duas manus vel duos pedes habentem mitti in ignem aeternum. (9) Et si oculus tuus scandalizat te, erue eum, et proiice abs te; bonum tibi est cum uno oculo in vitam intrare, quam duos oculos habentem mitti in gehennam ignis. (10) Videte ne contemnatis unum ex his pusillis; dico enim vobis, quia angeli eorum in caelis semper vident faciem Patris mei, qui in caelis est.

Here and again in CH II.14.69–78 Ælfric uses forms of *æswician* and *æswicung* to render Latin *scandalizare* and *scandalum*. Neither pair is easily glossed. Modern Bibles tend to use 'offend' and 'offence', but Ælfric's terms seem, as the element *-swic-* would suggest, to carry a sense of failure or disloyalty and also deceit; cf esp. 217 ff.

155–66 Cf Haymo, *Hom. Mich.*, PL 95, 1525D:

> Ut supra evangelista retulit, accesserunt ad Petrum qui didrachma accipiebant, et dixerunt ei: Magister vester non solvit didrachma? Ait etiam. Et cum intrasset domum, praevenit eum Iesus, dicens: Quid tibi videtur, Simon? Reges terrae a quibus suscipiunt tributum vel censum? A filiis suis, an ab alienis? Et ille dixit: Ab alienis. Dixit illi Iesus: Ergo liberi sunt filii. Ne autem scandalizemus eos, vade ad mare, et mitte hamum, et eum piscem qui primus ascenderit, tolle, et aperto eius ore invenies staterem, illum sumens, da eis pro me et te (Mt 17.24–6).

Stater is generally understood to be a coin and is so rendered in the Lindisfarne Gospels (*trymes*) and Rushworth (*scilling*) and in one manuscript of the *OE Gospels* (*penig*); but the other manuscript has *wecg*, like Ælfric, presumably meaning a gold piece (cf CH I.4.42 and I.27.144). One would like to think Ælfric saw a link between the golden *wecg* found in the fish's mouth and the golden *wecg* cast into the sea by secular philosophers in I.4 and I.27. There is again close agreement between Ælfric and the *OE Gospels* in rendering *didrachma* by *gafol oððe tol*. Ælfric is, however, alone in rendering *filiis* by the more general *gesiblingum*.

167–72 Cf Haymo, *Hom. Mich.*, PL 95, 1525D-6A:

> Quia ergo alii discipuli viderant Petrum in redditione census Domino coaequari, computantes eum illis omnibus esse praelatum, in illa hora accesserunt ad Iesum, dicentes: 'Quis putas maior est in regno coelorum?'.

For 167–8 cf Jerome, *Commentarii in Evangelium Matthaei*, 3.483–5 (CCSL 77):

> Videns Iesus cogitationes eorum, et causas erroris intellegens, vult desiderium gloriae, humilitatis contentione sanare.

(Repeated by Smaragdus, *Collectiones*, PL 102, 478A.)

172–7 Cf Haymo, *Hom. Mich.*, PL 95, 1526BC:

> Ac si diceret: Sicut parvulus iste cuius vobis exemplum proposui, videns mulierem pulchram non concupiscit, non alienas divitias appetit, laesus non relaedit, non aliud cogitat, et aliud loquitur, et iratus non perpetuas tenet discordias, ita et vos nisi talem habueritis innocentiam in mente, qualem iste habet in corpore, regnum coelorum . . . intrare nequaquam potestis.

178–86 Cf Haymo, *Hom. Mich.*, PL 95, 1526CD:

Cum ergo ait: 'Nisi conversi, etc.' . . . tale est si dixisset . . . non quod apostolos corpore vellet esse parvulos, sed ut innocentiam parvulorum in mente possiderent. Huiuscemodi parvulos Dominus suos volebat esse discipulos, quibus dicebat: 'Sinite parvulos venire ad me, talium est enim regnum coelorum' (Mt 19.14). Et Paulus apostolus talium innocentiam parvulorum suos volebat habere discipulos, quibus per epistolam praecipiebat: 'Nolite pueri effici sensibus, sed malitia parvuli estote, sensibus autem perfecti sitis' (1 Cor 14.20).

188–91 Cf Haymo, *Hom. Mich.*, PL 95, 1526D-7A:

Habeamus ergo virtutem humilitatis, si volumus habere in regno coelorum locum celsitudinis, quoniam, sicut Salvator ait in evangelio: 'Omnis qui se humiliat exaltabitur, et qui se exaltat humiliabitur' (Lc 14.11, *reversed*).

191–4 Cf Haymo, *Hom. Mich.*, PL 95, 1526D:

Parvulus enim est qui sibi displicet ut Deo placeat, tantoque ante Deum erit pulchrior, quanto apud semetipsum erit humilior.

195–8 Cf Haymo, *Hom. Mich.*, PL 95, 1527B:

Quamvis non sit eligendum cui iuxta scripturae vocem benefacere debeamus, illis tamen qui propter Deum parvi et humiles esse eligunt, in cuius vitae moribus Christum esse cognoscimus, specialem benevolentiam impendere debemus.

199–204 Cf Haymo, *Hom. Mich.*, PL 95, 1527C:

Et ipse alibi dicit: 'Qui suscipit prophetam in nomine prophetae, mercedem prophetae accipiet; et qui suscipit iustum in nomine iusti, mercedem iusti accipiet' (Mt 10.41).

But the exposition Ælfric gives is not in Haymo. In defining the righteous who is received or welcomed like the *lytlingas* as a minister of God (line 201) Ælfric perhaps makes for difficulties in his argument, since he goes on to identify as clerics those who offend or mislead the *lytlingas* (lines 211 ff).

208–10 Cf Haymo, *Hom. Mich.*, PL 95, 1528A:

Per molam asinariam quae pondus habet, sed nullum iter explicat, volubilis amor saeculi exprimitur.

210–11 Ps 11.9: *In circuitu impii ambulant*. (Not cited by Haymo.)

211–16 Cf Bede, *Commentarius in Marcum*, 3.471–6 (CCSL 120):

Qui ad sanctitatis speciem deductus vel verbo ceteros destruit vel exemplo, melius profecto erat ut hunc ad mortem sub exteriori habitu terrena acta constringerent, quam sacra officia in culpa ceteris imitabilem demonstrarent, quia nimirum, si solus caderet, utcumque hunc tolerabilior inferni poena cruciaret.

Repeated by Smaragdus, *Collectiones*, PL 102, 478D-9A. Haymo (*Hom. Mich.*, PL 95, 1528B) draws on Bede but is less close to Ælfric. The punctus versus at 215 is evidently not a sentence end, since *þonne* here is the conjunction 'than'.

217–24 Cf Haymo, *Hom. Mich.*, PL 95, 1528C:

> Mundus . . . id est mundi amatores . . . Mundi enim amatores dum propter cupiditates saeculi alios non metuunt scandalizare, tamen ipsi scandalum sustinent.

There is no equivalent in any of the commentators for 221–4. Ælfric is here continuing the critique of corrupt clerics begun at 211 ff. He seems to understand *scandalis* as betrayals and deceits.

225–37 Cf Haymo, *Hom. Mich.*, PL 95, 1529BC:

> Cum a littera excludimur, spiritualis sensus est requirendus. Per hoc quod manus, pes, oculus, nostris necessitatibus necessariora sunt, propinquorum et carissimorum affectus in hoc loco designatur, ac si diceret Dominus: 'Si quis tibi fuerit pretiosus ut oculus, propinquus ut pes, necessarius ut manus, et a via Dei te recedere persuaserit, huius amorem abscinde, et abs te proiice. Melius est te solum intrare ad vitam, quam cum multa turba propinquorum mitti in ignem aeternum'.

But 227–8 is much closer to Bede, *Commentarius in Marcum*, 3.483–4 (CCSL 120):

> Manum nostram appellat necessarium amicum cuius opere atque auxilio cotidiano opus habemus.

(Repeated by Smaragdus, *Collectiones*, PL 102, 479B).

238–40 Cf Haymo, *Hom. Mich.*, PL 95, 1530A:

> Quisquis tales scandalizare non metuit, offendit Deum qui habitat in illis, sicut ipse per prophetam dicit: 'Qui tangit vos, quasi qui tangit pupillam oculi mei' (Zach 2.8).

241–7 Cf Haymo, *Hom. Mich.*, PL 95, 1530AB:

> In hoc loco discimus, quia unusquisque fidelium angelum ob sui custodiam deputatum habet, qui et eum a tentationibus defendit, et in virtutibus iuvat. . . . Et psalmista de iusto quolibet: 'Angelis suis mandavit de te, ut custodiant te in omnibus viis tuis, et in manibus tollent te, ne forte offendas ad lapidem pedem tuum' (Ps 90.11–12).

247–8 Cf Jerome, *Commentarii in Evangelium Matthaei*, 3.570–2 (CCSL 77):

> Magna dignitas animarum, ut unaquaeque habeat ab ortu nativitatis in custodiam sui angelum delegatum.

(Repeated by Smaragdus, *Collectiones*, PL 102, 479D.)

249–58 Cf Haymo, *Hom. Mich.*, PL 95, 1530BC:

> Hinc de Petro in Actibus apostolorum legimus, quia cum ab angelo de carcere eductus, ianuam pulsare coepisset, fideles qui convenerant, dicebant: 'Non est Petrus, sed angelus eius' (Acts 12.6–15). Angeli ergo

> parvulorum semper vident faciem patris, quia sic propter nos foras exeunt, ut ab eius visione nunquam recedant. . . . Angeli qui custodes sunt vitae nostrae, orationes et opera nostra Deo nuntiare creduntur, sicut angelus ait Tobiae: 'Cum orares, ego obtuli orationes tuas ante Deum' (Tob 12.12).

259–78 This final discussion of angels as guardians of nations has no parallel in Haymo or the other possible sources for the homily, but it seems likely that Ælfric was drawing on some earlier discussion. Lines 262–3 draw on Deuteronomy 32.8, though not in the standard Vulgate form (which has *iuxta numerum filiorum Israhel* rather than *secundum numerum angelorum*) but in a form which is much cited as a variant in commentaries, going back to Jerome (cited here from his *Commentarii in Ezechiel*, 9.28.96–8 (CCSL 75)):

> Quando dividebat altissimus gentes, disseminabat filios Adam, constituit terminos nationum iuxta numerum angelorum Dei.

Gregory the Great reads this quite differently, as evidence that the number of the saved will equal the number of angels remaining in heaven, but Ælfric's interpretation resembles, e.g., that of Haymo in his *Commentaria in Cantica Canticorum* (PL 116, 711A):

> Sub divisione iuxta numerum angelorum Dei ponunt alii, quia singulis populis delegati angeli ad custodiam, et iuxta numerum illorum angelorum est numerus populorum maiorum.

Lines 266–9 cite verses from Dan 10:

> (20) Et nunc revertar ut praelier adversum principem Persarum. Cum ego egrederer, apparuit princeps Graecorum veniens. (21) . . . et nemo est adiutor meus in omnibus his nisi Michael princeps vester. . . . (13) Princeps autem regni Persarum restitit mihi viginti et uno diebus; et ecce Michael, unus de principibus primis, venit in adiutorium meum; et ego remansi ibi iuxta regem Persarum.

The verses are similarly used by Gregory the Great in his *Moralia siue Expositio in Iob*, XVII.xii.16–73, which may have been Ælfric's source. The idea that St Michael transferred his protection from the Jews to the Christians is particularly striking.

35 TWENTY-FIRST SUNDAY AFTER PENTECOST

The homily offers a fairly close allegorical commentary on the parable of the wedding-feast for the king's son in Matthew 22.1–14, which forms the Gospel for the day. The parable sets up a series of sharp distinctions between the rejected and the chosen: first between those who, refusing the king's invitation, are destroyed by his armies and those who are gathered into the feast from the streets, and then between the one man who has no wedding-garment and is cast into outer darkness and the other guests who are properly clothed; the sequence culminates in the dreadful warning that many are called but few are chosen. Patristic commentators and their successors found the parable both troubling and challenging: it suggested both a mingling of good and evil within the church and an apparent severity in the operation of salvation. Ælfric follows the main outlines of the exegetical tradition, interpreting the feast as the marriage of church and Christ and the wedding-garment as charity and showing how the parable can be reconciled to both justice and mercy; he emphasises the possibility of mercy and repentance (cf esp. 212 ff) and illustrates this with a long exemplum, telling the story of a recalcitrant monk saved on his death-bed by the prayers of his fellow-monks and turning to repentance. But he seems particularly interested in the eschatological implications of the passage, adding details on the nature of judgement and the after-life (lines 122–33, 193–207) and in a closing section emphasising the multitude of the saved (lines 274–84). There are several parallels with his homily for the third Sunday after Epiphany (CH I.8), which partly uses the same sources.

Ælfric identifies his source as Gregory, and does indeed draw mainly on Gregory's homily 38, the only item provided for this occasion in Paul the Deacon's homiliary.[1] There are a few points where he seems also to be influenced by Haymo's homily 135, an adaptation and expansion of Gregory's, and there are other debts to Haymo's homily 19, Gregory's homily 19 and probably Gregory's *Dialogues*. He mostly handles his sources rather freely, though the general argument is similar.

Sources and Notes

The following texts are cited below:

1. Alcuin, *Interrogationes et Responsiones in Genesim*, PL 100, cols. 516–66.
2. Augustine, *Sermones*, PL 38, Serm. 90, cols. 559–66.
3. Gregory the Great, *Dialogi*, ed. A. de Vogüé and P. Antin, 3 vols., Sources Chrétiennes 251, 260 and 265 (Paris, 1978–80).
4. Gregory the Great, *Homiliae in Evangelia*, PL 76, Hom. 19 and 38, cols. 1153–9 and 1281–93.
5. Haymo of Auxerre, *Homiliae de Tempore*, PL 118, Hom. 19 and 135, cols. 137–47 and 717–26.

4–25 Mt 22.1–14:

(1) Et respondens Iesus, dixit iterum in parabolis eis, dicens: (2) Simile factum est regnum caelorum homini regi, qui fecit nuptias filio suo. (3) Et misit servos suos vocare invitatos ad nuptias, et nolebant venire. (4) Iterum misit alios servos, dicens: Dicite invitatis: Ecce prandium meum paravi, tauri mei et altilia occisa sunt, et omnia parata; venite ad nuptias. (5) Illi

[1] See Förster 1894, pp. 5 and 29, and Smetana 1959, p. 194.

autem neglexerunt; et abierunt, alius [*var.* alii] in villam suam, alius [*var.* alii] vero ad negotiationem suam; (6) reliqui vero tenuerunt servos eius, et contumeliis affectos occiderunt. (7) Rex autem cum audisset, iratus est; et missis exercitibus suis, perdidit homicidas illos, et civitatem illorum succendit. (8) Tunc ait servis suis: Nuptiae quidem paratae sunt, sed qui invitati erant, non fuerunt digni; (9) ite ergo ad exitus viarum, et quoscumque inveneritis, vocate ad nuptias. (10) Et egressi servi eius in vias, congregaverunt omnes quos invenerunt, malos et bonos; et impletae sunt nuptiae discumbentium. (11) Intravit autem rex ut videret discumbentes, et vidit ibi hominem non vestitum veste nuptiali. (12) Et ait illi: Amice, quomodo huc intrasti non habens vestem nuptialem? At ille obmutuit. (13) Tunc dixit rex ministris: Ligatis manibus et pedibus eius, mittite eum in tenebras exteriores; ibi erit fletus et stridor dentium. (14) Multi enim sunt vocati, pauci vero electi.

The rendering of *invitatos* (v.3) as *underþeodan* (line 7) is perhaps just an attempt to lend clarity to the situation; there is no relevant variant reading in the Latin Bible, and the OE Gospels have nothing similar.

27–35 Gregory, Hom. 38, PL 76, 1282D-3A:

Saepe iam me dixisse memini quod plerumque in sancto evangelio regnum coelorum praesens ecclesia nominatur. Congregatio quippe iustorum regnum coelorum dicitur. Quia enim per prophetam Dominus dicit: 'Coelum mihi sedes est' (Is 66.1); et Salomon ait: 'Anima iusti sedes est sapientiae' [*not in fact a Biblical quotation, but PL suggests an allusion to Sap 7.27*: (Sapientia) in animas sanctas se transfert]; Paulus etiam dicit: 'Christum Dei virtutem et Dei sapientiam' (1 Cor 1.24); siquido colligere debemus quia si Deus sapientia, anima autem iusti sedes sapientiae, dum coelum dicitur sedes Dei, coelum ergo est anima iusti.

35–41 Gregory, Hom. 38, PL 76, 1283AB:

Hinc per psalmistam de sanctis praedicatoribus dicitur: 'Coeli enarrant gloriam Dei' (Ps 18.2). Regnum ergo coelorum est ecclesia iustorum, quia dum eorum corda in terra nil ambiunt, per hoc quod ad superna suspirant, iam in eis Dominus quasi in coelestibus regnat. . . . Deus pater Deo filio suo nuptias fecit . . . quo ei per incarnationis mysterium sanctam ecclesiam sociavit.

41–6 The specific points about the church as bride and mother are not in Gregory; similar expressions appear in CH I.33.19–23 and II.1.91–109.

46–50 Gregory, Hom. 38, PL 76, 1283C:

Misit semel, misit iterum quia incarnationis dominicae praedicatores et prius prophetas, et postmodum apostolos fecit. Bis itaque servos ad invitandum misit, quia incarnationem unigeniti et per prophetas dixit futuram, et per apostolos nuntiavit factam.

54–68 Gregory, Hom. 38, PL 76, 1284A:

Qui per tauros nisi patres testamenti veteris significantur? Nam dum ex permissione legis acceperant quatenus adversarios suos odii retributione percuterent . . . quid aliud quam tauri erant, qui inimicos suos virtutis corporeae cornu feriebant? [*earlier*] Cum vero in lege scriptum sit: 'Diliges amicum tuum, et odio habebis inimicum tuum' [*in fact from Christ's summary of the old law at Mt 5.43, though the first part is in Lev 19.18*], accepta tunc iustis licentia fuerat ut Dei suosque adversarios quanta possent virtute comprimerent, eosque iure gladii ferirent. Quod in novo procul dubio testamento compescitur, cum per semetipsam veritas praedicat, dicens: 'Diligite inimicos vestros, benefacite his qui oderunt vos [*Ælfric completes the quotation:* et orate pro persequentibus et calumniantibus vos; ut sitis filii Patris vestri, qui in caelis est; qui solem suum oriri facit super bonos et malos; et pluit super iustos et iniustos.]' (Mt 5.44–5).

69–76 Cf Gregory, Hom. 38, PL 76, 1284AB:

Quid vero per altilia nisi patres testamenti novi figurantur, qui dum gratiam pinguedinis internae percipiunt, a terrenis desideriis enitentes, ad sublimia contemplationis suae pennis sublevantur? In imo quippe cogitationem ponere, quid est aliud quam quaedam ariditas mentis? Qui autem intellectu coelestium iam per sancta desideria de supernis delectationis intimae cibo pascuntur, quasi largiori alimento pinguescunt. Hac enim pinguedine saginari propheta concupierat, cum dicebat: 'Sicut adipe et pinguedine repleatur anima mea' (Ps 62.6).

76–82 There is a basis in Gregory, Hom. 38, PL 76, 1284BC:

Ac si apertius dicatur: Patrum praecedentium mortes aspicite, et remedia vitae vestrae cogitate.

But Ælfric is concerned not with deaths but with the lives of the fathers and the words of prophets and apostles about Christ.

83–93 Gregory, Hom. 38, PL 76, 1284C–5A (rather freely adapted):

In villam ire est labori terreno immoderate incumbere, in negotiationem vero ire est actionum saecularium lucris inhiare. Quia enim alius intentus labori terreno, alius vero mundi huius actionibus deditus, mysterium incarnationis dominicae pensare et secundum illud vivere dissimulat. . . . Et plerumque, quod est gravius, nonnulli vocantis gratiam non solum respuunt, sed etiam persequuntur.

98–109 The starting-point for this discussion is probably Gregory, Hom. 38, PL 76, 1285A: *Homicidas perdit, quia persequentes interimit*. Ælfric develops this into a point about the martyred apostles and their particular persecutors; he may have been prompted by Haymo's reference to the martyrdom of Peter and Paul, commenting on an earlier verse in the Gospel (Hom. 135, PL 118, 720A), *alii crucifixi sunt . . . ut Paulus*, or by Gregory's later reference (Hom. 38, PL 76, 1285B), *ubi sunt superbi illi martyrum persecutores*. The persecutors named are those who appear in Ælfric's own accounts of the apostles elsewhere (CH I.26, CH II.27, CH II.24, CH I.31, CH I.38) and presumably reflect his familiarity with the legends which he used for those accounts. Ælfric shows a similar concern to specify God's vengeance on those who persecute the faithful in the long excursus at I.37.148–280.

109–14 Gregory, Hom. 38, PL 76, 1285A:

> Civitatem eorum igni succendit, quia illorum non solum animae, sed et caro quoque in qua habitaverant, aeterna gehennae flamma cruciatur. Missis vero exercitibus exstinxisse homicidas dicitur, quia in hominibus omne iudicium per angelos exhibetur. Quid namque sunt illa angelorum agmina nisi exercitus regis nostri? Unde et idem rex Dominus sabaoth dicitur. Sabaoth quippe exercituum interpretatur.

117–20 Gregory, Hom. 38, PL 76, 1285C:

> Si in scriptura sacra vias actiones accipimus, exitus viarum intelligimus defectus actionum, quia illi plerumque facile ad Deum veniunt, quos in terrenis actibus prospera nulla comitantur.

122–32 The starting-point is Gregory, Hom. 38, PL 76, 1285C:

> Per has regis nuptias praesens ecclesia designatur, in qua cum bonis et mali conveniunt.

Ælfric then develops this through the parable of the wheat and the tares from Mt 13.24–43:

> (26) Cum autem crevisset herba, et fructum fecisset, tunc apparuerunt et zizania. . . . (30) Colligite primum zizania, et alligate ea in fasciculos ad comburendum, triticum autem congregate in horreum meum. . . . (39) Messis vero, consummatio saeculi est. Messores autem, angeli sunt. (40) Sicut ergo colliguntur zizania, et igni comburuntur; sic erit in consummatione saeculi. (41) Mittet Filius hominis angelos suos, et colligent de regno eius omnia scandala, et eos qui faciunt iniquitatem; (42) et mittent eos in caminum ignis.

Cross (1963a, pp. 336–7) suggests that Ælfric took his explanation of the bundles, lines 125–30, from Gregory's *Dialogues*, IV.36.99–104, though the examples are different:

> Messores quippe angeli zizania ad conburendum in fasciculis ligant, cum pares paribus in tormentis similibus sociant, ut superbi cum superbis, luxuriosi cum luxuriosis, avari cum avaris, fallaces cum fallacibus, invidi cum invidis, infideles cum infidelibus ardeant.

Ælfric's examples correspond better with the longer list he gives at CH I.8.191 ff.

134–6 Cf Gregory, Hom. 38, PL 76, 1285D-6A:

> Boni enim soli nusquam sunt, nisi in coelo; et mali soli nusquam sunt, nisi in inferno. . . . Si ergo boni estis, quamdiu in hac vita subsistitis,

aequanimiter tolerate malos. Nam quisquis malos non tolerat, ipse sibi per intolerantiam suam testis est quia bonus non est.

136–41 Gregory, Hom. 38, PL 76, 1286C:

Hinc ad Ezechielem Dominus dicit: 'Fili hominis, increduli et subversores sunt tecum, et cum scorpionibus habitas' (Ez 2.6). . . . Hinc Paulus discipulorum vitam et laudat et roborat, dicens: 'In medio nationis pravae et perversae, inter quos lucetis sicut luminaria in mundo, verbum vitae continentes' (Phil 2.15–16).

143–52 Gregory, Hom. 38, PL 76, 1287CD:

Recte caritas nuptialis vestis vocatur, quia hanc in se conditor noster habuit, dum ad sociandae sibi ecclesiae nuptias venit. . . . Unde et Iohannes dicit: 'Sic enim dilexit Deus mundum, ut filium suum unigenitum daret pro nobis' (Jn 3.16). Qui ergo per caritatem venit ad homines, eamdem caritatem innotuit vestem esse nuptialem. Omnis vestrum qui in ecclesia positus Deo credidit, iam ad nuptias intravit; sed cum nuptiali veste non venit, si caritatis gratiam non custodit.

Ælfric's reference to faith and baptism relates to a slightly earlier point by Gregory, raising but dismissing a possible identification of the wedding garment.

152–8 Possibly prompted by a hint in Gregory, Hom. 38, PL 76, 1287D-8A:

Si quis ad carnales nuptias esset invitatus . . . inter gaudentes et festa celebrantes despectis vestibus apparere erubesceret. . . . Qua ergo mente haec spiritalia festa conspicimus, qui nuptialem vestem, id est caritatem, quae sola nos speciosos exhibet, non habemus?

Cross (1963a, p. 345) suggests a possible influence from Haymo, Hom. 135 (PL 118, 724B), *sive aliter . . . ornat*. Ælfric's neat antitheses are not to be found in either source.

158–62 The ultimate source is 1 Cor 13.2–3:

(2) Si habuero omnem fidem . . . (3) et si distribuero in cibos pauperum omnes facultates meas, et si tradidero corpus meum ita ut ardeam, caritatem autem non habuero, nihil mihi prodest.

The following sentence is from Gregory, Hom. 38, PL 76, 1289A: *Caritas vera est cum et in Deo diligitur amicus, et propter Deum diligitur inimicus*. The quotation from Corinthians is not in Gregory, though it does appear in Haymo's homily for the same occasion at an earlier point. But it may be that Ælfric picked up the phrasing from some other text: he does not signal it as a Biblical quotation, as he normally does, and the adaptation of St Paul's words is strangely similar to the *Ancrene Riwle*: cf esp. *ȝef ich nefde luue þerwið to Godd & to alle men, in him & for him, al were ispillet* (*Ancrene Wisse*, ed. J. R. R. Tolkien, EETS os 249 (1962), p. 196).

162–8 Gregory, Hom. 38, PL 76, 1289C:

Rex ad nuptias ingreditur, et cordis nostri habitum contemplatur, atque ei quem caritate vestitum non invenit, protinus iratus dicit. . . . Mirandum valde est . . . quod hunc et amicum vocat, et reprobat . . . amice per fidem, sed non amice per operationem.

169–74 Gregory, Hom. 38, PL 76, 1289CD:

At ille obmutuit, quia . . . in illa districtione ultimae increpationis omne argumentum cessat excusationis, quippe quia ille foris increpat, qui testis conscientiae intus animum accusat. Sed inter haec sciendum est quia quisquis hanc vestem virtutis habet, sed tamen adhuc perfecte non habet, ad pii regis ingressum desperare veniam non debet, quia ipse quoque spem nobis per psalmistam tribuens, dicit: 'Imperfectum meum viderunt oculi tui, et in libro tuo omnes scribentur' (Ps 138.16).

174–81 Gregory, Hom. 38, PL 76, 1290A:

Ligantur tunc pedes et manus per districtionem sententiae, qui modo a pravis operibus ligari noluerunt per meliorationem vitae. . . . Pedes qui visitare aegrum negligunt, manus quae nihil indigentibus tribuunt a bono opere iam ex voluntate ligatae sunt. Qui ergo nunc sponte ligantur in vitio, tunc in supplicio ligantur invite.

182–8 Gregory, Hom. 38, PL 76, 1290AB:

Interiores tenebras dicimus caecitatem cordis, exteriores tenebras aeternam noctem damnationis. . . . Invitus proiicitur in noctem damnationis, qui hic sponte cecidit in caecitatem cordis.

Ælfric goes on to cite Jn 8.12 (not used by Gregory):

Ego sum lux mundi; qui sequitur me non ambulat in tenebris, sed habebit lumen vitae.

189–93 Cf Gregory, Hom. 38, PL 76, 1290B:

Ubi fletus quoque et stridor dentium esse perhibetur, ut illic dentes strideant, qui hic de edacitate gaudebant; illic oculi defleant, qui hic per illicitas concupiscentias versabantur.

193–207 As Cross (1963a, pp. 339–40) demonstrates, the passage was probably prompted by Haymo's homily 19, where he comments on a parallel Biblical phrase (Hom. 19, PL 118 146BC):

Oculi enim prae nimio fumo solent lacrymari, et dentes prae nimio frigore stridescere. . . . Reprobi in poena et frigus inaestimabile, et calorem intolerabilem sustinebunt. . . . Si quis autem de resurrectione sui corporis dubitat, ipsam per hunc locum fieri intelligere valet. Oculi enim carnei sunt, et dentes ex ossibus. . . . [*The intervening sentences roughly parallel Ælfric in sense.*] Unde alibi beatus Iob dicit: 'Credo quod Redemptor meus vivit, et in novissimo die de terra surrecturus sum. Et rursum circumdabor pelle mea, et in carne mea videbo Deum, quem visurus sum ego ipse, et non alius, et oculi mei conspecturi sunt' (Job 19.25–7), id est, non alia figura pro me, sed ego ipse eum videbo.

For 195–7, on the absence of light in hell, cf above CH I.8.186–7 and note.

208–11 In exploring this final verse Ælfric draws additionally on Gregory's homily 19, which treats the same verse where it is repeated in Mt 20.16 and was to be used as his source for exegesis of that verse in CH II.5; cf Gregory, Hom. 19, PL 76, 1157AB:

> Sed post haec terribile est valde quod sequitur. . . . Ecce vox omnium Christum clamat, sed vita omnium non clamat. Plerique Deum vocibus sequuntur, moribus fugiunt.

211–3 Gregory, Hom. 38, PL 76, 1290C:

> Nonnulli in bonis quae incoeperunt minime persistunt. Alter pene totam vitam ducere in pravitate conspicitur, sed iuxta finem vitae a pravitate sua per districtae poenitentiae lamenta revocatur. . . . Alius bonum bene inchoat, melius consummat.

214–8 Gregory, Hom. 19, PL 76, 1158A:

> Duo sunt quae sollicite pensare debemus. . . . Primum est ut de se quisque minime praesumat, quia etsi iam ad fidem vocatus est, utrum perenni regno dignus sit nescit. Secundum vero est ut unusquisque proximum, quem fortasse iacere in vitiis conspicit, desperare non audeat, quia divinae misericordiae divitias ignorat.

219–26 Gregory, Hom. 38, PL 76, 1292BC:

> Frater quidam in monasterium meum . . . gratia conversationis venit, qui diu regulariter protractus, quandoque susceptus est. Quem frater suus ad monasterium non conversationis studio, sed carnali amore secutus est. Is autem qui ad conversationem venerat valde fratribus placebat; at contra, frater illius longe a vita eius ac moribus discrepabat. Vivebat tamen in monasterio necessitate potius quam voluntate.

226–30 Gregory, Hom. 38, PL 76, 1292CD:

> Et cum in cunctis actibus perversus existeret, pro fratre suo ab omnibus aequanimiter tolerabatur. Erat enim levis eloquio, pravus actione, cultus vestibus, moribus incultus; ferre vero non poterat si quisquam illi de sancti habitus conversatione loqueretur. Facta autem fuerat vita illius cunctis fratribus visu gravis sed tamen ut dictum est pro fratris sui gratia erat cunctis tolerabilis. . . . Bona non solum facere sed etiam audire non poterat.

230–6 Gregory, Hom. 38, PL 76, 1292D-3A:

> In hac pestilentia . . . percussus in inguine, perductus est ad mortem. Cumque extremum spiritum ageret, convenerunt fratres, ut egressum illius orando protegerent. Iam corpus eius ab extrema fuerat parte praemortuum, in solo tantummodo pectore vitalis adhuc calor anhelabat. Cuncti fratres tanto pro eo coeperunt enixius orare, quanto eum iam videbant sub celeritate discedere.

236–43 Gregory, Hom. 38, PL 76, 1293A:

Cum repente coepit . . . clamare . . . dicens: 'Recedite, recedite, ecce draconi ad devorandum datus sum, qui propter vestram praesentiam devorare me non potest. Caput meum iam in suo ore absorbuit; date locum ut me amplius non cruciet. . . . Si ei ad devorandum datus sum, quare propter vos moras patior?' Tunc fratres coeperunt ei dicere: 'Quid est quod loqueris, frater? Signum tibi sanctae crucis imprime.'

243–53 Gregory, Hom. 38, PL 76, 1293AB:

Respondebat ille ut poterat, dicens: 'Volo me signare, sed non possum, quia a dracone premor.' Cumque hoc fratres audirent, prostrati in terra cum lacrymis coeperunt pro ereptione illius vehementius orare. Et ecce subito coepit melioratus aeger quibus valebat vocibus exsultare, dicens: 'Gratias deo, ecce draco qui me ad devorandum acceperat fugit, orationibus vestris expulsus stare non potuit. Pro peccatis meis modo intercedite, quia converti paratus sum, et saecularem vitam funditus relinquere.'

There is nothing in Gregory's account here to explain Ælfric's reference to the brother as a *cniht* or youth (line 248). But Gregory retold the story in very similar words in his *Dialogues*, IV.40 (p. 140), and there identified him as a *puer*; the Old English version several times calls him a *cniht* (Hecht, p. 324). Ælfric presumably recalled the *Dialogues* version (unless he had a copy of the homily in which the detail had been added).

253–8 Gregory, Hom. 38, PL 76, 1293B:

Homo ergo qui . . . ab extrema corporis fuerat parte praemortuus, reservatus ad vitam, toto ad Deum corde conversus est. Longis et continuis in conversatione eadem flagellis eruditus, atque ante paucos dies excrescente corporis molestia defunctus est. Qui iam moriens draconem non vidit, quia illum per cordis immutationem vicit.

259–73 The main argument is from Gregory, Hom. 38, PL 76, 1286D-7B:

Terrere vos non debet quod in ecclesia et multi mali et pauci sunt boni, quia arca in undis diluvii, quae huius ecclesiae typum gessit, et ampla in inferioribus, et angusta in superioribus fuit. . . . Inferius quippe quadrupedia atque reptilia, superius vero aves et homines habuisse credenda est. Ibi lata exstitit, ubi bestias habuit; ibi angusta, ubi homines servavit, quia nimirum sancta ecclesia in carnalibus ampla est, in spiritalibus angusta. Ubi enim bestiales hominum mores tolerat, illic latius sinum laxat. . . . Eo autem usque arca angustatur in summis . . . quia in sancta ecclesia quanto sanctiores quique sunt, tanto pauciores.

But Gregory describes two floors while Ælfric distinguishes three, in accordance with the Vulgate (Gen 6.16), and distributes the species differently. Förster suggested Bede's *Hexameron* as a source, but although this does specify three floors the account is not otherwise close. As Cross (1963a, pp. 343–4) suggests, Ælfric was perhaps combining Gregory, the Vulgate and Alcuin's *Interrogationes et Responsiones* (PL 100, 528), where the lowest of the three levels contains wild animals and reptiles, the next tame animals and the highest humans.

274–84 Ælfric now develops in characteristic fashion (cf CH II.5.183 ff) and in opposition to Gregory the argument for the multitude of those who are saved, though they seem few. With 274–5 cf CH II.6.123–5. The precise sense of 276–7 is unclear. With 277–84 esp. cf Augustine, Serm. 90, §4, PL 38, 561 (though the parallel is not close):

> Iidem ipsi in se ipsis multi, in comparatione malorum pauci. Quomodo probamus quia in se ipsis multi? 'Multi ab oriente et ab occidente venient, [et recumbent cum Abraham, et Isaac, et Iacob in regno caelorum]. (Mt 8.11)

The quotation at 280–1 is Ps 138.18: *Dinumerabo eos, et super arenam multiplicabuntur*. As Cross (1969, p. 152) notes, it is used in a similar context in Gregory's homily 27 (PL 76, 1207B) and borrowed from there by Ælfric for CH II.35.61–2. Ælfric was probably also responsible for adding the quotation when revising the similar discussion at CH II.5.194.

285 A surprisingly early use of the poetic word *metod*, which is otherwise used by Ælfric only in his experiments with rhythmical and alliterative prose in CH II and the addition to I.38 (see Godden 1980, pp. 217–9, and CH I.38.351 and note). The sense, if there is a precise one, is presumably either 'God of gods' or 'God of the fates' or perhaps 'Lord God'. As usual, Ælfric replaced it with a more prosaic equivalent in the course of revision.

36 ALL SAINTS

The feast of All Saints seems to go back to at least the fourth century and to have been established at Rome in the early seventh century, with the dedication of the former Pantheon by Pope Boniface IV (an event recorded in Bede's *Historia Ecclesiastica*, II.iv). Its association with 1 November is first recorded at York in the mid-eighth century and seems to have become general at the end of the century.[1] It is mentioned in the *Old English Martyrology* under that day, and in the verse *Menologium.* It was not covered in the homiliaries of Smaragdus or Haymo, or in the original homiliary of Paul the Deacon, but later versions include it. The reading from Matthew 5.1–12 which Ælfric uses is given for the feast-day of martyrs in Smaragdus and the later versions of PD, but it seems to have been the established reading for All Saints' Day in England, since it is marked for that occasion in the margins of two manuscripts of the *Old English Gospels* (Cambridge, University Library, MS Ii.2.11 and Bodleian, MS Bodley 441).[2]

In the first part of his homily Ælfric describes in turn all the different kinds of

[1] See Cross 1977, p. 127. [2] Cf too Lenker, p. 370.

saint: angels (lines 16–37), patriarchs (lines 37–41), prophets (lines 41–51), John the Baptist and the twelve apostles (lines 52–70), martyrs (lines 71–88), confessors (lines 89–103), anchorites (lines 104–117) and virgins, led by the Virgin Mary (lines 118–36). For the second part he expounds the Gospel reading for the occasion and the list of the beatitudes from Matthew 5.1–12, which he sees as particularly appropriate to the saint. The main source for the first part of the homily is a sermon on the foundation of the feast and the different categories of saints, beginning 'Legimus in ecclesiasticis historiis': it appears among the homilies attributed to Bede in PL 94, cols. 452–5, but is of unknown authorship. J. E. Cross identified it as a source in 1958, and elaborated the argument in 1963.[3] He printed a critical text of the sermon, with further discussion, in 1977 (see below), noting that manuscripts preserved a fuller version than that printed in PL 94. Mary Clayton shows that Ælfric used some material from the *De Assumptione* of Paschasius Radbertus, material that he also used in his homily on the assumption of the Virgin (CH I.30).[4] For the second part, the commentary on the pericope, the main source, as Förster demonstrated,[5] is Augustine's commentary, *De Sermone Domini in Monte*. Smetana pointed out that both the relevant part of this commentary and the Ps-Bede sermon occurred in the late version of Paul the Deacon's homiliary printed in PL 95.[6] Smetana also showed that Ælfric used Haymo's homily on the parallel Gospel text at Luke 6 as an additional source for the second part;[7] this occurs in versions of Paul the Deacon's homiliary, for the common of martyrs, though Ælfric also knew Haymo's own homiliary.

Sources and Notes

The following texts are cited below:

1. Anon., Homily on All Saints, beginning 'Legimus in ecclesiasticis historiis', ed. J. E. Cross in '*Legimus in ecclesiasticis historicis*: A Sermon for All Saints and its use in Old English Prose,' *Traditio* 33 (1977), 101–35 (text, pp. 105–21) [source passages are cited by line numbers].
2. Augustine, *De Sermone Domini in Monte*, ed. A. Mutzenbecher, CCSL 35 (Turnhout, 1967).
3. Haymo of Auxerre, *Homiliae de Sanctis*, PL 118, Hom. 8, cols. 776–81.
4. Paschasius Radbertus, *De Assumptione Sanctae Mariae Virginis*, ed. A. Ripberger, CCCM 56C (Turnhout, 1985), pp. 109–62.

[3] J. E. Cross, 'A source for one of Ælfric's Catholic Homilies', *English Studies* 39 (1958), 248–51 and Cross 1963b.

[4] Clayton 1983, pp. 350–1.

[5] Förster 1894, p. 37.

[6] Smetana 1959, pp. 194–5.

[7] Smetana 1961, p. 458.

3–6 Perhaps prompted by the opening account of the origins of the feast in the sermon *Legimus*, quoted below for lines 142–6.

6–15 Apoc 7.9–12:

> (9) Post haec vidi turbam magnam quam dinumerare nemo poterat ex omnibus gentibus et tribubus et populis et linguis stantes ante thronum et in conspectu agni amicti stolas albas et palmae in manibus eorum. (10) Et clamabant voce magna dicentes salus Deo nostro qui sedet super thronum et agno. (11) Et omnes angeli stabant in circuitu throni et seniorum et quattuor animalium et ceciderunt in conspectu throni in facies suas et adoraverunt Deum. (12) Dicentes amen benedictio et claritas et sapientia et gratiarum actio et honor et virtus et fortitudo Deo nostro in saecula saeculorum amen.

17–26 *Legimus*, 37–42:

> Qui superna caelorum regna spiritibus angelicis ad laudem et gloriam atque honorem sui nominis ac maiestatis in perpetuum miro ordine collocavit. De quibus plura loqui pertimescimus quia soli deo scire est quomodo vel quemadmodum eorum nobis invisibilis absque contagione seu diminutione in sua sola puritate consistat natura. Sed tamen novem esse angelorum ordines ad dei iudicia ac ministeria complenda, testante sacro eloquio, cognovimus.

Ælfric adds the reference to the fallen angels, 24–6.

27–34 *Legimus*, 44–53:

> Alii ex illis ad nos in mundum missi futura predicando perveniunt; alii ad haec sunt constituti ut per eos signa et miracula frequentius fiant; alii subiectis angelorum spiritibus praesunt eisque ad explenda divina mysteria disponenda principantur; . . . alii tanta divinitatis gratia replentur ut in eis dominus sedeat et per eos sua iudicia decernat; . . . alia vero ita deo coniuncta sunt agmina angelorum ut inter haec et deum nulli alii intersint, tanto magis ardent amore quanto subtilius claritatem divinitatis eius aspiciunt.

The close parallels between Ælfric's wording here and his account of the angels at CH I.24.85–102 seem to be due to the anonymous homilist's use of the same material from Gregory that Ælfric had followed there.

34–41 *Legimus*, 61–9:

> Adhuc tamen aliquid de hac eadem tam pulchra atque praeclara festivitate loqui incipiamus quae, non solum angelorum, ut praediximus, spiritibus, verumetiam sanctis omnibus qui in terra sunt ab exordio mundi procreati honorabiliter dedicata consistit. E quibus primi fuerunt patriarchae, viri religiosi atque gloriosi in vita sua, patres prophetarum et apostolorum, quorum memoria non dereliquetur, et nomen eorum manet in eternum quia deo digni inventi sunt, fide praeclari, . . . iustitia insignes . . . obedientes in praeceptis.

41–4 *Legimus*, 75–8:

Hos sequitur electio prophetarum cum quibus loqutus est deus et ostendit illis secreta sua ut ea, quae ventura erant quasi praesentia, spiritu sancto inluminati, agnoscere atque enarrare potuerunt, principes populorum ventura praedicando facti.

44–7 *Legimus*, 84–6:

Multis quoque miraculorum signis effulsere. Hominum infirmitates curabant, mortuorum corpora resuscitabant.

47–9 *Legimus*, 82–4:

Clauserunt refrenatis imbribus caelum, iterum parcendo aperuerunt. Peccata populi plangentes eorum se ultioni opponentes.

49–51 *Legimus*, 86–8:

Christi vero per virginem nativitatem ac passionem vel resurrectionem sive ascensionem et spiritus sancti adventum futurum in consummatione mundi iudicium dei edocti clara voce praedixere.

52–5 *Legimus*, 97–104:

In novo testamento . . . Iohannes Baptista . . . qui Ihesum peccata mundi tollentem videndo agnovit ac digito demonstravit (Jn 1.29) cui inter natos mulierum non surrexit, Christo attestante, maior (Mt 11.11) . . . Christum mundo venturum prophetavit.

55–9 *Legimus*, 106–10:

Huic athlete dei electo concordat duodenus apostolorum numerus, quos . . . elegit, ut in omnem terram sonus eorum praedicationis exiret et in fines orbis terrae eorum procederent verba.

59–70 *Legimus*, 112–22:

Quibus ipse dominus locutus est dicens: 'Vos estis lux mundi . . . sic luceat lux vestra coram hominibus, ut videant opera vestra bona et glorificent patrem vestrum qui in celis est' (Mt 5.14, 16). Et iterum. '. . .Vos autem dixi amicos, quia omnia quaecumque audivi a patre meo nota feci vobis' (Jn 15.15). Et quodcumque ligare voluissent super terram, ligatum esse in caelis et quodcumque solverent super terram solutum in caelis esse promisit (Mt 18.18). Et iterum cum venisset ad iudicandum seculum eos super sedes duodecium esse sessuros et secum iudicaturos orbem terrae praedixerat (cf Mt 19.28).

Ælfric apparently adds the reference to the apostles working miracles (line 65).

71–80 *Legimus*, 124–30:

His subiectum est triumphale martyrum nomen qui per diversa tormentorum genera Christi passionem non lassescentibus praecordiorum mentibus imitabantur; alii ferro perempti, alii flammis exusti, alii flagris verberati, alii vectibus perforati, alii cruciati patibulo, alii pelagi periculo [demersi], alii vivi decoriati, alii vinculis mancipati, alii linguis privati, alii lapidibus obruti, alii frigore adflicti, alii fame cruciati, alii vero truncatis manibus sive ceteris caesis membris spectaculum contumeliae in populis nudi propter nomen domini portantes.

80–84 *Legimus*, 130–32, 142:

Hi sunt triumphatores et amici dei qui, contemnentes sceleratorum iussa principum, modo coronantur et accipiunt palmas laborum. . . . 'Occidi possunt et flecti nequeunt' [*explicitly quoting Gregory the Great, Hom. 27, PL 76, 1207*].

84–8 *Legimus*, 142–6, quoting Sap 3.4–6:

'Et si coram hominibus tormenta passi sunt, spes illorum inmortalitate plena est. In paucis vexati, in multis bene disponentur, quoniam deus temptavit eos et invenit illos dignos se. Tamquam aurum in fornace probavit illos et quasi holocausta hostiam accepit illos.'

89–92 Loosely paraphrases *Legimus*, 150–2:

Christi vero sacerdotibus atque doctoribus sive confessoribus huius festivitatem diei non ignotam esse credimus. Qui corda fidelium spiritaliter quasi imbribus inrigant caelestibus.

The odd expression *folces men* at 91, also used at CH I.38.20, presumably means something like 'ordinary people'; cf too CH II.10.17.

92–6 Renders more closely *Legimus*, 158–61:

Quorum mens lucidissima, manus vero plene sunt munditia; eo quod in mensa altaris sacrosancta Christi corporis et sanguinis mysteria celebrantes et in sui cordis penetrabilibus hostiam vivam, deoque placentem, id est, semetipsos, sine macula atque admixtione pravi operis offerre non desistant.

96–8 Cf *Legimus*, 153–7:

Qui talenta sibi credita non solum reddere verum etiam cum usura sine fraude amplificare procuraverunt quia bonum quod per gratiam spiritus sancti intellegendo didicere, non sibimet tantummodo sed et aliis subiectorum mentibus profuturum secundum apostoli praeceptum, arguendo, obsecrando, increpando, curamque faciendo, inserere nitebantur.

The allusion is to the parable of the talents, Mt 25.14–30; for the interpretation, cf CH II.38.112–29.

99–103 From *Legimus*, 161–4:

Et licet persecutorum non sensissent gladium, tamen per vitae meritum, deo digni, martyrio non privantur. Quia martyrium non sola sanguinis effusione, sed abstinentia peccatorum et exercitatione dei praeceptorum perficitur.

104–11 A rearrangement of details from *Legimus*, 182–9:

Sic et anachoritarum singulare propositum . . . qui per singula heremi loca in speluncis et exiguis cellarum tuguriis unici . . . bestiis sociati, multi

> avibus subministrati, ciborum spernentes dilicias, luxus seculi calcantes, laudem temporalem non amantes, visus hominum fugientes, angelorum adsueti loquelis, plurimis virtutum effulsere signis, caecis visum innovant, claudis gressum firmant, surdis auditum tribuunt, superantes daemonia, . . . mortuos suscitant.

In the Latin sermon, as edited, this account of the hermits comes after the celebration of the Virgin Mary and the virgin saints which Ælfric gives at 118–36, but at least one manuscript of the sermon shows the same order as his (see Cross 1977, p. 125).

111–17 Presumably a reminiscence of Ælfric's own reading in the *Vitae Patrum*, by which he probably meant the material printed as books 5 and 6 in Migne's version, PL 73, cols. 851–1022B (see J. E. Cross, 'On the Library of the Old English Martyrologist', in Lapidge and Gneuss 1985, pp. 227–49, at 244, n.84).

118–20 A close rendering of *Legimus*, 165–7:

> Beata Dei genetrix et semper virgo Maria, templum domini, sacrarium spiritus sancti, virgo ante partum, virgo in partu, virgo post partum, praesentis solemnitate diei, cum suis virginibus, expers nullo modo credenda est.

The cross-sign here and at 167 seems to be just a paragraph marker (for a different function see CH I.20.150 and note).

121–3 Ælfric adds the justification for Mary's status, 121–2. His explanation that the Virgin Mary, though she is herself greater than all the angels and other saints, is placed last in the list *endebyrdlice æfter wifhade*, 'in order according to her female gender', presumably means that the preceding groups, including martyrs and anchorites, are to be understood as exclusively male, and perhaps that the virgins who follow her are all female and embrace all varieties of female sanctity. The Latin sermon emphasises that the virgins following Mary are of both sexes, but Ælfric does not make the same point here, though he does emphasise in other homilies that the virtue of virginity is manifest in both men and women; and his additional reference to virgin martyrs at 133–6 perhaps serves to separate female saints from the general body of martyrs described at 71–88.

124–7 Based, as Mary Clayton pointed out, on Paschasius Radbertus's *De Assumptione*, 302–3, 308–13:

> Haec est dies praeclara, in qua meruit exaltari super choros angelorum . . . Haec est, inquam, dies in qua usque ad throni celsitudinem intemerata mater et virgo processit atque in regni solio sublimata post Christum gloriosa resedit. Sic itaque ubique confidenter sancta Dei canit ecclesia, quod de nullo alio sanctorum fas est credere, ut ultra angelorum vel archangelorum merita transcenderit.

127–36 Ælfric develops the encomium on virginity from *Legimus*, 170–4:

Eamque omnium virtutum reginam, fructum salutis perpetuae, sociam esse angelorum suis adfirmabat exemplis, ita ut innumerabilis utriusque sexus multitudo eius sequebatur vestigia, ut relictis nuptiarum copulationibus spretoque liberorum propagine, sponso, qui in caelis est, perenni mente, actu, abitu et gestu, adplicare maluerint.

The reference to those who were martyred in defence of their virginity (lines 133–6) does not have a parallel in any of the manuscripts of the *Legimus* sermon so far analysed.

137–42 The general account of the festival is perhaps loosely based on *Legimus*, 189–94:

Verum quia his omnibus non mediocriter sed perfecte huius sacratissime atque excellentissime solemnitas diei maximo sine fine constat honore, nos ergo, fratres carissimi, tantorum patrocinia intercessorum de quibus locuti sumus, tota mentis intentione, queramus ut, per temporalia festa quae gerimus, eorum meritis intercedentibus ad aeterna pervenire valeamus.

142–6 From the introductory part of *Legimus*, 12–16:

Decretum est ut in ecclesiis dei que per orbem terrarum longe lateque construuntur, honor et memoria omnium sanctorum in die qua praediximus haberetur ut quicquid humana fragilitas per ignorantiam vel neglegentiam seu per occupationem rei secularis in solemnitate sanctorum minus plene peregisset in hac sancta observatione solveretur.

(Perhaps a little from the previous passage too.)

152–66 Mt 5.1–12:

(1) Videns autem turbas ascendit in montem et cum sedisset accesserunt ad eum discipuli eius; (2) et aperiens os suum docebat eos dicens: (3) beati pauperes spiritu quoniam ipsorum est regnum caelorum; (4) beati mites quoniam ipsi possidebunt terram; (5) beati qui lugent quoniam ipsi consolabuntur; (6) beati qui esuriunt et sitiunt iustitiam quoniam ipsi saturabuntur; (7) beati misericordes quia ipsi misericordiam consequentur; (8) beati mundo corde quoniam ipsi Deum videbunt; (9) beati pacifici quoniam filii Dei vocabuntur; (10) beati qui persecutionem patiuntur propter iustitiam quoniam ipsorum est regnum caelorum; (11) beati estis cum maledixerint vobis et persecuti vos fuerint et dixerint omne malum adversum vos mentientes propter me. (12) Gaudete et exultate quoniam merces vestra copiosa est in caelis sic enim persecuti sunt prophetas qui fuerunt ante vos.

167–73 Augustine, *Sermone Domini*, 1.32–8:

Si quaeritur, quid significet mons, bene intellegitur significare maiora praecepta iustitiae, quia minora erant quae Iudaeis data sunt. Unus tamen deus per sanctos prophetas et famulos suos secundum ordinatissimam distributionem temporum dedit minora praecepta populo quem timore adhuc alligari oportebat, et per filium suum maiora populo quem caritate iam liberari convenerat.

173–9 Augustine, *Sermone Domini*, 1.47–55:

Sedens autem docet, quod pertinet ad dignitatem magistri. Et accedunt ad eum discipuli eius, ut audiendis illius verbis hi essent etiam corpore viciniores, qui praeceptis implendis animo propinquabant. . . . et aperiens os suum, fortasse ipsa mora commendat aliquanto longiorem futurum esse sermonem, nisi forte non vacet quod nunc eum dictum est aperuisse os suum, quod ipse in lege veteri aperire soleret ora prophetarum.

181–3 Augustine, *Sermone Domini*, 1.65–70:

Recte hic intelleguntur pauperes spiritu humiles et timentes deum, id est non habentes inflantem spiritum. . . . Initium autem sapientiae timor domini (Sir 1.16), quoniam et e contrario initium omnis peccati superbia scribitur (Sir 10.15).

183–97 Haymo, Hom. 8, PL 118, 779CD:

Rebus sunt pauperes et non spiritu, qui nihil habentes, multa habere concupiscunt. Spiritu sunt pauperes et non rebus, sicut illi qui secundum Apostolum, tanquam nihil habentes, et omnia possidentes sunt, quales fuerunt Abraham, Iacob et David: qui regali solio sublimatus erat, pauperem se ostendit spiritu, dicens: Ego autem mendicus sum et pauper (Ps 39.18). . . . Nec rebus nec spiritu sunt pauperes, divites superbi, qui facultatibus locupletati, nihilominus mente sunt turgidi. . . . Rebus et spiritu sunt pauperes perfecti monachi, qui propter Deum omnia relinquentes, nec corporis proprii potestatem in suo arbitrio relinquunt, et ideo quanto hic propter Deum sunt pauperiores, tanto in futura gloria erunt ditiores.

198–204 Augustine, *Sermone Domini*, reordered:

[1.80–82] Mites autem sunt qui cedunt inprobitatibus et non resistunt malo, sed vincunt in bono malum (Rom 12.21). . . . [1.75–80] Illam credo terram de qua in psalmis dicitur, 'Spes mea es tu, portio mea in terra viventium' (Ps 141.6). Significat enim quamdam soliditatem et stabilitatem hereditatis perpetuae, ubi anima per bonum affectum tamquam loco suo requiescit sicut corpus in terra, et inde cibo suo alitur sicut corpus ex terra. Ipsa est requies et vita sanctorum.

205–10 Ælfric uses Haymo's interpretation, but adds the reference to the comfort of the Holy Spirit from Augustine:

[Haymo, Hom. 8, PL 118, 780A] Beati dicuntur flentes, non illi qui flent propter temporalium damna commodorum, propter amissionem carorum, sed qui flent propter remissionem peccatorum.

[Augustine, *Sermone Domini*, 1.90–92] Consolabuntur ergo spiritu sancto, qui maxime propterea paraclytus nominatur, id est consolator, ut temporalem amittentes aeterna laetitia perfruantur.

212–18 Ælfric again combines Haymo and Augustine:

[Haymo, Hom. 8, PL 118, 779D-80A] Iustitiam quippe esurire et sitire, est praecepta Dei libenter audire, et libentius opere implere. Tales enim saturabuntur, quando ad videndum Deum cuius hic mandata cum magna mentis esurie susceperunt, perducentur, dicentes cum Psalmista: 'Ego autem in iustitia apparebo, et in conspectu tuo satiabor dum manifestabitur gloria tua' (Ps 16.15).

[Augustine, *Sermone Domini*, 1.95–7] Illo ergo cibo saturabuntur de quo ipse dominus dicit: 'Meus cibus est ut faciam voluntatem patris mei, quod est iustitia' (Jn 4.34).

220–1 From Augustine, *Sermone Domini*, 1.100–1:

Beatos esse dicit qui subveniunt miseris, quoniam eis ita rependitur, ut de miseria liberentur.

222–7 Augustine, *Sermone Domini*, 1.103–8:

Quam ergo stulti sunt qui deum istis exterioribus oculis quaerunt, cum corde videatur, sicut alibi scriptum est, 'Et in simplicitate cordis quaerite illum' (Sap 1.1). Hoc est enim mundum cor, quod est simplex cor. Et quemadmodum lumen hoc videri non potest nisi oculis mundis, ita nec deus videtur, nisi mundum sit illud quo videri potest.

228–35 Augustine, *Sermone Domini*, 1.110–15, 121–2:

In pace perfectio est, ubi nihil repugnat; et ideo filii dei pacifici, quoniam nihil resistit deo et utique filii similitudinem patris habere debent. Pacifici autem in semet ipsis sunt, qui omnes animi sui motus componentes et subicientes rationi, id est menti et spiritui, carnalesque concupiscentias habentes edomitas fiunt regnum dei. . . . Et haec est pax quae datur in terra hominibus bonae voluntatis (Lc 2.14).

237–48 Augustine has little specifically on this verse, and Ælfric instead uses some comments by Haymo on Luke 6.22 and Matthew 5.10–12 (Hom. 8, PL 118):

[780D] Sustinent enim multas tribulationes homicidae, adulteri, fures, alienarum rerum invasores. Nec tamen talis persecutio ad beatitudinem perducit, quae propter iustitiam sustinetur. [780C] Ubi ostenditur quia persecutio pravorum non est timenda, sed potius cum adfuerit, toleranda.

Lines 242–5 are Mt 10.28, not quoted by either Augustine or Haymo:

Et nolite timere eos qui occidunt corpus, animam autem non possunt occidere: sed potius timete eum, qui potest et animam et corpus perdere in gehennam.

For 245–8 cf Haymo, Hom. 8, PL 118, 780CD:

Non nos ad nostram persecutionem pravos homines commovere debemus, sed potius cum iustitia et rectitudine quantum possumus, cum fuerint commoti, mitigare. Quod si quiescere noluerint, magis persecutionem tolerandam, quam iustitiam relinquendam.

252–5 Augustine similarly notes that the final verse, though it seems to be addressed specifically to the disciples, in reality applies like the preceding verses to all Christians (*Sermone Domini*, 1.143–7):

> Inde iam incipit loqui praesentes conpellans, cum et illa, quae supra dicta sunt, ad eos etiam pertinerent, qui praesentes audiebant, et haec postea, quae videntur praesentibus specialiter dici, pertineant etiam ad illos qui absentes vel post futuri erant.

256–8 Mt 5.11 (from the pericope, see above). Ælfric presumably read the persecutors as hypocrites or dissimulators because of *mentientes*.

262–6 Rom 5.3–5 [cited later by Augustine at *Sermone Domini*, 1.274–8]:

> (3) Gloriamur in tribulationibus; scientes quod tribulatio patientiam operatur, (4) patientia autem probationem, probatio vero spem, (5) spes autem non confundit; quia caritas Dei diffusa est in cordibus nostris per Spiritum Sanctum qui datus est nobis.

266–74 Haymo, Hom. 8, PL 118, 781AB:

> Unde Iacobus admonet, dicens: 'Omne gaudium existimate, fratres, cum in tentationes varias incideritis, scientes quod probatio fidei vestrae multo pretiosor est auro, quod per ignem probatur'. Et alia scriptura: 'Vasa figuli probat fornax, et homines iustos tentatio tribulationis' (Sir 27.6). Hinc et Salvator cum discipulos ad persecutionem tolerandam hortaretur, sui exemplum posuit, dicens: 'Si me persecuti sunt, et vos persequentur. . . .' (Jn 15.20). Et iterum: 'Si de mundo fuissetis, mundus quod suum erat diligeret, quia vero de mundo non estis, sed ego elegi vos de mundo, propterea odit vos mundus' (Jn. 15.19).

But Ælfric quotes Jn 15.18 instead of 19: *Si mundus vos odit, scitote quia me priorem vobis odio habuit*. Haymo's quotation from James, followed by Ælfric, is in fact a curious amalgam, presumably quoted from memory, of Jac 1.2–3:

> (2) Omne gaudium existimate, fratres mei, cum in tentationes varias incideritis: (3) scientes quod probatio fidei vestrae patientiam operatur.

and 1 Petr 1.6–7:

> (6) In quo exultabitis, modicum nunc si oportet contristari in variis tentationibus: (7) ut probatio vestrae fidei multo pretiosior auro quod per ignem probatur inveniatur in laudem.

282 Augustine goes on to deal with the question of heretics who suffer persecution but not for righteousness, and are therefore excluded from bliss, and with the spiritual nature of the reward, but does not have a great deal more to say on the beatitudes at this point. Ælfric is perhaps referring rather to the earlier material in Augustine's sermon, on the ordering of the beatitudes and their relation to the principal virtues.

37 ST CLEMENT

Clement of Rome, or St Clement I, bishop of Rome from c. 92 to 101 AD, was honoured in the church from a very early date. He is mentioned in Bede's *Martyrology*, in the verse *Menologium* and in the *Old English Martyrology*.[1] Ælfric bases his account of the saint on a Latin *Passio*, BHL 1848, which circulated in a variety of versions and has been printed several times, all differing in matters of expression and occasionally substance. The closest printed version that I have found is that published by Diekamp in 1913 (see below). Patrick Zettel demonstrated that the Hereford MS (Hereford, Cathedral Library, MS P.7.vi) of the Cotton-Corpus legendary contained a number of variant readings which were evidently in the source used by Ælfric and did not appear in any other version investigated by him[2]; and although some of those readings do occur in the Diekamp text, and evidently had a wider circulation, there remain a few not so far found outside the Hereford MS; I print them below in italics, with a reference to Hereford in parentheses. (It is also the case that the Hereford MS has many variants that were evidently not in Ælfric's source.) The other manuscripts of the Cotton-Corpus legendary which contain this text show no particular resemblance to Ælfric's version or hence to the Hereford MS: presumably either they or the Hereford MS acquired a different version in the course of transmission.

Ælfric gives a heavily abridged version of the *Passio*, omitting the whole account of Clement's evangelism and miracle-working in Rome and his conflicts with authorities there, though adding from other sources a brief account of his meeting with St Dionisius, and focusing mainly on the story of his exile and death, for which he follows the *Passio* fairly closely. He follows this with an account of a post-mortem miracle which is based on a story told by Gregory of Tours (BHL 1855) but is attached to the *Passio* in a number of manuscripts, including those of the Cotton-Corpus legendary. I have given the version printed by Mombritius, since this is closer than Gregory's own account and Diekamp does not print the miracle. This narrative material amounts to barely more than half of the homily, however. The rest is taken up with a series of Biblical and hagiographical examples demonstrating that, despite the apparent implications of the Clement story, God often does rescue his adherents from warfare, persecution and imprisonment. I have found no source or prompting for this discussion in Ælfric's authorities; it is a striking testimony to the problems raised by adapting hagiographic material to a vernacular readership.

[1] And see also M. Lapidge, 'The Saintly Life', in *The Cambridge Companion to Old English Literature*, ed. M. Godden and M. Lapidge (Cambridge, 1991), for a brief discussion of the development of the cult in England.

[2] Zettel 1979, pp. 162–3, 241–4. The use of the *Passio* was first noted by Förster (1892, pp. 29–31).

Sources and Notes

The following texts are cited below:

1. Anon., *Passio Clementis*, ed. F. Diekamp in *Patres Apostolici*, ed. F. X. Funk and F. Diekamp, 2 vols. (3rd ed., Tübingen, 1901–13), II.51–81 [variants are printed in italics].
2. Gregory of Tours, *Miraculum eiusdem*, from Mombritius 1910, I.344–6.
3. Haymo of Auxerre, *Historiae Sacrae Epitome*, PL 118, cols. 817–74.
4. Hilduinus, *Passio Sanctorum Dionysii, Rustici et Eleuterii Martyrum*, in Mombritius 1910, I.394–409.
5. Jerome, *De Viris Inlustribus*, ed. E. C. Richardson, Texte und Untersuchungen 14.1 (Leipzig, 1896), pp. 1–56.

7–14 Note the briefer introduction in the *Passio Clementis* (Diekamp, 51.2–3):

> Tertius Romanae ecclesiae praefuit episcopus Clemens, qui disciplinam apostoli Petri secutus. . . .

Ælfric's wording seems to imply a claim that Clement was Peter's direct successor as bishop of Rome, and a hint that this was a controversial issue. All the authorities known to Ælfric seem to have agreed that Clement was the fourth pope, after Peter, Linus and Cletus (or Anacletus). This is the view of Jerome, Augustine and Haymo, and it also figures in early pontifical lists. Jerome does note that many 'Latins' treat Clement as the second pope (*De Viris Inlustribus*, c. 15):

> Clemens, de quo apostolus Paulus ad Philippenses scribens, ait, 'Cum Clemente et caeteris cooperatoribus meis, quorum nomina scripta sunt in libro vitae', quartus post Petrum Romae episcopus: siquidem secundus Linus fuit, tertius Anencletus, tametsi plerique Latinorum secundum post apostolum putent fuisse Clementem.

and Haymo records a variant view that Linus and Cletus did not hold office as bishops but only as assistants to Peter, though even so he considers they should retain their place in the list of popes (Haymo, *Epitome*, III.xii, PL 118, 834C):

> Cletus vero, Romanus pontifex, et ipse duodecim annis sedet, et transiens Clementi papatum reliquit. Aiunt autem qui de cathedra Romanae Ecclesiae perscrutati sunt, quod Linus et Cletus non sederunt ut pontifices, sed ut summi pontificis coadiutores, quibus beatus Petrus tradidit ecclesiasticarum rerum dispositionem: ipse vero tantum orationi et praedicationi vacabat. Unde tanta auctoritate donati, meruerunt in catalogo pontificum reponi.

The opening words of the *Passio* identify Clement as the third bishop of Rome, presumably after Linus and Cletus and not counting Peter himself, but the Hereford MS version of this *Passio* reads *secundus* instead of *tertius*, apparently making him next after Peter (and another manuscript cited by Diekamp reads *quartus*). Ælfric is presumably meaning to suggest that Linus and Cletus were indeed bishops but were not Peter's successors and were hence not popes. He would seem to be adopting a specifically Roman position against his usual authorities. The reason for his firm position on this subject is perhaps to be found in Bede's *Historia Ecclesiastica*, II.iv, where Bede records St Augustine of Canterbury's consecration of Laurence as his successor and cites as the precedent and authority for this action (normally frowned on by church canons) St Peter's consecration of Clement as his successor.

15–23 *Passio Clementis*, Diekamp, 51.3–53.2:

> Ita morum ornamentis pollebat, ut et Iudaeis et Gentilibus et omnibus Christianis populis complaceret. Diligebant enim eum Gentiles, quoniam non execrando, sed rationem reddendo ex eorum libris et caeremoniis ostendebat ubi nati et unde nati essent hi, quos deos putarent et colerent, et quid egissent et qualiter defecissent evidentissimis documentis adstruebat; ipsosque Gentiles posse indulgentiam a Deo consequi si ab eorum cultura recederent, edocebat.

The reading of all manuscripts of the Old English text except A in line 16, *hæþenum and cristenum* for *cristenum*, is clearly correct, since it agrees with the source and with the context, and would appear to be the original reading, with *hæþenum and* omitted in error in A and the omission not noticed by Ælfric or others when correcting the text. One might note too that the *Passio* makes it clear that Clement demonstrated the nature of the pagans' gods from the pagans' own books; Ælfric only says *mid boclicum gesceade*.

23–7 *Passio Clementis*, Diekamp, 53.3–6 :

> Iudaeorum vero hoc ordine gratia utebatur, quod patres eorum amicos Dei adsereret et legem eorum sanctam et sacratissimam memoraret primumque locum istos apud Deum habituros adstrueret, si legis suae sacramenta servarent.

27–33 *Passio Clementis*, Diekamp, 53.13–20:

> A Christianis vero ideo quam maxime diligebatur, quoniam singularum regionum inopes nominatim habebat scriptos et hos, quos baptismatis sanctificatione illuminaverat, non sinebat publicae fieri mendicitati subiectos. Quotidiana itaque praedicatione mediocres ac divites admonebat, ne paterentur baptizatos pauperes a Iudaeis vel Gentilibus stipem publicam accipere et vitam baptismatis sacrificatione mundatum donis Gentilium inquinari.

Clement's policy of compiling written records of the wealth of each region in order to provide for the poor becomes in Ælfric simply a habit of keeping all the regions in his memory, thus obscuring the connection with the subsequent clauses; possibly his copy of the source was corrupt at this point.

33–50 None of the extant versions of the Latin *Passio* has any reference to Dionysius here. Did Ælfric add the account just for completeness, or was he wishing to imply a point about the unity of the church and of Peter and Paul, or the backing of both Pauline and Petrine authority for the church of Rome, or the role of the church of Rome in the conversion of Francia and Spain? The material presumably comes from the *Passio Sanctorum Dionysii, Rustici et Eleuterii Martyrum* ascribed to Hilduin of St-Denis (Mombritius 1910, I.394–409), which Ælfric used as a source for his later account of St Dionysius, LS 29.[3] Ælfric passes over the long account of the conversion of Dionysius by St Paul, his teachings and writings, and takes up the narrative with the saint's arrival in Rome (*Passio Sanctorum*, Mombritius 1910, I):

> [402.21–403.1] Preciosus Dionysius arcis romanae moeniis sui auspice Christo praesentiam intulit . . . et beatum Clementem pontificem sanctae et summae apostolicae sedis iam apicem gubernantem invenit. A quo idem . . . Dionysius mox ut se potuerunt invicem salutare digno est cum honore susceptus, et pro sanctitatis ac eruditionis suae reverentia seu anterioris fraternitatis coniunctione loco maximae venerationis est habitus. Cum quo etiam pro mutua collocutione apostolicarum sanctionum et dulcedine spiritualis dilectionis aliquandiu familiarissime conversatus immodici amoris uterque vinculis sese constrinxerunt. . . . 'Perge in nomine domini partes aggrediens occidentis . . . et sicut dominus Iesus Christus magistro meo tradidit Petro, et ego sanctae haereditatis iura suscepi, cum alligandi solvendique auctoritate tibi semper presto sit divina potestas . . . omnem suscipiens Galliam opus fac evangelistae, ministerium tuum imple. . . .' Socios quoque ei et comministros verbi plures et probatos viros adhibuit. . . . Qui simul properantes et circum circa dominum praedicantes appulerunt portum arelatensium civitatis. . . . [403.51–404.2] Tantas enim per illum dominus dignabatur exercere virtutes ut rebellium corda gentilium non minus miraculis quam praedicationibus obtineret. . . . Mox ut illum videre poterant, tanta et ita ineffabiliter in eo lux caelestis gratiae radiabatur, ut aut omni ferocitate una cum armis deposita se illi prosternerent, aut qui compuncti spiritus sancti dono ad credendum non erant, pavore nimio solverentur et territi a presentia eius aufugerent.

There is no precise equivalent in the *Passio* to the statement that all Gaul was converted (lines 47–9; or indeed to the similar statement in the LS 29 version, at 193–4), but it is perhaps a permissible exaggeration of the narrative, and no reference to sending disciples to Spain (lines 49–50 of this text).

51–62 Ælfric now omits a long section of about 163 lines in the *Passio Clementis* (Diekamp, 55.1–71.17), on Clement's conversions and miracles among the Romans and the developing opposition to him, which seems to have been in all versions of the *Passio*. He picks up the story with the culmination of pressure against him (though the *Passio* represents Trajan as responding to reports of

[3] It was available in CC; see Zettel 1979, pp. 236, 309.

sedition and popular disturbance rather than to the growth of Christianity); *Passio Clementis*, Diekamp, 71.18–73.15:

> Tunc Mamertinus praefectus missa relatione ad Traianum imperatorem de Clemente dixit. . . . Tunc imperator Traianus rescripsit, debere eum aut sacrificiis consentire aut trans Ponticum mare in eremo, quae adiacet civitati Chersoni, subire exilium. . . . Tantam denique Dominus gratiam sancto Clementi attribuit, ut fleret praefectus et diceret: 'Deus tuus, quem tu pure colis, ipse te adiuvet in hac relegatione exilii.' Et delegavit ei navem et omnibus necessariis impositis dimisit eum. Repleta est autem navis, quia de populo religiosi viri multi secuti sunt eum.

Ælfric's description of the desert near Cersona as a wasteland to which Christians condemned for their faith were exiled is presumably deduced from the next section of the story.

63–7 *Passio Clementis*, Diekamp, 73.16–75.3:

> Cum autem pervenisset in locum exilii, illic erant in ergastulis ad secanda marmora amplius quam duo millia Christiani diuturna relegatione damnati. Qui videntes sanctum Clementem episcopum omnes una voce in fletu et gemitu proruperunt: '*Ecce pastor noster, ecce consolatio nostri operis ac laboris*' [*Hereford MS*].

In the standard version of the *Passio* the weeping of the Christian exiles is appropriate as they see Clement being exiled too, and the pope then offers them consolation and hope. The addition of the words *Ecce* ... in the Hereford version makes the weeping inappropriate and it may have been Ælfric who changed it to cries of joy.

67–82 *Passio Clementis*, Diekamp, 75.7–77.1:

> Et cum multam eis consolationis doctrinam et patientiae intimasset, didicit ab eis quod de sexto miliario aquam suis humeris adportarent. Tunc sanctus Clemens dixit ad eos: 'Oremus Dominum Iesum Christum, ut confessoribus suis fontis venam *prope* [*Hereford MS*] aperiat . . . ut de eius beneficio gratulemur.' Cumque oratione completa hinc inde circumspiceret, vidit agnum stantem, qui pede dextro erecto quasi locum sancto Clementi ostenderet. Tunc sanctus Clemens intellegens Dominum esse [*the Hereford MS here reads* intelligens misterium quod videbat] . . . perrexit ad locum et dixit: '. . . in isto loco percutite.' . . . [*The people fail to find water at the spot, and so Clement himself takes a spade:*] Sanctus Clemens levi ictu locum sub pede agni percussit, unde fons affluentibus venis ornatus apparuit, qui suo impetu evomens fluvium fecit. Tunc cunctis gaudentibus . . . *completum est itaque in illic quod dixerant: 'Ecce pastor noster, ecce consolatio nostri operis ac laboris'* [*Hereford MS*].

83–9 *Passio Clementis*, Diekamp, 77.4–11:

> Ad istam autem famam confluxit omnis provincia, et venientes universi ad doctrinam sancti Clementis convertebantur ad dominum, ita ut in die

quingenti et eo amplius baptizati recederent. Intra unum autem annum factae sunt ibi a credentibus septuaginta quinque ecclesiae et omnia idola confracta sunt, omnia templa per gyrum provinciae destructa luci etiam universi per trecenta milia in toto per gyrum excisi.

89–104 *Passio Clementis*, Diekamp, 77.12–79.5:

Tunc paganis insistentibus tam invidiosa relatio cucurrit ad imperatorem Traianum, ut dicerent ibi per Clementem *culturam deorum deperisse et* [*Hereford MS*] innumerabilem Christianorum populum accrevisse. Et missus est dux Aufidianus, qui multos Christianorum diversis poenis occidit. Et cum videret *eos nullo timore perterritos, sed* [*Hereford MS*] omnes gaudentes ad passionem accedere, cessit multitudini, solum sanctum Clementem cogens ad sacrificandum. Et cum videret eum sic fixum in Domino, ut penitus mutari non posset, dixit ad suos: 'Producatur in medio mari, et ligata ad collum eius ancora, praecipitetur, ut non possint Christiani hunc pro Deo colere.' Quod cum factum fuisset, omnis multitudo Christianorum coepit stare ad litus et flere.

In defining Trajan as *se hæðena casere* and his lieutenant as *wælhreowne*, and focusing on the decline in his own cults rather than the growth of Christianity as a provocation, Ælfric seems to be concerned to develop a picture of a tyrant emperor; one might contrast the more sympathetic view of Trajan in the Whitby Life of Gregory the Great. If the final words, *and biddende . . . behwyrfan*, are Ælfric's own addition (and there is no equivalent in any version I have seen) they perhaps stem from a wish to indicate that the people, having willingly embraced martyrdom themselves, were not grieving over the death of the pope but only over the removal of his body.

107–14 *Passio Clementis*, Diekamp, 79.5–12:

Tunc dixerunt Cornelius et Phoebus discipuli eius: '*Fratres* [*Hereford MS*], omnes unanimes oremus, ut ostendat nobis Dominus martyris sui exuvias.' Orantibus autem populis recessit mare in sinum suum per tria fere milia, et ingressi per siccum populi invenerunt in modum templi marmorei habitaculum a Deo paratum et ibi in arca saxea corpus sancti Clementis positum, *sine dubio ministerio angelorum* [*var. Diekamp*], ita ut ancora, cum qua missus fuerat, iuxta eum esset posita.

114–26 *Passio Clementis*, Diekamp, 79.13–81.2:

Revelatum est autem discipulis eius, ut non inde tollerent corpus eius. Quibus etiam hoc intimatum est, quod omni anno die passionis eius recedat mare, ut per septem dies advenientibus siccum iter praebeat. Quod ad laudem nominis sui facit Dominus fieri usque in hodiernum diem. Hoc autem facto omnes per gyrum gentes crediderunt Christo. Ubi nullus Gentilis, nullus Iudaeus, nullus prorsus invenitur haereticus. Et fiunt ibi multa beneficia orationibus eius; *nam et si quis his diebus quo natalis eius celebratur infirmus advenerit, sanus revertitur* [*Hereford MS*].

> Caeci illuminantur die natalis eius, daemones effugantur. . . . *Tribulantes letificantur, et omnes ibi cum pacis gaudio beneficia eius consequuntur* [*Hereford MS*].

The additional clause in Q and other manuscripts at 114 seems from its manuscript distribution to be authorial, and corresponds closely to the first sentence of the Latin passage here cited; one must presume that Ælfric consulted or recalled the source in the course of revision.

128–47 Ælfric now turns to the miracle story told by Gregory of Tours, which was attached to the *Passio* in a number of manuscripts. He omits Gregory's elaborate introduction and recapitulation of the *Passio*, and gives a succinct version, omitting the dramatic representation of the mother's grief.

Miraculum eiusdem, Mombritius 1910, I.345.13–46:

> Factum est autem ut in una solemnitatum quaedam mulier cum filio suo parvulo locum accederet . . . ecce factus est repente sonus innundantium aquarum et cohoperientium mare; ex quo terrefacta mulier oblita est sobolis suae et coepit velociter cum reliqua multitudine populi ripam petere. Igitur . . . postquam ad littus venisset, meminit se filium reliquisse.. . . . Totum autem annum in lamentationibus et eiulatu ducens . . . recurrente autem . . . solemnitatis die beati Clementis martyris, venit iterum mulier ad spectandum maris secessum . . . anticipat omnes ad ingrediendum et ipsa praecedit ad tumulum. . . . Ita dicebat: '. . . Tu domine qui filium unicum viduae . . . redonavit incolumem, et nunc domine respice ancillam tuam ut beati Clementis martyris tui suffragiis adiuta, impertiar insequenti quod obnixe peto'. Et dum haec et alia diceret, erecta in genua dum divertit se in partem aliam, vultum aspicit filii in eo loco ubi eum dormientem reliquaerat, in ipso adhuc sopore teneri. . . . Mulier autem prae gaudio . . . lachrymis irrigabat et osculabatur. Coepit autem eum interrogare ac dicere inter ipsa oscula ubi per totius anni fuisset spatia. At ille nescire se ait si annus integer praeterisset sed sic tantum dormisse suavi sopore quasi unius noctis spatio. Tunc . . . omnes populi qui aderant benedixerunt dominum nostrum Iesum christum qui tanta mirabilia ostendit servis suis.

The touching words of the child seem to be Ælfric's contribution; Latin versions of the miracle give it only as reported speech.

154–89 In his account of the Assyrian message to Hezekiah, the king's response and the prophesy of Isaiah, Ælfric conflates, perhaps from memory, the account given at Isaiah 36 and 37.1–7 with the very similar one given at Isaiah 37.8 ff, and rearranges some of the details.

154–63 Mainly from Is 36.1–20 but the *ærendgewritu* of 158 presumably come from 37.14 (see below):

> (1) Et factum est in quartodecimo anno regis Ezechiae ascendit Sennacherib rex Assyriorum super omnes civitates Iuda munitas et cepit eas. (2)

et misit rex Assyriorum Rabsacen de Lachis in Hierusalem ad regem Ezechiam in manu gravi. . . . (13) Et stetit Rabsaces et clamavit voce magna iudaice et dixit: 'Audite verba regis magni regis Assyriorum. (14) Haec dicit rex: non seducat vos Ezechias quia non poterit eruere vos. (15) et non vobis tribuat fiduciam Ezechias super Domino dicens eruens liberabit nos Dominus, non dabitur civitas ista in manu regis Assyriorum. . . . (18) Ne conturbet vos Ezechias dicens Dominus liberabit nos. Numquid liberaverunt dii gentium unusquisque terram suam de manu regis Assyriorum? (19) Ubi est deus Emath et Arfad? ubi est deus Seffarvaim? Numquid liberaverunt Samariam de manu mea? (20) Quis est ex omnibus diis terrarum istarum qui eruerit terram suam de manu mea ut eruat Dominus Hierusalem de manu mea?'

163–73 Is 37.1, 14–20:

(1) Et factum est cum audisset, rex Ezechias scidit vestimenta sua et obvolutus est sacco et intravit in domum Domini. . . . (14) et tulit Ezechias libros de manu nuntiorum et legit eos et ascendit in domum Domini et expandit eos Ezechias coram Domino. (15) Et oravit Ezechias ad Dominum dicens: (16) 'Domine exercituum Deus Israhel qui sedes super cherubin: tu es Deus solus omnium regnorum terrae; tu fecisti caelum et terram. (17) Inclina Domine aurem tuam et audi; aperi Domine oculos tuos et vide et audi omnia verba Sennacherib quae misit ad blasphemandum Deum viventem. . . . (19) Et dederunt deos earum igni, non enim erant dii sed opera manuum hominum, lignum et lapis, et comminuerunt eos. (20) Et nunc Domine Deus noster salva nos de manu eius et cognoscant omnia regna terrae quia tu es Dominus solus.'

174–83 Is 37.2–7, 29–35, re-ordered:

(2) Et misit Eliachim qui erat super domum et Sobnam scribam et seniores de sacerdotibus opertos saccis ad Isaiam filium Amos prophetam. (3) Et dixerunt ad eum: . . . (4) 'Si quo modo audiat Dominus Deus tuus verba Rabsaces quem misit rex Assyriorum dominus suus ad blasphemandum Deum viventem et obprobrandum sermonibus quos audivit Dominus Deus tuus, leva ergo orationem pro reliquiis quae reppertae sunt.' . . . (6) Et dixit ad eos Isaias: 'Haec dicetis domino vestro: haec dicit Dominus: ne timeas a facie verborum quae audisti quibus blasphemaverunt pueri regis Assyriorum me. (33) Propterea haec dicit Dominus de rege Assyriorum: non introibit civitatem hanc et non iaciet ibi sagittam et non occupabit eam clypeus et non mittet in circuitu eius aggerem. (29) Cum fureres adversum me superbia tua ascendit in aures meas; ponam ergo circulum in naribus tuis et frenum in labiis tuis et reducam te in viam per quam venisti. (7) Ecce ego dabo ei spiritum et audiet nuntium et revertetur ad terram suam et corruere eum faciam gladio in terra sua. (35) Et protegam civitatem istam ut salvem eam propter me et propter David servum meum.'

183–9 Is 37.36–8:

(36) Egressus est autem angelus Domini et percussit in castris Assyriorum centum octoginta quinque milia et surrexerunt mane et ecce omnes cadavera mortuorum. (37) Et egressus est et abiit et reversus est Sennacherib rex Assyriorum et habitavit in Nineve. (38) Et factum est cum adoraret in templo Nesrach deum suum Adramelech et Sarasar filii eius percusserunt eum gladio fugeruntque in terram Ararat et regnavit Asoraddon filius eius pro eo.

190–9 A summary account of the story of the three youths from Dan 3:

(12) 'Sunt ergo viri iudaei quos constituisti super opera regionis Babyloniae Sedrac Misac et Abdenago. Viri isti contempserunt rex decretum tuum; deos tuos non colunt et statuam auream quam erexisti non adorant.' . . . (19) Tunc Nabuchodonosor repletus est furore et aspectus faciei illius inmutatus est super Sedrac Misac et Abdenago et praecepit ut succenderetur fornax septuplum quam succendi consuerat. (20) Et viris fortissimis de exercitu suo iussit ut ligatis pedibus Sedrac Misac et Abdenago mitterent eos in fornacem ignis ardentem. (49) Angelus autem descendit cum Azaria et sociis eius in fornacem et excussit flammam ignis de fornace. (50) Et fecit medium fornacis quasi ventum roris flantem et non tetigit eos omnino ignis neque contristavit nec quicquam molestiae intulit. (47) Et effundebatur flamma super fornacem cubitis quadraginta novem. (48) Et erupit et incendit quos repperit iuxta fornacem de Chaldeis. (94) Et congregati satrapae magistratus et iudices et potentes regis contemplabantur viros illos quoniam nihil potestatis habuisset ignis in corporibus eorum et capillus capitis eorum non esset adustus. . . . (95) Et erumpens Nabuchodonosor ait: 'Benedictus Deus eorum Sedrac videlicet Misac et Abdenago qui misit angelum suum et eruit servos suos quia crediderunt in eo.'

The story is also told in CH II.1.

200–29 Dan 14.27–41, with a conclusion taken from Dan 6:

(27) Quod cum audissent Babylonii indignati sunt vehementer et congregati adversum regem dixerunt: 'Iudaeus factus est rex, Bel destruxit, draconem interfecit et sacerdotes occidit'. (28) Et dixerunt cum venissent ad regem: 'Trade nobis Danihelum alioquin interficiemus te et domum tuam.' (29) Vidit ergo rex quod inruerent in eum vehementer et necessitate conpulsus tradidit eis Danihelum. (30) Qui miserunt eum in lacum leonum et erat ibi diebus sex. (31) Porro in lacu erant septem leones et dabantur eis cotidie duo corpora et duae oves et tunc non data sunt eis ut devorarent Danihelum. (32) Erat autem Abacuc propheta in Iudaea et ipse coxerat pulmentum et intriverat panes in alveolo et ibat in campum ut ferret messoribus. (33) Dixitque angelus Domini ad Abacuc: 'Fer prandium quod habes in Babylonem Daniheli qui est in lacu leonum.' (34) Et dixit Abacuc:

'Domine, Babylonem non vidi et lacum nescio.' (35) Et adprehendit eum angelus Domini in vertice eius et portavit eum capillo capitis sui posuitque eum in Babylone supra lacum in impetu spiritus sui. (36) Et clamavit Abacuc dicens: 'Danihel tolle prandium quod misit tibi Deus.' (37) Et ait Danihel: 'Recordatus es enim mei Deus et non dereliquisti diligentes te.' (38) Surgensque Danihel comedit. Porro angelus Dei restituit Abacuc confestim in loco suo. (39) Venit ergo rex die septima ut lugeret Danihelum et venit ad lacum et introspexit et ecce Danihel sedens. (40) Et exclamavit rex voce magna dicens: 'Magnus es Domine Deus Danihelis'; et extraxit eum. (41) Porro illos qui perditionis eius causa fuerant intromisit et devorati sunt in momento coram eo. (6.26–7?) 'Tremescant et paveant Deum Danihelis. . . . Ipse liberator atque salvator faciens signa et mirabilia in caelo et in terra.'

230–9 Acts 5.17–23:

(17) Exsurgens autem princeps sacerdotum et omnes qui cum illo erant quae est heresis Sadducaeorum, repleti sunt zelo, (18) et iniecerunt manus in apostolos et posuerunt illos in custodia publica. (19) Angelus autem Domini per noctem aperiens ianuas carceris et educens eos dixit: (20) 'Ite et stantes loquimini in templo plebi omnia verba vitae huius.' (21) Qui cum audissent intraverunt diluculo in templum et docebant. Adveniens autem princeps sacerdotum et qui cum eo erant convocaverunt concilium et omnes seniores filiorum Israhel et miserunt in carcerem ut adducerentur. (22) Cum venissent autem ministri et aperto carcere non invenissent illos reversi nuntiaverunt, (23) dicentes: 'Carcerem quidem invenimus clausum cum omni diligentia et custodes stantes ad ianuas aperientes autem neminem intus invenimus.'

240–5 Acts 12.3–10:

(3) Videns autem quia placeret Iudaeis adposuit adprehendere et Petrum; erant autem dies azymorum. (4) Quem cum adprehendisset misit in carcerem, tradens quattuor quaternionibus militum custodire eum, volens post pascha producere eum populo. (6) Cum autem producturus eum esset Herodes in ipsa nocte erat Petrus dormiens inter duos milites vinctus catenis duabus et custodes ante ostium custodiebant carcerem. (7) Et ecce angelus Domini adstitit et lumen refulsit in habitaculo percussoque latere Petri suscitavit eum, dicens 'Surge velociter', et ceciderunt catenae de manibus eius. (10) Transeuntes autem primam et secundam custodiam venerunt ad portam ferream quae ducit ad civitatem quae ultro aperta est eis et exeuntes processerunt vicum unum et continuo discessit angelus ab eo.

The story is also told in CH II.24.

245–9 The two episodes from the story of John the Evangelist are included in Ælfric's full account at CH I.4.21–5 and 212–28; see above for the sources. For the first, Ælfric's wording here seems slightly closer to the source, Bede, than to the version in I.4.

249–50 2 Cor 11.25: *Nocte et die in profundo maris fui.*

251–2 Acts 28.3–5:

(3) Cum congregasset autem Paulus sarmentorum aliquantam multitudinem et inposuisset super ignem, vipera a calore cum processisset invasit manum eius. (4) Ut vero viderunt barbari pendentem bestiam de manu eius ad invicem dicebant utique homicida est homo hic qui cum evaserit de mari Ultio non sinit vivere. (5) Et ille quidem excutiens bestiam in ignem nihil mali passus est.

259–60 Ps 33.20: *Multae tribulationes iustorum et de omnibus his liberavit eos.*

270–4 Lc 23.41–3:

(41) 'Et nos quidem iuste nam digna factis recipimus; hic vero nihil mali gessit.' (42) Et dicebat ad Iesum 'Domine memento mei cum veneris in regnum tuum'. (43) Et dixit illi Iesus 'amen dico tibi hodie mecum eris in paradiso'.

38 ST ANDREW

A comment by Ælfric originally written as a conclusion to this homily, and erroneously preserved in the Royal MS (see Appendix A2, *CH I*, p. 531), shows that the homily was in its earliest form just an exposition of the Gospel passage for the day, Matthew 4.18–22, on the choosing of Andrew, Peter, James and John as disciples. Subsequently, though before MS A was produced and before the series was circulated, Ælfric added an account of the apostle's passion (lines 169–351), and some time later again added a brief alliterative linking sentence, preserved in the later versions of MS Q etc. (see 168 app. crit.), to join the two parts. The use of his alliterative style towards the end of the account of the passion raises at least the possibility that he wrote this second section around the time when he was completing work on the Second Series, which seems to be the period when he developed that style. Indeed, one interpretation of the cancelled conclusion is that he initially intended to cover the passion in the Second Series, rather as he divided Scriptural exegesis and hagiographical narrative for St Stephen's day between the two Series; the passion narrative may thus have been written for the Second Series and transferred to the First before the latter was circulated.

Ælfric's main concern in the first part is to explore the ways in which the four disciples can be seen as models and symbols for all true believers. He had available to him at least three Latin homilies on the Gospel text: one by Gregory which appears in Paul the Deacon's homiliary for the occasion, one by Hericus which closely follows it in later versions of the homiliary, and one by Haymo in his homiliary.[1] Gregory is primarily concerned with seeing the disciples as models of those who renounce the world, while Haymo and Hericus are more concerned with interpreting them as representatives of the Jews and the Gentiles. The central core of Ælfric's treatment (lines 44–150) is a detailed exposition of the Gospel text, closely based on the homily by Gregory and emphasising particularly the disciples' renunciation of possessions and earthly desires to follow Christ, as an example to others. Ælfric prefaces it however with some comments on the symbolism of the sea and the reasons for Christ's choice of humble fisherman as his apostles (lines 12–43); here he seems to be drawing, in part at least, on Haymo and Hericus. Haymo and Hericus seem again to be at least the inspiration behind Ælfric's exploration of the names of the four apostles at the end of the exposition, lines 151–69.

For the narrative Ælfric drew on a *Passio Andreae* which describes the apostle's debates with the proconsul Aegeas in Achaia and his subsequent martyrdom on the cross. It is a powerful narrative which seems to have been a major influence on *The Dream of the Rood*. The Latin text survives in a number of printed editions. Förster quoted from the version printed by Mombritius,[2] but the version edited by Bonnet is much closer. Ælfric probably found the source in his copy of the Cotton-Corpus legendary. MS F of this collection (Bodleian, MS Bodley 354) has a version similar to Mombritius, but Zettel has shown[3] that the later Hereford MS (Hereford, Cathedral Library, MS P.7.vi) has a different version which is very close to Ælfric; it is in fact virtually identical to that edited by Bonnet (though Zettel did not compare the two). The Hereford version differs, however, in having a conclusion, beyond the point where Ælfric and the Bonnet text end, describing the saint's burial by Maximilla and the miracles at his tomb. I have taken the source passages from Bonnet's text but incorporated readings from other manuscripts as recorded in his critical apparatus where these are closer to Ælfric. Ælfric seems to follow the Latin text very closely, omitting little apart from a brief debate on death and resurrection.[4]

Sources and Notes

The following texts are cited below:

1. Anon., *Passio Andreae*, ed. M. Bonnet, in Lipsius and Bonnet, II.1–37 [relevant variants from Bonnet's apparatus are incorporated in square brackets].

[1] Ælfric's use of Gregory was pointed out by C. R. Davis, 'Two new sources for Ælfric's Catholic Homilies', *JEGP* 41 (1942), 510–13, and Smetana (1959, p. 195) noted that it was included in Paul the Deacon's homiliary. In his later article (1961, p. 461) Smetana suggested the use of Haymo's homily for the introductory passage.

[2] Förster 1892, pp. 21–2.

[3] Zettel 1979, pp. 166–71 and 244–6.

[4] See further on this homily and its themes, Godden 1996, pp. 272–5.

2. Bede, *Commentarius in Marcum*, ed. D. Hurst, CCSL 120 (Turnhout, 1960), pp. 431–648.
3. Gregory the Great, *Homiliae in Evangelia*, PL 76, Hom. 5, cols. 1092–5.
4. Haymo of Auxerre, *Homiliae de Sanctis*, PL 118, Hom. 1, cols. 747–55.
5. Hericus, *Homiliae in Circulum Anni*, ed. R. Quadri, CCCM 116B (Turnhout, 1994), Hom. II.46 (pp. 446–51).
6. Jerome, *Commentarii in Evangelium Matthaei*, ed. D. Hurst and M. Adriaen, CCSL 77 (Turnhout, 1969).
7. Smaragdus, *Collectiones in Evangelia et Epistolas*, PL 102, cols 510–2.

4–11 Mt 4.18–22:

> (18) Ambulans autem iuxta mare Galilaeae vidit duos fratres, Simonem, qui vocatur Petrus, et Andream fratrem eius, mittentes rete in mare; erant enim piscatores, (19) et ait illis: Venite post me, et faciam vos fieri piscatores hominum. (20) At illi continuo relictis retibus secuti sunt eum. (21) Et procedens inde, vidit alios duos fratres, Iacobum Zebedaei, et Iohannem fratrem eius, in navi cum Zebedaeo patre eorum, reficientes retia sua; et vocavit eos. (22) Illi autem statim relictis retibus et patre, secuti sunt eum.

12–17 These lines are not printed in Thorpe's edition but would seem to have been accidentally omitted, since they occur in all manuscripts. This opening passage is not close to Gregory or Ælfric's other possible sources. For the parallel between the sea and the world one might compare Haymo, Hom. 1, PL 118, 748A:

> Mare ergo in hoc loco mundum significat. Et pulchre, quia sicut mare immobile esse non potest sed semper accedit et recedit, sic mundus diversis perturbationibus et fluctuationibus commovetur.

It is though a commonplace, as Ælfric remarks; he uses it himself at CH I.12.31, CH II.16.144 ff and 24.87 ff, always developing the equation somewhat independently of his immediate sources. The word *swangettunge* (line 13) is not otherwise recorded but presumably is equivalent to something like Latin *perturbatio* or *fluctuatio*. For 14–16 a possible influence is Hericus, though this relates to an interpretation of the four disciples as symbols of the Jews and the Gentiles (Hom. II.46, 129 ff):

> Quatuor discipuli a domino de mari vocati, duos significant populos, de sollicitudinibus et inquiete istius saeculi ad soliditatem spiritalis studii per gratiam Dei vocatos.

17–24 Possibly adapted from Haymo, Hom. 1, PL 118, 751BC:

> Sic isti in gremio ecclesiae recepti, navem fidei ascendentes, retia praedicationis in verbo et opere habentes, de amarissimis et tenebrosis mundi gurgitibus, multos homines ad veram lucem traxerunt. . . . 'Mittam piscatores meos, et piscabuntur eos; venatores meos et venabuntur eos de omni monte, et de omni colle' (Jer 16.16).

But for the phrase *to staþolfæstnysse lybbendra eorðan þæt is to þam ecan eðele* cf

CH I.36.202 *ðæra lybbendra eorþe is seo staðolfæstnys þæs ecan eardes*, explaining the *terra viventium* of Ps 141.6.

24–43 This powerful discussion of Christ choosing humble fishermen perhaps draws in part (lines 24 and 28–31) on Haymo (Hom. 1, PL 118, 750BC):

> Piscatores et illitterati a Domino eliguntur, ne fides credentium, quae per eorum doctrinam et praedicationem instruenda erat, in eloquentia verborum, et non in virtute Dei fieri putaretur. . . . Non elegit potentes vel filios regum, non philosophos vel sapientes mundi, sed pauperes simplices . . . per quorum tamen doctrinam et praedicationem potentes mundi et sapientes ad suam fidem vocavit.

The first sentence comes from Jerome's commentary on Matthew (*Comm. Matth.*, 1.404) and is also quoted by Bede (*Comm. Marc.*, 1.359) and by Smaragdus (*Collectiones*, PL 102, 511). There is a similar passage in Hericus, Hom. II.46, 51 ff; but if these are Ælfric's sources, he has insisted on the point that Christ chose emperors and other great men after the humble fisherman, where Haymo and Hericus assert that he chose fishermen and not nobles; and he has introduced the idea of the emperor bowing before the memorial to the fisherman. The quotation at 43 is 1 Cor 1.31: *Qui gloriatur, in Domino glorietur*.

44–51 Ælfric now begins with Gregory's exposition, Hom. 5, PL 76, 1093A:

> Nulla vero hunc facere adhuc miracula viderant, nihil ab eo de praemio aeternae retributionis audierant; et tamen ad unum Domini praeceptum [*cf earlier* ad unius iussionis vocem] hoc quod possidere videbantur obliti sunt. Quanta nos eius miracula videmus, quot flagellis affligimur, quantis minarum asperitatibus deterremur, et tamen vocantem sequi contemnimus?

51–60 Gregory, Hom. 5, PL 76, 1093AB:

> In coelo iam sedet, qui de conversione nos admonet; iam iugo fidei colla gentium subdidit, iam mundi gloriam stravit, iam, ruinis eius crebescentibus, districti sui iudicii diem propinquantem denuntiat; et tamen superba mens nostra non vult hoc sponte deserere quod quotidie perdit invita. Quid ergo, carissimi, quid in eius iudicio dicturi sumus, qui ab amore praesentis saeculi nec praeceptis flectimur, nec verberibus emendamur.

61–6 Gregory, Hom. 5, PL 76, 1093BC:

> Sed fortasse aliquis tacitis sibi cogitationibus dicat: 'Ad vocem dominicam uterque iste piscator quid aut quantum dimisit, qui pene nihil habuit?' Sed hac in re . . . affectum debemus potius pensare quam censum. Multum reliquit qui sibi nihil retinuit. . . . Certe nos et habita cum amore possidemus, et ea quae minime habemus ex desiderio quaerimus.

66–73 Gregory, Hom. 5, PL 76, 1093C:

> Multum ergo Petrus et Andreas dimisit, quando uterque etiam desideria habendi derelinquit. Multum dimisit, qui cum re possessa etiam concupiscentiis renuntiavit. . . . Nemo igitur . . . dicat: 'Imitari mundi huius

contemptores volo, sed quod relinquam non habeo.' . . . Exteriora etenim nostra Domino quamlibet parva sufficiunt. Cor namque, et non substantiam pensat; nec perpendit quantum in eius sacrificio, sed ex quanto proferatur.

73–9 Gregory, Hom. 5, PL 76, 1093C-1094A:

Ecce sancti negotiatores nostri perpetuam angelorum vitam datis retibus et navi mercati sunt. Aestimationem quippe pretii non habet, sed tamen regnum Dei tantum valet quantum habes. Valuit namque Zacchaeo dimidium substantiae. . . . Valuit Petro et Andreae dimissis retibus et navi, valuit viduae duobus minutis, valuit alteri calice aquae frigidae.

80–93 Ælfric now explains Gregory's three allusions by giving the appropriate Gospel passages. The first is Lc 19.2–10:

(2) Et ecce vir nomine Zaccheus; et hic princeps erat publicanorum, et ipse dives; (3) et quaerebat videre Iesum, quis esset; et non poterat prae turba, quia statura pusillus erat. (4) Et praecurrens ascendit in arborem sycomorum ut videret eum; quia inde erat transiturus. (5) Et cum venisset ad locum, suspiciens Iesus vidit illum, et dixit ad eum: Zacchee, festinans descende, quia hodie in domo tua oportet me manere. (6) Et festinans descendit, et excepit illum gaudens. . . . (8) Stans autem Zacchaeus, dixit ad Dominum: Ecce dimidium bonorum meorum. Domine, do pauperibus; et si quid aliquem defraudavi, reddo quadruplum. (9) Ait Iesus ad eum: Quia hodie salus domui huic facta est, eo quod et ipse filius sit Abrahae. (10) Venit enim Filius hominis quaerere, et salvum facere quod perierat.

96–103 Mc 12.41–4:

(41) Et sedens Iesus contra gazofilacium, aspiciebat quomodo turba iactaret aes in gazofilacium, et multi divites iactabant multa. (42) Cum venisset autem vidua una pauper, misit duo minuta, quod est quadrans, (43) et convocans discipulos suos, ait illis: Amen dico vobis, quoniam vidua haec pauper plus omnibus misit, qui miserunt in gazofilacium. (44) Omnes enim ex eo, quod abundabat illis, miserunt; haec vero de penuria sua omnia quae habuit, misit totum victum suum.

105–7 Mt 10.42:

Et quicumque potum dederit uni ex minimis istis calicem aquae frigidae tantum in nomine discipuli; amen dico vobis, non perdet mercedem suam.

107–116 Gregory, Hom. 5, PL 76, 1094AB:

Pensate igitur, fratres, quod vilius cum emitur, quid carius cum possidetur. . . . Redemptore etenim nato, coeli cives ostensi sunt, qui clamarent: 'Gloria in excelsis Deo, et in terra pax hominibus bonae voluntatis' (Lc 2.14). . . . Nihil quippe offertur Deo ditius voluntate bona.

119–25 Gregory, Hom. 5, PL 76, 1094BC:

Voluntas autem bona est sic adversa alterius sicut nostra pertimescere, sic de prosperitate proximi sicut de nostro profectu gratulari . . . amicum non propter mundum, sed propter Deum diligere, inimicum etiam amando tolerare, nulli quod pati non vis facere . . . necessitati proximi non solum iuxta vires concurrere, sed prodesse etiam ultra vires velle. Quid ergo isto holocausto locupletius, quando per hoc quod Deo immolat in ara cordis anima semetipsam mactat.

125–31 Gregory, Hom. 5, PL 76, 1094AB (earlier):

Hinc etenim psalmista dicit: 'In me sunt, Deus, vota tua quae reddam, laudationes tibi' (Ps 55.12). Ac si aperte dicat: Etsi exterius munera offerenda non habeo, intra memetipsum tamen invenio quod in ara tuae laudis impono, quia qui nostra datione non pasceris, oblatione cordis melius placaris.

131–6 Gregory, Hom. 5, PL 76, 1094C:

Sed hoc bonae voluntatis sacrificium nunquam plene persolvitur, nisi mundi huius cupiditas perfecte deseratur. . . . Et quia semper invidia a bona voluntate discordat, mox ut haec mentem ceperit, illa discedit. Unde praedicatores sancti ut possent proximos perfecte diligere studuerunt in hoc saeculo nihil amare, nihil umquam appetere, nihil vel sine appetitu possidere.

137–43 Gregory, Hom. 5, PL 76, 1094CD:

Quos bene Isaias intuens, ait: 'Qui sunt isti, qui ut nubes volant, et quasi columbae ad fenestras suas?' (Is 60.8). Vidit quippe terrena eos despicere, mente coelestibus propinquare, verbis pluere, miraculis coruscare. . . . Hos volantes pariter et nubes appellat. Fenestrae autem nostri sunt oculi, quia per ipsos anima respicit quod exterius concupiscit.

143–50 Gregory, Hom. 5, PL 76, 1094D-5A:

Columba vero simplex est animal, atque a malitia fellis alienum. Quasi columbae ergo ad fenestras suas sunt, qui nihil in hoc mundo concupiscunt, qui omnia simpliciter aspiciunt, et in his quae vident rapacitatis studio non trahuntur. At contra milvus et non columba ad fenestras suas est, qui ad ea quae oculis considerat rapinae desiderio anhelat.

153–68 Both Hericus and Haymo conclude with a discussion of the names of the four disciples, and the former seems quite close to Ælfric lines 155–9 (Hericus, Hom. II.46, 132 ff):

Simon Petrus, qui interpretatur oboediens, sive agnoscens, et Iacobus qui supplantator dicitur . . . Andreas, vero, qui virilis dicitur, et Iohannes, qui gratia Dei interpretatur. . . . Moraliter quatuor nomina ista in se unusquisque fidelium valet recognoscere, si illorum interpretationes in quatuor principalibus virtutibus studuerit observare.

Hericus identifies the *agnoscens* sense of the name Peter with acknowledging sins, but Haymo agrees with Ælfric (lines 157–9) in associating it with knowing God (Hom. 1, PL 118, 754C):

> Hanc virtutem in se habuit, qui corde, hominem videns, Deum cognovit, dicens: 'Tu es Christus filius Dei vivi' (Mt 16.16).

But he does not discuss the name Simon. On 161–8 cf Hericus, Hom. II.46, 148–59:

> Est Andreas, cum viriliter per temperantiam sustinet temptationes sibi illatas. Iacobus quoque non indebite supplantator dicitur, si per fortitudinem vitia supplantare probatur. Convenienter etiam Iohannes nominari potest, si per iustitiam mandata creatoris adimplens. . . . Curet etiam cum Andrea virili temptationibus diaboli viriliter resistere.

As Fred Robinson has shown,[5] such name-etymologies are recurrent in Ælfric and he would probably have known other authorities, such as Jerome's *Liber Interpretationis Hebraicorum Nominum* (CCSL 72) and the Ps-Isidore, *Liber de Ortu et Obitu Patrum*, PL 83, 1286, both of which give the same etymologies, though neither in fact has similar discussions of them. Ælfric gives a different interpretation of the name Peter at CH II.24.165 ff.

170–2 At CH I.21.238 Ælfric mentions Andrew preaching in Scythia, but seems to have overlooked that tradition here. The *Passio* opens with an address from the deacons of the church of Achaia to all other churches, and refers to the faith which they had been taught by the apostle.

172–7 *Passio Andreae*, Bonnet, 3.3–8:

> Proconsul Aegeas Patras civitatem ingressus coepit compellere credentes Christum ad sacrificia idolorum. Cui occurrens sanctus Andreas dixit: 'Oportebat ut tu qui iudex esse hominum meruisti, iudicem tuum qui est in caelo cognosceres et agnitum coleres et colendo eum qui verus deus est ab his qui veri dii non sunt animum revocares.'

177–85 *Passio Andreae*, Bonnet, 3.8–5.3:

> Cui Aegeas dixit: 'Tu es Andreas qui destruis templa deorum et suades hominibus ad superstitiosam sectam quam nuper detectam Romani principes exterminari iusserunt?' Andreas respondit: 'Romani principes nondum cognoverunt [veritatem, et] hoc quod pro salute hominum veniens dei filius docuerit ista idola non solum deos non esse, sed esse daemonia pessima et inimica humano generi, quae hoc docent homines unde offendatur deus et . . . cum aversus fuerit . . . habeantur a diabolo ipsi captivi et tamdiu eos deludat quamdiu de corpore exeant rei et nudi, nihil secum praeter peccata portantes.'

185–90 *Passio Andreae*, Bonnet, 5.4–9:

> Aegeas dixit: 'Ista superstitiosa et vana verba [sunt, nam] Iesus vester dum [haec] praedicaret, Iudaei illum crucis patibulum affixerunt.' Andreas

[5] Fred Robinson, 'The significance of names in Old English literature', *Anglia* 86 (1968), 14–58.

respondit: 'O si velis scire mysterium crucis, quam rationabili caritate auctor humani generis pro restauratione nostra hoc crucis patibulum non invitus sed sponte suscepit.'

191–7 *Passio Andreae*, Bonnet, 5.9–7.5:

Aegeas dixit: 'Cum traditus asseratur a suo discipulo, et . . . ad petitionem Iudaeorum a militibus praesidis crucifixus, quomodo tu dicis eum spontaneum crucis subisse patibulum?' Andreas respondit: 'Ideo ego dico spontaneum, quoniam simul cum ipso fui cum a suo discipulo traderetur, et antequam traderetur dixit nobis quod tradendus esset et crucifigendus pro salute hominum et die tertia resurrecturum se esse praedixit. . . . Dicebat nobis: "Potestatem habeo ponendi animam meam, et potestatem habeo iterum adsumendi eam" (Jn 10.18).'

197–203 *Passio Andreae*, Bonnet, 8.5–9.3:

Aegeas dixit: 'Miror te prudentem virum istum velle sectari quem quoquo pacto, aut sponte aut invitum, cruci tamen confiteris affixum.' Andreas respondit: '. . . magnum est mysterium crucis. Quod si forte volueris audire retexam.' Aegeas dixit: 'Mysterium non potest dici sed supplicium.' Andreas respondit: 'Ipsum supplicium mysterium restaurationis [humani generis] si patienter audias comprobabis.'

203–11 *Passio Andreae*, Bonnet, 9.3–10.2:

Aegeas dixit: 'Ego quidem patienter te audiam. Sed tu si me obtemperanter non audias, ipsum crucis mysterium in te ipsum [excipies].' Andreas respondit: 'Ego si crucis patibulum expavescerem, crucis gloriam non praedicarem.' Aegeas dixit: 'Insanus sermo tuus praedicat gloriam supplicii, [quia] per audaciam poenam non times mortis.' Andreas respondit: 'Non per audaciam sed per fidem poenam non timeo mortis; mors enim iustorum pretiosa est, mors vero peccatorum pessima.'

(Despite the manuscript punctuation, *rode wite* at 207 would seem to mean 'the punishment of the cross'.)

211–17 *Passio Andreae*, Bonnet, 13.1–14.1:

Aegeas dixit: '. . . Mihi autem nisi hoc consentias ut sacrificium diis omnipotentibus offeras, in ipsa cruce quam laudas te fustigatum affigi praecipiam.' Andreas respondit: 'Omnipotenti deo qui unus et verus est ego [quotidie] die sacrifico, non . . . taurorum mugientium carnes nec hyrcorum sanguinem sed immaculatum agnum quotidie in altare crucis sacrifico; cuius carnes posteaquam omnis populus credentium manducaverit et eius sanguinem biberit, agnus qui sacrificatus est integer perseverat et vivus.'

The verb *ett* seems necessary to the sense at 217 but its absence from not only MS A but also D suggests that it was omitted by Ælfric or his own scribe.

217–30 *Passio Andreae*, Bonnet, 14.4–15.8:

Aegeas dixit: 'Quomodo potest hoc fieri?' Andreas respondit: 'Si vis discere quomodo potest hoc fieri, adsume formam discipuli, ut possis [discere] quod quaeris.' Aegeas dixit: 'Ego a te tormentis exigo huius rei notitiam.' Andreas respondit: 'Miror te hominem prudentem [ad tantam stultitiam devolutum, ut putes] tormentis me tibi divina pandere sacrificia. Audisti mysterium crucis, audisti mysterium sacrificii. Si credideris Christum filium dei qui crucifixus est a Iudaeis, verum deum esse, pandam tibi quo ordine occisus vivat agnus qui cum sacrificatus fuerit et comestus integer tamen et immaculatus in suo regno permaneat'. . . . Si non credideris, penitus numquam tu ad indaginem huius veritatis attinges.

231–40 *Passio Andreae*, Bonnet, 16.1–17.5:

Tunc iratus Aegeas iussit eum in carcerem trudi. Ubi cum esset clausus, venit ad eum multitudo paene totius provinciae ita, ut Aegeam vellent occidere et Andream apostolum fractis ianuis carceris liberare. Quos sanctus Andreas his verbis ammonuit: 'Nolite quietem domini nostri Iesu Christi in seditionem diabolicam excitare. Nam traditus dominus omnem patientiam praebuit; non contendit, non clamavit, nec in plateis aliquis eum clamantem audivit (Mt 12.19). Habete silentium, quietem et pacem, et non solum meum martyrium nolite impedire, verum etiam vos ipsos quasi athletas domini praeparate, ut vincatis minas intrepido animo, plagas autem per tollerantiam corporis superetis.'

241–50 *Passio Andreae*, Bonnet, 17.5–18.7:

'Si enim terror timendus est, ille est utique metuendus qui finem non habet. Nam humanus timor fumo similis est, et subito cum excitatus fuerit evanescit. . . . Isti enim dolores aut leves sunt et tolerari possunt, aut graves sunt et cito animam eiiciunt. Illi autem dolores aeterni sunt ubi est quotidianus fletus et mugitus et luctus et sine fine cruciatus, ad quem Aegeas proconsul ire non timet. Estote ergo magis parati ad hoc, ut per tribulationes temporales ad aeterna gaudia pertingatis, ubi semper laetemini, semper floreatis, semperque cum Christo regnetis.'

251–57 *Passio Andreae*, Bonnet, 18.8–19.4:

Haec et his similia sancto Andrea apostolo per totam noctem populum ammonente, dum lux diei in matutino prorumperet, misit Aegeas et adduxit ad se sanctum Andream, ac sedens pro tribunali dixit: 'Existimavi te nocturna cogitatione revocare animum tuum ab stultitia et a Christi tui laude cessare, ut possis nobiscum non amittere gaudia vitae. Stultum est enim ultro velle ad passionem crucis ire, et ignibus ac flammis [se] ipsum pessimis destinare.'

257–67 *Passio Andreae*, Bonnet, 19.4–20.6:

Andreas respondit: 'Gaudia tecum habere potero si credens Christum amittas culturas idolorum. Christus enim me misit ad istam provinciam in qua non parvum populum ei adquisivi.' Aegeas dixit: 'Ideo te sacrificare compello, ut isti qui per te decepti sunt populi relinquant vanitatem tuae doctrinae et ipsi diis offerant grata libamina. Nulla enim remansit in Achaia civitas in qua non templa deorum derelicta sint et deserta. Nunc ergo per te iterum restauretur cultura deorum, ut et dii qui contra te irati sunt placari possint, et in nostra possis amicitia permanere. Sin alias, diversa pro defensione deorum patieris supplicia, et post omnia crucis quam laudasti patibulo suspensus deficies.'

267–75 *Passio Andreae*, Bonnet, 20.6–21.7:

Andreas respondit: 'Audi filius mortis et stipula aeternis parata incendiis, audi me servum domini et apostolum Iesu Christi. Nunc usque mitius tecum egi censura fidei, ut rationis capax veritatis defensor effectus. . . . Sed quia in impudentia tua perdurans me putas minas tuas posse formidare, quidquid tibi videtur in suppliciis magis excogita. Tanto enim meo regi ero acceptior, quanto pro eius nomine fuero permanens in tormenta confessor.'

276–87 *Passio Andreae*, Bonnet, 22.1–23.7:

Tunc Aegeas iussit eum flagellis caedi extensum, quique cum septem terniones transisset, elevatus est atque adductus ante eum. Cui Aegeas dixit: 'Audi me Andrea, et ab effusione tui sanguinis consilium revoca. Quod si non feceris, crucis te faciam interire patibulo.' Andreas respondit: 'Ego crucis Christi servus sum, et crucis tropheum optare potius debeo quam timere. [Tu] autem cruciatus aeternus qui debetur poteris evadere, si postquam probaveris perseverantiam meam vel sic credideris Christum. Ego enim de tuo interitu timeo, non de mea passione conturbor. Passio enim mea aut unius diei spatium occupat aut duorum [aut ut multum trium]. Tuus autem cruciatus nec per milia annorum potest pervenire ad finem. Unde desine iam miserias tuas augmentare, et ignem tibi tu ipse aeternum accendere.'

288–95 *Passio Andreae*, Bonnet, 23.8–24.6:

Tunc indignatus Aegeas cruci eum affigi praecepit, mandans hoc quaestionariis ut ligatis pedibus et manibus quasi in eculeo tenderetur, ne clavis affixus cito deficeret, sed cruciaretur potius longo cruciatu. Cumque eum carnifices ducerent, concursus factus est populorum clamantium ac dicentium: 'Iustus homo et amicus dei quid fecit, ut ducatur ad crucem.' Andreas vero rogabat populum ut non impedirent passionem eius, gaudens enim et exultans ibat et a doctrina non cessans.

295–307 *Passio Andreae*, Bonnet, 24.7–26.1:

Cumque pervenisset ad locum ubi crux parata erat, videns eam a longe exclamavit voce magna dicens: 'Salve crux, quae in corpore Christi dedicata es et ex [membris eius tanquam] margaritis ornata; antequam te ascenderet dominus timorem terrenum habuisti, modo vero amorem caelestem obtinens pro voto susciperis. . . . Securus ergo et gaudens venio ad te; ita ut et tu exultans suscipias me discipulum eius qui pependit in te, quia amator tuus semper fui et desideravi amplecti te. O bona crux quae decorem et pulchritudinem de membris domini suscepisti, diu desiderata, sollicite amata, sine intermissione quaesita et aliquando iam concupiscenti animo praeparata accipe me ab hominibus et redde me magistro meo ut per te me recipiat qui per te redemit me.

308–15 *Passio Andreae*, Bonnet, 26.1–27.4:

Et haec dicens exspoliavit se et vestimenta sua tradidit carnificibus, qui accedentes levaverunt eum in crucem et extendentes funibus totum corpus eius sicut eis iussum fuerat suspenderunt. Adstantes vero turbae ad viginti milia hominum, inter quos frater Aegeae nomine Stratocles simul clamabat cum populo iniusto iudicio sanctum virum hoc pati. Sanctus vero Andreas confortabat mentes credentium Christum, hortabatur tollerantiam temporalem, docens nihil esse dignum passionis ad remunerationis compensationem aeternam.

315–23 *Passio Andreae*, Bonnet, 28.1–29.5:

Interea vadit omnis populus cum clamore ad domum Aegeae omnes pariter clamantes dicebant virum sanctum, pudicum, ornatum moribus, bonum doctorem, pium, modestum, rationabilem, non debere hoc pati, sed debere deponi de cruce, quia iam secunda die in cruce positus veritatem praedicare non cessat. Tunc Aegeas pavescens populum promittens se eum deponere simul coepit ire.

323–30 *Passio Andreae*, Bonnet, 29.5–31.4:

Quem videns sanctus Andreas dixit: 'Quid tu ad nos Aegea venisti? Si vis credere Christum, sicut promisi aperietur tibi via indulgentiae; si autem venisti ad hoc tantum ut me solvas, ego penitus hinc de ista cruce vivens in corpore deponi non potero. Iam enim regem meum video, iam adoro, iam in conspectu eius consisto. Et tuis miseriis doleo, quia paratus te expectat aeternus interitus. Curre pro te miser, dum adhuc potes, ne tunc incipias velle cum non poteris.'

331–7 *Passio Andreae*, Bonnet, 32.1–34.2:

Mittentes autem manus ad crucem carnifices non poterant penitus contingere eum . . . Stupebant enim brachia eorum quicumque se extendissent ad solvendum eum. Tunc voce magna sanctus Andreas dixit: 'Domine Iesu Christe, magister bone, iube me de ista cruce non deponi, nisi ante spiritum meum susceperis.' Et cum haec dixisset videntibus cunctis splendor nimius sicut fulgor de caelo veniens, ita circumdedit eum ut penitus prae ipso splendore oculi eum non possent humani aspicere.

337–51 *Passio Andreae*, Bonnet, 34.2–36.2:

> Cumque permansisset splendor fere dimidiae horae spatio, abscedente lumine emisit spiritum, simul cum ipso lumine pergens ad dominum, cui est gloria in saecula saeculorum. Aegeas vero areptus a daemonio antequam perveniret ad domum suam in via, in conspectu omnium a daemonio vexatus expiravit. Frater vero eius tenens corpus sancti Andreae evasit. Tantus autem timor invasit universos ut nullus remaneret qui non crederet salvatori nostro deo.

Lines 347–8 come from *Passio Andreae*, Bonnet, 1.1–2.1:

> Passionem sancti Andreae apostoli quam oculis nostris vidimus omnes presbiteri et diacones ecclesiarum Achaiae scribimus universis ecclesiis.

These final lines, esp. 341–51, seem to be written in the rhythmical and alliterative style that normally marks Ælfric's later work.[6] In the final sentence, 349–51, Ælfric was evidently recasting part of the original ending preserved in MS A, printed at App. A2.4–7, and although this sentence is less clearly alliterative than the rest of the final section it is noticeable that in rewriting Ælfric has strengthened the two-stress pattern and substituted the poetic word *metod* (cf CH I.35.285 and note) for the original *scyppend*.

39 FIRST SUNDAY IN ADVENT

The Gospel reading for the first Sunday in Advent was Matthew 21.1–9, on Christ's entry into Jerusalem,[1] but Ælfric chose to use this, more appropriately, on Palm Sunday itself (CH I.14). Instead he used for this occasion the epistle for the day, Romans 13.11–17, St Paul's warning that the hour has come and it is time to arise. It was an appropriate text to announce the second coming of Christ and the end of the world, a traditional theme of Advent and the major concern of the next homily, but in this case Ælfric's treatment is mainly at the tropological level, dealing with the preparation for Christmas and the celebration of Christ's first advent. As originally written it was a very short homily, and Ælfric later[2] added at the end a slightly revised version of the discussion of Antichrist and the end of the world originally used in the preface to the Series (see line 111, and above, commentary on CH I.praef.). Though not closely related to any of the issues discussed in the original homily, the addition was

[6] Pope, who has given the fullest account of the alliterative style, casts doubt (p.113 and n.2) on the use of the form at all in the First Series, but the whole of the passage 341–51 falls naturally into pairs of two-stressed phrases, almost all of them linked by alliteration (*Egeas . . . atelicum, hamwerd . . . huse, awedde . . . aworpen, manna . . . mid, gewat . . . worulde . . . wælhreow, heold . . . halgan, micelre . . . moste, micel oga . . . eallum þam mennisce, belaf . . . gelyfde*, etc.).

[1] Lenker, p. 342.

[2] Clemoes' arguments would suggest a date of approximately 1005; see *CH I*, pp. 161–2.

clearly appropriate to the expectations and celebrations of the second coming associated with the Advent period.

The sources if any are hard to find. Ælfric's usual homiletic source-book, Paul the Deacon's homiliary, had nothing on the epistle for the day. Förster noted some points of overlap with Smaragdus's discussion of the epistle, though they are brief and not wholly compelling;[3] as far as I know no further suggestions have been made. There are some points of similarity with Haymo's commentary on the Epistles (PL 117), and some with Rabanus Maurus's commentary (PL 111), though there is no reason to suppose that Ælfric knew the latter. There are however some striking similarities with the commentary on the epistles by Pelagius (which often went under the name of Jerome in the Middle Ages) and the revised version of this by Cassiodorus (printed as the work of Primasius in PL 68). Though in its pure form the work of Pelagius has survived in very few cases, and may already have been rare in Ælfric's time, it seems to have had a wide circulation in adapted forms[4] and to have been used by Haymo and Smaragdus, so it is not unlikely that Ælfric could have known it in some form. There is some slight evidence, at 39–41, that he may have used a version containing early interpolations by one Iohannes Diaconus.[5] There are perhaps, too, sufficient similarities to Haymo's exposition to suggest that Ælfric read that as well; but there is little evidence for Smaragdus. There is also much independent quotation from the Bible, especially the epistles.

Sources and Notes

The following texts are cited below:

1. Cassiodorus, *Commentaria in Epistolas S. Pauli*, printed under Primasius, PL 68, cols. 415–794.
2. Haymo of Auxerre, *Expositio in Pauli Epistolas*, PL 117, cols. 361–938.
3. *Pelagius's Expositions of Thirteen Epistles of St Paul*, ed. A. Souter, Texts and Studies IX, 3 parts (Cambridge, 1922–31). The main text is in pt. 2, *Text and Apparatus Criticus* (1926) and the interpolations by John the Deacon, referred to as 'Ps-Jerome', are printed separately in pt. 3, *Pseudo-Jerome Interpolations* (1931).
4. Smaragdus, *Collectiones in Evangelia et Epistolas*, PL 102, cols. 512–3.

[3] Förster 1894, pp. 40–41.

[4] See Souter, *Pelagius's Expositions*, part 1, *Introduction* (for details, see list of texts cited below) and A. Souter, *The Earliest Latin Commentaries on the Epistles of St Paul* (Oxford, 1927).

[5] See Souter, *Pelagius's Expositions*, part 3, *Pseudo-Jerome Interpolations* (for details, see list of texts cited below), for the text and discussion of these interpolations, and G. Morin, 'Jean Diacre et le pseudo-Jérôme sur les épîtres de S. Paulin,' *RB* 27 (1910), 113–7, for the attribution.

6–13 Ælfric is presumably here referring to the use of readings from the prophets in the daily office, not the mass to which the laity had access, since it is only in the office that Old Testament readings were used. In his letter to the monks of Eynsham he mentions only reading from Isaiah in the Advent period (Jones 1998, §75), and Isaiah does indeed provide all the readings in the Leofric Collectar,[6] for the first two Sundays in Advent at least, apart from Romans 13.11–14. By *ealle godes þeowan* he presumably means secular clerics as well as monks, since he makes it clear in his pastoral letters that he expects the former as well to celebrate the offices. In citing the sayings of the prophets and the 'harmonious songs of praise' as foretelling Christ's advent he is perhaps recalling his interpretation of the two fishes in CH I.12.102–4:

> Ða twegen fixas getacnodon. sealmsang. and þæra witigena cwydas: an ðære gecydde. and bodode cristes tocyme mid sealmsange: and oðer mid witegunge.

15–16 Mt 28.20: *Et ecce ego vobiscum sum omnibus diebus, usque ad consummationem saeculi.*

20–25 Ælfric seems here to be speaking as a minister of God to other clerics—'We ministers of God strengthen our faith . . . and exhort ourselves . . .' . But the reason may simply be that the point he is making applies only to clerics, since the services in question are those of the office.

26–7 For the phrase 'to the Romans and also to all faithful people': cf Haymo (*Expositio*, PL 117, 483C): *Dicit apostolus Romanis et omnibus credentibus, etiam necdum credentibus.*

27–33 Rom 13.11–14:

> (11) Et hoc scientes tempus: quia hora est iam nos de somno surgere. Nunc enim propior est nostra salus, quam cum credidimus. (12) Nox praecessit, dies autem appropinquavit. Abiiciamus ergo opera tenebrarum, et induamur arma lucis. (13) Sicut in die honeste ambulemus: non in comesationibus et ebrietatibus, non in cubilibus et inpudicitiis, non in contentione et aemulatione. (14) sed induimini Dominum Iesum Christum.

34–6 The sleep of sloth and lack of faith: Pelagius relates the sleep to sloth and ignorance (Pelagius, *Expositiones*, 104.12: *De somno inertiae et ignorantiae*), and Smaragdus to sloth (*Collectiones*, PL 102, 512C: *In somno desidiae*); cf too *nox est infidelitas* (*Collectiones* , PL 102, 512D). Only Haymo identifies it also with lack of faith (*Expositio*, PL 117, 483C):

> Quia hora est sive tempus, iam nos de somno pigritiae et desidiae surgere, de somno quoque infidelitatis et vitiorum atque ignorantiae.

[6] *The Leofric Collectar*, ed. E. S. Dewick and W. H. Frere, 2 vols., Henry Bradshaw Society 45 and 56 (London, 1914–21).

37–9 Pelagius, *Expositiones*, 104.8–11:

Hora est ut ad perfectiora tendatis: non enim debetis semper parvuli esse et lactantes, sicut alibi idem dicit: 'Etenim deberetis magistri [*var.* perfecti] esse propter tempus,' et cetera (Hebr 5.12).

39–41 Possibly prompted by Pelagius as interpolated by Iohannes Diaconus (Souter, pt. 3, 24.19–21):

Item hortatur apostolus, ut tenebrosa et somni torpore depressa opera relinquentes, in lumine, hoc est, in bonis operibus ambulemus.

41–4 The meaning is not entirely clear, but Ælfric seems to be elaborating the image of the light to refer both to the incarnation and to the present state of the virtuous. Something resembling the second part of Ælfric's explanation is to be found in Haymo (*Expositio*, PL 117, 483C–4A):

Ista nox quotidie praecedit in electis, et ad vitam aeternam praedestinatis appropinquat dies, illuminatio videlicet fidei, cognitio sanctae Trinitatis, et splendor virtutum, quoniam dum transeunt quotidie per mortem corporis ab aerumnis huius saeculi, in lucem supernae claritatis colliguntur.

44–55 Ælfric offers two interpretations for the second part of verse 11: salvation is closer for individuals because they grow in understanding and faith, but also because both the individual end of life and the general end is always getting closer. Something like those two senses are set out by Smaragdus (*Collectiones*, PL 102, 512D):

Verum sciendum est adventum lucis huius, et diei duplici modo accipiendum. Generaliter omnibus, et unicuique specialiter. Generaliter cum dies futuri saeculi advenerit, ad cuius comparationem praesentis huius mundi spatium tenebrae appellantur. Singulariter unicuique, cum Christus in corde est, diem illi facit, cum ignorantia tenebras illi generat.

But for the wording of the first part, lines 44–6, Ælfric seems to be closest to Pelagius (*Expositiones*, 104.14–15):

Scientia proficiente, propior est nostra salus, quam [*var.* quando primum] credidimus.

He then quotes Ps 83.8, *Ibunt de virtute in virtutem*, which is not cited by any of his possible sources and seems to refer back to the image of the journey at 43. Then, in 50–55, he gives the second interpretation of the coming of the day or light, viz. Christ's second coming or advent (the first or *generaliter* sense of Smaragdus). Cf too Haymo (*Expositio*, PL 117, 483D):

Dum finis mundi magis ac magis appropinquat, vita futura et salus aeterna magis ac magis festinat.

But both refer to the end of the world, not the individual end which Ælfric also signals at 50. At 51–2 there is an echo of 2 Cor 5.10:

Omnes enim nos manifestari oportet ante tribunal Christi, ut referat unusquisque propria corporis, prout gessit, sive bonum sive malum.

(Cf the rendering at CH II.19.239–41.)

56–61 Possibly an expansion of Pelagius, *Expositiones*, 104.16–17: *Comparat diei scientiam et ignorantiam nocti.*

63–8 Both Pelagius and Cassiodorus interpret the works of darkness as ignorance, Smaragdus and Haymo as sin. Only Haymo refers to the devil (*Expositio*, PL 117, 484B):

> Induamur arma lucis, hoc est, undique muniamus nos omnibus virtutibus, ut simus protecti et tuti contra adversa diaboli.

But none of the texts agree with Ælfric in citing Jac 4.7–8:

> (7) Resistite autem diabolo, et fugiet a vobis. (8) Appropinquate Deo, et appropinquabit vobis.

On Ælfric's error in implying that this is a quotation from St Paul, see Sarah Larrat Keefer, 'An interesting error in Ælfric's Dominica I in Adventu Domini', *Neophilologus* 60 (1976), 138–9. The weapons of light are defined as good works by Cassiodorus and Rabanus, as virtues by Smaragdus and Haymo. Ælfric's 'works of righteousness and truth' is perhaps prompted by Pelagius's *luminis opera* (*Expositiones*, 104.21) or Cassiodorus's *arma scientiae, hoc est opera bona* (*Comm. Epist.*, PL 68, 498B).

70–75 Pelagius, *Expositiones*, 105.2–5:

> Sicut lux diei prohibet unum quemque agere quod nocte libere committebat, ita et scientia nos prohibet legis mandata contemnere. Sive: quod sciamus nos a Deo semper videri.

Cassiodorus is less close but similar.

75–9 Pelagius, *Expositiones*, 105.7–10:

> Comisatio est mensae collatio: nos vero habemus spiritale convivium, [apostolo] dicente: 'cum convenitis, unus quisque [vestrum] psalmum habet' (1 Cor 14.26), et cetera. Ebrietatem vero pernitiosam esse et luxuriae materiam.

Cf too Cassiodorus, *Comm. Epist.*, PL 68, 498C, though this is less close:

> Comessatio est collatio convivii. Nos igitur non tales, sed spirituales de Apostolo habemus comessationes. Cum convenitis, inquit, invicem, unusquisque vestrum psalmum habet, et reliqua.

Ælfric's *halwende lar on muþe* presumably renders the next phrase of the quotation from 1 Cor 14.26, *doctrinam habet*, while his *hæbbe* presumably renders a variant *habeat* for *habet* (which occurs for instance in PL 30's version of this passage, at 706C.) Ælfric seems to understand 1 Cor 14.26 as a reference, figuratively at least, to a meal, an assembly that involves eating and drinking, since he uses it to comment on the phrase *na on oferætum and druncennyssum*; *gastlice gereordunge* presumably means 'spiritual meals or banquets', and when he translates Paul's *convenitis* as *eow to gereorde gadriað* he presumably means 'when you gather for a meal'. Modern translations do not seem to interpret it as a meal, and in context it does not sound at all like one, but Pelagius seems to have understood it in the same way as Ælfric. The association may have been prompted by the *Cum convenitis ad manducandum* . . . of 1 Cor 11.33, which is a meal.

79–80 Prov 31.4: *Quia nullum secretum est ubi regnat ebrietas.*

81–2 Phil 3.19: *Quorum finis interitus, quorum Deus venter est, et gloria in confusione ipsorum.*

83–5 There is nothing resembling this reference to marriage in the Latin texts: Pelagius and Cassiodorus pass over the phrase, the others have a little on sexual licence but no reference to marriage and nothing similar. I am not sure what Ælfric means by 'let there be honourable marriage amongst the faithful, so that no fornication or uncleanness be *named* in God's church'—perhaps 'spoken of'.

85–93 No parallels in the Latin commentaries. Line 86 refers to Mt 5.9: *Beati pacifici, quoniam filii Dei vocabuntur.* For 88–9, *anda is derigendlic leahtor*, cf Pelagius, *Expositiones*, 105.13: *Contentionem et invidiam criminosas esse* . . . (citing the epistle of St. James). Cf the treatment of *anda* at CH II.4.39 ff.

95–6 Gal 3.27 [cited in the same context by Haymo, *Expositio*, PL 117, 485B]: *Quicumque enim in Christo baptizati estis, Christum induistis.*

98–108 Col 3.12–17 (not cited by any of the Latin texts):

> (12) Induite vos ergo, sicut electi Dei sancti et dilecti, viscera misericordiae, benignitatem, humilitatem, modestiam, patientiam; (13) subportantes invicem et donantes vobis ipsis si quis adversus aliquem habet querellam, sicut et Dominus donavit vobis ita et vos. (14) Super omnia autem haec caritatem quod est vinculum perfectionis. (15) Et pax Christi exultet in cordibus vestris in qua et vocati estis in uno corpore; et grati estote. (16) Verbum Christi habitet in vobis abundanter in omni sapientia docentes et commonentes vosmet ipsos psalmis, hymnis, canticis spiritalibus in gratia cantantes in cordibus vestris Deo. (17) Omne quodcumque facitis in verbo aut in opere omnia in nomine Domini Iesu gratias agentes Deo et Patri per ipsum.

40 SECOND SUNDAY IN ADVENT

A homily on the end of the world and the last judgement, based on the Gospel reading for the day, Luke 21.25–33. Ælfric's main source, as he indicates, is Gregory the Great, specifically the first of his homilies on the Gospels, which is given in Paul the Deacon's homiliary.[1] But he draws on a number of other historical and exegetical works, especially in exploring the complex eschatological issues associated with the fate of those living at the time of the end (lines

[1] Förster 1894 and Smetana 1959, p. 195; Smetana also suggested (1961, p. 467) the use of Haymo.

131–55), and writes with considerable authority and assurance on points which others had found difficult and controversial. On the question of the imminence of the end he is inclined to be cautious, suggesting a longer time-scheme than Gregory would imply (note that Gregory mentions current natural disasters as a prelude to the end of the world, but Ælfric offers no equivalent), discounting Haymo's view that the signs in the heavens had already appeared and hesitating noticeably in his conclusion. His firm insistence at the outset of the homily that he is quoting Gregory's words on the imminence of the end (without ever signalling at what point, if at all, his own voice takes over) adds a further level of ambiguity to his own position; Gregory had, after all, been writing four centuries earlier when he said that the end was at hand. If the homilies were written in something like the order in which they appear in the collection, this one may have closely preceded the writing of the preface in which Ælfric draws attention to the imminence of Antichrist.

Sources and Notes

The following texts are cited below:

1. Ælfric's *Excerpts* from the *Prognosticon Futuri Saeculi* of Julian of Toledo, ed. Gatch 1977, pp. 129–46.
2. Bede, *Commentarius in Lucam*, ed. D. Hurst, CCSL 120 (Turnhout, 1960), pp. 5–425.
3. Bede, *De Natura Rerum*, ed. C.W. Jones, CCSL 123A (Turnhout, 1975), pp. 189–234.
4. Bede, *De Temporum Ratione*, ed. C. W. Jones in *Bedae Opera De Temporibus*, CCSL 123B (Turnhout, 1977), pp. 263–460.
5. Gregory the Great, *Homiliae in Evangelia*, PL 76, Hom. 1, cols. 1077–81.
6. Gregory the Great, *Moralia siue Expositio in Iob*, ed. M. Adriaen, 3 vols., CCSL 143–143B (Turnhout, 1979–85).
7. Haymo of Auxerre, *Homiliae de Tempore*, PL 118, Hom. 2, cols. 17–25.
8. Haymo (or Remigius) of Auxerre, *Commentarius in Apocalypsin*, PL 117, cols. 937–1220.
9. Julian of Toledo, *Prognosticon Futuri Saeculi*, ed. J. Hillgarth, CCSL 115 (Turnhout, 1976), pp. 11–126.

3–19 Lc 21.25–33:

(25) Et erunt signa in sole et luna et stellis, et in terris pressura gentium prae confusione sonitus maris et fluctuum; (26) arescentibus hominibus prae timore et expectatione quae supervenient universo orbi. Nam virtutes caelorum movebuntur. (27) Et tunc videbunt Filium hominis venientem in nube cum potestate magna et maiestate. (28) His autem fieri incipientibus respicite et levate capita vestra quoniam appropinquat redemptio vestra. (29) Et dixit illis similitudinem. Videte ficulneam et omnes arbores. (30)

Cum producunt iam ex se fructum, scitis quoniam prope est aestas. (31) Ita et vos cum videritis haec fieri scitote quoniam prope est regnum Dei. (32) Amen dico vobis quia non praeteribit generatio haec donec omnia fiant. (33) Caelum et terra transibunt verba autem mea non transient.

20–26 Gregory, Hom. 1, PL 76, 1077C:

Dominus ac Redemptor noster, fratres carissimi, paratos nos invenire desiderans, senescentem mundum quae mala sequantur denuntiat, ut nos ab eius amore compescat. Appropinquantem eius terminum quantae percussiones praeveniant innotescit, ut si Deum metuere in tranquillitate non volumus, vicinum eius iudicium vel percussionibus attriti timeamus.

26–31 Gregory, Hom. 1, PL 76, 1077C–8B:

Huic etenim lectioni sancti Evangelii, quam modo vestra fraternitas audivit, paulo superius Dominus praemisit, dicens: 'Exsurget gens contra gentem, et regnum adversus regnum; et erunt terrae motus magni per loca, et pestilentiae, et fames' (Lc 21.10). Et quibusdam interpositis, hoc quod modo audistis adiunxit: 'Erunt signa in sole, et luna, et stellis, et in terris pressura gentium, prae confusione sonitus maris et fluctuum' (Lc 21.25).

32–7 Cf Gregory, Hom. 1, PL 76, 1078B:

Ex quibus profecto omnibus alia iam facta cernimus, alia e proximo ventura formidamus. Nam gentem super gentem exsurgere, earumque pressuram terris insistere, plus iam in nostris temporibus cernimus quam in codicibus legimus. Quod terrae motus urbes innumeras subruat, ex aliis mundi partibus scitis quam frequenter audivimus.

The curious detail of the thirteen cities destroyed by earthquake in the time of Tiberius, which does not appear in Gregory or any of the other commentaries on this text that Ælfric is likely to have consulted, and which scarcely qualifies as a recent sign, is mentioned in the *Chronicon* of Jerome (ed. R. Helm, in *Eusebius Werke*, vol. 7, GCS 47 (Berlin, 1984), p. 172): *xiii urbes terrae motu corruerunt*. The detail also appears, no doubt borrowed from Jerome, in the *Epitoma Chronicon* attributed to Prosper of Aquitaine (ed. T. Mommsen, MGH, Auctores Antiquissimi 9 (Berlin, 1892), pp. 385–485, at 408): *Huius imperii anno quinto tredecim urbes terrae motu corruerunt*. Neither text is otherwise known to have been used by Ælfric. In the face of Gregory's reference to recent times Ælfric seems to be deliberately extending the time-scheme that is at issue.

37–51 Cf Gregory, Hom. 1, PL 76, 1078BC:

Pestilentias sine cessatione patimur. Signa vero in sole, et luna, et stellis, adhuc aperte minime videmus, sed quia et haec non longe sint, ex ipsa iam aeris immutatione colligimus.

Gregory goes on to mention the fiery armies seen in the heavens before the invasion of the Goths. Ælfric's discussion (lines 39–46) of signs in the sun, moon and stars which are natural phenomena and should decidedly not be confused with the signs that are due to precede the end of time seems to refer to the more specific description of those signs in Mt 24.29–30 which he goes on to quote at lines 46–51:

> (29) Statim autem post tribulationem dierum illorum sol obscurabitur, et luna non dabit lumen suum, et stellae cadent de caelo, et virtutes caelorum commovebuntur. (30) Et tunc parebit signum Filii hominis in caelo, et tunc plangent omnes tribus terrae.

That the sign of the son of man is the cross is a detail that figures in Ælfric's excerpts from Julian of Toledo's *Prognosticon* (*Excerpts*, 204–5, from *Prognosticon*, III.v.29–31). The verses from Matthew are also quoted in support by Bede in his commentary on Luke and by Haymo in his homily on the Luke text (Haymo, Hom. 2, PL 118, 18C); it may have been Haymo's subsequent remark that such signs had already frequently been seen (*Signa in sole et luna et stellis, a quibusdam frequenter visa esse referuntur*, Hom. 2, PL 118, 19D; and again, *praedicta sunt signa in sole et luna et stellis, impleta sunt*, Hom. 2, PL 118, 24C) which in part prompted Ælfric to make his rebuttal and explain the phenomena in question. The eclipse of the sun by the moon, and of the moon by the earth's shadow, is discussed in similar words in Ælfric's *De Temporibus Anni* (3.15 and 16), where his sources seem to be Bede:

> [*De Natura Rerum*, 22.2–4] Solem interventu lunae, lunamque terrae obiectu nobis perhibent occultari. Sed solis defectum non nisi novissima primave fieri luna, quod vocant coitum, lunae autem non nisi plena. [*De Temporum Ratione*, 7.17–20] quam videlicet umbram noctis ad aeris usque et aetheris confinium philosophi dicunt exaltari, et . . . lunam . . . aliquando contingi atque obscurari.

Comets are discussed similarly at *De Temporibus Anni*, 9.13, drawing on Bede again:

> [*De Natura Rerum*, 24.2–8] Cometae sunt stellae flammis crinitae, repente nascentes, regni mutationem, aut pestilentiam aut bella, vel ventos aestusve, portendentes. . . . Brevissimum quo cernerentur spatium septem dierum adnotatum est, longissimum lxxx.

In omitting Gregory's reference to the fiery armies and silently rebutting Haymo's identification of the apocalyptic signs with eclipses and comets, Ælfric is perhaps betraying a concern to present the end as less imminent than it was for either Gregory or Haymo.

51–4 Cf Gregory, Hom. 1, PL 76, 1078C:

> Confusio autem maris et fluctuum necdum nova exorta est. Sed cum multa praenuntiata iam completa sint, dubium non est quin sequantur etiam pauca quae restant.

As they stand in the printed text, lines 51–2 presumably mean 'the turbulence of the sea and the noise of the waves have not yet arisen in unaccustomed form'. The reading of some other manuscripts allows a sense 'the turbulence of the sea and the noise(s) of the waves have not yet generally arisen', but MS A has the support of the other generally reliable manuscript, K, and Q's *swegunge* is unlikely as a np.

55–64 Gregory, Hom. 1, PL 76, 1078C–79A:

> Haec nos, fratres carissimi, idcirco dicimus, ut ad cautelae studium vestrae mentes evigilent, ne securitate torpeant, ne ignorantia languescant, sed semper eas et timor sollicitet, et in bono opere sollicitudo confirmet, pensantes hoc quod Redemptoris nostri voce subiungitur: 'Arescentibus hominibus prae timore et exspectatione quae supervenient universo orbi. Nam virtutes coelorum movebuntur.' Quid etenim Dominus virtutes coelorum nisi angelos, archangelos, thronos, dominationes, principatus et potestates appellat, quae in adventu districti iudicis nostris tunc oculis visibiliter apparebunt, ut districte tunc a nobis exigant hoc, quod nos modo invisibilis conditor aequanimiter portat?

65–9 Christ as son of man. There is no parallel in Gregory, but a faint one in Haymo (Hom. 2, PL 118, 22A):

> Filium ergo hominis in iudicio visuri sunt, quia in forma servi, id est in forma hominis quam pro nobis assumpsit, ad iudicium venturus est. . . .

For the point at 68–9, that Christ was uniquely *mannes bearn*, see my note on CH I.3.73–4.

69–73 Gregory, Hom. 1, PL 76, 1079A:

> Ubi et subditur: 'Et tunc videbunt Filium hominis venientem in nubibus cum potestate magna et maiestate.' Ac si aperte diceretur: In potestate et maiestate visuri sunt quem in humilitate positum audire noluerunt, ut virtutem eius tanto tunc districtius sentiant, quanto nunc cervicem cordis ad eius patientiam non inclinant.

73–87 Gregory, Hom. 1, PL 76, 1079ABC:

> Sed quia haec contra reprobos dicta sunt, mox ad electorum consolationem verba vertuntur. Nam et subditur: 'His autem fieri incipientibus, respicite et levate vos capita vestra, quoniam appropinquat redemptio vestra.' Ac si aperte Veritas electos suos admoneat, dicens: Cum plagae mundi crebrescunt, cum terror iudicii virtutibus commotis ostenditur, levate capita, id est exhilarate corda, quia dum finitur mundus, cui amici non estis, prope fit redemptio quam quaesistis. In scriptura etenim sacra saepe caput pro mente ponitur, quia sicut capite reguntur membra, ita et cogitationes mente disponuntur. Levare itaque capita est mentes nostras ad gaudia patriae coelestis erigere. Qui ergo Deum diligunt ex mundi fine gaudere atque hilarescere iubentur, quia videlicet eum quem amant mox inveniunt, dum transit is quem non amaverunt.

88–104 Gregory, Hom. 1, PL 76, 1079BCD:

> Absit enim ut fidelis quisque qui Deum videre desiderat de mundi percussionibus lugeat, quem finiri eisdem suis percussionibus non ignorat.

Scriptum namque est: 'Quicunque voluerit amicus esse saeculi huius, inimicus Dei constituitur' (Jac 4.4). Qui ergo appropinquante mundi fine non gaudet, amicum se illius esse testatur, atque per hoc inimicus Dei esse convincitur. Sed absit hoc a fidelium cordibus, absit ab his qui et esse aliam vitam per fidem credunt, et eam per operationem diligunt. Ex mundi enim destructione lugere eorum est qui radices cordis in eius amore plantaverunt, qui sequentem vitam non quaerunt, qui illam neque esse suspicantur. Nos autem qui coelestis patriae gaudia aeterna cognovimus, festinare ad ea quantocius debemus. Optandum nobis est citius pergere, atque ad illam breviore via pervenire. Quibus enim malis mundus non urgetur? Quae nos tristitia, quae adversitas non angustat? Quid est vita mortalis, nisi via? Et quale sit, fratres mei, perpendite, in labore viae lassescere, et tamen eamdem viam nolle finiri.

108–10 Gregory, Hom. 1, PL 76, 1080A:

Quibus profecto verbis ostenditur quia fructus mundi ruina est. Ad hoc enim crescit, ut cadat. Ad hoc germinat, ut quaecunque germinaverit, cladibus consumat.

110–20 The discussion of the world's youth and age is evidently prompted by a slightly later passage in Gregory, Hom. 1, PL 76, 1080C:

Sicut enim in iuventute viget corpus, forte et incolume manet pectus, torosa cervix, plena sunt bronchia; in annis autem senilibus statura curvatur, cervix exsiccata deponitur, frequentibus suspiriis pectus urgetur, virtus deficit, loquentis verba anhelitus intercidit; nam etsi languor desit, plerumque sensibus ipsa sua salus aegritudo est: ita mundus in annis prioribus velut in iuventute viguit, ad propagandam humani generis prolem robustus fuit, salute corporum viridis, opulentia rerum pinguis; at nunc ipsa sua senectute deprimitur, et quasi ad vicinam mortem molestiis crescentibus urgetur.

But Ælfric's wording is significantly different at points. His phrase *langsum on life. stille on langsumere sibbe* seems to reflect the words *erat vita longa . . . tranquillitas in diuturna pace* which Gregory uses in another passage on the world's youth and age (Hom. 28, PL 76, 1212D). J. E. Cross[2] cites the latter passage as a source for the references to the topos in Blickling homily 10 and Ælfric's *Passio Mauricii* (LS 28.160 ff) and it may be that Ælfric was combining the two passages from memory; or that he was using a variant text of Gregory's first homily which contained elements from his twenty-eighth.

121–4 Gregory, Hom. 1, PL 76, 1080CD:

Nolite ergo, fratres mei, diligere quem videtis diu stare non posse. Praecepta apostolica in animo ponite, quibus nos admonet, dicens:

[2] J. E. Cross, 'Gregory, Blickling Homily X and Ælfric's Passio S. Mauricii on the world's youth and age', *Neuphilologische Mitteilungen* 66 (1965), 327–30.

'Nolite diligere mundum, neque ea quae in mundo sunt, quia si quis diligit mundum, non est caritas patris in eo' (1 Jn 2.15).

124–6 Gregory, Hom. 1, PL 76, 1080A:

Bene autem regnum Dei aestati comparatur, quia tunc moeroris nostri nubila transeunt, et vitae dies aeterni solis claritate fulgescunt.

127–31 Gregory, Hom. 1, PL 76, 1080A:

Quae omnia sub magna certitudine confirmantur, cum sententia subiungitur qua dicitur: Amen dico vobis, quia non praeteribit generatio haec, donec omnia fiant. Coelum et terra transibunt, verba autem mea non transibunt.

The interpretation is not from Gregory, who deals only with the latter part of the verse, but both Bede and Haymo suggest that the *generatio* could be either the Jews or mankind in general; Bede, *Comm. Luc.*, 6.312–3:

Generationem autem aut omne hominum genus dicit aut specialiter Iudaeorum.

Haymo, Hom. 2, PL 118, 24B:

Generatio autem haec, si de Iudaeorum gente intelligatur, non praeteribit, ut plures illorum non sint, quoadusque omnia quae a Domino praedicta sunt, impleantur.

131–47 This section has no parallel in Gregory and it is hard at first sight to see how it connects with the preceding material. The phrase *be þysum andgite* seems on reflection to refer not to the point about the Jews which Ælfric has just made but to the other meaning of *generatio* offered by Bede and Haymo, mankind in general, an interpretation which Ælfric belatedly refers to at 142. Neither Bede nor Haymo comment on the words beyond the brief explanation above, but for Ælfric they evidently raised important issues. In part he seems anxious to repudiate a notion that humanity might simply die out before the world ends—a view that seems to play no part in earlier patristic exegesis but might well have been familiar to those who knew Old English poems such as *The Wanderer*. But pursuing this argument, and citing texts in support, leads him on to the complex eschatological issue of the fate of those who are still living when the day of judgement comes (an issue no doubt of particular moment in his time). The quotation from St Paul, lines 132–6, is from 1 Thess 4.16–18:

(16) Quoniam ipse Dominus in iussu et in voce archangeli et in tuba Dei descendet de caelo, et mortui qui in Christo sunt resurgent primi. (17) Deinde nos qui vivimus qui relinquimur simul rapiemur cum illis in nubibus obviam Domino in aera, et sic semper cum Domino erimus. (18) Itaque consolamini invicem in verbis istis.

It is followed by Mt 24.31:

Et mittet angelos suos cum tuba et voce magna, et congregabunt electos eius a quattuor ventis, a summis coelorum usque ad terminos eorum.

(Cook (1898, p. 167, n.2) suggests that there is influence from Mc 13.27: *a summo terrae usque ad summum caeli.*) The two quotations also occur together in Ælfric's excerpts from the *Prognosticon* of Julian of Toledo (*Excerpts*, 186–90 and 197–9), where they are used, as in the *Prognosticon* itself, as part of the narrative of the last judgement, not apparently in support of any particular point of doctrine. Haymo also cites the two passages together, in his commentary on the epistle to the Thessalonians (PL 117, 771D), but only to support the detail of the trumpet sounding. Ælfric's two references to *þysum andgite* (lines 131, 136) indicate that he sees the two passages as lending support to a particular argument: he is presumably suggesting that Matthew's reference to the angels gathering the elect from all the bounds of the earth and bringing them to heaven (though that is not in fact what Matthew's Gospel itself says) supports the testimony of St Paul that the elect who are living at the end of the world will join the resurrected saints and be carried in clouds to heaven. Ælfric does in fact allude to 1 Thess 4.17 again at a later point in the *Excerpts*, at 270–4, in support of his argument there that those who are found alive at the day of judgement will taste a momentary death and then immediately be resurrected in the clouds which carry them to the place of judgement (*Excerpts*, 270–4):

> Ipsi vero qui viventes repperiuntur in die iudicii, sicut docet pater Agustinus, in ipso raptu nubium momentaneam mortem gustabunt, et sic in terram ibunt quia corpus exanime terra est, et iterum statim in ipsis nubibus spiritum vite accipient.

This seems to lie behind lines 142–4 of the present homily. The passage in the Excerpts is an Ælfrician addition, not from the *Prognosticon* itself. The passage by Augustine to which he refers is probably in the *De Civitate Dei*, discussing whether the righteous will suffer death at the end of time (*De Civitate Dei*, XX.20.56–9, CCSL 48):

> Si ergo sanctos, qui reperientur Christo veniente viventes eique in obviam rapientur, crediderimus in eodem raptu de mortalibus corporibus exituros et ad eadem mox inmortalia redituros. . . .

But it looks as if his actual source was a passage from the commentary on the Apocalypse printed in PL 117 (composed by either Haymo or Remigius of Auxerre), which similarly cites Augustine (*Comm. Apoc.*, PL 117, 1076C):

> . . . Quia et vivi reperientur homines, ex quorum persona hoc apostolus loquitur; et tamen scire debet ut beatus Augustinus dicit, in ipso raptu nubium, etsi momentaneam, mortem tamen gustabunt. In terram ergo revertentur, quia hoc est corpus in terram reverti, quod est exeunte anima remanere corpus, quod utique terra est. Itaque securi dicimus, quia in momento et in ictu oculi, in ipsis nubibus, spiritum vitae accipient hi, qui in adventu Domini vivi reperientur.

(Alcuin has very similar material in his commentary on the Apocalypse, PL 100, 1150A, but is less close, though he does refer to his authority, like Ælfric, as

Pater Augustinus.) Haymo's clause, *ex quorum . . . loquitur*, may also have prompted Ælfric's point (lines 140–1) that St Paul's phrase *nos qui vivimus* refers not to himself but to those who will live at the end of time.

That the righteous still living will die through the fire that destroys the earth (lines 144–7) is also said at Pope 11.302–4, but it is not in the *Excerpts* passage or in its sources.

147–55 The location of the last judgement is briefly discussed in the *Excerpts* at 179–86, following *Prognosticon*, III.ii; Julian notes the difficulty of the issue and cites Jerome's argument that Joel's reference to the vale of Josaphat should not be understood literally, which may lie behind Ælfric's firm dismissal of an earthly location, but there is no further parallel. I think it probable that for the homily he was drawing on the discussion in Bede's *De Temporum Ratione*, a text which he had already used earlier in the homily. Bede too notes the controversial nature of the subject, but, like Ælfric, cites 1 Thessalonians as evidence that the righteous at least are raised into the air for the judgement (*De Temporum Ratione*, 70.46–54):

> Constat namque quia cum descendente domino ad iudicium in ictu oculi fuerit omnium resurrectio celebrata mortuorum, sancti confestim rapiantur obviam illi in aera: hoc etenim intellegitur apostolus indicare cum ait, 'Quoniam ipse Dominus in iussu et in voce archangeli et in tuba Dei descendet de caelo, et mortui qui in Christo sunt, resurgent primi; deinde nos qui vivimus, qui relinquimur, simul rapiemur cum illis in nubibus obviam Domino in aera (1 Thess 4.16–17).'

Ælfric's next point, that the righteous subsequently reside nowhere but in heaven with God, probably reflects Bede's subsequent argument that St Paul's words are to be understood as implying not that the righteous remain in the air but that after the judgement they reside with God (*De Temporum Ratione*, 70.80–85):

> Non sic accipiendum est, tamquam in aere nos dixerit semper cum domino esse mansuros. Quia nec ipse utique ibi manebit, quia veniens transiturus est. Venienti quippe ibitur obviam, non manenti. Sed ita cum domino erimus, id est sic erimus habentes corpora sempiterna ubicumque cum illo fuerimus.

Ælfric's preceding point (lines 147–50) that the righteous who have previously been cleansed from sin are not harmed by the fire but those who have not been cleansed do feel its (presumably purging) heat may reflect Bede's arguments too, though Bede is I think talking about the living while Ælfric's references to cleansing suggests he may be thinking of those who have already experienced the purgatorial fires (*De Temporum Ratione*, 70.65–8, 72–4):

> Namque aliquos electorum eo purgari a levioribus quibusdam admissis, et beatus Augustinus in libro de Civitate Dei XX ex prophetarum dictis intellegit. Et sanctus papa Gregorius. . . . Satis autem clarum est, quia raptis ad vocem tubae obviam domino in aera perfectis servis illius conflagratio mundana non noceat.

157–65 Perhaps drawing mainly, as Förster suggested, on a passage which he identified in Bede's commentary on Luke (*Comm. Luc.*, 6.332–6), though it is taken verbatim from Gregory's *Moralia* and is repeated in the homily by Smaragdus for this occasion (*Collectiones*, PL 102, 519CD). I quote from the *Moralia* (XVII.ix.21–5):

> Hinc ad Ioannem angelica voce perhibetur: 'Erit caelum novum et terra nova'. Quae quidem non alia condenda sunt, sed haec ipsa renovantur. Caelum igitur et terra et transit et erit quia et ab ea quam nunc habet specie per ignem tergitur et tamen in sua semper natura servatur.

The citation of Isaiah at 163–5 may have been prompted by Bede's comments in the chapter on the day of judgement in *De Temporum Ratione*, 70.31–5:

> Cum autem peracto iudicio fuerit caelum novum et terra nova, id est non alia pro aliis, sed haec ipsa per ignem innovata et quasi quadam resurrectionis virtute glorificata claruerint, tunc, ut Isaias praedixit: 'Erit lux lunae sicut lux solis et lux solis septempliciter sicut lux septem dierum' (Is 30.26).

There is perhaps a little from Haymo's homily too (Hom. 2, PL 118, 25A):

> Non ut omnino non sint, sed ut in melius immutanda sint. Ipsa ergo immutatio transitus appellatur. Transire uero dicitur non solum id quod ita perit quod nunquam sit, sed quod immutatur ut melius sit.

165–8 Ælfric seems now to return to Gregory's homily, though he also uses the passage in the Excerpts (*Excerpts*, 208–11), in a very similar context (Hom. 1, PL 76, 1081AB):

> Hanc psalmista exprimit, dicens: 'Deus manifeste veniet, Deus noster, et non silebit. Ignis in conspectu eius ardebit, et in circuitu eius tempestas valida' (Ps 49.3). Districtionem quippe tantae iustitiae tempestas ignisque comitantur, quia tempestas examinat, quos ignis exurat.

168–72 Gregory, Hom. 1, PL 76, 1081B [citing Soph 1.14–16, though not by name]:

> De illo etenim die per prophetam dicitur: 'Iuxta est dies Domini magnus, iuxta et velox nimis. Vox diei Domini amara, tribulabitur ibi fortis. Dies irae, dies illa, dies tribulationis et angustiae, dies calamitatis et miseriae, dies tenebrarum et caliginis, dies nebulae et turbinis, dies tubae et clangoris'.

173–5 Gregory, Hom. 1, PL 76, 1081B:

> Illum ergo diem, fratres carissimi, ante oculos ponite, et quidquid modo grave creditur in eius comparatione levigatur.

175–9 Gregory, Hom. 1, PL 76, 1081C:

> Vitam corrigite, mores mutate, mala tentantia resistendo vincite, perpetrata autem fletibus punite. Adventum namque aeterni iudicis tanto

securiores quandoque videbitis, quanto nunc districtionem illius timendo praevenitis.

Interpolating Ps 36.27: *Declina a malo et fac bonum.*

179–87 The final comments, delicately balancing the idea of imminence against the possibility of a long delay before the end, seem to be entirely Ælfric's own.

Appendices A and B

For notes on these passages, see the relevant homilies above (CH I.12, 38, 8, 16 and 17, respectively).

CATHOLIC HOMILIES II

PREFACE

The preface survives only in MS K, as part of the two-series set, but presumably accompanied the original publication of the Series on its own, and subsequent copies. The Latin part is here apparently addressed exclusively to Sigeric, and much more fulsomely than in CH I, while the Old English addresses users. The individual points are mostly those made in the earlier preface, mainly in more summary fashion.[1]

Notes

9–13 Ælfric's insistence on the simple and clear language he has used in the homilies, in contrast to a more verbose or obscure diction that he might have used instead, is noticeably more emphatic than in the CH I preface; on its relationship to the contemporary enthusiasm for esoteric diction in Latin writing, see above on the earlier preface, and also, with reference to this passage, Michael Lapidge, 'Æthelwold as Scholar and Teacher', in *Bishop Æthelwold: his Career and Influence*, ed. B. Yorke (Woodbridge, 1988), pp. 89–117, at 107–8. Lapidge notes that Ælfric's dismissive phrase *garrula verbositate* may have been taken from Aldhelm's prose *De Virginitate*, c.19, where it occurs at the end of a discussion of the division of society between virginity, chastity and matrimony.

13–14 The 'injuries caused by hostile pirates' are presumably the Viking raids in the south of England in the early 990s, perhaps 994; see above, pp. xxxii–xxxv.

40 *þæra anra þe angelcynn mid freolsdagum wurðað.* Exceptions to this are Alexander, Eventius and Theodolus in II.18 and the Seven Sleepers in II.27, both presumably to be understood as appendages to the main items.

The comments at 37–43 imply that a user of the collection should have no difficulty in identifying the forty items and their occasion. But it is hard to find a criterion in MS K at least which would make the numbering and ascriptions unambiguous; see Godden 1973.

AMMONITIO

This warning against drunkenness survives only in MS K. Being in Latin, it is presumably addressed to the better-educated among his readers, and it ends, rather disturbingly, with a fresh address to Sigeric himself. There is an equally

[1] See also the edition and notes in Wilcox 1994.

prominent complaint of drunkenness at the end of Ælfric's treatise On the Old and New Testament (Crawford, pp. 74–5), but there addressed to his friend the layman Sigeweard. There is also an attack on the vice (as Wilcox points out, 1994, pp. 148–9) in his pastoral letter for Wulfsige, this time addressed to secular priests (Fehr I, §§74–6). It was clearly a matter of considerable concern to Ælfric, but not apparently a vice that marked one class rather than another.

Notes

52–7 is from Leviticus 10.8–10.

59–61 is Luke 21.34.

62–3 draws on 1 Cor 6.10: *Neque ebriosi . . . regnum Dei possidebunt.*

I NATIVITY OF CHRIST

This is one of the most independent of the Second Series homilies, relying little on direct translation from Latin sources (apart from the Bible) but showing the sort of parallels with Ælfric's own earlier homilies and their sources that suggests further reflection on earlier work. The core of the homily, as the title indicates, is the list of prophecies or testimonies of Christ (lines 121–272). Ælfric had already emphasised the multitude of Old Testament prophecies of Christ's birth and Mary's virginity in his homily for the Purification (CH I.13.35–8):

> þa witegunga be cristes acennednysse. and be þære eadigan marian mægðhade sindon swiðe menigfealdlice on ðære ealdan æ. gesette. and se ðe hi asmeagan wile: þær he hi afint mid micelre genihtsumnysse.

Although many of the testimonies in this homily are not specifically about the incarnation, it was perhaps felt to be highly appropriate for a Christmas sermon because of the liturgical emphasis on prophecies of Christ at this period, which Ælfric notes at CH I.39.6–13. Indeed the homily might be seen as an attempt to give the laity access to the prophetic texts which Ælfric had mentioned in the CH I homilies. The list is preceded by a free-ranging discussion of the nativity, the incarnation and the virgin birth (lines 1–120) and followed by some general precepts (lines 272–303).

The question of sources is peculiarly complicated. Förster could find no specific source, and Smetana made no suggestions in his seminal articles of 1959 and 1961. For the first section, on the incarnation and the virgin birth, J. E. Cross identified a range of sources which seem to have contributed elements to the homily[1]: an extract from Isidore's *De Ecclesiasticis Officiis* excerpted in Paul the Deacon's homiliary for the Vigil of the Nativity; a Ps-Augustine sermon, number 245, now attributed to Ildefonsus of Seville, which appears under the

[1] Cross 1963b.

nativity in the late version of the homiliary printed in PL 95; and a sermon printed as possibly Augustine's, number 370, and perhaps partly by him, part of which (though not the relevant part) appears in the homiliary for the Purification. For the sequence of Old Testament prophecies Cross suggested as source an excerpt from a Ps-Augustinian sermon, now attributed to Quodvultdeus, which appears in PL 95. The parallels in the final 'heathen' testimonies from the Sybil and Nebuchadnezzar suggest that this was indeed a source, but it provides at best only six of the twenty-four prophecies given by Ælfric. A more substantial source for the prophecies is the anonymous legend of St James the Apostle which Ælfric used for his own homily on St James (CH II.27) and which includes a lengthy sermon by the apostle on the prophecies of Christ. It gives eleven of the prophecies used by Ælfric, often in the same sequence, and shows the same habit of grouping them by topics such as the birth or ascension. But there remain seven testimonies not derived from either source: that Ælfric did have a source for these, and did not derive them from his own familiarity with the Bible, is indicated by the fact that they include an untraceable and almost certainly misascribed quotation from 'Jeremiah'. The quotations are a particular problem, since they show a surprising amount of misattribution, unusual wording, untraceable citations and odd interpretations. This is partly due to the sources but affects the other quotations just as much.

The sermon attributed to St James may have been significant for Ælfric not only in suggesting appropriate prophecies but also in providing a model and inspiration for his own sermon; but, like the piece by Quodvultdeus and other texts containing such prophecies, it is significantly different in being apparently directed at unbelieving Jews who need to be persuaded that Christ was the Messiah whom their own texts predicted, whereas the prophecies in Ælfric's text are directed at Christians, though their function too is to strengthen belief in Christ as God (lines 122, 267–70).

Sources and Notes

The following texts are cited below:

1. Anon., *Passio Iacobi Apostoli*, in Mombritius 1910, II.37–40.
2. Augustine, *Sermones*, PL 39, Serm. 370 [= *Sermones dubii*], cols. 1657–9.
3. Ps-Augustine, *Sermones*, PL 39, Serm. 245 [= Augustine, *Sermones suppositi*], cols. 2196–8 (now attributed to Ildefonsus of Seville).
4. Isidore, *De Ecclesiasticis Officiis*, ed. C. M. Lawson, CCSL 113 (Turnhout, 1989).
5. Quodvultdeus, *Contra Iudaeos, Paganos et Arrianos*, ed. R. Braun, CCSL 60 (Turnhout, 1976), pp. 227–58.

Rubrics. By *catholicus*, used in both the heading to the Series and the title of the first homily, and indeed in the preface, Ælfric seems to mean orthodox, that is, free from heresy. Its emphatic placing underlines the importance he attached in the CH I preface to the reliable authorities on which he had drawn and his concern to replace the erroneous teaching available previously in the vernacular.

1–46 A general resemblance to the extract from Isidore's *De Ecclesiasticis Officiis*; cf esp. with 1–5 the opening of Isidore (I.26.2–5):

> Natalis Domini dies ea de causa a patribus votivae solemnitatis institutus est, quia in eo Christus pro redemptione mundi nasci corporaliter voluit, prodiens ex virginis utero, qui erat in patris imperio.

On the implications of God pondering how to redeem mankind (esp. *smeade* line 18) see Grundy 1992. Lines 28–9 allude to Phil 2.8: *Humiliavit semet ipsum factus oboediens usque ad mortem, mortem autem crucis.* With 41–2 cf Isidore, *De Ecclesiasticis Officiis*, I.26.16–22:

> Ut autem videretur, Verbum caro factum est, adsumendo carnem, non mutatum in carne. Assumpsit enim humanitatem, non amisit divinitatem; ita idem Deus et idem homo, in natura Dei aequalis patri, in natura hominis factus mortalis in nobis pro nobis, de nobis, manens quod erat, suscipiens quod non erat, ut liberaret quod fecerat.

47–58 Cf Ps-Augustine, Serm. 245, PL 39, 2197:

> [§3] Dominus Moysi sancto praecepit, de singulis tribus virgas afferri. Allatae sunt duodecim virgae, inter quas etiam una erat quae Aaron fuerat sacerdotis: positae sunt a sancto Moyse in tabernaculo testimonii. Virga autem Aaron post alterum diem invenitur subito produxisse flores et frondes, et peperisse nuces (Num 17.6–8). Delectat hoc mysterium cum caritate vestra contra perfidiam Iudaicam commiscere, ubi maxime figura intervenit sacramenti. Virga ecce protulit quod ante non habuit, non radicata plantatione, non defossa sarculo, non animata succo, non fecundata seminario: et tamen cum illic deessent universa iura naturae, protulit virga quod nec semine suggeri potuit, nec radice. Virga ergo potuit contra naturam nuces educere: virgo non potuit contra naturae iura Dei filium generare? Dicat igitur mihi Iudaeus incredulus, quemadmodum arida virga floruit et fronduit et nuces protulit; et ego dicam illi quemadmodum virgo conceperit et pepererit. . . . [§5] Virga illa, unde agebamus, Aaron virgo Maria fuit, quae nobis Christum verum sacerdotem concepit et peperit, de quo modo David cecinit, 'Tu es sacerdos in aeternum secundum ordinem Melchisedech' (Ps 109.4).

59–69 Cf Augustine, Serm. 370, §1, PL 39, 1657:

> Hodiernus dies ad habendam spem vitae aeternae, magnum contulit gaudium generi humano. Primus enim homo . . . non est natus, sed factus; patre nullo, nulla matre, sed Deo operante. Haec est hominis prima conditio. Adam de terra. Secunda conditio est hominis, qua creatur femina de latere viri. Tertia conditio est hominis, qua natus est homo ex viro et

femina. Quarta conditio est Dei et hominis, qua natus est Christus sine viro de femina. In istis quatuor conditionibus una sola nobis usitata est, caeterae tres non sunt in oculis carnis, sed in fide cordis. De terra factum hominem sine patre, sine matre, non novimus; factam feminam de latere viri non novimus, lectam et auditam credidimus. Tertia illa usitata est nobis ipsa quotidiana de complexu maris et feminae quotidie nascuntur homines. Iam ergo erat una sine viro et femina, iam erat altera de viro sine femina, iam erat tertia de viro et femina, quarta restabat sine viro de femina. Sed ista quarta liberavit tres. Prima enim et secunda ruerunt, tertiam de ruina genuerunt, in quarta salutem invenerunt.

86–90 The supposed virginity of bees is cited as an analogy for the virgin birth by Rufinus (*De Symbolo*, PL 21, 350) and Augustine (*De Trinitate*, III.vii.52–4, CCSL 50), as Cross points out, and it also figures, as Mary Clayton noted (1990, pp. 258–9), in the liturgy for Easter; but none provides the degree of detail provided by Ælfric. Another relevant instance is the *De Mirabilibus Sacrae Scripturae* (PL 35, 2193), but this does not look close enough either. None of these sources seems to mention honey.

91–3 For the church as virgin bride, cf CH I.33.19–23, drawing on Bede.

93–4 2 Cor 11.2: *Despondi enim vos uni viro virginem castam exhibere Christo.*

94–6 Jn 3.29: *Qui habet sponsam sponsus est.*

96–8 Ps 18.6: *Et ipse tamquam sponsus procedens de thalamo suo.*

103–4 Jn 3.3: *Nisi quis natus fuerit denuo non potest videre regnum Dei.*

107–9 Jn 3.5: *Respondit Iesus: amen amen dico tibi nisi quis renatus fuerit ex aqua et Spiritu, non potest introire in regnum Dei.*

127–33 Perhaps prompted by the reference to God's promises to Abraham at the beginning of St James's sermon in the *Passio Iacobi* (Mombritius 1910, II.38.41–2), but Ælfric had already made the same point, in a similar context and in very similar wording, in his homily for the annunciation (CH I.13.213–6). For the descent of Mary from David, not mentioned at that point, cf CH I.13.43–4 and note. Ælfric's reference here is to Gen 22.18: *Et benedicentur in semine tuo omnes gentes terrae* (or Gen 26.4).

134–7 Quodvultdeus, *Contra Iudaeos*, 11.20–25:

> Accedat et alius testis. Dic et tu, Hieremia, testimonium Christo. 'Hic est, inquit, Deus noster, et non aestimabitur alius absque illo, qui invenit omnem viam scientiae, et dedit eam Iacob puero suo, et Israhel dilecto sibi. Post haec in terris visus est, et cum hominibus conversatus est.'

The citation is in fact from Baruch 3.36–8, not the Book of Jeremiah, but the attribution to the latter seems to have been fairly general, as indeed Augustine notes (*De Civitate Dei*, XVIII.33.19–21, CCSL 48):

> Hoc testimonium quidam non Hieremiae, sed scribae eius attribuunt, qui vocabatur Baruch: sed Hieremiae celebratius habetur.

The Vulgate text is somewhat different in wording and Ælfric's *steore and þeawfæstnysse* (lines 135–6) perhaps reflects Vulgate *viam disciplinae* rather than *viam scientiae*.

137–40 Presumably Mich 5.5, but in a curiously distorted form:

> Et erit iste pax Assyrius cum venerit in terram nostram et quando calcaverit in domibus nostris.

The verse, or at least the first part, does seem to have been read as a prophecy of Christ (Julian of Toledo, *Commentarius in Nahum Prophetam*, PL 96, 742B), but the Assyrian is interpreted as the devil by Jerome (*Commentarii in Prophetas Minores*, 2.5.192–204, CCSL 76) and Haymo (*Commentarius in Prophetas Minores*, PL 117, 158B) whereas Ælfric seems to convert him into Christ, and the trampling of the invader into the visit of the Lord; I have found no precedent for this.

140–3 Is 7.14 [cited in the *Passio Iacobi* (Mombritius 1910, II.38.53–5), and in Quodvultdeus (*Contra Iudaeos*, 11.18–20)]: *Ecce virgo concipiet et pariet filium et vocabitis nomen eius Emmanuhel.*

143–5 Probably from *Passio Iacobi*, Mombritius 1910, II.38.57–8:

> Ezechiel autem assignat dicens: 'Veniet rex tuus Syon humilis ut restauret te.'

The quotation is not however in Ezechiel, or indeed anywhere else in the Vulgate. The nearest I can find is Zach 9.9 in the form in which it is cited by Christ himself as a prophecy at Mt 21.4–5:

> (4) Hoc autem factus est ut impleretur quod dictum est per prophetam dicentem: (5) dicite filiae Sion, ecce rex tuus venit tibi mansuetus. . . .

(The Vulgate text of Zachariah itself reads: *Exsulta . . . filia Sion . . . rex tuus veniet tibi iustus.*) But there is nothing there to prompt the phrase *ut restauret te* or Ælfric's *and geedstaðelað þe*.

146–55 Dan 9.21–4:

> (21) Ecce vir Gabrihel quem videram in visione principio cito volans tetigit me . . . (22) et docuit me et locutus est mihi dixitque Danihel nunc egressus sum ut docerem te et intellegeres (23) . . . tu ergo animadverte sermonem et intellege visionem. (24) Septuaginta ebdomades adbreviatae sunt super populum tuum et super urbem sanctam tuam ut consummetur praevaricatio et finem accipiat peccatum et deleatur iniquitas et adducatur iustitia sempiterna et impleatur visio et prophetes et unguatur sanctus sanctorum.

Ælfric's rendering silently assumes the exegetical tradition (cf Jerome, *Commentarii in Danielem*, 3.9.158–9, CCSL 75A and Julian of Toledo, *De Comprobatione Aetatis*, PL 96, 556) that seventy weeks mean seventy weeks of years, that is, 490 years. The passage is discussed as a prophecy of Christ by Jerome, in his commentary on Daniel (*Comm. Dan.*, 3.9.149–59, CCSL 75A):

> Nullique dubium quin de adventu Christi praedicatio sit; qui post septuaginta hebdomadas mundo apparuit, post quem consummata sunt delicta, et finem accepit peccatum, et deleta est iniquitas, et annuntiata iustitia sempiterna quae legis iustitiam vinceret, et impleta est visio et prophetia quia 'lex et prophetae usque ad Ioannis baptisma', et unctus sanctus sanctorum, quae omnia, priusquam Christus humanum corpus assumeret, sperabantur magis quam tenebantur. Dicit autem ipse angelus: 'septuaginta annorum hebdomadas', id est annos quadringentos nonaginta. . . .

But there is nothing very close to Ælfric's account.

170–6 Apparently drawing on the *Passio Iacobi*, Mombritius 1910, II.39.1–4:

> David autem dicit vocem filii dei dicentis: 'Dominus dixit ad me: filius meus es tu.' Et patris vox de filio dicit: 'Ipse invocabit me; pater meus es tu, et ego primogenitum ponam illum excelsum apud reges terrae.'

The first citation is Ps 2.7, given in full by Ælfric: *Dominus dixit ad me filius meus es tu, ego hodie genui te* (though since the anonymous Old English version of the *Passio Iacobi* (Warner, 22.3) gives a version of the last part, it may have been given in full in Ælfric's copy). The second is an abridged version of Ps 88.27–8:

> (27) Ipse invocabit me pater meus es tu, Deus meus et susceptor salutis meae.
> (28) Et ego primogenitum ponam illum excelsum prae regibus terrae.

But Ælfric's additional words *and eft se fæder be him cwæð; Ic beo him fæder. and he bið me sunu* bear no resemblance to the second part of verse 27 (which is in any case omitted in the *Passio Iacobi*) or as far as I can discover to anything else in the Psalms, or indeed the Bible. He presents the words as if they are part of verse 28 but it is hard to imagine how he came to do so; perhaps they originated as a marginal addition, drawing on memory, and were incorporated at slightly the wrong point.

177–81 Is 9.6–7 (a familiar Messianic prophecy, but curiously not used by either the *Passio Iacobi* or Quodvultdeus):

> (6) Parvulus enim natus est nobis, filius datus est nobis, et factus est principatus super umerum eius, et vocabitur nomen eius Admirabilis, consiliarius, Deus fortis, Pater futuri saeculi, Princeps pacis. (7) Multiplicabitur eius imperium et pacis non erit finis.

182–6 The prophecy from 'Jeremiah' is not in the *Passio Iacobi* or Quodvultdeus, nor, curiously, in Jeremiah. Cook listed this as an untraced passage, and I have had no more success in locating it. It is decidedly not in Jeremiah and I can find nothing like it in any other Biblical book. I can only assume that it is a garbled and misattributed version of the subsequent quotation from Isaiah, which it somewhat resembles, presumably corrupted by transmission through written sources or memory.

186–91 Is 35.4–6 (not used by the *Passio Iacobi* or Quodvultdeus):

(4) Dicite pusillanimis confortamini nolite timere. Ecce Deus vester . . . veniet et salvabit vos. (5) Tunc aperientur oculi caecorum et aures surdorum patebunt. (6) Tunc saliet sicut cervus claudus et aperta erit lingua mutorum.

191–5 closely following *Passio Iacobi*, Mombritius 1910, II.39.5–8:

De passione autem eius dicit Isaias: 'sicut ovis ad occisionem ductus est' (Is 53.7); et David in persona eius dicit: 'foderunt manus meas et pedes meos; dinumeraverunt omnia ossa mea . . . diviserunt sibi vestimenta mea' (Ps 21.17–19).

Ælfric gives more of Is 53.7:

Sicut ovis ad occisionem ducetur, et quasi agnus coram tondente se obmutescet, et non aperiet os suum.

But he omits Ps 21.18.

195–200 *Passio Iacobi*, Mombritius 1910, II.39.10–12:

De morte autem eius dicit: 'Caro mea requiescet in spe, quia non derelinques animam meam in inferno nec dabis sanctum tuum videre corruptionem' (Ps 15.9–10). Vox autem filii ad patrem dicit: 'Exurgam et adhuc tecum sum' (Ps 138.18).

The *Passio Iacobi* seems to attribute only the second quotation specifically to Christ's own voice, but apparently understands him as the speaker of the first one too.

200–1 *Passio Iacobi*, Mombritius 1910, II.39.14–16:

De ascensione autem eius dicit . . . 'Ascendit deus in iubilatione' (Ps 46.6)

201–3 Ps 67.33–4: *Psallite Deo qui ascendit super caelum caeli ad orientem.*

204–5 *Passio Iacobi*, Mombritius 1910, II.39.17–19:

Nam quod sedeat ad dexteram patris idem dicit per David: 'Dixit dominus domino meo: sede a dextris meis' (Ps 109.1).

205–7 Quodvultdeus, *Contra Iudaeos*, 13.6–9:

Accedat etiam David sanctus . . . dicat et ipse de Christo: 'Adorabunt, inquit, eum omnes reges terrae; omnes gentes servient illi' (Ps 71.11).

207–10 *Passio Iacobi*, Mombritius 1910, II.39.19–21:

Quod venturus sit iudicare terram per ignem, dicit propheta: 'Deus manifeste veniet deus noster, et non silebit. Ignis in conspectu eius ardebit et in circuitu eius tempestas valida' (Ps 49.3).

210–13 *Passio Iacobi*, Mombritius 1910, II.39.23–7:

Ait enim Isaias: 'surgent mortui et resurgent omnes qui in monumentis sunt' (*perhaps* Is 26.19). Si interroges quid erit cum resurrexerit, dicit

David . . . 'et tibi domine misericordia, quia tu reddes singulis secundum opera eorum' (Ps 61.13).

The Vulgate reading for Is 26.19 is rather different: *Vivent mortui tui, interfecti mei resurgent*.

214–5 Quodvultdeus, *Contra Iudaeos*, 13.38–40:

Quod si velim ex lege et ex prophetis omnia quae de Christo dicta sunt colligere, facilius me tempus quam copia deserit.

217–8 Quodvultdeus, *Contra Iudaeos*, 15.10–12:

Demonstremus etiam nos ex gentibus testimonium Christo fuisse prolatum; quoniam veritas non tacuit clamando etiam per linguas inimicorum suorum.

219–22 Quodvultdeus, *Contra Iudaeos*:

[16.6–7] Quid Sibylla vaticinando etiam de Christo clamaverit, in medium proferamus . . . [*Quodvultdeus quotes the verses.*] . . . [16.38–9] Haec de Christi nativitate, passione et resurrectione atque secundo eius adventu ita dicta sunt.

224–46 The use of Daniel was prompted by Quodvultdeus who refers more briefly to the episode (*Contra Iudaeos*, 15.18–25):

Nabuchodonosor, regem scilicet Babylonis non praetermittamus. Dic, Nabuchodonosor, quid in fornace, quo tres viros iustos iniuste miseris, vidisti? dic, dic quid tibi fuerit revelatum. Nonne, inquit suis, tres viros misimus in fornace ligatos? Et aiunt ei, Vere, rex. Ecce, inquit, ego video quatuor viros solutos deambulantes in medio ignis, et corruptio in illis nulla est, et aspectus quarti similitudo est filii Dei.

Ælfric gives a fuller account. The opening summarises Dan 1.1–4, and then proceeds with Dan 3.1–24 and 47–50:

(1) Nabuchodonosor rex fecit statuam auream . . . (4) et praeco clamabat valenter vobis dicitur populis tribubus et linguis (5) in hora qua audieritis sonitum tubae . . . cadentes adorate statuam auream quam constituit Nabuchodonosor rex (6) si quis autem non prostratus adoraverit eadem hora mittetur in fornacem ignis ardentis . . . (12) 'sunt ergo viri iudaei quos constituisti super opera regionis Babyloniae Sedrac Misac et Abdenago viri isti contempserunt rex decretum tuum deos tuos non colunt et statuam auream quam erexisti non adorant' . . . (15) 'quis est Deus qui eripiat vos de manu mea'. (16) Respondentes Sedrac Misac et Abdenago dixerunt regi Nabuchodonosor . . . (17) 'ecce enim Deus noster quem colimus potest eripere nos de camino ignis ardentis et de manibus tuis rex liberare (18) quod si noluerit notum tibi sit rex quia deos tuos non colimus et statuam auream quam erexisti non adoramus.' (19) Tunc Nabuchodonosor repletus est furore et aspectus faciei illius inmutatus est super Sedrac Misac et Abdenago et praecepit ut succenderetur fornax

septuplum quam succendi consuerat. (20) Et viris fortissimis de exercitu suo iussit ut ligatis pedibus Sedrac Misac et Abdenago mitterent eos in fornacem ignis ardentem. (21) Et confestim viri illi vincti cum bracis suis et tiaris et calciamentis et vestibus missi sunt in medium fornacis ignis ardentis. . . . (47) Et effundebatur flamma super fornacem cubitis quadraginta novem (48) et erupit et incendit quos repperit iuxta fornacem de Chaldeis. . . . (50) Et non tetigit eos omnino ignis neque contristavit nec quicquam molestiae intulit. (24) Et ambulabant in medio flammae, laudantes Deum et benedicentes Domino.

247–66 Dan 3.91–6:

(91) Tunc Nabuchodonosor rex obstipuit et surrexit propere et ait optimatibus suis: Nonne tres viros misimus in medio ignis conpeditos? Qui respondentes dixerunt regi: vere rex. (92) Respondit et ait: ecce ego video viros quattuor solutos et ambulantes in medio ignis et nihil corruptionis in eis est et species quarti similis filio Dei. (93) Tunc accessit Nabuchodonosor ad ostium fornacis ignis ardentis et ait: Sedrac Misac et Abdenago servi Dei excelsi egredimini et venite; statimque egressi sunt Sedrac Misac et Abdenago de medio ignis. (94) Et congregati satrapae magistratus et iudices et potentes regis contemplabantur viros illos quoniam nihil potestatis habuisset ignis in corporibus eorum et capillus capitis eorum non esset adustus et sarabara eorum non fuissent inmutata et odor ignis non transisset per eos. (95) Et erumpens Nabuchodonosor ait benedictus Deus eorum Sedrac videlicet Misac et Abdenago qui misit angelum suum et eruit servos suos . . . (96) A me ergo positum est hoc decretum ut omnis populus et tribus et lingua quaecumque locuta fuerit blasphemiam contra Deum Sedrac Misac et Abdenago dispereat et domus eius vastetur; neque enim est Deus alius qui possit ita salvare.

For 254 cf Quodvultdeus, *Contra Iudaeos*, 15.28–29 (addressing Nebuchadnezzar):

Quis tibi istud annuntiavit? nisi quia sic te divinus ignis intus illuminavit.

270–2 Ps 85.9–10:

(9) Omnes gentes quascumque fecisti venient et adorabunt coram te Domine et glorificabunt nomen tuum, (10) quoniam magnus es tu et faciens mirabilia; tu es Deus solus.

277–91 Ælfric perhaps has in mind, in these final injunctions, the ways in which the laity normally celebrated Christmas, but the emphasis on chastity as the key virtue at 283–7, though perhaps justified by the earlier discussion of the virgin birth, sounds more like an allusion to his criticisms of the secular clergy.

289–91 Lc 21.34:

Adtendite autem vobis ne forte graventur corda vestra in crapula et ebrietate et curis huius vitae et superveniat in vos repentina dies illa.

293–4 An allusion to Lc 1.28: *Benedicta tu in mulieribus.*

2 STEPHEN

It is not clear why Ælfric chose to produce a second homily for St Stephen, after writing about his martyrdom and the example of brotherly love for this occasion in the First Series: presumably either the feast-day was for him as important as the other occasions which are covered in both Series (Christmas, Epiphany, Lent, Easter, Rogationtide, the Assumption of the Virgin, SS Peter and Paul), or the subject-matter seemed imperative—though it is striking that this item appears in only one other collection apart from the complete set of the series in K. The subject, miracles worked by Stephen's relics in the vicinity of St Augustine's seat at Hippo, was presumably prompted by the inclusion of Augustine's account of these events for the same occasion in versions of Paul the Deacon's homiliary. The narrative as Ælfric gives it highlights the particular miracle of the children cursed by their mother (lines 98–176), and this prompts an interesting discussion of the topic of cursing (lines 190–217).

Förster demonstrated that Ælfric's account was drawn primarily from Augustine's discussion of miracles in *De Civitate Dei*, and especially miracles associated with the relics of St Stephen which were brought to North Africa in the saint's time.[1] Augustine's account refers at a number of points to the *libelli* of contemporary testimony which he assiduously commissioned, and Ælfric's version incorporates substantial additional material apparently taken from the *Libellus* which gave the testimony of Paulus about the miracle by which he was healed (the *Libellus* survives as Augustine's Serm. 322, PL 38, 1443 ff). Since Ælfric's account differs even from this in some significant points of detail, especially the direct speech of the devil, and begins with a homiletic address which he quotes as Augustine's but is not in either of these sources, Förster argued that his actual source was a lost or untraced sermon attributed to Augustine, in which material from the two texts had already been combined and adapted. His arguments have proved remarkably accurate. Precisely such a sermon appears in the eighth-century Fleury homiliary, printed in 1967 from a transcription by Reginald Gregoire in PLS 4, cols. 1903–10. This has the material from *De Civitate Dei* prefaced by a homiletic address that closely resembles Ælfric's opening, and followed by the relevant material from the *Libellus* of Paulus, recast in a form much closer to Ælfric, including direct speech by the devil, and a concluding discussion of cursing that corresponds in part to his. Parts at least of the sermon have been linked to Caesarius of Arles.[2] The particular copy printed in PLS is extremely corrupt, at times reduced to nonsense (and I have for that reason quoted from *De Civitate Dei* below, rather than the sermon, whenever possible), and omits one of the miracles in *De Civitate Dei* which Ælfric uses, but there can be little doubt that his source was a

[1] Förster 1892, pp. 31–4.

[2] See Caesarius of Arles, *Sermones*, ed. G. Morin, CCSL 103 (Turnhout, 1953), p. cix, and PLS 4, col. 1903.

version of this sermon. Where he found it is not clear, but given the Fleury origins of the English monastic reform movement, and Ælfric's use of work by Abbo of Fleury, it would hardly be surprising if he had seen material from the Fleury homiliary. It may be significant that the sermon is immediately followed in the manuscript by another text on Stephen, an abridged version of sermon 382 from the *Sermones dubii* of Augustine, since Ælfric seems to have used material from this sermon both here and in the First Series homily on St Stephen. As noted above, some versions of Paul the Deacon's homiliary give Augustine's account of the miracles from *De Civitate Dei* as a text for the occasion, but none of the copies that I have seen contains the material from the *Libellus* and the homiletic opening, or indeed all the *De Civitate Dei* material which Ælfric used. One minor feature of his version worth noting is Ælfric's tendency to associate all the miracles with a single shrine or church of St Stephen in Hippo, whereas Augustine associates them with a number of different shrines.

Sources and Notes

The following texts are cited below:

1. Anon., *Homiliare Floriacense*, PLS 4, Hom. 15, cols. 1903–10.
2. Augustine, *De Civitate Dei*, ed. B. Dombart and A. Kalb, 2 vols., CCSL 47–8 (Turnhout, 1955).
3. Augustine(?), *Sermones*, PL 39, Serm. 382 [=Augustine, *Sermones dubii*], cols. 1684–6.

1–10 Cf *Hom. Flor.*, 15, PLS 4, 1903:

> Dum frequenter auribus vestris insignia miraculorum sancti Stephani protomartyris, fratres carissimi, recensentur, confidimus quod plurima ex eis iam vestrae memoriae fuerint commendata. Miracula ergo ipsa, ut optime nostis, beatus Augustinus Hipponae regensis episcopus in libris quos De civitate Dei conscripsit inseruit dicens: Hipponiensem quendam virginem scio quae cum se oleo domni Stephani perunxisset, cui pro illa orans presbyter instillaverat lacrimas suas mox a daemonio fuisse sanatam.

In this Fleury version the opening address is evidently in the adapter's voice, not as Ælfric has it in the voice of Augustine. The miracle is from *De Civitate Dei*, XXII.8.243–5, but as Förster pointed out, it is not associated there with St Stephen, and occurs before Augustine turns to the miracles of Stephen.

10–13 Cf Augustine, *De Civitate Dei*, XXII.8.267–71 [= *Hom. Flor.*, 15, PLS 4, 1904], where a blind woman asks to be led to meet a bishop who is carrying a relic of St Stephen to Aquae Tibilitanae:

> Ibi caeca mulier ut ad episcopum portantem duceretur oravit . . . protinus vidit. Stupentibus qui aderant praeibat exultans, viam carpens et viae ducem ulterius non requirens.

14–21 Cf *De Civitate Dei*, XXII.8.279–85 [= *Hom. Flor.*, 15, PLS 4, 1904]:

Eucharius est presbyter ex Hispania, Calamae habitat. Vetere morbo calculi laborabat. Per memoriam supradicti martyris, quam Possidius illo advexit episcopus, salvus factus est. Idem ipse postea morbo alio praevalescente mortuus sic iacebat ut ei iam pollices ligarentur. Opitulatione memorati martyris cum de memoria eius reportata esset et super iacentis corpus missa ipsius presbyteri tunica suscitatus est.

Augustine locates the miracle at Calama near Hippo, but Ælfric seems to place it in Spain (despite his opening remark that Augustine was presenting miracles which occurred in his own vicinity).

22–47 Cf *De Civitate Dei*, XXII.8.286–305 [= *Hom. Flor.*, 15, PLS 4, 1904]:

Fuit ibi vir in ordine suo primarius, nomine Martialis, aevo iam gravis et multum abhorrens a religione Christiana. Habebat sane fidelem filiam et generum eodem anno baptizatum. Qui cum eum aegrotantem multis et magnis lacrimis rogarent, ut fieret Christianus, prorsus abnuit eosque a se turbida indignatione submovit. Visum est genero eius, ut iret ad memoriam sancti Stephani et illic pro eo quantum posset oraret, ut Deus illi daret mentem bonam, qua credere non differret in Christum. Fecit hoc ingenti gemitu et fletu et sinceriter ardente pietatis affectu; deinde abscedens aliquid de altari florum, quod occurrit, tulit eique, cum iam nox esset, ad caput posuit; tum dormitum est. Et ecce ante diluculum clamat, ut ad episcopum curreretur qui mecum forte tunc erat apud Hipponem. Cum ergo eum audisset absentem, venire presbyteros postulavit. Venerunt, credere se dixit, admirantibus atque gaudentibus omnibus baptizatus est. Hoc, quamdiu vixit, in ore habebat: 'Christe, accipe spiritum meum'; cum haec verba beatissimi Stephani, quando lapidatus est a Iudaeis, ultima fuisse nesciret; quae huic quoque ultima fuerunt; nam non multo post etiam ipse defunctus est.

48–52 *De Civitate Dei*, XXII.8.306–9 [omitted in *Hom. Flor.*, 15]:

Sanati sunt illic per eundem martyrem etiam podagri duo cives, peregrinus unus: sed cives omni modo; peregrinus autem per revelationem, quid adhiberet quando doleret, audivit; et cum hoc fecerit, dolor continuo conquiescit.

52–6 *De Civitate Dei*, XXII.8.311–5 [= *Hom. Flor.*, 15, PLS 4, 1905]:

Puerum quendam parvulum, cum in area luderet, exorbitantes boves, qui vehiculum trahebant, rota obtriverunt, et confestim palpitavit expirans. Hunc mater abreptum ad eandem memoriam posuit, et non solum revixit, verum etiam inlaesus apparuit.

(It is in fact a different shrine in the Latin versions.)

56–61 *De Civitate Dei*, XXII.8.316–20 [= *Hom. Flor.*, 15, PLS 4, 1905]:

Sanctimonialis quaedam in vicina possessione, quae Caspaliana dicitur, cum aegritudine laboraret ac desperaretur, ad eandem memoriam tunica eius adlata est; quae antequam revocaretur, illa defuncta est. Hac tamen tunica operuerunt cadaver eius parentes, et recepto spiritu salva facta est.

62–6 *De Civitate Dei*, XXII.8.321–8 [= *Hom. Flor.*, 15, PLS 4, 1905]: Apud Hipponem Bassus quidam Syrus ad memoriam eiusdem martyris orabat pro aegrotante et periclitante filia eoque secum vestem eius adtulerat, cum ecce pueri de domo cucurrerunt, qui ei mortuam nuntiarent. [*But the servants are prevented from telling the father. Hom. Flor. reads* nuntiaverunt, *which may explain Ælfric's version.*] . . . Qui cum domum redisset iam suorum eiulatibus personantem et vestem filiae, quam ferebat, super eam proiecisset, reddita est vitae.

66–70 *De Civitate Dei*, XXII.8.329–34 [= *Hom. Flor.*, 15, PLS 4, 1905]: Rursus ibidem apud nos Irenaei cuiusdam collectarii filius aegritudine extinctus est. Cumque corpus iaceret exanime atque a lugentibus et lamentantibus exequiae pararentur, amicorum eius quidam inter aliorum consolantium verba suggessit, ut eiusdem martyris oleo corpus perungueretur. Factum est, et revixit.

70–73 *De Civitate Dei*, XXII.8.335–8 [= *Hom. Flor.*, 15, PLS 4, 1905]: Itemque apud nos vir tribunicius Eleusinus super memoriam martyrum, quae in suburbano eius est, aegritudine exanimatum posuit infantulum filium, et post orationem, quam multis cum lacrimis ibi fudit, viventem levavit.

(Ælfric again relocates the miracle at the same shrine as the preceding ones.)

74–8 *De Civitate Dei*, XXII.8.345–9 [= *Hom. Flor.*, 15, PLS 4, 1905]: Si enim miracula sanitatum, ut alia taceam, ea tantummodo velim scribere, quae per hunc martyrem, id est gloriosissimum Stephanum, facta sunt in Colonia Calamensi et in nostra, plurimi conficiendi sunt libri, nec tamen omnia colligi poterunt.

79–97 *De Civitate Dei*, XXII.8.365–85, 390–1 [= *Hom. Flor.*, 15, PLS 4, 1906]: Petroniam, clarissimam feminam, quae ibi mirabiliter ex magno atque diuturno, in quo medicorum adiutoria cuncta defecerant, languore sanata est, hortati sumus . . . ut libellum daret, qui recitaretur in populo. . . . A quodam Iudaeo dixit sibi fuisse persuasum, ut anulum capillacio vinculo insereret, quo sub omni veste ad nuda corporis cingeretur; qui anulus haberet sub gemma lapidem in renibus inventum bovis. Hoc alligata quasi remedio ad sancti martyris limina veniebat. Sed profecta a Carthagine, cum in confinio fluminis Bagradae in sua possessione mansisset, surgens ut iter perageret ante pedes suos illum iacentem anulum vidit et capillaciam zonam, qua fuerat alligatus, mirata temptavit. Quam cum omnino suis nodis firmissimis, sicut erat, comperisset astrictam, crepuisse atque exiluisse anulum suspicata est; qui etiam ipse cum integerrimus fuisset inventus, futurae salutis quodam modo pignus de tanto miraculo se accepisse praesumpsit atque illud vinculum solvens simul cum eodem anulo proiecit in flumen. . . . Martyr certe ipse, quo inpetrante illa sanata est. . . .

Instead of the kidney-stone mentioned by Augustine, Ælfric has a *wernægel*, rendered 'wart' by Thorpe, which seems to be 'a hard lump found on the back of cattle' produced by the larvae of the gadfly (Audrey Meaney, *Anglo-Saxon Amulets and Curing Stones* (Oxford, 1981), p. 109, and further references in BT s.v. *wernægel*). On its use as an amulet see Meaney, pp. 108–13, who notes that Ælfric's source may not have been identical to the *De Civitate Dei* at this point but argues that 'he probably effected a deliberate change here, describing a custom known to him in order to give the passage more force' (p. 109). She suggests that the first element of the word is *wær* meaning 'protective, guardian' and the second element 'nail' (p. 113). The *capillacium vinculum* of Augustine's narrative would seem to be a girdle made of hair (cf Lewis and Short, s.v. *capillaceus* and the translation by Henry Bettenson,[3] but Ælfric seems to have understood it as a band for fastening the hair, hence *snodu*, which in this case is somehow used by the woman to fasten the *wernægel* to a ring and both to her body. She then finds the *snodu* and the ring lying on the ground before her, miraculously detached from her body, whereas in Augustine's account the ring is on the ground and the girdle still round her body (though the Latin construction readily lends itself to misinterpretation). The completion of the journey and the healing are not narrated in the Latin.

98–113 *De Civitate Dei*, XXII.8.407–15 [= *Hom. Flor.*, 15, PLS 4, 1906–7]:

Unum est apud nos factum, non maius quam illa quae dixi, sed tam clarum atque inlustre miraculum, ut nullum arbitrer esse Hipponiensium, qui hoc non vel viderit vel didicerit, nullum qui oblivisci ulla ratione potuerit. Decem quidam fratres (quorum septem sunt mares, tres feminae) de Caesarea Cappadociae, suorum civium non ignobiles, maledicto matris recenti patris eorum obitu destitutae, quae iniuriam sibi ab eis factam acerbissime tulit, tali poena sunt divinitus coherciti, ut horribiliter quaterentur omnes tremore membrorum.

Ælfric presumably understood Cappadocia to be the name of the city rather than the region (see above, note on CH I.30.199 ff). The cursing episode is narrated more fully by one of the sons in the *Libellus* (PL 38, 1443) but Ælfric was evidently using the adaptation given in the Fleury homily (*Hom. Flor.*, 15, PLS 4, 1909):

Diebus enim Paschae . . . mulier illa ab uno de filiis suis legitur non parvam iniuriam pertulisse. Quae dum nimio amaro animo ut eis malediceret ad baptisterium cucurrerit, obviam habuit personam quandam quae ab illa quo pergeret inquisivit. Illa vero dixit ei: Ad ecclesiam vado ut pro iniuria quam a filio pertuli, ipsum filium maledicam. Tunc respondit illi persona illa, quae sine dubio in figura hominis diabolus fuit: Quia

[3] Henry Bettenson, trans., *Concerning the City of God against the Pagans* (Harmondsworth, 1972), p. 1044.

quando iniuriam pertulisti, toti filii tui in praesenti fuerunt, et nec eis doluit tua iniuria nec defensuri te a suo fratre voluerunt, iuste et bene facis ut eis omnibus maledicas.

114–23 *Hom. Flor.*, 15, PLS 4, 1909 [based on the *Libellus*, PL 38, 1443–4]: Illa audito crudeli et nefando consilio atque maiori furore suae insaniae, ingressa est baptisterium. Et solvens crines suos deposuit eos in aqua quae in fontibus erat, et cum grandi furore maledicente filiis suis. Post hoc factum ad domum reversa, invenit eos omnibus membris cum ingenti cruciatu trementes. Tunc pro eo quod tantum male fecerat, nimio dolore percussa abiit et laqueo se suspendit. Quam rem sine dubio ille persuasit qui prius ut filiis suis malediceret consilium dedit.

124–37 *De Civitate Dei*, XXII.8.416–35 [= *Hom. Flor.*, 15, PLS 4, 1907]: In qua foedissima specie oculos suorum civium non ferentes, quaqua versum cuique ire visum est, toto paene vagabantur orbe Romano. Ex his etiam ad nos venerunt duo, frater et soror, Paulus et Palladia, multis aliis locis miseria diffamante iam cogniti. Venerunt autem ante Pascha ferme dies quindecim, ecclesiam cotidie et in ea memoriam gloriosissimi Stephani frequentabant, orantes ut iam sibi placaretur Deus et salutem pristinam redderet. . . . Venit et Pascha, atque ipso die dominico mane, cum iam frequens populus praesens esset et loci sancti cancellos, ubi martyrium erat, idem iuvenis orans teneret, repente prostratus est et dormienti simillimus iacuit, non tamen tremens, sicut etiam per somnum solebant. . . . Et ecce surrexit, et non tremebat, quoniam sanatus erat, et stabat incolumis, intuens intuentes.

138–48 *De Civitate Dei*, XXII.8.435–52 [= *Hom. Flor.*, 15, PLS 4, 1907–8]: Quis ergo se tenuit a laudibus Dei? Clamantium gratulantiumque vocibus ecclesia usquequaque completa est. Inde ad me curritur, ubi sedebam iam processurus: inruit alter quisque post alterum, omnis posterior quasi novum, quod alius prior dixerat, nuntiantes: meque gaudente et apud me Deo gratias agente, ingreditur etiam ipse cum pluribus, inclinatur ad genua mea, erigitur ad osculum meum. Procedimus ad populum, plena erat ecclesia. . . . Salutavi populum . . . [*Augustine then mentions the reading from Scripture and his preaching.*] Nobiscum homo prandit, et diligenter nobis omnem suae fraternaeque ac maternae calamitatis indicavit historiam.

148–76 *De Civitate Dei*, XXII.8.454–81, XXII.9.1–6 [= *Hom. Flor.*, 15, PLS 4, 1908–9]:

Quod cum ex dominico Paschae die tertio fieret in gradibus exedrae . . . feci stare ambos fratres, cum eorum legeretur libellus. Intuebatur populus universus sexus utriusque, unum stantem sine deformi motu, alteram membris omnibus contrementem. Et qui ipsum non viderant, quid in eo divinae misericordiae factum esset, in eius sorore cernebant. . . . Inter haec recitato eorum libello de conspectu populi eos abire praecepi, et de tota ipsa causa aliquanto diligentius coeperam disputare, cum ecce me disputante voces aliae de memoria martyris novae gratulationis audiuntur. Conversi sunt eo, qui me audiebant, coeperuntque concurrere. Illa enim, ubi de gradibus descendit in quibus steterat, ad sanctum martyrem orare perrexerat; quae mox ut cancellos adtigit, conlapsa similiter velut in somnum sana surrexit. Dum ergo requireremus quid factum fuerit, unde ille strepitus laetus extiterit, ingressi sunt cum illa in basilicam, in qua eramus, adducentes eam sanam de martyris loco. Tum vero tantus ab utroque sexu admirationis clamor exortus est, ut vox continuata cum lacrimis non videretur posse finiri. Perducta est ad eum locum, ubi paulo ante steterat tremens. Exultabant eam similem fratri, cui doluerant remansisse dissimilem. . . . Exultabant in Dei laudem voce sine verbis, tanto sonitu, quantum nostrae aures ferre vix possent. Quid erat in cordibus exultantium, nisi fides Christi, pro qua Stephani sanguis effusus est? Cui, nisi huic fidei adtestantur ista miracula, in qua praedicatur Christus resurrexisse in carne et in caelum ascendisse cum carne? quia et ipsi martyres huius fidei martyres, id est huius fidei testes, fuerunt; huic fidei testimonium perhibentes mundum inimicissimum et crudelissimum pertulerunt eumque non repugnando, sed moriendo vicerunt.

181–6 Lc 23.34: *Iesus autem dicebat: Pater dimitte illis non enim sciunt quid faciunt*, followed by Acts 7.59: *Positis autem genibus clamavit voce magna: Domine ne statuas illis hoc peccatum.* The two quotations are frequently associated, as in the Augustinian sermon cited below.

190–200 *Hom. Flor.*, 15, PLS 4, 1909–10:

Nemo ergo maledicat quia scriptum est: 'Neque maledici regnum Dei possidebunt' (1 Cor 6.9–10). Nemo umquam ulli hominum maledicat aut aliquid mali venire desideret, ne forte per ipsam maledictionem vel odium quasi quibusdam diabolicis funibus collum animae suae ligans, non solum se ab aeterna vita faciat alienum, sed etiam infernalibus poenis faciat obnoxium. Observent ergo omnes filii ne despiciant et ad iracundiam excitent parentes suos ut eos ad se maledicendos incipiant provocare. Similiter et omnes patres vel matres faciant.

200–1 Exod 20.12: *Honora patrem tuum et matrem tuam, ut sis longaevus super terram, quam Dominus Deus tuus dabit tibi.*

207–8 Cf Jac 3.10: *Ex ipso ore procedit benedictio et maledictio. Non oportet, fratres mei, haec ita fieri.*

208–13 Corresponds fairly closely to a passage in Augustine, Serm. 382, §5, PL 39, 1686:

Advertat Sanctitas vestra. Iudex homo per se ipsum reum non occidit, sed iubet, et spiculator occidit. Iudex dicit, Occide: et tortor occidit. Et tu quando dicis, Occide inimicum meum, te facis iudicem, et Deum quaeris esse tortorem.

The context is not quite the same (it is concerned with the sinfulness of praying God to kill one's enemies rather than specifically with cursing) but it is a homily on Stephen and brotherly love and another passage corresponds closely with lines in Ælfric's first homily on Stephen, so there is some likelihood that this was his source. But Ælfric's adaptation of the argument and the overall difference of context do raise problems. Ælfric seems to be suggesting that to curse one's enemies is to ask God to injure them, but he does not explain whether he means to imply that a curse which takes effect is therefore the work of God, and this becomes a significant question because of his detailed account of the mother's curse and its effect. In a sermon which Augustine is represented as having delivered after the healing of the son and just before the healing of the daughter, indeed while it is taking place, he makes it clear that he considers God to have given effect to the mother's curse: the mother was justified in her resentment of her children, and the just God heard her prayer, he says (Serm. 323, PL 38, 1445). The testimony of the son Paulus given in Serm. 322 acknowledges the guilt of the children and the extreme provocation of their mother, and his account of the curse (which is not described at all by Augustine) identifies it as a religious ritual performed in church; but he complicates the interpretation by emphasising the extremity of the mother's grief and anger and representing her as being led astray by the devil, or a diabolic person, who encourages her to extend the curse to the other children. The Fleury adaptation, followed by Ælfric's homily, shifts the balance further, by omitting the details of the original provocation by the son, transferring to the devil's speech the reference to the other children's failure to intervene, emphasising further the extreme nature of the mother's reaction (*nimio amaro animo*, *cum grandi furore*), and making the devil responsible for her suicide. Instead of Augustine's theory of God's role in an *imprecatio* which takes effect, the Fleury sermon appropriately ends with an attack on *maledictio* or cursing which again emphasises the devil's involvement, and Ælfric pursues the same line, repeatedly stressing the diabolic associations of cursing (lines 192–207). The Latin sermon, though taking a totally different line from Augustine in its interpretation of the story of the mother's curse, is at least consistent in reading it as an irrational and sinful act that was prompted by the devil and consigned her to the devil's power. Though Ælfric seems to share that reading, his final sentences (lines 208–13), in which he apparently returns to an Augustinian doctrine of God's involvement and adapts Augustine's discussion of prayer to include malediction, seem to introduce a new complication in the theorizing of the curse and leaves open the difficult doctrinal issue of why God should have given effect to the mother's curse.

214–7 Mt 5.44–5 [also cited in Augustine's, Serm. 382, §1, PL 39]:

(44) Ego autem dico vobis: Diligite inimicos vestros, benefacite his qui oderunt vos, et orate pro persequentibus et calumniantibus vos, (45) ut sitis filii Patris vestri, qui in caelis est.

3 EPIPHANY

Epiphany, as Ælfric explains both here and in his earlier piece for the occasion, marks both Christ's revelation to the magi and the later revelation of his divinity at his baptism. The first occasion is covered in the First Series, and he turns here to the second. The account of the baptism in Matthew 3.13–17 was appointed for Wednesday after Epiphany and the one in John 1.29–34 for the Octave, but Ælfric offers instead (lines 14–75) a conflated account of John the Baptist and the baptism of Christ, combining these two versions with the narrative from Luke and other Biblical and exegetical material. He then discusses various aspects of the text (lines 76–133), before turning to a more detailed discussion of the two appearances of the Holy Spirit, as dove and as fire (lines 134–91), the nature of John's baptism (lines 192–218) and finally the contemporary role of baptism and the justification for baptizing infants. A principal concern is baptism—its origins, functions, and the important question of its sacramental quality, which, Ælfric insists, is not affected by the character of the celebrant. Two of the small authorial additions found in MSS B and R, at 196 and 212, show him continuing to refine the argument in later revision.

Ælfric's reference to 'wisra lareowa trahtnunga' (line 77) implies the use of more than one source for the exegesis. Förster pointed to Ælfric's use of Augustine's Tractates on John, and Smetana added Bede's homily on Matthew 3.13–17 (Hom. I.12), noting also some similarities to Bede's homilies I.11 and I.15 (all three were included in Paul the Deacon's homiliary).[1] The homily also reworks material from two earlier pieces, the homily for the Nativity of John the Baptist (CH I.25) and the homily for Pentecost (CH I.22), and in the process brings in material from Gregory the Great. There may also be some material from Haymo (homilies 16 and 108). But this is a homily in which Ælfric selects and rewrites very freely, and none of the sources acted as a model for the piece as a whole. For the concluding discussion of baptism, Fehr noted parallels in Theodulfus of Orleans and Amalarius of Metz,[2] but there is no convincing evidence of a debt.

Sources and Notes

The following texts are cited below:

1. Amalarius, *Liber Officialis*, ed. J. Hanssens in *Amalarii Episcopi Opera Liturgica Omnia*, Studi e Testi 139 (Vatican City, 1948).
2. Augustine, *In Iohannis Evangelium Tractatus CXXIV*, ed. R. Willems, CCSL 36 (Turnhout, 1954).

[1] Förster 1894, p. 36; Smetana 1959, pp. 195–6.

[2] B. Fehr, 'Über einige Quellen zu Ælfrics *Homiliae Catholicae*', *Archiv* 130 (1913), 378–81.

3. Bede, *Homiliae*, ed. D. Hurst, CCSL 122 (Turnhout, 1955), Hom. I.12 (pp. 80–87) and Hom. I.15 (pp. 105–10).
4. Gregory the Great, *Homiliae in Evangelia*, PL 76, Hom. 20, cols. 1159–70.
5. Haymo of Auxerre, *Homiliae de Tempore*, PL 118, Hom. 108, cols. 578–84.
6. Theodulfus of Orleans, *De Ordine Baptismi*, PL 105, cols. 223–40.

1–4 Cf the similar passage at CH I.7.37–51, and the note on it above.

10–11 Mt 11.11: *Non surrexit inter natos mulierum maior Iohanne Baptista*. For the interpretation, cf CH I.25.103–8, possibly drawing on Ps-Augustine, Serm. 197 (PL 39, 2114): *Iohannes enim natus mulieris, Christus autem virginis natus est*.

14–23 Repeats in slightly different words, presumably from memory, the resumé of John's early life given at CH I.25.41–9, which is in turn pieced together from a variety of Biblical references and exegetical traditions. The reference to him eating *þæt þæt he on wuda findan mihte* presumably refers to the *wudehunig and oþre waclice þigene* of I.25.46. By *gestiþod* (line 14) Ælfric presumably means something like 'grown strong or hardy' rather than 'grown up, matured', since in CH I.25 he says that John departed for the wilderness when he became *gewittig* (line 41) and in his youth (line 109).

23–5 Cf CH I.25.50–54, drawing on Gregory's Hom. 20, PL 76, 1159–68 (and see further below on lines 55–60).

26–34 Mt 3.1–2, 10, 5–6:

> (1) In diebus autem illis venit Iohannes Baptista praedicans in deserto Iudaeae (2) et dicens: paenitentiam agite adpropinquavit enim regnum caelorum. . . . (10) Omnis ergo arbor quae non facit fructum bonum exciditur et in ignem mittitur. (5) Tunc exiebat ad eum Hierosolyma et omnis Iudaea et omnis regio circa Iordanen (6) et baptizabantur in Iordane ab eo confitentes peccata sua.

For the comment at 30–2, cf Gregory, Hom. 20, PL 76, 1164D:

> Omnis enim arbor non faciens fructum bonum, excidetur, et in ignem mittetur, quia unusquisque perversus paratam citius gehennae concremationem invenit, qui hic fructum boni operis facere contemnit.

34–55 Lc 3.10–16, with interjected comments:

> (10) Et interrogabant eum turbae dicentes quid ergo faciemus. (11) Respondens autem dicebat illis qui habet duas tunicas det non habenti et qui habet escas similiter faciat. (12) Venerunt autem et publicani ut baptizarentur et dixerunt ad illum magister quid faciemus. (13) At ille dixit ad eos nihil amplius quam quod constitutum est vobis faciatis. (14) Interrogabant autem eum et milites dicentes quid faciemus et nos et ait illis neminem concutiatis neque calumniam faciatis et contenti estote stipendiis vestris. (15) Existimante autem populo et cogitantibus omnibus in cordibus suis de Iohanne ne forte ipse esset Christus. (16) Respondit

Iohannes dicens omnibus: (*Jn 1.20:* non sum ego Christus;) ego quidem aqua baptizo vos, venit autem fortior me cuius non sum dignus solvere corrigiam calciamentorum eius; ipse vos baptizabit in Spiritu Sancto et igni.

The clause *to ði . . . behreowsian* (lines 51–2) perhaps alludes to the phrase *baptismum poenitentiae* at Luke 3.3. For the emphasis on Christ not beginning his ministry until the age of 30 cf CH I.1.249–50 and I.25.124–5; it presumably relates to arguments about the proper age for ordination.

55–60 Cf Haymo, Hom. 108, PL 118, 580CD [a source used for Pope 12]:

Et convenienter in ordine baptizandi utrumque posuit, aquam scilicet et spiritum sanctum. Quia aqua corpus lavat, sed spiritus sanctus mentem renovat. Superflue enim aqua esset, nisi spiritus sanctus peccata remitteret. Aqua igitur exterius significat quod spiritus sanctus interius operatur, id est, mundationem peccatorum. Ergo aqua proficit ad lavacrum, spiritus autem ad gratiam. Siquidem Iohannes baptizabat populum aqua, non in remissionem peccatorum, sed in poenitentiam, dicens: 'Ego baptizo in aqua, medius autem vestrum stetit quem vos nescitis. Hic est qui baptizat in spiritu sancto et igni'.

The argument that John's baptism did not actually convey the forgiveness of sins, despite the implications of the Gospels, is reiterated both in this homily and in CH I.25; the main source for this distinction seems to be Gregory's Hom. 20, used as a source for CH I.25; cf esp. PL 76, 1160–1.[3]

61–75 A conflation of Mt 3.13–17 and Jn 1.29–30:

(Mt 3.13) Tunc venit Iesus a Galilaea in Iordanen ad Iohannem ut baptizaretur ab eo. (Jn 1.29) Videt Iohannes Iesum venientem ad se et ait: ecce agnus Dei qui tollit peccatum mundi. (30) Hic est de quo dixi: post me venit vir qui ante me factus est quia prior me erat. (Mt 3.14) Iohannes autem prohibebat eum dicens ego a te debeo baptizari et tu venis ad me. (15) Respondens autem Iesus dixit ei: Sine modo; sic enim decet nos implere omnem iustitiam. Tunc dimisit eum. (16) Baptizatus autem confestim ascendit de aqua et ecce aperti sunt ei caeli et vidit Spiritum Dei descendentem sicut columbam venientem super se. (17) Et ecce vox de caelis dicens hic est Filius meus dilectus in quo mihi conplacui.

79–84 A summary of Exod 12.1–10, in very similar words to CH II.15.8–18:

(1) Dixit quoque Dominus ad Mosen et Aaron in terra Aegypti. (3) Loquimini ad universum coetum filiorum Israhel et dicite eis: decima die mensis huius tollat unusquisque agnum per familias et domos suas, (6) et servabitis eum usque ad quartamdecimam diem mensis huius immolabitque eum universa multitudo filiorum Israhel ad vesperam; (7) et sument de sanguine ac ponent super utrumque postem et in superliminaribus

[3] Cf Jerome Oetgen, 'Another source for Ælfric's Second Epiphany homily (CH II, 3)', *Notes and Queries* 227 (June 1982), 198–9.

domorum in quibus comedent illum; (8) et edent carnes nocte illa assas igni. (10) Nec remanebit ex eo quicquam usque mane; si quid residui fuerit igne conburetis.

Bede (Hom. I.15, 28–36) refers to the Old Testament parallel but not in similar words. For the sign of the cross see the note on CH II.15.50–9.

86–8 Probably an allusion to Is 53.7: *Sicut ovis ad occisionem ducetur, et quasi angus coram tondente obmutescet et non aperiet os suum*, a common Christological citation used at CH II.1.192–3 and cited in a similar context by Bede (Hom. I.16, 40) and Haymo (Hom. 16, PL 118, 115–6). It resembles a comment in the anonymous *Breviarium in Psalmos* printed as Jerome's at PL 26, 1215B: '*Et omnis mansuetudinis eius.' Non contendit, neque clamavit: sed sicut agnus mansuetus deductus est ad victimam*; the first part, *non contendit, neque clamavit*, is from Mt 12.19. Cf too Smaragdus (*Collectiones*, PL 102, 251–2).

91–6 cf Bede, Hom. I.12, 72–6 (in the voice of Christ):

> Nulla personarum maiorum contemnat ab humilibus meis in remissionem peccatorum baptizari, cum meminerint dominum qui in spiritu sancto baptizans peccata dimittere solet suum baptizandum in aqua submisisse servi manibus caput.

The first part perhaps reflects Bede, Hom. I.12, 22–24:

> Venit filius Dei baptizari ab homine non anxia necessitate abluendi alicuius sui peccati 'qui peccatum non fecit ullum . . .'.

96–8 Cf Pope 11.17–19.

98–101 Bede, Hom. I.12, 1–8:

> Lectio sancti evangelii . . . magnum nobis et in domino et in servo dat perfectae humilitatis exemplum. In domino quidem quia cum sit dominus Deus non solum ab homine servo baptizari sed etiam ipse ad hunc baptizandus venire dignatus est. In servo autem quia cum sciret praecursorem se ac baptistam sui salvatoris esse destinatum memor tamen propriae fragilitatis iniunctum sibi humiliter excusavit officium. . . .

101–3 Bede, Hom. I.12, 56–7:

> Sed quia vera humilitas ipsa est quam oboedientia comes non deserit quod prius officium expavit humiliter implevit.

104–7 Bede, Hom. I.12, 63–5:

> Sine me modo, inquit, sine me modo ut iussi a te baptizari in aqua et tu postmodum a me quod quaeris baptizaberis in spiritu.

Combined with Augustine, *Tract.*, 4.14.8:

> Quid est: 'impleatur omnis iustitia'? Impleatur omnis humilitas.

109–14 A succinct rendering of Bede, Hom I.12, 83–94:

> Numquid enim credi decet domino tunc primum caelestia patuisse secreta cum recta fides habet non minus tempore quo cum hominibus conversatus

est quam post et antea patris in sinu mansisse et sedem tenuisse caelestem? Aut a tricesimo aetatis anno quando baptizatus est spiritus sancti dona percepit qui a prima conceptione spiritu sancto plenus semper existit? Nobis ergo . . . sunt haec celebrata mysteria. Quia enim nobis dominus sacrosancto sui corporis intinctu baptismi lavacrum dedicavit nobis quoque post acceptum baptisma caeli aditum patere et spiritum sanctum dari monstravit.

115–8 Ps 92.5: *Testimonia tua credibilia facta sunt nimis* (or *testimonia tua fide digna sunt valde*).

118–21 Cf Bede, Hom. I.12, 135–8:

Filius Dei baptizatur in homine, spiritus Dei descendit in columba, pater Deus adest in voce; sanctae et individuae trinitatis in baptismo declaratur mysterium.

It is followed by one of Ælfric's characteristic formulations of trinitarian belief (lines 121–33).

137–8 Sap 1.7: *Quoniam spiritus Domini replevit orbem terrarum.*

138–49 A resumé of Acts 2.1–11.

150–67 Primarily a recasting of passages from the earlier Pentecost homily, CH I.22, viz. 128–30, 173–5, 130–2, 138–42, 145–55, which are in turn drawn mainly from Gregory the Great's homily 30 and follow his application of the dove to the peaceful nature of Christ and the fire to the zeal of the apostles. (Haymo also contrasts the two appearances of the Spirit in his homily for Epiphany, but there is no close parallel to Ælfric.) Bede's interpretation is very different, focusing mainly on the application to the individual Christian, but Ælfric uses some of his details to develop the interpretation of the dove (Hom. I.12, 201–11):

A malitia aliena est; omnis amaritudo et ira et indignatio tollatur a nobis cum omni malitia. Nullum ore vel unguibus laedit ne minimas quidem musculas vel vermiculos quibus minores paene omnes aviculae se suosque pullos nutriunt . . . ipsa terrae fructibus et semine pascitur.

For 155–8 cf Mt 12.19: *Non contendet, neque clamabit, neque audiet aliquis in plateis vocem eius,* and CH I.22.140–1.

168–78 An expansion and recasting of CH I.22.156–65, applying the imagery of both the dove and the fire to the individual Christian; the ultimate source is again Gregory, Hom. 30. The details at 172–3 may also be influenced by the Bede passage used for 150–67 (Hom. I.12, 205–7):

Videamus ne dentes nostri sint arma et sagittae ne mordentes et comedentes invicem consumamur ab inivicem; contineamus manus a rapinis.

For 170–71 cf also Augustine, *Tract.*, 6.4.2–4:

Intellegat unusquisque, si habet Spiritum sanctum, simplicem se esse debere sicut columbam; habere cum fratribus veram pacem.

179–81 Augustine, *Tract.*, 6.3.14–16:

> Sunt enim qui dicuntur simplices, et pigri sunt; vocantur simplices, sunt autem segnes.

181–2 Rom 8.9 (not in Augustine): *Si quis Spiritum Christi non habet, hic non est eius.*

182–7 Probably influenced by Augustine's long discussion of the dove and comparisons with the raven and kite and other birds, but the parallels are not close. Cf Augustine, *Tract.*, 6.4.5–12, 6.12.11, 5.12.1–6 and esp. 6.12.10–12:

> Milvi rapiunt, accipitres rapiunt, corvi rapiunt; columbae non rapiunt.

and *Tract.*, 6.4.14–16:

> Sunt passeres brevissimi, vel muscas occidunt: nihil horum columba; non enim de morte pascitur.

(Cf too Bede's reference to the raven at Hom. I.15, 86–9.) Lines 184–5 repeat CH I.38.148–9, derived from Gregory.

188–91 Recasting CH I.22.156–8.

192–205 The ideas are in the main Augustinian, reiterated at length and in many shapes over Tractates 4–6. The closest parallels seem to be (Augustine, *Tract.*):

> [5.5.13–20] Si ergo solus Dominus baptizatus esset baptismo Iohannis, non deessent qui sic eum haberent, ut putarent baptismum Iohannis maiorem esse, quam est baptismus Christi. Dicerent enim: Usque adeo illud baptisma maius est, ut solus Christus eo baptizari meruisset. Ergo ut daretur nobis a Domino exemplum humilitatis . . . Christus suscepit quod ei opus non erat.
>
> [5.3.7–9] Sed quare missus est Iohannes baptizans? Quia oportebat baptizari Christum.
>
> [5.5.3–5] Sed quare non solus ipse baptizatus est a Iohanne, si ad hoc missus erat Iohannes, per quem baptizaretur Christus?
>
> [5.5.20–22] Et rursus, ne hoc ipsum quod accepit a Iohanne Christus, praeponeretur baptismati Christi, permissi sunt et alii baptizari a Iohanne.
>
> [5.4.6–14] Unde accepit, nisi a Domino Iesu Christo? . . . De Christo enim dictum est: 'Omnia per ipsum facta sunt': . . . Quomodo creavit Mariam, et creatus est per Mariam, sic dedit baptismum Iohanni, et baptizatus est a Iohanne.

I am not sure who the heretics mentioned at 192 are; Augustine seems to be talking hypothetically. And the reasons which Ælfric gives for the inferiority of John's baptism are Gregory's not Augustine's; cf above on lines 55–60 and CH I.25.

206–8 Cf Augustine, *Tract.*, 5.4.2–5:

> Baptismus quem accepit Iohannes, baptismus Iohannis dictus est; solus tale donum accepit: nullus ante illum iustorum, nullus post illum, ut acciperet baptismum, qui baptismus illius diceretur.

210–2 Augustine, *Tract.*, 5.5.22–4:

> Sed qui baptizati sunt a Iohanne, non eis suffecit: baptizati sunt enim baptismo Christi.

214–8 Perhaps following *Tract.*, 5.6.2–7, though I think Augustine's point is that Christ baptized no-one, rather than just a few:

> Dominus autem Iesus Christus noluit baptismum suum alicui dare, non ut nemo baptizaretur baptismo Domini, sed ut semper ipse Dominus baptizaret: id actum est, ut et per ministros Dominus baptizaret, id est, ut quos ministri Domini baptizaturi erant, Dominus baptizaret, non illi.

This is something of a Biblical crux; Jn 3.22 seems to describe Christ as baptizing, but Jn 4.2 corrects this: *Quamquam Iesus non baptizaret sed discipuli eius*. The warning against repeated baptism, a fundamental point of orthodox dogma since Augustine, is also made at CH I.20.257–9 and Pope 12.78–94.

219–28 Augustine, *Tract.*, 6.8.8–13:

> Sunt alii aliis sanctiores, sunt alii aliis meliores. Quare ergo si unus ab illo . . . iusto sancto baptizetur, alius ab alio inferioris meriti . . . unum tamen et par et aequale est quod acceperunt, nisi quia 'hic est qui baptizat'?

Cf too Haymo, Hom. 108, PL 118, 580C:

> Hoc autem sacramentum nec malus peius, nec bonus melius implere potest. Quia qualiscunque sit minister exterior, spiritus sanctus operator est interior. Unde post baptismum ecclesia peccantibus poenitentiam indicit, non autem baptismum iterat.

233–44 Apparently Ælfric's extension and summary of the argument about the doctrinal aspects of baptism, and the question of the unworthy priest. Lines 235–6 are probably Mt 23.3. Lines 243–4 are Lc 10.16: *Qui vos audit me audit, et qui vos spernit me spernit*.

245–99 A discussion of infant baptism. Fehr cited Theodulfus of Orleans and Amalarius of Metz, both of whom discuss the issues in detail, but neither has much in common with Ælfric's account. Theodulfus begins his *De Ordine Baptismi* with a chapter justifying infant baptism as a way of preserving an ancient custom of teaching and then baptising adults, going back to the apostles (*De Ordine*, PL 105, 224BC):

> Quod modo infantes catechumeni efficiuntur antiquus mos servatur. Quicunque enim ad apostolos credentes baptizandi adveniebant, instruebantur et docebantur ab eis, et instructi et docti de sacramento baptismatis et de caeteris regulis fidei, accipiebant sacrosanctum mysterium baptismatis. . . . Infantes ergo et audientes et catechumeni fiunt, non quo in eadem aetate et instrui et doceri possint, sed ut antiquus mos servetur, quo apostoli eos quos baptizaturi erant primum docebant et instruebant, sicut iam dictum est.

Ælfric instead refers to the old practice of the *halgan lareowas* baptizing infants by virtue of the faith of their parents and with the guarantee of their godfathers, though his justification by reference to original sin does resemble that in Theodulfus (*De Ordine*, PL 105, 228B):

> Quamvis illi necdum loqui possint, pro illis et confitentur et loquuntur qui eos de lavacro fontis suscipiunt. Nec immerito dignum est, ut qui aliorum peccatis obnoxii sunt, aliorum etiam confessione per mysterium baptismatis remissionem originalium percipiant peccatorum.

(Amalarius, *Liber Officialis*, I.24 is similar.) Lines 255–7 are John 3.3, cited Theodulfus, *De Ordine*, PL 105, 231.

For the practice of baptism in the early church see J. D. C. Fisher, *Christian Initiation: Baptism in the Medieval West* (London, 1965); and Sarah Foot, '"By water and by spirit": the administration of baptism in early Anglo-Saxon England', in *Pastoral Care before the Parish*, ed. John Blair and Richard Sharpe (Leicester, 1992), pp. 171–92.

262–72 Ælfric gives the story of the woman with a possessed daughter (Mc 7.25–30) as a justification and precedent for the child being saved by the parent's faith; it is also used by Amalarius, but the parallels are not close (*Liber Officialis*, I.24):

> [I.24.1] Scriptum est in evangelio Marci venisse syrofenissam mulierem ad Christum rogantem pro filia quae habebat spiritum inmundum. Cui Dominus dixit: 'Sine prius saturari filios: non est enim bonum sumere panem filiorum, et mittere canibus. At illa respondit et dicit ei: Utique, Domine; nam et catelli sub mensa comedunt de micis puerorum. Et ait illi: Propter hunc sermonem, vade; exiit daemonium de filia tua.' . . . [I.24.3] Ubi datur exemplum catechizando et baptizando infantes, quia videlicet per fidem et confessionem parentum in baptismo liberantur a diabolo parvuli, qui necdum per se sapere vel aliquid cogitare boni possunt aut mali.

287–98 A brief conclusion on the need for the baptized infant to learn about the faith when he matures. The Biblical quotations are:

> Rom 2.12: *Quicumque enim sine lege peccaverunt, sine lege et peribunt.*
> 1 Cor 14.38: *Si quis autem ignorat ignorabitur.*
> Jac 4.8: *Adpropinquate Domino et adpropinquabit vobis.*
> Ps 111.1: *Beatus vir qui timet Dominum; in mandatis eius volet nimis.*

The additional quotation in MSS B and R at 294, an Ælfrician addition, is probably based on Ps 48.13:

> Et homo cum in honore esset non intellexit conparatus est iumentis insipientibus et similis factus est illis.

Cf the reworking of this at Pope 16.59 ff.

4 SECOND SUNDAY AFTER EPIPHANY

The homily expounds the Gospel for the day, John 2.1–11, on the marriage at Cana and Christ's first miracle. Interpreting the six water-vessels as the six ages of the world and the wine as the spiritual truth hidden in the events of those ages, Ælfric is able to use the occasion to convey the major events of the Old Testament—the creation of Adam, the killing of Abel, the flood, the sacrifice of Isaac, the conflict of Saul and David, and the Babylonian exile—and their significance for the Christian faith.

Ælfric specifies Bede as source at the beginning of his exposition, and does seem to have drawn extensively on his homily on the Gospel passage, Hom. I.14; it is given for the occasion in Paul the Deacon's homiliary. But he would also have known two adaptations of Bede, by Smaragdus and Haymo, and could have consulted one of Bede's own sources, Augustine's Tractates on John: Smaragdus repeats, often in abridged form, most of Bede's points but supplements them with other material, while Haymo characteristically expands the exegesis, using more Biblical material and some other sources, and both draw independently on Augustine's Tractates. It is hard to say which was the precise source at any particular point, since Ælfric often abbreviates material in a similar way to Smaragdus and expands in a manner resembling Haymo, but there are occasional points which suggest a debt to both as well as Bede. The *trahtnere* to whom he refers at 297 is in fact Haymo not Bede. If Ælfric consulted the Tractates directly, there is no sign of it. But he does seem to have drawn on Augustine, perhaps the *De Catechizandis Rudibus*, in developing the idea of the two cities, Jerusalem and Babylon.[1]

Bede methodically interprets the events of each age first in a literal or moral sense (represented by the water) and then in an allegorical or anagogical sense (represented by the wine), and in this he is followed by Smaragdus and Haymo; Ælfric confines his interpretation to the allegorical level.

Sources and Notes

The following texts are cited below:

1. Augustine, *De Catechizandis Rudibus*, ed. J. B. Bauer, CCSL 46 (Turnhout, 1969), pp. 121–78.
2. Bede, *Homiliae*, ed. D. Hurst, CCSL 122 (Turnhout, 1955), Hom. I.14 (pp. 95–104).
3. Haymo of Auxerre, *Homiliae de Tempore*, PL 118, Hom. 18, cols. 126–37.
4. Smaragdus, *Collectiones in Evangelia et Epistolas*, PL 102, cols. 84–90.

[1] Förster (1894, pp. 22–3) identified the Bede homily, and noted its close agreement with Smaragdus. Smetana (1959, p. 34) pointed out the inclusion of the Bede homily in Paul the Deacon's homiliary, and (1961, pp. 463–4) suggested the use of Haymo. Joyce Hill (1992) has made a strong case for the importance of Smaragdus as a source, arguing that Ælfric took from his exposition most of the material that is also in Bede as well as some material that is also in Haymo. Since, as Hill agrees, it is likely that Ælfric had consulted all three expositions it is perhaps a scholastic nicety to try to define which one provided material that is in two or three of them; but Hill seems to me mistaken in attributing 297–305 to Smaragdus, for the reasons given in the note below, and she does not mention the passage at 111–22, in which Ælfric is closer to Bede than to Smaragdus.

1–24 Jn 2.1–11:

(1) Et die tertio nuptiae factae sunt in Cana Galilaeae et erat mater Iesu ibi. (2) Vocatus est autem ibi et Iesus et discipuli eius ad nuptias. (3) Et deficiente vino dicit mater Iesu ad eum: vinum non habent. (4) Et dicit ei Iesus: quid mihi et tibi est mulier, nondum venit hora mea. (5) Dicit mater eius ministris: quodcumque dixerit vobis facite. (6) Erant autem ibi lapideae hydriae sex positae secundum purificationem Iudaeorum, capientes singulae metretas binas vel ternas. (7) Dicit eis Iesus: implete hydrias aqua, et impleverunt eas usque ad summum. (8) Et dicit eis Iesus: haurite nunc et ferte architriclino, et tulerunt. (9) Ut autem gustavit architriclinus aquam vinum factam et non sciebat unde esset, ministri autem sciebant qui haurierant aquam, vocat sponsum architriclinus. (10) et dicit ei: omnis homo primum bonum vinum ponit et cum inebriati fuerint tunc id quod deterius est; tu servasti bonum vinum usque adhuc. (11) Hoc fecit initium signorum Iesus in Cana Galilaeae et manifestavit gloriam suam et crediderunt in eum discipuli eius.

25–9 A succinct summary of Bede's long-winded argument at Hom. I.14, 1–9:

Quod dominus noster atque salvator ad nuptias vocatus non solum venire sed et miraculum ibidem quo convivas laetificaret facere dignatus est . . . fidem recte credentium confirmat. . . . Si enim thoro inmaculato et nuptiis debita castitate celebratis culpa inesset, nequaquam dominus ad has venire nequaquam eas signorum suorum initiis consecrare voluisset.

Ælfric's qualification in the justification of marriage at 28–9, repeated at 300–1 and more fully at CH II.6.118–27, is perhaps his own interpretation of Bede's 'due chastity'; Haymo's citation (Hom. 18, PL 118, 126D–7A) of Paul, esp. 1 Cor 7.2–4, points if anything the opposite way to Ælfric's comment.

29–36 Cf Bede, Hom. I.14, 31–3:

Sponsus ergo Christus, sponsa eius est ecclesia, filii sponsi vel nuptiarum singuli quique fidelium eius sunt

and Smaragdus (apparently based on Jerome), *Collectiones*, PL 102, 85AB:

Dominus ad nuptias in hunc mundum venit, quia sanctam ecclesiam sibi copulavit. De qua apostolus ait: 'Aptavi vos uni viro virginem castam exhibere Christo' (2 Cor 11.2), habet ergo sponsam ecclesiam.

For the reference to the church as virgin mother (lines 34–6), cf CH I.33.19–23 and II.1.115–7.

37–44 Cf Bede, Hom. I.14, 53–9:

Sed et hoc quod in Cana Galilaeae, id est in zelo transmigrationis eaedem nuptiae factae perhibentur typice denuntiat eos maxime gratia Christi dignos existere qui zelo fervere piae devotionis et aemulari carismata maiora ac de vitiis ad virtutes bona operando de terrenis ad aeterna norunt sperando et amando transmigrare.

(Repeated by Smaragdus, *Collectiones*, PL 102, 85B.) Haymo spells out the details on Cana more closely, Hom. 18, PL 118, 127D–8A:

> Cana quippe viculus Galilaeae, zelus interpretatur. Galilaea namque transmigratio facta in nostra lingua dicitur. Ex qua interpretatione ostenditur, quia ille feliciter ad has nuptias discumbit, qui zelo amoris Dei tactus, de terreno amore ad coeleste desiderium transmigraverit.

Ælfric's use of *anda* for *zelum* is puzzling. Bede and Haymo interpret Cana as zeal in a positive sense, a passion *for* God. Ælfric interprets it as *anda* in an adverse sense, as a passion *against* wrong. The word seems otherwise always to have a derogatory sense in his writings, often being used for one of the deadly sins, and nearly always in other Old English works, though there is some use of it in the *Pastoral Care* as righteous indignation; his argument for a favourable sense here perhaps owes something to Alfred, but it remains surprising that he should substitute a hostile emotion for the devotion and love defined by his sources.

45–7 Cf Bede, Hom. I.14, 59–62:

> Discumbente autem ad nuptias domino vinum defecit ut vino meliore per ipsum mirabili ordine facto manifestaretur gloria latentis in homine Dei et credentium in eum fides aucta proficeret.

(Repeated by Smaragdus, *Collectiones*, PL 102, 85CD.)

48–51 Bede, Hom. I.14, 78–86 [= Smaragdus, *Collectiones*, PL 102, 86A]:

> Sed in eo quod miraculum facturus ait, 'Quid mihi et tibi est, mulier?' significat se divinitatis, qua miraculum erat patrandum, non principium temporaliter accepisse de matre, sed aeternitatem semper habuisse de patre. 'Quid mihi, inquit, et tibi est, mulier? nondum venit hora mea.' Cui divinitati quam ex patre semper habui, cum tua carne, ex qua carnem suscepi, commune non est, nondum venit hora mea, ut fragilitatem sumptae ex te humanitatis moriendo demonstrem.

Put more succinctly and pointedly by Ælfric, in the form of an imagined answer to Mary, a form perhaps prompted by Haymo, Hom. 18, PL 118, 129D.

52–5 Bede, Hom. I.14, 97–100 [= Smaragdus, *Collectiones*, PL 102, 86B]:

> Hydriae vocantur vasa aquarum receptui parata; Graece enim aqua ydor dicitur. Aqua autem scripturae sacrae scientiam designat, quae suos auditores et a peccatorum sorde abluere et divinae cognitionis solet fonte potare.

The comment is oddly placed in the Old English text. The word *hydriae* has not been used by Ælfric and does not strictly need to be explained, and in any case the point should properly come later, at line 70 where the vessels are mentioned. Perhaps he was interested in the possibility of a word-play on Greek *hydriae* and *ydor* and Old English *ingehyd*; one can imagine his pleasure at a piece of exegesis which works better in Old English than in Latin.

55–7 Cf Haymo, Hom. 18, PL 118, 131A:

> Quae bene lapideae esse referuntur, quia contra tentationes diaboli firma et fixa sunt praecordia sanctorum.

58–60 Cf Bede, Hom. I.14, 62–8:

Quod si mysterium quaerimus, apparente in carne Domino, meraca illa legalis sensus suavitas paulatim coeperat ob carnalem Pharisaeorum interpretationem, a prisca sua virtute deficere, qui mox ea quae carnalia videbantur mandata ad spiritalem convertit doctrinam, cunctamque litterae legalis superficiem evangelica caelestis gratiae virtute mutavit, quod est vinum fecisse de aqua.

(Repeated Smaragdus, *Collectiones*, PL 102, 85D.) The sense is difficult, in both source and Old English, partly because both conflate the image of the wine that runs short with the water that is turned into wine. Bede redefines the wine running short as the old law losing its 'sweetness' through its corruption into fleshly senses by the Pharisees; Ælfric interprets it as the old law coming to an end as regards (or perhaps because of) fleshly works, through Christ's coming, and being changed into spiritual senses. Bede, followed by Smaragdus and Haymo, sees the fleshly nature of the Old Law as due to its corruption by the Pharisees; Ælfric seems to see it as innate to the Old Law.

60–67 Bede, Hom. I.14, 124–7:

Quantum inter aquam et vinum tantum distare inter sensum illum quo scripturae ante adventum salvatoris intellegebantur et eum quem veniens ipse revelavit apostolis eorumque discipulis perpetuo sequendum.

For 65–7 cf CH I.25.98–100.

70–78 Cf Smaragdus, *Collectiones*, PL 102, 86D-87A:

Non enim dictum est, capientes metretas, aliae binas, aliae ternas, sed ipsae sex hydriae capiebant metretas binas vel ternas . . . quia scripturae sanctae auctores, modo de patre tantum loquuntur et filio, modo etiam spiritus sancti faciunt mentionem. In binis vel ternis, totamque, unus est Deus, intellige trinitatem.

The first part is from Augustine's Tractates and also occurs in Haymo, Hom.18, PL 118, 135D, the rest is abridged from Bede, Hom. I.14, 116–24.

79–83 Haymo, Hom. 18, PL 118, 130BC:

Quoniam autem secundum purificationem Iudaeorum positae referuntur, traditio habebat Iudaeorum, et maxime Pharisaeorum, ut in conviviis et nuptiis vasa cum aqua haberentur, propter purificationem Iudaeorum, vel lavationem manuum, vel quidquid necesse esset.

(The reference to the floor is Ælfric's own detail.)

83–91 Bede, Hom. I.14 at 103, followed by Smaragdus, *Collectiones*, PL 102, 86C, mentions the six ages at this point, but they are listed in detail by Haymo, Hom. 18, PL 118, 131AB:

Bene autem sex fuisse referuntur, quia sex sunt mundi huius aetates, in quibus Deus omnipotens hydrias spirituales, id est sanctos viros ad nostram eruditionem et ablutionem mittere dignatus est. Prima mundi aetas fuit ab Adam usque ad Noe, secunda a Noe usque ad Abraham, tertia ab Abraham usque ad David, quarta a David usque ad transmigrationem Babyloniae, quinta a transmigratione Babyloniae usque ad adventum Christi in carne, sexta a primo adventu Domini, quo venit redimere mundum, usque ad secundum eius adventum, quo venturus est mundum iudicare.

Both Haymo and Smaragdus end the sixth age with Christ's second coming; Ælfric ends it with the coming of Antichrist.

92–9 Bede, Hom. I.14, 134–6, 127–32 [= Smaragdus, *Collectiones*, PL 102, 87B]:

Videamus ergo, fratres, sex hydrias scripturarum aqua salutari repletas, videamus eamdem aquam in suavissimum vini odorem gustumque conversam. . . . Et quidem potuit Dominus vacuas implere hydrias vino, qui in exordio mundanae creationis cuncta creavit ex nihilo; sed maluit de aqua facere vinum, quo typice doceret non se ad solvendum inprobandumque, sed ad implendum potius legem prophetasque venisse.

The description of the water as *wann*, a word not otherwise found in Ælfric, presumably contrasts it with the bright or colourful appearance of the wine, and can perhaps be related to the earlier description of the old law as a *sceadu*.

100–4 Bede does not refer to Adam; Ælfric takes the comment from Smaragdus (who took it from Augustine); Smaragdus, *Collectiones*, PL 102, 90A:

Prima ergo hydria impleta est in Adam, quando de latere eius, illo dormiente, fabricata est Eva. Dormivit in cruce Christus, et de latere eius formatur ecclesia.

104–10 Bede, Hom. I.14, 136–7, 145–7, 150–1:

In prima aetate saeculi Abel iustum frater invidens occidit. . . . Sed si intellexerint Cain homicidam Iudaeorum esse perfidiam, occisionem Abel passionem esse domini salvatoris . . . nimirum aquam in vinum mutatam repperiunt, quia sacrae dicta legis sacratius intellegunt.

(Repeated Smaragdus, *Collectiones*, PL 102, 87C, and expanded Haymo, Hom. 18, PL 118, 132A-C.)

111–22 Bede, Hom. I.14, 152–4, 158–61, 164–167 [= Smaragdus, *Collectiones*, PL 102, 87D]:

Secunda aetate saeculi inchoante deletus est aquis diluvii mundus ob peccatorum magnitudinem, sed solus Noe est propter iustitiam cum domo sua liberatus in archa. . . . At vero dum altius aspicere coeperit, et in archa ecclesiam, in Noe Christum, in aqua diluente peccatores aquam baptismi, quae peccata diluit . . . intellexerit, vinum profecto de aqua factum miratur, quia in veteris historia facti suam ablutionem, sanctificationem, iustificationem prophetari contemplatur.

122–8 Ælfric's own expansion, it seems.

129–30 The apologetic note presumably refers to the following retelling of the Abraham and Isaac story, since Ælfric's version of the preceding Noah story is as brief as Bede's. (He had told the Noah story at some length in CH I.1.176–201, but this is his first account of Abraham and Isaac.)

131–60 The story is summarised by Bede, Hom. I.14, 167–72, and Smaragdus, and given more fully by Haymo, but in more detail by Ælfric, drawing on Gen 22.1–19:

> (1) Temptavit Deus Abraham et . . . (2) ait ei: tolle filium tuum unigenitum quem diligis Isaac et vade in terram Visionis atque offer eum ibi holocaustum super unum montium quem monstravero tibi. (3) Igitur Abraham de nocte consurgens stravit asinum suum, ducens secum duos iuvenes et Isaac filium suum, cumque concidisset ligna in holocaustum abiit ad locum quem praeceperat ei Deus. (4) Die autem tertio elevatis oculis vidit locum procul. (5) Dixitque ad pueros suos: expectate hic cum asino ego et puer illuc usque properantes postquam adoraverimus revertemur ad vos. (6) Tulit quoque ligna holocausti et inposuit super Isaac filium suum; ipse vero portabat in manibus ignem et gladium cumque duo pergerent simul (7) dixit Isaac patri suo: pater mi . . . ecce inquit ignis et ligna. Ubi est victima holocausti? (8) Dixit Abraham: Deus providebit sibi victimam holocausti fili mi. Pergebant ergo pariter (9) veneruntque ad locum quem ostenderat ei Deus in quo aedificavit altare et desuper ligna conposuit, cumque conligasset Isaac filium suum posuit eum in altari super struem lignorum. (10) Extenditque manum et arripuit gladium ut immolaret filium. (11) Et ecce angelus Domini de caelo clamavit dicens Abraham, Abraham, qui respondit adsum. (12) Dixitque ei: non extendas manum tuam super puerum neque facias illi quicquam. Nunc cognovi quod timeas Dominum et non peperceris filio tuo unigenito propter me. (13) Levavit Abraham oculos viditque post tergum arietem inter vepres herentem cornibus quem adsumens obtulit holocaustum pro filio. . . . (15) Vocavit autem angelus Domini Abraham secundo de caelo dicens: (16) per memet ipsum iuravi dicit Dominus quia fecisti rem hanc et non pepercisti filio tuo unigenito (17) benedicam tibi et multiplicabo semen tuum sicut stellas caeli et velut harenam quae est in litore maris. Possidebit semen tuum portas inimicorum suorum (18) et benedicentur in semine tuo omnes gentes terrae quia oboedisti voci meae. (19) Reversus est Abraham ad pueros suos abieruntque Bersabee simul et habitavit ibi.

161–78 Bede, Hom. I.14, 174–82:

> Quod si in immolatione filii unici dilecti passionem eius intellegis, de quo dicit pater: 'Hic est filius meus dilectus, in quo mihi complacui' (Mt 3.17); in quo quia divinitate inpassibili permanente, sola humanitas mortem passa est et dolorem, quasi filius offertur, sed aries mactatur; si intellegis benedictionem, quae promissa est Abrahae, in te de gentibus credendis

munus esse completum, nimirum de aqua tibi vinum fecit, quia spiritalem sensum, cuius nova flagrantia debriaris, aperuit.

Haymo's adaptation may have furnished some details of phrasing and interpretation as well (Hom. 18, PL 118, 133D):

. . . Ut intelligat per Abraham Deum Patrem, et per Isaac unigenitum filium eius, Dominum Iesum Christum, qui est unigenitus filius patris, per immolationem Isaac Domini passionem, qui pro nobis passurus, lignum in quo pateretur ipse portavit. . . .

Ælfric seems to have added the reference to Isaac's and Christ's acceptance of their fate, lines 166–7, and the quotations from St Paul. Lines 165–6 are Rom 8.32:

Qui etiam Filio suo non pepercit sed pro nobis omnibus tradidit illum quomodo non etiam cum illo omnia nobis donabit.

Line 168 is Phil 2.8: *Humiliavit semet ipsum factus oboediens usque ad mortem mortem autem crucis.* Lines 175–6 are Gal 3.29: *Si autem vos Christi ergo Abrahae semen estis secundum promissionem heredes* (cf CH I.6.115–6).

179–99 The story of Saul and David is briefly alluded to by Bede, and told in more detail by Haymo (Hom. 18, PL 118, 134A). Ælfric gives a fuller account, from 1 Samuel; cf esp. 1 Sam 16:

(1) Dixitque Dominus ad Samuelem: Usquequo tu luges Saul, cum ego proiecerim eum ne regnet super Israhel? Imple cornu tuum oleo, et veni, ut mittam te ad Isai Bethleemitem: providi enim in filiis eius mihi regem. . . . (3) Et vocabis Isai ad victimam, et ego ostendam tibi quid facias, et ungues quemcumque monstravero tibi. (4) Fecit ergo Samuel, sicut locutus est ei Dominus. Venitque in Bethleem . . . (12) et ait Dominus: Surge, ungue eum, ipse est enim. (13) Tulit ergo Samuel cornu olei, et unxit eum in medio fratrum eius: et directus est Spiritus Domini a die illa in David, et deinceps. . . . (14) Spiritus autem Domini recessit a Saul, et exagitabat eum spiritus nequam, a Domino.

The enmity of Saul and David's flight is in 1 Samuel 18.6 ff, and Saul's death is at 1 Samuel 31.1–7.

200–209 Bede, Hom. I.14, 188–95:

At si in Saule Iudaeos persequentes, in David Christum et ecclesiam significari cognoverit, illorum ob perfidiam et carnale simul imperium et spiritale destructum, Christi autem et ecclesiae regnum semper esse mansurum, poculum utique vini de aqua factum sentiet; quia se suamque vitam et regnum, sed et ipsum regem ibi scriptum legere novit, ubi prius quasi de aliis veterem legebat historiam.

210–29 The Babylonian exile is summarised by Bede (Hom. I.14, 195–9) and Smaragdus and a little more fully by Haymo (Hom. 18, PL 118, 134BC). Ælfric draws on 4 Reg 25 for the beginning of the exile and Ezra for the restoration.

230–39 Bede (Hom. I.14, 202–14) interprets Jerusalem as the church, Babylon as 'confusion of sinners', Nebuchadnezzar as the devil and Jesus as Christ. In taking Jerusalem as heaven and Babylon as hell Ælfric agrees with Haymo (Hom. 18, PL 118, 134CD):

> Si vero ad altiorem intellectum mentem tuam transtuleris, ut intelligas per populum Israeliticum genus humanum; per Nabuchodonosor, qui populum captivavit, diabolum figurari, per Babyloniam, quae confusio interpretatur, infernum; ubi diabolus genus humanum post praevaricationem captivum traxit; per Ierusalem, quae visio pacis interpretatur, coelestem patriam.

But Haymo appears to read the story as referring typologically to the fall and redemption of mankind, and Ælfric agrees with Bede in reading it morally, with reference to the recurrent 'capture' of souls.

239–67 Here Ælfric digresses from the close exegesis of the Gospel passage to explore the idea of the two cities, symbolized by Jerusalem and Babylon, warring eternally against each other. The idea is Augustinian, developed in *De Civitate Dei*. Closest, perhaps, to Ælfric's development of this idea is Augustine's *De Catechizandis Rudibus*, cc.19–21:

> [20.54–62] Ibi Ierusalem condita est famosissima civitas dei, serviens in signo liberae civitatis, quae caelestis Ierusalem dicitur, quod verbum est hebraeum, et interpretatur visio pacis. Cuius cives sunt omnes sanctificati homines qui fuerunt, et qui sunt, et qui futuri sunt; et omnes sanctificati spiritus, etiam quicumque in excelsis caelorum partibus pia devotione obtemperant Deo, nec imitantur impiam diaboli superbiam et angelorum eius. Huius civitatis rex est dominus Iesus Christus. . . . [21.3–9] Sicut autem Ierusalem significat civitatem societatemque sanctorum, sic Babylonia significat civitatem societatemque iniquorum, quoniam dicitur interpretari confusio. De quibus duabus civitatibus, ab exordio generis humani usque in finem saeculi permixte temporum varietate currentibus, et ultimo iudicio separandis, paulo ante iam diximus.

The nearest to Ælfric's discussion of those who appear to serve the other city (lines 247–67) that I can find is in Augustine's *De Catechizandis Rudibus*, 21.20–37:

> Hoc autem totum figurate significat ecclesiam Christi in omnibus sanctis eius, qui sunt cives Ierusalem caelestis, servituram fuisse sub regibus huius saeculi. Dicit enim et apostolica doctrina, 'ut omnis anima sublimioribus potestatibus subdita sit'; et 'ut reddantur omnibus omnia; cui tributum, tributum; cui vectigal, vectigal' (Rom 13.1, 7); et caetera quae salvo Dei nostri cultu, constitutionis humanae principibus reddimus; quando et ipse Dominus, ut nobis huius sanae doctrinae praeberet exemplum, pro capite hominis quo erat indutus, tributum solvere non dedignatus est. Iubentur autem etiam servi christiani et boni fideles dominis suis temporalibus aequanimiter fideliterque servire: quos iudicaturi sunt, si usque in finem iniquos invenerint; aut cum quibus aequaliter regnaturi sunt, si et illi ad

verum Deum conversi fuerint. Omnibus tamen praecipitur servire humanis potestatibus atque terrenis, quo usque post tempus praefinitum, quod significant septuaginta anni, ab istius saeculi confusione tanquam de captivitate Babyloniae, sicut Ierusalem liberetur ecclesia.

Ælfric alludes at 252–4 to Mt 22.21, perhaps expanding on the allusion to tribute in the *De Catechizandis Rudibus* passage: *Tunc ait illis: Reddite ergo quae sunt Caesaris, Caesari; et quae sunt Dei, Deo*. Lines 254–6 are 1 Petr 2.18 (*Servi, subditi estote in omni timore dominis, non tantum bonis et modestis, sed etiam dyscolis*), perhaps expanding on the reference to *servi* above (though PL identifies the reference there as Eph 6.5). Lines 261–2 are presumably based on Mt 23.3:

Omnia ergo quaecumque dixerint vobis, servate, et facite; secundum opera vero eorum nolite facere; dicunt enim, et non faciunt.

and 264–5 probably alludes to Mt 3.12 (or Lc 3.17):

et congregabit triticum suum in horreum, paleas autem comburet igni inextinguibili.

268–76 Cf Haymo, Hom. 18, PL 118, 134D:

Per Iesum sacerdotem magnum, Dominum nostrum Iesum Christum, qui factus est sacerdos in aeternum secundum ordinem Melchiscdech, qui electos suos de captivitate Babyloniae ad coelestem patriam revocavit: hydria tua, quae prius aquam habebat, conversa est tibi in vinum.

276–81 Bede, Hom. I.14, 214–7 [= Smaragdus, *Collectiones*, PL 102, 88C]:

Sexta inchoante saeculi aetate dominus in carne apparens octava die nativitatis iuxta legem circumcisus est, tricesima et tertia post haec ad templum delatus, et legalia pro eo sunt munera oblata.

281–93 Bede suggests baptism as the first allegorical reading, but then the general resurrection (Hom. I.14, 231–9):

Porro si circumcisionis diem ad generalem humani generis resurrectionem, quando mortalis propago cessabit, mortalitas tota in immortalitatem mutabitur, interpretaris: et circumcisos induci in templum cum hostiis intellexeris, quando post resurrectionem universali expleto iudicio sancti iam incorruptibiles facti, ad contemplandam perpetuo speciem divinae maiestatis cum bonorum operum muneribus intrabunt: mirandum profecto, vinum de aqua fieri videbis.

Ælfric's *seo galnys forðwyrt and ablinð ælc hæmed* (line 284) presumably expands Bede's *mortalis propago cessabit*. Lines 291–3 allude to Jn 2.10, not cited at this point in the sources. Ælfric's comment on other interpretations at 281–2 may also refer to his moral interpretation in CH I.6.

294–7 Bede does not in fact offer much further exposition beyond this point, but Ælfric may be referring to the literal or moral interpretations which he has given throughout, and which Ælfric has omitted; or, as Hill suggests, to the material which Smaragdus added from Augustine.

297–305 Haymo, Hom. 18, PL 118, 136BC:

> Architriclinus dicitur princeps triclinii . . . triclinium autem est domus tres ordines habens. . . . Spiritaliter vero sicut per architriclinum magistri ecclesiae designantur, sic per triclinium ipsa ecclesia exprimitur, quae tres habet ordines, coniugatorum, continentium atque virginum.

A somewhat similar passage occurs at this point in two manuscripts of Bede, but it differs significantly in defining the three orders as married, chaste and *doctores* rather than *virgines* (as too does Smaragdus, *Collectiones*, PL 102, 89A). For the three orders cf esp. CH II.6.115 ff.

308–311 Cf Bede, Hom. I.14, 277–8:

> Doctorum est cognoscere distantiam legis et evangelii, veritatis et umbrae.

and perhaps Haymo's *magistri ecclesiae* above.

320–3 Bede, Hom. I.14, 282–5:

> Manifestavit hoc signo quia ipse esset rex gloriae, et ideo sponsus ecclesiae, qui ut homo communis veniret ad nuptias, sed quasi dominus caeli et terrae elementa prout voluisset, converteret.

5 SEPTUAGESIMA

The homily expounds the Gospel passage for the day, the parable of the vineyard from Matthew 20.1–16, with a brief excursus at the end on the meaning of Septuagesima and the liturgical practice of the period. Ælfric follows Gregory in offering a threefold interpretation, though the first and second are not explicitly distinguished: firstly, the vineyard is the church, the vines are the righteous from Abel onwards, and the workers called at various hours of the day are the preachers sent to educate the people at different periods of history (lines 36–71); secondly, the workers are themselves the righteous, cultivating the true faith at different times in the past, firstly the Hebrews and then the Gentiles (lines 71–90); thirdly, the workers are individuals called to the faith at different times of their life (lines 90–142). The subsequent discussion contrasting the patriarchs and prophets who had to wait in limbo and the Christians of the present who go direct to heaven (lines 143–68) seems to revert to the second. The primary source is Gregory the Great's homily on the parable, which Ælfric probably found in Paul the Deacon's homiliary for this occasion and generally follows very closely indeed, with often close imitation of his syntax and wording. The one major omission is the exemplum in section 7, which he had already used in CH I.35.[1] Yet in small ways there are signs of his interest in pursuing a slightly different line from Gregory, especially in dealing with the knotty issues

[1] The sources are discussed by Förster (1894, pp. 3, 49), Smetana (1959, p. 196), Smetana (1961, p. 466, suggesting Haymo), D. Whitelock, in *Sweet's Anglo-Saxon Reader* (rev. ed., Oxford, 1967), pp. 249–51, and Cross 1969.

of merit and grace. In emphasising that the thief on the cross was justly saved before the apostles because of his superior belief, he gives greater weight to merit and justice, and the same concern perhaps lies behind his greater emphasis on the limbo in which the patriarchs and prophets rested before redemption (lines 152–4). His firm insistence on the multitude of those who are saved, in contrast to Gregory's insistence on only a few, repeats a position he had taken in an earlier homily, CH I.35, also in opposition to Gregory, and seems to work in the direction of an acceptance of merit rather than the arbitrariness of divine grace. Yet as if to balance that emphasis, Ælfric develops further the role of grace in fostering the will to good, at 228–32.

Some of the Biblical quotations which he adds in support of the argument are also to be found in Haymo's reworking of Gregory, but I am not sure that this is more than coincidental agreement. There are though occasional points for which he might be indebted to other works of Gregory, Bede and Augustine. For the excursus on the liturgy there are, as Förster showed, close parallels with the *Liber Officialis* of Amalarius of Metz, though rearranged in ways which suggest he might have been relying on material absorbed and remembered long before rather than working directly from the Latin text.[2]

Sources and Notes

The following texts are cited below:

1. Amalarius, *Liber Officialis*, ed. J. Hanssens in *Amalarii Episcopi Opera Liturgica Omnia*, Studi e Testi 139 (Vatican City, 1948).
2. Gregory the Great, *Homiliae in Evangelia*, PL 76, Hom. 19, cols. 1153–9.
3. Haymo of Auxerre, *Homiliae de Tempore*, PL 118, Hom. 21, cols.154–63.

1–33 Mt 20.1–16:

> (1) Simile est enim regnum caelorum homini patri familias qui exiit primo mane conducere operarios in vineam suam. (2) Conventione autem facta cum operariis ex denario diurno misit eos in vineam suam. (3) Et egressus circa horam tertiam vidit alios stantes in foro otiosos. (4) Et illis dixit ite et vos in vineam et quod iustum fuerit dabo vobis. (5) Illi autem abierunt. Iterum autem exiit circa sextam et nonam horam et fecit similiter. (6) Circa undecimam vero exiit et invenit alios stantes et dicit illis: quid hic statis tota die otiosi. (7) Dicunt ei: quia nemo nos conduxit. Dicit illis: ite et vos in vineam. (8) Cum sero autem factum esset dicit dominus vineae procuratori suo: voca operarios et redde illis mercedem incipiens a novissimis usque ad primos. (9) Cum venissent ergo qui circa undecimam horam venerant, acceperunt singulos denarios. (10) Venientes autem et

[2] There is a similar discussion of Septuagesima in Ælfric's Letter to the Monks of Eynsham, written around 1005, but he seems to have gone back to Amalarius for the material rather than using this vernacular account; see Jones 1998, pp. 118–20 and 172–6, for an excellent account of Ælfric's treatment of the material.

primi, arbitrati sunt quod plus essent accepturi; acceperunt autem et ipsi singulos denarios. (11) Et accipientes murmurabant adversus patrem familias (12) dicentes: hii novissimi una hora fecerunt et pares illos nobis fecisti qui portavimus pondus diei et aestus. (13) At ille respondens uni eorum dixit: amice non facio tibi iniuriam; nonne ex denario convenisti mecum? (14) Tolle quod tuum est et vade; volo autem et huic novissimo dare sicut et tibi. (15) Aut non licet mihi quod volo facere, an oculus tuus nequam est quia ego bonus sum? (16) Sic erunt novissimi primi et primi novissimi; multi sunt enim vocati pauci autem electi.

34–6 Gregory, Hom. 19, PL 76, 1154B:

In explanatione sua multa ad loquendum sancti Evangelii lectio postulat, quam volo, si possum, sub brevitate perstringere, ne vos et extensa processio, et prolixa expositio videatur onerare.

36–9 Though presented in Gregory's voice, the opening words of the exposition are not in fact from the main source (at least in the form of it that has come down) but are repeated from CH I.35.27–8, which drew in turn on Gregory's homily 28.

39–50 Gregory, Hom. 19, PL 76, 1154BC:

Quis vero patrisfamilias similitudinem rectius tenet quam conditor noster, qui regit quos condidit, et electos suos sic in hoc mundo possidet, quasi subiectos dominus in domo? Qui habet vineam, universalem scilicet ecclesiam, quae, ab Abel iusto usque ad ultimum electum qui in fine mundi nasciturus est, quot sanctos protulit, quasi tot palmites misit.

Ælfric interpolates two Biblical quotations which are also used, among many others, by Haymo (Homily 21, PL 118, 155B) in his adaptation of Gregory's argument; Is 5.7: *Vinea enim Domini exercituum domus Israhel est*, and Mt 21.43: *Ideo dico vobis, quia auferetur a vobis regnum Dei, et dabitur genti facienti fructus eius.*

50–61 Gregory, Hom. 19, PL 76, 1154C:

Hic itaque paterfamilias ad excolendam vineam suam mane, hora tertia, sexta, nona, et undecima operarios conducit, quia a mundi huius initio usque in finem ad erudiendam plebem fidelium praedicatores congregare non destitit.

Ælfric develops Gregory's vague reference to cultivating the vines into a more detailed image of pruning away the ill-growing shoots (the vices), so that new shots may grow and the vines be fruitful in good works. None of the commentaries that I have seen goes into this kind of detail, and Ælfric may have simply been drawing on his own understanding of vine-cultivation and its symbolism (somewhat as he does with trees in CH II.26); a slight parallel can be found in Gregory's *Regula Pastoralis*, PL 77, 76C:

Magnus quippe susceptae Ecclesiae colonus [= *St Paul*], alios palmites ut crescere debeant rigat; alios cum plus iusto crescere conspicit resecat, ne

> aut non crescendo non ferant fructus, aut, immoderate crescendo, quos protulerint amittant.

Thorpe translates *ymbhwyrft* 'compass', but BT suggests 'care, attention', citing King Alfred's use of *ymbhweorfan* in a similar sense at *Pastoral Care*, c.40 (293.3, translating the passage quoted above).

62–71 A close rendering of Gregory, Hom. 19, PL 76, 1154CD:

> Mane etenim mundi fuit ab Adam usque ad Noe, hora vero tertia a Noe usque ad Abraham, sexta quoque ab Abraham usque ad Moysen, nona autem a Moyse usque ad adventum Domini, undecima vero ab adventu Domini usque ad finem mundi. . . . Ad erudiendam ergo Dominus plebem suam, quasi ad excolendam vineam suam, nullo tempore destitit operarios mittere, quia et prius per patres, et postmodum per legis doctores et prophetas, ad extremum vero per apostolos, dum plebis suae mores excoluit, quasi per operarios in vineae cultura laboravit.

71–90 Ælfric now moves to the second interpretation of the parable, in which the workers are individual believers rather than teachers; he follows Gregory in this but ignores the latter's concessionary *quamvis* which signals the shift. Gregory, Hom. 19, PL 76, 1154D-5B:

> Quamvis, in quolibet modulo vel mensura, quisquis cum fide recta bonae actionis exstitit huius vineae operarius fuit. Operator ergo mane, hora tertia, sexta et nona, antiquus ille Hebraicus populus designatur, qui in electis suis ab ipso mundi exordio, dum recta fide Deum studuit colere, quasi non destitit in vineae cultura laborare. Ad undecimam vero gentiles vocantur, quibus et dicitur: Quid hic statis tota die otiosi? Qui enim, transacto tam longo mundi tempore, pro vita sua laborare neglexerant, quasi tota die otiosi stabant. Sed pensate, fratres, quid inquisiti respondeant: Dicunt enim: Quia nemo nos conduxit. Nullus quippe ad eos patriarcha, nullus propheta venerat. Et quid est dicere: Ad laborem nos nemo conduxit, nisi, vitae nobis vias nullus praedicavit? Quid ergo nos, a bono opere cessantes, in excusatione nostra dicturi sumus, qui pene a matris utero ad fidem venimus, qui verba vitae ab ipsis cunabulis audivimus, qui ab uberibus sanctae ecclesiae potum supernae praedicationis sumpsimus cum lacte carnis?

90–106 Gregory, Hom. 19, PL 76, 1155BC:

> Possumus vero et easdem diversitates horarum, etiam ad unumquemque hominem per aetatum momenta distinguere. Mane quippe intellectus nostri pueritia est. Hora autem tertia adolescentia intelligi potest, quia quasi iam sol in altum proficit, dum calor aetatis crescit. Sexta vero iuventus est, quia velut in centro sol figitur, dum in ea plenitudo roboris solidatur. Nona autem senectus intelligitur, in qua sol velut ab alto axe descendit, quia ea aetas a calore iuventutis deficit. Undecima vero hora ea est aetas quae decrepita vel veterana dicitur. . . . Quia ergo ad vitam bonam

alius in pueritia, alius in adolescentia, alius in iuventute, alius in senectute, alius in decrepita aetate perducitur, quasi diversis horis operarii ad vineam vocantur.

107–21 Gregory, Hom. 19, PL 76, 1155CD:

Mores ergo vestros, fratres carissimi, aspicite, et si iam Dei operarii estis videte. Penset unusquisque quid agat, et consideret si in Domini vinea laboret. Qui enim in hac vita ea quae sua sunt quaerit adhuc ad Dominicam vineam non venit. Illi namque Domino laborant, qui non sua, sed lucra dominica cogitant, qui zelo caritatis, studio pietatis inserviunt, animabus lucrandis invigilant, perducere et alios secum ad vitam festinant. Nam qui sibi vivit, qui carnis suae voluptatibus pascitur, recte otiosus redarguitur, quia fructum divini operis non sectatur. Qui vero et usque ad aetatem ultimam Deo vivere neglexerit, quasi usque ad undecimam otiosus stetit.

122–42 Gregory, Hom. 19, PL 76, 1155D-6A:

Unde recte usque ad undecimam torpentibus dicitur: Quid hic statis tota die otiosi? Ac si aperte dicatur: Et si Deo vivere in pueritia et iuventute noluistis, saltem in ultima aetate resipiscite, et ad vitae vias cum iam laboraturi multum non estis, vel sero venite. Et tales ergo paterfamilias vocat, et plerumque ante remunerantur, quia prius ad regnum de corpore exeunt quam hi qui iam a pueritia vocati esse videbantur. An non ad undecimam horam venit latro, qui etsi non habuit per aetatem, habuit tamen sero per poenam, qui Deum in cruce confessus est, et pene cum voce sententiae spiritum exhalavit vitae? A novissimo autem reddere denarium paterfamilias coepit, quia ad paradisi requiem prius latronem quam Petrum perduxit.

Ælfric adds the actual words of Christ and the thief, from Lc 23.42–3:

(42) Et dicebat ad Iesum: Domine, memento mei cum veneris in regnum tuum. (43) Et dixit illi Iesus: Amen dico tibi: Hodie mecum eris in paradiso.

The comment at 140–2 is not from Gregory's homily 19; Cross (1969) suggests either his homily 30, PL 76, 1225, *Et tunc Petrus negavit in terra, cum latro confiteretur in cruce* or Bede's commentary on Luke, *Commentarius in Lucam*, 6.1697–9 (CCSL 120):

Confitebatur dominum quem videbat secum humana infirmitate morientem, quando negabant apostoli eum, quem miracula viderant divina virtute facientem.

At 137 and 146 *neorxna wang*, 'paradise', has been altered to *heofonan rice* in both MS F and the antecedent of M: whether because the corrector was unfamiliar with the phrase itself, or identified it with Eden only, or with an interim place distinct from heaven,[3] one cannot tell.

[3] Cf the prose Phoenix, in *The Phoenix*, ed. N. F. Blake (rev. ed., Exeter, 1990), pp. 98–100. On the general problem of the location of paradise in Old English, and esp. in Ælfric,

143–9 Gregory, Hom. 19, PL 76, 1156A-D:

Quanti patres ante legem, quanti sub lege fuerunt. . . . Sed quia antiqui patres usque ad adventum Domini, quantumlibet iuste vixerint, ducti ad regnum non sunt, nisi ille descenderet qui paradisi claustra hominibus interpositione suae mortis aperiret, eorum hoc ipsum murmurasse est quod et recte pro percipiendo regno vixerunt, et tamen diu ad percipiendum regnum dilati sunt. . . . Nos autem qui ad undecimam venimus, post laborem non murmuramus, et denarium accipimus, quia post Mediatoris adventum, in hoc mundo venientes, ad regnum ducimur mox ut de corpore eximus, et illud sine mora percipimus, quod antiqui patres cum magna percipere dilatione meruerunt.

It is striking that neither Ælfric nor Gregory give any hint of an alternative to heaven as a resting-place after death for the righteous, prior to the last judgement. In CH II.21, 83–9, Ælfric distinguishes between the perfect who go directly to heaven and the less than perfect who go to an intermediate paradise.[4]

149–55 Cf Gregory, Hom. 19, PL 76, 1156BC:

Pondus enim diei et aestus portaverunt hi quos a mundi initio, quia diu hic contigit vivere, necesse fuit etiam longiora carnis tentamenta tolerare. . . . Quos enim post peractam iustitiam inferni loca quamvis tranquilla susceperunt, eis profecto et laborasse fuit in vinea, et murmurasse. Quasi ergo post murmurationem denarium accipiunt, qui post longa inferni tempore ad gaudia regni pervenerunt.

156–7 Gregory, Hom. 19, PL 76, 1156B:

Sed quaeri potest quomodo murmurasse dicti sunt, qui saltem sero ad regnum vocantur? Coelorum etenim regnum nullus murmurans accipit, nullus qui accipit murmurare potest.

157–60 Gregory, Hom. 19, PL 76, 1156C:

Eorum hoc ipsum murmurasse est quod et recte pro percipiendo regno vixerunt, et tamen diu ad percipiendum regnum dilati sunt.

160–84 Gregory, Hom. 19, PL 76, 1156C-7A:

Nos autem [*as above under 143–9*] . . . meruerunt. Unde et idem paterfamilias dicit: 'Volo et huic novissimo dare sicut et tibi.' Et quia ipsa regni perceptio eius est bonitas voluntatis, recte subiungit: 'Aut non licet mihi quod volo facere?' Stulta enim quaestio est hominis contra benignitatem Dei. Non querendum quippe esset si non dat quod non debet, sed si non daret quod deberet. Unde apte subditur: 'An oculus tuus nequam est quia ego bonus sum?' Nemo autem se de opere, nemo de

see further A. Kabir, 'Interim Paradises and Anglo-Saxon Literature' (unpubl. Ph.D. thesis, Cambridge Univ., 1998).

[4] On the problem of resting-places after death, see A. Kabir, 'Interim Paradises'.

tempore extollat, cum hac expleta sententia subsequenter Veritas clamet: 'Sic erunt novissimi primi, et primi novissimi.' Ecce enim etsi iam scimus quae vel quanta bona egimus, adhuc supernus iudex qua subtilitate haec examinet ignoramus. Et quidem gaudendum cuique summopere est in regno Dei esse vel ultimum. Sed post haec terribile est valde quod sequitur: 'Multi enim sunt vocati, pauci vero electi.'

184–7 Gregory now develops (§ 5) the implications of the Biblical verse, arguing that though there are many believers and they fill the church in which he is speaking, few will be among the elect who are saved. Ælfric substitutes, in 184–95, an opposing line that he had already pursued in the same context in CH I.35 (and characteristically invokes Gregory himself in doing so), urging that very many will be saved though they may seem few. The citation is Mt 8.11: *Dico autem vobis, quod multi ab oriente et occidente venient, et recumbent cum Abraham, et Isaac, et Iacob in regno caelorum.* The verse is quoted in Haymo's homily on the parable, but had already been used by Ælfric in a similar context at CH I.35.278–80.

187–91 The reference is to Gregory's Hom. 34, PL 76, 1252BC:

Quia enim superna illa civitas ex angelis et hominibus constat, ad quam tantum credimus humanum genus ascendere, quantos illic contigit electos angelos remansisse.

Ælfric had already used it in CH I 24.103–6, in wording probably recalled here. In the same homily he comments on the multitude of angels, giving the number as a thousand and one millions (lines 157–60).

191–4 The main point is repeated from CH I.35.281–3, where Ælfric may have been recalling Augustine's Serm. 90 (see note); there is perhaps also an echo of a phrase from Gregory's homily 19, his main source for the present homily (Hom. 19, PL 76, 1157C): *Neque etenim possunt qui hic carnis suae voluptatibus serviunt, illic in ovium grege numerari.* The additional clause in MS M at 194 (quoting Ps 138.17) closely matches the next clause in the passage from CH I.35.283–4, and is probably Ælfric's own addition.

195–209 Ælfric now returns to Gregory's main discussion of the problem of identifying the called and chosen; Gregory, Hom. 19, PL 76, 1157C–8A:

Et multos tales intra ecclesiam, fratres carissimi, cernitis, sed eos nec imitari nec desperare debetis. Quid enim sit hodie aspicimus, sed quid cras futurus sit unusquisque nescimus. Plerumque et qui post nos venire cernitur per agilitatem nos boni operis antecedit, et vix eum cras sequimur quem hodie praeire videbamur. Certe cum Stephanus pro fide moreretur, Saulus lapidantium vestimenta servabat. Omnium ergo lapidantium manibus ipse lapidavit, qui ad lapidandum omnes exertos reddidit, et tamen eumdem ipsum in sancta ecclesia laboribus antecessit quem persequendo martyrem fecit. Duo ergo sunt quae sollicite pensare debemus. Quia enim multi vocati, sed pauci electi sunt, primum est ut de se quisque minime praesumat, quia etsi iam ad fidem vocatus est, utrum perenni regno dignus sit nescit. Secundum vero est ut unusquisque proximum, quem fortasse iacere in vitiis conspicit, desperare non audeat, quia divinae misericordiae divitias ignorat.

210–27 Gregory, Hom. 19, PL 76, 1159BC (Ælfric omits the intervening exemplum):

Has divinae pietatis divitias consideravit psalmista, cum diceret: 'Adiutor meus, tibi psallam, quia tu Deus susceptor meus es, Deus meus misericordia mea' (Ps 58.18). Ecce perpendens in quibus laboribus humana sit vita constituta, Deum appellavit adiutorem; et quia a tribulatione praesenti in requiem aeternam nos suscipit, appellat etiam susceptorem. Sed considerans quod mala nostra aspicit et portat, culpas nostras tolerat, et tamen nos per poenitentiam ad praemia reservat, noluit Deum misericordem dicere, sed hunc ipsam misericordiam vocavit, dicens: 'Deus meus misericordia mea.' Revocemus ergo ante oculos mala quae fecimus, pensemus ex quanta Dei benignitate toleramur, consideremus quae sunt pietatis eius viscera, ut non solum culpas indulgeat, sed coeleste regnum poenitentibus etiam post culpas promittat. Atque ex omnibus medullis cordis dicamus singuli, dicamus omens: 'Deus meus misericordia mea.'

227–33 Gregory's homily ends at this point, and Ælfric concludes with a brief comment on mercy and grace, quoting (without attribution) Ps 58.11: *Misericordia eius praeveniet me*, and Ps 22.6: *Et misericordia tua subsequetur me*. The two verses are frequently quoted together in discussions of grace; the nearest I have found to Ælfric is in Augustine's *Enchiridion* (IX.98–104, CCSL 46, pp. 23–114):

. . . [Deus] qui hominis voluntatem bonam et praeparat adiuvandam, et adiuvat praeparatam. Praecedit enim bona voluntas hominis multa Dei dona, sed non omnia: quae autem non praecedit ipsa, in eis est et ipsa. Nam utrumque legitur in sanctis eloquiis; et, 'Misericordia eius praeveniet me' (Ps 58.11); et, 'Misericordia eius subsequetur me' (Ps 22.6); nolentem praevenit, ut velit; volentem subsequitur, ne frustra velit.

240–8 Amalarius, *Liber Officialis*, I.1.1–2:

Septuagesima computatur secundum titulationem sacramentarii et antiphonarii novem ebdomadibus ante pascha Domini et finitur post pascha Domini in septima sabbati. Die dominica habet initium et in sabbato finem. Populi Dei tempus captivitatis significat, qui peccando recessit a Deo, et per misericordiam eius revertitur ad requiem. Populus Dei in Babilonia detentus est captivus sub numero septuagenario; quo numero completo reversus est in Hierusalem.

249–52 Amalarius, *Liber Officialis*, I.1.6:

Fors dictator septuagesimae novit per Christi gratiam nobis peccata dimissa, septuaginta annos mutavit, quia in aliquibus criminibus communicamus priori populo, septuaginta diebus, et quod illi inviti sustinuerunt, quia servi erant, nos voluntarie pro peccatis nostris sustineamus.

253–69 Corresponds to various points made by Amalarius, *Liber Officialis*:

[I.1.5] Quanto tempore in captivitate fuerit, Hieremias manifestat dicens: 'Perdam ex eis vocem gaudii et laetitiae, vocem sponsi et vocem sponsae . . . et servient omnes gentes istae regi Babilonis septuaginta annis' [Jer 25.10–11].

[I.1.16] Quapropter alleluia in illo tempore non cantatur apud nos et dulcissimus ymnus angelorum 'Gloria in excelsis Deo'.

[I.1.19] Propter hos dolores non possumus laetari et securi esse, sed praeparare debemus nos ad bellum.

[I.1.19] In introitu dicit:'Circumdederunt me gemitus mortis, dolores inferni circumdederunt me'.

[I.1.19] ipsud ieiunium quod prius dictum est, intimavit in prima oratione missae, dicens: 'ut qui iuste pro peccatis nostris affligimur'.

[I.1.19] ut apostolus: 'Omnis autem, inquit, qui in agone contendit, ab omnibus se abstinet' (1 Cor 9.25).

For the introit Ælfric gives a fuller quotation, Ps 17.5–7:

(5) Circumdederunt me dolores mortis et torrentes iniquitatis conturbaverunt me. (6) Dolores inferni circumdederunt me praeoccupaverunt me laquei mortis. (7) Cum tribularer invocavi Dominum et ad Deum meum clamavi exaudivit de templo sancto suo vocem meam et clamor meus in conspectu eius introibit in aures eius.

272–82 Amalarius, *Liber Officialis*, I.1.16–17:

Alleluia propter honorem et latitudinem primae linguae praeclarius est. . . . Ad comparationem enim linguae hebraicae tam graeci quam latini sermonis pauper est. Pauperem linguam in supradictis diebus frequentamus, 'Laus tibi, Domine, rex aeternae gloriae'. . . . Alleluia, et Gloria in excelsis Deo, cantica coelestia sunt. Unde Iohannes in Apocalypsi: 'Post haec audivi quasi vocem magnam turbarum multarum in caelo dicentium: Alleluia' (Apoc 19.1). De gloria in excelsis Deo nulli dubium quin angelorum cantus sit.

6 SEXAGESIMA

An exposition of the Gospel for the day, the parable of the sower from Luke 8.4–15. Ælfric's account follows in the main Christ's own exposition and the commentaries of Gregory and Bede, but he takes the opportunity of the reference to the three-fold crop (from Matthew or Mark rather than Luke) to develop his own discussion of the three orders of Christian society, married, widowed and virgin, and the forms of chastity appropriate to each (lines 115–66).

Ælfric identifies his source at the outset as Gregory, and certainly much of the material comes from his homily 15, which is given for the occasion in Paul the Deacon's homiliary.[1] But Gregory's exegesis was also used by other writers known to Ælfric: much of it appears in Bede's commentary on Luke, most of which is in turn copied verbatim by Smaragdus, along with material from Gregory not used by Bede, and Bede and Gregory were recast into a longer piece by Haymo. It is clear that Ælfric did use Gregory directly, since he takes material not found in the others, and there is no trace of distinctive material from Haymo. He also used material from Bede's commentary, but whether directly from Bede or via Smaragdus is impossible to say, since the latter copies verbatim. Joyce Hill argues that Smaragdus 'is a much more likely immediate source' than Bede,[2] presumably because the material was conveniently to hand under the same occasion in his homiliary. I have cited from Bede if only because it is the prior text, there is some reason to think that Ælfric knew the text directly and Smaragdus has nothing of his own to add in this case.

For the excursus on chastity Ælfric cites both Augustine and Gregory as authorities (lines 117 and 143), though in neither case has it proved possible to identify a precise source.

Sources and Notes

The following texts are cited below:

1. Bede, *Commentarius in Lucam*, ed. D. Hurst, CCSL 120 (Turnhout, 1960), pp. 5–425.
2. Gregory the Great, *Homiliae in Evangelia*, PL 76, Hom. 15, cols. 1131–4.
3. Smaragdus, *Collectiones in Evangelia et Epistolas*, PL 102, cols. 109–12.

1–32 Mainly from Lc 8.4–15 but with some readings from the parallel accounts of Mt 13.1–23 and Mc 4.1–20:

> (Lc 8.4) Cum autem turba plurima conveniret, et de civitatibus properarent ad eum, dixit per similitudinem: (5) Exiit qui seminat seminare semen suum. Et, dum seminat, aliud cecidit secus viam, et conculcatum est, et volucres coeli comederunt illud. (6) Et aliud cecidit supra petram, et natum aruit, quia non habebat humorem. (7) Et aliud cecidit inter spinas, et simul exortae spinae suffocaverunt illud. (8) Et aliud cecidit in terram bonam, et ortum fecit fructum centuplum (*Mc 4.8*: et adferebat unum

[1] Förster 1894, pp. 13–14; Smetana 1959, pp. 196–7; Smetana 1961, p. 467.
[2] Hill 1992, p. 227.

triginta et unum sexaginta et unum centum; *cf too Mt 13.8*). Haec dicens, clamabat: Qui habet aures audiendi audiat. (9) Interrogabant autem eum discipuli eius quae esset haec parabola. (10) Quibus ipse dixit: Vobis datum est nosse mysterium regni Dei, caeteris autem (*Mc 4.11*: illis autem qui foris sunt) in parabolis, ut videntes non videant, et audientes non intellegant. (11) Est autem haec parabola: Semen est verbum Dei. (12) Qui autem secus viam, hi sunt qui audiunt, deinde venit diabolus, et tollit verbum de corde eorum, ne credentes salvi fiant. (13) Nam qui supra petram, qui cum audierint, cum gaudio suscipiunt verbum. Et hi radices non habent, qui ad tempus credunt, et in tempore tentationis recedunt. (14) Quod autem in spinas cecidit, hi sunt qui audierunt, et a sollicitudinibus, et divitiis, et voluptatibus vitae euntes suffocantur, et non referunt fructum. (15) Quod autem in bonam terram, hi sunt qui in corde bono et optimo audientes verbum retinent, et fructum afferunt in patientia (*Mc 4.20:* unum triginta et unum sexaginta et unum centum; *cf too Mt 13.23*).

33–52 Gregory, Hom. 15, PL 76, 1131C–2A:
Unde et idem Dominus per semetipsum dignatus est exponere quod dicebat, ut sciatis rerum significationes quaerere in iis etiam quae per semetipsum noluit explanare. Exponendo ergo quod dixit figurate se loqui innotuit, quatenus certos vos redderet cum vobis nostra fragilitas verborum illius figuras aperiret. Quis enim mihi unquam crederet, si spinas divitias interpretari voluissem, maxime cum illae pungant, istae delectent? Et tamen spinae sunt, quia cogitationum suarum punctionibus mentem lacerant, et cum usque ad peccatum pertrahunt, quasi inflicto vulnere cruentant. Quas bene hoc in loco, alio evangelista attestante, nequaquam Dominus divitias, sed fallaces divitias appellat (Mt 13.22). Fallaces enim sunt quae nobiscum diu permanere non possunt, fallaces sunt quae mentis nostrae inopiam non expellunt. Solae autem divitiae verae sunt quae nos divites virtutibus faciunt. Si ergo, fratres carissimi, divites esse cupitis, veras divitias amate. Si culmen veri honoris quaeritis, ad coeleste regnum tendite. Si gloriam dignitatum diligitis, in illa superna angelorum curia ascribi festinate.
(No precise equivalent for 45–7.)

53–5 Bede, *Comm. Luc.*, 3.323–5 [= Smaragdus, *Collectiones*, PL 102, 109D]:
Quae Dominus exposuit, pia fide suscipienda sunt. Quae autem tacita nostrae intellegentiae dereliquit, perstringenda sunt breviter.

55–64 Bede, *Comm. Luc.*, 3.312–8 [= Smaragdus, *Collectiones*, PL 102, 109CD]:
Sed quia semen, quod verbum Dei sit, terramque variam, quod diversum cor auditorum significet, ipse Dominus aperuit, satorem quem nobis quaerendum reliquit, nullum melius quam filium Dei intellegere possumus, qui exiit seminare semen suum, quia de sinu patris, qua creaturae non

erat accessus, egrediens, ad hoc venit in mundum ut testimonium perhiberet veritati.

64–72 Bede, *Comm. Luc.*, 3.325–33:

Semen quod secus viam cecidit, duplici laesura disperiit, et a viantibus scilicet conculcatum, et a volucribus raptum. Via est ergo cor, sedulo malarum cogitationum transitu attritum atque arefactum, ne verbi semen excipere ac germinare sufficiat. Atque ideo quicquid boni seminis vicinia talis viae contingit, pessimae cogitationis meatu conculcatum, a daemonibus eripitur. Qui volucres caeli, sive quia caelestis spiritalisque sint naturae, seu quia per aera volitant, appellantur.

72–8 Bede, *Comm. Luc.*, 3.379–86:

De hoc semine . . . Matheus ita: 'Omnis qui audit verbum regni, et non intellegit, venit malus et rapit' (Mt 13.19). Ex quo manifeste docetur eos circa viam seminatos, qui verbum quod audiunt nulla fide, nullo intellectu, nulla saltim temptandae utilitatis occasione percipere dignantur.

(The final clause is a version of Lc 8.12)

79–89 Paraphrasing Lc 8.6 and 13, and then Bede, *Comm. Luc.*, 3.335–9 [= Smaragdus, *Collectiones*, PL 102, 110A]:

Petram dicit, durum et indomitum cor, ac nullo verae fidei vomere penetratum. Hoc est autem umor ad radicem seminis quod iuxta aliam parabolam, oleum ad lampades virginum nutriendas, id est, amor et perseverantia virtutis.

90–105 Gregory, Hom. 15, PL 76, 1133AB:

Notandum vero est quod exponens Dominus dicit quia sollicitudines, et voluptates, et divitiae suffocant verbum. Suffocant enim, quia importunis cogitationibus suis guttur mentis strangulant; et dum bonum desiderium intrare ad cor non sinunt, quasi aditum flatus vitalis necant. Notandum etiam quod duo sunt quae divitiis iungit, sollicitudines videlicet et voluptates, quia profecto et per curam mentem opprimunt, et per affluentiam resolvunt. Re enim contraria possessores suos et afflictos et lubricos faciunt. Sed quia voluptas convenire non potest cum afflictione, alio quidem tempore per custodiae suae sollicitudinem affligunt, atque alio per abundantiam ad voluptates emolliunt.

(Repeated verbatim by Bede, *Comm. Luc.*, 3.409–19 and Smaragdus, *Collectiones*, PL 102, 111CD.)

108–14 There is a slight resemblance to Gregory's comments on bearing patiently the tribulations of the world (repeated by Bede and Smaragdus), but no real parallel. Lines 109–10 are Lc 21.19: *In patientia vestra possidebitis animas vestras.*

115–35 The discussion of the three orders was probably prompted by Bede, *Comm. Luc.*, 3.435–47 [= Smaragdus, *Collectiones*, PL 102, 112AB]:

> Quod vero secundum Matheum dicitur: 'Et fructum affert, et facit aliud quidem centum, aliud autem sexaginta, porro aliud triginta'. Triginta referuntur ad nuptias. . . . Sexaginta ad viduas, eo quod in angustia et tribulatione sint positae. . . . Porro centesimus numerus . . . exprimit virginitatis coronam.

The Latin note citing Augustine as authority occurs only in MS K, like the other Latin notes in CH II, but is presumably Ælfric's, perhaps originating as a marginal comment, perhaps prompted by either a query from a reader or an awareness that the argument needed buttressing. But what text is Ælfric citing, and with reference to which part of his argument? The identification of the threefold crop with marriage, widowhood and virginity is to be found in a sermon formerly attributed to Augustine (Ps-Augustine, Serm. 303, PL 39, 2327), but is something of a commonplace, going back beyond Bede to Jerome (cf Hurst's notes to Bede), and hardly controversial. It seems more likely that the Latin note is to be linked with the sentence on the *læwedra regol* at 125–7, also found only in K, and that Ælfric was seeking to invoke Augustine's authority for his definition of the 'rule' for the laity at 118–25, reinforcing the two-fold reference to *boclicum gesetnyssum*. But I cannot find a close parallel for his definition. The Ps-Augustine sermon does not have much to say on the subject (Serm. 303, §7, PL 39, 2327):

> Tres enim professiones sunt in sancta ecclesia catholica. Sunt virgines, sunt viduae, sunt etiam coniugati. Virgines exhibent centesimum, viduae sexagesimum, coniugati vero trigesimum. . . . Coniugati vero qui sibi invicem fidem servaverint, et extra se nihil agnoverint, se ipsos tantum nonnisi pro desiderio filiorum agnoverint, assidue eleemosynas fecerint, et in quantum possunt Dei praecepta servaverint, sancto Iob, sanctae Sarae, vel sanctae Susannae cum sanctis Patriarchis et Prophetis merebuntur feliciter sociari.

Ælfric may have been thinking of Augustine's treatise *De Bono Coniugali*, though if so only for its general approval of marriage. A Ps-Augustine sermon, number 292 (PL 39, 2300), now edited as Caesarius, Serm. 44 (CCSL 103), urges against intercourse with a wife who is pregnant or menstruating. The reference to *scrift* suggests that when he specifies *boclic* teaching he may also have been thinking of confessional and penitential texts, but although prescriptions against intercourse during menstruation and pregnancy are common enough (cf Pierre Payer, *Sex and the Penitentials* (Toronto, 1984), esp. pp. 23–8), I have found no reference to abstinence after child-bearing age. Ælfric's heavy insistence on bookish authority for his views suggests that they may have been both unusual and controversial. (Cf too Ælfric's earlier reference to the three orders, CH I.9.198–220, and note.)

136–66 For 146–50 cf Concilium Nicaenum I, canon 3 (*Decrees of the Ecumenical Councils*, ed. N. Tanner (London and Washington, 1990), vol. 1, pp. 5–19, at 7):

> Interdixit per omnia magna synodus, nec episcope nec presbytero nec alicui prorus, qui est in clero, licere subintroductam habere mulierem, nisi forte matrem aut sororem aut amitam vel eas tantum personas quae suspicionem effugiunt.

Ælfric's *faðu oððe modrie* presumably reflects the variant reading *amitam vel matertam* (see Whitelock in *Councils and Synods*, vol. 1, part 1, ed. D. Whitelock *et al.* (Oxford, 1981), p. 198, n.2). The number of 318 bishops present at the synod is a piece of general tradition, but it does seem to have formed a rubric to the Nicene creed. Although Ælfric often writes against the marriage of priests, this is I think the only time that he mentions, and accepts, the marriage of those in clerical orders below that of deacon; I do not know what text by Gregory he is citing as authority.[3] The warning against priests engaging in business is repeated at Fehr I, § 77; Whitelock cites as a parallel a clause in the *Capitula* of Ghaerbald, bishop of Liège, printed in MGH, Legum Sectio II, Capitularia regum Francorum I, ed. A. Boretius (Hanover, 1883), pp. 242–44, at 244:

> (c.16) Ut presbyter negotiator non sit nec per ullum turpe lucrum pecunias congreget.

161–2 is Mt 19.27: *Tunc respondens Petrus dixit ei: ecce nos reliquimus omnia et secuti sumus te.*

167–98 Gregory, Hom. 15, PL 76, 1133C-4B:

> In ea porticu quae euntibus ad ecclesiam beati Clementis est pervia fuit quidam Servulus nomine, quem multi vestrum mecum noverunt, rebus pauper, meritis dives, quem longa aegritudo dissolverat. Nam a primaeva aetate usque ad finem vitae paralyticus iacebat. Quid dicam quia stare non poterat? Qui nunquam in lecto suo surgere vel ad sedendum valebat, nunquam manum suam ad os ducere, nunquam se potuit in latus aliud declinare. Huic ad serviendum mater cum fratre aderat, et quidquid ex eleemosyna potuisset accipere, hoc eorum manibus pauperibus erogabat. Nequaquam litteras noverat, sed scripturae sacrae sibimet codices emerat, et religiosos quosque in hospitalitate suscipiens, hos coram se legere sine intermissione faciebat. Factumque est ut, quantum ad mensuram propriam, plene sacram scripturam disceret, cum, sicut dixi, litteras funditus ignoraret. Studebat in dolore semper gratias agere, hymnis Deo et laudibus diebus ac noctibus vacare. Sed cum iam tempus esset ut tanta eius patientia remunerari debuisset, membrorum dolor ad vitalia rediit.

[3] But Aaron Kleist of Cambridge University suggests in a forthcoming article, surely rightly, that Ælfric was thinking of the answers supposedly given by Gregory to Augustine of Canterbury, as reported in Bede's *Historia Ecclesiastica*; see esp. *Historia*, I.xxvii (Colgrave and Mynors 1969, 80.14–16):

> Siqui vero sunt clerici extra sacros ordines constituti, qui se continere non possunt, sortire uxores debent.

Cumque se iam morti proximum agnovit, peregrinos viros atque in hospitalitate susceptos admonuit ut surgerent, et cum eo psalmos pro exspectatione exitus sui decantarent. Cumque cum eis et ipse moriens psalleret, voces psallentium repente compescuit, cum terrore magni clamoris, dicens: Tacete, nunquid non auditis quantae resonant laudes in coelo? Cumque ad easdem laudes quas intus audierat aurem cordis intenderet, sancta illa anima a carne soluta est. Sed exeunte illa tanta illic fragrantia odoris aspersa est, ut omnes illi qui aderant inaestimabili suavitate replerentur, ita ut per hoc patenter agnoscerent quod eam laudes in coelo suscepissent. Cui rei monachus noster interfuit, qui nunc usque vivit, et cum magno fletu attestari solet quia quousque corpus eius sepulturae traderetur, ab eorum naribus odoris illius fragrantia non recessit. Ecce quo fine ex hac vita exiit qui in hac vita aequanimiter flagella toleravit. Iuxta vocem ergo dominicam, bona terra fructum per patientiam reddidit, quae, exarata disciplinae vomere, ad remunerationis segetem pervenit.

199–206 Gregory, Hom. 15, PL 76, 1134BC:

Sed vos rogo, fratres carissimi, attendite quod excusationis argumentum in illo districto iudicio habituri sumus nos, qui, a bono opere torpentes, et res et manus accepimus, si praecepta dominica egenus et sine manibus impleverit. . . . Haec vobiscum, fratres, agite, sic vos ad studium boni operis instigate, ut cum bonos vobis modo ad imitandum proponitis, eorum consortes tunc esse valeatis.

7 FIRST SUNDAY IN LENT

Ælfric had already covered the Gospel for the day in his First Series homily for this occasion, CH I.11, and here he offers a general sermon on Lenten themes, and particularly alms-giving. It seems to be especially addressed to the rich, though in ways that repeatedly and sympathetically acknowledge their due place in the Christian world rather than deriding them; and it also insists that even the poor have opportunities for charitable giving.

Förster could find no source for most of the homily, suggesting only a passage from Gregory for the introductory material on Lent (which is in any case transmitted through Ælfric's earlier homily for this occasion, CH I.11) and a possible borrowing from Cassian's Collations.[1] Smetana could add nothing further.[2] Pope, however, in a note on a passage in his homily 13 which adapts this text, commented that 'a good deal of Ælfric's doctrine on alms in the earlier homily corresponds to what is said in the pseudo-Augustinian *Sermo* cccx, *De*

[1] Förster 1894, pp. 16–17, 48.
[2] Smetana 1959, p. 197.

Eleemosynis, PL xxxix. 2340–2'.[3] Subsequently, in an article published in 1976, Wolfgang Becker independently identified this sermon as a source for both Ælfric and Vercelli 10 (= Napier 49), and described and printed a variant text, based on manuscripts at Münich and Vienna, which was distinctly closer to Ælfric than the PL version; and in a supplementary note in 1979 he cited some further manuscripts containing this variant, including Salisbury Cathedral MS 9.[4] In 1990 J. E. Cross identified and printed (with variants from Salisbury MS 9 and the Vienna MS) a further copy, in Salisbury Cathedral MS 179, which was still closer to Ælfric;[5] the manuscript, written at Salisbury in the later eleventh century, contains the second part of an augmented version of Paul the Deacon's homiliary, and this makes it all the more likely that this version of the *Sermo* was indeed Ælfric's source, and that he found it in his copy of PD. The text as printed by Cross closely parallels lines 46–125 of Ælfric. To this central core of admonition, Ælfric appropriately adds the dramatic confrontation between Christ and the righteous and sinners from Matthew 25, which focuses on charity. (At least, his words imply that he has added it. The fact that Vercelli 10 also has a scene from the last judgement, though a more colourful and apocryphal one, and placed before rather than after the section on alms-giving, makes one wonder whether there was not something similar in the version of Serm. 310 which Ælfric saw.) There are also some slight parallels, not previously noted, with Augustine's Serm. 206, on Lent.

Sources and Notes

The following texts are cited below:

1. Anon., *Sermo de Misericordia*, ed. J. E. Cross, in 'A *Sermo de Misericordia* in Old English Prose', *Anglia* 108 (1990), 429–40 (text, pp. 431–33).
2. Augustine, *Sermones*, PL 38, Serm. 206, cols. 1041–2.

1–9 For the association of Easter with the eucharist cf the introduction to CH II.15 below, and Pope 19.119–30, which specifies the five Sundays of Lent and the four days culminating in Easter Sunday as appropriate days for taking the eucharist.

10–25 Recasts CH I.11.177–89 (itself derived in part from Gregory's homily 16 and/or Haymo's homily 28). For Ælfric's tendency to cite Enoch in association with Elijah, see R. K. Emmerson, *Antichrist in the Middle Ages* (Manchester, 1981).

[3] Pope, p. 509.

[4] W. Becker, 'The Latin Manuscript Sources of the Old English Translations of the Sermon *Remedia Peccatorum*', *Medium Ævum* 45 (1976), 145–52; and 'The Manuscript Source of Ælfric's Catholic Homily II 7—a Supplementary Note', *Medium Ævum* 48 (1979), 105–6.

[5] J. E. Cross, 'A *Sermo de Misericordia* in Old English Prose', *Anglia* 108 (1990), 429–40.

25–8 For the emphasis on sexual abstinence during Lent, cf the *Capitula* of Theodulf of Orleans (Sauer, *Theodulfi Capitula*), c. 43:

> Abstinendum est enim in his sacratissimis diebus a coniugibus, et caste et pie vivendum, . . . quia pene nihil valet ieiunium, quod coniugali opere polluitur.

28–33 Cf Augustine, Serm. 206, §1, PL 38, 1041:

> Orationibus, ieiuniis, eleemosynis et alia quidem tempora debent christiano fervere: verumtamen et illos qui diebus aliis in his pigri sunt, debet ista solemnitas excitare; et ii qui per alios dies ad ista sunt alacres, nunc ea debent ferventius exercere.

38–41 Augustine, Serm. 206, §2, PL 38, 1041:

> Dominus dicit: 'Date et dabitur vobis; dimittite et dimittetur vobis' (Lc 6.37–8). Haec duo genera eleemosynarum, tribuendi et ignoscendi, clementer et ferventer operemur.

46–51 *Sermo de Misericordia*, 1–5:

> Misericordia, fratres, peccatorum sunt remedia; ipsa est quae a morte liberat et non patitur hominem ire interitum. Haec enim solo patrocinatur in die iudicii . . . 'Iudicium enim sine misericordia illi, qui non fecit misericordiam' (Jac 2.13).

(The final sentence is identified as a quotation from James in Salisbury MS 179 but not in Salisbury MS 9.)

52–4 *Sermo de Misericordia*, 5–6, 8–10 :

> Talis debet esse misericordia . . . De iustis laboribus tuis non de rebus alienigenis, audi Salomonem dicentem: 'Honora dominum de tuis iustis laboribus' (cf Prov 3.9).

54–7 No source known.

57–66 *Sermo de Misericordia*, 17–18, 20–27 (part of an imagined speech by God at the last judgement):

> Ego misericordiam fieri iussi, non fraudes et rapinas mandavi. . . . Rapis aliena et gaudes; pauper misericordiam rogat et contristaris, et faciem tuam avertis. Oblitus es dictum prophete: Qui avertit faciem suam a paupere et ipse invocabit dominum 'et non exaudietur' (Prov 21.13). Inclina aurem ad egenum et fame deficientem, ut et tuam vocem exaudiat deus. Eroga unde tibi dedit, tu inde si feceris multiplicaberis. Quod si neglexeris dare, auferet ea que donavit, et egenus remanebis.

67–79 *Sermo de Misericordia*, 45–58:

> Tibi dedi ut haberes, pauperi non dedi. Quare? Ut te probarem, non quia unde darem non habui, sed per pauperes probare te volui. Ego sum deus qui divitem et pauperem feci; per te divitem pauperes pascere volui. Prerogatorem te in meis bonis constitui. . . . Quid tibi soli v[i]ndicas quod ambobus dedi? Quod solus comedis quod ambobus creavi? . . . Si tuo labori

> hoc quod habes adsignas, aut si tuos esse putas ipsos fructus quos terra producit, ecce, aufero auxilium meum et habeto laborem tuum. Subduco pluviam et sterilem faciam terram tuam. . . . Si terra tua est, mea est pluvia. Plue super terram tuam si potes, producat germen suum. Si vales, oriri fac solem, excoquat tuas messes.

80–5 *Sermo de Misericordia*, 59–63:

> Nam ipsa terra quam dicis tua non est. Aut non audisti dicentem: 'Domini est terra et plenitudo eius' (Ps 23.1). . . . Pauperes mei vivent sine te. Tu, si potes, vive sine me. Pauperes mei, habentes me, omnia habent. Tu quid habes, qui me non habes?

85–7 Not in any version of the *Sermo ad Misericordia* so far identified. The quotation is Ps 38.7: *Frustra conturbatur, thesaurizat et ignorat cui congregabit ea.*

87–99 *Sermo de Misericordia*, 67–72:

> Si pecunia non finitur, vita tamen finitur, quando non speras. Sic consideravit ille dives qui in habundantia torquebatur et quasi de inopia conqueri videbatur. 'Quid', inquit, 'faciam quia non habeo ubi fructus meos congregem?' (Lc 12.17). Et audivit vocem domini dicentem: 'Stulte, hac nocte anima tua auferetur a te; quae parasti cuius erunt?' (Lc 12.20)

Ælfric gives a fuller quotation from Lc 12.16–21:

> (16) Dixit autem similitudinem ad illos dicens hominis cuiusdam divitis uberes fructus ager adtulit (17) et cogitabat intra se dicens quid faciam quod non habeo quo congregem fructus meos. (18) Et dixit: hoc faciam destruam horrea mea et maiora faciam et illuc congregabo omnia quae nata sunt mihi et bona mea (19) et dicam animae meae anima habes multa bona posita in annos plurimos requiesce comede bibe epulare. (20) Dixit autem illi Deus: stulte hac nocte animam tuam repetunt a te quae autem parasti cuius erunt. (21) Sic est qui sibi thesaurizat et non est in Deum dives.

100–12 *Sermo de Misericordia*, 75–83:

> Ecce, tu times dare, ne timeas qui nescis in crastinum diem supervenias. Fac misericordiam quia non te deserit qui te prerogatorem constituit. . . . dicente domino: 'Thesaurizate vobis thesauros in caelo ubi neque erugo, neque tinea demolitur; et ubi fures non effodiunt, nec furantur, ubi enim est thesaurus tuus, ibi est et cor tuum' (Mt 6.20–1). Ergo ad hoc nobis dominus egentes homines dimisit in terris quo nobis liceat quicquid impendimus illis pro amore eius centuplicatum invenire in caelis.

Ælfric adds Mt 6.19:

> Nolite thesaurizare vobis thesauros in terra, ubi erugo et tinea demolitur, ubi fures effodiunt et furantur.

The sentence at 110–12 is one of Ælfric's favourite sayings (cf note on CH I.11.225–7; there are twelve examples in his works). It somewhat resembles Mt 19.29 (*Et omnis qui reliquit domum . . . propter nomen meum centuplum accipiet et vitam aeternam possidebit*) but the characteristic notion of hundredfold repayment for what one has done for others is not really close to Mt 19.29. It is sometimes presented as if it is part of a Biblical quotation (e.g. St Paul at CH I.18.203 and Matthew at Brotanek 1.240), but misleadingly. In most cases there is no equivalent in the sources from which Ælfric appears to be working; the only exception apart from this one is in the sermon by St Thomas the apostle given in LS 37.192. The sentence from *Sermo de Misericordia* cited here is close to the present example and to CH I.11.225 and I.18.203 and I.27.208 and Brotanek 1.240. Yet it looks more like an allusion to the saying than the source itself for the other versions. It seems to be an established saying that may be ultimately based on Mt 19.29 (it even appears in the *Ayenbite of Inwit* and its French source[6]).

113–6 *Sermo de Misericordia*, 84–6:

> Si omnibus nobis in hoc seculo fuisset habundantia, non haberet locum misericordia, ut peccatorum nostrorum flammas munus panis extingueret.

Ælfric adds the implied quotation from Sir 3.33: *Sicut aqua extinguit ignem, ita elimosina peccata* (cited in this form earlier, at 37–8 of the *Sermo de Misericordia*).

116–25 *Sermo de Misericordia*, 89–98 (with the citations reversed):

> Dominus Christus in elimosina facienda omnes conclusit nec pauperibus ut excusarent permisit dicens: 'Qui dederit calicem aquae frigidae tantum in nomine meo non perdit mercedem suam' (*cf* Mc 9.40, Mt 10.42). . . . Nam et vidua illa a domino Christo ideo laudatur quia duo minuta quae habuit dare non est morata. . . . Ideoque illam dominus conlaudans dixit: 'Amen, dico vobis plus omnibus haec vidua in gazofilacium misit' quia nichil substantiae dereliquit.

Ælfric gives a fuller quotation from Mc 12.41–4:

> (41) Et sedens Iesus contra gazofilacium aspiciebat quomodo turba iactaret aes in gazofilacium et multi divites iactabant multa. (42) Cum venisset autem una vidua pauper misit duo minuta quod est quadrans. (43) Et convocans discipulos suos ait illis: amen dico vobis quoniam vidua haec pauper plus omnibus misit qui miserunt in gazofilacium. (44) Omnes enim ex eo quod abundabat illis miserunt haec vero de penuria sua omnia quae habuit misit totum victum suum.

125–8 Not in any version of the *Sermo de Misericordia*.

130–77 Mt 25.31–46 (not in the *Sermo de Misericordia*):

> (31) Cum autem venerit Filius hominis in maiestate sua et omnes angeli cum eo, tunc sedebit super sedem maiestatis suae. (32) Et congregabuntur

[6] Cf Kenneth Sisam, *Fourteenth-Century Prose and Verse* (Oxford, 1921), pp. 35 and 213. Asser perhaps alludes to the same pseudo-scriptural saying in his *Life of King Alfred*; see *Alfred the Great: Asser's Life of King Alfred and other contemporary sources*, translated with an introduction and notes by Simon Keynes and Michael Lapidge (Harmondsworth, 1983), pp. 105 and 273.

ante eum omnes gentes et separabit eos ab invicem sicut pastor segregat oves ab hedis. (33) Et statuet oves quidem a dextris suis, hedos autem a sinistris. (34) Tunc dicet rex his qui a dextris eius erunt: venite benedicti Patris mei, possidete paratum vobis regnum a constitutione mundi. (35) Esurivi enim et dedistis mihi manducare; sitivi et dedistis mihi bibere; hospes eram et collexistis me; (36) nudus et operuistis me; infirmus et visitastis me; in carcere eram et venistis ad me. (37) Tunc respondebunt ei iusti dicentes: Domine quando te vidimus esurientem et pavimus; sitientem et dedimus tibi potum; (38) quando autem te vidimus hospitem et colleximus te aut nudum et cooperuimus; (39) aut quando te vidimus infirmum aut in carcere et venimus ad te? (40) Et respondens rex dicet illis: amen dico vobis quamdiu fecistis uni de his fratribus meis minimis, mihi fecistis. (41) Tunc dicet et his qui a sinistris erunt: discedite a me maledicti in ignem aeternum qui paratus est diabolo et angelis eius. (42) Esurivi enim et non dedistis mihi manducare; sitivi et non dedistis mihi potum; (43) hospes eram et non collexistis me; nudus et non operuistis me; infirmus et in carcere et non visitastis me. (44) Tunc respondebunt et ipsi dicentes: Domine quando te vidimus esurientem aut sitientem aut hospitem aut nudum aut infirmum vel in carcere et non ministravimus tibi. (45) Tunc respondebit illis dicens: amen dico vobis quamdiu non fecistis uni de minoribus his nec mihi fecistis. (46) Et ibunt hii in supplicium aeternum; iusti autem in vitam aeternam.

For 138–43 cf CH I.3.73 ff, I.40.64 ff.

8 SECOND SUNDAY IN LENT

A short exposition of the Gospel for the day, the story from Matthew 15.21–8 of the Canaanite woman with a daughter possessed by the devil. Exegetical tradition, from Jerome onward, mingled literal readings of the woman as an exemplar of faith with a variety of more allegorical interpretations. Although there are occasional touches of a moral (tropological) interpretation in Ælfric's version, his primary concern is an allegorical reading which interprets the woman as the church and focuses (rather more comprehensively and coherently than his predecessors) on the contrast between the Jews and the Gentiles; the story is for Ælfric the point at which Christ proclaims the *transmigratio* of the faith from Jews to heathens which is to take effect after his death.

Förster found parallels with Jerome's commentary on Matthew, Bede's commentaries on Matthew and on Mark, and Smaragdus.[1] Since all the material from Jerome and the Mark commentary is in Smaragdus, he suggested that Ælfric just used the latter and the Bedan commentary on Matthew. Smetana suggested

[1] Förster 1894, p. 41.

that Ælfric used Bede's homily I.22, which appears in some versions of PD, including that in PL 95, rather than the commentary on Matthew.[2] In his later article, he notes that 'there is a great deal of similarity in word and phrase among Ælfric's sources for this homily' but 'there are scattered passages which are closer in thought and expression to Haymo than to Bede'.[3] Smaragdus, with occasional passages from Haymo, does seem to have provided most of the material. I find nothing to suggest direct use of Bede's homily; although the commentary on Matthew is not in fact by Bede, and Pope expresses strong doubt whether Ælfric ever used it, there is one point where it seems to be much the closest (lines 37–44).

Sources and Notes

The following texts are cited below:

1. Ps-Bede, *In Matthaei Evangelium Expositio*, PL 92, cols. 9–132.
2. Haymo of Auxerre, *Homiliae de Tempore*, PL 118, Hom. 35, cols. 226–32.
3. Smaragdus, *Collectiones in Evangelia et Epistolas*, PL 102, cols. 130–2.

3–4 Ælfric's own summary of the preceding narrative in the Gospel.

4–21 Mt 15.21–8:

(21) Et egressus inde Iesus secessit in partes Tyri et Sidonis. (22) Et ecce mulier chananea a finibus illis egressa clamavit dicens ei: miserere mei Domine Fili David filia mea male a daemonio vexatur. (23) Qui non respondit ei verbum et accedentes discipuli eius rogabant eum dicentes: dimitte eam quia clamat post nos. (24) Ipse autem respondens ait: non sum missus nisi ad oves quae perierunt domus Israhel. (25) At illa venit et adoravit eum dicens: Domine adiuva me. (26) Qui respondens ait: non est bonum sumere panem filiorum et mittere canibus. (27) At illa dixit: etiam Domine nam et catelli edunt de micis quae cadunt de mensa dominorum suorum. (28) Tunc respondens Iesus ait illi: o mulier magna est fides tua fiat; tibi sicut vis. Et sanata est filia illius ex illa hora.

22–8 Smaragdus, *Collectiones*, PL 102, 132BC (derived from Bede's commentary on Mark):

Typice autem mulier haec gentilis, sed cum fide ad Dominum veniens Ecclesiam designat de gentibus collectam; quae et Chananaea vocatur, quia zelo fidei commota ad Dominum veniens, idola dereliquit. . . . Quod vero de finibus suis egressam eam dicit Matthaeus, hoc signat, quod illi solum fideliter ac recte properantibus orant, qui priscas suae perfidiae mansiones relinquunt, atque in domum Domini, videlicet ecclesiam, pia se devotione transferunt.

[2] Smetana 1959, p. 197.
[3] Smetana 1961, p. 464.

30–33 Smaragdus, *Collectiones*, PL 102, 131A (from Jerome's commentary on Matthew):

Ego filiam ecclesiae puto animas esse credentium, quae male a daemonio vexabantur, ignorantes creatorem, et adorantes lapidem.

34–7 Haymo, Hom. 35, PL 118, 228A (expanded from Bede's homily):

Nam sic Deum credidit ut hominem non negaret, sic hominem confitetur ut eumdem verum Deum credat. Verum enim Deum credidit, cum dixit: 'Miserere mei.' Verum hominem, cum adiunxit: Fili David. Filium David vocat, quia de stirpe David Salvator noster carnem assumpsit.

37–44 Cf Ps-Bede commentary on Matthew (*Expos. Matth.*, PL 92, 75D):

Tropologice vero filia a daemonio vexata cuiuslibet est conscientia, sordibus vitiorum polluta, cuius emendationem a pio Conditore debet continuis flagitare lamentis.

Probably from Bede's homily, I.22, 106–13, but Ælfric's *æfter ðeawlicum andgite* does seem to point to Ps-Bede's *tropologice* (though he does use the phrase without specific prompting at CH I.8.227).

45–51 Smaragdus, *Collectiones*, PL 102, 131AB (from Jerome):

'Qui non respondit ei verbum.' Non de superbia Pharisaica, nec de Scribarum supercilio, sed ne ipse sententiae suae videretur contrarius, per quam iusserat: 'In viam gentium, ne abieritis, et in civitates Samaritanorum ne intraveritis' (Mt 10.5). Nolebat enim occasionem calumniatoribus dare, perfectamque salutem gentium passionis et resurrectionis tempore reservabat.

Combined with Haymo, Hom. 35, PL 118, 228CD [from Bede, Hom. I.22, 31–4]:

Non est hoc ex supercilio Scribarum et Pharisaeorum, quod Dominus mulieri clamanti non respondit, sed . . . ut occasionem non credendi Iudaeis auferret, ne forte dicerent: Christus nobis promissus est, et iste gentes docet, gentes curat, et ideo nolumus credere in ipsum.

51–7 A summary of Haymo, Hom. 35, PL 118, 229B:

Ad quod dicendum, quia de praesentia sua corporali dixit: quoniam neminem gentilium per semetipsum docuisse legitur, exceptis duobus diebus in Samaria, ut occasionem non credendi (sicut supra dictum est) Iudaeis auferret. . . . Et ideo qui prius dicebat: 'In viam gentium ne abieritis, et in civitates Samaritanorum ne introieritis' (Mt 10.5), postea dixit: 'Euntes in mundum universum, praedicate evangelium omni creaturae' (Mc 16.15). Quod impletum est post eius ascensionem, ad apostolorum praedicationem.

Ælfric replaces Mc 16.15 with the text from Mt 28.19–20:

(19) Euntes ergo docete omnes gentes, baptizantes eos in nomine Patris, et Filii, et Spiritus Sancti; (20) docentes eos servare omnia quaecumque mandavi vobis.

60–65 There is no parallel to this in the commentaries, and it is not clear what point Ælfric is making; is he perhaps suggesting that even the intercession of the whole group of apostles is useless without the willingness of Christ?

68–79 No parallels. It looks like Ælfric's own expression of the kind of points being made by the commentators. Cf Smaragdus, *Collectiones*, PL 102, 131BC:

Non quod et ad gentes non missus sit, sed primum ad Israel missus sit, ut illis non recipientibus evangelium, iuste fieret ad gentes transmigratio.

80–87 Smaragdus, *Collectiones*, PL 102, 131C (from Bede on Mark):

Mira sub persona mulieris Chananitidis, ecclesiae fides, patientia, humilitas, praedicatur. Fides, qua crediderit sanari posse filiam suam: patientia, qua toties contempta in precibus perseverat: humilitas, qua se catulis comparat.

88–98 Smaragdus, *Collectiones*, PL 102, 131CD (from Bede on Mark):

O mira rerum conversio, Israel quondam filius, nos canes, pro diversitate fidei ordo nominum commutatur. De illis postea dicitur: 'Circumdederunt me canes multi' (Ps 21.17). . . . De nobis autem, ad pietatis gratiam conversis, dicit: 'Et alias oves habeo, quae non sunt ex hoc ovili, et illas oportet me adducere, et vocem meam audient' (Jn 10.16).

101–19 Smaragdus, *Collectiones*, PL 102, 131D-2A (from Bede on Mark):

Notandum sane quod mystice loquitur credens ex gentibus mulier. Qui catelli sub mensa comedunt de micis puerorum? Mensa quippe est scriptura sancta, quae nobis panem vitae ministrat, hinc etenim dicit ecclesia: 'Parasti in conspectu meo mensam adversus eos qui tribulant me' (Ps 22.5). Micae puerorum interna sunt mysteria scripturarum, quibus humilium solent corda refici. Non ergo crustas, sed micas de pane puerorum edunt catelli, quia conversi ad fidem gentiles, non litterae superficiem in scripturis, sed spiritalium medullam sensuum, quam bonis actibus proficere videant inquirunt. Et hoc sub mensa dominorum, dum verbis sacri eloquii humiliter subditi ad implenda quae praecepta sunt, cuncta sui cordis et corporis officia subponunt, quatenus ad speranda quae a Domino promissa sunt praemia in coelis, merito se debitae humilitatis erigant.

Ælfric adds a pointed application to the Jews and the Gentiles.

122–7 Smaragdus, *Collectiones*, PL 102, 132AB (from Bede on Mark):

Propter magnam matris fidem filiam deseruit daemonium. Ubi datur exemplum catechizandi infantes, quia videlicet per fidem et confessionem parentum in baptismo, liberantur a diabolo parvuli, qui nec dum per se sapere, vel aliquid agere boni possunt aut mali.

128–30 An odd conclusion to this homily. Given its similarity to the conclusion to his Life of St Edmund (LS 32.267–75), with its explicit contrast between

Jews and Christians, and the prominent initial position of the word *cristenra* here, it may be meant as a last and understated comment on the shift of divine favour from Jews to Gentiles.

9 ST GREGORY THE GREAT

The feast-day of Gregory the Great is mentioned in the verse *Menologium* as an occasion celebrated by the whole nation, and he was recognised, as Ælfric says, as the apostle of the English. There were many accounts of his life, including two early ones from England, and Ælfric here supplies his own version. The homiletic collections which Ælfric used did not cover this occasion, but the Cotton-Corpus legendary provided a Life of Gregory written by Paul the Deacon, which drew mainly on Gregory of Tours' *Historia Francorum* and Bede's *Historia Ecclesiastica* and Gregory's own writings (the version of Paul the Deacon's Life printed in PL 75 is a later interpolated text; Ælfric used the original version which was edited by H. Grisar in 1887[1]). Ælfric used this text for the structure of his account, and for its material on Gregory's life in Rome, but omitted the account of his writings and his embassy to Constantinople and greatly expanded the account of the mission to England. This is covered only briefly by Paul and Ælfric used instead the account in the *Historia Ecclesiastica*. Mostly he worked from the Latin text, but curiously, as Dorothy Whitelock pointed out, for the famous passage on the slave-boys in the market-place he seems to have chosen to rewrite the Old English version (which he attributes to Alfred).[2] It is difficult to imagine that he admired its style, or found it easier to update its English than to translate Bede's Latin himself, but perhaps it was a passage he had come to know well (so well, indeed, that he may have unconsciously changed some of the details). In selecting and adapting material from his two main sources Ælfric reshaped the story considerably, placing the market-place story in its chronological position (it is an appendage in the *Vita* and in the *Historia Ecclesiastica*) and making the mission to England the focus of Gregory's career. His use in full of Gregory's great sermon to the Roman people in the time of plague (lines 111–55) and his letter of admonition against pride to Augustine (lines 239–46) indicates an interest in maintaining the homiletic role of his work even within hagiographic writing, and the suppression of what is a central concern in the *Vita*, Gregory's strong preference for the

[1] The version in the surviving manuscripts of CC mostly shares the variants recorded by Grisar that were evidently in Ælfric's version, but has no other variants that are significant for Ælfric; see Zettel 1979, p. 185.

[2] On sources see: Förster 1892, pp. 34–5; A. Stephan, 'Eine weitere Quelle von Ælfrics Gregorhomilie', *Beiblatt zur Anglia* 14 (1903), 315–20; M. R. Godden, 'The sources for Ælfric's homily on St Gregory', *Anglia* 86 (1968), 79–88; Zettel 1979, pp. 144, 184–6. More generally, see Godden 1996, pp. 275–6. For the use of the *Old English Bede*, see D. Whitelock, 'The Old English Bede', *Proceedings of the British Academy* 48 (1962), 57–90, at p. 58 and n.10, and Godden 1978, pp. 102–3.

monastic life of contemplation over the pastoral work of teaching and administration, no doubt reflects Ælfric's own views on this issue, which is also a key concern in the next homily, on St Cuthbert. His reshaping of the story of the mission disguises all evidence of the reluctance of the missionaries, and omits the references to the prior existence of Christianity in Britain.

Sources and Notes

The following texts are cited below:

1. Bede, *Historia Ecclesiastica Gentis Anglorum*, ed. B. Colgrave and R. A. B. Mynors (Oxford, 1969).
2. *The Old English Version of Bede's Ecclesiastical History of the English People*, ed. T. A. Miller, EETS os 95 and 96 (1890–91).
3. Paulus Diaconus, *Vita Gregorii*, ed. H. Grisar, 'Die Gregorbiographie des Paulus Diakonus in ihrer ursprünglichen Gestalt, nach italienischen Handschriften', *Zeitschrift für katholische Theologie* 11 (1887), 158–73 (text, pp. 162–73) [cited by chapter and lines]. (I have normalised the eccentric spelling of Grisar's text and variant readings taken from Grisar's apparatus are printed in italics.)

3–5 Cf Bede, *Historia Ecclesiastica*, II.i (122.7–11):

Quem recte nostrum appellare possumus et debemus apostolum, quia . . . nostram gentem eatenus idolis mancipatam Christi fecit ecclesiam.

6–11 The 'many holy books' which tell St Gregory's life perhaps include the anonymous Whitby life and the one by John the Deacon;[3] Ælfric shows no evidence of knowing any specific version, but a familiarity with others might explain his reference to miracle-working at 256. The belief that King Alfred was the author of the Old English translation of Bede was shared by William of Malmesbury (cf Whitelock, 'Old English Bede', 1962), but there is nothing to indicate why either thought this.

12–21 *Vita Gregorii*, 1.1–12:

Gregorius, urbe *Roma* patre Gordiano editus, non solum nobilem de spectabili senatorum prosapia, verum etiam religiosam originem duxit. Nam Felix, eiusdem apostolice sedis antistes, vir magnae in Christo et ecclesia gloriae, eius atavus fuit. Sed tamen hanc Gregorius tantae nobilitatis lineam moribus extulit, probis actibus decoravit. . . . Gregorius namque ex Graeco eloquio in nostram linguam Vigilantius sonat. Re etenim vera vigilavit sibi, dum divinis inhaerendo praeceptis laudabiliter vixit; vigilavit et fidelium populis, dum doctrinae affluentis ingenio eis, quo tramite celestia scanderent, patefecit.

[3] The Whitby life is edited by B. Colgrave, *The Earliest Life of Gregory the Great* (Lawrence, Kansas, 1968, repr. Cambridge, 1985); John the Deacon's *Vita* is printed in PL 75, cols. 59–240.

22–31 *Vita Gregorii*, 2.1–11:

Disciplinis vero liberalibus, hoc est grammatica, rhetorica, dialectica, ita a *pupericia* est institutus, ut quamvis eo tempore florerent adhuc Romae studia litterarum, nulli in urbe ipsa putaretur esse secundus. Inerat ei in parva adhuc aetate maturum iam studium, adherere scilicet dictis maiorum, et si quid dignum potuisset auditu percipere, non segniter oblivioni tradere, sed tenaci potius memoriae commendare; hauriebatque iam tunc sitibundo fluenta pectore doctrinae, quae post congruenti tempore mellito gutture eructaret. Hic in annis adolescentiae, quibus solet ea aetas seculi vias ingredi, deo coepit devotus existere et ad supernae vitae patriam totis desideriis anhelare.

32–42 *Vita Gregorii*, 3.6: Parentum . . . post obitu.
and *Vita Gregorii*, 4.1–12:

Sex denique in Sicilia monasteria construens . . . septimum vero intra urbis muros instituit, in quo et ipse postmodum regulari tramite . . . sub abbatis imperio militavit. Quibus monasteriis tantum de redditibus praediorum delegavit, quantum posset illic commorantibus ad cotidianum victum sufficere; reliqua vero cum omni domo praedia vendidit ac pauperibus erogavit, nobilitatemque illam, quam ad saeculum videbatur habere, totam ad nanciscendam supernae gloriam dignitatis . . . convertit. Et qui ante serico contextu ac gemmis micantibus solitus erat per urbem procedere trabeatus, post vili contectus tegmine, ministrabat pauper ipse pauperibus.

Ælfric's *readum golde* has no parallel in the *Vita*. The adjective is one he commonly applies; cf CH I.4.87 and 93 and notes.

42–8 *Vita Gregorii*, 5.2–7:

In quo tanta perfectionis gratia coepit conversari, ut iam tunc in ipsis initiis perfectorum posset numero deputari. Inerat denique ei tanta abstinentia in cibis, vigilantia in orationibus. . . . Sustinebat preterea assiduas corporis infirmitates.

combined with *Vita Gregorii*, 13.8–9:

Quo malis praesentibus durius deprimebatur, eo de aeterna certius praesumtione respirabat.

49–52 *Vita Gregorii*, 7.3–6:

Denique cernens Romanus pontifex, qui tunc ecclesiae praeerat, virtutum gradibus Gregorium ad alta conscendere, eum abstractum a monasterio, ecclesiastici ordinis officio sublimavit levitamque septimum ad suum adiutorium ascivit. [*Goes on to describe his mission to Constantinople.*]

53–80 The account of the slave-boys shows close correspondence with the account in the *Old English Bede*, as Whitelock pointed out; OE Bede, 96.6–33:

Sume dæge þider niwan come cypemen of Brytene ond monig cepe þing on ceapstowe brohte, ond eac monige cwomon to bicgenne þa ðing. Þa

> gelomp þætte Gregorius betweoh oðre eac þider cwom, ond þa geseah betweoh oðer þing cype cneohtas þær gesette: wæron hwites lichoman ond fægres ondwlitan men ond æðellice gefeaxe. Ða he ða heo geseah ond beheold, þa frægn he, of hwelcon londe oðþe of hwylcre þeode hy brohte wæron. Sægde him mon, þæt heo of Breotone ealonde brohte wæron, ond þæs ealondes bigengan swelcre onsyne men wæron. Eft he frægn, hwæðer þa ilcan londleode cristne wæron þe hi þa gen in hæðennesse gedwolan lifden. Cwæð him mon to ond sægde, þæt heo hæðne wæron; ond he ða of inneweardre heortan swiðe sworette ond þus cwæð: Wala wa: þæt is sarlic, þætte swa fæger feorh ond swa leohtes ondwlitan men scyle agan ond besittan þeostra aldor.
>
> Eft he frægn, hwæt seo þeod nemned wære, þe heo of cwomon. Ondswarede him mon þæt heo Ongle nemde wæron. Cwæð he: Wel þæt swa mæg: forðon heo ænlice onsyne habbað, ond eac swylce gedafonað, þæt heo engla æfenerfeweardas in heofonum sy. Þa gyt he furðor frægn ond cwæð: Hwæt hatte seo mægð, þe þa cneohtas hider of lædde wæron. Þa ondswarede him mon ond cwæð, þæt heo Dere nemde wæron. Cwæð he: Wel þæt is cweden Dere, *de ira eruti*; heo sculon of Godes yrre beon abrogdene, ond to Cristes mildheortnesse gecegde. Ða gyt he ahsode hwæt heora cyning haten wære: ond him mon ondswarade ond cwæð, þætte he Æll haten wære. Ond þa plegode he mid his wordum to þæm noman ond cwæð: Alleluia, þæt gedafenað, þætte Godes lof usses scyppendes in þæm dælum sungen sy.

Ælfric's rewriting of it no doubt reflects the Latin account, reproduced in the *Vita* from the *Historia*, as well. Cf esp. the beginning, *Vita Gregorii*, 15.9–13 [= *Historia Ecclesiastica*, II.i]:

> Dum die quadam advenientibus nuper mercatoribus multa venalia in forum Rome conlata fuissent multique ad emendum hinc inde confluerent, contigit et Gregorium . . . cum ceteris advenisse ac vidisse inter alia pueros venales positos. . . .

None of the three earlier versions suggests that the merchants were themselves English and it seems somewhat implausible of Ælfric to say they were (lines 54–5) since the questions and answers would then have applied as much to the merchants as to the slave-boys. The *Old English Bede's cypemen of Brytene* perhaps suggested it to him. For *engla lande* (line 61) all three versions have Britain; Ælfric's *engla* rather spoils the point of the question and answer at 66–70. For *engla wlite* (line 69) cf *Historia* and *Vita*, *angelicam faciem*, as against the *Old English Bede*, *ænlice onsyne* (but some manuscripts have *englelice* or *engceli*). At 73–5 Ælfric seems to lose the point by not citing the Latin base of the pun, *de ira*.

81–8 The wording suggests a continued debt to the *Old English Bede* (OE Bede, 96.33–98.7):

> Ond he þa sona eode to ðæm biscope ond to ðam papan þæs apostolican seðles . . . bæd hine þæt he Ongolþeode onsende in Breotene hwelcehwego

lareowas, þætte þurh þa heo to Criste gecyrrede wæron; ond cwæð þæt he selfa geara wære mid Godes fultome þæt weorc to fremmenne, gif þæm apostolican papan þæt licade, ond ðæt his willa ond his leafnis wære. Þa ne wolde se papa þæt þafian ne þa burgware þon ma, þætte swa æðele wer ond swa geþungen ond swa gelæred swa feor fram him gewite.

Neither Latin version has any equivalent to these epithets for Gregory. But the Old English translator differs from them in suggesting that the pope was also unwilling to let him go, and in this point Ælfric agrees with the *Vita Gregorii*, 15.31–8 [= *Historia Ecclesiastica*, II.i]:

Accedensque ad pontificem Romanae et apostolicae sedis rogavit, ut genti Anglorum in Britanniam aliquos verbi ministros, per quos ad Christum converteretur, mitteret, asserens se ipsum in hoc opus, domino cooperante, perficiendum paratum esse, si tamen eidem apostolico pape hoc ut fieret placeret. Quod dum perficere non posset quia, etsi pontifex concedere illi quod petierat vellet, non tamen cives Romani, ut tam longe ab urbe secederet permitterent. . . .

89–106 *Vita Gregorii*, 10.11–30 (following an account of other disasters):

Subsecuta est e vestigio clades quam inguinariam vocant. Nam . . . primum omnium . . . Pelagium papam perculit et sine mora exstinxit. Quo defuncto tanta strages populi facta est, ut passim subtractis habitatoribus domus in urbe plurimae vacuae remanerent. Sed quia ecclesia Dei sine rectore esse non poterat, beatum Gregorium, licet totis viribus renitentem, plebs tamen omnis elegit. . . . Unde factum est, ut epistolam ad imperatorem Mauricium dirigeret, cuius filium ex lavacro sancto susceperat, adiurans et multa prece deposcens, ne unquam adsensum populis praeberet, ut se huius honoris gloria sublimaret. [*previous sentence:*] . . . metuens ne mundi gloria quam prius abiecerat ei sub ecclesiastici colore regiminis aliquo modo subripere posset. . . . Sed prefectus urbis, Germanus nomine, eius nuntium anticipavit comprehensumque ac disruptis epistolis consensum, *quid* populus fecerat imperatori direxit. At ille gratias deo agens . . . ipsum instituti praecepit.

106–8 *Vita Gregorii*, 11.50–54 (after the sermon and penance, i.e. after Ælfric's 163):

Cumque adhuc futurus antistes fuge latibula praepararet, capitur, trahitur et ad beati Petri apostoli basilicam ducitur, ibique ad pontificalis gratiae officium consecratus papa urbis efficitur.

109–22 *Vita Gregorii*, 11.1–13:

Cumque in hoc res staret ut benediceretur, et lues populum devastaret, verbum ad plebem pro agenda penitentia hoc modo exorsus est: 'Oportet, fratres dilectissimi, ut flagella dei, quae metuere ventura debuimus, saltem praesentia, et experta timeamus. Conversionis nobis aditum dolor aperiat et cordis nostri duritiam ipsa quam patimur pena dissolvat. . . . Ecce etenim cuncta plebs celestis irae mucrone percutitur et repentina singuli caede vastantur. Nec languor mortem praevenit, sed languoris moras, ut cernitis, mors ipsa praecurrit. Percussus quisque ante rapitur, quam ad lamenta penitentiae convertatur. Pensate ergo, qualis ad conspectum districti iudicis pervenit, cui non vacat flere quod fecit.'

123–35 *Vita Gregorii*, 11.13–24:

Habitatores quique . . . corruunt, domus vacuae relinquuntur, filiorum funera parentes aspiciunt et sui eos ad interitum heredes praecedunt. Unusquisque ergo nostrum ad poenitentiae lamenta confugiat, dum flere ante percussionem vacat. Revocemus ante oculos mentis quidquid errando commisimus et quod nequiter egimus flendo puniamus. Praeveniamus faciem eius in confessione, et sicut propheta admonet, 'Levemus corda nostra cum manibus ad Deum' (Lam 3.41). Ad Deum quippe corda cum manibus levare, est orationis nostrae studium cum merito bonae operationis erigere. Dat profecto, dat tremori nostro fiduciam, qui per prophetam clamat: 'Nolo mortem peccatoris, sed ut convertatur et vivat' (Ez 33.11).

136–55 *Vita Gregorii*, 11.24–41:

Nullus autem de iniquitatum suarum immanitate desperet. Veternosas namque Ninivitarum culpas triduana poenitentia abstersit: et conversus latro vitae praemia, etiam in ipsa sententia suae mortis, emeruit. Mutemus igitur corda, . . . citius ad precem iudex flectitur, si a pravitate sua petitor corrigatur. Imminente ergo tantae animadversionis gladio, nos importunis *fletibus* insistamus. Ea namque quae ingrata esse hominibus importunitas solet, *iudici* veritatis placet, quia pius ac misericors Dominus vult a se precibus exigi, qui quantum meremur, non vult irasci. Hinc etenim per psalmistam dicit: 'Invoca me in die tribulationis tuae, *et* eripiam te, et magnificabis me' (Ps 49.15). Ipse ergo sibi testis est quia invocantibus misereri desiderat, qui admonet ut invocetur. Proinde, fratres carissimi, contrito corde, et correctis operibus, *ab ipso feriae quartae diluculo* ad septiformem letaniam devota cum lacrimis mente veniamus; ut districtus iudex dum culpas nostras nos punire considerat, ipse a sententia propositae damnationis parcat.'

156–63 *Vita Gregorii*, 11.43–50:

Igitur dum magna multitudo sacerdotum, monachorum, diversique sexus et aetatis, iuxta praeceptionem beati Gregorii die constituta Dominum rogatura venisset, intantum lues ipsa divino iudicio desaeviit, ut intra unius horae spatium, dum voces plebs ad dominum supplicationis emitteret, octoginta homines ad terram corruentes spiritum exhalarent. Sed non destitit sacerdos tantus populo praedicare, ne ab oratione cessarent, donec miseratione divina pestis ipsa quiesceret.

The *Vita* does not mention the laity in the procession, unless they are implied by *diversique sexus et aetatis*. Chapters 12–14 deal with Gregory's writings, his ill-health and his pastoral work.

164–73 *Vita Gregorii*, 15.38–41 and 16.1–3:

> Mox ut ipse pontificatus officio functus est, opus diu desideratum perfecit, alios quidem praedicatores mittens sed ipse praedicationem, ut fructificaret, suis exhortationibus ac precibus fulciens. Denique direxit ad eandem insulam servos dei Mellitum, Augustinum et Iohannem cum multis aliis deum timentibus monachis.

The explanation that Gregory himself was unable to leave Rome, not in any of the sources, was perhaps obvious enough, but it underlies his comments to Augustine at 186–7. Paul gives the names of just three missionaries, implying that they were all part of the original mission. Ælfric adds three others, Laurentius, Petrus and Justus, presumably taken from the *Historia Ecclesiastica* or tradition. Laurentius and Petrus are mentioned in the *Historia Ecclesiastica*, I.xxvii as the messengers sent from England by Augustine to Gregory. According to Bede, in a passage in *Historia Ecclesiastica*, I.xxix which Ælfric uses later (lines 247–53), Mellitus and Justus were not on the original mission but were sent by Gregory later; they are mentioned several times together, or in association with Laurentius, in the early chapters of *Historia Ecclesiastica*, II, and that may have prompted Ælfric to add Justus to the original mission, despite the clear contrary evidence of both the Latin and the English versions of the *Historia*.

175–87 The *Vita* records the conversion in one sentence, and goes on to report Gregory's own comments. Ælfric now turns to the *Historia Ecclesiastica*, converting Gregory's letter of exhortation, sent after the missionaries have attempted to abandon their journey, into a speech of encouragement as they leave (*Historia Ecclesiastica*, I.xxiii, 70.4–14):

> Nec labor vos ergo itineris nec maledicorum hominum linguae deterreant, sed omni instantia omnique fervore, quae inchoastis, Deo auctore peragite, scientes quod laborem magnum maior aeternae retributionis gloria sequitur. Remeanti autem Augustino praeposito vestro, quem et abbatem vobis constituimus, in omnibus humiliter oboedite, scientes hoc vestris animabus per omnia profuturum, quicquid a vobis fuerit in eius admonitione conpletum. Omnipotens Deus sua vos gratia protegat, et vestri laboris fructum in aeterna me patria videre concedat, quatinus etsi vobiscum laborare nequeo, simul in gaudio retributionis inveniar, quia laborare scilicet volo.

The text is slightly adapted to avoid reference to Augustine's return from the mission.

188–204 Bede, *Historia Ecclesiastica*, I.xxv (72.10–15, 20–27, 74.13–18, 21–5):

> Roboratus ergo confirmatione beati patris Gregorii, Augustinus cum famulis Christi, qui erant cum eo, rediit in opus Verbi pervenitque Brittaniam. Erat eo tempore rex Aedilberct in Cantia potentissimus, qui ad confinium usque Humbrae fluminis maximi, quo meridiani et septentrionales Anglorum populi dirimuntur, fines imperii tetenderat. . . . In hac

ergo adplicuit servus Domini Augustinus et socii eius, viri ut ferunt ferme xl. Acceperant autem, praecipiente beato papa Gregorio, de gente Francorum interpretes; et mittens ad Aedilberctum, mandavit se venisse de Roma ac nuntium ferre optimum, qui sibi obtemperantibus aeterna in caelis gaudia et regnum sine fine cum Deo vivo et vero futurum sine ulla dubietate promitteret. . . . Cumque ad iussionem regis residentes verbum ei vitae una cum omnibus qui aderant eius comitibus praedicarent, respondit ille dicens: 'Pulchra sunt quidem verba et promissa quae adfertis; sed quia nova sunt et incerta, non his possum adsensum tribuere relictis eis, quae tanto tempore cum omni Anglorum gente servavi. Verum . . . benigno vos hospitio recipere et, quae victui sunt vestro necessaria, ministrare curamus, nec prohibemus quin omnes quos potestis fidei vestrae religionis praedicando sociatis.' Dedit ergo eis mansionem in civitate Doruvernensi, quae imperii sui totius erat metropolis.

The omitted material includes an account of Æthelberht's Christian wife and his familiarity with Christian doctrine.

205–15 Bede, *Historia Ecclesiastica*, I.xxvi (76.3–12):

Coeperunt apostolicam primitivae ecclesiae vitam imitari, orationibus videlicet assiduis vigiliis ac ieiuniis serviendo, verbum vitae quibus poterant praedicando, cuncta huius mundi velut aliena spernendo, ea tantum quae victui necessaria videbantur ab eis quos docebant accipiendo, secundum ea quae docebant ipsi per omnia vivendo, et paratum ad patiendum adversa quaeque vel etiam moriendum pro ea quam praedicabant veritate animum habendo. Quid mora? Crediderunt nonnulli et baptizabantur, mirantes simplicitatem innocentis vitae ac dulcedinem doctrinae eorum caelestis.

216–25 Bede, *Historia Ecclesiastica*, I.xxvi (76.20–78.4, re-ordered):

At ubi ipse etiam inter alios delectatus vita mundissima sanctorum et promissis eorum suavissimis, quae vera esse miraculorum quoque multorum ostensione firmaverunt, credens baptizatus est, coepere plures cotidie ad audiendum Verbum confluere, ac relicto gentilitatis ritu unitati se sanctae Christi ecclesiae credendo sociare. Quorum fidei et conversioni ita congratulatus esse rex perhibetur, ut nullum tamen cogeret ad Christianismum, sed tantummodo credentes artiori dilectione, quasi concives sibi regni caelestis, amplecteretur. Didicerat enim a doctoribus auctoribusque suae salutis servitium Christi voluntarium, non coacticium esse debere.

Perhaps deliberately, the re-ordering of sentences has the multitude of new converts appearing to respond to the king's affection for converts and his policy of voluntarism rather than to his own conversion.

226–32 Bede, *Historia Ecclesiastica*, I.xxvii (78.7–14):

Interea vir Domini Augustinus venit Arelas, et ab archiepiscopo eiusdem civitatis Aetherio, iuxta quod iussa sancti patris Gregorii acceperant, archiepiscopus genti Anglorum ordinatus est; reversusque Brittaniam misit continuo Romam Laurentium presbyterum et Petrum monachum, qui beato pontifici Gregorio gentem Anglorum fidem Christi suscepisse ac se episcopum factum esse referrent, simul et de eis quae necessariae videbantur quaestionibus eius consulta flagitans.

232–8 Bede goes on to give the questions and answers which followed (i.e. the *Liber Responsionum*); Ælfric presumably alludes to this at 237–8, but does not use it. Lines 235–6 refer to *Historia Ecclesiastica*, I.xxxii (110.23–5):

Misit idem beatus papa Gregorius eodem tempore etiam regi Aedilbercto epistulam, simul et dona in diversis speciebus perplura.

There is, curiously, nothing to parallel Ælfric's reference to Gregory's pleasure at the news, though he may be alluding to the passage from the *Moralia* quoted at this point in the *Vita Gregorii* (16.11–21), in which Gregory celebrates the conversion of the English.

239–46 Bede, *Historia Ecclesiastica,* I.xxxi (108.26–110.2)

Scio, frater carissime, quia omnipotens Deus per dilectionem tuam in gentem, quam eligi voluit, magna miracula ostendit: unde necesse est, ut de eodem dono caelesti et timendo gaudeas et gaudendo pertimescas. Gaudeas videlicet, quia Anglorum animae per exteriora miracula ad interiorem gratiam pertrahuntur; pertimescas vero, ne inter signa, quae fiunt, infirmus animus in sui praesumtione se elevet, et unde foras in honorem tollitur, inde per inanem gloriam intus cadat.

247–53 Cf Bede, *Historia Ecclesiastica,* I.xxix (104.1–9):

Praeterea idem papa Gregorius Augustino episcopo . . . misit . . . vasa videlicet sacra et vestimenta altarium, ornamenta quoque ecclesiarum et sacerdotalia vel clericilia indumenta, sanctorum etiam apostolorum ac martyrum reliquias, necnon et codices plurimos.

The letter that follows in *Historia Ecclesiastica*, I.xxix, says that the bishop of London (rather than Augustine's successors or the archbishops of Canterbury) should in future receive the pallium from the Roman see. But if, as Colgrave and Mynors comment, 'it is clear that Gregory expected Augustine to make his seat at London rather than Canterbury', in spirit at least the passage does mean what Ælfric takes it to mean. The letter also instructs Augustine to ordain twelve bishops who are to be subject to his jurisdiction, which no doubt prompted Ælfric's 251–2. But his words are 'bishops in every city in England', whereas Gregory's letter says that Augustine is to choose a bishop for York, who will himself appoint twelve bishops for his region. The *Historia Ecclesiastica* actually records Augustine consecrating only two bishops, Mellitus and Justus (II.iii), despite Ælfric's statement.

254–60 The writings of Gregory are discussed at length in *Historia Ecclesiastica*, II.i and *Vita Gregorii*, 12. Neither Paul nor Bede ascribe any miracles to

Gregory, and Paul's comments suggest that none are known (*Vita Gregorii*, 16.25–9):

> Iam vero utrum aliquibus vir iste tanti meriti miraculis claruerit, superfluo quaeritur, cum luce clarius constet quod is qui virtutum signa suis meritis valuit aliis quoque Christo largiente adquirere, si exegisset oportunitas, facilius poterat haec etiam ipse promereri.

The interpolated version adds a long series of miracles at this point, and Ælfric evidently knew at least one of them (see CH II.15.167–73). For the final lines, cf *Vita Gregorii*, 17.7–11:

> Qui beatissimus pontifex, postquam sedem Romanae et apostolicae ecclesiae annis tredecim mensibus sex et diebus decem gloriosissime rexit, ex hac luce subtractus atque ad eternam est regni celestis sedem translatus.

10 ST CUTHBERT

Cuthbert is the only English saint covered in the Catholic Homilies and, apart from St Augustine of Canterbury, the only one whose feast-day was widely celebrated in English churches and acknowledged as a secular feast-day. Four accounts of his life were written soon after his death, and a further one in the tenth century. Ælfric gives a long account of his life written in a new and apparently experimental style, marked by passages with a regular rhythm and alliteration in a manner resembling Old English verse, together with a sprinkling of poetic words and occasional rhyme (e.g. 72–3).

Ælfric mentions the prose and verse lives by Bede at the beginning of the homily. Förster argued that he used both as sources, and also noted a parallel with the relevant parts of the *Historia Ecclesiastica*, which mostly repeats material from Bede's earlier lives but has some additional material. Gordon Whatley has convincingly shown that there are also traces of the influence of the earlier anonymous life composed at Lindisfarne, which Bede used as a source.[1] More recently, B. A. Blokhuis has published a very detailed and thorough analysis of the question of sources[2] (she does not refer to Förster's analysis and presumably was unaware of Whatley's). She argues that Ælfric used Bede's verse Life and the *Historia Ecclesiastica* but not the anonymous Life or Bede's prose Life; all the parallels with the anonymous Life are coincidental and those with Bede's prose Life, she thinks, are either coincidental or borrowings from the *Historia*'s revision of material from the prose Life. Having reviewed the material again, my own view is that the parallels with the anonymous Life

[1] Whatley, *Acta* (forthcoming).

[2] 'Bede and Ælfric: the Sources of the Homily on St Cuthbert', in *Beda Venerabilis: Historian, Monk and Northumbrian*, ed. L. A. J. R. Houwen and A. A. Macdonald, Mediaevalia Groningana 19, Groningen 1996, pp. 107–38

adduced by Whatley (mostly not noted by Blokhuis) are clearly there, and that there are also definite borrowings from Bede's prose Life for the material that is not reproduced in the *Historia*. But Blokhuis is clearly right in emphasising the primary use of Bede's verse Life and the use of the *Historia*, and she identifies some further parallels, especially with the *Historia*, which I had not noticed before. The situation is an extraordinary one for a number of reasons: why did Ælfric use all these sources, since they contain largely the same material; why in particular did he choose to make such extensive use of the very difficult metrical life; how did he acquire copies of these lives, especially the anonymous life; how much did the different structures and stylistic techniques of the three lives affect his own writing?

The metrical life of Cuthbert is an extremely difficult poem,[3] full of rare poetic or esoteric vocabulary, convoluted syntax and oblique expressions; it is also very allusive in its treatment of the story, and Michael Lapidge argues that it was designed as a meditation on a familiar story rather than as a substitute for the anonymous Life. Yet Ælfric uses it not simply for the occasional episodes and passages which are not in the other lives, but extensively for stories which are covered in detail by the other two; often it seems to have been his preferred source. Part of the attraction may have been that it often dealt more succinctly with the story than Bede's prose Life, which adds a great deal of circumstantial detail and a number of additional miracles, most of which Ælfric omits; but he was by this stage experienced at reducing hagiographic texts and would hardly have needed the help of Bede's verse Life to do it. It would also seem that the style itself interested Ælfric, since his own version is so marked by poetic language and techniques. This is the first, and I think possibly the only case, in which Ælfric made substantial use of a poem as source, and it would seem that the example of Bede's metrical life inspired him to experiment with poetic techniques in his own writing. The homily is striking evidence of his grasp both of Latin poetic language and of Old English poetic diction.

The anonymous Life seems to have provided mainly isolated phrases and details, which do not significantly affect the narrative but presumably struck Ælfric as more appropriate or more telling: thus in the account of the angel who rides by and heals his swollen knee (lines 28–47), the phrase *ana under sunnbeame*, the peaceful words and the brave reply are from the anonymous Life, the crutches and the snow-white horse probably from Bede's verse Life, and the nature of the swelling, the pleasant greeting and the allusion to Raphael from Bede's prose Life. Given the rarity of the anonymous Life, and the fact that some copies of Bede's prose Life have details from the anonymous Life added as glosses, it seems possible that Ælfric used a copy of Bede's prose Life

[3] Cf M. Lapidge, 'Bede's Metrical *Vita S. Cuthberti*', in *St Cuthbert, his Cult and his Community to A.D. 1200*, ed. G. Bonner, C. Stancliffe and D. Rollason (Woodbridge, 1989), pp. 77–93, at 93.

that already included these phrases from the anonymous Life; but there are a few signs that he may have known rather more of the story than added glosses would account for.

The three *Vitae* structure the story of Cuthbert differently. The anonymous Life has a four book structure, book I covering his early life as a layman, including spells as a shepherd and a soldier, book II his early years as a monk, first at Ripon and then at Melrose, book III the move to Lindisfarne and his solitary life on Farne, and book IV his period as a bishop, his death on Farne and the subsequent miracles. It is primarily an account of miracles of healing and prophecy, but does tell a story of his career. Bede's verse Life is written in 46 chapters which focus on individual miracles and omit most of the context of events, though it does allude to the main events in his career—Ripon, Lindisfarne, Farne, the episcopate and finally Farne again. As Lapidge says, 'it is part of Bede's purpose to remove the episodes of Cuthbert's life from the temporal and local and to situate them in a timeless, placeless framework'.[4] In Bede's prose Life, which also tells the story in 46 chapters, though they do not all match those in the verse Life, Bede restores and indeed greatly extends the circumstantial detail and tries to place the miracles in a biographical context. He tells how the vision of Aidan's death prompted him to abandon his sheep and seek out the monastic life; Cuthbert became a monk at Melrose because of the reputation of Boisil, was taken by his abbot to Ripon but then returned when the monks were expelled from there, was sent by his abbot to be prior at Lindisfarne because of his virtue, retired to Farne, became bishop and then returned to Farne to die. The events are placed in a historical and political context. Ælfric clearly follows the model of Bede's verse Life as much as possible. He focuses on the miracles and gives very little sense of the context and place: there is no hint that the miracle of the seals takes place at Coldingham, not Cuthbert's own monastery, for instance. He does not say where he became a monk and never mentions Melrose or Ripon, though he does note, 140–1, that Cuthbert was then prior at Lindisfarne. Though Bede's verse Life may have been conceived, as Lapidge suggests, for those who already knew the Cuthbert story, this would probably not be the case for Ælfric's account and he presumably expected his readers to focus on the miracles and the general spiritual and exemplary character of the life rather than its historical and geographical context (and perhaps these would in any case have meant less to his readers than to Bede's). As in the *Vitae* Cuthbert's role as a preacher to the people of the surrounding region, despite his status as a monk and his fondness for the solitary life, is strongly emphasised, an aspect that would have had particular significance for Ælfric and his contemporaries. Though Ælfric makes extensive use of the *Vitae* he changes or adds a few details, perhaps unconsciously. The most puzzling is the statement that

[4] Lapidge, 'Bede's Metrical *Vita*', p. 91.

Cuthbert was preaching before he became a monk (line 52): Ælfric seems to envisage him having an earlier status as a cleric.

The Cotton-Corpus legendary did not include any material on Cuthbert, it would appear. Presumably Ælfric had a separate collection of Cuthbert material; several extant manuscripts include both Bede's prose Life and his verse Life,[5] and sometimes chapters from the *Historia* are included as well (though not, I think, the ones that Ælfric uses), but there is no evidence of the anonymous Life circulating with these other texts: the seven extant manuscripts containing the anonymous Life are all of Continental origin and none of them contains the other Lives.[6]

In the notes below I have printed the version that seems to me closest in each case, though often the different versions are very similar and one could not be always sure that Ælfric used the passage quoted; it would appear that he had in any case read all three *Vitae* and the *Historia* before he started. Though Bede's verse Life often provides the closest verbal parallel, the fuller context provided by the other two must have informed the way Ælfric transformed it.

There is a useful but brief account of the rhythm and alliteration of this piece in Pope, pp. 113–4. On the use of poetic vocabulary see Godden 1980 and Frank 1994; more generally see Godden 1996, pp. 276–81.

Sources and Notes

The following texts are cited below:

1. Anon., *Vita Cuthberti*, ed. and trans. B. Colgrave in *Two Lives of Saint Cuthbert* (Cambridge, 1940), pp. 60–138. [= VCA]
2. Bede, *Historia Ecclesiastica Gentis Anglorum*, ed. B. Colgrave and R. A. B. Mynors (Oxford, 1969). [=*Historia*]
3. Bede, *Vita Cuthberti Metrica*, ed. W. Jaager in *Bedas metrische Vita sancti Cuthberti* (Leipzig, 1935). [= VCM]
4. Bede, *Vita Cuthberti Prosa*, ed. and trans. B. Colgrave in *Two Lives of Saint Cuthbert* (Cambridge, 1940), pp. 142–306. [= VCP]

[5] See Colgrave, *Two Lives*, pp. 45–50.

[6] Michael Lapidge (*Wulfstan of Winchester: Life of St Æthelwold*, ed. M. Lapidge and M. Winterbottom (Oxford, 1991)) notes a collection of Cuthbert material in a later manuscript with possibly Ælfrician connections, viz. Paris, Bibliothèque Nationale, lat. 5362. He sees the manuscript as 'arguably a later copy of a hagiographical commonplace-book compiled by Ælfric himself' (p. cxlviii), and remarks that 'nearly all these contents' of the Paris MS were used in some way by Ælfric, citing as one example 'Bede's prose *Vita S. Cuthberti* [which] forms the basis of Catholic Homilies II, no. x.' Unfortunately the collection turns out not to be very apposite to Ælfric's account of Cuthbert: it has Bede's prose life in a form very close to that printed by Colgrave (i.e. with no apparent additions corresponding to the *Historia* or VCA), followed by two post-mortem miracles from the *Historia Ecclesiastica*, IV.xxxi–xxxii and one from the *Historia de S. Cuthberto*, none of them used by Ælfric; and it does not have the relevant bits from the *Historia Ecclesiastica* or Ælfric's primary source, the metrical life, or the anonymous life.

7–27 The first episode is in VCA I.3, VCM c.1 and VCP c.1. For the beginning, esp. *efenealdum*, cf VCA I.3, 64.8–10 (or VCP, but less clearly, even though Ælfric does mention Bede as the source):

> Dum ergo puer esset annorum octo, omnes coaetaneos in agilitate et petulantia superans. . . .

For the rest Ælfric seems to draw primarily on Bede's VCM, c.1, 46–61, 63–9, though the details are in a different order:

> [46] Forte vago gracilis dum gramine luderet aetas,
> [49–51] . . . dominus digno puerilia sensa magistro
> Correxit, tenero nam de grege parvulus instans
> Viribus admonuit dubiis ne fidere mallet . . .
> [63–64] 'Quid te, care, levi subdis per inania ludo,
> Quem deus aetherio sublimis honore sacravit . . .
> [67–69] Fas erit aut vulgi antistes similabitur actis?
> Linque tuis ergo tam dissona frivola fatis
> Devotusque deo sacrum coniungere pectus.
> [65] . . . Praeficiens populis, caeli quibus atria pandas?'
> [54–61] At puer infantis risit sacra famina, nolens
> Octennis trimum despectus habere magistrum.
> Qui gemit et luctu faciem perfundit amaro.
> Solvitur in lacrimas ludus cunctique vicissim
> Unius incertos satagunt abstergere fletus,
> Nec valuere tamen solacia rapta novari.
> Hunc pia complexum Cuthbertus ad oscula mulcet,
> Obsecrans siccare genas, deponere luctus.

The last detail is from the VCP, c.1, 158.5–7:

> relicta continuo ludendi vanitate domum rediit, ac stabilior iam ex illo tempore animoque adolescentior existere coepit.

28–47 The second episode is found in all three *Vitae*, VCP c.2, 158–60, VCM c.2, and VCA I.4. Lines 28–35 are a curious mixture of phrases from all of them:

> [VCP] Subito dolore genu correptum illius, acri coepit tumore grossescere . . . [VCM] atque regit vestigia languida pino. Cumque die quadam sub divo fessa locasset Membra dolens solus [VCA] in solis ardore iacens [VCM] ecce repente Venit eques niveo venerandus tegmine nec non Gratia cornipedi similis, recubumque salutat, Obsequium sibi ferre rogans. [VCA] salutansque verbis pacificis [VCP] mansueto illum salutaret alloquio.

Ælfric's apparent additions are the detail of warming his limbs and *dægwistes* (line 35); his *snawhwitum* horse presumably derives from the *niveo* garment of Bede's verse Life and the 'not dissimilar' appearance of the horse.

35–9 Cf VCM c.2, 81–5:

Cui talia reddit:
'Obsequiis nunc ipse tuis adsistere promtus
Vellem, ni diro premeretur compede gressus;
Nam tumet ecce genu, nullis quod cura medentum
Tempore iam multo valuit mollire lagonis'.

VCP is much the same; Ælfric's *læcewyrt* was perhaps suggested by VCM's *lagonis* (flasks?) rather than VCP's *industria medicorum*. For *anmodlice* cf VCA *intrepida mente*.

39–43 VCM c.2, 86–91:

Desilit hospes equo, palpat genu sedulus aegrum,
Sic fatus: 'Similae nitidam cum lacte farinam
Olla coquat pariter ferventis in igne culinae,
Hocque istum calido sanandus inunge tumorem.'
Haec memorans conscendit equum, quo venerat illo
Calle domum remeans.

(Note the VCM's reference to the angel returning on the track by which he came.)

44–7 VCP c.2, 160.13–16:

> Ille iussis obtemperans, post dies paucos sanatus est, agnovitque angelum fuisse qui haec sibi monita dedisset, mittente illo qui quondam Raphaelem archangelum ad sanandos Tobiae visus destinare dignatus est.

Ælfric's firm statement that God has visited Cuthbert through his angel gives the agency to God more clearly than in the *Vitae*.

Ælfric does not use the next episode in VCP and VCM (c.3) where Cuthbert saves some monks being carried out to sea on rafts; it is not in VCA.

48–51 A brief summary of VCP and VCM cc.4, VCA I.5; cf VCA which seems closest (VCA I.5, 68.15–70.3):

> Alia quoque tempore in adolescentia sua . . . quando in montanis . . . cum aliis pastoribus pecora domini sui pascebat . . . vidit visionem quam ei Dominus revelavit, hoc est coelo aperto . . . angelos ascendentes et descendentes viderat, et inter manus eorum animam sanctam . . . Post paucos dies, celeberrime obitum sancti episcopi nostri Aegdani . . . nuntiatum esse audierunt.

VCP presents the event as a conversion experience for Cuthbert, leading him to seek the monastic life. All three locate the event in the hills (*montanis, collibus*) rather than Ælfric's *felda*. Ælfric omits a miracle of Aidan given in VCM c.5.

51–8 In VCA I.6, VCP c.5, VCM c.6, but no version suggests that Cuthbert was preaching; the VCA and VCM locate the event in his youth, implicitly while still in secular life, the VCP places it immediately after his decision to enter a monastery (because of his vision of Aidan) but before he does so. The bad weather is specified in the VCA and (in graphic detail) in the VCM. The *westen* is suggested by the VCP only (where the fall of night and the absence of human habitation, rather than bad weather, are mentioned to explain Cuthbert's need to seek shelter in a hut, and provide a more appropriate context for the miraculous provision of food, since Cuthbert has been fasting all day). The shepherd's hut is from VCP or VCM. The VCM gives the details succinctly (where the VCP is curiously concerned with feeding the horse), c.6, 165–78:

Ingrediens itiner pluvio concluditur euro,
Frigora quaque volant, percurrit sidera nimbus,
Divertitque rigens veteris sub tecta tabernae,
Condiderat pecorum quam sola per avia custos,
Parieti et adnectit quo venerat ipse caballum. . . .
Divinis horam dum sacrat laudibus almus,
Cernit equum subito ipsius decerpere morsu
Tecta casae, feniqne fluunt in fasce cadentis
Missa pio iuveni summo convivia dono . . .
Ergo sacer calidi panis carnisque superna
Iam dape pastus, agit grates. . . .

All three specify meat, *caro*, as well as bread; Ælfric's vaguer *syfling* ('relish'?) may reflect sensitivity about fasting, especially since he presents Cuthbert as already a cleric; VCP has the event occurring on a Friday, i.e. a fast day, but there is no hint of that in Ælfric's version.

59–73 VCA II.2, VCM c.7, VCP cc.6–7. The VCP gives a long account of Cuthbert joining the monastery at Melrose and then moving to Ripon some years later. The VCA gives a brief chapter on him becoming a monk. The VCM, like Ælfric, goes quickly to the next miracle (c.7, 180–4):

Hinc maiora petens monachis Hrypensibus almus
Corpore, mente, habitu, factisque adiungitur et mox
Ponitur hospitibus famulus, iussoque libenter
Subditus obsequio, celsae de moenibus aulae
Cernere promeruit gaudens et pascere civem.

But VCP's *relictis seculi rebus* may be the source of 59–60 *ealle woruldðing forlet*. For 63–6 cf VCA II.2, which sets the scene and identifies the visitor as an angel at the outset; VCA II.2 (76.18–78.9):

> Quadam die in matutina hora hiemali et nivali tempore, apparuit ei angelus Domini in forma stabilis viri. . . . Deinde ergo suscepto eo secundum morem eius benigne. . . . Revertens ad monasterium querens panem . . . reversus vero ad hospitem.

The VCP c.7 is perhaps nearest for the rest of the story, but the details are rearranged:

> [176.23–4] At ubi rediit, non invenit hospitem quem edentem reliquerat.
> [178.2–3] vidit iuxta positos tres panes calidos insoliti candoris et gratiae,
> [178.6–7] Nam et lilia candore, et rosas odore, et mella praecellunt sapore.

> [176.24–5] Explorat vestigia qua iret, sed nulla uspiam invenit. Recens autem nix terram texerat . . . [178.3–10] pavensque talia secum loquitur, 'Cerno quod angelus Dei erat quem suscepi, pascere non pasci veniens. En panes attulit, quales terra gignere nequit.' . . . Unde constat quia non de nostra tellure orti, sed de paradiso voluptatis sunt allati. Nec mirum quod epulas in terris sumere respuerit humanas, qui aeterno vitae pane fruitur in coelis.

Ælfric reverses the details of the snow and the loaves. The VCA does not have the images of lily, rose and honey. Note the rhyme which Ælfric introduces in the last sentence.

74–94 VCA II.3 and VCP c.10 locate this story at the double monastery of Coldingham, when Cuthbert was on a visit from Melrose; VCM c.8, like Ælfric, omits all details of the context, leaving it to be assumed that it was at his own monastery (Ripon [!] in VCM, unspecified in Ælfric). Ælfric's account seems close to the VCM, though with a bit of detail from the VCP (e.g. that the spy is a monk); VCM c.8, 220–47:

> Interea iuvenis solitos nocturnus ad hymnos
> Digreditur, lento quidam quem calle secutus
> Illius incertos studuit dinoscere gressus.
> Ad mare deveniunt; collo tenus inditus undis
> Marmoreo Cuthbertus agit sub carmine noctem.
> Egreditur ponto genibusque in litore fixis
> Expandit geminas supplex ad sidera palmas.
> Tum maris ecce duo veniunt animalia fundo
> Vatis et ante pedes fulva sternuntur harena;
> Hinc gelidas villo flatuque foventia plantas
> Aequoreum tergunt sancto de corpore frigus;
> Supplice tum nutu sese benedicier orant.
> Qui parens votis verbo dextraque ministris
> Impendit grates patriasque remittit ad undas
> Ac matutino tectis se tempore reddit.
> Haec comes ut vidit perculsus corda pavore . . .
> At revoluta dies noctis cum pelleret umbras,
> Aeger adest vati, supplex genibusque volutus
> Se poscit domino prece commendare profusa, . . .
> 'sed nunc donabitur error
> Iam tibi poscenti, retices si visa, quousque
> Decedam mundo.' . . .
> Tum prece languorem pellit culpamque relaxat.

Ælfric is insistent that this asceticism is Cuthbert's normal practice; the *Vitae* imply only that it was his custom to pray on the shore at night. He identifies the animals as seals; the VCM and VCA do not specify, the VCP says otters, *lutraeae* (= OE *oter*). The *Vitae* hint that Cuthbert guessed the monk's crime without being told.

95–7 Ælfric in fact omits only one miracle at this point, the story of being marooned on the Pictish coast (VCA II.5, VCP c.11, VCM c.9).

97–112 VCA II.5, VCP c.12, VCM c.10; VCM seems closest (c.10, 291–308):

Inde sacerdotis meritoque graduque potitus
Tendebat populos vitae renovare fluentis.
Forte viae comiti, sed praescius ipse futuri,
'Fare, sodalis', ait, 'quo fercula sumere mens sit.'
'Haec et ego', dixit, 'dubio sub pectore mecum;
Prandia non tulimus vasis, domus hospita non est. . . .'
Respondit senior: 'Domino si fidere discas!
Providet ille dapes, vatem qui pascere corvos
Iussit; iam aspectas aquilam vaga flabra secantem
Nos valet hac etiam omnipotens satiare ministra.'
Dumque iter inceptum peragunt, venere sub amnem,
Et volucrem rubro, quae celsa sub axe volarat,
Marmoris in ripa residere tuentur, at altus
'Cernis', ait vates, 'nostram super aequora servam?
Curre, rogo, et dominus misit quae munera defer.'
Attulit ast piscem, medium secat atque ministrae
Parte famem pellit, firmant sua pectora parte.

But for *to ðam dæge* (line 100) cf VCA II.5 (84.29) *quis tibi hodie prandium preparavit* or VCP c.12 (194.27–8) *dic age sodalis ubi hodie refici disponas*. Both VCA and VCP identify the companion as a boy or servant, *puer*. Ælfric places the eagle a little earlier in the story than any of the *Vitae*.

112–26 Ælfric presents the next miracle as part of the same journey; in the *Vitae* (VCA II.6, VCP c.13, VCM c.11) it is more vaguely placed 'at the same period'. Cf VCM c.11, 311–2:

Tempore non alio pandens caelestia terris
Impia iam pulchre ludibria prodidit anguis.

Ælfric's account corresponds loosely to the narrative in the *Vitae*: fire breaks out, the people rush off to try to extinguish it with water, but it disappears again [through Cuthbert's prayers in VCP] and the people return ashamed to the saint; but there are no close parallels of phrasing. Cf VCP c.13, 198.14–25:

> Statimque hostis ille nequissimus fantasticum deferens ignem, domum iuxta positam incendit. . . . Tum exiliens quasi ad extinguendum ignem turba pene tota quam docebat . . . certatim aquas iactabat. Nec tamen unda vera falsas potuit restinguere flammas, donec orante viro Dei Cuthberto fugatus auctor fallaciarum ficta secum incendia vacuas reportaret in auras. Quod videns turba multum salubriter erubuit, rursusque ad virum Dei ingressa, flexis genibus instabilis animi veniam precabatur.

In all three the saint's warning is followed by the illusory fire breaking out; Ælfric seems to describe the people rushing away *before* the fire.

127–31 VCA II.7, VCP c.14, VCM c.12; cf VCM c.12, 333–9:

> Quin etiam veri flammis crepitantibus ignes
> Arida deriperent tecti dum culmina quondam,
> Incubuit precibus, ventosque laresque retorquens
> Voce pericla fugat, iuvenum quae dextra nequibat.
> Nec mirum vati fragilem cessisse caminum,
> Igniferis satanae qui spicula torta pharetris
> Aetherio suerat umbone relidere(?) Christi.

131–6 The three *Vitae* pass on to the next miracle, described in lines 137–57. Ælfric's brief intervening comment on Cuthbert's preaching is perhaps based on an earlier chapter found only in VCP c.9, which describes his preaching in the countryside, though there is little close parallel; cf esp., with 133–6, VCP c.9, 186.9–15:

> Porro Cuthberto tanta erat docendi peritia . . . ut nullus praesentium latebras ei sui cordis celare praesumeret, omnes palam quae gesserant confitendo proferrent, quia nimirum haec eadem illum latere nullomodo putabant, et confessa dignis ut imperabat poenitentiae fructibus abstergerent.

The passage is oddly placed in Ælfric's version, in the middle of a sequence of miracle stories; possibly it marks the end of a sequence of events associated with Cuthbert's preaching expeditions. Ælfric's comment that the people *secretly* or in private made amends for their sins is striking: Bede's *palam* might be taken to refer to public confession (cf Colgrave's rendering 'made open confession of what they had done') and it may be that Ælfric wanted to emphasise private confession and penance instead. Blokhuis suggests that Ælfric was here following the *Historia Ecclesiastica* version of this passage, which reads (in most manuscripts) *dicendi peritia* rather than *docendi peritia*, perhaps prompting his *fægre getingnysse*.

137–57 All three *Vitae* have a similar story to Ælfric's (VCA II.8, VCP c.15, VCM c.13), but he must have used more than one, taking, for instance, the references to the wife's previous virtue and Cuthbert's visits from VCP, but the fact that Cuthbert was then prior at Lindisfarne from VCA or VCM. VCM is very close for the last sentence. The nearest passages seem to be:

> [VCP c.15, 204.1–7, 12–13] Erat praefectus Ecgfridi regis Hildmer nomine, vir religiosis cum omni domo sua deditus operibus, ideoque a beato Cuthberto specialiter dilectus, et cum itineris propinquitas congrueret, crebro ab eo visitatus. Cuius uxor cum elemosinis et caeteris virtutum fructibus esset intenta, subito correpta a demone acerrime coepit vexari. . . . Ascendit vir eius equum et concitus venit ad hominem Dei. [VCM c.13, 347–8] Tempore namque fuit Lindisfarnensis in illo

Praepositus cellae. [VCA II.8, 92.2–3] Erubescebat illam olim religiosam, tamen a demonio vexatam indicare. [VCP c.15, 204.13–206.3] Precatusque est eum dicens, Obsecro . . . ut mittas presbiterum qui illam priusquam moriatur visitet, eique dominici corporis et sanguinis sacramenta ministret. . . . Cognovit repente in spiritu quia . . . demonis infestatione premeretur coniux . . . 'ipse ad visitandam eam tecum pergere debeo'. [*Cf* Cuius uxor . . . *above*] Cunque agerent iter coepit flere homo, et dolorem cordis profluentibus in maxillam prodere lacrimis. . . . Quem vir Domini blande consolatus, Noli inquit plorare . . . scio etiam quia priusquam illo pervenerimus, fugato demonio liberabitur, ac nobis advenientibus cum gaudio occurrens, has ipsa habenas sanissima mente excipiet. . . . [VCM c.13, 369–72] Occurrit mulier sospes dextraque prehendens Frena, rogat vatem descendere adireque tecta Dignetur famulae, pandens nova dona salutis, Eius ad adventum fugiens ut cesserit hydros.

In the VCA the wife is cured as she touches Cuthbert's bridle; in having her cured while Cuthbert and the husband are approaching the house, so that she is not in fact seen in her frenzy, Ælfric is perhaps following VCM (the VCP confusedly includes both details).

158–9 The *Vitae* now describe Cuthbert's move from Melrose to Lindisfarne (VCA III.1, VCP c.16, VCM c.14), his way of life there and (VCA) his wish to move to Farne. Ælfric makes no reference to Melrose or indeed Ripon, and his brief comment on the miracles which Cuthbert performed within the monastery presumably refers to Lindisfarne; all three *Vitae* mention miracles of healing and driving out devils at Lindisfarne.

159–62 The decision to move to solitude is covered in VCA III.1, VCP c.17, VCM c.14. On Cuthbert's motives, cf VCM c.14, 373–6:

Talia mirantum fragili ne laude supernae
Caelestisque exsors famae foret, abdita mavult
Secreti lustrare, deo qua teste valeret
Laudis ab humanae liber munirier aura.

162–70 VCP c.17, 214.16–30:

Longinquiorem ac remotiorem ab hominibus locum certaminis petiit. Farne dicitur insula medio in mari posita . . . et hinc altissimo, et inde infinito clauditur oceano. Nullus hanc facile ante famulum Domini Cuthbertum solus valebat inhabitare colonus, propter videlicet demorantium ibi phantasias demonum. Verum intrante eam milite Christi . . . omnia tela nequissimi ignea extincta et ipse nequissimus cum omni satellitum suorum turba porro fugatus est hostis.

171–6 VCA II.3, VCP c.18, VCM c.16; cf VCM c.16, 406–12:

Fontis inops fuerat locus hic, sed sanctus amoenam
Excutit insolita precibus dulcedine limpham.

> . . . Nec mirum haec domini famulum potuisse mereri,
> Qui quondam, saliente sitim dum pelleret unda,
> In meracum latices valuit convertere nectar.

and VCP c.18, 216.28–218.7:

> At vero ipsa eius mansio aquae erat indiga, utpote in durissima et prope saxea rupe condita. . . . 'Fodiamus in medio tuguriunculi mei, credo torrente voluptatis suae potabit nos.'

176–83 The growing of crops is described in VCP c.19 and more briefly VCM c.17; it is not in VCA; cf VCP c.19, 220.14–28:

> Proprio manuum labore iuxta exempla patrum vivere magis aptum ducebat. Rogavit ergo afferri sibi . . . triticum quod sereret. Sed seminata verno tempore terra, nullos usque ad medium aestatis reddidit fructus. Unde visitantibus se iuxta morem fratribus aiebat vir Dei, 'Forsitan aut telluris huiusce natura, aut voluntas Dei non est ut hoc in loco mihi triticum nascatur. Afferte rogo ordeum, si forte vel illud fructum facere possit. . . .' Allatumque ordeum dum ultra omne tempus serendi, ultra omnem spem fructificandi terrae commendaret, mox abundanter exortum fecit fructum copiosum.

Ælfric's comment that the wheat-seed would not even produce shoots (lines 180–1) is not in VCP or VCM but is in the *Historia*, IV.xxviii (436.12–14):

> Nil omnino non dico spicarum, sed ne herbae quidem ex eo germinari usque ad aestatis tempora contigit.

Ælfric's *ofer ælcne timan* presumably means 'beyond any appropriate period for sowing', translating *ultra omne tempus serendi*.

184–90 VCP c.19, 220.28–222.9:

> Qui dum maturescere coepisset, venere volucres, et huic depascendo certatim insistebant. Ad quos piissimus Christi servus . . . inquit: '. . . Si tamen a Deo licentiam accepistis, facite quod ipse permisit. Sin autem, recedite neque ulterius aliena ledatis.' Dixerat, et ad primam iubentis vocem universa volucrum multitudo recessit, seque per omnia deinceps ab eiusdem messis invasione continuit.

Not in VCA, and neither VCP nor VCM identifies the birds as ravens at this point; the VCM begins the next miracle with words that could be taken to imply that the ravens of that story were the same birds as in this ('the ravens rescind the agreement . . .'), but Ælfric's phrasing implies they were different—'two other dark ravens'.

190–200 VCA III.5, VCP c.20, VCM c.18; cf VCM c.18, 431–44:

> Rescindunt corvi nigro sub crimine pactum
> Effringuntque domus ruptoque e culmine culmos
> In propriae gaudent transferre cubilia prolis.
> Hos vatis cessare monet . . . Abite . . .
> Dixerat et tristes abeunt, triduoque peracto

Alter adest vati pedibusque volutus et alas
Lugubre sparsus veniam reditumque precatur.
Patrata qui pace redit sociumque revisit.
Tandem ambo veniunt alacres adipemque suillam
Secum digna ferunt vati dona, unguine cuius
Calciamenta pius mollire valeret et exin
Innocuo condunt illic sua tecta paratu.

201–9 VCA III.4, VCP c.21, VCM c.19; cf VCP c.21, 226.2–26:

Disponebat parvulam sibi . . . cotidianis necessitatibus aptam condere casulam, cui a parte maris . . . basis supponenda erat. . . . Rogavit ergo fratres qui se visitaturi advenerant, ut cum redire vellent, lignum sibi . . . ad faciendam domunculae basim deferrent. Qui promiserunt se libentissime facturos quod petiit . . . reversique die debito ad eum non attulere quod rogabantur. . . . At vir . . . dicens: 'Credo quia Deus non obliviscatur meae voluntatis et necessitatis'. Fecerunt ut dixerat, et exurgentes mane viderunt quia nocturnus oceani estus lignum memoratae longitudinis attulit, et in ipso insuper loco deposuit, ubi in aedificium desuper erat imponendum.

The three *Vitae* and Ælfric are all equally vague about the function of this little room.

210–12 Summarises a chapter on his pastoral work with visitors (VCM c.20, VCP c.22).

212–25 Ælfric passes over a chapter in VCP, 23, on the healing of one of Ælflæd's nuns by his girdle. The story of his meeting with Ælflæd and prophecy is in VCA III.6 and VCP c.24, but VCM c.21, 492–517, is closest:

Dumque pium cuncti gauderent visere vatem
Eius et ortatu cordis conponere fluctus,
Ecce alios inter signis sublimibus acta
Regia virgo venit . . .
dictisque illam dum affatur amicis,
Femineis subito rogitat sic anxia curis:
'. . . Dic ergo, adiuro summi per regna tonantis,
Ecgfridus imperium quod sit recturus in aevum.'
Vera cui dubio pandit sermone prophetes:
'. . . Et nihili unius luxus reputabitur anni,
Mors ubi languentes diffunditur atra per artus.'
Quae gemit et lacrimis praesagia tristia deflens
'Quem, rogo, linquet' ait, 'regni qui sceptra gubernet,
Cum fratre et nato careat?' Cui talia vatis:
'. . . Forsan et haec inter dominus sibi servat et huius
Qui regat imperii lectus moderator habenas,
Ecgfridus utque tibi fratris nectatur amore.'

Both VCA and VCP report that Cuthbert visited Ælflæd at Coquet; the VCM tells that she visited him, apparently at Farne, and asked him to advise her; the ensuing discussion takes place after he has made a sea-journey. Ælfric seems to place the whole occasion at Farne (confirmed by 230 *on ðisum wacum scræfum*, 236 *ðis igland*); either he was misled by a casual reading of the VCM, or he thought it inappropriate that Cuthbert should have journeyed to meet royal abbesses after forsaking Lindisfarne for the life of a solitary hermit. Her name and relationship to Ecgfrid are curiously not given in the VCM (though her role as abbess is, and her name is used by Cuthbert later); they are given in the VCP version, c.24, and VCA II.6.

226–38 Closely follows VCM c.21, 518–35:

> Audet adhuc supplex virgo pulsare propheten:
> 'O variis hominum finduntur pectora curis!
> Pars nacto gaudet mortalis culmine pompae,
> Pars cupiens gazas luxu populante fugaces
> Pauperiem nullo deponit fine perennem.
> Tu licet oblatum mundi contemnis honorem
> Vilibus et mavis secretus condier antris,
> Pontificis summi quam vis potiundus honore . . .'
> 'Non ego', respondit, 'dignum me tanta subire
> Culmina iam fateor, domini sed dextera nullis
> Effugitur caeli terraeve marisve latebris;
> Qui si tanta gradus iubeat me pondera ferre,
> Credo brevi laxet, transacto et forte duorum
> Curriculo annorum absolvar rursumque adamatis
> Gaudens secretis reddar. Sed tu quoque nostrum,
> Aelffleda, conloquium perpes reticere memento,
> Absolvar donec vinclis et carcere carnis.'

239–252 VCP c.24, 238.4–18 (VCA and VCM are briefer):

> Nec multo post congregata sinodo non parva sub praesentia piissimi ac Deo dilecti regis Egfridi, cui beatae memoriae Theodorus archiepiscopus praesidebat unanimo omnium consensu ad episcopatum ecclesiae Lindisfarnensis electus est. Qui cum multis legatariis ac litteris ad se praemissis nequaquam suo loco posset erui, tandem rex ipse praefatus una cum sanctissimo antistite Trumwine nec non et aliis quam plurimis religiosis ac potentibus viris ad insulam navigavit, genuflectunt omnes, adiurant per Dominum, lacrimas fundunt, obsecrant, donec ipsum quoque lacrimis plenum dulcibus extrahunt latebris, atque ad sinodum pertrahunt. . . . atque ad suscipiendum episcopatus officium collum summittere compellitur.

The prophecy of the child has been told earlier, 17–19; the prophecy of Boisil is mentioned at VCP cc.8 and 22. Presumably *ðises iglandes* at 240 means Britain, even though *ðis igland* at 236 is Farne. And *his mynstre* at 244 must refer to his hermitage on Farne rather than a monastery; Blokhuis points out that the *Historia* version of this passage reads *suo monasterio* for *suo loco*.

252–8 VCP c.24, 238.20–25:

> Ut verbis eius propheticis per omnia satisfieret, Egfridus post annum Pictorum gladio trucidatur, et Aldfridus in regnum frater eius nothus substituitur, qui non paucis ante temporibus in regionibus Scottorum lectioni operam dabat, ibi ob amorem sapientiae spontaneum passus exilium.

VCP c.27 describes Ecgfrith's attack on the Picts as rash and cruel (242.20–22): *Dum Egfridus rex ausu temerario exercitum in Pictos duceret, eorumque regna atroci ac feroci sevicia devastaret.* The *Historia*, IV.xxvi records strong criticism of the attack. That it was against God's will is perhaps suggested by VCA IV.8, *Secundum praedestinatum iudicium Dei superandus et occidendus* or VCM c.19, 615–6, *noster miles sortitur domino decretum iudice finem*; though Ælfric would not presumably confuse a predestined end with an act of divine punishment, and he may have just been elaborating on his own account. Both VCP and VCM locate the king's death a year or so after Cuthbert's election.

259–71 VCA IV.1, VCM c.22, VCP c.26; Ælfric's account seems to combine VCP c.22, 240.29–242.5:

> Susceptum autem episcopatus ordinem venerabilis vir Domini Cuthbertus, iuxta praecepta et exempla apostolica virtutum ornabat operibus. Commissam nanque sibi plebem et orationibus protegebat assiduis, et ammonitionibus saluberrimis ad coelestia vocabat, et quod maxime doctores iuvat, ea quae agenda docebat, ipse prius agendo praemonstrabat.

and VCM c.22, 559–61:

> Pauperibus qui dives, inops sibi, blandus amaris,
> In turbis monachus, neque enim vel tegmina sueta
> Arida vel heremi mutari fercula curat.

and, for 265–7, the account in the *Historia*, IV.xxviii (438.20–2):

> Erat quippe ante omnia divinae caritatis igne fervidus, patientiae virtute modestus, orationum devotioni sollertissime intentus. . . .

Historia, IV.xxviii repeats much of the passage in VCP but also has additional material. Ælfric's *to geefenlæcunge* . . . may reflect the *Historia's ad imitationem beatorum apostolorum* rather than VCP's *iuxta praecepta* . . . .

272–5 Ælfric briefly narrates a series of miracles described at length in VCA and VCP and more briefly in VCM. The healing of a gesith's wife is in VCA IV.3, VCP c.29, VCM c.23; cf VCM c.23, 565–70:

> Doctor ubique pius caelestia dona ministrans,
> Per comitis tulis arva gradus, quem languida coniunx
> Tristabat perpessa luem loetoque propinquans.
> Alma salutiferae cui vatis munera limphae
> Presbytero famulante dedit tabemque removit,
> Moxque illi obsequium praebebat femina sospes.

275–7 VCA IV.4, VCM c.24, VCP c.30; cf VCM c.24, 571–4:

Tempore non alio laterali tacta dolore
Virgo premebatur capitisque gravidine fessa
Aegra diu gemuit; sacro quam crismate tinctam
Antistes rediviva novat per dona salutis.

The girl is identified as a nun in VCA and VCP.

277–81 VCM c.25, VCP c.31 (not in VCA); cf VCM c.25, 575–82:

Vir pater ipse domus morbo depressus acerbo
Cogit amicorum suprema ad fata cohortes.
Conveniunt plures; cui forte ibi protulit unus,
Quem sibi quondam almi doctoris dextra roganti
Sacrarat dederatque pio pro munere, panem.
Intingunt limphis, potandum suscipit aeger;
Moxque medellifero morbi cessere sub haustu
Laxatosque salus rediviva subintrat in artus.

VCP identifies the man as Hildmer, the *praefectus* who figures in lines 137–57.

282–6 VCA IV.5, VCM c.26, VCP c.32; cf VCP c.32, 256.28–258.23:

Quodam quoque tempore dum sanctissimus gregis dominici pastor sua lustrando circuiret ovilia . . . ecce subito apparuerunt mulieres ferentes in grabato iuvenem longae egritudinis acerbitate tabefactum . . . miserunt ad episcopum rogantes ut ad accipiendam benedictionem ad se hunc afferri permitteret. . . . Et . . . pepulit pestem . . . Denique eadem hora surgens . . . regressus est ad eas quae se portaverant feminas. Sicque factum est ut quae eum illo tristes languidum advexerant, cum eis inde gaudentibus et ipse sospes ac laetabundus domum rediret.

(The VCM version lacks some of Ælfric's details.)

286–91 VCA IV.6, VCM c.27, VCP c.33; cf VCM c.27, 591–6:

Ferre videt maestam nati moritura parentem
Funera seminecis; conpassus et ipse dolenti
Bassia dat puero matremque affatur amaram:
'Linque metum lacrimasque, puer sanabitur iste,
Et tua tota domus mortis hac sorte carebit.'
Cuius dicta salus puerique domusque secuta est.

(The VCP makes it clearer that Cuthbert is travelling around his diocese at the time.)

292–303 VCA IV.9, VCM c.31, VCP c.34; cf VCP c.34, 262.2–13:

Rogatus a nobilissima et sanctissima virgine Christi Elffledae abbatissa . . . venit ad possessionem monasterii ipsius. . . . Ubi dum hora refectionis ad mensam consedissent, subito venerabilis pater Cuthbertus aversam a carnalibus epulis mentem ad spiritualia contemplanda contulit . . . cultellus quoque quem tenebat decidit in mensam.

followed by VCM c.31, 664–79:

Aelffleda perquirit . . .
Forte recens veniat tanti quo causa tremoris.
'Venerat angelicus', respondit, 'ab aethere coetus,
Deque tuis secum praelecto milite castris
Aurea dulcisonis remeabat ad astra triumphis.'
Inquirit nomen. 'Cras mystica', dixit, 'ad altar
Obtulero cum sacra, mihi nomenque modusque,
Quo petit astra, tuis pandetur in ordine dictis.'
[*Ælfflæd sends messengers and discovers that* . . .]
Frondiferi quendam nemoris dum scanderet alta,
Caederet ut pecori arboreo de pabula cono,
Deciduum membris animam posuisse solutis,
Illoque humanis ablatum in tempore rebus,
Quo sacer aetherias raptum cernebat ad auras.

Only the VCM mentions the song and explains why the man was climbing the tree; Ælfric identifies the tree as an oak, and twice emphasises that the man died in the service of his employer and his cattle. In all three *Vitae* Cuthbert prophesies that Ælfflæd will name the man to Cuthbert the next morning when he is celebrating mass, and the VCA and VCP show that happening; Ælfric says that the name will be reported to *her* at that moment.

304–7 This brief summary of Cuthbert's miracles may have been prompted by a rather flowery short chapter earlier in VCM; there is no equivalent in VCA and VCP; VCM, c.28, 597–609:

Dicere quid coner, quae nullo edicere versu
Sufficiam, quoties languorum tabe peresos
Invalidosque potens iam verbo erexerit artus . . .
Spirituum quoties per devia fugerit horror
Cuthberti consueta minis se linquere fassus
Pectora et ignivomas baratri sub cogier umbras
Absentisque etiam poenis se plectier atris.
Virtutesque sacri numero quid prendere certem,
Tanta prophetalis quem gratia fulcit honoris,
Tam puroque poli qui pervolat aethera visu.

The VCM does not specify prophesying the deaths of 'the doomed' (assuming that *fægra* is the genitive plural of the poetic word *fæge*), but the final lines refer to his prophetic powers and Ælfric was no doubt thinking especially of the prophecy of Ecgfrith's death (which immediately follows this passage in the VCM), and perhaps Hereberht's and his own.

308–322 VCA IV.9, VCM c.30, VCP c.28; cf VCP c.28, 248.20–250.17:

Erat autem presbiter vitae venerabilis nomine Herebertus . . . vitam solitariam ducens, annis singulis ad eum venire, et monita ab eo perpetuae salutis accipere consueverat. . . . Dixit inter alia Cuthbertus, 'Memento frater Hereberte ut modo quicquid opus habes me interroges, mecumque loquaris, quia postquam ab invicem digressi fuerimus, non ultra nos invicem in hoc saeculo carneis oculis videbimus. Certus sum enim quia tempus meae resolutionis instat.' . . . Qui haec audiens provolutus eius pedibus, fusisque cum gemitu lacrimis, 'Obsecro inquit per Dominum ne me derelinquas, sed tui sodalis memineris, rogesque supernam pietatem ut cui pariter in terris servivimus, ad eius videndam claritatem pariter transeamus ad coelos. Nosti enim quia ad tui oris imperium semper vivere studui'. . . . Incubuit precibus episcopus . . . 'Surge', inquit, 'frater mi et noli plorare, sed gaudio gaude, quia donavit nobis superna clementia quod rogavimus eam'.

VCM and VCP go on to report that Hereberht and Cuthbert did indeed eventually die on the same day, though the former first suffered a long illness to make him worthy to die with the greater saint. Ælfric moves the meeting to a slightly later position, just before the end, and creates a moving conclusion in which the two men depart from their last meeting to return to their homes and await death.

324–31 A summary of the long description of Cuthbert's last miracles and death, VCP cc.37–40 or VCM cc.32–7. (There is no further reference to Hereberht.)

331–3 The burial is described at the end of VCP c.40. The post-mortem miracles are described in VCP cc.41–6.

333–8 The discovery of the uncorrupt body is described in detail at VCP c.42 (making it clear that the initiative came from the monks, not bishop Eadberht).

11 ST BENEDICT

Perhaps fittingly for the work of a Benedictine monk, this is the longest piece in the Catholic Homilies, far exceeding any other hagiographic item and resembling in its length and manner the texts in Ælfric's next main collection, the Lives of Saints. Though it refers to the festival on 'this present day', it makes no concessions to the preaching function of the Catholic Homilies.

The Cotton-Corpus legendary has nothing for St Benedict, but Ælfric would have been familiar with the standard account of the saint, since it forms book II of the *Dialogues* of Gregory the Great.[1] Ælfric does not in fact name his source (though he does identify Gregory as its author late on, at 326–7), and retains nothing of the dialogue structure and very little of the discussion of the doctrinal significance of the miracle stories which alternates with the narratives;

[1] Identified as the source by Förster (1892), p. 37.

when he does use such material, he carefully disguises its dialogue origins (lines 326–33, 536–46). Instead he focuses on the narrative of Benedict's life and, particularly, the series of miracles which reveal his glory. The rule for monks which must have been his main grounds for fame in late Anglo-Saxon England is only touched on very briefly at the end, though it is true that the narrative provides a series of representative stories about the governance of monasteries. For Gregory, the mass of circumstantial detail, giving locations, names of participants, names of witnesses, historical references and a variety of other realistic details, was an important part of his claim that miracles did occur in the here and now of sixth-century Italy. For Ælfric, such details had less significance. He reduces Gregory's narrative radically, retaining the essentials of the stories (and omitting very few of them) but telling them much more succinctly. The historical context was evidently not important to his task: he omits the stories which prophesy the Goths' destruction of Rome and the Lombards' destruction of Cassino (*Dialogues*, II.15.17–33, II.17.1–24) and does not identify Totilla and Zalla, or the convert at 135–9, as Goths. His concern seems to have been to create a context-free narrative of sanctity, exemplifying divine power working through Benedict in miracles of healing, prophecy and defeat of the devil. The only material not from the *Dialogues* is some details from the Rule silently incorporated into lines 219–33, a brief description of Benedict from an unknown source, and the details of his post-mortem translation to Fleury. Ælfric evidently knew of Wærferth's translation of the *Dialogues* but there is no trace of its influence on his own rendering.

Sources and Notes

The following texts are cited below:

1. Benedict of Nursia, *Regula*, ed. R. Hanslik, CSEL 75 (2nd ed., Vienna, 1977).
2. Gregory the Great, *Dialogi*, ed. A. de Vogüé and P. Antin, 3 vols., Sources Chrétiennes 251, 260 and 265 (Paris, 1978–80).

3–7 A very free paraphrase of *Dialogues*, II.prol.6–14:

> Qui liberiori genere ex provincia Nursiae exortus, Romae liberalibus litterarum studiis traditus fuerat. Sed cum in eis multos ire per abrupta vitiorum cerneret, eum, quem quasi in ingressum mundi posuerat, retraxit pedem, ne si quid de scientia eius adtingeret, ipse quoque postmodum in inmane praecipitium totus iret. Despectis itaque litterarum studiis, relicta domo rebusque patris, soli Deo placere desiderans, sanctae conversationis habitum quaesivit.

Ælfric seems to have invented the nobility and piety of Benedict's parents, his philosopher-teachers, his advanced stage of learning, the secrecy of his departure, and the departure from Rome rather than his parental home.

Otherwise it is fairly close. But note that Wærferth also refers to the nobility of his parentage—*he wæs geboren of freon and of æþelum cynne*[2]—and Moricca records a variant *nobiliori* for *liberiori* from a tenth-century manuscript, Rome, Vatic. Palat. MS 262.[3]

8–10 *Dialogues*, II.1.2–5:

Nutrix . . . sola secuta est. Cumque ad locum venissent, qui Effide dicitur, multisque honestioribus viris caritate se illic detinentibus. . . .

11–22 *Dialogues*, II.1.6–24:

Nutrix illius . . . a vicinis mulieribus praestari sibi capisterium petiit, quod . . . casu accidente fractum est, sicque ut in duabus partibus inveniretur divisum. . . . Nutrix illius . . . vehementissime flere coepit, quia vas quod praestitum acceperat, fractum videbat. Benedictus autem religiosus et pius puer cum nutricem suam flere conspiceret, eius dolori compassus, ablatis secum utrisque fracti capisterii partibus, sese cum lacrimis in orationem dedit. Qui ab oratione surgens, ita iuxta se vas sanum repperit ut in eo fracturae inveniri vestigia nulla potuissent. . . . Quae res in loco eodem a cunctis est agnita, atque in tanta admiratione habita, ut hoc ipsum capisterium eius loci incolae in ecclesiae ingressu suspenderent quatenus et praesentes et secuturi omnes agnoscerent, Benedictus puer conversationis gratiam a quanta perfectione coepisset.

23–36 *Dialogues*, II.1.27–56:

Sed Benedictus plus appetens mala mundi perpeti quam laudes, pro Deo laboribus fatigari quam vitae huius favoribus extolli, nutricem suam occulte fugiens, deserti loci secessum petiit cui Sublacus vocabulum est, qui a Romana urbe quadraginta fere millibus distans. . . . Quo dum fugiens pergeret, monachus quidam Romanus nomine, . . . eique sanctae conversationis habitum tradidit, et in quantum licuit, ministravit . . . tribus annis. . . . Ad eumdem vero specum a Romani cella iter non erat, quia excelsa desuper rupis eminebat; sed ex eadem rupe in longissimo fune religatum Romanus deponere panem consueverat; in qua etiam resti parvum tintinabulum inseruit, ut ad sonum tintinabuli vir Dei cognosceret quando sibi Romanus panem praeberet, quem exiens acciperet. Sed antiquus hostis unius caritati invidens, alterius refectioni, cum quadam die submitti panem conspiceret, iactavit lapidem, et tintinabulum fregit. Romanus tamen modis congruentibus ministrare non desiit.

37–44 Summarises from *Dialogues*, II.1:

[57–69] Omnipotens Deus . . . cuidam presbitero . . . per visum . . . apparere dignatus est, dicens: 'Tu tibi delicias praeparas, et servus meus illo in loco fame cruciatur.' Qui protinus surrexit, atque in ipsa sollemnitate paschali

[2] Hecht, p. 95.

[3] *Gregorii Magni Dialogi Libri IV*, ed. Umberto Moricca (Rome 1924).

cum alimentis quae sibi paraverat, ad locum tetendit, et virum Dei . . . latere in specu repperit. [83–4] Eodem quoque tempore hunc in specu latitantem etiam pastores invenerunt. . . . [87–91] Nomen itaque eius per vicina loca cunctis innotuit, factumque est ut ex illo iam tempore a multis frequentari coepisset, qui cum ei cibos deferrent corporis, ab eius ore in suo pectore alimenta referebant vitae.

45–60 *Dialogues*, II.2.1–24:

Quadam vero die dum solus esset, temptator adfuit. Nam nigra parvaque avis, quae vulgo merola vocatur, circa eius faciem volitare coepit, eiusque vultui importune insistere, ita ut capi manu posset, si hanc vir sanctus tenere voluisset. Sed signo crucis edito, recessit avis. Tanta autem carnis temptatio, avi eadem recedente, secuta est, quantam vir sanctus numquam fuerat expertus. Quandam namque aliquando feminam viderat, quam malignus spiritus ante eius mentis oculos reduxit: tantoque igne servi Dei animum in specie illius accendit, ut se in eius pectore amoris flamma vix caperet, et iam paene deserere heremum voluptate victus deliberaret. Cum subito superna gratia respectus, ad semetipsum reversus est, atque urticarum et veprium iuxta densa succrescere frutecta conspiciens, exutus indumento nudum se in illis spinarum aculeis et urticarum incendiis proiecit, ibique diu volutatus, toto ex eis corpore vulneratus exiit, et per cutis vulnera eduxit a corpore vulnus mentis, quia voluptatem traxit in dolorem, cumque bene poenaliter arderet foris, extinxit quod inlicite ardebat intus. Vicit itaque peccatum, quia mutavit incendium. Ex quo videlicet tempore, sicut post discipulis ipse perhibebat, ita in illo est temptatio voluptatis edomita, ut tale in se aliquid minime sentiret.

It is perhaps in the interests of a more heroic picture of the saint that Ælfric does not tell us that Benedict was inflamed by an image of a woman he had once seen, or that he contemplated giving up the ascetic life, almost overcome by desire.

61–86 *Dialogues*, II.3.5–39:

Non longe autem monasterium fuit, cuius congregationis pater defunctus est, omnisque ex illo congregatio ad eundem venerabilem Benedictum venit, et magnis precibus, ut eis praeesse deberet, petiit. Qui diu negando distulit, suis illorumque fratrum moribus convenire non posse praedixit, sed victus quandoque precibus, adsensum dedit. Cumque in eodem monasterio regularis vitae custodiam teneret, nullique, ut prius, per actus inlicitos in dextram laevamque partem deflectere a conversationis itinere liceret, suscepti fratres insane saevientes semetipsos prius accusare coeperunt, quia hunc sibi praeesse poposcerant, quorum scilicet tortitudo in norma eius rectitudinis offendebat. . . . Tractare de eius aliquid morte conati sunt. Qui, inito consilio, venenum vino miscuerunt. Et cum vas vitreum, in quo ille pestifer potus habebatur, recumbenti patri ex more monasterii ad benedicendum fuisset oblatum, Benedictus, extensa manu, signum crucis edidit, et vas quod longius tenebatur eodem signo rupit, sicque confractum est, ac si in illo vase mortis pro cruce lapidem dedisset. Intellexit protinus vir Dei quia potum mortis habuerat, quod portare non potuit signum vitae, atque ilico surrexit, et vultu placido, mente tranquilla, convocatos fratres allocutus est, dicens: 'Misereatur vestri, fratres, omnipotens Deus. Quare in me facere ista voluistis? Numquid non prius dixi quia vestris ac meis moribus non conveniret? Ite, et iuxta mores vestros vobis patrem quaerite, quia me post haec habere minime potestis.' Tunc ad locum dilectae solitudinis rediit, et solus in superni spectatoris oculis habitavit secum.

87–94 *Dialogues*, II.3.114–26:

Cum sanctus vir in eadem solitudine virtutibus signisque succresceret, multi ab eo in loco eodem ad omnipotentis Dei sunt servitium congregati, ita ut illic duodecim monasteria cum omnipotentis Iesu Christi Domini opitulatione construeret, in quibus statutis patribus duodenos monachos deputavit, paucos vero secum retinuit, quos adhuc in sua praesentia aptius erudiri iudicavit. Coepere etiam tunc ad eum Romanae urbis nobiles et religiosi concurrere, suosque ei filios omnipotenti Domino nutriendos dare. Tunc quoque bonae spei suas soboles, Euthicius Maurum, Tertullus vero patricius Placidum tradidit.

94–108 *Dialogues*, II.7.1–28:

Quadam vero die . . . praedictus Placidus puer sancti viri monachus ad hauriendam de lacu aquam egressus est. Qui vas quod tenuerat in aqua incaute submittens, ipse quoque cadendo secutus est. . . . Vir autem Dei intra cellam positus, hoc protinus agnovit, et Maurum festine vocavit, dicens: 'Frater Maure, curre, quia puer ille . . . in lacum cecidit, iamque eum longius unda trahit.' . . . Benedictione etenim postulata atque percepta . . . perrexit Maurus, atque usque ad eum locum, quo ab unda ducebatur puer, per terram se ire existimans, super aquam cucurrit, eumque per capillos tenuit, rapido quoque cursu rediit. Qui mox ut terram tetigit, ad se reversus post terga respexit, et quia super aquas cucurrisset agnovit, et quod praesumere non potuisset ut fieret, miratus extremuit factum. Reversus ad Patrem, rem gestam retulit. Vir autem venerabilis Benedictus hoc non suis meritis, sed oboedientiae illius deputare coepit. At contra Maurus pro solo eius imperio factum dicebat, seque conscium in illa virtute non esse, quam nesciens fecisset. Sed . . . puer qui ereptus est . . . dicebat: 'Ego cum ex aqua traherer, super caput meum abbatis melotem videbam, atque ipsum me ex aquis educere considerabam.'

109–17 *Dialogues*, II.4.2–32 (much abridged):

Quidam monachus erat qui ad orationem stare non poterat, sed mox ut se fratres ad orationis studium inclinassent, ipse egrediebatur foras, et mente vaga terrena aliqua et transitoria agebat. . . . Vir Dei . . . aspexit quod eundem monachum qui manere in oratione non poterat, quidam niger puerulus per vestimenti fimbriam foras trahebat. . . . Die igitur alia, expleta oratione vir Dei oratorium egressus, stantem foris monachum repperit, quem pro caecitate cordis sui virga percussit, qui ex illo die nihil persuasionis ulterius a nigro iam puerulo pertulit, sed ad orationis studium immobilis permansit, sicque antiquus hostis dominari non ausus est in eius cogitatione, ac si ipse percussus fuisset ex verbere.

118–34 *Dialogues*, II.5.1–27:
Ex his autem monasteriis quae in eodem loco construxerat, tria sursum in rupibus montis erant, et valde erat fratribus laboriosum, semper ad lacum descendere, ut aquam haurire debuissent, maxime quia ex devexo montis latere erat grave descendentibus in timore periculum. Tunc . . . ad Dei famulum Benedictum venerunt, dicentes: 'Laboriosum nobis est propter aquam cotidie usque ad lacum descendere, et idcirco necesse est ex eodem loco monasteria mutari.' Quos blande consolatus dimisit, et nocte eadem cum parvo puerulo nomine Placido, cuius superius memoriam feci, eiusdem montis ascendit rupem, ibique diutius oravit, et oratione completa, tres petras in loco eodem pro signo posuit, atque ad suum cunctis illic nescientibus monasterium rediit. Cumque die alio ad eum pro necessitate aquae praedicti fratres redissent, dixit: 'Ite, et rupem illam, in qua tres super invicem positas petras invenitis, in modico cavate. Valet enim omnipotens Deus etiam in illo montis cacumine aquam producere, ut vobis laborem tanti itineris dignetur auferre.' Qui euntes, rupem montis quam Benedictus praedixerat iam sudantem invenerunt, cumque in ea concavum locum fecissent, statim aqua repletus est, quae tam sufficienter emanavit, ut nunc usque ubertim defluat, atque ab illo montis cacumine usque ad inferiora derivetur.

135–9 A summary of the story of the Gothic convert at *Dialogues*, II.6.1–20:
Alio quoque tempore Gothus quidam pauper spiritu ad conversationem venit. . . . Quadam vero die ei dari ferramentum iussit, quod a falcis similitudine falcastrum vocatur . . . ferrum de manubrio prosiliens in lacum cecidit, ubi scilicet tanta erat aquarum profunditas. . . . Benedictus haec audiens accessit ad locum, tulit de manu Gothi manubrium, et misit in lacum, et mox ferrum de profundo rediit atque in manubrium intravit. Qui statim ferramentum Gotho reddidit, dicens: 'Ecce labora, et noli contristari.'

The point of Gregory's story is perhaps that the barbarian warrior shows his true humility by becoming a monk, engaging in manual labour and offering to do penance for the loss of the tool; Ælfric's summary perhaps leaves the reader to suppose the man is a labourer on the monastic estate. In the Latin Benedict holds the handle *in* the water, not over it.

140–52 *Dialogues*, II.8.6–37:

Vicinae ecclesiae presbiter, Florentius nomine, . . . antiqui hostis malitia perculsus . . . invidiae facibus magis magisque succensus deterior fiebat, quia conversationis illius habere appetebat laudem, sed habere laudabilem vitam nolebat. Qui . . . servo omnipotentis Domini infectum veneno panem quasi pro benedictione transmitteret. . . . Ad horam vero refectionis illius ex vicina silva corvus venire consueverat, et panem de manu eius accipere. Qui cum more solito venisset, panem quem presbiter transmiserat, vir Dei ante corvum proiecit, eique praecepit, dicens: 'In nomine Iesu Christi Domini tolle hunc panem, et tali eum in loco proice, ubi a nullo homine possit inveniri.' . . . Quandoque corvus momordit, levavit, et recessit. Post trium vero horarum spatium abiecto pane rediit, et de manu hominis Dei annonam quam consueverat accepit.

153–70 *Dialogues*, II.8.40–67:

Sed praedictus Florentius, quia magistri corpus necare non potuit, se ad extinguendas discipulorum animas accendit, ita ut in horto cellae, cui Benedictus inerat, ante eorum oculos nudas septem puellas mitteret, quae coram eis, sibi invicem manus tenentes et diutius ludentes, illorum mentem ad perversitatem libidinis inflammarent. Quod sanctus vir de cella conspiciens, lapsumque adhuc tenerioribus discipulis pertimescens, idque pro sua solius fieri persecutione pertractans, invidiae locum dedit . . . et paucis secum monachis ablatis habitationem mutavit loci. . . . Nam cum praedictus presbiter stans in solario Benedictum discessisse cognosceret et exultaret, perdurante immobiliter tota domus fabrica, hoc ipsum in quo stabat solarium cecidit, et Benedicti hostem conterens extinxit. Quod viri Dei discipulus, Maurus nomine, statim venerabili patri Benedicto, qui adhuc a loco eodem vix decem millibus aberat, aestimavit esse nuntiandum, dicens: 'Revertere, quia presbiter qui te persequebatur, extinctus est.' Quod vir Dei Benedictus audiens, sese in gravibus lamentis dedit, vel quia inimicus occubuit, vel quia de inimici morte discipulus exultavit. Qua de re factum est, ut eidem quoque discipulo paenitentiam indiceret, quod mandans talia, gaudere de inimici interitu praesumpsisset.

171–86 *Dialogues*, II.8.94–123:

Castrum namque quod Casinum dicitur, in excelsi montis latere situm est. Qui videlicet mons . . . per tria millia in altum se subrigens, velut ad aera cacumen tendit. Ubi vetustissimum fanum fuit, in quo ex antiquorum more gentilium ab stulto rusticorum populo Apollo colebatur. Circumquaque etiam in cultu daemonum luci succreverant, in quibus adhuc eodem tempore infidelium insana multitudo sacrificiis sacrilegis insudabat. Ibi itaque vir Dei perveniens, contrivit idolum, subvertit aram, succidit lucos, atque in ipso templo Apollinis oraculum beati Martini, ubi vero ara eiusdem Apollinis fuit, oraculum sancti construxit Iohannis, et commorantem circumquaque multitudinem praedicatione continua ad fidem vocabat. Sed haec antiquus hostis tacite non ferens, non occulte vel per somnium, sed aperta visione eiusdem patris se oculis ingerebat, et magnis clamoribus vim se perpeti conquerebatur, ita ut voces illius etiam fratres audirent, quamvis imaginem minime cernerent. Ut enim discipulis suis venerabilis pater dicebat, corporalibus eius oculis isdem antiquus hostis teterrimus et succensus apparebat, qui in eum ore oculisque flammantibus saevire videbatur. Iam vero quae diceret audiebant omnes. Prius enim hunc vocabat ex nomine . . . dicens: 'Benedicte, Benedicte', et eum sibi nullo modo respondere conspiceret, protinus adiungebat: 'Maledicte, non Benedicte, quid mecum habes, quid me persequeris?'

187–93 *Dialogues*, II.9.1–12:

Quadam die dum fratres habitacula eiusdem cellae construerent, lapis in medio iacebat quem in aedificio levare decreverunt. Cumque eum duo vel tres movere non possent, plures adiuncti sunt, sed ita immobilis mansit . . . quod super eum ipse per se antiquus hostis sederet. . . . Ad virum Dei missum est ut veniret. . . . Qui mox venit, orationem faciens benedictionem dedit, et tanta lapis celeritate levatus est, ac si nullum prius pondus habuisset.

193–204 *Dialogues*, II.10.1–13:

Tunc in conspectu viri Dei placuit ut in loco eodem terram foderent. Quam dum fodiendo altius penetrarent, aereum illic idolum fratres invenerunt. Quo ad horam casu in coquina proiecto, exire ignis repente visus est, atque in cunctorum monachorum oculis quia omne eiusdem coquinae aedificium consumeretur ostendit. Cumque iaciendo aquam, et ignem quasi extinguendo perstreperent, pulsatus eodem tumultu vir Domini advenit. Qui eumdem ignem in oculis fratrum esse, in suis vero non esse considerans, caput protinus in orationem flexit, et eos quos phantastico repperit igne deludi, revocavit fratres ad oculos suos, ut et sanum illud coquinae aedificium adsistere cernerent.

Note Ælfric's explanation that the devil was protecting the brazen image (line 195).

205–18 *Dialogues*, II.11.1–25:

Rursum dum fratres parietem . . . paulo altius aedificarent, vir Dei in orationis studio intra cellulae suae claustra morabatur. Cui antiquus hostis insultans apparuit, et quia ad laborantes fratres pergeret indicavit. Quod vir Dei per nuntium celerrime fratribus indicavit, dicens: 'Fratres, caute vos agite, quia ad vos hac hora malignus spiritus venit.' Is qui mandatum detulit, vix verba compleverat, et malignus spiritus eumdem parietem qui aedificabatur evertit, atque unum puerulum monachum . . . opprimens, ruina conteruit. . . . Tunc isdem pater ad se dilaceratum puerum deferri iubet. Quem portare non nisi in sago potuerunt, quia conlapsi saxa parietis eius non solum membra, sed etiam ossa contriverant. Eumque vir Dei praecepit

> statim in cella sua . . . proici, missisque foras fratribus cellam clausit. Qui orationi instantius quam solebat incubuit. Mira res, hora eadem hunc incolumem, atque ut prius valentem ad eundem iterum laborem misit . . . de cuius se interitu antiquus hostis Benedicto insultare credidisset.

Ælfric has the devil acting before the messenger arrives.

219–33 *Dialogues*, II.11.26–8, II.12.1–19:

> Coepit vero inter ista vir Dei prophetiae spiritu pollere, ventura praedicere, praesentibus absentia nuntiare. Mos etenim cellae fuit, ut quotiens ad responsum aliquod egrederentur fratres, cibum potumque extra cellam minime sumerent. . . . Quadam die ad responsum fratres egressi sunt, in quo tardiori compulsi sunt hora demorari. Qui manere iuxta religiosam feminam noverant, cuius ingressi habitaculum sumpserunt cibum. Cumque iam tardius ad cellam redissent, benedictionem patris ex more petierunt. Quos ille protinus percontatus est, dicens: 'Ubi comedistis?' Qui responderunt, dicentes: 'Nusquam.' Quibus ille ait: 'Quare ita mentimini? Numquid illius talis feminae habitaculum non intrastis? Numquid hos atque illos cibos non accepistis? Numquid tot calices non bibistis?' Cumque eis venerabilis pater et hospitium mulieris, et genera ciborum, et numerum potionum diceret, recognoscentes cuncta quae egerant, ad eius pedes tremefacti ceciderunt, se deliquisse confessi sunt. Ipse autem protinus culpam pepercit.

Ælfric has considerably rewritten this account (unless he had a very different text of it): the simple rule that the monks might not eat when away from the monastery becomes a rule that they might not eat without Benedict's permission if they were able to return the same day; the errant monks are numbered two; their half-justification, that they had been delayed to a late hour, is replaced by a firm statement that they broke the rule; and the pious woman's house is defined as a *gesthus* (perhaps prompted by Gregory's *hospitium*). The recasting of the regulation reflects the provision of chapter 51 of the Rule of St Benedict (*Regula*, 51.1–2):

> Frater qui pro quovis responso dirigitur, et ea die speratur reverti ad monasterium, non praesumat foris manducare, etiamsi omnino rogetur a quovis, nisi forte ei ab abbate suo praecipiatur.

Ælfric omits a further miracle of this kind (*Dialogues*, II.13).

234–47 *Dialogues*, II.14.1–27:

> Gothorum namque temporibus, cum rex eorum Totila sanctum virum prophetiae habere spiritum audisset, ad eius monasterium pergens, paulo longius substitit eique se venturum esse nuntiavit. Cui dum protinus mandatum de monasterio fuisset ut veniret, ipse, sicut perfidae mentis fuit, an vir Domini prophetiae spiritum haberet explorare conatus est. Quidam vero eius spatarius Riggo dicebatur, cui calciamenta sua praebuit, eumque indui regalibus vestibus fecit, quem quasi in persona sua pergere ad Dei hominem praecepit. In cuius obsequio tres qui sibi prae caeteris adhaerere

> consueverant, comites misit. . . . Cumque isdem Riggo decoratus vestibus, obsequentum frequentia comitatus monasterium fuisset ingressus, vir Dei eminus sedebat. Quem venientem conspiciens, cum iam ab eo audiri potuisset, clamavit, dicens: 'Pone, fili, pone hoc quod portas: non est tuum.' Qui Riggo protinus in terram cecidit, et quia tanto viro inludere praesumpsisset, expavit, omnesque qui cum eo ad Dei hominem veniebant, terrae consternati sunt. Surgentes autem, ad eum propinquare minime praesumpserunt, sed ad suum regem reversi, nuntiaverunt trepidi in quanta velocitate fuerant deprehensi.

Note that Ælfric does not identify the king as a Goth, leaving it unclear what or whom he ruled.

247–61 *Dialogues*, II.15.1–16:

> Tunc per se isdem Totila ad Dei hominem accessit. Quem cum longe sedentem cerneret, non ausus accedere sese in terram dedit. Cui dum vir Dei bis et ter diceret: 'Surge', sed ipse ante eum erigi de terra non auderet, Benedictus . . . per semetipsum dignatus est accedere ad regem prostratum. Quem de terra levavit, de suis actibus increpavit, atque in paucis sermonibus cuncta quae illi erant ventura praenuntiavit, dicens: 'Multa mala facis, multa fecisti. Iam aliquando ab iniquitate compescere. Et quidem Romam ingressurus es, mare transiturus, novem annis regnas, decimo morieris.' Quibus auditis rex vehementer territus, oratione petita recessit, atque ex illo iam tempore minus crudelis fuit. Cum non multo post Romam adiit, ad Siciliam perrexit, anno autem regni sui decimo omnipotentis Dei iudicio regnum cum vita perdidit.

262–73 *Dialogues*, II.16.1–22:

> Eodem quoque tempore quidam Aquinensis ecclesiae clericus daemonio vexabatur. . . . Ductus itaque est ad omnipotentis Dei famulum Benedictum, qui Iesu Christo Domino preces fundens, antiquum hostem de obsesso homine protinus expulit. Cui sanato praecepit, dicens: 'Vade, et post haec carnem non comedas, ad sacrum vero ordinem nunquam accedere praesumas. Quacumque autem die sacrum ordinem temerare praesumpseris, statim iuri diaboli iterum manciparis.' Discessit igitur clericus sanus, et . . . ea quae vir Dei praeceperat, interim custodivit. . . . post annos multos . . . verba viri Dei quasi ex longo tempore oblitus postposuit, atque ad sacrum ordinem accessit. Quem mox is qui reliquerat diabolus tenuit, eumque vexare quousque animam eius excuteret, non cessavit.

274–82 *Dialogues*, II.18.1–13:

> Quodam quoque tempore Exhilaratus noster, quem ipse conversum nosti, transmissus a domino suo fuerat, ut Dei viro in monasterium vino plena duo lignea vascula quae vulgo flascones vocantur, deferret. Qui unum detulit, alterum vero pergens in itinere abscondit. Vir autem Domini . . . unum cum gratiarum actione suscepit, et discedentem puerum monuit,

> dicens: 'Vide, fili, de illo flascone quem abscondisti iam non bibas, sed inclina illum caute, et invenis quid intus habet.' Qui confusus valde a Dei homine exivit, et reversus volens adhuc probare quod audierat, cum flasconem inclinasset, de eo protinus serpens egressus est.

By *puer* the Latin probably means 'servant'. Without apparent prompting Ælfric describes the snake as *fah*, which could be either the adjective *fag* 'variegated, dappled' or the adjective *fah* 'dangerous, deadly'.

283–5 Not from the source, but presumably referring to the miracles of prophecy and vision omitted by Ælfric, *Dialogues*, II.15.3, 17, 19.

286–91 *Dialogues*, II.20.1–18:

> Quadam quoque die dum venerabilis pater vespertina iam hora corporis alimenta perciperet, eius monachus cuiusdam defensoris filius fuerat, qui ei ante mensam lucernam tenebat. Cumque vir Dei ederet, ipse autem cum lucernae ministerio adstaret, coepit per superbiae spiritum in mente sua tacitus volvere, et per cogitationem dicere: 'Quis est hic cui ego manducanti adsisto, lucernam teneo, servitium impendo? Quis sum ego, ut isti serviam?' Ad quem vir Dei statim conversus, vehementer eum coepit increpare, dicens: 'Signa cor tuum, frater. Quid est quod loqueris?' . . . Vocatisque statim fratribus, praecepit ei lucernam de manibus tolli, ipsum vero iussit a ministerio recedere, et sibi hora eadem quietum sedere. Qui requisitus a fratribus quid habuerit in corde, per ordinem narravit quanto superbiae spiritu intumuerat, et quae contra virum Dei verba per cogitationem tacitus dicebat.

The Latin identifies the monk as a *cild* (cf 286) only in so far as he is the son of a *defensor*.

292–301 *Dialogues*, II.21.1–14:

> Alio igitur tempore in eadem Campaniae regione famis incubuerat, magnaque omnes alimentorum indigentia coangustabat. Iamque in Benedicti monasterio triticum deerat, panes vero paene omnes consumpti fuerant, ut non plus quam quinque ad refectionis horam fratribus inveniri potuissent. Cumque eos venerabilis pater contristatos cerneret, eorum pusillanimitatem studuit modesta increpatione corrigere, et rursum promissione sublevare, dicens: 'Quare de panis inopia vester animus contristatur? Hodie quidem minus est, sed die crastina abundanter habebitis.' Sequenti autem die ducenti farinae modii ante fores cellae in saccis inventi sunt, quos omnipotens Deus quibus deferentibus transmisisset, nunc usque manet incognitum.

behlaf at 297 is hard to explain. The only other possible occurrence is in the anonymous Old English account of the Seven Sleepers (Magennis 1994, lines 425–7), which reads:

> And bige us swa ðeah rumlicor todæg be hlafe þonne ðu gebohtest gyrstandæg and bring us bet behlaf[.] þonne ðu ær brohtest.

Magennis reports an erasure of one letter after *behlaf*, and given the parallelism of the two clauses it is perhaps easiest to read *be hlafe* in both and assume a sense 'with regard to bread', since the first instance can hardly be a noun. The current instance, in II.11, is strikingly similar in construction to the first of these, and one should perhaps interpret it similarly and read it as *be hlaf* or *be hlafe*. Ælfric does not otherwise use *be* with the accusative, except once apparently in error, but the fact that all four manuscripts here read *behlaf* (or *be hlaf*) and that the second instance in the Seven Sleepers has apparently been corrected to *behlaf* suggests that it did make sense to contemporary scribes. The alternative to reading it as *be hlaf(e)* is to interpret it as a spelling for an otherwise unrecorded noun *belaf* (f.) meaning 'remnant', or perhaps as a cognate of *bileofa* 'provisions', with intrusive *h* from association with *hlaf*.

302–25 *Dialogues*, II.22.1–33:

> Alio quoque tempore a quodam fideli viro fuerat rogatus ut in eius praedio iuxta Terracinensem urbem missis discipulis suis construere monasterium debuisset. Qui roganti consentiens, deputatis fratribus patrem constituit, et quis eis secundus esset ordinavit. Quibus euntibus spondit dicens: 'Ite, et die illo ego venio, et ostendo vobis in quo loco . . . aedificare debeatis.' Qui benedictione percepta ilico perrexerunt, et constitutum diem magnopere praestolantes. . . . Nocte vero eadem qua promissus inlucescebat dies, eidem servo Dei quem illic patrem constituerat, atque eius praeposito vir Domini in somnis apparuit, et loca singula ubi quid aedificari debuisset subtiliter designavit. Cumque utrique a somno surgerent, sibi invicem quod viderant, retulerunt. . . . Cumque vir Dei constituto die minime venisset, ad eum cum moerore reversi sunt, dicentes: 'Expectavimus, pater, ut venires sicut promiseras, et nobis ostenderes ubi quid aedificare deberemus, et non venisti.' Quibus ipse ait: 'Quare, fratres, quare ista dicitis? Numquid sicut promisi, non veni? . . . Numquid utrisque vobis dormientibus non apparui, et loca singula designavi? Ite, et sicut per visionem audistis, omne habitaculum monasterii ita construite.' Qui haec audientes, vehementer admirati, ad praedictum praedium sunt reversi, et cuncta habitacula sicut ex revelatione didicerant construxerunt.

326–33 For once, Ælfric uses the intervening discussion of the miracle, presumably reflecting an interest in the nature of dream-visions; the significant point is that Benedict actually came in spirit to the monks, as Abacuc journeyed in the body to Daniel. *Dialogues*, II.22.39–48:

> Et certe scriptura teste novimus quod propheta ex Iudaea sublevatus, repente est cum prandio in Chaldaea depositus, quo videlicet prandio prophetam refecit, seque repente in Iudaea iterum invenit. Si igitur tam longe Abacuc potuit sub momento corporaliter ire et prandium deferre, quid mirum si Benedictus pater obtinuit quatenus iret per spiritum, et fratrum quiescentium spiritibus necessaria narraret, ut sicut ille ad cibum

corporis corporaliter perrexit, ita iste ad institutionem spiritalis vitae spiritaliter pergeret?

334–61 *Dialogues*, II.23.8–47:

Nam non longe ab eius monasterio duae quaedam sanctimoniales feminae nobiliori genere exortae, in loco proprio conversabantur, quibus quidam religiosus vir ad exterioris vitae usum praebebat obsequium. Sed sicut nonnullis solet nobilitas generis parere ignobilitatem mentis, ut minus se in hoc mundo despiciant, qui plus se ceteris aliquid fuisse meminerunt, necdum praedictae sanctimoniales feminae perfecte linguam sub habitus sui freno restrinxerant, et eumdem religiosum virum . . . incautis saepe sermonibus ad iracundiam provocabant. Qui cum diu ista toleraret, perrexit ad Dei hominem, quantasque pateretur verborum contumelias, enarravit. Vir autem Dei haec de illis audiens, eis protinus mandavit, dicens: 'Corrigite linguam vestram, quia si non emendaveritis, excommunico vos.' . . . Illae autem a pristinis moribus nihil mutatae, intra paucos dies defunctae sunt, atque in ecclesia sepultae. Cumque in eadem ecclesia missarum sollemnia celebrarentur, atque ex more diaconus clamaret: 'Si quis non communicat, det locum', nutrix earum quae pro eis oblationem Domino deferre consueverat, eas de sepulcris suis progredi et exire ecclesiam videbat. Quod dum saepius cerneret, quia ad vocem diaconi clamantis exiebant foras, atque intra ecclesiam permanere non poterant, ad memoriam rediit quae vir Dei illis adhuc viventibus mandavit. Eas quippe se communione privare dixerat, nisi mores suos et verba corrigerent. Tunc servo Dei cum gravi moerore indicatum est, qui manu sua protinus oblationem dedit, dicens: 'Ite et hanc oblationem pro eis offerri Domino facite, et ulterius excommunicatae non erunt.' Quae dum oblatio pro eis fuisset immolata, et a diacone iuxta morem clamatum est, ut non communicantes ab ecclesia exirent, et illae exire ab ecclesia ulterius visae non sunt. Qua ex re indubitanter patuit quia dum inter eos qui communione privati sunt, minime recederent, communionem a Domino per servum Domini recepissent.

It is not clear what Ælfric means by calling the servant *æðele* (line 337), but perhaps it is meant as a moral quality contrasting with the merely social aspect of *æðelborennyss*. His version of the deacon's words, 'let anyone who is not fit to communicate leave the church' is rather sharper than Gregory's 'if anyone is not communicating, go out of the place'.

362–75 *Dialogues*, II.24.1–16:

Quadam quoque die dum quidam eius puerulus monachus parentes suos ultra quam debebat diligens, atque ad eorum habitaculum tendens, sine benedictione de monasterio exisset, eodem die mox ut ad eos pervenit, defunctus est. Cumque esset sepultus, die altero proiectum foras corpus eius inventum est. Quod rursus tradere sepulturae curaverunt, sed

> sequenti die iterum proiectum exterius atque inhumatum sicut prius invenerunt. Tunc concite ad Benedicti patris vestigia currentes, cum magno fletu petierunt ut ei suam gratiam largiri dignaretur. Quibus vir Dei manu sua protinus communionem dominici corporis dedit dicens: 'Ite, atque hoc dominicum corpus super pectus eius ponite, eumque sepulturae sic tradite.' Quod cum factum fuisset, susceptum corpus eius terra tenuit, nec ultra proiecit.

Ælfric expands Gregory's brief reference to the boy 'loving his parents more than he ought', apparently to explain in what ways this might be sinful and make his fate more justifiable (lines 362–4).

376–92 *Dialogues*, II.25.1–19:

> Quidam autem eius monachus mobilitati mentem dederat, et permanere in monasterio nolebat. Cumque eum vir Dei adsidue corriperet, frequenter admoneret, ipse vero nullo modo consentiret in congregatione persistere, atque importunis precibus ut relaxaretur immineret, quadam die isdem venerabilis pater, nimietatis eius taedio affectus, iratus iussit ut discederet. Qui mox ut monasterium exiit, contra se adsistere aperto ore draconem in itinere invenit. Cumque eum isdem draco qui apparuerat devorare vellet, coepit ipse tremens et palpitans magnis vocibus clamare, dicens: 'Currite, currite, quia draco iste me devorare vult.' Currentes autem fratres draconem minime viderunt, sed trementem atque palpitantem monachum ad monasterium reduxerunt. Qui statim promisit nunquam se esse iam a monasterio recessurum, atque ex hora eadem in sua promissione permansit, quippe qui sancti viri orationibus contra se adsistere draconem viderat, quem prius non videndo sequebatur.

393–5 *Dialogues*, II.26.1–7:

> Sed neque hoc silendum puto, quod illustri viro Aptonio narrante cognovi. Qui aiebat patris sui puerum morbo elefantino fuisse correptum. . . . Qui ad virum Dei ab eodem patre eius missus est et saluti pristinae sub omni celeritate restitutus.

396–407 *Dialogues*, II.27.2–17:

> Die quadam fidelis vir quidam necessitate debiti compulsus . . . venit itaque ad monasterium, omnipotentis Dei famulum repperit, quia a creditore suo pro duodecim solidis graviter adfligeretur, intimavit. Cui venerabilis pater nequaquam se habere duodecim solidos respondit, sed tamen eius inopiam blanda locutione consolatus, ait: 'Vade, et post biduum revertere, quia deest hodie quod tibi debeam dare.' In ipso autem biduo more suo in oratione fuit occupatus. Cum die tertio is qui necessitate debiti affligebatur rediit, super arcam vero monasterii, quae erat frumento plena, subito tredecim solidi sunt inventi. Quos vir Dei deferri iussit, et adflicto petitori tribuit, dicens, ut duodecim redderet, et unum in expensis propriis haberet.

Ælfric has, unusually, converted the Latin coins into English money, at the rate of twenty-four *solidi* to the pound and twenty pence to the *solidus*.

408–12 *Dialogues*, II.27.19–26:

Quidam vir gravissima adversarii sui aemulatione laborabat, cuius ad hoc usque odium prorupit, ut ei nescienti in potu venenum daret. Qui quamvis vitam auferre non valuit, cutis tamen colorem mutavit, ita ut diffusa in corpore eius varietas leprae morem imitari videretur. Sed ad Dei hominem deductus salutem pristinam citius recepit. Nam mox ut eum contigit, omnem cutis illius varietatem fugavit.

413–33 *Dialogues*, II:

[28.1–25] Eo quoque tempore quo alimentorum inopia Campaniam graviter affligebat, vir Dei diversis indigentibus monasterii sui cuncta tribuerat, ut paene nihil in cellario nisi parum quid olei in vitreo vase remaneret. Tunc quidam subdiaconus Agapitus nomine advenit, magnopere postulans ut sibi aliquantulum oleum dari debuisset. Vir autem Domini . . . hoc ipsum parum quod remanserat olei, iussit petenti dari. Monachus vero qui cellarium tenebat audivit quidem iubentis verba, sed implere distulit. . . . respondit monachus se minime dedisse, quia si illud tribueret, omnino nihil fratribus remaneret. Tunc iratus, aliis praecepit ut hoc ipsum vas vitreum in quo parum olei remansisse videbatur, per fenestram proicerent, ne in cella aliquid per inoboedientiam remaneret. Factumque est. Sub fenestra autem eadem ingens praecipitium patebat saxorum molibus asperum. Proiectum itaque vas vitreum venit in saxis, sed sic mansit incolume ac si proiectum minime fuisset, ita ut neque frangi, neque effundi oleum potuisset. Quod vir Domini praecepit levari, atque, ut erat integrum, petenti tribuit. Tunc collectis fratribus, inoboedientem monachum de infidelitate sua et superbia coram omnibus increpavit.

[29.1–10] Qua increpatione completa, sese cum iisdem fratribus in orationem dedit. In eo autem loco ubi cum fratribus orabat, vacuus erat ab oleo doleus et coopertus. Cumque sanctus vir in oratione persisteret, coepit operimentum eiusdem dolei oleo excrescente sublevari. Quo commoto atque sublevato, oleum quod excreverat, ora dolei transiens, pavimentum loci in quo incubuerant inundabat. Quod Benedictus Dei famulus ut aspexit, protinus orationem complevit, atque in pavimentum oleum defluere cessavit.

434–42 *Dialogues*, II.30.1–14:

Quadam die dum ad beati Iohannis oratorium . . . pergeret, ei antiquus hostis in mulomedici specie obviam factus est, cornu et tripedicam ferens. Quem cum requisisset, dicens: 'Ubi vadis?' ille respondit: 'Ecce ad fratres vado potionem eis dare.' Itaque perrexit venerabilis Benedictus ad orationem; qua completa concitus rediit. Malignus vero spiritus unum seniorem monachum invenit aquam haurientem, in quo statim ingressus est, eumque in terram proiecit, et vehementissime vexavit. . . . Vir Dei . . . ei solummodo

> alapam dedit, et malignum ab eo spiritum protinus excussit, ita ut ad eum redire ulterius non auderet.

Ælfric has, sadly, omitted the devil's disguise as a veterinary surgeon taking a potion to the monks and thus, presumably, an implicit demonstration of Benedict's ability to see through diabolic disguises.

443–69 *Dialogues*, II.31.1–41:

> Gothorum quidam Zalla nomine perfidiae fuit arrianae, qui Totilae regis eorum temporibus, contra catholicae ecclesiae religiosos viros ardore immanissimae crudelitatis exarsit, ita ut quisquis ei clericus monachusve ante faciem venisset, ab eius manibus vivus nullo modo exiret. Quadam vero die avaritiae suae aestu succensus, in rapinam rerum inhians, dum quemdam rusticum tormentis crudelibus affligeret eumque per supplicia diversa laniaret, victus poenis rusticus, sese res suas Benedicto Dei famulo commendasse professus est. . . . Tunc isdem Zalla cessavit rusticum tormentis affligere, sed eius brachia loris fortibus adstringens, ante equum suum coepit impellere, ut quis esset Benedictus qui eius res susceperat demonstraret. Quem ligatis brachiis rusticus antecedens duxit ad sancti viri monasterium, eumque ante ingressum cellae solum sedentem repperit et legentem. . . . Quem dum fervido spiritu . . . eo terrore quo consueverat, acturum se existimans, magnis coepit vocibus clamare, dicens: 'Surge, surge, et res istius rustici redde quas accepisti.' Ad cuius vocem vir Dei protinus oculos levavit a lectione, eumque intuitus, mox etiam rusticum qui ligatus tenebatur, attendit. Ad cuius brachia dum oculos deflexisset, miro modo tanta se celeritate coeperunt illigata brachiis lora devolvere, ut dissolvi tam concite nulla hominum festinatione potuissent. . . . Ad tantae potestatis vim tremefactus Zalla ad terram corruit, et cervicem crudelitatis rigidae ad eius vestigia inclinans, orationibus se illius commendavit. Vir autem sanctus a lectione minime surrexit, sed vocatis fratribus, eum introrsus tolli, ut benedictionem acciperet, praecepit. Quem ad se reductum, ut a tantae crudelitatis insania quiescere deberet, admonuit. Qui fractus recedens, nil ulterius petere a rustico praesumpsit, quem vir Dei non tangendo, sed respiciendo solverat.

Note that again Ælfric does not identify Zalla as a Goth, only as a heretic. The form *Thesalla*, found in MSS K and D, is interpreted in my edition as an error for *Salla*, prompted by a scribal misunderstanding of the construction *þe salla hatte*, 'who was called Salla' (see *CH II*, p. 355), but David Yerkes[4] argues that Thesalla is Ælfric's rendering of a Latin variant such as *tzalla*. If so then the phrase *Thesalla hatte* is to be read as an example of either the paratactic clause with *hatte* described by Mitchell (OES §1475), '—he was called Thesalla—' or the clause with apparent omission of the relative (OES §2305), '(who) was called Thesalla'. This is an extremely rare construction in Ælfric, indeed Mitchell says Ælfric

[4] David Yerkes, 'Ælfric's *thesalla*', *Notes and Queries* 227 (1982), 397–9.

avoids it with *hatte*, but there is one probable instance, in this very homily, at 28 (*romanus hatte*). This is supported by all the manuscripts and the two instances could be explained as an experimental usage. Even so, Thesalla does not seem a likely rendering of *tzalla* or even *tezalla*; the Old English version of the *Dialogues* has Zalla. It may be that Ælfric originally wrote *salla hatte* and either he or one of his scribes then normalised the construction by adding *þe* above the line, and this was then misunderstood by copyists who produced *thesalla hatte*.

470–85 *Dialogues*, II.32.2–33:

> Quidam vero rusticus defuncti filii corpus in ulnis ferens, orbitatis luctu aestuans, ad monasterium venit, Benedictum patrem quaesivit. . . . Quem mox ut orbatus rusticus aspexit, clamare coepit: 'Redde filium meum, redde filium meum.' Vir autem Dei in hac voce substitit, dicens: 'Numquid ego tibi filium tuum abstuli?' Cui ille respondit: 'Mortuus est, veni, resuscita eum.' Quod mox ut Dei famulus audivit, valde contristatus est, dicens: 'Recedite, fratres, recedite. Haec nostra non sunt, sed sanctorum apostolorum sunt.' . . . At ille, quem nimius cogebat dolor, in sua petitione perstitit, iurans quod non recederet, nisi eius filium resuscitaret. . . . Dum Dei vir cum fratribus pervenisset, flexit genua, et super corpusculum infantis incubuit, seseque erigens, ad caelum palmas tetendit dicens: 'Domine, non aspicias peccata mea, sed fidem huius hominis, qui resuscitari filium suum rogat, et redde in hoc corpusculo animam quam abstulisti.' Vix in oratione verba compleverat, et regrediente anima ita corpusculum pueri omne contremuit, ut sub oculis omnium qui aderant, apparuerit concussione mirifica tremendo palpitasse. Cuius mox manum tenuit, et eum patri viventem atque incolumem dedit.

Note Ælfric's emphasis at the outset on the *geleafful* status of the peasant, in contrast presumably to Zalla (and cf too the *cristenne mannan* of 446), as if it is important to stress that the miracles are worked on behalf of devout believers.

486–512 *Dialogues*, II.33.7–47:

> Soror namque eius, Scolastica nomine, omnipotenti Domino ab ipso infantiae tempore dicata, ad eum semel per annum venire consueverat, ad quam vir Dei non longe extra ianuam in possessione monasterii descendebat. Quadam vero die venit ex more, atque ad eam cum discipulis venerabilis eius descendit frater. Qui totum diem in Dei laudibus sacrisque colloquiis ducentes, incumbentibus iam noctis tenebris simul acceperunt cibos. Cumque adhuc ad mensam sederent, et inter sacra colloquia tardior se hora protraheret, eadem sanctimonialis femina soror eius eum rogavit, dicens: 'Quaeso te ne ista nocte me deseras, ut usque mane aliquid de caelestis vitae gaudiis loquamur.' Cui ille respondit: 'Quid est quod loqueris, soror? Manere extra cellam nullatenus possum.' Tanta vero erat caeli serenitas, ut nulla in aere nubes appareret. Sanctimonialis autem femina, cum verba fratris negantis audisset, insertas digitis manus

> super mensam posuit, et caput in manibus omnipotentem Dominum rogatura declinavit. Cumque levaret de mensa caput, tanta coruscationis et tonitrui virtus, tantaque inundatio pluviae erupit, ut neque venerabilis Benedictus, neque fratres qui cum eo aderant, extra loci limen quo consederant, pedem movere potuissent. . . . Tunc vir Dei inter coruscos et tonitruos atque ingentis pluviae inundationem videns se ad monasterium non posse remeare, coepit conqueri contristatus, dicens: 'Parcat tibi omnipotens Deus, soror. Quid est quod fecisti?' Cui illa respondit: 'Ecce te rogavi, et audire me noluisti. Rogavi Dominum meum, et audivit me. Modo ergo si potes egredere, et me dimissa ad monasterium recede.' Ipse autem exire extra tectum non valens, qui remanere sponte noluit, in loco mansit invitus, sicque factum est ut totam noctem pervigilem ducerent, atque per sacra spiritalis vitae colloquia sese vicaria relatione satiarent.

Gregory reports that Scholastica visited her brother once a year, and that he met her at a property of the monastery not far from his gate (since she would not be allowed in the monastery itself); Ælfric says that she lived near the monastery and that Benedict visited her once a year, at her *cyte*, apparently identifying the residence near the monastery with her own home. Possibly he had a variant text (though the beginning of the next chapter in Gregory again makes it clear that the meeting-place was not her own *cella*). Or perhaps he allowed himself to misread or adapt the source because he did not approve of a *mynecyne* freely travelling from her place of seclusion.

512–21 *Dialogues*, II.34.3–13:

> Cum ecce post triduum in cella consistens, elevatis in aera oculis, vidit eiusdem sororis suae animam de eius corpore egressam, in columbae specie caeli secreta penetrare. Qui tantae eius gloriae congaudens, omnipotenti Deo in hymnis et laudibus gratias reddidit, eiusque obitum fratribus denuntiavit. Quos etiam protinus misit, ut eius corpus ad monasterium deferrent, atque in sepulcro quod sibi ipse paraverat, ponerent. Quo facto contigit ut quorum mens una semper in Deo fuerat, eorum quoque corpora nec sepultura separaret.

In identifying Scholastica as a *mynecyne* Ælfric is perhaps translating the *sanctimonialis* of *Dialogues*, II.33.22 (above); he adds the point that she is dedicated to virginity at 487–8. Cf the *mynecyne* of 334 ff. In neither case are the women apparently part of a community.

522–36 *Dialogues*, II.35.1–43:

> Alio quoque tempore . . . in cuius turris superioribus se venerabilis Benedictus . . . collocavit. . . . Cumque vir Domini Benedictus . . . ad fenestram stans, et omnipotentem Dominum deprecans, subito intempesta noctis hora respiciens, vidit fusam lucem desuper cunctas noctis tenebras exfugasse, tantoque splendore clarescere, ut diem vinceret lux illa . . . Omnis etiam mundus velut sub uno solis radio collectus, ante oculos eius adductus

> est. Qui venerabilis pater, dum intentam oculorum aciem in hoc splendore coruscae lucis infigeret, vidit Germani Capuani episcopi animam in spera ignea ab angelis in caelum ferri. Tunc tanti sibi testem volens adhibere miraculi, Servandum diaconum iterato bis terque eius nomine, cum clamoris magnitudine vocavit. Cumque ille . . . respexit, partemque lucis exiguam vidit. . . . Vir Dei . . . statim in Casinum castrum religioso viro Theopropo mandavit ut ad Capuanam urbem sub eadem nocte transmitteret, et quid de Germano episcopo ageretur agnosceret et indicaret. Factumque est, et reverentissimum virum Germanum episcopum is qui missus fuerat iam defunctum repperit, et requirens subtiliter agnovit eodem momento fuisse illius obitum quo vir Domini eius cognovit ascensum.

536–46 Ælfric uses the subsequent discussion between Peter and Gregory, though avoiding the dialogue form (*Dialogues*, II.35.44–71):

> [Petr.] Mira res valde, et vehementer stupenda . . . ut mundus omnis ab homine uno videatur. [Gregor.] . . . Animae videnti creatorem angusta est omnis creatura. Quamlibet etenim parum de luce creatoris aspexerit, breve ei fit omne quod creatum est, quia ipsa luce visionis intimae, mentis laxatur sinus, tantumque expanditur in Deo, ut superior existat mundo. Fit vero ipsa videntis anima etiam super semetipsam. . . . Quid itaque mirum si mundum ante se collectum vidit, qui sublevatus in mentis lumine extra mundum fuit? . . . In illa ergo luce quae exterioribus oculis fulsit, lux interior in mente fuit, quae videntis animum quia ad superiora rapuit, ei quam angusta essent omnia inferiora monstravit.

547–53 *Dialogues*, II.36.6–11:

> Nam scripsit monachorum regulam discretione praecipuam, sermone luculentam. Cuius si quis velit subtilius mores vitamque cognoscere, potest in eadem institutione regulae omnes magisterii illius actus invenire, quia sanctus vir nullo modo potuit aliter docere quam vixit.

The brief description, lines 550–3, is not in the Dialogues and I have not found its source.

554–72 *Dialogues*, II.37.1–28:

> Eodem vero anno quo de hac vita erat exiturus, quibusdam discipulis secum conversantibus, quibusdam longe manentibus, sanctissimi sui obitus denuntiavit diem. . . . Ante sextum vero sui exitus diem aperiri sibi sepulturam iubet. Qui mox correptus febribus, acri coepit ardore fatigari. Cumque per dies singulos languor ingravesceret, sexto die portari se in oratorium a discipulis fecit, ibique exitum suum dominici corporis et sanguinis perceptione munivit, atque inter discipulorum manus imbecilla membra sustentans, erectis in caelum manibus stetit, et ultimum spiritum inter verba orationis efflavit. Qua scilicet die duobus de eo fratribus . . . revelatio unius atque indissimilis visionis apparuit. Viderunt namque quia strata palliis atque innumeris corusca lampadibus via recto orientis tramite

> ab eius cella in caelum usque tendebatur. Cui venerando habitu vir desuper clarus adsistens, cuius esset via quam cernerent, inquisivit. Illi autem se nescire professi sunt. Quibus ipse ait: 'Haec est via qua dilectus Domino caelum Benedictus ascendit.' . . . Sepultus vero est in oratorio beati Baptistae Iohannis, quod destructa ara Apollinis ipse construxit.

572–7 The subsequent translation of the body to Fleury is not, of course, in the *Dialogues*. There are a number of early references to this event and some more detailed narratives; see Walter Goffart, 'Le Mans, St. Scholastica and the literary tradition of the Translation of St Benedict', *RB* 77 (1967), 104–41. Förster suggested that Ælfric may have got the information from Bede's Martyrology; it certainly occurs, under 11 July, in the adaptation by Florus of Lyons.[5] But Ælfric perhaps needed no written source for so familiar a detail and so brief a reference. Förster suggested that Ælfric may have had an interpolated copy of the *Dialogues* which might explain his additional material here and perhaps elsewhere, but I have found no trace of such interpolations, and later translations of the bodies of saints are the sort of material that Ælfric adds elsewhere, e.g. with St Oswald.

577–84 *Dialogues*, II.38.1–12:

> Qui et in eo specu in quo prius Sublacu habitavit, nunc usque si petentium fides exigat, miraculis coruscat. . . . Quaedam mulier mente capta, dum sensum funditus perdidisset, per montes et valles, silvas et campos die noctuque vagabatur, ibique tantummodo quiescebat, ubi hanc quiescere lassitudo coegisset. Quadam vero die dum vaga nimium erraret, ad beati viri Benedicti patris specum devenit, ibique nesciens ingressa mansit. Facto autem mane, ita sanato sensu egressa est, ac si eam numquam insania capitis ulla tenuisset. Quae omni vitae suae tempore in eadem quam acceperat salute permansit.

585–7 Ælfric's peroration is in alliterative prose, as in several other homilies (see above, Introduction, pp. xxxvi–vii). There is a similar *occupatio* trope in the previous homily, II.10.304–7, but in fact the incident above is the last miracle described by Gregory; he concludes with a brief discussion about miracles which occur away from a saint's tomb.

12 MID-LENT SUNDAY

This is another very long piece, twice as long as most of the exegetical homilies, and a very substantial one, covering the whole story of the exodus from Egypt and the journey to the promised land, and taking in two major pastoral topics, the ten commandments and the eight chief sins, with their matching virtues. The earlier

[5] *Edition pratique des martyrologes de Bède, de l'Anonyme lyonnais et de Florus*, ed. J. Dubois and G. Renaud (Paris, 1976), p. 125.

homily for this occasion, CH I.12, covers the Gospel reading for the day, on the feeding of the 5000. The five loaves are there interpreted as the Pentateuch, converted by Christ into spiritual nourishment for all, and this prompted Ælfric to give a brief twenty-line summary of the story of Moses, the exodus and the ten commandments, for those who 'do not know who Moses is'. Ælfric cancelled this passage shortly afterwards, noting in the margin of the Royal MS that it 'is more fully dealt with in the second book', and the first part of the current homily is indeed a long expansion of the topics covered in that earlier passage, justified by the fact that, as he notes (lines 1–2), Exodus is read in the monastic office during Lent. The second part, entitled *Secunda Sententia* or *Secundus Sermo* in the manuscripts, takes the story on into the Book of Joshua and the arrival in the promised land. It was presumably written some time after the first, since it is marked by a sustained use of the alliterative style which is quite absent from the first part. A third major homiletic account of the Hebrews' period in the desert is Pope 20, *De Populo Israhel*, which begins by referring back to the first part of the present homily and summarising its contents; indeed its opening words suggest that it was written as a sequel to this first part. Possibly Ælfric at some stage devised a sequence of texts on the exodus, running from CH II.12a to Pope 20 and then CH II.12b, though the texts do not survive together in any manuscript.

Förster suggested that Ælfric had used the Ps-Bede commentary on the Pentateuch for the first part and the commentary on Joshua attributed to Isidore or Bede for the second part, plus Alcuin's *Liber de Virtutibus et Vitiis* and Cassian's *Conlationes* for the analysis of the deadly sins.[1] Fehr argued for the use of Alcuin's exposition of the ten commandments and Alcuin's source in Isidore.[2] The Ps-Bede material on Exodus and Leviticus relevant to Ælfric is all to be found in Isidore's *Quaestiones in Vetus Testamentum*, which is probably a more likely source. But it has to be said that Ælfric's interpretation of the narrative from Exodus, Leviticus and Joshua, while evidently in the Isidorean tradition, seldom bears a very close resemblance. His use of two stray passages from Augustine and Gregory, taken from texts primarily concerned with quite different subjects, suggests that Ælfric may have been primarily drawing on a range of reading stored in his memory. The brief Alcuinian exposition of the ten commandments cited by Fehr seems to have nothing that is not in Isidore.

Sources and Notes

The following texts are cited below:

1. Alcuin, *De Virtutibus et Vitiis*, PL 101, cols. 613–38.
2. Augustine, *In Iohannis Evangelium Tractatus CXXIV*, ed. R. Willems, CCSL 36 (Turnhout, 1954).

[1] Förster 1894, pp. 25–6 and 46–8.

[2] B. Fehr, 'Über einige Quellen zu Ælfrics *Homiliae Catholicae*', *Archiv* 130 (1913), 378–81.

3. Bede, *Commentarius in Genesim*, ed. C.W. Jones, CCSL 118A (Turnhout, 1967).
4. John Cassian, *Conlationes*, ed. M. Petschenig, CSEL 13 (Vienna, 1886).
5. *Excerptiones Ps-Egberti*, printed in B. Thorpe, ed., *Ancient Laws and Institutes*, 2 vols. (London, 1840), II.97–127.
6. Gregory the Great, *Homiliae in Evangelia*, PL 76, Hom. 21, cols. 1169–74.
7. Haymo of Auxerre, *Homiliae de Tempore*, PL 118, Hom. 33, cols. 217–21.
8. Isidore, *Quaestiones in Vetus Testamentum*, PL 83, cols. 207–424.
9. Theodulf of Orleans, *Capitula*, in H. Sauer, ed., *Theodulfi Capitula in England*, Texte und Untersuchungen zur englischen Philologie, Bd. 8 (Münich, 1978).

1–6 The *we* of line 1 presumably refers to the monks and clerics who read Exodus in the office, i.e. the private services, and the *ge* and *eow* of 2–5 to the laity to whom the story is told and expounded in the public service, the mass.

7–16 The three ages. A patristic commonplace which Ælfric might have first met in Augustine, Gregory, Isidore, Bede or a number of other writers. For references see the helpful note in *Byrhtferth's Enchiridion*, ed. P. S. Baker and M. Lapidge, EETS ss 15 (1995), p. 338. It is noted in similar terms at CH I.22.33–8. What Ælfric implies he is offering here is an allegorical reading of the Old Testament teachings (cf *bebead* 16) rather than its narrative; most of the homily is in fact concerned with allegorical interpretation of Old Testament narrative or with literal interpretation of Old Testament teachings, but there is some allegorical reading of the instructions on sacrifices.

17–27 A resumé of Old Testament history from Abraham to Jacob. Ælfric uses Abraham to present the exodus as the fulfilment of the promise and prophecy which God made to him. By the building of Jerusalem 'in another fashion now' (lines 21–2) Ælfric presumably means its rebuilding after the destruction of Jerusalem by the Romans; cf CH I.28.58–9.

22–7 Gen 15.13–16:

> (13) Dictumque est ad eum: scito praenoscens quod peregrinum futurum sit semen tuum in terra non sua et subicient eos servituti et adfligent quadringentis annis. (14) Verumtamen gentem cui servituri sunt ego iudicabo et post haec egredientur cum magna substantia. . . . (16) Generatione autem quarta revertentur huc.

28–40 Summary from Genesis and Exodus; close parallels are:

> (Gen 41.54) Coeperunt venire septem anni inopiae . . . et in universo orbe fames praevaluit in cuncta autem terra Aegypti erat panis. (49) Tantaque fuit multitudo tritici ut harenae maris coaequaretur et copia mensuram excederet. (46.27) Omnis anima domus Iacob quae ingressa est Aegyptum fuere septuaginta. (Exod 1.8) Surrexit interea rex novus super Aegyptum qui ignorabat Ioseph. (11) Praeposuit itaque eis magistros operum ut

adfligerent eos oneribus aedificaveruntque urbes tabernaculorum Pharaoni Phiton et Ramesses. (13) Oderantque filios Israhel Aegyptii et adfligebant inludentes eis. (16) Hebraeas et partus tempus advenerit si masculus fuerit interficite illum.

41–54 Summary account of Moses from Exodus; cf esp. Exod 3.7–8, 10: (7) Cui ait Dominus: vidi adflictionem populi mei in Aegypto et clamorem eius audivi . . . (8) et sciens dolorem eius descendi ut liberarem eum de manibus Aegyptiorum et educerem de terra illa in terram bonam et spatiosam in terram quae fluit lacte et melle . . . (10) Sed veni mittam te ad Pharaonem ut educas populum meum filios Israhel de Aegypto. (5.1–2) Post haec ingressi sunt Moses et Aaron et dixerunt Pharaoni: haec dicit Dominus Deus Israhel, dimitte populum meum ut sacrificet mihi in deserto. (2) At ille respondit: quis est Dominus ut audiam vocem eius et dimittam Israhel; nescio Dominum et Israhel non dimittam.

55–80 The account of the plagues summarises Exod 7–12: (7.19) Dixit quoque Dominus ad Mosen: dic ad Aaron tolle virgam tuam et extende manum tuam super aquas Aegypti et super fluvios eorum et rivos ac paludes et omnes lacus aquarum ut vertantur in sanguinem. (8.6) Et ascenderunt ranae operueruntque terram Aegypti. (17) Et facti sunt scinifes in hominibus et in iumentis. (22) Faciamque mirabilem in die illa terram Gessen in qua populus meus est ut non sint ibi muscae. (24) Fecitque Dominus ita et venit musca gravissima in domos Pharaonis et servorum eius et in omnem terram Aegypti corruptaque est terra ab huiuscemodi muscis. (9.6) Mortuaque sunt omnia animantia Aegyptiorum de animalibus vero filiorum Israhel nihil omnino periit. (7) Et misit Pharao ad videndum nec erat quicquam mortuum de his quae possidebat Israhel ingravatumque est cor Pharaonis et non dimisit populum. (10) Factaque sunt vulnera vesicarum turgentium in hominibus et in iumentis. (23) Et Dominus dedit tonitrua et grandinem ac discurrentia fulgura super terram pluitque Dominus grandinem super terram Aegypti. (24) Et grando et ignis inmixta pariter ferebantur tantaeque fuit magnitudinis quanta ante numquam apparuit in universa terra Aegypti ex quo gens illa condita est. (25) Et percussit grando in omni terra Aegypti cuncta quae fuerunt in agris ab homine usque ad iumentum cunctam herbam agri percussit grando et omne lignum regionis confregit. (10.13) Et mane facto ventus urens levavit lucustas (14) quae ascenderunt super universam terram Aegypti et sederunt in cunctis finibus Aegyptiorum innumerabiles quales ante illud tempus non fuerant nec postea futurae sunt. (15) Operueruntque universam superficiem terrae vastantes omnia devorata est igitur herba terrae et quicquid pomorum in arboribus fuit quae grando dimiserat nihilque omnino virens relictum est in lignis et in herbis terrae in cuncta Aegypto. (22) Et factae sunt tenebrae horribiles in universa terra Aegypti tribus

> diebus. (23) Nemo vidit fratrem suum nec movit se de loco in quo erat; ubicumque autem habitabant filii Israhel lux erat. (12.29) Factum est autem in noctis medio percussit Dominus omne primogenitum in terra Aegypti. . . . (30) Surrexitque Pharao nocte et omnes servi eius cunctaque Aegyptus et ortus est clamor magnus in Aegypto neque enim erat domus in qua non iaceret mortuus.

Ælfric's *gnættum* and *hundes lusum* (line 59) presumably translate *sciniphes* and *muscae* respectively: *gnættas* refer to *sciniphes* at Pope 4.142, and Isidore reports that the Septuagint has *cynomyiam, id est, caninam muscam* for Vulgate *musca*, which may have prompted *hundes lys*; *gnættum and fleogum* at Pope 1.230 appears to translate *muscas*, but Ælfric may there be thinking of both *sciniphes* and *muscae* rather than Augustine's *muscas et ranas*. *Cinifes* is a kind of stinging insect according to Lewis and Short; but the Authorised Version has 'lice'.
The comment at 60–2 is from Augustine's *Tract.*, 1.15.16–19:

> Populum Pharaonis superbum potuit Deus domare de ursis, de leonibus, de serpentibus; muscas et ranas illis immisit, ut rebus vilissimis superbia domaretur.

It is used as source for Pope 1.228–46. The detail of *hundes lys* flying into mouths and nostrils seems to be Ælfric's own; it is partially repeated at Pope 1.233.

81–6 From Exod 12–15; cf esp.:

> (12.37) Profectique sunt filii Israhel de Ramesse in Soccoth sescenta ferme milia peditum virorum absque parvulis. (14.5) Et nuntiatum est regi Aegyptiorum quod fugisset populus; immutatumque est cor Pharaonis. . . . (6) Iunxit ergo currum, et omnem populum suum assumpsit secum. (15) Dixitque Dominus ad Mosen . . . (16) Tu autem eleva virgam tuam et extende manum super mare et divide illud . . . (21) Cumque extendisset Moses manum super mare abstulit illud Dominus flante vento vehementi et urente tota nocte et vertit in siccum divisaque est aqua. (22) Et ingressi sunt filii Israhel per medium maris sicci; erat enim aqua quasi murus a dextra eorum et leva. (23) Persequentesque Aegyptii ingressi sunt post eos omnis equitatus Pharaonis currus eius et equites per medium maris. (26) Et ait Dominus ad Mosen extende manum tuam super mare ut revertantur aquae ad Aegyptios super currus et equites eorum. (27) Cumque extendisset Moses manum contra mare reversum est primo diluculo ad priorem locum fugientibusque Aegyptiis occurrerunt aquae et involvit eos Dominus in mediis fluctibus. (28) Reversaeque sunt aquae et operuerunt currus et equites cuncti exercitus Pharaonis qui sequentes ingressi fuerant mare ne unus quidem superfuit ex eis. (29) Filii autem Israhel perrexerunt per medium sicci maris et aquae eis erant quasi pro muro a dextris et a sinistris. (15.1) Tunc cecinit Moses et filii Israhel carmen hoc Domino et dixerunt cantemus Domino gloriose enim magnificatus est equum et ascensorem deiecit in mare.

102–10 summarises Exod 16.14–35 and 17.1–6.

110–15 Exod 13.21–2:

> (21) Dominus autem praecedebat eos ad ostendendam viam per diem in columna nubis, et per noctem in columna ignis, ut dux esset itineris utroque tempore. (22) Numquam defuit columna nubis per diem, nec columna ignis per noctem coram populo.

and Deut 1.33:

> qui praecessit vos in via et metatus est locum in quo tentoria figere deberetis, nocte ostendens vobis iter per ignem et die per columnam nubis.

115–19 Exod 16.35: *Filii autem Israhel comederunt man quadraginta annis donec venirent in terram habitabilem*, and Deut 8.4: *Vestimentum tuum quo operiebaris nequaquam vetustate defecit, et pes tuus non est subtritus en quadragesimus annus est.*

120–34 Exod:

> (19.9) Ait ei Dominus iam nunc veniam ad te in caligine nubis ut audiat me populus loquentem ad te et credat tibi in perpetuum. . . . (11) Et sint parati in diem tertium die enim tertio descendet Dominus coram omni plebe super montem Sinai. . . . (16) Iam advenerat tertius dies. (24.16) Et habitavit gloria Domini super Sinai. (19.16) Et mane inclaruerat et ecce coeperunt audiri tonitrua ac micare fulgura et nubes densissima operire montem clangorque bucinae vehementius perstrepebat. . . . (21) Dixit ad eum descende et contestare populum ne forte velint transcendere terminos ad videndum Dominum et pereat ex eis plurima multitudo. . . . (24) Cui ait Dominus vade descende ascendesque tu et Aaron tecum sacerdotes autem et populus ne transeant terminos nec ascendant ad Dominum ne forte interficiat illos.

135–48 That the ten commandments can be divided into three and seven, and were thus divided between the two tablets, is not Biblical but traditional; it is noted by Isidore (*Quaestiones*, PL 83, 301AB, 302BC; see note on 255 ff). The first commandment as given by Ælfric is not in fact from Exodus but from Christ's formulation of the first of the two great commandments at Mc 12.29: *Iesus autem respondit ei quia primum omnium mandatum est audi Israhel Dominus Deus noster Deus unus est.* The same form is cited by Isidore. The remaining commandments generally follow Exod 20.7–17, but reverse verses 13 and 14, putting adultery before murder, and rearrange verse 17 into two distinct commands:

> (7) Non adsumes nomen Domini Dei tui in vanum. . . . (8) Memento ut diem sabbati sanctifices. . . . (12) Honora patrem tuum et matrem tuam. (13) Non occides. (14) Non moechaberis. (15) Non furtum facies. (16) Non loqueris contra proximum tuum falsum testimonium. (17) Non concupisces domum proximi tui nec desiderabis uxorem eius non servum non ancillam non bovem non asinum nec omnia quae illius sunt.

The rearrangement of verse 17 into the ninth and tenth commandments is in Isidore (and traditional), and similar in wording.

149–51 Exod 24.18:

Ingressusque Moses medium nebulae ascendit in montem et fuit ibi quadraginta diebus et quadraginta noctibus.

and 34.28:

Fecit ergo ibi cum Domino quadraginta dies et quadraginta noctes; panem non comedit et aquam non bibit, et scripsit in tabulis verba foederis decem.

151–8 Moses' responsibility for the Pentateuch is a matter of tradition.

158–64 Summarising Exod 25–30.

169–73 Mt 5.17–18:

(17) Nolite putare quoniam veni solvere legem aut prophetas; non veni solvere sed adimplere. (18) Amen quippe dico vobis donec transeat caelum et terra iota unum aut unus apex non praeteribit a lege donec omnia fiant.

175–7 If the promise of a further exposition on another occasion means further allegorical interpretation of the narrative given here, there is no obvious text that fits the bill, though some parts of Pope 20, *De Populo Israhel* might; but further narrative from Exodus, with commentary, is found in the second half of this homily (for the same occasion, but written later), CH II.13 and LS 13.

178–86 Cf Isidore, *Quaestiones*, PL 83:

[*In Exodum*, c. 1.2, 287C] Aegyptus enim hic mundus esse figuraliter multis prophetarum vocibus approbatur. . . . [*In Exodum*, c. 3.1, 288A] Affligit Pharao filios Israel luto, et latere. Israel similitudo est populi nostri. Pharao autem est diaboli.

186–9 Isidore, *In Exodum*, c. 19.1–20.3, *Quaestiones*, PL 83:

[296BC] Quid mare Rubrum, nisi baptismus est Christi sanguine consecratus? Hostes sequentes cum rege, qui a tergo moriuntur, peccata sunt praeterita, quae delentur, et diabolus, qui in spirituali baptismo suffocatur. . . . Post transitum Rubri maris canit canticum populus Deo, Aegyptiis et Pharaone submersis. Non aliter et fideles, postquam de lavacro conscendunt, exstinctis peccatis, hymnum in voce gratulationis emittunt. . . . [296D] et per patientiam exspectando.

192–5 Slightly resembles Isidore, *In Exodum*, c. 20.3, *Quaestiones*, PL 83, 296D:

Iam dehinc ducitur post maris transitum populus per desertum. Baptizati scilicet omnes per mundum, non perfruentes promissa patria; sed quod non vident, sperando, et per patientiam exspectando, tanquam in deserto sunt, et illic laboriosae et periculosae tentationes, ne revertantur corde in Aegyptum, nec ibi tandem Christus deserit, nam et illa columna non recedit.

195–205 Not really close to the relevant chapter in Isidore, *In Exodum*, c. 18. Ælfric seems instead to be recalling a passage in Gregory the Great's homily on the resurrection, already used in part for CH I.17 (Gregory, Hom. 21, PL 76, 1171BC):

> Unde recte quoque populum per deserta gradientem columna ignis in nocte et columna nubis praeibat in die. In igne enim terror est, in nube autem visionis lene blandimentum; dies vero vita iusti, et nox accipitur vita peccatoris. . . . In die ergo per nubem columna monstrata est, et in nocte per ignem, quia omnipotens Deus et blandus iustis, et terribilis apparebit iniustis. Istos in iudicio veniens per lenitatis mansuetudinem demulcet, illos vero per iustitiae districtionem terret.

206–8 1 Cor 10.1–3:

> (1) Nolo enim vos ignorare fratres quoniam patres nostri omnes sub nube fuerunt et omnes mare transierunt. (2) Et omnes in Mose baptizati sunt in nube et in mari. (3) Et omnes eandem escam spiritalem manducaverunt.

208–10 Isidore, *In Exodum*, c. 23.3, *Quaestiones*, PL 83, 298A: *Manna utique, quod est Christus, qui tanquam panis vivus de coelo descendit.*

210–12 Jn 6.51–2:

> (51) Ego sum panis vivus qui de caelo descendi. (52) Si quis manducaverit ex hoc pane vivet in aeternum et panis quem ego dabo caro mea est pro mundi vita.

215–8 Isidore, *In Exodum*, c. 24.1–2, *Quaestiones*, PL 83, 299AB:

> Percussa enim petra fons manavit. Percussus in cruce Christus sitientibus lavacri gratiam, et donum Spiritus sancti effudit. Petram enim istam figuram habuisse Christi probat Apostolus, cum dixit: 'Bibebant autem de spirituali consequenti eos petra, petra autem erat Christus' (1 Cor 10.4).

218–20 Cf CH II.14.319–23.

221–5 Isidore, *In Exodum*, c. 28.1, *Quaestiones*, PL 83, 300BC:

> Iam deinde quinquagesima die post actum pascha data est lex Moysi. Ita et quinquagesima die post passionem Domini, quam pascha illud praefigurabat, datus est Spiritus sanctus, promissus Paracletus, descendens super apostolos . . . et divisis linguis credentium, totus evangelica praedicatione mundus impletus est.

But Ælfric had already drawn this comparison at CH I.22.1–38.

226–39 Isidore, *In Exodum*, c. 28.2–3, *Quaestiones*, PL 83, 300C-301A:

> Aspicit illuc cunctus populus voces, et lampades, montemque fumantem, tonitrua, et fulgura, clangoremque buccinae perstrepentem [*alluding mainly to Exod 20.18, not used earlier by Ælfric*]. In vocibus namque et tonitruis clamor praedicantium intelligitur, in lampadibus claritas miraculorum, in sonitu buccinae fortis praedicatio sanctorum. . . . Quod autem

> legem daturus Dominus, in igne et fumo descendit, hoc significat, quia et fideles claritatis suae ostensione illuminat, et infidelium oculos per fumum erroris obscurat.

240–50 Isidore, *In Exodum*, c. 28.2, *Quaestiones*, PL 83, 300C:

> Dicitur illic lex scripta digito Dei. Et Dominus dicit de Spiritu sancto: 'In digito Dei eiicio daemonia' (Lc 11.20).

Ælfric adds Mt 12.28: *In spiritu Dei eiicio daemones*. Lines 243–8 are repeated at Pope 4.158–62, as part of a commentary on the Luke passage; Pope cites Bede and Haymo as sources, but they do not provide the salient details here.

250–4 Isidore, *In Exodum*, c. 31.1, *Quaestiones*, PL 83, 303CD:

> Sed cur lapideae eaedem tabulae fuerint, nisi ad significandum cor Iudaeorum lapideum? Per lapidis insensibilitatem demonstravit duram eorum mentis stoliditatem, de qua propheta dicit: 'Auferam ab eis cor lapideum, et dabo eis cor carneum' (Ez 11.19).

255–60 Isidore, *In Exodum*, c. 30.1, *Quaestiones*, PL 83, 303C:

> Cur autem in duabus tabulis scripta est lex, nisi aut propter duo Testamenta significanda, aut propter illa duo praecepta dilectionis Dei, et dilectionis proximi, in quibus tota lex pendet et prophetae? Haec enim in tabulis singulis explicata sunt. In una enim tria praecepta ad Dei pertinentia charitatem; in altera vero septem pertinentia ad proximi societatem.

260–7 A characteristic trinitarian passage by Ælfric; Isidore has a quite different commentary, on worshipping other gods.

267–73 Isidore, *In Exodum*, c. 29.3, *Quaestiones*, PL 83:

> [301C] Non accipies in vanum nomen Domini Dei tui; id est, ne aestimes creaturam esse filium Dei, quoniam omnis creatura vanitati subiecta est (Rom 8.20); sed credas eum esse aequalem patri, Deum de Deo, verum verbum, per quem omnia facta sunt. . . . [*earlier*, 301B] Creatura enim mutabilis est.

273–311 Exod 20.11:

> Sex enim diebus fecit Dominus caelum et terram et mare et omnia quae in eis sunt et requievit in die septimo idcirco benedixit Dominus diei sabbati et sanctificavit eum.

The third commandment, on the sabbath, prompts Ælfric into a substantial excursus on matters of fundamental doctrine. The sabbath was evidently a matter of some interest, since he returns to it in several later works—Pope 2, Irvine 3, and the second pastoral letter for Wulfstan, Fehr III (see Irvine, pp. 52–6). It has no parallel in Isidore, who identifies the commandment with the Holy Spirit (as the first two refer to the Father and the Son). There is a very closely parallel passage, entitled *De Sabbato*, in the so-called *Excerptiones Ps-Egberti*, c. 36:

> Deus creator omnium creavit hominem in sexta feria, et in sabbato requievit ab operibus suis, et sanctificavit sabbatum propter futuram significationem passionis Christi, et quietis in sepulchro. Non ideo requievit quia lassus esset, qui omnia sine labore fecit, cuius omnipotentia non potest lassari; et sic requievit ab operibus suis, ut non alias creaturas quam antea fecerat postea fecisset. Non fecit alias creaturas postea, sed ipsas quas tunc fecit, omni anno usque in finem saeculi facit. Homines creat in animabus et corporibus, et animalia et bestias sine animabus; omnis anima hominis a Deo datur, et ipse renovat creaturas suas, sicut Christus in Evangelio ait: 'Pater meus usque modo operatur, et ego operor' (Jn 5.17). Christus pro nobis passus est in sexta aetate mundi, in sexta feria; et reformavit perditum hominem passione sua et operatis miraculis suis. Requievit in sepulchro per sabbatum, et sanctificavit Dominicam diem resurrectione sua; nam Dominica dies prima dies saeculi est, et dies resurrectionis Christi, et dies Pentecostes, et ideo sancta est, et nos ipsi debemus esse spiritaliter sabbatum sabbatizantes, id est, vacantes ab operibus servitutis, id est, peccatis.

The passage occurs in only one manuscript of this late Anglo-Saxon collection, a manuscript closely associated with Wulfstan, and has no attribution. Although the *Excerptiones* have often been cited as a source for Ælfric, especially the pastoral letters, Cross and Hamer have persuasively argued that the debt is the other way round.[3] The *De sabbato* passage is remarkably close in expression and thought to Ælfric, and as I argued in 1985,[4] it seems likely that it is by Ælfric himself. Some of the ideas can be found in earlier writings, especially Augustine and Bede. For the explanation of God resting and the contrast between Gen 1.2–3 and Jn 5.17 cf esp. Augustine's *Tract.*, 17.14.7–12:

> Deus requievit in die septimo. Non enim defecerat Deus operando creaturam suam, et indigebat requie sicut homo. Quomodo defecerat qui verbo fecerat? Tamen et illud verum est, quia requievit Deus ab operibus suis in die septimo; et hoc verum est quod ait Iesus, Pater meus usque modo operatur.

and Bede, *Comm. Gen.*:

> [1.1023–7] 'Et requievit die septimo ab universo opere suo quod patrarat.' Non quasi lassus ex nimio labore Deus instar humanae fragilitatis completa mundi fabrica requievit; sed requievisse ab universo opere suo dicitur, quia novam creaturam ultra instituere aliquam cessavit. . . . [1.1080–4] Id est, completo mundi ornatu, cessaverat ab instituendis

[3] J. E. Cross and A. Hamer, 'Ælfric's *Letters* and the *Excerptiones Ecgberhti*', in *Alfred the Wise*, ed. Jane Roberts and Janet Nelson with Malcolm Godden (Cambridge, 1997), pp. 5–13.

[4] Godden 1985a, p. 283.

> ultra novis rerum generibus. Neque huic sententiae contrarium debet illud estimari, quod in evangelio dicit: 'Ipse Pater meus usque modo operatur, et ego operor.'

The contrast between the two texts also furnishes the first question and answer in Alcuin's *Interrogationes et Responsiones*. But whereas Augustine, Bede and Alcuin all reconcile the two by explaining that God ceased to create new kinds of creature but continued to govern and administer creation, Ælfric (and the *Excerptiones*) explains God's continuing work as the daily task of multiplying fresh examples of each species, including man. (There is a faint hint of this idea in Haymo's adaptation of Bede or Augustine; Haymo, Hom. 33, PL 118, 221:

> Neque enim advertentes quia Conditor in die septima, non ab opere mundanae gubernationis et animae, imo quotidianarum creaturarum substitutione, sed a nova creaturarum institutione cessavit. Quod vero dicitur requievit Deus die septimo ab omnibus operibus suis, ita intelligendum est cessasse Deum a novarum conditione creaturarum.)

This idea leads Ælfric into the issue of predestination and one of his favourite topics, the origin of the soul,[5] since his strong belief in the creationist theory requires him to see God as continuing to create new souls in the present, and to reject the belief that all souls were created at the beginning of time. Underlying the reference to God continuing to create animals and plants (lines 296–9) may be the important distinction he draws so frequently elsewhere, that humans have souls but the others do not.

Lines 300–311 briefly and elegantly outline the significance of the sabbath, interweaving the typological, anagogical and tropological senses: referring, that is, to Christ's own rest in the tomb (lines 300–1, 304–7), to the future rest of all good Christians in heaven (lines 308–10), and to the present abstention from sinful works (lines 304–5, 310–11). All three senses are touched on by Augustine in *De Genesi ad Litteram*, c. 13 (CSEL 28.1), though not in wording at all close to Ælfric. The tropological and anagogical senses are also in Bede's *Comm. Gen.*, 1.1062–75:

> Per requiem diei septimi, quae post opera sex dierum semper celebrari solebat, praefigurabatur magnus ille dies sabbati, in quo Dominus semel in sepulchro erat requieturus, completis ac perfectis in die sexto omnibus operibus suis. . . . Sed et haec sanctificatio ac benedictio septimi diei, et requies in illa Dei post opera sua valde bona designavit quod nos singuli post opera bona quae in nobis ipse operatur et velle et perficere, ad requiem tendimus vitae celestis, in qua aeterna eius sanctificatione et benedictione perfruamur.

The tropological reference to abstention from sin is developed more fully in Augustine's Tractates on John (44.9), which is the source for Irvine 3 and

[5] See Godden 1985a, pp. 283–5.

(perhaps indirectly) Pope 2; both works focus mainly on this sense (cf Irvine, p. 54).

312–6 The formulation of the fourth commandment probably draws on Mt 15.3–4: *Deus dixit: honora patrem et matrem, et qui maledixerit patri vel matri morte moriatur*, which combines Exod 20.12 and 21.17. For the interpretation of this as angering or cursing, cf CH II.2.196 ff and II.19.186–91. For the comments cf Isidore, *In Exodum*, c. 29.9, *Quaestiones*, PL 83, 302C:

> Iubetur ergo in hoc praecepto filiis honorare parentes, neque contumeliosos illis existere, sed officio pietatis reverentiam debitam praestare. Nam qui parentibus honorem deferre non novit, quibus parcere poterit, aut quomodo alios diligere poterit, qui suos odit?

But Isidore does not mention the allegorical interpretation at 316–7.

317–20 Ælfric seems to follow Isidore in distinguishing between non-marital and extra-marital sexual relations (*In Exodum*, c. 29.11, *Quaestiones*, PL 83, 302D-3A):

> Sextum: Non moechaberis, id est, ne quisquam praeter matrimonii foedus aliid feminis misceatur ad explendam libidinem. Nam specialiter adulterium facit qui praeter suam coniugem ad alteram accedit.

Both seem to understand this as a male sin.

320–5 Isidore, *In Exodum*, c. 29.10, *Quaestiones*, PL 83, 302CD:

> Quintum: Non occides. Etenim non solum opere perpetrans homicidium facit, sed etiam et qui incurrit in eum esurientem, vel nudum, qui mori possit, nisi indumentum cibumque porrigendo subveniat, et idem homicida tenebitur.

But Ælfric adds as further examples of homicide causing death by false accusation (*forsegð*) and destroying someone's soul. On the latter cf CH II.13.63–5.

325–6 Isidore is similarly brief (*In Exodum*, c. 29.12, *Quaestiones*, PL 83, 303A): *Septimum: Non furtum facies, quod est vitium rapacitatis.*

326–8 Isidore, *In Exodum*, c. 29.13, *Quaestiones*, PL 83, 303A: *Octavum: Non falsum testimonium dices, quod est crimen mendacii et falsitatis.*

328–31 Isidore briefly distinguishes this from his sixth commandment (*In Exodum*, c. 29.14, *Quaestiones*, PL 83, 303A):

> Nonum: Non concupisces uxorem proximi tui. In hoc praecepto vetat intentionem adulterinae cogitationis. Nam aliud est facere aliquid tale praeter uxorem, aliud non appetere alienam uxorem. Ideo duo praecepta sunt, Non moechaberis, et, Non concupisces uxorem proximi tui.

Ælfric's language perhaps implies that the distinction is not so much between act and desire but between the fornication of a married man with another woman (the sixth commandment) and the fornication of a man with a married woman (the ninth).

331–3 Cf Isidore, *In Exodum*, c. 29.15, *Quaestiones*, PL 83, 303AB:

> Decimum: Non concupisces rem proximi tui. In quo praecepto damnat ambitionem saeculi, et refrenat concupiscentiam rerum.

334–7 Isidore, *In Exodum*, c. 29.16, *Quaestiones*, PL 83, 303BC:

> Et notandum quia sicut decem plagis percutiuntur Aegyptii, sic decem praeceptis conscribuntur tabulae, quibus regantur populi Dei.

Isidore offers a final comment that only the third commandment is to be understood figuratively, the rest are all literal (*In Exodum*, c. 29.16).

337–43 Cf Isidore, *In Exodum*, c. 50.1, *Quaestiones*, PL 83, 313B: *Tabernaculum hoc per allegoriam ecclesia est in huius vitae eremo constituta* and *In Exodum*, c. 44.1, *Quaestiones*, PL 83, 310AB:

> Per hanc arcam . . . ecclesia Christi significatur, aedificata ex omnibus sanctis. . . . Intus autem ac foris inauratur arca; sic et ecclesia, quasi aurum radiare debet, tam interius vitae splendore quam exterius doctrinae et sapientiae claritate.

Ælfric returned to this subject later in his Preface to Genesis.

344–56 Cf Isidore, *In Leviticum*, c. 1.1–2, *Quaestiones*, PL 83, 321B:

> Sequens Leviticus liber hostiarum diversitates exsequitur, quarum typus imaginem passionis Christi praeferebat. Nam postquam ipse oblatus est, omnes illae hostiae cessaverunt. . . . Ipse enim in vitulo propter virtutem crucis offerebatur; ipse in agno propter innocentiam, in ariete propter principatum, in hirco propter similitudinem carnis peccati, ut de peccato damnaret peccatum; idem in turture et columba propter Deum et hominem, quia mediator Dei et hominum in duarum substantiarum coniunctione ostendebatur.

357–66 Isidore, *In Leviticum*, c. 1.3, *Quaestiones*, PL 83, 321CD:

> Nos autem moraliter munus Deo offerimus vitulum, cum carnis superbiam vincimus; agnum, cum irrationabiles motus et insipientes corrigimus; haedum, dum lasciviam superamus; columbam, dum simplicitatem mentis retinemus; turturem, dum carnis servamus castitatem; panes azymos, dum 'non in fermento malitiae, sed in azymis sinceritatis et veritatis ambulamus' (1 Cor 5.8).

366–73 Isidore, *In Leviticum*, cc. 3–5, *Quaestiones*, PL 83, 322C-3A:

> Quod autem mel in Dei sacrificio non offertur, indicat apud Deum nihil voluptuosum, nihil suave huius mundi placere. . . . E contrario admisceri in omnibus sacrificiis sal iubetur, scilicet, ut omnia quae in Christi honorem offerimus, sal rationis ac discretionis semper accipiant. . . . Quod vero in sacrificio oleum offerebatur, significat ut quidquid ad cultum

> Christi et devotionem sanctorum impendimus, totum hilariter faciamus. . . . 'Hilarem enim datorem diligit Deus' (2 Cor 9.7).

375–81 Summarises the death of Moses (Deut 34.5–8), and of Aaron and the succession of his son Eleazar (Num 20.22–30), the succession of Joshua (Num 27.12–23) and God's promise to Joshua (Jos 1.1–9, 17).

386–9 Crossing the Jordan: from Joshua 3–4.

389–97 The fall of Jericho is from Joshua 6. But although the figure seven occurs repeatedly, it is nowhere said that the city had seven walls.

398–413 Draws on Jos 10–13. The stones falling from heaven and the sun standing still are at Jos 10.11–13. The list of thirty-two defeated kings is at Jos 12 and the division of the land at Jos 13. For the seven defeated nations see below under 477 ff.

416–24 Cf Isidore, *In Iosue*, c. 1.2, *Quaestiones*, PL 83, 371A, but it is not close:

> Defunctus est ergo Moyses, defuncta est lex, legalia praecepta iam cessant, et obtinet Iesus, id est Salvator Christus Filius Dei, principatum: introducit populum in terram de qua dicit Dominus: 'Beati mites, quoniam ipsi possidebunt terram' (Mt 5.4).

425–38 Isidore has a slightly similar passage, identifying Jericho as the world because its name means moon and the Hebrews went round it seven times, and interpreting its fall as the end of the world's pride and faithlessness (*In Iosue*, c. 7.1, *Quaestiones*, PL 83, 374ABC):

> Circumdatur post haec Iericho, expugnaturque, adversus quam gladius non educitur, aries non dirigitur, nec tela vibrantur. Tubae solummodo sacerdotales septem diebus continuis adhibentur, sicque circumacta arca, muri Iericho subruuntur. Iericho autem per interpretationem luna dicitur. . . . Hanc ergo urbem Iericho diebus septem ferentes arcam Israelitae aeneis tubis clangentibus circumeunt, et muri eius per arcae praesentiam atque ad aerearum tubarum sonitum cadunt, quia in hoc tempore, quod septem dierum vicissitudine volvitur, dum fertur arca, id est, dum orbem terrarum circumiens movetur ecclesia ad praedicantium voces, quasi ad tubarum sonitum muri Iericho, id est, elatio mundi, ac superba infidelitatis obstacula corruunt, donec in fine temporum mors novissima inimica destruatur.

439–76 Isidore has no equivalent to this excursus in which Ælfric emphasises the gulf between the old law which justified, even celebrated, the killing of enemies, and the new law of love and peace. It bears some resemblance to the discussion, in a similar context, at the end of his later piece on the Macchabees (LS 25), though there Ælfric is careful to qualify his argument by adding a passage on the just war which justifies Christian warfare, and another that distinguishes between the monks and the *bellatores* (LS 25.684–714 and 812–32). The irruptions of the Vikings perhaps made a difference. Lines 443–51 are from Mt 5.43–6:

> (43) Audistis quia dictum est diliges proximum tuum et odio habebis inimicum tuum. (44) Ego autem dico vobis diligite inimicos vestros, benefacite his qui oderunt vos et orate pro persequentibus et calumniantibus vos, (45) ut sitis filii Patris vestri qui in caelis est qui solem suum oriri facit super bonos et malos et pluit super iustos et iniustos. (46) Si enim diligatis eos qui vos diligunt, quam mercedem habebitis?

Lines 455–7 cite Mt 5.20:

> Dico enim vobis quia nisi abundaverit iustitia vestra plus quam scribarum et Pharisaeorum non intrabitis in regnum caelorum.

Lines 466–73 are from Eph 6:

> (11) Induite vos armaturam Dei, ut possitis stare adversus insidias diaboli; (12) Quia non est nobis conluctatio adversus carnem et sanguinem sed adversus principes et potestates, adversus mundi rectores tenebrarum harum, contra spiritalia nequitiae in caelestibus. . . . (14) State ergo succincti lumbos vestros in veritate et induti loricam iustitiae . . . (16) in omnibus sumentes scutum fidei . . . (17) et galeam salutis adsumite et gladium Spiritus quod est verbum Dei.

477–92 The identification of Joshua's opponents with the eight chief sins is not suggested by Isidore. Ælfric seems to be following Cassian, *Conlationes*, V.16–19. The number of seven defeated nations is probably derived from Deut 7.1, cited by Cassian, *Conlationes*, V.16 (141.2–9):

> Cum introduxerit te dominus deus tuus in terram quam possessurus ingrederis, et deleverit gentes multas coram te, Chettaeum et Gergesaeum et Amorraeum, Chananaeum et Ferezaeum et Evaeum et Iebusaeum, septem gentes multo maioris numeri quam tu es, et robustiores te, tradideritque eas dominus tibi, percuties eas usque ad internicionem.

The addition of the Egyptians to make eight follows Cassian, cc. 17–19. But Cassian has a more detailed argument applying specifically to monks: just as, according to Deuteronomy, the Hebrews were liberated from the Egyptians and went on to confront seven further nations, so the monk, having been liberated from gluttony, confronts seven further vices; and just as the Egyptians were left behind but not said to have been destroyed like the other seven, so the monk must destroy the other seven vices in himself but cannot expect to destroy the physical needs underlying gluttony. Ælfric, on the other hand, implies by his wording that the Egyptians stand for pride, the eighth sin in his list, and has no suggestion of a distinction in their fates. Cassian's list of the sins is as follows (*Conlationes*, V.2, 121.11–16):

> Octo sunt principalia vitia, quae humanum infestant genus, id est, primum gastrimargia, quod sonat ventris ingluvies; secundum fornicatio; tertium filargyria, id est, avaritia sive amor pecuniae; quartum ira;

quintum tristitia; sextum acedia, id est, anxietas, seu taedium cordis; septimum cenodoxia, id est, iactantia, seu vana gloria; octavum superbia.

Ælfric follows this order, but for his analysis mainly follows Alcuin's *De Virtutibus et Vitiis* (PL 101, 632–7), which has a different order, beginning with *superbia*, then *gula*, *fornicatio, avaritia, ira, acedia, tristitia*, and *cenodoxia* or *vana gloria*. The significance of the identifications, and particularly their order, has been discussed by Clemoes (1959, pp. 225–6), and Pope (pp. 284–5).[6] Another list, also rendered into Old English, is given in the *Capitula* of Theodulf of Orleans (Sauer, c. 31): *gastrimargia, fornicatio, accidia siue tristitia, avaritia, vana gloria, invidia, ira, superbia*. For the explanation at 488–91, cf Cassian, *Conlationes*, V.16 (141.11–16):

> Et ideo in catalogo quidem dinumerantur septem nationes, in expugnatione vero earum sine numeri adscriptione ponuntur. Ita enim dicitur: 'Et deleverit gentes multas coram te.' Numerosior enim est quam Israhel, carnalium passionum populus, qui de hoc septenario fomite vitiorum ac radice procedit.

and *Conlationes*, V.16 (142.14–18):

> Quae cum sint multo maioris numeri quam virtutes, devictis tamen illis octo principalibus vitiis, ex quorum natura eas certum est emanare, omnes protinus conquiescunt, ac perpetua pariter cum his internicione delentur.

For the military imagery at 479–81, cf Alcuin, *De Virtutibus*, c. 34, PL 101, 636D:

> Hi sunt octo totius impietatis duces cum exercitibus suis, et fortissimi contra humanum genus diabolicae fraudis bellatores.

493–500 *gifernys* = *gula* or *gastrimargia*. Alcuin, *De Virtutibus*, c. 28, PL 101, 633CD:

> Primum est corporale peccatum gula, id est, intemperans cibi vel potus voluptas, per quam primi parentes humani generis paradisi felicitatem perdiderunt. . . . Quae tribus modis regnare videtur in homine; id est, dum homo horam canonicam et statutam gulae causa anticipare cupit, aut exquisitiores cibos sibi praeparare iubet, quam necessitas corporis, vel suae qualitas personae exigat, vel si plus accipiet in edendo vel bibendo propter desiderium intemperantiae suae, quam suae proficiat saluti. De qua gula nascitur inepta laetitia, scurrilitas, levitas, vaniloquium, immunditia corporis, instabilitas mentis, ebrietas, libido.

500–505 *forliger oððe galnyss* = *fornicatio*. Based on Alcuin, *De Virtutibus*, c. 29, PL 101, 633D-4A:

> Fornicatio est omnis corporalis immunditia, quae solet fieri ex incontinentia libidinis, et mollitia animae, quae consentit suae carni peccare. . . . De qua [fornicatione] nascitur caecitas mentis, inconstantia oculorum vel totius corporis amor immoderatus; saepe periculum vitae, lascivia, ioca,

[6] Cf too M. Bloomfield, *The Seven Deadly Sins* (Michigan, 1952), pp. 112 ff.

petulantia, et omnis incontinentia; odium mandatorum Dei, mentis enervatio, et iniustae cupiditates.

505–10 *gitsung* = *avaritia*. Alcuin, *De Virtutibus*, c. 30, PL 101, 634B:

Avaritia est nimia divitiarum acquirendi, habendi, vel tenendi cupiditas, quae pestis inexplebilis est. Sicut hydropicus, qui quanto plus bibit, tanto plus illi sitis accrescit: sic avaritia quanto magis habet, tanto plus [habere] desiderat. . . . Cuius genera [*var.* germina] sunt invidia, furta, latrocinia, homicidia, mendacia, periuria, rapinae, violentiae, inquietudo, iniusta iudicia. . . .

510–13 *weamet* = *ira*. Alcuin, *De Virtutibus*, c. 31, PL 101, 634CD:

Ira una est de octo vitiis principalibus, quae si ratione non regitur, in furorem vertitur: ita ut homo sui animi impotens erit, faciens quae non convenit. Haec enim si cordi insidit, omnem eximit ab eo providentiam facti, . . . sed omnia per praecipitium quoddam facere videtur. De qua, id est ira, pullulat tumor mentis, rixae et contumeliae, clamor, indignatio, praesumptio, blasphemiae, sanguinis effusio, homicidia, ulciscendi cupiditas, iniuriarum memoria.

514–9 *unrotnys* = *tristitia*. Cf Alcuin, *De Virtutibus*, c. 33 (PL 101, 635BC):

Tristitiae duo sunt genera: unum salutiferum, alterum pestiferum. Tristitia salutaris est, quando de peccatis suis animus contristatur peccatoris, et ita contristatur, ut confessionem et poenitentiam agere quaerat, et converti se ad Deum desideret. Alia est tristitia huius saeculi . . . quae animum perturbat, et saepe in desperationem mittit. . . . Ex ipsa nascitur malitia, rancor, animi pusillanimitas, amaritudo, desperatio.

But Ælfric's definition of *unrotnys* as grief (or resentment?) directed against God because of misfortunes in the world is not from Alcuin. For Ælfric's *unrotnys ðissere worulde* cf the A version of the *Capitula* of Theodulf (Sauer, p. 357), *worulde unrotnes*.

519–24 *asolcennys* or *æmelnys* = *acedia* or *anxietas* or *tedium cordis*. Cf Alcuin, *De Virtutibus*, c. 32, PL 101, 635AB (but not close):

Acedia est pestis, quae Deo famulantibus multum nocere probatur, dum otiosus homo torpescit in desideriis carnalibus, nec in opere gaudet spirituali. . . . De qua nascitur somnolentia, pigritia operis boni, instabilitas loci, pervagatio de loco in locum, tepiditas laborandi, taedium cordis, murmuratio et inaniloquia.

The vices of *gemagnys* (persistence, importunity), *wordlung* (talkativeness?), *worung* (restlessness, wandering) and *fyrwitnys* (curiosity) seem odd as manifestations of sloth, but Ælfric, and no doubt Alcuin too, was presumably thinking of the failings shown by monks with an inadequate commitment to their vocation; cf especially the vices shown by reluctant monks at CH II.11.362–92.

524–31 *idel wuldor* = *cenodoxia* or *vana gloria*. Perhaps based on Alcuin, *De Virtutibus*, c. 34 PL 101, 635D-6A, but expanded:

Vana gloria est, dum homo appetit in bonis suis laudari, . . . Ex cuius vitii radice multi malitiae germinare videntur ramusculi: inde iactantia, arrogantia, indignatio, discordia, inanis gloriae cupido, et hypocrisis.

531–41 *modignys = superbia*. Alcuin, *De Virtutibus*, c. 27, PL 101, 633AB:

Primum vitium est spirituale, superbia, de qua dicitur: 'Initium omnis peccati superbia' (Sir 10.15), quae regina est omnium malorum, per quam angeli ceciderunt de coelo, quae fit ex contemptu mandatorum Dei. . . . Ex ipsa vero nascitur omnis inobedientia, et omnis praesumptio, et omnis pertinacia, contentiones, haereses, arrogantia.

Ælfric's list of progeny perhaps owes something to Cassian (*Conlationes*, V.16, 143.3–4): *De superbia, contemptus, invidia, inobedientia, blasphemia, murmuratio, detractatio*. His description of pride as *ord and ende* of the list, and justification for its final placing, perhaps reflects his awareness of Alcuin's list in which pride is placed first.

548–59 Alcuin, *De Virtutibus*, c. 34, PL 101, 637A:

Isti vero bellatores Deo auxiliante facillime vincuntur a bellatoribus Christi per virtutes sanctas. Prima superbia per humilitatem, gula per abstinentiam, fornicatio per castitatem, avaritia per abstinentiam [*var.* largitatem et contemptum mundi], ira per patientiam, acedia per instantiam boni operis, tristitia mala per laetitiam spiritualem, vana gloria per charitatem Dei vincitur.

For the expansion of *castitatem* at 550–2, cf CH II.6.115–57.

560–5 The narrative detail is from the account of the Gibeonites at Joshua 9, esp. 9.22–3, but Ælfric's commentary bears no resemblance to Isidore's comments on that episode (*In Iosue*, c. 11) and a fair amount of resemblance instead to Isidore's comments on the Hebrews' making some of the Canaanites tributaries at Judges 1 (*In Iosue*, c. 18.1–2, *Quaestiones*, PL 83, 379B-8A):

Illud autem, quod cum Israelitico populo percepta repromissionis terra partiretur, Ephraim tamen tribui Chananaeus gentilis populus non occisus, sed factus tributarius dicitur. . . . Qui tamen tributarius efficitur, quia hoc ipsum vitium quod subiugare non possumus, ad usum nostrae utilitatis humiliter retorquemus.

565–71 Isidore, *In Iosue*, c. 12.2, *Quaestiones*, PL 83, 377B:

Iesus igitur noster solem stare fecit, non tunc solum, sed multo magis modo in adventu suo, dum nos bellum gerimus adversus vitiorum gentes. . . . Sol nobis iustitiae indesinenter assistit, nec deserit unquam nos, nec festinat occumbere, quia ipse dixit: 'Ecce ego vobiscum sum omnibus diebus usque ad consummationem saeculi' (Mt 28.20).

571–9 Isidore, *In Iosue*, c. 15.1, *Quaestiones*, PL 83, 378C:

Cur vero Levitae non acceperunt haereditatem terrae? Utique quia Dominus noster Iesus Christus ipse est haereditas eorum, sicut scriptum est: 'Ego haereditas eorum, et possessio non dabitur eis in Israel' (cf Num. 18.20). Ego enim sum possessio eorum. Clericorum enim haereditas et possessio ob hoc se dici voluit Deus, quia ministri altaris ipsius effecti sunt.

580–2 Cf the curiously similar peroration on the miracles of Benedict at CH II.11.585.

13 FIFTH SUNDAY IN LENT (PASSION SUNDAY)

This is the only Sunday in Lent not already covered in CH I. The homily is primarily an exposition of the long Gospel passage for the day, John 8.46–59, on Christ's arguments with the Jews about his divinity and his relation to God the Father; but Ælfric introduces at the end, in recognition of the approaching time of the passion, a short passage from John 3 together with the text from Numbers to which it alludes, on the brazen serpent erected by Moses in the desert. The text from John was a reading for the Easter period (as well as for the Sunday after Pentecost), and Ælfric evidently chose it for its typological reference to the contemplation of the crucified Christ and the healing properties of Christ's death. But the story of the brazen serpent from Numbers was clearly a text that meant much to him: he was to introduce and discuss it again in the homily *De Populo Israhel* (Pope 20.304–52), and again more briefly at Pope 12.227–38. Both the Gospel texts discussed here are relatively challenging to exposition and understanding, and Ælfric seems in his opening remarks to have the monks and clergy as much in mind as the laity.

Ælfric cites Augustine and Gregory as his sources at the outset, and the exposition of the Gospel text does indeed show close parallels with the relevant portion of Augustine's Tractates on John (42 and 43) and Gregory's homily 18 on the Gospel text (which appears in Paul the Deacon's homiliary for the occasion).[1] As Förster says, Ælfric interweaves phrases from both, often within the same sentence.[2] He seems also to have consulted Haymo's homily for the occasion (line 56), itself drawing heavily on Augustine and Gregory, and probably also a homily on the same text by Hericus, which appears in the PL 95 version of PD for the first Thursday in Lent; Smaragdus reproduces much of Gregory's material but does not seem to have been used. For the brief exposition of John 3.14–15, and the associated text from Numbers, he used Augustine's Tractates again and Haymo's homily 108 for the Sunday after Pentecost (which seems closer for the relevant passage than Bede's Hom II.18 which Förster cited). Ælfric uses the source material very freely, especially Augustine, and the parallels are seldom very close.

[1] So Smetana (1959, p. 197); but his statement that Tractates 42 and 43 are also in PD is, I think, a confusion with Tractate 12 used later.

[2] Förster 1894, pp. 14–15.

Sources and Notes

The following texts are cited below:

1. Amalarius, *Liber Officialis*, ed. J. Hanssens in *Amalarii Episcopi Opera Liturgica Omnia*, Studi e Testi 139 (Vatican City, 1948).
2. Augustine, *In Iohannis Evangelium Tractatus CXXIV*, ed. R. Willems, CCSL 36 (Turnhout, 1954).
3. Gregory the Great, *Homiliae in Evangelia*, PL 76, Hom. 18, cols. 1149–53.
4. Haymo of Auxerre, *Homiliae de Tempore*, PL 118, Hom. 56 and 108, cols. 327–36 and 578–84.
5. Hericus, *Homiliae in Circulum Anni*, ed. R. Quadri, CCCM 116 (Turnhout, 1992), Hom. I.32 (pp. 270–81).

1–10 Cf Amalarius, *Liber officialis*, IV.20.1–2, 5:

> Dies passionis Domini computantur duabus ebdomadibus ante pascha Domini. Neque enim ab re est, quod in duabus ebdomadibus recolitur eius passio. . . . In illis diebus amittimus per undecim dies in solis responsoriis gloriam sanctae trinitatis, quoniam per humilitatem veniendum est ad passionem Christi. . . . Ab illo die quando amittimus Gloria Patri, duae ebdomadae sunt, hoc est, quattuordecim dies usque in pascha Domini.

Ælfric is evidently describing the private offices of monks and clerics, perhaps for the instruction of the clerics.

13–41 Jn 8.46–59:

> (46) Quis ex vobis arguit me de peccato? si veritatem dico quare vos non creditis mihi? (47) Qui est ex Deo verba Dei audit; propterea vos non auditis quia ex Deo non estis. (48) Responderunt igitur Iudaei et dixerunt ei: nonne bene dicimus nos quia Samaritanus es tu et daemonium habes. (49) Respondit Iesus: ego daemonium non habeo sed honorifico Patrem meum et vos inhonoratis me. (50) Ego autem non quaero gloriam meam; est qui quaerit et iudicat. (51) Amen amen dico vobis si quis sermonem meum servaverit mortem non videbit in aeternum. (52) Dixerunt ergo Iudaei: nunc cognovimus quia daemonium habes. Abraham mortuus est et prophetae et tu dicis si quis sermonem meum servaverit non gustabit mortem in aeternum. (53) Numquid tu maior es patre nostro Abraham qui mortuus est et prophetae mortui sunt; quem te ipsum facis? (54) Respondit Iesus: si ego glorifico me ipsum gloria mea nihil est; est Pater meus qui glorificat me quem vos dicitis quia Deus noster est (55) et non cognovistis eum. Ego autem novi eum et si dixero quia non scio eum ero similis vobis mendax; sed scio eum et sermonem eius servo. (56) Abraham pater vester exultavit ut videret diem meum et vidit et gavisus est. (57) Dixerunt ergo Iudaei ad eum: quinquaginta annos nondum habes et Abraham vidisti? (58) Dixit eis Iesus: amen amen dico vobis antequam

Abraham fieret ego sum. (59) Tulerunt ergo lapides ut iacerent in eum. Iesus autem abscondit se et exivit de templo.

43–8 Gregory, Hom. 18, PL 76, 1150B:

Pensate, fratres charissimi, mansuetudinem Dei. Relaxare peccata venerat, et dicebat: 'Quis ex vobis arguet me de peccato?' Non dedignatur ex ratione ostendere se peccatorem non esse, qui ex virtute divinitatis poterat peccatores iustificare.

50–9 Augustine, *Tract.*, 42.15.11–14, 37:

Et ex Deo sunt, et ex Deo non sunt; natura ex Deo sunt, vitio non sunt ex Deo: natura enim bona quae ex Deo est, peccavit voluntate, credendo quod diabolus persuasit, et vitiata est. . . . imitando diabolum, filii diaboli facti erant.

Ælfric elucidates by quoting Jn 8.44 (and paraphrasing v.45):

(44) Vos ex patre diabolo estis, et desideria patris vestri vultis facere. Ille homicida erat ab initio, et in veritate non stetit, quia non est veritas in eo. Cum loquitur mendacium, ex propriis loquitur, quia mendax est, et pater eius. (45) Ego autem quia veritatem dico non creditis mihi.

59–65 Augustine, *Tract.*, 42 [commenting on Jn 8.44]:

[12.5–6] 'Ille homicida erat ab initio,' verum est; nam primum hominem occidit. [11.5–6] Ecce quod est: 'desideria patris vestri facere vultis; Quaeritis me occidere . . .'. . . . [11.14–18] Homicidia dicitur diabolus, non gladio armatus, non ferro accinctus . . . Noli ergo putare te non esse homicidam, quando fratri tuo mala persuades: si fratri tuo mala persuades, occidis.

But cf Hericus, Hom. I.32, 225–9:

Diabolus contra primum hominem non ferro accinctus sed letifera persuasione armatus venit, nec eum gladio sed verbo necavit; omnis ergo qui alicui homini mala persuadet, dum illum ad peccatum pertrahit occidit.

66–74 Cf Augustine, *Tract.*, 42.10.12–14, 24–5:

Bona est enim omnis natura; sed vitiata est hominis natura per voluntatem malam. . . . Unde ergo Iudaei filii diaboli? Imitando, non nascendo.

and Haymo, Hom. 56, PL 118, 328C:

Ergo per propaginem carnis filii erant Abrahae, sed per imitationem humilitatis et fidei, non erant filii Abrahae. Sic ergo, ut dictum est, natura ex Deo erant, sed vitio ex Deo non erant.

and Hericus, Hom I.32, 204–6:

Unde sequitur: Vos ex patre diabolo estis. Filios diaboli dicit Iudaeos, non nascendo sed imitando; nam consuetudo est sacrae scripturae ex imitatione vel similitudine filios appellare.

74–80 Jn 8.34: *Respondit eis Iesus: amen amen dico vobis, quia omnis qui facit peccatum servus est peccati.* Not quoted or discussed by the main sources here;

perhaps influenced by Augustine's comments, at *Tract.*, 41.4.6–18: *O miserabilis servitus! . . . Mala servitus!*

81–94 Ælfric seems to be drawing on Haymo, Hom. 56, PL 118, 328AB:

> In his verbis unusquisque suam conscientiam probare potest, utrum ex Deo sit an non. Qui enim verbum Dei libenter audit, et libentius opere complet, nullo modo se ex Deo esse dubitet. . . . Qui vero vecors et durus verbum Dei audire contemnit, vel si cum aure corporis audierit, illud nullo studio vel labore in opere mittere conatur, profecto se ex Deo non esse manifestat; quales erant isti, quibus a Domino dicitur: 'Propterea vos non auditis, quia ex Deo non estis.'

and Haymo's source, Gregory, Hom. 18, PL 76, 1150BC:

> Si enim ipse verba Dei audit qui ex Deo est, et audire verba eius non potest quisquis ex illo non est, interroget se unusquisque si verba Dei in aure cordis percipit, et intelliget unde sit. Coelestem patriam desiderare Veritas iubet, carnis desideria conteri, mundi gloriam declinare, aliena non appetere, propria largiri. Penset ergo apud se unusquisque vestrum si haec vox Dei in cordis eius aure convaluit, et quia iam ex Deo sit agnoscit. Nam sunt nonnulli qui praecepta Dei nec aure corporis percipere dignantur. Et sunt nonnulli qui haec quidem corporis aure percipiunt, sed nullo ea mentis desiderio complectuntur. Et sunt nonnulli qui libenter verba Dei suscipiunt, ita ut etiam in fletibus compungantur, sed post lacrymarum tempus ad iniquitatem redeunt. Hi profecto verba Dei non audiunt, qui haec exercere opere contemnunt.

For the passages added in MS F by another hand, drawn from the same passage of Gregory, see *CH II*, p. 357.

96–9 Haymo, Hom. 56, PL 118, 329C:

> Tanta igitur discordia inter Iudaeos et praedictos Samaritanos excrevit . . . quemcunque autem Iudaei improperio lacessere volebant, illum Samaritanum vocabant.

99–107 Augustine, *Tract.*, 43.2.3–13:

> Horum duorum sibi obiectorum unum negavit, alterum non negavit. 'Respondit enim, et ait: Ego daemonium non habeo.' Non dixit, Samaritanus non sum: . . . Samaritanus enim interpretatur custos. Noverat se ille nostrum esse custodem. 'Non enim dormit neque dormitat qui custodit Israel' (Ps 120.4): et, 'Nisi Dominus custodierit civitatem, in vanum vigilabunt qui custodiunt' (Ps 126.1). Est ergo ille custos noster, qui creator noster.

107–17 Gregory, Hom. 18, PL 76, 1151AB:

> Duo quippe ei illata fuerunt: unum negavit, aliud tacendo consensit. . . . Sed tacuit quod recognovit, et patienter repulit quod dictum fallaciter audivit, dicens: 'Ego daemonium non habeo.' . . . Qui si eisdem ista

dicentibus respondere voluisset: Daemonium vos habetis, verum profecto diceret, quia nisi impleti essent daemonio, tam perversa de Deo loqui non possent. Sed accepta iniuria etiam quod verum erat dicere Veritas noluit, ne non dixisse veritatem, sed provocatus contumeliam reddidisse videretur. Ex qua re quid nobis innuitur, nisi ut eo tempore quo a proximis ex falsitate contumelias accipimus, eorum etiam vera mala taceamus, ne ministerium iustae correptionis in arma vertamus furoris? Sed quia quisquis Dei zelo utitur a pravis hominibus dehonestatur, in semetipso nobis Dominus patientiae praebuit exemplum.

118–22 Augustine, *Tract.*, 43.3.3–6:

Hoc est: Ego me non honorifico, ne vobis arrogans videar, . . . sed si vos me agnosceretis . . . vos honorificaretis me.

123–36 Augustine, *Tract.*, 43.9.25–39:

Non enim quia homo factus est, iam comparandus est nobis. Nos homines cum peccato, ille sine peccato; . . . nos nec quia volumus nati sumus, nec quamdiu volumus vivimus, nec quomodo volumus morimur; ille antequam nasceretur elegit de qua nasceretur, . . . et miraculis se Deum ostendebat. . . . Postremo elegit et genus mortis, hoc est, ut in cruce penderet, et . . . in ipsa cruce quando voluit, corpus dimisit, et abscessit; in ipso sepulcro quamdiu voluit, iacuit; quando voluit, tamquam de lecto surrexit.

137–45 cf Augustine, *Tract.*, 43.9.42–10.3:

Secundum ipsam formam servi multum interest inter gloriam Christi, et gloriam hominum ceterorum. De ipsa gloria dicebat, quando quod daemonium haberet audiebat: 'ego non quaero gloriam meam; est qui quaerat et iudicet'. Tu autem de te, Domine, quid dicis? 'Amen, amen dico vobis, si quis sermonem meum servaverit, mortem non videbit in aeternum.'

145–9 Gregory, Hom. 18, PL 76, 1151C:

Cum vero malorum perversitas crescit non solum praedicatio frangi [*var.* minui] non debet, sed etiam augeri. Quod suo Dominus exemplo nos admonet, qui postquam habere daemonium dictus est praedicationis suae beneficia largius impendit.

152–68 Cf Augustine, *Tract.*:

[43.11.6–9] Videbat Dominus aliam mortem, de qua nos liberare venerat, mortem secundam, mortem aeternam . . . Ipsa est vera mors, nam ista migratio est. . . . [43.13.1–6] Isti autem indignantes mortui, et morti sempiternae praedestinati, respondebant conviciose . . . Sed ista morte quam Dominus vult intellegi, nec Abraham mortuus est, nec prophetae. Illi enim mortui sunt, et vivunt; isti vivebant, et mortui erant.

But Ælfric characteristically develops the topic of the after-life of the body and the soul (lines 156–9). In describing the good soul awaiting the general resurrection in glory with the saints, he is perhaps alluding to the place of rest described in Drihthelm's vision, CH II.21.83 ff.

172–4 Augustine, *Tract.*, 43.14.4–9:

Refert enim gloriam suam ad Patrem, de quo est quod Deus est. . . . Si et ille Filium glorificat, et Filius Patrem glorificat.

177–83 Augustine, *Tract.*, 43.15.12–19:

Eum dicit Patrem suum Dominus Christus, quem illi dicebant Deum suum, et non cognoverunt; si enim ipsum cognovissent, eius Filium recepissent. . . . Secundum carnem iudicantibus potuit et hinc arrogans videri, quia dixit: 'ego novi eum'. Sed videte quid sequatur: 'si dixero quia non novi eum, ero similis vobis mendax.' Ergo arrogantia non ita caveatur, ut veritas relinquatur.

185–90 Gregory cites Abraham's meeting with three angels (from Gen 18) in support of Jn 8.56, and Augustine cites the strange oath about Isaac's marriage at Gen 24; Ælfric, like Haymo, uses both. Gregory, Hom. 18, PL 76, 1152A:

Tunc quippe diem Domini Abraham vidit, cum in figura summae Trinitatis tres angelos hospitio suscepit; quibus profecto susceptis, sic tribus quasi uni locutus est, quia etsi in personis numerus Trinitatis est, in natura unitas divinitatis est.

190–204 Cf Augustine, *Tract.*, 43.16.27–46:

Pater Abraham quando misit servum suum, ut peteret uxorem filio suo Isaac . . . Quid vult Deus caeli ad femur Abrahae? Iam intelligitis sacramentum: per femur, genus. Ergo quae fuit illa iuratio, nisi quia significabatur de genere Abrahae venturum in carne Deum caeli? . . . Etenim propheta erat Abraham. . . . Semen suum significavit dicendo: 'Mitte manum sub femore meo'; Dominum suum significavit addendo: 'et iura per Deum caeli'.

But the first part includes wording either from Gen 24.1–4 or from Haymo's adaptation of Augustine (Haymo, Hom. 56, PL 118, 334D–5A):

Legimus enim in Genesi quia, cum esset senex provectaeque aetatis, servum seniorem domus suae vocavit ad se, et ait illi: 'Mitte manum tuam sub femore meo, et iura mihi per Deum coeli, quod non accipias uxorem filio meo de filiabus Chanaan, inter quos habito, sed proficiscaris ad terram et cognationem meam, et inde filio meo Isaac accipias uxorem (Gen 24.1–4).' Quid sibi vult talis adiuratio? Quid Deus coeli ad femur Abrahae pertinet, aut femur Abrahae ad Deum coeli?

205–20 Augustine, Gregory and Haymo have similar arguments. Cf esp. Augustine, *Tract.*, 43.17.5–13:

Intellege, *fieret* ad humanam facturam, *sum* vero ad divinam pertinere substantiam. *Fieret* quia creatura est Abraham. Non dixit: antequam

> Abraham esset, ego eram; sed: 'antequam Abraham fieret', qui nisi per me non fieret, 'ego sum'. . . . agnoscite Creatorem, discernite creaturam.

Gregory and Haymo both cite Exodus and the appropriateness of the present tense to God; cf Gregory, Hom. 18, PL 76, 1152B:

> Ante enim praeteriti temporis est, Sum praesentis. Et quia praeteritum et futurum tempus Divinitas non habet, sed semper esse habet, non ait: Ante Abraham ego fui, sed 'Ante Abraham ego sum.' Unde et ad Moysen dicitur: 'Ego sum qui sum.' Et, 'Dices aliis Israel: Qui est misit me ad vos' (Exod 3.14).

(Cf Haymo, Hom. 56, PL 118, 335D.) But Ælfric's argument that only God truly *is* because creatures derive their being from him is a different point.

221–3 Cf Haymo, Hom. 56, PL 118, 336A:

> 'Tulerunt ergo lapides, ut iacerent in eum.' Recte ad lapides cucurrerunt, qui lapideum cor habebant, quibus bene congruit.

224–8 A combination of Augustine, *Tract.*, 43.18.5–11:

> Iesus autem, tamquam homo . . . tamquam humilis . . . quid magnum erat ut eos continuo dehiscens terra sorberet.

and Gregory, Hom. 18, PL 76, 1152C:

> Mirum valde est, fratres charissimi, cur persecutores suos Dominus se abscondendo declinaverit, qui si divinitatis suae potentiam exercere voluisset, tacito nutu mentis in suis eos ictibus ligaret, aut in poena subitae mortis obrueret. Sed quia pati venerat, exercere iudicium nolebat.

228–36 No very close parallels, but cf Gregory, Hom. 18, PL 76, 1153B:

> Hoc autem quod de Domino scriptum est, Abscondit se, intelligi et aliter potest. . . . Quid abscondendo se Dominus significat, nisi quod eis ipsa veritas absconditur, qui eius verba sequi contemnunt?

Haymo also cites Luke 4.28 (Hom. 56, PL 118):

> [336BC] Legimus enim quia cum ducerent eum usque ad supercilium montis, super quem civitas eorum aedificata erat, ut inde eum praecipitarent, ipse transiens per medium illorum ibat. . . . [336B] Non enim Dominus ante manus persequentium sese abscondit, ut mori timeret, qui pro nobis mori venerat, sed humilitatis gratia, ut congruo tempore congruam mortem susciperet, videlicet crucis.

237–41 None of the sources for the main part have anything corresponding to this concluding section; it is in some respect introduced, elegantly, by the preceding statement that Christ evaded the Jews on this occasion in order to die by the death that he had chosen and that had been prophesied for him. The opening text is Jn 3.14–15:

> (14) Et sicut Moses exaltavit serpentem in deserto, ita exaltari oportet Filium hominis, (15) ut omnis qui credit in ipso non pereat sed habeat vitam aeternam.

241–56 Cf Augustine, *Tract.*, 12.11.7–9, commenting on this text:

Magnum sacramentum, et qui legerunt, noverunt. Deinde audiant vel qui non legerunt, vel qui forte lectum sive auditum obliti sunt.

Ælfric goes on to cite Num 21.6–9:

(6) Quam ob rem misit Dominus in populum ignitos serpentes ad quorum plagas et mortes plurimorum (7) venerunt ad Mosen atque dixerunt; peccavimus quia locuti sumus contra Dominum et te; ora ut tollat a nobis serpentes. Oravit Moses pro populo, (8) et locutus est Dominus ad eum: fac serpentem [aerenum] et pone eum pro signo; qui percussus aspexerit eum vivet. (9) Fecit ergo Moses serpentem aeneum et posuit pro signo; quem cum percussi aspicerent sanabantur.

257–9 Augustine, *Tract.*, 12.11.19–21:

Quid sunt serpentes mordentes? peccata de mortalitate carnis. Quis est serpens exaltatus: mors Domini in cruce.

259–64 Cf Haymo, Hom. 108, PL 118, 583D:

Sicut enim serpens ille similitudinem habebat ignitorum serpentium, sed tamen a veneno serpentium alienus erat: sic Dominus Iesus Christus apparuit in similitudine carnis peccati, nullam tamen maculam traxit peccati.

264–76 Augustine, *Tract.*, 12.11.22–32:

Morsus serpentis lethalis, mors Domini vitalis. Adtenditur serpens, ut nihil valeat serpens. Quid est hoc? Adtenditur mors, ut nihil valeat mors. Sed cuius mors? Mors vitae. . . . Nonne vita Christus? et tamen in cruce Christus. Nonne vita Christus? et tamen mortuus Christus. Sed in morte Christi mors mortua est; quia vita mortua occidit mortem, plenitudo vitae deglutivit mortem; absorpta est mors in Christi corpore.

Ælfric supports the identification of Christ with life by quoting Jn 11.25–6:

(25) Dixit ei Iesus ego sum resurrectio et vita qui credit in me etsi mortuus fuerit vivet. (26) Et omnis qui vivit et credit in me non morietur in aeternum.

277–88 Augustine, *Tract.*, 12.11.34–46:

Interim modo, fratres, ut a peccato sanemur, Christum crucifixum intueamur. . . . Quomodo qui intuebantur illum serpentem, non peribant morsibus serpentum, sic qui intuentur fide mortem Christi, sanantur a morsibus peccatorum. Sed illi sanabantur a morte ad vitam temporalem, hic autem ait: 'ut habeant vitam aeternam'. Hoc enim interest inter figuratam imaginem et rem ipsam; figura praestabat vitam temporalem; res ipsa cuius illa figura erat, praestat vitam aeternam.

288–90 Haymo, Hom. 56, PL 118, 336B:

Dignum namque erat ut, quia primus homo per lignum vetitum ceciderat, per lignum sanctae crucis restauraretur.

14 PALM SUNDAY

The First Series homily for this occasion, I.14, covers the triumphal entry into Jerusalem on Palm Sunday itself. For the Second Series Ælfric gives an account of the last supper and the passion: in Ælfric's view at least preaching was not permitted on the days which actually commemorate these events (Maundy Thursday, Good Friday and Holy Saturday), but the Gospel narratives were appointed to be read on Palm Sunday and the succeeding days. It is striking that so central an event of Christian story had not been covered in the First Series, except for very brief summaries in CH I.1 and I.14, given that the First Series does cover Christ's nativity, the main events of his infancy, his resurrection and ascension; but the sustained use of rhythm and alliteration makes it certain that this is indeed a comparatively late composition. The homily is mainly narrative, but narrative alternates throughout with points of literal explanation or allegorical interpretation. It is for Ælfric a somewhat unusual structure, contrasting with his more common practice of giving the full Gospel narrative first before turning back for interpretation.

For the narrative Ælfric drew extensively on all four Gospels but managed to produce a coherent account of events from the Conspiracy onwards, selecting freely and often combining details from several versions within the same sentence or passage. No doubt considerable thought was involved in choosing a single narrative line, but he does not allude to the differences between the versions or to any principles of selection.[1] Striking perhaps is the absence of the moments which might suggest Christ's own reluctance—the prayer in the garden of Gethsemane, the final cry to God the Father on the cross—and perhaps the emphasis on verses which suggest Christ's full control over events, such as the opening section of prophecy and the verse from John at 45–7. For the interpretative material, identifying precise sources presents a problem. Paul the Deacon's homiliary gives a commentary on the entry into Jerusalem for Palm Sunday and has no homiletic commentary on the passion itself. The ultimate sources for much of Ælfric's exposition are Jerome's commentary on Matthew and Augustine's Tractates on John, but much of their material is incorporated into Bede's commentaries on Mark and Luke and the Ps-Bede commentary on Matthew, and all three fathers are heavily used in the very long homily by Smaragdus for this occasion and the one by Haymo. Ælfric certainly knew the latter two homilists as well as Augustine's Tractates and probably the Bede commentaries. The evidence (outside this particular homily) for his direct knowledge of Jerome's commentary is much slighter, and for the Ps-Bede commentary very slight. Förster thought that Ælfric took all his material from Smaragdus, who presents an extremely long narrative based on the three

[1] See Raw 1990, esp. chapters 4–8, on the aspects emphasised by Ælfric and his contemporaries.

synoptic Gospels and an extensive commentary.[2] But all of the material in Smaragdus is taken verbatim from earlier commentaries which Ælfric could have known, principally those by Bede and Jerome, and there is also much overlap with Haymo's homily; and Smaragdus does not include by any means all the earlier material used by Ælfric. Smaragdus is an almost certain source for 298–301, however. No single commentary provides all the identifiable material used by Ælfric, and apart from the Augustine passages there is nothing for which there is only one possible source. Following Pope's practice, where there is nothing to choose between texts containing the same material I have cited the earliest likely source in each case (i.e. Jerome, Augustine, Bede) and noted where it is reproduced in later commentaries that Ælfric might have consulted. At a few points I have cited the brief commentary on the passion (printed in PL 106) by Candidus Fuldensis, a little-known figure from the early ninth century; I have no great confidence that Ælfric knew this work, but it does provide parallels that are not in the other commentaries. But this is a homily, like CH II.12, in which parallels are seldom verbally close; this may be due to the transforming effect of the rhythmical style, but it might also suggest that Ælfric was working as much from memory and his trained understanding of this central narrative as from direct sources. Many small points of interpretation, mainly at the literal level, are embedded in the paraphrase of the Gospel narrative. There are also a number of points for which I can find no source. Much of the Gospel material is of course the same in Matthew, Mark and Luke; I have cited Matthew in such cases.

Sources and Notes

The following texts are cited below:

1. Augustine, *In Iohannis Evangelium Tractatus CXXIV*, ed. R. Willems, CCSL 36 (Turnhout, 1954).
2. Augustine, *Sermones*, ed. C. Lambot, CCSL 41 (Turnhout, 1961), Serm. 5 (pp. 50–60).
3. Bede, *Commentarius in Lucam*, ed. D. Hurst, CCSL 120 (Turnhout, 1960), pp. 5–425. [= BedeL]
4. Bede, *Commentarius in Marcum*, ed. D. Hurst, CCSL 120 (Turnhout, 1960), pp. 431–648. [= BedeM]
5. Bede, *Expositio Actuum Apostolorum*, ed. M. Laistner, CCSL 121 (Turnhout, 1983), pp. 3–99.
6. Candidus Fuldensis, *De Passione Domini*, PL 106, cols. 57–104.
7. Haymo of Auxerre, *Homiliae de Tempore*, PL 118, Hom. 64, cols. 358–81. [= H]

[2] Förster 1894, p. 42. (Smetana does not discuss this text.)

8. Jerome, *Commentarii in Evangelium Matthaei*, ed. D. Hurst and M. Adriaen, CCSL 77 (Turnhout, 1969).
9. Smaragdus, *Collectiones in Evangelia et Epistolas*, PL 102, cols. 169–99. [= Sm]

3–6 Cf CH I.10, esp. 23–9.

6–13 Gospels (Mt and Lc):

(Mt 17.1) Et post dies sex adsumpsit Iesus Petrum et Iacobum et Iohannem fratrem eius et ducit illos in montem excelsum seorsum (2) et transfiguratus est ante eos et resplenduit facies eius sicut sol; vestimenta autem eius facta sunt alba sicut nix. (3) Et ecce apparuit illis Moses et Helias cum eo loquentes. (Lc 9.31) Et dicebant excessum eius quem conpleturus erat in Hierusalem. (Mt 17.4) Respondens autem Petrus dixit ad Iesum: Domine bonum est nos hic esse si vis faciamus hic tria tabernacula. . . . (5) Ecce nubes lucida obumbravit eos et ecce vox de nube dicens: hic est Filius meus dilectus in quo mihi bene conplacuit; ipsum audite.

14–22 Gospels (Lc, Mt, Mc):

(Lc 22.1) Adpropinquabat autem dies festus azymorum qui dicitur pascha. (2) Et quaerebant principes sacerdotum et scribae quomodo eum interficerent timebant vero plebem. (3) Intravit autem Satanas in Iudam qui cognominatur Scarioth unum de duodecim. (Mt 26.15) Et ait illis quid vultis mihi dare et ego vobis eum tradam at illi constituerunt ei triginta argenteos. (Mc 14.11) qui audientes gavisi sunt.

23–5 Ælfric seems to place Christ's triumphal entry into Jerusalem, on Palm Sunday, after Judas's betrayal, contrary to the order of events in all the Gospels. Perhaps he was influenced by the sequence in John's Gospel, where the plotting of the chief priests and the resentment of Judas are described just before the entry into Jerusalem (Jn 11.55–7, 12.1–6).

25–31 Gospels (Mt, Jn):

(Mt 26.20) Vespere autem facto discumbebat cum duodecim discipulis. (Jn 13.4) Surgit a cena et ponit vestimenta sua et cum accepisset linteum praecinxit se. (5) Deinde mittit aquam in pelvem et coepit lavare pedes discipulorum. . . . (12) Et accepit vestimenta sua cum recubuisset iterum dixit eis. . . . (14) Si ergo ego lavi vestros pedes Dominus et magister et vos debetis alter alterius lavare pedes. (15) Exemplum enim dedi vobis ut quemadmodum ego feci vobis ita et vos faciatis.

31–7 The main points are present, at great length, in Augustine's exposition, the Tractates on John, 54–6, but there are no close parallels.

38–53 Gospels (Jn, Mt, Lc):

(Jn 13.21) Cum haec dixisset Iesus turbatus est spiritu et protestatus est et dixit amen amen dico vobis quia unus ex vobis tradet me. (Mt 26.22) Et contristati valde coeperunt singuli dicere: numquid ego sum Domine? (23) At ipse respondens ait: qui intinguit mecum manum in parapside hic me tradet. (24) . . . vae autem homini illi per quem Filius hominis traditur bonum erat ei si natus non fuisset homo ille. (25) Respondens autem Iudas qui tradidit eum dixit: numquid ego sum rabbi? ait illi: tu dixisti. (Jn 10.18) Potestatem habeo ponendi eam et potestatem habeo iterum sumendi eam. (Mt 26.26) Cenantibus autem eis accepit Iesus panem et benedixit ac fregit deditque discipulis suis et ait: accipite et comedite hoc est corpus meum. (27) Et accipiens calicem gratias egit et dedit illis dicens: bibite ex hoc omnes; (28) Hic est enim sanguis meus novi testamenti qui pro multis effunditur in remissionem peccatorum (*Cf too Lc 22.20:* similiter et calicem postquam cenavit . . .).

54–8 Jerome, *Comm. Matth.*, 4.1125–8:
'Bonum erat illi, si natus non fuisset homo ille,' non ideo putandus est ante fuisse quam nasceretur . . . sed simpliciter dictum est, multo melius esse, non subsistere, quam male subsistere. [= *BedeM, Sm, H*]

58–63 Cf Haymo, Hom. 64, PL 118, 363A:
Multi sunt qui scelus Iudae detestantur, quod impie egerit, quod magistrum suum tradiderit: illum autem reprehendentes, ipsi reprehensionem minime in semetipsis cavent. Dum enim veritatem pro pecunia subvertunt, quid aliud quam Christum tradunt? Ipse enim dixit: 'Ego sum veritas' (Jn 14.6). [= *BedeL, BedeM, Sm, but perhaps closer*]

63–8 Smaragdus, *Collectiones*, PL 102, 178BC:
Postquam typicum Pascha fuerat impletum, et agni carnes cum apostolis comederat, assumpsit panem, qui confortat cor hominis, et ad verum Paschae transgreditur sacramentum. Ut quomodo in praefiguratione eius Melchisedech summi Dei sacerdos panem et vinum offerens fecerat, ipse quoque in veritate sui corporis et sanguinis repraesentaret. [*From BedeM, but marginally closer*]

69–78 Mt 26:
(31) Tunc dicit illis Iesus: omnes vos scandalum patiemini in me in ista nocte; scriptum est enim percutiam pastorem et dispergentur oves gregis. (32) Postquam autem resurrexero praecedam vos in Galilaeam. (33) Respondens autem Petrus ait illi: et si omnes scandalizati fuerint in te ego numquam scandalizabor. (34) Ait illi Iesus: amen dico tibi quia in hac nocte antequam gallus cantet ter me negabis. (35) Ait illi Petrus etiam si oportuerit me mori tecum non te negabo; similiter et omnes discipuli dixerunt.

Ælfric's *æswiciað* presumably means 'fail, fall away from', reflecting an interpretation of *scandalum* in verse 31, literally a stumbling-block, as 'a cause of failure or fall'. (BT says 'offend' but BTS suggests 'desert'.)

78–97 Judas's departure is not mentioned in the synoptic gospels; John places it earlier, during the last supper (13.30): *Cum ergo accepisset ille buccellam exivit continuo erat autem nox*.

The rest is from John, Matthew and Luke:

(Jn 18.3) Iudas ergo cum accepisset cohortem et a pontificibus et Pharisaeis ministros venit illuc cum lanternis et facibus et armis. (Mt 26.48) Qui autem tradidit eum dedit illis signum dicens: quemcumque osculatus fuero ipse est tenete eum. (49) Et confestim accedens ad Iesum dixit: have rabbi et osculatus est eum. (Jn 18.4) Iesus itaque sciens omnia quae ventura erant super eum processit et dicit eis quem quaeritis. (5) Responderunt ei Iesum Nazarenum. Dicit eis Iesus ego sum. . . . (6) Abierunt retrorsum et ceciderunt in terram. (7) Iterum ergo eos interrogavit quem quaeritis; illi autem dixerunt Iesum Nazarenum. (8) Respondit Iesus: dixi vobis quia ego sum; si ergo me quaeritis sinite hos abire. . . . (10) Simon ergo Petrus habens gladium eduxit eum et percussit pontificis servum et abscidit eius auriculam dextram. . . . (11) Dixit ergo Iesus Petro mitte gladium in vaginam. (Mt 26.53) An putas quia non possum rogare Patrem meum et exhibebit mihi modo plus quam duodecim legiones angelorum. (54) Quomodo ergo implebuntur scripturae quia sic oportet fieri. (Lc 22.51) Et cum tetigisset auriculam eius sanavit eum.

98–113 For the details on a legion, cf Jerome, *Comm. Matth.*, 4.1345–50:

Una legio apud veteres sex milibus complebatur hominum. . . . dixisse sufficiat septuaginta duo milia angelorum . . . de duodecim legionibus fieri. [=*Sm and H*].

Lines 107–9 allude to Lc 22.38: *At illi dixerunt Domine ecce gladii duo hic at ille dixit eis satis est*. For 101–3 cf Candidus Fuldensis, *De Passione*, PL 106, 77B:

Sed et aliud potest intelligi his verbis Dominum significasse, ac si aperte diceret eis: Sinite istos primum ire, et praedicare gentibus.

For 103–5 cf Candidus Fuldensis, *De Passione*, PL 106, 76D, or perhaps 86B:

Cum enim Iudaeis tradi vellet, apparuit, quantum ille tunc valebat, potestas eius, cum audito uno eius verbo abierunt retrorsum, et ceciderunt in terram.

114–28 Gospels (Mt, Lc, Mc):

(Mt 26.56) Tunc discipuli omnes relicto eo fugerunt. (57) At illi tenentes Iesum duxerunt ad Caiaphan principem sacerdotum ubi scribae et seniores convenerant. (58) Petrus autem sequebatur eum a longe. (Lc 22.63) Et viri qui tenebant illum inludebant ei caedentes. (64) Et velaverunt eum et percutiebant faciem eius et interrogabant eum dicentes: prophetiza quis est qui te percussit. (65) Et alia multa blasphemantes dicebant in eum. (Mc 14.56) Multi enim testimonium falsum dicebant adversus eum. (Mt 26.63) Et princeps sacerdotum ait illi: adiuro te per Deum vivum ut dicas nobis si tu es Christus Filius Dei. (64) Dicit illi Iesus tu dixisti (*cf* Mc 14.62 Iesus autem dixit illi: ego sum); verumtamen dico vobis amodo videbitis Filium hominis sedentem a dextris virtutis et venientem in nubibus caeli. (65) Tunc princeps sacerdotum scidit vestimenta sua dicens: blasphemavit. . . . (66) Quid vobis videtur? At illi respondentes dixerunt: reus est mortis. (67) Tunc expuerunt in faciem eius . . . (Mc 14.65) et coeperunt . . . dicere ei prophetiza.

No source for 128–30.

131–9 Gospels (Lc, Jn, Mt):

(Lc 22.55) Accenso autem igni in medio atrio et circumsedentibus illis erat Petrus in medio eorum. (Jn 18.18) Stabant autem servi et ministri ad prunas quia frigus erat et calefiebant erat autem cum eis et Petrus stans et calefaciens se. (Mt 26.69) Et accessit ad eum una ancilla dicens et tu cum Iesu Galilaeo eras. (70) At ille negavit coram omnibus dicens nescio quid dicis. (71) Exeunte autem illo ianuam vidit eum alia et ait his qui erant ibi: et hic erat cum Iesu Nazareno. (72) Et iterum negavit cum iuramento quia non novi hominem. (73) Et post pusillum accesserunt qui stabant et dixerunt Petro vere et tu ex illis es. . . . (74) Tunc coepit detestari et iurare quia non novisset hominem et continuo gallus cantavit. (Lc 22.61) Et conversus Dominus respexit Petrum et recordatus est Petrus verbi Domini. . . . (62) Et egressus foras Petrus flevit amare.

139–47 Cf Candidus Fuldensis, *De Passione*, PL 106, 82D:

Quod Petrus princeps apostolorum et primus ecclesiae post Dominum pastor constitutus permissus est ut negaret, non frustra actum est.

and 73D:

Permisit eum tunc negare, ut postea ecclesiae princeps futurus delinquentibus ipse dimitteret, cum sibi a Domino dimissum peccatum negationis videret.

Or Gregory, Hom. 21 (a source for CH I.15), PL 76, 1172A:

Qua in re considerandum nobis est cur omnipotens Deus eum quem cunctae Ecclesiae praeferre disposuerat ancillae vocem pertimescere et seipsum negare permisit. Quod nimirum magnae actum esse pietatis dispensatione cognoscimus, ut is qui futurus erat pastor Ecclesiae in sua culpa disceret qualiter aliis misereri debuisset. Prius itaque eum ostendit sibi, et tunc praeposuit caeteris, ut ex sua infirmitate cognosceret quam misericorditer aliena infirma toleraret.

148–59 Luke and Matthew:

(Lc 22.66) Et ut factus est dies convenerunt seniores plebis et principes sacerdotum et scribae et duxerunt illum in concilium suum dicentes si tu es Christus dic nobis. (23.1) Et surgens omnis multitudo eorum duxerunt illum ad Pilatum. (2) Coeperunt autem accusare illum. (Mt 27.12) Et cum accusaretur a principibus sacerdotum et senioribus nihil respondit. (3) Tunc videns Iudas qui eum tradidit quod damnatus esset, paenitentia ductus rettulit triginta argenteos principibus sacerdotum et senioribus. . . . (5) Et proiectis argenteis in templo recessit et abiens laqueo se suspendit. (6) Principes autem sacerdotum acceptis argenteis dixerunt non licet mittere eos in corbanan quia pretium sanguinis est. (7) Consilio autem inito emerunt ex illis agrum figuli in sepulturam peregrinorum. . . . (9) Tunc impletum est quod dictum est per Hieremiam prophetam dicentem et acceperunt triginta argenteos. . . .

Ælfric's *gebolgen* (line 153) presumably means something like 'repentant, grief-stricken' rather than the usual 'angry' here; there is nothing in the Gospel account to suggest anger on the part of Judas, and the commentaries agree in seeing it as an attempt at repentance, as indeed does Ælfric at 159; cf Alfred's rendering of Ps 41.7 *anima mea conturbata est* as *wæs min sawl and min mod gebolgen and gedrefed*, where the context implies grief. On 154–5 cf Bede, *Expos. Act.*, 1.198–200:

Dignam sibi poenam traditor amens invenit, ut videlicet guttur quo vox proditionis exierat laquei nodus necaret.

159–62 Jerome, *Comm. Matth.*, 4.1494–1501 (but not very similar):

Nihil profuit egisse paenitentiam per quam scelus corrigere non potuit. . . . ut non solum emendare nequiverit proditionis nefas, sed ad prius scelus etiam proprii homicidii crimen addiderit.

Cf too Bede, *Expos. Act.*, 1.193–4: *Qui, relatis triginta argenteis, traditionis crimen criminosiori in se protinus morte multavit* (taken verbatim from Gregory's *Moralia siue Expositio in Iob*).

162–4 Cf Jerome, *Comm. Matth.*, 4.1513–5 (but making a different point):

Nos qui peregrini eramus a lege et prophetis . . . in pretio sanguinis eius requiescimus. [= *Sm*]

164–6 Acts 1.18: *Et hic quidem possedit agrum de mercede iniquitatis et suspensus crepuit medius et diffusa sunt omnia viscera eius.* Ælfric's closing phrases on Judas, 'not at all lodged in any grave' perhaps reflects Bede's fanciful notion that Judas, being loathsome to both heaven and earth, dissolved into the air (*Expos. Act.*, 1.200–6).

167–82 From Matthew and Luke:

(Mt 27.11) Iesus autem stetit ante praesidem et interrogavit eum praeses dicens: tu es rex Iudaeorum? Dicit ei Iesus: tu dicis. (Lc 23.7) Et ut cognovit quod de Herodis potestate esset remisit eum ad Herodem qui et ipse Hierosolymis erat illis diebus. (8) Herodes autem viso Iesu gavisus est valde erat enim cupiens ex multo tempore videre eum eo quod audiret multa de illo et sperabat signum aliquod videre ab eo fieri. (9) Interrogabat autem illum multis sermonibus at ipse nihil illi respondebat. (11) Sprevit autem illum Herodes cum exercitu suo et inlusit indutum veste alba et remisit ad Pilatum, (12) et facti sunt amici Herodes et Pilatus in ipsa die nam antea inimici erant ad invicem. (13) Pilatus autem convocatis principibus sacerdotum et magistratibus et plebe (14) dixit ad illos: obtulistis mihi hunc hominem quasi avertentem populum et ecce ego coram vobis interrogans nullam causam inveni in homine isto ex his in quibus eum accusatis (15) sed neque Herodes; nam remisi vos ad illum et ecce nihil dignum morte actum est ei. (16) Emendatum ergo illum dimittam.

183–204 From Matthew and Luke:

(Mt 27.15) Per diem autem sollemnem consueverat praeses dimittere populo unum vinctum quem voluissent. (16) Habebat autem tunc vinctum insignem qui dicebatur Barabbas. (Lc 23.19) Qui erat propter seditionem quandam factam in civitate et homicidium missus in carcerem. (Mt 27.17) Congregatis ergo illis dixit Pilatus: quem vultis dimittam vobis Barabban an Iesum qui dicitur Christus? (21) At illi dixerunt Barabban. (22) Dicit illis Pilatus quid igitur faciam de Iesu qui dicitur Christus. (23) Dicunt omnes crucifigatur. . . (24) Videns autem Pilatus quia nihil proficeret sed magis tumultus fieret, accepta aqua lavit manus coram populo dicens innocens ego sum a sanguine iusti huius. . . . (25) Et respondens universus populus dixit: sanguis eius super nos et super filios nostros. (26) Tunc dimisit illis Barabban; Iesum autem flagellatum tradidit eis ut crucifigeretur. (27) Tunc milites praesidis suscipientes Iesum in praetorio congregaverunt ad eum universam cohortem. (28) Et exuentes eum clamydem coccineam circumdederunt ei. (29) Et plectentes coronam de spinis posuerunt super caput eius et harundinem in dextera eius et genu flexo ante eum inludebant dicentes have rex Iudaeorum. (31) Et postquam inluserunt ei exuerunt eum clamydem et induerunt eum vestimentis eius et duxerunt eum ut crucifigerent.

205–8 Cf Haymo, Hom. 64, PL 118, 374B:

Haec maledictio perseverat in Iudaeis usque hodie, et usque in diem iudicii perseverabit. Non enim sufficit eis ut semetipsos, qui tunc temporis erant, damnarent, sed etiam omnem progeniem, quae necdum nata erat, sub hac maledictionis noxa constringerent. [*Adapted from Jerome, Comm. Matth., 4.1595–7.*]

208–10 Augustine, *Tract.*, 116.1.1–3:

Cum Iudaei clamassent, non Iesum sibi a Pilato dimitti velle per Pascha, sed Barabbam latronem; non salvatorem, sed interfectorem; non datorem vitae, sed ademtorem.

and Jerome, *Comm. Matth.*, 4.1603–6:

Barabbas latro . . . qui homicidiorum auctor erat, dimissus est populo Iudaeorum, id est diabolus qui usque hodie regnat in eis.

(The two points are also combined in BedeL and Sm., but less close.)

210–18 Cf Bede, *Comm. Marc.*, 4.1253–85 *passim*:

[1253] Nos autem omnia haec intellegamus mystice. . . . [1265–6] Mystice ergo in purpura qua indutus est Dominus, ipsa eius caro quam passionibus obiecit, insinuatur. . . . [1282–5] Sicut enim purpura colorem sanguinis qui pro nobis effusus est imitatur, ita et habitum regni quod post passionem intravit . . . insinuat. . . . [1268–70] In corona vero quam portabat spinea, nostrorum susceptio peccatorum, pro qua mortalis fieri dignatus est, ostenditur. . . . [1272–4] Namque spinas in significatione peccatorum poni solere testatur ipse Dominus, qui protoplasto in peccatum prolapso dicebat: 'Terra tua spinas et tribulos germinabit tibi' (Gen 3.18, *to which Ælfric adds v.17*: quia audisti vocem uxoris tuae et comedisti de ligno ex quo praeceperam tibi ne comederes . . .).

218–9 No source known.

219–21 Cf Haymo, Hom. 64, PL 118, 375BC:

Quandiu Dominus illusionem passus est, et sputa sustinuit, et coronam spineam in capite habuit, non propria vestimenta habuit induta, sed aliena. Mox autem ut hora despectionis transiit, propria vestimenta resumpsit. Quia quod passus est, et quod flagellatus est, non fuit proprium Divinitatis illius. Quod autem die tertia resurrexit, quasi proprium vestimentum resumpsit, per quod significabatur, quod horam mortem erat gustaturus, et iterum ad tempus peracta passione de sepulcro resurrecturus.

222–5 From Mc 15.22–3:

(22) Et perducunt illum in Golgotha locum quod est interpretatum Calvariae locus. (23) Et dabant ei bibere murratum vinum et non accepit.

225–7 Jerome, *Comm. Matth.*, 4.1691–4:

Quod autem dicitur 'cum gustasset noluit bibere', hoc indicat quod gustaverit quidem pro nobis mortis amaritudinem, sed tertia die resurrexit. [= *Sm*]

227–34 From John:

(19.18) Ubi eum crucifixerunt et cum eo alios duos hinc et hinc medium autem Iesum, (19) scripsit autem et titulum Pilatus et posuit super crucem erat autem scriptum Iesus Nazarenus rex Iudaeorum. (20) Hunc ergo titulum multi legerunt Iudaeorum quia prope civitatem erat locus ubi crucifixus est Iesus et erat scriptum hebraice graece et latine.

236–8 Jn 19.23–4:

(23) Milites ergo cum crucifixissent eum acceperunt vestimenta eius et fecerunt quattuor partes unicuique militi partem et tunicam erat autem tunica inconsutilis desuper contexta per totum. (24) Dixerunt ergo ad invicem non scindamus eam sed sortiamur de illa.

238–40 Cf Haymo, Hom. 64, PL 118, 376C:

> Tunica autem illius inconsutilis desuper texta, unitatem ipsius ecclesiae designat, quia omnis unitas regni in corpore sanctae ecclesiae consistit. Quae unitas non humano arbitrio, sed divina dispensatione regitur.

241–4 This rhetorical sentence was perhaps inspired by the verses of Caelius Sedulius, *Carmen Paschale*, 5.188–95 (CSEL 10) [quoted by Bede, *Comm. Luc.*, 6.1533–44]:

> Qualiter sane Dominus in cruce sit positus, quidve eadem sacratissimi corporis positio regalis in se typi contineat, Sedulius in paschali carmine pulchre versibus dixit:
>
> Neve quis ignoret speciem crucis esse colendam,
> Quae Dominum portavit ovans ratione potenti,
> Quattuor inde plagas quadrati colligit orbis.
> Splendidus auctoris de vertice fulget Eous,
> Occiduo sacrae lambuntur sidere plantae.
> Arcton dextra tenet, medium laeva erigit axem,
> Cunctaque de membris vivit natura creantis,
> Et cruce complexum Christus regit undique mundum.

Sedulius's description of the hands pointing north and south, and the head and feet pointing west and east, would seem to view Christ in a prone position. Ælfric imagines Christ raised on the cross, facing west but with the crown of his head (*hnol* presumably rendering Sedulius's *vertice*) somehow tilted to point to the east. (None of the visual representations that I have seen match such an image: they show Christ's head either upright or bent in the direction of one arm.) The detail of four nails is curiously not mentioned by the commentaries, though it is discussed, with reference to the legend of the finding of the cross, by Gregory of Tours, *Libri Miraculorum*, PL 71, 710. Ælfric perhaps uses the number to support the typology of the four corners of the world, though the nails are not of course aligned to the four quarters. The use of the detail may reflect their prominence in art; the shift to three nails probably started too late to be an issue here.[3]

244–57 Gospels (Mt and Lc):

> (Mt 27.39) Praetereuntes autem blasphemabant eum moventes capita sua. (40) Et dicentes: qui destruit templum et in triduo illud reaedificat salva temet ipsum; si Filius Dei es descende de cruce. (41) Similiter et principes sacerdotum inludentes cum scribis et senioribus dicentes: (42) Alios salvos fecit se ipsum non potest salvum facere; si rex Israhel est descendat nunc de cruce et credemus ei. (Lc 23.34) Iesus autem dicebat Pater dimitte illis non enim sciunt quid faciunt. (39) Unus autem de his qui pendebant latronibus blasphemabat eum dicens: si tu es Christus salvum fac temet ipsum et nos. (40) Respondens autem alter increpabat illum dicens: neque

[3] Cf *Ancrene Wisse: Parts Six and Seven*, ed. G. Shepherd (London, 1959), p. 57.

tu times Deum quod in eadem damnatione es. (41) Et nos quidem iuste nam digna factis recipimus; hic vero nihil mali gessit. (42) Et dicebat ad Iesum Domine memento mei cum veneris in regnum tuum. (43) Et dixit illi Iesus: amen dico tibi hodie mecum eris in paradiso.

258–62 Jerome, *Comm. Matth.*, 4.1745–9:
In duobus latronibus uterque populus et gentilium et Iudaeorum primum Dominum blasphemavit, postea signorum magnitudine alter exterritus egit paenitentiam et usque hodie Iudaeos increpat blasphemantes.

263–6 Jn 19.25–6:
(25) Stabant autem iuxta crucem Iesu mater eius et soror matris eius Maria Cleopae et Maria Magdalene. (26) Cum vidisset ergo Iesus matrem et discipulum stantem quem diligebat dicit matri suae: mulier ecce filius tuus.

266–7 Cf Augustine, *Tract.*, 119.1.12–14 (referring to the marriage at Cana):
Hanc itaque horam praedixerat quae tunc nondum venerat, in qua deberet agnoscere moriturus, de qua fuerat mortaliter natus.

267–71 Jn 19.27–9:
(27) Deinde dicit discipulo: ecce mater tua et ex illa hora accepit eam discipulus in sua. (28) Postea sciens Iesus quia iam omnia consummata sunt ut consummaretur scriptura dicit sitio. (29) Vas ergo positum erat aceto plenum; illi autem spongiam plenam aceto hysopo circumponentes obtulerunt ori eius.

271–5 Lc 23.44–6:
(44) Erat autem fere hora sexta et tenebrae factae sunt in universa terra usque in nonam horam. (45) Et obscuratus est sol. . . . (46) Et clamans voce magna Iesus ait: Pater in manus tuas commendo spiritum meum; et haec dicens exspiravit.

276–83 From Matthew and Luke:
(Mt 27.51) Et ecce velum templi scissum est in duas partes a summo usque deorsum et terra mota est et petrae scissae sunt. (52) Et monumenta aperta sunt et multa corpora sanctorum qui dormierant surrexerunt. (53) Et exeuntes de monumentis post resurrectionem eius venerunt in sanctam civitatem et apparuerunt multis. (54) Centurio autem et qui cum eo erant custodientes Iesum viso terraemotu et his quae fiebant timuerunt valde dicentes vere Dei Filius erat iste. (Lc 23.48) Et omnis turba eorum qui simul aderant ad spectaculum istud et videbant quae fiebant percutientes pectora sua revertebantur.

284–7 Cf Augustine, *Tract.*, 119.4.18–20: *Iudaei quippe ipsi erant acetum, degenerantes a vino patriarcharum et prophetarum.*

289–91 Cf Jerome, *Comm. Matth.*, 4.1795: *Divinae potestatis indicium est emittere spiritum.* [= *Sm, H; the same point is in BedeM.*]

291–5 Cf Jerome, *Comm. Matth.*, 4.1809–13 (though it is not very close):

Sed mihi videtur terrae motus et reliqua typum ferre credentium, quod pristinis errorum vitiis derelictis et cordis emollita duritia, qui prius similes erant tumulis mortuorum, postea agnoverint creatorem.

295–8 Jerome, *Comm. Matth.*, 4.1799–1801:

Velum templi scissum est et omnia legis sacramenta quae prius tegebantur prodita sunt atque ad gentilium populum transierunt. [= *BedeL, BedeM, Sm, H.*]

298–301 The same point is made at CH I.30.76–80 and I.15.133–9, both drawing on Paschasius Radbertus.

301–9 Cf Bede, *Comm. Luc.*, 6.1587–9:

Neque enim putandum est eum haec patrem frustra orasse, sed in eis nimirum qui post eius passionem credidere quod orabat impetrasse.

Ælfric has not in fact cited Luke 23.34 on forgiveness from the cross. For the eight thousand, see Acts 2.41, 4.4. They are cited as part of the same argument, perhaps adapted from Bede, by Candidus Fuldensis, *De Passione*, PL 106, 92CD:

Iesus autem dicebat: 'Pater, dimitte illis, nesciunt enim quid faciunt' (Lc 23.34). Implevit Dominus quod ante discipulis praecepit: Orate, inquit, pro persequentibus et calumniantibus vobis. Et utique non irrita potuit esse eius oratio; multi enim Iudaeorum, pro quibus tunc oravit, nescientes quod Filius Dei erat quem morte damnabant, postea conversi crediderunt, et fidelium numero additi sunt, sicut uno die tria millia, et altero quinque millia eorum credidisse referuntur.

310–19 Jn 19.31–4:

(31) Iudaei ergo quoniam parasceve erat ut non remanerent in cruce corpora; sabbato erat enim magnus dies ille sabbati; rogaverunt Pilatum ut frangerentur eorum crura et tollerentur. (32) Venerunt ergo milites et primi quidem fregerunt crura et alterius qui crucifixus est cum eo. (33) Ad Iesum autem cum venissent ut viderunt eum iam mortuum non fregerunt eius crura. (34) Sed unus militum lancea latus eius aperuit et continuo exivit sanguis et aqua.

The *cwylmbærum tolum* at 314, not specified in the Gospels, perhaps allude to pictorial representations of the instruments of the passion (e.g. Tiberius Psalter f.13r, Raw 1990, pl.xiii; ivory plaque in the Victoria and Albert Museum, London, Gameson 1995, pl.5b). Admittedly the instruments are the lance, scourge and sponge, but pictorially they suggest the soldiers with weapons.

319–27 Cf Augustine, *Tract.*, 120.2.10–12:

Ille sanguis in remissionem fusus est peccatorum: aqua illa salutare temperat poculum; haec et lavacrum praestat, et potum.

And Augustine, Serm. 5, 104–8:

De ipso sanguine et aqua significatur nata ecclesia. Et quando exiit sanguis et aqua de latere? Cum iam dormiret Christus in cruce, quia et Adam in paradiso somnum accepit, et sic illi de latere Eva producta est.

Cf also Candidus Fuldensis, *De Passione*, PL 106, 101B:

Quod latus lancea perforatur, unde exivit unda et sanguis, significat unum esse ecclesiae catholicae ingressum, aquam scilicet et baptismi, vel baptismum sanguinis. 'Nisi, inquit, quis renatus fuerit ex aqua et Spiritu, non potest introire in regnum Dei.' Vel aqua igitur, vel sanguine quis baptizetur, baptismus tamen ingressus ecclesiae est.

327–34 Haymo, Hom. 64, PL 118, 380CD:

Siquidem sexta feria Dominus crucifixus est, sabbato quievit in sepulcro, octavo, qui est primus, resurrexit. Et pulchro ordine, quia homo sexta die factus est, et Deus septimo requievit die ab omnibus operibus suis, pulchra ratione Dominus sexta feria genus humanum sua passione redemit, sabbato in sepulcro quievit, octavo die resurrexit.

335–45 From Mark and John:

(Mc 15.42) Et cum iam sero esset factum quia erat parasceve quod est ante sabbatum. (43) Venit Ioseph ab Arimathia nobilis decurio, (Jn 19.38) eo quod esset discipulus Iesu, occultus autem propter metum Iudaeorum. (Mc 15.43) Et audacter introiit ad Pilatum et petiit corpus Iesu. (44) Pilatus autem mirabatur si iam obisset. (Jn 19.38) Et permisit Pilatus; venit ergo et tulit corpus Iesu. (39) Venit autem et Nicodemus qui venerat ad Iesum nocte primum ferens mixturam murrae et aloes quasi libras centum. (40) Acceperunt ergo corpus Iesu et ligaverunt eum linteis cum aromatibus sicut mos Iudaeis est sepelire. (41) Erat autem in loco ubi crucifixus est hortus et in horto monumentum novum in quo nondum quisquam positus erat. (42) Ibi ergo propter parasceven Iudaeorum quia iuxta erat monumentum posuerunt Iesum.

346–8 Augustine, *Tract.*, 120.5.3–5:

Sicut in Mariae virginis utero nemo ante illum, nemo post illum conceptus est; ita in hoc monumento nemo ante illum, nemo post illum sepultus est.

348–52 Mt 27.62–6:

(62) Altera autem die quae est post parasceven convenerunt principes sacerdotum et Pharisaei ad Pilatum, (63) dicentes: domine recordati sumus quia seductor ille dixit adhuc vivens post tres dies resurgam; (64) iube ergo custodiri sepulchrum usque in diem tertium ne forte veniant discipuli eius et furentur eum et dicant plebi surrexit a mortuis et erit novissimus error peior priore. (65) Ait illis Pilatus: habetis custodiam, ite custodite sicut scitis. (66) Illi autem abeuntes munierunt sepulchrum signantes lapidem cum custodibus.

357 See the note on the similar comment at the end of CH I.14.

15 EASTER DAY

This is the most celebrated and discussed of all Ælfric's homilies, having been printed by Archbishop Parker and his associates in 1565 as evidence of the agreement between the Protestant reformers and the Anglo-Saxon church on eucharistic doctrine, and argued about repeatedly by Catholic and Protestant polemicists from then until well into the nineteenth century, with occasional later returns.[1] When Ælfric wrote, the eucharistic issue had not acquired such notoriety as a shibboleth, though views similar to his were condemned as heretical a century later. It was even so a challenging topic to embark on in a vernacular sermon, and although Ælfric acknowledges that it was an area of doubt and disagreement he gives no hint that he thought it too dangerous or too difficult for such an occasion, though his reference to divine grace as his guide (lines 3–4) may be significant.

The First Series homily for Easter Sunday had already covered the events commemorated on that day, the Gospel account of the resurrection. In the Second Series Ælfric provided two, possibly three, more homilies for the occasion, testifying to its importance as a major preaching day. He was perhaps prompted to devote a sermon to the Biblical establishment of the eucharist and its theory by the example of Gregory the Great, who concludes his exposition of the Gospel account of the resurrection, in his homily for the occasion (Hom. 22), with a brief discussion of the first passover in Exodus and its significance for the Christian eucharist, though he does not embark on eucharistic theory. But a stronger reason was probably the close association of Easter with the taking of the sacrament by the laity. Urging the laity in a later text to take the sacrament more frequently than they do, Ælfric lists the fifteen days in the year when the pious can do so, and these begin with the five Sundays of Lent and the four days culminating in Easter Sunday (Pope 19.119–30); and he urges those who are unwilling to take the sacrament so frequently to do so at least three times a year. The second sentence of the present homily (lines 3–4) implies that all those present are expected to take the sacrament after the completion of the homily.[2]

Ælfric's use of the treatise *De Corpore et Sanguine Domini* by Ratramnus of Corbie as a source for the central, doctrinal, part of the homily (lines 86–254) has been recognised since the seventeenth century.[3] Förster added Gregory's

[1] See especially the two articles by T. H. Leinbaugh, 'Ælfric's *Sermo de Sacrificio in Die Pascae*: Anglican Polemic in the Sixteenth and Seventeenth Centuries', in *Anglo-Saxon Scholarship: the First Three Centuries*, ed. M. McC. Gatch and C. Berkhout (Boston, Mass., 1982), pp. 51–68; and 'The Sources for Ælfric's Easter Sermon: the History of the Controversy and a New Source', *Notes and Queries* 231 (1986), 294–311.

[2] A contemporary Lenten confessional text specifies Easter as the time for taking the sacrament; see N. R. Ker, 'Three Old English Texts in a Salisbury Pontifical, Cotton Tiberius C i', in *The Anglo-Saxons: Studies in some Aspects of their History and Culture presented to Bruce Dickins*, ed. P. Clemoes (London, 1959), pp. 262–79, at 277, lines 17–18.

[3] See Leinbaugh, 'Ælfric's Easter Sermon'.

homily 22, for Easter Day, as a source for the exposition of the passover from Exodus (it is assigned to Easter in Paul the Deacon's homiliary), and identified the source for the miracle narrated at 159–67 in the *Vitae Patrum*.[4] For the Exodus material at the beginning he suggested Bede's Commentary on Exodus, though this is in fact only a copy of one attributed to Isidore. More recently Leinbaugh has pointed to some use of Augustine's Tractates on John for the passage at 324–36 (he suggests also for 52–9, though I am less convinced),[5] and Bakhuizen, in his edition of Ratramnus, noted a case where Ælfric seemed to have gone back to a sermon of Augustine to fill out a quotation by Ratramnus (lines 225–44); there is probably another case of this, involving Augustine's Tractates again, at 199–208. Leinbaugh also pointed out that the two miracles used by Ælfric at 159–73, which have an important part in the historical controversy about this text since they seem to reflect a more realist view of the eucharist and were often treated by early commentators as spurious, are to be found together, though in reverse order, in the treatise *De Corpore et Sanguine Domini* of Paschasius Radbertus. If this was indeed Ælfric's source it is particularly striking, since Paschasius's views were so opposed to those of Ratramnus. But the two exempla also appear in the *Exaggeratio Plurimorum Auctorum De Corpore et Sanguine Domini*, a collection of patristic and other proof-texts on the subject which is now attributed to Paschasius himself,[6] and thence in later treatises, and it may be that Ælfric drew on such a collection rather than Paschasius's treatise.[7] Even so, the context is likely to have been firmly realist rather than figural.

In using Ratramnus Ælfric's method was apparently to work first through the treatise from beginning to end, selecting the main points and conclusions and omitting most of the argument and evidence; this forms the first part of his discussion (lines 90–158), analysing in what sense and how the bread and wine become Christ's body and blood. He then introduces the two exempla from other sources. Then he returns to the treatise to pick out and develop several points which were used by Ratramnus as part of his main argument about the symbolic nature of the sacrament but are used by Ælfric as distinct aspects of the eucharist. These are: the prefiguration of the sacrament by the manna in the desert and the water from the rock (lines 174–214); the sacrament as a memorial and renewal of Christ's sacrifice (lines 214–24); the sacrament as a symbol of all Christians, who are spiritually all the body of Christ (lines 225–49); and the sacrament as a symbol of the union of all Christians with Christ through the mixing of wine and water (lines 249–54).

The precise nature of Ælfric's stance on eucharistic theory has been discussed repeatedly since the seventeenth century, and it is not feasible to do it justice

[4] Förster 1894, pp. 12–13, 56; Smetana 1959, p. 197.

[5] See Leinbaugh, 'Ælfric's Easter Sermon'.

[6] See Bakhuizen 1974, pp. 29–32 (see list of texts cited below).

[7] Cf Leinbaugh, 'Ælfric's Easter Sermon'.

here.[8] Ratramnus argues that the bread which is called the body of Christ is a *figura* or *mysterium*, and not a truth, which he defines as something apprehensible to the senses. Ælfric at the outset seems to accept his distinction between truth and figure and the implication that the bread is not 'truly' Christ's body (lines 90–101); but his opening statement of the issue seems to indicate some kind of transformation of the bread and wine (lines 86–90) and his preferred formulation is that the bread *is* 'truly' Christ's body, but spiritually rather than physically (cf 104–7, 126–8, 156–7). Nowhere does he quite say that the eucharistic bread is Christ's body through *getacnung* in the way that the terms lamb or lion signify Christ. And the two miracles which he adds at the centre of the arguments drawn from Ratramnus push strongly towards a more realist view. If at first sight it seems perverse to have chosen Ratramnus as his model, since the essential arguments are so different, it is also important to note that Ratramnus's formulations are often closer to Ælfric's main line than the former's introductory and concluding remarks would suggest; cf especially the passage from chapter 49 quoted as source for lines 124–8. And Ratramnus's secondary argument, that the body represented by the eucharist is to be distinguished from the body in which Christ was born, crucified and buried, is one that Ælfric appears happy to follow, even though the two miracle stories seem to argue against it.

Sources and Notes

The following texts are cited below:

1. Augustine, *In Iohannis Evangelium Tractatus CXXIV*, ed. R. Willems, CCSL 36 (Turnhout, 1954).
2. Augustine, *Sermones*, PL 38, Serm. 272, cols. 1246–8.
3. Gregory the Great, *Homiliae in Evangelia*, PL 76, Hom. 22, cols. 1174–81.
4. Isidore, *Quaestiones in Vetus Testamentum*, PL 83, cols. 207–424.
5. Paschasius Radbertus, *De Corpore et Sanguine Domini*, ed. B. Paulus, CCCM 16 (Turnhout, 1969), pp. 1–131.
6. Ratramnus, *De Corpore et Sanguine Domini*, ed. J. N. Bakhuizen van den Brink (Amsterdam, 1974).

8–28 Exod 12.1–15:

(1) Dixit quoque Dominus ad Mosen et Aaron in terra Aegypti . . . (3) loquimini ad universum coetum filiorum Israhel et dicite eis: decima die mensis huius tollat unusquisque agnum per familias et domos suas. (6) . . . Immolabitque eum universa multitudo filiorum Israhel ad vesperam. (7) Et

[8] See Bakhuizen and Leinbaugh for the history, and also C. L. Wrenn, 'Some Aspects of Anglo-Saxon Theology', in *Studies in Language, Literature and Culture of the Middle Ages and Later*, ed. E. B. Atwood and A. A. Hill (Austin, Texas, 1969), pp. 182–9; and A. Crépin, 'Ælfric et les controverses sur l'eucharistie: étude de vocabulaire' in *Vivante Tradition*, ed. O. Lutaud *et al.* (Paris, 1982), pp. 67–72.

sument de sanguine ac ponent super utrumque postem et in superliminaribus domorum in quibus comedent illum. (8) Et edent carnes nocte illa assas igni et azymos panes cum lactucis agrestibus. (9) Non comedetis ex eo crudum quid nec coctum aqua sed assum tantum igni. Caput cum pedibus eius et intestinis vorabitis. (10) Nec remanebit ex eo quicquam usque mane; si quid residuum fuerit igne conburetis. (11) Sic autem comedetis illum: renes vestros accingetis, calciamenta habebitis in pedibus, tenentes baculos in manibus, et comedetis festinantes; est enim phase id est transitus Domini. (12) Et transibo per terram Aegypti nocte illa percutiamque omne primogenitum in terra Aegypti. . . . (13) Erit autem sanguis vobis in signum in aedibus in quibus eritis et videbo sanguinem ac transibo vos nec erit in vobis plaga disperdens quando percussero terram Aegypti. (14) Habebitis autem hanc diem in monumentum et celebrabitis eam sollemnem Domino in generationibus vestris cultu sempiterno. (15) Septem diebus azyma comedetis.

34 Presumably a reference back to CH II.12 (or at least to the first part—the second part seems a later composition).

38–43 Cf Isidore, *In Exodum*, c. 15.1, *Quaestiones,* PL 83, 294D:

Interea fit pascha: in occisione agni occiditur Christus, de quo in Evangelio dicitur: 'Ecce agnus Dei, ecce qui tollit peccata mundi' (Jn 1.29, *though Ælfric is quoting the liturgical version*).

50–9 Isidore, *In Exodum*, c. 15.1–2, *Quaestiones*, PL 83, 294D-5A:

Vespere immolatur agnus, in vespera mundi passus est Dominus. . . . Sanguine agni illiniuntur Israelitarum postes, ne vastator angelus audeat inferre perniciem. Signantur signo dominicae passionis in frontibus fideles populi ad tutelam salutis, ut hi soli ab interitu liberentur, qui cruore dominicae passionis corde et fronte signati sunt.

(Leinbaugh cites as source for this the passage from Augustine given below for 324–36, but Isidore seems closer and more probable.) For the (non-Biblical) detail that the Israelites marked their doors with the sign of the cross, cf CH I.22.7 and II.3.81–2. I can find no trace of this in earlier writers, though the identification of the Greek letter *tau* with the sign of the cross is common in patristic exegesis. Is it possible that Ælfric has assumed it from the allegorical link (made by Augustine, Tractates 55, Gregory, Hom. 22, and Isidore for instance) between the marking of the door posts with the blood of the lamb and the marking of the forehead of Christians with the sign of the cross in baptism?

59–85 The re-enactment of the Hebrew passover in the Christian eucharist seems not to have a specific source. Lines 70–76 are from Jn 6.54–59:

(54) Dixit ergo eis Iesus amen amen dico vobis nisi manducaveritis carnem Filii hominis et biberitis eius sanguinem non habetis vitam in vobis. (55)

Qui manducat meam carnem et bibit meum sanguinem habet vitam aeternam et ego resuscitabo eum in novissimo die. . . . (57) Qui manducat meam carnem et bibit meum sanguinem in me manet et ego in illo. . . . (59) Hic est panis qui de caelo descendit non sicut manducaverunt patres vestri manna et mortui sunt. Qui manducat hunc panem vivet in aeternum.

Lines 76–81 are from Matthew and Luke:

(Mt 26.26) Cenantibus autem eis accepit Iesus panem et benedixit ac fregit deditque discipulis suis et ait accipite et comedite hoc est corpus meum. (Lc 22.19) Hoc facite in meam commemorationem. (Mt 26.27) Et accipiens calicem gratias egit et dedit illis dicens bibite ex hoc omnes. (28) Hic est enim sanguis meus novi testamenti qui pro multis effunditur in remissionem peccatorum.

86–90 Ratramnus takes as his starting point two questions: whether the eucharistic bread and wine is Christ's body and blood in truth, that is, in a manner apprehensible to the senses, or in mystery, that is, apprehensible only to the eyes of faith; and whether it is the same body as that which was born of the virgin Mary and was crucified and buried. Ælfric takes a different starting point, focusing on how the bread and wine can become Christ's body and blood; though he does go on to confront the questions raised by Ratramnus.

90–92 Cf Ratramnus, *De Corpore et Sanguine*, cc. 6,8,7 (44.13–14, 23–6, 16–22, 29–30), drawing the same distinction between truth and figure but using mainly different examples:

[c.6] Harum duarum quaestionum primam inspiciamus; et ne dubietatis ambage detineamur, definiamus quid sit figura, quid veritas. [c.8] Veritas vero est, rei manifestae demonstratio, nullis umbrarum imaginibus obvelatae, sed puris et apertis, utque planius eloquamur, naturalibus significationibus insinuatae; ut pote cum dicitur Christus natus de virgine, passus, crucifixus, mortuus et sepultus. [c.7] Figura est obumbratio quaedam, quibusdam velaminibus quod intendit ostendens; verbi gratia, verbum volentes dicere, panem nuncupamus: sicut in oratione dominica panem cotidianum dari nobis expostulamus; vel cum Christus in evangelio loquitur dicens: 'Ego sum panis vivus, qui de coelo descendi' (Jn 6.41) ; vel cum seipsum vitem, discipulos autem palmites appellat: 'Ego sum dicens vitis vera, vos autem palmites' (Jn 15.5). Haec enim omnia aliud dicunt et aliud innuunt. [c.8] Nam substantialiter, nec panis Christus, nec vitis Christus, nec palmites apostoli.

For Christ as the bread which feeds both men and angels, lines 95–6, cf CH II.16.189–90; it seems not to be Biblical. The lamb and lion are used as examples by Ælfric in a similar passage at CH I.25.138–48 (possibly drawing in turn on Augustine's Tractates on John).

100–7 Following Ratramnus, *De Corpore et Sanguine*, cc. 9 and 10 (45.1–6, 15–20) in part, but Ratramnus concludes that the bread and wine are Christ's body and blood *figurate*, Ælfric that they are so *soðlice* through a spiritual mystery:

> [c.9] At ille panis qui per sacerdotis ministerium Christi corpus conficitur, aliud exterius humanis sensibus ostendit, et aliud interius fidelium mentibus clamat. Exterius quidem panis, quod ante fuerat, forma pretenditur, color ostenditur, sapor accipitur: ast interius . . . Christi corpus ostenditur. . . . [c.10] Haec ita esse dum nemo potest abnegare, claret quia panis ille vinumque figurate Christi corpus et sanguis existit. Non enim secundum quod videtur vel carnis species in illo pane cognoscitur, vel in illo vino cruoris unda monstratur; cum tamen post misticam consecrationem nec panis iam dicitur nec vinum, sed Christi corpus et sanguis.

Ælfric ignores cc. 11–16 in which Ratramnus argues against the view that the bread and wine are physically transformed into the body and blood, and substitutes an analogy with the baptism of a child.

111–6 Ratramnus, *De Corpore et Sanguine*, c. 17 (47.16–17, 22–7):

> Consideremus sacri fontem baptismatis, qui fons vitae non immerito nuncupatur. . . . In eo tamen fonte si consideretur solummodo quod corporeus aspicit sensus, elementum fluidum conspicitur, corruptioni subiectum, nec nisi corpora lavandi potentiam optinere. Sed accessit sancti Spiritus per sacerdotis consecrationem virtus, et efficax facta est non solum corpora, verum etiam animas diluere, et spiritales sordes spiritali potentia dimovere.

117–24 Ratramnus, *De Corpore et Sanguine*, cc. 18–19 (47.28, 47.35–48.2):

> [c.18] Ecce in uno eodemque elemento duo videmus inesse.. . . . . Igitur in proprietate humor corruptibilis, in misterio vero virtus sanabilis. [c.19] Sic itaque Christi corpus et sanguis superficietenus considerata, creatura est mutabilitati corruptelaeque subiecta. Si misterii vero perpendas virtutem, vita est participantibus se tribuens immortalitatem.

124–8 Cf Ratramnus, *De Corpore et Sanguine*, c. 49 (55.11–15):

> Ex his omnibus quae sunt actenus dicta monstratum est quod corpus et sanguis Christi, quae fidelium ore in ecclesia percipiuntur, figurae sint secundum speciem visibilem; at vero secundum invisibilem substantiam, id est divini potentiam verbi, corpus et sanguis vere Christi existunt.

128–30 Ratramnus, *De Corpore et Sanguine*, c. 69 (60.1–6):

> Huius doctissimi viri auctoritate perdocemur quod multa differentia separantur corpus in quo passus est Christus, et sanguis quem pendens in cruce de latere suo profudit, et hoc corpus quod in misterio passionis Christi cotidie a fidelibus celebratur, et ille quoque sanguis qui fidelium ore sumitur, misterium sit illius sanguinis quo totus redemptus est mundus.

130–8 Ratramnus, *De Corpore et Sanguine*, c. 72 (60.32–61.6):

Illa namque caro quae crucifixa est, de virginis carne facta est, ossibus et nervis compacta, et humanorum membrorum liniamentis distincta, rationalis animae spiritu vivificata in propriam vitam et congruentes motus. At vero caro spiritalis quae populum credentem spiritaliter pascit, secundum speciem quam gerit exterius, frumenti granis manu artificis consistit, nullis nervis ossibusque compacta, nulla membrorum varietate distincta, nulla rationali substantia vegetata, nullos proprios potens motus exercere. Quicquid enim in ea vitae praebet substantiam, spiritalis est potentiae et invisibilis efficientiae, divinaeque virtutis: atque aliud longe consistit secundum quod exterius conspicitur, atque aliud secundum quod in misterio creditur.

Cf too c. 74 (61.16–18):

Et sicut non corporaliter sed spiritaliter panis ille credentium corpus dicitur, sic quoque Christi corpus non corporaliter sed spiritaliter necesse est intellegatur.

138–42 Ratramnus, *De Corpore et Sanguine*, c. 93 (67.2–5):

Ista, fratres, ideo dicuntur sacramenta, quia in eis aliud videtur et aliud intellegitur: quod videtur, speciem habet corporalem; quod intellegitur, fructum habet spiritalem.

(Quoting Augustine, Serm. 272, PL 38, 1247.)

143–7 Ratramnus, *De Corpore et Sanguine*, cc. 76–7 (61.32–6, 62.7–8):

[c.76] Corpus Christi quod mortuum est et resurrexit, et immortale factum 'iam non moritur, et mors illi ultra non dominabitur' (Rom 6.9), aeternum est, nec iam passibile: hoc autem quod in ecclesia celebratur, temporale est, non aeternum; corruptibile est, non incorruptum; [c.77] per partes comminutum dispertitur sumendum, et dentibus commolitum in corpus traicitur.

147–53 This passage on the wholeness of Christ's body in the eucharist seems not to be from Ratramnus.

153–7 Ratramnus, *De Corpore et Sanguine*, c. 88 (64.32–65.2):

Et hoc corpus pignus est et species; illud vero ipsa veritas. Hoc enim geretur donec ad illud perveniatur; ubi vero ad illud perventum fuerit, hoc removebitur.

c. 60 (58.12–13):

Est quidem corpus Christi; sed non corporale, sed spiritale: est sanguis Christi; sed non corporalis, sed spiritalis.

and c. 25 (49.23–4), but in a different context:

Non istic racio qua fieri potuerit, disquirenda; sed fides quod factum sit, adhibenda.

159–67 The story is told in the so-called *Verba Seniorum* attributed to Pelagius, which went under the name of the *Vitae Patrum* (PL 73, 978D–980A):

> Dixit Pater noster abbas Arsenius de quodam sene, qui erat magnus in hac vita, simplex autem in fide, et errabat pro eo quod erat idiota, et dicebat, non esse naturaliter corpus Christi panem quem sumimus, sed figuram eius esse. Hoc autem audientes duo senes quod diceret hunc sermonem, et scientes quia magna esset vita et conversatio eius, cogitaverunt quia innocenter et simpliciter diceret hoc, et venerunt ad eum, et dicunt ei: 'Abba, audivimus sermonem cuiusdam infidelis, qui dicit quia panis quem sumimus, non natura corpus Christi, sed figura est eius.' Senex autem ait eis: 'Ego sum qui hoc dixi.' . . . Sed et illi senes abeuntes in cella sua, rogabant et ipsi, dicentes: 'Domine Iesu Christe, revela seni mysterium hoc, ut credat et non perdat laborem suum.' Exaudivit autem Deus utrosque: et hebdomada completa venerunt Dominico die in ecclesia, et sederunt ipsi tres soli super sedile de scirpo, quod in modum fascis erat ligatum, medius autem sedebat senex ille. Aperti sunt autem oculi eorum intellectuales; et quando positi sunt panes in altari, videbatur illis tantummodo tribus tanquam puerulus iacens super altare. Et cum extendisset presbyter manus, ut frangeret panem, descendit angelus Domini de coelo habens cultrum in manu, et secavit puerulum illum, sanguinem vero excipiebat in calice. Cum autem presbyter frangeret in partibus parvis panem, etiam et angelus incidebat pueri membra in modicis partibus. Cum autem accessisset senex, ut acciperet sanctam communionem, data est ipsi soli caro sanguine cruentata. Quod cum vidisset, pertimuit, et clamavit, dicens: 'Credo, Domine, quia panis qui in altari ponitur, corpus tuum est, et calix tuus est sanguis.' Et statim facta est pars illa in manu eius panis, secundum mysterium, et sumpsit illud in ore, gratias agens Deo. Dixerunt autem ei senes: 'Deus scit humanam naturam; quia non potest vesci carnibus crudis, et propterea transformat corpus suum in panem, et sanguinem suum in vinum, his qui illud cum fide suscipiunt.' Et egerunt gratias Deo de sene illo; quia non permisit Deus perire labores eius, et reversi sunt cum gaudio ad cellas suas.

It also appears, in virtually the same words, as an exemplum in the *De Corpore et Sanguine Domini* of Paschasius Radbertus, c. 14, and similarly in the work of the same title by Durandus (PL 149, 1419). Paschasius does not attribute it specifically to the *Vitae Patrum*, as Durandus does, but Ælfric could perhaps have recognised its source from the opening reference to Abbot Arsenius as the authority for the story. Ælfric gives an abridged account that does not quite accord with these versions, which tell how two monks ask for a revelation on behalf of a third who disbelieves in the *veritas* of the body and blood in the eucharist, thinking it to be a *figura;* all three see the miracle, but only the disbeliever is described as partaking of the eucharist.

167–73 The second miracle, concerning Gregory the Great, is to be found in at least three early lives of the pope (the Whitby version, the one by John the Deacon and the interpolated version of Paul the Deacon's Life), and in the eucharistic treatises of Paschasius Radbertus (*De Corpore et Sanguine*) and Durandus (PL 149, 1418), preceding the miracle from the *Vitae Patrum*, though John the Deacon and Durandus fail to mention the gory detail of the finger-joint. I give the text from Paschasius, which seems the likeliest source (*De Corpore et Sanguine*, c. 14, 44–70):

> Sed et illud ex vita beati Gregorii addendum. Cum matrona quaedam nobilis singulis diebus Dominicis oblationes facere consuevisset more ecclesiastico atque offerre, quadam die cum ad communionem sanctam inter alias venisset, ut corpus Christi acciperet; illi autem beatus pontifex offam Dominici corporis porrexit, dicens: Corpus Domini nostri Iesu Christi prosit tibi in remissionem omnium peccatorum; continuo subrisit; quod vir Dei videns, ab ea communionem sacram retraxit, et super altare posuit, donec, explicito ministerio sacro, interrogavit eam cur riserit. At illa: Recognovi, inquit, portiunculam oblationis meae fuisse quam corpus Domini te appellasse audivi, et ideo risi. Tunc sanctus vir Gregorius loquens ad populum, exhortatus est eos Deum exorare precibus ad corroborandam fidem mulieris, ut visibili specie Dominus demonstraret, quod oculis mentis illa credere non valebat. Quod cum oratum fuisset, surgens una cum populo, mox cernentibus cunctis pallam revolvit altaris, contuente etiam illa, invenit partem quam posuerat in modum digiti auricularis sanguine superfusam. Tunc mulieri sacerdos inquit: Disce verum esse quod Veritas ait, quia panis quem nos offerimus, vere est corpus Christi, iuxta ipsius vocem, et sanguis vere est potus. Crede iam tandem quod aliud esse non potest, nisi quod divina maiestas voluit. Deinde sacerdos Christi continuo precibus egit, ut eadem caro et sanguis pristinam reciperet formam; sicque factum est, ut omnes glorificarent Deum, et infidelitas pelleretur feminae, sacroque sancto communicata misterio sanaretur.

174–80 Ratramnus, *De Corpore et Sanguine*, c. 20 (48.7–11):

> Apostolus quoque scribens Corinthiis ait: 'Nescitis quoniam patres nostri omnes sub nube fuerunt, et omnes mare transierunt, et omnes in moysen baptizati sunt, in nube, et in mari, et omnes eandem escam spiritalem manducaverunt; et omnes eundem potum spiritalem biberunt? Bibebant autem de spiritali consequenti eos petra. Petra autem erat Christus' (1 Cor 10.1–4).

180–4 Not from Ratramnus. Cf CH II.12.215–8. The quotation is from Jn 7.37–9:

> (37) In novissimo autem die magno festivitatis stabat Iesus et clamabat dicens si quis sitit veniat ad me et bibat. (38) Qui credit in me sicut dixit scriptura flumina de ventre eius fluent aquae vivae. (39) Hoc autem dixit de Spiritu quem accepturi erant credentes in eum.

184–90 Ratramnus, *De Corpore et Sanguine*, cc. 22–3 (48.34–49.2, 5–8):

> [c.22] Et cum cibus vel potus ille futuri corporis Christi sanguinisque misterium, quod caelebrat ecclesia, premonstraret, eandem tamen escam spiritalem manducasse, eundem potum spiritalem bibisse patres nostros sanctus Paulus asseverat. [c.23] Unus idemque Christus est, qui et populum in deserto, in nube et in mari baptizatum, sua carne pavit, suo sanguine tunc potavit, et in ecclesia nunc credentium populum sui corporis pane, sui sanguinis unda pascit atque potat.

191–8 Ratramnus, *De Corpore et Sanguine*, cc. 27–8 (50.5–11, 16–21):

> [c.27] Et, evangelista narrante, cognovimus quod Dominus Ihesus Christus priusquam pateretur, 'accepto pane, gratias egit, et dedit discipulis suis dicens: Hoc est corpus meum quod pro vobis datur: hoc facite in meam commemorationem. Similiter et calicem, postquam cenavit, dicens: Hic est calix novum testamentum in sanguine meo, qui pro vobis fundetur' (Lc 22.19–20). Videmus nondum passum esse Christum, et iam tamen sui corporis et sanguinis misterium operatum fuisse. [c.28] Sicut ergo paulo antequam pateretur, panis substantiam et vini creaturam convertere potuit in proprium corpus quod passurum erat, et in suum sanguinem qui post fundendus exstabat; sic etiam in deserto manna et aqua[m] de petra in suam carnem et sanguinem convertere prevaluit, quamvis longe post et caro illius in cruce pro nobis pendenda, et sanguis eius in ablutionem nostram fundendus superabat.

199–208 The prompt for this passage is Ratramnus, *De Corpore et Sanguine*, c. 78 (62.13–19):

> Hinc beatus Agustinus in evangelii Iohannis expositione, dum de corpore Christi loqueretur et sanguine, sic ait: 'Manducavit et Moyses manna, manducavit et Aaron, manducavit et Finees, manducaverunt ibi multi qui Deo placuerunt, et mortui non sunt. Quare? Quia visibilem cibum spiritaliter intellexerunt, spiritaliter esurierunt, spiritaliter gustaverunt, ut spiritaliter satiarentur.'

Ratramnus is here quoting Augustine's *Tract.*, 26.11.14–18, but Ælfric has gone behind Ratramnus to paraphrase the Biblical verse which prompted that discussion, Jn 6.49: *Patres vestri manducaverunt in deserto manna et mortui sunt*; and in his explanation of that verse was probably influenced by Augustine's remarks, which are not cited by Ratramnus (Augustine, *Tract.*, 26.11.4–6): *Quare manducaverunt, et mortui sunt? Quia quod videbant, credebant; quod non videbant, non intellegebant.*

208–10 Jn 6.55: *Qui manducat meam carnem et bibit meum sanguinem habet vitam aeternam.*

210–14 Cf Ratramnus, commenting on the similar Jn 6.54 (*De Corpore et Sanguine*, c. 29, 50.24–7):

Non enim dicit quod caro ipsius quae pependit in cruce, particulatim concidenda foret et a discipulis manducanda; vel sanguis ipsius, quem fusurus erat pro mundi redemptione, discipulis dandus esset in potum.

214–7 Not from Ratramnus, but cf CH II.12.160–4, 344–73.

217–20 Ratramnus, *De Corpore et Sanguine*, c. 99 (68.21–4):

Addamus etiam quod iste panis et calix, qui corpus et sanguis Christi nominatur et existit, memoriam representat Dominicae passionis sive mortis, quemadmodum ipse in evangelio dixit: 'Hoc facite in meam commemorationem' (Lc 22.19).

220–2 Cf Ratramnus, *De Corpore et Sanguine*, c. 39 (53.18–22):

Quod semel fecit, [nunc] cotidie frequentat: semel enim pro peccatis populi se obtulit, celebratur tamen haec eadem oblatio singulis per fideles diebus, sed in misterio, ut quod Dominus Iesus Christus semel se offerens adimplevit, hoc in eius passionis memoriam cotidie geritur per misteriorum celebrationem.

As Bakhuizen points out, Ratramnus's original text read *non* rather than *nunc*, appropriately to his argument that the body represented by the eucharist is not the body in which Christ suffered but celebrates its memory. The more 'realist' reading *nunc* seems to have become part of the received text of Ratramnus, and was evidently in Ælfric's version.

222–4 Not from Ratramnus, but cf CH II.21.140–2.

225–44 Ratramnus, *De Corpore et Sanguine*, c. 73 (61.10–11) and c. 95 (67.15–26):

[c.73] Considerandum quoque quod in pane illo non solum corpus Christi, verum corpus etiam in eum credentis populi figuretur. . . . [c.95] Et de hoc mistico corpore volens aliquid apertius et manifestius loqui, sic dicit in consequentibus: 'Corpus ergo Christi si vultis intellegere, apostolum audite dicentem: "Vos estis corpus Christi et membra" (1 Cor 12.27) . . . misterium vestrum in mensa Domini positum est. Misterium vestrum accipitis, ad id quod estis . . . ipsum apostolum dicentem audiamus, cum de isto sacramento loqueretur, ait: "Unus panis, unum corpus multi in Christo" (1 Cor 10.17), et reliqua'.

Ratramnus makes it clear that he is quoting Augustine (in fact, Serm. 272, PL 38, 1246) but as Bakhuizen points out Ælfric seems to have consulted more of that sermon than Ratramnus quotes; Augustine continues after the quotation from 1 Cor 10 (Serm. 272, PL 38, 1247–8):

Intelligite et gaudete; unitas, veritas, pietas, charitas. Unus panis: quis est iste unus panis? Unum corpus multi. Recolite quia panis non fit de uno grano, sed de multis. . . . Estote quod videtis, et accipite quod estis [*cf Ælfric 231–3*]. . . . Sicut enim ut sit species visibilis panis, multa grana in unum consperguntur, tanquam illud fiat, quod de fidelibus ait Scriptura sancta, 'Erat illis anima una, et cor unum in Deum' (Acts 4.32): sic et de vino. Fratres, recolite unde fit vinum. Grana multa pendent ad botrum, sed liquor granorum in unitate confunditur. Ita et Dominus Christus nos significavit nos ad se pertinere voluit, misterium pacis et unitatis nostrae in sua mensa consecravit. Qui accipit misterium unitatis, et non tenet vinculum pacis, non misterium accipit pro se, sed testimonium contra se.

247–9 Cf 1 Cor 11.29: *Qui enim manducat et bibit indigne iudicium sibi manducat et bibit non diiudicans corpus.*

249–54 Ratramnus, *De Corpore et Sanguine*, c. 75 (61.19–26):

Sic et in vino qui sanguis Christi dicitur, aqua misceri iubetur, nec unum sine altero permittitur offerri, quia nec populus sine Christo, nec Christus sine populo; sicut nec caput sine corpore, vel corpus sine capite, valet existere. Aqua denique in illo sacramento populi gestat imaginem. Igitur si vinum illud sanctificatum per ministrorum officium, in Christi sanguinem corporaliter convertitur; aqua quoque, quae pariter admixta est, in sanguinem populi credentis necesse est corporaliter convertatur.

258–69 Ælfric is elaborating, as he says, part of the epistle for the day, 1 Cor. 5.7–8:

(7) Expurgate vetus fermentum ut sitis nova consparsio sicut estis azymi. Etenim pascha nostrum immolatus est Christus. (8) Itaque epulemur non in fermento veteri neque in fermento malitiae et nequitiae sed in azymis sinceritatis et veritatis.

For the comments cf Smaragdus's exposition of the epistle (*Collectiones*, PL 102, 224CD):

Etenim Pascha nostrum immolatus est Christus. Ac si diceret, non a nobis in figura agnus, sicut Iudaeis, sed in veritate nobis quotidie occiditur Christus, et Pascha quotidie celebramus, si fermentum malitiae et nequitiae non habemus. Et Iudaei quidem septem diebus azyma comedebant, et quia in septem diebus mundus est factus, qui semper in suo ordine revolvitur. Nos simpliciter Pascha celebramus si in his diebus pure et sinceriter versamur. Quod est enim aliud fermentum, nisi corruptio naturae, quod et ipsum prius a naturali dulcedine recedens, adulterino acrore corruptum est.

269–72 Gregory, Hom. 22, PL 76, 1179AB:

Lactucae vero agrestes valde amarae sunt. Carnes ergo Agni cum lactucis agrestibus sunt edendae, ut cum corpus Redemptoris accipimus, nos pro peccatis nostris in fletibus affligamus, quatenus ipsa amaritudo poenitentiae abstergat a mentis stomacho perversae humorem vitae.

273–84 Gregory, Hom. 22, PL 76, 1179BCD:

Nunquid, fratres charissimi, Israeliticus ille populus in Aegypto constitutus comedere agnum crudum consueverat . . . Nec coctum aqua. Sed quid aqua, nisi humanam scientiam designat . . . Quid crudae Agni carnes nisi inconsideratam ac sine reverentia cogitationis relictam illius humanitatem significant? . . . Omnis enim qui Redemptorem nostrum purum hominem credit, quid iste aliud quam agni carnes crudas comedit, quas videlicet coquere per divinitatis eius intelligentiam noluit? Omnis vero qui incarnationis eius mysteria iuxta humanam sapientiam discutere conatur, carnes agni aqua vult coquere,. . . . Qui ergo Paschalis gaudii solemnitatem celebrare desiderat . . . assas igni carnes comedat, ut dispensari omnia per sancti Spiritus potentiam sciat.

284–7 Exod 12.9–10, quoted above, but with the added detail of the bones taken from God's instructions for the future observance of the passover at Exod 12.46: *In una domo comedetur nec efferetis de carnibus eius foras nec os illius confringetis.*

287–302 Gregory, Hom. 22, PL 76, 1179D-80AB:

De quo adhuc recte subiungitur: 'Caput cum pedibus et intestinis vorabitis' quia Redemptor noster est α et ω, Deus videlicet ante saecula, et homo in fine saeculorum. . . . Caput ergo agni vorare, est divinitatem illius fide percipere. . . . Quid vero sunt intestina, nisi verborum illius occulta et mystica mandata? Quae tunc voramus, cum verba vitae cum aviditate sumimus. . . . 'Non remanebit ex eo quidquam usque mane', quia eius dicta magna sunt sollicitudine discutienda, quatenus priusquam dies resurrectionis appareat, in hac praesentis vitae nocte omnia illius mandata intelligendo et operando penetrentur. . . . Quod ex agno remanet igne comburimus quando hoc quod de mysterio incarnationis eius intelligere et penetrare non possumus potestati sancti Spiritus humiliter reservamus, ut non superbe quis audeat vel contemnere vel denuntiare quod non intelligit, sed hoc igni tradit cum sancto Spiritui reservat.

303–9 Cf Gregory, Hom. 22, PL 76, 1180B-81A:

Quid in renibus nisi delectatio carnis accipitur? . . . Qui ergo pascha comedit, habere renes accinctos debet, ut . . . carnem a luxuria restringat. . . . Calceamenta habebitis in pedibus. . . . Quid vero calceamenta, nisi pelles mortuorum animalium? Calceamenta autem pedes muniunt. Quae vero sunt mortua animalia, ex quorum pellibus nostri muniuntur pedes, nisi antiqui patres, qui nos ad aeternam patriam praecesserunt? Quorum dum exempla conspicimus, nostri operis pedes munimus. Calceamenta ergo in pedibus habere est mortuorum vitam conspicere, et nostra vestigia a peccati vulnere custodire.

309–13 Cf Gregory, Hom. 22, PL 76, 1181A: *Quid lex per baculum nisi pastoralem custodiam designat?*

313–17 Cf Gregory, Hom. 22, PL 76, 1181AB:

Mandata Dei, mysteria Redemptoris, coelestis patriae gaudia, cum festinatione cognoscite, et praecepta vitae cum festinatione implere curate. . . . Festinantes ergo pascha comedite, id est ad solemnitatem patriae coelestis anhelate. Nemo in huius vitae itinere torpeat, ne in patria locum perdat.

For 316–7 Cook (1898) cites Sir 5.8–9:

> (8) Non tardes converti ad Deum et ne differas de die in diem. (9) Subito enim venit ira illius et in tempore vindictae disperdet te.

317–23 Not mentioned by Gregory, and it is not part of the text from Exodus 12 which he is expounding. Isidore has something similar in the paragraph on the passover already cited (*In Exodum*, c. 15.1, *Quaestiones*, PL 83, 294D):

> Prohibentur qui pascha faciunt ossa frangere; non franguntur in cruce ossa Domini, attestante evangelista, qui ait: 'Os eius non comminuetis.'

But Jn 19.36 might have been sufficient prompting. Those who will see whom they wounded at the last judgement are presumably specifically the Roman *cempan*.

324–35 Cf Augustine, *Tract.*, 55.1.11–31:

> In sua vero lingua, hoc est in hebraea, Pascha transitus dicitur; propterea tunc primum Pascha celebravit populus Dei, quando ex Aegypto fugientes, rubrum mare transierunt. Nunc ergo figura illa prophetica in veritate completa est, cum . . . a perditione huius saeculi tamquam a captivitate vel interemtione Aegyptia liberamur; et agimus saluberrimum transitum, cum a diabolo transimus ad Christum, et ab isto instabili saeculo ad eius fundatissimum regnum. . . . Hoc itaque nomen, id est, Pascha, quod latine . . . transitus nuncupatur, velut interpretans nobis beatus evangelista: 'Ante diem', inquit, 'festum Paschae, sciens Iesus quia venit hora eius ut transeat ex hoc mundo ad Patrem' (Jn 13.1). . . . Spes membris in capite data est, quod essent illo transeunte sine dubio secutura.

Leinbaugh[9] argues that Ælfric was also influenced by Bede's briefer adaptation of this passage, in Homily II.5 (CCSL 122), but it is hard to see any very convincing parallels; though there is a fleeting reference to the tropological level, which Augustine neglects (Bede, Hom. II.5, 13–16):

> . . . Quod eius exemplo fideles abiectis temporalibus desideriis, abiecta vitiorum servitute, continuis virtutum studiis transire debeant ad promissionem patriae caelestis.

The passage from Augustine is repeated in Haymo's homily 67, but less closely.

16 EASTER

The two parts of this homily deal with two appearances of Christ to his disciples after the resurrection. Christ's appearance to two disciples on the road to Emmaus, Luke 24.13–35, was the reading for Monday in Easter week, and his appearance to the disciples fishing, John 21.1–12, was the reading for Wednesday. But the first part of the homily is clearly intended to be read on Easter Day

[9] See Leinbaugh, 'Ælfric's Easter Sermon'.

as the title and opening words show (cf too lines 39–40); the second part, which has no separate rubric in most manuscripts, seems to be intended likewise for Easter Day (cf esp. 102–4). Each part has its own introduction and conclusion and may once have figured as an independent (though very short) address, as Thorpe prints them; but as they stand in the Second Series collection they seem intended to form a single composite item (Ælfric says in the preface that he has put a Latin rubric before each of the forty items in the collection), though Ælfric may have had it in mind that they could be used as alternatives, both to each other and to the longer and more abstruse homily 15. Easter is the only occasion in the Series for which there is double provision. The first part of II.16 seems to have been conceived as a homily on hospitality.

In both parts Ælfric cites Gregory as his source; the texts in question are homilies 23 and 24, both appointed for the Easter period in Paul the Deacon's homiliary.[1] For the first part there seems also to have been some use, as Förster suggested, of Bede's commentary on Luke, or perhaps Smaragdus who copies all the relevant material from Bede for his homily for Monday in Easter Week; both recycle Gregory's material, but do not have all the material from him that Ælfric used. For the second part, Förster noted one sentence which seems to match the homily by Smaragdus, who otherwise agrees very closely with Gregory, and suggested that this comes from an untraced variant version of Gregory's homily which both Ælfric and Smaragdus used. Joyce Hill has argued more recently that, despite his own claims, Ælfric did not use Gregory's homily directly but relied on Smaragdus's text and cited Gregory as source because it was so marked in the margins of his copy of Smaragdus.[2] Since the Gregory text was in Paul the Deacon's homiliary for the Easter period, however, it seems highly likely that Ælfric had at least read it as well as Smaragdus, and there is nothing to indicate reliance on the latter apart from the single sentence cited by Förster. In general Ælfric follows Gregory's wording closely for both parts, focusing closely on the Gospel text.

Sources and Notes

The following texts are cited below:

1. Amalarius, *Liber Officialis*, ed. J. Hanssens in *Amalarii Episcopi Opera Liturgica Omnia*, Studi e Testi 139 (Vatican City, 1948).
2. Bede, *Commentarius in Lucam*, ed. D. Hurst, CCSL 120 (Turnhout, 1960), pp. 5–425.
3. Gregory the Great, *Homiliae in Evangelia*, PL 76, Hom. 23 and 24, cols. 1181–3 and 1183–8.
4. Smaragdus, *Collectiones in Evangelia et Epistolas*, PL 102, cols. 230–4 and 242–7.

[1] See Förster 1894, pp. 6–7, and Smetana 1959, p. 198.
[2] Hill 1992, pp. 228–32.

1–2 A strikingly alliterative sentence.

2–38 Lc 24.13–35:

(13) Et ecce duo ex illis ibant ipsa die in castellum quod erat in spatio stadiorum sexaginta ab Hierusalem nomine Emmaus. (14) Et ipsi loquebantur ad invicem de his omnibus quae acciderant. (15) Et factum est dum fabularentur et secum quaererent et ipse Iesus adpropinquans ibat cum illis. (16) Oculi autem illorum tenebantur ne eum agnoscerent. (17) Et ait ad illos: qui sunt hii sermones quos confertis ad invicem ambulantes et estis tristes? (18) Et respondens unus cui nomen Cleopas dixit ei: tu solus peregrinus es in Hierusalem et non cognovisti quae facta sunt in illa his diebus? (19) Quibus ille dixit quae? Et dixerunt: de Iesu Nazareno qui fuit vir propheta potens in opere et sermone coram Deo et omni populo. (20) Et quomodo eum tradiderunt summi sacerdotum et principes nostri in damnationem mortis et crucifixerunt eum. (21) Nos autem sperabamus quia ipse esset redempturus Israhel et nunc super haec omnia tertia dies hodie quod haec facta sunt. (22) Sed et mulieres quaedam ex nostris terruerunt nos quae ante lucem fuerunt ad monumentum (23) et non invento corpore eius venerunt dicentes se etiam visionem angelorum vidisse qui dicunt eum vivere. (24) Et abierunt quidam ex nostris ad monumentum et ita invenerunt sicut mulieres dixerunt, ipsum vero non viderunt. (25) Et ipse dixit ad eos: o stulti et tardi corde ad credendum in omnibus quae locuti sunt prophetae. (26) Nonne haec oportuit pati Christum et ita intrare in gloriam suam? (27) Et incipiens a Mose et omnibus prophetis interpretabatur illis in omnibus scripturis quae de ipso erant. (28) Et adpropinquaverunt castello quo ibant et ipse se finxit longius ire. (29) Et coegerunt illum dicentes: mane nobiscum quoniam advesperascit et inclinata est iam dies; et intravit cum illis. (30) Et factum est dum recumberet cum illis accepit panem et benedixit ac fregit et porrigebat illis. (31) Et aperti sunt oculi eorum et cognoverunt eum et ipse evanuit ex oculis eorum. (32) Et dixerunt ad invicem: nonne cor nostrum ardens erat in nobis dum loqueretur in via et aperiret nobis scripturas? (33) Et surgentes eadem hora regressi sunt in Hierusalem et invenerunt congregatos undecim et eos qui cum ipsis erant, (34) dicentes quod surrexit Dominus vere et apparuit Simoni. (35) Et ipsi narrabant quae gesta erant in via et quomodo cognoverunt eum in fractione panis.

Ælfric's *fif mila* (line 5) for the sixty *stadia* of verse 13 implies a calculation of twelve stadia to the mile, rather than the usual eight stadia to the mile which Bede specifies in his commentary (*Comm. Luc.*, 6.2014 ff); the same equation is apparently used at Pope 14.44 (though see Pope's note).

40–50 Gregory, Hom. 23, PL 76, 1182BC:

Ecce audistis, fratres charissimi, quia duobus discipulis ambulantibus in via, non quidem credentibus, sed tamen de se loquentibus Dominus apparuit, sed eis speciem quam recognoscerent non ostendit. Hoc ergo egit foris Dominus in oculis corporis quod apud ipsos agebatur intus in oculis cordis. Ipsi namque apud semetipsos intus et amabant et dubitabant, eis autem Dominus foris et praesens aderat, et quis esset non ostendebat. De se ergo loquentibus praesentiam exhibuit, sed de se dubitantibus cognitionis suae speciem abscondit.

50–52 Cf Bede, *Comm. Luc.*, 6.2035–6 [= Smaragdus, *Collectiones*, PL 102, 231D]:

Semper se quod promisit impleturum designet: 'Ubi enim sunt duo vel tres congregati in nomine meo ibi sum in medio eorum' (Mt 18.20).

52–5 Gregory, Hom. 23, PL 76, 1182C:

Duritiam intellectus increpavit; sacrae Scripturae mysteria quae de seipso erant aperuit, et tamen quia adhuc in eorum cordibus peregrinus erat a fide, se ire longius finxit.

55–63 Cf Bede's more negative formulation, *Comm. Luc.*, 6.2086–96 [= Smaragdus, *Collectiones*, PL 102, 232–3]:

Hoc nobis in loco non ulla scripturam interpretandi, sed gemina nos ipsos humiliandi necessitas incumbit, qui neque in scripturis quantum oportet edocti, neque ad implenda quae discere forte potuimus quantum decet simus intenti. Nam si Moyses et omnes prophetae Christum locuti sunt, et hunc per angustiam passionis in gloriam suam intraturum, qua ratione se gloriantur esse Christianos, qui iuxta virium suarum modulum neque scripturas qualiter ad Christum pertineant investigare, neque ad gloriam quam cum Christo habere cupiunt, per passiones tribulationum desiderant attingere?

64–72 Gregory, Hom. 23, PL 76, 1182D-3A [= Bede, *Comm. Luc.*, 6.2111–5]:

Mensam ponunt, cibos offerunt, et Deum quem in Scripturae sacrae expositione non cognoverant, in panis fractione cognoscunt. Audiendo ergo praecepta Dei illuminati non sunt, faciendo illuminati sunt, quia scriptum est: 'Non auditores legis iusti sunt apud Deum, sed factores legis iustificabuntur' (Rom 2.13).

72–96 Gregory, Hom. 23, PL 76, 1183ABC:

Ecce Dominus non est cognitus dum loqueretur, et dignatus est cognosci dum pascitur. Hospitalitatem ergo, fratres charissimi, diligite, charitatis opera amate. Hinc enim per Paulum dicitur: 'Caritas fraternitatis maneat in vobis, et hospitalitatem nolite oblivisci. Per hanc enim placuerunt [*Vulgate* latuerunt] quidam angelis hospitio receptis' (Hebr 13.1–2). Hinc Petrus ait: 'Hospitales invicem sine murmuratione' (1 Petr 4.9). Hinc ipsa Veritas dicit: 'Hospes fui, et suscepistis me' (Mt 25.35). Opinata res est valde, et seniorum nostrorum nobis relatione tradita. Quidam paterfamilias cum tota domo sua magno hospitalitatis studio serviebat;

> cumque quotidie ad mensam suam peregrinos susciperet, quodam die peregrinus quidam inter alios venit, ad mensam ductus est. Dumque paterfamilias ex humilitatis consuetudine aquam vellet in eius manibus fundere, conversus urceum accepit, sed repente eum in cuius manibus aquam fundere voluerat non invenit. Cumque hoc factum secum ipse miraretur, eadem nocte ei Dominus per visionem dixit: 'Caeteris diebus me in membris meis, hesterno autem die me in memetipso suscepisti.' Ecce in iudicium veniens, dicet: 'Quod uni ex minimis meis fecistis, mihi fecistis' (Mt 25.40). . . . Pensate, fratres, quanta hospitalitatis virtus sit.

By *heahfæderum* (line 83) Ælfric would normally mean patriarchs, but the story which he, drawing on Gregory, goes on to tell is obviously not from the Old Testament and Gregory's *seniorum nostrorum nobis relatione tradita* probably means something like 'reported in a story told to us by our predecessors or elders'. If Ælfric, missing this, did indeed mean patriarchs he was perhaps thinking of Abraham entertaining the three angels in Genesis, or Lot in Sodom.

98–104 A reference back perhaps to CH I.16 and possibly I.15. The passage also links the two parts of this homily. On Christ's eating physical food after the resurrection, see the note to I.21.38–47.

105–29 Jn 21.1–13:

> (1) Postea manifestavit se iterum Iesus ad mare Tiberiadis; manifestavit autem sic. (2) Erant simul Simon Petrus et Thomas qui dicitur Didymus et Nathanahel qui erat a Cana Galilaeae et filii Zebedaei et alii ex discipulis eius duo. (3) Dicit eis Simon Petrus; vado piscari. Dicunt ei: venimus et nos tecum; et exierunt et ascenderunt in navem et illa nocte nihil prendiderunt. (4) Mane autem iam facto stetit Iesus in litore; non tamen cognoverunt discipuli quia Iesus est. (5) Dicit ergo eis Iesus: pueri numquid pulmentarium habetis? Responderunt ei non. (6) Dixit eis: mittite in dexteram navigii rete et invenietis. Miserunt ergo et iam non valebant illud trahere a multitudine piscium. (7) Dicit ergo discipulus ille quem diligebat Iesus Petro: Dominus est. Simon Petrus cum audisset quia Dominus est tunicam succinxit se erat enim nudus et misit se in mare. (8) Alii autem discipuli navigio venerunt, non enim longe erant a terra, sed quasi a cubitis ducentis trahentes rete piscium. (9) Ut ergo descenderunt in terram viderunt prunas positas et piscem superpositum et panem. (10) Dicit eis Iesus: adferte de piscibus quos prendidistis nunc. (11) Ascendit Simon Petrus et traxit rete in terram plenum magnis piscibus centum quinquaginta tribus et cum tanti essent non est scissum rete. (12) Dicit eis Iesus: venite prandete; et nemo audebat discentium interrogare eum tu quis es, scientes quia Dominus esset. (13) Et venit Iesus et accepit panem et dat eis et piscem similiter.

Ælfric's *hlaf ðær onem*, 'bread near by', perhaps reflects Augustine's argument (Tractates on John, 123.2.9 ff, repeated by Smaragdus, *Collectiones*, PL 102,

244D) that the bread in verse 9 should not be understood as being *on* the fire because of the allegorical significance, though Ælfric does not in fact use that distinction between the fish and the bread.

130–42 Gregory, Hom. 24, PL 76, 1184BC [= Smaragdus, *Collectiones*, PL 102, 243C]:

Quaeri etenim potest cur Petrus, qui piscator ante conversionem fuit, post conversionem ad piscationem rediit; . . . Nam piscatorem Petrum, Matthaeum vero telonearium scimus; et post conversionem suam ad piscationem Petrus rediit, Matthaeus vero ad telonei negotium non resedit, quia aliud est victum per piscationem quaerere, aliud autem telonei lucris pecunias augere. Sunt enim pleraque negotia, quae sine peccatis exhiberi aut vix aut nullatenus possunt. Quae ergo ad peccatum implicant, ad haec necesse est ut post conversionem animus non recurrat. [*earlier*] Sed si virtus discretionis inspicitur, citius videtur quia nimirum negotium quod ante conversionem sine peccato exstitit, hoc etiam post conversionem repetere culpa non fuit.

142–52 Gregory, Hom. 24, PL 76, 1184C-85A [= Smaragdus, *Collectiones*, PL 102, 243D]:

Quaeri etiam potest cur, discipulis in mari laborantibus, post resurrectionem suam Dominus in littore stetit, qui ante resurrectionem suam coram discipulis in fluctibus maris ambulavit (Mt 14.23–6). . . . . Quid enim mare nisi praesens saeculum signat . . . ? Quid per soliditatem littoris nisi illa perpetuitas quietis aeternae figuratur? Quia ergo discipuli adhuc fluctibus mortalis vitae inerant, in mari laborabant. Quia autem Redemptor noster iam corruptionem carnis excesserat, post resurrectionem suam in littore stabat. Ac si ipsum resurrectionis suae mysterium rebus discipulis loqueretur, dicens: Iam vobis in mari non appareo, quia vobiscum in perturbationis fluctibus non sum.

153–72 Gregory, Hom. 24, PL 76, 1185BCD [= Smaragdus, *Collectiones*, PL 102, 244AB]:

Facta est autem discipulis piscationis magna difficultas, ut magistro veniente fieret admirationis magna sublimitas. . . . Bis in sancto Evangelio legitur, quia Dominus iussit ut ad piscandum retia mitterentur, ante passionem videlicet (Lc 5.4–11), et post resurrectionem. Sed priusquam Redemptor noster pateretur et resurgeret, mitti quidem rete ad piscandum iubet, sed utrum in dexteram, an in sinistram mitti debuisset, non iubet; post resurrectionem vero discipulis apparens, mitti rete in dexteram iubet. . . . Quis vero nesciat bonos dextera, et malos sinistra figurari? Illa ergo piscatio . . . praesentem ecclesiam designat. . . . Haec autem piscatio post Domini resurrectionem facta, in solam dexteram missa est, quia ad videndam claritatis eius gloriam sola electorum ecclesia pertingit. . . . In illa piscatione prae multitudine piscium rete rumpitur, quia nunc ad

> confessionem fidei etiam cum electis reprobi tanti intrant qui ipsam quoque ecclesiam haeresibus scindant. In ista vero piscatione et multi pisces et magni capiuntur, et rete non rumpitur, quia sancta electorum ecclesia, in continua auctoris sui pace requiescens, nullis iam dissensionibus dilaniatur.

The final point is rather differently put: in describing the breaking of the net, Ælfric thinks of apostates leaving the church rather than heretics damaging it. The same striking difference of emphasis is evident in Ælfric's later homily on the fishing episode from Luke 5.4–11, Pope 14.147 ff., where Ælfric develops further the theme of those who 'escape' from the church, identifying them with those in his own time who side with the Vikings. (Smaragdus here reproduces Gregory verbatim but omits some intervening material after the previous passage, not used by Ælfric. Augustine's series of sermons on the two stories of fishing, Serm. 248–52, show the same emphasis as Gregory on heresies and schisms.)

173–84 Gregory, Hom. 24, PL 76, 1185D-6A [= Smaragdus, *Collectiones*, PL 102, 245A]:

> Captis autem tam magnis piscibus, 'Ascendit Simon Petrus, et traxit rete in terram.' . . . Ipsi quippe sancta ecclesia est commissa, ipsi specialiter dicitur: 'Simon Ioannis amas me? Pasce oves meas' (Jn 21.15; *Ælfric adds v.17:* et dicit ei Domine tu omnia scis tu scis quia amo te). . . . Quia ergo praedicator ecclesiae nos a mundi huius fluctibus separat, . . . quia sanctae praedicationis voce stabilitatem aeternae patriae fidelibus ostendit. Hoc egit verbis, hoc epistolis, hoc agit quotidie miraculorum signis.

But Gregory's argument that Peter *showed* heaven to the faithful through his teachings and miracles is rather different from Ælfric's notion that he brings them to heaven through his intercession and the power of forgiveness granted to him; Ælfric seems to be thinking more of Peter's control over the gates of heaven.

184–5 Gregory gives two elaborate numerological explanations of the number of fishes: the substitute sentence in MS U here, almost certainly added by Ælfric himself in the course of revision and using his characteristic late rhythmical style, summarises the second of these explanations (Hom. 24, PL 76, 1186), which identifies the number with the Trinity and the elect in heaven.

186–99 Close to Gregory, Hom. 24, PL 76, 1186D, but as Förster showed, the slight recasting in Smaragdus seems to match Ælfric's wording more closely (*Collectiones*, PL 102, 247AB):

> Quid est quod Redemptor noster piscem assum post resurrectionem manducavit, et in alio Evangelio dicitur, cum pisce asso favum mellis, in isto vero panem cum pisce? Quid enim piscis assus significat, nisi Christum passum, quid in favo mellis, nisi divinitatis dulcedinem. . . . An qui in pisce asso figurari voluit tribulationem passionis suae, in favo mellis utramque

naturam exprimere voluit personae suae. Favus quippe mel in cera est, mel vero in cera, est divinitas in humanitate, quod ab hac quoque lectione non discrepat, nam piscem comedit et panem qui enim assari ut piscis potuit ex humanitate, pane nos reficit ex divinitate, qui ait: 'Ego sum panis vivus qui de coelo descendi' (Jn 6.35). Assum vero piscem comedit et panem, ut ipso suo cibo nobis ostenderet, quia et passionem ex nostra humanitate pertulit, et resurrectionem nostram ex sua divinitate procuravit.

The same wording is found in Alcuin's Commentary on John's Gospel (PL 100, 998AB), but Smaragdus seems a more likely source for Ælfric. Förster's suggestion that both Smaragdus and Ælfric were drawing on a variant version of Gregory seems not unlikely. None of the commentators seem to interpret the fire.

200–6 Gregory, Hom. 24, PL 76 [= Smaragdus, *Collectiones*, PL 102, 246C]:

[1187C] Cur cum septem discipulis ultimum convivium celebrat, nisi quod eos tantummodo qui septiformi gratia sancti Spiritus pleni sunt futuros secum in aeterna refectione denuntiat? . . . [1188A] Mementote quid de eodem spiritu Paulus dicat: 'Si quis spiritum Christi non habet, hic non est eius' (Rom 8.9).

The list of the seven gifts of the Spirit is from Is 11.2–3:

(2) Et requiescet super eum spiritus Domini spiritus sapientiae et intellectus spiritus consilii et fortitudinis spiritus scientiae et pietatis (3) et replebit eum spiritus timoris Domini.

The list is given earlier by Gregory (Hom. 24, PL 76, 1186B) and Smaragdus (*Collectiones*, PL 102, 245).

208–25 Not in Gregory or Smaragdus. The Psalm verse (117.24) features prominently in the Easter liturgy. Cf Amalarius, *Liber Officialis*, IV.23.12:

Igitur quia una die resurrexit Dominus, sic currunt officia nostra per illos septem dies, quasi adhuc sit dies dominica. . . . cantores quotidie cantant: 'Haec dies quam fecit Dominus.'

Line 218 is conceivably an allusion to Amos 5.18: *Vae desiderantibus diem Domini; ad quid eam vobis? Dies Domini ista tenebrae et non lux.*

Ælfric seems to be alluding to traditions of general celebration and recreation during Easter week, and contrasting them with the more measured celebration of the monastic liturgy.

17 PHILIP AND JAMES

The two apostles have quite distinct histories but share a feast-day and, according to the Old English verse *Menologium* at least, died on the same day.

St Philip is mentioned once in a list of the apostles in the synoptic Gospels, and several times in St John's Gospel, but Ælfric does not discuss these earlier appearances. The *Old English Martyrology* gives his feast-day under 1 May, and a few details from the legend used by Ælfric (OE Martyrology, II.72–3). Cynewulf mentions his martyrdom amongst the Asians (*Fates of the Apostles*, 37–41).

St James is a more difficult figure to identify. 'James the son of Alphaeus' is listed as one of the apostles at Mark 3.18, in addition to James the brother of John. A 'James the less' is mentioned at Mark 15.40, simply as the son of one of the three Maries at the tomb. And a James is mentioned as the brother of Christ at Mark 6.3, and then as a leading figure in the church in Jerusalem in Acts. Isidore identifies the apostle of Mark 3.18 with James the Just, the brother of the Lord and leader of the church, though redefining him as cousin (*De Ortu et Obitu*, 76.1, Chaparro Gómez, 1985): *Iacobus Alfei, episcopus Hierosolimorum primus, cognomento Iustus, sororis matris Domini filius, unde et Domini frater vocatus*. The *Old English Martyrology* similarly identifies the two and summarises the story told by Ælfric, but gives the feast under 22 June. Ælfric evidently follows this tradition of identifying the apostle with the leader of the church in Jerusalem, but says nothing of his relationship to Christ either here or when he refers to James the Just in other texts (e.g. CH I.22.102, 28.28, On the Old and New Testament, 1000, Crawford, p. 60). He identified the other apostle James, the brother of John the Evangelist, as a cousin of Christ, but since (as Pope has shown, pp. 217–20) he probably knew a comment by Haymo identifying both James's as cousins of Christ (i.e. as the sons of two sisters of the Virgin Mary), this should not have prevented him seeing James the Just as Christ's cousin as well. Since Ælfric refers to James the brother of John as James *se gingra*, he may have identified him, rather than James the Just, with James the less, *Iacobus minor*, the son of Mary, thus removing some of the evidence for identifying James the Just as a cousin of Christ.

The reading appointed for this occasion was John 14.1 ff (which mentions Philip but not James), and Paul the Deacon's homiliary provided an extract from Augustine's Tractates for the purpose. (Smaragdus and Haymo do not provide for the occasion.) But Ælfric has chosen instead to give the legends of the apostles' preaching and death. For the brief account of Philip, Förster[1] identified as Ælfric's source the short account of Philip's teaching and death printed by Mombritius (BHL 6814). It is a fairly close rendering. The one substantial difference is that whereas Ælfric's account implies a peaceful death, the *Passio* ends with a brief account of the apostle's martyrdom at the hands of unbelievers:

> Post haec infideles ipsum tenuerunt et cruci instar magistri eius quem praedicabat affixerunt.

Traditions seem to have been variable on this point. Aldhelm, in his *Carmina Ecclesiastica*, seems to hint at his martyrdom, and *The Fates of the Apostles* refers explicitly to his death on a cross (lines 37–41), but the *Old English Martyrology* does not mention it (OE Martyrology, II.72–3) and the Martyrology attributed to Bede says only *et apud Hierapolim dormivit in pace*. Philip's death on the cross is reported

[1] Förster 1892, p. 22.

as early as Jerome's *Chronicon*, but it is not in the Ps-Abdias version of his life (printed Fabricius, II.738). More relevantly, it is not in all versions of the legend printed by Mombritius: Zettel reports that the two manuscripts of the Cotton-Corpus legendary which contain the legend lack the relevant sentence, reading simply *perrexit ad Dominum*, as printed below;[2] the same variant is also noted in the ASS, and occurs in the copy in an early manuscript from England, Cambridge, Pembroke College, MS 24, f.8. Ælfric presumably found the legend in his copy of the Cotton-Corpus legendary, and accepted its account of a peaceful end.

For St James, the legendary provided a brief account of the apostle's martyrdom (BHL 4093, as printed in Fábrega Grau and Mombritius),[3] drawn verbatim from the narrative in the *Historia Ecclesiastica* of Eusebius, as translated by Rufinus (II.xxiii). Ælfric's account corresponds quite closely with this, but he supplemented it with further material adapted from later in the *Historia Ecclesiastica* (III.viii), describing various miraculous signs which followed in Jerusalem, sent to warn the Jews of the divine wrath and allow them opportunity to repent, and culminating in a brief reference to the consequent destruction of Jerusalem.[4] He is here developing a theme and subject already explored in CH I.28, where he describes the Jews' persecution of Stephen and the two James, their failure to respond to the forty years' opportunity for repentance which God offered them, and then the destruction of their city by the Romans as divine punishment for their crimes. He presumably took the material directly from the *Historia Ecclesiastica*.

The style of the first part is intermittently rhythmical, and almost entirely so from line 26 onwards, with frequent alliteration; the second part is rhythmical throughout, and often alliterative.

Sources and Notes

The following texts are cited below:

1. Anon., *Passio Philippi*, in Mombritius 1910, II.385.
2. Rufinus, *Historia Ecclesiastica*, ed. T. Mommsen, in *Eusebius Werke*, ed. E. Klostermann, vol. 2, 2 parts, GCS 9.1 and 9.2 (Leipzig, 1903–8).

1–16 *Passio Philippi*, Mombritius 1910, II.385.2–13:

Sanctus Philippus apostolus domini nostri Iesu Christi post ascensum salvatoris per annos viginti instanter praedicavit gentibus per Scythiam evangelium. Ubi cum tentus esset a gentibus, adductus est ad statuam Martis, et cum compelleretur ad sacrificandum, exiit de basi in qua statua Martis stabat draco ingens, et percussit filium pontificis qui ministrabat ignem sacrificii. Percussit etiam duos tribunos qui praeerant provinciae,

[2] Zettel 1979, pp. 186–7.
[3] Cf Zettel 1979, p. 19, Jackson and Lapidge 1996, p. 137.
[4] Förster 1892, p. 23.

cuius officiales in vinculis tenebant sanctum Philippum apostolum. De flatu autem draconis omnes morbidi redditi vehementer aegrotare coeperunt. Quare Philippus omnibus ait: 'Audite consilium meum, et recuperabitis sanitatem, sed et isti qui sunt mortui suscitabuntur. Draco quoque qui pro vobis est noxius in dei mei nomine fugabitur.' Dicunt ei omnes: 'Dic nobis quid faciamus'. Dicit ei[s] apostolus: 'Deiicite hunc Martem et confringite, et in loco in quo fixus stat crucem Dei mei Iesu Christi affigite, et hanc adorate.'

16–25 *Passio Philippi*, Mombritius 1910, II.385.13–21:
Tunc illi qui cruciabantur coeperunt clamare: 'Recuperetur in nobis virtus, et deiicimus hunc Martem.' Facto itaque silentio apostolus dixit: 'Praecipio tibi draco in nomine Domini nostri Iesu Christi: exi de loc isto, et vade, et morare in loco deserto ubi non est accessus hominum et nulla utilitas humanis commodis commoratur, ita ut vadens nemini noceas.' Tunc draco ille saevissimus exiens coepit ire festinus, et ultra nusquam comparuit. Filium autem pontificis qui ministrabat ignem sacrificii et duos tribunos qui mortui fuerant suscitavit, omnemque turbam quae mortua [*presumably an error for* morbida *or some such*] fuerat draconis flatu sanitati restituit.

26–40 *Passio Philippi*, Mombritius 1910, II.385.21–31:
Unde factum est ut universi Philippum apostolum qui persequebantur poenitentiam agentes deum hunc extimantes adorarent. Ipse autem per unum annum iugiter docebat eos quomodo periclitanti mundo adventus Domini subvenisset, quomodo natus ex virgine, quomodo passus, quomodo sepultus die tertia resurrexisset, quomodo post resurrectionem eadem quae ante passionem suam docuerat iterasset, quomodo videntibus apostolis ascendisset in caelos, quomodo misisset spiritum sanctum quem promisit, et veniens sedit super apostolos duodecim et omnium linguas et sermocinationes mentibus apostolorum suorum inseruit. 'Ex quorum ipse numero huc missus scire vos feci ista ydola vana esse et cultoribus suis inimica.' Haec et his similia docente Philippo crediderunt, et multa millia hominum baptizati sunt.

41–60 *Passio Philippi*, Mombritius 1910, II.385.31–46:
Ordinatis autem clericis, episcopo et presbyteris et diaconibus, atque ecclesiis multis instructis, ipse per revelationem ad Asiam reversus et in civitate Hierapoly commoratus haeresem malignam hebionitarum extinxit, qui docebant non verum natum ex virgine dei filium hominem assumpsisse. Erant autem duae filiae eius sacratissimae virgines, per quas Dominus multitudinem virginum lucratus est. Ipse autem Philippus ante septem dies migrationis suae vocavit ad se omnes presbyteros et diaconos, sed et vicinarum urbium episcopos, et dixit eis: 'Hos septem dies mihi Dominus in ista vita concessit. Memores estote doctrinae Domini nostri Iesu Christi, et state viriliter. Dominus autem complebit promissa sua, et corroborabit ecclesiam suam.' Haec et his similia praedicans apostolus Domini annorum octoginta septem [*the text printed by Mombritius here*

describes his martyrdom; other versions read instead perrexit ad Dominum] . . . et in ea civitate positum est sanctum corpus eius. Et post aliquot annos duae sacratae virgines dextra laevaque parte eius sepultae sunt. Ubi praestantur beneficia dei orante apostolo Philippo omnibus qui credunt regnum patris et filii et spiritus sancti regnare in saecula saeculorum.

Ælfric seems to have more information on the daughters than the *Passio* provides.

64–73 Rufinus, *Historia Ecclesiastica*, II.xxiii.4–6 (167.7–16):

Suscepit ecclesiam cum apostolis frater Domini Iacobus, qui ab omnibus cognominatus est Iustus, ab ipsius Domini temporibus perdurans usque ad nos. Et multi quidem Iacobi vocati sunt, sed hic ex utero matris suae sanctus fuit. Vinum et siceram non bibit neque animal manducavit, ferrum in caput eius non ascendit, oleo non est perunctus, balneis non est usus. . . . Solus ingrediebatur templum et iacebat super genua sua orans pro populi indulgentia, ita ut orando callos faceret in genibus ad modum cameli semper genua flectendo.

The thirty years' duration of his rule is noted in CH I.22, probably drawn from Haymo's *Historiae Sacrae Epitome*, II.xxvi (PL 118, 830A): *Tricesimo episcopatus sui anno.*

74–84 Rufinus, *Historia Ecclesiastica*, II.xxiii.9–12 (169.5–23):

Illae autem haereses . . . non crediderunt neque surrexisse eum neque venturum . . . Qui vero crediderunt, per Iacobum crediderunt. In quibus cum multi etiam ex principibus credidissent, perturbatio erat Iudaeorum et scribarum ac Pharisaeorum . . . Convenientes igitur ad Iacobum dicebant ei: '. . . deprecamur ergo te, ut suadeas omnibus convenientibus in die paschae de Iesu. . . . quia iustus es et personam nullius accipis. . . . Ascende itaque in excelsum locum pinnae templi, ut in edito positus appareas omnibus, et verba tua audiantur a cunctis.' . . . Statuerunt igitur supradicti scribae et Pharisaei Iacobum supra pinnam templi et voce magna clamantes ad eum dicunt: 'virorum iustissime, cui omnes nos obtemperare debemus, quoniam populus errat post Iesum qui crucifixus est, enuntia nobis, quod sit ostium Iesu.'

Rufinus makes it clear that the Pharisees are asking James to dissuade the people from their belief in Jesus as the Messiah. Ælfric instead presents the citizens in general asking him to tell them the truth about the Saviour, though he then goes on to give the scribes a more central role.

84–90 Rufinus, *Historia Ecclesiastica*, II.xxiii.13–14 (169.23–171.4):

Tum Iacobus ad eos ingenti voce respondit: 'Quid me interrogatis de filio hominis? Et ecce ipse sedet in caelo a dextris summae virtutis, et ipse venturus est in nubibus caeli.' Cumque hac responsione et testimonio Iacobi multis satisfactum esset et libenter audissent, quae Iacobus protestatus est, coeperunt glorificare deum et dicere: 'Osanna filio David'.

91–104 Rufinus, *Historia Ecclesiastica*, II.xxiii.15–18 (171.5–21):

Tunc rursum ipsi scribae et Pharisaei coeperunt ad invicem dicere: 'Male fecimus tale testimonium praestare Iesu, sed ascendamus et praecipitemus hunc deorsum, ut ceteri terreantur et non credant ei.' Simul et voce magna exclamaverunt dicentes: 'O O et Iustus erravit'. . . . Ascenderunt ergo et praecipitaverunt eum et . . . coeperunt eum urgere lapidibus, quia deiectus non solum mori non potuit, sed conversus et super genua sua procumbens dicebat: 'Rogo, Domine deus pater, remitte eis peccatum . . .'. Cumque eum talia orantem desuper lapidibus perurgerent . . . et unus ex ipsis fullo arrepto fuste . . . cerebro eius inlisit, et tali martyrio consummatus est ac sepultus in eodem loco prope templum.

105–10 Cf Rufinus, *Historia Ecclesiastica*, III.viii.1–2 (215.24–217.5):

Sed infelicem plebem deterrimi quidam homines . . . suadebant ut evidentibus signis et indiciis iracundiae et indignationis divinae non crederent, quibus aperte futurum et urbis et gentis praesagabatur excidium. . . . etenim stella praefulgens gladio per omnia similis imminere desuper civitati et cometes praeterea exitialibus flammis ardere per totum visus est annum.

110–13 Rufinus, *Historia Ecclesiastica*, III.viii.3 (217.12–13):

Vitula sacrificiis admota et aris adsistens inter ipsas ministrorum manus enixa est agnam.

113–15 Rufinus, *Historia Ecclesiastica*, III.viii.5 (217.21–3):

Etenim prope solis occasum visi sunt currus et quadrigae in omni regione per aerem ferri et armatorum cohortes misceri nubibus.

115–24 Rufinus, *Historia Ecclesiastica*, III.viii.7–9 (219.5–221.2):

Etenim quidam Ananiae filius Iesus nomine vir plebeius et rusticus . . . repente clamare coepit: 'Vox ab oriente, vox ab occidente, vox a quattuor ventis, vox super Hierusolyma et super templum . . . vox super populum.' Et indesinenter die noctuque per omnes plateas circumiens haec clamabat, usque quo quidam primores ex populo viri . . . correptum hominem multis verberibus adficiunt. At ille nequaquam pro se aliquid loquens, sed ne eos quidem qui circumsteterant deprecans, easdem voces pari obstinatione et clamore repetebat. . . . flagris ad ossa usque laniatus neque preces neque lacrimas fudit, sed eandem vocem miserabiliter et cum quodam ululatu emittens per singula paene verbera proferebat, addens etiam hoc: 'Vae vae Hierusolymis'.

124–32 Refers generally to the events described in Rufinus's *Historia Ecclesiastica*, III.v–vii—the persecution of Christ, Stephen and the two James, and then the siege and destruction of the city, no doubt recalling the earlier account in CH I.28.23–59.

18 INVENTION OF THE CROSS AND ALEXANDER, EVENTIUS AND THEODOLUS

For the third of May Ælfric gives narratives for two distinct feasts, the Invention of the Cross and the martyrdom of Alexander, Eventius and Theodolus. The Invention is the major feast, noted in the verse *Menologium* among the occasions celebrated nationally, by the laity as well as monks, and given a high ranking in calendars; the martyrdom of Alexander (the fifth pope after Peter, according to legend) and his companions at the hands of Aurelianus is a feast of lower ranking, normally celebrated by the monasteries only.[1] The two texts are not specifically connected in the manuscripts and there is nothing to suggest that Ælfric meant them to be read consecutively, though there is no closing Amen to the first in MS K; but, as Sisam pointed out, as a monastic observance the martyrdom of Alexander has no claim to be included in the Catholic Homilies in its own right and it seems likely that Ælfric at least counted the two texts together in his calculation of forty homilies in the Series. Presumably Ælfric thought the story of St Alexander sufficiently interesting or the feast sufficiently important to include a truncated version of the legend nevertheless, but it is hard to see why.

Ælfric gives a remarkably brief account of the discovery of the cross. His comment on other versions at 51–3 suggests that he was familiar with the traditional legend (BHL 4169) which survives in a number of Anglo-Saxon manuscripts, including copies of the Cotton-Corpus legendary, was retold by Cynewulf in *Elene* and in an Old English prose account[2] and drawn on by the *Old English Martyrology*.[3] But he evidently preferred the account given in the *Historia Ecclesiastica* of Eusebius and Rufinus (which he habitually, and conventionally, attributes to Jerome), which describes Constantine's vision of the cross before a battle in Book IX and Helena's journey to Jerusalem to find the cross in Book X.[4] Even so he radically abridges this account, ignoring, for instance, the account of Constantine's establishment of Christian worship in Rome and the miracle by which the true cross is revealed after Helena found the three crosses. The brevity is puzzling, given the prominence of the feast and the story; perhaps Ælfric's awareness of rival versions made him reluctant to go into detail. In combining and shaping the material from the *Historia* Ælfric seems to have been influenced by the other version of the story; his use of the vision of the cross as a starting-point, leading directly to Helena's search for the cross, is particularly reminiscent of the legend, and the presentation of Maxentius as a cruel aggressor and invader recalls the barbarians who play a similar role in the

[1] Cf Sisam, *Studies*, p. 164, and the figures showing the relative status of feasts given by Zettel (1979, pp. 76–7).

[2] *The Old English Finding of the True Cross*, ed. M.-C. Bodden (Cambridge, 1987).

[3] See the entry by Fred Biggs in SASLC 1990, pp. 12–13.

[4] Förster 1892, p. 37.

other version. Ælfric retells the story of Constantine's battle with Maxentius in graphic fashion, emphasising in particular his anxiety not to shed the blood of his own people; note especially Ælfric's insistence that Maxentius alone was killed (26, 29–30—according to Rufinus his entourage died with him).

For the second narrative, Ælfric used a traditional and familiar legend (BHL 266) which describes a series of miracles and martyrdoms associated with Alexander, culminating in Alexander's own death.[5] The legend was included in the Cotton-Corpus legendary and drawn on for instance for Bede's Martyrology.[6] Perhaps because the other martyrs involved, whose deaths preceded that of the pope himself, had their own entries in martyrologies under other dates (e.g. that of Ado, and the *Old English Martryology*, II.190 ff) Ælfric gives only the last part of the legend, chapter 4, when the persecutor Aurelianus finally turns to Alexander himself and the two priests Eventius and Theodolus, producing a somewhat abrupt starting-point. At some later date, however, he added a prequel covering the rest of the story, which survives only in one manuscript and was printed from there by Pope as item 23. Given the slightly different wording of the one clause that overlaps, 69–70 of this homily and line 208 of Pope's, it is likely that Ælfric revised the present homily and issued a full version rather than just the prequel, but if so it has not survived. Both parts of the present homily are written in Ælfric's alliterative style, apart from the first sentence of each.

Sources and Notes

The following texts are cited below:

1. Anon., *Acta Alexandri*, ASS Maii I.374–5.
2. Rufinus, *Historia Ecclesiastica*, ed. T. Mommsen, in *Eusebius Werke*, ed. E. Klostermann, vol. 2, 2 parts, GCS 9.1 and 9.2 (Leipzig, 1903–8).

3–22 Rufinus, *Historia Ecclesiastica*, IX.i–iv (827.26–829.24):

Etenim cum religiosissimus imperator Constantinus . . . adversum Maxentium urbis Romae tyrannum bellum pararet atque exercitum duceret (erat quidem iam tunc Christianae religionis fautor verique dei venerator, nondum tamen, ut est sollemne nostris initiari, signum dominicae passionis acceperat), cum igitur anxius . . . iter ageret atque ad caelum saepius oculos elevaret et inde sibi divinum precaretur auxilium, videt per soporem ad orientis partem in caelo signum crucis igneo fulgore rutilare. . . . adstare sibi videt angelos dicentes: 'Constantine . . . in hoc vince.' Tum vero laetus redditus et de victoria iam securus, signum crucis, quod in caelo viderat, in sua fronte designat. . . . exin signum, quod in

[5] See Förster (1892, pp. 38–39), Pope (pp. 734–35, 737–46), and Zettel (1979, pp. 187–89).

[6] See Whatley, *Acta*. On the origins of the legend see P. A. B. Llewellyn, 'The passion of St. Alexander and his Companions, St. Hermes and St. Quirinus: a Suggested Date and Author', *Vetera Christianorum* 13 (1976), 289–96. (Reference from Whatley.)

> caelo sibi fuerat demonstratum, in militaria vexilla transformat ac labarum, quem dicunt, in speciem crucis dominicae exaptat. . . . sed et in dextera sua manu signum nihilominus crucis ex auro fabrefactum habuisse perhibetur. . . . deum . . . precabatur, ne dexteram suam, quam signo muniverat salutari, cruore Romani sanguinis macularet.

Lines 21–2 seem to be Ælfric's own formulation, building perhaps on Rufinus's *Historia Ecclesiastica*, IX.iii (829.20–21): *Nec sine oppugnatione patriae, quam tyrannus obsederat, reddere poterat patriae libertatem.*

23–37 Rufinus, *Historia Ecclesiastica*, IX.iv–v, ix (829.25–33, 831.3–5, 831.18–833.2):

> Ecce subito velut vi divina correptus Maxentius agitur in occursum et proruens urbis Romae portis sequi se reliquum exercitum iubet, prior ipse obvius praecurrit armatus. Iusserat autem navibus ad decipulam conpositis fluvium sterni et superpositis pontibus exaequari. Ut ergo ipse eques ac praecursor, oblitus operis sui, cum paucis ingressus est pontem, subsedere naves et in profundum demersus totius belli futuras caedes unius nefandi capitis sui diremit interitu atque inpollutam religiosi principis dexteram a civili cruore servavit. . . . Ita namque Maxentius atque hi qui cum ipso erant armati satellites demersi sunt in profundum pontibusque his devolutus est, quos ad religiosi principis aptarat exitium. . . . Tum vero laeti omnes cum coniugibus ac liberis, senatus populusque Romanus . . . Constantinum velut salutis auctorem ac restitutorem libertatis excipiunt.

Rufinus describes Constantine's triumphant entry into Rome and his promulgation of honours to the Christian God, but does not mention his baptism. The current view is that he was not baptized until just before his death.

38–51 Rufinus, *Historia Ecclesiastica*, X.vii–viii (969.11–26, 970.19–22, 24–5):

> Per idem tempus Helena Constantini mater, femina inconparabilis fide religione animi ac magnificentia singulari . . . Hierusolyma petit atque ibi locum, in quo sacrosanctum corpus Christi patibulo adfixum pependerat, ab incolis perquirit. . . . Sed cum . . . religiosa femina properasset ad locum caelesti sibi indicio designatum . . . in altum purgatis ruderibus tres confuso ordine repperit cruces. Sed obturbabat reperti muneris laetitiam uniuscuiusque crucis indiscreta proprietas. . . . Hic iam humanae ambiguitatis incertum divinum flagitat testimonium. [*the Historia now describes the healing of a dying woman by the cross, at the instance of Macarius, bishop in Jerusalem.*] Sic evidenti indicio regina voti compos effecta templum mirificum in eo loco, in quo crucem reppererat, regia ambitione construxit. Clavos quoque, quibus corpus dominicum fuerat adfixum, portat ad filium [*who uses them in trappings for his warhorse and in his helmet*]. . . . Ligni vero ipsius salutaris partem detulit filio, partem vero thecis argenteis conditam dereliquit in loco.

Alliteration perhaps explains Ælfric's reference to Christ's hands alone (*folman* 51); the Latin implies that it is all the nails.

55 Ælfric's comment that 'we do not have the cross on which Christ suffered' may only mean that it does not survive whole, but it is a very striking remark given the references in late Anglo-Saxon England to the possession of fragments of the true cross:[7] the *Anglo-Saxon Chronicle* records under 885 that the pope sent a fragment to King Alfred; the Chronicle of Ælfric's patron Æthelweard elaborates the detail; King Athelstan gave fragments to Malmesbury and Exeter;[8] and a (presumed) fragment in a reliquary from Ælfric's own time survives in Brussels. Ælfric comments in a later text (LS 27.143–4) that parts of the cross are now distributed to every land.

67–8 Possibly a reference to the martyrdom of Hermes and Quirinus, and other Christians, in the earlier part of the legend. But the reference, here and subsequently, to Aurelianus as a *casere* is puzzling. He is consistently described as a *comes* in the Latin source. At the beginning of the story, in the part not used by Ælfric for this homily, the Latin explains that he was sent to Rome to persecute the Christians by the emperor Trajan, but that Trajan then died and Aurelianus on entering Rome was welcomed by the senate 'as if (or as) they thought him to be their emperor Trajan' [*omnis senatus ita famulatus est ei, ut ipsum Principem crederent esse Traianum*]. Ælfric may have been influenced by this, and perhaps also by the story recorded by Orosius (*Historia Aduersum Paganos*, VII.xxiii) and others, that the somewhat later emperor Aurelianus began to persecute the Christians, whereupon a thunderbolt struck before him and he shortly afterwards died. It is always possible that Ælfric had a version of the source which represented Aurelianus as an emperor; the persecutor certainly speaks as if he is an emperor (cf 83 and its source). By the time he came to write his later prequel, however, Ælfric had evidently changed his mind. He renders the sentence quoted above in cautious fashion as: *Ac Traianus gewat on þæm ilcan geare. Aurelianus þa ferde mid mycelre fare to Rome, and he hæfde ðone anwald þe se oðer ær hæfde* (Pope 23.48–50), a formulation presumably designed to allow for the uncertainty about the persecutor's status; and he calls Aurelianus *cwellere* and *manfulla* but not *casere*.

68–77 *Acta Alexandri*, ASS Maii I.374–5, c. 15:

Deinde sanctum Alexandrum Papam iussit sibi exhiberi, dixitque ei: Exquiro a te prius, ut omnia sectae vestrae mihi mysteria manifestes, ut sciam cur pro Christo nescio quo, occidi quam vinci optetis. S. Alexander dixit: Quod quaeris sanctum est, et non permittimur a Christo sanctum dare canibus. Aurelianus comes dixit: Ergo ego canis sum? S. Alexander respondit: Utinam canis esses, sed quod tibi peius est, etiam cane deterior: canis enim pro factis malis in ignem aeternum non mittetur, sed semel

[7] For an account see M. Swanton, *The Dream of the Rood* (Manchester, 1970), pp. 48–9.
[8] See B. Harbert, 'King Alfred's *æstel*', *ASE* 3 (1974), 103–10, at 109.

mortuus, et corpore simul moritur et flatu. Homo autem, qui ad Dei similitudinem factus est, si per iniqua opera a Dei cultura recesserit, aeternis suppliciis subiacebit.

For Ælfric's characteristic interjection about dogs having no souls, see Godden 1985a.

78–82 *Acta Alexandri*, ASS Maii I.374–5, c. 15:

Aurelianus comes dixit: Si interrogationibus meis satis non feceris, scias te verberibus attrectandum. S. Alexander dixit: Aureliane tyranne, quid est quod talia temerario ausu perquiris? et hoc a me, qui praeter regem meum, qui est in caelis, alterum omnino non timeo? Erras, si te putas, non credendo, sed discutiendo a Christianis hominibus erudiri.

82–9 *Acta Alexandri*, ASS Maii I.374–5, c. 16:

Aurelianus comes dixit: Artificiosa loquacitas tua cesset, non enim ante iudicem qualemcumque loqueris, sed ante eum, cuius potentiam totus mundus expertus est. . . . Ideo permitteris loqui, miserrime, quia vario tormentorum genere cito anima tua extorquenda est. Alexander dixit: Nihil novum facturus es: quis enim innocens manus tuas evasit? Soli illi apud te vivunt, qui negaverunt se servos esse Domini Iesu Christi. Ego autem, quia certus sum me Dominum meum numquam negaturum, necesse est ut a te interficiar.

89–97 *Acta Alexandri*, ASS Maii I.374–5, c. 17:

Tunc iratus Aurelianus iussit eum in eculeo levari, et torqueri ungulis, atque lampadibus attrectari. Cumque diu haec faceret, et ille nullam emitteret vocem, dixit ei Aurelianus: Quare taces? S. Alexander dixit: Quia tempore orationis homo Christianus cum Deo loquitur. . . . Aurelianus comes dixit: Considera quia triginta annorum aetas tibi est, quare tuam perdere vis iuventutem? S. Alexander dixit: Utinam animam tuam non perderes.

98–113 *Acta Alexandri*, ASS Maii I.374–5, cc. 17–18:

[c.17] Et cum esset in eculeo suspensus sanctus Alexander, misit ad Aurelianum uxor eius dicens, Libera te, et dimitte istum sanctum Alexandrum, quia et tu mala morte moriturus es, et me viduam derelinques. Aurelianus dixit: Nonne amicus tuus est, et ideo talia verba pro ipso loqueris? [c.18] Et deposito sancto Alexandro iussit applicari Eventium et Theodolum: et interrogans beatum Alexandrum dixit: Dic mihi, Alexander, isti qui sunt? Alexander respondit: Ambo viri sancti, ambo presbyteri. Applicato igitur sancto Eventio Aurelianus dixit: Quis diceris? Sanctus Eventius respondit: Nomine carnali Eventius dicor, nomine spirituali Christianus sum. Aurelianus dixit: Et tu quando factus es Christianus? Sanctus Eventius dixit: Ante hos annos septuaginta, quia cum annorum essem undecim baptizatus sum, cum autem essem viginti annorum, presbyter ordinatus sum. . . . Aurelianus dixit: Consule senectuti tuae; nega Christum esse Deum tuum, et amicum meum te faciam et divitem comitemque. Eventius dixit. . . . age poenitentiam, et crede Christum Dei filium esse verum Deum, ut possis eius misericordiam invenire.

114–21 *Acta Alexandri*, ASS Maii I.374–5, c. 18:
Tunc amoveri fecit et hunc Aurelianus, et iussit sibi Theodolum applicari, cui et dixit; Tu es Theodolus, qui iussa mea pro nihilo computasti? Sanctus Theodolus dixit: Etiam pro nihilo teipsum semper computabo, qui sanctos Dei his suppliciis maceras. . . . Aurelianus dixit: Quasi tu immunis eris? Theodolus dixit: Credo de misericordia Dei mei, quia non separabor a societate sanctorum martyrum eius.

121–36 *Acta Alexandri*, ASS Maii I.374–5, c. 19:
Tunc Aurelianus iussit fortiter incendi furnum, et iussit Alexandrum et Eventium dorsum ad dorsum ligari, et sic praecipitari in *furnum*[9] candentem. Theodolum vero ante ipsum furnum stare praecepit, ut quasi eorum territus passione ad sacrificandum idolis consentiret. [*Nothing for 125–7*] Sanctus vero Alexander clamavit dicens: Frater Theodole, festina venire huc, et age [*var.* vade] nobiscum, quia ille quartus, qui inter tres pueros Hebraeos apparuit, nunc hic nobiscum est. Et exiliens in ignem Sanctus Theodolus ingressus est furnum, et gratias agentes Deo pariter dicebant: 'Igne nos examinasti Domine, et non est inventa in nobis iniquitas' (Ps 16.3). Quod cum nuntiatum fuisset Aureliano, iratus ingemuit, et angustiatus prae furore, iussit Eventium et Theodolum decollari, Alexandrum vero punctim per tota membra transfigi.

137–44 *Acta Alexandri*, ASS Maii I.374–5, c. 20:
Cumque eis quasi mortuis insultaret, vox facta est repente ad eum de caelo dicens: Aureliane, istis, quibus insultas, apertus est paradisus deliciarum, tibi autem apertus est tartarus et infernus. Ad haec verba tremor corripuit Aurelianum, et coepit dicere ad Severinam uxorem suam, Venit ad me quidam iuvenis cum virga ferrea ignita, et iactavit eam ante pedes meos, dicens: Habes Aureliane quod egisti. Et ex illa hora totus contremui, et in febre sum devolutus, et quid faciam nescio; ora pro me, Severina, Deum tuum, ut indulgeat mihi.

144–56 *Acta Alexandri*, ASS Maii I.374–5, c. 20:
Severina vero dixit ei: Ego vadam et per me sepeliam eos, ne et mihi similiter contingat. Vadens autem in septimo milliario ab urbe Roma via Numentana in praedium suum, Eventium et Alexandrum in uno posuit monumento, Theodolum vere solum in loco altero sepelivit. . . . Severina autem festinans rediit, invenitque Aurelianum loquentem aliena, canden-

[9] ASS version prints *futurum*.

tem febribus, ac sibi omnes miserias reputantem. Cui respondens Severina dixit: Noluisti audire vocem meam, et ecce ipse mala morte morieris, et me viduam derelinques. Qui mox expiravit masticans linguam suam; Severina vero uxor eius vestivit se cilicio, et tam diu iacuit ante limina sanctorum quos ipsa sepelierat, donec venisset ab oriente sanctus Sixtus episcopus, a quo impetravit Severina ut in eodem loco praedii ipsius ordinaretur episcopus, qui omni die quae sunt sancta martyribus celebraret; ideoque locus ipse habet proprium sacerdotem usque in hodiernum diem. Sanctorum autem ipsorum natilitia cum omni gloria et honore celebrantur quinto nonas Maii, benedictus Deus in secula seculorum. Amen.

19 MONDAY IN ROGATIONTIDE

The provision of three more homilies for Rogationtide in the Second Series, following the three in the First Series, testifies to the importance of the period for preaching to the laity. On the period in general, see above under CH I.18 and the introduction to the collection by Bazire and Cross. The present sermon deals widely with the relations of society, beginning with the theme of brotherly love and then turning to the moral duties of the different orders of society—kings, bishops and clerics, judges, husbands and wives, parents and children, servants and masters, rich, merchants, middling classes and poor, the sick and suffering—before ending with some brief comments, relevant to Rogationtide, on prayer and fasting. It is more closely engaged with contemporary social issues than anything else in Ælfric's work, and remarkably hard-hitting on those in authority; the critique of judges is particularly sharp.

There is no real model or particular source for this homily. One striking influence, as J. E. Cross brilliantly observed,[1] is a brief paragraph from the legend of the martyrdom of St Peter and St Paul, in which St Paul explains to the emperor Nero the nature of his preaching, and in particular emphasises that he has taught people to respect authority and support society. Ælfric had used the passage in his account of the martyrdom (see above, CH I.26.206–20 and notes), and it evidently appealed to him both as a justification of Christian teaching as a social force and as a model for his own use. It provides a basis primarily for the account of social classes at 91–251, but its opening reference to brotherly love may also have prompted Ælfric's opening discussion of love, lines 1–90. The anonymous author of the legend presumably had in mind St Paul's teaching as articulated in his epistles, and Ælfric has evidently drawn on his familiarity with the epistles to give substance to the headings suggested by the legend, though in some cases he seems to have reproduced the wording without having particular Biblical citations in mind. The passage in the legend refers, in this order, to: the

[1] Cross 1972, pp. 26–8, 33–6.

rich, middling and poor; fathers and children; husbands and wives; masters and servants. Ælfric adds the three authorities at the beginning—kings, bishops and clergy, and judges—, the merchants after the rich, and the sick and suffering at the end; and rather surprisingly shifts the three classes of rich, middling and poor to the end. In commenting on the duties of the king and the bishop he may have been thinking of the Irish-Latin tract *De Duodecim Abusivis*, which he adapted into English at some stage and used as a source for later work.[2] The ninth abuse is a wicked king (*rex iniquus*) and the tenth a negligent bishop (*episcopus neglegens*), and there are similarities of thought, though rather more with his own adaptation than with the Latin text.[3] There are also signs of influence from two homilies of Gregory, 27 and 30,[4] assigned in Paul the Deacon's homiliary to the Common of Apostles and Pentecost respectively, Augustine's sermon 350 and the Rule of St Benedict. But the main source is the Bible, furnishing a wide range of citations which testify to Ælfric's detailed recall of Scripture.

The homily is written throughout in Ælfric's rhythmical alliterative style. MSS P and f[b] show further revision and expansion by Ælfric, in at least two stages (perhaps dating after 1005), reinforcing especially the critique of judges, merchants and the wealthy.

Sources and Notes

The following texts are cited below:

1. Anon., *Passio Sanctorum Apostolorum Petri et Pauli*, ed. R. A. Lipsius, in Lipsius and Bonnet, I.119–77.
2. Augustine (?), *Sermones*, PL 39, Serm. 350 [=Augustine, *Sermones dubii*], cols. 1533–5.
3. Augustine, *Sermones inediti*, PL 46, Serm. 10, cols. 843–6.
4. Benedict of Nursia, *Regula*, ed. R. Hanslik, CSEL 75 (2nd ed., Vienna, 1977).
5. Ps-Cyprian, *De Duodecim Abusivis*, ed. S. Hellman, Texte und Untersuchungen 4.1 (Leipzig 1909), pp. 1–62. Ælfric's adaptation is printed by Morris, pp. 299–304.
6. Gregory the Great, *Homiliae in Evangelia*, PL 76, Hom. 27 and 30, cols. 1204–10 and 1220–7.
7. Gregory the Great, *Dialogi*, ed. A. de Vogüé and P. Antin, 3 vols., Sources Chrétiennes 251, 260 and 265 (Paris, 1978–80).
8. Paulus Diaconus, *Vita Gregorii*, ed. H. Grisar, 'Die Gregorbiographie des Paulus Diakonus in ihrer ursprünglichen Gestalt, nach italienischen Hands-

[2] See Pope, pp. 373–4.

[3] Jost (p. 37) argued that Ælfric had produced his own English version at an early stage and used it as a source for the present homily; that certainly seems possible, though the sustained use of rhythm and alliteration in the translation would suggest it is not an early text and the parallels are no more than one would expect in the work of the same author.

[4] For the latter see Pope, p. 405.

chriften', *Zeitschrift für katholische Theologie* 11 (1887), 158–73 (text, pp. 162–73) [cited by chapter and lines]. (I have normalised the eccentric spelling of Grisar's text.)

3–7 Mt 22.35–40:

(35) Et interrogavit eum unus ex eis legis doctor temptans eum: (36) Magister quod est mandatum magnum in lege? (37) Ait illi Iesus: diliges Dominum Deum tuum ex toto corde tuo et in tota anima tua et in tota mente tua. (38) Hoc est maximum et primum mandatum. (39) Secundum autem simile est huic: diliges proximum tuum sicut te ipsum. (40) In his duobus mandatis universa lex pendet et prophetae.

12–16 Cf Augustine, Serm. 350, §2 (PL 39, 1534), commenting on the same verses from Matthew:

Si ergo non vacat omnes paginas sanctas perscrutari, omnia involucra sermonum evolvere, omnia scripturarum secreta penetrare; tene charitatem, ubi pendent omnia. . . . Ille itaque tenet et quod patet et quod latet in divinis sermonibus, qui charitatem tenet in moribus.

16–18 Alluding to 1 Cor 13.3:

Et si distribuero in cibos pauperum omnes facultates meas et si tradidero corpus meum ut ardeam caritatem autem non habuero nihil mihi prodest.

18–21 Cf Gregory, commenting on Jn 14.12 ff (Hom. 27, PL 76, 1205AB):

Omne mandatum de sola dilectione est, et omnia unum praeceptum sunt, quia quidquid praecipitur, in sola charitate solidatur. Ut enim multi arboris rami ex una radice prodeunt, sic multae virtutes ex una charitate generantur.

22–4 Jn 14.23:

Respondit Iesus et dixit ei si quis diligit me sermonem meum servabit et Pater meus diliget eum et ad eum veniemus et mansiones apud eum faciemus.

25–32 Gregory, Hom. 30, PL 76, 1220C:

In ipso autem lectionis exordio audistis quid Veritas dicat: 'Si quis diligit me, sermonem meum servabit.' Probatio ergo dilectionis, exhibitio est operis. Hinc in Epistola sua idem Iohannes dicit: 'Qui dicit, Diligo Deum, et mandata eius non custodit, mendax est' (1 Jn 2.4, *perhaps influenced by 1 Jn 4.20*). Vere etenim Deum diligimus, si ad mandata eius nos a nostris voluptatibus coarctamus. Nam qui adhuc per illicita desideria diffluit, profecto Deum non amat, quia ei in sua voluntate contradicit.

Jn 14.23–4, and Gregory's commentary on it, are used more fully by Ælfric in a later homily, Pope 10.29–64.

36–45 Gregory, Hom. 30, PL 76, 1220D–21B:

Certe si domum vestram quisquam dives ac praepotens amicus intraret, omni festinantia domus tota mundaretur, ne quid fortasse esset quod

> oculos amici intrantis offenderet. Tergat ergo sordes pravi operis, qui Deo praeparat domum mentis. Sed videte quid Veritas dicat: Veniemus, et mansionem apud eum faciemus.. . . . Unde et adhuc subditur: 'Qui non diligit me, sermones meos non servat.' . . . Nunquam est Dei amor otiosus. Operatur etenim magna, si est; si vero operari renuit, amor non est.

47–54 Gregory, commenting on Jn 15.14 (Hom. 27, PL 76, 1206BC):

> 'Vos amici mei estis.' O quanta est misericordia conditoris nostri. Servi digni non sumus, et amici vocamur. Quanta est dignitas hominum esse amicos Dei? Sed audistis gloriam dignitatis, audite et laborem certaminis. 'Si feceritis quae ego praecipio vobis.' Amici mei estis, si ea quae praecipio vobis facitis. Ac si aperte dicat: Gaudetis de culmine, pensate quibus laboribus pervenitur ad culmen.

54–9 Cf perhaps a sentence from the sermon addressed by Gregory to the Roman people in time of plague, incorporated in Paul the Deacon's Life of the pope and taken thence by Ælfric in CH II.9 (*Vita Gregorii*, 11.24): *Nullus autem de iniquitatum suarum immanitate desperet.*

60–63 Paraphrasing Mt 22.37–8 again, followed by 1 Jn 4.12: *Si diligamus invicem Deus in nobis manet et caritas eius in nobis perfecta est*, and Rom 13.10: *Plenitudo ergo legis est dilectio.*

64–6 Mt 23.8–9: (8) *Omnes autem vos fratres estis* (9) *et . . . unus enim est Pater vester qui in caelis est.*

69–73 Cf 1 Jn 3.16–17:

> (16) In hoc cognovimus caritatem quoniam ille pro nobis animam suam posuit et nos debemus pro fratribus animas ponere. (17) Qui habuerit substantiam mundi et viderit fratrem suum necesse habere et clauserit viscera sua ab eo, quomodo caritas Dei manet in eo?

73–80 Gregory, Hom 27, PL 76, 1206B (after quoting 1 Jn 3.17):

> Hinc etiam Iohannes Baptista ait: 'Qui habet duas tunicas, det non habenti' (Lc 3.11). Qui ergo tranquillitatis tempore non dat pro Deo tunicam suam, quando in persecutione daturus est animam suam? Virtus ergo charitatis ut invicta sit in perturbatione, nutriatur per misericordiam in tranquillitate, quatenus omnipotenti Deo primum discat sua impendere, postmodum semetipsum.

81–85 Cf Gregory, Hom. 27, PL 76, 1205CD:

> Qua in re, fratres charissimi, solerter intuendum est quod antiquus hostis, dum mentem nostram ad rerum temporalium delectationem trahit, infirmiorem contra nos proximum excitat, qui ea ipsa quae diligimus auferre moliatur. . . . Nam in odium repente exardescimus; et dum foris invicti esse cupimus, intus graviter ferimur; dum parva foris defendimus,

intus amittimus maxima, quia dum rem diligimus temporalem, veram amittimus dilectionem.

87–90 For the image cf Augustine, *Sermones inediti* 10, §3, PL 46, 845 (apparently authentic):

Qui ergo in hac vita gemunt, et desiderant illam patriam, currant, non pedibus corporis, sed affectibus cordis. Non quaerant naves, sed pennas charitatis apprehendant. Quae sunt duae alae charitatis? Dilectio Dei, et dilectio proximi.

93–6 Cf *De Duodecim Abusivis*, 51.5–9:

Nomen enim regis intellectualiter hoc retinet, ut subiectis omnibus rectoris officium procuret. Sed qualiter alios corrigere poterit qui proprios mores ne iniqui sint non corrigit? Quoniam in iustitia regis exaltatur solium, et in veritate solidantur gubernacula populorum.

96–9 The *De Duodecim Abusivis* lists the actions of a good king and the misfortunes caused by a bad one; cf esp. the summary sentence (52.7–10):

Haec regni prosperitatem in praesenti faciunt, et regem ad caelestia regna meliora perducunt. Qui vero regnum secundum hanc legem non dispensat, multas nimirum adversitates imperii tolerat.

100–4 For the etymology of the word *episcopus*, cf *De Duodecim Abusivis*, 53.19–21, 54.9–11:

Primum namque ab episcopo quid sui nominis dignitas tenet inquiratur, quoniam episcopus cum Grecum nomen sit, speculator interpretatur.. . . . Decet ergo episcopum omnium quibus in specula positus est, peccata diligenter attendere et postquam attenderit, sermone, si poterit et actu corrigere.

There is little similarity otherwise; closer to Ælfric's emphasis is the account of the first abuse (*De Duodecim Abusivis*, 32.10–33.2):

Primus abusionis gradus est, si sine operibus bonis sapiens et praedicator fuerit, qui quod sermone docet, actibus explere neglegit.

109–11 Mt 15.14: *Caecus autem si caeco ducatum praestet ambo in foveam cadunt.*

121–2 Lc 10.16: *Qui vos audit me audit et qui vos spernit me spernit.*

123–7 The quotation of Ps 39.11 seems to reflect the way it is used in the Rule of St Benedict (cf esp. Ælfric's 126–7); *Regula*, 2.8–9:

Tantundem iterum erit, ut si inquieto vel inoboedienti gregi pastoris fuerit omnis diligentia attributa, et morbidis earum actibus universa fuerit cura exhibita, pastor eorum in iudicio Domini absolutus, dicat cum Propheta Domino: 'Iustitiam tuam non abscondi in corde meo, veritatem tuam et salutare tuum dixi (Ps 39.11): ipsi autem contemnentes spreverunt me' [*a combination of Is 1.2 and Ez 20.27*].

128–52 The long and forceful passage on judges has no equivalent in either the *De Duodecim Abusivis* or the *Passio Petri et Pauli*, and draws mainly on Scripture (though the quotations at 136–42 and 148–52 are not obviously directed at judges in the Bible). If, as I think, the additions in MSS P and f[b] are indeed by Ælfric, they show a particular concern to sharpen the attack in this section. Lines 128–30 are Sap 1.1: *Diligite iustitiam qui iudicatis terram, sentite de Domino in bonitate et in simplicitate cordis quaerite illum.* Lines 130–2 are Ps 57.2: *Si vere utique iustitiam loquimini recta iudicate filii hominum.* The additional quotation in MSS Pf[b] at 132 is from Ps 10.6: *Qui autem diligit iniquitatem odit animam suam.*

132–4 Lc 6.36, 38:

> (36) Estote ergo misericordes sicut et Pater vester misericors est. . . . (38) Eadem quippe mensura qua mensi fueritis remetietur vobis.

(Omitting verse 37, which would have been awkward in this context: *Nolite iudicare et non iudicabimini; nolite condemnare et non condemnabimini; dimittite et dimittemini.*)

134–6 Jac 2.13: *Iudicium enim sine misericordia illi qui non fecit misericordiam.*

136–42 Is 1.17–20:

> (17) Discite benefacere, quaerite iudicium, subvenite oppresso, iudicate pupillo, defendite viduam, (18) et venite et arguite me dicit Dominus; si fuerint peccata vestra ut coccinum quasi nix dealbabuntur. . . . (19) Si volueritis et audieritis bona terrae comedetis. (20) Quod si nolueritis et me provocaveritis ad iracundiam gladius devorabit vos.

142–8 Is 5.20–24:

> (20) Vae qui dicitis malum bonum et bonum malum, ponentes tenebras lucem et lucem tenebras. . . . (22) Vae qui potentes estis ad bibendum vinum et viri fortes ad miscendam ebrietatem. (23) Qui iustificatis impium pro muneribus et iustitiam iusti aufertis ab eo. (24) Propter hoc, sicut devorat stipulam lingua ignis, et calor flammae exurit, sic radix eorum quasi favilla erit.

148–52 From Proverbs:

> (2.14) Qui laetantur cum malefecerint et exultant in rebus pessimis. . . . (4.16) Non enim dormiunt nisi malefecerint et rapitur somnus ab eis nisi subplantaverint. . . . (18) Iustorum autem semita quasi lux splendens procedit et crescit usque ad perfectam diem.

153–4 Col 3.19: *Viri diligite uxores et nolite amari esse ad illas.*

154–7 Cf CH I.26.213–5, from *Passio Petri et Pauli*, Lipsius, c.37:

> Docui viros fidem servare coniugibus, sicut illi sibi servare pudorem omnimodis volunt. Quod enim punit maritus in uxore adultera, hoc punit in marito adultero ipse pater et conditor rerum deus.

There is no Scriptural basis according to Cross, and I cannot find any either, or indeed any verbal parallels in other texts. There is perhaps a vague reminiscence of 1 Cor 7.3: *Uxori vir debitum reddat similiter autem et uxor viro.*

157–9 Cf *Passio Petri et Pauli*, Lipsius, c.37: *Docui uxores diligere viros suos et timere eos quasi dominos.* Cross suggests a reference to Eph 5.22: *Mulieres viris suis subditae sint sicut Domino*, or perhaps Col 3.18: *Mulieres subditae estote viris sicut oportet in Domino.* But in either case there is a curious shift from *Domino* to *dominis* (which does not figure in the recorded Vulgate variants). Ælfric's *gehyrsumian* for *diligere* perhaps reflects the Biblical texts.

159–66 A combination of Mark, Matthew and 1 Corinthians:

> (Mc 10.11) Et dicit illis quicumque dimiserit uxorem suam et aliam duxerit, adulterium committit super eam. (Mt 5.32) Et qui dimissam duxerit adulterat. (Mc 10.12) Et si uxor dimiserit virum suum et alii nupserit moechatur. (1 Cor 7.10) His autem qui matrimonio iuncti sunt praecipio non ego sed Dominus uxorem a viro non discedere. (11) Quod si discesserit manere innuptam aut viro suo reconciliari et vir uxorem ne dimittat.

For 160–5 cf too the similar verse at Mt 19.9:

> Dico autem vobis quia quicumque dimiserit uxorem suam nisi ob fornicationem et aliam duxerit moechatur et qui dimissam duxerit moechatur.

166–85 For the rest of this extended discussion of marital relations I know of no sources or relevant parallels. Some of the points are raised more briefly at CH II.6.118–27; see the notes there. On 178–9, *nytenu sindon sawullease*, cf Godden 1985a, pp. 280–3.

186–91 Cf *Passio Petri et Pauli*, Lipsius, c.37: *Docui filios obtemperare parentibus et monitis salutaribus.* The underlying reference is Eph 6.1, and Ælfric continues from this passage:

> (1) Filii oboedite parentibus vestris in Domino hoc enim est iustum. (2) Honora patrem tuum et matrem quod est mandatum primum in promissione. (4) Et patres nolite ad iracundiam provocare filios vestros sed educate illos in disciplina et correptione Domini.

and from Mt 15.4: *Nam Deus dixit honora patrem et matrem et qui maledixerit patri vel matri morte moriatur.* Lines 187–9 seem to mean: 'he urged fathers not to anger their children, lest they become weakened (or oppressed) through faintheartedness'; but it is not clear what exactly Ælfric means by this.

192–5 From Proverbs:

> (23.13) Noli subtrahere a puero disciplinam. . . . (14) Tu virga percuties eum et animam eius de inferno liberabis. (13.24) Qui parcit virgae suae odit filium suum; qui autem diligit illum instanter erudit.

195–200 Cf perhaps Prov 29.15: *Virga atque correptio tribuet sapientiam*; and Sap 1.4–5:

> (4) Quoniam in malivolam animam non intrabit sapientia nec habitabit in corpore subdito peccatis; (5) sanctus enim spiritus disciplinae effugiet

fictum et auferet se a cogitationibus quae sunt sine intellectu et corripietur superveniente iniquitate.

200–4 Referring to 1 Sam 3.13, 4.11, 18. The tract *De Duodecim Abusivis* cites Eli's failure to correct his sons as an example of the sixth abuse, *dominus sine virtute* (43.11–14), but it is not used in Ælfric's adaptation.

204–11 Gregory, *Dialogues*, IV.19.7–22:

Nam quidam vir cunctis in hac urbe notissimus, ante triennium filium habuit annorum, sicut arbitror, quinque; quem nimis carnaliter diligens remisse nutriebat, atque isdem parvulus, quod dictu grave est, mox eius animo aliquid obstitisset, maiestatem Dei blasphemare consueverat. Qui in hac ante triennium mortalitate percussus, venit ad mortem. Cumque eum suus pater in sinum teneret, sicut hii testati sunt qui praesentes fuerunt, malignos ad se venisse spiritus trementibus oculis puer aspiciens, coepit clamare: Obsta, pater. Obsta, pater. Qui clamans declinabat faciem, ut se ab eis in sinu patris absconderet. Quem cum ille trementem requireret quid videret, puer adiunxit, dicens: Mauri homines venerunt, qui me tollere volunt. Qui cum hoc dixisset, maiestatis nomen protinus blasphemavit, et animam reddidit.

211–4 Cf Mt 19.14: *Iesus vero ait eis sinite parvulos et nolite eos prohibere ad me venire talium est enim regnum caelorum.*

215–20 Prompted by *Passio Petri et Pauli*, Lipsius, c.37: *Docui servos ut fideliter et quasi deo ita serviant dominis suis.* But essentially an adaptation of Col 3.22–4:

(22) Servi oboedite per omnia dominis carnalibus non ad oculum servientes quasi hominibus placentes sed in simplicitate cordis timentes Dominum. (23) Quodcumque facitis ex animo operamini sicut Domino et non hominibus. (24) Scientes quod a Domino accipietis retributionem hereditatis Domino Christo servite.

The additional sentence in MSS P and f[b] at 220 was almost certainly added by Ælfric and uses his rhythmical style. Assuming that *scæcð* is the pres. ind. 3s of *sceacan* 'to shake, flee, run away' (for the particular sense cf CH II.11.389, though one would expect a preposition such as *of*), the meaning is presumably something like: '(the servant) who runs away from his master and carries off his property is not worthy of any Christian sacrament or sanctified burial'. The need for a moral censure and religious sanction suggests that this is a misdemeanour which a servant might well get away with in terms of law (and indeed implies a class of servants who might be addressed by Ælfric's sermon); and it all reminds one strongly of Wulfstan's impassioned account of slaves who turn viking and dominate and mock their old masters.

220–7 Cf *Passio Petri et Pauli*, Lipsius, c.37: *Docui dominos ut mitius cum servis suis agant*; perhaps drawing on Col 4.1: *Domini quod iustum est et aequum servis praestate scientes quoniam et vos Dominum habetis in caelo*. But, as the reference to the pater noster suggests, Ælfric is also thinking of the discussion at CH I.19.41 (possibly influenced in turn by Augustine): *Se hlaford and se þeowa ealle hi sind gebroðra and ealle hi habbað ænne fæder on heofonum.* On *ðeowt*, cf the similar discussion above at CH II.13.74–80.

228–35 Cf *Passio Petri et Pauli*, Lipsius, c.37:

> Docui sublimes et divites non se extollere et sperare in incerto divitiarum, sed in deo ponere spem suam.

Referring to 1 Tim 6.17:

> Divitibus huius saeculi praecipe non sublime sapere neque sperare in incerto divitiarum sed in Deo.

Ælfric continues with Lc 11.41 (addressed in fact to the Pharisees rather than the rich):

> Verumtamen quod superest date elemosynam et ecce omnia munda sunt vobis.

And Mt 16.26:

> Quid enim prodest homini si mundum universum lucretur animae vero suae detrimentum patiatur?

235–41 There seems to be no Biblical basis for the passage on merchants, but Ælfric does not in fact claim it as St Paul's teaching. The *Passio Petri* has a reference to *negotiatores* but Ælfric does not quote it in CH I.26 and it is about paying taxes not about honest trading: *Docui negotiatores reddere vectigalia ministris reipublicae.* For 238–9 cf Rom 14.10: *Omnes enim stabimus ante tribunal Dei.* One might note that Ælfric's Colloquy also shows an interest in the moral status of the merchant.[5] The fourteen-line passage which Ælfric added later at 238 continues the critique of merchants, including an attack on usury; see Pope, pp. 749–52.

241–2 Cf *Passio Petri et Pauli*, Lipsius, c.37: *Docui mediocres victu et vestimento contentos esse.* Cross cites 1 Tim 6.8: *Habentes autem alimenta et quibus tegamur his contenti sumus.*

242–6 Cf *Passio Petri et Pauli*, Lipsius, c.37: *Docui pauperes in sua egestate gaudere.* Not Biblical; Cross suggests a confusion of two clauses in 2 Cor 6.10, with Ælfric's adaptation here influenced by the phrasing of Rom 12.12: *Spe gaudentes, in tribulatione patientes.* Neither is very convincing, but I cannot find anything else.

246–51 Apoc 3.19: *Ego quos amo arguo et castigo*, and Hebr 12.5–6:

> (5) Fili mi, noli neglegere disciplinam Domini, neque fatigeris cum ab eo argueris. (6) Quem enim diligit Dominus castigat, flagellat autem omnem filium quem recipit.

[5] Stéphane Lebecq emphasises the sympathetic attitude to merchants shown by Ælfric in the Colloquy, describing it as the first clerical defence of the mercantile profession, in 'Ælfric et Alpert: Existe-t-il un discours clerical sur les marchands dans l'Europe du Nord à l'aube du XIe siècle?', *Cahiers de civilisation médiévale* 27 (1984), 85–93.

The two quotations are similarly cited together in a passage on advising the sick by Gregory the Great, *Regula Pastoralis*, III.12 (PL 77, 67–8).

252–9 Job 1.20: *Dominus dedit, Dominus abstulit; sit nomen Domini benedictum.* Ælfric similarly cites Job as a model for patience in sickness at CH I.31.279–87 and CH II.30, esp. 234–8. *We rædað þis eft* (line 254) presumably refers to the reading from Job as part of the monastic and clerical office in September, but the implication is that this will be an occasion for a fuller account of Job's story to those for whom it is unfamiliar; Ælfric is no doubt referring to his provision of a homiletic account of Job for the first Sunday in September, CH II.30, probably written before the present one since it is in plain prose.

259–70 The subject opens out into the more general topic of tribulation. With 259–60 and 266–7 cf Ps 33.20: *Multae tribulationes iustorum et de omnibus his liberavit eos* (quoted by Gregory immediately after the two quotations noted above at 246–51). Lines 268–70 perhaps allude to Mt 10.22: *Et eritis odio omnibus propter nomen meum; qui autem perseveraverit in finem hic salvus erit*. Note the use of rhyme in 263–4.

271–4 Lc 21.36: *Vigilate itaque omni tempore orantes ut digni habeamini fugere ista omnia quae futura sunt et stare ante Filium hominis.*

274–84 Jac 5.16–20:

> (16) Confitemini ergo alterutrum peccata vestra et orate pro invicem ut salvemini. Multum enim valet deprecatio iusti adsidua. (17) Helias homo erat similis nobis passibilis et oratione oravit ut non plueret super terram et non pluit annos tres et menses sex. (18) Et rursum oravit et caelum dedit pluviam et terra dedit fructum suum. (19) Fratres mei si quis ex vobis erraverit a veritate et converterit quis eum, (20) scire debet quoniam qui converti fecerit peccatorem ab errore viae suae salvabit animam eius a morte et operit multitudinem peccatorum.

285–8 Cf 1 Cor 6.9–10:

> (9) Neque fornicarii neque idolis servientes neque adulteri (10) neque molles neque masculorum concubitores neque fures neque avari neque ebriosi neque maledici neque rapaces regnum Dei possidebunt.

If this is what Ælfric had in mind, he has omitted the *molles neque masculorum concubitores*, usually understood now as referring to homosexuality, and the *maledici*. When he cites and translates the list more fully at LS 17.34–44, the omitted phrase is rendered simply (and perhaps evasively): *Ða hnescan vel wacmod, þæt synd þa ðe nane stiðnysse nabbað ongean leahtras.*

288–90 Witches and *wigeleras* figure frequently in Ælfric's lists or denunciations of sins, and in those of Wulfstan and the laws and penitentials, but I cannot find any particular Biblical authority that Ælfric might be alluding to, though it may be a reference to Exodus 22.18 on witches (*maleficos*) or Deuteronomy 18.10.

When Ælfric deals with the subject at length in LS 17 he cites Augustine as his authority rather than the Bible.

290–98 Some concluding remarks about fasting, appropriate to Rogationtide. Ælfric is presumably objecting to the notion that eating fish was a form of fasting.

20 TUESDAY IN ROGATIONTIDE (FURSEY)

For Tuesday in Rogationtide Ælfric gives two visions of the otherworld, those of Fursey and Drihthelm, followed by two further brief stories, from Gregory's *Dialogues* and Bede's *Historia Ecclesiastica*, which also relate to the afterlife and the otherworld. They are printed as items 20 (Fursey) and 21 (Drihthelm etc.) in this edition; whether Ælfric meant them to be read as one sermon or more is not made clear; the items printed together as II.21 have the air of being appendages to the account of Fursey.[1] None of them makes any reference to Rogationtide, though it is possible that the idea of intercession for the dead which becomes prominent in the appended pieces was felt to be appropriate to this time of prayer.

Although Fursey was recognised as a saint in Anglo-Saxon England and his story appears in contemporary legendaries, his feast-day was not of major status and Ælfric's concern seems to be with his vision of the otherworld more than the sanctity of his life. He was perhaps led to this choice of material by a familiarity with (and a wish to counter) a vernacular tradition of giving eschatological sermons, often of a sensational kind using apocryphal legends, in the Rogationtide period (see the items in the collection by Bazire and Cross, especially 5, which shows parallels with the *Visio Pauli*, and 3 and 10 which draw on the Apocalypse of Thomas). Hence the opening attack on the apocryphal *Visio Pauli*. But though he had, and cited, the authority of St Augustine for repudiating the latter, his preference for the vision of Fursey presumably rested less on its authority, since it is an anonymous piece (though it does have the support of Bede who retells the story in his *Historia Ecclesiastica*), than on its content, and specifically its focus on moral issues, articulated through the dialogue with the accusing devils and the exhortations of Beanus and Meldanus. Its eschatology is in fact very unspecific: while it describes the four fires of punishment, it does not distinguish hell from purgatory or paradise from heaven, as the next piece does, or discriminate the kinds of punishments in relation to particular sins.

Ælfric would have known the summary account of Fursey given by Bede, but his source was the fuller anonymous *Vita Fursei* mentioned, and summarized, by

[1] See Godden 1973 on the problem of numbering the homilies and defining their boundaries.

Bede.[2] The closest printed version is that in the ASS (Jan II.36–41), but the copies found in manuscripts of the Cotton-Corpus legendary contain variant readings closer to Ælfric's version at a number of points[3] and I have incorporated these in brackets. I have also supplied two readings from the version edited by Krusch in 1902; Krusch printed only excerpts, but for these gives full collations.[4] Ælfric gives a fairly full rendering of the vision and the moral debates, but severely reduces the preaching of the two priests and the account of Fursey's waking life.

Sources and Notes

The following texts are cited below:

1. Anon., *Vita Fursei*, ASS Jan. II.36–41.
2. Anon., *Vita Fursei*, ed. B. Krusch, MGH, Scriptores rerum Merovingicarum, 4 (Hanover and Leipzig, 1902), pp. 434–40.
3. Augustine, *In Iohannis Evangelium Tractatus CXXIV*, ed. R. Willems, CCSL 36 (Turnhout, 1954).
4. Bede, *Historia Ecclesiastica Gentis Anglorum*, ed. B. Colgrave and R. A. B. Mynors (Oxford, 1969).

1–16 2 Cor 12.2, 4, with the Latin unusually quoted in full, presumably as a testimony to its importance. Ælfric's use of it to reject the apocryphal *Visio Pauli* may owe something to Augustine's rejection in his *Tract.*, 98.8.13–21:

> Qua occasione vani quidam Apocalypsim Pauli, quam sana non recipit ecclesia, nescio quibus fabulis plenam, stultissima praesumptione finxerunt; dicentes hanc esse unde dixerat raptum se fuisse in tertium caelum, et illic audisse ineffabilia verba quae non licet homini loqui. Utcumque illorum tolerabilis esset audacia, si se audisse dixisset quae adhuc non licet homini loqui: cum vero dixerit, quae non licet homini loqui; isti qui sunt qui haec audeant impudenter et infeliciter loqui?

19–25 *Vita Fursei*, ASS Jan. II.36–41, c. 1:

> [§1] Fuit vir vitae venerabilis, Furseus nomine, nobilis quidem genere sed nobilior fide. . . . Huius viri infantia . . . sacris litteris, et monasticis erudiebatur disciplinis. [§2] Crescente vero aetate . . . corpore castus, mente devotus, affabilis colloquio, amabilis adspectu . . . et ita in eo omnium virtutum decorem sapientia adornabat . . . Patriam parentesque relinquens, sacrae Scripturae studiis aliquot vacabat annis; ac sufficienter instructus monasterium in quodam construxit loco, ubi, undique religiosis

[2] Identified by Förster (1892, p. 39).

[3] See Zettel 1979, pp. 152–4, 190–1, 271–2.

[4] Maria Ciccarese gives a full discussion and a text in 'Le Visioni di S. Fursa', *Romana Barbarica* 8 (1984–5), 231–303, but her text is in general less close to Ælfric than that in ASS.

confluentibus viris, aliquos etiam de parentibus suis pia sollicitudine evocare curavit.

The *Vita*, somewhat surprisingly, does not identify Fursey's nationality or native land, though both ASS and Krusch record a variant *in Hibernia* after the opening *Fuit*; but Bede refers to Fursey as *de nobilissimo genere Scottorum* (*Historia Ecclesiastica*, III.xix, 270.13), which may have prompted Ælfric's *Scyttisc*. This is the only occurrence of the word in his work, and could perhaps have meant Scottish rather than Irish (cf 252 and 258), though Bede clearly meant Irish. Neither the *Vita* nor Ælfric identify the other land to which Fursey went on leaving his family and native land, and in which he built a monastery and received his vision. The *Vita* seems to place him in Ireland immediately after the vision, and Ælfric implies he was either in Ireland or Scotland at that time (see 252 and notes); Bede's account, in *Historia Ecclesiastica*, III.xix, is ambiguous but could be seen to locate the monastery and vision in England (*Historia Ecclesiastica*, III.xix, 268–70, 274).

25–38 *Vita Fursei*, ASS Jan. II.36–41, c. 1:

[§3] Quadam die corporis aegrotantis molestia corripitur . . . quasi iam mortuus ad proximam deportatus est casam. [§4] Et cum se tenebrarum caligine circumdari vidisset, quatuor manus desuper ad se extensas conspexit; tenentesque illum per brachia, niveis subvolabant pennis. . . . et quasi per caliginem angelica cernebat corpora. . . . Tertium quoque angelum, armatum scuto candido, et fulgureo nimium gladio, claritate perspicuum, se praecedere conspexit. Hi tres caelicolae, splendentes pari fulgore, mirae suavitatis dulcedinem alarum sonitu, carminum modulamine, conspectusque pulchritudine, illius animae inferebant. Canebant autem uno incipiente: 'ibunt sancti de virtute in virtutem; videbitur Deus deorum in Sion' (Ps 83.8). . . . Audiebat quoque aliud quasi ignotum canticum multorum millium angelorum, unde pauca vix poterat intelligere, hoc est: 'Exierunt autem obviam Christo' [*an allusion to Mt 25.1* exierunt obviam sponso?].

The sense of the last sentence is perhaps that in the dream the second song seemed unfamiliar; in abbreviating the point Ælfric implies that the three words were the whole of the song.

39–56 *Vita Fursei*, ASS Jan. II.36–41, c. 1:

[§5] Tunc unus ex supernis agminibus armato praecedentique angelo iussit, ad corpus venerandum reducere virum . . . sanctus angelus a dextris consistens, dixit ei: 'Oportet te proprium corpus suscipere, quoadusque debitam reportes sollicitudinem.' Tunc vir sanctus taedio separandae societatis angelicae affectus, dixit se ab eis separari noluisse. Angelus vero Domini sanctus respondit: 'Ad te, completa praedicta sollicitudine, suscipiendum revertemur, cantabantque dimidium versiculum.' . . . Tunc qualiter anima corpus intraverit huius carminis suavitate laetificata, intelligere non potuit. [§6] Tuncque in pullorum cantu, roseo colore vultum perfusus, in momento temporis . . . audivit verba admirantium ac plangentium, qui paulatim vestimentis superpositis moventibus denudaverunt faciem eius. Tunc vir Dei circumstantibus dixit: 'Quid, stupentes sonitus inquietos emittitis?' At illi respondentes, omnem rei referebant ei ordinem, qualiter vespertinali hora transisset, et usque ad gallorum cantus corpus exanime in medio servassent. At ille sedens, angelicamque claritatem ac dulcedinem mente revolvens . . . petivitque et accepit sacri corporis et sanguinis communionem, vixitque infirmus ipso die et altero.

57–73 *Vita Fursei*, ASS Jan. II.36–41, c. 2:
[§7] Media vero nocte tertiae feriae . . . manibusque in oratione extensis, laetus excepit mortem. . . . apertis oculis, nullum nisi tres supradictos sanctos vidit angelos, . . . [§8] ululatus et clamores daemonum . . . audivit, ex quibus unus dixit; 'Antecedamus, et ante faciem illius bella commoveamus.' . . . Corpora autem daemonum . . . plena deformitate et nigredine erant. . . . [§9] Bellantia vero daemonia ignitas sagittas iactabant contra illum, sed angelico scuto omnia tela nequissima extinguebantur. Cadebant vero adversarii ante conspectum pugnantis angeli, qui . . . dixit: 'Nolite tardare iter nostrum, quia hic homo non est particeps perditionis vestrae.' Contradicente adversario ac blasphemante, iniustum esse Deo, hominem peccatoribus consentientem, nihil damnationis habere, cum scriptum sit: 'Non solum qui faciunt, sed etiam qui consentiunt facientibus, digni sunt morte' (Rom 1.32). Pugnante vero angelo, existimabat vir sanctus clamorem pugnae, et vociferantium daemoniorum in omnem terram audiri.

74–92 *Vita Fursei*, ASS Jan. II.36–41, c. 2:
[§10] Cumque victus Satanas . . . dixit: 'Otiosos sermones saepe protulit, et ideo non debet illaesus vita perfrui beata.' Sanctus angelus dixit: 'Nisi principalia protuleris crimina, propter minima non peribit.' [§11] Accusator antiquus dixit: 'Scriptum est [*omitted CC*], "Nisi remiseritis hominibus peccata eorum, nec pater vester caelestis dimittet vobis peccata vestra" (Mc 11.26).' Sanctus angelus respondit: 'Ubi se vindicavit, vel cui iniuriam fecit?' Diabolus dixit: 'Non est scriptum: Si non vindicetis, sed si non remiseritis de cordibus vestris (Mt 18.35).' . . . Sanctus angelus dixit: 'Iudicemur ante Dominum.' [§12] Ter victus inimicus, viperea restaurat venena, dicens: '. . . Scriptum est enim: "Nisi conversi fueritis, et efficiamini sicut parvuli, non intrabitis in regnum caelorum" (Mt 18.3). Hoc verbum minime implevit.' [*The following passage comes next in the CC version, but earlier, in §11, in the ASS text:*] Sanctus angelus excusans, dixit: 'Indulgentiam in corde habuit, sed consuetudine humana continuit.' Diabolus respondit: 'Sicut accepit malum ex consuetudine, ita accipiet

vindictam a superno Iudice.' . . . [§12] Angelus domini dixit: 'Iudicemur ante Dominum.' Praeliante sancto angelo contriti sunt adversarii.

93–111 *Vita Fursei*, ASS Jan. II.36–41, c. 3:
[§13] Tunc sanctus angelus, qui a dextris eius erat, dixit: 'Respice in mundum.' Tunc vir sanctus respexit, et vidit vallem tenebrosam sub se in imo positam, et vidit quatuor ignes ibidem in aere incendi aliquibus spatiis a se distantes. . . . sanctus angelus dixit: 'Hi sunt quatuor ignes, qui mundum succendunt, postquam in baptismo omnia peccata dimissa sunt . . . [mentientes ea que promiserunt *CC*]. Unus enim est mendacii . . . alter cupiditatis . . . tertius dissensionis . . . quartus impietatis, cum infirmiores spoliare et eis fraudem facere pro nihilo ducunt.' . . . Ignibus vero crescentibus in maius, effectus est unus, et illi appropinquabat. Timensque vir Dei ignem minacem, sancto angelo secum loquenti ait: 'Ignis mihi appropinquat.' Cui respondit angelus: 'Quod non accendisti, non ardebit in te. Licet enim terribilis fit et grandis ignis iste, tamen secundum merita operum singulos examinat:. . . . Sicut enim corpus ardet per illicitam voluptatem, ita et anima ardebit per debitam poenam.' Tunc vidit sanctum angelum praecedentem, et ignem flammae dividentem in duos muros utroque latere; et duo sancti angeli utroque latere ab igne eum defendebant.

112–22 *Vita Fursei*, ASS Jan. II.36–41, c. 3:
[§14] Vidit quoque quatuor daemonia immunda per ignem volantia, et bellum horribile in medio ignis construentia. Et dixit unus ex illis: 'Servus qui scit voluntatem Domini sui, et non facit digna, plagis vapulabit multis' (Lc 12.47). Sanctus angelus respondit: 'Quid enim iste de voluntate Domini sui non adimplevit?' Satanas respondit: 'Scriptum est: "Dona iniquorum reprobat Altissimus" (Sir 34.23), iste dona iniquorum recepit.' Sanctus angelus respondit: 'Credidit enim quod unusquisque eorum egisset poenitentiam.' Diabolus dixit: 'Ante debuit probare poenitentiae perseverantiam, et sic fructum suscipere.' . . . Sanctus angelus respondit: 'Iudicemur ante Dominum.'

Lines 117–8 are Ælfric's comment, derived in part from *Vita Fursei*, ASS Jan. II.36–41, c. 6, §29.

122–33 *Vita Fursei*, ASS Jan. II.36–41, c. 3:
[§15] Daemon dixit: 'Quia omne delictum, quod non purgatur super terram, de caelo promisit esse vindicandum . . . Hic autem homo non purgavit delicta sua in terra, nec vindictam hic recipit. Ubi est ergo iustitia Dei?' Sanctus angelus increpans eos dixit: 'Nolite blasphemare dum nescitis occulta Dei iudicia.' Diabolus respondit: 'Quid enim hic occultum?' Sanctus angelus dixit: 'Quamdiu speratur poenitentia, comitatur hominem divina misericordia.' Satanas respondit: 'Sed nullus tamen hic

locus poenitentiae.' Angelus respondit: 'Profunditatem mysteriorum Dei ignoratis; fortasse etenim hic erit.'

Lines 123–4, marked as an untraced Biblical quotation by Cook (1898, p. 257), do not seem to be Biblical and are not specifically claimed as God's words by the devil.

134–45 *Vita Fursei*, ASS Jan. II.36–41, c. 3:

[§16] Alius vero satellitum eius dixit: '. . . Diliges proximum tuum sicut te ipsum' (Mt 22.39). Sanctus angelus respondit: 'Vir iste in proximos suos operatus est bona.' Adversarius respondit: 'Non sufficit operari bona, nisi etiam proximum sicut semetipsum dilexerit.' Sanctus angelus respondit: 'Fructus dilectionis, est bona operari: quia Deus reddet unicuique secundum opera sua.' . . . [§17] Victus sex vicibus diabolus more suo in blasphemiam erupit, dicens '. . . vir iste . . . promisit enim seculo abrenuntiare, et e contrario iste seculum dilexit, contra apostoli praeceptum dicentis: "Nolite diligere mundum, neque ea quae in mundo sunt" (1 Jn 2.15). Virum ergo hunc nec propriae sponsionis sermo, nec apostoli prohibuit sententia.' Sanctus angelus respondit: 'Non sibi soli ea quae sunt seculi, sed omnibus indigentibus dispensanda dilexit. . . .'

146–51 *Vita Fursei*, ASS Jan. II.36–41, c. 3:

[§18] Victis adversariis, angelis vincentibus, rursus diabolus ad callidas convertitur accusationes, dicens: 'Scriptum est: "Nisi annuntiaveris iniquo iniquitate[m] suam, sanguinem eius requiram de manu tua" (Ez 3.18). Hic non annuntiavit digne poenitentiam peccantibus.' Sanctus angelus respondit: 'De hoc enim tempore scriptum est: "prudens in tempore illo tacebit, quia tempus pessimum est" (cf Amos 5.13). . . . dum videt quod audita praedicatio despicitur.'

152–61 *Vita Fursei*, ASS Jan. II.36–41, c. 4:

[§19] In omni vero contradictione daemonum praevalida nimis extitit pugna, donec iudice Domino triumphantibus sanctis angelis, contritis devictisque adversariis, immensa claritate vir sanctus circumfusus est. . . . Tunc sursum adspiciens, vidit immensa agmina, eximia claritate fulgentia, angelorum ac praecedentium sanctorum hominum, qui advolantes, quasi alis, immensa coruscatione circumdederunt eum, omnem formidinem ignis ac daemoniorum terrores procul abigentes. Conspicit quoque duos venerabiles viros illius provinciae, in qua ipse vir Domini Furseus natus erat, quorum unus Beanus, alter Meldanus vocabatur. Haec videns quasi obiisse credebat . . . qui propius ad illum accedentes loqui ad illum familiariter coeperunt.

162–71 *Vita Fursei*, ASS Jan. II.36–41, c. 4:

[§20] Tunc adspiciebat magnam caeli serenitatem, et duos angelos proximam caeli iucunditatem repetentes, et quasi per ostium aethereum intrantes, et erumpente circa illos mira magnitudine claritatis audiebantur quasi per quatuor choros cantantium multitudines angelorum, ac dicentium: 'Sanctus, sanctus, sanctus, Dominus Deus Sabaoth' (cf Apoc 4.8). . . . de quibus [angelis] unus ait: 'Scis ubi agitur haec laetitia et gaudium?' Illo respondente se nescire, sanctus angelus respondit: 'Apud supernum conventum, unde et nos sumus.' . . . Rursumque angelus Domini beato viro ad carmina caelestia audienda intento loquitur, dicens: 'In hoc caelesti regno nulla unquam tristitia nisi de hominum perditione fieri potest.'

172–77 The *Vita* is confusing at this point, reporting that 'the aforesaid priests', radiant in angelic form, approached from the mysteries of heaven, and told Fursey that he must return to the world; he is immediately led back, but Meldanus and Beanus then obtain a respite in order to address him, which they do in a lengthy exhortation over §§21–28; the two men and the angelic host then disappear into heaven and Fursey with the three original angels departs on the return journey to earth; cf *Vita Fursei*, ASS Jan. II.36–41, c. 5, §21 for the first part:

[§21] Tunc praedictos sacerdotes cum ingenti claritate a secreto caeli procedere, angelica forma radiantes, ad se venire conspicit, ac sibi ad seculum redire praecipiunt. At ille tacens, et huius nuntii tristitia stupefactus, in momento reversus est, sanctis angelis eum reducentibus. Praefati vero viri venerabiles spatium poscunt cum eo loquendi, et dicunt: 'Quid times? Unius diei iter est, quo laboraturus es.'

No *sacerdotes* have in fact been mentioned before, and although Beanus and Meldanus are probably priests, as Bede and Ælfric say, they are already with Fursey when the *sacerdotes* arrive from the inner heaven with the message; and the journey to earth seems to be enacted twice. Ælfric has a much more coherent version, in which it is angels who bring the message and the journey back does not begin until after the two priests have completed their exhortations. It seems likely that he had a Latin text which gave this version, but the extant manuscripts of the CC have the same reading as the ASS.

177–98 Combining a series of points from the exhortations and advice of the two priests, *Vita Fursei*, ASS Jan. II.36–41, cc. 5 and 6:

[§21] Beato Furseo interrogante de mundi fine, aiunt finem creaturae iam tunc non esse, quamvis in proximo sit; sed famis et mortalitatis plagis humanum genus esse vexandum. . . . [§22] '. . . Per quatuor res pereunt animae fidelium; per huius mundi illecebrosa vitia, per suggestionem militantis diaboli, per negligentiam doctorum, per mala exempla pravorum principum. . . . [§25] Contra doctores irascitur Dominus, eo quod divinos libros negligentes, curas huius mundi cum omni dilectione agunt. . . . [§26] . . . Nulla vero discordia in ecclesia Dei sit sed qui in plebe praesunt, apostolico ordini, et doctrinae sanctae insistant; qui vero in monasteriis degunt, cum silentio operantes, suum panem manducent. . . . [§27] Te ergo ipsum nec semper remotum, nec semper in publico decernas; sed quando te remotum esse volueris, omni custodia te ipsum serva, omnia divina observando praecepta. Et quando in publicum processeris, ad animarum salutem, non ad huius mundi inhianda lucra, animum intentum adhibeto. . . . Nullam quoque patrimonio custodiam, nullam curis huius seculi intenti cordis diligentiam adhibeas; sed omnibus adversantibus vel contrariis, puri pectoris indulgentia, bona pro malis rependens, pro inimicis supplica Domino. . . . [§26] Esto sicut fidelis dispensator, nihil tibi praeter victum et vestitum vendicans. [*previous sentence*] Vitam tuam, creaturis Dei utendo, serva; omne quod malum est, abnegando respue.'

Ælfric's selection and adaptation here creates a striking and well-organised passage on the role of clerics, and especially the relationship of monks to the world.

199–218 *Vita Fursei*, ASS Jan. II.36–41, c. 6:

[§29] His dictis a beato Beano et Meldano, supernum illud angelorum simul cum ipso Beano et Meldano in caelum receptum est agmen; beatoque Furseo cum tribus angelis solis ad terram reversuro, maximus appropinquabat ignis. Sed angelus Domini, sicut et ante, medium dividens findebat ignem. At daemones arreptum de mediis ignibus virum unum proiecerunt super humerum beati Fursei, et maxillam maxillae eius impresserunt, humerum et maxillam eius incendentes. Cognoscebat quoque sanctus Furseus virum, quod ei vestimentum proprium moriens perdonavit; humerumque eius ac maxillam incendens, ab angelo sancto in ignem, unde exiit, proiectus est. . . . Tunc diabolus antiquas repetens fallacias dixit . . .'sicut enim eius bona suscepisti, sic de poenis eius particeps esse debes.' Angelus Domini respondit: 'non propter avaritiam sed propter animam eius liberandam suscepit.' Cessavitque ignis. Tunc dixit angelus Domini: 'Quod accendisti, hoc arsit in te. Si enim huius viri in peccatis suis mortui vestimenta non suscepisses, nec poenae illius in corpore tuo arderent.'

Ælfric again has information about the burning soul which is not in the extant versions—that the person was Fursey's *tunman*.

218–27 *Vita Fursei*, ASS Jan. II.36–41, c. 6:

[§30] 'Praedica ergo omnibus, quod poenitentia agenda est, et a sacerdote suscipienda, usque in extremam horam; sed tamen nisi poenituerit, nihil substantiae eius suscipiendum, nec corpus eius in sancto sepeliendum est loco. Vivo tamen praedicetur acrius, quatenus cor illius amaritudo compunctionis tangat, ut tactum quandoque purgetur, omnibusque pristinis renuntians iniquitatibus, eleemosynas ubertim pauperibus distribuat. Nihil tamen exinde a sacerdote ei praedicante suscipiatur, sed iuxta sepulchrum eius bona illius pauperibus dividantur. . . .'

228–37 *Vita Fursei*, ASS Jan. II.36–41, c. 7:

[§31] His atque aliis sanctae exhortationis sermonibus vir Domini instructus, super tectum ecclesiae inter sanctos constitit angelos, suumque corpus considerans, nec parietes domus nec turbam lugentium, nec ipsa corporis indumenta videre potuit; iubeturque ab angelo proprium cognoscere et resumere corpus. Tunc ille quasi ignotum cadaver timens, nolle se ibidem appropinquare respondit. Cui sanctus angelus: 'Noli timere inquit hoc suscipere corpus, quod sine ulla repugnatione infirmitatis vel vitiorum expugnantium, quamvis invalidum, habere potes. Concupiscentias enim illicitas in hac tribulatione superasti, ut ultra contra te non praevaleant.'

237–51 *Vita Fursei*, ASS Jan. II.36–41, c. 7:

[§32] Tunc vidit [sub] pectore illius corpus aperiri. Dixitque ei angelus: 'Reviviscens corpus tuum aqua fontis superfundatur, et nullum dolorem, nisi tantum concremationis sentire poteris. Benefaciens, omnem gressum tuum usque in finem videbimus, et sic te laetum beneque operantem suscipiemus.' Exurgens autem vir sanctus quasi ex profunda mortis quiete, conspiciensque parentum multitudinem vel vicinorum sive etiam clericorum, ingemiscensque magnitudinem humanae stultitiae, arduumque et difficilem transitum admirans . . . singula per ordinem annuntiabat. Atque viva superfusus aqua, incendium inter scapulas sensit, quod de iniquo sumpsit viro, et in facie eius apparuit; mirumque in modum quod anima sola sustinuit, in carne demonstrabatur.

252–68 A much abbreviated account of *Vita Fursei*, ASS Jan. II.36–41, c. 7:

[§33] Egressus inde verbum Dei per universam Hiberniam praedicabat, et ea quae viderat vel audierat, omnibus populis Scotorum annuntiabat; erat vero in illo incomparabilis gratia, nihil terrenum cuiquam petens, . . . omnibus bonis amabilis, iniquis et peccatoribus terribilis, divinis virtutibus clarus. Ex obsessis enim corporibus daemonia fugabat, et pauperes recreabat. [§34] . . . ac duodecim annos in opere suae praedicationis complendos praedicentem, quod ita factum est. [§35] . . . . Atque exinde non multo post de Hibernia peregrina littora petens, per Britannos in Saxoniam transvectus est . . . [§36] Completis vero duodecim annis, quos angelus praedixerat, sanctus quadam infirmitate correptus, . . . locum monasterii a praedicto sibi rege Sigeberto traditum acceleravit construere. [§38] . . . ad Galliarum littora . . . navigavit; ibique a Francorum rege Clodoveo et Patricio Erchenaldo honorifice susceptus, monasterium in loco . . . construxit. At non multo post . . . infirmitate corripitur . . . et sic praesentia relinquens . . . ad aeterna commivit regna. [§39] Corpus vero illius ab illustri viro Erchenaldo Patricio retentum . . . in villa cui Perona vocabulum est ponitur. . . . reverenter ergo . . . prope altare reconditur, ibique annis fere quatuor demoratur. . . . ibi post tot annos immaculatum et integrum corpus . . . transfertur sine ulla putredine. Ubi etiam recta fide petentibus merita illius clarescunt divinis virtutibus, adiuvante Domino nostro Iesu Christo. . . .

On Ælfric's introduction of *Scotland* as an area where Fursey preached, presumably meaning modern Scotland, see *CH II*, p. 366; similarly, *scottum* at 258 presumably means inhabitants of Scotland.

21 TUESDAY IN ROGATIONTIDE

The account of Dryhthelm's vision is evidently a companion piece to the preceding account of Fursey, offering a more detailed exposition of the doctrine of purgatory and the interim paradise. Ælfric follows Bede's account in *Historia Ecclesiastica*, V.xii fairly closely, though in a more concise style; he omits the passage towards the end (496.8–27) which tells how Dryhthelm described his experiences to a hermit and the king, but includes the salient points of that passage at the beginning of his own version. The Old English translation of Bede's work seems here to have had no influence on his rendering (cf above under CH II.9).

The vision is followed by two rather puzzling short passages beginning in the same way, *we rædað gehwær*. . . . The first notes the frequency of visions of this kind, and briefly describes one from Gregory's *Dialogues* which illustrates the rewards of alms-giving; it finishes with a comment on the importance of intercession between the living and the dead, an issue not illustrated by the Gregorian story but touched on previously in the account of Dryhthelm (lines 77–9). The passage is concluded with a formal peroration, but there is then a further rubric and another short passage, beginning with the same introductory phrase, this time on the role of the mass in releasing the living and the dead, illustrated by a story from Bede's *Historia Ecclesiastica*. The passage is evidently developing the point made earlier at lines 77–9, about the release of souls from punishment by means of the mass, though this is in fact only a marginal aspect of the story from Bede. The introductory comment, on the efficacy of the mass, almost exactly repeats Ælfric's comment in the earlier homily on the mass, II.15.222–4. Perhaps writing that prompted him to write up the Imma story, and then to attach it to the Drihthelm story.

A number of the points made in this text, and especially at 130–7 (the different fates of souls, the efficacy of intercession and the mass) are repeated in a later homily, Pope 11, esp. lines 200–42. The main source there is Julian of Toledo's *Prognosticon*, partly as mediated through Ælfric's excerpts, but the parallels with the Dryhthelm text seem to owe little to Julian. Ælfric was evidently engaged from an early period in collecting and adapting texts which related to the fate of the soul after death and particularly the question of subsequent intercession. The excerpts from Julian are one example of this, and the present curious sequence of texts, somewhat uncertainly related to the occasion and to each other, are another.

Sources and Notes

The following texts are cited below:

1. Bede, *Historia Ecclesiastica Gentis Anglorum*, ed. B. Colgrave and R. A. B. Mynors (Oxford, 1969).
2. Gregory the Great, *Dialogi*, ed. A. de Vogüé and P. Antin, 3 vols., Sources Chrétiennes 251, 260 and 265 (Paris, 1978–80).
3. *The Old English Version of Bede's Ecclesiastical History of the English People*, ed. T. A. Miller, EETS os 95 and 96 (1890–91).

3–20 Bede, *Historia Ecclesiastica*, V.xii (488.1–25):

> His temporibus . . . erat ergo pater familias in regione Nordanhymbrorum . . . religiosam cum domu sua gerens vitam. Qui infirmitate corporis tactus, et hac crescente per dies ad extrema perductus, primo tempore noctis defunctus est, sed diluculo revivescens ac repente residens, omnes qui corpori flentes adsederant, timore immenso perculsos in fugam convertit: uxor tantum quae amplius amabat, quamvis multum tremens et pavida, remansit. Quam ille consolatus: 'Noli, inquit, timere, quia iam vere surrexi a morte qua tenebar, et apud homines sum iterum vivere permissus; non tamen ea mihi qua ante consueram conversatione. . . .' Statimque surgens abiit ad villulae oratorium, et usque ad diem in oratione persistens, mox omnem quam possederat substantiam in tres divisit portiones, e quibus unam coniugi, alteram filiis tradidit, tertiam sibi ipse retentans, statim pauperibus distribuit. Nec multo post saeculi curis absolutus ad monasterium Mailros . . . pervenit, acceptaque tonsura locum secretae mansionis quam praeviderat abbas, intravit: et ibi usque ad diem mortis in tanta mentis et corporis contritione duravit. . . .

The comment on Dryhthelm's character at 4–5 is drawn in part from a parenthetic remark at the end of the story (498.8–9), referring to the period after his vision: *Erat namque homo simplicis ingenii ac moderatae naturae*. The name of the abbot (Ediluald) is given later, at 496.25, but Bede says nothing about Dryhthelm following the abbot's guidance; the notion of a monk having a special status and privacy within the monastery was perhaps a delicate issue for Ælfric.

21–33 Bede, *Historia Ecclesiastica*, V.xii (488.27–490.14):

> Narrabat autem hoc modo quod viderat: 'Lucidus, inquiens, aspectu et clarus erat indumento, qui me ducebat. Incedebamus autem tacentes, ut videbatur mihi, contra ortum solis solstitialem; cumque ambularemus, devenimus ad vallem multae latitudinis ac profunditatis, infinitae autem longitudinis, quae ad levam nobis sita, unum latus flammis ferventibus nimium terribile, alterum furenti grandine ac frigore nivium omnia perflante

atque verrente non minus intolerabile praeferebat. Utrumque autem erat animabus hominum plenum, quae vicissim huc inde videbantur quasi tempestatis impetu iactari. Cum enim vim fervoris immensi tolerare non possent, prosiliebant miserae in medium rigoris infesti; et cum neque ibi quippiam requiei invenire valerent, resiliebant rursus urendae in medium flammarum inextinguibilium. Cumque hac infelici vicissitudine longe lateque, prout aspicere poteram, sine ulla quietis intercapedine innumerabilis spirituum deformium multitudo torqueretur, cogitare coepi quod hic fortasse esset infernus, de cuius tormentis intolerabilibus narrari saepius audivi. Respondit cogitationi meae ductor, qui me praecedebat: "Non hoc, inquiens, suspiceris; non enim hic infernus est ille, quem putas."'

That Dryhthelm told his story to King Aldfrith and other virtuous people is noted later by Bede, at 496.8–27; Bede mentions especially the monk Hæmgisl, who was still living at the time of writing and whose account was Bede's source.

34–54 Bede, *Historia Ecclesiastica*, V.xii (490.15–492.12):

'At cum me hoc spectaculo tam horrendo perterritum paulatim in ulteriora produceret, vidi subito ante nos obscurari incipere loca, et tenebris omnia repleri. Quas cum intraremus, in tantum paulisper condensatae sunt, ut nihil praeter ipsas aspicerem, excepta dumtaxat specie et veste eius, qui me ducebat. Et cum progrederemur sola sub nocte per umbras, ecce subito apparent ante nos crebri flammarum tetrarum globi ascendentes quasi de puteo magno, rursumque decidentes in eundem. Quo cum perductus essem, repente ductor meus disparuit, ac me solum in medio tenebrarum et horridae visionis reliquit. At . . . cerno omnia quae ascendebant fastigia flammarum plena esse spiritibus hominum, qui instar favillarum cum fumo ascendentium nunc ad sublimiora proicerentur, nunc retractis ignium vaporibus relaberentur in profunda. Sed et fetor incomparabilis cum eisdem vaporibus ebulliens omnia illa tenebrarum loca replebat. Et cum diutius ibi pavidus consisterem, utpote incertus quid agerem, quo verterem gressum, qui me finis maneret, audio subitum . . . turbam malignorum spirituum, quae quinque animas hominum merentes heiulantesque, ipsa multum exultans et cachinnans, medias illas trahebat in tenebras; e quibus videlicet hominibus, ut dinoscere potui, quidam erat adtonsus ut clericus, quidam laicus, quaedam femina. . . . Interea ascenderunt quidam spirituum obscurorum de abysso illa flammivoma, et adcurrentes circumdederunt me, atque oculis flammantibus, et de ore ac naribus ignem putidum efflantes angebant; forcipibus quoque igneis, quos tenebant in manibus, minitabantur me comprehendere, nec tamen me ullatenus contingere, tametsi terrere, praesumebant.'

Note Ælfric's graphic detail of black fire, at 37 and 47 (and cf further, for the topos of a fire that is black and gives no light, CH I.8.186 and I.35.195, and notes). Darkness is a distinguishing feature of hell in this vision; cf again 80–81. On *scegdon* (line 48), 'jeered', see N. R. Ker, 'Old English *Scægan*', *Medium Ævum* 1 (1932), 137–8.

55–79 Bede, *Historia Ecclesiastica*, V.xii (492.15–494.22):

'Apparuit retro via qua veneram quasi fulgor stellae micantis inter tenebras, qui paulatim crescens, et ad me ocius festinans, ubi adpropinquavit, dispersi sunt et aufugerunt omnes qui me forcipibus rapere quaerebant spiritus infesti. Ille autem, qui adveniens eos fugavit, erat ipse qui me ante ducebat; qui mox conversus ad dextrum iter quasi contra ortum solis brumalem me ducere coepit. Nec mora, exemtum tenebris in auras me serenae lucis eduxit . . . [*They then approach a long wall with no gates or windows, and suddenly find themselves on top of it.*] Et ecce ibi campus erat latissimus ac laetissimus, tantaque flagrantia vernantium flosculorum plenus. . . . Tanta autem lux cuncta ea loca perfuderat, ut omni splendore diei sive solis meridiani radiis videretur esse praeclarior. Erantque in hoc campo innumera hominum albatorum conventicula sedesque plurimae agminum laetantium. Cumque inter choros felicium incolarum medios me duceret, cogitare coepi quod hoc fortasse esse regnum caelorum, de quo praedicari saepius audivi. Respondit ille cogitatui meo: "Non, inquiens, non hoc est regnum caelorum quod autumas". Cumque procedentes transissemus et has beatorum mansiones spirituum, aspicio ante nos multo maiorem luminis gratiam quam prius, in qua etiam vocem cantantium dulcissimam audivi; sed et odoris flagrantia miri tanta de loco effundebatur. . . . Repente ductor substitit; nec mora, gressum retorquens ipsa me, qua venimus, via reduxit. Cumque reversi perveniremus ad mansiones illas laetas spirituum candidatorum, dixit mihi: "Scis, quae sint ista omnia, quae vidisti?" Respondi ego. Non. Et ait: "Vallis illa, quam aspexisti flammis ferventibus et frigoribus horrenda rigidis, ipse est locus in quo examinandae et castigandae sunt animae illorum, qui differentes confiteri et emendare scelera quae fecerunt, in ipso tandem mortis articulo ad paenitentiam confugiunt, et sic de corpore exeunt; qui tamen, quia confessionem et paenitentiam vel in morte habuerunt, omnes in die iudicii ad regnum caelorum perveniunt. Multos autem preces viventium et elimosynae et ieiunia et maxime celebratio missarum, ut etiam ante diem iudicii liberentur, adiuvant."'

80–100 Bede, *Historia Ecclesiastica*, V.xii (494.22–496.7):

'"Porro puteus ille flammivomus ac putidus, quem vidisti, ipsum est os gehennae, in quo quicumque semel inciderit numquam inde liberabitur in aevum. Locus vero iste florifer, in quo pulcherrimam hanc iuventutem iucundari ac fulgere conspicis, ipse est in quo recipiuntur animae eorum qui in bonis quidem operibus de corpore exeunt; non tamen sunt tantae perfectionis, ut in regnum caelorum statim mereantur introduci; qui tamen omnes in die iudicii ad visionem Christi et gaudia regni caelestis intrabunt. Nam quicumque in omni verbo et opere et cogitatione perfecti sunt, mox de corpore egressi ad regnum caeleste perveniunt; ad cuius vicinia pertinet locus ille, ubi sonum cantilenae dulcis cum odore suavitatis ac splendore lucis audisti. Tu autem, quia nunc ad corpus reverti et rursum inter homines vivere debes, si actus tuos curiosius discutere, et mores sermonesque tuos in rectitudine ac simplicitate servare studueris, accipies et ipse post mortem locum mansionis inter haec quae cernis agmina laetabunda spirituum beatorum. Namque ego, cum ad tempus abscessissem a te, ad hoc feci, ut quid de te fieri deberet agnoscerem." Haec mihi cum dixisset, multum detestatus sum reverti ad corpus, delectatus nimirum suavitate ac decore loci illius quem intuebar, simul et consortio eorum quos in illo videbam. Nec tamen aliquid ductorem meum rogare audebam; sed inter haec nescio quo ordine repente me inter homines vivere cerno.'

101–11 Bede, *Historia Ecclesiastica*, V.xii (496.28–498.13):

Accepit autem in eodem monasterio locum mansionis secretiorem, ubi liberius continuis in orationibus famulatui sui Conditoris vacaret. Et quia locus ipse super ripam fluminis erat situs, solebat hoc creber ob magnum castigandi corporis affectum ingredi, ac saepius in eo supermeantibus undis immergi; sicque ibidem quamdiu sustinere posse videbatur, psalmis vel precibus insistere, fixusque manere ascendente aqua fluminis usque ad lumbos, aliquando et usque ad collum; atque inde egrediens ad terram numquam ipsa vestimenta uda atque algida deponere curabat, donec ex suo corpore calefierent et siccarentur. Cumque tempore hiemali . . . dicerent qui videbant: 'Mirum, frater Drycthelme (hoc enim erat viro nomen), quod tantam frigoris asperitatem ulla ratione tolerare praevales', respondebat ille simpliciter (erat namque homo simplicis ingenii ac moderatae naturae): 'Frigidiora ego vidi.' Et cum dicerent: 'Mirum quod tam austeram tenere continentiam velis', respondebat: 'Austeriora ego vidi.' Sicque usque ad diem suae vocationis infatigabili caelestium bonorum desiderio corpus senile inter cotidiana ieiunia domabat, multisque et verbo et conversatione saluti fuit.

112–30 A lively elaboration of one of the stories of otherworld visions told in Book IV of Gregory's *Dialogues*, but Ælfric seems to have conflated, perhaps from memory, the vision of a soldier, who saw amongst many other sights houses being built of gold in the other world (c. 37, and a further detail in c. 38), with the vision of a monk called Deusdedit, who saw a house being built for a shoemaker (c. 38); Gregory, *Dialogues*:

[IV.37.70–72:] Ibi quaedam mirae potentiae aedificabatur domus, quae aureis videbatur laterculis construi, sed cuius esset non potuit agnosci.

[IV.38.1–11:] Sic etiam quidam iuxta nos, Deusdedit nomine, religiosus habitabat, qui calciamenta solebat operari. De quo alter per revelationem vidit quod eius domus aedificabatur, sed in ea constructores sui solo die sabbati videbantur operari. Qui eiusdem viri postmodum subtiliter vitam requirens, invenit quia ex his quae diebus singulis laborabat, quicquid ex victu atque vestitu superesse potuisset, die sabbato ad beati Petri ecclesiam deferre consueverat, atque indigentibus erogare. Qua ex re perpende, quia non immerito domus ipsius fabrica sabbato crescebat.

In the *Dialogues*, the celebration of the shoemaker, whose future celestial home only advances towards completion on one day a week, is perhaps rather muted in contrast to the other sights and buildings; Ælfric's picture, with the house being built of gold and being almost complete, and apparently being worked on most of all on Saturdays, but not only then, is altogether more enthusiastic about the shoemaker's status.

143–50 From Bede, *Historia Ecclesiastica*, IV.xxii (400.24–402.4):

> In praefato autem proelio, quo occisus est rex Aelfuini, . . . occisus est ibi inter alios, de militia eius iuvenis, vocabulo Imma; qui cum die illo et nocte sequenti inter cadavera occisorum similis mortuo iaceret, tandem recepto spiritu revixit, ac residens sua vulnera, prout potuit, ipse alligavit; dein modicum requietus levavit se et coepit abire, sicubi amicos, qui sui curam agerent, posset invenire. Quod dum faceret, inventus est et captus a viris hostilis exercitus et ad dominum ipsorum, comitem videlicet Aedilredi regis, adductus.

That the battle was between the forces of Ecgfrith of Northumbria and Æthelred of Mercia is taken from the previous chapter in Bede, *Historia*, IV.xxi. But Bede identifies Imma as a retainer of Ælfwine, brother of Ecgfrith and apparently an under-king, who was killed in the battle; Ælfric seems to identify him as a thegn of the Mercian Æthelred, and hence identifies the enemies who capture him as northerners (lines 149–50), i.e. Northumbrians, despite the clear statement in Bede that their leader was a *comes* of Æthelred. Perhaps he was drawing on memory of the story.[1]

150–66 Bede, *Historia Ecclesiastica*, IV.xxii (402.8–27):

> At ille suscipiens eum curam vulneribus egit, et ubi sanescere coepit, noctu eum ne aufugeret vinciri praecepit. Nec tamen vinciri potuit; nam mox ut abiere qui vincierant, eadem eius sunt vincula soluta. Habebat enim germanum fratrem, cui nomen erat Tunna, presbyterum et abbatem monasterii. . . . Qui cum eum in pugna peremtum audiret, venit quaerere, si forte corpus eius invenire posset; inventumque alium illi per omnia simillimum, putavit ipsum esse, quem ad monasterium suum deferens honorifice sepelivit, et pro absolutione animae eius sepius missas facere curavit. Quarum celebratione factum est quod dixi, ut nullus eum posset vincire, quin continuo solveretur. Interea comes qui eum tenebat mirari et interrogare coepit, quare ligari non posset, an forte litteras solutorias, de qualibus fabulae ferunt, apud se haberet, propter quas ligari non posset. At ille respondit nil se talium artium nosse: 'Sed habeo fratrem, inquit, presbyterum in mea provincia, et scio quia ille me interfectum putans, pro me missas crebras facit; et si nunc in alia vita essem, ibi anima mea per intercessiones eius solveretur a poenis.'

[1] The *Old English Bede* identifies Imma as a thegn of Ecgfrith (OE Bede, 326.3–5).

There is an extensive literature on the reference to magic and runic letters in this passage. See R. I. Page, 'Anglo-Saxon runes and magic', *Journal of the British Archaeological Association* 27 (1964), 14–31, reprinted in his *Runes and Runic Inscriptions*, ed. D. Parsons (Woodbridge, 1995), pp. 105–25; Joel Rosenthal, 'Bede's use of miracles in the Ecclesiastical History', *Traditio* 31 (1975), 328–35; Seth Lerer, *Literacy and Power in Anglo-Saxon Literature* (Lincoln, Nebraska and London, 1984), chapter 1. Page concludes:

> Thus the Anglo-Saxon evidence for rune-magic, though not negligible, is slight. The only certain point is Ælfric's unambiguous reference. Without it the existence of rune-magic would hardly have been deduced from the English material alone.

See further Christine Fell, 'Runes and semantics' in *Old English Runes and their Continental Background*, ed. Alfred Bammesberger (Heidelberg 1991), pp. 195–229, demonstrating that the word *run* generally refers to words and discourse in Ælfric, and Old English generally, and has no evident implications of magic, except for this one example. Bede refers only to 'releasing letters', but the Old English translation renders this as *alysendlecan rune* (OE Bede, 328.6). Ælfric's *runstafum* seems definitely to mean 'runic letters' (cf Exeter Book riddles 42 and 58, and the less conclusive *Beowulf*,1695), and it does appear that Bede's reference to 'releasing letters' naturally suggested to Ælfric (with or without the help of the *Old English Bede*[2]) an inscription in the runic script, with magical powers presumably associated with that script.

167–76 *Historia Ecclesiastica*, IV.xxii (404.4–11, 16–20):

> Ut ergo convaluit, vendidit eum Lundoniam Freso cuidam; sed nec ab illo nec cum illuc duceretur ullatinus potuit alligari. Verum cum alia atque alia vinculorum ei genera hostes imponerent, cumque vidisset, qui emerat, vinculis eum non potuisse cohiberi, donavit ei facultatem sese redimendi, si posset. A tertia autem hora, quando missae fieri solebant, sepissime vincula solvebantur. At ille dato iureiurando ut rediret, vel pecuniam illi pro se mitteret, venit Cantiam ad regem Hlotheri. [*Imma then obtains the ransom from King Hlothere of Kent* . . . .] Qui post haec patriam reversus atque ad suum fratrem perveniens, replicavit ex ordine cuncta quae sibi adversa, quaeve in adversis solacia provenissent; cognovitque, referente eo, illis maxime temporibus sua fuisse vincula soluta, quibus pro se missarum fuerant celebrata sollemnia.

176–80 The final chapter of the *Dialogues*, Book IV chapter 12, is devoted to the question of the role of the Mass in helping the living and the dead.

[2] Lerer (p. 52) says: 'The similarity of his [Ælfric's] account to that of the Old English Bede has led most modern readers to assume a direct borrowing from the translation.' The comment is not footnoted and I do not know of the evidence for it; Page had already dismissed the notion in his 1964 article (p. 114), though Elliott's brief comment in his book on runes might be taken as implying such a view (R.W.V. Elliott, *Runes: an Introduction* (2nd ed., Manchester and New York, 1989), p. 81).

22 WEDNESDAY IN ROGATIONTIDE

The reading for the occasion, John 17.1–11, is one of the densest Gospel texts tackled by Ælfric, and the exegesis is equally challenging, as he comments himself (lines 32–3). Yet the homily is clearly addressed to the laity (line 191 ff), whom he presumably expected to follow the difficult argument. He notes that he draws on Augustine's exposition, and probably found the relevant parts of Augustine's Tractates on John (104–7) assigned to this occasion in his version of Paul the Deacon's homiliary.[1] But the material there was far too long and dense for the purpose, and relied too heavily on the whole extent of the Tractates for its arguments, and Ælfric evidently selected and rewrote very freely in developing his own exposition. If, as he argues, the Gospel text was highly appropriate to the Vigil of the Ascension, since Christ speaks to the Father about the completion of his task and his return to the Father, it was also full of difficult implications for the nature of Christ and his relationship to time. Ælfric focuses primarily on the problems posed by the text concerning the nature of Christ, distinguishing repeatedly between the divinity which existed outside time and was equal with the Father and the humanity which sought at this moment to be glorified by the Father.

The commentary on the final verses is fairly brief and at some later stage Ælfric added three further passages of comment, at 162, 172 and 179 (printed by Pope as 25a, b and c). All three seem to deal not so much with the main concerns of the Gospel passage and the original exposition but, in various ways, with the nature of God's continued involvement with the world and the elect, after creation, after the ascension, and after death. They are all in plain prose but their absence from MS M as well as K and others would suggest that they were added some considerable time after the completion of the Catholic Homilies.

Sources and Notes

The following text is cited below:

1. Augustine, *In Iohannis Evangelium Tractatus CXXIV*, ed. R. Willems, CCSL 36 (Turnhout, 1954).

3–24 Jn 17.1–11:

(1) Haec locutus est Iesus et sublevatis oculis in caelum dixit: Pater venit hora, clarifica Filium tuum ut Filius tuus clarificet te (2) sicut dedisti ei potestatem omnis carnis ut omne quod dedisti ei det eis vitam aeternam. (3) Haec est autem vita aeterna ut cognoscant te solum verum Deum et quem misisti Iesum Christum. (4) Ego te clarificavi super terram, opus

[1] Förster (1894, p. 35) identified Augustine, Tractates, 104–7 and 110–11 as source; Smetana (1959, p. 198) pointed out that Tractates 104–7 are in the late version of PD printed at PL 95.142 ff (there is no evident use of Tractates 110–11 in fact).

consummavi quod dedisti mihi ut faciam. (5) Et nunc clarifica me tu Pater apud temet ipsum claritatem quam habui priusquam mundus esset apud te. (6) Manifestavi nomen tuum hominibus quos dedisti mihi de mundo; tui erant et mihi eos dedisti et sermonem tuum servaverunt. (7) Nunc cognoverunt quia omnia quae dedisti mihi abs te sunt (8) quia verba quae dedisti mihi dedi eis et ipsi acceperunt et cognoverunt vere quia a te exivi et crediderunt quia tu me misisti. (9) Ego pro eis rogo non pro mundo rogo sed pro his quos dedisti mihi quia tui sunt. (10) Et mea omnia tua sunt et tua mea sunt et clarificatus sum in eis. (11) Et iam non sum in mundo et hii in mundo sunt et ego ad te venio Pater sancte.

25–31 Christ's words are spoken (as Ælfric perhaps deliberately fails to mention) during the last supper rather than prior to the ascension, but the repeated reference, in John 14 and 16, to his imminent departure no doubt justified the application to the ascension.

34–49 Adapted in part from points in Augustine's *Tract.*, 104.2 and 105.1, but focusing on the distinction between what is said of the Son's divinity and what is said with reference to his humanity.:

[104.2.32–3] Dicat ergo Pater, venit hora, qui cum Patre disposuit omnes horas . . . [104.2.17–19] ostendit omne tempus . . . ab illo esse dispositum qui tempori subditus non est; . . . [104.2.25–7] tempus Christus quo moreretur elegit, qui etiam tempus quo de uirgine natus est, cum Patre constituit, de quo sine tempore natus est.

[105.1.1–3] Glorificatum a Patre Filium secundum formam servi, quam Pater suscitavit a mortuis, et ad suam dexteram collocavit, res ipsa indicat . . . [104.3.7–12] 'Propter quod et Deus illum exaltavit, et donavit ei nomen quod est super omne nomen, ut in nomine Iesu omne genu flectatur caelestium, terrestrium, et infernorum' (Phil 2.9–10). . . . Haec est clarificatio Domini nostri Iesu Christi.

50–58 Based on Augustine, *Tract.*, 105.1.5–14:

Merito quaeritur quomodo Patrem clarificaverit Filius, cum sempiterna claritas Patris nec diminuta fuerit in forma humana, nec augeri potuerit in sua perfectione divina. Sed in seipsa claritas Patris nec minui nec augeri potest; apud homines autem procul dubio minor erat, quando in Iudaea tantummodo Deus notus erat, nondum a solis ortu usque ad occasum laudabant pueri nomen Domini. Hoc autem quia per evangelium Christi factum est, ut per filium Pater innotesceret gentibus, profecto Patrem clarificavit et Filius.

59–67 Fairly closely based on Augustine, *Tract.*, 105.2.4–10:

Omnem carnem dixit omnem hominem, a parte totum significans, quemadmodum rursus a parte superiore significatus est homo totus, ubi ait apostolus: 'Omnis anima potestatibus sublimioribus subdita sit' (Rom

13.1). Quid enim dixit 'omnis anima', nisi omnis homo? Et hoc autem quod potestas Christo a Patre data est omnis carnis, secundum hominem intellegendum est, nam secundum Deum omnia per ipsum facta sunt.

68–88 Adapted from Augustine, *Tract.*, 105.3.3–29, with a more pointed conclusion:

Ordo verborum est: 'ut te et quem misisti Iesum Christum cognoscant solum verum Deum'. Consequenter enim et Spiritus sanctus intellegitur, quia Spiritus est Patris et Filii, tamquam caritas substantialis et consubstantialis amborum. Quoniam non duo dii Pater et Filius, nec tres dii Pater et Filius et Spiritus sanctus, sed ipsa Trinitas unus solus verus Deus. Nec idem tamen pater qui Filius, nec idem Filius qui Pater, nec idem Spiritus sanctus qui Pater et Filius, quoniam tres sunt Pater et Filius et Spiritus sanctus, sed ipsa Trinitas unus est Deus. . . . Porro si cognitio Dei est vita aeterna, tanto magis vivere tendimus, quanto magis in hac cognitione proficimus. Non autem moriemur in vita aeterna, tunc ergo Dei cognitio perfecta erit, quando nulla mors erit. . . . Ibi erit Dei sine fine laudatio, ubi erit Dei plena cognitio.

89–99 Ælfric turns into clear positive statements Augustine's series of tricky questions, Augustine, *Tract.*, 105.4.4–10:

Non ait iussisti sed dedisti; ubi commendatur evidens gratia. Quid enim habet quod non accepit, etiam in unigenito humana natura? An non accepit, ut nihil mali, sed bona faceret omnia, quando in unitatem personae suscepta est a Verbo, per quod facta sunt omnia? Sed quomodo consummavit opus quod accepit ut faciat, cum restet adhuc passionis experimentum.

101–17 Adapted from phrases and Biblical quotations in Augustine, *Tract.*, 105.7 and 8:

[105.7.4–8] Intellegamus praedestinationem claritatis humanae quae in illo est naturae, ex mortali immortalis apud Patrem futurae, et hoc iam praedestinando factum fuisse antequam mundus esset, quod in mundo etiam suo tempore fieret. . . . [105.8.19–23:] 'qui predestinatus est Filius Dei in virtute' (Rom 1.4). . . . Secundum hanc ergo praedestinationem etiam clarificatus est antequam mundus esset, ut esset claritas eius ex resurrectione mortuorum apud Patrem, ad cuius dexteram sedet. [*Back to 105.7.19, 23–4*:] Tunc elegit etiam nos in ipso. Quid enim dicit apostolus? . . . 'Quos autem praedestinavit, illos et vocavit' (Rom 8.30). [*Ælfric continues with the rest of the verse*: et quos vocavit hos et iustificavit; quos autem iustificavit illos et glorificavit.] [*Back to 105.7.8–10, quoting Eph 1.4*:] Si enim de nobis dixit apostolus: 'Sicut elegit nos in ipso ante mundi constitutionem.'

118–22 Cf Augustine, *Tract.*, 106.1:

[106.1.3–4] Quod si de his tantum dicit discipulis cum quibus coenavit . . . [106.1.11–12] omnes intellegi voluit, etiam qui in eum fuerant credituri. . . .

122–7 Cf Augustine, *Tract.*, 106.5.4–9:

An aliquando erant Patris, quando non erant unigeniti Filii eius, et habuit aliquando Pater aliquid sine Filio? Absit. Verumtamen habuit aliquid aliquando Deus Filius, quod nondum habuit idem ipse homo Filius, quia nondum erat homo factus ex matre, quando tamen habebat universa cum Patre.

132–6 Cf Augustine, *Tract.*, 106.5.32–7:

Iam superius eisdem discipulis dixerat: 'Ego vos de mundo elegi' (Jn 15.19). . . . Quos Deus Filius de mundo elegit cum Patre, idem ipse homo Filius de mundo eos accepit a Patre.

141–5 Ælfric's own brief explication.

146–50 Cf Augustine, *Tract.*, 107.1.4–6:

Mundum vult modo intellegi, qui vivunt secundum concupiscentiam mundi, et non sunt in ea sorte gratiae, ut ab illo eligantur ex mundo.

150–3 The words in fact come later in the Gospel, not earlier (Jn 17.20), but they have been quoted earlier by Augustine, *Tract.*, 106.2.34–6 (though making a different point):

Non pro his autem rogo tantum sed et pro his qui credituri sunt per verbum eorum in me.

156–9 Jn 17.24:

Pater quos dedisti mihi volo ut ubi ego sum et illi sint mecum ut videant claritatem meam quam dedisti mihi quia dilexisti me ante constitutionem mundi.

165–79 Developed perhaps from Augustine, *Tract.*, 107.2.4–6:

Ubi satis apparet quomodo unigeniti Filii sint omnia quae sunt Patris; per hoc utique quod etiam ipse Deus est, et de Patre Patri est natus aequalis.

and supported by Mt 28.20:

Ecce ego vobiscum sum omnibus diebus usque ad consummationem saeculi.

The brief addition by Ælfric at 172 (printed Pope 25b), commenting that it is as great a *cræft* to hold and guide the creatures which he created as to make them in the first place, evidently refers back to the statement at line 168 that the Trinity 'holds' the whole of creation, though the wording is awkward since there is no proper referent for the *he*. The comment seems curiously unnecessary, but perhaps Ælfric was concerned to stress the continued role of God, or the Trinity, in the world.

180–204 The long peroration has of course no equivalent in Augustine. The reference to those who do not know Latin remaining silent about Christian doctrine (line 191) seems curiously barbed. For the notion of the world's tribulations as a sign of its approaching end, cf esp. LS 27.157 ff.

23 THIRD SUNDAY AFTER PENTECOST

This is the first of five homilies for Sundays after Pentecost in which Ælfric focuses on exegesis of the Gospel passage appointed for the occasion. In it he develops particularly the theme of the call to the Gentiles, which had played an important part in his homilies for Septuagesima and Sexagesima and was to recur in homilies 25 and 28. He cites Gregory as the source for his exposition of the pericope, the parable of the feast from Luke 14.16–24, and Gregory the Great's homily on the Gospel (Hom. 36)[1] does provide most of the details of Ælfric's interpretation, but the latter is considerably shorter and offers a rather different slant. Gregory's is primarily a moral or tropological interpretation concerned with pride, curiosity and lust: it begins with a distinction between corporal and mental appetites, goes on to discuss the priestly role, the uses of the senses and the moral effects of tribulation, and ends with an exemplum on withdrawal from the world. Ælfric omits most of this moral analysis, but he also gives the parable a historical dimension, using the allegorical level, that is scarcely present in Gregory's reading. For him, the preparation of the feast is the passion (cf 24, 30–32), and the series of summons to the guests represents a historical sequence, the calls first to the Jews under the Old Law, and then to the Gentiles, 'us' (note the fulfilment of prophecies at 32, the historical sequence at 96–8, and the *ær—nu* contrast at 101–3). He stresses too the geographical spread of the summons (*geond ealne middangeard* 26, *eallum geleaffullum* 33, *of eallum middangearde* 98–9 and again 105), and uses the first person plural in discussing the call to the Gentiles (*we* 98, *us* 113, 115). As in homilies 5 and 6, Ælfric sees the parable as an image of the historical movement from the call to the Jews to the call to the Anglo-Saxons at the end of time.

Some of Ælfric's changes were possibly influenced by other Latin homilies on the parable. The piece by Gregory is the only item for the occasion in PD,[2] but other authorities named by Ælfric in his preface, Augustine, Haymo and Smaragdus, have expositions of the parable and the first two at least appear to have contributed something. Both Augustine (Serm. 112) and Haymo (Hom. 112)[3] emphasise at the outset the historical or allegorical dimension of the parable, with Augustine, like Ælfric, distinguishing between the calls to the Jews and the call to 'us' the Gentiles, and both interpret the preparations for the feast as Christ's sacrifice. Ælfric's discussion of the five senses, for which Gregory provides no help, seems to owe something to Augustine and possibly Haymo as well. The homily by Smaragdus (*Collectiones*, PL 102, 355–8) is primarily a condensation of Gregory's, however, and seems to have contributed nothing.

One other respect in which Ælfric's handling of the parable seems distinctive

[1] Cf Förster 1894, p. 5.
[2] Cf Smetana 1959, pp. 174 and 198.
[3] Noted as a source by Smetana (1961, pp. 467–8).

is a tendency towards a specifically monastic idealism that is not evident in previous treatments of the text. When one of the invited guests excuses himself on the grounds of his marriage, Gregory, Haymo and Smaragdus all feel it incumbent on them to explain that marriage itself is good and ordained by God, though it is here used as an image of being wedded to the flesh. Ælfric does not feel the same necessity (though he had made that point at CH II.4.25–9), or the need to explain that there are good as well as bad uses of the senses, and it is noticeable that he adds a reference to 'the purity which God loves' (lines 74–5) and defines the sin of touch at 60–1 as 'foul and sinful touchings' (whereas for Haymo it is striking a neighbour). The anxiety of earlier writers to counter any latent suggestions in the parable that life in the world, ploughing and wiving, is inherently sinful, which is particularly noticeable in Gregory (it is the point of his final exemplum), gives way in small respects to a delicate acceptance of the ascetic implications in Ælfric's version.

Ælfric's exposition of the parable is, as he acknowledges, a brief one, and at some stage before he issued the Series he added a further section, lines 126 ff, drawing mainly on Gospel narrative. This appears as an appendage to the main part in four manuscripts apart from MS K, though the separate title appears only in K; it also appears as an independent item for the Fourth Sunday after Epiphany in MS M, perhaps by Ælfric's own decision, and was later detached from the rest of this homily, almost certainly by Ælfric, and incorporated into a new one for the Twelfth Sunday after Pentecost, printed as Pope 17; there is a detailed discussion in Pope, pp. 563–6. The first part (lines 131–41) is basically a translation of Matthew 8.23–7, the story of Christ quelling a storm at sea. This was the pericope for the fourth Sunday after Epiphany (an occasion not covered in the Catholic Homilies), to which Ælfric is presumably referring in his second sentence: *We sind gecnæwe þæt we hit forgymeleasodon on ðam dæge þe mann þæt godspel rædde.* However a few details seem to come from the parallel story in Mark 4, and when Ælfric continues the story beyond the pericope it is the version in Mark 5 that he uses for his account of the madman and the Gadarene swine, rather than the one in Matthew 8, though the latter supplies one or two details. Ælfric's reason for using Mark is perhaps something to do with his sources for the brief passages of exegesis, lines 142–6 and 177–98 (discussed by Pope, pp. 565–6). He would presumably have known the Latin version of Origen's homily on Matthew 8.23–7, since it is the one piece for the fourth Sunday after Epiphany in PD. He probably knew as well the homilies of Haymo and Smaragdus for the same occasion. However, the closest source for his comment on the pericope seems to be none of these but Bede's commentary on the Gospel of Mark, as Pope showed; the other commentaries have similar ideas but Bede's *verbo* (rendered as *anre hæse*) and *furorem* (rendered as *yðigendan*) seem decisive, though the last part of 142–6 probably comes from Haymo. Bede's commentary on Mark is used by Smaragdus in his homily, and although the latter cannot have supplied Ælfric with all that he used from Bede it may have drawn his attention to the Mark commentary and hence prompted his use of the Mark narrative for part of his text; but it is equally possible that the genesis of the Old English piece was Ælfric's reading in Mark and Bede's commentary on it, and that he substituted the Matthew text for the first part because it was the pericope for an earlier occasion that he had not covered. For his comments on the second part, the story of the madman, Bede's commentary on Mark seems again to be the main influence, though the only parallel I have found for the exegesis of the swine at the end is King Alfred's translation of Gregory the Great's *Regula Pastoralis*.

Yet if Bede supplies most of the details of Ælfric's exegesis, the general direction of his comments is not that of Bede or, indeed, of Haymo, Origen or Jerome. Bede treats the story of the storm as an allegory of the passion, with the ship as the cross, and the story of the madman as an allegory of the conversion of the heathen. There is no trace of either interpretation in Ælfric (despite the obvious links they would have offered with the main part of his homily), or of the concern of the other commentators on Matthew with the theme of the disciples' doubt. Ælfric's concern is with the illumination of God's power, recognised by the sea and wind, the oarsmen, the devils and the witnesses to the healing of the madman. Neither this theme nor the Gospel text itself seems closely connected with the main part of the homily. One can only assume that it was a text which interested Ælfric and that he added it here simply because the rest of the homily was brief. The fact that part of the *Alia Narratio* is in alliterative prose (see lines 151–4 and 179–98) suggests that it was written some time after the main homily.

Sources and Notes

The following texts are cited below:

1. Augustine, *Sermones*, PL 38, Serm. 112, cols. 643–8.
2. Bede, *Commentarius in Marcum*, ed. D. Hurst, CCSL 120 (Turnhout, 1960), pp. 431–648.
3. Gregory the Great, *Homiliae in Evangelia*, PL 76, Hom. 36, cols. 1265–74.
4. Haymo of Auxerre, *Homiliae de Tempore*, PL 118, Hom. 20 and 112, cols. 147–54 and 601–8.
5. *King Alfred's West-Saxon Version of Gregory's Pastoral Care*, ed. H. Sweet, EETS os 45 and 50 (1871–2, repr. 1996).

3–20 A close translation of Lc 14.16–24, except that Ælfric adds *nu niwan* (line 11) and renders *servus* as *bydel*, 'messenger', at line 12:

(16) At ipse dixit ei: Homo quidam fecit cenam magnam et vocavit multos.
(17) Et misit servum suum hora cenae dicere invitatis ut venirent, quia iam parata sunt omnia. (18) Et coeperunt simul omnes excusare. Primus dixit ei: Villam emi et necesse habeo exire et videre illam; rogo te habe me

excusatum. (19) Et alter dixit: Iuga boum emi quinque et eo probare illa; rogo te habe me excusatum. (20) Et alius dixit: Uxorem duxi et ideo non possum venire. (21) Et reversus servus nuntiavit haec domino suo. Tunc iratus paterfamilias dixit servo suo: Exi cito in plateas et vicos civitatis, et pauperes ac debiles et caecos et claudos introduc huc. (22) Et ait servus: Domine factum est ut imperasti et adhuc locus est. (23) Et ait dominus servo: exi in vias et sepes et conpelle intrare ut impleatur domus mea. (24) Dico autem vobis quod nemo virorum illorum qui vocati sunt gustabit cenam meam.

21–4 None of the commentaries is particularly close here.

24–8 Loosely based on Gregory the Great, Hom. 36, PL 76, 1267B:

> Sed quis per hunc servum .. nisi praedicatorum ordo designatur? De quo videlicet ordine quamvis adhuc indigni existimus . . . hoc est quod ago, servus enim sum summi patrisfamilias. Cum vos admoneo ad contemptum saeculi, invitare vos venio ad coenam Dei.

But line 26 resembles rather Haymo, Hom. 112, PL 118, 601D:

> Vocavit autem multos . . . postmodum per praedicationem apostolorum ex quatuor mundi partibus populum gentium ad fidem vocando.

28–30 Follows Gregory, Hom. 36, PL 76, 1267A:

> Quid hora coenae, nisi finis est mundi? In quo nimirum nos sumus, sicut iam dudum Paulus testatur, dicens: 'Nos sumus in quos fines saeculorum devenerunt' (1 Cor 10.11).

The quotation from St Paul troubled the Old English scribes but accurately renders the Latin.

30–33 No parallel in Gregory; the nearest is Haymo, Hom. 112, PL 118, 602D:

> Omnia enim parata sunt, quia ille singularis agnus occisus est, in cuius praeparatione omnia praecesserunt. Sive omnia parata sunt, quia nullum exemplum virtutis est quod ad nostram imitationem in operibus sanctorum non sit declaratum. Iam enim innocentiam Abel audivimus, obedientiam Abrahae, constantiam Isaac . . . et finem Domini vidimus.

Haymo is not concerned with prophecy but he does identify the Old Testament figures as the preparations and Christ's passion as the fulfillment of them. Augustine too relates the verse to Christ's sacrifice, Serm. 112, §1, PL 38, 643: *Parata iam coena, immolato Christo. . . .*

33–7 Follows Gregory fairly closely, Hom. 36, PL 76, 1267D:

> Offert Deus quod rogari debuit; non rogatus dare vult quod vix sperari poterat . . .; paratas vero delicias refectionis aeternae denuntiat, et tamen simul omnes excusant.

The first part, however, is recast in apparent echo of Mt 7.7 or Lc 11.9: *Petite et dabitur vobis; quaerite et invenietis.*

39–42 From Gregory, Hom. 36, PL 76, 1268B:

> Quid per villam nisi terrena substantia designatur? Exiit ergo videre villam qui sola exteriora cogitat propter substantiam.

44–62 The basic exegesis is probably from Gregory, Hom. 36, PL 76, 1268BC:

> Quid in quinque iugis boum nisi quinque corporis sensus accepimus? Qui recte quoque iuga vocati sunt, quia in utroque sexu geminantur. Qui videlicet corporales sensus, quia interna comprehendere nesciunt, sed sola exteriora cognoscunt, et, deserentes intima, ea quae extra sunt tangunt, recte per eos curiositatis designatur. . . . Grave namque curiositatis est vitium. . . . Eo probare illa, quia videlicet aliquando pertinere probatio ad curiositatem solet.

Gregory does not, however, elaborate on the five senses and Ælfric seems to have been influenced here by Augustine, whose exegesis of the verse is otherwise not close to Ælfric (Augustine, Serm. 112, §3, PL 38, 644–5):

> In oculis visus est, auditus in auribus, odoratus in naribus, gustatus in faucibus, tactus in omnibus membris. Alba et nigra et quoquo modo colorata, lucida et obscura videndo sentimus. Rauca et canora, audiendo sentimus. Suave olentia et grave olentia, odorando sentimus. Dulcia et amara, gustando sentimus. Dura et mollia, lenia et aspera, calida et frigida, gravia et levia, tangendo sentimus. . . . Bene olet, male olet; scio, sentio. Hoc dulce est, hoc amarum; hoc salsum, hoc fatuum. . . . Tangendo novi quid durum est, quid molle sit; quid lene sit, quid asperum sit.

Haymo also names the five senses and discusses their corruption (Hom. 112, PL 118, 603), but his ideas are different from Ælfric's.

63–70 Close to Gregory, Hom. 36, PL 76, 1268D:

> Dum enim dicit Rogo te, et tamen venire contemnit, humilitas sonat in voce, superbia in actione. . . . Nam dum cuilibet perverse agenti dicimus Convertere, Deum sequere, mundum relinque, ubi hunc nisi ad dominicam coenam vocamus? Sed cum respondet: Ora pro me, quia peccator sum, hoc facere non possum, quid aliud agit, nisi et rogat et excusat?

71–6 Cf Gregory, Hom. 36, PL 76, 1269A: *Quid per uxorem nisi voluptas carnis accipitur?*

80–94 Mostly from Gregory though the points are re-ordered (Hom. 36, PL 76):

> [1269C] Pauperes et debiles dicuntur, qui iudicio suo apud semetipsos infirmi sunt. . . . Caeci vero sunt, qui nullum ingenii lumen habent. Claudi quoque sunt, qui rectos gressus in operatione non habent. Sed dum morum vitia in membrorum debilitate signantur, profecto liquet quia sicut illi peccatores fuerunt qui vocati venire noluerunt, ita hi quoque peccatores sunt qui invitantur et veniunt. Sed peccatores superbi respuuntur, ut peccatores humiles eligantur. Hos itaque elegit Deus quos despicit

> mundus, quia plerumque ipsa despectio hominem revocat ad semetipsum. [1269B] Venire superbi renuunt, pauperes eliguntur. Cur hoc? Quia, iuxta Pauli vocem, 'Infirma mundi eligit Deus, ut confundat fortia' (1 Cor 1.27).

Ælfric does not use the long parallel with the story of the Amalekites, 1 Samuel 30.11 ff, which follows in Gregory.

96–110 Mostly from Gregory, Hom. 36, PL 76, 1270C-1B:

> Intravit iam frequentia Iudaeorum, sed adhuc locus vacat in regno, ubi suscipi debeat numerositas gentium. Unde et eidem servo dicitur: 'Exi in vias et sepes, et compelle intrare, ut impleatur domus mea.' Cum de vicis et plateis ad coenam quosdam Dominus invitat, illum videlicet populum designat qui tenere legem sub urbana conversatione noverat; cum vero convivas suos colligi ex viis et sepibus praecipit, nimirum agrestem populum colligere, id est gentilem, quaerit. . . . Alii enim vocantur, et venire contemnunt; alii vocantur et veniunt; alii autem nequaquam dicitur quia vocantur, sed compelluntur ut intrent. . . . Saepe namque nonnulli ad temporalem gloriam proficere volentes, aut longa aegritudine tabescunt, aut afflicti iniuriis concidunt, aut percussi gravibus damnis affliguntur, et in mundi dolore vident quia nihil confidere de eius voluptate debuerunt, seque ipsos in suis desideriis reprehendentes, ad Deum corda convertunt.

Ælfric's *wilde* at 104, meaning presumably untamed and therefore uncivilised, does not exactly correspond to Gregory's *agrestem*; but similar imagery contrasting the Jews and Gentiles is used at CH I.14.61–3.

113–22 Follows Gregory very closely, Hom. 36, PL 76, 1272BC:

> Ecce vocat per se, vocat per angelos, vocat per patres, vocat per prophetas, vocat per apostolos, vocat per pastores, vocat etiam per nos, vocat plerumque per miracula, vocat plerumque per flagella, vocat aliquando per hujus mundi prospera, vocat aliquando per adversa. Nemo contemnat, ne, dum vocatus excusat, cum voluerit intrare non valeat. Audite quid Sapientia per Salomonem dicat: 'Tunc invocabunt me, et non exaudiam; mane consurgent, et non invenient me' (Prov 1.28).

126 ff The sources for the *Alia Narratio* are printed by Pope in his edition of Pope 17 and therefore not repeated here.

131–41 A close translation of the Vulgate text of Mt 8.23–7, except that 133–4, *Se wind . . . blæde*, is not in Mt and perhaps renders Mc 4.37 *procella magna venti*; 134–5 *on ðam steorsetle* is from Mc 4.38 *in puppi*; 138 *het hi stille beon* probably reflects the *Tace, obmutesce* of Mc 4.39; and 140 *ða reðran* probably comes from Bede's explanation in his commentary on Mark (*Comm. Marc.*, 2.75–6), *Non ergo discipuli sed nautae et ceteri qui in navi erant mirabantur*, though as Pope notes, the point is originally Jerome's.

142–6 The commentary follows Bede on Mark and then, briefly, Haymo, PL 118, Hom. 20.

147–76 A close rendering of Mc 5.1–20 except that instead of 5.4 *et nemo poterat eum domare* Ælfric has, a sentence later, *and nan man ne mihte ðæs weges faran*, from Mt 8.28; where Mark has the herdsmen report the event *in civitatem et in agros* Ælfric, like Matthew, has only the city; and Ælfric omits the citizens' request to Christ to leave them (Mc 5.16–17 = Mt 8.34).

177 For the explanation of a *legio* cf CH II.14.98 and commentary.

179–85 Loosely parallel to Bede on Mark, though the last part (*ne into . . . genumen*) has no equivalent there.

186–94 The passage from Bede cited by Pope is not at all similar to Ælfric's comment on the habits of pigs. The nearest parallel I have found is, curiously, in King Alfred's Old English version of Gregory the Great's *Regula Pastoralis*, c.54 (*Pastoral Care*, 421.2–6):

> Swa ðet swin, ðeah hit aðwægen sie, gif hit eft filð on ðæt sol, ðonne bið hit fulre ðonne hit ær wæs, & ne forstent ðæt ðweal nauht, ðeah hit ær aðwægen wære; swa bið ðæm ðe his gedonan synna wepeð, & hi swaðeah ne forlæt; hefigran scylde & hefigran witum he hine underðiet, gif he hit ne forlæt.

Gregory himself (PL 77, 110A) is less close since he writes of the pig being washed in the wallowing-pool of mud and therefore returning dirtier than it went, whereas Alfred pictures the pig returning to the mud after being washed clean. The king makes the same adaptation in his rendering of Boethius's *De Consolatione* (OE Boethius, 115.5–10). Ælfric seems to have known both of these Old English texts.[4] Neither Bede nor Alfred offers a parallel for his reference to the dark colour of the pigs.

24 ST PETER

Ælfric had already written one homily for this occasion, CH I.26, where he expounded the Gospel text for the day (Matthew 16.13–21, on the naming of Simon Peter) and then narrated the martyrdom of Peter and Paul. A second homily is perhaps a testimony to the importance of the occasion (the only other saint's day to be covered in both Series is the Assumption of the Virgin). For this homily Ælfric takes the epistle for the day, Acts 12.1–23 on Peter's release from prison by an angel, and the Gospel reading for the octave, Matthew 14.22–36, telling of Peter walking on the waves. On the former he offers little more than a paraphrase of the Biblical narrative, adding some historical information

[4] See Godden 1978.

on Herod and Pilate but resolutely avoiding the allegorical interpretation which he probably knew from Bede's commentary on Acts and the homily on the epistle by Smaragdus,[1] and insisting that his concern is with the simple understanding of the laity (lines 48–50). His treatment of the Gospel text is a very different matter. He ventures deep into allegorical interpretation and problems of dogma, draws on a wide range of sources for his exposition as well as developing it in ways of his own, and three times turns away from the text in question to discuss other Biblical texts in detail. There is a willingness in this part of the homily to explore difficult concepts and employ challengingly complex formulations (e.g. 167–73). This is particularly noticeable where he is treating texts that he also expounded elsewhere. Possibly associated with this is the use of Biblical quotations in Latin (lines 95–6, 202–3) and two Latin notes citing St Augustine as authority for points of interpretation (lines 128–30, 163–4), though these are only in MS K. He seems to have written the second part with a quite different audience in mind from the *læwede men* of the first part who need no more than a simple narrative.

The use of sources is more complicated than Ælfric's opening reference to St Augustine suggests.[2] He knew both a genuine homily by Augustine on the Gospel text, his sermon 76, probably available in his copy of PD, and another homily on the same text which went under Augustine's name, Ps-Augustine, Serm. 72 (which is not found in any homiliary, according to Smetana). Both influenced his treatment of the Gospel text and passages are at times translated very closely, but Ælfric is highly selective in his use of them and draws on at least three other sources as well. Ps-Augustine, Serm. 72, which probably provided him with his starting-point, turns almost immediately to the words 'Christ went up into a mountain to pray alone' and the idea of Christ's solitary ascension. The author quotes in support John 3.13, 'No man ascends[3] up to heaven but he that came down from heaven, the son of man, who is in heaven', and explains briefly that even at the day of judgement Christ can be said to ascend alone, since Christ the head and the church as the limbs make one body,

[1] Smaragdus, *Collectiones in Evangelia et Epistolas*, PL 102, cols. 389–90.

[2] Förster (1892, pp. 33–4) suggested Augustine's sermons 75 and 76 (PL 38, cols. 474–9 and 479–83) as sources, but the former offers nothing for which Ps-Augustine, Serm. 72 is not a better source. The latter was identified by Smetana (1959, pp. 198–9), who also pointed out that Serm. 76 was to be found in a later version of PD. There is a further detailed discussion of sources by J. E. Cross (1968).

[3] The Latin sermon reads *ascendit*, as does the Vulgate. The author clearly understands this as present tense, and so does Ælfric (*astihð*). The commentaries by Augustine, Bede and Haymo make it clear that they too took it as a present tense. However, the Greek text apparently uses the perfect tense, and the Authorized Version accordingly reads 'no man hath ascended'. It appears then that part at least of the dogmatic crux with which Augustine and his successors were wrestling here was based on a misunderstanding of an ambiguous reading present not only in the Vulgate but also in the older Latin version of the Bible which Augustine used (though a misunderstanding perhaps more fruitful for theological discussion than the correct reading).

but earlier Christ ascended literally alone in order to intercede with God for man. Ælfric, however, is not satisfied with this brief explanation and develops the problems raised by John 3.13 at some length (lines 98–130). The verse forms part of the pericope for the Sunday after Pentecost and he was therefore able to use material from two homilies for that occasion, Bede's Hom. II.18 (included in PD) and Haymo's Hom. 108, as well as, probably, Augustine's Tractates on John.[4] He follows Bede most closely, exploring not only the Christological issues but also the apparent contradictions between the statement in John and Biblical texts which insist that others have ascended or will ascend. At the end he returns neatly to the Ps-Augustine sermon for its concluding statement on the problem and cites its authority (lines 125–30). This was not, however, the end of his interest in the verse. Much later he composed a full homily on John 3.1–15 for the Sunday after Pentecost (Pope 12), using again the sermons by Bede and Haymo and Augustine's Tractates; there he treats verse 13 once more, but this time more briefly and simply, and drawing on this earlier commentary as well as his Latin sources.

After pursuing this particular 'knot' Ælfric returns to his main text in Matthew and starts afresh, interpreting the first five verses (lines 22–7) with the help of Ps-Augustine, Serm. 72 (lines 131–55). This source has, however, little to say on the remaining verses of the pericope and Ælfric then turns to Augustine's Serm. 76 for the rest of the exposition. Once again, following his source, he turns away from the pericope to discuss another germane text, Matthew 16.13–19, where Christ names Peter as the rock. This was a text which Ælfric had already expounded in CH I.26. His source there was Bede, and his concern was largely with St Peter as an archetype of the bishop or priest and as a model of Christian faith; here his source is Augustine (though there is some reminiscence of the earlier homily) and his emphasis on St Peter as a figure for the church. The name Petrus or *stænen*, 'made of rock', earlier seen as testifying to the strength of Peter's faith and the steadfastness of his profession, is here seen to signify his relationship to Christ, the true *stan*, and hence his symbolic role as the church, and Ælfric quotes his source in Latin to emphasise the point (lines 163–4). He then turns back once again to his main text and continues his exposition for a further sixty lines (lines 174–233), mainly following Augustine's Serm. 76 to the end of his sermon but occasionally developing rather different ideas of his own.

The two Augustinian sermons both end their exposition with Matthew 14.33, which is in fact the end of the episode. It is also the normal end of the pericope[5] but in his translation of the Gospel at the beginning Ælfric continues for three more verses, to tell of Christ's healing of the diseased. He returns to this section

[4] All that Ælfric used from Bede is in fact excerpted by Smaragdus in his sermon (*Collectiones*, PL 102, 341–2), but there is nothing specific to point to Smaragdus rather than Bede.

[5] So Lenker, p. 361.

with a brief comment near the end of his homily, but then turns aside to the parallel story of the woman healed by touching Christ's clothing from Mark 5.25 ff and Luke 8.43 ff.

Clearly much thought has gone into this homily, combining as it does discussion of five different Biblical texts and expository material drawing on at least six different sources. The immediate concern influencing the choice of texts was perhaps the role of St Peter. Yet there seems to be something deeper than this, not only a willingness to explore issues incidentally touched on by the text, but also an interest in generalising Peter as a figure for the church and exemplar of faith and doubt. The concept of the body of the church and its unity plays a part in the excursus on John 3.13 and Matthew 16.13–19; and the one comment that Ælfric makes on the concluding miracle is to underline the faith which distinguishes the woman from the crowd thronging around Christ—*synderlice mid geleafan*.

Sources and Notes

The following texts are cited below:

1. Augustine, *In Iohannis Evangelium Tractatus CXXIV*, ed. R. Willems, CCSL 36 (Turnhout, 1954).
2. Augustine, *Sermones*, PL 38, Serm. 76, cols. 479–83.
3. Ps-Augustine, *Sermones*, PL 39, Serm. 72 [= Augustine, *Sermones suppositíti*], cols. 1884–6.
4. Bede, *Commentarius in Marcum*, ed. D. Hurst, CCSL 120 (Turnhout, 1960), pp. 431–648.
5. Bede, *Expositio Actuum Apostolorum*, ed. M. Laistner, CCSL 121 (Turnhout, 1983), pp. 3–99.
6. Bede, *Homiliae*, ed. D. Hurst, CCSL 122 (Turnhout, 1955), Hom. II.18 (pp. 311–17).
7. Haymo of Auxerre, *Homiliae de Tempore*, PL 118, Hom. 108, cols. 578–84.
8. Rufinus, *Historia Ecclesiastica*, ed. T. Mommsen, in *Eusebius Werke*, ed. E. Klostermann, vol. 2, 2 parts, GCS 9.1 and 9.2 (Leipzig, 1903–8).

1–41 A rendering, sometimes close, sometimes abbreviated, of Acts 12.1–23: (1) Eodem autem tempore misit Herodes rex manus ut adfligeret quosdam de ecclesia. (2) Occidit autem Iacobum fratrem Iohannis gladio. (3) Videns autem quia placeret Iudaeis adposuit adprehendere et Petrum; erant autem dies azymorum. (4) Quem cum adprehendisset misit in carcerem tradens quattuor quaternionibus militum custodire eum, volens post pascha producere eum populo. (5) Et Petrus quidem servabatur in carcere; oratio autem fiebat sine intermissione ab ecclesia ad Deum pro eo. (6) Cum autem producturus eum esset Herodes in ipsa nocte erat Petrus dormiens inter duos milites vinctus catenis duabus et custodes ante ostium custodiebant carcerem. (7) Et ecce angelus Domini adstitit et lumen refulsit in habitaculo percussoque latere Petri suscitavit eum dicens: surge velociter; et ceciderunt catenae de manibus eius. (8) Dixit autem angelus ad eum: praecingere et calcia te gallicas tuas. Et fecit sic et dixit illi: circumda tibi vestimentum tuum et sequere me. (9) Et exiens sequebatur et nesciebat quia verum est quod fiebat per angelum, aestimabat autem se visum videre. (10) Transeuntes autem primam et secundam custodiam venerunt ad portam ferream quae ducit ad civitatem quae ultro aperta est eis et exeuntes processerunt vicum unum; et continuo discessit angelus ab eo. (11) Et Petrus ad se reversus dixit: nunc scio vere quia misit Dominus angelum suum et eripuit me de manu Herodis et de omni expectatione plebis Iudaeorum. (12) Consideransque venit ad domum Mariae matris Iohannis qui cognominatus est Marcus ubi erant multi congregati et orantes. (13) Pulsante autem eo ostium ianuae processit puella ad audiendum nomine Rhode. (14) Et ut cognovit vocem Petri prae gaudio non aperuit ianuam sed intro currens nuntiavit stare Petrum ante ianuam. (15) At illi dixerunt ad eam: insanis. Illa autem adfirmabat sic se habere. Illi autem dicebant: angelus eius est. (16) Petrus autem perseverabat pulsans cum autem aperuissent viderunt eum et obstipuerunt. (17) Annuens autem eis manu ut tacerent enarravit quomodo Dominus eduxisset eum de carcere dixitque: nuntiate Iacobo et fratribus haec et egressus abiit in alium locum. (18) Facta autem die erat non parva turbatio inter milites quidnam de Petro factum esset. (19) Herodes autem . . . descendens a Iudaea in Caesaream ibi commoratus est. (20) Erat autem iratus Tyriis et Sidoniis. . . . (21) Statuto autem die Herodes vestitus veste regia sedit pro tribunali et contionabatur ad eos. . . . (23) Confestim autem percussit eum angelus Domini eo quod non dedisset honorem Deo et consumptus a vermibus exspiravit.

42–8 The information on Pilate presumably comes from the *Historia Ecclesiastica* of Rufinus (II.vii), referred to by Ælfric at 48, and the details on the three Herods may have come from there too (I.vii-viii, xiii, II.iv), as Förster suggested (1894, p. 53). But Bede's comments on this passage in his *Expositio Actuum Apostolorum* give the requisite details of the three Herods, and Ælfric had already discussed the first two in detail in CH I.32.33–54, which is verbally quite close.

50–2 A cautious formulation. Lammas Day, or 1 August, was indeed the festival of St Peter in Chains, or St Peter ad Vincula, on which Peter's release was celebrated, even though the narrative from Acts was used as the epistle for St Peter's day in June. Whether the release was to be supposed to have happened on 1 August was a moot issue, since the narrative apparently places it soon after Easter; the version of PD in PL 95 includes a sermon discussing the problems.

Ælfric's comment does not quite say that the release did happen at Lammas, though the adaptation to Lammas in MS G is not so careful.

54–85 A fairly free translation of the Vulgate text of Mt 14.22–36:

> (22) Et statim iussit discipulos ascendere in navicula et praecedere eum trans fretum, donec dimitteret turbas. (23) Et dimissa turba ascendit in montem solus orare; vespere autem facto solus erat ibi. (24) Navicula autem in medio mari iactabatur fluctibus; erat enim contrarius ventus. (25) Quarta autem vigilia noctis venit ad eos ambulans supra mare. (26) Et videntes eum supra mare ambulantem turbati sunt dicentes quia fantasma est, et prae timore clamaverunt. (27) Statimque Iesus locutus est eis dicens: habete fiduciam; ego sum; nolite timere. (28) Respondens autem Petrus dixit: Domine si tu es iube me venire ad te super aquas. (29) At ipse ait veni; et descendens Petrus de navicula ambulabat super aquam ut veniret ad Iesum. (30) Videns vero ventum validum timuit et cum coepisset mergi clamavit dicens: Domine salvum me fac. (31) Et continuo Iesus extendens manum adprehendit eum et ait illi: modicae fidei quare dubitasti. (32) Et cum ascendissent in naviculam cessavit ventus. (33) Qui autem in navicula erant venerunt et adoraverunt eum dicentes: vere Filius Dei es. (34) Et cum transfretassent venerunt in terram Gennesar. (35) Et cum cognovissent eum viri loci illius miserunt in universam regionem illam et obtulerunt ei omnes male habentes. (36) Et rogabant eum ut vel fimbriam vestimenti eius tangerent et quicumque tetigerunt salvi facti sunt.

The one substantial difference is *Se hælend þæt geðafode* (line 84), which is not in the Biblical text.

86–92 No close parallels, despite the attribution. Cf Ps-Augustine, Serm. 72, §2, PL 39, 1884:

> Navicellam quippe istam, fratres, ecclesiam cogitate; turbulentum mare, hoc saeculum.

The phrase *þæra lybbendra eorðan* (line 92) renders the Biblical phrase *terra viventium*, as Cross noted (1968, p. 60), but it is not used in any of the relevant sources; Ælfric was perhaps recalling his own phrasing at CH I.36.202, derived from Augustine. For the image cf perhaps Bede's commentary on Mark (*Comm. Marc.*, 2.1083–7):

> Labor discipulorum in remigando et contrarius eis ventus labores sanctae ecclesiae varios designat, quae inter undas saeculi adversantis et immundorum flatus spirituum ad quietem patriae caelestis quasi ad fidam litoris stationem pervenire conatur.

92–8 From Ps-Augustine, Serm. 72, §1, PL 39, 1884:

> Mons altitudo est: quid enim in hoc mundo altius coelo? Quis vero in coelum ascendit, novit optime fides vestra. Cur autem solus ascendit? Quia 'nemo ascendit in coelum, nisi qui de coelo descendit, Filius hominis, qui est in coelo' (Jn 3.13).

99–100 A favourite Ælfrician comment: cf CH I.40.68–9, II.7.138–40.

100–106 From Bede, Hom. II.18, 119–21, 125–8:

Merito autem quaeritur, quomodo dicatur filius hominis vel descendisse de caelo, vel eo quo haec in terra loquebatur iam fuisse in caelo. . . . Non ergo caro Christi descendit de caelo, neque ante tempus ascensionis erat in caelo. Et qua ratione dicitur, nisi qui descendit de caelo, filius hominis, qui est in caelo, nisi quia una Christi persona est in duabus existens naturis?

106–8 From Haymo's homily for the Sunday after Pentecost, Hom. 108, PL 118, 582D:

Ad quod dicendum quia mediator Dei et hominum Dominus Iesus Christus, in una eademque persona ex duabus substantiis creditur, divina scilicet et humana. Quia idem est filius Dei, qui et filius hominis: et idem filius hominis, qui et Filius Dei.

109–13 Returns to Bede, Hom. II.18, 128–31:

Atque ideo filius hominis recte dicitur et descendisse de caelo, et ante passionem fuisse in caelo, quia quod in sua natura habere non potuit, hoc in filio Dei a quo assumptus est, habuit.

113–15 Bede and Haymo both insist that the divinity was always in heaven but say nothing of earth; Ælfric here parallels Augustine, whose Tractates on John he had used before, and was to use again when expounding this text in Pope 12 (Augustine, *Tract.*, 12.8.3–4):

Ecce hic erat, et in caelo erat, hic erat carne, in caelo erat divinitate; immo, ubique divinitate.

116–25 Mostly from Bede, Hom. II.18, 139–53:

Sed et hoc quaerendum quomodo dictum sit: 'Et nemo ascendit in caelum, nisi qui descendit de caelo', cum omnes electi se veraciter confidant ascensuros in caelum, promittente sibi Domino quia 'ubi sum ego, illic et minister meus erit' (Jn 12.26). Cuius tamen nodum quaestionis apertissima ratio solvit quia videlicet mediator Dei et hominum homo Christus Iesus electorum omnium caput est; itemque omnes electi eiusdem capitis membra sunt, dicente apostolo . . .: 'Vos enim estis corpus Christi et membra de membro' (1 Cor 12.27). . . . Nemo ascendit in caelum, nisi Christus in corpore suo, quod est ecclesia, qui in se ipso quidem primum, cernentibus apostolis eminentioribus nimirum membris suis, ascendit, et exinde in membris suis cotidie ascendens se colligit in caelum.

125–30 Ælfric now returns, in mid-sentence, to Ps-Augustine, Serm. 72, §1, picking up where he left it at line 98 (PL 39, 1884):

Quamvis et in fine cum venerit, et nos omnes sua membra collegerit, ac levaverit in coelum, etiam tunc solus ascendet: quia caput cum corpore suo unus est Christus. Nunc autem solum caput ascendit.

The Latin note in MS K, quoting his source, was presumably a marginal citation giving his authority for a difficult point of doctrine.

131–9 Continues with Ps-Augustine, Serm. 72, §§1 and 2, PL 39, 1884–5:

> Ipse ascendit solus orare; quia ipse ascendit ad Patrem pro nobis interpellare. . . . Dum ille orat in excelso, navicula turbatur fluctibus in profundo. Quia insurgunt fluctus, potest ipsa navicula turbari: sed quia Christus orat, non potest mergi. Navicellam quippe istam, fratres, ecclesiam cogitate; turbulentum mare, hoc saeculum. Quando aliquis impiae voluntatis, maximae potestatis, persecutionem indicit ecclesiae . . . super naviculam Christi grandis unda consurgit. . . . Quantumlibet mare saeviat, ventus incumbat, inter flatus et fluctus navis ista turbetur: tantum non mergatur.

139–49 Very close to Ps-Augustine, Serm. 72, §4, though line 149 is Ælfric's own qualification (PL 39, 1886):

> Venit ergo Christus ad navim suam quarta vigilia noctis, et visitavit eam. Quarta vigilia noctis, extrema pars noctis est. Vigilia una tres horas habet, ac per hoc nox quatuor vigilias habet, ternis horis per singulas vigilias distributis. Quarta ergo vigilia noctis, hoc est pene iam nocte finita. Sic veniet in fine saeculi, iniquitatis nocte transacta, ad iudicandos vivos et mortuos. Venit enim nunc, sicut audistis, valde mirabiliter ambulans super aquas. Surgebant fluctus; sed calcabantur: fremens pelagus sub Domini vestigiis murmurabat; sed tamen eum volens nolens portabat. Quantumlibet tumores saeculi potestatesque consurgant, premit eorum caput, nostrum Caput.

150–55 From Ps-Augustine, Serm. 72, §4, PL 39, 1886:

> Cum vero appropinquaret naviculae, turbati sunt prae timore discipuli, et exclamaverunt, putantes phantasma esse. Quibus Dominus ait: 'Habete fiduciam; ego sum, nolite timere.' Quid est, Ego sum? Non sum phantasma quod putatis, agnoscite quem videtis.

155–73 Ælfric now turns to Augustine's, Serm. 76, §1, PL 38, 479:

> Evangelium . . . admonet nos intelligere mare praesens saeculum esse, Petrum vero apostolum ecclesiae unicae typum. Ipse enim Petrus in Apostolorum ordine primus, in Christi amore promptissimus, saepe unus respondet pro omnibus. Ipse denique Domino Iesu Christo requirente, quemnam homines dicerent eum esse, et opiniones varias hominum discipulis respondentibus, rursusque Domino interrogante et dicente, 'Vos autem quem me esse dicitis?' respondit Petrus, 'Tu es Christus filius Dei vivi' (Mt 16.15–16). Unus pro multis dedit responsum, unitas in multis. . . . Simon quippe antea vocabatur. Hoc autem ei nomen, ut Petrus appellaretur, a Domino impositum est: et hoc in ea figura, ut significaret ecclesiam. Quia enim Christus petra, Petrus populus christianus. . . . 'Tu es ergo',

inquit, 'Petrus; et super hanc petram' quam confessus es, super hanc petram quam cognovisti, dicens, 'Tu es Christus filius Dei vivi', 'aedificabo ecclesiam meam' (Mt 16.18), id est, Super me ipsum filium Dei vivi, aedificabo ecclesiam meam. Super me aedificabo te, non me super te.

Lines 169–70 recall Ælfric's earlier treatment of this verse, at CH I.26.63–4. Lines 172–3, with no parallel in Augustine, perhaps draw on the same earlier text, 66: *He is se grundweal ealra þæra getimbrunga his agenre cyrcan.* The Latin note, repeating the point already made in the original Old English text at 174, evidently refers to the opening of this passage in Augustine. On the implication that this was the moment at which Simon received the name Peter, cf CH I.26.60–73 and note.

175–88 Mostly based on Augustine, but selective, and the interpretation of the strong and the weak (lines 181–4) seems to be Ælfric's own (Serm. 76, §4, PL 38, 480–1):

Illum tamen videte Petrum, qui tunc erat figura nostra: modo fidit, modo titubat. . . . Proinde quia ecclesia Christi habet firmos, habet et infirmos; nec sine firmis potest esse, nec sine infirmis: unde dicit Paulus apostolus, 'Debemus autem nos firmi, infirmorum onera sustinere' (Rom 15.1). . . . In illo ergo uno apostolo . . . utrumque genus significandum fuit, id est, firmi et infirmi: quia sine utroque non est ecclesia.

Augustine defines Peter's weakness as his fear of Christ's death.

189–212 Draws together points from §§ 5, 8 and 6 of Augustine's sermon, but there is no parallel to lines 207–12 (Serm. 76, PL 38):

[§5, 481] Non enim possum hoc in me, sed in te. . . . quia cum iusseris, fiet. . . . Et Dominus, Veni, inquit. Et sine ulla dubitatione Petrus ad verbum iubentis . . . desiluit in aquas, et ambulare coepit. Potuit quod Dominus, non in se, sed in Domino. . . . [§8, 482] Praesumpsit de Domino, potuit de Domino: titubavit ut homo, rediit ad Dominum. . . . [§6, 481] Nemo a Deo fit firmus, nisi qui se a se ipso sentit infirmum. . . . [§8, 482] Si dicebam, 'Motus est pes meus'. Psalmus loquitur, . . . 'Misericordia tua, Domine, adiuvabat me' (Ps 93.18). . . . Et 'omnis qui invocaverit nomen Domini, salvus erit' (Joel 2.32). Continuo porrigens adiutorium dexterae suae, levavit mergentem, increpavit diffidentem.

213–29 Mainly from Augustine, Serm. 76, §9 (PL 38, 482–3), but with possibly some points prompted by Ps-Augustine, Serm. 72, §§3 and 5 (PL 39, 1884–6):

[Augustine, §9] Attendite saeculum quasi mare. [Ps-Augustine, §3] Adulatores vestros tanquam latentes sub undis scopulos observate. Quando enim mare tranquillum est, tunc saxa latentia non videntur. [Augustine, §9] Amas Deum; ambulas super mare, sub pedibus tuis est saeculi tumor. Amas saeculum; absorbebit te. Amatores suos vorare novit, non portare. Sed cum fluctuat cupiditate cor tuum, ut vincas tuam cupiditatem, invoca Christi divinitatem. . . . Noli hinc interrogare temporis tranquillitatem: interroga, sed tuam cupiditatem. Vide si tranquillitas est in te; vide si non te subvertit ventus interior: hoc vide. . . . Magnae felicitatis est, a felicitate non vinci. Disce calcare saeculum: memento fidere in Christo. Et si . . . mergi incipis, dic: Domine, pereo, libera me. Dic, Pereo; ne pereas. [Ps-Augustine, §5] Porriget ille manum; et eruet de profundo. Etenim manus eius deducet nos, et continebit nos dextera eius.

233–48 Ælfric combines two versions of the healing, Mc 5.25–34 and Lc 8.43–8; the use of Lc 8.45, slightly cut, enables him to emphasise the role of Peter:

(Mc 5.25) Et mulier quae erat in profluvio sanguinis annis duodecim. . . . (27) Cum audisset de Iesu venit in turba retro et tetigit vestimentum eius; (28) dicebat enim quia si vel vestimentum eius (Lc 8.44 fimbriam vestimenti eius) tetigero salva ero. (29) Et confestim siccatus est fons sanguinis eius, et sensit corpore quod sanata esset a plaga. (Lc 8.45) Et ait Iesus: quis est qui me tetigit? Negantibus autem omnibus dixit Petrus et qui cum illo erant: praeceptor turbae te conprimunt et adfligunt et dicis quis me tetigit. (46) Et dixit Iesus: tetigit me aliquis nam ego novi virtutem de me exisse. (47) Videns autem mulier quia non latuit, tremens venit et procidit ante pedes illius et ob quam causam tetigerit eum indicavit coram omni populo et quemadmodum confestim sanata sit. (48) At ipse dixit illi: filia, fides tua te salvam fecit; vade in pace.

Lines 242–3 are Ælfric's comment.

25 EIGHTH SUNDAY AFTER PENTECOST

Ælfric here offers a fairly straightforward exposition of the feeding of the four thousand, taken from Mark 8.1–9, the Gospel passage for the day. He had already discussed the story of Christ feeding the five thousand in CH I.12, and examined there some of the larger implications of the story, and here confines himself to noting the differences between the two miracles and explaining the allegorical significance of the salient details. The one substantial point which catches his attention and interest is the distinction between the ordinary faithful and the perfect or elect who follow a higher ideal. Bede, his main source, interprets the few fishes of the story as the saints whose lives and passions serve as a model for others. The detail of the food which is left over represents for him the higher teachings of perfection which only the *sancti* can follow, not the ordinary faithful, and the baskets in which it is collected symbolise, through the rushes and palm-leaves of which they are made, the qualities possessed by the *sancti* or *electi*. (In the earlier miracle Bede, followed by Ælfric, had interpreted the fishes as the psalms and sayings of the prophets and the left-over food as difficult teachings which needed to be explained to the people by the learned.)

Ælfric refuses to follow Bede in any of these interpretations, avoiding reference to the left-over food and explaining the fishes as the teachers who wrote the Scriptures. Yet he does raise the question of the perfect at a different point. Bede had argued that whereas the earlier miracle represented the Old Testament teaching to suppress carnal desires, this one embodied the New Testament teaching to abandon the world and its possessions. Ælfric, perhaps following a hint from Haymo, pauses to assert that this is a teaching for the perfect few rather than a rule for all, and develops the point by discussing the story from Matthew 19 of the rich man whom Christ urges to sell all his possessions if he wished to be perfect. Ælfric is clearly aware of the distinctions which Bede is trying to find in the text but prefers to express it in his own terms and to concentrate on the ways in which the miracle applies to the multitude of faithful rather than the perfect few. Something of Bede's tone and focus does come over, however, in Ælfric's repeated use of the term *gecorenan*, 'the elect', at 36, 66, 68, 71, 125 (the first and last translate Bede's *electi* but the others are not derived from his sources).

Ælfric's main source was Bede's commentary on Mark, perhaps in the form of the adapted commentary on the pericope found as a homily in PD.[1] He possibly took a hint or two from Haymo's homily 119, which is based on Bede's commentary but adds further alternative exegesis of detail and much supporting Biblical quotation.[2] He seems, however, not to have used the homily by Smaragdus, or the Ps-Augustine sermon which occurs for this occasion in the PL 95 version of PD, or Augustine's Serm. 95 on Mark 8.1–9. Most of the points of interpretation are to be found in Bede but the wording is not at all close and the more impressive pieces of phrasing are generally Ælfric's own (e.g. 32–5, 129–34).

Sources and Notes

The following texts are cited below:

1. Bede, *Commentarius in Marcum*, ed. D. Hurst, CCSL 120 (Turnhout, 1960), pp. 431–648.
2. Haymo of Auxerre, *Homiliae de Tempore*, PL 118, Hom. 119, cols. 634–40.

1–18 A close rendering of Mc 8.1–9:

> (1) In illis diebus iterum cum turba multa esset nec haberent quod manducarent convocatis discipulis ait illis. (2) Misereor super turba quia ecce iam triduo sustinent me nec habent quod manducent. (3) Et si dimisero eos ieiunos in domum suam deficient in via quidam enim ex eis de longe venerunt. (4) Et responderunt ei discipuli sui: unde istos poterit quis hic saturare panibus in solitudine. (5) Et interrogavit eos quot panes

[1] See Förster 1894, p. 26, and Smetana 1959, p. 199.
[2] Cf Smetana 1961, pp. 464–5.

habetis? qui dixerunt septem. (6) Et praecepit turbae discumbere supra terram et accipiens septem panes, gratias agens fregit et dabat discipulis suis ut adponerent et adposuerunt turbae. (7) Et habebant pisciculos paucos et ipsos benedixit et iussit adponi. (8) Et manducaverunt et saturati sunt et sustulerunt quod superaverat de fragmentis septem sportas. (9) Erant autem qui manducaverunt quasi quattuor milia et dimisit eos.

Bede (*Comm. Marc.*, 2.1530 ff) locates the miracle on a mountain, following Mt 15.29; Ælfric's *westen* is presumably derived from the *solitudo* of verse 4. The last phrase, *buton wifum and cildum,* is from the parallel version in Mt 15.38 (*quattuor milia hominum extra parvulos et mulieres*), not from Mark.

19–30 Bede compares the two miracles and there is a fuller comparison, as Smetana notes, in Haymo, who may have influenced Ælfric here; but the details probably come from CH I.12 and, for 28–30, from Bede, *Comm. Marc.*, 2.1529–30:

Hic autem novi veritas ac gratia testamenti fidelibus ministranda monstrata est.

32–4 The idea is in Bede, but not the concise phrasing (*Comm. Marc.*, 2.1515–23):

In hac lectione consideranda est in uno eodemque redemptore nostro distincta operatio divinitatis et humanitatis . . . Quis enim non videat hoc quod super turbam miseretur dominus . . . affectum esse et compassionem humanae fragilitatis? quod vero de septem panibus et pisciculis paucis quattuor hominum milia saturavit divinae opus esse virtutis?

35–9 Based on Bede, who cites Mt 15.29–30 for the crowd's purpose [= *for hælðe heora untrumra*] and then comments (*Comm. Marc.*, 2.1548–54):

Turba ergo triduo dominum propter sanationem infirmorum suorum sustinet cum electi quique fide sanctae trinitatis lucidi domino pro suis suorumque peccatis animae videlicet languoribus perseveranti instantia supplicant. Item turba triduo dominum sustinet quando multitudo fidelium peccata quae perpetravit per paenitentiam declinans ad dominum se in opere in locutione atque in cogitatione convertit.

39–45 Fairly close to Bede, *Comm. Marc.*, 2.1554–58:

Quos dimittere ieiunos in domum suam dominus non vult, ne deficiant in via quia videlicet conversi peccatores in praesentis vitae via deficiunt, si in sua conscientia sine doctrinae sanctae pabulo dimittantur.

46–63 Follows Bede which, but for the last two sentences, in turn follows Gregory the Great (Bede, *Comm. Marc.*, 2.1561–4, 1568–81):

Quidam enim ex eis de longe venerunt. Est autem qui nihil fraudis et nihil carnalis corruptionis expertus ad omnipotentis Dei servitium festinavit; iste de longinquo non venit, quia per incorruptionem et innocentiam proximus fuit. . . . Alii vero post carnis flagitia, alii post falsa testimonia, alii post facta furta, alii post illatas violentias, alii post perpetrata homicidia, ad paenitentiam redeunt, atque ad omnipotentis Dei servitium convertuntur; hi videlicet ad Dominum de longinquo veniunt. Quanto etenim quisque plus in pravo opere erravit, tanto ab omnipotente Domino longius recessit. Dentur alimenta eis etiam qui de longinquo veniunt, quia conversis peccatoribus doctrinae sanctae cibi praebendi sunt, ut in Deum vires reparent, quas in flagitiis amiserunt. Item Iudaei quicumque in Christo crediderunt, de prope ad illum venerunt, quia legis et prophetarum erant litteris edocti de illo. Credentes vero ex gentibus de longe utique venerunt ad Christum, quia nullis paginarum sanctarum monumentis de eius erant fide praemoniti.

64–71 Bede, *Comm. Marc.*, 2.1583–5:

Bene septem panes in mysterio novi testamenti ponuntur, in quo septiformis gratia spiritus sancti plenius fidelibus cunctis et credenda revelatur et credita datur.

Ælfric's back-reference is presumably to CH II.16.200 ff, though he had also listed the sevenfold gifts of the Spirit at CH I.22.229–31. The ultimate source for the list is Is 11.2–3:

Et requiescet super eum spiritus Domini, spiritus sapientiae et intellectus, spiritus consilii et fortitudinis, spiritus scientiae et pietatis. Et replebit eum spiritus timoris Domini.

72–83 The initial point, to 77, is from Bede, *Comm. Marc.*, 2.1590–7:

Supra in refectione quinque panum turba super faenum viride discumbebat, nunc ubi septem panibus reficienda est, supra terram discumbere praecipitur, quia per scripturam legis carnis desideria calcare et comprimere iubemur. . . . In novo autem testamento ipsam quoque terram ac facultates temporales derelinquere praecipimur.

Haymo, who has pursued the same general argument without any verbal similarity to Ælfric up to this point, seems to have prompted what follows with his reference to this as the more perfect way (Hom. 119, PL 118, 637C):

. . . Sed etiam ad perfectionem tendentes proprias facultates cum ipsa terra relinquere monet, Domino dicente: 'Si vis perfectus esse, vade vende omnia quae habes et da pauperibus, et habebis thesaurum in coelo, et veni sequere me' (Mt 19.21).

Haymo goes on to cite the similar text from Lc 14.26. Bede quotes Mt 19.21 later as part of his interpretation of the leftover food, and his reference to levels of attainment may have influenced Ælfric (Bede, *Comm. Marc.*, 2.1655–7):

Sunt altiora perfectionis praecepta vel potius exhortamenta et consilia quae generalis fidelium multitudo nequit servando et implendo attingere.

Ælfric's emphasis on the renunciation of the world and possessions as teaching only for the perfect few is very much his own, however. Lines 79–82 seem to echo 1 Tim 6.17–18:

(17) Divitibus huius saeculi praecipe non sublime sapere neque sperare in incerto divitiarum sed in Deo qui praestat nobis omnia abunde ad

> fruendum. (18) Bene agere divites fieri in operibus bonis facile tribuere communicare.

On his sensitivity generally over the question of the virtuous rich, see Godden 1990.

83–96 Ælfric's version of the story of the rich man (lines 84–95) is not from Matthew, from which Haymo and Bede quote, but from the parallel version in Mc 10.17–22:

> (17) Procurrens quidam genu flexo ante eum rogabat eum: magister bone, quid faciam ut vitam aeternam percipiam? (18) Iesus autem dixit ei: Quid me dicis bonum? Nemo bonus nisi unus Deus. (19) Praecepta nosti: ne adulteres, ne occidas, ne fureris, ne falsum testimonium dixeris, ne fraudem feceris, honora patrem tuum et matrem. (20) Et ille respondens ait illi: magister omnia haec conservavi a iuventute mea. (21) Iesus autem intuitus eum dilexit eum et dixit illi: Unum tibi deest: vade quaecumque habes vende et da pauperibus, et habebis thesaurum in caelo, et veni sequere me. (22) Qui contristatus in verbo abiit maerens: erat enim habens possessiones multas.

His use of *fulfremed* at 78 and 96 makes it clear, however, that he has the *perfectus* of Matthew 19 in mind as well.

97–101 Very close to Bede, *Comm. Marc.*, 2.1622–6:

> Acceptis autem ad frangendum panibus Dominus gratias agit, ut et ipse quantum de salute generis humani congaudeat ostendat, et nos ad agendas semper Deo gratias informet, cum vel terreno pane carnem, vel animam caelesti superna gratia largiente reficimus.

101–10 Ælfric's only use of the word *leornere*; his usual word for disciple is *leorningcniht* or *discipuli*, though he also experiments at this time with *leorningman*, which occurs only in this homily (line 27) and the next two (CH II.26.2 var., II.27.27 and 42). The exposition is loosely based on Bede, *Comm. Marc.*, 2.1606–10, 1616–22:

> Dominus accipiens panes dabat discipulis, ut ipsi acceptos turbae apponerent, quia spiritalis dona scientiae tribuens apostolis, per eorum ministerium voluit ecclesiae suae, per orbem vitae cibaria distribui. . . . Cui contra propheta miserabilem quorundam famem deplorans aiebat: 'Parvuli petierunt panem, nec erat qui frangeret eis' (Lam 4.4), quod est aliis verbis dicere: Indocti quaesierunt pabulo verbi Dei, quo ad virtutem bonae operationis convalescerent refici, nec erat, magistris deficientibus, qui eis scripturae archana patefaceret, eosque ad viam veritatis institueret.

Ælfric omits a sentence interpreting the bread as the sacraments.

111–13 An odd detail. Bede interprets the fishes as the saints living at the time of the New Testament whose lives are recorded there, not the saints who wrote it (*Comm. Marc.*, 2.1630–3):

> Quid in pisciculis . . . nisi sanctos accipimus illius temporis quo eadem est condita scriptura vel quorum ipsa scriptura fidem, vitam et passiones continet?

The Ps-Bede commentary on Matthew adapts Bede's words to give the same sense as Ælfric (PL 92, 77A):

> In pisciculis vero sanctos accipimus per quos fit eadem condita scriptura. . . .

The commentary on Matthew attributed to Rabanus Maurus gives the same reading (PL 107, 983D), with rather more of Bede, though his homily on the text reads as Bede does. There is little evidence that Ælfric knew either of these commentaries (see Pope, p. 162 on Ps-Bede), but the agreement perhaps reflects a variant version of Bede. Yet the interpretation of the fishes as the lives and passions of the saints is in any case so clear from the rest of Bede's commentary, and from Haymo's homily, that Ælfric must have knowingly rejected it.

114–20 Bede, *Comm. Marc.*, 2.1638–41, 1649–52:

> Manducant de panibus domini ac piscibus et saturantur qui audientes verba Dei et exempla intuentes ad profectum vitae correctioris per haec excitari atque adsurgere festinant. . . . Manducant namque et non saturantur qui panem verbi Dei audiendo degustant, sed non faciendo quae audiunt, nihil ex his internae dulcedinis quo cor ipsorum confirmetur in ventre memoriae recipiunt.

121–34 Bede now considers the detail of the left-over food, which he interprets as the teaching of a higher perfection which only the perfect or elect could follow, transcending the ordinary faithful, and he relates the symbolism of the baskets to these *sancti* or *electi*. Ælfric omits altogether the first point, then equates the seven baskets with the seven loaves which were offered to all, and while following Bede and then Haymo in his interpretation of the rushes and palms of which the baskets are made leaves it to be understood that the symbolism applies to all the faithful, not just the perfect. Lines 121–7 roughly parallel Bede, *Comm. Marc.*, 2.1661–9:

> Unde bene sportae, quibus dominicorum sunt condita fragmenta ciborum, propter septiformem spiritus gratiam, septem fuisse memorantur. Nam quia sportae iunco et palmarum foliis solent contexi, merito in sanctorum significatione ponuntur; iuncus quippe super aquas nasci consuevit, palma vero victricem ornat manum. Et iunceis vasis recte comparantur electi, cum radicem cordis, ne forte ab amore aeternitatis arescat, in ipso vitae fonte collocant.

Lines 129–34 depart from Bede, who associates the palm of victory with the hope of eternal reward, and are perhaps influenced by Haymo's reference to spiritual warfare, Hom. 119, PL 118, 640A:

> Quasi autem cum iunco palma in sporta contexitur, quando iidem sancti viri contra carnis vitia et cogitationum spiritale bellum suscipiunt. . . .

135–7 The commentators offer a great variety of explanations for the number 4000; Ælfric is perhaps following Bede, *Comm. Marc.*, 2.1679–80:

> Bene quattuor milia ut ipso etiam numero docerent evangelicis se pastos esse cibariis.

140–43 1 Cor 2.9:

> Quod oculus non vidit nec auris audivit nec in cor hominis ascendit, quae praeparavit Deus his qui diligunt illum.

26 NINTH SUNDAY AFTER PENTECOST

This is a wide-ranging homily which starts with the Gospel passage for the day, Christ's warning from Matthew 7.15–21 against false prophets, the seeming religious, and the trees which do not bear good fruit; from the latter image Ælfric moves to the parable of the fruitless tree in Luke 13.6–9 and from there to a dramatic and highly rhetorical denunciation of avarice, before returning briefly to the pericope. Christ's warning was directed against heretics, Ælfric tells us, while the Luke parable was understood by some commentators to refer to the destruction of the Jews; but he ignores these more historical readings and directs his interpretation firmly towards a moral reading, focusing on good works, true goodness and penitence.

For his exposition of the pericope he seems to have used a homily attributed to Origen (in an anonymous Latin version), which was assigned to this occasion in PD, and possibly also one by Haymo.[1] Both read the false prophets primarily as heretics, and Ælfric is very selective in his use of them. There are possible touches from the Jerome tradition, and Ælfric enriches the exposition with additional quotations from Genesis, Matthew, Luke and Jude. His other major source is Augustine's Serm. 72, which starts with the similar passage on trees and fruit from Matthew 12.33 ff but then turns, like Ælfric, to the parable from Luke 13. Ælfric follows Augustine closely, evidently relishing the rhetorical passages on avarice which he uses for lines 106–33, though there may be touches from Gregory's homily on the same parable. Augustine's sermon does not appear in PD, and has no evident connection with the occasion or the pericope; Ælfric's use of it suggests some considerable familiarity with Augustinian material beyond that used in PD.[2]

Sources and Notes

The following texts are cited below:

1. Augustine, *Sermones*, PL 38, Serm. 72, cols. 467–70.
2. Gregory, *Homiliae in Evangelia*, PL 76, Hom. 31, cols. 1227–32.

[1] See Smetana 1959, p. 199, and Smetana 1961, p. 467.

[2] Much of the material on Matthew appears also in the commentary of Rabanus Maurus, PL 107, 845–9, and in his homily on the passage, PL 110, but not all, and there is no other evidence of Ælfric's use of Rabanus.

3. Haymo of Auxerre, *Homiliae de Tempore*, PL 118, Hom. 120, cols. 640–6.
4. Ps-Origen, *Homiliae in Matthaeum*, PLS 4, Hom. 5, cols. 872–8.

1–13 Mt 7.15–21:

> (15) Adtendite a falsis prophetis qui veniunt ad vos in vestimentis ovium. Intrinsecus autem sunt lupi rapaces. (16) A fructibus eorum cognoscetis eos. Numquid colligunt de spinis uvas aut de tribulis ficus? (17) Sic omnis arbor bona fructus bonos facit; mala autem arbor fructus malos facit. (18) Non potest arbor bona fructus malos facere, neque arbor mala fructus bonos facere. (19) Omnis arbor quae non facit fructum bonum exciditur et in ignem mittitur. (20) Igitur ex fructibus eorum cognoscetis eos. (21) Non omnis qui dicit mihi Domine Domine intrabit in regnum caelorum sed qui facit voluntatem Patris mei qui in caelis est, ipse intrabit in regnum caelorum.

14–22 The false prophets were once heretics, Ælfric says; now they are to be identified with hypocrites, sinners under a veil of religion. Ps-Origen also has a then-and-now opening, but his is between those who persecuted the Old Testament prophets and those who now persecute Christians, under the guise of religion, whom he goes on to identify with heretics. There is a faint resemblance (cf esp. the word *geættrode* and *venenatum*) to a passage in Jerome's commentary on Matthew (*Commentarii in Evangelium Matthaei*, 1.946–51, CCSL 77), repeated by Smaragdus, *Collectiones in Evangelia et Epistolas*, PL 102, 413BC:

> Et de omnibus quidem intelligi potest, qui aliud habitu ac sermone promittunt, aliud opere demonstrant. Sed specialiter de hereticis intelligendum, qui videntur continentia, castitate, ieiunio, quasi quadam pietatis se veste circumdari, intrinsecus vero habentes animum venenatum, simpliciora fratrum corda decipiunt.

Haymo, Hom. 120, PL 118, also reads them as heretics, but only as such.

23–9 Lc 16.15:

> Et ait illis: vos estis qui iustificatis vos coram hominibus; Deus autem novit corda vestra.

and Mt 23.27–8:

> (27) Vae vobis scribae et Pharisaei hypocritae quia similes estis sepulchris dealbatis quae a foris parent hominibus speciosa, intus vero plena sunt ossibus mortuorum et omni spurcitia. (28) Sic et vos a foris quidem paretis hominibus iusti; intus autem pleni estis hypocrisi et iniquitate.

Neither is quoted in Ps-Origen. They are repeated by Ælfric at Pope 15.72–9, preserving there the specific reference to the scribes and Pharisees that is omitted here.

30–34 Cf Ps-Origen, *Hom. Matth.*, 5, §1, PLS 4, 872–3:

> Attendite ergo, hoc est, considerate quia non sunt oves, sed lupi in vestimento ovium; quia non sunt religiosi sed irreligiosi in figura

religiositatis: quod non sunt Christiani, sed veritate vacui Christianorum persecutores. . . . Lupi vero graves nominantur omnes infideles haeretici, qui graviter sanctam ecclesiam opprimunt et persequuntur, vel molestare frequentant, qui sine misericordia rapere et coacervare non desinunt.

35–41 Cf Ps-Origen, *Hom. Matth.*, 5, §1, PLS 4, 873:

Nolite ad vultum attendere, sed ad opera, nolite vestimentum considerare, sed inspicite figuram fallaciae. Apostolos praedicant, sed apostolis contraria adnuntiant, martyres magnificant, sed martyrum persecutores probantur. . . . sanctos persequuntur, fideles opprimunt, deum etiam si non verbis, moribus blasphemant.

44–7 Gen 3.17–18 [also quoted by Haymo in this context, Hom. 120, PL 118, 642–3]:

(17) Ad Adam vero dixit: quia audisti vocem uxoris tuae et comedisti de ligno ex quo praeceperam tibi ne comederes, maledicta terra in opere tuo. . . . (18) Spinas et tribulos germinabit tibi.

48–52 Ps-Origen, *Hom. Matth.*, 5, §2, PLS 4, 874:

Arbores hic nominans dominus non arbores vere significat istas in terra fixas, non de arboribus his talibus loquitur. Istae enim sunt sine spiritu, sine anima, sine vita . . . sed per earum figuram homines significat et de hominibus loquitur, qui propria voluntate seu bonum fructum seu malum proferunt.

52–9 A threefold distinction that is not found in any of the possible sources, though Haymo does distinguish between those who fail to do good and those who do evil (Hom. 120, PL 118, 645A):

Non dicit, quae facit fructum malum, sed quae non facit fructum bonum. Ubi e diverso colligere possumus, quae poena praeparata sit mala operantibus, quando poena praedicitur etiam a bono opere torpentibus. Si enim in ignem mittitur qui nudum non vestivit, in quem ignem mittendus est, qui vestitum exspoliavit?

Lines 57–8 refer to Jude 1.12: *Arbores autumnales infructuosae bis mortuae eradicatae*. I have found no other use of this rare quotation in a context that is at all similar to Ælfric.

61–9 A combination of points made by Ps-Origen (*Hom. Matth.*, 5, PLS 4) and Augustine (Serm. 72, PL 38):

[Ps-Origen, §3, 874] Non dixit enim: non potest iste malus converti et effici bonus, sed usque quo est malus, usque hoc bonum fructum non potest facere. [Augustine, §1, 467] Prius est enim mutandus homo, ut opera mutentur. Si enim manet homo in eo quod malus est, bona opera habere non potest: si manet in eo quod bonus est, mala opera habere non potest. [Ps-Origen, §3, 875] Propterea utique docentur homines a lege et prophetis, ab evangelistis et apostolis, ab ipso etiam Domino et ab his qui ecclesiae doctores sunt, ut malum derelinquant et ad bonum sese convertant.

70–80 Augustine, Serm. 72, §3, PL 38, 467:

'Omnis arbor quae non facit fructum bonum, excidetur, et in ignem mittetur' (Mt 3.10). De hac securi comminatur paterfamilias in Evangelio, dicens: 'Ecce triennium est quod venio ad hanc arborem, et fructum in ea non invenio. Nunc debeo locum evacuare: proinde amputetur. Et intercedit colonus, dicens: Domine, dimitte illam et hoc anno; circumfodiam illam, et adhibebo cophinum stercoris: si fecerit fructum, bene; sin minus, venies et amputabis eam' (Lc 13.7–9).

Ælfric gives the whole parable, Lc 13.6–9, but presumably takes *hiredes hlaford* from Augustine's *paterfamilias*:

(6) Dicebat autem hanc similitudinem. Arborem fici habebat quidam plantatam in vinea sua et venit quaerens fructum in illa et non invenit. (7) Dixit autem ad cultorem vineae: ecce anni tres sunt ex quo venio quaerens fructum in ficulnea hac et non invenio. Succide ergo illam ut quid etiam terram occupat. (8) At ille respondens dixit illi: Domine dimitte illam et hoc anno usque dum fodiam circa illam et mittam stercora. (9) Et si quidem fecerit fructum; sin autem in futurum succides eam.

80–88 Augustine, Serm. 72, §3, PL 38, 467–8:

Tanquam per triennium Dominus visitavit genus humanum, hoc est, tribus quibusdam temporibus. Primum tempus, ante Legem; secundum, in Lege; tertium modo est, quod tempus est gratiae.

The reading of the three years as the three ages is common, but it prompts some variation in the interpretation of the tree. Augustine reads the unfruitful tree as the Gentiles, still remaining to be converted while the Jews had responded to God's earlier 'visits' (and he avoids comment on the failure of the tree to produce fruit in the past). Ælfric's image of God waiting for mankind's conversion is perhaps closer to Gregory (Hom. 31, PL 76, 1229A), who sees the tree as human nature, remaining unconverted through the three ages; Bede (*Commentarius in Lucam*, 4.1380, CCSL 120) adapts Gregory's argument into an interpretation of the Jews, still failing to respond in the third age and being doomed therefore to destruction by the Romans.

89–100 Augustine, Serm. 72, §3, PL 38, 468:

Intercedit colonus; pro plebe orat apostolus: 'Flecto, inquit, genua mea pro vobis ad patrem, ut in caritate radicati et fundati, valeatis apprehendere cum omnibus sanctis quae sit latitudo et longitudo, altitudo et profundum; cognoscere etiam supereminentem scientiam charitatis Christi, ut impleamini in omnem plenitudinem Dei' (Eph 3.14–19). Flectendo genua, pro nobis intercedit apud patremfamilias, ne eradicemur. Ergo quia necesse est ut veniat, agamus ut fructuosos nos inveniat.

101–6 Cf Augustine (Serm. 72, PL 38) and Gregory (Hom. 31, PL 76):

[Augustine, §3, 468] Circumfossio arboris, est humilitas poenitentis. Omnis enim fossa humilis. Cophinus stercoris, sordes poenitentiae.

[Gregory, 1229D] Quid est cophinus stercoris, nisi memoria peccatorum? [Augustine, §3, 468] Quid enim stercore sordidius? et tamen, si bene utaris, quid fructuosius?

106–16 Augustine, Serm. 72, §4, PL 38, 468:

Muta cor, et mutabitur opus. Exstirpa cupiditatem, planta charitatem. Sicut enim 'radix est omnium malorum cupiditas' (1 Tim 6.10); sic et radix omnium bonorum charitas. . . . Quod habere vis, non est valde bonum: quod esse non vis, hoc est bonum. Vis enim habere sanitatem corporis; hoc est bonum: nec tamen putes magnum bonum esse, quod habet et malus. Aurum et argentum habere vis; ecce et hoc dico, bonum est; sed si bene usus fueris: bene autem non uteris, si malus fueris. Ac per hoc aurum et argentum malis malum est, bonis bonum est.

116–29 Augustine, Serm. 72, §5, PL 38, 469:

Quid prodest plena bonis arca, inani conscientia? Bona vis habere, et bonus non vis esse? Non vides te erubescere debere de bonis tuis, si domus tua plena est bonis, et te habet malum? Quid enim est quod velis habere malum? Dic mihi. Nihil omnino; non uxorem, non filium, non filiam, non servum, non ancillam, non villam, non tunicam, postremo non caligam: et tamen vis habere malam vitam. Rogo te, praepone vitam tuam caligae tuae. Omnia quae circumiacent oculis tuis, elegantia et pulchra tibi chara sunt; et tibi ipse vilis es ac foedus? Si tibi possent respondere bona quibus est plena domus tua, . . . Tacita voce interpellant contra te Dominum tuum: 'Ecce bona tanta dedisti huic, et ipse malus est! Quid ei prodest quod habet, quando eum qui omnia dedit, non habet?'

129–33 Augustine, Serm. 72, §6, PL 38, 469:

Quaerit ergo aliquis admonitus his verbis meis, et forte compunctus, quaerit quid sit bonum, quale bonum, unde bonum. . . . Respondebo quaerenti, et dicam: Hoc est bonum, quod non potes invitus amittere. Potes enim aurum perdere, et nolens; potes domum, potes honores, potes ipsam carnis salutem: bonum vero quo vere bonus es, nec invitus accipis, nec invitus amittis.

133–47 Finally Ælfric returns to the last verse of the pericope, Matthew 7.21. His commentary is based on Ps-Origen, *Hom. Matth.*, 5, PLS 4 (reflecting the interpretation of the false prophets as heretics):

[§6, 877] Audiant hoc mobiles et nutantes isti, qui duplici sunt corde. Illi qui Christum nominant nomine sed abnegant substantia, nominant nomine sed negant in virtute. . . . 'Hoc est enim opus Dei, ut credatis ei, quem misit ille' (Jn 6.29), ait Dominus. . . . Prima voluntas dei haec est, ut credatur filius, ut unigenitus confiteatur . . . [§7, 878] Non te iuvat . . . nisi ab omni te inmunditia et inreligiositate abstinueris.

27 ST JAMES THE APOSTLE, AND THE SEVEN SLEEPERS

The main part of the text is a straightforward narrative of the passion of St James the apostle, brother of John the Evangelist, whose death at the hands of Herod is mentioned at Acts 12.1–2. The Gospel text appointed for the occasion was Matthew 20.20–23, where the mother of James and John asks Christ whether her sons will sit at his side in heaven. Ælfric probably knew Bede's homily on this text (Hom. II.21),[1] which is prescribed for St James's day in PDM, and perhaps the one included in Haymo's homiliary too.[2] The Gospel text itself is touched on briefly in CH II.37. Here, however, Ælfric chooses not to discuss the pericope but offers instead an account of the passion. The narrative focuses on the apostle's conflict first with a magician or *dry* and then with the Jews and their leaders, both being converted by a combination of miracle-working and citing of Scriptural testimonies to Christ's divinity. The apostle's death is scarcely described.

Ælfric used as source a Latin *Passio* (BHL 4057) similar to that printed by Mombritius.[3] The version printed by Fabricius is generally less close but occasionally provides a reading closer to Ælfric. The manuscripts of the Cotton-Corpus legendary have a version similar to Mombritius but show no variations that particularly resemble Ælfric's version and lack the relevant variants from the Fabricius version;[4] presumably his copy of the legendary had a different version of the legend, perhaps the result of conflation with another copy. Ælfric follows the narrative of his source fairly closely from beginning to end, but summarises in one sentence (lines 122–4) the very long list of Old Testament testimonies to Christ given by the apostle in his sermon, which forms the central third of the Latin *Passio* and plays a key role in the text's doctrinal concerns with the defeat of Judaism by Christianity. This may be because he had already used (or decided to use) this material as a source for his own similar sermon and list of testimonies in CH II.1, but he shows a tendency to omit such sermon material and concentrate on narrative in the hagiographic pieces in his Lives of Saints collection,[5] and there are signs of similar tendencies in the later pieces for saints' days in CH II; possibly it is this which explains his exclusion of both the sermon material and the exposition of the pericope.

The Mombritius version seems also to have been the source for the anonymous Old English narrative found in BL, MS Cotton Vespasian D.xiv.[6]

[1] It possibly influenced his treatment of the verses from Matthew in CH II.37.

[2] PL 118, 238 ff. See Pope, p. 218 for Ælfric's possible use of this homily, which is appointed for the Wednesday after the Second Sunday in Lent.

[3] The source was identified by Förster (1892, p. 23).

[4] Cf Zettel 1979, pp. 191–2.

[5] See Dorothy Bethurum, 'The form of Ælfric's *Lives of Saints*', *Studies in Philology* 29 (1932), 515–43.

[6] Warner, pp. 21–5.

This starts at a later point in the story, equivalent to line 111 in Ælfric's version, and rather abruptly; many of the other pieces in this manuscript are excerpts selected for their doctrinal content and it is likely that this too is an incomplete text, excerpted to concentrate on the list of testimonies to Christ which Ælfric omits. The *Old English Martyrology* briefly records a quite different tradition, about St James preaching in Spain (OE Martyrology, II.158–9). This seems to have been unknown to Ælfric, or at least unaccepted; he speaks only of James preaching among the Jews in his treatise on the Old and New Testament, 988–90 (Crawford, p. 59).

Ælfric's account of St James is complete in itself, though it ends rather abruptly, but at some stage before circulating the series Ælfric wrote a brief account of the Seven Sleepers as a pendant to it, in anticipation of the feast-day which occurs two days later. Like SS Alexander, Eventius and Theodolus, whose story is covered in CH II.18, the Seven Sleepers are not among the saints whose feasts were normally observed by the laity and would not properly have a place in the Catholic Homilies. Ælfric does not explain whether he included them for the importance of their festival or for the sake of the story, though evidence for the latter is the weight he gives to the legend as proof of the resurrection of the body both here (lines 220–3) and in his later use of the story, in an addition to CH I.16.[7]

Ælfric's source seems to have been a long, florid Latin narrative (BHL 2316) which appears in the Cotton-Corpus legendary and was translated in full by another, unidentified Anglo-Saxon author of Ælfric's time, whose version appears among his works in the Julius MS of the Lives of Saints.[8] Ælfric's version is extremely abridged, barely more than a summary, its 47 lines in print contrasting with the 770 needed to render the source in full by the other translator (or 870 lines originally, since the printed copy is truncated at the end and the lost copy in BL, MS Cotton Otho B.x was 100 lines longer).[9] Only at the end does Ælfric translate rather than summarise. The Latin text sets the first part of the story in a context of fierce persecution by the Emperor Decius, and the second part, the reawakening of the saints, in a context of bitter theological dispute over the question of bodily resurrection. The former is mentioned briefly by Ælfric, the latter not at all, but the doctrinal issue is clear enough in the conclusion of the story. Though the account is brief, it shows Ælfric's characteristic tendency in hagiographic narrative to turn it into a conflict of heroic saints and cruel tyrants, in contrast to the Latin narrative which

[7] See Gatch 1977, p. 87. There is an excellent account of Ælfric's treatment of the Seven Sleepers by Hugh Magennis (see Magennis 1996).

[8] BL, MS Cotton Julius E.vii. The Latin text was printed by Huber in 1903 (for details see below). Huber identified this as Ælfric's source in his study, *Die Wanderlegende von den Siebenschlafern* (Leipzig, 1910). The Old English legend has been edited with a thorough discussion and an account of the origin and significance of the story by Hugh Magennis (see Magennis 1994).

[9] See Ker 1957, p. 226.

represents Decius as curiously sympathetic to the young men. Magennis (1996, pp. 319–20), pointing out this feature, persuasively argues that Ælfric's wording is influenced at times by the version of the story given by Gregory of Tours (BHL 2312).[10] The similarities of approach may be coincidental, but there certainly is a striking parallel between Ælfric's *þas seofon geleaffullan godes cempan* 187–8 and Gregory's *hii septem adletae Christi* (*Passio*, I.762.7).

Sources and Notes

The following texts are cited below:

1. Anon., *Passio Iacobi Apostoli*, in Fabricius, II.516–31.
2. Anon., *Passio Iacobi Apostoli*, in Mombritius 1910, II.37–40.
3. Anon., *Passio S. Iacobi*, in Salisbury Cathedral MS 222, ff. 33r-35v and BL, MS Cotton Nero E.i, ff. 52r-53v. [= CC]
4. Anon., *Passio Septem Dormientium*, ed. M. Huber, 'Beitrag zur Visionsliteratur und Siebenschläferlegende des Mittelalters, I Teil: Text', *Beilage zum Jahresbericht des humanistischen Gymnasiums Metten* (1902–3), 39–78.
5. Bede, *Homiliae*, ed. D. Hurst, CCSL 122 (Turnhout, 1955), Hom. II.21 (pp. 335–41).

1–5 On Ælfric's belief that James and John were sons of the Virgin Mary's sister (also Mary), see Pope's lengthy note to his homily 1, line 5. He points out that Ælfric's main authorities for his work, Jerome, Augustine, Gregory and Bede, all differ from him on this, but suggests that he may have been influenced by an anonymous homily on the Gospel for the day, Mt 20.20–23, which occurs in Haymo's homiliary. A source for the idea of Christ's special concern with James, John and Peter is scarcely needed, but there is a close parallel in the Bede homily on Mt 20.20–23 (Hom. II.21, 48–51):

> . . . Nossent se inter discipulos specialius a domino diligi, se specialius cum beato Petro conscios saepe factos archanorum quae ignorarent ceteri quod frequens sancti evangelii textus indicat.

6–14 *Passio Iacobi*, Mombritius 1910, II.37.18–26:

> Apostolus . . . Iacobus frater beati Iohannis . . . omnem Iudaeam et Samariam visitabat. . . . Accidit autem ut quidam Hermogenes magus discipulum suum [Ph]iletum nomine mitteret ad eum, qui cum venisset cum aliquantis pharisaeis ad Iacobum conabatur asserere quod non verus esset dei filius Iesus Christus nazarenus cuius se Iacobus apostolum memorabat. Iacobus autem in spiritu sancto confidenter agens omnes assertiones eius evacuabat, ostendens ei ex scripturis divinis hunc esse verum filium dei.

[10] Ed. B. Krusch in *Passiones Vitaeque Sanctorum Aevi Merovingici*, ed. B. Krusch and W. Levison, MGH, Scriptores rerum Merovingicarum, 7.1 (Hanover and Leipzig, 1919–20), I.757–69.

Hermogenes' role as magician is heavily stressed by Ælfric, who adds *þurh drycræft* here (though no magic seems in fact involved in challenging St James) and again at 16, and associates it closely with false belief through expressions such as *dwollicum* (line 15) and *þines gedwyldes*. By *Samaria* the source no doubt meant the province, but here and at II.13.96 Ælfric designates it a city.

14–28 *Passio Iacobi*, Mombritius 1910, II.37.26–34:

Reversus autem ad Hermogenem [Ph]iletus dixit ei: 'Iacobum qui se servum Christi Iesu nazareni asserit et apostolum esse eius scias superari non posse. Nam in nomine eius vidi eum [daemones ex obsessis corporibus eiicientem *not in Momb. or CC, but in Fab., II.517*], caecos illuminare, leprososque mundare. Asserunt etiam iam amicissimi mei vidisse se Iacobum mortuos suscitantem. Sed quid multis moramur, omnes scripturas sanctas memoriter retinet, ex quibus ostendit non esse alterum filium dei nisi hunc quem Iudaei crucifixerunt. Placeat ergo tibi consilium meum, et veni ad ipsum, et postula tibi indulgentiam ab eo. Quod si non feceris, scias artem tuam magicam in nullo penitus profuturam. Me autem scias ad ipsum reverti et petere ut eius merear esse discipulus.'

29–38 *Passio Iacobi*, Mombritius 1910, II.37.34–40:

Hermogenes autem hoc audiens repletus est zelo et fixit [Ph]iletum ita ut se movere non posset et dicebat ei: 'Videamus si Iacobus tuus solvet te ab his vinculis.' Tunc festinanter puerum suum ad Iacobum misit. Cui cum venisset et nuntiasset ei, statim sudarium suum misit ad eum dicens: 'Accipiat eum et dicat: Dominus Iesus christus erigit elisos et ipse solvit compeditos' [*probably a version of Ps 144.14* Dominus . . . erigit omnes elisos *or 145.8* Dominus erigit adlisos, *combined with 145.7* Dominus solvit conpeditos.] Statim autem ut de sudario suo tetigit eum is qui eum attulerat, resolutus a vinculo magi, currens venit ad Iacobum insultans maleficiis eius.

38–54 *Passio Iacobi*, Mombritius 1910, II.37.40–51:

Hermogenes autem magus dolens quod ei insultaret de arte sua, excitavit daemones et misit eos ad Iacobum dicens: 'Ite et ipsum Iacobum mihi huc adducite, simul etiam et Philetum discipulum meum, et vindicem me in eo, ne mihi caeteri discipuli mei taliter incipiant insultare.' Venientia autem daemonia ubi Iacobus orabat, ululatum in aera habere coeperunt dicentia: 'Iacobe apostole dei, miserere nostri quia antequam veniat tempus incendii nostri iam ardemus.' Dicit eis Iacobus: 'Ut quid venistis ad me?' Dicunt ei daemones: 'Misit nos Hermogenes ut te et Philetum ad ipsum perduceremus. Mox autem ut ingressi sumus, angelus dei sanctus cathenis igneis religavit nos et cruciamur.' Dicit eis Iacobus: 'In nomine patris et filii et spiritus sancti, exsolvat vos angelus domini ita ut revertentes ad Hermogenem non eum laedatis sed vinctum huc eum ad me adducatis.'

55–68 *Passio Iacobi*, Mombritius 1910, II.37.51–38.6:

Qui cum abissent, ligaverunt eum restibus manus a tergo et ita eum adduxerunt ad Iacobum dicentes: 'Misisti nos ubi incensi sumus et torti et intolerabiliter consumati.' Interea cum ad Iacobum fuisset adductus, dicit ei Iacobus apostolus dei: 'Stultissime hominum cum inimico generis humani rationem te habere, non consideras quem rogasti ut mitteret tibi angelos suos ad laesionem meam, quos ego adhuc non permitto ut furorem suum tibi ostendant?' Clamant quoque ipsa daemonia dicentia: 'Da nobis eum in potestatem, ut possimus et tuas iniurias vindicare et nostra incendia'. Dicit eis Iacobus: 'Ecce Philetus ante vos est, cur eum non tenetis?' Dicunt ei daemones: 'Nos non possumus nec formicam quae in cubiculo tuo est manu contingere.'

68–81 *Passio Iacobi*, Mombritius 1910, II.38.6–14:

Tunc beatus Iacobus dicit ad Philetum: 'Ut cognoscas scholam Domini nostri Iesu Christi hanc esse, discant homines bona pro malis reddere; ille te ligavit, tu eum solve. Ille te vinctum a daemoniis ad se conatus est adducere, tu eum captum a daemoniis liberum ire permitte.' At ubi solvit eum Philetus, confussus, humilis et deiectus Hermogenes coepit stare. Dicit ei Iacobus: 'Vade liber quocumque volueris. Non est enim disciplinae nostrae ut invitus aliquis convertatur.' Dicit ei Hermogenes: 'Ego novi iras daemonum. Nisi mihi dederis aliquid quod mecum habeam, tenent me et diversis poenis interficiunt.' Tunc dicit ei Iacobus: 'Accipe tibi baculum itineris mei, et cum eo perge securus quocumque volueris.'

82–9 *Passio Iacobi*, Mombritius 1910, II.38.14–21:

Et accipiens baculum apostoli domum suam ivit et posuit super cervicem suam et super cervices discipulorum suorum et zabernas plenas codicibus attulit ad apostolum Dei et coepit eos ignibus concremare. Dicit ei Iacobus: 'Ne forte odor incendii eorum vexet incautos, mitte intra zabernas petras simul et plumbum, et fac eas demergi in mari.' Quod cum fecisset Hermogenes reversus tenere coepit plantas apostoli, rogans eum et dicens: 'Animarum liberator accipe poenitentem quem invidentem et detrahentem hactenus sustinuisti.'

89–108 *Passio Iacobi*, Mombritius 1910, II.38.21–34:

Respondit Iacobus et dixit: 'Si veram deo poenitentiam obtuleris, veram eius indulgentiam consequeris.' Dicit ei Hermogenes: 'Adeo enim veram deo poenitentiam offerro, ut omnes codices meos in quibus erat illicita praesumptio abiecerim, et omnibus simul abrenuntiaverim artibus inimici.' Dicit ei apostolus: 'Nunc vade per domos eorum quos evertisti [ut et revoces Domino quae tulisti. Doce hoc esse verum, quod antea docebas esse falsum . . . *not in Momb.; from Fab., II.520; CC has a corrupt version of it.*] Doce esse falsum quod dicebas esse verum. Idolum quoque quod adorabas . . . confringe. Pecunias quas de malo opere acquisisti in bonis operibus expende. [E]t sicut fuisti filius diaboli imitando diabolum, efficiaris filius dei imitando deum, qui quottidie ingratis praestat beneficia et se blasphemantibus exhibet alimenta. Si enim cum malus esses apud deum bonus circa te extitit dominus, quantomagis erit circa te benignior si malus esse cessaveris et bonis coeperis operibus placere?' Haec et his similia dicente Iacobo in omnibus obtemperavit Hermogenes, et ita coepit in dei esse timore perfectus ut et virtutes per eum plurimas faceret dominus.

Momb., Fab. and CC agree in attributing the miracles more directly to God than Ælfric does.

109–35 *Passio Iacobi*, Mombritius 1910, II.38.34–39.49:

Videntes igitur Iudaei quia hunc magum quem invictum putabant ita convertisset, ut etiam omnes discipuli et amici eius . . . Iesu Christo per Iacobum credidissent, obtulerunt pecunias centurionibus duobus qui praeerant Hierosolimis. Lisias et Theochlytus tenuerunt eum et miserunt eum in custodiam. Facta autem sedicione de apostolo, dictum est debere eum educi et secundum legem audiri. Tunc pharisaei dicebant: 'Ut quid praedicas Iesum hominem quem inter latrones crucifixum omnes scimus?' Tunc Iacobus repletus spiritu sancto dixit: 'Audite viri fratres . . . [*omitting a long series of Old Testament prophecies, II.38.41–39.42*] Haec omnia viri fratres filii abrahae praedixerunt, loquente per os eorum spiritu sancto. Numquid si hoc non credimus poterimus evadere perpetui ignis supplicia aut non merito puniendi erimus, cum gentes credant vocibus prophetarum . . .? . . . Crimina lachrymosis vocibus lugeamus, ut poenitentiam nostram pius indultor accipiat, ne illa nobis eveniant contemptoribus quae in Moise leguntur et in David: "aperta est terra et deglutivit datham et operuit super synagogam Abiron; exarsit ignis in synagoga eorum et flamma combussit peccatores" (Ps 105.17–18, *alluding to Num 16.31–5, which lies behind Ælfric's explanation at 131–2*).'

136–55 *Passio Iacobi*, Mombritius 1910, II.39.49–40.4:

Haec et his similia dicente Iacobo, tantam dominus gratiam apostolo suo contulit ut omnes una voce clamarent: 'Peccavimus, iniuste egimus, da remedium quid faciamus.' Quibus Iacobus ait: 'Viri fratres, nolite desperare; credite tantum et baptizemini, et delebuntur omnia peccata vestra.' Post aliquot dies Abiatar pontifex anni illius videns tantum populum domino credidisse, repletus zelo per pecunias excitavit sedicionem gravissimam, ita ut vir unus scriba phariseorum mitteret funem in collo eius et perduceret eum ad praetorium herodis regis. Herodes autem filius Archelai regis iussit decollari eum. [*On the relationship of this Herod, son of Archelaeus, to Herod the Great, cf CH I.32.33–54.*] Cumque duceretur ad decollationem vidit paralyticum iacentem et clamantem: 'Sancte Iacobe apostole Iesu Christi, libera me a doloribus quibus omnia membra mea cruciantur', et ait ad eum: 'In nomine Domini nostri Iesu Christi . . . exurge sanus et benedic salvatorem tuum.' Et protinus surrexit et gaudens cucurrit et benedixit nomen Domini nostri Iesu Christi.

156–80 *Passio Iacobi*, Mombritius 1910, II.40.4–21:

Tunc ille scriba pharisaeorum . . . mittens se ad pedes eius . . . Iosias . . . 'Obsecro te' ait 'des mihi indulgentiam et facias me nominis sancti participem.' Intelligens autem Iacobus visitatum cor eius a domino dixit ei: 'Tu credis quia dominus Iesus Christus quem crucifixerunt Iudaei ipse sit verus filius Dei vivi?' Et ait Iosias: 'Ego credo et haec est fides mea ex hac hora quia ipse est filius Dei.' Tunc Abiatar pontifex fecit eum teneri et dixit ei: 'Si non discesseris a Iacobo et maledixeris nomen Iesu cum ipso decolaberis.' Dicit ei Iosias: 'Maledictus tu et maledicti omnes dies tui. Nomen autem domini Iesu Christi . . . est benedictum in saecula.' Tunc Abiatar iussit pugnis caedi os eius et missa de eo legatione ad Herodem impetravit ut simul cum Iacobo decollaretur. Ventum est autem ad locum ubi capite plectendi erant et dixit Iacobus spiculatori: 'Priusquam nos decolles facito nobis aquam dari.' Et allata est ei lagena aqua plena. Tunc dixit ad Iosiam: 'Credis in patrem et filium et spiritum sanctum?' At ubi dixit Iosias 'Credo' perfudit eum Iacobus et dixit ei: 'Da mihi pacis osculum.' Cumque osculatus esset eum, posuit manum suam super caput eius et benedixit eum. Et fecit signaculum crucis Christi in frontem eius atque ita perfectus in fide Domini nostri Iesu Christi cum apostolo eadem hora martyr effectus perrexit ad dominum, cui est honor et gloria in saecula saeculorum.

184–205 *Passio Septem Dormientium*, Huber:

[§1] In illo tempore regnavit Decius imperator, et descendit in . . . Ephesum. . . . [§3] Fides vero in his deprehendebatur, Maximianus, Malchus, Martinianus, Dionysius, Iohannes, Seraphin et Constantinus . . . erant officiales palatii, et primi et nobiles ex senatu. [*Other attendants betray them to the emperor (§4), who gives them time to reconsider (though the only reason he cites is their beauty), §5:*] 'Non enim iustum est perdere aetates vestras in tormentis et tabefieri decorem pulchritudinis vestrae, sed ecce do vobis tempus, ut sapiatis et vivatis.' . . . Decius autem imperator ingressus est alias civitates facere eadem. . . . [§6] Sanctus Maximianus et socii eius perfecerunt opera iustitiae in fide. Tollentes autem aurum et argentum a parentibus suis, dabant mendicis occulte et aperte consilium fecerunt, omnes dicentes: 'Eruamus nos ipsos de habitatione civitatis istius, et eamus in speluncam grandem in monte Celio, et ibi deprecemur Deum incessanter. . . .' [§7] Post dies autem aliquos reversus est Decius imperator in Ephesorum civitatem, et in ipsa hora praecepit summatibus suis immolare, sanctum Maximianum et socios eius requirens. . . . [*Decius expresses grief for their loss because they are of distinguished family, and forces their parents to reveal their hiding-place.*] [§9] Et cum nollet laedere eos, inmisit Deus in corde eius ut obturaret os speluncae lapidibus. [§8] Deus autem misericors . . . praecepit illis mortem quietis eorum . . . Et non senserunt quomodo dormierunt neque ubi animas eorum deposuit Deus.

The *Passio Septem Dormientium* records the death of Decius, the eventual accession of Theodosius after many other emperors, and the rise of heretical disputes about the resurrection. The period of 372 years (cf 204–5) is mentioned by the proconsul who interrogates Malchus, as the age of the coins which he is carrying [§16]; it thus covers the time until the saints are discovered, not until the establishment of Christianity over the whole world.

206–225 *Passio Septem Dormientium*, Huber:

[§12] In diebus Theodosii imperatoris, cum perfectus esset fide patrum suorum . . . contigit pueri . . . cum aliis operariis fatigari duobus diebus et volvere lapides ex ore speluncae. . . . Contigit autem ex voluntate Dei dare vitam sanctis, qui fuerant in spelunca. [*Malchus goes into Ephesus for food and the story is revealed.*] [§18] Et ibit [Theodosius] cum curribus suis cum multa festinatione de Constantinopoli in Epheso. Et egressa est omnis civitas in occursum eius, et episcopus cum primatibus civitatis. Et ascenderunt ad sanctos martyres in spelunca . . . et egressi sunt sancti martyres in occursum imperatoris, et mox ut viderunt eum splenduerunt facies eorum tamquam sol. Et ingressus est imperator, et cecidit ante eos, et amplexus est eos, et super cervicem uniuscuiusque flebat. Et cor eius exsultabat, et dicebat ad eos: 'Sic vos video ante me tamquam si video regem Christum Dominum Deum nostrum, cum revocaret Lazarum de monumento. . . .' Et dixit Maximianus imperatori: 'At nunc permaneat in pace imperium tuum, et in fortitudine fidei tuae. Iesus Christus custodiat imperium tuum in nomine suo a tentationibus et laqueis Satanae. Et crede nobis quoniam propter te suscitavit nos Deus a terra ante diem magnum resurrectionis, ut credas sine dubitatione quoniam est resurrectio mortuorum. Et resurreximus et [vivimus]. . . .'

225–230 *Passio Septem Dormientium*, Huber, §19:

Et omnibus videntibus inclinata capita sua in terra dormierunt, et tradiderunt spiritus suos secundum praeceptum Dei. . . . Et [imperator] praecepit fieri loculos aureos in quibus mitterentur corpora eorum. Et in ipsa nocte apparuerunt imperatori, et dixerunt ei: '[Ex] terra surreximus, neque ex auro neque ex argento. Et nunc unde surreximus dimitte nos. Deus iterum suscitabit nos.' . . . Et dimisit eos in loco eorum. Et facta est congregatio multa episcoporum, et fecerunt ibi memoriam [*var.* maximam].

28 TWELFTH SUNDAY AFTER PENTECOST

Ælfric takes as his starting-point the Gospel for the day, Luke 18.9–14, the brief parable about the Pharisee and the publican who went to the temple to pray, and develops out of it the themes of prayer and particularly pride; nearly half the homily is taken up with the stories of Nebuchadnezzar and Balthasar as examples of fallen pride, and to these he added, at some later stage of revision, a further long exemplum about the emperor Theodosius and St Ambrose (printed as Pope 26). His particular interest seems to be less the type of the religious enthusiast suggested by the Pharisee than the rich and powerful ruler who needs to recognise the power of God and his church. Hence, too, the references to feeding the poor and building churches as examples of good works which men should not boast about (lines 59–63). Nebuchadnezzar excellently suits the theme of the pericope and Ælfric's exegesis: he is undoubtedly an example of pride, a great king who attributes his grandeur to himself, and is humbled by God. Balthasar, however, though Ælfric refers to his pride, is more evidently an example of blasphemy, feasting from the holy vessels of the temple, while Theodosius is an example of humility rather than pride, his initial crime being presumably vengefulness or excessive cruelty in the administration of imperial power. In extrapolating from the example of Nebuchadnezzar Ælfric's mind was perhaps running more on the theme of great kings being brought low by God than on the original theme of pride in attributing virtue to oneself. Even more loosely connected, as Ælfric's wording seems to acknowledge, is the additional discussion of tithing found in MS R at line 167 (printed as Pope 30.75–114), but there seems little doubt, as Pope argues, that this was genuinely added by Ælfric himself, on at least one occasion, even if it was not written for this homily. Both this and the section on Theodosius may reflect Ælfric's response to issues developing in England since the early 990s.[1]

Ælfric seems to have known and consulted a number of commentaries on the Gospel text included in versions of Paul the Deacon's homiliary: Bede's commentary on Luke (the relevant part is in PD), Augustine's Serm. 115 (in PDM), and a sermon by Hericus (also in PDM), which is mostly an expansion of the first two but may have influenced Ælfric in a few places.[2] Haymo's homily mostly draws on Bede and offers nothing new that is relevant, except perhaps in its reference to great men destroyed for their pride. (The homily by Smaragdus

[1] Mary Clayton persuasively argues ('Ælfric's *Esther*: a *speculum reginae*', in *Text and Gloss: Studies in Insular Learning and Literature presented to Joseph Donovan Pheifer*, ed. H. O'Briain, Anne d'Arcy and John Scattergood (Dublin, 1999), pp. 89–101) that in adding the story of Theodosius's penance for massacring the inhabitants of a city Ælfric was thinking of the St Brice's day massacre of the Danes in England in 1002.

[2] Förster (1894, p. 26) identified Bede; Smetana (1959, p. 200) noted the use of Augustine and the presence of both this and the relevant excerpt from Bede in PDM and PD respectively. The Hericus sermon appears at PL 95, 1375 ff, but is cited here from the more recent edition in CCCM 116B.

was no doubt known to Ælfric but draws heavily on Bede and has contributed nothing.)

For the passages on Nebuchadnezzar and Balthasar he seems to have relied on the Bible; for the sources of the additions, see Pope, pp. 759–61 and 803–12.

Sources and Notes

The following texts are cited below:

1. Augustine, *Sermones*, PL 38, Serm. 115, cols. 655–7.
2. Bede, *Commentarius in Lucam*, ed. D. Hurst, CCSL 120 (Turnhout, 1960), pp. 5–425.
3. Haymo of Auxerre, *Homiliae de Tempore*, PL 118, Hom. 123, cols. 661–4.
4. Hericus, *Homiliae in Circulum Anni*, ed. R. Quadri, CCCM 116B (Turnhout, 1994), Hom. II.30 (pp. 283–90).
5. *King Alfred's West-Saxon Version of Gregory's Pastoral Care*, ed. H. Sweet, EETS os 45 and 50 (1871–2, repr. 1996).
6. Smaragdus, *Collectiones in Evangelia et Epistolas*, PL 102, cols. 435–6.

1–16 Lc 18.9–14:

> (9) Dixit autem et ad quosdam qui in se confidebant tamquam iusti et aspernabantur ceteros parabolam istam. (10) Duo homines ascenderunt in templum ut orarent, unus Pharisaeus et alter publicanus. (11) Pharisaeus stans haec apud se orabat: Deus gratias ago tibi quia non sum sicut ceteri hominum, raptores, iniusti, adulteri vel ut etiam hic publicanus. (12) Ieiuno bis in sabbato, decimas do omnium quae possideo. (13) Et publicanus a longe stans nolebat nec oculos ad caelum levare sed percutiebat pectus suum dicens: Deus propitius esto mihi peccatori. (14) Dico vobis descendit hic iustificatus in domum suam ab illo quia omnis qui se exaltat humiliabitur et qui se humiliat exaltabitur.

For the translation of *publicanus* as *openlice synful* cf Hericus, Hom. II.30, 53–6:

> Publicani autem dicebantur, vel qui publicis flagitiis incumbebant, vel qui publicis negotiis inserviebant, vectigalia reipublicae persolventes, id est telonearii, vel etiam qui per fas et nefas divitias sibi accumulabant.

Elsewhere, e.g. CH I.24.3 and II.32.18, Ælfric uses the term *gerefa*, but here the sinfulness of the *publicanus* is crucial. The sense 'openly sinful' is well established in Old English renderings of the Gospels (see Godden 1990, pp. 62–4). The clause *swiðor þonne se sunderhalga* perhaps reflects a reading of *ab illo* as 'from him' rather than 'from the temple' (cf 46–7).

17–25 Characteristically, Ælfric gives initial prominence to the historical allegory by which Pharisee and publican represent Jews and Gentiles, which is a minor and secondary interpretation in the Latin commentaries. His words correspond loosely to Bede's interpretation, repeated by Hericus and Smaragdus (Bede, *Comm. Luc.*, 5.1171–8):

> Typice autem Pharisaeus iudaeorum est populus qui ex iustificationibus legis extollit merita sua, publicanus vero gentilis est qui longe a Deo positus confitetur peccata sua, quorum unus superbiendo recessit humiliatus alter lamentando appropinquare meruit exaltatus. . . . Et de utroque populo praefato et de omni superbo vel humili recte potest intellegi.

25–8 Bede begins by distinguishing four aspects of pride, and attributes to the Pharisee his last kind, believing oneself unique in one's virtue (*Comm. Luc.*, 5.1143–8):

> Quattuor sunt species, quibus omnis tumor arrogantium demonstratur, cum bonum aut a semetipsis habere se aestimant, aut si sibi datum desuper credunt, pro suis se hoc accepisse meritis putant, aut certe cum iactant se habere, quod non habent, aut, despectis caeteris, singulariter videri appetunt habere quod habent.

Ælfric seems to be thinking rather of the second aspect, attributing one's virtue to one's own merits.

28–37 Cf Augustine, Serm. 115, §2, PL 38, 656:

> Ascendit orare: noluit Deum rogare, sed se laudare. [*earlier*] Diceret saltem, Sicut multi homines. Quid est, sicut caeteri homines, nisi omnes praeter ipsum? Ego, inquit, iustus sum, caeteri peccatores. . . . Ego solus sum, iste de caeteris est. . . .

38–63 There is nothing similar in the sources to these comments on prayer and boasting, though cf perhaps Hericus on the brevity of the publican's prayer (Hom. II.30, 160–1):

> Magna precis brevitas, sed mira robustaque devotione commendata.

The preceding verses in Luke 18 have emphasised the value of insistent praying. The remarks on *gylp* show some similarities to other comments by Ælfric, e.g. CH I.8.54 ff, I.11.220 ff, II.39.214 ff.

64–82 Ezekiel's vision of the four beasts with eyes is linked to the moral blindness of the Pharisee by Gregory in his commentary on Ezekiel (PL 76, 842C-3A). The passage is repeated, selectively, by Bede in his commentary on Luke, and thence by Hericus, Haymo and Smaragdus; Ælfric follows Bede, *Comm. Luc.*, 5.1152–64, very closely:

> Iezechiel propheta de ostensis sibi caeli animalibus scribit: 'Et totum corpus plenum oculis in circuitu ipsorum quattuor' (Ez 1.18). Corpora quippe animalium idcirco plena oculis describuntur quia sanctorum actio ab omni parte circumspecta est, bona desiderabiliter providens, mala sollerter cavens. Sed nos saepe dum aliis rebus intendimus fit ut alia neglegamus, et ubi neglegimus ibi procul dubio oculum non habemus. Nam ecce Pharisaeus ad exhibendam abstinentiam ad impendendam misericordiam, ad referendas Deo gratias oculum habuerat, sed ad humilitatis custodiam non habebat. Et quid prodest quod contra hostium

insidias paene tota civitas caute custoditur, si unum foramen apertum relinquitur unde ab hostibus intretur?

The interpretation of the four beasts as the evangelists is traditional; when Ælfric discusses it in more detail, in LS 15.178 ff, his source is the prologue to Jerome's commentary on Matthew (*Commentarii in Evangelium Matthaei*, Praef.55 ff., CCSL 77). Ælfric's use of the rare term *port* for *civitas*, rather than the more usual *burh*, is hard to explain, but he does use *portgeat* in a somewhat similar context at CH I.33.6 and 28 and it may be that *port* for him particularly signified a defended and walled city with gates.

83–91 The Pharisee's pride in his works takes Ælfric into a brief discussion of the role played by divine grace in initiating good works, quoting 1 Cor 4.7: *Quid autem habes quod non accepisti? Si autem accepisti quid gloriaris quasi non acceperis?* and Jn 15.5: *Quia sine me nihil potestis facere*. The first is much quoted by Augustine in his discussions of grace (see Grundy 1991, p. 143), but Ælfric is perhaps responding here to the reworking by Hericus of Bede's discussion of the four kinds of pride. Hericus quotes the first part of the quotation from Corinthians in describing the belief that virtue comes from oneself (Hom II.30, 72–6):

Secunda species est cum aliquis bonum quod habet a seipso se arbitratur habere, diabolum profecto imitans qui per elationem dixit: Nescio dominum, et ego feci memetipsum, quem redarguit apostoli sententia dicentis: 'Quid enim habes quod non accepisti?'

It is clearly this type of pride which Ælfric has in mind as the distinguishing mark of the Pharisee, as indeed it is of Nebuchadnezzar in his treatment.

92–6 Hericus focuses on the punishment of the proud in the next world, but Ælfric may have noticed Haymo's comment on the verse, which touches on their humiliation in this world and mentions Nebuchadnezzar as an example (Hom. 123, PL 118, 664B):

Dicendum est, quia variis modis homines in hoc saeculo et in futuro exaltantur, et humiliantur. Alii hic et in futuro exaltantur sicut fuit rex David, Job, Ezechias, Josias et caeteri tales, qui gloriosi in hoc saeculo fuerunt, et gloriosiores in futuro. Alii hic et in futuro humiliantur, sicut sunt superbi homines, qui sunt pauperes: vel certe illi, qui in hoc saeculo de peccatis vindictam recipiunt, et in futuro ad poenam perpetuam transeunt, quales fuerunt Herodes et Antiochus, Nabuchodonosor et Pilatus, et multi tales.

96–133 The account of Nebuchadnezzar summarises Dan 1.1–2 and 4.1–24 and then translates fairly closely Dan 4.25–34:

(1.1) Venit Nabuchodonosor rex Babylonis Hierusalem et obsedit eam. (2) Et tradidit Dominus in manu eius Ioachim regem Iudae et partem vasorum domus Dei et asportavit ea in terram Sennaar in domum dei sui et vasa intulit in domum thesauri dei sui. . . . (4.25) Omnia venerunt super Nabuchodonosor regem. (26) Post finem mensuum duodecim in aula Babylonis deambulabat. (27) Responditque rex et ait: nonne haec est Babylon magna quam ego aedificavi in domum regni in robore fortitudinis meae et in gloria decoris mei? (28) Cum adhuc sermo esset in ore regis vox de caelo ruit: tibi dicitur Nabuchodonosor rex regnum transiit a te. (29) Et ab hominibus te eicient et cum bestiis feris erit habitatio tua; faenum quasi bos comedes et septem tempora mutabuntur super te donec scias quod dominetur Excelsus in regno hominum et cuicumque voluerit det illud. (30) Eadem hora sermo conpletus est super Nabuchodonosor. Ex hominibus abiectus est et faenum ut bos comedit, et rore caeli corpus eius infectum est, donec capilli eius in similitudinem aquilarum crescerent et ungues eius quasi avium. (31) Igitur post finem dierum ego Nabuchodonosor oculos meos ad caelum levavi et sensus meus redditus est mihi et Altissimo benedixi et viventem in sempiternum laudavi et glorificavi quia potestas eius potestas sempiterna et regnum eius in generationem et generationem. (32) Et omnes habitatores terrae apud eum in nihilum reputati sunt. Iuxta voluntatem enim suam facit tam in virtutibus caeli quam in habitatoribus terrae et non est qui resistat manui eius et dicat ei quare fecisti. (33) In ipso tempore sensus meus reversus est ad me et ad honorem regni mei decoremque perveni et figura mea reversa est ad me et optimates mei et magistratus mei requisierunt me et in regno meo constitutus sum et magnificentia amplior addita est mihi. (34) Nunc igitur ego Nabuchodonosor laudo et magnifico et glorifico Regem caeli quia omnia opera eius vera et viae eius iudicia et gradientes in superbia potest humiliare.

However, the powerful sentence at 106–9 is actually an almost verbatim repetition of King Alfred's rendering of Nebuchadnezzar's words in the *Pastoral Care*, 39.16–18:

Hu ne is ðis sio micle Babilon ðe ic self atimbrede to kynestole and to ðrymme, me selfum to wlite and wuldre mid mine agne mægene and strengo?

Ælfric perhaps recalled not only Alfred's wording but also his use of Nebuchadnezzar as an example of pride. His reading at 117, 'his hair grew like that of women, and his nails like the claws of an eagle', for verse 31, 'his hair grew like (the feathers) of eagles and his nails like those of birds' is puzzling. I can find no trace of a relevant alternative to the Vulgate reading. Perhaps it is his own substitution for the curious Biblical image, reflecting the differences between male and female hairstyles in his own time, though if so it is an odd one, since long hair may have become a female feature in late Anglo-Saxon England but had been a traditional feature of Germanic kings and still appeared in contemporary illustration, e.g. for Pharaoh and Abraham in the Hexateuch manuscript, BL, MS Cotton Claudius B.iv.

134–59 The story of Balthasar, 134–59, renders Dan 5:

(1) Balthasar rex fecit grande convivium optimatibus suis mille. . . . (2) Praecepit ergo iam temulentus ut adferrentur vasa aurea et argentea quae

asportaverat Nabuchodonosor pater eius de templo quod fuit in Hierusalem. . . . (4) Bibebant vinum et laudabant deos suos aureos et argenteos et aereos ferreos ligneosque et lapideos. (5) In eadem hora apparuerunt digiti quasi manus hominis scribentis contra candelabrum in superficie parietis aulae regiae et rex aspiciebat articulos manus scribentis. (6) Tunc regis facies commutata est et cogitationes eius conturbabant eum et conpages renum eius solvebantur et genua eius ad se invicem conlidebantur. . . . (13) Igitur introductus est Danihel coram rege ad quem praefatus rex ait: . . . (16) Si ergo vales scripturam legere et interpretationem indicare mihi purpura vestieris et torquem auream circa collum tuum habebis et tertius in regno meo princeps eris. (17) Ad quae respondens Danihel ait coram rege: munera tua sint tibi et dona domus tuae alteri da; scripturam autem legam tibi rex et interpretationem eius ostendam tibi. [*He rehearses the fall of Nebuchadnezzar.*] (22) Tu quoque filius eius Balthasar non humiliasti cor tuum cum scires haec omnia. (23) Sed adversum Dominatorem caeli elevatus es et vasa domus eius adlata sunt coram te et tu et optimates tui et uxores tuae et concubinae vinum bibistis in eis. Deos quoque . . . qui non vident neque audiunt neque sentiunt laudasti. Porro Deum . . . non glorificasti. (24) Idcirco ab eo missus est articulus manus quae scripsit hoc quod exaratum est. (25) Haec est autem scriptura quae digesta est: mane thecel fares. (26) Et haec interpretatio sermonis. Mane: numeravit Deus regnum tuum et conplevit illud. (27) Thecel: adpensum est in statera et inventus est minus habens. (28) Fares: divisum est regnum tuum et datum est Medis et Persis. (29) Tunc iubente rege indutus est Danihel purpura et circumdata est torques aurea collo eius et praedicatum est de eo quod haberet potestatem tertius in regno. (30) Eadem nocte interfectus est Balthasar rex Chaldeus (31) et Darius Medus successit in regnum.

Ælfric follows the reading *est* rather than *es* in verse 27.

29 ASSUMPTION OF THE VIRGIN

In his First Series homily for the festival Ælfric had given a cautious discussion of the assumption followed by an account of two miracles of the Virgin. Here he gives a further homily for the occasion, briefly expounding the Gospel for the day, the story of Martha and Mary from Luke 10.38–43; whether prompted by the interest of the text or the importance of the occasion he does not explain, though no other Marian feast-day is covered in both Series. He uses the story in strikingly independent fashion, as an argument for the superiority of the religious life, both teaching and worship, over the secular life of providing for the material needs of others.[1] Gregory the Great had discussed the story in his Moralia on Job and in

[1] There is an excellent discussion of the sources and treatment of them by Mary Clayton in her Oxford D.Phil. thesis (Clayton 1983), and a more summary but equally

his homilies on Ezekiel, and in both cases interpreted the two sisters as symbols of the active and contemplative life, the active being spent in helping the needy, teaching the ignorant and correcting the sinful, and the contemplative in separation from anxieties and concentration on God.[2] Bede repeated the passage from the homilies on Ezekiel when discussing the Martha and Mary story in his commentary on Luke,[3] and Haymo made the same identifications in his homily for the Assumption, although for him the active life appears not to include the work of teaching and guiding others.[4] Ælfric knew the *Moralia*,[5] Bede's commentary on Luke (probably) and the homilies of Haymo, but silently rejects their views, choosing instead, as he says (line 20), to follow Augustine. The latter discusses the story at length in his sermons 103 and 104, and for him the two sisters represent the present life and the future life, the former spent in the toil of serving and feeding others, the latter in the peace of being fed and served by God, though he adds that a foretaste of the future life may be had in the present when worshipping God. Sermon 103 concentrates on showing how Martha's life is the way to Mary's, while the particular concern of Sermon 104 is to justify Martha's life of toil and service as the necessary life of this world. These two sermons, which are combined as one item for the occasion in versions of PD, are clearly Ælfric's source[6] and he accepts much of Augustine's argument, but he is inclined to stress the value of Mary's life rather more and, beginning at line 72, departs radically from Augustine in his characteristic apologia for the life of the teacher and scholar. Whereas Augustine had distinguished between serving others and being served by God, Ælfric here distinguishes between serving others, including the clergy, with material things and the better life of serving others with spiritual food through the work of teaching. For Augustine the preacher and teacher is represented by Martha, and he modestly hints that the congregation listening to him are, for the moment, closer to Mary than he is; for Ælfric the teacher is here represented by Mary, because of his concern with *heofenlican lare*. In his use of the two sisters as symbols of two lives which can be followed in the world Ælfric is perhaps after all indebted to the Gregorian tradition, but neither Gregory nor Bede offers any support for identifying the better life of Mary with the life of studying and teaching.

valuable one in her article 'Hermits and the Contemplative Life in Anglo-Saxon England', in Szarmach 1996, pp. 147–75. My account is indebted to both.

[2] *Moralia siue Expositio in Iob*, VI.xxxvii.160–215, ed. M. Adriaen, CCSL 143 (Turnhout, 1979); *Homiliae in Ezechielem*, II.2.178–291, ed. M. Adriaen, CCSL 142 (Turnhout, 1971).

[3] *Commentarius in Lucam*, 3.2311–77, ed. D. Hurst, CCSL 120 (Turnhout, 1960), pp. 5–425.

[4] PL 118, 768 ff.

[5] See notes to CH II.30.

[6] Identified by Förster (1894, p. 34); Smetana (1959, p. 200) mistakenly represents the source as Augustine's Tractates on John 103 and 104 but does note that the two pieces occur together in PDM.

Sources and Notes

The following texts are cited below:

1. Augustine, *Sermones*, PL 38, Serm. 103 and 104, cols. 613–8.

7–17 Lc 10.38–42:

> (38) Et ipse intravit in quoddam castellum et mulier quaedam Martha nomine excepit illum in domum suam. (39) Et huic erat soror nomine Maria quae etiam sedens secus pedes Domini audiebat verbum illius. (40) Martha autem satagebat circa frequens ministerium quae stetit et ait: Domine non est tibi curae quod soror mea reliquit me solam ministrare? Dic ergo illi ut me adiuvet. (41) Et respondens dixit illi Dominus: Martha Martha sollicita es et turbaris erga plurima. (42) Porro unum est necessarium; Maria optimam partem elegit quae non auferetur ab ea.

The strange phrase *eaðelican byrig* for *castellum* (cf Thorpe's baffled comment) is presumably used to stress the diminutive element in the Latin word, with *eaðelic* in its sense 'small, slight' (cf CH II.12.61 and 31.67); for *castellum* cf Ælfric's Glossary, 318.9: *castellum: wic oððe litel port*.

20–26 Despite the reference to Augustine, the general account of Martha and Mary seems to be based simply on Ælfric's own reading of the New Testament, esp. Jn 11.1–45 and 12.1–11. The former passage, on the raising of Lazarus, is discussed at length in a later homily, Pope 6. As Pope notes (p. 331), Ælfric silently rejects the tradition, mooted by Augustine and approved by Gregory and Bede among others, that this Mary, who anoints Christ's feet in Jn 12, is to be identified with the prostitute who anoints Christ's feet in Lc 7.37.

26–35 Loosely based on Augustine, Serm.103, §2, PL 38, 613:

> Nam et ista dignatio fuit, se praebere pascendum. Habebat carnem, in qua esuriret quidem, et sitiret: sed nescitis quia in eremo esurienti angeli ministrabant (Mt 4.11)? . . . Ne quis tamen vestrum forsitan dicat: O beati qui Christum suscipere in domum propriam meruerunt! Noli dolere, noli murmurare quia temporibus natus es, quando iam Dominum non vides in carne: non tibi abstulit istam dignationem. 'Cum uni, inquit, ex minimis meis fecistis, mihi fecistis' (Mt 25.40).

A very similar passage, but with Zacheus instead of Martha and Mary, occurs in Ælfric's later homily for the dedication of a church, Brotanek (p. 13); cf too Pope's comments, p. 561.

36–41 Augustine, Serm. 104, PL 38:

> [§1, 616] Laborabat illa, vacabat ista. . . . [§4, 617–8] In his duabus mulieribus, duas vitas esse figuratas, praesentem et futuram, laboriosam et quietam, aerumnosam et beatam, temporalem et aeternam. . . . Quod agebat Martha, ibi sumus: quod agebat Maria, hoc speramus.

46–53 Augustine, Serm. 104, §3, PL 38, 617:

> Praeponitur unum multis. Non enim a multis unum, sed multa ab uno. Multa sunt quae facta sunt, unus est qui fecit. Coelum, terra, mare, et omnia quae in eis sunt, quam multa sunt! . . . Bona valde quae fecit: quanto melior ille qui fecit?

54–70 Augustine, Serm. 104, PL 38:

> [§1, 616] Intenta erat Martha quomodo pasceret Dominum: intenta Maria quomodo pasceretur a Domino. . . . Mira enim suavitate tenebatur: quae profecto maior est mentis quam ventris. Excusata est, sedit securior. . . . [§3, 617] Bene ergo Martha circa corporalem Domini . . . necessitatem ministrabat. . . . Ergo Maria meliorem partem elegit, quae non auferetur ab ea. Hoc enim elegit, quod semper manebit: non auferetur ab ea. . . . Auferetur enim a te [= Martha] labor, ut requies detur. Tu navigas, illa iam in portu est. . . . [*earlier*] Circa unum se voluit occupari. Iam tenebat: 'Mihi autem adhaerere Deo, bonum est' (Ps 72.28).

Ælfric adds the quotation from Jn 12.26: *Ubi sum ego, illic et minister meus erit.*

70–82 This section on the superiority of the teaching life is largely independent. Ælfric's starting point is perhaps Augustine, Serm. 103, §5, 615:

> Bona sunt ministeria circa pauperes, et maxime circa sanctos Dei servitia debita, obsequia religiosa. . . . Melius est tamen quod elegit Maria.

But where Augustine goes on to define the better part as the sweetness of heaven and divine love, Ælfric urges the importance of teaching and knowing the divine law, quoting 1 Cor 14.38: *Si quis autem ignorat ignorabitur*, and Rom 2.12: *Quicumque enim sine lege peccaverunt sine lege et peribunt* (texts which he had used in a similar context at CH II.3.292 ff). The distinction between man whose erect posture invites him to look up to heaven and animals whose eyes naturally turn to the ground (lines 75–80), is something of a classical commonplace, but is used by King Alfred in his version of Boethius, and thence by Ælfric in a much adapted passage in LS 1.49–61.[7]

83–92 Ælfric's list of the works of mercy reflects those implied by Augustine, Serm. 104, PL 38:

> [§3, 617] Misericordia miseris necessaria est. Frangis panem esurienti; quia invenisti esurientem: tolle famem; cui frangis panem? Tolle peregrinationem; cui exhibes hospitalitatem? Tolle nuditatem; cui praeparas vestem? Non sit aegritudo; quem visitas? Non sit captivitas; quem redimis? Non sit rixa; quem concordas? Non sit mors; quem sepelis? [*The next few lines of exposition draw on both pieces:* Serm.104, §3, 617] In illo saeculo futuro non erunt ista mala; ergo nec ista ministeria. [Serm.103, §6, 615] Ibi pascemur, non pascemus. Ideo hoc ibi erit plenum atque perfectum, quod hic elegit

[7] Cf Godden 1985a, pp. 296–8.

Maria. . . . Dominus ipse dicit de servis suis: 'amen dico vobis, quia faciet eos recumbere, et transibit, et ministrabit illis' (Lc 12.37).

92–109 Ælfric reiterates his own interpretation (lines 92–6) and then returns to Augustine's Serm. 104, §4, PL 38, 618:

> Erant ergo in illa domo istae duae vitae, et ipse fons vitae. In Martha erat imago praesentium, in Maria futurorum. Quod agebat Martha, ibi sumus: quod agebat Maria, hoc speramus. . . . [*earlier*] Ambae innocentes, ambae, inquam, laudabiles, sed una laboriosa, altera otiosa: nulla facinorosa, quam cavere debet laboriosa; nulla desidiosa, quam cavere debet otiosa. . . . Remoti a negotiis, sepositis familiaribus curis, convenistis, statis, auditis. In quantum hoc agitis, Mariae similes estis.

Ælfric has here slightly shifted his ground, identifying Mary's life not with the clerical role of teaching but (following Augustine) with the shared experience of worship and prayer, and he picks up the point in his subsequent remarks on the importance of participation in that worship (lines 110–15).

115–33 Ælfric concludes by repeating the warnings already given, in the CH I homily and again at the beginning of this one, against apocryphal accounts of the assumption of the Virgin. When he mentions Augustine, Jerome and Gregory 'and many others', he perhaps means as opponents of apocryphal literature in general rather than specifically assumption narratives; he cites 'Jerome' against apocryphal legends of the assumption in I.30 and Augustine against the *Visio Pauli* in II.20. I know of no evidence for Ælfric's implication that some of the apocryphal narratives were based on dreams (line 122), unless he means vision narratives. The reference to English versions (line 126) suggests familiarity with those that survive among the Blickling homilies and in Cambridge, Corpus Christi College, MS 41.

134–7 Clayton (1983, p. 367) suggests an echo of a liturgical respond for the feast of the Assumption (PL 78, 798C): *Ecce exaltata es super choros angelorum, intercede pro nobis ad Dominum Deum nostrum.*

30 JOB

Ælfric's usual sources offer no precedent for this account of Job and his sufferings and patience; none of the homiliaries, or indeed sanctorale collections, contains a homily on Job or life of Job, though there do exist two brief sermons by Caesarius and one by Augustine,[1] none at all similar to Ælfric's. His interest in the patriarch as an exemplary figure of patience is, however, clear enough from his use of him in other homilies, such as CH I.31.279–87, CH II.19.252–9,

[1] Caesarius of Arles, *Sermones*, ed. G. Morin, CCSL 103 (Turnhout, 1953), Serm. 131 and 132; Augustine, *Sermones*, ed. C. Lambot, CCSL 41 (Turnhout, 1961), Serm. 12.

LS 16.36–54. At the end he refers briefly to the allegorical application of Job's story to Christ and the church, which is developed at length in Gregory's *Moralia* and in compilations based on that work. Ælfric occasionally uses parts of this interpretation in other works (see, e.g. CH I.14, Pope 1 and Pope 18) but only for isolated images or ideas and not with reference to Job himself. His many references to Job all confine themselves, as here, to the literal aspect; possibly his resistance to allegorising Job's experiences extended beyond the inappropriateness to the unlearned which he adduces here. Indeed, for all the complexity of the allegorical interpretation, to produce a brief and coherent moral reading of Job's story at the literal level was itself no small task. The explanation which Ælfric offers at the outset for his unusual choice of subject perhaps begs more questions than it answers. He is providing an account of Job for the laity, he says, because it is the time of year when the Book of Job is read in church services; but such Old Testament readings were part of the special monastic and clerical offices, not of the mass which the laity attended.[2]

The homily takes the main story from the first two chapters and the last of the Book of Job, but draws on the rest of the book to give an account of Job's life before his trials (lines 40–51) and the flavour of his argument with the comforters (lines 142–51) and of Job's own response of grief and faith (lines 166–75). Interwoven through the account are Ælfric's comments on the moral implications and doctrinal issues raised by the Biblical text, and on aspects of Old Testament custom. Some of these have parallels in Gregory the Great's enormous commentary, the Moralia on Job, a work which Ælfric evidently knew well.[3] As Besserman points out, the character of the debt suggests rather Ælfric's general familiarity with the *Moralia* than its immediate use while composing the homily. The other comments, however, are not to be found in Gregory. Ælfric's reference to *lareowas* at 233 suggests that he knew other allegorical commentaries, but none that I have found shows any parallel (apart from a presumably coincidental match in a twelfth-century work, see note on 34–7).

Ælfric's view of Job's experiences also differs significantly from Gregory's. The latter had seen them as God's trial of Job, to test whether his virtues and faith would survive under vicissitude, a test justified in part because Job's

[2] Cf Gatch 1977, p. 203, n. 53. Ælfric lists the Old Testament readings in his letter for the monks of Eynsham (Jones 1998).

[3] The use of the *Moralia* in this homily was demonstrated, with some specific parallels noted, by L. L. Besserman in 'A note on the source of Ælfric's homily on the Book of Job', *English Language Notes* 10 (1973), 248–52. Förster (1894) had originally not thought that the *Moralia* was known to Ælfric, but Arvid Gabrielson pointed to some parallels with CH I.11 and 14 (Gabrielson 1912), and Förster himself later suggested the use of the *Moralia* in the Job homily in 'Der Inhalt der altenglischen Handschrift Vespasianus D. XIV', *Englische Studien* 54 (1920), 46–68, at 57, n.1. Pope cites the *Moralia* as source for his homilies 1 and 18. Cf also notes to CH I.31.276 ff. Ælfric seems to have known the *Moralia* itself rather than any of the abbreviations and compilations described by Rene Wasselynck, 'Les compilations des *Moralia in Job* du VIIe and VIIe siècle', *Recherches de theologie ancienne et médiévale* (Louvain) 29 (1962), 5–32.

perseverance exalts him still higher than his initial righteousness. This is how Ælfric normally understands Job's story too (cf esp. CH I.31, but also LS 16). Here, however, the concept of trial is absent; the key words *fandian* and *fandung* do not appear, and the concept seems virtually ruled out by Ælfric's assurance that God had preserved Job from defeat (lines 127–9). Ælfric presents the story instead as an episode in the continual warfare waged by Satan against man, emphasising the devil's role and his separation from God (lines 26–37, 52–4, 87–97, 161–6), and is at pains to deny that the fire which destroys Job's sheep comes from God (lines 90–97). He acknowledges that Job's tribulations are specifically permitted by God, but the reason, he suggests, is not to try him but to provide for future generations a model of patience and righteousness (lines 51–2, 113–6). For Ælfric, Job's experiences reflect not so much God's testing of men as the truth which Job articulates at the height of them, *mannes lif is campdom ofer eorðan* (cf 150–60, 234–8). Ælfric seems slightly uncertain over the question whether Job's sins play any part in his sufferings. He stresses his righteousness (lines 38–9, 52–3) and criticises the comforters' arguments that Job is being punished for his sins (lines 140–2) but at times seems to come to the same view himself, both here (see 146–8 and 201–2 and the comments below) and in CH II.19.251–62.

In drawing on the Bible, Ælfric seems to have used a number of readings that are not to be found in the standard Vulgate text, or in the version used by Gregory (see lines 20, 69, 83–4, 104, 130, 146, 192–3, 223–5). It is clear from the last instance that we are not dealing with stray readings picked up from commentaries using other versions but with features of a full text of the book of Job, and equally clear from Ælfric's comment at 19, on variant readings of Job 1.6, that he was aware of diverging translations. Most of the distinctive readings, perhaps all, are characteristic of the Septuagint. C. R. Davis[4] suggested in 1949 that the *altera translatio* to which Ælfric refers at line 19 was Jerome's first version of Job, a rendering based mainly on the Septuagint but with an elaborate apparatus of signs to show words and phrases that are not in the Hebrew text or are in the Hebrew but not in the Greek text (printed PL 29, cols. 61–114). Further examination indicates that nearly all the other non-Vulgate readings can be found in this version, and it seems extremely probable that Ælfric did indeed use it, quite extensively. At the same time, there are places where Ælfric's rendering is clearly based on Jerome's second version, that of the Vulgate, and not the first. It would seem that he worked from both versions, perhaps prompted in the first instance by Gregory's note in the *Moralia* that he too had drawn on both the new and the old translations, and that in some places at least Ælfric chose the readings which best supported his attempt to offer a literal interpretation of the story of Job, and in particular one which lent itself to a depiction of Job as exemplary moral figure.

[4] C. R. Davis, 'A note on Ælfric's translation of *Job* I, 6', *Modern Language Notes* 60 (1945), 494–5.

Sources and Notes

The following texts are cited below:

1. Augustine, *Sermones*, ed. C. Lambot, CCSL 41 (Turnhout, 1961), Serm. 12 (pp. 164–74).
2. Gregory the Great, *Moralia siue Expositio in Iob*, ed. M. Adriaen, 3 vols., CCSL 143–143B (Turnhout 1979–85).
3. Jerome's first version of the Book of Job, *Liber Iob*, PL 29, cols. 61–114.

7–26 Job 1.1–8 (Vulgate):

> (1) Vir erat in terra Hus nomine Iob et erat vir ille simplex et rectus ac timens Deum et recedens a malo. (2) Natique sunt ei septem filii et tres filiae (3) et fuit possessio eius septem milia ovium et tria milia camelorum, quingenta quoque iuga boum et quingentae asinae ac familia multa nimis eratque vir ille magnus inter omnes Orientales. (4) Et ibant filii eius et faciebant convivium per domos unusquisque in die suo et mittentes vocabant tres sorores suas ut comederent et biberent cum eis. (5) Cumque in orbem transissent dies convivii mittebat ad eos Iob et sanctificabat illos consurgensque diluculo offerebat holocausta per singulos. Dicebat enim ne forte peccaverint filii mei et benedixerint Deo in cordibus suis. Sic faciebat Iob cunctis diebus. (6) Quadam autem die cum venissent filii Dei ut adsisterent coram Domino, adfuit inter eos etiam Satan. (7) Cui dixit Dominus: Unde venis? Qui respondens ait: Circuivi terram et perambulavi eam. (8) Dixitque Dominus ad eum: Numquid considerasti servum meum Iob quod non sit ei similis in terra, homo simplex et rectus et timens Deum ac recedens a malo?

Ælfric's note at line 19 (perhaps a marginalium originally) draws attention to the variant reading for verse 6. Jerome (*Liber Iob*, PL 29, 63B) in fact has *angeli* rather than *angeli Dei*, but Ælfric may have been familiar with the latter reading from elsewhere; it occurs in the commentary by Jerome's pupil, Philippus Presbyter (printed PL 23, 1409C), and also in Augustine's Annotations on Job (PL 34, 825).[5] The reading is also recorded from Vulgate manuscripts in the apparatus of the Rome 1951 edition of the Vulgate.

26–37 Augustine (Serm. 12) and Gregory similarly try to explain Satan's apparent presence in heaven. Ælfric's image of the blind man and the sun closely parallels Gregory, although Augustine uses it too; Gregory, *Moralia*, II.iv.18–21:

> Ipse in conspectu Domini, non autem in conspectu eius Dominus fuit; sicut caecus cum in sole consistit, ipse quidem radiis solis perfunditur sed tamen lumen non videt quo illustratur.

Ælfric's explanation that Satan is in fact on earth is, I think, entirely his own, although the quotation from Isaiah 66.1 at 30–31 (*haec dicit Dominus: caelum*

[5] Davis, 'Ælfric's translation', notes these two.

sedis mea et terra scabillum pedum meorum) is used by Gregory in a different context a little later (*Moralia*, II.xii.7–8). The quotation from 1 Petr 5.8–9 at 34–7 (*sobrii estote vigilate quia adversarius vester diabolus tamquam leo rugiens circuit quaerens quem devoret. Cui resistite fortes fide*) is also used at the same point in a twelfth-century commentary on Job (PL 164, 555) but not in earlier commentaries.

38–52 Ælfric's account of Job's good works is a tissue of quotations from the Book of Job:

> (29.12) Quod liberassem pauperem vociferantem et pupillum cui non esset adiutor. (13) . . . et cor viduae consolatus sum. (14) Iustitia indutus sum. . . . (15) Oculus fui caeco et pes claudo. (16) Pater eram pauperum. . . . [*Ælfric then converts the following sequence of conditional clauses into positive statements.*] (31.20) Si non . . . de velleribus ovium mearum calefactus est. (16) Si negavi quod volebant pauperibus. . . . (17) Si comedi buccellam meam solus et non comedit pupillus ex ea (18) quia ab infantia mea crevit mecum miseratio et de utero matris meae egressa est mecum. (25) Si laetatus sum super multis divitiis meis. . . . (29) Si gavisus sum ad ruinam eius qui me oderat. . . . (32) Foris non mansit peregrinus; ostium meum viatori patuit. (33) Si abscondi quasi homo peccatum meum et celavi in sinu meo iniquitatem meam. . . .

Gregory has a similar account of Job in his preface, using different verses, and follows it with a similar defence of Job against the appearance of boasting, although his explanation that Job tells of his good deeds to restore his own morale is not Ælfric's (*Moralia*, Praef.III.54–63):

> Si vero hoc quibusdam displicet, quod bona sua ipse narravit, sciendum est quia inter tot rerum damna, inter tot corporis vulnera, inter tot pignorum funera, amicis ad consolationem venientibus et ad increpationem erumpentibus de vita sua desperare cogebatur. . . . Hi namque, qui ad consolandum venerant dum quasi eius iniustitiae exprobrabant, desperare eum de semetipso funditus compellebant. Quod ergo bona sua ad mentem revocat, non se per iactantiam elevat.

52–86 Ælfric returns to the Biblical narrative, translating Job 1.9–22:

> (9) Cui respondens Satan ait: Numquid frustra timet Iob Deum. (10) Nonne tu vallasti eum ac domum eius universamque substantiam per circuitum operibus manuum eius benedixisti, et possessio illius crevit in terra? (11) Sed extende paululum manum tuam et tange cuncta quae possidet, nisi in facie tua benedixerit tibi. (12) Dixit ergo Dominus ad Satan: Ecce universa quae habet in manu tua sunt; tantum in eum ne extendas manum tuam. Egressusque est Satan a facie Domini. (13) Cum autem quadam die filii et filiae eius comederent et biberent vinum in domo fratris sui primogeniti, (14) nuntius venit ad Iob qui diceret: Boves arabant et asinae pascebantur iuxta eos, (15) et inruerunt Sabei tuleruntque omnia

et pueros percusserunt gladio et evasi ego solus ut nuntiarem tibi. (16) Cumque adhuc ille loqueretur venit alter et dixit: Ignis Dei cecidit e caelo et tactas oves puerosque consumpsit et effugi ego solus ut nuntiarem tibi. (17) Sed et illo adhuc loquente venit alius et dixit: Chaldei fecerunt tres turmas et invaserunt camelos et tulerunt eos necnon et pueros percusserunt gladio et ego fugi solus ut nuntiarem tibi. (18) Loquebatur ille et ecce alius intravit et dixit: Filiis tuis et filiabus vescentibus et bibentibus vinum in domo fratris sui primogeniti, (19) repente ventus vehemens inruit a regione deserti et concussit quattuor angulos domus quae corruens oppressit liberos tuos et mortui sunt et effugi ego solus ut nuntiarem tibi. (20) Tunc surrexit Iob et scidit tunicam suam et tonso capite corruens in terram adoravit, (21) et dixit: Nudus egressus sum de utero matris meae et nudus revertar illuc; Dominus dedit, Dominus abstulit; sit nomen Domini benedictum. (22) In omnibus his non peccavit Iob [labiis suis] neque stultum quid contra Deum locutus est.

Ælfric's *fyr* at 69 renders not the Vulgate *Ignis Dei* but the variant *Ignis*, which is crucial for his argument in the next paragraph. *Liber Iob* reads *Ignis Dei* but with a sign indicating that *Dei* is not in the Greek but imported from the Hebrew. *Ignis* is also found as a Vulgate variant. At 83–4, *swa swa* etc. is from *Liber Iob* (PL 29, 65A): *Sicut Domino placuit ita factum est*. The words *labiis suis* are not found in verse 22 in either the Vulgate text or *Liber Iob*, but they do occur as a Vulgate variant, probably imported from Job 2.10. Ælfric's one intervening comment, lines 61–3, implicitly defending God's benevolence, parallels generally Gregory's exposition but there is no close link.

87–103 Ælfric's argument (lines 90–97) that the fire which destroys Job's sheep, like the fire sent by Antichrist, cannot really come from heaven is one he had already deployed in similar terms in the preface to CH I, but I know of no source. Gregory acknowledges that it is God's fire, explaining that God permitted it, but concentrates on an allegorical reading. Ælfric's explanation (lines 97–101) of verse 22, Job sinned not with his lips (itself dependent on a variant reading), is loosely parallel to Gregory (*Moralia*, III.x.2–3): *Duobus modis labiis delinquimus, cum aut iniusta dicimus aut iusta reticemus.*

104–29 From Job 2.1–10:

(1) Factum est autem cum quadam die venissent filii Dei et starent coram Domino, venisset quoque Satan inter eos et staret in conspectu eius. (3) Et dixit Dominus ad Satan: Numquid considerasti servum meum Iob quod non sit ei similis in terra . . . et adhuc retinens innocentiam? Tu autem commovisti me adversus eum ut adfligerem illum frustra. (4) Cui respondens Satan ait: Pellem pro pelle et cuncta quae habet homo dabit pro anima sua. (5) Alioquin mitte manum tuam et tange os eius et carnem et tunc videbis quod in facie benedicat tibi. (6) Dixit ergo Dominus ad Satan: Ecce in manu tua est, verumtamen animam illius serva. (7) Egressus igitur Satan a facie Domini, percussit Iob ulcere pessimo a planta pedis

usque ad verticem eius. (8) Qui testa saniem deradebat sedens in sterquilinio. (9) Dixit autem illi uxor sua: Adhuc tu permanes in simplicitate tua. Benedic Deo et morere. (10) Qui ait ad illam: Quasi una de stultis locuta es. Si bona suscepimus de manu Domini quare mala non suscipiamus? In omnibus his non peccavit Iob labiis suis.

Liber Iob has *filii Dei* without comment at verse 1, but Ælfric presumably felt justified in persevering with the *angeli Dei* reading of Job 1.6. He renders *anima* as *life* at 110 but, crucially, as *sawle* at 113, a point developed at 129. The parallel between Satan's use of Job's wife and his earlier use of Eve is made by Gregory at *Moralia*, III.viii.13–15, 21:

Nam antiquae artis insidias repetit, et quia scit quomodo Adam decipi soleat, ad Evam recurrit. . . . Cor igitur mulieris tenuit.

130–46 The account of the three comforters comes from Job 2.11–13:

(11) Igitur audientes tres amici Iob omne malum quod accidisset, ei venerunt singuli de loco suo, Eliphaz Themanites et Baldad Suites et Sophar Naamathites. Condixerant enim ut pariter venientes visitarent eum et consolarentur. (12) Cumque levassent procul oculos suos non cognoverunt eum et exclamantes ploraverunt scissisque vestibus sparserunt pulverem super caput suum in caelum. (13) Et sederunt cum eo in terram septem diebus et septem noctibus et nemo loquebatur ei verbum; videbant enim dolorem esse vehementem.

That the comforters are kings is a Septuagint reading transmitted by *Liber Iob*, PL 29, 67A:

Ut audierunt tres amici eius omnia mala haec quae acciderunt illi, convenerunt unusquisque de regione sua ad eum Eliphaz Themanites rex, Baldad Sauchites tyrannus et Sophor . . . Mineorum rex.

The terms *gesibbe* at 130 and *mæg* at 191 and 197 would seem to identify them also as kinsmen of Job, though the Vulgate (and *Liber Iob*) only calls them *amici*. I can find no source for this idea: a relationship with Eliphaz is deducible from Genesis 36 and 46.13, but hardly seems adequate to explain Ælfric's emphasis. Since Ælfric elsewhere uses both Old English words to render *amicus* (see glossary), and uses *mæg* and *freond* interchangeably at 190–201, we should perhaps conclude that he used *gesibb* and *mæg* in a wider sense than the dictionaries suggest, and that they just mean 'friends' here; or perhaps that he understood *amicus* as having a possible sense of kin. The comforters' shift from consolation to criticism for his sins (lines 140–2) is noted by Gregory in the passage already quoted from his preface, and again later. Their actual words, lines 142–5, come from Job 4.5–6:

(5) Nunc autem venit super te plaga et defecisti; tetigit te et conturbatus es. (6) [Ubi est] timor tuus, fortitudo tua, patientia tua et perfectio viarum tuarum?

146–60 Job's reply, lines 146–51, selects from cc. 6 and 7:

(6.1) Respondens autem Iob dixit: (2) Utinam adpenderentur peccata mea quibus iram merui et calamitas quam patior in statera. (3) Quasi harena maris haec gravior appareret; unde et verba mea dolore sunt plena. (26) Ad increpandum tantum eloquia concinnatis. . . . (27) . . . et subvertere nitimini amicum vestrum. (7.1) Militia est vita hominis super terram et sicut dies mercennarii dies eius.

Job 6.2–3 is a troubling passage that appears in many forms. The Vulgate has Job apparently complaining that his misfortunes far outweigh any sins by which he might have deserved punishment (cf Rheims-Douay 'Would God my sinnes were weyed, wherby I haue deserued wrath, and the calamitie, which I suffer in a balance. 3 As the sand of the sea this would appeare heauier, wherfore my wordes also are ful of sorrow'), but there is a variant reading *haec graviora apparent* (referring to *peccata*) giving the opposite (and safer) sense. *Liber Iob's* rendering is obscure but certainly identifies something (probably Job's words) as heavier than sand and may have influenced Ælfric's rendering (*Liber Iob*, PL 29, 71A):

Si quis appendens ponderet iram meam, et sermones meos ponat in statera simul, arena littorum inveniet graviores.

The Old English presumably means either that Job's sins and misery together weigh more than the sands of the sea-shore, or that his sins weigh far more than his sufferings (following the Vulgate variant). If Job, in the Old English, is asserting the weight of his sins, it justifies God but conflicts somewhat with the preceding criticism of the comforters for speaking as if Job had been punished for sins. Gregory follows the Vulgate but avoids the problem by allegorising the verse. Ælfric's elaboration of 7.1, in lines 151–60, has a general resemblance to Gregory's exposition, *Moralia*, VIII.vi–vii, although Gregory is more interested in the variant reading *temptatio est vita* than *militia est vita*.

161–75 Ælfric's summary of Job's afflictions and insistence that they failed to turn him from his faith have some similarity to Gregory's preface, *Moralia*, Praef.III.54–63 (the passage quoted above at lines 38–52), but it is Ælfric who stresses the devil's part in this. The words of Job that follow, lines 166–75, are selected to trace the course of Job's triumph, drawing on various verses:

(7.5) Induta est caro mea putredine et sordibus pulveris. Cutis mea aruit et contracta est. (30.16) . . . et possident me dies adflictionis. (17) Nocte os meum perforatur doloribus, et qui me comedunt non dormiunt. (19) Conparatus sum luto et adsimilatus favillae et cineri. (7.16) . . . Parce mihi, nihil enim sunt dies mei. (19.25) Scio enim quod redemptor meus vivat et in novissimo de terra surrecturus sim. (26) Et rursum circumdabor pelle mea et in carne mea videbo Deum. (27) Quem visurus sum ego ipse et oculi mei conspecturi sunt et non alius. Reposita est haec spes mea in sinu meo.

176–203 Ælfric now turns to the end of the story, paraphrasing Job 42.7–10:

(7) Postquam autem locutus est Dominus verba haec ad Iob, dixit ad Eliphaz Themaniten: Iratus est furor meus in te et in duos amicos tuos quoniam non estis locuti coram me rectum sicut servus meus Iob. (8) Sumite igitur vobis septem tauros et septem arietes, et ite ad servum meum Iob et offerte holocaustum pro vobis. Iob autem servus meus orabit

> pro vobis. Faciem eius suscipiam ut non vobis inputetur stultitia, neque enim locuti estis ad me recta sicut servus meus Iob. (9) Abierunt ergo Eliphaz Themanites et Baldad Suites et Sophar Naamathites et fecerunt sicut locutus fuerat ad eos Dominus et suscepit Dominus faciem Iob. (10) Dominus quoque conversus est ad paenitentiam Iob cum oraret ille pro amicis suis, et addidit Dominus omnia quaecumque fuerant Iob duplicia.

For 192–3 cf *Liber Iob*, PL 29, 112B: *Et cum orasset etiam pro amicis, remisit illis peccatum.* His comments on the value of prayer have an approximate parallel in Gregory, *Moralia*, XXXV.xi. The word *behreowsunge* at 202, rendering *paenitentiam*, is presumably to be understood here as 'grief' rather than 'penitence' or 'repentance', the usual sense, if we are not meant to see Job as a sinner.

204–26 Ælfric concludes the story with the last verses of the Vulgate book:

> (42.12) Dominus autem benedixit novissimis Iob magis quam principio eius et facta sunt ei quattuordecim milia ovium et sex milia camelorum et mille iuga boum et mille asinae. (13) Et fuerunt ei septem filii et filiae tres. (11) Venerunt autem ad eum omnes fratres sui et universae sorores suae et cuncti qui noverant eum prius et comederunt cum eo panem in domo eius et moverunt super eum caput et consolati sunt eum super omni malo quod intulerat Dominus super eum et dederunt ei unusquisque ovem unam et inaurem auream unam. (15) Non sunt autem inventae mulieres speciosae sicut filiae Iob in universa terra deditque eis pater suus hereditatem inter fratres earum. (16) Vixit autem Iob post haec centum quadraginta annis et vidit filios suos et filios filiorum suorum usque ad quartam generationem et mortuus est senex et plenus dierum.

The change of order, placing verse 11 after 12–13, leaves Job's recovery of fortune appearing as unmistakably the gift of God, avoiding any of the Biblical implication that the gifts of his kindred and neighbours contributed. The explanation for Job's children not being restored twofold is from Gregory, *Moralia*, XXXV.xvi; cf esp. lines 13–15, *decem postmodum in carne restituit, decem vero qui amissi fuerant in occulta animarum vita servavit* with *on ðam digelan life* (line 214). The final information, on Job's age and his descent from Abraham, is derived from the Septuagint via *Liber Iob*, PL 29, 113A, 114A:

> Et omnes anni vitae eius fuerunt ducenti quadraginta octo . . . Erat autem ipse filius quidem Zarae, de Esau filiis filius, de matre vero Bosram, ita ut sit quintus ab Abraham.

31 SIXTEENTH SUNDAY AFTER PENTECOST

Ælfric's text is the Gospel for the day, from the Sermon on the Mount, Matthew 6.24–33, 'No man can serve two masters'. His source, as he says, is Bede, not the Ps-Bede commentary on Matthew but the authentic commentary on Luke, for the Gospel passage is closely parallel to Luke 16.13 and 12.22–31;

the relevant part of Bede's commentary on Luke is excerpted and used for this occasion in Paul the Deacon's homiliary.[1] Bede's exposition is in fact almost entirely derived, word-for-word, from Augustine's commentary on the sermon on the Mount and Jerome's commentary on Matthew,[2] but it is Bede that he specifies and there is no sign that he has gone behind Bede to consult his sources. He probably also knew the more extended allegorical treatments by Hericus (included in PDM) and Haymo, but shows little if any sign of influence from them.[3]

The general line of argument is similar to Bede's, but Ælfric does not follow him at all closely and gradually moves further away as the homily develops. Bede is chiefly concerned to explain away the possible implications of the text, arguing that man is meant to take reasonable thought for food and clothing, though as necessities rather than an end in themselves. Ælfric accepts this point but uses the text to illustrate the divine scheme more as it applies to the after-life and the beauty of eternity. In doing so, he seems to acknowledge that this teaching will find little favour with his readers: 'this Gospel will seem *sellic* to foolish men, but I tell it nevertheless, in case someone likes it', he says at the end (lines 103–4). *Sellic* or *syllic* normally means '(attractively) strange, wonderful, rare' in Ælfric's works and elsewhere, and is applied to miracles, buildings, even silkworms and their products, but the context here suggests something more like '(repellently) strange, absurd, odd'. The nearest parallels are at Pope 13.34: *Her syndon syllice word samlæredum mannum; nu wylle we eow geopenian þæt andgit þærto* (referring to the Gospel passage on beams and motes which he is about to expound) and the Letter for Wulfsige (Fehr I, §14), where he has been discussing the canonical decrees against the marriage or concubinage of priests:

> Nu þincð eow þis syllic to gehyrenne, forþanþe ge habbað eowre yrmðe swa on gewunan gebroht, swylce hit nan pleoh ne sy, þæt se preost libbe swa swa ceorl.
>
> [Now this will seem strange to you to hear, because you have brought your wretched ways into common practice, as if there is no problem in a priest living like a married man.][4]

Ælfric seems, in his homily, to be confessing that not just the Gospel text but the lessons that he draws from it will seem absurdly unrealistic to his audience. As he notes at the outset, Bede's exposition is brief, and Ælfric's own more succinct phrasing makes it even briefer; it is easily the shortest piece in the

[1] Förster (1894, p. 26) suggested the Matthew commentary as source. Smetana (1959, p. 200) pointed out that an excerpt from the Luke commentary was in PD and contained 'much the same material'; in fact it contains much more material that Ælfric used.

[2] See Hurst's notes in the CCSL edition of Bede.

[3] Smetana (1961, p. 465) suggests that Ælfric turned to Haymo for two passages (lines 37–9, 93–6) but in both cases the material is in Bede as well. There is however a parallel not in Bede at 47–9 (see below).

[4] Cf too LS 25.564 and Warner, 135.11.

Series, and rivalled only by CH I.17. Yet since he is selective in his coverage of Sundays after Pentecost, he presumably thought this an important text to provide.

Sources and Notes

The following texts are cited below:

1. Bede, *Commentarius in Lucam*, ed. D. Hurst, CCSL 120 (Turnhout, 1960), pp. 5–425.
2. Haymo of Auxerre, *Homiliae de Tempore*, PL 118, Hom. 127, cols. 680–4.

1–23 A free paraphrase of Mt 6.24–33:

> (24) Nemo potest duobus dominis servire: aut enim unum odio habebit et alterum diliget aut unum sustinebit et alterum contemnet. Non potestis Deo servire et mamonae. (25) Ideo dico vobis ne solliciti sitis animae vestrae quid manducetis, neque corpori vestro quid induamini. Nonne anima plus est quam esca et corpus plus est quam vestimentum? (26) Respicite volatilia caeli quoniam non serunt neque metunt neque congregant in horrea et Pater vester caelestis pascit illa. Nonne vos magis pluris estis illis? (27) Quis autem vestrum cogitans potest adicere ad staturam suam cubitum unum? (28) Et de vestimento quid solliciti estis? Considerate lilia agri quomodo crescunt; non laborant nec nent. (29) Dico autem vobis quoniam nec Salomon in omni gloria sua coopertus est sicut unum ex istis. (30) Si autem faenum agri quod hodie est et cras in clibanum mittitur Deus sic vestit, quanto magis vos minimae fidei? (31) Nolite ergo solliciti esse dicentes quid manducabimus aut quid bibemus aut quo operiemur. (32) Haec enim omnia gentes inquirunt. Scit enim Pater vester quia his omnibus indigetis. (33) Quaerite autem primum regnum et iustitiam eius et omnia haec adicientur vobis.

Ælfric silently omits the *neque congregant in horrea* of verse 26 and the *vos minime fidei* of verse 30; *geðeot* at line 5 renders not the *unum sustinebit* of Mt 6.24 but the *uni adherebit* of the parallel text Lc 16.13; and his rendering of *mamonae* as *eowres feos gestreone* perhaps reflects Bede's gloss *divitias*.

24–34 Ælfric follows Bede fairly closely in his discussion of riches (*Comm. Luc.*, 5.154–65):

> Nemo servus potest duobus dominis servire, quia non valet simul transitoria et aeterna diligere. Si enim aeternitatem diligimus, cuncta temporalia in usu non in affectu possidemus. . . . Nam qui sint duo domini consequenter exponit dicens. . . . Audiat hoc avarus, audiat qui censetur vocabulo christiano non posse simul mammonae, hoc est divitiis . . . sed qui servit divitiis. Qui enim divitiarum servus est, divitias custodit ut servus; qui autem servitutis excussit iugum, distribuit eas ut dominus.

34–49 The antithetical development of the opening verses is Ælfric's own, with a passing allusion to 1 Tim 6.10: *Radix omnium malorum est cupiditas*. Lines 38–40, on the need for labour, come from Bede's comment on Lc 12, citing Gen 3.19 (*Comm. Luc.*, 4.853–4):

> Et quia in sudore vultus praeparamus nobis panem, labor exercendus est, sollicitudo tollenda.

(Haymo's elaboration of this, suggested by Smetana, does not seem any closer.) Lines 41–7 parallel Bede, but are much more concise (*Comm. Luc.*, 4.855–64):

> Ammonet ut meminerimus multo amplius nobis Deum dedisse quod nos fecit et composuit ex anima et corpore quam est alimentum atque tegumentum, ut intellegas eum qui dedit animam multo facilius escam esse daturum similiter eum qui corpus dedit, multo facilius daturum esse vestimentum. Quo loco quaeri solet utrum ad animam cibus iste perveniat, cum anima incorporea sit, iste autem cibus corporeus. Sed animam hoc loco pro ista vita positam noverimus, cuius retinaculum est alimentum istud corporeum.

Ælfric characteristically shifts from Bede's 'God will give' to 'God can give . . . if you do his will'. His qualifying reminder, lines 47–9, that although God can provide he sometimes sends famine instead as a punishment has no parallel in Bede or his sources, although the same idea is in Haymo at this point (Hom. 127, PL 118, 682D): *Nisi forte peccatis abundantibus sterilitas terrae iusto Dei iudicio contra naturam accidat*. There is however nothing to match Ælfric's argument that anyone who starves to death as a result of such famine nevertheless comes to God unless irretrievably damned. There may have been a topical relevance to this point.

50–66 The main points of Ælfric's discussion of the birds are in Bede (*Comm. Luc.*, 4.871–88):

> Quod si volatilia absque cura et aerumnis Dei aluntur providentia, quae hodie sunt et cras non erunt . . . quanto magis homines quibus aeternitas promittitur Dei reguntur imperio. Quanto magis pluris estis illis, id est carius vos valetis, quia rationale utique animal, sicuti est homo, sublimius ordinatum est in rerum natura quam irrationabilia, sicuti sunt aves. . . . Non autem vestra cura factum esse ut ad hanc staturam veniret corpus vestrum. . . . Illi ergo etiam tegendi corporis curam relinquite, cuius videtis cura factum esse ut tantae staturae corpus habeatis.

Ælfric characteristically adds the angels to this picture of the chain of being, as he does also in his adaptation of King Alfred's contrast between man and beasts for LS 1 (cf Godden 1985a, pp. 296–8), and alludes to the role of the incarnation in elevating man's position in the chain (a point developed more fully at CH I.2.141–62).

67–84 In translating the Gospel passage Ælfric had paraphrased the strange image of the lilies being cast into the oven with the word *forswælede*, 'burnt up'.

Here, however, he creates a more familiar (to the English) picture of the fragile beauty of the lilies being withered by winter cold (lines 67–70). His use of this to suggest both God's generosity as Creator and the transience of earthly things, in contrast to the beauty promised in the afterlife, is very much his own, although Bede, following Jerome, had mentioned the rose, the lily and violet and glossed 'tomorrow' as future time (*Comm. Luc.*, 4.897–904):

> Et re vera quod sericum, quae regum purpura, quae pictura textricum, potest floribus comparari? Quid ita rubet ut rosa? Quid ita candet ut lilium? Violae vero purpuram nullo superari murice. . . . Cras in scripturis futurum tempus intellegitur.

85–102 The last part of Ælfric's exposition, returning to the distinction between the eternal life which is the true aim and reward and the earthly provision which is a transitory loan, owes a little to Bede (*Comm. Luc.*, 4.934–8):

> Qui enim non ait, dabuntur, sed adicientur, profecto indicat aliud esse quod principaliter datur, aliud quod superadditur. Quia nobis in intentione aeternitas, in usu vero temporalitas esse debet, et illud datur et hoc nimirum ex abundanti superadditur.

The form of the concluding exhortation (lines 99–102) was perhaps prompted by Sir 5.5, *ne adiicias peccatum super peccatum,* which is quoted by Bede in a different context as part of his gloss to Lc 16.13 (*Comm. Luc.*, 5.174). Ælfric ends with a proverb not recorded before his time, though the *Ancrene Riwle* a little later has a parallel of sorts: *And of a drope waxeth a muche flod and adrencheth the soule.*[5]

DE SANCTA MARIA

The feast of the Nativity of the Virgin had been established in England since the eighth century, and is listed in the *Menologium* as one of the occasions celebrated by the whole church. As with the apostle Thomas later (see the *Excusatio Dictantis*), Ælfric offers two distinct reasons for excluding the occasion from his collection: the danger of heresy, and the difficulty of the pericope.[1] The first objection is apparently directed at the apocryphal legends about the Virgin's conception, birth and childhood, which circulated in several versions in this period; the Gospel of Ps-Matthew was included in the Cotton-Corpus legendary, and the *De Nativitate Mariae* appeared in some versions of Paul the Deacon's

[5] *The English Text of the Ancrene Riwle: BM MS Cotton Nero A. xiv*, ed. Mabel Day, EETS os 225 (1952), p. 32. See B. J. Whiting and H.W. Whiting, *Proverbs, Sentences and Proverbial Phrases* (Cambridge, Mass., 1968), p. 481 (R22). Further examples are given by M. P. Tilley, *A Dictionary of the Proverbs in England in the Sixteenth and Seventeenth Centuries* (Ann Arbor, Mich., 1950), D617.

[1] There is an excellent and comprehensive discussion of this passage by Mary Clayton in 'Ælfric and the Nativity of the Blessed Virgin Mary', *Anglia* 104 (1986), 286–315. My comments are based almost entirely on her article.

homiliary for this occasion. The reference to the nature of her birth and the identity and quality of her parents seems to point to such narratives, and Ælfric refers to them more explicitly but in similar terms in the introduction to his later homily for the occasion, Assmann 3. Ælfric would have known of their questionable status from the Gelasian decree, and presumably found it impossible to disentangle the safe from the unsafe elements.

The pericope for the occasion was Matthew 1.1–16,[2] which gives the genealogy of Joseph. Although the original homiliary of Paul the Deacon had a different reading for this occasion, later copies, including some from Ælfric's time, did provide allegorical interpretations of the Matthew reading for this occasion, usually a long extract from Rabanus Maurus's Commentary on Matthew. Given the fact that Ælfric found it possible to produce two sermons for the Assumption in the Catholic Homilies without touching on the dangerous matter of the apocryphal legends which he rejected, and that he later produced a homily for the Nativity too, his excuses for not covering the occasion here seem less than compelling.

32 ST MATTHEW

Ælfric returns to the pattern of the First Series homilies on St Peter and St Andrew, expounding the Gospel text for the day and then telling the story of the apostle's martyrdom. The text is Matthew 9.9–13, the calling of Matthew from his toll-booth to be a disciple. The details of his exposition mostly come from Bede's sermon I.21, a source identified by Förster and shown by Smetana to have been included in Paul the Deacon's homiliary for the occasion.[1] Bede takes the Gospel story as an example of God's grace to sinners, which transforms Matthew from tax-collector to apostle and evangelist and offers thereby hope to the sinners who congregate in Matthew's house. Ælfric shares Bede's general view and had already used Matthew as an example of divine grace in CH I.22, but he takes the notion rather further, passing over Bede's arguments that the sinners had already begun to follow Christ of themselves and instead developing the concept of a salvation wrought by divine grace rather than human merits (lines 68–78). Perhaps associated with this is a difference of attitude to publicans. Bede acknowledges that Matthew is a publican (citing Matthew 10.3), like those who attend his house, and explains that the word means one who is publicly disgraced by his crimes or involved in public business which can scarcely, if at all, be conducted without sin; presumably, although he does not say so, he sees Matthew's tax-collecting as falling into the latter category. 'Publicans and sinners' is thus a tautology for Bede,

[2] Lenker, p. 367.

[1] See Förster's review of Cook 1898, in *Englische Studien* 28 (1900), 419–30, at 423; C. R. Davis, 'Two new sources for Ælfric's Catholic Homilies', *JEGP* 41 (1942), 510–13; Smetana 1959, p. 200.

and he remarks on the kindness shown by Luke and Mark in not identifying Matthew as a publican. Elsewhere Ælfric seems to share this view: in CH II.28 he translates *publicanus* as *openlice synful* (lines 6–7), and in II.16 he refers to Matthew's tax-collecting as an occupation scarcely possible without sin (lines 130–42). Here, however, he translates *publicani* as *gerefan*, 'officers', and leaves it to be supposed that these may be distinct from the sinners of whom the Pharisees complain. He says nothing against Matthew's occupation, and omits all Bede's references to Matthew as a publican. Matthew's sins are those of 'all mankind', indeed a kind of ignorance (*nytennysse*, 75). This may simply reflect a wish to see the apostle as a type of ordinary humanity rather than more narrowly as a representative of a social class, but there is perhaps too a reluctance to blacken the moral status of tax-collectors. (And perhaps also a reluctance to denigrate future apostles even before their conversion; cf the similar treatment of St Paul in CH II.27.)

For the story of the apostle's preaching among the Ethiopians, Ælfric uses a Latin legend which was widely disseminated, particularly in the Ps-Abdias compilation, and has been printed in numerous versions. None represents exactly what Ælfric was using, but marginally the closest seems to be that reproduced by Fabricius, identified by Förster,[2] though in a number of places it is necessary to invoke readings from two others, those by Mombritius and Atenolfi. Here as elsewhere Ælfric was evidently using a text that had experienced a fair amount of conflation; the versions surviving in manuscripts of the Cotton-Corpus legendary are not particularly close.[3] It is a somewhat extravagant legend, including a lively scene with dragons and a loving account of the earthly paradise, as well as some lengthy accounts of doctrine. Ælfric gives a very succinct version, omitting the dragons and most of the sermons. The one aspect which particularly catches his attention is the crisis over the new king's attempt to obtain as a wife his predecessor's daughter, now a nun and abbess. Ælfric recounts this episode in some detail, including the essence of the apostle's objections. The story is also summarised, even more briefly, in the *Old English Martyrology* (OE Martyrology, II.212–4), but Ælfric seems to know nothing, or perhaps believe nothing, of the tradition recorded there that St Matthew also preached in Macedonia.

Sources and Notes

The following texts are cited below:

1. Anon., *Passio Matthaei*, in G. T. Atenolfi, *I Testi medioevali degli atti di S. Matteo l'evangelista* (Rome, 1958), pp. 58–80. [= Aten.]
2. Anon., *Passio Matthaei*, in Fabricius, II.636–68.
3. Anon., *Passio Matthaei*, in Mombritius 1910, II.257–63.
4. Bede, *Homiliae*, ed. D. Hurst, CCSL 122 (Turnhout, 1955), Hom. I.21 (pp. 148–55).

[2] Förster 1892, p. 24.
[3] See Zettel 1979, p. 58.

1–20 The text mainly follows Mt 9.9–13, but with a few details from the parallel account in Lc 5.27–32:

(Mt 9.9) Et cum transiret inde Iesus, vidit hominem sedentem in teloneo, Mattheum nomine, et ait illi: sequere me; et surgens secutus est eum. [Lc 5.29: Et fecit ei convivium magnum Levi in domo sua.] (Mt 9.10) Et factum est, discumbente eo in domo, ecce multi publicani et peccatores venientes discumbebant cum Iesu et discipulis eius. (11) Et videntes Pharisaei dicebant discipulis eius [Lc 5.30: et murmurabant Pharisaei et scribae]: quare cum publicanis et peccatoribus manducat magister vester? (12) At Iesus audiens ait: non est opus valentibus medico sed male habentibus. (13) Euntes autem, discite quid est misericordiam volo et non sacrificium. Non enim veni vocare iustos sed peccatores [Lc 5.32: ad paenitentiam].

Ælfric's opening comment at 19–20 presumably means that his interpretation will be based in part on the details taken from Luke's version, as to a small extent it is. Bede begins with a fairly detailed comparison of the two accounts.

20–33 In discussing the significance of Matthew's name and his conversion Ælfric takes points from various places in Bede's homily I.21:

[32–4] Matheus Hebraice, Latine dicitur donatus, quod profecto nomen illi apte congruit qui tantum gratiae supernae munus accepit. . . . [9–14] De publicano iustum de telonеario discipulum fecit, quem etiam, proficientibus eiusdem gratiae incrementis, de communi discipulorum numero ad apostolatus gradum promovit; nec solum praedicandi verum etiam scribendi evangelium illi ministerium commisit. . . . [22–3] Vidit autem non tam corporei intuitus quam internae miserationis aspectibus. . . . [55–9] Vidit ergo publicanum, et quia miserando atque eligendo vidit, ait illi: Sequere me. Sequere autem dixit imitare, sequere dixit non tam incessu pedum quam exsecutione morum. 'Qui enim dicit se in Christo manere, debet sicut ille ambulavit et ipse ambulare' (1 Jn 2.6). . . . [72–3] Dominus qui eum foris verbo vocavit, intus invisibili instinctu ut sequeretur edocuit.

34–54 Bede cites Luke for the detail of the great feast at Matthew's house, and then, like Ælfric, develops the idea of an inner spiritual feast (Hom. I.21, 109–14):

Non tantum in domo sua terrestri convivium domino corporale exhibuit, sed multo gratius illi convivium in domo pectoris sui per fidem ac dilectionem paravit, ipso adtestante qui ait: 'ecce ego sto ad ostium et pulso; si quis audierit vocem meam et aperuerit ianuam, intrabo ad illum et caenabo cum illo et ipse mecum' (Apoc 3.20).

For Ælfric's development of this image (lines 40–44), not from Bede, cf passages in his own writings, at CH I.20.186–9, CH II.19.32–4, Pope 10.49 ff. For 44–8, on the Pharisees, cf Bede, Hom. I.21, 127–31:

Duplici errore tenebantur Pharisaei, cum magistro veritatis de susceptione peccatorum derogabant, quia et se iustos arbitrabantur . . . et eos criminabantur iniustos.

But the discussion of *hælend* and healing (lines 48–54) owes nothing to Bede. The striking, if characteristic, note that Christ heals men's bodies as well as souls is also made at Pope 2.91–7, where Ælfric is drawing on Augustine. Cook (1898, p. 257) cites line 52 as an untraced Biblical quotation, but it may be Ælfric's own. For the comment cf Bede, Hom. I.21, 148–51:

> In eo autem quod valentibus non opus esse medico dicit, illorum temeritatem redarguit qui, de sua iustitia praesumentes, gratiae caelestis auxilium quaerere detractabant.

55–67 Ælfric's development of Christ's quotation from Hosea 6.6 seems to be his own. For the identification of the Pharisees with the Jews and their pride in the Old Law, cf CH II.28.

68–78 A slight similarity to Bede at first, Hom. I.21, 204–10:

> Vocat peccatores ut per paenitentiam corrigantur, vocat iustos ut magis magisque iustificentur. Quamvis et ita recte intellegi possit quod ait: 'Non veni vocare iustos, sed peccatores', quia non illos vocaverit qui, suam iustitiam volentes constituere, iustitiae Dei non sunt subiecti, sed eos potius qui fragilitatis suae conscii non erubescunt profiteri, quia 'in multis offendimus omnes'.

But Ælfric gives the point a strongly Augustinian cast, forsaking the *vocat*, 'calls', of Bede and the Gospel for stronger language: 'God turns the sinful to repentance and fills the righteous with more righteousness'. The note continues in lines 72 ff, which are more difficult than at first appears. *Eal mennisc wæs synfull* perhaps reflects James 3.2, *in multis offendimus omnes*, quoted by Bede (Hom. I.21, 210), but Ælfric absorbs into it the quotation from Romans 3.23–4 with which Bede had opened his homily: (23) *Omnes enim peccaverunt et egent gloriam Dei.* (24) *Iustificati gratis per gratiam ipsius*. Thorpe (II.473) reads at 73–4 *ða ðe he geceas* and translates: 'the Lord justified, without merits, through his grace, those whom he chose, as he did this evangelist Matthew'. The sense is plausible, but the manuscripts all have *ða ða he geceas* = 'when he chose'. Though there is an awkwardness in not having an object for *gerihtwisode* (MS G supplies *hit*), this reading makes reasonable sense; Ælfric is referring to the redemption of all mankind, not the election of the chosen. For the use of the temporal clause to emphasise Christ's free choice of time, cf lines 98–9, *þa ða he wolde, com to middanearde*. Ælfric is apparently comparing the act of grace involved in redeeming all men from original sin (partially in answer to the Pharisees' or Jews' claim to be righteous at 70–72) with the individual act of grace shown in the elevation of Matthew. The imagery of the last sentence recalls a similar context at CH II.23.186 ff.

81–105 Ælfric now turns to the *Passio Matthaei*, which begins, after an introductory sentence on his calling to be an apostle, as follows (*Passio Matth.*, Fabricius):

[§1] Postquam spiritum sanctum inluminatorem una cum caeteris accepisset, et in orbem terrarum ad praedicandum evangelium esset directus, Aethiopiam . . . provinciam suscepit. In quam profectus ipse . . . contigit ut duo magi, Zaroes et Arphaxat, simul essent.[*They claim to be gods and are worshipped by the Ethiopians; they perform wonders (of the kind attributed to them in CH II.33) but are countered by St Matthew.*] [§2] Hunc cum vidisset Aethiops eunuchus, Candacis nomine, qui fuerat a Philippo apostolo diacono baptizatus, procidit ad pedes eius, et adorans dixit. . . . [*Candacis welcomes St Matthew to his house, where many others come to be baptized or healed.*] [§3] Tum Candacis eunuchus, qui eum susceperat omni affectione, interrogavit eum dicens: 'Obsecro te, ut digneris indicare mihi, quomodo cum sis Hebraeus, nosti Graecam, Aegyptiacam et Aethiopicam sermocinationem . . . ?' Respondit apostolus: 'Totus mundus unam sermocinationem habuisse omnium hominum dignoscitur. Sed nata est praesumptio omnium hominum talis, quae eos turrim tantae magnitudinis facere hortaretur, ita ut cacumen eius pervenisset ad coelum. Hanc praesumptionem Deus omnipotens hoc ordine repressit, ut alter alterum tum non potuerit loquentem advertere. . . . Veniens autem filius Dei omnipotentis, ostendere voluit quo ordine aedificando perveniremus ad coelum; et nobis duodecim discipulis suis misit spiritum sanctum de coelo, cum sederemus in uno loco, venitque supra unumquemque nostrum, et inflammati sumus sicuti ferrum inflammatur ab igne. Posthaec cum a nobis pavor simul et splendor discessisset, coepimus variis linguis loqui gentibus. [*Describes in detail their teaching on the nature and life of Christ.*] . . . Omnium gentium etiam linguas scimus . . . non mediocriter sed perfecte. Et ad quamcumque gentem pervenire potuerimus, iam loquelam eius perfecte cognoscimus.'

For *Silhearwe* as a term for the Ethiopians, see J. R. R. Tolkien, 'Sigelwara land', *Medium Ævum* 1 (1932), 183–96, and continued in *Medium Ævum* 3 (1934), 95–111. The identification of Candacis as one of the king's servants and the reference to his journey to Jerusalem are added from Acts 8.26 ff (though Acts actually identify him as one of the queen's servants). The Latin text's reference to Philip as *apostolo diacono* conflates Philip the apostle, mentioned in the Gospels and Acts 1.13, with Philip the deacon whose appointment is recorded at Acts 6 and subsequent preaching in Acts 8. The conversion of the Ethiopian eunuch seems to belong to the deacon, but Ælfric firmly ascribes it to the apostle.

106–22 *Passio Matth.*, Fabricius:

[§4] Haec et his similia multa mystico sermone apostolus cum dissereret, venit qui diceret magos illos cum singulis draconibus advenire. Dracones autem erant galeati, et flatus eorum flammiferum ardorem emittebat, sulphureasque spargebant auras e naribus, quorum odor homines interficiebat. . . . [*Matthew approaches the dragons and puts them to sleep; after the magi have failed to rouse them, Matthew himself wakes the dragons and orders them to return to their own place.*] Ad hanc vocem elevantes capita serpentes coeperunt ire, atque . . . nunquam amplius comparuerunt. [*In §§ 5 and 6 Matthew gives to the spectators a lavish and exuberant description of the earthly paradise, and explains how man lost it through the fall but, through the redemption, the souls of the good now pass there after death, beginning with the good thief on the cross.*] [§7] Cum haec et similia loqueretur apostolus, ecce tumultus luctuosus subito ortus est, in quo regis filius mortuus plangebatur. Ad cuius funus stabant magi, qui cum non possent suscitare eum, conabantur regi persuadere, hunc a diis raptum esse in collegium suum, ut sit unus ex diis, cui oporteat et simulachrum fabricari, et templum. Quae cum audivisset Candacis eunuchus, ingressus ad reginam, dixit illi: '. . . rogo te, ut veniat ad nos apostolus Dei Matthaeus.' . . . Tunc missi sunt per Candacem [honorati viri a latere regis],[4] qui rogantes apostolum cum honore introduxerunt ad regem. [*Queen Euphroenissa begs him to save her son, and Matthew prays.*] 'In nomine Domini mei Iesu Christi crucifixi, exsurge Eufranon[5]' Et confestim exsurrexit puer. Ad hoc factum, expavit cor regis . . . et praecones misit per civitatem, et diversas provincias Aethiopiae, dicentes: 'Venite ad civitatem, et videte Deum in effigie hominis latentem.'

122–30 *Passio Matth.*, Fabricius, §8:

Cumque venisset omnis multitudo cum cereis et lampadibus[6] et cum thymiamate, ac diverso sacrificiorum ritu, Matthaeus apostolus domini hac voce omnes alloquitur: 'Ego Deus non sum, sed servus Domini mei Iesu Christi, filii Dei omnipotentis, qui me misit ad vos, ut relicto errore simulachrorum vestrorum, ad verum Deum convertamini. . . . Et nunc . . . aurum et coronas aureas et argentum ab oculis meis tollite, et iis divenditis templum Domino extruite, atque ibi congregemini ad audiendum verbum Domini.'

131–49 *Passio Matth.*, Fabricius, §8:

Quo audito, intra triginta dies sexaginta[7] millia hominum congregata, fabricantes ecclesiam sanctam consummaverunt. Et vocavit nomen templi Matthaeus Resurrectio, quoniam per resurrectionem occasio aedificationis extiterat. Sedit autem in ecclesia illa Matthaeus annis xxiii. Et constituit presbyteros ac diaconos, et per civitates et castella ordinavit episcopos, et multas construxit per loca diversa ecclesias. Et baptizatus est rex Aeglippus et regina Euphoenissa, et filius eius qui suscitatus erat Eufranon; et filia eius Effigenia[8] baptizata, et virgo Christi permansit. Interea, magi timentes fugerunt ad Persas. Caeterum longum est narrare, quanti caeci inluminati, quanti paralytici curati, [quanti leprosi mundati,][9] quot denique a daemoniis

[4] From Aten.; Fab. has *virum honoratum a latere regis aliqui* for *honorati . . . regis.*

[5] From Aten.(and so henceforth); Fab. *Euphranor*, Momb. *Euphranon.*

[6] From Aten.; Fab. *lapidibus.*

[7] From Momb.; Fab. *undecim.*

[8] From Aten. (and so henceforth); Fab. *Iphigenia*, Momb. *Ephigenia.*

[9] Clause from Aten., Momb.; not in Fab.

> liberati, et quot mortui suscitati, quam[10] christianissimus rex iste fuit, et religiosissima[11] eius coniunx, devotus quoque omnis exercitus et populus[12] Aethiopiae. . . . Quae omnia propter copiam rerum praeteriens, quo ordine passionem sanctam celebraverit, retexam.

Only the Fabricius version has the sentence about the flight of the magi at this point, cf Old English lines 141–2, but the Atenolfi and Mombritius versions instead have a sentence at the very end of the text, which does come a little closer in wording to Ælfric:

> Zaroes et arfaxat illi duo magi ab ea hora qua suscitavit Matheus . . . filium regis mortuum fugientes ab Aethiopia in persidem devoluti sunt.

150–67 *Passio Matth.*, Fabricius:

> [§9] Non multo post enim rex Aeglippus, senectute expleta, perrexit ad Dominum, et accepit Hyrtacus exadelphus [*Fab.* rex adelphus] imperium eius. Hic cum vellet accipere Effigeniam filiam defuncti regis uxorem, iam Christo dicatam, et quae sacrum velamen acceperat de manu apostoli, praeposita iam virginum amplius quam ducentarum, sperabat tum rex Hyrtacus, quod per apostolum posset eius animum commovere. Quare coepit cum sancto Matthaeo agere, dicens: 'Dimidium regni mei accipe, tantum ut Effigeniam queam matrimonio meo copulare.' Cui beatus apostolus ait: 'Iuxta bonum propositum praedecessoris tui regis, qui omni die sabbato conveniebat, ubi verbum Domini praedicabam, iube illic et tu convenire universas virgines, quae cum Effigenia sunt. . . . [§10] Facto autem in congregatione magno silentio, aperiens os suum apostolus dixit: [*A long sermon follows, demonstrating that God has blessed marriage, but that all good things can be wrong in certain conditions, just as evils, even murder and perjury, can be good in some circumstances. Ælfric's account of Matthew's sermon at 158–60 corresponds better to some of his own preaching (e.g. CH II.6) than to anything in the sermon as reported by the Latin texts, which have little on widowhood or virginity at this point.*] [§11] Nam si hodie desponsatam regis, servus regis usurpare audeat, non solum offensam, sed etiam crimen tam grande incurrisse dignoscitur, ut merito vivens tradatur flammarum incendiis. . . . Ita etiam tu, o fili charissime rex Hyrtace, sciens Effigeniam filiam regis decessoris tui, sponsam regis caelestis esse effectam, et sacra velamine consecratam, quomodo quaeso poteris sponsam potentioris te tollere, et tuo eam matrimonio copulare?' Ad hunc sermonem Hyrtacus rex . . . ira accensus abscessit.

Matthew continues his sermon, urging them not to fear mortal kings.

168–90 *Passio Matth.*, Fabricius:

> [§13] Tunc Effigenia prostravit se coram omni populo ad pedes apostoli, et dixit: 'Obsecro te per ipsum, cuius apostolus es, ut imponas super me et

[10] From Aten., Momb.
[11] Fab. *gloriosissima*.
[12] *et populus* not in Aten., Momb.

super has virgines manus, ut per verbum tuum sint Domino consecratae, ut possimus evadere minas illius.. . . .' Tum apostolus, confidentiam habens in Dominum suum . . . imponens velamen super caput eius, et supra capita omnium virginum quae cum ea erant, hanc benedictionem dixit: 'Deus plasmator corporum, afflator animarum, qui nunquam spernis aetatem, non sexum reprobas, non ullam conditionem gratia tua ducis indignam, sed omnium aequalis creator es et redemptor: tu has famulas tuas, quas . . . ad conservandem coronam perpetuae virginitatis [et ad] castimoniam conservare animae dignatus es, tuae protectionis scuto circumtege, ut quas ad omne opus virtutis et gloriae . . . praeparasti . . . insolubilem filii tui domini nostri Iesu Christi copulam mereantur. . . . [*Matthew continues on the virtues of virginity.*]' [§14] Cumque respondissent Amen, et mysteria Domini celebrata, et missam suscepisset omnis ecclesia [et unusquisque ad domum propriam remearet *Aten., Momb.*] retinuit se ut iuxta altare . . . illic martyrium apostolicum exultaret. Itaque non multo post expansis manibus orantem, spiculator missus ab Hyrtaco, a tergo punctim, unius gladii ictu feriens apostolum, martyrem Christi effecit.

191–223 *Passio Matth.*, Fabricius:

[§14] Quo audito, omnis populus ad palatium cum igne pergebat. Cui furenti populo occurrerunt omnes presbyteri, et omnes diaconi ac clerici. . . . 'Nolite fratres (dicebant) contra praeceptum Domini agere.' [*They cite the example of St Peter.*] [§15] Interea Effigenia, sacratissima virgo Christi, quod in auro et argento ac gemmis habere potuerat, hoc totum sacerdotibus contulit, et omni clero, dicens: 'Postquam dignam apostolo Christi fabricaveritis ecclesiam, quicquid superfuerit, pauperibus erogabitis . . .' Factum est autem post haec . . . ut omnium nobilium uxores miserit rex Hyrtacus ad eam, sperans quod aliqua ratione posset ad eius consensum pervenire. Quod cum penitus non posset, convocavit magos ut daemonum illam ministerio raperent. Qui cum et ipsi nulla hoc possent consequi ratione, fecit circumdari ignem praetorio, in quo cum virginibus Christi commanens, Domino suo die noctuque famulabatur. Sed cum per circuitum ignis arderet, apparuit angelus Domini cum Matthaeo apostolo et dixit: 'Effigenia firma esto, et noli expavescere hos ignes. Ad illum enim a quo tibi sunt suppositi, revertentur.' . . . Excitavit Deus ventum validissimum, et mutavit omne illud incendium a domo virginis suae, et ita consumpsit palatium Hyrtaci, ut non inde potuerit aliquid ex facultatibus liberari. Ipse autem Hyrtacus cum suo filio unico vix evasit; sed melius fuerat incendio interisse. Caeterum filium eius vehementissimus mox daemon implevit. . . . Ipsum autem Hyrtacum elephantiae vulnera a capite usque ad ultima pedum vestigia ligaverunt. Quod cum medici curare non possent, ipse in se gladium ponens, illi incubuit, digno supplicio: ut quo a tergo apostolum Domini percusserat, ipse a recto seipsum stomacho perforaret. Quo facto, omnis populus . . . apprehenderunt cum omni exercitu fratrem Effigeniae, nomine Beor,[13] qui . . . de manu Matthaei fuerat gratiam Domini consecutus. Is itaque . . . regnavit per annos lxiii. . . . Et se vivente, constituit unum ex filiis suis ducem omnis exercitus, alterum vero regem. . . . Omnes quoque provinciae Aethiopum ecclesiis repletae sunt catholicis, usque in hodiernum diem. . . . Et fiunt ibi mirabilia magna, ad confessionem beati apostoli.

33 SS SIMON AND JUDE

The reading for this occasion was apparently John 15.17–25,[1] on the persecution of the apostles, but Ælfric evidently preferred to focus on the narrative of the two apostles' preaching, miracle-working and eventual martyrdom in Persia. Striking is the absence of any reference to their earlier history or role during Christ's life, such as Ælfric gives for most of the other apostles. The *Old English Martyrology* (OE Martyrology, II.240) records a tradition identifying Simon as Christ's cousin, son of Mary's sister Mary Cleophas, before briefly summarising the story told by Ælfric, and Cynewulf's *Fates of the Apostles* mentions their martyrdom in Persia. Ælfric evidently used a Latin narrative of the acts and martyrdom which exists in a number of forms, none of them quite identical with his.[2] The narrative is found as part of the ten-book Ps-Abdias collection (as printed by Fabricius, de la Barré[3] and others), but also on its own in legendaries (as printed by Mombritius). Ælfric probably knew the text in the latter form, for the format of the Abdias compilation leaves no traces on this or other apostolic narratives by him, and the account of Abdias and his writings is given at the end of his piece, as in Mombritius, whereas in the Ps-Abdias collection it is given in a preface at the head of the whole work. In matters of detail Ælfric is generally closest to Mombritius of the printed versions, but for some readings it is necessary to turn to the Ps-Abdias texts. Zettel has shown that, although the *Passio* does not survive in the early manuscripts of the Cotton-Corpus legendary (though it is mentioned in the table of contents of Salisbury Cathedral MS 222), it does occur in a twelfth-century derivative, Bodleian, MS Bodley 354, and that this copy, though late and often corrupt, is in several respects closer to Ælfric than any single printed version, combining readings found in Mombritius and others, as well as offering one individual reading clearly used by him.[4] Even so there are a few places where it lacks the particular variant used by Ælfric, as well as some details (esp. names and numbers) which he evidently got from his source

[13] The form *Ueor* (line 218) does not occur in any of the versions I have seen: Fab., Momb., Aten. and others have *Beor*, the ASS version has *Ugor*.

[1] Lenker, p. 370.

[2] So Förster 1892, pp. 24–5.

[3] R. L. de la Barré, *Historia Christiana Veterum Patrum* (Paris, 1583).

[4] Zettel 1979, pp. 28, 154–6, 195–8.

but are not to be found in any version that I have seen. The actual version which he used was no doubt the result of conflation between several versions, of both the Ps-Abdias and the separate type (like the Bodley MS version indeed, which has further variants written in early hands in the margins).

Ælfric's handling of the source is a mixture of free translation and summary, omitting none of the incidents but curtailing some of the arguments and sermons, straightening or bypassing some confusions in the narrative, and passing over the initial account of the Manichaean doctrines taught by the magi. He retains the strong vein of Christian ethics which pervades the story—the apostles' refusal to allow the execution of the heathen priests or the killing or forcible conversion of the magi, their contempt for wealth and idealisation of poverty, their refusal to name the true culprit when the miraculously articulate infant has cleared the deacon of the charge of being its father, their choice of martyrdom in preference to the death of their persecutors.

The occasion does not seem to have figured prominently in Anglo-Saxon church practice. Ælfric's version occurs in two legendaries, MSS L and f^{k}, amongst other lives and passions of apostles, but in no other MS apart from K itself, not even in MSS such as D, E and T which give fairly full coverage to saints' days.

Sources and Notes

The following texts are cited below:

1. Anon., *Passio Simonis et Iudae*, in Bodleian, MS Bodley 354, ff. 11r–16v. [= B354]
2. Anon., *Passio Simonis et Iudae*, in Fabricius, II.608–36.
3. Anon., *Passio Simonis et Iudae*, in Mombritius 1910, II.534–9.

2–17 From the *Passio*, Mombritius 1910, II:

[534.2–4:] Simeon chananeus et Iudas Zelotes apostoli domini nostri Iesu Christi, cum per revelationem spiritus sancti Persidem regionem fuissent ingressi, invenerunt ibi duos magos Zaroen et Arphaxar [Arfaxat *Fab.*], qui a facie sancti Mathei apostoli de Ethiopia fugerant. [*The Passio then describes the mixture of Manichaean and pagan doctrines taught by the magi.*] [534.19–29:] Sancti apostoli . . . cum ingressi essent persidem, occurrit eis praefectus Baradach [*so Momb.;* Caradac/Waradac *in B354, but* Varardach *in Fab. and other Ps-Abdias versions*] dux regis babyloniorum, cui nomen Xerxes. Hic autem contra Indos qui fines persidis invaserant susceperat bellum. In comitatu autem eius erant sacrificatores et Arioli et magi . . . qui per singulas mansiones sacrificantes daemoniis dabant responsa falaciae suae. Illo autem die . . . nullum penitus potuerunt dare responsum. Perrexerunt autem ad fanum vicinae civitatis et illic consulentes daemonia, dedit mugitum daemon et dixit: 'Dii qui vos comitabantur euntes in praelium non possunt dare responsa quia apostoli dei ibi

> sunt; unus dicitur Simon, alter Iudas. Isti autem hanc virtutem consecuti sunt a deo ut nullus deus audeat illis presentibus loqui.'

Note Ælfric's careful distinction between the gods which the Persians believe themselves to be worshipping and the devils who in fact occupy the shrines and speak for them.

18–40 *Passio*, Mombritius 1910, II:

> [534.29–33] Tunc Baradach dux exercitus regis Xerxis fecit eos inquiri; quos cum invenisset coepit ab eis inquirere qui essent aut unde essent aut quare venissent. Cui sanctus apostolus Simon dixit: 'Si genus quaeris, hebrei sumus. Si conditionem, servi sumus Iesu Christi. Si causam quaeris, salutis vestrae causa venimus, ut relicto errore simulachrorum Deum qui est in caelis possitis agnoscere.' [*At the general's request, the apostles pray to God to let the demons speak.*] [534.48–535.4] Coeperunt fanatici eorum aripi et dicere: 'Grande bellum futurum esse, et ex utraque parte posse interfici preliantes.' Tunc apostoli ex abundanti laetitia in risum excitati sunt. Dicit eis dux: 'Me timor invasit, et vos ridetis?' Dicunt ei apostoli: 'Cesset timor tuus, quia in ingressu nostro pax nobiscum intravit in istam provinciam. Nam hodie intermitte profectionem, et crastino die hac hora diei id est tertia venient ad te quos praemisisti cum legatis Indorum, qui vobis et terras invasas restitutas vestro imperio nuntiabunt, et in solitis tributis additum referent, et paci vestrae ad quascumque conditiones volueritis gratanter consentientes pactum firmissimum stabilibunt.' Simili modo pontifices risum levaverunt, dicentes duci: 'Domine dux, noli credere istis hominibus vanis mendacibus, advenis et ignotis . . . Isti autem dii qui nunquam fallunt dederunt tibi responsa. . . . [535.18–22:] Iube eos custodiri ne fugiant.' Respondens dux dixit: 'Ego non solum eos iubeo custodiri, sed etiam et vos eritis in custodia in crastinum. . . . Post haec iudicabitur qui sint, qui merito debeant honorari, quique merito debeant condemnari.'

41–54 *Passio*, Mombritius 1910, II.535.22–36:

> Factum est autem in crastinum iuxta verbum apostolorum. Venerunt nuntii qui missi fuerant cursu velocissimo in dromedariis et nuntiaverunt omnia ita esse sicut apostoli fuerant prosecuti. Tunc iratus pontificibus dux iussit ignem copiosum accendi, ut ibi pontifices praecipitarentur et omnes qui apostolorum dei effuscare nitebantur predicationem. Apostoli autem prostraverunt se duci dicentes: 'Obsecramus te domine, ne efficiamur nos causa interitus eorum, ut qui pro salute hominum huc missi sumus non vivificare mortuos sed viventes occidere videamur.' Et cum pulverem super caput suum mitterent prostrati duci Barach, dixit: 'Miror vos ita pro his intervenire, qui nihil aliud egerunt per omnes comites meos . . . quibus etiam premia contulerunt ingentia, nisi ut vos incenderent vivos.' Dicunt ei ambo apostoli: 'Disciplina magistri nostri

hanc regulam tenet, ut non solum malum pro malo non reddat, sed etiam bona pro malis restituat. Hanc solam distantiam novi inter nos esse et caeteras disciplinas, quod omnes reddunt pro malo malum, omnesque odio habentes se odio habent, nos autem diligimus inimicos nostros et benefacimus iis qui nos oderunt.'

54–69 *Passio*, Mombritius 1910, II:
[535.37–44] Dux autem dixit eis: 'Vel hoc facere me permittite, ut omnia bona eorum vobis tradantur.' Et cum haec diceret iussit inquiri quanta esset facultas pontificum. [*It is found that each priest has an income of a pound of gold each month.*] . . . Et computati sunt pontifices et inventi sunt centumviginti [*so Momb. and B354, in contrast to Ælfric's 100; Fab. and De la Barré have 120 talents instead.*] . . . Congregatae sunt autem familiae eorum et vestes et ministeria et argentum et aurum et iumenta et omnia quae habere poterant [nec poterat dinumerari facultas eorum *from Fab. 616; not in B354*]. Apostoli vero nihil omnino accipere voluerunt. [*At this point all versions seem awkward and probably corrupt. In Momb. the general suddenly addresses the king, who has not been present hitherto, and the return to the king (cf Ælfric, 70–72) is never mentioned. Other versions have the general returning to the king with the apostles at this point and reporting the events, without apparently waiting to hear their reply to the preceding question, though able to report it to the king. Ælfric either had a superior text or made sense for himself out of the confusion by giving the apostles' argument with the general in direct narrative first and then having them brought to the king and their story reported. The reply here is in the general's subsequent report in all versions.*] [*Passio*, Mombritius 1910, II.535.52–536.4:] Et quae eis offerebantur contempserunt dicentes: 'Non nobis licet aliquid possidere super terram, quia possessio nostra in caelis est, quae est aeterna, ubi immortalitas regnat. . . .' Quibus cum dicerem 'aliquantulum accipite, quia peregrini [pauperes et peregrini *Fab.*] estis', isti dixerunt: 'Non sumus pauperes quia divitias caelestes habemus. Sed si vis ut ad salutem animae tuae proficiat census, eroga eum debilibus, eroga tribulatis, eroga viduis et orphanis, eroga infirmantibus, libera debitores qui a creditoribus exiguntur et quod reddere possint non habent, eroga publice manum porrigentibus et omnibus qui his opibus indigent. Nos enim terreno penitus non egemus [et morientem hominem non sequuntur *from an earlier point, at Passio*, Mombritius 1910, II.535.55–6].'

70–85 After the general returns to the king with the apostles (not in Momb.), there is a confused sequence, omitted by Ælfric, in which the magi urge the king to force the apostles to worship his gods, the king proposes a debate but instead the magi offer to dispute with some *advocati* so that they can show their own power; the text continues (*Passio*, Mombritius 1910, II.536.15–25):

Tunc iussu regis et ducis omnes advocati praesto facti sunt. Isti sunt a duce admoniti ut quanta possent constantia haberent cum his magis contentionem. . . . Et cum in praesentia regis et ducis cunctorumque magi loquuti essent, omnis illa advocatio ita muta facta est, ut nec quod loqui non poterant indicarent. Et cum unius hore fere spatium transisset, dixerunt magi ad regem: 'Ut scia[s] [*Fab.*, *B354*] nos ex deorum numero esse, permittemus eos loqui quidem posse, sed ambulare non posse.' Quod cum fecissent, adiecerunt iterum dicentes regi: 'Ecce reddimus eis gressum, sed facimus eos apertis oculis non videre.' Cumque et hoc fecissent, expavit cor regis et ducis, dicentibus amicis eorum non debere contemni hos magos, ne et regi et duci hanc inferrent debilitatem in membris.

The sense of *unbesorge* (line 76) is uncertain. If *besorg* at App. B3.44 means 'dear, beloved, precious (to God)' the sense here might be that the men summoned by the king to be targets for the magi's powers must have been people who were dispensable to him, though the Latin legend seems to identify them as counsellors. Alternatively, the context might suggest that Ælfric was identifying them as healthy or whole before the magi's incapacitating tricks took effect, or possibly carefree.

86–109 A summary and free paraphrase of *Passio*, Mombritius 1910, II.536.32–537.18:

[536.32–8:] Convocavit autem dux omnem illam advocationem in domum suam et . . . dixit: '. . . Sciatis me invenisse homines qui vos muniant et doceant qualiter non solum vobis non praevaleant sed etiam a vobis superati discendat.' Tunc omnis illa multitudo advocatorum prostrata duci gratias agens coepit precibus agere ut dictum facto compleret. At ille produxit eis apostolos dei Simonem et Iudam. . . . [536.48–537.18:] 'Nos enim omnes homines de uno patre et de una matre nati sumus qui cum facti essent et positi in regione vivorum, suadente angelo invidiae praevaricati sunt in lege quam a suo conditore acceperant et servi facti eius cui suadenti obtemperaverunt. . . . Sic tamen exilio damnatis misericordiam suam Deus in parte constituit, ut si homo creatorem suum solum deum excoleret, inimicus ille angelus ei nocere non posset. Egit autem hic ipse pessimus homo ut a creatore suo recedens idola coleret, et elementa adoraret. . . . Hunc autem errorem in omnibus hic angelus princeps invidiae ideo nutriit ut ipse eis dominetur . . . Hac de causa fecit vos per magos suos quandiu voluit tacere et iterum fecit vos immobiles permanere. [*The reference to blessing seems to be Ælfric's.*] . . . Venite ad nos et promittite ab idolorum cultura discedere, et deum solum invisibilem colere et adorare, et cum haec feceritis, imponimus nostras manus super capita vestra et signum Christi facimus in frontibus vestris, et si non confutaveritis eos, credite nos fallere omnia quaecumque asserimus.' Tunc universi illi advocati . . . prostraverunt se apostolis [ad pedes apostolorum *B354*] dicentes: 'Vos facite ut non nobis possint linguae impedire officia, nec aliqua in membris nostris impedimenta inferre, et sit super nos ira dei si ultra nos idolis crediderimus.' Tunc oraverunt simul sancti apostoli . . . signati sunt in frontibus et abierunt. Ingressi autem cum duce ad regem, assunt magi volentes facere quae fecerunt et nulla poterant ratione praevalere.

110–33 Summarises *Passio*, Mombritius 1910, II.537.18–40: Unus autem ex advocatis nomine Zeus [*So Momb.; B354* Zeveus*; Fab. et al.* Zebeus] dixit: 'Audi domine rex ista stercora abiicienda sunt ex tuo regno et emundanda ne forte omnibus putredinem generent. Habent enim secum angelum humani generis inimicum, et ludificant de his hominibus quos ipse angelus malus poterat habere subiectos, qui non deo omnipotenti subiecti sed illos habent deos quos ipsi custodiunt. . . . Denique [apostoli] signum Dei sui in frontibus nostris suis digitis facientes . . . ecce in Dei nomine insultamus eis.' Tunc universi advocati insultant eisdem magis dicentes: 'Si potestis agite quae heri gessistis.' Illico irati magi multitudinem serpentium fecerunt. Tunc dixerunt omnes regi: 'Domine rex voca apostolos dei' et cursim miserunt ad apostolos dei. Et venientes apostoli impleverunt pallia sua serpentibus et miserunt in eosdem magos dicentes: [*All Latin versions agree that the apostles filled their own cloaks with the snakes and sent them back to the magi; Ælfric's notion that they found the snakes in the magi's cloaks perhaps reflects an unrecorded reading* invenerunt *for* impleverunt.] 'In nomine Domini nostri Iesu Christi non morte eos afficite sed morsibus eos attractantes. . . .' Statimque serpentes comedere coeperunt carnes eorum, et coeperunt hululare sicut lupi. Rex autem et omnes dicebant apostolis: 'Permittite eos ut moriantur ab eis.' At illi dixerunt: 'Nos missi sumus a morte ad vitam reducere, non a vita praecipitare ad mortem.' Tunc oratione facta dixerunt apostoli serpentibus: 'Recedite in nomine Domini nostri Iesu Christi ad loca vestra. Omne autem venenum quod infudistis istis magis auferte.' . . . Universi serpentes iterum morsibus edebant carnes eorum, ut venena sua traherent suggentes sanguinem eorum.

134–51 Corresponds fairly closely to *Passio*, Mombritius 1910, II.537.40–53: Cumque abiissent omnes serpentes, dixerunt apostoli magis: 'Audite sanctam scripturam o impii dicentem qui proximo suo parat foveam, ipse prior cadit in eam. [*Cf Prov 26.27:* qui fodit foveam incidet in eam.] Vos quidem parastis nobis mortem, nos autem rogavimus Dominum nostrum . . . ut vos a morte eriperet. Et qui per multos annos debuistis vulneribus his serpentinis affligi, tercio die transacto recuperata vobis sanitas renovabitur. Forsitan vel ab impietate vestra cessabitis, dum bonitatem dei circa vos exhuberare probaveritis. In istis autem tribus diebus ideo permittimus vobis dominari dolores, ut poeniteat vos erroris vestri.' Tunc apostoli Dei iusserunt eos . . . duci ad hospitia sua, et per triduum non manducare non bibere neque dormire illis possibile fuit [sed in his sola vociferatio doloribus extorta incessabilis extitit *from Fab. 625;*

also in B354, but not in Momb.]. Sed cum iam in eo essent ut simul pariter expirarent, venerunt apostoli ad eos et dixerunt: 'Non dignatur deus habere servitia coacta. Ideoque surgite sani habentes liberam facultatem convertendi de malo in bonum. . . .' Illi autem permanentes in perfidia sua, sicut a facie Mathei fugerant, sic ab his duobus apostolis fugientes . . . [*the magi proceed to stir up pagan priests elsewhere against the apostles*].

152–69 *Passio*, Mombritius 1910, II.538.1–17:

Apostoli autem a rege et duce rogati morabantur in Babylonia facientes mirabilia magna, illuminantes caecos, surdis reddentes auditum, gressum claudis, mundantes leprosos, fugantes daemonia ex obsessis corporibus. Habebant autem discipulos multos, ex quibus presbyteros, diaconos et clericos ecclesiasque ordinabant. Factum est autem ut unus ex diaconibus pateretur crimen incestus. . . . virum sanctum et castum diaconem Euphrosynen nomine impetebat. . . . Tunc ambo apostoli dixerunt: 'Quando natus est puer?' Responderunt 'heri'. . . . Dicunt eis apostoli dei: 'Perducite huc infantem et diaconem quem accusatis huc adducite.' Cumque in praesentia essent, dicunt apostoli ad infantem: 'In nomine Domini nostri Iesu Christi loquere et dic si iste diaconus praesumpsit hanc iniquitatem.' Infans autem absolutissimo sermone ait: 'diaconus iste vir sanctus et castus est, et nunquam inquinavit carnem suam.' Insistebant autem parentes ut de persona culpabili interrogarent. Qui dixerunt: 'Nos innocentes absolvere decet, nocentes prodere non decet.'

170–88 *Passio*, Mombritius 1910, II.538.18–38, but summarising the apostles' sermon:

Post haec autem contigit dum exercitum agerent ut amicus regis Nicanor nomine in ipso genu sagittam acciperet, quae de osse illius nulla poterat evelli ratione. Tunc beatus Simon apostolus Christi invocato nomine Iesu mox ut manum applicuit eam abstulit, statimque sanatus est ut nec signum vulneris remaneret. Item evenit ut duae tygres ferocissimae in singulis caveis clausae fugerent, et quidquid invenire poterant devorarent. [Omnis populus ad apostolos Dei confugit *Fab. 626; also in B354*.] Tunc sancti apostoli invocantes nomen Domini nostri Iesu Christi iusserunt ut sequerentur eos domum in qua manebant, et per triduum ibi manserunt et convocantes omnem populum dixerunt: 'Audite omnes filii . . . considerate feras quae nunquam mansuescere poterant; quoniam audito nomine Domini nostri Iesu Christi in agnos conversae sunt . . . Deum autem qui nos creavit ignoratis, qui dat nobis pluviam de caelo et producit nobis panem de terra et vinum et oleum de surculis lignum. Ut autem sciatis quia ipse est verus Deus, erunt vobis in testimonium tygres istae, ut ipsae vos ammoneant quodam modo ut non alterum colatis deum nisi Dominum nostrum Iesum Christum, in cuius nomine istae mansuetae factae sunt, quasi oves in medio vestri conversabuntur. . . .Nos autem oportet peragrare civitates universas et provincias, ut praedicatio evangelii Domini nostri Iesu Christi possit agnosci.'

189–212 Summarises the substance of *Passio*, Mombritius 1910, II.538.38–539.5: Flaebant autem populi rogantes eos ut non discederent, quibus petentibus uno anno et mensibus tribus remorati sunt [*so all versions, in contrast to Ælfric's fourteen months*], in quo amplius quadraginta millibus hominum baptizati sunt . . . videntes omnes infirmitates verbo curari, illuminari caecos, etiam mortuos suscitari. . . . Ordinaverunt ex civitate episcopum nomine Abdiam, qui cum ipsis venerat qui et ipse viderat oculis suis Dominum. Et repleta est civitas ecclesiis. . . . Circumierunt autem duodecim provincias persidis et civitates eorum, in quibus quae egerint et quae passi sint per annos tredecim [*so all versions*] longa narratione scripsit Craton. . . . Igitur magi Zaroes et Arfaxar facientes scelera pereuntates et dicentes se ex genere deorum semper a facie apostolorum fugientes, tandiu erant in quacumque civitate quandiu agnoscerent eos advenire. . . . Erant autem in civitate Suamnir [Suanir *in other versions*] septuaginta templorum pontifices [qui solebant singulas libras auri a rege consequi, quando solis epulas celebrabant *Fab.; not in B354*], quos hac locutione magi in apostolos incitaverunt: 'Venturi sunt duo hebrei deorum omnium inimici. At ubi docuerint deum alterum adorari debere, vos exclusi eritis a facultatibus vestris, et pro purgamento eritis abiecti. Alloquimini ergo populum ut mox cum urbem istam intraverint teneantur ad sacrificandum. Si consenserint pacem habebunt cum diis vestris; si vero contempserint, sciatis illos ipsos ad subversionem vestram ingressuros ad depredationem et mortem.'

213–34 Corresponds to *Passio*, Mombritius 1910, II.539.5–26, slightly abridged: Factum est autem ut cum peragrassent universas provincias venerunt ad Suamnir civitatem magnam. In quam cum ingressi fuissent et mansissent apud discipulum suum virorum nomine Sennen [*var.* Semnes]. Ecce circa horam primam venerunt omnes pontifices cum populo innumerabili clamantes ad Sennen: 'Produc ad nos inimicos deorum nostrorum, cum quibus si non sacrificaveris incendemus te et domum tuam cum ipsis.' Interea tenentur apostoli Dei et ducuntur ad templum solis. Quod ingredientes coeperunt clamare daemones per erguminos: 'Quid nobis et vobis apostoli Dei vivi, ut in ingressu vestro flammis exuramur?' Stabat autem in una aede templi ab oriente quadriga equorum fusilis ex auro, in qua sol radiabat. In alia autem stabat luna fusilis ex argento habens bigam boum fusilem similiter ex argento. Coeperunt ergo pontifices apostolis Dei vim facere cum populo ut adorarent eos. Simul et illi duo magi qui hanc ipsam violentiam excitarant. Tunc dixit Iudas ad Simonem: 'Frater Simon, video Dominum Iesum Christum vocantem nos.' Similiter et Simon respondit: 'Diu est quod intueor aspectum Domini in medio angelorum . . . .' Apparuit eis angelus Domini dicens: 'Confortamini, et unum ex duobus eligite: aut istorum repentinum interitum, aut ad palmam martyrii vestri cum fiducia boni certaminis praeparate.' Cui respondentes dixerunt: 'Oranda est misericordia Domini nostri Iesu Christi, ut et istis propitietur et nos adiuvet ut possimus pertingere ad coronam.' Hoc autem soli apostoli videntes et audientes. . . .

Neither the legend nor Ælfric explain how this exchange came to be recorded.

235–59 *Passio*, Mombritius 1910, II.539.27–44:

Compellebantur a pontificibus adorare simulacra solis et lunae. Quibus apostoli dixerunt: 'Facite fieri silentium, ut demus responsum omni populo. . . . Audite omnes et videte. Solem nos scimus esse servum Dei, et lunam similiter praecepto sui creatoris esse subiectam, in caeli tamen firmamento consistentes. . . . Ut sciatis autem quia simulachra eorum non sole sed daemoniis plena sunt, iubemus nunc huic daemonio quod in simulacris solis et lunae vos ludificat [ut egrediatur ex eis, et ipsi ea comminuat *B354*].' Et stupentibus dixit Simon ad simulacrum solis: 'Praecipio tibi ludificator huius populi daemon pessime, exi de simulacro solis et comminue ipsum et quadrigam eius.' Similiter cum hoc Iudas ad simulacrum lunae dixisset, visi sunt ab omni populo duo ethiopes nigri nudi horribili habitu egressi, et confringentes ea hululatum dirae vocis emiserunt. Tunc omnes pontifices irruentes in apostolos Christi interfecerunt eos. Erant autem gaudentes et alacres, gratias deo agentes quia digni habiti sunt pro nomine Domini pati. Passi sunt autem quinto calendas novembres. Simul quoque passus est Sennes hospes eorum, quoniam idolis sacrificare contempsit. Ipsa autem hora cum nimia fuisset caeli serenitas fulgora steterunt nimia ita ut trifarium templum ipsum inciderent a summo tecti fastigio usque ad ultimum fundamentum. Illi autem magi Zaroes et Arfaxar ictu corruscationis adusti in carbones conversi sunt.

260–74 *Passio*, Mombritius 1910, II.539.44–53:

Post menses autem tres misit rex et confiscavit omnes pontifices; corpora autem apostolorum cum ingenti honore ad suam transtulit civitatem, in qua instruxit basilicam in octogeno ciclo [octo *Fab.*, *B354*] angulorum, ut octogenorum pedum [octies octogenos pedes *Fab.*] numerus numeretur per gyrum. In altum autem pedum centum viginti. Omnia ex quadratis marmoribus simmaticis extruxit. Cameram vero laminis aureis affixit. In medio autem octogeno sarcophagum ex argento puro instituit. Per tres autem annos fabricam incessanter exercuit et consumans eam die natalis eorum, id est quinto calendas novembres, meruit dedicare loca eorum. In quo loco beneficia consequuntur qui credentes in Dominum Iesum Christum illuc meruerunt pervenire.

275–82 *Passio*, Mombritius 1910, II.539.53–8:

Scripsit autem gesta apostolorum Abdias episcopus Babylonis, qui ab ipsis apostolis ordinatus, hebreo sermone, quae omnia a discipulo eiusdem

Abdiae Europio [Eutropio *Fab.*, *B354*] nomine in grecum translata sunt, quae universa nihilominus ab Aphricano in decem librorum volumina latino sunt translata sermone. Ex quibus decem libris ista descripsimus, initia de primo et ultima de decimo, agentes deo gratias, qui vivit et regnat in secula saeculorum. Amen.

34 ST MARTIN

St Martin is prominent in Anglo-Saxon hagiography, one of the few non-Biblical saints listed by the Old English verse *Menologium* among those celebrated by all the English and figuring in both the Vercelli and Blickling collections of homilies. A life of him was probably an obligatory feature of the Catholic Homilies therefore. Its sustained use of alliterative prose suggests that it was one of the last to be written in the Series; even so, the extensive abbreviation of the voluminous materials available on St Martin which the homiletic form required evidently led to pressure soon afterwards for the second and much longer version which Ælfric wrote for his Lives of Saints collection (LS 31).

For his narrative of the life and death of Martin Ælfric drew on a number of overlapping sources, probably already collected together, as Zettel has shown,[1] in the copy of the Cotton-Corpus legendary which he used. For the life he used the standard *Vita* by Sulpicius Severus (also used by the author of the Blickling/Vercelli life), but also included a few episodes which are not in the *Vita* but occur in the *Dialogues* of Sulpicius. For the saint's death he turned to the Epistle to Bassula by Sulpicius, and for the final passage on the saint's burial he used an excerpt from the *Historia Francorum* of Gregory of Tours. But he also had available to him a summary of the life and death of St Martin by Alcuin, based on the writings of Sulpicius and Gregory of Tours, and in matters of detail, phrasing and arrangement Ælfric is often closer to Alcuin. He clearly found Alcuin's method of summary a convenient guide for his own condensation of the long narrative by Sulpicius, as well as finding occasional inspiration in his language, and used his work alongside the others. Zettel questions, indeed, whether Ælfric used the *Dialogues* at all for this piece, but he certainly knew them when he wrote his later life of Martin, and there is at least one detail which seems to come from the *Dialogues* rather than Alcuin's version.

Ælfric's technique, rather like that used in his lives of St Cuthbert and St Benedict, was to abridge by summarising most of the incident and omitting much of the contextual detail; in particular the background of ecclesiastical

[1] Zettel 1979, pp. 106–10, 247–9, 268–70; see also Zettel 1982, pp. 24–7. Ælfric's use of the texts by Sulpicius and Gregory of Tours was identified by Förster (1892, pp. 41–2). There is an excellent detailed account of Ælfric's treatment of his sources in his lives of St Martin by Fred Biggs, 'Ælfric as Historian: his Use of Alcuin's *Laudationes* and Sulpicius' *Dialogues* in his Two Lives of Martin', in Szarmach 1996, pp. 289–315.

history (the exile of Hilarius by Arians, their oppression of Martin, his conflict with other bishops and clergy, the gradual evangelisation of areas surrounding Tours) mostly disappears, though some aspects, such as the qualities of the monastic life which Martin sustained while bishop of Tours, are given fuller treatment. What Ælfric produces is an account of Martin's virtues and miracles rather than a sequential history. At the same time, he renders his sources very freely, even loosely, and imports a range of colourful language and emotive comments that is not characteristic of the two preceding homilies, but seems to be associated with the use of alliterative prose (see 53–4, 61, 191, 308 for example). Much of this colour was eliminated when he later wrote a fresh and longer version of the life, as LS 31, where he drew on the same sources (and one or two more) but translated them more closely and fully. The later version is also more faithful to the sources, in several places where Ælfric had, deliberately or not, varied from the strict sense of Sulpicius in this version (see 48, 102–3, 185–6 and notes).

The homily survives in only two copies apart from MS K but not necessarily because of any preference, by Ælfric or others, for the LS version. The inclusion of LS 31 in MS B may be a sign of such preference, but the compilers of MSS E (section b) and f^{k} had access to the Lives collection and yet chose the CH II homily for St Martin; MSS such as D, L and T which might have been expected to include this homily do not have LS 31 either.

Sources and Notes

The following texts are cited below:

1. Alcuin, *Vita Sancti Martini Turonensis*, PL 101, cols. 657–64.
2. Gregory of Tours, *Historia Francorum*, ed. B. Krusch and W. Levison, MGH, Scriptores rerum Merovingicarum, 1.1 (Berlin, 1937–51).
3. Sulpicius Severus, *Dialogi*, ed. K. Halm, CSEL 1 (Vienna, 1866), pp. 152–216.
4. Sulpicius Severus, *Epistula Tertia* (*Epistula ad Bassulam*), ed. K. Halm, CSEL 1 (Vienna, 1866), pp. 146–51.
5. Sulpicius Severus, *Vita Sancti Martini*, ed. K. Halm, CSEL 1 (Vienna, 1866), pp. 109–37.

1–18 Follows Sulpicius, *Vita*, c. 2:

> [111.26–9] Martinus Sabaria Pannoniarum oppido oriundus fuit, sed intra Italiam Ticini altus est, parentibus secundum saeculi dignitatem non infimis, gentilibus tamen. Pater eius miles primum, post tribunus militum fuit. . . . [112.2–13] Cum esset annorum decem, invitis parentibus ad ecclesiam confugit seque catechumenum fieri postulavit. Mox mirum in modum totus in Dei opere conversus, cum esset annorum duodecim, eremum concupivit. . . . Sed cum edictum esset a regibus ut veteranorum

filii ad militiam scriberentur, prodente patre qui felicibus eius actibus invidebat, cum esset annorum quindecim, captus et catenatus sacramentis militaribus inplicatus est, uno tantum servo comite contentus, cui tamen versa vice dominus serviebat.

The distinction between being *gecristnod* (line 10) and being *gefullod* (line 26) reflects one made several times by Sulpicius but not discussed by Ælfric, indeed evaded. According to Sulpicius, Martin sought to be made a catechumen at this point, and apparently was, but did not receive baptism until eight years later. Ælfric says that Martin sought baptism, *fulluht*, and was *gecristnod*, which he evidently distinguishes from being *gefullod*. The word *gecristnod* refers in his time to the ritual of preparation for baptism, but it is clear that this immediately preceded baptism proper at that period, and the practice of a long delay between *cristnung* or becoming a catechumen and baptism had ceased, or at least ceased to be approved (see Wulfstan homilies VIIIa, b and c, especialy VIIIb line 38 and VIIIc lines 69–71). Ælfric does not mention *cristnung* when he discusses baptism in CH II.3 but takes infant baptism for granted. Here too after this first instance he avoids reference to *cristnung* and the status of catechumen, and seems to allow it no value. Thus when Christ refers to Martin in a vision as *adhuc catechumen* Ælfric renders it *ungefullod gyt*, 'still unbaptised' (line 42). Subsequently the catechumen who dies before baptism is simply described as a *hæðen wer* who *on fulluhte underfangen næs* (lines 95–6), and is not only taken to hell, as in Sulpicius, but consigned to torment. (In the later version, LS 31, Ælfric explains that the man is *gecristnod* and had sought instruction in the faith from Martin, but retains the reference to *witnungum* at 231.) The statement later that Tetradius became first a catechumen and then baptized is omitted by Ælfric (lines 198–203). It is pleasing to note that the anonymous author of the Vercelli version of the story does pause to explain that *gecristnod* means the first stage of baptism (Vercelli 18.17), but the explanation has been badly mangled in the other two manuscripts, including Blickling, and the force of Christ's *adhuc catechumen* is misunderstood.

19–26 From Sulpicius, *Vita*, c. 2:

[111.29–31] Ipse, armatam militiam in adulescentia secutus, inter scolares alas sub rege Constantio [*var.* Constantino], deinde sub Iuliano Caesare militavit . . . [112.16–25] Integer tamen ab iis vitiis quibus illud hominum genus implicari solet. Multa illius circa commilitones benignitas, mira caritas, patientia vero atque humilitas . . . ut iam illo tempore non miles sed monachus putaretur. Pro quibus rebus ita sibi omnes commilitones devinxerat ut eum miro adfectu venerarentur. Necdum tamen regeneratus in Christo, agebat quendam bonis operibus baptismi candidatum: adsistere scilicet laborantibus, opem ferre miseris, alere egentes, vestire nudos.

At line 19 the manuscript reading *constantium* should perhaps have been allowed to stand in the Old English text, as in the standard Latin texts, rather than emending to the variant *constantinum*, but the latter does appear in the Latin tradition and seems to characterise the English tradition, being the reading of both Ælfric's later version and the Vercelli/Blickling version.

27–44 Sulpicius, *Vita*, c. 3 (113.1–114.1):

> Quodam itaque tempore, cum iam nihil praeter arma et simplicem militiae vestem haberet, media hieme quae solito asperior inhorruerat . . . obvium habet in porta Ambianensium civitatis pauperem nudum. Qui cum praetereuntes ut sui misererentur oraret omnesque miserum praeterirent, intellexit vir Deo plenus sibi illum . . . reservari. . . . Nihil praeter chlamydem, qua indutus erat, habebat; iam enim reliqua in opus simile consumpserat. Arrepto itaque ferro quo accinctus erat, mediam dividit partemque eius pauperi tribuit, reliqua rursus induitur. Interea de circumstantibus ridere nonnulli, quia deformis esse truncatus habitu videretur; multi tamen . . . altius gemere, quod nihil simile fecissent, cum utique plus habentes vestire pauperem sine sua nuditate potuissent. Nocte igitur insecuta, cum se sopori dedisset, vidit Christum chlamydis suae, qua pauperem texerat, parte vestitum. Intueri diligentissime Dominum vestemque, quam dederat, iubetur agnoscere. Mox ad angelorum circumstantium multitudinem audit Iesum clara voce dicentem: 'Martinus adhuc catechumenus hac me veste contexit.' . . . Quo viso, vir beatissimus non in gloriam est elatus humanam, sed bonitatem Dei in suo opere cognoscens, cum esset annorum duodeviginti, ad baptismum convolavit. [*Martin decides to continue in the army for two more years.*]

45–58 Sulpicius, *Vita*, c. 4 (114.7–29):

> Interea inruentibus intra Gallias barbaris, Iulianus Caesar, coacto in unum exercitu . . . donativum coepit erogare militibus, et, ut est consuetudinis, singuli citabantur donec ad Martinum ventum est. . . . 'Hactenus, inquit ad Caesarem, militavi tibi; patere ut nunc militem Deo. Donativum tuum pugnaturus accipiat; Christi ego miles sum; pugnare mihi non licet.' Tum vero adversus hanc vocem tyrannus infremuit, dicens eum metu pugnae, quae postero die erat futura, non religionis gratia detractare militiam. At Martinus intrepidus . . . 'crastina die ante aciem inermis adstabo et in nomine Domini Iesu, signo crucis, non clipeo protectus aut galea, hostium cuneos penetrabo securus.' Retrudi ergo in custodiam iubetur, facturus fidem dictis, ut inermis barbaris obiceretur. Postero die hostes legatos de pace miserunt, sua omnia seque dedentes. . . . Et quamvis pius Dominus servare militem suum licet inter hostium gladios et tela potuisset, tamen, ne vel aliorum mortibus sancti violarentur obtutus, exemit pugnae necessitatem.

The red shield, heavy helm and hard mail-shirt of Ælfric's version correspond simply to Latin *clipeus* 'shield' and *galea* 'helmet.

59–74 Sulpicius, *Vita*, c. 5:

[115.3–5] Exinde, relicta militia, sanctum Hilarium Pictavae episcopum civitatis, cuius tunc in Dei rebus spectata et cognita fides habebatur, expetiit et aliquamdiu apud eum commoratus est. [*Hilarius tries to involve him in divine service, as deacon or priest, but Martin resists.*] [115.12–116.5] Nec multo post admonitus per soporem ut patriam parentesque, quos adhuc gentilitas detinebat, religiosa sollicitudine visitaret, . . . profectus est multis ab eo obstrictus precibus et lacrimis ut rediret. . . . Primum inter Alpes devia secutus incidit in latrones. Cumque unus securi elevata in caput eius librasset ictum, ferientis dexteram sustinuit alter; vinctis tamen post tergum manibus, uni adservandus et spoliandus traditur. Qui cum eum ad remotiora duxisset, percontari ab eo coepit quisnam esset. Respondit Christianum se esse. Quaerebat etiam ab eo an timeret. Tum vero constantissime profitetur numquam se tam fuisse securum. . . . Ingressusque evangelicam disputationem verbum Dei latroni praedicabat. . . . Latro credidit prosecutusque Martinum viae reddidit. . . . Idemque postea religiosam agens vitam visus est.

The image of Hilarius shining like a star in true learning (line 61) seems to be from Alcuin (*Vita*, PL 101, 659C):

Quasi Lucifer in coelo stellis clarior caeteris clarescit, ita ille sanctus vir in Ecclesia Christi, omnibus famae magnitudine, et sanctitate vitae, et doctrinarum veritate sanctarum excellentior effulsit.

The axe-blow to Martin's head is warded off in the *Vita*, but seems to strike home in the Old English.

74–85 Sulpicius, *Vita*, c. 6 (116.7–16):

Igitur Martinus inde progressus cum Mediolanum praeterisset, diabolus in itinere, humana specie adsumpta, se ei obvium tulit, quo tenderet quaerens. . . . Ait ad eum: 'Quocumque ieris vel quaecumque temptaveris, diabolus tibi adversabitur.' Tunc ei prophetica voce respondens: 'Dominus mihi, inquit, adiutor est; non timebo quid faciat mihi homo' (Ps 117.6). Statimque de conspectu eius inimicus evanuit. Itaque . . . matrem a gentilitatis absolvit errore, patre in malis perseverante; plures tamen suo salvavit exemplo.

Ælfric adds the striking comment that Martin's failure to convert his own father shows us that many people may go to heaven even though their relatives are damned; it is difficult to imagine why the point needed making.

86–109 A summary account of events in Sulpicius, *Vita*, cc. 6–8:

[116.17–21] Dehinc cum haeresis Arriana per totum orbem et maxime intra Illyricum pullulasset, cum adversus perfidiam sacerdotum solus paene acerrime repugnaret, multisque suppliciis esset adfectus—nam et publice virgis caesus est . . . Italiam repetens. [*Martin returns to Italy from his homeland and learns that Hilary has been exiled by the Arians; he establishes a monastery at Milan, but he too is driven into exile.*] [117.1–118.21] Hic aliquamdiu radicibus vixit herbarum. Quo tempore helleborum, venenatum, ut ferunt, gramen, in cibum sumpsit. Sed cum vim veneni in se grassantis vicina iam morte sensisset, imminens periculum oratione repulit statimque omnis dolor fugatus est. . . . Cum iam Hilarius praeterisset, ita eum est vestigiis prosecutus; cumque ab eo gratissime fuisset susceptus, haut longe sibi ab oppido monasterium conlocavit. Quo tempore se ei quidam catechumenus iunxit, cupiens sanctissimi viri institui disciplinis. Paucisque interpositis diebus, languore correptus vi febrium laborabat. Ac tum Martinus forte discesserat. Et cum per triduum defuisset, regressus exanime corpus invenit: ita subita mors fuerat, ut absque baptismate humanis rebus excederet. . . . Martinus flens et eiulans accurrit . . . super exanimata defuncti fratris membra prosternitur. Et cum aliquamdiu orationi incubuisset . . . vixque duarum fere horarum spatium intercesserat, videt defunctum paulatim membris omnibus commoveri. . . . Ita redditus vitae, statim baptismum consecutus, plures postea vixit annos . . . Idem tamen referre erat solitus se corpore exutum ad tribunal iudicis ductum, deputandumque obscuris locis et vulgaribus turbis tristem excepisse sententiam; tum per duos angelos iudici fuisse suggestum, hunc esse pro quo Martinus oraret; ita per eosdem angelos se iussum reduci, et Martino redditum. . . . Nec multo post . . . clamore et luctu turbae plangentis excipitur . . . indicatur unum ex familia servulum laqueo sibi vitam extorsisse. . . . ingreditur . . . oravit, mox vivescente vultu, marcescentibus oculis in ora illius defunctus erigitur.

In his account of the final miracle, Ælfric stresses his opposition to suicide with the details *ungesceadwis* and *unwurðne*; for *fotum span* cf CH II.2.121–2.

110–32 Sulpicius, *Vita*, cc. 9–10:

[118.25–119.5] Sub idem fere tempus, ad episcopatum Turonicae ecclesiae petebatur; sed cum erui monasterio suo non facile posset, Rusticius quidam, unus e civibus, uxoris languore simulato ad genua illius provolutus ut egrederetur obtinuit. Ita, dispositis iam in itinere civium turbis, sub quadam custodia ad civitatem usque deducitur. . . . Una omnium voluntas, eadem vota eademque sententia: Martinum episcopatus esse dignissimum; felicem fore tali ecclesiam sacerdote. [*The Vita describes the opposition of other bishops; Ælfric simply reports his ordination.*] [119.26–120.27] Iam vero, sumpto episcopatu . . . idem constantissime perseverabat qui prius fuerat. Eadem in corde eius humilitas, eadem in vestitu eius vilitas erat; atque ita, plenus auctoritatis et gratiae, inplebat episcopi dignitatem, ut non tamen propositum monachi virtutemque desereret. . . . Duobus fere extra civitatem milibus monasterium sibi statuit. . . . Discipuli fere octoginta erant, qui ad exemplum beati magistri instituebantur. Nemo ibi quicquam proprium habebat, omnia in medium conferebantur. Non emere aut vendere, ut plerisque monachis moris est, quicquam licebat; ars ibi, exceptis scriptoribus, nulla habebatur, cui tamen operi minor aetas deputabatur; maiores orationi vacabant. Rarus cuiquam

> extra cellulam suam egressus, nisi cum ad locum orationis conveniebant. Cibum una omnes post horam ieiunii accipiebant. Vinum nemo noverat, nisi quem infirmitas coegisset. Plerique camelorum saetis vestiebantur: mollior ibi habitus pro crimine erat. . . . Multi inter eos nobiles habebantur, qui longe aliter educati . . . pluresque ex eis postea episcopos vidimus. Quae enim esset civitas aut ecclesia, quae non sibi de Martini monasterio cuperet sacerdotem?

Note Ælfric's reference to monastic rule at 124–5. The one detail which he omits from this glowing tribute to monasticism is the sentence *Rarus* . . . which reveals that the monks had separate cells, contrary to Anglo-Saxon practice.

133–46 Sulpicius, *Vita*, c. 11 (121.2–23):

> Erat haud longe ab oppido proximus monasterio locus quem falsa hominum opinio velut consepultis ibi martyribus sacraverat; nam et altare ibi a superioribus episcopis constitutum habebatur. Sed Martinus . . . ab his qui maiores natu erant presbyteris vel clericis flagitabat nomen sibi martyris, tempus passionis ostendi: grandi se scrupulo permoveri, quod nihil certi constans sibi maiorum memoria tradidisset. . . . Quodam die paucis secum adhibitis fratribus ad locum pergit. Dehinc super sepulchrum ipsum adstans oravit ad Dominum, ut quis esset vel cuius meriti esset sepultus ostenderet. Tum conversus ad laevam videt prope adsistere umbram sordidam, trucem; . . . nomen edicit, de crimine confitetur: latronem se fuisse, ob scelera percussum . . . sibi nihil cum martyribus esse commune, cum illos gloria, se poena retineret. . . . Tum Martinus . . . iussit ex eo loco altare . . . submoveri atque ita populum superstitionis illius absolvit errore.

146–54 Ælfric inserts here two episodes not in the *Vita*. They occur in Sulpicius's *Dialogues*, at II.4 and III.2 respectively, but probably come, as Zettel says, from Alcuin, who summarises them together (*Vita*, PL 101, 660AB):

> Tertium ab eodem sancto viro, in Carnoteno oppido, cuiusdam mulieris flent[is] filium sola oratione in conspectu populi resuscitavit. Quo miraculo viso, plurimi ex populo crediderunt Christo. Succedente itidem tempore, in eodem oppido, mutam ab infantia puellam benedicti olei inunctione sanavit.

Ælfric's *fram cildhade* accords with Alcuin's *de infantia* rather than the *ab utero* of Sulpicius.

154–60 Ælfric returns to Sulpicius's *Vita*, though failing to explain that Martin spellbound the heathens not in a gratuitous display of power but in the mistaken belief that they were engaging in devil-worship rather than a funeral (Sulpicius, *Vita*, c. 12, 121.24–122.12):

> Accidit autem insequenti tempore, dum iter ageret, ut gentilis cuiusdam corpus, quod ad sepulchrum cum superstitioso funere deferebatur, obvium haberet; . . . levato ergo in adversos signo crucis, imperat turbae non moveri loco onusque deponere. Hic vero . . . videres miseros primum velut

saxa riguisse. Dein, cum promovere se summo conamine niterentur, ultra accedere non valentes ridiculam in vertiginem rotabantur, donec victi corporis onus ponunt. . . . Elevata rursum manu dat eis abeundi et tollendi corporis potestatem.

But the reference to their noise, lines 155–6, is perhaps due to Alcuin's brief summary, *Vita*, PL 101, 660C:

Nam turbam paganorum ritu tumultuantem in obsequio cuiusdam corporis, verbo orationis, uno ligavit in loco; iterumque resolvens suis permisit dominari vestigiis.

161–77 Sulpicius, *Vita*, c. 13 (122.15–123.21):

Item cum in vico quodam templum antiquissimum diruisset et arborem pinum, quae fano erat proxima, esset adgressus excidere, tum vero antistes loci illius ceteraque gentilium turba coepit obsistere. Et cum idem illi, dum templum evertitur, imperante Domino quievissent, succidi arborem non patiebantur. . . . arborem illam succidi oportere, quia esset daemoni dedicata. Tum unus ex illis, qui erat audacior ceteris: 'si habes, inquit, aliquam de Deo tuo . . . fiduciam, nosmet ipsi succidemus hanc arborem, tu ruentem excipe; et si tecum est tuus . . . Dominus, evades.' Tum ille, intrepide confisus in Domino, facturum se pollicetur. . . . Itaque, cum unam in partem pinus illa esset adclinis, ut non esset dubium quam in partem succisa corrueret, eo loci vinctus statuitur pro arbitrio rusticorum, quo arborem esse casuram nemo dubitabat. Succidere igitur ipsi suam pinum cum ingenti gaudio laetitiaque coeperunt. . . . At ille confisus in Domino, intrepidus opperiens, cum iam fragorem sui pinus concidens edidisset, iam cadenti, iam super se ruenti, elevata obviam manu, signum salutis opponit. Tum vero . . . diversam in partem ruit, adeo ut rusticos, qui tuto in loco steterant, paene prostraverit. . . . Nemo fere ex inmani illa multitudine gentilium fuit, qui non impositione manus desiderata Dominum Iesum, relicto impietatis errore, crediderit.

178–89 Mainly from Sulpicius's *Vita*, c. 14, but Ælfric's version of the second incident is strikingly different: in the *Vita*, Martin cannot destroy the temple because the heathens resist, and the angels simply keep them at bay while he demolishes it, whereas Ælfric says Martin cannot destroy the temple because of its strong construction, and the angels do the work for him (Sulpicius, *Vita*, c. 14, 123.28–124.17):

Cum . . . fano antiquissimo et celeberrimo ignem inmisisset, in proximam . . . domum agente vento flammarum globi ferebantur. Quod ubi Martinus advertit, rapido cursu tectum domus scandit, obvium se advenientibus flammis inferens. Tum vero . . . cerneres contra vim venti ignem retorqueri, ut compugnantium inter se elementorum quidam conflictus videretur. . . . Cum itidem templum . . . voluisset evertere, restitit ei multitudo gentilium. . . . Itaque . . . precabatur ad Dominum ut, quia

> templum illud evertere humana manus non potuisset, virtus illud divina dirueret. Tum subito ei duo angeli hastati atque scutati . . . se obtulerunt . . . ne quis dum templum dirueretur, obsisteret; rediret ergo et opus coeptum devotus impleret.

Some of the phrasing seems to come from Alcuin's summary of the incidents (*Vita*, PL 101, 660C; cf esp. *unscyldigum, mid gedwylde deoflum gehalgod, an eald hus*):

> Seipsum in tecto cuiusdam domus flammis opposuit, ne innocua laederet ignis tecta, qui fanum incendit idololatriae. Aliud quoque templum antiquo errore daemonibus dedicatum, dum manu non potuit humana, angelico fultus auxilio subvertit.

189–96 The substance is in Sulpicius's *Vita*, c. 15, but Ælfric seems to have relied on Alcuin, *Vita*, PL 101, 660D:

> Nec non alio loco gentilium sacra subvertens, a quodam pagano gladio appetitus, ille nudum ferientis ictui collum opposuit; sed impius retro cadens, suam intelligens impietatem, veniam postulavit a sancto; alteroque librante ictum in sanctum caput, ferrum effugit de manibus.

Neither source has anything as colourful as *scinendan brande* (line 191).

196–211 Ælfric seems to have drawn on Alcuin, *Vita*, PL 101, 660D-1A:

> Treveris paralyticam puellam, totisque resolutam membris, sacra benedicti olei infusione, astante populo, pristinae reddidit sanitati. Tetradii proconsularis viri servum manus impositione a daemonio liberavit. Unde et ille Tetradius cum tota domo sua ad Christianam conversus est professionem. Cuiusdam quoque patrisfamilias puerum a daemone arreptum atrocissimo, digitos in os mittens, spiritum malignum per pudenda patientis exire compulit.

But he filled out the first and third miracles with a little more detail from the much longer account in Sulpicius's *Vita*, cc. 16 and 17:

> [125.15–18] Puella quaedam dira paralysis aegritudine tenebatur, ita ut iam per multum tempus nullo ad humanos usus corporis officio fungeretur; omni ex parte praemortua vix tenui spiritu palpitabat. . . . [126.24–127.11] Ingressus patris familias cuiusdam domum . . . saevire dentibus miser coepit . . . sed cum dentibus fremeret hiantique ore morsum minaretur, digitos ei Martinus in os intulit: 'Si habes, inquit, aliquid potestatis, hos devora.' Tum vero, ac si candens ferrum faucibus accepisset, longe reductis dentibus digitos beati viri vitabat attingere; et . . . foeda relinquens vestigia fluxu ventris egestus est.

211–28 Corresponding to parts of Sulpicius's *Vita*, cc. 18–21, but drawn entirely from Alcuin, *Vita*, PL 101, 661AB (and thus omitting Sulpicius's account of Martin's relationship with emperors and usurpers in c. 20):

> Leprosum in porta Parisiacae civitatis a deformitate sui corporis solo salvavit osculo; sed et fimbrias vestimenti eius, et fila cilicii multos sanare morbos compertum est. Filia Arborii praefecti per impositionem epistolae sancti

Martini a gravissimis liberata est febribus. . . . Idem quoque sanctus Martinus cadens per gradus, graviter pene totus attritus membris, nocte ab angelo ad integram recreatus est sanitatem: saepiusque angelicis visitationibus et familiari locutione fruebatur. Quodam vero die beatissimae Genitricis Dei et Domini nostri Iesu Christi, et sanctorum apostolorum Petri et Pauli; nec non sanctarum virginum Theclae et Agnetis visitatione vir Dei honoratus et confortatus est. Nam daemonum phantasmata, et in diversis figuris horribiles aspectus nihil metuens, nec ullis eorum fallaciis illudi potuit.

229–38 Ælfric omits various delusions of the devil, but returns to Sulpicius's *Vita*, c. 24 for this one (134.2–20):

Quodam enim die . . . veste etiam regia indutus, diademate ex gemmis auroque redimitus . . . oranti in cellula adstitit. . . . 'Agnosce, inquit, Martine quem cernis? Christus ego sum.' . . . 'Non se, inquit, Iesus Dominus purpuratum nec diademate renidentem venturum esse praedixit; ego Christum, nisi in eo habitu formaque qua passus est . . . venisse non credam.' Ad hanc ille vocem statim ut fumus evanuit et cellulam tanto foetore conplevit ut indubia indicia relinqueret diabolum se fuisse.

239–68 Sulpicius now ends with a personal conclusion about his own knowledge of the saint and his character, but Ælfric adds several more incidents which come ultimately from various points in the Dialogues but are summarised at this point by Alcuin (*Vita*, PL 101, 661BCD):

Spiritu vero prophetarum ita claruit, ut multis multa praedixerit futura. . . . Et eodem beato viro celebrante sanctum mysterium ad altare, globus igneus subito de vertice fulsit illius. Evantius quidam aegrotus, properante ad se beato viro, prius sanitatem recepit, quam sanctus Martinus domum intraret. In eadem quoque domo puerum a serpente percussum, sanctorum tactu digitorum a periculo mortis eruit. Nam tantae fuit vir Dei patientiae, ut convicia non doluerit, opprobria non senserit. . . . Nemini adulando blandiebatur; principi nulli veritatis verba tacuit, ad nota semper orationum subsidia recurrens. Unde si quid ei potestas renuit saecularis, mox divina praestitit pietas. Quaedam puella [*but var.* persona] daemoniaco arrepta spiritu, stramine, ubi sanctus Martinus sedebat, a potestate erepta est inimica. Non solum homines, sed etiam animalia a daemonum liberans potestate, et mansueta in suum redire gregem mandavit. Etiam fuit tantae misericordiae, ut canibus sequentibus lepusculum imperaverit stare; et miseram bestiolam a praesenti morte eripuit. . . . Mulier a sanguinis fluxu vestimentorum illius tactu sanata est.

Alcuin is very close to Ælfric's version and would seem to be his sole source but for a few details. The fiery ball is in Alcuin but not the detail of it drawing up Martin's hair (lines 242–3), and this is in Sulpicius's *Dialogues*, II.2 (181.28–182.2):

Globum ignis de capite illius vidimus emicare, ita ut in sublime contendens longum admodum crinem flamma produceret.

The *wod man* of 256 is a *puella* in Alcuin but a madman (*energumeno*) in the *Dialogues*, II.8 (190.22), although the latter account is otherwise so unlike Ælfric's that it is difficult to believe he was using it (the episode is not in LS 31) and Ælfric may have seen the variant *persona* in his copy. And the *sona hal* of 266 could reflect the *sub momento temporis fuisse sanatum* of *Dialogues*, III.9 (207.8–9). The phrase *þurh þæs hælendes gife* at 245 is not from either source, but a similar addition comes at 89–90.

270–95 From Sulpicius, *Epistula* III.6–13:

> [147.14–148.17] Martinus igitur obitum suum longe ante praesciit dixitque fratribus dissolutionem sui corporis inminere. Interea causa extitit qua Condacensem dioecesim visitaret. Nam, clericis inter se ecclesiae illius discordantibus, pacem cupiens reformare. . . . Ita profectus cum suo illo . . . discipulorum . . . comitatu, mergos in flumine conspicatur piscium praedam sequi et rapacem ingluviem adsiduis urguere capturis. 'Forma, inquit, haec daemonum est: insidiantur incautis, capiunt nescientes, captos devorant. . . .' Imperat deinde potenti verbo ut eum cui innatabant gurgitem relinquentes aridas peterent desertasque regiones. . . . Ita grege facto, omnes in unum illae volucres congregatae, relicto flumine montes silvasque petierunt. . . . Aliquandiu ergo in vico illo vel in ecclesia ad quam ierat commoratus, pace inter clericos restituta cum iam regredi ad monasterium cogitaret, viribus corporis coepit repente destitui convocatisque fratribus indicat se iam resolvi. Tunc vero maeror et luctus omnium et vox una plangentium: 'Cur nos, pater deseris? Aut cui nos desolatos relinquis? Invadent gregem tuum lupi rapaces: quis nos a morsibus eorum . . . prohibebit? Scimus quidem desiderare te Christum, sed salva tibi sunt tua praemia nec dilata minuentur; nostri potius miserere, quos deseris.' Tunc ille . . . conversus ad Dominum . . . respondit: 'Domine, si adhuc populo tuo sum necessarius, non recuso laborem; fiat voluntas tua . . . [148.24] nec fatiscentem causabor aetatem.'

296–313 Mainly from Sulpicius, *Epistula* III.14–17 (149.4–150.4):

> Itaque cum iam per aliquot dies vi febrium teneretur, non tamen ab opere Dei cessabat; pernoctans in orationibus et vigiliis . . . nobili illo strato suo in cinere et cilicio recubans. . . . Oculis tamen ac manibus in caelum semper intentis, invictum ab oratione spiritum non relaxabat. . . . Diabolum vidit prope adsistere. 'Quid hic, inquit, adstas, cruenta bestia? Nihil in me, funeste, reperies. Abrahae me sinus recipit.' Cum hac ergo voce spiritum caelo reddidit. Testatique nobis sunt qui ibidem fuerunt vidisse se vultum eius tamquam vultum angeli; membra autem eius candida tamquam nix videbantur. . . . Iam enim sic videbatur, quasi in futurae resurrectionis gloria et natura demutatae carnis ostensus esset.

Lines 305–7, on the angels singing, and lines 310–13, on the saint's age and the lamentation for him, are probably from Alcuin (*Vita*, PL 101, 664AB):

> Anno igitur aetatis suae LXXXI, et episcopatus sui XXVI, maturus annis et moribus apud Condatensem dioecesis suae vicum, ut diximus, feliciter recessit a saeculo. Sed inter divina sacrae praedicationis verba, cum angelicis coelestium hymnorum vocibus, circumstantibus suis discipulis, gratia plenus et sanctitate, sanctam Iesu Christo tradidit animam. Multi enim in eius transitu voces audierunt angelorum sanctum Martinum laudantium.. . . . quantus erat luctus omnium! quanta praecipue lamenta monachorum et virginum dicentium, quia pium est gaudere Martino, et pium est flere Martinum.

The colourful description of Martin's body, brighter than glass, whiter than milk, and his face shining more brightly than light (lines 307–10) derives originally from the *De Virtutibus* of Gregory of Tours, but is found in some manuscripts of Sulpicius at this point (cf CSEL 1, 149.19 variant and Zettel 1982, p. 26): *Vultus luce clarior renitebat . . . vitro purior, lacte candidior iam in quadam futurae resurrectionis.*

314–32 Ælfric finally turns to Gregory of Tours, or rather the extract from his *Historia Francorum* I.48 (32.8–33.14) which he probably found in his legendary, for an account of the contest over his body:

> Pectavi populi ad eius transitum sicut Toronici convenerunt. Quo migrante, grandis altercatio in utrumque surrexit populum. Dicebant enim Pectavi: 'Noster est monachus, nobis abba extitit, nos requiremus commendatum. Sufficiat vobis quod dum esset in mundo episcopus, usi fuistis eius conloquium . . . nobis liciat auferre vel cadaver exanimum.' . . . His ergo litigantibus, sol ruente nox clauditur, corpusque in medio positum . . . ab utroque populo custoditur. . . . Denique nocte media omnes Pectavi somno falanga compraemitur, nec ullus superfuit qui ex hac multitudine vigilaret. Igitur . . . Toronici . . . adprehensam sanctissimi corporis glebam . . . suscipiunt, positumque in navi . . . ad urbem Toronicam cum magnis laudibus psallentioque dirigunt copioso. De quorum vocibus Pectavi expergefacti . . . cum magna confusione ad propria sunt reversi.

Ælfric's much abridged version of the life of Martin has not in fact identified the place where he built his monastery near St Hilary (lines 93–4), so that the reference here to the Pictavians or people of Poitiers is somewhat abrupt.

EXCUSATIO DICTANTIS

In concluding his homiliary with a set of homilies for the common of saints, Ælfric was following the practice of Latin collections, such as those of Paul the Deacon, Smaragdus and Haymo. The usefulness of such sets in these collections is clear enough: the homiliaries make very limited provision for specific saints, and since they were written primarily for monastic use the potential need for homilies on saints' days was very high. Their value in Ælfric's collection is less clear, since he provides specific homilies, mostly narrative, for virtually all the saints' days which would be needed in a collection designed for preaching to the laity. The only apostles not covered, for which CH II.35 might be used, are Thomas and perhaps Matthias. The occasions on which two apostles are celebrated, for which CH II.36 might be used, have all been covered already (CH I.26, II.17 and 33). Presumably these, together with CH II.38, were to be used to provide alternatives to the more specific homilies elsewhere in the collection (just as two alternative homilies are provided for the feast-days of St Stephen and St Peter). But there are no occasions in the secular calendar on which several martyrs or virgins might be celebrated. There are perhaps signs here of a wider function for at least some of the texts than that sketched in the prefaces.

No other record survives of the poem on St Thomas to which Ælfric refers here. He can hardly have been very serious in offering the existence of a vernacular poem as a justification for not providing a sermon for use on the feast-day, but his second reason, a doubt about the authenticity of one incident in the story, scarcely serves any better; he later produced a version of the apostle's life, in LS 36, and omitted the offending episode. The objections of St Augustine to which he refers are presumably those which he quotes when he makes a similar point in the introduction to his later account (LS 36.1–12), from the *De Sermone Domini in Monte*, 1.1635–9 (CCSL 35):

> Cui scripturae licet nobis non credere. Non enim est in catholico canone. Illi tamen eam et legunt et tamquam incorruptissimam verissimamque honorant qui adversus corporales vindictas quae sunt in veteri testamento nescio qua caecitate acerrime saeviunt.

But in fact Augustine's reservations are about the credibility and canonicity of the whole text, not just this episode, and it is those who rage *against* the vengefulness of the Old Testament (i.e. the Manichaeans), not those who love vengeance, who read it with zeal. Ælfric's memory evidently played him convenient tricks.[1]

35 ON THE FEAST-DAY OF ONE APOSTLE

Ælfric takes as his subject for II.35 Christ's words to the apostles at John 15.12–16, which is the text used for the Common of an Apostle in PD. The introductory paragraph on the apostles shows that the homily was specifically written for use on an apostle's day, and Ælfric frequently recalls in the course of the homily that the Gospel verses were originally addressed to the apostles (lines 14, 38, 52, 55, 87). In every case, however, he goes on to argue for an application to all the faithful (cf especially 55–8) and his main concern seems to be not with the apostles, or even their successors, but with a series of topics prompted by the text: true love, Christ's distinction between servants and friends, grace, rewards, and prayer. He had clearly consulted Gregory the Great's homily on the text,

[1] See the fuller discussion in Godden 1985b, pp. 88–90.

which is given in PD, but used it comparatively little.[1] The first three sections are altogether ignored here, although they are used, extensively and often verbatim, in the Rogationtide homily CH II.19 (whose alliterative prose suggests that it was probably a later composition than this one). Instead, Ælfric makes his own brief comments on true love, interwoven with Biblical references, and then develops the distinction between friends and servants with the help of a point made in Augustine's Tractates on John.[2] He then draws on Gregory for two brief points (lines 51–4, 58–62) before developing a long discussion of the role of divine grace which owes nothing to either source, and then returning to Gregory for much of the last two sections, on heavenly rewards and prayer.

Sources and Notes

The following texts are cited below:

1. Augustine, *In Iohannis Evangelium Tractatus CXXIV*, ed. R. Willems, CCSL 36 (Turnhout, 1954).
2. Gregory the Great, *Homiliae in Evangelia*, PL 76, Hom. 27, cols. 1204–10.

14–25 Corresponds verbatim with Jn 15.12–16:

> (12) Hoc est praeceptum meum ut diligatis invicem sicut dilexi vos. (13) Maiorem hac dilectionem nemo habet ut animam suam quis ponat pro amicis suis. (14) Vos amici mei estis si feceritis quae ego praecipio vobis. (15) Iam non dico vos servos quia servus nescit quid facit dominus eius. Vos autem dixi amicos quia omnia quaecumque audivi a Patre meo nota feci vobis. (16) Non vos me elegistis sed ego elegi vos et posui vos ut eatis et fructum adferatis, et fructus vester maneat ut quodcumque petieritis Patrem in nomine meo det vobis.

25–36 A reference back to such discussions of true love as that at CH I.3.118–85. Ælfric here uses allusively a series of Biblical texts:

> (Rom 13.10) Plenitudo ergo legis est dilectio; (Mt 22.37–40) diliges Dominum . . . diliges proximum tuum . . . In his duobus mandatis universa lex pendet, et prophetae; (Jn 13.35) in hoc cognoscent omnes quia mei discipuli estis si dilectionem habueritis ad invicem.

Lines 34–5 perhaps allude to 1 Cor 13.1–3, and lines 35–6, while echoing the pericope (v.13), perhaps also allude to 1 Jn 3.16: *In hoc cognovimus caritatem quoniam ille pro nobis animam suam posuit.*

41–49 For 45–6 cf Augustine, *Tract.*, 85.3.5–9:

> Sicut enim duo sunt timores, qui faciunt duo genera timentium, sic duae sunt servitutes, quae faciunt duo genera servorum. Est timor quem perfecta caritas foras mittit, et est alius timor castus permanens in saeculum saeculi.

[1] Cited by Förster (1894, p. 12); Smetana (1959, p. 201) noted its inclusion in PD, but his comment that Ælfric's homily 'is for the most part merely a translation of the 27th homily of Gregory' seems wide of the mark.

[2] Cf Smetana 1959, who notes that the relevant excerpt was in PD for this occasion.

But the rest of Augustine's discussion is different. He takes it for granted that to be a *servus* is good, and tries to explain why Christ should repudiate the name for his followers, whereas Ælfric takes it for granted that a *servus* is lowly, defining him as one enslaved to sin, and then needs to qualify that to allow for the clergy's title of *Godes þeowas*.

51–62 Loosely based on Gregory, Hom. 27, PL 76, 1206D-7B:

> Quae sunt omnia quae audivit a Patre suo, quae nota fieri voluit servis suis, ut eos efficeret amicos suos, nisi gaudia internae charitatis, nisi illa festa supernae patriae, quae nostris quotidie mentibus per aspirationem sui amoris imprimit? . . . Istos vero amicos Dei aspexerat propheta, cum dicebat: 'Mihi autem nimis honorificati sunt amici tui, Deus . . . Nimis confortatus est principatus eorum' (Ps 138.17). . . . Sed sic magni forsitan pauci sunt? Subiunxit: 'Dinumerabo eos, et super arenam multiplicabuntur' (Ps 138.18).

But Ælfric omits the intervening passage in which Gregory applies the psalm quotations to the elect who suffer torments and martyrdom to win heaven, and substitutes Mark 13.37 (lines 55–8) to make them apply to all Christians. The point about the great numbers who will be saved is a favourite one with Ælfric, and frequently in opposition to Gregory; cf CH I.35.277–84, and CH II.5.183–94 (including the additional clause in MS M).

63–87 The discussion of grace recalls the accounts in CH I.7.172–98 and II.28.83–91 but is fuller and different in detail, and no source has been found, though there are faint similarities to the discussion in Augustine's Tractate 86.2. The initial statements come surprisingly close to picturing Christ as a man purified by grace, and Ælfric is quick to correct this impression with his explanation of the divinity and humanity of Christ (lines 74–81), though at the cost of some digression from his theme. The quotation at 67–8 is probably from Eph 2.8: *Gratia enim estis salvati per fidem* (or possibly 1 Petr 1.5: *Qui in virtute Dei custodimini per fidem in salutem*) which is also used, in a similar context, at CH I.7.180–81. The next sentence, with the statement that 'every Christian is chosen by God from the beginning of his faith' (lines 69–70), seems at odds with the more orthodox Pauline view, expressed for instance in CH II.22, that the elect are chosen from the beginning of time. (Cf Grundy 1991, p. 116.)

87–108 Ælfric here silently takes up the next and final words of the Gospel text (the rest of v.16). He applies this first to the apostles while at the same time sustaining the discussion of grace; hence the conjunction of *sylfwilles* and *be godes hæse*. Gregory provides a starting-point and a basis for the subsequent application to all men (Hom. 27, PL 76, 1207CD, 1208A):

> Posui ad gratiam, plantavi ut eatis volendo, fructum afferatis operando. . . . Mors namque interveniens fructum nostri laboris abscidit. Quod vero pro aeterna vita agitur etiam post mortem servatur; et tunc apparere incipit, cum laborum carnalium fructus coeperit non videri. Ibi ergo illa retributio inchoat, ubi ista terminatur. . . . Nam quod a morte incipiat fructus Dei,

> testatur propheta, qui dicit: 'Cum dederit dilectis suis somnum, haec est haereditas Domini' (Ps 126.2–3) . . . electi Dei postquam pervenerint ad mortem, tunc invenient haereditatem.

The intervening quotation from Ezekiel at 91, *ic do þæt ge doð*, is presumably a variant reading of Ez 24.22, where the Vulgate has *Et facietis sicut feci*. The last two sentences (lines 105–8) are repeated at Pope 11.153–9 and correspond, as Pope has shown, to a passage in Ælfric's excerpts from Julian of Toledo's *Prognosticon* (*Excerpts*, 65–9):

> Quid non properamus et currimus, ut patriam nostram videre et parentes salutare possimus? Magnus illic nos carorum numerus expectat, parentum, fratrum, filiorum sequens nos et copiosa turba desiderat, iam de sua incolomitate secura, adhuc de nostra salute sollicita.

This corresponds almost exactly with Julian's own text (*Prognosticon*, I.xv.103–8), and Ælfric could have been drawing on the *Prognosticon* directly in this homily. The context there (the persecutions at the end of the world) is quite dissimilar.

109–30 The discussion of prayer follows Gregory at first (Hom. 27, PL 76, 1208BC):

> Sed quia nomen filii Iesus est, Iesus autem salvator, vel etiam salutaris dicitur, ille ergo in nomine salvatoris petit, qui illud petit quod ad veram salutem pertinet. Nam si id quod non expedit petitur, non in nomine Iesu petitur pater. . . . Hinc est quod et Paulus non exauditur quia si liberaretur a tentatione, ei non proderat ad salutem. [*Referring to 2 Cor 12.9.*]

The rest seems to be Ælfric's own, with a buried quotation from Prov 28:9 at 118–9, *qui declinat aurem suam ne audiat legem, oratio eius erit execrabilis*, and an explicit one from 1 Jn 5.16 at 125. (Gregory here discusses in some detail questions of what may be properly asked for in prayer.)

36 ON THE FEAST-DAY OF SEVERAL APOSTLES

Ælfric's subject is the clergy in their role as teachers; his text, Luke 10.1–7 on Christ's instructions to the disciples to preach, is to be taken as a model for all teachers, he insists (lines 22–6), bishops, mass-priests and other clerics (lines 120–22). The use of the Luke text for the common of apostles seems to have been unusual[1] and the rubric may not reflect Ælfric's original intention. The text does not appear as a Gospel reading in the original PD, or in the homiliaries of Smaragdus and Haymo, but occurs in later versions of PD for St Luke's day. Ælfric seems to have circulated his homily at some stage without a rubric (see *CH II*, p. 377) and there is nothing in the text to associate it with a particular occasion, as there is in the preceding homily.

[1] Lenker (p. 374) lists a range of other readings but not this one.

His sole source is a homily on the text by Gregory the Great, used in late versions of PD.[2] This is a long and often acutely critical piece on the failings of the clergy in the pope's time, contrasted with the model of the Gospel text, understood both literally and allegorically. Ælfric reduces the criticism to a minimum, though lines 34–6 acknowledge its justice, and concentrates instead on the positive aspects of the relationship between clergy and laity. He omits altogether the second half of the sermon, which is devoted entirely to the clergy's deficiencies; he reverses the two points at 40–52, so that the failings of the laity precede those of the clergy; and in his interpretation of verse 3, 'I send you as lambs amongst wolves', he virtually eliminates Gregory's account of the wolvishness of the clergy and counters his insistence on the need for mildness in guiding the laity with his own insistence on the need for strictness (lines 64–6). Gregory's sermon addresses the laity (or perhaps the non-teaching monks and clerics) but also at times the negligent pastors directly. Ælfric avoids the awkwardness, and leaves the status of his own audience unspecified, by using third-person forms for clergy and laity throughout. Otherwise he follows Gregory closely where he uses him; the significant departures are 22–6, 64–6, 77–80, 117–8 and 135–7.

Sources and Notes

The following text is cited below:

1. Gregory the Great, *Homiliae in Evangelia*, PL 76, Hom. 17, cols. 1138–49.

1–15 Corresponds closely to the Vulgate text of Lc 10.1–7:

> (1) Post haec autem designavit Dominus et alios septuaginta duos et misit illos binos ante faciem suam in omnem civitatem et locum quo erat ipse venturus. (2) Et dicebat illis: messis quidem multa operarii autem pauci rogate ergo Dominum messis ut mittat operarios in messem. (3) Ite ecce ego mitto vos sicut agnos inter lupos. (4) Nolite portare sacculum neque peram neque calciamenta et neminem per viam salutaveritis. (5) In quamcumque domum intraveritis primum dicite pax huic domui. (6) Et si ibi fuerit filius pacis requiescet super illam pax vestra; sin autem ad vos revertetur. (7) In eadem autem domo manete edentes et bibentes quae apud illos sunt; dignus enim est operarius mercede sua.

Puse and *codd* (line 8) render *sacculum* and *pera*; Gregory takes *sacculum* as a bag containing money, and that seems to be the sense of *puse* at CH I.18.177. *Gecyrran* at 9 corresponds to Vulgate *salutaveritis* and clearly carries the meaning 'to greet' at 87.

16–22 Closely follows Gregory, Hom. 17, PL 76, 1139AB:

> Dominus et Salvator noster, fratres charissimi, aliquando nos sermonibus, aliquando vero operibus admonet. . . . Ecce enim binos in praedicationem

[2] Förster 1894, p. 7; Smetana 1959, p. 201.

> discipulos mittit, quia duo sunt praecepta charitatis, Dei videlicet amor, et proximi . . . qui charitatem erga alterum non habet, praedicationis officium suscipere nullatenus debet.

With 22–6 contrast the distinction which Bede draws, *Comm. Luc.*, 3.1872–5, between the apostles signifying the bishops and the 72 disciples who represent the priests.

26–32 Closely follows Gregory, Hom. 17, PL 76, 1139BC:

> Praedicatores enim suos Dominus sequitur, quia praedicatio praevenit, et tunc ad mentis nostrae habitaculum Dominus venit. . . . Hinc namque eisdem praedicatoribus Isaias dicit: 'Parate viam Domini, rectas facite semitas Dei nostri' (Is 40.3). . . . Iter facimus cum nos eius gloriam vestris mentibus praedicamus, ut eas et ipse post veniens per amoris sui praesentiam illustret.

33–56 From Gregory but with some rearrangement and the Psalm quotation extended (Hom. 17, PL 76, 1139C-40A):

> Ad messem multam operarii pauci sunt, quod sine gravi moerore loqui non possumus. . . . Ecce mundus sacerdotibus plenus est, sed tamen in messe Dei rarus valde invenitur operator. . . . Vos pro nobis petite, ut digna vobis operari valeamus. . . . Saepe enim pro sua nequitia praedicantium lingua restringitur: saepe vero ex subiectorum culpa agitur ut eis qui praesunt, praedicationis sermo subtrahatur. . . . Ex vitio subiectorum, vox praedicantium prohibetur sicut ad Ezechielem Dominus dicit: 'Linguam tuam adhaerescere faciam palato tuo, et eris mutus, nec quasi vir obiurgans, quia domus exasperans est' (Ez 3.26). Ac si aperte dicat: Idcirco tibi praedicationis sermo tollitur, quia dum me in suis actibus plebs exasperat, non est digna cui exhortatio veritatis fiat. [*earlier*] Ex sua quippe nequitia praedicantium lingua restringitur, sicut Psalmista ait: 'Peccatori autem dixit Deus: Quare tu enarras iustitias meas? [*Ælfric completes the quotation:* et assumis testamentum meum per os tuum? Tu vero odisti disciplinam, et proiecisti sermones meos retrorsum' (Ps 49.16–17).] . . . Quia vero Pastoris taciturnitas aliquando sibi, semper autem subiectis noceat, certissime scitur.

57–68 Draws on Gregory (Hom. 17, PL 76, 1140BC) in part, but not close:

> Utinam si ad praedicationis virtutem non sufficimus, loci nostri officium in innocentia vitae teneamus. . . . Qui enim locum praedicationis suscipit, mala inferre non debet, sed tolerare, ut ex ipsa sua mansuetudine iram saevientium mitiget. . . . Quem et si quando zelus rectitudinis exigit ut erga subiectos saeviat, furor ipse de amore sit, non de crudelitate.

For the quotation which Ælfric uses to support his qualification, 65–6, Cook (1898) suggests Prov 29.19: *Servus verbis non potest erudiri*; there is perhaps an echo of Prov 18.2, *non recipit stultus verba prudentiae* as well.

69–90 Follows Gregory, Hom. 17, PL 76, 1140D-41B, fairly closely:
Praedicatori etenim tanta debet in Deo esse fiducia, ut praesentis vitae sumptus quamvis non provideat, tamen sibi hos non deesse certissime sciat, ne dum mens eius occupatur ad temporalia, minus aliis provideat aeterna. [*Ælfric omits Gregory's interpretation of the* sacculum *(seen as a purse in which the treasure of wisdom is locked up), but adds his own sharp remark on clerical avarice at 77–80.*] . . . Quid vero per peram, nisi onera saeculi; et quid hoc loco per calceamenta, nisi mortuorum operum exempla signantur? Qui ergo officium praedicationis suscipit, dignum non est ut onus saecularium negotiorum portet, ne dum hoc eius colla deprimit, ad praedicanda coelestia non assurgat. Nec debet stultorum operum exempla conspicere, ne sua opera quasi ex mortuis pellibus credat munire. Sunt etenim multi qui pravitatem suam ex alienis pravitatibus tuentur. Quia enim alios talia fecisse considerant, se haec facere licenter putant. Hi quid aliud faciunt, nisi pedes suos ex mortuorum animalium munire pellibus conantur?

87–90 Gregory, Hom. 17, PL 76 (earlier, 1140D):
Cui etiam per viam neminem salutare conceditur, ut sub quanta festinatione iter praedicationis pergere debeat ostendatur.

93–99 Gregory, Hom. 17, PL 76, 1141BC:
Pax quae ab ore praedicatoris offertur, aut requiescit in domo, si in ea filius pacis fuerit, aut ad eumdem praedicatorem revertitur; quia aut erit quisque praedestinatus ad vitam, et coeleste verbum sequitur quod audit; aut si nullus audire voluerit, ipse praedicator sine fructu non erit, quia ad eum pax revertitur, quoniam ei a Domino pro labore sui operis merces recompensatur.

101–20 Gregory, Hom. 17, PL 76, 1141C-42A:
Ecce autem qui peram et sacculum portare prohibuit sumptus et alimenta ex eadem praedicatione concedit. . . . Si pax nostra recipitur, dignum est ut in eadem domo maneamus edentes et bibentes quae apud illos sunt, ut ab eis terrena stipendia consequamur, quibus praemia patriae coelestis offerimus. Unde etiam Paulus haec ipsa pro minimo suscipiens, dicit: 'Si nos vobis spiritalia seminavimus, magnum est si vestra carnalia metamus?' (1 Cor 9.11). . . . Qua in re considerandum est quod uni nostro operi duae mercedes debentur, una in via, altera in patria; una quae nos in labore sustentat, alia quae nos in resurrectione remunerat. . . . Vetus ergo quisque praedicator non ideo praedicare debet, ut in hoc tempore mercedem recipiat, sed ideo mercedem recipere, ut praedicare subsistat. Quisquis namque ideo praedicat ut hic vel laudis vel muneris mercedem recipiat, aeterna procul dubio mercede se privat. Quisquis vero vel ea quae dicit, ideo placere hominibus appetit, ut, dum placet quod dicitur, per eadem dicta non ipse, sed Dominus ametur [*Ælfric substitutes doing the Lord's will for this justification of rhetoric*], vel idcirco terrena stipendia in praedicatione consequitur, ne a

> praedicationis voce per indigentiam lassetur, huic procul dubio ad recipiendam mercedem nil obstat in patria, quia sumptus sumpsit in via.

120–30 Gregory, Hom. 17, PL 76, 1142C-43A (but omitting the discussion of the failings of the clergy which occupies most of this section):

> Sed debemus sine cessatione meminisse quod de quibusdam scriptum est: 'Peccata Populi mei comedent' (Os 4.8). . . . Sed et nos qui ex oblationibus fidelium vivimus, quas illi pro peccatis suis obtulerunt, si comedimus et tacemus, eorum procul dubio peccata manducamus. . . . Praecones namque venturi iudicis sumus. Quis ergo venturum iudicem nuntiet, si praeco tacet?

131–7 Partly from Gregory, Hom. 17, PL 76, 1143AB:

> Debemus namque pensare continuo quod sanctis apostolis dicitur, et per apostolos nobis: 'Vos estis sal terrae' (Mt 5.13). Si ergo sal sumus, condire mentes fidelium debemus. . . . Curare namque sacerdotem necesse est, quae singulis dicat, unumquemque qualiter admoneat, ut quisquis sacerdoti iungitur, quasi ex salis tactu, aeternae vitae sapore condiatur. Sal etenim terrae non sumus, si corda audientium non condimus.

But where Gregory thinks of animals being given rock-salt to lick, Ælfric thinks rather (lines 135–7) of salt as a preservative for food. The identification of salt with wisdom is not in Gregory's homily; cf however his *Regula Pastoralis*, PL 77, 31C: *Per sal quippe, verbi sapientia designatur.*

37 ON THE FEAST-DAY OF HOLY MARTYRS

Luke 21.9–19, in which Christ warns the disciples of the persecutions which they will suffer and the subsequent tribulations and signs marking the approaching end of the world, is one of several texts used for the common of martyrs in Paul the Deacon's homiliary. The signs are those which Wulfstan applied to his own time—the raids of the Vikings, the collapse of social bonds and the imminence of the end of the world—and Ælfric himself had seen some of the signs in an apocalyptic light when he discussed them at the end of the First Series (CH I.40.20 ff). Here, however, he makes no explicit reference to current events or the approach of the apocalypse and reads the text as referring as much to the past persecutions of the early martyrs and the ordinary tribulations of contemporary existence as to the future signs and terrors of the reign of Antichrist. The final verse, on patience, leads him into a discussion of spiritual martyrdom achieved through the patient endurance of the characteristic afflictions of life in the world.

His source is Gregory the Great's homily 35, found in PD.[1] Gregory's particular concern is with the contemporary application of the text to problems of harmony and dissension in communities; he discusses at length aspects of

[1] See Förster 1894, pp. 4–5; Smetana 1959, p. 201.

forgiveness and revenge, and ends with a story of an exemplary monk who treated those who harrassed him with perfect patience and mildness. Ælfric announces in his first sentence his own concern with real martyrs, *ðæra martira gewinn*, and writes with feeling of their experiences in passages at 68–83 and 101–12; cf too 115–22. He too then focuses on the possibilities of an inner martyrdom for those living in present times, in the peace of God's church, but turns from Gregory's emphasis on patience in the face of afflictions from others to include also zeal in resistance to temptation (lines 135–6) but especially patience in the face of God's afflictions, which he gives first place in the discussion at 155–63. Appropriately, therefore, he adds to Gregory's story of Stephen's patience in response to harassment the story of Romula's patience in response to illness and paralysis, and concludes with his own topos, that God 'chastises and rebukes those whom he loves' (line 202). The homily may have been intended for preaching on the festival of a martyr-saint, as the rubric argues, but there is no specific application in the text and the final concern is with the less heroic role of the ordinary sufferer.

Sources and Notes

The following texts are cited below:

1. Bede, *Homiliae*, ed. D. Hurst, CCSL 122 (Turnhout, 1955), Hom. II.21 (pp. 335–48).
2. Gregory the Great, *Homiliae in Evangelia*, PL 76, Hom. 35 and 40, cols. 1259–65 and 1301–12.

3–20 Lc 21.9–19:

(9) Cum autem audieritis proelia et seditiones, nolite terreri. Oportet primum haec fieri sed non statim finis. (10) Tunc dicebat illis: Surget gens contra gentem et regnum adversus regnum; (11) terraemotus magni erunt per loca et pestilentiae et fames terroresque de caelo et signa magna erunt. (12) Sed ante haec omnia inicient vobis manus suas et persequentur, tradentes in synagogas et custodias, trahentes ad reges et praesides propter nomen meum. (13) Continget autem vobis in testimonium. (14) Ponite ergo in cordibus vestris non praemeditari quemadmodum respondeatis. (15) Ego enim dabo vobis os et sapientiam cui non poterunt resistere et contradicere omnes adversarii vestri. (16) Trademini autem a parentibus et fratribus et cognatis et amicis et morte adficient ex vobis. (17) Et eritis odio omnibus propter nomen meum. (18) Et capillus de capite vestro non peribit. (19) In patientia vestra possidebitis animas vestras.

The *amici* of verse 16 are either omitted or incorporated into the *magum* of line 17.

22–33 From Gregory, Hom. 35, PL 76, 1259BC:

Dominus ac Redemptor noster perituri mundi praecurrentia mala denuntiat, ut eo minus perturbent venientia, quo fuerint praescita. Minus enim

> iacula feriunt quae praevidentur; et nos tolerabilius mundi mala suscipimus, si contra haec per praescientiae clypeum munimur. Ecce enim dicit: Cum audieritis. . . . Bella quippe ad hostes pertinent, seditiones ad cives. Ut ergo nos indicet interius exteriusque turbari, aliud nos fatetur ab hostibus, aliud a fratribus perpeti.

33–5 Ælfric's comment that God does not cause these afflictions presumably applies not to the whole catalogue of tribulations but specifically to *gefeoht and sacu*, since he goes on to acknowledge that the others are due to God (implicitly at 44–56, explicitly at 155–63 and 202–5). He is apparently taking a stand against the view, later to be voiced by Wulfstan, that the troubles caused by Viking raids and internal treachery are divine punishments.

37–40 Cf Gregory, Hom. 35, PL 76, 1259D:

> Ultima tribulatio multis tribulationibus praevenitur, et per crebra mala quae praeveniunt indicantur mala perpetua quae subsequentur.

The wording is close to that of the CH I.praef.69–73.

41–65 Gregory, Hom. 35, PL 76, 1260AB:

> Surget gens contra gentem, ecce perturbatio hominum; erunt terrae motus magni per loca, ecce respectus irae desuper; erunt pestilentiae, ecce inaequalitas corporum; erit fames, ecce sterilitas terrae; terroresque de coelo et tempestates, ecce inaequalitas aeris. Quia ergo omnia consummanda sunt, ante consummationem omnia perturbantur; et qui in cunctis deliquimus, in cunctis ferimur, ut impleatur quod dicitur: 'Et pugnabit pro eo orbis terrarum contra insensatos' (Sap 5.21). Omnia namque quae ad usum vitae accepimus ad usum convertimus culpae, sed cuncta quae ad usum pravitatis infleximus ad usum nobis vertuntur ultionis. Tranquillitatem quippe humanae pacis ad usum vertimus vanae securitatis, peregrinationem terrae pro habitatione dileximus patriae; salutem corporum redegimus in usum vitiorum; ubertatis abundantiam non ad necessitatem carnis, sed ad perversitatem intorsimus voluptatis; ipsa serena blandimenta aeris ad amorem nobis servire coegimus terrenae delectationis. Iure ergo restat ut simul nos omnia feriant, quae simul omnia vitiis nostris male subacta serviebant.

The phrase *et tempestates* (after *de coelo*) is a Biblical variant which Gregory mentions earlier, and is implicit in Ælfric's exposition.

66–83 The impassioned account of the early martyrdoms is not from Gregory. Ælfric was perhaps drawing on his own familiarity with legends of apostles and martyrs.

85–8 From Gregory, Hom. 35, PL 76, 1261A:

> Mors quippe iustorum bonis in adiutorium est, malis in testimonium, ut inde perversi sine excusatione pereant, unde electi exemplum capiunt [*var.* salutis] ut vivant.

91–9 Gregory, Hom. 35, PL 76, 1261AB:

. . . Ac si aperte membris suis infirmantibus dicat: Nolite terreri, nolite pertimescere; vos ad certamen acceditis, sed ego praelior; vos verba editis, sed ego sum qui loquor.

Ælfric adds in support Lc 12.4–5:

(4) Dico autem vobis amicis meis ne terreamini ab his qui occidunt corpus et post haec non habent amplius quod faciant. (5) Ostendam autem vobis quem timeatis: timete eum qui postquam occiderit habet potestatem mittere in gehennam. Ita dico vobis: hunc timete.

99–112 Mostly Ælfric's own comments on betrayal by kin, apparently, drawing on his reading of the stories of martyrs; lines 107–10 are from Mt 24.12–13:

(12) Et quoniam abundavit iniquitas, refrigescet caritas multorum; (13) qui autem perseveraverit usque in finem, hic salvus erit.

With the sentiment at 110–2, cf Gregory, Hom. 35, PL 76, 1261B:

Minorem dolorem mala ingerunt quae ab extraneis inferuntur. Plus vero in nobis ea tormenta saeviunt quae ab illis patimur de quorum mentibus praesumebamus, quia cum damno corporis mala nos cruciant amissae charitatis.

113–22 Cf Gregory, Hom. 35, PL 76, 1261CD:

Sed quia dura sunt quae praedicuntur de afflictione mortis, protinus consolatio subditur de gaudio resurrectionis, cum dicitur: Capillus. . . . videlicet aperte dicens: Cur timetis ne pereat quod incisum dolet, quando et illud in vobis perire non potest quod incisum non dolet?

Lines 118–22 are a characteristic saying of Ælfric; cf esp. his comment at CH I.16.124 ff, starting from the same verse, and Pope 11.32 ff.

123–9 From Gregory, Hom. 35, PL 76, 1261D, 1262BC:

Idcirco possessio animae in virtute patientiae ponitur, quia radix omnium custosque virtutum patientia est. . . . Per impatientiae autem vitium ipsa virtutum nutrix doctrina dissipatur. Scriptum namque est: 'Doctrina viri per patientiam noscitur' (Prov 19.11). . . . Rursus Salomon indicat, dicens: 'Melior est patiens viro forti, et qui dominatur animo suo expugnatore urbium' (Prov 16.32). Minor est ergo victoria urbes expugnare, quia extra sunt quae vincuntur. Maius autem est quod per patientiam vincitur, quia ipse a se animus superatur, et semetipsum sibimetipsi subiicit, quando eum patientia in humilitate tolerantiae sternit.

129–54 Follows Gregory, Hom. 35, PL 76, 1263B-D, closely:

Si enim, adiuvante nos Domino, virtutem patientiae servare contendimus, et in pace ecclesiae vivimus, et tamen martyrii palmam tenemus. Duo quippe sunt martyrii genera, [*var.* unum in publico, aliud in occulto] unum in mente, aliud in mente simul et actione. . . . Mori quippe a persequente martyrium in aperto opere est; ferre vero contumelias, odientem diligere, martyrium est in occulta cogitatione. Nam quia duo sunt martyrii genera, unum in occulto opere, aliud in publico, testatur veritas, quae Zebedaei filios requirit, dicens: 'Potestis bibere calicem quem ego bibiturus sum?' (Mt 20.22). Cui cum protinus responderent: 'Possumus', illico Dominus respondit, dicens: 'Calicem quidem meum bibetis.' Quid enim per calicem, nisi dolorem passionis accipimus? De quo alias dicit: 'Pater, si fieri potest, transeat a me calix iste' (Mt 26.39). Et Zebedaei filii, id est Iacobus et Ioannes, non uterque per martyrium occubuit, et tamen quod uterque calicem biberet audivit. Ioannes namque nequaquam per martyrium vitam finivit, sed tamen martyr exstitit, quia passionem quam non suscepit in corpore servavit in mente. Et nos ergo hoc exemplo sine ferro esse possumus martyres, si patientiam veraciter in animo custodimus.

The detail of St James's end (line 147) derives from the legend which Ælfric gives in CH II.27, cf II.27.169–79. The phrase *on sibbe* at 148 perhaps shows the influence of Bede's *in pace* in his similar exposition of the Matthew text (Hom. II.21, 185). The final sentence is from the end of Gregory (Hom. 35, PL 76, 1264C):

Sancta ecclesia, electorum floribus plena, habet in pace lilia, in bello rosas.

155–63 From Gregory, Hom. 35, PL 76, 1264C-5A:

Sciendum praeterea est quod tribus modis virtus patientiae exerceri solet. Alia namque sunt quae a Deo, alia quae ab antiquo adversario, alia quae a proximo sustinemus. A proximo namque persecutiones, damna et contumelias; ab antiquo vero adversario tentamenta; a Deo autem flagella toleramus. Sed in his omnibus tribus modis vigilanti oculo semetipsam debet mens circumspicere, ne contra mala proximi pertrahatur ad retributionem mali, ne contra tentamenta adversarii seducatur ad delectationem vel consensum delicti, ne contra flagella opificis ad excessum proruat murmurationis.

164–75 From Gregory, Hom. 35, PL 76, 1263D-4B:

Fuit quidam diebus nostris Stephanus nomine, pater monasterii iuxta Reatinae urbis moenia constituti, vir valde sanctus, virtute patientiae singularis. . . . Hic pro amore coelestis patriae cuncta despexerat, possidere aliquid in hoc mundo fugiebat; tumultus devitabat hominum, crebris ac prolixioribus orationibus intentus erat. Virtus tamen patientiae in eo vehementer excreverat, ita ut eum sibi amicum crederet, qui sibi molestiae aliquid irrogasset; reddebat contumeliis gratias; si quod in ipsa sua inopia damnum ei fuisset illatum, hoc maximum lucrum putabat; omnes suos adversarios nihil aliud quam adiutores aestimabat. Hunc cum dies mortis egredi de corpore urgeret, convenerunt multi, ut tam sanctae animae de hoc mundo recedenti suas animas commendarent. Cumque circa lectum illius hi qui convenerant omnes assisterent, alii corporeis oculis ingredientes angelos viderunt, sed dicere aliquid nullo modo potuerunt; alii omnino nihil viderunt; sed omnes qui aderant ita vehementissimus timor perculit, ut nullus, egrediente illa sancta anima, illic stare potuisset. Et hi ergo qui viderant, et hi qui omnino nihil viderant, uno omnes timore perculsi et territi fugerunt.

176–201 An abridged version of another story which Gregory gives in his homily 40. He describes the small community in Rome comprising Redempta, her disciple Romula and one other, and continues, of Romula (Hom. 40, PL 76, 1310C–12A):

Erat quippe mirae patientiae, summae obedientiae, custos oris sui ad silentium, studiosa valde ad continuae orationis usum. . . . Haec quam praediximus Romula ea quam Graeco vocabulo medici paralysin vocant molestia corporali percussa est, multisque annis in lectulo decubans pene omnium iacebat membrorum officio destituta, nec tamen haec eadem eius mentem ad impatientiam flagella perduxerant. Nam ipsa ei detrimenta membrorum facta fuerant incrementa virtutum, quia tanto sollicitius ad usum orationis succreverat, quanto et aliud quodlibet agere nequaquam valebat. Nocte ergo quadam eamdem Redemptam . . . vocavit dicens: 'Mater, veni, mater, veni.' Quae mox cum alia eius discipula surrexit. . . . Cumque noctis medio, lectulo iacentis assisterent, subito coelitus lux emissa omne illius cellulae spatium implevit; et splendor tantae claritatis emicuit, ut corda assistentium inaestimabili pavore perstringeret. . . . Coepit namque quasi cuiusdam magnae multitudinis ingredientis sonitus audiri, ostium cellulae concuti, ac si ingredientium turba premeretur. . . . Quam lucem protinus miri odoris est fragrantia subsecuta, ita ut earum animum, quia lux emissa terruerat, odoris suavitas refoveret. Sed cum vim claritatis illius ferre non possent, coepit eadem Romula assistentem sibi et trementem Redemptam, suorum morum magistram, blanda voce consolari, dicens: noli timere, mater, non morior modo. Cumque hoc illa crebro diceret, paulatim lux quae fuerat immissa subtracta est, sed is qui subsecutus est odor remansit. . . . Nocte ergo quarta eamdem magistram suam iterum vocavit. Qua veniente viaticum petiit, et accepit. . . . Ecce subito in platea ante eiusdem cellulae ostium duo chori psallentium constiterunt, et sicut ipsae se dicebant sexus ex vocibus discrevisse, psalmodiae cantus dicebant viri, et feminae respondebant. Cumque ante fores cellulae exhiberentur coelestes exsequiae, sancta illa anima carne soluta est. Qua ad coelum ducta, quanto chori psallentium altius ascendebant, tanto coepit psalmodia lenius audiri, quousque et eiusdem psalmodiae sonitus, et odoris suavitas elongata finiretur.

202 From Apoc 3.19: *Ego quos amo, arguo et castigo.*

38 ON THE FEAST-DAY OF A CONFESSOR

Ælfric's avowed subject is the teacher-saint who performs spiritual miracles by his preaching and guidance (lines 192–end), but in working towards this topic he dwells on layman as well as cleric, and on good living as well as good teaching, so that the teacher-saint or holy confessor comes to stand as a model of the Christian who puts God's talents to work. His text is the parable of the talents from Matthew 25.14–30, conflated with the parallel version in Luke 19.12–26. Neither version seems otherwise to have been in use in Anglo-Saxon England for the common of a confessor[1] but both are used for the occasion in the late version of PD printed in PL 95, and Matthew in Haymo's homiliary. The authorities with whom Ælfric was familiar varied in their precise interpretation of the parable but seem to have agreed in applying it primarily to the clergy as teachers. This is so in Jerome's commentary on Matthew, Augustine's Serm. 94 on the Matthew version, and Bede's commentary on Luke, which draws on Jerome.[2] It is less explicitly so in Gregory's homily 9 (Ælfric's main source) and Haymo's homily 9, both on Matthew 25,[3] though it becomes clear in both as the interpretation proceeds. Gregory interprets the three servants who receive the talents as, firstly, those who have understanding of external things only but bring people to God by teaching as best they can; secondly, those who understand internal mysteries and perform wonders, by both of which they bring men to God; and thirdly, those who have internal understanding but fail to use it for others. Ælfric adopts much of Gregory's wording but conveys a significantly different reading of the text. He interprets the first servant as the laity or unlearned (*læwed* 55) who are given the outer senses which enable them to bring others to God by the righteousness of their lives. The second servant, by implication representing the clergy or *læred*, uses the outer senses to live the good life and also has the inner understanding, later defined as book learning (line 166), to perceive heavenly wisdom, so that he can bring men to God both by preaching and by example. The third servant receives only one *andgit* or sense, but Ælfric is careful not to specify which, the outer or inner, and presumably intends him therefore to stand freely for both the *læwed* and the *læred* who apply their understanding to things of the flesh. As the homily develops, however, the third servant comes increasingly to stand for the slothful cleric, who should have used his intellect to preach to others so that his treasure might be multiplied by their zeal and turned by them into action. The identification of the third servant and his talent becomes clearer when the pound is taken from him and given to the first servant, the layman who had originally

[1] Cf Lenker, p. 375.

[2] Augustine's sermon is at PL 38, 580; for the others see below. The relevant part of Bede's commentary is included as a sermon for the common of a confessor in PDM.

[3] Förster (1894, p. 3) identified Gregory as the source; Smetana (1959, p. 201) notes its inclusion in PD. The Haymo homily is at PL 118, cols. 781–5.

only the outer understanding but is subsequently granted the inner one too. Ælfric is perhaps thinking of the intelligent and spiritual layman such as his patrons Æthelweard and Æthelmær.

Having completed his exposition of the parable, Ælfric then develops the theme of the teacher using his talents with an account of the last judgement, drawn from a different sermon by Gregory, depicting the apostles leading those whom they have converted into the presence of God. It is perhaps significant of Ælfric's continuing concern with the *læwed* and the *læred* that whereas Gregory pictures the apostles as an object-lesson for the contemporary clergy who have no sheep to lead, Ælfric describes the apostles and other *godes bydela* as an object-lesson for men in general. For the final passage, on the specific concern of the feast-day, confessors, and the praises of the unspecified confessor for whom the homily is to be used, he seems to have drawn on a sermon included in PDM for the common of a confessor.[4] PL attributes it to Maximus and prints it in the collection of sermons by that saint in PL 57 (Hom. 78, cols. 417–20). More recently it has been printed as homily 51 of the *Collectio Homiliarum* tentatively attributed to a Eusebius Gallicanus, a shadowy sixth-century writer from Gaul who may have written the homilies or collected and adapted the work of earlier writers.

Ælfric has evidently devised his homily for use on a confessor's feast-day, leaving a blank for the name at 229. The likeliest confessor-saint for which the homily might have been needed is perhaps St Augustine of Canterbury, since his feast was among those observed by the laity and he is not otherwise provided for, but the last section is perhaps more appropriate to a recent saint and Ælfric may have been thinking of the needs of individual churches to celebrate particular saints.

Sources and Notes

The following texts are cited below:

1. Bede, *Commentarius in Lucam*, ed. D. Hurst, CCSL 120 (Turnhout, 1960), pp. 5–425.
2. Eusebius Gallicanus, *Collectio Homiliarum*, ed. F. Glorie, CCSL 101A (Turnhout, 1971), Hom. 51 (pp. 593–603).
3. Gregory the Great, *Homiliae in Evangelia*, PL 76, Hom. 9 and 17, cols. 1105–9 and 1138–49.
4. Jerome, *Commentarii in Evangelium Matthaei*, ed. D. Hurst and M. Adriaen, CCSL 77 (Turnhout, 1969).

1–37 A conflation of Mt 25.14–29 and Lc 19.15–26:

(Mt 25.14) Sicut enim homo proficiscens vocavit servos suos et tradidit illis bona sua. [*But* rice *at line 3 reflects the* nobilis *of Lc 19.12.*] (15) Et uni dedit

[4] Identified by Cross (1963b, pp. 4–8).

quinque talenta alii autem duo alii vero unum unicuique secundum propriam virtutem et profectus est statim. (16) Abiit autem qui quinque talenta acceperat et operatus est in eis et lucratus est alia quinque. (17) Similiter qui duo acceperat lucratus est alia duo. (18) Qui autem unum acceperat abiens fodit in terra et abscondit pecuniam domini sui. (19) Post multum vero temporis venit dominus servorum illorum et posuit rationem cum eis. (Lc 19.15) Iussit vocari servos quibus dedit pecuniam, ut sciret quantum quisque negotiatus esset. (Mt 25.20) Et accedens qui quinque talenta acceperat obtulit alia quinque talenta dicens domine quinque talenta mihi tradidisti ecce alia quinque superlucratus sum. (21) Ait illi dominus eius: Euge bone serve et fidelis, quia super pauca fuisti fidelis, super multa te constituam; intra in gaudium domini tui. (22) Accessit autem et qui duo talenta acceperat et ait: domine duo talenta tradidisti mihi, ecce alia duo lucratus sum. (23) Ait illi dominus eius: Euge serve bone et fidelis, quia super pauca fuisti fidelis, supra multa te constituam; intra in gaudium domini tui. (Lc 19.20) Et alter venit dicens: Domine, ecce mna tua, quam habui repositam in sudario. (21) Timui enim te, quia homo austeris es, tollis quod non posuisti, et metis quod non seminasti. (22) Dicit ei: De ore tuo te iudico, serve nequam. Sciebas quod ego austeris homo sum, tollens quod non posui et metens quod non seminavi? (23) Et quare non dedisti pecuniam meam ad mensam [Mt 25.27 nummulariis] et ego veniens cum usuris utique exegissem illud? (24) Et adstantibus dixit: Auferte ab illo mnam et date illi qui decem mnas habet. (25) Et dixerunt ei: Domine habet decem mnas. (26) Dico autem vobis quia omni habenti dabitur. . . . (Mt 25.29) Omni enim habenti dabitur et abundabit; ei autem qui non habet et quod videtur habere auferetur ab eo.

Ælfric's conflation of the two versions is puzzling, since it merely serves to create a contradiction over the fate of the one pound (cf line 11 from Mt with 25 from Lc, and also line 104) and does not accord with his exposition, which mainly follows Matthew. Gregory uses Matthew exclusively and includes verse 30 as well. Perhaps Ælfric originally intended to use Luke and incompletely altered it to Matthew to match Gregory's commentary. The one striking feature otherwise of the passage is the phrase *myneterum to sleanne*, 'to moneyers to strike (coins)', rendering Mt 25.27 *nummulariis* or Lc 19.23 *ad mensam.* The OE Gospels agree in using *myneterum*, perhaps because Anglo-Saxon moneyers exchanged and lent money as well as coining it,[5] perhaps because *nummularius* could be an official of the mint (cf Lewis and Short s.v.). But Ælfric's reference to striking coins is harder to explain. It seems to suggest that the servant was to give a pound of gold or silver to the moneyers to be turned into coins (or conceivably a pound's worth of old coins to be turned into new ones) and expect some profit in return, whereas normally it would result in profit to the moneyer.

[5] Cf Henry Loyn's comments on Anglo-Saxon and Continental moneyers, in his *Anglo-Saxon England and the Norman Conquest* (2nd ed., London, 1991), pp. 129–32.

Perhaps what is implied is a practice of lending money, or bullion, to the moneyer to be turned into coins which are then supplied to others, with the moneyer passing a share of his profit to the original lender as interest.

38–53 Gregory, Hom. 9, PL 76, 1106BC:

> Quis itaque iste homo est qui peregre proficiscitur, nisi Redemptor noster, qui in ea carne quam assumpserat abiit in coelum? Carnis enim locus proprius terra est, quae quasi ad peregrina ducitur, dum per Redemptorem nostrum in coelo collocatur. Sed homo iste peregre proficiscens servis suis bona sua tradidit, quia fidelibus suis spiritalia dona concessit. Et uni quidem quinque talenta, alii duo, alii vero commisit unum. Quinque etenim sunt corporis sensus, videlicet visus, auditus, gustus, odoratus et tactus. Quinque ergo talentis donum quinque sensuum, id est exteriorum scientia, exprimitur. Duobus vero intellectus et operatio designatur. Unius autem talenti nomine intellectus tantummodo designatur.

The superiority of the two talents to the five is noted by Gregory later, in the passage quoted at 132–49. Whereas in Gregory the *intellectum* represented by the single talent evidently refers to the understanding of spiritual things also received by the second servant, the *an andgit* of Ælfric could refer to either the external or internal understanding.

54–66 Gregory, Hom. 9, PL 76, 1106C:

> Sed is qui quinque talenta acceperat alia quinque lucratus est, quia sunt nonnulli qui, etsi interna ac mystica penetrare nesciunt, pro intentione tamen supernae patriae docent recta quos possunt de ipsis exterioribus quae acceperunt; dumque se a carnis petulantia et a terrenarum rerum ambitu, atque a visibilium voluptate, custodiunt, ab his etiam alios admonendo compescunt.

But Ælfric emphatically reads the man with five talents as a layman who teaches others primarily by the example of his life, rather than one who, while living rightly, teaches and admonishes others to the right way as well as he can through his own limited understanding.

66–76 Gregory, Hom. 9, PL 76, 1106CD:

> Et sunt nonnulli qui, quasi duobus talentis ditati, intellectum atque operationem percipiunt, subtilia de internis intelligunt, mira in exterioribus operantur; cumque et intelligendo et operando aliis praedicant, quasi duplicatum de negotio lucrum reportant. Bene autem alia quinque vel alia duo in lucrum venisse referuntur, quia dum utrique sexui praedicatio impenditur, quasi accepta talenta geminantur.

Gregory's *mira operantur*, 'perform wonderful things', presumably alludes to miracle-working, rather different from Ælfric's picture of the teacher who wins others to the faith by setting the example of a good life, through the proper use of the outer senses. But Haymo, reworking Gregory, makes it an issue of good living too. The *an underfenge* of 74 presumably refers to the doubling of the capital rather than the original gift.

77–85 Gregory, Hom. 9, PL 76, 1106D-7A:

Sed is qui unum talentum acceperat, abiens, fodit in terram, et abscondit pecuniam domini sui. Talentum in terra abscondere est acceptum ingenium in terrenis actibus implicare, lucrum spiritale non quaerere, cor a terrenis cogitationibus nunquam levare. Sunt namque nonnulli qui donum intelligentiae perceperunt, sed tamen sola quae carnis sunt sapiunt. De quibus per prophetam dicitur: 'Sapientes sunt ut faciant mala, bene autem facere nescierunt' (Jer 4.22).

86–99 Gregory, Hom. 9, PL 76, 1107AB:

Sed Dominus, qui talenta contulit, rationem positurus redit, quia is qui nunc pie spiritalia dona tribuit districte in iudicio merita exquirit, quid quisque accepit considerat, et quod lucrum de acceptis reportet pensat. Servus qui geminata talenta retulit a domino laudatur, atque ad aeternam remunerationem perducitur, cum ei voce dominica dicitur: Euge serve bone et fidelis, quia super pauca fuisti fidelis, super multa te constituam, intra in gaudium domini tui. Pauca quippe bona sunt omnia praesentis vitae, quamlibet multa esse videantur, comparatione retributionis aeternae. Sed tunc fidelis servus super multa constituitur quando, devicta omni corruptionis molestia, de aeternis gaudiis in illa coelesti sede gloriatur. Tunc ad domini sui gaudium perfecte intromittitur, quando in aeterna illa patria assumptus, atque angelorum coetibus admistus, sic interius gaudet de munere, ut non sit iam quod exterius doleat de corruptione.

99–111 Gregory, Hom. 9, PL 76, 1107BCD:

Servus autem qui operari de talento noluit, ad dominum cum verbis excusationis redit, dicens: Domine, scio quia . . . Sunt enim plerique intra sanctam Ecclesiam, quorum iste servus imaginem tenet, qui melioris vitae vias aggredi metuunt, et tamen iacere in sui torporis ignavia non pertimescunt; cumque se peccatores considerant, sanctitatis vias arripere trepidant, et remanere in suis iniquitatibus non formidant . . . velut in perturbatione consilium non habent, dum moriuntur, et vitam timent.

Ælfric's *lifes wegas* are not clearly the same as *melioris vitae vias*.

115–18 None of the commentaries I have seen give such a warning about usury. The Biblical reference is perhaps esp. to Ezekiel 18.

118–29 Cf Gregory, Hom. 9, PL 76, 1108AB:

Pecuniam vero dare nummulariis est eis scientiam praedicationis impendere qui hanc valeant exercere. Sed sicut nostrum periculum aspicitis si dominicam pecuniam teneamus, ita vestrum, fratres carissimi, sollicite pensate, quia a vobis cum usura exigitur quod auditis. . . . Pensate ergo, fratres carissimi, quia de accepta hac verbi pecunia usuras solvetis, et curate ut ex eo quod auditis etiam alia studeatis intelligere quae non auditis.

Gregory understands the interest only as an increase in understanding; Ælfric's notion of both a multiplying of knowledge and an expression of that knowledge in the way of life probably proceeds from his own general understanding of the parable, but the emphasis on works is also to be found in Jerome's commentary on Matthew (*Comm. Matth.*, 4.882–8):

Pecunia ergo et argentum praedicatio evangelii est et sermo divinus qui dari debuit nummulariis et trapizetis, id est vel ceteris doctoribus . . . vel cunctis credentibus qui possunt pecuniam duplicare et cum usuris reddere, ut quicquid sermone didicerant opere explerent.

Bede offers a similar idea (*Comm. Luc.*, 5.1780–3):

Qui verbi pecuniam a doctore percipit emitque credendo necesse est eam cum usuris solvat operando, ut quod auditu didicit exsequatur et actu.

132–49 Gregory, Hom. 9, PL 76, 1108BC:

Opportunum valde videbatur ut cum malo servo unum talentum tollitur, ei potius qui duo quam qui quinque talenta acceperat daretur. Illi enim dari debuit qui minus quam qui plus habuit. Sed, sicut superius diximus, per quinque talenta, quinque videlicet sensus, id est exteriorum scientia designatur, per duo autem intellectus et operatio exprimitur. Plus ergo habuit qui duo quam qui quinque talenta perceperat, quia qui per quinque talenta exteriorum administrationem meruit, ab intellectu interiorum adhuc vacuus fuit. Unum ergo talentum, quod intellectum significare diximus, illi dari debuit qui bene exteriora quae acceperat ministravit. Quod quotidie in sancta ecclesia cernimus, quia plerique dum bene ministrant exteriora quae accipiunt, per adiunctam gratiam ad intellectum quoque mysticum perducuntur, ut etiam de interna intelligentia polleant qui exteriora fideliter administrant.

152–61 Gregory, Hom. 9, PL 76, 1108D-9A:

Habenti namque dabitur, et abundabit, quia quisquis charitatem habet etiam dona alia percipit. Quisquis charitatem non habet etiam dona quae percepisse videbatur amittit. Unde necesse est, fratres mei, ut per omne quod agitis erga charitatis custodiam vigiletis. Charitas autem vera est amicum diligere in Deo, et inimicum diligere propter Deum. Quam quisquis non habet omne bonum amittit quod habet, talento quod acceperat privatur, et iuxta Dominicam sententiam in exteriores tenebras mittitur. Per poenam quippe in exteriores tenebras cadit, qui per culpam suam sponte in interiores tenebras cecidit; et illic coactus patitur tenebras ultionis, qui hic libenter sustinuit tenebras voluptatis.

162–75 Gregory, Hom. 9, PL 76, 1109AB:

Sciendum vero est quod nullus piger ab hac talenti acceptione securus est. Nullus namque est qui veraciter dicat: Talentum minime accepi, non est

> unde rationes ponere cogar. Talenti enim nomine cuilibet pauperi etiam hoc ipsum reputabitur, quod vel minimum accepit. Alius namque accepit intelligentiam, praedicationis ministerium debet ex talento. Alius terrenam substantiam accepit, erogationem talenti debet ex rebus. Alius nec internorum intelligentiam, nec rerum affluentiam accepit, sed tamen didicit artem qua pascitur, ipsa ars ei in talenti acceptione reputatur. Alius nihil horum assecutus est, sed tamen fortasse familiaritatis locum apud divitem meruit, talentum profecto familiaritatis accepit. Si ergo nihil ei pro indigentibus loquitur, pro talenti retentione damnatur.

179–89 From Gregory's homily 17 (PL 76, 1148BC), where it forms part of a long critique of the contemporary clergy (omitted by Ælfric when he used Hom. 17 as a source for CH II.36):

> Ecce in maiestate terribili, inter angelorum atque archangelorum choros videbitur. In illo tanto examine electorum omnium et reproborum multitudo deducetur, et unusquisque quid sit operatus ostendetur. Ibi Petrus cum Iudaea conversa, quam post se traxit, apparebit. Ibi Paulus conversum, ut ita dixerim, mundum ducens. Ibi Andreas post se Achaiam, ibi Ioannes Asiam, Thomas Indiam, in conspectum sui regis conversam ducet. Ibi omnes dominici gregis arietes cum animarum lucris apparebunt, qui sanctis suis praedicationibus Deo post se subditum gregem trahunt. Cum igitur tot pastores cum gregibus suis ante aeterni pastoris oculos venerint, nos miseri quid dicturi sumus, qui ad Dominum nostrum post negotium vacui redimus, qui pastorum nomen habuimus et oves quas ex nutrimento nostro debeamus ostendere non habemus? Hic pastores vocati sumus, et ibi gregem non ducimus.

Gregory introduces the passage with a reference to the image of the talents, but using Luke 19 rather than Matthew 25. Ælfric generalises Gregory's last sentences to refer to all men, not only clerics.

192–215 Apparently Ælfric's own, with a quotation at 196–9 from Mt 10.32: *Omnis ergo qui confitebitur me coram hominibus confitebor et ego eum coram Patre meo qui est in caelis.* There is some resemblance to the passage on confessor-saints in his earlier homily on All Saints, CH I.36.89–103.

215–28 From Eusebius Gallicanus, Hom. 51, 20–34:

> Digne enim in memoria vertitur hominum: qui ad gaudium transiit angelorum . . . Dicit sermo divinus: 'Ne laudaveris hominem in vita sua' [*conflating Sir 11.2 and 11.30?*]—tamquam si diceret: 'lauda post vitam; magnifica post consummationem'—, duplici enim ex causa utilius est hominum magis memoriae laudem dare quam vitae, ut illo potissimum tempore merita sanctitatis extollas: quando nec laudantem adulatio notet, nec laudatum tentet elatio. Lauda ergo post periculum, praedica securum! lauda non navigantis felicitatem, sed, cum pervenit ad portum: lauda ducis virtutem, sed cum perductus est ad triumphum! quis autem vivens, tuto

possit ac sine trepidatione laudari: qui et de praeterito meminit se habere quod doleat, et de futuro videt sibi superesse quod timeat?

229–38 Eusebius Gallicanus, Hom. 51, 50–69:
Beati autem patris merita, iam in tuto posita securi, magnificemus: qui, gubernaculum fidei viriliter tenens, ancoram spei tranquilla iam in statione composuit, et, plenam caelestibus divitiis et aeternis mercibus, navem optato in littore collocavit; qui contra omnes adversarios scutum timoris dei tamdiu infatigabiliter tenuit, donec ad victoriam perveniret. Quid enim fuit totus vitae illius cursus, nisi unus cum [per]vigili hoste conflictus? . . . Quantis hic caecis a via veritatis errantibus et de summa iam in profundum rupe pendentibus, amissum reddidit visum, et illum, quo christus videretur, reparavit intuitum! quantorum auribus surdis et infidelitatis obduratione damnatis, ad percipiendam vocem caelestium mandatorum pretiosum infudit auditum, ut vocanti deo ad misericordiam, responderent per oboedientiam! quantos intrinsecus vulneratos, angelici oris arte ab orationum infirmitate curavit!

240–5 The peroration is in the alliterative style.

39 ON THE FEAST-DAY OF HOLY VIRGINS

Ælfric takes the parable of the five wise and five foolish virgins as his text, from Matthew 25.1–13, the standard reading for the occasion. He cites Augustine and Gregory as his sources, and his main source is indeed a sermon by Augustine,[1] who delicately and gradually teases out the meaning of the different features of the parable: the virgins are all who abstain from illicit pleasures, the lamps are good works, the oil is charity, the sleep is death, the clamour when the bridegroom comes is the universal resurrection, the vessels of oil are human hearts, the foolish virgins who have no oil are those who lead the good life only to impress others, and the merchants who sell oil are flatterers. Augustine's theme is a Pauline one, that the life of ascetic virtue and good works is worthless at the last judgement unless kindled by *caritas*. Gregory the Great, whose sermon on the text is also used by Ælfric, interprets the details in much the same way but gives more prominence to the theme of the transitory glory pursued by the foolish virgins and to the terrors of death and judgement. The one specific point of difference between the two authorities is the interpretation of the oil which distinguishes the wise from the foolish virgins. Whereas Augustine sees it as *caritas*, Gregory interprets it, rather awkwardly, as *nitor gloriae*, the lustre of glory, which the wise virgins

[1] The two sources were identified by Förster (1894, p. 15); Smetana (1959, p. 202) shows that both occur in PDM.

retain in their hearts or conscience while the foolish ones seek it in the adulation of others.

Ælfric draws extensively on both, interweaving and rearranging their points to an unusual degree and occasionally using their words to make rather different points. He takes most from Augustine but minimises his tendency to treat the parable as a riddle or puzzle and omits much of the detailed proof of his interpretation. His own theme is a synthesis and development of the two sources, posing a contrast between the inner quality which makes the wise virgins' life acceptable at the last judgement and the pursuit of empty reputation which makes the foolish virgins' life lustreless when it comes to doomsday. He initially follows Augustine in interpreting the oil as true love (line 48) but as the homily proceeds he speaks not so much of love (the one further reference is at 73) but of the *god ingehyd* in the heart or mind, which motivates action on earth and is judged by God on doomsday (lines 64–7, 143–4, 150–3, 171–4). *Ingehyd* has a variety of meanings, even within Ælfric's own work, sometimes rendering *scientia* and sometimes *conscientia*. Here he seems to mean by it something like an inner will or disposition. The lamps of the virgins are fired by the *god ingehyd* or inner desire to please God, and it is this rather than the works themselves that God judges at doomsday (lines 150–5). At the same time as adapting Augustine's reading in this way, Ælfric absorbs Gregory's interpretation by contrasting this love or *ingehyd* with the pursuit of idle adulation which motivates the foolish virgins (lines 67, 70–78, 139–46, 157–63, 169–71, 215–16, mostly Ælfrician additions).

At the end of the homily Ælfric excludes Gregory's long and terrifying exemplum of the death of a sinner, having already used it in CH I.28, but he does add a warning against the apocryphal legend that the Virgin Mary and other saints would intercede for the damned at the last judgement (lines 184–98). In contrast to the strong apocalyptic warnings of the preface to CH I, and the more ambiguous ones in CH I.40, the emphasis here is on the complete uncertainty of when the end will come and the frequently defeated expectations of the end in the past (lines 111–21); but the fact that the issue was still a live one for Ælfric is evident from the passage on this subject that he added, probably some time around 1005, at 121.

Although the rubric, and indeed the earlier note headed *Excusatio Dictantis*, assign the homily to the feast-day of holy virgins, Ælfric follows the patristic tradition in applying the text to all the faithful, not just women in religious orders,[2] and the avowed subject of the homily is not mentioned again after the rubric. There was indeed no occasion in the secular calendar when such a homily might be needed; but perhaps Ælfric anticipated local needs for the

[2] Cf Jerome's commentary on Matthew (*Commentarii in Evangelium Matthaei*, CCSL 77), as well as Augustine's Serm. 93. Gregory applies it to both sexes, but his references to the *continentes* and to abstinence suggest he may have been thinking particularly of monks and nuns.

festivals of such as St Agnes or St Æthelthryth and left it to the individual preacher to provide an appropriate link.

Sources and Notes

The following texts are cited below:
1. Augustine, *Sermones*, PL 38, Serm. 93, cols. 573–80.
2. Gregory the Great, *Homiliae in Evangelia*, PL 76, Hom. 12, cols. 1118–23.

1–24 Corresponds closely to Mt 25.1–13:

(1) Tunc simile erit regnum coelorum decem virginibus quae, accipientes lampades suas, exierunt obviam sponso et sponsae. (2) Quinque autem ex eis erant fatuae, et quinque prudentes. (3) Sed quinque fatuae, acceptis lampadibus, non sumpserunt oleum secum; (4) prudentes vero acceperunt oleum in vasis suis cum lampadibus. (5) Moram autem faciente sponso, dormitaverunt omnes, et dormierunt. (6) Media autem nocte clamor factus est: Ecce sponsus venit, exite obviam ei. (7) Tunc surrexerunt omnes virgines illae, et ornaverunt lampades suas. (8) Fatuae autem sapientibus dixerunt: Date nobis de oleo vestro, quia lampades nostrae exstinguntur. (9) Responderunt prudentes, dicentes: Ne forte non sufficiat nobis et vobis, ite potius ad vendentes, et emite vobis. (10) Dum autem irent emere, venit sponsus, et quae paratae erant intraverunt cum eo ad nuptias, et clausa est ianua. (11) Novissime vero veniunt et reliquae virgines, dicentes: Domine, Domine, aperi nobis. (12) At ille respondens, ait: Amen dico vobis, nescio vos. (13) Vigilate itaque, quia nescitis diem neque horam.

27–40 Follows Gregory, Hom. 12, PL 76, 1118C–9B:

Sed sciendum nobis est quod saepe in sacro eloquio regnum coelorum praesentis temporis ecclesia dicitur. De quo alio in loco Dominus dicit: 'Mittet filius hominis angelos suos, et colligent de regno eius omnia scandala' (Mt 13.41). Neque enim in illo regno beatitudinis, in quo pax summa est, inveniri scandala poterunt quae colligantur. . . . In qua quia mali cum bonis et reprobi cum electis admisti sunt, recte similis virginibus prudentibus et fatuis esse perhibetur. . . . [*earlier*] In quinque autem corporis sensibus unusquisque subsistit, geminatus autem quinarius denarium perficit. Et quia ex utroque sexu fidelium multitudo colligitur, sancta ecclesia decem virginibus similis denuntiatur.

For heaven as the church, cf CH I.35.27–8 and II.5.36–8, both times following Gregory. The reference at 35 to earlier accounts of the five senses is presumably to CH II.23.44 ff and II.38.46 ff.

40–48 From Augustine, Serm. 93, §§2–3, PL 38, 574:

[§2] Qui ergo se abstinet ab illicito visu, ab illicito auditu, ab illicito odoratu, ab illicito gustatu, ab illicito tactu, propter ipsam integritatem, virginis nomen accepit. [§3] Sed si bonum est abstinere ab illicitis sentiendi motibus, et ideo unaquaeque anima christiana virginis nomen accepit; quare quinque admittuntur, et quinque repelluntur?

with a further sentence from Gregory, Hom. 12, PL 76, 1119C:

Notandum vero quod omnes lampades habent sed omnes oleum non habent.

48–54 From Augustine, Serm. 93, §5, PL 38, 575:

Caritas, quae merito oleo significatur. Omnibus enim humoribus oleum supereminet. Mitte aquam, et superinfunde oleum, oleum supereminet. Mitte oleum, superinfunde aquam, oleum supereminet. Si ordinem servaveris, vincit: si ordinem mutaveris, vincit. 'Caritas nunquam cadit' (1 Cor 13.8).

54–64 Augustine, Serm. 93, §3, PL 38, 574:

Virgines, propter abstinentiam ab illicitis sensibus; lampades habent, propter opera bona. De quibus operibus Dominus dicit: 'Luceant opera vestra coram hominibus, ut videant bona facta vestra, et glorificent Patrem vestrum qui in coelis est' (Mt 5.16). Item discipulis dicit: 'Sint lumbi vestri accincti, et lucernae ardentes' (Lc 12.35). In lumbis accinctis, virginitas: in lucernis ardentibus, opera bona.

64–71 Partially as Gregory, Hom. 12, PL 76, 1119CD:

Prudentes ergo oleum in vasis habent, quia nitorem gloriae intra conscientiam retinent, Paulo attestante, qui ait: 'Gloria nostra haec est, testimonium conscientiae nostrae' (2 Cor 1.12). . . . Unde per psalmistam quoque de sancta electorum ecclesia dicitur: 'Omnis gloria eius filiae regis ab intus' (Ps 44.14).

The phrases *and na cepan dysegra manna herunge* (line 67) and *na on ydelra manna herunge* (lines 70–71) reflect, like the subsequent passage, an earlier part of Gregory's discussion; cf Hom. 12 (PL 76, 1119B): *Humanos favores expetunt* and *solam laudis transitoriae retributionem quaerunt.*

71–8 Not directly from either source, but similar to a passage (based on Haymo) at CH I.28.169–72, where the same quotation from Mt 6.2 is used.

78–86 From Augustine, Serm. 93, §4, though Ælfric's justification for the identification of virgins with all Christians (because they do not fornicate with false pagan gods) is strikingly different from Augustine (PL 38, 574–5):

Non solet dici virginitas utique in coniugatis: tamen etiam ibi est fidei virginitas, quae exhibet pudicitiam coniugalem. Nam ut noverit sanctitas vestra, non importune secundum animam et secundum integritatem fidei, qua etiam fide ab illicitis abstinetur, et bona opera fiunt, unumquemque vel unamquamque animam virginem dici; tota Ecclesia quae constat ex virginibus et pueris, et maritatis feminis et uxoratis viris, uno nomine virgo est appellata. Unde hoc probamus? Apostolum audi dicentem, non solis sanctimonialibus, sed universae prorsus ecclesiae: 'Desponsavi vos uni viro virginem castam exhibere Christo' (2 Cor 11.2).

87–92 A conflation of points made by Ælfric in earlier homilies, CH II.1.100–2 and 4.32–6.

92–103 From Augustine, Serm. 93, §6, PL 38, 575–6:

> Quid est, ire obviam sponso? Corde ire, exspectare eius adventum. Sed ille tardabat. Dum tardat ille, dormierunt omnes. . . . Non recordamini Apostolum dicentem, 'De dormientibus autem nolo vos ignorare, fratres' (1 Thess 4.13), id est, de his qui mortui sunt? Quare enim dormientes vocantur, nisi quia suo die resuscitantur? . . . Fatua sit virgo, prudens sit virgo, somnum mortis omnes patiuntur.

Despite Ælfric's remark that the equation of sleep with death is a commonplace, Augustine gives only the one citation (having first discussed at length the possibility that sleep may stand for the reign of sin) and Gregory none; but Ælfric had given another example at CH II.35.102 ff.

107–11 Augustine, Serm. 93, §8, PL 38, 576–7:

> Quid est, media nocte? Quando non speratur, quando omnino non creditur. Noctem posuit pro ignorantia. . . . 'Dies Domini, ait Apostolus, tanquam fur in nocte, ita veniet' (1 Thess 5.2).

111–15 Augustine, Serm. 93, §7, PL 38, 576:

> Aliquando autem dicunt sibi homines: Ecce iam dies iudicii venit, tanta mala fiunt, tantae tribulationes crebrescunt; ecce omnia quae prophetae dixerunt, pene completa sunt; iam dies iudicii instat. Qui hoc dicunt, et fideliter dicunt, tanquam obviam eunt sponso cogitationibus talibus. Sed ecce bellum super bellum, tribulatio super tribulationem, terrae motus super terrae motum, fames super famem, gens super gentem, et nondum venit sponsus.

Augustine presents these anticipations of the end as a positive feature of the faithful, using them to explain the phrase 'they went to meet the bridegroom'; Ælfric's use of them to gloss midnight, meaning an unknown time, perhaps presents millennialist expectations in a more negative light.

115–21 Augustine, Serm. 93, §8, PL 38, 576–7:

> Ecce ab Adam tot anni transierunt, et ecce complentur sex millia annorum, et continuo, quomodo quidam tractatores computaverunt, continuo veniet dies iudicii: et veniunt, et transeunt computationes, et adhuc remoratur sponsi adventus, et dormiunt virgines quae obviam ierant. Et ecce dum non speratur, dum dicitur, sex millia annorum exspectabantur, et ecce transierunt, unde scimus iam quando veniet? media nocte veniet. Quid est, Media nocte veniet? Dum nescis, veniet. Quare dum nescis, veniet? Ipsum Dominum audi: 'Non est vestrum scire tempora, quae Pater posuit in sua potestate' (Acts 1.7).

The seven-line passage which Ælfric added at this point, in the course of later revision, together with a Latin note on the same issue (Pope 28), is puzzling. It notes, as if to counter Ælfric's original assurance that no-one knows when the world will end, a prophecy, based on 2 Thessalonians 2.7–8 and a discussion by Jerome, that Antichrist will not come and hence the world will not end until the Roman empire falls. Given his apparent move away from apocalyptic expectations after his early work, one would expect this to be intended as an assurance that the end is not all that imminent, but Ælfric does not say so; presumably he saw the Byzantine empire as a guarantee of the continuing stability of the Roman empire.

121–31 Augustine, Serm. 93, §9, PL 38, 577:

> Quis iste clamor, nisi de quo apostolus dicit, 'In ictu oculi, in novissima tuba? Canet enim tuba, et mortui resurgent incorrupti, et nos immutabimur' (1 Cor 15.52). Denique clamore facto media nocte, quo clamabitur, Ecce sponsus venit, quid sequitur? Surrexerunt omnes. Quid est, Surrexerunt omnes? Veniet hora, dixit ipse Dominus, 'quando omnes qui sunt in monumentis, audient vocem eius, et procedent' (Jn 5.28–9).

Ælfric glosses *immutabimur* (lines 126–7) and, at lines 130–1, completes the verse from Jn 5.29: *Qui bona fecerunt in resurrectionem vitae; qui vero mala egerunt in resurrectionem iudicii.*

134–6 Gregory, Hom. 12, PL 76, 1120A:

> Tunc omnes virgines surgunt, quia et electi et reprobi a somno suae mortis excitantur.

136–8 Augustine, Serm. 93, §10, PL 38, 577:

> Coeperunt aptare lampades suas, id est praeparare Deo operum suorum reddere rationem.

138–44 Gregory, Hom. 12, PL 76, 1120AB:

> Sed lampades fatuarum virginum exstinguuntur . . . et a Deo retributionem non inveniunt, quia pro eis receperunt ab hominibus laudes quas amaverunt. Quid est autem quod tunc a prudentibus oleum petunt, nisi quod in adventu iudicis cum se intus vacuas invenerint, testimonium foris quaerunt?

144–6 Augustine, Serm. 93, §10, PL 38, 577–8:

> Hoc quaerebant quod consueverant, id est, alieno oleo lucere, ad alienas laudes ambulare.

146–53 Gregory, Hom. 12, PL 76, 1120B:

> Ac si a sua fiducia deceptae proximis dicant: Quia nos quasi sine opere repelli conspicitis, dicite de nostris operibus quid vidistis. Sed prudentes virgines respondent, dicentes: 'Ne forte non sufficiat nobis et vobis.' In illo enim die (quod tamen de quibusdam in pace ecclesiae quiescentibus

loquor) sibimetipsi testimonium uniuscuiusque vix sufficit; quanto minus et sibi et proximo?

But Ælfric here speaks explicitly of the inner quality, *ingehyd*, and its absence, where Gregory is concerned with the way that the earlier pursuit of praise negates the value of works.

153–5 Cf Augustine, Serm. 93, §14 (PL 38, 578), although he is making a different point:

Forte tu non invenis aliquid in conscientia tua; et invenit ille qui melius videt, cuius acies divina penetrat altiora.

156–7 Augustine, Serm. 93, §11, PL 38, 578:

Non consulentium, sed irridentium est ista responsio.

157–74 Mainly Ælfric's own, developing the contrast between inner disposition, *ingehyd*, and reliance on outward prestige. The identification of merchants as flatterers (*adulatores*) is in both Gregory and Augustine, and the latter offers a partial parallel for 167–8 and 171–4 (Serm. 93, PL 38):

[§15, 579] Et illae fatuae postea venerunt: sed numquid oleum emerunt, aut a quibus emerent invenerunt? [§13, 578] De oleo interiore fecit opera bona, et tamen in illo iudicio trepidat ipsa bona conscientia.

176–83 Developed from Augustine, Serm. 93, §16, PL 38, 579:

Dictum est, 'Pulsate et aperietur vobis' (Mt 7.7): sed modo quando tempus est misericordiae, non quando tempus est iudicii. . . . Tempus est misericordiae; age poenitentiam. . . . Et quid illis profuit sera poenitentia.

184–98 The familiarity of this particular false belief is evident from the account of precisely such intercession in two vernacular homilies, Vercelli 15 (Vercelli Homilies, pp. 259–60) and a homily from Cambridge, Corpus Christi College, MS 41 printed by Hulme.[3] Mary Clayton suggests that the motif derives from the Apocalypse of Mary but notes that it is itself found only in Old English and may be an Anglo-Saxon development.[4] Tom Hill subsequently found a late Icelandic parallel, which may itself derive from Old English sources.[5] The quotation at 195–8 is from Mt 26.41.

200–205 Based on Augustine, Serm. 93, §16, PL 38, 579:

Non illas novit, qui omnia novit? . . . In arte mea non vos agnosco; ars mea nescit vitia: hoc est autem magnum, et nescit vitia, et iudicat vitia. Nescit faciendo, iudicat arguendo.

[3] W. H. Hulme, 'The Old English Gospel of Nicodemus', *Modern Philology* 1 (1903–4), 579–614.

[4] Mary Clayton, 'Delivering the damned: a motif in Old English homiletic prose', *Medium Ævum* 55 (1986), 92–101.

[5] Thomas D. Hill, 'Delivering the damned in Old English anonymous homilies and Jón Arason's *Ljómur*', *Medium Ævum* 61 (1992), 75–82.

208–12 Cf Gregory, Hom. 12, PL 76, 1121D–2A:

Quia post peccata Deus poenitentiam suscipit, si sciret quisque de praesenti saeculo quo tempore exiret, aliud tempus voluptatibus, atque aliud poenitentiae aptare potuisset. Sed qui poenitenti veniam spopondit, peccanti diem crastinum non promisit. Semper ergo extremum diem debemus metuere, quem nunquam possumus praevidere.

213–15 From Augustine's peroration, Serm. 93, §17, PL 38, 580:

Corde vigila, fide vigila, spe vigila, charitate vigila, operibus vigila.

40 DEDICATION OF A CHURCH

Ælfric's subject is not primarily the church as a physical building, the *cyrce*, but the church or temple as an image for man and for the congregation of all the faithful, the *gelaðung*. He weaves together a series of Biblical texts which use the imagery of temple, foundations and building, drawing out their spiritual implications but relying on the continued metaphor rather than a particular issue to sustain the coherence of his discussion. The first 223 lines are mainly concerned with the Old Testament account of Solomon and his temple, and its spiritual significance, though with a substantial excursus on a text from 1 Peter; the next 70 lines turn to St Paul's epistle to the Corinthians, leading into an important discussion of eschatological issues. Only in the last twenty lines does he turn to the practical questions of the treatment of churches.

No obvious model exists for this type of sermon, though for the general shape one might compare the Easter Day homily CH II.15, which similarly combines allegorical exegesis of the Old Testament with the exploration of salient texts from the Gospels and epistles. The use of Solomon's temple as a subject perhaps owes something to Bede's homily for the dedication, which deals mainly with the reading from John 10 but goes on to comment on the temple as a figure for the church. But rather than following any particular source Ælfric seems to be drawing on familiarity with a wide range of authorities, and frequently not the obvious ones such as homilies for the dedication in the homiliaries of Paul the Deacon and others. For the exposition of the Old Testament account he seems to have used Bede's homily for the dedication (Hom. II.24) and a homily for the occasion by Eusebius Gallicanus, both found in versions of PD, but also Augustine and Isidore, plus commentaries on the epistles by Bede and Haymo for the intervening material; and for the discussion of the text from St Paul he used Haymo's commentary and a sermon on the text by Caesarius.

The dedication of churches was the duty of bishops, and Ælfric perhaps wrote this piece with their use in mind; the adaptation by Wulfstan proves that one at least found it useful, and the only copies that survive, outside the complete set in MS K, are two in episcopal collections. But Ælfric may also have intended it for use by ordinary preachers on the anniversary of the dedication of a church.

Sources and Notes

The following texts are cited below:

1. Augustine, *Enarrationes in Psalmos*, ed. E. Dekkers and J. Fraipont, 3 vols., CCSL 38–40 (Turnhout, 1956).
2. Bede, *Commentarius in Epistolas Septem Catholicas*, ed. D. Hurst, CCSL 121 (Turnhout, 1983), pp. 181–342.
3. Bede, *Homiliae*, ed. D. Hurst, CCSL 122 (Turnhout, 1955), Hom. II.24 (pp. 358–67).
4. Caesarius of Arles, *Sermones*, ed. G. Morin, CCSL 104 (Turnhout, 1953), Serm. 179 (pp. 724–29) [cited by section and line numbers].
5. Eusebius Gallicanus, *Collectio Homiliarum*, ed. F. Glorie, CCSL 101A (Turnhout, 1971), Hom. 47 (pp. 555–63).
6. Haymo of Auxerre, *Expositio in Pauli Epistolas*, PL 117, cols. 361–938.
7. Isidore, *Etymologiae*, ed. W. M. Lindsay (Oxford, 1911).
8. Theodulf of Orleans, *Capitula*, in H. Sauer, ed., *Theodulfi Capitula in England*, Texte und Untersuchungen zur englischen Philologie, Bd. 8 (Münich, 1978).

10–15 Summarising 2 Sam 7. The length of David's reign is given at 2 Sam 5.4 (or 3 Reg 2.11)

17–40 From 3 Reg 3.4–15, 4.29:

> (4) Abiit itaque in Gabaon ut immolaret ibi; illud quippe erat excelsum maximum; mille hostias in holocaustum obtulit Salomon super altare illud in Gabaon. (5) Apparuit Dominus Salomoni per somnium nocte dicens: Postula quod vis ut dem tibi. (6) Et ait Salomon: Tu fecisti cum servo tuo David patre meo misericordiam magnam sicut ambulavit in conspectu tuo in veritate et iustitia et recto corde tecum; custodisti ei misericordiam tuam grandem et dedisti ei filium sedentem super thronum eius sicut et hodie. (7) Et nunc Domine Deus tu regnare fecisti servum tuum pro David patre meo; ego autem sum puer parvus, et ignorans egressum et introitum meum. (8) Et servus tuus in medio est populi quem elegisti, populi infiniti qui numerari et supputari non potest prae multitudine. (9) Dabis ergo servo tuo cor docile ut iudicare possit populum tuum et discernere inter malum et bonum. . . . (10) Placuit ergo sermo coram Domino quod Salomon rem huiuscemodi postulasset. (11) Et dixit Deus Salomoni: Quia postulasti verbum hoc et non petisti tibi dies multos nec divitias aut animam inimicorum tuorum, sed postulasti tibi sapientiam ad discernendum iudicium. (12) Ecce feci tibi secundum sermones tuos et dedi tibi cor sapiens et intellegens in tantum, ut nullus ante te similis tui fuerit nec post te surrecturus sit. (13) Sed et haec quae non postulasti dedi tibi, divitias scilicet et gloriam ut nemo fuerit similis tui in regibus cunctis retro diebus. (14) Si autem ambulaveris in viis meis et custodieris

praecepta mea et mandata mea sicut ambulavit pater tuus, longos faciam dies tuos. (15) Igitur evigilavit Salomon et intellexit quod esset somnium. . . . (4.29) Dedit quoque Deus sapientiam Salomoni et prudentiam multam nimis et latitudinem cordis quasi harenam quae est in litore maris.

40–47 From 3 Reg 4.21–4, 11.42:

(21) Salomon autem erat in dicione sua habens omnia regna sicut a flumine terrae Philisthim usque ad terminum Aegypti, offerentium sibi munera et servientium ei cunctis diebus vitae eius. (22) Erat autem cibus Salomonis per dies singulos triginta chori similae et sexaginta chori farinae; (23) Decem [*Ælfric has* twelf] boves pingues et viginti boves pascuales et centum arietes, excepta venatione cervorum caprearum atque bubalorum et avium altilium. (24) Ipse enim . . . habebat pacem ex omni parte in circuitu. (11.42) Dies autem quos regnavit Salomon in Hierusalem super omnem Israhel, quadraginta anni sunt.

47–52 3 Reg 4:

(32) Locutus est quoque Salomon tria milia parabolas et fuerunt carmina eius quinque et mille. (33) Et disputavit super lignis a cedro quae est in Libano usque ad hysopum quae egreditur de pariete; et disseruit de iumentis et volucribus et reptilibus et piscibus. (34) Et veniebant de cunctis populis ad audiendam sapientiam Salomonis.

52–60 3 Reg 6:

(2) Domus autem quam aedificabat rex Salomon Domino habebat sexaginta cubitos in longitudine et viginti cubitos in latitudine et triginta cubitos in altitudine. (3) Et porticus erat ante templum viginti cubitorum longitudinis iuxta mensuram latitudinis templi et habebat decem cubitos latitudinis ante faciem templi. (38) . . . Aedificavitque eam annis septem.

The gold and precious stones are mentioned in cc. 6 and 7. I do not know why Ælfric says the *porticus* or porch was on the east; it is not so specified in the Bible.

60–73 3 Reg 8:

(1) Tunc congregavit omnes maiores natu Israhel. (62) Igitur rex et omnis Israhel cum eo immolabant victimas coram Domino. (63) Mactavitque Salomon hostias pacificas quas immolavit Domino boum viginti duo milia, ovium centum viginti milia, et dedicaverunt templum Domini rex et filii Israhel. (22) Stetit autem Salomon ante altare Domini . . . [*Ælfric summarises the long prayer at 8.23–53.*] (54) Factum est autem cum conplesset Salomon orans Dominum omnem orationem et deprecationem hanc, surrexit de conspectu altaris Domini utrumque enim genu in terram fixerat et manus expanderat ad caelum. (55) Stetit ergo et benedixit omni ecclesiae Israhel voce magna dicens: (56) Benedictus Dominus qui dedit requiem populo suo Israhel iuxta omnia quae locutus est . . . per Mosen servum suum. (66) Et in die octava dimisit populos qui benedicentes regi

profecti sunt in tabernacula sua laetantes et alacri corde super omnibus bonis quae fecerat Dominus David servo suo et Israhel populo suo.

74–85 The interpretation of Solomon as peace is common, but of the writings Ælfric is likely to have known only Isidore's *Etymologies* parallels the reason he gives (*Etymologiae*, VII.6.65): *Salomon . . . id est pacificus, eo quod in regno eius pax fuerit*. The identification with Christ is also common, but the supporting links with other Biblical texts are more varied. Bede cites Isaiah (Hom. II.24, 231–4):

> Salomon quippe rex qui interpretatur pacificus ipsum redemptorem nostrum typice designat de quo Isaias ait: 'Multiplicabitur eius imperium, et pacis non erit finis' (Is 9.7).

Ælfric's use of Eph 2.14 (lines 80–81) and Jn 14.27 (lines 83–5) is paralleled in Augustine's *Enarrationes in Psalmos*, Ps 71, 1.7–17:

> Salomon quippe interpretatur pacificus; ac per hoc, tale vocabulum illi verissime atque optime congruit, per quem mediatorem ex inimicis, accepta remissione peccatorum, reconciliamur Deo. . . . Idem ipse est ille pacificus, 'qui fecit utraque unum. . . .' Ipse in evangelio dicit: 'pacem relinquo vobis, pacem meam do vobis.'

Augustine's comment is recycled in the Ps-Bede *Quaestiones in Libros Regum* (PL 93, 444–5) and, partially, in the homily by Eusebius Gallicanus cited below, lines 175–87. But Augustine focuses on peace-making between God and man. Ælfric's reference to peace between men and angels uses again the interpretation of Eph 2.14 which he used at CH I.2.51–2, following Bede's Hom. I.6.

85–98 Cf Bede Hom. II.24, 234–7:

> Templum quod aedificavit catholica eius ecclesia est quam de universis per orbem credentibus quasi de vivis lapidibus in unam suae fidei et caritatis conpagem adgregat.

The reference to living stones prompts Ælfric to cite (lines 89–93) the underlying text, 1 Petr 2.4–5:

> (4) Ad quem accedentes lapidem vivum ab hominibus quidem reprobatum, a Deo autem electum honorificatum. (5) Et ipsi tamquam lapides vivi superaedificamini domus spiritalis.

Lines 87–8 and 96–7 repeat material from CH I.26.64 ff.

98–108 Drawing on 1 Cor 3.17 (quoted at 100–1) and 1 Cor 6.19:

> An nescitis quoniam membra vestra templum est Spiritus Sancti qui in vobis est.

Lines 103–4 repeat a comment on this verse in Haymo's commentary on the Pauline epistles (*Expositio*, PL 117, 527A):

> A tempore baptismatis incipit habitare in nobis Spiritus sanctus, et templum illius sunt omnes angeli et omnes iusti.

108–17 Cf Bede's commentary on 1 Peter (*Comm. Epist.*, 2.5.93–8):

> Ita illos domus spiritales dicit fieri debere, cum sit una domus Christi ex electis omnibus angelis et hominibus condita, quo modo cum sit una

ecclesia catholica toto orbe diffusa saepe pluraliter appellantur ecclesiae propter multifaria scilicet fidelium conventicula variis tribubus linguis et populis discreta.

117–24 This seems to be Ælfric's own attempt to deal with literal-minded readers, but the reinterpretation of 'house' as household rather than building does seem to run against the preceding and subsequent use of stones as images for men. The distinction between *weallum* and *wagum* (line 121) is perhaps between stone and wooden walls, or possibly between foundation walls and others.

125–31 Bede on 1 Peter (*Comm. Epist.*, 2.5.61–7):

> Et sicut ordines lapidum in pariete portantur alii ab aliis, ita portantur fideles quique a praecedentibus in ecclesia iustis, portant ipsi sequentes per doctrinam et tolerantiam usque ad ultimum iustum, qui cum a prioribus portetur quem portare debeat ipse sequentem non habebit, qui autem omne aedificium portat et ipse a nemine portatur dominus est Christus.

133–44 No apparent parallel for this distinctive interpretation of the offerings as liturgical praise. The reference to *clænum* servants of God at 142 suggests that Ælfric wishes particularly to emphasise the importance of a liturgy conducted by monks or at least celibate priests. Ps 92.5, quoted at 138–40, is an antiphon for the occasion (cf Gregory, *Liber Responsalis,* PL 78, 830). It is also quoted by Haymo in his homily for the occasion (Hom. 141, PL 118, 746B).

147–75 From 3 Reg 10:

> (1) Sed et regina Saba audita fama Salomonis in nomine Domini venit temptare eum in enigmatibus. (2) Et ingressa Hierusalem multo comitatu et divitiis, camelis portantibus aromata et aurum infinitum nimis et gemmas pretiosas; venit ad Salomonem et locuta est ei universa quae habebat in corde suo. (3) Et docuit eam Salomon omnia verba quae proposuerat; non fuit sermo qui regem posset latere et non responderet ei. (4) Videns autem regina Saba omnem sapientiam Salomonis et domum quam aedificaverat, (5) et cibos mensae eius et habitacula servorum et ordinem ministrantium vestesque eorum et pincernas et holocausta quae offerebat in domo Domini, non habebat ultra spiritum. (6) Dixitque ad regem: verus est sermo quem audivi in terra mea (7) super sermonibus tuis et super sapientia tua, et non credebam narrantibus mihi donec ipsa veni et vidi oculis meis, et probavi quod media pars mihi nuntiata non fuerit. Maior est sapientia et opera tua quam rumor quem audivi. (8) Beati viri tui et beati servi tui hii qui stant coram te semper et audiunt sapientiam tuam. (9) Sit Dominus Deus tuus benedictus cui placuisti et posuit te super thronum Israhel . . . et constituit te regem ut faceres iudicium et iustitiam. (10) Dedit ergo regi centum viginti talenta auri et aromata multa nimis et gemmas pretiosas. . . . (13) Rex autem Salomon dedit reginae Saba omnia quae voluit et petivit ab eo exceptis his quae ultro obtulerat ei munere

regio; quae reversa est et abiit in terram suam cum servis suis. . . . (23) Magnificatus est ergo rex Salomon super omnes reges terrae divitiis et sapientia. (24) Et universa terra desiderabat vultum Salomonis ut audiret sapientiam eius quam dederat Deus in corde eius; (25) et singuli deferebant ei munera vasa argentea et aurea vestes et arma bellica aromata quoque et equos et mulos per annos singulos.

175–87 Eusebius Gallicanus, Hom. 47:

[33–46] Ergo in figura reginae huius ecclesia venit . . . audire sapientiam Salomonis, id est, veri pacifici Domini nostri Iesu Christi, qui 'fecit utraque unum, solvens inimicitias' inter Deum et hominem 'in carne sua' (Eph 2.14). Venit, post veteres et profanas superstitiones audire et discere de fidei illuminatione et iudicio futuro, de animae immortalitate, de spe resurrectionis et gloria. . . . Venit exhibens munera digna Christo, aurum et gemmas pretiosas; et hoc camelis portantibus. . . . [50–53] Cum his tamquam muneribus regina haec ingreditur ad pacificum regem Christum, exhibens secum fidei aurum, puritatis incensa, pretiosas splendorisque gemmas, morum scilicet insignia et ornamenta virtutum.

Ælfric's substitution of prayer for purity as the interpretation of incense (line 186), if it is not due to a variant in the Latin, may be prompted by his interpretation at CH I.7.230.

187–93 Eusebius Gallicanus, Hom. 47, 18–20:

Haec est regina illa de qua ad Dominum dicitur, 'Astitit regina a dextris tuis in vestitu deaurato, circumamicta varietate' (Ps 44.10); id est, diversarum circumdata pretioso decore virtutum.

193–9 Eusebius Gallicanus, Hom. 47:

[53–6] 'Et locuta est ei universa quae habebat in corde suo'; id est, aperuit ei cor suum, manifestavit ei occulta conscientiae suae in confessione et paenitudine praecedentium delictorum. [46–9] Et hoc camelis portantibus, id est, ex gentili populo venientibus, qui prius fuerant vitiorum foeditate distorti, et malorum onere curvi, ac peccatorum pravitate deformes.

199–208 Eusebius Gallicanus, Hom. 47:

[61–5] Quid erat rationis, ut praepotens regina domum, expensas, et cibos regios tantopere miraretur? Ergo hoc loco aliqua maiora nos oportet inquirere. Vidit ergo ecclesia ex gentibus congregata sapientiam Christi. [68–70] Agnovit verum fabricatorem caeli et terrae, et potentissimum humani generis conditorem; de cuius sapientia dicitur, 'Omnia in mensura et pondere et numero constituisti' (Sap 11.21). [76] Cibus enim Christi est salus nostra.

208–17 Eusebius Gallicanus, Hom. 47:

[90–95] Cum ergo pervenerit regina haec, sive ecclesia, sive quaeque anima sancta, cum pervenerit in aeternam Hierusalem . . . multo plura et magnificentiora perspiciet, quam ei sunt in hac terra per sacra eloquia, per prophetas atque apostolos nuntiata. [*Eusebius then quotes 1 Cor 13.12, but Ælfric uses 1 Cor 2.9 (alluded to in the next passage):* sed sicut scriptum est, quod oculus non vidit nec auris audivit nec in cor hominis ascendit quae praeparavit Deus his qui diligunt illum.] [Hom. 47, 118–23] Et revera id 'quod parat Deus diligentibus se' . . . acquiri potest, aestimari non potest. . . . Habebit de perceptione fructum, non habebit de satietate fastidium.

For 217–23 cf the passage from Eusebius cited at 175–87.

223–38 Ælfric now turns to 1 Cor 3.11–15:

(11) Fundamentum enim aliud nemo potest ponere praeter id quod positum est qui est Christus Iesus. (12) Si quis autem superaedificat supra fundamentum hoc aurum, argentum, lapides pretiosos, ligna, faenum, stipulam, (13) uniuscuiusque opus manifestum erit. Dies enim declarabit quia in igne revelabitur et uniuscuiusque opus quale sit ignis probabit. (14) Si cuius opus manserit quod superaedificavit, mercedem accipiet. (15) Si cuius opus arserit, detrimentum patietur; ipse autem salvus erit sic tamen, quasi per ignem.

239–50 For commentary on these fearful words, Ælfric seems at first to use Haymo's commentary on 1 Corinthians (*Expositio*, PL 117):

[525CD] Si quis autem superaedificat supra fundamentum hoc, id est supra fidem Christi, aurum, id est doctrinam sanctam et rectum sensum, argentum, id est eloquia divina . . . et lapides pretiosos, id est diversa genera virtutum . . . nec consumentur ab igne die iudicii. . . . [526A] Igitur sicut aurum, et argentum, et lapides pretiosi igne probantur, et tamen non consumuntur, ita in die iudicii qui habuerint bona opera et bonam praedicationem, licet per ignem transeant, tamen nullam poenam neque laesuram sustinebunt.

The nature of the fire is a significant issue and Ælfric, with his eschatological interests, articulates it carefully. For St Paul it may have been only an element of his metaphor. Haymo interprets it literally, as a fire that purges or expiates on the day of judgement, though it is perhaps also eternal, since those guilty of capital sins remain in it. Ælfric defines it more explicitly as the fire which envelops the whole world at the end of time (lines 248, 274–5; cf too CH I.40.140–55 and Pope 11.296 ff). It is a purgatorial fire, apparently purging or cleansing both those who are still living at the end of time and those who are dead (cf 275–9 and CH I.40.145–6), and differentiated from the eternal fire in which the damned burn for ever (*ðam ecum fyre*, 259; Caesarius makes the same distinction). He then goes on to distinguish it also from the purgatorial places in which the souls of the dead are purged prior to the last judgement (lines 275–9).

254–8 Cf Haymo, *Expositio*, PL 117, 525D-6A:

Per fenum vero, lignum, stipulam, levia peccata, sicut est otiosus sermo, risus inhonestus, et caetera talia. . . . Qui vero habuerint levia peccata,

> transeundo per ignem expiabuntur, quia consumentur ibi sicut fenum vel stipula, sive ut ligna comburentur ab igne, tamen ipsi non remanebunt in igne, sed mandati et probati ascendent ad Dominum.

258–61 Cf Haymo, *Expositio*, PL 117, 526AB:

> At qui habuerint gravia peccata, quae a regno coelorum separant . . . illi pondere peccatorum gravati, remanebunt in igne, et sustinebunt poenas non deficientes.

and Caesarius, Serm. 179, 2.10–12:

> Illo transitorio igne, de quo dixit apostolus, purgari non poterit, sed aeterna illum flamma sine ullo remedio cruciabit.

261–67 Haymo (above) cites only idle speech and laughter as minor sins. Caesarius gives a fuller list, Serm. 179, 3.3–14:

> Quotiens aliquis aut in cibo aut in potu plus accipit quam necesse est, ad minuta peccata noverit pertinere: quotiens plus loquitur quam oportet . . .; quotiens pauperem inportune petentem exasperat; . . . quotiens excepto desiderio filiorum uxorem suam agnoverit . . . si plus aut proximum aut uxorem aut filium aut servum exasperaverit quam oportet, si amplius fuerit blanditus quam expedit.

The last two in Ælfric's list, eating before time and immoderate play, are not in either source.

267–72 Caesarius, Serm. 179:

> [3.29–31] Quibus peccatis licet occidi animam non credamus, tamen ita eam velud quibusdam pustulis et quasi horrenda scabie replentes deformem faciunt. [4.4–6] Quicquid enim de istis peccatis a nobis redemptum non fuerit, illo igne purgandum est.

272–5 Caesarius, Serm. 179, 5.9–11:

> Et qui modo nec unum digitum suum in ignem vult mittere, quare non timeat ne necesse sit tunc non parvo tempore cum anima et corpore cruciari?

275–9 The notion of many distinct purgatorial places recalls especially the account of Fursey, CH II.20.

279–82 Haymo cites only adultery, fornication and murder as deadly sins. Caesarius again gives a fuller list, similar to Ælfric's (Serm. 179, 2.3–6):

> Sacrilegium, homicidium, adulterium, falsum testimonium, furtum, rapina, superbia, invidia, avaritia, et, si longo tempore teneatur, iracundia, ebrietas, si assidua sit, et detractio in eorum numero computantur.

Ælfric has a further three, pagan worship, sorcery and witchcraft.

282–7 Caesarius, Serm. 179, 5.15–21:

> Illi enim qui capitalia peccata committunt, si ea, dum vivunt, emendare paenitentiae medicamento noluerint, ad illum ignem . . . venire non

poterunt, sed magis illam duram et inrevocabilem sententiam audituri sunt: 'discedite a me, maledicti in ignem aeternum' (Mt 25.41).

293–311 The final set of injunctions on the proper treatment of churches and clergy has no parallel in the sources Ælfric had been using for this homily. For 293–8 cf the injunction against a priest buying a church in the *Capitula* of Theodulf of Orleans (Sauer, c.16).

EXPLICIT AND ORATIO

While the prefaces seem to have been composed originally to accompany separate copies of CH I and CH II, the concluding prayer was evidently written to accompany the two-Series set that we find in MS K, which Ælfric presumably put together after completing the Second Series and circulating copies of it to Sigeric and others who had previously been sent the First Series. Note how he refers here to 'these two books' but to 'this book' in the singular in the preface to CH II (line 44). If he was serious about his promise not to translate Gospel texts or expositions ever again he soon changed his mind, since his five homilies for Fridays in Lent and the homily for the third Sunday in Lent, all focusing on the Gospel passages for the occasions, are thought to be relatively early work, prior to the completion of the Lives of Saints collection (itself finished by 1001 at the latest),[1] and he continued to produce such homilies through the rest of his career. There are similar disclaimers in the prefaces to the Grammar and the Lives of Saints. The final sentence refers to the item which follows next in MS K, Ælfric's *De Temporibus Anni*, but the sentence is not an integral part of the *Oratio* and we do not need to assume that the tract appeared in all copies of the two-Series set issued by Ælfric.

[1] See Clemoes 1959, pp. 220–1, and Pope 1967–8, pp. 226–7.

GLOSSARY

Procedures and conventions

1. Headword

There are about 5056 separate headwords in the text, ranging from 536 for the letter S to 36 for I. There are also 430 proper names, which are included with the other words but followed by brief identifications rather than glosses. Æ is placed after **A**, and **þ** after **T**, and the **ge-** prefix is ignored in the ordering; **þ** is always used in the headword and citations rather than **ð**. The commonest spelling is given first, citing nouns by nominative singular and verbs by infinitive, except in a few instances when using a slightly less common variant spelling places the word with closely related words. Variant spellings of the headword or the stem are listed immediately after it if relatively common, e.g. **agifan, agyfan**, but towards the end if not (and in that case, usually with an indication of frequency in the form 2x = twice), e.g. **acyn-** for **acennan**, or **aflyg-** for **afligan**. In the case of verbs which occur both with and without the prefix **ge-**, and apparently with the same meaning, both forms are given in the headword unless one is relatively rare, when the latter is cited near the end of the entry; past participles in **ge-** are assumed to derive from the only or commonest form of the verb otherwise evidenced in the CH unless there are differences of meaning. Nouns ending in **-nyss, -nys, -nes** etc. are always listed as **-nyss**. In cases where words that are formally past participles occur only adjectivally and no other forms of the putative verb occur in the text, I normally cite them in the pp. form, since it is not clear that the verb has any independent existence for Ælfric (this is esp. true with prefixed forms such as **asolcen**). Where the headword form does not occur and is in doubt, it is placed in square brackets.

2. Gender and class of Nouns

The gender of nouns is specified on the basis of usage in the text or, if that is not clear, the dictionaries. If the gender of a noun is not clear from the instances in the text and the dictionaries record variation, I give the possibilities, in the form **mn**, etc. If there are clear signs in the text of more than one gender, I give the evidence (but I have not taken such features as, e.g., plural endings in **-u** as evidence in itself of neuter gender). I have marked feminine and neuter nouns (but not masculines) as weak if the text or dictionaries so indicate; but I have given the forms if the evidence is contradictory.

3. Classes of Verbs

Classes of strong verbs, as defined by the standard grammars, are indicated by arabic numerals. Classes of weak verbs, as traditionally defined, are indicated by roman numerals, as I, II and III, but it needs to be noted that Ælfric's usage does not accord with these classifications in many cases. Class I verbs of the **herian** type are indistinguishable from Class II verbs, since the present tense forms are generally those of Class II and the past tense and past participle of both types vary freely between **-ed-**, **-od-** and **-ad-**; I have marked the former as I/II. Class I verbs that had **-gan** or **-wan** in the infinitive in earlier OE, such as **bebyrgan** and **awilwan**, often appear here with regular **-ian** (and **-iað** in the present plural); but their preterites are distinct and I have marked them as Class I (and generally given their forms).

4. Meanings

I give the meanings which seem to be active for examples in the text. Where possible I distinguish examples of distinct senses; but not in cases where, though there are important distinctions of sense, the particular sense of individual examples might be a matter of opinion, and indeed where more than one sense may be present, e.g. with the senses 'pre-ordain, foresee, provide, scrutinize' for **foresceawian**.

My aim is to give the sense in MnE terms. I try to give the range of MnE equivalents for a particular word, and to distinguish different senses where these are differently expressed in MnE; but not, generally, to distinguish different senses and uses which are still current with the same word in MnE, e.g. **nama** meaning appellation, reputation, 'in God's name'.

5. Examples

I normally give four examples, two from each series, if they occur; they are not necessarily the first two occurrences, but are often chosen to illustrate a range of uses or forms. Where it is necessary to distinguish different senses of the word, I illustrate each one, but not necessarily with four examples of each subsidiary sense. Where not all examples have been cited, I conclude with an indication of the number of occurrences, in the form [234 ex.]; it is an approximate number in some cases, e.g. with frequently occurring words which have homonyms such as **to** prep. and adv. Expressions like 'I.3.47, etc' mean there are several more examples in that homily; 'I.3.47 ff' means there are several more examples in the succeeding lines.

6. Variant spellings and grammatical forms

For variations in the spelling of the stem see above under Headwords. For strong verbs I have indicated the forms taken by the preterite and the past participle, and also the pres.s. where it involves a change in the stem or might cause difficulty. For weak verbs I have cited any irregular or unexpected forms, but have not reported the regular alternation between **-ed-**, **-od-** and **-ad-** in the preterite and pp., or that between **-gende**, **-giende**, **-iende** and **-igende** in the present participle of verbs in **-ian**, or the similar variations between **-i-** and **-ig-** etc. in the present tenses of such verbs. Verb inflexions are on the whole those cited in the grammars for late West Saxon, but note that subjunctive plurals are **-on** or occasionally **-an** rather than **-en**, that **-an** can occur as well as **-on** for indicative plurals, and **-on** and even **-en** for infinitives. For neuter nouns I have reported the instances of plurals in **-a** and **-u**, since there is much variation here. Where forms of verbs or nouns are cited I have generally indicated their grammatical function, but I have not attempted a comprehensive parsing of all forms that occur in the text. Variations in medial vowels (e.g. **leofesta, leofosta**), or their suppression, and doubling of consonants (e.g. **licmen, licmenn**) are not generally noted.

7. Cross-references

Cross-references from one word to another related word are marked by 'cf'; cross-references from a variant spelling to the head-word are marked by 'see'. I have cross-referred from simplex forms to all prefixed forms (except of course **ge-** and, for the most part, **un-**), but not from the prefixed forms to the simplex. Where there is no simplex but several prefixed forms, I have given the full list under the first example (alphabetically) and cross-referred from the others, in the form: cf. **be-** etc. I have not given cross-references for standard grammatical forms (e.g. **bead** for **beodan**) and not always for standard spelling variations, such as **-i-** for **-y-**.

Abbreviations

After head-word: adj. = adjective; adv. = adverb; f. = feminine (noun); m. = masculine (noun); n. = neuter (noun); prep. = preposition; interj. = interjection; vb 1–7 = strong verb, class 1–7; vb I–III = weak verb class I–III; anom. vb = anomalous verb; pret.pres.vb = preterite present verb; uninfl. = uninflected.

In citing forms, case is shown as nom., acc., gen., dat., instr.; case and number as, e.g., ds. = dative singular, nap. = nom. and acc. plural.

Other common abbreviations are:

app.cr. = apparatus criticus
comp. = comparative
correl. = correlative
excl. = excluding
fig. = figuratively
imper. = imperative
impers. = impersonal
inf. = infinitive
intrans. = intransitive
lit. = literally
pres. = present
pres.pt. = present participle
pp. = past participle
pret. = preterite
subj. = subjunctive
sup. = superlative
trans. = transitive
usu. = usually
var. variant(s)
voc. = vocative
w. = with
wk = weak

a adv. *for ever.* I.1.293, 296; 19.194; II.1.303; 14.269. [84 ex.]

Aaron half-brother of Moses. II.1.52; 12.41, 49, etc; 15.203. [8 ex.]

abacan vb 6. *to bake.* II.15.87 (pp. **abacen**).

Abacuc, Abbacuc the prophet Habbakuk. I.37.210 ff; II.11.330.

abbud m. *abbot.* I.23.137 ff; II.9.34; 11.1, 61, etc; 21.17, 154. **abbod-** 3x. [9 ex.]

abbudisse wk f. *abbess.* II.10.213; 32.153, 168.

Abdenago one of the three 'children of Israel' persecuted by Nebuchadnezzar; also called **Azarias**. II.4.251.

Abdias St Abdias of Babylon, said to have been one of Christ's 72 disciples; supposed follower of SS Simon and Jude, credited with a collection of acts of the apostles. II.33.275.

Abel son of Adam and Eve. II.4.104, 109; 5.49.

aberan vb 4. *to bear, give birth to.* I.13.106; 25.86; II.1.58; 29.118; *to carry* I.15.166; 23.8; II.2.63; 22.182; *to sustain, endure* II.1.33; 11.80. Pret.s. **abær**; pp. **aboren**. [22 ex.]

aberstan vb 3. *to break out.* II.11.503 (pret.s. **abærst**).

Abiathar highpriest in Jerusalem at the time of the apostles. II.27.142, 164, 169.

abidan vb 1. *to await.* I.9.129; II.10.322; *to wait, remain* I.9.6; 15.148; II.24.62; 34.296. Pret.s. **abad**.

abiddan vb 5. *to obtain by asking or praying* (w. acc. or gen.). I.11.84; 37.114; II.1.298; 14.96; *to ask for, pray for* II.14.184; 27.172 (two senses not always distinct). Pret. **abæd, abæd-**. [15 ex.]

Abigail wife of Nabal and subsequently of King David. I.32.115.

Abiron rebel against Moses in the wilderness. II.27.130, 133.

abitan vb 1. *to bite, devour.* I.17.44; 26.136; II.13.252; 30.36. Pret.pl. **abiton**; pp. **abiten**. [9 ex.]

ablawan vb 1. *to blow, breathe.* I.1.67; 16.9; 22.214; II.11.562; *to blow away* I.32.153. Pret.s. **ableow**. [10 ex.]

ablendan vb I. *to blind.* I.8.185; 10.39; 39.90; II.4.219. Pres.s.3 **ablent**; pp. **ablend**. [8 ex.]

ablicged pp. as adj. *stupefied, shocked, amazed.* I.22.52; 26.226; II.11.467; 20.174. [9 ex.]

ablinnan vb 3. *to cease, stop.* trans., w. acc. or gen., and intrans. I.4.152; 29.154, 274; II.4.285; 33.28. Pp. **ablunnen**. [7 ex.]

Abraham the patriarch. I.3.32; 6.12, etc; II.1.128; 4.131 ff. [89 ex.]

Abram the original name of Abraham. I.6.25, 33.

abrecan vb 4. *to break free, to break away, escape*. I.15.149–50; 23.89; II.39.51. Pret.s.3 subj. **abræce**.

abredan vb 3. *to pull, draw, take away*. I.10.47; 27.146; 28.47; II.10.116; 11.544; 14.92. Pret. **abræd, abrud-**; pp. **abroden**.

abreoþan vb 2. *to fall, fail*. I.1.27; 18.108; 19.151, 167; II.6.84. Pres.s.3 **abryþ**; pret.s. **abreaþ**.

abugan vb 2. *to bow down, turn away*. I.1.222; 11.125; 14.51; 21.70; II.18.22, 54–6, 124. Pret.s. **abeah**.

abutan, -on adv. *around*. I.20.173; 28.203 (prep.?).

abyrian vb I. *to taste*. w. gen. I.16.137; 25.14 (pres.s.3 **abyrigð**). Cf **on-**.

ac conj. *but*. I.praef.50; 1.19; II.praef.38; 1.28. [1277 ex.]

ac f. *oaktree*. II.10.301.

acealdod pp. as adj. *chilled*. I.35.233.

acennan vb I. *to bear (a child), give birth to*. I.1.241; 2.5–6, 86; II.1.3 ff, 39–40; 34.1; *to bring forth, give forth* I.20.62–4; II.12.523. **acyn-** 2x. (Mainly used in pp., 124x, = *born*.) [156 ex.] Cf **cynnan**.

acennednyss f. *birth*. I.2.105; 5.100; II.1.2, etc.; 4.90. **acened-** 1x, **acynned-** 1x. [71 ex.]

aceocian vb II. *to choke*. I.14.178.

aceorfan vb 3. *to cut, cut away*. I.34.148, 230.

Achaia province in southern part of Greece. I.38.171; II.38.185.

aclænsian vb II. *to purge, cleanse*. I.praef.92; 23.78.

acolian vb II. *to cool off*. II.37.109.

acoren pp. as adj. *select, well-chosen*. II.26.124. Cf **geceosan**.

acs- see **ax-**.

acucian vb II. *to revive, come back to life*. I.AppB2.14, 17 ff; II.1.55; 7.32.

acuman vb 4. *to bear, endure*. I.praef.67; *to come, descend, go* I.1.151 (pret.s. **acom**); II.11.510.

acumendlic adj. *bearable*. I.38.244; comp. adv. (w. adjectival function?) I.6.89. Cf **un-**.

acweccan vb I. *to shake, quiver*. I.5.164 (pret. **acwehte**).

acwelan vb 4. *to die*. I.4.28 (pret.s.3 subj. **acwæle**); II.12.323; 31.48.

acwellan vb I. *to kill*. I.1.196; 3.44; II.2.196; 4.195. Pret. **acweald-**; pp. **acweald**. [92 ex.]

acwencan vb I. *to extinguish, quench*. II.10.122; 11.56; 16.221; 39.15, 138, 142.

acyn- see **acen-**

ad n. *pyre*. II.33.43.

Adam the first man. I.1.68, etc; 11.154; II.1.60; 4.100 ff. [64 ex.]

adeadian vb II. *to die*. I.10.131; 11.55.

adela m. *muck*. II.23.187; 32.77.

adelfan vb 3. *to dig*. II.7.106; 11.127.

adil- see **adyl-**.

adl f. *sickness*. I.5.127; 31.93; II.9.117–8; 10.89. [8 ex.] Cf **feorh-**.

(ge)adlian vb II. *to be ill, grow faint*. I.5.143; 40.57.

adlig adj. *sick, diseased*. I.praef.78; 21.104; II.2.62; 10.37. [18 ex.] Cf **fot-**.

adlung f. *sickness*. I.8.53.

adrædan vb I. *to fear*. II.37.97. Cf **on-**.

adræfan vb I. *to drive out, expel*. I.1.44; 4.172; II.6.45; 11.265. [23 ex.] Cf **to-**.

adrencan vb I. *to drown* (trans.). I.1.194, 200; 14.124; II.15.29. pp. **adrengt, adrenct**. Cf **for-**.

adreogan vb 2. *to live, experience* (w. **lif** as object). I.30.259; AppB3.110; II.10.162; 20.188; *to live through, endure, spend* I.5.139; 37.133, 250; II.11.492; *to do, perform, commit* I.24.54; II.9.129; *to earn?* II.19.240. Pres.s.3 **adrihð**; pret. **adreah, adrug-**. [15 ex.]

Adriaticum Adriatic (sea). I.34.6.

adrifan vb 1. *to drive (nails)*. I.9.172; II.18.50; *to drive away* II.2.27. Pret.s. **adraf**; pp. **adrifen**.

adrincan vb 3. *to drown* (intrans.). II.12.187, 478; 23.167. Pret. **adranc, adruncon**.

adruwian vb II. *to dry*. I.AppB2.11; II.21.106.

adumbian vb II. *to be or become dumb*. I.13.168; 31.52; II.33.77; 39.169. [9 ex.]

adun, adune adv. *down, downwards*. I.10.124; 11.17, etc; II.12.130; 34.276. [13 ex.]

adwæscan vb I. *to extinguish, eliminate,*

destroy. I.3.40; 9.72; II.6.63; 7.115–6. [30 ex.]

adwellan vb I. *to destroy, prevent*. II.27.9.

adwelian vb II. *to wander, stray*. II.34.261.

adydan vb I. *to kill*. I.28.53; 33.19; II.4.125; 11.409. [13 ex.]

adyligian vb II. *to eliminate, erase, destroy*. I.4.155; 21.81; II.1.159; 2.7. Inf. **adiligian, adyligian**; pres.s.3 **adilegað, adylegað**; pret.s. **adilegode, adilogode, adylegode**; pp. **adylegod. adil-** 6x. [22 ex.] Cf **for-**.

afandian vb II. *to test, assay, try* (often with implications of trial by suffering). I.praef.93; 7.184; II.4.131; 7.68; perhaps extending to the sense *to improve, harden, make strong, or prove to be strong*, e.g. I.36.270; 38.283; *to discover, experience* II.9.113; 33.140; 40.162. [31 ex.]

afandung f. *testing, proving*. I.36.263–4, 268.

afaran vb 6. *to go, pass, travel*. pp. **afaren** I.11.175; 15.118; II.8.25; 32.88.

afæran vb I. *to frighten*. I.7.76; 15.51–2; II.21.11; 37.95. [6 ex.]

afæstnian vb II. *to fix, fasten*. I.38.212.

afeallan vb 7. *to fall*. I.1.81; 4.198; 27.223; II.30.93. Pret. **afeol(l), afeollon**. [6 ex.]

afedan vb I. *to feed, nourish, support, bring up (a child)*. I.1.233; 4.41; II.13.196; 19.205; 34.3. Pres.s.3 **afet(t)**. [23 ex.]

afeormian vb II. *to purge, purify*. I.6.128; 23.79, 82; II.40.256–60.

afindan vb 3. *to find*. I.13.37; 36.87; II.14.180; 27.208; 34.32. Pres.s.3 **afint**; pret. **afund-**; pp. **afunden**. [12 ex.]

afligan vb I. *to cast out, expel*. I.4.104; 24.118; II.10.89; 24.232. **aflyg-** 2x. [16 ex.]

aflowan vb 7. *to flow*. II.12.215 (pret.s. **afleow**).

aflyman vb I. *to put to flight, expel*. I.35.101; II.4.196.

Africanus supposed translator of Abdias' account of SS Simon and Jude. II.33.278.

afundennyss f. *working? devising?* I.7.186.

afylan vb I. *to defile*. II.34.48. Cf **be-**.

afyllan vb I. *to fill*. I.4.11; 29.173; II.12.58; 24.15. Pret. **afyld-**. [69 ex.]

afyllan vb I. *to fell, cause to fall*. I.26.238; II.21.146.

afyrht adj. *frightened*. I.2.23; 5.68; II.10.87; 11.233. [40 ex.]

afyrsian vb II. *to remove, expel*. I.8.82; 21.103; II.13.249; 37.143. [8 ex.]

agan pret.pres. vb. *to have, possess*. I.praef.98; 10.149; 11.94; 31.16; II.30.58–9. **geagenne** I.4.102; 38.109. Pres.s.3 **ah**; pret.s. **ahte**. Cf **nagan**.

agan anom. vb. *to go, pass*. I.22.13; II.11.315; 26.83; 39.112; impers., *to happen* II.11.259; 28.104. Pret.s. **aeode**.

Agapitus deacon of Bishop Sixtus (3rd century). I.29.10, 73.

agean adv. *back*. I.14.11, 81. Cf **ongean**.

agen adj. *own*. I.1.122; 5.161; II.1.24; 2.20; **agen cyre** *free will* I.1.28, 53; II.33.147. [192 ex.]

agennyss f. *property, quality*. I.20.101.

agenslaga m. *self-slayer, one who commits suicide*. II.14.161.

ageotan vb 2. *to pour, infuse, spill, shed* (blood or tears). I.4.141; 32.132; 36.265; II.11.427; 15.81; 39.50–1; *cast* (from molten metal) II.33.220–2. Pret. **ageat, agut-**; pp. **agoten**. [20 ex.]

agifan, agyfan vb 5. *to give*. I.2.74; 3.89; II.6.110; 14.275. Pret. **ageaf, agef** (1x), **ageafon**. [30 ex.]

Agna St Agnes, virgin martyr of Rome (d. c305). II.34.223.

geagnian vb II. *to possess, appropriate, take possession of*. I.31.205; II.4.157; 5.41; 7.72. **geahn-** 4x. [13 ex.]

agotennyss f. *shedding*. I.38.278.

agrafan vb 6. *to engrave, carve*. I.29.124; 31.179. Pret.s. **agrof**; pp. **agrafen**.

Agripina wife of Agrippa, prefect of the emperor Nero. I.26.161.

Agrippa prefect of the emperor Nero. I.26.255.

Agust- see **August-**.

agyldan vb 3. *to pay, return*. II.5.18; 11.396; 20.195; 27.70. **agyldan gescead** *to give account, make a reckoning* I.6.101; 19.232; II.3.238; 39.137. **agild-** 1x. [13 ex.] Cf **for-**.

agyltan vb I. *to do wrong, to sin* (usu. w. **wiþ**). I.3.136; 21.83; II.1.15; 25.47; trans.(?), *to do wrongly* I.4.168; II.9.128; 27.158. [13 ex.]

aheardian vb II. *to be hard, unforgiving*. I.16.80; II.4.56.

aheawan vb 7. *to cut down*. II.34.161, 170 (pret. **aheowon**).

ahebban vb 6. *to raise, lift up*. I.praef.117; 11.18; II.2.72; 9.131. Pres.s.3 **ahefþ**; imper. **ahefe**; pret. **ahof, ahefde** (1x), **ahofon**; pp. **ahafen**. [49 ex.]

ahon vb 7. *to hang, crucify*. I.10.158; 11.36; II.2.121; 11.29. Pret. **aheng, ahencg; ahengon**; pp. **ahangen**. [24 ex.]

ahreddan vb I. *to rescue, save*. I.13.20; 26.290; II.1.26; 5.252. Pres.s.3 **arett** 1x. [41 ex.]

ahreosan vb 2. *to fall*. I.4.206–8; 11.111; 13.16. Pret.s. **ahreas**.

aht n. *anything*. I.19.152; II.33.118; 34.302.

ahwar adv. *in any way*. I.3.163; 32.124; 33.141; II.7.42; 40.14; *anywhere* II.14.56 (or perhaps *in any way*); 34.169. **awar** 2x.

ahwænan vb I. *to grieve*. I.32.24.

ahyldan vb I. *to bend, incline, lay, tilt*. I.10.147; 37.168; II.11.279–80; 34.170. [9 ex.]

Aidan monk of Iona, bishop of Lindisfarne (635–51). II.10.50.

alædan vb I. *to lead, take*. I.29.276; 37.233; 38.233; II.9.72; 27.72.

alænan vb I. *to lend, supply*. I.18.47; 19.232; II.7.45; 11.400; 34.318. (Not clear from examples whether loan and repayment is necessarily implied.)

alætan vb 7. *to give, grant*. I.38.76; *to lose, give up* II.7.98; 37.133; *to let down, to lower* I.27.48, 96; *to set free, release* II.14.181. Pret. **alet, aleton**; pp. **alæten**.

alecgan vb I. *to lay, lay down, place*. I.2.19; 4.235; II.1.50; 18.28; *to suppress, destroy* I.4.26; 19.144; II.5.113; 12.406; *to abandon* II.13.147. Pret. **aled-**. [11 ex.]

alefian vb II. *to enfeeble, injure, make ill or incapable*. I.praef.79 (**aleu-**); 16.131–4; II.10.29; 23.80. [11 ex.]

aleogan vb 2. *to deceive, lie to*. I.22.93 (pp. **alogen**).

Alexander (a) husband of Salome, sister of Herod the Great. I.5.151. (b) bishop of Constantinople, opposed to Arius the heresiarch. I.20.214, 218 (perhaps confused with St Alexander of Alexandria). (c) St Alexander, pope and martyr at the time of the emperor Trajan (AD 98–117), reputedly the fifth pope after St Peter. II.18.64, etc.

Alexandria city of Egypt. I.32.162.

alihtan vb I. *to descend, alight*. I.27.244; 38.86.

alutan vb 2. *to bow, bend down*. I.20.15; 36.13; II.11.76; 34.190. Pret. **aleat, aluton**; pp. **aloten**. [7 ex.]

[alwe] wk f. *aloe*. II.14.341.

alyfed pp. as adj. *permitted*. I.6.79; 9.109; II.2.190; 6.121. [24 ex.] Cf **una-**.

alyfedlic adj. *permitted*. I.24.55. Cf **una-**.

alyfedlice adv. *allowably, in the permitted manner*. II.6.138.

alysan vb I. *to release, redeem*. I.1.272; 9.60; II.9.196; 14.243. [95 ex.] Cf **to-**.

alysednyss f. *redemption*. I.1.230; 2.222; II.1.20; 12.219. [59 ex.]

alysend m. *redeemer*. I.6.59; 9.31; II.1.58; 8.37. [20 ex.]

Amalarius of Metz (d. 850), pupil of Alcuin, and author of *De ecclesiasticis officiis*. II.5.237.

amansumian vb II. *to excommunicate*. I.8.80; II.11.342, 347, 361.

ameldian vb II. *to reveal, betray*. II.10.238; 20.18; 27.211; 34.14. [6 ex.]

amen used as concluding formula, 81x. cf also I.31.177. **amenn** 8x.

ametan vb 5. *to mete out, allot*. II.19.133–4. Pret. **amæton**; pp. **ameten**. Cf **wiþ-**.

Amos the prophet. I.22.188.

amyrran vb I. *to destroy, ruin*. I.26.109; 31.208–9; II.11.137; 19.183. [12 ex.]

an num., article, adj. *one*. I.1.6; 2.183; II.1.40; 2.49; *a, an* I.12.15; 14.93; II.2.79; 8.6; after noun or pron., *alone* I.11.164; 36.127; II.12.450; 18.86 (not found in nom.s., for which **ana** is apparently used instead). asm. **ænne, anne** (2x). [800 ex.]

ana adv. *alone, only*. I.1.87; 4.127; II.1.30; 4.171. [86 ex.]

anb- see **andb-**.

[anccleow] n.(?) *ankle*. I.31.189 (dp. **-um**).

ancenned adj. *only-begotten, only-born*. I.2.91; 33.8; II.1.26; 4.154. [21 ex.]

ancerlif n. *solitary life, life as a recluse*. II.10.162, 210.

ancersetl n. *hermitage, place of solitude*. II.10.308, 324.

ancersetla m. *anchorite, solitary hermit*. I.36.104, 112.

ancra m. *anchor*. I.37.101, 113.

and conj. *and*. Usually written as 7. [9530 ex.]

anda m. *hostility, malice, spite, envy(?)*. I.1.128; 14.160; 39.85 ff; II.4.38 ff(n); 11.160; 12.508. [28 ex.] (Sense is hard to pin down; cf esp. II.4.38 ff and note.)

andaga m. *appointed day, specified time*. II.1.157; 11.308 ff.

andbidian, an- vb II. *to wait, await* (usu w. gen.). I.2.205; 40.185 (w. acc.); II.11.317; 25.7. **gean-** 1x; **geand-** 1x. [32 ex.]

andbidung, an- f. *waiting, enduring, expectation*. I.40.9, 58; II.12.193; 24.24; 39.95.

andetere m. *confessor, one who testifies to the true faith*. I.31.329; 37.71; II.24.120; 38.193 ff. **andett-** 1x. [9 ex.]

andetnyss f. *confession, testifying*. I.26.25; 38.274; II.9.130; 20.219. [12 ex.]

(ge)andettan vb I. *to profess, confess, acknowledge, testify to*. I.2.15; 5.97; II.3.33; 24.170. **andd-** 1x. [38 ex.]

andfenga m. *receiver*. II.5.212, 215.

andfenge adj. *welcome, acceptable*. I.11.205; 32.101; II.4.105; 32.59. [8 ex.]

andgit n. *understanding, sense (as a quality or power of the mind)*. I.5.147; 20.197, etc; II.30.3–5; 38.166; *one of the five outer senses (sight, etc)* I.9.69; II.23.44; *meaning (of a text, etc), interpretation, the general sense of a text* I.12.70 ff; 40.131; II.24.86; 25.26. nap. **-gitu**. **andgyt-** 8x. [126 ex.]

andgitful adj. *having understanding*. II.12.253.

andgitleas adj. *lacking understanding or sense*. II.26.50; 37.56; 40.8.

andgitleast f. *lack of understanding*. II.29.78.

andian vb II. *to be hostile or envious*. I.24.153; II.4.40 ff; 11.33; 27.89; 34.15.

andlyfa m. *sustenance*. II.19.245.

andlyfen f. *sustenance, food*. I.27.220; 30.215; II.36.120.

Andreas St Andrew the apostle. I.12.14; 21.30, 238; 35.106; 38.passim; I.AppA2.2; II.8.63; 35.4; 38.184. gs. **andrees**.

andsæc m. *refusal*. II.11.500.

andsæte adj. *repugnant, unpleasing, hated (by)*. I.32.131; II.35.119; 37.18, 113.

andswarian vb II. *to answer*. II.7.151, 167; 9.76; 37.196.

andswaru f. *answer*. I.9.26, 44; 29.159; II.9.237; 16.18. [16 ex.]

andweald see **anweald**.

andwerd, andweard adj. *present (in time or place), belonging to here or now*. I.4.280; 5.94; II.5.38; 22.173. **andwyrd-** 1x. [90 ex.] Cf **unandwerd**.

geandwerdian vb II. *to present, to bring before someone*. I.29.5.

andwerdnyss, andweard- f. *presence*. I.6.56; 19.61; II.2.110; 4.59. **anwerd-** 1x. [35 ex.]

andwlita m. *face*. I.4.84, 227; 31.49; II.9.58; 11.550; 34.308.

andwyrdan vb I. *to answer*. I.4.169; 8.90; II.3.35; 4.141. Pres.s.3 **andwyrd, -wyrt, -werd**. **geand-** 8x (excl. pp.). [228 ex.]

anegede adj. *one-eyed*. I.34.151.

anfeald adj. *simple, ordinary, single*. I.15.142; II.3.9; 15.276; 16.56; 24.49; *honest, not duplicitous* II.19.219; **be anfealdan, -um** *'onefold', singly* I.8.174; II.7.110; etc. [11 ex.]

anfealdlice adv. *simply, straightforwardly*. I.21.109; 23.29; II.12.414; 14.57; *singly, one-for-one* I.2.59; *once, singly* I.9.152. [8 ex.]

anfealdnyss f. *singleness*. II.19.130.

anfeng m. *receiving, welcoming*. I.8.52; 23.132; 34.198.

angean prep. *opposite, facing*. I.30.139.

angel m. *hook*. I.14.173–7, 190; 34.164.

Angelcynn n. the English nation, England. II.praef.40; 9.82, 165, 173, 200, etc; 20.259; Explicit.3.

angenga m. *solitary voyager*. I.7.72. Cf **æfter-, big-, fore-**.

angencga adj. *solitary, inclined to wandering alone*. I.34.11, 15.

angin, anginn n. *beginning, start, origin*. I.1.6; 6.146; II.4.100; 15.291; *enterprise, undertaking, action* I.3.190; 38.236; II.14.198; 20.245. **angyn(n)** 8x, **annginn** 1x. [72 ex.]

Angle npl. the Angles. II.9.68.

geangsumian vb II. *to afflict*. I.28.140; 29.164; II.11.293; 18.134. [12 ex.]

angsum adj. *troubled, afflicted*. II.14.40.

angsumlic adj. *painful*. I.5.131.

angsumnyss f. *anguish, pain*. I.5.160; 23.52, 105; 28.49; 40.171. [6 ex.]

anhebban vb 6. *to exalt, raise*. I.13.196.

animan vb 4. *to take*. I.1.278; 14.188; II.10.109; 11.290. Pret.s. **anam**.

geanlæcan vb I. *to unite*. I.22.120 (pret. -læhte).

geanlician vb II. *to compare*. II.30.170.

anlicnyss f. *image*. I.1.112, 212; 4.209; II.13.284–5; 18.55. [63 ex.]

anlipig see **ænlipig**.

anmod adj. *of one mind*. I.22.75, 240; 37.205.

anmodlice adv. *with one mind, unanimously*. I.3.51; 4.158; II.9.95; 10.241; *resolutely, boldly* I.7.257; 38.88; 40.99(?); II.10.36. [19 ex.]

anmodnyss f. *boldness, determination*. I.25.166.

Anna (a) mother of the virgin Mary. II.DSM.4. (b) the widow who greets the Christ-child in the temple. I.9.182 ff.

Annania the priest of Damascus who helps St Paul. I.8.74; 27.26 ff, 90.

Annanias (a) one of the three children of Israel persecuted by Nebuchadnezzar. I.37.191; II.1.231 ff. = **Sidrac**. (b) follower of the apostles who is punished for keeping back some of his wealth. I.22.88 ff; 27.212, 221. voc. **-ia**; ads. **-ian**.

annyss f. *unity*. I.2.223; 7.70; II.3.280; 15.238 ff. [36 ex.]

anræd adj. *resolute*. I.19.155; AppB3.68; II.32.204; 37.71. [8 ex.]

anrædlice adv. *resolutely, persistently*. I.7.113; 8.49; II.11.66; 17.2. [11 ex.]

anrædnyss f. *constancy, perseverance*. I.26.61; 27.44; II.6.86; 12.555. [14 ex.]

anstandende adj. *living alone, on one's own*. I.1.69; 10.153; II.10.162.

ansund adj. *sound, unharmed, intact*. I.4.6; 30.46; II.2.56; 11.163. [23 ex.]

ansundnyss f. *wholeness, unharmed condition*. I.4.63.

ansyn f. *face, appearance, sight*. I.3.27; 9.36; II.14.8; 19.218. [16 ex.]

antecrist m. *antichrist*. I.praef.73 ff; 21.201; II.4.91; 7.16. (Used with or without article.) [11 ex.]

antimber mn. *material (from which something is made)*. I.1.101; 20.262–3; 26.79; II.40.86; *cause* I.praef.56; 39.79. [9 ex.]

Antipater son of Herod the Great (presumably distinct from Antipas—see under **Herodes**). I.5.161.

anþracian vb II. *to fear, dread*. I.5.68; II.10.148 (w. gen.); 38.106.

anþræce adj. *terrible, dreadful*. I.4.152; 30.251; II.21.26, 29; 34.156.

anwalhnyss f. *integrity, purity*. II.39.44.

anweald m. *power, control, rule*. I.1.33; 8.19; II.1.181; 3.214. **and-** 6x. [40 ex.]

anwerd- see **andweard-**.

anwille adj. *wilful, obstinate*. II.37.39.

anwilnyss f. *obstinacy*. I.29.112.

aplantian vb II. *to plant*. I.40.97; II.1.54; 26.73, 108.

Apollo the sun-god of Greek paganism. II.11.173.

apostol m. *apostle*. I.1.252; 3.4; II.5.267, 279; 9.1. np. **-li** 53x, **-las** 13x; ap. **-las**; dp. **-lon** 17x, **-lum** 51x. [510 ex.]

apostolic adj. *of the apostle(s)*. I.26.243; 31.244; II.8.64; 9.81. [13 ex.]

Aquinenscisc of Aquino in southern Italy. II.11.262.

ar f. *wealth, property*. I.2.12; 4.51.

Arabisc Arabian. I.32.50; AppB2.25.

arasian vb II. *to reveal, discover*. II.11.247; 32.85.

aræcan vb I. *to give, supply*. I.5.163.

aræfnian vb II. *to ponder*. I.2.38, 204 (**aref-**), 214; *to endure* II.2.168.

aræran vb I. *to raise, build, erect*. I.1.260; 3.41; II.1.226; 2.144. [139 ex.]

aræsan vb I(?). *to rush*. II.10.117.

arc m. *ark (of Noah)*. I.1.185 ff; 35.260, 266; II.4.113, 116.

Archelaus son of Herod the Great and ethnarch of Judaea (4BC-6AD). I.5.172, 182 (app.crit.); 32.43.

ardlice adv. *quickly, hastily, immediately*. I.5.22, 92; 23.143; II.10.298; 11.437. [15 ex.] Cf **arodlice**.

areccan vb I. *to recount, narrate*. I.12.79; 20.166; II.1.214.

Arethe king of Arabia, father of Herodias the wife of Herod II. I.32.50–51.

arett see **ahreddan**.

Arfaxaþ (a) son of Noah's son Shem. I.1.225. (b) one of the magi opposed to SS Matthew, Simon and Jude. II.32.84, 141; 33.4, 73, 199.

arfæst adj. *kindly, virtuous, gracious* (often translating Lat. *pius*). I.3.111; 4.34; II.9.144; 18.6. [14 ex.]

arfæstlice adv. *virtuously, mercifully, with*

kindness. I.36.275; AppB3.102; II.2.180; 5.218; 11.14.

arfæstnyss f. *kindliness, graciousness, virtue*. I.21.189; 24.112; II.2.33; 5.223. [13 ex.]

arian vb II. *to protect, spare*. w. dat. I.praef.95; 4.167; II.4.148, 154; 9.154 (**gearige**); 11.506; 30.171.

arisan vb 1. *to arise, get up, return to life*. I.1.166; 4.136; II.1.211; 11.250. Pres.s.3 **arist**; pret. **aras, aris-**; pp. **arisen**. **arys-** IX. [188 ex.]

arist see **ærist**

Aristodemus chief priest of the pagans at Ephesus in the time of St John. I.4.216 ff.

arleas adj. *wicked (often with implications of cruelty)*. I.praef.113; 3.111; II.11.158; 14.106. [64 ex.]

arleaslice adv. *wickedly*. I.5.161, 166; 24.195.

arleasnyss f. *wickedness*. I.praef.112, 115; 3.105; II.20.102; 26.22. [12 ex.]

arn see **yrnan**.

arodlice adv. *quickly, hastily*. II.4.134. Cf **ardlice**.

Arrius the heretic Arius (c.250–c.336). I.20.213, 224. **Arrianes** II.34.86 (false formation from Lat. adj. **arriana**?).

arwurþe adj. *distinguished, worthy, deserving of respect or worship*. I.23.135; 39.83; II.10.32; 20.20. [15 ex.]

arwurþful adj. *distinguished, worthy, deserving of respect or honour*. I.5.153; 6.111; II.11.494; 13.7. [7 ex.]

(ge)arwurþian vb II. *to honour, respect*. I.26.207; 30.102–5; II.12.143, 312 ff; 13.22; 19.158. [29 ex.]

arwurþlice adv. *honourably, worthily*. I.25.88; 31.229; 36.4; 39.31. **arwyrþ-** IX. [8 ex.]

arwurþnyss f. *honour*. I.22.15; 26.278; II.18.147; 20.261. **arwyrþ-** IX. [18 ex.]

asawan vb 7. *to sow*. II.10.182 (pret.s. **aseow**).

asceacan vb 6. *to remove, shake off*. I.14.115; 37.252; 39.40. Pret.s. **ascoc**.

asceofan, ascufan vb 2. *to push, remove, repel*. I.10.39; 37.102; II.11.332; 14.224. Pres.pl. **ascufaþ**; pret. **asceaf, ascufon**; pp. **ascofen**. [14 ex.]

asceotan vb 2. *to fall, leap, shoot (up or down)*. I.11.78, 80; II.11.139; 21.49; trans., *to shoot (an arrow)* I.37.179. Pres.s.3 **ascyt**; pret. **asceat, ascuton**.

asciran vb I. *to distinguish, specify*. I.21.75. (Apparently distinct from **ascyrian**.)

ascortian vb II. *to run short*. II.4.6, 58.

ascreadian vb II. *to cut (away)*. II.5.56.

ascrepan vb 5. *to scrape*. II.30.119 (pret.s. **ascræp**).

ascunian vb II. *to shun, avoid*. I.20.189. Cf **on-**.

ascyndan vb I. *to drive away*. I.28.80.

ascyrian vb I/II. *to separate, exclude*. I.6.123; 8.61, 77, 80; II.7.117; 11.351. [9 ex.]

asecgan vb III. *to describe, report*. I.20.166.

asendan vb I. *to send*. I.praef.45; 1.189; II.1.20; 5.83. Pres.s.3 **asent**. [128 ex.]

asettan vb I. *to place, set, set down, put*. I.2.9; 29.95; II.3.145; 11.119. [10 ex.]

Asia the region or continent of Asia (described as amounting to half the world at I.4.174 but generally seeming to designate Asia Minor). I.21.238; 26.102; II.17.43; 38.185.

asigan vb 1. *to sink, decline*. II.5.98 (pres.s.3 **asihþ**).

asincan vb 3. *to sink*. II.11.138 (pret.s. **asanc**).

asleacian vb II. *to slacken*. I.40.56, 113 (**aslacod**); II.6.200; 29.94.

aslidan vb 1. *to slip, fall*. I.11.74, 144; 20.258; 33.25; II.24.204. Pres.s.3 **aslit**; pret. **aslad, aslid-**. Cf **æt-**.

asmeagan vb II. *to devise, conceive, consider, comprehend, interpret, examine*. I.13.15, 37; 24.114; 38.273; II.praef.32; 15.297; 24.222. Imper. **asmea**; pret. **asmead-**; pp. **asmead**. **asmeg-** IX. [21 ex.]

asolcen adj. *slackened, slothful, idle*. I.21.175; 24.61; II.12.521; 38.99, 162.

asolcennyss f. *sloth, idleness*. I.39.34; II.3.180; 12.519; 38.108. [6 ex.]

aspendan vb I. *to spend*. I.3.144; 8.185; II.5.120; 19.73. Pres.s.3 **aspent**. [18 ex.]

aspide m. *asp*. I.32.178.

aspiwan vb 1. *to spew, vomit*. I.18.29 (pret.s. **aspaw**).

aspringan vb 3. *to spring up, originate, descend*. I.1.223; 2.65; II.6.116; 10.174. Pret. **asprang, asprung-**; pp. **asprungen**. [34 ex.]

aspyrian vb I/II. *to study, examine.* II.16.62.

assa m. *donkey.* I.2.210–2; 14.9, etc; II.14.23; 30.11. [29 ex.]

astandan vb 6. *to stand up.* I.3.191; 19.158; II.6.186; 11.560; *to stand* II.2.160; *to rise, arise* I.3.17. Pret. **astod, astodon**. [9 ex.]

Astaroþ a demon in a temple in India. I.31.9, 19, 47.

astellan vb I. *to establish, initiate.* I.3.84; 19.8; II.1.285; 3.93. Pret. **asteald-, astalde** (1x). [20 ex.]

astifian vb II. *to become rigid.* I.38.331.

astigan vb 1. *to ascend, descend.* I.9.57; 15.145–6; II.17.79; 24.97–8 ff; trans., *to ascend to, to climb* I.10.176; 26.229; II.5.189; 14.301; 24.201. Pres.s.3 **astihþ**; imper. **astih**; pret. **astah, astig-**; pp. **astigen**. [105 ex.]

astreccan vb I. *to stretch, extend, lay low.* I.4.135; 8.9; II.4.146; 8.14. Pret. **astreht-**; pp. **astreht**. [62 ex.]

Astriges brother of Polimius king of India, and king of an adjacent territory, responsible for the death of St Bartholomew. I.31.203, 206, 230; 35.105.

astyrian vb I/II. *to stir, move, agitate, arouse.* I.3.46; 23.109; II.3.156; 11.505. [34 ex.]

aswindan vb 3. *to fade, weaken.* I.19.113.

asyndrian vb II. *to separate, exclude.* I.27.169, 182.

atelic adj. *horrible.* I.1.120; 8.31; II.2.125; 34.142. [15 ex.]

atelice adv. *horribly.* I.8.41; II.30.194.

atendan vb I. *to kindle, set on fire.* II.20.96. Cf **on-**.

ateon vb 2. *to draw, drag.* I.37.223; 38.15; II.10.248; 11.129; *to deal with, use* I.19.232. Pres.pl.**ateoþ**; pret. **ateah, atug-**; pp. **atogen**. [16 ex.]

ateorian vb II. *to fail, fade, become weary, cease.* I.5.65; 10.134; II.4.45; 7.88. [33 ex.]

ateorigendlic adj. *fleeting, fading, transient.* I.3.185; 24.142; II.12.426; 15.52. [13 ex.] Cf **una-**.

ateorung f. *transience, fading, weariness.* I.10.54; 30.119; 31.40; 32.213. [6 ex.]

Atticus a disciple of St John the evangelist. I.4.74, 143.

attor n. *poison.* I.4.213; 5.133; II.11.72; 33.131 (**atter**). [15 ex.]

attorbære adj. *poisonous.* I.4.223.

aþ m. *oath.* I.32.18, 23, etc; II.13.197; 14.122; 19.237. [12 ex.]

Aþelwold (a) St Athelwold of Winchester (c.908–84). I.praef.3 (Lat. **adelwoldi**), 46. (b) seventh-century abbot of Melrose. II.21.18.

aþened adj. *outstretched.* I.26.123.

aþeostrian, aþyst- vb II. *to darken.* I.15.177; 40.40, 48; II.12.239; 14.272, 288.

aþolian vb II. *to endure, remain, survive.* II.2.125; 3.260; 11.163; 16.125, 169.

aþrawan vb 7. *to turn, twist.* I.34.18 (pp. **aþrawen**).

aþryt see **æþryttan**.

aþswaru f. *oath-swearing.* I.32.89.

aþum m. *son-in-law.* I.32.52; II.2.28, 32.

aþwean vb 6. *to wash, wash away, wash clean.* I.29.283; 31.153; II.14.28; 19.119. Pres.s.3 **aþweahþ, aþwehþ, aþwyhþ**; pret. **aþwoh, aþwogon**; pp. **aþwogen**. [23 ex.]

Aufidianus persecutor of St Clement. I.37.94–6.

Augustinus (a) St Augustine of Hippo (354–430). I.praef.15; 18.61; 20.6; II.2.1; 13.42. **Ag-** 3x. [20 ex.] (b) St Augustine of Canterbury (d. 604/5). II.9.171, etc.

Augustus title or name given to Octavius Caesar. I.2.54.

Aurelianus Roman 'emperor' and persecutor of St Alexander. II.18.66, etc.; see notes.

awacan vb 6. *to waken* (intrans.). II.11.312; 18.15; 40.38. Pret. **awoc, awocon**.

awacian vb II. *to weaken.* I.12.55.

awar see **ahwar**.

awægan vb I. *to deny, repudiate.* I.7.146; 32.24; II.20.98; 27.97.

awecgan vb I. *to move, dislodge.* I.25.214(?); II.11.189; 30.163. Pret. **awegd-**.

awedan vb I. *to be or go mad.* I.29.273; 31.55; II.11.262; 23.171; *to rage, act fiercely* II.9.159. pp. **awed(d)** *mad, maddened* II.8.9; 34.200; etc. [18 ex.]

awefan vb 5. *to weave.* I.25.43 (pp. **awefen**).

aweg adv. *away*. I.28.217; 31.197; II.1.225; 5.60. **aweig** 3x; **onweg** I.37.131. [38 ex.]

awegan vb 5. *to transport* I.21.209–10; *to weigh* II.28.153, 30.147; *to lift up(?)* I.1.11. Pres.s **awyhþ**; pret.s. **awæh**; pp. **awegen**. Cf **uta-**.

awendan vb I. *to change, turn, translate*. I.1.147; 6.48; II.praef.29; 4.16; intrans., I.1.27; 40.157; II.6.183; 15.111. Pres.s.2 **awendest, awentst, awenst**; 3 **awent**. [154 ex.]

awendedlic adj. *changeable*. II.15.121.

awendedlicnyss f. *mutability*. II.12.272.

awendednyss f. *change, transformation*. II.13.156.

awerian vb I/II. *to protect*. I.AppB3.2; II.25.139–40.

awestan vb I. *to destroy*. II.7.105; 9.117; pp. **awest** *empty, uninhabited* II.9.93, 124.

awiht adv. *in any way*. II.10.38.

awildian vb II. *to grow wild*. II.5.58.

awilian vb I. *to roll away*. I.15.21; II.27.208 (pret.pl. **awiligdon**). Cf **awyltan, wylian**.

awlætan vb I. *to make loathsome, disfigure*. II.40.270.

aworpennyss f. *damnation, rejection*. I.23.49.

awrecan vb 5. *to avenge*. II.20.79 (pret.s. **awræc**).

awreccan vb I. *to arouse, awaken*. I.4.44; 14.32; II.23.136; 34.326. Pret. **awreht-**, pp. **awreht**. [8 ex.]

awringan vb 3. *to squeeze out*. II.15.89 (pp. **awrungen**).

awritan vb 1. *to write, copy*. I.praef.129; 2.8, 62; II.10.6; 12.240; *to describe, set down in writing* I.39.97; 40.47; II.2.74; 34.266. Pret. **awrat, awrit-**. [82 ex.]

awurpan vb 3. *to throw, cast, reject*. I.4.53; 8.167–9; II.1.240; 16.155. Pres.s.3 **awyrpþ**; pret. **awearp, awerp** (1x), **awurp-**; pp. **aworpen**. [80 ex.]

awyllan vb I. *to boil*. II.10.41.

awyltan vb I. *to roll away*. I.15.24, 85. Cf **awilian**.

awyrdan vb I. *to injure, damage*. I.praef.81; 31.11, 19; II.10.115; 11.13. [10 ex.]

awyrdnyss f. *injury*. I.11.78; 16.133; 31.132, 141–2.

awyrian vb I. *to curse*. I.1.145; II.2.108; 26.46; 27.168. pp. as adj, *accursed* I.4.147; 7.154; II.4.193; 7.161–2; etc. (49x). pp. **awyrged, awyried, awyriged, awir-** (2x), **awrig-** (1x). [53 ex.]

awyrigednyss f. *curse*. I.6.174.

awyrpan vb I. *to recover*. I.35.248 (pret.s. **-pte**).

awyrtwalian vb II. *to root out, uproot*. II.26.107.

axe wk f. *ash*. I.18.34; II.30.170; 34.298.

axian vb II. *to ask*. I.1.90; 34.81; II.3.34; 16.127. **acsode** 2x. [49 ex.] Cf **of-**.

geaxian vb II. *to discover, learn*. I.5.50, 56; 14.19; II.11.164; 24.81. [18 ex.]

axung f. *asking, questioning*. I.12.100 (**acsunge**); II.17.92.

aydlian vb II. *to annul, cancel, refute*. I.4.33; 6.25, 65; 20.71; 31.31; II.27.13.

Azarias one of the three children of Israel persecuted by Nebuchadnezzar. I.37.191; II.1.231 ff. Also called Abdenago.

æ f.(indecl.) *law* (always with ref. to law of God). (a) specifically Old Testament law, often called **seo ealde æ** or **Moyses æ**. I.1.232; 2.147; II.4.99; 12.10. (b) God's law more generally, or Christian law. I.11.196; 29.194; II.3.292; 19.63. [145 ex.]

[geæbiligian] vb I. *to anger*. I.34.238; 38.288; II.7.42; 19.188; 40.291. Pres.s.3 **geæbilihþ**; pret. **-biligd-**; pp. **-bylid**.

æbilignyss f. *anger, indignation*. II.2.27; 12.512, 530. (Translates **indignatio**.)

æcer m. *field*. I.24.66; 37.210; II.7.78–9; 14.157. [9 ex.]

æddre wk f. *spring, source*. I.37.71. Cf **wæteræddre**.

geædlæcan see **geedlæcan**.

æfen m. *evening, eve*. I.6.151; 14.182 (**frige æfen** = evening preceding Friday), 185; II.22.180; 24.62. [7 ex.]

æfenlæcan vb I. *to approach evening*. II.16.26.

æfensang m. *(office of) evensong*. I.13.184.

æfnung f. *evening*. I.30.240; II.5.17, 20; 11.492; 15.50. [9 ex.]

æfre adv. *ever, always, eternally*. I.1.7–8; 2.6; II.17.66; 39.52. [168 ex.]

æftemysta adj. *final, last*. I.13.219; 36.253.

æfter prep. w. dat. *after, according to, in consequence of*. I.2.154; 3.66; 6.116; II.praef.31; 2.178; 11.336. [417 ex.]

æfterfylian vb I. *to follow, succeed.* I.16.103 (perhaps better divided as **heræfter fyliað**); 32.77. pres.pt. as adj., *succeeding, subsequent* I.8.166; 21.108; 28.112; II.15.179. [9 ex.]

æftergenga m. *successor.* I.praef.46; 37.36; II.9.249; 15.83. **-gencg-** 2x. [12 ex.]

æftergengnyss f. *succession, posterity.* II.12.280.

æfterweard adj. *following.* I.26.140.

æftra adj. *subsequent, later.* I.22.144; 25.118; II.praef.37; 16.162. [9 ex.]

æg n. *egg.* I.2.182–3; 18.57, 109 ff. **æig** 2x. [12 ex.]

æghwær, æighwær adv. *everywhere.* I.8.110; 15.110; 19.54; 20.161. **æighwar** 2x. [13 ex., CH I only]

æghwylc pron. *everyone, each one.* I.22.184. adj. *every.* I.30.23; AppB3.225; II.15.152. **æig-** 2x, **-hwilc** 1x.

ægþer conj. **ægþer ge . . . ge** *both . . . and.* I.6.23; 7.163; II.1.40; 10.5; **ægþer . . . and** II.1.272. **æig-** 23x. [85 ex.]

ægþer pron. *each of two.* I.7.65; 19.103; II.praef.37; 11.313. adj., *each of two.* I.33.148; II.1.5; 29.101; 33.25. [16 ex.]

æht f. *wealth, possessions, property.* I.3.183; 4.49; II.6.170; 19.82–5. Always pl. except I.18.199; II.12.507. **hæhtum** 1x. [105 ex.]

ælc pron. *each, each one.* I.12.13; 30.150; II.2.141; 19.276. adj. *each, every, all* I.6.21; 7.175; II.3.166; 4.285. **ælce dæg(e)** *(on) every day* I.11.188, etc. (5x); **ælce geare** *(in) every year* II.12.298, etc. (3x). dsn. **-on** 1x. [303 ex.]

ælcung, ælcygendum see **elcung, elcian.**

ælemidde wk f. *middle.* II.14.229.

Ælfeah Ælfeah I bishop of Winchester 934–51. I.praef.46 (**ælfeage**).

Ælflæd abbess of Whitby 680–713 and sister of Kings Ecgfrith and Aldfrith of Northumbria. II.10.213, 237, 292.

Ælfred Alfred the Great, king of Wessex 871–99. I.praef.55; II.9.7.

ælfremed adj. *free (from), estranged.* I.2.143; 4.276; 38.144; *foreign, alien* I.11.208; II.9.208; as noun, *stranger, foreigner* I.5.67; 34.162.

geælfremed adj. *estranged, alienated.* I.23.92; 24.190.

Ælfric monk of Cerne and abbot of Eynsham. I.praef.3 (Lat. **ælfricus**), 44; II.praef.1 (Lat. **ælfricus**), 29.

Ælfrid Aldfrith, king of Northumbria 685–704. II.21.21.

ælic adj. *of the (OT) law, prescribed by the (OT) law.* I.6.144; 12.106; II.4.280; 5.68; 12.137, 152; 32.61. **ænlice** I.AppA1.9.

ælincg f. *burning, kindling.* II.40.261.

Ælle king of Deira 560–c590. II.9.77.

ælmesdæd f. *act of almsgiving.* I.3.152; AppB3.232; II.1.282; 7.5. **ælmys-** 1x. [11 ex.]

ælmesgeorn adj. *eager in almsgiving.* I.4.40.

ælmesse wk f. *alms, almsgiving, charitable gifts.* I.11.210; 35.159; II.6.174; 7.40, 52, etc. **ælmys-** 3x. [17 ex.]

ælmihtig adj. *almighty (as epithet for God or gods).* I.praef.65; 1.6; II.1.25; 3.4. In phrase **god ælmihtig** 25x. [345 ex.]

æltewe adj. *sound.* I.18.108.

ælþeodig adj. *foreign, as a stranger.* I.29.43; 31.9, 48; II.2.49; 14.157, 163; 16.10. [21 ex.]

ælþeodignyss f. *foreign parts.* II.38.7, 39, 42.

æmelnyss f. *sloth.* II.12.485, 520.

æmod adj. *disheartened.* II.30.6.

geæmtian vb II. *to empty.* I.20.228.

æmtig adj. *empty, void, idle.* I.13.209; 15.30; II.4.95; 5.15. [15 ex.]

æne adv. *once, on one occasion.* I.5.120; 9.241; II.11.489; 16.155. [14 ex.]

ænig adj. *any.* I.1.42; 2.189; II.1.264; 3.91. as pron., I.38.101; II.11.159; etc. [75 ex.]

ænlic adj. *peerless, unique.* I.AppB2.24, 26. See also **ælic.**

ænlipig adj. and pron. *individual, single, each* (often with adverbial sense, *singly, one at a time*). I.2.71; II.4.69, 72; 5.23; 11.90; 34.211. **anlipig** 2x. [11 ex.]

æppel m. *a fruit.* I.5.163; 11.158; II.12.500; 13.289; 19.294. (All refer to Eden except the first, = Lat. **pomum.**) Cf **fic-**.

æppeltun m. *orchard.* II.26.49.

ær adv. *previously.* I.praef.81; 1.56; II.1.121; 2.13. [c290 ex.] See also **ærest, æror.**

ær prep. w. dat. *before.* I.2.142; 14.140; II.12.8; 16.155. **ær þan, þon** *before that, previously* I.37.13; etc. [c81 ex.]

ær conj. *before*. I.4.179; 20.216; II.3.67; 6.159; 10.258. [c8 ex.]

ær þan þe conj. *before*. I.praef.59; 1.249; II.2.76; 4.81. [76 ex.]

æren adj. *brazen, of brass*. I.26.165; II.11.194; 13.250 ff.

ærende n. *errand, message*. I.23.137; 34.77; II.10.243; 12.50. [7 ex.]

ærendgewrit n. *letter*. I.27.62; 37.158; II.34.215. nap. **-gewritu**.

ærendraca m. *messenger*. I.1.252; 32.71 (**ærenddracum**); 35.12; II.2.59; 9.103. [16 ex.]

ærest adv. *first, at first*. I.1.130; 3.95; II.2.178; 4.20. **ærst** 1x. [66 ex.]

ærist mn. *resurrection*. I.4.249; 8.198; II.1.220; 15.66. (Mostly m. or n., but f. at I.30.81 and perhaps alt. from f. at I.1.285, 15.36, 140, etc.) **ariste** 1x. [112 ex.]

ærmerigen m. *dawn, daybreak*. I.15.20; 20.180; II.2.86; 5.5, 62. (Mainly in phrase **on ærnemerigen**, printed as 2 words at I.20.180 and 31.65, but **se ærmerigen** at II.5.62.) [15 ex.]

æror adv. (comp. of **ær**). *previously, earlier*. I.4.177; 20.264; 21.182; 25.150; 30.203.

ærra adj. *previous, former*. I.4.71; 7.66; II.praef.33; 2.131. [29 ex.]

ærwacel adj. *awake early*. I.4.251.

æs n. *food, bait*. I.14.173–4.

(ge)æswician vb II. *to fail, desert, undermine*. w. acc. or dat. I.32.74; 33.116; 34.143, 148–50, 204–7; II.14.69n, 74. [11 ex.]

æswicung f. *undermining, betrayal, deceit?* I.34.146–7n, 217–22; II.39.30–31.

æt prep. w. dat. *at, from, of, by* (referring to location in place or time, person etc. from whom something is taken or sought). I.praef.99; 1.236; 37.276; II.1.49, 204; 3.205; 16.2. [c350 ex.]

æt mn. *food*. I.4.123; 11.10; II.7.163; 10.104. [10 ex.] Cf **ofer-**.

æt, æton (vb) see **etan**.

ætberstan vb 3. *to escape from*. w. dat. or of. I.26.144; 38.281; II.16.169; 32.172. Pret. ætbærst, ætburst-. [13 ex.]

ætbredan vb 3. *to remove*. I.4.16; 8.53; II.5.46; 7.108. Pres.s. **ætbretst, ætbret(t) ætbryt**; pret. **ætbræd, ætbrud-**; pp. **ætbroden**. [44 ex.]

æteowian vb I/II. trans., *to reveal, display*. I.28.138; 29.130; II.14.143; 16.43–5; intrans., *to appear* I.4.244; 5.22; II.15.298; 16.150. Pret. **æteowd-, -wed-, -wod-**; pp. **-wed, -wod. ætywed** 2x. [104 ex.]

ætfleon vb 2. *to escape, flee from*. w. dat. or acc. I.32.127; 34.59; II.30.74; 33.5, 149–50. Pret. **-fleah, -flugon**.

ætforan prep. w. dat. *before, in front of, in the presence of, in advance of*. I.1.181; 4.221; II.praef.41; 8.80. [99 ex.]

ætforeweardan see **foreweard**.

ætgædere adv. *together*. I.20.116–7, 177, 181.

æthabban vb III. *to withhold, retain*. I.22.91 (**-hæfdon**).

æthleapan vb 7. *to run away from*. w. dat. I.AppB3.195.

ætlutian vb II. *to hide*. II.9.107.

ætslidan vb 1. *to slip*. II.34.216 (pret.s. **-slad**).

ætsomne adv. *together*. II.10.320; 12.176; 14.25; 34.128.

ætspurnan vb 3. *to stumble (over)*. I.11.19 (**-spyrnan**), 62; 34.247; II.11.69. Pret.s. **-spearn**.

ætstandan vb 6. *to stand still, stop*. I.7.110; 25.210; II.12.114; 34.263. **ætstandenum** (var. **ætstandendum**) for pres.pt. *standing by, supporting* I.34.88; cf. also next word. Pres.s.3 **-stent**; pret. **-stod, stodon**. [12 ex.]

ætstandend m. *attendant*. I.30.234 (**-standenum**, var. **-standendum**).

ættren adj. *poisonous*. I.18.125.

geættrian vb II. *to poison*. I.18.129, 131; 34.16; II.13.246; 26.22. [9 ex.]

ættrig adj. *poisonous*. II.10.129; 13.278.

ætwindan vb 3. *to escape, get away from*. w. acc. or dat. I.5.121; 24.30, 65; II.11.446; 13.155. Pres.s. 3 **-wint**; pret. **-wand, -wundon**; pp. **-wunden**. [12 ex.]

ætwitan vb 1. *to reproach, blame*. I.AppB3.36 (pres.s.3 **ætwat**).

æþelboren adj. *of high birth*. I.5.62; 6.24; II.2.79; 9.12. [16 ex.]

æþelborennyss f. *noble birth, high rank*. II.9.16, 38; 11.336; 27.192.

Æþelbriht, -byrht king of Kent converted by St Augustine's mission; d. 616. II.9.190, 198, 216, 236.

æþele adj. *noble, excellent, splendid*. I.3.123; 21.27; II.10.168; 12.399. [19 ex.]

æþeling m. *prince*. I.7.134; 8.136; II.1.26; 32.118. [13 ex.]

æþellice adv. *splendidly, nobly, finely*. II.9.58; 11.4.

Æþelmær thegn and later ealdorman under Ethelred II and patron of Ælfric. I.praef.47.

Æþelred (a) Ethelred II, king of England 978–1016. I.praef.45. (b) king of Mercia c674–704. II.21.144–6.

æþm m. *blast (of fire)*. I.40.149; II.21.43.

æþryt adj. *tedious*. I.5.183; II.23.74.

æþryt n. *tedium*. II.praef.35(?); ExDict.4.

(ge)æþryttan vb I. *to weary, bore*. II.30.6; 40.216 (**aðryt**).

æwbræce, eawbræce adj. *adulterous, in breach of marriage bond*. I.26.215; II.19.156–65.

æwbrice m. *adultery*. II.12.320.

æwe fn. *spouse*; *marriage law, marital rule or propriety*. I.2.190; 13.83; 32.53; II.4.302; 6.119; 13.83; 19.154–5, 160. (Both senses evident, but individual examples are hard to differentiate.) **eawe** 1x. [17 ex.]

æx f. *axe*. II.26.88, 99; 34.66.

Babilon, Babylon, Babilonia the city or region of Babylon. I.37.212, 215; II.4.88, 219, 233–69; 28.106; 33.154.

Babilonisc of Babylon. I.37.200; II.4.88, 230, 257; 5.241, 248.

bacan vb 6. *to bake*. I.32.200 (pres.s.2 **bæcst**). Cf **a-**.

Bagrade river near Carthage (modern Mejerdah). II.2.86.

Baldaþ (a) Baldach, a god of the Indians. I.31.223. (b) Baldad, one of the three comforters of Job. II.30.132, 190.

Balthasar king of Babylon (or the Chaldees), and son of Nebuchadnezzar; aka Belshazaar. II.28.134, 158.

bam see **begen**

ban n. *bone*. I.1.91; 15.55; II.11.574; 15.131–4. [23 ex.]

geban, gebann n. *decree*. I.2.9, 62; 25.157; II.1.263; 34.12. [7 ex.]

baptista m. epithet of John the Baptist. II.4.313.

barn see **byrnan**

Barnabas companion of St Paul on his mission. I.27.52, 56.

Barrabas the murderer released in place of Christ. II.14.186–8.

Bartholomeus the apostle. I.21.30, 238; 31.passim; 35.105; II.35.6.

Basilius St Basil of Cappadocia (c.330–79). I.30.200–22.

basing m. *cloak*. II.33.123; 34.33–9.

batian vb II. *to improve, grow strong*. I.18.106.

baþian vb II. *to bathe*. II.17.67.

bæc n. *back*. I.14.110; 23.144; 26.143; 31.191; II.32.217.

bæftan adv. *behind*. I.7.90; 14.23; II.5.198; 32.187. prep. w. dat. *behind, away from* I.14.140; 20.126; II.11.221; 24.237. [14 ex.]

bænen adj. *made of bone*. I.35.200.

bær f. *bier*. I.4.42; 26.112; 33.10, 39; II.10.286.

bærman m. *person carrying a bier*. I.33.10, 39, 54; II.10.284.

bærnan vb I. *to burn*. I.31.270; II.18.91. Cf **for-**.

bærnet n. *burn, burning*. I.31.269; II.4.167; 20.240, 248.

bæþ n. *bath*. I.4.25; 5.143; 29.184. Pl. **baþu, baþum**. Cf **fulluht-**.

be prep. w. dat. *concerning, about, by, by means of, according to* (w. ref. to a topic of discussion, agency, authority, etc.). I.praef.130; 2.36; 6.166; II.1.134; 11.275; 25.112; 26.52; w. acc. I.32.163–4. **be anfealdon, be dæle** etc., see under relevant adj. or noun. [762 ex.]

(ge)beacn n. *sign*. I.34.84; II.10.84. Cf **fore-, sige-**.

bealcettan vb I. *to emit, spew out*. II.9.28.

beald adj. *bold, fervent*. II.14.185; 19.272.

bealdlice adv. *bravely, confidently*. I.3.126; 16.67; II.7.6; 14.92. [9 ex.]

bealdwyrde adj. *bold-speaking, arrogant*. I.29.59.

bealu f. *ruin, destruction*. I.19.122.

beam m. *tree*. I.AppB2.3; II.34.168. Cf **ceder-, pin-**; cf also **sunn-**.

Beanus one of the priests whose souls St Fursey meets in the otherworld. II.20.162, 201.

beard m. *beard*. I.31.35, 189.

bearn n. *child*. I.1.167; 3.61–3; II.1.24; 6.120. [192 ex.] Cf **steop-**.

bearneaca adj. *pregnant*. I.2.16.

bearneacnigende adj. *pregnant*. II.6.121.

bearnteam m. *procreation of children.* II.4.28, 301; 6.131.

gebeat n. *beating.* I.28.80; 29.143.

beatan vb 7. *to beat.* I.29.180, 243–4; 31.224; II.14.282; 23.154. Pret. **beot, beoton**; pp. **gebeaten**. [8 ex.] Cf **of-**.

bebeodan vb 2. *to command, instruct.* I.1.190; 4.159; II.1.48; 15.8–9. Pres.s.3 **bebyt(t)**; pret. **bebead, bebud-**; pp. **beboden**. [88 ex.]

bebindan vb 3. *to bind, fetter.* I.14.46, 117; 23.98; II.14.205. Pres.s.3 **bebint**; pp. **bebunden**.

bebod n. *command, commandment, instruction.* I.1.82; 6.90; II.1.16; 6.202. nap. **-a, -u**. [127 ex.]

bebyrian vb I. *to bury.* I.1.277; 26.278; II.6.195; 11.367–74. Infl.inf. **bebyrgenne**; pret. **bebyrgd-, bebyrigd-**; pp. **bebyriged**. **bebir-** 3x. [36 ex.]

beceapian vb II. *to sell.* I.4.60; 22.97; II.14.61; 25.93; *to buy* I.13.206; 31.309, 328; 38.93. [11 ex.]

beceorfan vb 3. *to deprive by cutting.* **heafde becorfen** *beheaded* I.29.61.

becidan vb I. *to complain.* II.32.44.

beclyppan vb I. *to clasp.* II.11.500. Cf **ymb-**.

beclysan vb I. *to enclose, close.* I.5.151; 13.30; 25.62; II.11.213. [18 ex.]

becnyttan vb I. *to tie, fasten.* I.31.321; II.2.82.

becuman vb 4. *to come, go.* I.praef.70; 1.36; II.1.71; 2.18. Pres.s. **becymst, becymþ**; pret. **becom, becom-**. [201 ex.]

becweþan vb 5. *to bequeath.* I.18.197; *to pray over, to protect by praying?* I.35.233. Pret.pl. **becwædon**.

becyrran vb I. *to turn.* II.14.137.

bed n. *bed.* I.9.7; 18.49; 29.132; II.13.136. [9 ex.] Cf **bryd-, forlir-, leger-**.

gebed n. *prayer or other religious utterance (e.g. song of praise).* I.3.113; 4.136; II.2.72; 10.55. nap. **-a, -u**. [105 ex.]

Beda the venerable Bede (c.673–735). I.praef.16; 6.157; 26.17; 33.16; II.4.25; 10.3, 7; 21.1, 142; 31.24.

bedælan vb I. *to deprive.* I.8.112; 21.191; II.10.171; 19.41. [15 ex., pp. only.]

gebedda m. *spouse, consort.* I.6.40; 9.10; 25.5; 26.161; II.32.138.

gebeddæg m. *day of prayer (i.e. Rogationtide or greater litany).* I.18.2.

gebedhus n. *house of prayer, oratory.* I.28.14, 75; II.11.175, 213; 40.65, 114. [9 ex.]

bedelfan vb 3. *to dig around.* II.26.79, 101; *to bury* II.38.11, 78. Pret.s. **bedealf**; pp. **bedolfen**.

bediglian vb II. *to hide.* I.2.80; 16.86; II.19.168 (**bedyg-**); 38.12. **bedigel-** 7x, **bedigolode** 1x, **bidig-** 1x. [21 ex.]

bedreda adj. *bedridden.* I.8.89, 204; 31.277; II.6.171 (**bedryda**); 27.149, 156. **bedd-** 1x. [9 ex.]

bedufan vb 2. *to sink.* II.24.205; 32.75 (pp. **bedofen**).

bedydrian vb II. *to deceive, delude.* II.10.119; 11.201.

bedydrung f. *deception, illusion.* I.praef.106 (app.crit.).

bedyppan vb I. *to dip.* II.2.116; 10.280; 14.42, 271.

bedyrnan vb I. *to hide.* II.12.415; 14.296.

beeod- see **began**.

befæstan vb I. *to entrust.* I.4.17; 26.270; II.11.92; 38.14, etc. [12 ex.]

befæstnian vb II. *to fix.* II.20.76.

befeallan vb 7. *to fall.* I.1.44; 24.51; II.5.207; 6.6. Pres.s.3 **befylþ**; pret. **befeol(l), befeollon**. [25 ex.]

befeolan vb 3. *to devote oneself to.* w. dat. II.23.69.

befon vb 7. *to encompass, encircle, encase, cover, clothe.* I.2.95; 10.159; II.5.35; 14.200. Pret. **befeng, -on**; pp. **befangen**. Inf. **befoon** 1x. [26 ex.]

beforan prep. w. dat. *before (in place or time), in front of.* I.5.26; 6.15; II.1.75; 3.66; **her beforan** *previous to this* II.22.151. as adv. I.14.22. [19 ex.]

befrinan vb 3. *to ask.* I.5.11 ff; 8.123; II.2.106; 6.15. Pret. **befran, befrunon**; pp. **befrynen**. [72 ex.]

befylan vb I. *to defile.* I.7.128; 32.134; II.7.26; 23.188. Cf **a-**.

began anom. vb. *to practise, engage in, devote oneself to, cultivate.* I.10.174; 18.40; II.6.121; 7.30; *to reach, arrive at* II.11.580; *to go around* II.5.263; 12.431; 30.23. Pres.s.3 **begæþ**; pl. **begaþ**; pret. **beeod-**. [43 ex.] See also **beginnan**.

begangan vb 7. *to commit, engage in.* I.10.180; II.3.172.

begeat m. *obtaining, acquisition*. I.17.29; II.4.302; 7.102.

begen pron. and adj. *both*. I.4.239; 29.93; II.10.78; 19.201. **begra, beigra, beira; bam**. [38 ex.]

begeotan vb 2. *to pour, sprinkle*. II.10.281; 20.247; 27.176. Pret.s. **begeat**; pp. **begoten**.

beginnan vb 3. *to begin* (w. inf. or **to** + infl. inf.). I.1.30; 3.31; II.10.215; 11.6. Pret. **began(n), begunnon**; pp. **begunnen**. [23 ex.] Cf **on-, under-**.

begleddian vb II. *to stain*. I.30.244.

begriwen pp. as adj. *enveloped, immersed*. I.8.47; 17.38; 27.8; II.22.148.

begyman vb I. *to attend to, look after*. w. gen. II.33.204.

begyrdan vb I. *to fasten, gird, clothe (esp. by wearing or fastening a belt?)*. II.2.83–4; 12.470; 15.19, 303; 16.120; 24.17. Cf **ymb-**.

begytan vb 5. *to obtain*. I.9.78; 27.225; II.6.176; 19.54; *to beget* I.praef.74 (app.crit.). Pres.s.2 **begytst**; 3 **begiit, begyt(t)**; pl. **begitaþ, begytaþ**; pret. **begeat, beget**; **begeat-**; pp. **begiten, begyten**. [29 ex.] Cf **for-, on-, under-**.

behabban vb III. *to contain, include*. I.15.72 (pres.s.3 **behæfþ**).

behat n. *promise*. I.4.250; 13.220; II.3.252; 5.11. [31 ex.]

behatan vb 7. *to promise*. I.1.195; 3.33; II.3.246; 5.224. Pres.s.3 **behæt**; pret. **behet, behet-**; pp. **behaten**. [74 ex.]

beheafdian vb II. *to behead*. I.26.255; 29.261; II.18.135; 24.44. [15 ex.]

beheafdung f. *beheading*. I.29.63; 32.179; II.27.178.

behealdan vb 7. *to consider, look at, take care*. I.1.99; 2.151; II.2.150; 5.109; refl., *to watch out* II.26.2, 30. Pres.s. **behylt**; pret. **beheold, beheold-**. [51 ex.]

behefe adj. *necessary*. I.34.234. Cf **nyd-**.

behlaf see II.11.297n.

behofian vb II. *to need*. w. gen. I.praef.58, 126; 14.11; II.3.77; 9.209. w.acc. I.31.73. [41 ex.]

behreowsian vb II. *to repent of*. I.9.68; 24.14; II.3.28; 14.139. [29 ex.]

behreowsung f. *repentance*. I.4.160; 16.80; II.3.209; 5.218. **bereow-** 3x. [32 ex.] Cf **bereowsungtid**.

behwyrfan vb 3? *to attend to (a dead body)*. I.7.206 (**bewyrfð**); 15.20; 37.106; II.14.339 (pret.s.3 subj. **behwurfe**); 18.153.

behwyrfan vb I. *to change, convert*. I.4.47, 51; 9.71 (**behwurfan**; possibly a separate strong verb); 27.144; 36.25.

behydan vb I. *to hide*. I.7.97; 20.109; II.7.104; 11.275. Pres.s.3 **behit**. [20 ex.]

behyld pp. *flayed*. I.36.76.

Bel Bel or Baal, god of the Babylonians. I.37.203.

beladian vb II. *to excuse*. II.20.86; 23.7, etc; 29.44; 34.294. [12 ex.]

beladung f. *excuse*. I.23.50; 35.170; II.5.88; 6.199. [7 ex.]

belædan vb I. *to bring, cause, impose*. II.20.32; 37.169.

belæfan vb I. *to leave (behind), spare*. II.6.58; 10.223; 11.417; 12.73; *to remain* II.32.207.

belæwa m. *betrayer*. I.27.212.

belæwan vb I. *to betray*. I.21.181; 32.186; II.14.20; 37.16. [22 ex.]

belæwing f. *treachery*. II.14.59.

beleafe (I.35.55) see Errata.

belean vb 6. *to censure*. II.5.84 (pret.s. subj. **beloge**).

gebelgan vb 3. refl., *to become angry*. I.26.121, 189; 29.58, 125; 38.231; *to repent, grieve?* II.14.153n. Pret.s. **gebealh**; pp. **gebolgen**.

gebelh m. *anger*. I.6.89.

belifan vb 1. *to remain*. I.2.61; 7.90; II.5.190; 7.66. Pret. **belaf, belif-**. [29 ex.]

belifian vb II. *to deprive of life*. II.2.210; 18.67.

belimpan vb 3. *to pertain, refer, belong*. I.7.227; 12.113; II.4.43; 12.256. Pret.s. **belamp**. [39 ex.]

belle wk f. *bell*. II.11.29–30, 34.

belucan vb 2. trans., *to lock, close*. I.1.190; 13.27, 30; II.1.296–8; 14.345; *to comprehend, encompass, include, conclude* I.6.3; 19.213–4; 39.94; II.22.153; intrans., *to end* II.39.205. Pres.s.3 **belicþ**; pret. **beleac, belucon**; pp. **belocen**. [36 ex.]

belyfan vb I. *to believe*. I.6.52; 7.178; II.1.245; 27.207. (Always with **on**.) [11 ex.]

bemænan vb I. *to complain (of), lament (for, over)*. I.28.110; 29.34; II.11.181; 20.245. [9 ex.]

ben f. *petition*. I.3.110; 24.119; II.14.305; 18.32. [45 ex.]

benæman vb I. *to deprive*. w. gen. object and dat. of person. I.14.178; 37.277; II.7.65; 18.9. [7 ex.]

bend m. *bond, fetter, chain*. I.16.83–4; 19.49; II.21.152; 27.74. [28 ex.]

gebendan vb I. *to bend*. I.34.16.

Benedictus St Benedict of Nursia (c.480–c.550). I.6.159; II.11.passim.

beneoþon prep. w. dat. *beneath*. I.5.132.

Beneuentani the people of Beneventum in southern Italy. I.34.42.

beniman vb 4. *to take away*. II.30.67, 83; 32.166. Pret. **benam, benam-**.

beo f. *bee*. II.1.88; 10.69.

beobread n. *honeycomb*. II.16.193–9.

beod m. *table*. I.23.8; II.3.267; 8.106; 15.241.

beodan vb 2. *to urge, bid, instruct, decree*. I.14.67; 23.129; II.4.254; 8.46; *to offer, proffer, inflict* I.14.129; 30.212; II.32.128; 33.59. Pres.s.3 **byt**; pret. **bead, bud-**; pp. **geboden**. [21 ex.] Cf **be-, for-**.

gebeodan vb 2. *to offer, proffer, propose*. I.19.50–1; 31.46–7; 38.122; II.11.82; 14.286. Pret. **gebud-**. [10 ex.]

beon anom. vb. *to be*. Forms (with totals, but not divided by function): **beo** (180), **bio** (1); **bist** (17), **byst** (8); **biþ** (801), **byþ** (4); **beoþ** (489); **eom** (92); **eart** (77); **is** (1973), **ys** (1); **sind** (517), **sindon** (44), **sint** (12), **synd** (44), **syndon** (18), **synt** (9); **si** (10), **sy** (225); **sin** (1), **syn** (4); **beon** (303), **beonne** (2); **wesan** (1, I.3.87); **wæs** (1987), **wære** (296), **wæron** (415); negative, **neom** (1); **nis** (199), **nys** (8); **næs** (118), **nære** (45), **næron** (37). (Some tendency to use **beon** forms for future sense, e.g. I.praef.58–61, 73–4.) **hwæs beoþ**, *of what value will be . . .?* II.7.98.

beor n. *beer*. II.3.17.

gebeor m. *companion at drink or feast*. I.32.16, 23; 35.19, 22; II.4.7, 46, 307. [10 ex.]

gebeorg n. *protection*. I.2.188.

(ge)beorgan vb 3. *to protect, defend, safeguard* (w. dat.). I.3.187; 29.16, 254; II.2.203; 18.98. Imper. **gebeorh**; pret. pl. **burgon**; pp. **geboregen**. [8 ex.]

beorht adj. *bright*. I.7.50; 39.59; II.21.61; 34.308; of voices, sounds, written discourse *clear, penetrating?* I.4.205; 29.102; II.11.548. **beortre** 1x. [14 ex.]

beorhte adv. *brightly*. I.4.272; II.17.109.

beorhtlice adv. *clearly*. I.29.49, 93.

beorhtnyss f. *brightness, splendour*. I.2.22; 4.110; II.10.67; 12.233. **beoht-** 2x, **beorhnysse** 1x. [30 ex.]

beorma m. *yeast, leaven*. II.12.365; 15.264–8.

gebeorscipe m. *banquet, party*. I.4.247; 19.230; II.4.80; 23.124. **beorscipe** 1x. [8 ex.]

gebeot n. *boast, boasting*. I.37.172; II.14.73, 138.

gebeotlic adj. *boastful, exultant*. II.12.93.

beotlice adv. *boastfully*. I.26.246.

bepæcan vb I. *to deceive, delude*. I.praef.64; 3.141; II.24.219; 26.19. Pret. **bepæht-**, pp. **bepæht**. [29 ex.]

bepæcend m. *deceiver*. I.6.177; II.33.245.

bera m. *bear*. I.18.7; II.12.62.

beran vb 4. *to carry, bear (fruit)*. I.4.129; 9.11; II.1.53–6; 4.17. Pres.s.3 **berþ, byrþ**; pret. **bær, bær-**; pp. **geboren**. [95 ex.] Cf **a-, for-, to-**.

geberan vb 4. *to give birth to, bear (a child)*. I.9.5; 31.80; II.1.85; 3.204. *to carry* I.9.33; II.11.231. Pret.s. **gebær**; pp. **geboren**. [32 ex.]

bere m. *barley*. I.12.91; II.10.181.

bereafian vb II. *to rob, plunder, strip* (w. dat. or gen. of object taken, or æt). I.17.55; 29.180; 37.276; II.10.184; 33.261. [7 ex.]

[bern] n. *barn*. I.35.130; II.4.264; 7.94. Pl. **bernu**.

beren adj. *of barley*. I.12.47, 91; 26.187; 30.210; II.25.20. **berne** 1x. [9 ex.]

bereowsungtid f. *time of repentance*. II.5.271, 283. Cf **behreow-**.

berie wk f. *berry*. II.15.89, 237. Cf **win-**.

Beriþ a god of the Indians. I.31.24–33.

berstan vb 3. *to break, break out* (intrans.). II.12.395 (**burston**); 16.166. Cf **æt-, to-**.

bertun m. *storehouse, granary*. II.7.93.

berypan vb I. *to despoil, rob, extort*. I.4.125; 10.180; 23.33; 38.90; II.7.58.

besargian vb II. *to pity, feel sorry for* (w.

object in acc., but gen. if a person). I.10.95; 19.239; II.10.288; 11.13. [14 ex.]

besargung f. *grieving for, pitying*. I.23.110.

besawan vb 7. *to sow*. I.12.63. pp. **besawen**.

besceawian vb II. *to look at, consider*. I.1.10; 32.196; 38.143; II.5.210, 222; 27.62. [7 ex.]

besceofan vb 2. *to despatch, send*. I.4.24 (inf. **besceofon**); 24.80; II.1.25; 19.290. Pret.s.subj. **bescufe**; pp. **bescofen**. [6 ex.]

besceotan vb 2. *to happen, occur*. II.13.10.

bescinan vb 1. *to shine around* (trans.). I.2.22 (pret.s. **bescean**).

bescyran vb 4. *to cut (hair), to tonsure*. pp. **bescoren** I.30.203; 32.186; II.17.67; 21.17.

bescyrian vb I/II. *to exclude, deprive*. I.17.41; II.36.116.

besecgan vb III. *to allege, say in accusation*. I.3.23 (pret.pl. **besædon**).

besencan vb I. *to sink* (trans.). I.22.13; 23.34; II.24.137, 218; 27.86. [14 ex.]

besendan vb I. *to send, impose*. II.30.236.

beseon vb 5. *to look, gaze*. I.4.65; 37.136; II.11.469; 20.93. **wel besewen** *refined, well presented*? I.35.227. Pres.s.3 **besyhþ**; imper. **beseoh**; pret. **beseah, beseh, besaw-**. [28 ex.]

besettan vb I. *to set, place, impose*. I.13.208; 31.322; II.12.294; 35.54; *to guard, attend* I.26.251; II.14.349; 20.230; 21.7 (all ref. to corpses). [22 ex.]

besingan vb 3. *to sing over, enchant*? I.31.324.

besittan vb 5. *to guard, attend*. I.15.9; 28.136; II.14.351; 34.321. Pret.pl. **besæton**.

beslean vb 6. *to fix, fasten*. pp. **beslagen** II.14.218. Cf. **geslean**.

besmitan vb 1. *to defile, pollute*. I.8.82–3; 37.33; II.18.32; 33.113, 166. Pret.s. **besmat**; pp. **besmiten**.

besmitennyss f. *pollution*. I.4.259; 36.20.

besorg adj. *dear, beloved*. I.AppB3.44.

bespætan vb I. *to spit upon*. II.14.128.

besprecan vb 5. *to intercede for, speak on behalf of*. I.26.147 (pret.s. **bespræc**).

bestandan vb 6. *to stand around, attend*. II.9.124.

bestingan vb 3. *to thrust, cram*. II.19.292; 34.206 (pret.s. **bestang**). Cf **of-**.

bestæppan vb 6. *to enter, pass*. II.14.17 (pret.s. **bestop**).

bestridan vb 1. *to bestride, mount (a horse)*. I.14.15; II.10.43 (pret.s. **bestrad**).

bestreowian vb II. *to strew, sprinkle*. II.30.136; 34.298.

beswican vb 1. *to deceive, trick*. I.1.120; 7.187; II.30.126–7; 33.136; **beswican æt** *to trick out of, to deprive of by deceit* I.34.223. Pret. **beswac, beswic-**; pp. **beswicen**. [21 ex.]

beswincan vb 3. *to cultivate, till*. pp. **beswuncenum** II.10.179.

beswingan vb 3. *to scourge, chastise*. I.10.8; 31.249–50; II.14.181; 19.250. Pres.s. **beswingþ, beswincþ**; pret.s. **beswang**; pp. **beswungen**. [13 ex.]

bet comp. adv. *better*. I.20.62; 30.254; 35.213; II.10.277; 15.311.

gebetan vb I. *to make amends for, atone for, remedy*. I.9.220; 10.72; 19.240; II.3.227; 10.136. **bet-** 4x. [25 ex.] Cf **dæd-**.

betæcan vb I. *to commit, entrust, deliver*. I.1.291; 3.166; II.1.17; 2.198. Pres.s.2 **betæhst**; 3 **betæcþ, betæhþ**; pret. **betæht-**; pp. **betæht**. [65 ex.]

betellan vb I. *to excuse, exculpate, defend*. I.5.43; II.13.46; 14.151; 27.114. Pret.s. **betealde**. [6 ex.]

beteon vb 2. *to cover*. II.36.86; *to accuse* II.33.159 (pp. **betogen**).

betera comp. adj. *better*. I.10.85; 12.138; II.3.193, 219–22; 31.8–9. [30 ex.]

gebeterian vb II. *to make better, improve*. I.28.101.

beterung f. *improvement*. I.19.201; 24.203; 25.186; 30.188 (**gebetrunge**). [6 ex.]

Bethleem the town of Bethlehem in Judaea. I.2.14, 33, etc; 5.9, etc; 7.9, etc; II.4.185, 189. **beþleem** 1x. [21 ex.]

betsta superl. adj. *best*. I.9.117; II.4.22.

betweonan, betwynan prep. w. dat. *between, among*; **him betwynan** *to each other*. I.2.33; 19.210; II.13.233; 16.6. [29 ex., all except II.13.233 governing a pron.] Cf. **betwux**.

betwux prep. w. dat. *between, among*. I.praef.89; 1.36; II.1.195; 13.138. **betux** 2x. [161 ex.]

beþencan vb I. *to consider*. I.AppB2.51; refl., *to reflect, to return to one's senses or reason*. I.30.193; II.11.51; 24.22; 27.192. Pret.s. **beþohte**; pp. **beþoht**.

(ge)beþian vb II. *to warm.* I.5.144; II.10.31, 44, 83.

beþung f. *warming.* I.5.145.

beþurfan pret.pres. vb. *to need.* II.10.139 (**beþorfte**); Expl.4.

bewæfan vb I. *to clothe, wrap.* I.2.92; 3.198; II.14.27, 199; 34.35, 41.

beweddian vb II. *to betrothe, marry.* I.2.188; 13.45, 79–86; II.1.93; 4.32. [8 ex.]

bewendan vb I. refl., *to turn, move.* I.26.199; II.6.172; 27.30.

beweorpan vb 3. *to wrap, surround.* I.31.154; II.10.164; 26.79, 101; *to throw* II.11.79. Pret. **bewurp-**; pp. **beworpen.**

bewepan vb 7. *to lament, weep over.* I.5.52; 9.90; II.3.226; 4.183. Pret. **beweop, beweop-.** [13 ex.]

bewerian vb I/II. *to protect, defend.* I.37.163; II.14.100; 19.138; 34.290; 36.82.

bewerigend m. *defender.* I.27.68.

bewindan vb 3. *to wrap.* I.2.18; 15.113; 23.140; II.18.48. Pret. **bewand, bewund-**; pp. **bewunden.** [14 ex.]

bewitan pret.pres. vb. *to watch over, govern.* I.1.35; 34.266; II.27.112. Pret. **bewist-.**

bewyrcan vb I. *to construct.* II.12.390; 33.268. Pret.s. **beworhte**; pp. **beworht.**

bewyrfþ see **behwyrfan** (1)

beyrnan vb 3. *to run, pass.* I.praef.48; 4.141; 23.94; II.2.53. Pret. **bearn, beurne.**

bibliothece wk f. *bible.* I.30.11, 14.

(ge)bicgan vb I. *to buy.* I.4.96–7; 12.10, 45; II.23.8; 39.17. Pret. **boht-, geboht-**; pp. **geboht.** [22 ex.]

gebicnian vb II. *to indicate, point, signify.* I.7.73; 25.137; II.4.118; 26.51. **bic-** 2x. (Cf. also **togebicnode** I.37.77, perhaps better printed as 2 words.) [14 ex.]

gebicnung f. *sign.* I.7.102; 34.30; 37.76; II.18.42; 34.140. Cf **fore-.**

gebidan vb 1. *to experience, live to see.* w. gen. or acc. I.praef.108; 15.153; 16.130; II.7.101. Pret.s. **gebad.** Cf **a-.**

biddan vb 5. *to pray, beseech.* w. gen. or acc. of thing asked for. I.praef.128; 3.101; 14.84; II.praef.43; 2.36; 17.121. Pres.s.2 **bitst**; 3 **bit, bitt**; pret. **bæd, bæd-, bede** (1x). **bydde** 1x. [279 ex.] Cf **a-.**

gebiddan vb 5. *to pray, pray for.* w. gen. of thing asked for. I.3.129; 13.222; 18.3; II.2.62; 12.446; refl., *to pray* I.2.150; 5.29; II.1.228; 2.160. Pres.s.3 **gebit(t)**; pret. **gebæd, gebæd-.** [102 ex.]

bifian, biuian vb II. *to tremble, quake.* I.15.176; 21.143; II.11.388; 14.277; 24.244. [10 ex.]

bifung f. *trembling, shaking.* II.2.154, 166.

gebigan vb I. *to bend, turn, convert.* I.praef.133; 1.54; II.1.93; 3.96. **big-, bihþ** 9x. Pres.s.2 **gebihst**; 3 **gebigþ, (ge)bihþ, gebyhþ.** [82 ex.]

bigels m. *vault, arch.* I.11.79; II.33.268.

bigeng, biggencg m. *worship, rite, observance.* I.4.207; 37.22; II.4.229; 15.26; *practice* I.6.88; 36.103; II.3.230; 12.355; *cultivation, tilling* II.5.70, 76. [22 ex.]

biggenga m. *worshipper.* I.29.237; *cultivator* II.26.75, 77, 89.

bigleofa m. *sustenance, food.* I.3.144; 4.279; II.9.36; 10.102. **bileof-** 3x, **byleof-** 1x. [64 ex.]

bigspel n. *parable, exemplary story.* I.23.4; 24.76; II.5.1; 23.3. **bisp-** 1x, **bysp-** 1x. [22 ex.]

bigwist m. *sustenance, food.* I.24.28; 25.150; 26.210; 28.46. **biwiste** 1x. [7 ex.]

bile m. *beak.* II.10.192.

bilewite, byle- adj. *innocent, gentle, simple.* I.1.137; 9.110–12; II.3.179; 20.84. [18 ex.]

bilewitlice adv. *innocently.* I.38.146.

bilewitnyss, byle- f. *simplicity, gentleness.* I.praef.52; 22.140; II.3.170; 9.214. [17 ex.]

(ge)bindan vb 3. *to bind, fetter.* I.1.275; 35.175; II.1.240; 2.105. Pres.s.2 **bintst**; pret. **geband, gebund-.** (**bind-** 6x, present tense only.) [50 ex.] Cf **be-, un-.**

binn f. *manger.* I.2.19, 27, 35, 95, etc.

binnon, binnan prep. w. dat. *within.* I.1.205; 28.16; II.1.50; 5.111. **bynnan** 2x. [76 ex.]

birg-, birig- see **byrgen**

biscop m. *bishop.* I.praef.46; 17.23; II.1.51 (of the old law); 2.1. **bisceope** 1x; **byscop** 1x. [109 ex.] Cf **erce-, heafod-, leod-.**

biscopdom m. *bishopric, episcopal office.* I.31.241; II.34.318.

biscophad m. *episcopal office or order.* I.31.237; II.1.164; 10.329.

biscopsetl n. *episcopal see or throne.* I.26.104; 29.291; 37.11.

biscopstol m. *episcopal see or throne.* II.9.167, 229.

biscopung, biscepung f. *rite of confirmation.* I.22.252–3.

bism-, bisn- see **bysm-, bysn-**; **bispel** see **bigspel**

gebit n. *biting, gnashing.* I.8.101, 167–70; 35.24, 176, 189.

bita m. *morsel, bite.* I.12.13.

bitan vb 1. *to bite, gnash.* I.3.46; 31.61; II.18.149; 36.60. Pret.s. **bat**. Cf **a-**.

biter adj. *bitter, painful.* I.29.280; 40.169; II.10.21; 15.270. [9 ex.]

biterlice adv. *bitterly*. II.2.102.

biternyss f. *bitterness* (ref. figuratively mainly to pain or anger). I.21.170; 28.126; II.3.172; 12.107. [11 ex.]

gebiterod pp. as adj. *bitter, embittered.* II.14.223–5.

biterwyrde adj. *bitter or hostile in speech.* I.22.141; II.3.157 (**byt-**).

Biþþinia Bithynia, a region of NW Asia Minor. I.26.102.

biuian see **bifian**.

biwiste see **bigwist**

blac adj. *black.* I.23.112; 28.216; 32.106; II.3.184; 33.249. [7 ex.]

blacian vb II. *to turn pale.* I.28.205.

blacung f. *turning pale.* I.4.227.

blawan vb 7. *to blow (of breath, wind, trumpets, etc.*; intrans.*).* I.16.54; 22.19; II.12.127, 393; 21.27; 39.125. Pres.s.3 **blæwþ**; pret. **bleow, bleow-**. (For **bleow** see also **blowan**.) Cf **a-, to-**.

blawend m. *'inspirer', one who creates by breathing?* II.32.176.

blawung f. *blowing.* II.12.434; 39.123.

blæcfexede adj. *black-haired.* I.31.33.

blæd m. *breath, blast.* I.22.169; 34.18; II.6.97; 10.83, 129. [10 ex.]

blædre wk f. *blister.* II.12.67.

bleo, gebleoh n. *colour, appearance.* II.31.70; 40.193.

(ge)bletsian vb II. *to bless.* I.4.87; 6.171; II.2.208; 4.154. **geblætsode** 1x. [77 ex.]

bletsung f. *blessing.* I.4.12; 6.174; II.4.160; 11.76. [39 ex.]

blind adj. *blind.* I.1.256; 4.172; II.1.184; 2.10. (Often used as noun, w. def. art.) [68 ex.]

blindnyss f. *blindness.* I.8.181–2; 10.96; II.11.115; 38.158. [9 ex.]

blis f. *bliss, joy, pleasure, cause of joy.* I.9.145; 24.13; II.2.158; 5.248. [65 ex.] Cf **un-**.

blissian vb II. intrans., *to be happy, rejoice (at)* (w. gen.). I.3.202; 5.152; II.2.41; 13.36; trans., *to make happy, to please* I.16.103. **geblissode** 1x. [73 ex.]

blissigendlic adj. *joyful.* I.25.78.

bliþe adj. *happy, cheerful.* I.9.27; 12.36; II.2.96; 10.318. (Some examples of **bliþe** may be adverbial.) [18 ex.]

bliþelice adv. *cheerfully, happily.* I.AppB3.244; II.12.483; 34.251.

blod n. *blood.* I.praef.114; 1.109; II.2.169; 15.13. [69 ex.]

geblodigian vb II. *to make bloody, to stain with blood.* II.6.42; 15.173.

blostm m? *blossom, flower.* I.5.105–6; 12.108; II.2.33; 31.84. ns. **blostm** (2x); nap. **blostman** (6x); dp. **blostmum** (1x). [9 ex.]

blostmbære adj. *blossoming, flowery.* II.21.68, 83.

blowan vb 7. *to blossom, flourish.* I.4.98; 38.250; II.1.53, 56 (pret.s. **bleow**); 21.60; 31.73.

boc f. *book.* I.praef.49, 129; 4.30, 175, 180; II.praef.29, 33–7; 9.6–8. gds., nap. **bec**. [135 ex.] Cf **dom-, gerim-, sealm-, traht-, þening-**.

bocere m. *'scribe' (of the Jewish community, as representative of Jewish law and religion).* I.3.22; 5.15; II.12.456; 32.11. [12 ex.]

bocland n. *estate.* II.10.297.

boclic adj. *of books, derived from books.* I.praef.68; 7.90; II.4.93; 6.120. [22 ex.]

boda m. *messenger.* I.24.85, 115; 37.178; II.33.42.

bodian vb II. *to preach, proclaim.* I.2.24; 4.74; II.1.268; 3.21. [122 ex.]

bodig n. *body.* I.26.42; II.34.158.

bodung f. *preaching, proclamation, announcement, prophecy.* I.2.214; 3.13; II.9.224; 19.47. [71 ex.] Cf **godspel-**.

bodungdæg m. *day of annunciation.* I.13.153.

boga m. *bow* (the weapon). I.34.16. Cf **ren-**.

[bog] m. *bough, branch.* I.14.21, 133; 16.122;

II.1.53; 5.56. **bogas, bogum**. [7 ex.] Cf **win-**.

bogian vb II. *to inhabit*. II.12.20.

bogung f. *arrogance?* II.28.25.

boht- see **bicgan**; **bord** n. see **oforbord**.

Boisil (d. c.660) prior of Melrose Abbey; described as a bishop by Ælfric. II.10.251.

borh m. *pledge*. II.3.254.

bosm m. *hold of a ship*. I.35.269; II.4.123; *bosom, lap, loving embrace* I.5.102; 20.96; II.6.61; 19.210; *heart* II.30.50, 175.

bot f. *remedy, atonement*. I.19.160, 240; II.6.164. Cf **dæd-**.

botl n. *palace, residence of king or other authority-figure*. I.18.8; 29.224; 38.316; II.32.207; *monastic residence* I.34.112; II.10.174 (Cuthbert's hermitage); 32.201; *residence or mansion in Heaven* I.30.163. [10 ex.]

brad adj. *wide, extensive, vast*. I.8.194; 10.177; II.4.124; 12.46. [10 ex.]

bradnyss f. *breadth, extent*. II.26.92; 40.40.

bragen n. *brain*. II.17.102.

brand m. *flame* II.10.120; *sword* II.34.191.

brastlian vb II. *to roar, crackle*. I.4.151; II.10.120; 12.126.

brædan vb I. *to roast*. I.15.59; 29.218; II.3.82; 15.14, 275; 16.187 ff. [12 ex.]

bræþ m. *scent*. I.15.81–3; 30.126; II.6.193; 10.68. [12 ex.] Cf **wyrt-**.

brecan vb 4. *to burst, break (out)* (intrans.). I.11.115. Cf **a-**, **to-**.

bredan vb I. *to hatch, produce (young)*. I.18.111; II.1.89.

[bredan] vb 3. *to change* (trans.). I.26.172 (pret.s. **bræd**); II.15.108 (pres.s.3 **bret**); *to lift, remove* II.11.431 (pret.pl. **brudon**). Cf **a-**, **æt-**, **wiþ-**

[gebredan] vb 3. *to weave*. pp. **gebroden** II.25.123.

breden adj. *wooden?* I.20.184.

bregan vb I. *to frighten*. I.10.85; 38.50.

bremblas, bremelas m.pl. *brambles*. I.1.146; 29.263; II.4.150; 26.6. [11 ex.]

breost n. *breast, lungs, chest*. I.5.101; 35.234; II.9.26; 11.373. nap. **breost**. [11 ex.]

brerd m. *brim*. II.4.15.

brice m. *fragment*. I.4.63–5; 12.23, 122, 127; II.25.24.

brice n. *use, enjoyment*. I.9.97; 23.78; II.10.175; 11.407. [12 ex.] Cf **ned-**.

bricg f. *bridge*. II.18.24, 28.

bricgian vb II. *to provide a smooth or decorous path for* (w. dat.). I.14.21; pp. **gebricgod** *provided with such a path, paved* II.11.565. Cf **ofer-**.

bridd m. *chick, young bird*. I.9.79, 88, 114; 18.111; II.10.192.

bridel m. *curb, bridle*. I.37.181; II.10.153.

(ge)bringan vb I. *to bring, produce, put, lead*. I.4.86; 9.76; II.6.31; 7.2. Pres.s.3 **(ge)brincþ**; pret. **(ge)broht-**; pp. **gebroht**. [142 ex.] Cf **forþ-**.

broc n. *disease*. I.31.273, 282; 35.255; II.2.15; 11.394.

gebrocian vb II. *to afflict with disease*. I.31.259, 303, 332 (all pp.).

brocung f. *disease, suffering from disease*. I.31.263, 275.

brod f. *brood*. II.1.89.

broga m. *terror*. II.39.173.

gebrosnian vb II. *to corrupt, decay*. II.1.198.

brosniendlic adj. *corruptible, perishable*. I.18.173; II.15.114, etc; 29.75; 31.83. Cf **un-**.

brosnung f. *corruption, decay, corruptibility*. I.6.123; 15.92; II.12.273; 15.113. [9 ex.] Cf **un-**.

broþor, broþer m. *brother, fellow-man, member of a monastic community*. I.3.169; 7.130; II.2.112; 9.239; 11.425. **broþur** 1x; ds.**breþer**; np. **broþru** (1x, I.20.17; error for **gebroþru**?—cf. app. crit.). [83 ex.]

gebroþra, gebroþru m.pl. *brothers, fellow-Christians (esp. as term of address), members of a monastic community*. I.2.42; 4.47, 74; 23.95; II.1.30; 11.417. [145 ex.]

broþorlic, broþer- adj. *brotherly*. I.3.166; 16.142; *of brothers or siblings* II.2.147.

broþorræden, broþer- f. *brotherhood, brotherliness*. I.9.112; 19.31–3; II.19.67.

gebrowen pp. (of **breowan**) as adj. *brewed*. I.25.45.

brucan vb 2. *to use, enjoy, have use or pleasure of, possess* (w. gen.). I.1.71; 4.123; II.10.217; 20.75. w. acc. I.23.54. Pres.s.3 **bricþ, brihþ, brycþ**; pret.s **breac**. [48 ex.]

bryd f. *bride*. I.4.14; 35.81; II.1.95, 100; 32.161. [17 ex.]

brydbed n. *marriage-bed, the bed of a bride*. I.13.151; II.1.98.

brydguma m. *bridegroom.* I.13.151; 36.132; II.1.96–7; 4.33. [24 ex.]

brym m. *sea.* II.10.75, 164, 190; 23.147; 24.60, 146.

bryne m. *burning, conflagration, fervour.* I.8.195; 24.143–5; 40.145; II.3.189; 40.292.

buc m. *stomach.* II.15.146.

bucca m. *male goat.* I.38.215; II.12.352, 361.

bucful m.? *bucketfull* (or perhaps 2 words). II.27.173.

bufon, bufan prep. w. dat. *above.* I.2.156; 4.271; II.3.108; 4.146. w. acc. I.4.232. adv. II.39.51–2. [30 ex.]

(ge)bugan vb 2. *to turn* (intrans.), *submit.* I.praef.84; 1.46, 49; II.1.232; 26.68. Pres.s.3 **gebyhþ**; pret. **(ge)beah, (ge)bug-**; pp. **gebogen**. [56 ex.] Cf **a-, for-, on-, under-**.

bugian vb I(?). *to inhabit.* II.10.167.

bugigend m. *inhabitant, occupant.* II.9.93. Cf **eorþbugend**.

bur n. *chamber.* I.31.71.

burh f. *city, town.* I.1.205; 2.12–13; II.4.233–4; 6.3. **buruh** 1x; gds. **byrig, birig** (1x), **byri** (6x); nagp. **burga**; dp. **burgum**. [167 ex.] Cf **heafod-**.

burhgeat n. *city gate.* I.15.162.

burhscir f. *district centring on a town?.* I.5.73; 26.5, 23; II.8.5; 34.318. (No Latin equivalent; the sources generally refer only to specific towns.)

burhwaru f. *body of inhabitants of a town.* I.5.14; 28.69; II.17.117–8; 28.80. Mainly in sing.; np. **-ra** I.18.38; II.34.321 (both ref. to citizens of 2 cities); dp. **-um** I.34.34; II.17.117; 27.211. **buruh-** 3x. [27 ex.] Cf **ceasterge-, eorþ-, hel-, heofen-, leden-**.

burhweall m. *city wall.* II.4.228; 12.39.

buton, butan prep.w. dat. *without, except for, outside.* I.praef.102; 1.7; II.1.9–10; 2.151; 11.497. conj. (a) *apart from, but, except, if not* (after questions or negatives, followed by noun in apposition or phrase or clause) I.7.182; 8.142; II.6.85–6; 23.70; (b) *unless* (w. subjunctive) I.praef.65; 11.129; II.1.106 ff; 20.137. [531 ex.]

butere wk f. *butter.* II.11.415.

butruc m. *cask, flagon* (source refers to a wooden container). II.11.274.

butu pron. *both.* I.1.140; 25.5, 8; II.29.22; 34.321. **buta** 1x. [8 ex.]

by- see also **bi-, big-**.

bydel m. *herald, messenger, announcer, forerunner.* I.praef.71; 25.53, 98; II.3.5–7; 9.167–70; 23.12. [50 ex.]

gebyldan vb I. *to embolden, make bold.* I.29.195; pp. **gebyld** I.3.126; 4.225; II.24.192; 27.12. [9 ex.]

[(ge)byldu] f. *confidence.* I.praef.50; 27.40; II.33.229; 34.167.

byme wk f. *trumpet.* I.praef.118; 22.19; II.5.280; 39.125. [13 ex.]

gebyrd f. *ancestry, lineage.* I.praef.47; 2.12; 7.134; II.13.68. [6 ex.]

gebyrdtid f. *birth, birthday, time of birth.* I.5.8; 7.47; II.1.277; DSM.1. [18 ex.]

byrgels m. *grave, burial-place.* II.14.157.

byrgen fn. *grave, tomb.* I.4.254–5; 15.149; II.11.367; 14.166, 278, 299. **birg-** 4x, **birig-** 2x. nap. **byrgenu**. [68 ex.]

gebyrian vb I/II. *to befit, belong, pertain.* w. dat. or **to**. I.praef.45; 5.63; II.4.253–4; 12.257. Pres.s.3 **-aþ, -eþ**; pl. **-iaþ**; pret.s. **-ode**. [12 ex.]

[byrle] m. *cupbearer, steward, servant.* II.4.19; ExDict.11.

byrnan vb 3. *to burn.* I.22.168–70; 35.196; II.1.209; 3.141; 20.216. Pret. **barn, burne**. [50 ex.] Cf **for-**.

byrne wk f. *mailshirt.* II.12.471; 34.54.

byrþen f. *burden, load.* I.4.85; 14.110; II.5.26; 24.186. [11 ex.]

byrþenmælum adv. *in bundles.* I.35.125.

byrþenstrang adj. *strong for bearing burdens.* I.14.55.

byrþere m. *carrier, bearer, mount.* I.14.88; 21.206; 33.41.

[bysegu] f. *labour.* I.35.90 (ds. **bysga**); II.29.57 (ds **bysegan**).

(ge)bysgian vb II. *to occupy, busy.* I.35.89; 40.57; II.26.56; 36.76. [14 ex.]

bysig adj. *busy.* II.29.15, 36, etc; 31.85.

bysmor, bism- mfn. *scorn, mockery, disgrace.* I.10.8; 15.162; II.34.251.

bysmorful adj. *shameful.* I.26.39.

bysmorlic adj. *shameful, contemptuous.* I.20.230; 21.167; 28.52 **(bysmer-)**; II.13.99.

bysmorlice adv. *with disgrace, in a manner conferring shame.* I.37.154; II.12.39.

gebysmrian vb II. *to despise, shame, dis-*

grace. w. acc. or dat. I.29.150–1; 37.18; II.11.218; 12.329. **bysm-** 1x. [11 ex.]

bysen f. *example, model*. I.praef.130; 31.315; II.28.160; 37.85. **bisne** 2x. [36 ex.]

(ge)bysnian vb II. *to set an example*. I.praef.110; 14.39; II.3.237, 240; 19.253. [17 ex.] Cf **mis-**.

gebysnung f. *example, precedent*. I.3.30; 8.73; II.3.237; 9.25. **bys-** 1x; **gebis-** 1x. [24 ex.]

bytlian vb II. *to build*. I.26.65, 71; II.21.118.

gebytlu n. *a building*. I.4.125, 148; 27.132; II.11.318; 21.118–20; 40.95, 130. **gebytlu** is the only form used (11 ex.); includes nap., as. (II.21.118), gs. or gp. (I.4.125).

gebytlung f. *building, design of a building*. II.11.311, 321, 324; 40.122; **bytlung** I.26.69.

bytming f. *bottom*. I.35.263, 266.

caflice adv. *quickly, boldly*. I.31.154; 33.57; II.15.313; 18.29; 24.179.

cafnyss f. *promptness, speed*. II.15.315.

caf adj. *prompt*. II.3.166 (**caue**); 24.156.

Cain son of Adam and Eve. II.4.105, 108.

calic m. *cup, chalice*. II.14.50; 15.79, 165; 37.139–45.

gecamp mn. *conflict, warfare*. I.5.120; 24.65; II.5.268; 34.16. [10 ex.]

Campania region of central Italy. I.34.5.

campdom m. *conflict, warfare*. I.29.36; II.30.150–2.

campian vb II. *to fight, wage war*. I.25.174; II.25.129.

canon m. *canon, article of ecclesiastical decrees*. II.6.147; 12.552.

canonic adj. *canonical, pertaining to ecclesiastical decrees*. II.6.164.

Cantwareburh Canterbury. II.9.191, 203.

Capharnaum city in Galilee. I.8.88.

capitulas m.pl. *headings, rubrics* (in a table of contents). II.praef.42.

Cappadocia region of Asia Minor. I.26.102; a city of that name (the sources in both cases refer to the city of Caesarea in Cappadocia) I.30.202; II.2.101.

carful adj. *anxious, thoughtful, attentive*. I.4.45; 24.51; II.18.10; 20.193. [17 ex.]

carfullice adv. *carefully, attentively*. I.26.92; 32.124; II.5.205; 38.123. [6 ex.]

carfulnyss f. *attention, thoughtfulness, dedication*. I.28.128; II.15.296; 20.44–6.

carian vb II. *to care, be anxious*. I.4.123; 17.61; AppB3.143; II.5.115. [6 ex.]

caru f. *care, anxiety*. I.28.122; 34.270; II.6.101; 30.237; 31.53. Cf **woruld-**.

casere m. *emperor*. I.2.9; 4.22; II.9.97 ff; 18.5 ff. [105 ex.]

Casinum Monte Cassino in Italy, south-east of Rome. II.11.171, 572.

cauertun m. *palace*. I.29.108; II.14.131 (translating **atrium** but perhaps referring to the whole building, the bishop's palace).

cæg f. *key*. I.26.14, 78, 93; II.14.145. **cæig** 2x.

cæppe wk f. *cloak*. I.23.141; II.11.107–8.

ceac m. *vessel (for water)* (no equivalent in source). I.29.177.

ceaf n. *chaff*. I.38.268; II.4.263–5; 19.148; 40.232 etc.

ceafl m. *jaw*. I.35.239; 37.226; II.34.208.

ceald adj. *cold*. I.22.149, 171; 35.254; 38.106; II.7.124.

cealf mn. *calf*. II.12.348–9, 357; 28.67.

cealfian vb II. *to calve, to give birth (to a calf)*. II.17.112.

ceap m. *purchase, purchasing*. I.28.86, 92, 174–5; 35.11, 84; II.39.18, 164. **cype**(?) I.28.9.

geceapian vb II. *to buy*. I.38.74, 104. Cf **be-**.

cearcian vb II. *to gnash*. I.8.199; 35.192.

ceas f. *questioning, complaint*. II.5.172.

ceast f. *conflict, strife*. I.28.126; 39.88; II.20.100; 27.145.

ceaster f. *city*. I.2.26; 38.262; II.11.532; 34.121. [12 ex.]

ceastergewaran m.pl. *citizens*. I.2.159; 24.185; II.4.247–8; 9.86. [16 ex.] Cf **burh-** etc.

cederbeam m. *cedar-tree*. II.40.49.

gecelan vb I. *to cool*. I.23.14.

celing f. *cooling*. I.29.215.

cempa m. *soldier, warrior (often in a spiritual sense)*. I.3.197; 8.94; II.3.42; 5.191. [47 ex.] Cf **efen-**.

cene adj. *brave*. I.16.71; 29.295.

cennan vb I. *to declare*. I.2.11, 69–71.

cennestre wk f. *mother*. I.25.29 (**cynnystre**), 62, 85; 30.5, 31, 41, 121; 36.118 (= Lat. **genetrix**). Cf **cynnan**.

cenning f. *birth, giving birth*. I.7.130; 9.6; 13.34–5; II.1.75–7. **cynn-** 2x. [10 ex.]

cenningstow f. *birthplace*. I.5.16, 56; 7.19, 86, 90.

ceorfan vb 3. *to cut*. I.31.269 (pres.s.3 **cyrfþ**); 34.225. Cf **a-, for-, to-**.

ceorfseax n. *knife*. I.31.269.

ceorian vb II. *to complain, murmur*. I.24.4; 31.264; II.5.156 ff; 29.32. [8 ex.]

ceorl m. *rustic, peasant*. II.11.457, 476; 17.118; *husband* II.39.82.

ceorlian vb II. *to marry, take a husband*. I.16.137.

ceorung f. *complaining*. I.30.156; 31.266; II.5.154, 158; 16.80. [8 ex.]

geceosan vb 2. *to choose*. I.1.235, 251; 3.33; II.1.38; 14.187–8. pp. as adj. or noun, **gecoren** *chosen, precious, elect* I.2.64; 3.81; II.4.186; 22.134. **ceos-** 2x, **cure** 1x. Pres.s.3 **gecyst**; pret. **geceas, gecur-**; pp. **gecoren**. [200 ex.]

ceosl n. *sand*. II.10.80, 85.

ceowan vb 2. *to chew, bite*. I.28.47 (**cuwon**); II.33.125, 132; 34.207.

cepan vb I. *to heed, pay attention to, care for, desire* (w. gen.). I.3.174; 17.40; II.11.24; 39.73; *to regulate, arrange, choose* (w. gen. or acc.) I.6.166, 190; II.19.178; *to pick, select, take* (w. gen.) I.23.7; II.14.83; **fleames cepan** *to take flight, run away* I.34.56; II.9.106; 21.152; 33.37. [30 ex.]

Cernel Cerne Abbas in Dorset. I.praef.47.

Cesarea, Cesarea Philippi a town in northern Palestine. I.26.5,18–21; II.24.37.

[Chaldei] the Chaldees or Babylonians. **chaldea rice** II.4.218; 11.330.

Chaldeisca Babylonian. I.37.190; II.4.214; 30.72.

Cham Ham son of Noah. I.1.184.

Chana town of Galilee. II.4.3, 37–8, 319.

Chananeisc Canaanite, of Canaan (province of Syria). II.8.6, 22, 44, 120.

cherubim order of angels. I.1.23; 24.82, 95, etc.

Chithia Scythia. I.21.238.

cidan vb I. *to complain (against), criticise*. w. dat. or prep. I.6.85; 10.15, 68; II.3.156; 11.71. **cyde** 1x. [7 ex.] Cf **be-**.

gecigan vb I. *to call, name*. I.2.14; 6.25, 28; II.4.3; 5.215; *to summon, invite* I.35.208; 39.102; II.5.33; 33.122, 128 (all). **gecyg-** 3x. [67 ex.]

cild, cyld n. *child*. I.1.240 ff; 2.19; II.3.246 ff; 11.93 ff. [220 ex.] Cf **fostor-, hyse-, leorning-, munuc-, steop-**.

cildclaþas m.pl. *swaddling-clothes, clothing for a baby*. I.2.18, 26, 92, etc.

cildcradol m. *cradle*. I.5.89; 29.195; 5.89.

cildhad m. *childhood*. I.27.7; 32.209; II.4.304; 5.92. **cyld-** 1x. [17 ex.]

cildlic adj. *of children*. II.10.22.

cing see **cyning**.

cinu f. *crack*. II.11.17.

cir- see **cyr-**.

Cirinus Quirinius, governor of Syria at the time of Christ's birth. I.2.11, 66.

ciþ m. *seed?* I.6.160.

ciþfæst adj. *firm-rooted*. I.21.159.

claþ m. *cloth, piece of cloth*. I.20.172; II.11.432; 20.118, 210; 27.34; in pl., *clothes* II.21.105. Cf **cild-, hand-, swat-**.

clawa m. *claw, hook*. I.29.131; 36.77; II.3.160; 28.118.

geclæman vb I. *to caulk, seal*. I.1.186.

clæne adj. *clean, chaste, pure*. I.1.154, 243; 4.93; II.4.263; 9.217. [60 ex.] Cf **un-**.

clænheort adj. *pure of heart*. I.36.161, 222; II.40.107.

clænlice adv. *chastely, in a state of innocence*. I.29.256; II.4.304; 6.127, 134.

clænnyss f. *chastity, virginity, purity*. I.4.6; 9.188; II.1.88, 283–5; 12.550. [41 ex.] Cf **un-**.

(ge)clænsian vb II. *to cleanse, purify, purge, heal (of leprosy)*. I.19.120; 20.188; II.15.271; 19.38. [37 ex.] Cf **a-, un-**.

clænsung f. *cleansing, purification*. I.8.43, 65; 23.57; II.3.228; 4.121. [7 ex.]

Clemens St Clement I, pope. I.37 *passim*. ds. **clemente, -tem**.

Cleophas one of the disciples on the road to Emmaus. II.16.10.

Cletus the third bishop in Rome (but not, according to Ælfric, pope). I.37.13.

clifian vb II. *to cleave, stick*. I.26.242; II.36.44.

clif n. *cliff, promontory*. II.13.232.

cliþa m. *poultice*. I.31.318.

clud m. *rock, hill*. I.AppB3.16, 85, 134; II.10.172; 11.120, 131. Cf **stan-**.

clut m. *plate*. I.29.145.

clyfa m. *bedchamber*. II.27.68.

clypian vb II. intrans., *to call, call out, exclaim, say;* trans., *to summon, call upon, name*. I.3.99; 4.197, 205; II.3.55; 5.21; 11.190. **cleop-** 3x, **clip-** 3x, **geclyp-** 3x. [153 ex.] Cf **of-, to-**.

clypung f. *calling, calling out, exclaiming, speech*. I.10.82, 94; 27.21; II.2.157; 8.52. [18 ex.]

clysing, clysung f. *imprisonment*. I.23.88; 28.204; II.5.152.

clywen n. *ball, globe*. II.34.242.

cnapa m. *youth, servant*. I.26.173; 27.227–8; II.9.59, 71; 39.82. [26 ex.]

gecnæwe adj. *conscious of, acknowledging, confessing* (w. gen.). II.11.233; 23.128; 28.38; 34.192.

gecnawan vb 7. *to recognize*. I.9.31, 46, 125; 23.12; II.1.224, 254; 20.159. Pret.s. **gecneow**. Cf **on-, to-**.

cnæpling m. *youth*. II.40.26.

gecneord adj. *studious, diligent*. I.30.15.

gecneordlæcan, gecnyrd- vb I. *to study*. I.30.9; II.4.274; 9.24.

gecneordlic adj. *studious, zealous*. II.5.76.

gecneordlice adv. *zealously, with dedication*. I.2.107; 4.51; 25.181; 34.46; II.13.90.

gecneordnyss, gecnyrd- f. *zeal, diligence, dedication*. I.7.236; 15.78; II.5.114; 10.260. [22 ex.] Cf **un-**.

cneow n. *knee*. I.1.218; 3.56; II.10.28 ff; 33.171. *generation* II.12.27. [27 ex.]

(ge)cneowian vb II. *to kneel*. I.38.33–4; II.11.16, 201, 429.

cniht m. *young man, servant, follower*. I.4.72, 78, 137; 8.89, 107; II.2.143; 13.192. [47 ex.] Cf **cype-, hired-, in-, leorning-**.

cnihthad m. *youth, early manhood (***cniht** when referring to age seems to imply a stage marked by financial independence, marriage, etc.). I.26.174; 32.209–10; II.5.93, 103.

cnol m. *summit*. I.34.14, 54, 105; II.11.128.

cnotta m. *knot, puzzle*. II.2.91; 24.116.

cnucian vb II. *to knock, beat*. I.18.54–5, 92–4 (**cnukyað**); 29.202, 236; II.24.26; 32.38. [16 ex.]

cnucung f. *knocking*. I.18.51.

cnyssan vb I. *to strike*. II.24.15.

coccel m. *tares?* (Lat. **zizania**). I.35.123–4.

codd m. *bag*. II.36.8, 70, 102.

col n. *(burnt?) coal*. II.33.259.

collecta f. *collect (liturgical)*. II.5.265.

cometa m. *comet*. II.17.109.

Constantinus (a) the emperor Constantine I (306–37). II.18.5, 14; (b) one of the Seven Sleepers. II.27.187.

Constantius Roman emperor (337–61), son of Constantine I. II.34.19 (em. from **constantinum**).

gecoren see **ceosan**. Cf **acoren**.

gecorennyss f. *election, choice*. I.23.48; 27.54; 37.26; II.35.65; *elect status, preciousness?* I.36.41. Cf **wiþer-**.

corn n. *corn*. I.35.123, 132; II.4.263–4; 12.32; 15.87; *grain of corn* I.12.61; II.15.134, 236.

cornbære adj. *corn-bearing*. I.30.218.

Cornelius disciple of St Clement. I.37.107.

cornhwycce wk f. *cornbox*. II.11.404.

coss m. *kiss*. I.37.141; II.2.144; 10.25; 14.83. [6 ex.]

cossian vb II. *to kiss*. I.37.140.

costnere m. *tempter*. I.11.11; 24.120; II.11.45; 24.212.

(ge)costnian vb II. *to tempt, assail*. I.11.28 ff, 66; 19.148; II.30.128; 38.224, 231. [15 ex.]

costnung f. *temptation, tribulation*. I.10.78, 86; 11.31; II.6.25; 11.49. [43 ex.]

coþu f. *disease, illness*. I.27.231; 31.182; II.10.274; 32.211. [11 ex.] Cf **in-, un-**.

crawan vb 7. *to crow*. II.14.76.

cræft m. *power, art, skill, occupation*. I.praef.82; 4.242; II.21.127; 34.126. [26 ex.]

[cræftan] vb I. *to design, contrive*. pp. II.40.9.

cræt n. *chariot*. I.21.205 ff; 27.244; II.12.93–7; 33.220–2. Pl. **-u**. [14 ex.]

creda m. *the Creed*. I.3.77; 20.3–6.

creopan vb 2. *to creep*. I.32.173; 35.263; II.24.236 (pret.s. **creap**); 33.120. Cf **under-**.

cricc f. *crutch*. II.10.29.

Crisaurius nobleman in a story told by Gregory the Great. I.28.197.

Crist Christ (always treated as personal name). pl. **lease cristas** I.praef.62. [1101 ex.]

cristen adj. *Christian*. I.2.90; 6.79–81; II.1.295; 2.23–4. [175 ex.]

cristendom m. *Christianity, Christian*

faith. I.6.88; 14.129–30; II.3.254; 27.205. [24 ex.]

cristnian vb II. *to christen*. I.21.165 (as part of infant baptism); II.34.10 (as a prior stage).

crocsceard n. *potsherd*. II.30.120.

cruma m. *crumb*. I.23.7, 65–8; II.3.266; 8.18, 100 ff.

cu f. *cow*. II.17.100.

cucu adj. *alive, living*. I.1.194; 3.129; II.2.60; 14.311–5. [27 ex.] Cf **sam-**.

cucian vb II. *to come to life*. I.33.61; AppB2.3. Cf **a-**, **geed-**.

culfre wk f. *dove or pigeon*. I.9.77 ff; 22.129 ff; II.3.151 ff; 12.362. **culufran** 1x. [44 ex.]

cuma m. *visitor*. I.2.96; 18.47; II.7.148 ff; 10.39, 62 ff. [21 ex.]

cuman vb 4. *to come*. I.praef.62; 8.90, 94–5; II.1.257; 5.161. Pres.s. **cymst, cymþ**; pret. **com, com-**; pp. **cumen** 2x, **gecumen** 1x. **gecum-, gecom(-)** 13x. [606 ex.] Cf **a-**, **be-**.

cumliþe adj. *hospitable*. II.16.80.

cumliþnyss f. *hospitableness*. II.10.65; 16.69, 74 ff.

cunnan pret.pres. vb. *to know, be familiar with*. I.praef.107; 15.121; II.praef.31; 3.292; *to know how to, to have sufficient understanding to* I.9.247; 32.203; II.12.214; 40.29. Pres.s. **canst; can, cann**; pret. **cuþ-**. For pp. no ex. of **gecunnen** and Ælfric seems to use **cuþ** instead, e.g. I.15.43, II.22.56; see under **cuþ**. [88 ex.]

cunnian vb II. *to test, try out*. I.30.224; II.23.10 (w. gen.).

cuþ adj and ?pp. *known, familiar*. I.praef.48; 23.45; II.9.10; 11.41. [32 ex.] Cf **for-**, **nam-**, **selt-**, **un-**, **wid-**.

Cuþberhtus, Cuthberhtus St Cuthbert (d. 687), hermit and bishop of Lindisfarne. II.10.passim. as. **cuðberht, -um**; gs. **-es**; ds. **cuðberhte**.

gecuþlæcan vb I. *to make known, make familiar*. I.27.49.

cuþlice adv. *familiarly, intimately, informedly*. I.19.30; 37.6, 37; II.19.120; 20.161; 34.222; *with inward or intimate knowledge?* I.30.56; *openly, explicitly* II.12.552; 14.279; 29.42 (or *familiarly*?).

cwacian vb II. *to shake, tremble*. I.8.196; 35.194; II.2.119, 135 ff; 18.140, 143. [11 ex.]

cwacung f. *shaking, trembling*. I.34.53; II.2.125, 151.

cwalu f. *killing*. ds. **cwale** I.5.180; II.1.22, 26; 13.61; ds. **cweale** I.3.145; 14.165, 169; 26.281.

cwealm m. *plague, pestilence*. I.40.28, 37; II.9.92, 110; 12.64; 20.180. [8 ex.] Cf **mann-**.

cwealmbære, cwelm-, cwylm- adj. *deadly, death-bearing*. I.4.214; 25.180; II.14.314, 317; 26.57. [7 ex.]

cwealmstow f. *place of slaughter or execution*. II.14.222; 18.47; 27.149, 172.

cweartern n. *prison*. I.4.220; 5.156; II.7.150; 24.6. [49 ex.]

cwede see **cwyde**.

cwelan vb 4. *to die*. I.4.217. Cf **a-**.

cwellan vb I. *to kill*. II.14.223 (pret.s. **cwealde**). Cf **a-**.

cwellere m. *killer, executioner*. I.3.102; 5.48, 57; II.14.236; 18.67. [38 ex.]

cwelmbærnyss f. *mortification*. I.7.232.

gecweman vb I. *to please, serve*. I.1.51; 11.107; II.16.78; 19.93. **gecwæmde** 1x. [11 ex.]

gecweme adj. *pleasing, acceptable*. I.1.185; 9.203; II.7.36; 9.143. [15 ex.]

gecwemednyss f. *pleasure, satisfaction*. I.11.212; 32.85; II.8.38; 40.207.

gecwemlice adv. *pleasingly, acceptably*. I.10.194 (**gecwemelice**); II.4.198; 5.144; 40.16.

cwen f. *queen*. I.7.134; 13.144; II.32.146; 40.147. [31 ex.]

cweþan, gecweþan vb 5. *to say, speak, call, name*. I.praef.60; 1.56; 24.85; II.1.92; 14.173; DSM.3; *to proclaim* II.3.207 (**gecweþan**); **gecwæþ to gefeohte** *issued a call to battle* II.34.46. Pres.s.2 **cwest, cweþst, cwyst**; 3 **cweþ, cwiþ, cwyþ**; pres.pt. **cweþende, cwæþende** (1x); pret. **cwæþ, cwæd-**; pp. **gecweden**. **ge-** forms (apart from pp.) 24x. [1729 ex.] Cf **be-**, **wiþ-**.

cwicsusl f. *living torment*. I.23.35; II.7.175; 18.150.

cwyddian vb II. *to speak*. I.26.6, 23, 27; II.24.157.

cwyddung f. *saying, report*. I.26.24.

cwyde m. *saying, discourse*. I.1.294; 4.203;

II.3.255; 11.326; Expl.10. **cwede** 1x. [48 ex.]

cwydeleas adj. *speechless*. I.5.147.

cwyld mfn. *destruction, death*. I.40.110.

cwylman vb I. *to torment*. I.5.160; 23.15; II.11.447; 27.152. [8 ex.]

cwylmian vb II. *to suffer (torment), be in pain*. I.5.127; 8.192; II.13.162; 14.315. [11 ex.]

cwylming f. *torment*. I.38.247, 281, 285; II.2.119.

cwyrnstan m. *millstone*. I.34.145, 206–8.

cyd- see **cidan, cyþan**.

cyf f. *barrel*. I.4.23; II.11.430.

cyfesboren adj. *illegitimate*. II.10.254.

cyld see **cild**.

cyle m. *cold*. I.5.106; 8.196; II.21.103; 31.67. [16 ex.]

cyme m. *coming, arrival*. II.34.93. Cf **ham-, to-**.

gecynd n. *nature, natural state*. I.1.53; 2.172; II.3.127; 39.49; *species* II.12.281. [62 ex.]

gecynde adj. *natural*. II.18.36.

gecyndelic adj. *natural*. I.6.195; 9.130; II.32.66.

gecyndelice adv. *naturally, by virtue of one's nature or origin*. I.7.176; 17.13; 19.18, 37; II.13.74, 188. [8 ex.]

cynecynn n. *royal line or family*. I.5.63–5; 14.146; II.1.131.

cynedom m. *royal power, rule*. I.26.203; 28.38; 32.59, 194; II.27.223.

cynegyrd f. *sceptre*. I.25.179; II.14.200; 34.58.

cynehelm m. *royal crown*. I.10.159; 31.200; 38.33.

cynelic adj. *royal, befitting a king*. I.2.50; 5.64–6; II.11.239; 24.39. [8 ex.]

cynerice n. *rule, royal power or position*. I.5.123; 32.192; II.11.261; 28.127. [6 ex.]

cynescipe m. *royal status*. I.AppB1.4.

cynesetl n. *throne*. I.5.85; 7.135; 18.33; 32.44. [7 ex.]

cynestol m. *capital, royal city*. II.17.104; 18.36; 28.107.

cyning m. *king*. I.praef.45; 1.8–9; II.1.223; 4.211–4. nas. **cyning** 152x, **cyng** 1x, **cyningcg** 1x, **cynyng** 1x; gs. **cyninges** 35x, **cinges** 2x, **cynges** 7x; ds. **cyninge** 50x, **cinge** 1x, **cynge** 1x; nap. **cyningas** 7x; gp. **cyninga** 7x; dp. **cyningum** 1x, **cynegum** 8x, **cynengum** 1x. [275 ex.] Cf **under-**.

cynn, cyn n. *kin, kindred, line*. I.1.237; 40.130; II.12.23; 13.200; *kind, sort, species* I.25.170; 29.196; II.7.40; 37.132. [36 ex.]

cynnan vb I. *to give birth*. I.2.17; 13.128. Cf **cenn-, acenn-, ed-, ancenn-, frumcenn-, unacenn-**.

cynren n. *kin, descendants*. I.6.22; II.15.26.

cypa m. *trader, seller*. I.28.94, 163, 172, 178; 38.73. Cf **mynet-**.

cype see **ceap** and next.

gecype adj. *for sale*. I.28.88, 165; **cype(?)** I.AppB3.52.

cypecniht m. *youth for sale, young male slave*. II.9.57.

cyping f. *buying and selling*. I.28.78.

cypman m. *trader*. I.28.13, 74, 164; II.9.54; 19.235.

gecypsed pp. as adj. *fettered, shackled*. II.27.35.

cyrcbræce f. *sacrilege*. II.40.279.

cyrce wk f. *church (usu. as a building, though sometimes fig.)*. I.4.112, 197; 34.36, etc; II.2.132; 40.295–6. **circan** 1x, **cyrican** 3x, **cyrrcan** 1x. [111 ex.]

cyrchalgung f. *consecration of a church*. II.40.134.

cyrclic adj. *of a church, ecclesiastical*. I.29.69; 39.7; II.5.238; 29.20. **circ-** 1x, **cyric-** 1x. [10 ex.]

cyrcweard m. *churchwarden*. I.30.239.

cyre m. *choice*. I.14.112. All other instances are in the phrase **agen cyre**, *free choice* I.1.53; 7.141; 14.115; II.33.147. [20 ex.]

cyrf m. *cutting*. II.26.71. Cf **of-**.

Cyrilla daughter of the emperor Decius. I.29.280, 284.

cyrm m. *noise, clamour*. I.40.172; II.12.208.

cyrnel mn. *nut, seed (of tree)*. I.16.121 ff.

cyrograf n. *charter, contract*. I.21.81.

cyrps adj. *curly(-haired)*. I.31.33.

gecyrran vb I. *to turn (*intrans.*), turn aside, return, go*. I.praef.115; 7.106; II.2.63; 6.159; *to turn to, turn aside to, return to* (w. acc.) I.5.57; 7.105; II.36.9; pp. **gecyrred** as adj., *converted* I.27.210; II.9.138. **cyr-** 10x. [113 ex.] Cf **be-, for-**.

cyrre m. *occasion*. I.30.206.

gecyrrednyss f. *conversion, reform, turning (to Christianity, monasticism, virtue, etc)*. I.3.192; 8.175; II.9.39; 16.132. [20 ex.]

cyrten adj. *handsome?.* II.12.526.

cyrtel m. *tunic.* I.4.97.

Cyrus Cyrus the great, king of Babylon (d. 530BC). I.37.200 (**cires**), etc; II.4.223–7.

cyssan vb I. *to kiss.* II.10.289; 14.83; 27.177, 217; **gecyste** I.29.230. Cf **cossian**.

cyst f. *chest, coffer.* II.26.116.

cyst m. *election, choice.* II.32.24. Cf **un-**.

cystelice adv. *generously, liberally.* II.10.340; 13.85.

cystig adj. *generous.* I.4.41; 9.103; 18.202; 24.149. Cf **un-**.

cystignyss f. *generosity.* I.34.203; II.12.553; 31.68.

cyte wk f. *cell, hut.* II.10.53–5; 11.490, 505; 37.184, 194.

cyþan vb I. *to reveal, show, announce, report.* I.praef.102, 11; 5.6; II.1.268; 3.49. **ge-** 7x. Pret. **cydd-, cyþd-**; pp. **gecyd(d)**. [142 ex.]

cyþere m. *martyr.* I.3.61; 29.170; 36.72; II.2.5; 34.135. [38 ex.]

gecyþnyss f. *testimony, Testament.* I.9.198; 25.98, 100 (**gecydnys**); II.2.174; 4.58. **cyþnyss** 2x. [32 ex.]

[cyþþ] f. *familiarity, friendship, intimacy, knowledge.* I.7.67; 27.186; II.10.137; 19.12. **kyððe** 1x. [11 ex.] Cf **un-**.

gedafenian, gedafnian vb II. (a) *to suit, be appropriate to.* w.dat. I.3.77; 7.205; II.6.136; 40.137; (b) impers., with **hit** or no expressed subject, followed by **þæt** clause or infinitive, *to be fitting, appropriate* I.2.109; 3.64, II.5.195; 6.141. [54 ex.]

gedafenlic adj. *fitting, suitable.* I.1.86; 7.52; II.1.37; 16.1; **gedauenlic** I.11.5. [10 ex.]

gedafenlice adv. *suitably.* I.3.67; II.10.35; 14.1; 19.158. Cf **unge-**.

gedal n. *division, sharing.* II.7.100; 25.104.

Dalila Delilah wife of Samson. I.32.185.

Damascus city of Damascus (Syria). I.27.14.

Daniel, Danihel the prophet Daniel. I.24.158; 32.181; 34.264–5; 37.201 ff.; II.1.146 ff.; 11.332; 28.144 ff.

Darius king of the Medes (521–486BC). II.28.159.

daru f. *injury, damage.* I.6.182; 28.188; II.4.147; 6.64. [8 ex.]

Dathan a rebel against Moses (Num. 16.1). II.27.130 (ds. uninfl.), 133.

Dauid king David. I.2.14, 121; II.1.130, 170. ds. **-de** II.4.86 etc., **-d** I.37.183. [49 ex.]

dæd f. *act, action.* I.11.77; 15.78; II.11.476; 12.329. [90 ex.]

dædbeta m. *penitent.* I.24.71, 194.

dædbetan vb I. *to do penance.* pres. part. I.4.160 (**dædbætende**); 8.68; II.4.271; 5.224.

dædbot f. *penance.* I.15.65; 23.27; II.3.229; 11.169. *soðe dædbot* I.24.74; 33.123; II.3.232; 26.107 (16 ex.). [41 ex.]

(ge)dæftan vb I. *to prepare, make suitable.* I.14.134; 25.196; II.19.36.

dæg m. *day, time.* I.1.97; 6.132; II.3.2; 12.274; *reign* I.praef.45; I.5.9; II.27.188, 206; **on dæg(e)** *in the daytime, in a day* I.2.121; 31.37; AppB3.23; **dæges** *by day* I.4.123; II.6.180; 23.153; **dæg** (acc. or endingless locative) *by day* II.21.147; **anes dæges** *in one day* I.31.281; II.19.256; 30.65; **eallum dagum** *every day* I.21.242; II.22.178; 30.18; **þæs dæges** *on that day* II.32.8. nas. **dæg, dægi** (4x), **dæig** (26x, all in CH I); gp. **daga, dagena** (1x). [510 ex.]

dæghwomlic adj. *daily.* I.6.127; 19.15, 107; 37.30; 39.47 (**dæig-**); II.9.36.

dæghwomlice (dæig-, -hwam-) adv. *daily.* I.12.91; 35.162; II.1.116; 15.221. [64 ex.]

dæglanges adv. *for the space of a day.* II.33.29.

dægred n. *daybreak.* I.34.114; 38.252; II.14.148 (**dæge-**).

dægþerlic adj. *present, pertaining to the present day* (always with **þis**). I.5.60; 6.3; II.5.270; 13.11. **dægi-** 1x, **dæig-** 5x. [21 ex.]

dægwist m. *sustenance, food for the day.* II.10.35.

dæigrima m. *dawn.* I.30.115. [= **aurora**]

dæigsteorra m. *morning star.* I.25.97. [= **lucifer**]

dæl m. *part, portion, share.* I.6.53; 9.84; II.1.226; 4.217; **be dæle** *partially* I.24.172; 38.151; II.11.259; **be sumum (-on) dæle** *partly* I.3.131; II.22.54; 24.180. [81 ex.] Cf **east-** etc.

dælan vb I. *to distribute.* I.4.60; 14.197; II.7.52; 25.102; intrans. I.18.207; *share* (**wiþ**) I.11.90, 18.177; *divide* I.32.46; II.1.195; 12.410; 21.14. [42 ex.] Cf **be-**, **to-**.

dælere m. *distributor*. I.18.208; II.7.71, 103. [= **prerogator**]

dælnimend m. *sharer, participator; one who shares the same condition or fate*. I.2.126; 39.92; II.13.125 (**-nym-**); 20.66; 27.159.

dead adj. *dead* (often in a figurative or spiritual sense). I.9.193; 10.131; II.11.470; 13.30. [100 ex.]

deadbære adj. *poisonous, deadly*. I.4.217; 6.106; II.11.80; 13.255. Cf **cwealm-**.

deadlic adj. *mortal, subject to death*. I.1.73; 7.209; II.4.285; 11.536; *mortal (causing death)* II.13.265. [32 ex.] Cf **un-**.

deadlicnyss f. *mortality*. I.2.126; 7.218; 10.54, 57; II.16.149, 152. Cf **un-**.

deaf adj. *deaf*. I.26.42; II.1.189; 28.150; 38.234. [10 ex.] See also **dufan**.

deag f. *dye*. II.14.213.

deagung f. *colouring*. II.31.71.

dearnunga, -e adv. *secretly*. II.6.149; 10.91, 156; 11.25; 14.335; 37.132.

deaþ m. *death*. I.3.81; 4.234; II.1.29; 4.168. [315 ex.]

deaþlic adj. *mortal, subject to death*. I.15.87, 122; 40.102. Cf. **un-**, **deadlic**.

gedecan vb I. *to deck, anoint*. II.14.342.

Decius Roman emperor and persecutor (249–51AD). I.29.3 etc.; II.27.188, 195.

gedefe adj. *meek, gentle*. I.36.199; 38.318.

delfan vb 3. *to dig*. trans. I.4.254; II.11.193; intrans. II.7.107. Cf. **a-**, **be-**.

gedelf n. *digging, act of digging*. I.37.78. Cf **marmstangedelf**, **ymbgedelf**.

dema m. *judge*. I.3.79; 21.229; II.2.209; 4.264. [37 ex.]

deman vb I. *to judge, decree, determine, decide*. I.8.77; 29.119; II.2.213; 19.129; w.acc., I.21.229; 22.133–4; 24.134; w.dat., I.27.129, 155; II.17.87; *to pronounce judgement* (with **dom** as obj.) I.20.223; 22.143. [32 ex.] Cf **for-**.

demere m. *one who judges*. I.27.180.

dene mf. *valley*. I.25.188, etc.; 30.68; II.20.95; 21.24, etc. Mainly f., but I.25.207 np. **denas**, var. **dena**. [10 ex.]

deofellic, deoflic, deofollic adj. *devilish, belonging to the devil or devils*. I.6.187; 38.173; II.4.56; 7.9.

deofol, deofl, deofel, deoful m. in s., n. in pl. *devil, the devil*. In s. with masc. article, I.10.86; 11.62; II.7.162; 39.186 (c.140 ex.); without article, I.1.211; 11.73; II.3.250; 7.175 (c.200 ex.); pl. I.1.259; 29.162; II.10.167; 12.242 (81 ex.). nas. **deofol** (128x), **deofel** (4x), **deofl** (2x), **deoful** (43x); gs. **deofles, diofles** (I.11.98); ds. **deofle**; nap. **deofla** (7x), **deoflo** (II.23.163), **deoflu** (42x); gp. **deofla**; dp. **deoflum**.

deofolgyld (deofel-, deoful-, -gild-) n. *idol, pagan god or shrine*. I.29.24; 31.306; II.11.174; 17.14. nap. **-gild, gyld**. [38 ex.] (The evidence for an abstract sense, *idolatry, pagan worship* (cf Pope), rests on the phrase **deofolgyld began** at I.22.247, II.8.51; but the example at I.38.181 suggests that this means *worship idols*.)

deofolgylda (deoful-) m. *worshipper of pagan idol or god*. I.4.194; II.19.286. Cf **hæþen-**.

deofolseoc (deoful-) adj. *possessed by devils, suffering from lunacy*. I.1.258; 4.108; 22.85; 26.168; 37.125; II.2.8.

deop adj. *deep*. I.34.145, 206; II.11.135; 21.25; fig., *complex, hard to fathom, deep-rooted* I.12.64; 30.185; II.12.167; 17.28. [18 ex.]

deoplic adj. *complex, having depths of significance*. I.36.179; II.24.99.

deoplice adv. *fully*. II.11.2; 40.131.

deopnyss f. *depth, subtlety* (fig.). I.7.139; 12.123; II.4.127; 6.156. [19 ex.]

deopþancellice adv. *subtly*. I.30.16.

deor n. *(wild) animal*. I.10.146; 20.13; II.33.176, etc.; 34.264. [14 ex.; pl. only] Cf **wildeor**.

deorcynn n. *the range or genus of (wild) animals*. I.1.84, 106, 188; 6.179; 32.177.

deore adj. *precious*. comp. **deorre** II.26.123.

gedeorf n. *hardship, labour*. I.3.173, 174; II.5.213; 9.2; 10.184; 35.12.

deorfan vb 3. *to labour*. II.34.293.

deorwurþe, -wyrþe adj. *precious*. I.3.81; 4.68; II.4.61; 14.14. [49 ex.]

deorwurþlic adj. *precious, splendid*. I.18.85; 26.37.

deorwurþlice adv. *splendidly, richly*. I.23.54; II.18.13.

Dere the Deiri (AS people of Northumbria). II.9.72–3.

derian, derigan vb I/II. w.dat. *to injure*. I.1.123; 6.180; II.1.244; 12.438. Pres.s.3 **-aþ**; pl. **-iaþ**; pret. **-ed-**, **-od-**. [28 ex.]

derigendlic, deriendlic adj. *harmful*. I.13.66; 18.195; II.12.518; 17.12. [15 ex.] Cf **un-**.

diacon m. *deacon*. I.3.6; 10.4; II.6.145; 11.345. **deaconas** I.3.4. [38 ex.] Cf **erce-, sub-**.

diaconhad m. *deacon's orders*. II.1.164; 9.52.

Dialegorum Gregory the Great's *Liber Dialogorum*. II.21.115, 177.

digel adj. *secret, hidden, mysterious*. I.10.200; 12.93; II.12.417; 15.293. **digl-** 10x, **digolne** 1x, **dihle** 1x. [37 ex.]

digelice, digellice adv. *secretly, privately*. I.praef.82; 33.111; II.10.136; 11.7. **diglice** 1x, **dihlice** 1x. [12 ex.]

digelnyss f. *mystery, hidden meaning* I.2.205; 21.110; II.15.302; 35.52; *secret thought* I.26.190; 39.93; II.10.135; 40.194; *secret place* II.34.229; **on digelnysse** *in seclusion* II.10.163; 20.189; 21.19; 34.121. **digl-** 1x, **dygel-** 2x. [33 ex.]

diht n. *direction, disposition, dispensation*. I.2.187; 3.139; II.4.182; 8.113. [28 ex.]

gediht n. *(literary) work, composition*. II.ExDict.1.

(ge)dihtan vb I. *to dictate, compose*. I.12.80; 30.17; II.4.63; 9.254; *direct, ordain* I.31.248; 40.83; II.11.306, 318. pres.s.3 **gediht**. [14 ex.]

dihtnere m. *steward*. II.20.196. (= **dispensator**).

dimnyss f. *gloom*. I.40.172. [= **caligo**]

Dionisius. (a) bishop of Rome (260–68) in succession to Sixtus II. I.29.290. (b) disciple of St Paul and apostle of Gaul. I.37.33–50. (c) one of the Seven Sleepers. II.27.186.

disc m. *dish*. dat.pl. **dihsum** I.AppB2.14.

discipuli m.pl. *disciples*. I.praef.108; 1.253; II.15.77; 19.109. np. **-i**, dp. **-um**. [7 ex.]

discþen m. *servant (at table)*. **discten** I.37.219.

dohtor f. *daughter*. I.14.94; 29.284; II.1.87; 2.24. ns. **dohter**, ds. **dehter, dehtre**, nap. **dohtra, dohtru**. [48 ex.]

dolhswaþu, -swæþ(?) fn. *scar, wound*. ns. **-swaþu** II.33.175; nap. **-swaþu** I.16.15, 101; 21.114; **dolchswaþu** I.16.99; dp. **-swaþum** I.16.18, 99.

dolh m. or n. *wound, sore*. ds. **dolge** I.31.318, 321.

dollice see **dwollice**.

dom m. (a) *judgement, sentence*. I.7.183; 8.63; II.7.50; 14.152. (b) *(the Last) Judgement*. (often **se miccla dom**) I.36.69; 40.185; II.1.126; 7.131. **domes dæg** I.1.117; etc. (10 ex.). ds. **domo** I.App.B3.30, 211. [91 ex.]

domboc f. *(Old Testament) book of law or ordinances*. II.12.155.

domern n. *judgement hall*. II.14.167, 197; 27.146.

Domicianus the emperor Domitian (51–96AD). I.4.22, 31; 37.245.

domsetl n. *judgement seat*. I.27.128; 36.69; II.7.133; 24.38. [9 ex.]

don, gedon anom. vb. *to do* I.9.105; II.2.109; with adverbial **swa** or **þus** (very frequent) I.9.116; II.19.75; *act* I.16.76; II.40.308; substituting for preceding verb, I.14.172; II.3.87; *give* I.19.229; 33.157; II.7.43; *put* I.AppB2.12; *cause* I.Praef.96; II.17.36; *make, cause to be* I.20.229; 25.188; II.6.100; 19.118 (**gedeþ**); *take* I.11.193; **to gymeleaste don** *neglect* II.36.77. Forms: inf. **don, doon** (4x), **donne**; pres.s.2 **dest**; 3 **deþ**; pl. **doþ, dooþ** (I.10.175); pl. subj. **don, doon** (I.11.70); pres.pt. **donde**; pret. **dyd-, did-** (2x). Prefixed form occurs as **gedeþ, gedo, gedon, gedoon, gedoþ, gedyde, gedydon**, and in the same senses as unprefixed (37x, excl. pp.). [389 ex.] Cf **for-, ofer-, on-, un-**.

doppetan v.I *to plunge*. II.34.276.

draca m. *dragon*. I.4.150 (dp. **dracan**); 6.181; II.11.382, etc.; 17.5 etc. [26 ex.]

dræf f. *company?, movement of animals in a group*. I.34.11 (Lat. **consortium**); II.34.263.

gedræfdon see **gedrefan**

dream m. *music, song, melody*. I.38.113; II.5.281; 12.127; 20.32; *frenzy, delusion* (of madness) I.35.106, 107; II.3.263; 8.31, 43. [16 ex.]

(ge)dreccan vb I. *to afflict, torment*. I.5.140; 10.77; II.11.439; 17.22. Pp. as adj., I.37.125; II.30.179; 33.107. pret.

dreht- (gedrehte I.5.138); pp. **gedreht**. [25 ex.]

gedreccednyss, -dreced-. f. *affliction*. I.praef.69; 16.140; 18.10; 31.16 (CH I only). **dreced-** 1x. [13 ex.]

gedrefan vb I. *to afflict, trouble*. I.4.119; 28.120; II.24.135; 37.52. Pret. **gedræfdon** II.8.104. [17 ex.]

gedrefednyss f. *affliction*. I.6.119; 36.262; II.5.251; 9.148. [18 ex.]

gedreme adj. *melodious*. I.2.135; 39.8.

drenc m. *drink*. I.4.214; 25.44; II.9.45; 11.73. **drænc** (MS D) II.11.74, 79. [20 ex.] Cf **ofer-, win-**.

gedreog n. *easing, softening*? II.10.199.

gedreoglæcan vb I. *to make fitting, arrange*. II.19.36.

dreori(g) adj. *sad, mournful*. I.4.41; 13.88; II.2.54; 10.148. [21 ex.]

dreoriglice adv. *sorrowfully*. II.10.21, 221.

dreorignyss f. *grief, mournfulness*. I.4.135; 40.125; II.10.23–4; 11.354.

drifan vb 1. *to drive*. I.19.164; 26.143; II.3.113; 11.452; *pursue* (a business or occupation) II.6.151. Pret.s. **draf**. Cf **a-, ofer-, þurh-**.

drigan vb I. *to dry*. I.20.151; II.10.83 (drygdon).

drige adj. *dry*. I.1.232, 255; 7.95; II.1.49, 54; 12.91. **dryge** 1x. [14 ex.]

drihtealdor m. *master of the household* (= **architriclinus**). II.4.17–18, 306, 308.

drihten m. *the Lord*. Always of God, esp. Christ. Usu. without article or other modifier: I.8.71; 28.66; II.4.13; 6.13; often with possessive: I.16.20; II.23.131. **drihten crist** I.3.66; II.12.568 (8x); **drihten hælend** I.3.56; II.8.3 (11x). **dryhten** 2x. [567 ex.]

drihtenlic adj. *of the Lord*. I.8.197; 27.29; II.15.59; 16.1.

Drihthelm a Northumbrian thegn. II.21.3, 101 **(drihtelm)**.

drinca (?) m. *drink*. **drincan** II.7.164; 11.436. (Possibly an infinitive, but translates **potionem** at II.11.436; cf Pope.)

drincan vb 3. *to drink*. I.4.216; 21.154; II.7.96; 16.215. **druncene** *affected by drink?* (= **inebriati**) II.4.21. Pret. **dranc, drunc-**; pp. **gedruncen**. **gedranc** 1x. [41 ex.] Cf **a-**.

drincere m. *drunkard*. II.19.287.

drohtnian vb II. *to live, lead a life* (in a particular manner, often monastic or ascetic). I.21.199; 22.139; II.4.128; 6.135. [34 ex.]

drohtnung f. *life, way of life* (esp. religious). I.8.86; 24.70; II.9.6; 11.67; *habitation* I.31.195; II.17.21. [58 ex.]

dropa m. *drop* (of liquid). I.21.42; 34.117.

dropmælum adv. *drop by drop*. I.34.115.

druncennyss f. *drunkenness*. I.10.179; 25.165; II.1.290; 12.495. [11 ex.]

druncnian vb II. *to become drunk*. I.25.15; II.3.18; 4.308.

Drusiana a widow raised from the dead by St John the Evangelist. I.4.40, 43, 44, 134.

dry m. *magician, sorcerer* (= Lat. **magus**). I.26.106, etc.; 29.233, 235; II.27.7, etc.; 33.131. gs. **dryes, drys**. [28 ex.]

dry- see also **dri-**.

drycræft m. *magic, sorcery*. I.26.109; 29.116; II.21.160; 27.26. [21 ex.]

dryman m. *magician, sorcerer*. II.19.288; 32.83, etc.; 33.4, etc. Plural only. [22 ex.]

drypan vb.I. *to moisten* (with drops). I.23.67; *drip, cause drops to fall* I.7.233.

dufan vb.2. *to sink*. II.24.74, 181, 226. Pres.s.2 **dyfst**; pret.s. **deaf**. Cf **be-**.

duguþ f. *virtue, virtuous action, honour*. I.10.132; II.12.521; 18.21; 19.78, 106. (Mainly alliterative.)

dumb adj. *dumb*. I.1.258; 13.167; II.1.190; 28.150. [17 ex.]

dun f. *mountain, hill*. I.1.11; 8.6; II.4.133; 12.149. [51 ex.]

[durran] pret. pres. vb. *to dare*. I.2.156; 31.62–3; II.3.100; 39.169. Pres.s.3 **dear**; pret. **dorst-**. [38 ex.]

duru f. *door*. I.4.112; 16.29; II.11.214; 20.164. nas. **duru**; ds. **dura**; nap. **dura**. [19 ex.]

dust n. *dust*. I.1.147; 4.209; II.12.527; 30.136. [21 ex.]

gedwæsman m. *heretic, foolish or superstitious person*. I.6.171.

dwæsnyss f. *folly* (Lat. **stultitia**). I.38.254.

dwelian vb II. *to wander, err, be foolish*. I.3.125; 18.194; II.3.195; 8.31. [26 ex.] Cf **a-**.

gedwola m. *heretic, fool*. I.7.216; 20.220, etc.; II.6.78; 19.283. [7 ex.]

dwollic adj. *foolish, wicked, heretical*. I.26.73; 34.170; II.4.127; 29.3. [11 ex.]

dwollice adv. *foolishly, erroneously*. I.26.30; II.4.128; 10.123; 23.181. **dollice** II.19.287.

gedwolman m. *heretic*. I.1.118; 4.178; II.3.192; 11.443. **dwolmannum** II.29.121. [22 ex.]

gedwyld n. *heresy, false belief*. I.praef.51; 1.220; II.praef.47; 5.84. [51 ex.]

gedwymor, gedwimor n. *illusion, phantom*. I.5.140; II.24.68, 151; 34.227.

gedwymorlic adj. *illusory*. II.11.203.

gedwymorlice adv. *illusorily*. II.10.120.

dydrung f. *delusion* by devil or sorcerer. II.10.122 (**dyderunge**); 11.199; 19.288.

dymhof n. *hidden place (*Lat. **latibula**). II.9.107.

dymlic adj. *obscure*. I.39.59.

dype wk f. *deep sea*. I.37.102.

dyppan vb. I. *to dip*. I.23.14. Cf **be-**.

gedyre n. *door-post*. I.22.7; II.3.82; 15.13, 53.

dyrling m. *favourite, loved one*. I.4.2; II.11.569.

dyrne adj. *secret*. II.19.170, 285.

dyrstig adj. *rash, presumptuous*. I.32.89; 34.113; II.1.264; 14.198, 336; 39.168.

dyrstiglice, dyrstelice adv. *rashly, presumptuously*. I.11.89; II.5.206; 10.254; 17.45. [8 ex.]

dyrsti(g)nyss f. *presumption*. I.4.181; 11.91–2; II.9.244; 11.271. [11 ex.]

gedyrstlæcan vb. I. *to presume, dare*. I.praef.56; 3.151; II.10.226; 11.267. Pres.s.2 **-læhst**; 3 **-læcð, -læhð**; pret.s. **-læhte**. [10 ex.]

dysig adj. *foolish*. I.10.183; 19.143; II.27.59; 31.103. [7 ex.]

dysig n. *folly*. I.19.144; II.20.245; 30.186.

dysignyss f. *folly*. I.AppB3.180.

dyslic adj. *foolish* (applied to ideas, activities). I.4.54; 6.85; II.5.171; 10.12. [10 ex.]

dyslice adv. *foolishly*. I.11.84; AppB3.91; II.30.100.

ea f. *river*. I.5.142; 28.32; II.2.85; 3.26. sg. only, indecl. [15 ex.]

eac adv. *also*. I.2.37; 3.138; II.1.277; 2.48; **eac swa** *similarly, likewise, just so* I.9.69, 111; II.1.129; 14.207; 20.89; **eac swa gelice** *similarly* I.30.76; **eac swilce (swylce)** *also* I.2.59; 3.66; II.1.217; 10.137; etc. [465 ex.]

eaca m. *increase*. II.6.138. Cf **ofer-, toeacan**.

geeacnian vb. II. *to conceive, be pregnant*. I.6.11; 13.25, etc.; 25.26; II.1.141; *increase* I.14.154; 35.276; II.7.94; 28.129. **eacniende** I.2.191. [22 ex.]

(ge)eacnung f. *conception, pregnancy*. I.36.119–20; *increase* II.37.181.

Eadberht bishop at Lindisfarne (688–98) after Cuthbert. II.10.334.

eadig adj. *blessed*. I.5.96; 13.180; II.3.296; 29.41. [160 ex.]

eadignyss f. *bliss*. I.2.65, 199; 31.94; II.3.298; *beatitude* I.36.151, etc. [12 ex.]

geeadmettan vb. I. *to humble*. I.21.80; 24.57; II.10.88; 28.15, etc. **geed-** 1x, **geeaþ-** 2x. [22 ex.]

eadmod, eaþ- adj. *humble*. I.8.31; 22.111; II.1.144; 5.277. [37 ex.]

eadmodlice adv. *humbly*. I.25.202; 31.332; II.2.39; 3.103. [9 ex.]

eadmodnyss, eaþ- f. *humility*. I.6.117; 7.256; II.1.281; 3.99. **eadd-** 1x. [51 ex.]

eage wk.n. *eye*. I.1.135; 6.104; II.1.184; 5.31. [76 ex.]

eaghring m. *eyeball?* I.31.294.

eahta num. *eight*. I.6.8; 25.176; II.4.122; 12.480.

eahtahyrnede adj. *eight-cornered*. II.33.264.

eahtateoþa wk. adj. *eighteenth*. I.6.149.

eahtatyne num. *eighteen*. II.34.44.

eahtawintre adj. *eight-year old*. II.10.8.

eahteoþa wk. adj. *eighth*. I.6.31, etc.; 36.251; II.4.278; 12.70. **eahtoþe** II.12.478. [17 ex.]

geeahtian vb. II. *to value*. pp. **geeht** I.38.110.

eala interj. (a) introducing a direct address. I.4.139; 5.17; II.3.268; 23.156. [30 ex.] (b) introducing an exclamation expressing emotion (desire, wonder, etc.). I.2.165; 9.41; II.5.143; 18.75. [10 ex.]

eald adj. *old*. I.6.23; 9.29; II.1.117; 5.250. comp. **yldra**, sup. **yldest, yltst-**. [167 ex.] Cf **efen-**.

ealdfæder m. *patriarch* (or more generally, *one of the righteous living before the time of Christ*). I.35.78; II.5.157, 165.

ealdian vb. II. *to grow old*. I.20.60; 40.22, 111; II.5.98; 13.191. Cf **for-**.

ealdlic adj. *of old age*. I.40.112.

ealdnyss f. *elderliness, agedness.* I.13.66; II.5.100, 104.

ealdor m. *ruler* (of Creation, a nation, legion, abbey, estate, etc.). I.1.29; 2.46; II.5.4; 11.84. **ealld-** 2x. [70 ex.] Cf **driht-**.

ealdorbiscop m. *highpriest.* I.3.28; 5.15; II.13.14; 14.115. [14 ex.]

ealdordom m. *authority, seniority, rule.* I.2.134; 33.63; II.2.188; 11.71. **ealder-** 1x. [11 ex.]

ealdorman m. *governor, chief officer (of a king or emperor).* I.2.10; 25.157; II.14.184; 21.150. **ealder-** 1x. [40 ex.]

ealdorscipe m. *authority, rule.* I.24.89, 122; 40.61; II.40.299.

(ge)ealgian vb II. *to defend, protect.* I.34.29; II.2.111.

eall, eal. (a) adj. *all.* I.4.241; 10.201; II.1.91; 20.259. (Frequently used with pronoun or demonstrative.) (b) adv. *wholly.* I.23.138; II.9.85; 18.24. (c) n. *everything.* I.26.117; II.10.145; 28.157. (The 3 functions are often hard to distinguish.) **eal(l) swa** *just as, just so* (printed as one word in CH I); I.35.106; II.14.78; **mid ealle** *utterly, wholly* I.21.197; II.37.200; **ealles** *wholly* I.24.51; II.28.31. Forms: **eal, eall; ealle, ealla** (1x); **ealles; eallne, ealne; eallre, ealre; eallra, ealra; eallon, eallum.** [1531 ex.]

eallbyrnende adj. *on fire all over.* II.10.127.

eallunga, -ge adv. *entirely.* I.1.288; 7.158; II.6.140; 9.167. **ealunga** 2x. [34 ex.]

eallwealdende adj. *all-ruling.* I.24.94.

ealu n. *ale.* II.3.17.

eanian vb II. *to give birth to* (esp. of lambs). II.17.113.

eard m. *region, land.* I.3.39; 4.174; II.4.4; 5.252. [70 ex.]

eardian vb II. *to live (in a region or object), dwell.* I.4.207; 5.176; II.11.552; 12.36. [13 ex.] Cf **on-**.

eardungstow f. *dwelling-place* (used of Heaven). I.23.126; 24.44; 36.135.

eare wk n. *ear.* I.26.186; 33.33; II.7.62; 13.90. [20 ex.]

earfoþe adj. *difficult, painful.* I.4.66; 12.92; II.24.115; 37.110. [11 ex.]

earfoþhylde adj. *discontented, impatient with hardship?* I.27.224 (see note).

earfoþlic adj. *difficult, painful.* I.24.52.

earfoþlice adv. *with difficulty.* I.5.136;18.87; II.2.167; 5.199. [12 ex.]

earfoþnyss f. *hardship.* I.praef.70; 3.180; II.6.83; 11.23. [37 ex.]

earm adj. *poor.* I.18.190 [= *pauper*]; II.7.102; *miserable* I.31.103; II.10.286; *wretched, despicable* I.6.97; II.18.99. [44 ex.]

earm m. *arm.* I.9.32, 48; 26.123, 236.

earming m. *wretch* (derogatory, usu. a term of abuse). I.4.106; 29.57; II.14.251; 18.148. [10 ex.]

earmlic adj. *miserable.* I.14.210; 23.66; II.10.274.

earmlice adv. *miserably.* I.AppB3.120, 219.

earn m. *eagle.* II.10.99 ff; 28.67, 118.

geearnian vb II. *to earn, merit.* I.1.64; 3.122; II.3.284; 4.239. **gegearnað** I.14.121. [45 ex.]

geearnung f. *earning, meriting.* I.1.124; 7.122; II.2.94; 3.222. **gegearnungum** I.28.173. [51 ex.]

earplætt m. *blow on the ear.* II.14.129.

(ge)earplættan vb I. to *strike on the ear.* I.31.298; II.ExDict.11.

east adv. *eastwards* I.26.288. **be eastan** *to the east of* I.2.218. (**east portic** at II.40.56 is probably a compound).

eastdæl m. *eastern quarter, direction.* I.5.25; 8.98; II.11.564; 14.243. [30 ex.]

easterdæg m. *Easter Sunday.* I.11.193; 22.29; II.2.131; 11.40.

easterlic adj. *belonging to Easter.* I.14.191; 22.4; II.2.148; 5.244. [8 ex.]

easterne adj. *eastern.* I.7.71; 32.157; II.30.13 (*eastern regions or peoples*).

eastertid f. *period of Easter or Passover.* I.12.8; 22.16; II.3.81; 5.285. [20 ex.]

eastre wk f. *Easter.* dat.(pl?) **eastron** II.2.128; 5.244, 271.

eastweard adv. *to the east.* I.19.57.

eaþe adj. *easy.* I.16.118.

eaþe adv. *easily.* I.1.32; 7.83; II.1.236; 14.100. [12 ex.]

eaþelic adj. *easy.* I.1.80, 150; 23.120; 25.154; 36.117; *weak, small* II.12.61; 29.8; 31.67.

eaþelice adv. *easily.* I.3.181; 7.240; II.10.122; 14.106. **eþelicor** 1x. [25 ex.]

eaþm- see **eadm-**.

eawbræca m. *one guilty of sacrilege.* I.29.162.
eawbræce see **æwbræce.**
eawe see **æwe.**
eawfæst adj. *pious, devout.* I.22.49; 23.136; II.2.56; 9.14. [CH I: 5 ex., CH II: 38 ex.]
eawfæstnyss f. *religion, piety.* I.27.116; II.2.23; 29.25.
eawunge adv. *openly.* II.6.149; 37.132.
eaxlum see **exl.**
ebreisc, hebreisc adj. *Hebrew.* I.1.228; 6.133 ff; 22.124; 27.90; II.5.74; 12.420. [23 ex.]
Ecclesiastica historia the Ecclesiastical History of Eusebius, translated and continued by Rufinus, but attributed to Jerome. II.18.4; 24.48.
ece adj. *everlasting.* I.1.164; 3.107; II.1.154; 15.144. **ecean** 1x; **æcere** 1x. (*eternal* in the strict sense is never the required sense and generally inappropriate.) [351 ex.] Cf **efen-.**
eced mn. *vinegar.* II.14.270, 285–6.
ecelice adv. *everlastingly* I.praef.72; 5.126; II.5.286; 12.195; *eternally* I.4.190. [19 ex.]
ecg f. *edge (of sword).* I.26.256; 29.72; II.12.407; 19.201. [6 ex.]
Ecgfridus Ecgfrith, king of Northumbria 670–85AD. II.10.214, etc.; II.21.144 (**ehfrid**).
ecnyss f. *eternity.* **on ecnysse** *for ever* I.1.296; 2.185; II.4.267; 13.28. [83 ex.]
geedcennan, -cynnan vb I. *to give birth again.* pp. *born again, reborn* I.6.62; 27.156, etc.; II.1.108; 35.72; 39.91.
geedcucian vb II. *to revive, come to life again.* I.6.99; 26.253; II.1.212; 2.56. pp. *revived, brought to life again* I.16.113; 23.27; II.2.72; 34.100. [25 ex.]
edcynning f. *rebirth, reborn state.* I.27.128, 154–5.
Edissa City where John the Baptist's head was taken; for Emissa in Phoenicia. I.32.159.
geedlæcan vb I. *to repeat, renew, begin again.* I.6.140; 21.38; II.12.427; 16.139. **geæd-** 1x. [10 ex.]
edlean n. *reward, payment.* I.praef.96; 8.58; II.3.283; 5.127. [40 ex.]
edniwe adj.(?) *renewed, more of the same* (or adv., *newly, again*; cf Pope and BTS). II.12.105, 298.
geedniwian vb II. *to renew, restore.* I.33.27; 40.161; II.4.229; 17.11. [8 ex.]
edniwung f. *renewal.* I.38.202.
geedstaþelian vb II. *to restore.* I.4.66–8; 31.175; II.1.145; 4.228. **geetstaðolode** I.14.156. [10 ex.]
(ge)edstaþelung f. *restoration.* I.24.84; 38.189.
edwist f. *substance.* I.3.185; 20.28; II.15.137; 16.197. [11 ex.]
edwit n. *scorn, reproach.* I.10.157; 19.212; II.30.141; 39.157. [7 ex.]
edwyrping f. *recovery.* II.2.57.
efencempa m. *fellow-soldier.* II.34.23.
efeneald adj. *of the same age.* I.5.166; 20.57, 63; II.10.9. **euenealdan** I.5.80.
efenece adj. *equally eternal.* I.2.42; 13.116; 20.33, 53, etc. [7 ex.]
efenedwistlic adj. *of the same substance.* II.22.73.
efenhlytta m. *partner, one sharing the same fate or reward.* I.5.111; II.13.92; 20.213. **efenlyttan** I.2.68.
geefenlæcan vb I. *to emulate.* I.2.220; 3.131; II.5.195; 9.205; *make equal* I.24.72. **efenlæcendra** I.27.179; **geeuen-** 7x. [38 ex.]
(ge)efenlæcung f. *emulation, imitating.* I.19.35; II.10.261; 13.71; 32.28. **efen-** I.27.213; **euen-** II.13.69; **geeuen-** II.13.74.
efenþeowa m. *fellow-servant.* I.2.152
efesian vb II. *to shave.* II.17.67.
Efesum, Ephesum Ephesus. I.4.38; II.27.189.
Effigenia daughter of the king of Ethiopia. II.32.140, etc.
Efide, Effide, modern Affile in Italy, just south of Sublacus. II.11.9.
efne interj. *behold, see* (drawing attention to a particular point or action; often rendering *ecce*). I.2.24; 3.49; II.4.140; 7.75. [125 ex.]
efstan vb I. *to hasten.* I.10.163; 23.149; II.6.50; 9.223. pres.s.2 **efst.** [12 ex.]
eft adv. *afterwards, again.* I.1.104; 4.92; II.1.107; 4.225. [410 ex.]
Egeas proconsul of Achaia and persecutor of St Andrew. I.35.106; 38.172 etc.
ege m. *fear* (often with implications of reverence). I.1.203; 4.107; II.12.358; 35.45. [36 ex.]

egeful(l) adj. *frightening, terrifying*. I.8.166; 12.32; II.12.200, 204. [8 ex.]
egefullice adv. *terrifyingly*. I.6.61.
geegesian vb II. *to frighten*. I.28.118; 37.97.
egeslic adj. *terrifying*. I.22.19; 28.211; II.2.166; 3.255. [18 ex.]
egeslice adv. *terrifyingly*. I.5.130; 14.108; II.3.291; 17.116. [9 ex.]
egle adj. *painful*. I.27.83; 34.240.
eglian vb II. *to ail, trouble*. II.34.250; 38.98.
Eglippus king of Ethiopia converted by St Matthew. II.32.117 etc.
egsa m. *terror*. II.19.260.
Egypte m. *Egyptians*. Only in **egypta land** *Egypt*. I.5.34 ff., 168; 22.5; AppA1.3; II.12.32, etc.; 13.244; 15.8, 326; I.36.115 (**egipta**).
Egyptisc adj. *Egyptian* (people or language). I.6.135; 22.9, 125; II.12.38, 45, 334; 15.55; 32.92; **egiptiscum**, II.12.95.
Ehfrid see **Ecgfridus**.
ehsynes adv. *visibly*. II.1.223.
geeht see **geeahtian**.
ehtan vb I. *to persecute, attack, harass*. w.gen. I.22.190; 36.273; II.3.43; 4.196. pres.s.2 **ehtst**, 3 **eht**. [25 ex.]
ehtere m. *persecutor*. I.4.23; 5.103; II.11.451; 14.148. [31 ex.]
ehtnyss f. *persecution*. I.5.5; 14.131; II.4.201; 9.211. [53 ex.]
ehþyrl n. *window*. I.38.139 ff.; II.11.425, 524.
elcian vb II. *to delay, hesitate*. I.18.84; 21.201; II.2.31; 15.316. w.gen., II.24.8; 39.94. **ælcygendum** I.24.198. [11 ex.]
elcung f. *delay*. I.35.240 (**ælcunge**); II.4.134; 5.147 ff; 11.64; 15.317.
ele m. *oil*. I.4.24; 5.144; II.33.183; 39.48 ff. [43 ex.]
Eleazar son and successor to Aaron as priest of the Hebrews. II.12.380.
elefantinus morbus m. a disease affecting the skin (sometimes associated with leprosy; cf note to I.23 above). II.11.395; 32.211.
elefæt n. *oil-flask*. II.4.184; 11.427.
Elena St Helena, mother of the emperor Constantine. II.18.38.
Eli highpriest of Israel. II.19.200.
Elias see **Helias**.
Elifaz one of Job's comforters. II.30.132, 190.
Elisabeþ mother of John the Baptist. I.13.59, 161, 170; 25.5, 8; **helisabeð** I.25.27.
Eliseus the prophet Elisha. dat. **eliseum**, I.27.228, 231.
elles adv. *otherwise*. I.19.122; 31.136; II.10.135; 18.53. [14 ex.]
eln f. *ell* (a measure, = Latin **cubitum**). II.31.11, 62.
embe see **ymbe**.
emlice adv. *equably*. I.35.134, 229; 40.64; II.6.197; *equally* II.12.409.
Emmanuhel I.13.26; II.1.142.
Emmaus town outside Jerusalem. II.16.5.
geemnettan vb I. *to regulate*. I.35.91; II.19.30; *compare, liken* II.8.87.
geemnian vb II. *to regulate, make straight*. I.25.215.
emniht f. *equinox*. I.6.134, 148.
emtwa num. **on emtwa** *in two (equal) parts*. II.11.11; 12.386; 14.165; 20.205; 34.34.
ende m. *end*. I.praef.59; 1.6; II.2.43; 3.299. [74 ex.]
geendebyrdan vb I. *to arrange in order, ordain, reckon, place in rank*. I.7.184; 24.109 ff; 27.205; II.5.182; ExDict.5. [17 ex.]
(ge)endebyrdlice adv. *in order, point by point*. I.36.123; II.10.4; 11.291.
endebyrdnyss f. *narrative*. I.2.4; 7.5; II.5.170; *rank, order, group* I.3.86; 6.170; II.2.150; 19.92. [21 ex.]
endeleas adj. *endless*. I.15.157; 38.247; II.38.246.
endeleaslice adv. *endlessly*. II.6.52; 19.58.
endeman m. *one living at the end of time*. I.31.331.
endemes adv. *together, in a body, without exception* (usu. with **ealle**). I.4.197; 7.103; II.10.167; 14.288. [14 ex.]
endenext adj. *last, final*. I.21.15; 25.71; II.5.18; 20.219. [35 ex.]
geendian vb II. trans. *to finish, complete, reach the end of*. I.7.244; 40.104; II.10.326; 40.284; *bring to an end* I.21.56; 32.220; II.17.57; 36.139; intrans. *come to an end, die* I.1.165; 28.202; II.35.96. [70 ex.]
endlofan num. *eleven*. II.16.34.

endlyfta adj. *eleventh.* II.5.53, 64, 77, 99, 131, 160; 10.335. **endleoftan** I.21.51.

geendung f. *end, ending, conclusion.* I.praef.58; 3.194; II.1.153; 5.183. [69 ex.]

engel m. *angel.* I.1.22; 2.22; II.1.20; 4.145. [354 ex.] Cf **heah-**.

engel(l)ic adj. *of angels.* I.5.102; 36.108.

engle m.pl. *the English.* g.pl. II.9.61, 252; 10.4.

englisc adj. *English.* I.praef.49 ff.; 26.100; II.praef.29; 9.1; **on englisc** *in(to) the English language* I.praef.55; 3.93; II.9.8; 13.101. [31 ex.]

Enoh the prophet Enoch. I.21.196 (**henoh**), 208, 213; II.7.16 (**enoch**).

ent m. *giant* (of the past). I.1.214; 22.112, 127; 26.37; II.12.154.

eode, eodon see **gan**.

eom see **beon**.

eornost n. **on eornost** *really, seriously.* II.14.168.

eornost adj. *zealous, serious.* **eornystum** I.27.28.

eornostlice adv. as a loose connective opening a sentence (so always in CH I), *truly, indeed.* I.29.266; 38.248; II.2.138; 5.62. [20 ex.]; as a second element, *fervently, whole-heartedly?* II.9.126; 12.470; 28.129; 39.23, 206. [7 ex.]

eorod n. *legion.* II.14.95, 98; 23.161, 177.

eorþbugend m. *human being, dweller on earth.* I.37.227; **eorðbugigende** II.9.123; **eorðbugiende** II.28.123.

eorþe wk f. *earth, the earth, the world* (in contrast to heaven), *land* (in contrast to sea, or as that which gives crops), *ground.* I.6.192; 11.96; II.11.374; 14.277. Usually without article, but occas. (24 ex.) with; cf. I.11.96 with II.7.81; I.15.175 with I.7.98. [177 ex.]

eorþlic adj. *earthly, belonging to this world.* I.1.64; 2.145; II.1.176; 4.124. [90 ex.]

eorþstyrung f. *earth-quake.* I.15.23; 18.7; II.37.7; 39.114. [10 ex.]

eorþwara m.pl. *dwellers on earth.* I.2.120; II.22.47. Cf **burh-** etc.

eow see **þu**.

eowd f. *flock.* I.2.21; 17.82 ff; II.8.97; 34.261. **eowed** (1x), **eowede** (2x), **eowode** (2x). [27 ex.]

eower poss.adj. *your.* I.3.138; 4.83; II.1.262; 6.109. Forms: **eowere, eowre; eowerne; eoweres, eowres; eowera; eowerum, eowrum**. (For the pronoun see **þu**; the uninflected gpl. pronoun form **eower** is often used adjectivally, e.g. I.35.238; II.27.128.) [c.220 ex.]

Ephesum see **Ef-**.

ercebiscop m. *archbishop.* II.9.226–7; 10.240.

ercediacon m. *archdeacon.* I.29.27, 42 (**-dicon**), 50.

ercehad m. *office of archbishop.* II.9.250.

erian vb I/II. *to plough.* I.31.159; 32.199; AppA1.7. Pres.s.2 **erast**; 3 **eraþ**.

Esau son of Isaac. I.7.129 ff; II.12.29.

estas m.pl. *delicacies, luxurious foods.* I.36.105; AppB3.117; II.23.62.

estful adj. *devout, devoted.* I.2.73; 6.127; II.6.111; 9.152. [22 ex.]

estfulnyss f. *devotion.* I.30.173; II.32.90.

estmettas m. *rich or delicate foods.* I.9.192–3; 23.54; 29.135; II.23.36.

(ge)etan vb 5. *to eat.* I.11.158; 15.58; II.7.96; 15.13. Forms: pres. **etst, geetst; et, ett, geet, geett; etaþ, geetaþ; ete; eton; etende; etenne;** pret. **æt, ætt, geætt; æton; æte;** pp. **geeten**. [65 ex., incl. 8 with **ge-**]

Etherius archbishop of Arles (so Bede; actually bishop of Lyons, d. 602). II.9.227.

Ethiopia Ethiopia. I.21.239; II.32.82.

ethiopisc adj. *the Ethiopian language.* II.32.92.

geetstaþ- see **geedstaþ-**.

eþel m. *land, esp. homeland.* I.5.32; 10.162; II.9.30; 10.188. [36 ex.]

Eua Eve. I.1.125, 278; 7.151, 194; 13.72; 14.189; 15.167; 30.165; II.1.61, 295; 4.100; 14.323; 30.127. **aeua** I.1.93.

Euantius healed by St Martin. II.34.244.

Eucharius healed by St Stephen. II.2.14.

geeuen- see **geefen-**.

Euentius priest martyred with St Alexander. II.18.65 ff.

Eufenissa wife of King Eglippus of Ethiopia. II.32.139

Eufranon son of Eglippus of Ethiopia, restored to life by St Matthew. II.32.119, 139.

Eufrates river Euphrates (Mesopotamia). dat. **eufraten** I.30.248.

Eufrosinus deacon appointed by SS Simon and Jude in Babylonia. II.33.159.

Eugenius a rich young man converted by St John. I.4.74, 143.
Eustochium Roman virgin (370–c.419) addressed in a letter by Jerome. I.30.6, 18.
exl f. *shoulder*. I.24.10 (**eaxlum**), 31, 33; 37.69; II.1.178.
Ezechias Hezekiah king of the Jews (c.715–687BC). I.31.318; 37.155 ff.
Ezechiel the prophet. I.praef.111; 13.27; 17.59, 69; 35.137; AppB3.6, 21; II.1.143; 12.252; 28.64; 35.91; 36.42.

gefa m. *enemy*. dat.pl.(?) **gefan** I.15.163.
facenfull adj. *deceitful*. I.5.79; 7.260; II.8.96.
facenlice adv. *deceitfully*. II.34.112.
facn n. *treachery, guile, fraud*. I.4.83; 8.44; II.3.182; 14.153. [12 ex.]
gefadian vb II. *to arrange, design*. I.20.55; 28.224; II.11.324; 40.58. [7 ex.]
fadung f. *arrangement, design*. I.20.12; 34.276; 35.220.
[fagettian] vb II?. intrans. *to change in appearance*. I.40.41 (pres.s.3 **-að**); *to prevaricate?* I.29.115 (pres.s.2 **-est**).
fagetung f. *change in appearance*. II.37.48.
fagnyss f. *stain, variation in colour*. I.8.45, 48; II.11.409, 412.
fah adj. *variegated? dangerous, deadly?*. II.11.281.
fahnyss f. *variety of colour?* II.12.341; 40.191. (Possibly the same as **fagnyss**.)
fandian vb II. *to test, try*. w.gen. I.praef.100; 4.91; II.11.245; 23.44. [18 ex.] Cf **a-**.
fandung f. *testing*. I.12.11 (dat.s. **fandunga**); 19.148 ff; 31.279; II.19.26. [11 ex.] Cf **a-**.
fant m. *baptismal water*. I.29.101; II.2.116; 3.251.
fantfæt n. *baptismal font*. II.2.115; 15.109.
fantwæter n. *baptismal water*. II.15.112; 20.239, 248.
faran vb 6. *to go*. I.1.283; 2.33; II.1.104; 4.42; *behave* I.11.103; AppB3.220; II.4.181; *deal, engage?* II.11.70; 19.289. Pres. tense only. Pres.s.2 **færst**, 3 **færþ**. [163 ex.] Cf **a-**, **for-**, **forþ-**, **in-**, **mis-**, **ofer-**, **ut-**.
gefaran vb 6. *to go* I.2.164; *to go to, attain* I.6.55; *to go over, traverse* II.38.106.
Farne Farne island, Northumbria. II.10.163.
faru f. *journey*. I.5.38; 27.243; II.9.174; 12.161; *train, retinue* I.27.235; II.40.150. ads. **fare** only. [12 ex.] Cf **fær**.
faþu f. *paternal aunt*. II.6.149.
fæc n. *period of time*. I.4.161; 27.25; II.11.151; 12.192; *interval of space?* I.33.141. **fæcc** II.12.405. [15 ex.]
fæcne adj. *treacherous, malicious*. II.14.157.
fæder m. *father*. I.1.242; 2.67; II.1.4; 4.140; *forefather* I.13.193, 212; *patriarch*, I.35.66. **feder** I.30.104. [504 ex.] Cf **eald-**, **forþ-**, **foster-**, **god-**, **heah-**.
gefædera m. *'co-father' (godfather of someone's child)*. II.9.98.
fæderlic adj. *fatherly*. I.27.115; 28.22.
fæderlice adv. *in fatherly fashion*. II.10.90.
fæge adj. *doomed, destined to die*. II.10.306.
fægen adj. *glad, joyful*. II.34.93.
fæger adj. *beautiful, fine, attractive, excellent*. I.1.29; 12.65; II.9.57; 10.173; of music, II.21.91; of preaching or Scriptures, II.9.199; ExDict.1. **fægere** 4x, **fægre** 2x; gpl. **fægra**. [16 ex.] (This word and the next seem to be used in a more general sense in CH II, esp. in alliterative prose.)
fæg(e)re adv. *attractively, finely, well*. II.10.114; 11.551; 17.57; 19.109, 232; 31.15, 17.
fægernyss f. *beauty*. I.1.26; 12.67; II.12.342; 31.70. [13 ex.]
fægnian vb II. w.gen. *to rejoice, exult*. I.4.36; 5.157; II.11.161; 13.37. **fæign-** 3x. [25 ex.]
fægnung f. *rejoicing*. I.25.63; II.2.163; 5.255.
fæhþ f. *enmity, feud*. I.15.158.
fæmne wk f. *woman*. I.1.92; 30.35; II.4.8; 34.112. [10 ex.]
fær n. *journey, way, course of life*. I.5.58; 6.167; II.1.268; 40.26. s. only. **færr** 2x. [13 ex.] Cf **fram-**, **in-**.
færeld n or m. *journey, movement, course*. I.7.185; 15.84; II.9.175; 10.45. [21 ex.] Cf **fram-**, **ofer-**, **up-**.
færinga adv. *suddenly*. I.26.289.
færlic adj. *sudden*. I.27.222; 29.68; II.1.291; 15.44. [11 ex.]
færlice adv. *suddenly*. I.2.27; 4.126; II.2.134; 10.22. [50]
gefærr- see **geferr-**.

fæst adj. *firm*. I.26.76; 37.70; II.11.100; 34.186. [7 ex.]

fæstan vb I. *to fast*. I.11.9, 42; II.7.11; 28.10. [17 ex.]

fæste adv. *firmly*. I.7.172; 16.37; 31.26; II.2.91. [6 ex.]

fæsten n. *fast*. I.4.240; 9.194; II.7.21, 25. Pl. **-u**. [34 ex.]

fæsten n. *stronghold*. II.5.146.

fæstendæg m. *day of fasting*. II.19.292.

fæsthafol adj. *tenacious*. **-felum** II.9.26.

fæstlice *firmly*. I.34.67.

gefæstnian vb II. *to fix, fasten*. I.1.36; 26.142; II.6.84; 9.25. **fæstnodon** II.14.261. [20 ex.] Cf **a-, be-**.

(ge)fæstnung f. *bond* I.6.29; *fastening* I.23.88.

fæt n. *vessel* (usu. for liquids). I.34.117, 119; 36.270; II.4.15; 11.74 ff, 281, 418 ff; (a sieve) II.11.17. pl. **fatu, fatum**. [15 ex.] Cf **ele-, fant-, hord-, heoht-, maþm-, wæter-**.

fætels m. *vessel, sack, container*. I.12.125; 27.32; II.11.300; 14.156. [6 ex.]

fætnyss f. *fatness*. I.35.75.

fæt(t) adj. *fat*. I.40.118; AppB3.10, 30, etc.; II.40.43.

fæþm f. *fathom, cubit*. I.1.185–6; 37.196; II.40.55–7.

gefea m. *joy*. I.2.24; 24.45; II.6.132; 11.495. [20 ex.]

feallan vb 7. *to fall*. I.2.57; 3.191; II.1.227; 8.18. Pres.s.3 **fylþ**; pret. **feol(l), feoll-**. [69 ex.] Cf **a-, be-, of-, to-**.

fealwe adj. *yellow-brown, dark-coloured*? dsm. **fealwun** II.10.85.

fear m. *bull*. I.34.11, etc.; 35.9, etc.; 38.214; II.30.183. [14 ex.]

feawa adj. *few*. I.4.192; 7.3; II.5.33; 25.78; as pron. w.gen. I.27.39; AppB3.66; II.3.214; 25.14. [45 ex.]

feax, fex n. *hair*. I.32.106; 37.197; II.2.116; 28.117. [9 ex.]

Febus one of the disciples of St Clement. I.37.107.

(ge)feccan vb I. *to fetch*. I.4.88; I.9.51; II.9.250; 11.31, 146. Pret. **(ge)fette, -on**. [22 ex., 17 with prefix.]

fedan vb I. *to feed* (trans.). I.12.49; 18.70; II.10.110; 29.54. Pres.s.3 **fet, fett**. [18 ex.] Cf **a-**.

fefor m. *fever*. I.8.124; 34.122; II.11.558; 18.143; 34.215, 297.

gefeg n. *fastening, joining*. II.34.186.

gefegan vb I. *to join, assemble*. I.4.63; 7.60.

fela indecl. adj. and pron. *many*. with noun in nom. or acc., I.1.208; 29.160; II.32.143 ff; 33.158; with noun in gen., I.31.21; 37.94; II.23.177; 38.232; standing alone, I.4.190; II.5.183–5; etc. [149 ex.]

feld m. *field, open land*. II.11.579; 21.59; ds **felda** I.praef.101; 26.234; 34.107; 40.150; II.10.49.

feldlic adj. *of the field*? (= *agrestis*). II.15.14, 262.

feldoxa m. *ox of the field? (= boves pascuales)*. II.40.44.

Felicissimus deacon martyred with Pope Sixtus. I.29.10, 73.

Felix St Felix, pope and ancestor of Gregory the Great, 483–92AD. II.9.14.

fell n. *skin*. I.1.148–9; 6.53; II.15.132; 30.109 **(fel)**. [12 ex.]

felmen see **fylmen**.

felnyss f. *feeling*. I.21.124–6.

fenix m. *phoenix*. I.AppB2.25.

fenlic adj. *muddy*? II.14.32; 23.187; 32.77.

feoh n. *money, wealth*. I.4.123; 27.245; II.11.398; 16.136. gs. **feos**, ds. **feo**. (Generally refers specifically to coins or bullion, not other forms of wealth.) [48 ex.]

gefeoht n. *battle*. I.3.76; 13.76; II.12.567; 21.145. s. only. [28 ex.]

feohtan vb 3. *to fight*. I.3.78; II.2.175; 12.568; 25.131. Pres.s.3 **fiht**; pret. **feaht, fuhton**. [13 ex.] Cf **ofer-, wiþ-**.

feond m. *enemy, devil*. I.3.168 ff; 30.264; II.25.132; 34.200. nap. **fynd**. [61 ex.]

feondlic adj. *devilish, hostile, oppressive*. I.24.120; 28.142; II.12.437; 19.289. [10 ex.]

feondscipe m. *enmity*. I.7.66.

feor(r) adv. *far*. II.1.243; 28.22; comp. **fyrr** II.25.55.

feorh n. *life*. I.26.285; 29.254; II.34.106; 37.105. **feoroh** I.5.170,179; gs. **feores**; ds. **feore**; nap. **feore**. [10 ex.]

feorhadl f. *fatal illness*. I.32.41.

feorm f. *feast*. II.23.4, 12, etc.; 33.205. [10 ex.]

(ge)feormian vb II. *to feast* (trans.). I.32.82; II.28.137. Cf **a-**.

feorran adv. *far off, from far away*. I.7.64; 8.138; II.11.74; 14.116. [21 ex.]

feorþa adj. *fourth*. I.3.10; 4.175; II.1.252; 4.86. **to feorþan healfe geare** *for three and a half years*. I.praef.87. [28 ex.]

feorþling m. *farthing*. I.19.142; 38.78, 99, 104; II.7.118.

feower num. *four*. I.1.106; 6.198; II.1.149; 14.236. indecl. except gpl. **feowera** I.38.152. [49 ex.]

feowerfeald adj. *numbering four, fourfold*. II.25.135; **be feowerfealdum** *fourfold* (adv.). I.8.173; 38.90, 95.

feowerteogeþa (-tig-) adj. *fourtieth*. I.1.284; 15.69, 192; II.4.280.

feowerteoþa adj. *fourteenth*. I.37.154.

feowertig num. *fourty*. indecl., w. gen. I.1.282; 3.37; II.4.198; 7.11. [43 ex.]

feowertigfeald adj. *numbering fourty* (days). II.7.10.

feowertyne num. *fourteen*. II.13.5; 20.11; 30.206; 33.190, 197.

gefera m. *companion*. I.1.41; 5.111; II.1.285; 9.188. [45 ex.]

feran vb I. *to go*. I.2.12; 8.87; II.2.83; 8.5. Pret. only (cf **faran**) apart from **aweg ferende** II.10.43. [147 ex.] Cf **for-, forþ-, in-, of-, ofer-, to-, þurh-, up-**.

geferan vb. I. *to attain, go to*. I.25.70; 29.222; 36.73 (all pret.).

fercian vb II. *to sustain*. I.32.205; II.31.47.

ferian vb I/II. *to carry, transport*. I.4.127; 5.148; II.4.221; 10.297. Forms: inf. **ferian, ferigan** (1x); pres.pl. **feriað**; pres.pt. **ferigende**; pret. **fered-, ferod-**; pp. **fered** (1x), **gefered** (2x), **geferod**. [51 ex.] Cf **forþ-**.

geferlæcan vb I. *to associate, unite*. I.8.190; 28.225; 33.64, 97; 36.107, 140. Pres.s.3 -læcð; pret. -læhte; pp. -læht.

geferræden f. *company, companionship*. I.2.157; 3.201; II.12.257; 20.45. **gefærrædene** I.3.119. [15 ex.]

fers n. *verse* (of Scripture). II.24.98.

fette see **feccan**

feþe n. *movement, power of walking*. I.23.138; 26.42, 247.

feþerrica see **fiþerrica**.

feþung f. *walking, movement*. II.10.29, 37.

gefexod adj. *having hair*. **æðellice gefexode**, *having fine (noble-looking?) hair*, II.9.58. Cf **blæcfexede**.

ficæppel m. *fig*. II.26.6, 42.

fictreow n. *figtree*. I.40.15, 105; II.26.73, 76. ap. **-treowa**.

fif num. *five*. I.9.68; 12.15; II.12.152; 25.19. [88 ex.]

fifta adj. *fifth*. I.3.10; 19.127; II.4.88; 12.64. **fifta fæder,** *great-great-great--grandfather* II.9.14. [14 ex.]

fifteogoþa adj. *fiftieth*. I.22.3, 29; II.12.122, 221–2.

fifteoþa adj. *fifteenth*. I.25.46. Cf **fyftyne**.

fiftig num. *fifty*. I.1.202; 5.158; 22.2, 17, 27; II.13.38, 206. **fifti** I.1.186. uninfl., w. gen.

filian etc. see **fylian**.

Filistei the Philistines. See **philistei**.

findan vb 3. *to find*. I.31.44; 34.165; II.3.19; 11.149; *devise* I.34.22; II.14.346. Pres.s.2 **findst, fintst**; pret.s.3 **funde**, pl. **fundon**; pp. **gefunden**. [15 ex.] Cf **a-**.

finger m. *finger*. I.23.14; 25.137; II.12.136; 15.172. [15 ex.]

fisc m. *fish*. I.1.108; 14.172; II.10.107; 16.112. nap. **fixas,** gp. **fixa,** dp. **fixum**. [44 ex.] Cf **fix-**

fiscere m. *fisher, fisherman*. I.22.189; 26.178; 38.6 etc.; II.16.132. [15 ex.]

fiþere n. *wing*. I.35.71; II.19.88, 90; 20.32. np. **-a**.

fiþerfote adj? *four-footed*. **-um** I.32.172–3 (as sb. in dp.).

fiþerhama m. *wing*. I.26.246 (dp. **-an**); II.20.28 (dp. **fyðerhaman**).

gefiþerhamod adj. *furnished with wings*. I.31.191; AppB2.29.

fiþerrica m. *tetrarch, ruler of a fourth part*. I.32.48; **feþerrica** I.26.18.

fiþerscite adj. *squared* (marble). I.31.180 (**fyðerscytum**); II.33.266.

fixnoþ m. *fishing*. II.16.108, 111, 133, etc.; 34.280.

(ge)fixian vb. II. *to fish, to catch by fishing*. **fix-** I.38.18; II.16.109 (both intrans.); **gefix-** I.38.19, 23 (both trans.).

fla wk f. *arrow*. I.4.80; 34.16; II.10.129; 20.62. [12 ex.]

flæsc n. *flesh*. I.1.91; 2.174 ff; II.2.171; 15.60. (Usu. translating Lat. *caro*.) [59 ex.]

flæscen adj. *fleshly, made of flesh, bodily*. I.35.200; II.12.253.

geflæschamian vb II. *to invest with flesh*. pp. I.2.179; 8.18; 19.189; 20.139; II.4.277.

flæsclic adj. *fleshly, bodily, physical* (often

as opposite of *spiritual*). I.4.16; 6.87; II.4.64; 5.117. [43 ex.]

flæsclice adv. *physically, in a physical sense.* I.13.217.

flæsclicnyss f. *incarnation* (of Christ). I.8.50; 13.67; 14.140; 35.41; II.15.278, 299.

flæscmete m. *meat.* ap. **-mettas** II.7.28; 11.267.

fleam m. *flight.* I.5.87; 14.4; II.9.106; 10.156. [13 ex.]

fleding f. *flooding, overflowing.* II.11.433.

fleogan, fleon vb 2. *to fly* (as birds, angels, etc.). I.9.111; 26.236; II.1.147; 10.189. Inf. **fleogan, fleon, gefleon** (II.19.87); pres.s.3 **flihð, flyhð**; pl. **fleoð**; pres.pt. **fleonde**; pret.s. **fleah**; pl. **flugon**; pp. **geflogen**. [37 ex.] Cf **fleon** below.

fleoge wk f. *a fly.* I.AppB2.6; II.3.186 (= *muscae*).

fleon vb 2. *to flee, seek refuge.* I.18.24; 26.121; II.9.126; 10.152. Inf. **fleon**; pres.s.3 **flihð, flyhð**; pl. **fleoð**; imp. **fleo, fleoh**; pres.pt. **fleonde**; pret.s. **fleah**; pl. **flugon**. (Forms are indistinguishable from those of **fleogan** above, but the senses are generally distinct.) [23 ex.] Cf **æt-, for-, oþ-**.

fleotan vb 2. *to float.* Pres.s.3. **flyt** II.39.51.

flering f. *floor, deck, level.* I.27.112; 35.264–5; II.11.164. Cf **upflering**.

flicorian vb II. *to flutter, fly to and fro.* II.11.46.

fligan vb I. *to put to flight.* II.10.129. Cf **a-**.

fliht m. *flight.* I.1.108; 37.219; II.19.89.

flint m. *flint.* I.6.52.

geflit n. *dispute, contention.* I.11.204; 39.32, 85; AppB3.202; II.20.152; 33.76.

flitan vb 1. *to dispute.* Pret.s. **flat** I.20.213.

geflitful adj. *disputatious, contentious.* I.39.87.

flocc m. *company, troop.* II.14.82; 30.73.

flocmælum adv. *in flocks.* I.9.111.

flod n. *the Flood.* I.1.189 ff; 6.14; II.4.112; 12.153; *flow of water, tide* II.10.207–8; *stretch of water* II.34.275 (latter examples in alliterative prose). [17 ex.]

flor f. II.4.80; 10.173; 11.432; 14.277; 20.54; 34.297. ds. **flora, flore**. Cf **up-**.

Florege the monastery at Fleury on the Loire. II.11.574.

Florentius opponent of St Benedict. II.11.141.

floterian vb II. *to float up and down, to be tossed as by waves.* II.24.220.

flowan vb 7. *to flow.* I.5.134; 6.199; II.2.95; 12.387; *to flood, to become full or covered with liquid?* II.11.431; 31.102. Pres.s.3 **fleowþ, flewþ**; pret.s. **fleow**; pl. **fleowon**. [20 ex.] Cf **a-, of-, to-, ut-**.

flys n. *fleece, fur.* II.10.83; 30.44.

fnæd n. *hem, fringe.* II.11.113; 24.84, 232, 238; **ge-** II.24.236; nap. **-du**.

foca m. *loaf of bread.* II.11.144.

foda m. *food.* I.2.212; 12.43; II.10.72; 25.56. [17 ex.]

fola m. *foal.* I.14.9, 12, etc.

folc n. *people* (human beings en masse, from a crowd to a nation or all Christians or heathens). I.1.265; 4.158; II.1.91; 3.45. s. only except I.AppB3.25, 188; II.40.206; but often with pl. verb. [460 ex.] Cf **land-**.

folde wk f. *earth, ground.* II.34.165.

folgere m. *follower, adherent.* I.31.204; 32.28; 34.176; II.5.200; 35.32; 37.82.

folgian vb II. *to follow.* I.3.117; 4.15; II.6.162; 11.8. [22 ex.]

folma, folme wk mf. *hand, palm.* ap. **folman** II.18.51.

fon vb 7. *to succeed* (to an office or throne) I.32.43; II.4.198; 10.222; 17.68. **fon on** *(re-)turn to, take up (again), begin with,* I.7.200; 9.221; II.5.18; 16.131. Imper. **foh**; pret. **feng, feng-**. [14 ex.] Cf **be-, on-, under-**.

gefon vb 7. *to seize, catch.* II.10.108–9; 11.47; 24.6. Pret. **gefeng**; pp. **gefangen**.

for prep. w. dat. or acc. *for, on account of, for the sake of, in place of.* w.dat. (usual), I.5.4; 6.168; II.3.88; 4.11; w.acc., I.3.173; 37.175(?); II.2.185; 19.76, 276; 22.20; *as, as if,* w.acc., I.27.104; 31.132; with **dæg, gear**, etc, *ago*, e.g. **for feawum dagum** (I.26.265) *a few days ago*; **for þysum life** *in this life* I.17.40; 31.275; **for worulde** *in worldly terms, as regards this world* I.4.100; 10.151; II.9.15; 20.19; etc. **for nahte** *as nothing* I.10.107; II.10.218; 18.117. [686 ex.]

for þam þe conj. (or causal connective). *because, for.* I.praef.57; 4.127; II.21.11; 36.27. [6 ex.].

for þan (a) conj. or causal connective.

because, for. I.9.215; 28.119; II.2.200; 11.387 (cf app.cr.). [21 ex., all but two in CH I]; (b) adv., *therefore*, II.14.209.

for þan þe conj. or causal connective. *because, for*. I.2.119; 7.76; II.1.14; 14.161; [768 ex.]

for þi, for þy (a) conj. or causal connective. *because, for*. I.11.202; 22.31; II.1.84; 3.88; (b) adv., *therefore, for that reason* (i) I.3.67; 30.173; II.15.222; 19.147; (ii) correlating with a following conj., I.10.169; 27.96; II.13.18; 32.50. [**for þi** 150 ex., **for þy** 22 ex.].

for þi þæt, for þy þæt conj. *because*. I.11.30; 12.59; II.1.30; 3.154. [16 ex.]

for þi þe, for þy þe conj. *because*. I.1.52; 10.178; II.3.55; 30.211. [18 ex.]

for- see also under **fore-**.

foran adv. *in front, beforehand*. II.20.61; 33.210; **forn angean, forn ongean** *opposite*. I.30.138; II.11.240.

forandæg m. *early part of the day*. II.4.21, 307.

foranheafod n. *forehead*. II.15.58; 33.101. Pl. **-du**. Cf **foreheafod**.

forarn see **foreyrnan**.

forbærnan vb I. *to burn up, destroy with fire*. I.praef.101; 18.9; II.3.83; 32.192. [29 ex.]

forbeodan vb 2. *to forbid*. (w. acc. object and dat. of person) I.1.78; 8.30; II.6.145; 36.102. Pres.s.3 **-byt, -bytt**; pret.s. **-bead**; pp. **-boden**. [22 ex.]

forberan vb 4. *to endure, submit to*. I.3.181; 15.147; II.4.181; 6.197. Pret. **forbær, forbær-**. [28 ex.]

forbugan vb 2. *to shun, evade*. I.1.295; 5.87; II.1.119; 13.224. Pres.s.3 **-bihþ**; pret.s. **-beah**; pl. **-bugon**. [31 ex.]

forbyrnan vb 3. intrans. *to burn up, to be consumed by fire*. I.3.145; AppB3.152; II.6.8; 10.119. Pret.s.3 **forbarn**; subj. **-burne**. [9 ex.]

forceorfan vb 3. *to cut off*. I.6.52; 36.79; II.3.30; 26.80. Pres.s.2 **-cyrfst**; pret. **-cearf, -curf-**; pp. **-corfen, -coruen**. [13 ex.]

forc f.? *pitchfork*. dp. **forcum** I.29.213. (Cf Pope p. 858)

forcuþ adj. *wicked*. I.1.41; 19.168; 38.211.

forcuþe adv. *wickedly, badly*. I.AppB3.69

forcyrran vb I. *to avoid, turn aside from*. I.5.32; 7.35.

fordeman vb I. *to condemn*. I.9.152–3; 23.33; II.16.12; 19.170. [10 ex.]

fordon anom. vb. *to destroy, corrupt, ruin*. I.praef.77; I.1.59; II.2.204; 4.232. Pres.s.3 **fordeþ**; pl. **fordoþ**; pret. **fordyd-**; pp. **fordon**. [38 ex.]

fordrencan vb I. *to make drunk, intoxicate*. pp. **fordrencte** I.22.57–8. Cf **a-**.

fordwinan vb 1. *to vanish*. I.26.193; 30.250; 38.243; II.16.88; 34.78, 237. Pres.s.3 **fordwinð**; pret. **-dwan, -dwinon**.

fordyligian vb II. *to destroy*. I.37.204. Cf **a-**.

fordyttan vb I. *to block up*. II.27.201.

fore prep. *on behalf of, in exchange for*. I.17.30; 32.154; II.18.101; 21.172; 24.10. (Always preceded by the relative or the pronoun object in dat.)

forealdian vb II. *to grow old?*. pp. **forealdode** II.34.13.

foreaþe adv. *very easily*. II.10.104.

foreaþelice adv. *very easily*. I.18.185.

forebeacn n. *portent*. I.3.16; 22.61. ap. **-cn, -cena**.

forebicnung f. *portent*. I.36.45.

foredum see **forod**

foregenga m. *predecessor, ancestor*. I.3.36; II.32.164; 36.85. Cf **an-** etc.

foregleaw adj. *forseeing, wise about the future*. II.10.306.

foreheafod n. *forehead*. I.31.185. Cf **foranheafod**.

foresæd adj. *aforementioned*. I.3.153; 4.78; II.2.16; 4.296. [39 ex.]

foresceawian vb II. *to pre-ordain, provide, foresee, scrutinize*. I.1.236; 7.122; II.4.142; 10.104. [22 ex.]

foresceawung f. *pre-ordination, provision, foresight, knowledge*. I.6.42, 201; II.12.511; 31.53, 63; 34.9. **forescawung-** 2x. [9 ex.]

foresecgan vb III. *to predict*. I.38.195; AppB3.157; II.10.126; 14.3. Pret. **foresæd-**, pp. **foresæd**. [11 ex.]

foresendan vb I. *to send in advance*. I.2.46.

foresettan vb I. *to set above or before*. I.24.156.

foresewen see **forseon**

foresprǣc f. *preface*. II.praef.33, 38, 42; *promise on behalf of someone* or *in advance* (by a godfather), II.3.272.

forespreca m. *advocate*. I.27.73; II.29.58; **forspreca** II.3.254.

foresprecan vb 5. *to promise on behalf of someone*. pres.part. II.8.126.

forestæppan vb.6. *to go before, precede*. I.25.17; 40.24, 46; II.5.199, 203; 9.117, 125. Pret. **forestop, forestop-**. [17 ex.]

foresteall m. *resistance, prevention*. II.14.16.

forestihtan vb I. *to predestine*. I.7.166 ff; 32.164; II.13.165; 22.105 ff. [11 ex.]

forestihtung f. *predestination*. II.22.108, 111.

foreþeon vb 1. *to excel, surpass*. I.24.153. Pres.s.3.subj. **forþeo** I.19.45.

foreþingere m. *intercessor*. II.12.577.

foreþingung f. *intercession*. II.14.35.

foreweard adj. *front, facing forward*. **forewearde heafod** *forehead* II.15.56. **æt foreweardan his gesceapes** *at the front part of his penis* I.6.53 (printed as **ætforeweardan**, probably mistakenly).

forewitegian vb II. *to prophesy, predict*. I.3.94.

forewittig adj. *foreknowing*. I.28.72.

foreyrnan vb 3. *to run before*. w. dat. I.37.134; 38.83; *to occur beforehand* II.37.37. Pret.s.3 **forarn**.

forfaran vb 6. *to die*. II.24.225; 33.212.

forferan vb I. *to perish, fall*. I.24.107; II.24.46.

forfleon vb 2. *to flee from*. I.5.87; 10.157; II.4.275; 10.160. Pres.s.3 **-flihþ**; pl. **-fleoþ**; pret. **-fleah, -flug-**. [20 ex.]

forgan anom. vb. *to do without, refrain from*. I.1.79; II.7.28; 19.169. pret.s. **foreode** I.11.211.

forgangan vb 7. *to refrain from*. I.1.78–9.

forgægan vb I. *to reject, transgress against, break* (a commandment). I.6.24; 7.154; 39.75; II.12.172.

forgægednyss f. *transgression*. I.2.94; 7.171; II.1.152; 4.213. [13 ex.]

forgifan, forgyfan vb 5. *to give*. I.1.258; 2.99; II.2.30; 3.204; *to forgive* I.3.136; 16.10; II.10.94; 17.99. Pret. **forgeaf, forgeaf-**; pp. -**gifen, -gyfen**. [219 ex.]

forgifen(n)yss, forgyfen(n)yss f. *forgiveness*. I.15.65; 16.11; II.3.59; 7.43. [36 ex.]

forgitan, forgytan vb 5. *to forget*. I.9.101; 24.196; II.3.293; 7.60. Pres.s.2 **-gitst**, 3 **-gyt**; pret.pl. **-geaton**; pp. **-gyten**. [11 ex.]

forgnagan vb 6. *to consume, devour*. pret. **forgnogon** II.12.73.

forgyldan vb 3. *to repay*. I.18.203; 26.133; II.1.213; 20.139. Pres.s.2 **-gyltst**; 3 **-gilt, -gylt**; pl. **-gyldaþ**; pret. **-geald, -guld-**; pp. **-golden**. [15 ex.] Cf **a-**.

forgyman vb. I. *to neglect, overlook*. II.19.248.

forgymeleasian, -gime- vb II. *to neglect*. I.23.120; 28.159; II.5.80; 7.65. [12 ex.]

forgyttol adj. *forgetful*. II.9.25.

forhabban, -hæbban vb III refl. *to restrain oneself, abstain*. I.9.9; 25.180; II.5.268; 7.37. Pres.s.3 **forhæfð**. [7 ex.]

forhæfednyss f. *abstinence, restraint*. I.7.239; 11.199; II.7.24; 9.45. [20 ex.]

forhigan vb I. *to despise*. I.21.93.

forhogian vb II. *to spurn, despise*. I.2.157; 4.55; II.4.305; 9.209. [7 ex.]

forhradian vb II. *to prevent, forestall* I.5.90; 32.60; *prepare, prepare for* I.32.93; 40.179; II.5.228; *anticipate, precede* II.9.118; *approach, go in front of* II.9.129.

forhraþe adv. *very quickly, soon*. II.5.58; 34.44.

forht adj. *fearful, frightened*. II.14.105; 34.201. Cf **un-**.

forhtian vb II. *to fear, be frightened*. I.3.125; 4.217; II.3.103; 17.93. [19 ex.]

forhtmod adj. *frightened*. I.34.56; II.11.246.

forhtung f. *fear*. I.4.227; II.9.133; 38.220.

forlædan vb I. *to lead astray*. II.19.113.

forlæran vb I. *to deceive, seduce*. I.1.159–60; 13.15; II.27.95.

forlætan vb 7. *to abandon, relinquish, leave out, leave*. I.7.161; 10.128; II.5.256; 9.201; *allow* II.12.81. Pres.s.3 **forlæt, forlętt** (I.38.64); pret. **forlet, forlet-**; pp. **forlæten**. [187 ex.]

forleogan vb 2. *to slander, give false testimony against*. I.3.20 (pret. **forlugon**); II.14.121.

forleosan vb 2. *to lose*. I.7.143; 9.197; II.19.84; 26.131. pp. as adj. **forloren** *fallen, damned* I.24.84; 26.201; II.35.7. Pres.s.3 **forlyst**; pret. **forleas, forluron**; pp. **forloren**. [52 ex.]

forlig(e)r, -lir n. *fornication, adultery*. I.1.179; 17.45; II.12.501; 19.156. [11 ex.]

forlig(e)r, -lir m. *fornicator, adulterer*.

I.8.192; 35.128; II.19.162, 285; 28.9. [9 ex.]
forligerlice adv. *adulterously, with fornication.* I.32.53; II.39.81.
forlirbed n. *bed of adultery.* I.39.32, 83.
forma wk.adj. *first.* I.3.6; 5.7; II.1.15; 4.84. [33 ex.]
formete m. *food for a journey?* **formettum** I.18.176.
formolsnian vb II. *to decay, crumble.* I.14.216; 28.145.
forn see **foran**.
fornean adv. *nearly, almost.* I.1.230; 38.62; II.12.65; 21.25. [13 ex.]
forniman vb 4. *to destroy, overpower.* I.21.41; 22.166; II.3.166–7; 13.275. Pres.s.3 **-nimþ, -nymþ**; pret.s. **-nam**; pp. **-numen**. [24 ex.]
forod adj. *broken.* II.19.90, 202 (**foredum**). Cf **un-**.
foroft adv. *very often.* I.12.35; II.9.53; 10.129; 15.224. [7 ex.]
forpæran vb I. *to injure, ruin.* I.14.171; 34.219; II.3.241; 12.322. [8 ex.]
forridel m. *messenger, fore-runner.* II.11.236.
forrotian vb II. *to rot away, putrefy.* I.7.242–3.
forrotodnyss f. *corruption, putrefaction.* II.15.321; 26.27; 30.166; 36.136.
forrynel m. *fore-runner, herald.* I.25.117, 224; 32.148.
forsacan vb 6. *to reject, refuse.* pret.s.subj. **forsoce** II.1.229. Cf **wiþ-**.
forsceotan vb 2. *to forestall, anticipate.* I.34.159 (pret.s. **forsceat**).
forscrencan vb I. *to supplant, crush?* I.13.124; 38.165; II.27.35 (pp. **forscrenctan**).
forscrencend m. *supplanter, destroyer?* I.13.122; 38.154, 164.
forscrincan vb 3. *to shrink up, wither.* II.6.80 (pret.s. **forscranc**); 30.168 (pp. **forscruncen**).
forscyld(e)god pp. as adj. *utterly sinful or guilty, beset or corrupted by sin.* I.1.59; 4.126; II.2.209; 21.136. [16 ex.]
forscyttan vb I. *to ward off, prevent.* I.36.49; 37.269; II.19.261.
forsearian vb II. *to dry up, wither.* I.40.9, 58; II.6.88; 25.127; 30.167; 31.68.
forsecgan vb III. *to accuse, testify against.* I.3.95, 97 (pret. **forsæd-**); II.12.322 (pres.s. **forsegð**).
forseon vb 5. *to despise, scorn.* I.2.156; 8.134; II.5.196; 8.85. Pres.s.2 **forsihst**; 3 **forsihþ**; pl. **forseoþ**; imp. **forseo(h)**; pres.pt. **forseonde**; pret. **forseah, forsawon**; pp. **forsewen, foresewen**. [95 ex.]
forseoþan vb 2. *to consume, dry up?* pp. **forsodene** I.5.107.
forsewenlic adj. *despised.* II.23.92.
forsewenlice adv. *ignominiously.* comp., I.32.168.
forsewennyss f. *scorn.* I.4.49; II.12.539; 14.308; 23.78; 40.290.
forsmorian vb II. *to choke, destroy by choking.* II.6.10, 28, 94–5; 12.188.
[forspanan] vb 6. *to lead astray, seduce.* I.1.139; 21.172; 28.162; II.13.64, 268; 32.197. Pres.s.3 **-spenð**; pret. **forspeon, forspeon-**; pp. **-spanen**.
forspreca see **fore-**
forsprecan vb 5. *to denounce.* II.33.210.
forstandan vb 6. *to protect* I.37.204 (pres.s.2 **forstentst**); *stand against, resist* II.20.61.
forst m. *frost.* I.5.107.
forstelan vb 4. *to steal.* I.15.10, 43, 46; II.7.106; 14.350.; 24.237. Pret. **-stæl, -stęl-**; pp. **-stolen**.
forsuwian vb II. *to suppress by silence, pass over, fail to mention.* I.3.186; 6.90; II.2.78; 10.96. [15 ex.]
forswælan vb I. *to burn up.* I.5.128; 36.74; II.31.16; 33.219. [7 ex.]
forswelgan vb 3. *to swallow up.* I.14.174, 191; 34.164; II.11.383–5; 27.133. Pres.s.3 **forswylcð, forswylhð**; pret. **forswealh, forswulg-**. [11 ex.]
forsweltan vb 3(?). *to die.* I.30.251 (pret.s. **forsweolt**).
forswiþe adv. *greatly.* II.34.322.
forsworcennyss f. *darkness.* I.29.200.
forsworen pp. as adj. *perjured.* I.8.193 (2x).
forsworennyss f. *perjury.* II.12.509; 19.237.
fortredan vb 5. *to tread down, suppress.* II.6.6, 65–6; 24.217, 225; 25.75. Pres.s.2 **fortretst**; pret. pl. **fortrædon**; pp. **fortreden**. Cf next, and **oftredan**.
fortredan vb I. *to tread down, suppress.* pret.pl. **fortreddon** I.36.106.

forþ adv. *forward, out, into view, onward, further.* I.4.158; 6.151; II.1.97; 4.221; **oð forð nihtes,** *until a late hour of night* II.11.524. [48 ex.]

forþateon vb 2. *to bring forth, utter.* pret.s. **forðateah** I.36.179.

forþbringan vb I. *to bring forth, produce.* II.6.168; 26.53, 67. Pres.s. 3 **forðbrincð**.

forþdæd f. *necessity, thing needful for life?* I.27.116.

forþeo see **foreþeon**

forþfaran vb 6. *to die.* I.5.170; 10.55; II.11.62; 15.224. Pres.s.3 **-færð**; pp. **forþfaren** (no pret.). [16 ex.]

forþfæder m. *forefather.* I.3.30; 7.190; 37.24; II.15.74, 176.

forþferan vb I. *to die.* I.1.202; 14.184; II.2.19; 13.27. (pret. only) [11 ex.]

forþferian vb I/II. *to despatch* (in death). pp. **forðferede** II.11.343.

forþgan anom. vb. *to pass by, continue.* I.22.83 (**forðeode**); II.34.160.

forþgang m. *outcome, progress.* I.14.84; II.20.151.

forþgenge adj. *operative?* I.37.57 (**forð-gencge**); *thriving* II.9.170.

forþgewiten pp. as adj. *past.* I.39.64.

forþheonon adv. *away from here.* I.AppB3.155.

forþlædan vb I. *to bring forth, produce.* I.1.105.

forþræstan vb I. *to stifle.* pp. as adj. **forðræstne** II.6.97.

forþrihte adv. *plainly, simply.* I.6.39; 14.76.

forþrysmian vb II. *to choke.* II.6.91.

forþsiþ m. *death.* I.5.165; 7.98; II.2.42; 5.164. [48 ex.]

forþstæppan vb 6. *to proceed* (esp. in a theological sense), *advance.* I.13.151; 20.49; 25.7; II.6.61. Pret.s. **forðstop**. [8 ex.]

forþstæppung f. *proceeding, issuing forth.* I.33.144.

forþteon vb 2. *to produce, bring forth.* I.16.123 (pres.s. **forðtihð**).

forþwyrtan vb I. *to cut off.* II.4.284.

forþyldigian vb II. *to endure patiently.* I.3.185; 36.241; II.5.217; 11.339. (**-þyldg-, þyldeg-**).

forþyrnan vb 3. *to run forth.* I.37.79.

forwandian vb II. *to hesitate.* II.14.60.

forwel adv. *very* (only with **fela, menige, oft**). I.praef.123; 7.133; II.2.6; 9.223. [32 ex.]

forweornian vb II. *to decay, fade, decline.* I.4.98; 11.55; 19.113.

forwerod pp. as adj. *worn out, decayed through age.* I.13.163; 16.128; II.5.99; 6.129. (**-wered-**). [8 ex.]

forwundian vb II. *to wound.* pp. as adj. I.31.271.

forwurþan vb 3. *to perish.* I.20.234; 24.83; II.19.200; 34.84. Pres.s.3 **forwyrð**; pret. **forwearþ, forwurd-**. [13 ex.]

forwyrcan vb I. *to ruin.* I.19.24; 20.241; II.1.13; 24.149; *to forfeit* I.1.273; 13.8; 14.169; II.12.545. Pret. **forwyrht-**; pp. **-wyrht**. [15 ex.]

forwyrd n. *destruction, perdition, death.* I.praef.71; 4.154; II.4.259; 9.125. [38 ex.]

forwyrnan vb I. *to refuse.* w. gen. object, and dat. of person. I.1.74; 2.154; II.7.163; 19.278. [19 ex.]

fosterfæder m. *foster-father* (all refs. to Joseph). I.2.13, 192; 5.33, 91; 9.146 (**fostor-**), 222; 13.100.

fostermodor, fostor- f. *foster-mother, nurse.* II.11.8 ff.

fostorcild n. *nursling, pupil.* I.29.193; II.34.288.

fostor m. *feeding; reproducing?.* I.1.189; 12.53.

fot n. *foot.* I.11.18; 19.233; II.1.194; 2.88. ds. **fet**; nap. **fet**; gp. **fota**; dp. **fotum** (48x), **foton** (7x). [104 ex.]

fotadlig adj. *suffering from bad feet.* II.2.48.

fotcops m. *fetter.* II.23.151–2.

fotlæst f. *footprint.* I.34.66, 96.

fotlic adj. *with feet, on foot.* II.32.28.

fotsceamul, -el m. *foot-stool.* I.19.57; 22.66 (**-scam-**); 32.104; II.30.30–32.

[fotswaþu] f. *track, foot.* I.4.158; 26.266; II.2.180; 10.71, 77. (as. **-swaþe**, dp. **-swaþum** only).

fotþweal n. *foot-washing.* I.29.51.

fotwylm m. *foot, sole of foot?* I.6.105 (ap. **-wylmys**); 7.95; 26.262 (ap. **-welmas**); II.32.212; 34.159.

fracod adj. *wicked, sinful.* II.10.228 (apm. **fracedan**); 19.118.

fracodlic adj. *sinful, impudent?* II.12.505.

fracodlice adv. *sinfully.* II.16.216; 19.298.

fracodnyss f. *sinfulness.* II.19.41.

fram prep. w. dat. (a) *from.* Expressing separation or direction (temporal or spatial). I.praef.62; 2.13; II.1.18; 2.20. (b) *by*. I.praef.45; 10.110; II.8.9; 27.71. **from** I.4.107. [576 ex.]

framfær n. *departure*. II.11.161; 17.21.

framfæreld n. or m. *departure*. I.2.163 (printed as 2 words).

Francan the Franks. **francena rice**, the kingdom of the Franks or (earlier) the region of Gaul. I.37.41, 48; II.9.193; 11.573; 20.260.

Francland n. Gaul. I.37.43.

fræcednyss, frecednyss f. *danger*. I.17.52; 25.75; II.10.126; 11.120. (**fræced-** mainly in CH I, **freced-** spellings mainly in CH II). [31 ex.]

fræcenful, frecenful adj. *perilous*. I.28.224; AppB3.158.

fræc adj. *greedy*. dsf. **fræcere** II.19.292.

(ge)fræt(e)wian, gefreatewian vb II. *to adorn* I.4.79; 14.87; II.9.40; 19.107. pp. only apart from **frætewað** II.31.17. [9 ex.]

frætewung f. *adornment*. I.20.166; 34.105; II.31.79 ff; 40.192. Var. forms: **freatewunge, frætwunga, frætuwunge.**

gefredan vb I. *to feel*. I.5.162; 14.176; II.11.60; 23.51. Pres.s.2 **gefretst**, 3 **gefret**. [18 ex.]

(ge)frefrian vb II. *to comfort*. I.11.217; 22.176; II.10.23; 11.123. [42 ex., mainly with prefix]

frefri(g)end m. *comforter*. I.37.66, 82.

fremde adj. *estranged*. II.10.162. Cf **æl-**.

fremfullic adj. *beneficial*. II.28.47.

fremian vb II. *to help, benefit*, pers. and impers., w. dat. of person. I.3.146; 5.104; II.2.80; 5.114. [39 ex.]

gefremman vb I/II. *to perform, do*. I.2.221; 3.171; II.3.132; 7.27. Pres.s.3 **gefremaþ**; pl. **gefremmaþ**; pret. **gefremod-, -med-**; pp. **gefremmed, gefremod**. [69 ex.]

fremming f. *performance, action*. I.praef.127; 8.49; II.12.245; 15.138. **fremmincge** 2x; **gefremminge** I.21.240. [16 ex.]

fremu f. *benefit*. II.27.26.

freoh see **frig**.

freolice adv. *freely, without constraint*. I.15.168; 16.71; II.9.201; 12.86.

freols m. or n. *festival*. I.34.8; II.27.1.

freolsdæg m. *festival, feast-day*. I.7.46; 30.23; II.13.10; 22.180. **-dæig** 2x. [11 ex.]

freolsian vb II. *to honour, celebrate*. I.6.158; 25.67; II.12.141; 15.26. [7 ex.]

freolslic adj. *festive, pertaining to a feast-day*. I.39.111.

freolstid f. *festival*. I.5.4; 7.8; II.15.28; 17.62. [20 ex.]

freond m. *friend, kinsman*. I.3.177; 4.140; II.5.28; 6.174. nap. **frynd; gefrynd** II.14.177. (For sense *kinsman, relative* cf II.10.278–81.) [67 ex.]

freondræden f. *friendship*. I.18.89–90.

freondscipe m. *friendship, intimate circle*. I.18.52 (**-scype**); 26.149; 38.265; 40.94.

frig adj. *free*. I.1.156; 34.163; AppB3.34; II.19.226; 27.73–5. **freoh** I.4.275.

frige æfen m. *Thursday evening*. I.14.182.

gefrinan vb 3. *to discover, learn*. pret.s. **gefran** I.5.172. Cf **be-**.

friþ m. or n. *peace, truce*. II.10.195.

gefriþian vb II. *to protect*. II.11.195.

frofer n. *comfort*. I.9.19; 29.162 (**frofor**); II.1.295; 17.34. [13 ex.]

froforgast m. *comforting spirit*. I.20.84; 22.176.

frogga m. *frog*. dp. **froggon** II.12.58.

fruma m. *beginning*. **æt fruman**, *at first* I.6.33; 21.97; II.8.45; 11.182. [11 ex.] Cf **ord-**.

frumcenned adj. *firstborn*. I.2.86 ff; 9.60; II.1.175; 12.79. **-cynnedan** I.2.18. [12 ex.]

frumsceaft m. *creation*. II.12.152.

frumsceapen adj. *first-created*. I.2.93; 7.250; II.1.59; 12.499. **-scapenan** 2x. [12 ex.]

frumslæp m. *first sleep*. II.2.35.

frumwæstm m. *first fruit*. II.7.54.

frymþ mf. *beginning*. I.praef.62; 2.166; II.1.18; 5.53. **frimþ** 2x. [20 ex.]

Frysa m. *Friesian*. II.21.167 ff.

fugel, fugol m. *bird*. I.18.113; AppB2.25 ff; II.3.159; 6.65. [46 ex.]

fugelcyn(n) n. I.1.84, 188; 9.118; 22.131; AppB2.6 (**fugolcynne**).

fugoloþ f. *products of fowling or bird-catching*. II.40.44.

ful adj. *dirty, foul, wicked*. I.6.103; 14.107; II.11.441; 12.569. (Always with moral sense or overtones.) [24 ex.]

ful, full adj. *full, complete, perfect*. I.12.21; 21.38; II.16.117; 26.116. [25 ex.]

ful, full adv. *fully, very, completely*. I.8.86; 19.199; II.12.326, 383. [13 ex.]

fule adv. *foully*. I.33.101, 104.

fulfremed adj. *perfect, complete*. I.6.15; 11.71; II.3.102; 4.238. **full-** 2x. [33 ex.]

fulfremedlic adj. *perfect, pertaining to perfection*. I.27.142; 28.192.

fulfremedlice adv. *perfectly, fully*. I.1.13; 30.11; II.9.42; 16.44; **-fremodlice** I.24.172. [13 ex.]

fulfremednyss f. *perfection*. I.12.119; 27.170; II.19.152; 22.52. [8 ex.]

fulgan anom. vb. *to perform, carry out*. w. dat. Pres.s.3 **fulgæð** I.4.125; 11.104.

(ge)fullian vb II. *to baptize*. I.4.73; 14.66; II.3.22, 101; 8.55. **fulgiaþ** (imp.pl.) I.14.66; pp. **gefullud-** 2x. [76 ex.]

fullic adj. *foul, sinful*. II.23.60.

fullice adv. *foully, sinfully*. II.23.189.

fullice adv. *fully*. I.20.164, 169; 23.100; 25.193; II.40.278. [7 ex.]

fulluht n. *baptism*. I.1.284; 6.47; II.3.21; 4.36. [94 ex.]

fulluhtbæþ n. *baptismal font or bathing*. I.29.91, 101, 283 (**fullutbæðe**).

fulluhtere m. *baptiser, baptist*. I.9.200; 25.4; II.3.6; 11.572. [30 ex.]

fullweaxen adj. *fully grown*. II.3.16. Cf I.AppB2.16.

fulnyss f. *foulness, dirt, sinfulness*. I.31.182; 32.134; II.14.32; 23.187; 34.21.

fultum m. *help*. I.praef.68; 1.88; II.1.295; 4.226. **fultome** I.36.139; **fultummes** I.11.65. [53 ex.]

(ge)fultumian vb II. *to help* (w.dat., but see II.7.128 and var.). I.3.117; 34.244; 37.59; II.5.231; 7.128; 21.133–5; 33.232.

fultumigend m. *helper, supporter*. II.18.7.

fundian vb II. *to intend to go, prepare to go*. II.2.93; 22.2.

fundung f. *preparation for departure?* II.22.30.

Furseus Irish saint and visionary (d. 650). II.20.passim.

furþon adv. *even*. usu. with negative, *not even*. I.3.141; 4.70; II.3.53; 10.180. [24 ex.]

furþor adv. *further, ahead*. I.25.185; 32.53; II.6.162; 21.65. [10 ex.]

fus adj. *eager to go*. II.10.328; 11.380.

fyftyne num. *fifteen*. II.34.17.

fylian, filian vb I. *to follow*. I.8.21; 10.143; II.2.179; 5.199. Forms: inf. **filian, filigan, fylian, fyligan**; pres.s.3 **fyligð, filið**; pl. **filiað, filigað, fyliað, fyligað, fyligiað**; pres.pt **fyligende**; pret. **filid-, filigd-, fylid-, fyligd-**. [82 ex.] Cf **æfter-**.

gefyllan vb I. *to fill, fulfil*. I.1.62; 2.58; II.1.160; 4.15. Pres.s.2 **gefylst**; 3 **gefylþ**; pret. **gefyld-, gefylld-**; **fyll-** 2x. [131 ex.] Cf **a-**.

fyll mn. *fall*. I.26.245; II.17.97.

gefyllednyss f. *fulfilment, fullness, completion*. I.9.229; 13.39; II.1.169; 7.82. [12 ex.]

fylmen n. *skin, scale*. I.6.65, 82 (**felmenes**); 27.37 (np. **-mene**).

fylst m. *help*. I.11.6; 25.167; II.25.131.

gefylsta m. *helper*. I.praef.127; 3.80; II.5.211; 9.52. [13 ex.]

fylstan vb I. *to help*. w. dat. I.3.78; 34.70; II.5.231; 9.169. Pres.s.3 **fylst**; pret.s. **fylste**. [8 ex.]

fylþ f. *foulness, wickedness*. II.33.112.

fyr n. *fire*. I.praef.97; 8.187; II.1.209; 3.139. [171 ex.]

fyrd f. *army, military expedition*. I.22.12; 30.206, 217, 247; II.12.115; 18.10.

fyrding f. *army, military expedition*. II.4.215; 12.84; 33.30.

fyrdlic adj. *military, martial*. I.30.122.

fyrdtruma m. *military troop*. I.30.116.

fyren adj. *fiery*. I.22.45; 31.190; II.13.245; 14.62. [17 ex.]

fyrenful adj. *sinful*. I.6.97; 28.137; 36.238 (**fyrnfulle**).

[fyrhtu] f. *fear*. I.27.20; 28.117; II.10.151; 14.87. [10 ex.]

fyrlen adj. *distant*. I.7.68 (**fyrlyne**); II.9.88; 10.132; 11.556; 29.112; 34.63.

fyrmest adj. *first, foremost*. I.3.86; 6.130; II.2.186; 5.19. [29 ex.]

fyrmest adv. *best*. I.10.195.

gefyrn adv. *earlier, long before, long ago*. I.6.63; 39.41; II.1.121; 10.101; **gefyrn worulde** *long ago in time?* II.1.128. [15 ex.]

fyrnleahtor m. *sin*. II.27.128.

fyrnlic adj. *wicked*. II.14.322; 17.100; 25.50.

fyrnlice adv. *wickedly, sinfully*. II.23.191.

fyrst mn. *time, period*. I.1.282; 2.48; II.1.156; 4.114; f. **to langere fyrste** I.27.56 (but cf. var.). [57 ex.]

fyrst f. *roof, ceiling*. II.14.276.

fyrþrian vb II. *to promote, push forward.* I.14.85; II.5.114.
fyrwit n. *curiosity, inquisitiveness.* II.10.94.
fyrwitnyss f. *curiosity.* II.10.89; 12.524; 23.56–7.
fyþer- see **fiþer-**.

Gabao where the sun stands still in Joshua's wars, at Joshua 10.12. II.12.405.
Gabrihel the archangel Gabriel. I.2.212 (**gabriel**); 13.3, 42; 25.10; 30.29, 60; 31.82; II.1.157.
gad f. *goad.* I.27.19, 78–9.
(ge)gaderian vb II. *to gather, collect* (trans. and intrans.). I.1.188; 12.22; II.2.76; 26.5. [64 ex.]
gegaderung f. *assembly, company.* I.21.10; 22.50; 35.29; II.5.38; 27.134.
gaffetung f. *chattering, loquaciousness.* I.21.168; 23.70; II.12.497.
gafol n. *tribute, tax, interest.* I.2.50; 4.124; II.33.42; 38.32. [13 ex.]
gafolgyldere m. *tributary, tax-payer.* II.33.32, 67 (**gafel-**).
gegafspræc f. *chattering, idle talk.* I.23.71.
gegafspræce adj. *loquacious.* I.35.226.
galdor n. *charm, incantation.* I.31.305, 324.
gal adj. *lustful.* I.25.162; 33.31.
Galatia Roman province in Asia Minor where St Paul preached. I.26.102.
Galilea the region of Galilee (northern Palestine). I.5.174; 15.32, 39, 117; II.4.38.
Galileisc pertaining to Galilee. I.2.13; 12.4; 13.43; 21.21; 22.53; 38.4; II.4.4, 38, 319; 14.72.
gallic adj. *lustful.* II.11.59.
galnyss f. *lustfulness, sexual appetite or desire.* I.6.82; 7.242; II.4.29; 7.26. [26 ex.]
gamen n. *sport, entertainment.* II.14.211.
gamenode see **gæmnigan**.
gan anom. vb. *to go, walk.* I.2.84; 9.11; II.1.97; 2.104. Pres.s.3 **gæþ**; pl. **gaþ**; pret. **eod-**. **gaan** IX. [202 ex.] Cf **a-, be-, for-, forþ-, in-, nyþer-, of-, ofer-, to-, þurh-, gangan**.
gegan anom. vb. *to reach, come to.* II.11.32; 31.49; 38.128. Pres.s.3 **gegæþ**; pl. **gegaþ**.
gang m. *walking, power of walking.* I.1.257; 20.15; II.23.84; 33.81; *privy* I.20.226. [9 ex.] Cf **forþ-, husel-, in-, ut-, ym-**.
gangan vb 7. *to go.* I.3.159; 6.15; II.1.251; 11.346. Pres. tense only. **gegange** I.34.90. [18 ex.] Cf **be-, for-, of-, ut-**.
Garganus mountain in SE Italy where St Michael appeared. I.34.5 ff.
garsecg m. *ocean.* I.31.6–7.
gast m. *spirit* (usu. the Holy Spirit; also used of devils and angels, and occasionally of an individual, esp. at the moment of death). I.1.19, 25; 30.263; II.10.306; 31.45. [389 ex.] Cf **frofor-, þening-**.
gastlic adj. *spiritual.* I.2.90; 3.164; II.1.107; 4.60. [180 ex.]
gastlice adv. *spiritually, in a spiritual sense* (often close to *figuratively*). I.2.84; 7.245; II.1.118; 4.178. [36 ex.]
gat f.? *goat.* II.7.136–7 (ap. **gæt**).
gatu see **geat**.
Gaza city of the Philistines. I.15.160–3.
gælsa m. *sensual pleasure.* I.36.105; II.4.305.
gæmnigan vb II. *to play.* II.9.77 (**gamenode**); 10.13; 40.267.
gærs n. *grass.* I.12.17; 21.124; II.10.180 (the shoots of wheat); 25.72. [17 ex.]
gærstapa m. *locust.* II.12.71.
ge pron. *you* see **þu**.
ge conj. *and.* Usu. in construction **ægþer ge . . . ge**, *both . . . and*, for which see under **ægþer**. Only exceptions noticed are **ge . . . ge**, *both . . . and* at II.1.164; 15.223.
gea interj. *yes, certainly.* I.22.97; II.3.265; 8.17, 99. Cf **gyse**.
geaf(-) see **gifan**.
geafl m. *fork.* I.29.208.
gealg adj. *gloomy.* I.31.264.
gealga m. *gallows.* I.38.187, 189, 206, 256, etc.
gealla m. *gall, bile.* I.38.144; II.3.160, 172.
geancyrr m. *return.* I.30.225.
geaplice adv. *cunningly.* I.5.43.
gear mn. *year.* I.1.202; 9.189; II.4.114; 9.28. as. **ealne gear** II.17.109; nap. **gear**. [160 ex.] Cf **hunger-**.
(ge)gearcian vb II. *to prepare.* I.1.43; 11.199; II.1.94; 5.231. [79 ex., incl. 8 with **ge-** (apart from pp.)]
gearcung f. *preparation.* I.35.84, 166; II.3.210; 23.118.
geare adv. *clearly, well.* I.1.134; 38.326.
gearlanges adv. *for a year.* II.26.78.

gearlic adj. *annual, of the year*. I.6.148; 11.191; II.5.239; 7.1. [8 ex.]

gegearn- see **geearn-**

gearo adj. *ready*. I.8.135; 12.125; II.23.35; 39.19. ns.n. **gearu**; nap.mn. **gearwe, gearowe, gearuwe**. [23 ex.]

geat n. *gate*. I.4.266; 13.28; II.1.296; 4.157. as. **geat, get** (1x); ds **geate, gete** (2x); nap. **gatu**. [32 ex.] Cf **burh-, helle-, port-**.

Gelboe Mount Gilboa in Galilee where Saul killed himself, I Samuel 31.1–7. II.4.197.

Genesar the region of Galilee. II.24.81.

geoc n. *yoke*. I.14.114; 38.55; II.25.53.

geogoþ f. *youth*. I.8.163; 13.60; II.5.93; 9.28. **iuguð** II.34.127; ds. **iugeðe** II.18.108. [14 ex.]

geogoþhad m. *youth*. I.30.107; 40.117; II.25.91.

geolca m. *yolk*. I.2.183.

geom(e)rian vb II. *to lament, bewail, mourn*. I.9.118; 24.149, 185; 35.38; II.34.36.

geomerung f. *lamentation*. I.9.119; II.2.32; 5.262; 13.9; 20.244; 28.52.

geond prep. w. acc. (and occas. dat.). *throughout, over*. I.1.220; 5.3; II.2.126 (w. dat.); 3.145. [84 ex.]

geondstredan vb I. *to sprinkle, strew*. pp. **geondstred** II.36.135.

geong adj. *young*. I.3.53; 5.93; 29.38; II.1.89. comp. **gyngra** I.20.217.

geonglic adj. *youthful, of youth*. II.9.28.

georne adv. *eagerly, urgently, well, fully*. I.7.162; 9.21; II.10.284; 11.307. [20 ex.]

geornful adj. *eager, zealous*. I.17.70; 29.236; 33.90; II.29.54; 36.88.

geornfullice adv. *zealously*. comp. I.35.235; II.9.48.

geornfulnyss f. *zealousness, devotion, eagerness*. I.14.83; 18.64; II.1.299; 13.6. [8 ex.]

geornlice adv. *eagerly, urgently*. I.praef.129; 4.142; II.1.299; 2.38. [35 ex.]

geotan vb 2. *to pour*. II.39.52. Cf **a-, be-, of-, ofer-**.

Gerasenorum (territory) of the Gadarenes (Syria). II.23.148.

Germanus bishop of Capua in the early sixth century. II.11.528.

Geropolis Hierapolis, town in Asia Minor. II.17.44.

gesthus n. *inn, room for guests*. I.2.20; 5.26; II.11.228; 13.186. [13 ex.]

Gezabel Queen Jezabel, wife of Ahab king of Israel. I.32.183.

get see **geat**.

geu see **iu**.

gi- see also **gy-**.

Giezi servant of the prophet Elisha. I.27.212 ff.

gif conj. *if*. I.1.52; 2.99; II.praef.35; 1.228. **gyf** 6x. [691 ex.]

gifan vb 5. *to give*. II.30.220 (pret.pl. **geafon**); 40.171 (pret.s. **geaf**). Cf **a-, for-**.

gifernyss f. *greed, gluttony*. I.5.130; 11.38; II.12.484, 493. **gyfer-** 2x. [10 ex.]

gifta, gyfta n.pl. *wedding, marriage feast, marriage*. I.35.15, 40; 36.131; II.4.3; 6.130. nap. **-a, -u, -e** (I.35.6). [37 ex.]

giftlic, gyftlic adj. *nuptial, pertaining to a wedding*. I.35.20–22, 143, 151, etc; II.4.297.

gifu, gyfu f. *gift, grace*. I.praef.49; 9.230; II.1.168; 25.29; 34.48. nap **-e, -a** (I.13.106). [137 ex.]

gilp, gylp m. *boasting, showing-off*. I.8.57–9; 11.79 ff; II.12.525 ff; 13.182; **ydel gylp** *vain-glory* 12x. [26 ex.] Cf **gylpan**.

gilplic adj. *boastful*. I.11.77; II.12.93.

gingra, gyngra m. *disciple, follower*. I.praef.81; 21.4; II.14.28; 17.51. [20 ex.]

git see **gyt, þu**.

gitsere, gytsere m. *avaricious person, miser*. I.4.114–5; 8.192–3; II.19.287; 31.28. [9 ex.]

gitsiend, gyts- adj. *covetous, greedy*. I.4.168; 28.77.

gitsung, gyts- f. I.10.180; 11.105; II.5.112; 12.506. [41 ex.]

giu, iu adv. *formerly, long ago, already*. I.4.78; 22.111; II.10.46; 11.22. **geu** 1x, **giu** 6x, **gyo** 1x, **gyu** 1x, **iu** 6x. [15 ex.]

(ge)gladian vb II. *to be glad, rejoice*. I.3.119; 40.79; *appease, propitiate* I.3.162; II.2.131; *please, gladden* I.8.157; 24.74–5; II.4.178. [12 ex.]

glæd adj. *cheerful*. I.4.227; 30.225; 31.41; II.11.81; 12.373.

glædlice adv. *eagerly*. II.7.33.

glædnyss f. *gladness, delight*. II.12.372.

glæs n. *glass*. II.34.308.

glæsen adj. *glass, made of glass*. I.34.117; II.11.74, 418–9, 423–5.

gleaw adj. *wise*. I.18.145. Cf **fore-**.
gleawlice adv. *wisely, intelligently*. I.8.42; 26.93; II.4.115; 38.167.
gleawnyss f. *wisdom, intelligence*. I.20.150; 32.196; 38.165.
gled f. *burning coal*. I.29.208, 212–4; II.16.121.
gleng mfn? *adornment*. I.23.41.
geglengan vb I. *to adorn*. I.1.263; 6.112; II.1.279; 31.68. Pres.s.3 **geglencþ**; pp. **geglencged, geglengd, geglenged**. [21 ex.]
glida m. *kite* (bird, = Lat. *milvus*). I.38.149; II.3.184.
glidan vb 1. *to glide* (of a star). pret.s.3 **glad** I.5.25; 7.29, 108, 124. Cf **ofer-, to-**.
glig n. *entertainment*. I.32.122.
glowan vb 7. *to glow*. I.29.145.
gnagan vb 6. *to gnaw*. II.8.109. Cf **for-**.
gnæt m. *gnat, stinging insect*. II.12.59.
gnornian vb II. *to lament, grieve*. II.21.46.
gnornung f. *grieving*. II.5.158; 36.34.
god m. *God, a god*. referring to the Christian God, I.1.6; 2.22; II.1.9; 2.39; other gods, I.31.223; 37.203; II.28.140, 150; 33.9; in a more general attributive sense, I.22.201; 39.82; II.22.73; 32.125. nap. **godas**. [c.2600 ex.]
god n. (a) in sing., *good* (in abstract sense), *goodness, good action, benefit*. I.1.135; 28.191–3; II.20.135; 40.29. [c.67 ex.] (b) in pl., *goods, belongings, wealth, blessings*. I.4.269; 19.232; II.7.64, 66; 19.141. [c.20 ex.] (The two senses, together with the noun 'God' and the adjective, are frequently the subject of rhetorical and semantic play, and are not always easy to distinguish.) **good, good-** 5x; often written **gód** in MS K, and so printed in CH II.
god adj. *good*. I.1.27; 2.31; II.3.29; 4.39. **goddra** 13x, **goddre** 9x; **good, good-** 12x; often written **gód** in MS K, and so printed in CH II. [c.253 ex.]
godcund adj. *divine*. I.3.68; 7.54; II.3.8; 7.19. [35 ex.]
godcundlic adj. *divine, belonging to God*. I.2.173; 5.124; II.4.287; 5.119. [17 ex.]
godcundlice adv. *as God, in divine terms*. I.10.152.
godcundnyss f. *divinity*. I.2.184; 4.190; II.1.32; 3.127. [83 ex.]
godewebb n. *fine clothing*. I.4.79; 23.5, 39; AppB2.10.
godfæder m. *god-father*. II.3.253, 272–4; 8.126.
(ge)godian vb II. *to improve*. (intrans.) I.8.79, 84; *to bless, enrich, endow*. I.1.162; 30.257; II.9.36; 32.22; 40.305. [9 ex.]
godnyss f. *goodness, virtue*. I.2.46; 3.123; II.3.113; 4.40. **good-** 4x. [47 ex.]
godspel n. *Gospel, gospel teaching, gospel passage*. I.praef.60; 2.97; II.5.34; Explic.6. **godd-** I.AppB2.46; **gospel** I.6.3. [142 ex.]
godspelbodung f. *teaching expressed by the Gospels*. I.22.33; 25.83.
godspellere m. *evangelist*. I.2.8; 4.3; II.4.2; 6.115. [68 ex.]
godspellic adj. *evangelical, pertaining to the Gospels*. I.praef.53; 2.4; II.4.2; 7.129. [28 ex.]
godspeltraht m. *Gospel exposition*. II.Explic.6.
gold n. *gold*. I.praef.93; 4.87; II.7.87; 9.40. [51 ex.]
goldhord m. *treasure*. I.4.61; 7.229; II.4.221; 6.47. [11 ex.]
goldsmiþ m. *goldsmith*. I.4.93.
goma m. *gum, palate*. II.36.44.
Gomorra city of Gomorrah. I.18.38.
Gordianus Roman senator and father of Gregory the Great. II.9.14.
goretan vb I. *to gaze, stare about*? **goretende** I.35.191.
grad m? *step*. II.34.217.
gram adj. *angry*. II.30.181.
grama m. *anger*. I.praef.77; 1.36; II.1.239; 9.74. [22ex.]
gramlic adj. *angry*. I.29.141; II.2.197.
gramlice adv. *angrily, fiercely*. I.35.108.
granung f. *groaning*. I.4.152.
grapian vb II. *to touch, feel*. I.15.54; 16.18, 20, etc; 21.113; II.10.40.
grapiendlic adj. *palpable, capable of being touched and felt*. I.16.40–1.
grapung f. *touching*. I.16.95–7.
Graton a pagan philosopher; for Latin Craton. I.4.54 ff.
grædelice adv. *greedily*. I.4.124; 14.190; II.34.278.
grædig adj. *greedy, covetous*. I.14.172 (**grædian**), 174; 37.226; AppB3.160; II.12.507; 38.61.

grædignyss f. *avarice.* I.AppB3.147; II.15.294; 26.107–9.
græft m. *sculpture, carving.* I.31.160.
great adj. *large.* I.3.127.
Grecas the Greeks. I.26.287; 30.13.
Grecisc Greek (language or people). I.3.92; 6.134; 22.124, 176; 30.10; 32.47; 34.266; II.4.52; 9.17; 14.232; 32.92.
Grecland Greece. I.37.35.
Gregorius Gregory the Great, pope, c.540–604. I.praef.16; 15.74, 143; 16.27–9; 21.110; 23.29, 135, 155; 24.16, 147; 28.17, 106, 194; 35.26, 219; 40.20; II.5.34, 187; 6.33, 143, 167; 9 passim; 11.326; 13.43; 15.168–70; 16.40, 130; 21.115, 177; 23.21; 29.124; 36.16; 37.21, 164, 176; 38.38; 39.26. as. **gregorium**, gs. **gregories**. [66 ex.]
(ge)gremian vb II. *to anger.* I.6.165; 19.138; II.23.192; 30.87; *provoke, revile?* II.14.120. [15 ex.]
grene adj. *green.* I.4.87; 34.107.
grennyss f. *greenness.* I.21.125 (= Lat. *viriditas*); AppB3.207 (**grænnysse**); II.21.60 (= *green plants?*).
greot n. *grit, earth.* I.4.254.
(ge)gretan vb I. *to greet.* I.1.238; 13.103, 179; II.10.34, 154; 35.108. [9 ex.]
greting f. *greeting.* I.13.50, 171, 176; 27.35.
gretingword n. *word used for greeting, salutation.* I.13.47.
grim adj. *terrible.* II.34.279.
grimetian vb II. *to howl, roar.* II.21.46; 30.36 (**grym-**); 33.144, 218.
grimlic adj. *terrible, fierce.* I.31.7; II.21.27.
grin nf? *noose.* II.2.121, 196; 14.154.
grindan vb 3. *to grind.* I.32.200 (**grintst**).
(ge)gripan, gegrypan vb 1. *to seize, snatch.* I.5.101; 25.153, 181; II.9.119; 34.279. [9 ex.]
growan vb 7. *to grow.* I.21.159; 40.118; II.1.53, 55 (pret.s. **greow**); 10.180. [8 ex.]
grund m. *sea-bed, river-bottom, sea-depths.* I.37.116; II.10.82; 12.91, 100, 388; 18.30; 34.276. Cf **helle-, sæ-**.
grundlinga, grundlunga, -ge adv. *to the ground.* I.4.208; 28.54; II.4.215; 11.174.
grundweal m. *foundation.* I.26.66, 71; II.40.225–31, 251.
gryre m. *terror.* I.31.234.
guþfana m. *war-standard.* II.18.17.
gy- see also **gi-**.
gyddian vb II. *to prophesy?* I.28.147.
gyddung f. *prophetic saying.* I.35.79; 36.44; 39.9; II.23.32; 27.123; *discourse* (in verse) II.10.6.
gyden(u) f. *goddess.* I.29.151 (dp. **gydenum**).
gyhþa m. *itching.* I.5.134.
gyld n. *temple, shrine, worship* (in phrase **þæt hæþene gyld** etc.). I.29.267; 31.210; II.33.106; 34.184. See **deofol-, hæþen-**.
gylden adj. *golden.* I.4.161; 10.159; II.4.220; 28.101. [16 ex.]
gylpan vb 3. *to boast.* pres.pt. **gylpend-** II.13.120; 28.55.
gylt m. *sin, offence.* I.1.116; 3.171; II.5.223; 20.78–9. [45 ex.]
gyman vb I. *to take care (of), pay heed to.* w.gen.object. I.4.19; 24.21; II.2.196; 10.118. [29 ex.] Cf **be-, for-**.
gymeleas adj. *careless, negligent.* I.praef.130; 3.190; 17.71 (**gime-**); II.praef.45.
gymeleaslice adv. *carelessly.* II.2.53.
gymeleast f. *neglect, negligence.* I.4.29; 14.120; II.2.7; 4.296. **gime-** 2x. [21 ex.]
gymen f. *care, diligence.* I.1.294; 24.132; II.14.268; 15.311. **gim-** 3x. [16 ex.]
gymend m. *protector.* I.34.32.
gymm m. *gem, jewel.* I.4.90; 30.226; 31.69, 72; II.9.40; 40.186. (pl. only).
gymstan m. *jewel.* I.4.48 ff (11x); II.40.151, 182, 241. **gim-** 2x.
gymwyrhta m. *jewel-worker.* I.4.94.
gynan vb I. *to drive back.* I.AppB3.195.
gynian vb II. *to yawn, gape.* I.10.127 (**gin-**); II.11.383; 34.205.
gyrd f. *rod.* I.4.86–7; II.1.49 ff; 11.114; 12.90. [16 ex.] Cf **cyne-**.
gyrdel m. *girdle, belt.* I.5.132; II.21.104.
gyr(e)la m. *dress, garment.* I.5.185; 18.186; 21.21; II.11.113; 40.190. dp. **-um, -an**.
gyrnan vb I. *to desire.* w. gen. I.9.102, 124; 23.117; 27.224; II.30.46; 40.170.
gyrstandæg, gyrston- adv. *yesterday.* I.3.195, 199; 8.124; II.16.91; 33.118.
gyse interj. *truly?* I.1.75.
gysternlic adj. *previous* (day). I.32.224.
gyt adv. *yet, still.* I.1.86; 2.16; II.4.9; 5.107. **gyta** I.40.38. [110 ex.] See also **þu**.
gyte m. *shedding* (of blood). I.5.159; 36.102; II.14.194; 20.148; *pouring* II.11.505. [7 ex.]

gyts- see **gits-**.

habban vb III. *to have, hold, possess, preserve*. I.praef.95; 1.28; II.1.23–4; 2.41; **beon gehæfd**, *to be, to be considered to be, to be identified as* I.33.131, 134; II.18.104; 34.61; **yfele gehæfd**, *severely ill* II.10.37, 278; 32.15; as auxiliary with pp. I.1.84; 5.59; II.1.80; 3.278. Pres.s. **hæbbe, hæfst, hæfþ**; pl. **habbaþ**; subj. **hæbbe, habbon**; imp. **hafa, habbaþ**; pres.pt. **hæbbende**; infl.inf. **hæbben(n)e**; pret. **hæfde, hæfdon**; pp. **gehæfd**. [504 ex.] Cf **æt-, be-, for-, wiþ-**.

hacela m. *cloak, coat*. I.3.53; II.5.202.

had m. *office, rank, order, ordination, status, person (of Trinity etc.)*. I.1.20; 3.87; II.3.233; 19.91. [59 ex.]

gehadian vb II. *to appoint, ordain* (priests etc.). I.3.4, 12; 31.236; 37.11; II.9.106, 227; 17.41; pp. as adj., *clerical, religious, denoting those in holy orders (including nuns)* II.6.136; 20.244; 32.171; 40.302. **hadodon** (pret.pl.) II.33.157. [23 ex.]

hadung f. *ordination, appointment*. I.31.239; II.1.164; 9.109.

hafenleas adj. *destitute, poor*. II.10.271; 11.396, 403; 19.73; 25.83. [10 ex.]

hafenleast f. *poverty*. I.8.134; 23.56; II.6.45; 7.69. [14 ex.]

hafitian vb II. *to flap wings?* II.14.76.

hagelstan m. *hailstone* (but here denoting the stones used to kill St Stephen). I.3.128.

hagol m. *hail*. II.12.69, 73; 21.27.

hal adj. *healthy, healed*. I.praef.80; 8.86; II.2.162; 32.48; **sy ðu hal** as salutation, I.38.296; II.14.202. [20 ex.] Cf **un-, wan-**.

gehal adj. *whole, sound, undamaged*, (of objects) II.2.90; 11.17, 204; (of persons) II.1.260; **on gehalum þingum**, *in a healthy state, while healthy?* II.21.74.

(ge)halgian vb II. *to consecrate, sanctify, bless, treat as holy*. I.29.100; 31.151; II.1.163; 15.76, 82, etc. [69 ex.]

halgung f. *making holy, blessing, consecration*. I.19.188–90; 34.79; II.4.121; 15.106; 40.61.

halig adj. *holy*. I.1.19; 2.73; II.1.3; 2.2; **se halga**, *the holy one, the saint* (esp. in allit. prose); **se halga gast**, *the Holy Spirit* (238 ex.). **hali** I.31.314; wk. forms **halga**, etc; **helgan** I.35.46. [1012 ex.]

haligdom m. *relic*. I.18.41; *sanctuary* II.12.432.

halignyss f. *holiness*. I.22.212; 24.190; 25.83; II.40.137–9. [9 ex.]

haligreft n. *veil*. II.32.165, 173.

halsian vb II. *to beseech*. I.praef.129; 29.104, 172, 274; II.praef.43; 10.215; *exorcise?* I.4.225; *adjure, command on oath* I.26.240; II.14.122 (**gehalsode**); 33.162. [14 ex.]

halwenda m. *saviour*. I.9.36, 132.

halwende adj. *healing, salutary*. I.5.143; 25.63; II.14.326; 34.73. [24 ex.]

halwendlic adj. *healing, salutary*. I.14.153; II.12.518; 39.44.

halwendlice adv. *salutarily, with salutary effect*. I.6.61; II.14.65.

ham m. *home*. ds. **hame** I.29.45, 230, 276; otherwise always as endlingless locative **ham**, in adverbial function after verbs of motion, *home, homewards* I.4.43; 5.45; II.2.63; 4.159. [36 ex.]

hamcyme m. *homecoming, return*. I.5.62.

hamwerd adv. *on the way home*. I.38.341.

hana m. *cock*. II.14.76, 137.

hancred m. *cockcrow, dawn*. I.4.252; II.20.49, 54; 24.65.

hand f. *hand*. I.1.12; 5.159; II.1.194; 4.146; *side* I.21.225; II.20.42; etc.; *possession, control* I.19.173; 30.25; II.6.204; 30.59; **on hand gan**, *to yield* I.28.51. ds. **handa, hand** (I.21.106); nap. **handa**. [157 ex.]

hand adv. *exactly*. In phrase **hand swa gelice**, *exactly the same* II.3.38; 5.12.

handbred n. *palm of the hand*. II.10.81; 11.479; 14.118. ap. **-du**.

handclaþ n. *towel*. I.29.171.

handcræft m. *skill or power of the hands*. I.27.115; II.6.202.

handgeweorc n. *handiwork, creation, something made by the hands*. I.4.167; 13.12; 26.41; 37.171; II.14.331; 30.56.

handgewrit n. *signed agreement*. I.30.191.

handhwil f. *moment, point of time*. I.21.13.

handlinga, handlunge adv. *with his own hands*. I.27.12; II.11.469.

handsex n. *knife*. II.15.163.

hangian vb II. *to hang* (intrans.). I.26.260; 38.267; II.13.290; 14.244; *depend* II.19.19. [18 ex.]

harwenge adj. *grey-haired.* I.26.173; 31.35.
hat adj. *hot.* I.4.25; 28.49; II.1.229; 14.273. [9 ex.]
hatan vb 7. *to order, command.* I.1.78; 4.42; II.2.209; 10.235; *to name, call* I.1.251; 6.149; II.8.95; 35.19; *to be called* (**hatan**) I.1.90; *is called, was called* (**hatte**) I.1.225–6; 12.14; II.5.237; 13.96. Pres.s.1 **hate**; 2 **hætst**; 3 **hæt, hætt**; pl. **hataþ**; pret. **het, heton**; pp. **gehaten**; passive pres. and pret.s. **hatte**. Pret.s. **gehet** 2x (I.6.34; 38.157). [443 ex.] Cf **be-**.
hatheortnyss f. *rage, anger.* I.25.163; 29.155; II.2.117; 27.63, 78.
gehathyrtan vb I. *to become angry.* I.30.216; pp. **gehathyrt**, *angered, angry* I.29.54; 31.206; II.11.380; 23.78. [8 ex.]
hatian vb II. *to hate.* I.3.179; 7.132; II.19.194; 33.52. [22 ex.]
hatung f. *hatred.* I.5.105; II.12.504.
hawian vb II. *to look, take heed.* I.23.83; II.24.223; 29.77.
hæfen f. *possession, property, wealth.* I.38.76, 110, 140; II.25.83.
gehæftan vb I. *to make captive, take prisoner, fetter.* I.11.175–6; 15.131; II.4.231; 21.171. [15 ex.]
hæft m. *captivity, imprisonment.* II.24.7.
hæftling m. *captive, prisoner.* I.7.99; 15.179; II.4.87, 217; 21.159; 29.85.
hæftned f. *captivity, fetter.* I.23.165 (**-nydum**); 35.103; 36.142; AppB3.34; II.5.241; 17.8.
hæftnung f. *captivity, fettering.* II.5.251; 21.169.
Hægmon Haymo of Auxerre (d. 865–6). I.praef.16; 8.15; 34.155.
hæhtum see **æht**
hæl f. *health, salvation.* I.2.101; 8.113–4; II.2.85; 17.11. (On gender see Godden 1980.) [32 ex.]
gehælan vb I. *to heal.* I.praef.82; 4.57; II.2.154; 24.250. **hælð** II.32.50. [134 ex.]
hælend m. *the Saviour.* I.2.42; 3.64; II.1.2; 4.5. Used instead of the name Jesus; occasionally occurs without article or possessive. **hælend crist** I.2.25, II.4.162; etc. (60 ex.). Usu. declined as noun, but **hælendum criste** 8x and **hælendne crist** 1x. [505 ex.]
hælþ f. *health, healing, act of healing, salvation.* I.8.115; 27.232; II.2.74; 24.242. [24 ex.]
hælu f. *health, salvation.* I.1.257; II.14.129; 20.192; 24.238; 25.98. **sy hælu** (as salutation), I.14.23, 138, 151 (**hælo**); 36.11. nads. **hælu**. [10 ex.]
hæman vb I. *to have sexual intercourse.* I.AppA1.17; II.12.144, 318–9. Cf **unriht-**.
hæmed n. *sexual intercourse.* I.9.212 (**hæmeð**); 21.214–7; II.1.77, 87; 4.285. [15 ex.]
hær n. *hair.* I.16.125; 23.43; II.3.20; 11.551. [11 ex.]
hære wk f. *hairshirt, sackcloth.* I.18.35; 37.164, 174; II.18.151; 34.298.
hærfest m. *autumn.* I.6.135.
hæs f. *order, command.* I.1.256; 4.45; II.1.241; 4.14. [66 ex.]
hæte wk f. *heat.* I.5.128; II.5.27; 6.80, 83; 15.87. [12 ex.]
hæter n. *garment.* I.23.53; 26.143; 28.48 (**hętera**). ap. **-a, -u**.
hætu f. *heat.* I.20.103, 107, 151–3; 35.195. nas. **hætu**.
hæþen adj. *heathen, gentile* (i.e. non-believers in God; used in opposition to Jews or to Christians). I.3.39; 4.210; II.1.217, 222; 2.22. [101 ex.]
hæþengyld n. *idolatry* I.4.207; 30.204; II.4.212; 40.282; *heathen shrine.* I.31.31; II.1.226; 34.161; *heathen god?* II.11.173 (**-gild**). [15 ex.]
hæþengylda, -gilda m. *idolator, heathen priest.* I.4.196, 212 ff; 31.232; II.17.6; 33.33. [22 ex.] Cf **deofol-**.
hæþenscipe m. *heathen faith, paganism.* I.4.195; 14.44; II.1.238; 8.23. **-scype** 1x. [14 ex.]
hæþung f. *heating.* I.20.153.
he, heo, hit, hi pers. pron., 3. *he, she, it, they; himself, etc.* Forms: (m.) **he; hine** (**hyne** 8x); **his** (**hys** 3x); **him**; (f.) **heo** (**hio** 2x); **hi**; **hire**; **hire**; (pl.) **hi** (**hie** I.11.12, **hy** 3x); **heora** (**hera** I.33.133, **hiora** I.1.279), **hyra**; **him**. [c2000 ex.]
heafod n. *head, chief.* I.10.159; 11.35–6; II.1.161; 2.35. ap. **heafda** (4x), **heafdu** (1x). [77 ex.] Cf **foran-, fore-, ofer-**.
heafodbiscop m. *high-priest.* II.27.142.
heafodburh f. *capital town, chief town.* II.9.204; 33.202.

heafodece m. *pain or illness of the head.* I.29.47; II.10.277.

heafodleahter, -or m. *capital sin.* I.8.60; 24.69; II.3.225; 12.480 ff. [19 ex.]

heafodman m. *ruler, governor.* I.3.22; 14.70; II.14.307; 20.183. [12 ex.]

heafodwyrhta m. *chief builder.* II.36.25.

heah adj. *high.* I.1.186; 11.21; II.4.303; 24.93; wk. forms **heag-**; sup. **hehst-** (**hext-** 1x). [22 ex.] Cf **unhyhst.**

heage adv. *high.* I.20.177.

heahengel m. *archangel.* I.1.22; 34.24 etc; II.1.21; 10.47. [41 ex.]

heahfæder m. *patriarch.* I.1.228; 3.32, 34; II.1.128; 5.67. [39 ex.]

heahgerefa m. *chief officer, prefect* (= Lat. *prefectus*). I.4.220; 26.161; 29.59; II.9.102. **-gereuan** 2x. [11 ex.]

heahnyss, heannyss f. (a) *height, altitude.* I.34.102; II.24.94; 26.93; 40.55; spelt **heah-** except at II.11.172. (b) **on heannysse, -um** *on high, in the heavens* (= *in excelsis*). I.2.30, 139; 5.52; 14.25; 38.115; *aloud*? I.33.30. (c) *high place* II.24.133. [16 ex.]

heahsetl n. *throne.* I.19.230; 36.126; II.10.232.

heahþegen m. *chief follower, officer* (= apostle). II.35.4.

heal f. *hall.* I.3.129; II.5.41; 10.231; 28.105, 141, 151.

(ge)healdan vb 7. *to hold, keep, preserve, maintain, guard.* I.1.183; 2.161; II.3.288; 4.12; *to regard, consider* I.22.247. Pres.s.2 **hylst,** 3 **(ge)hylt;** pret. **(ge)heold-;** pp. **gehealden.** [271 ex.] Cf **be-, mis-.**

gehealdsumnyss f. *observance, practice, rule.* I.18.5; 22.106; II.12.194; 15.309. **gehealt-** 2x. [9 ex.] Cf **ungehealdsum.**

healf f. *side.* I.15.90; 28.9; II.12.92; 16.159; esp. in phrase **on . . . healfe** (as. or ds.), **on . . . healfa** (ap.). [25 ex.]

healf adj. *half.* I.4.175; 32.18; II.11.396; 40.162; with intervening possessive, I.8.172; II.32.155; in numbers, **to feorðan healfan geare,** *for three and a half years,* I.praef.87; etc. [17 ex.]

healfunga adv. *partially.* I.8.104.

healic adj. *high* (literally or figuratively), *heavenly, holy.* I.1.231; 7.69; II.3.228; 5.273; *chief, major, great* (in negative senses) I.19.120; 24.51–3; II.14.34; 34.134. [57 ex.]

healice adv. *majestically, supremely, on high.* I.17.15; II.12.538; 14.12, 234; 19.65.

healicnyss f. *height, majesty.* I.7.77.

healt adj. *lame, limping.* I.1.256 (apparently distinguished from **lama**); 14.72; II.1.190; 23.15. [16 ex.]

hean adj. *lowly, poor.* I.4.111; 19.40.

heannyss see **heahnyss.**

heap m. *crowd, troop, gathering.* I.21.55; 22.111; II.10.22; 35.105. [23 ex.]

heard adj. *hard.* I.3.55; 6.194; II.10.192; 14.94. [20 ex.]

hearde adv. *severely, heavily, strongly.* II.10.302; 14.270, 308; 34.98, 327. (All in alliterative prose.)

heardheort adj. *heard-hearted, stubborn.* I.7.100; 15.180; 18.138; 25.219; II.14.294.

heardheortnyss f. *hard-heartedness, stubbornness.* I.18.150; 33.153; II.6.85–7; 12.251.

heardmod adj. *stubborn, unfeeling.* I.28.129.

heardmodnyss f. *hard-heartedness, lack of feeling.* I.18.137.

heardnebb adj. *having a hard beak.* II.10.185.

heardnyss f. *hardness.* II.10.173; of hearts or minds, II.9.115; 13.222; 16.52.

hearm m. *harm, damage, injury.* I.3.174; AppB3.72; II.35.29; 40.237, 253.

hearmcwydol adj. *disparaging, inclined to malicious speech.* II.11.337.

hearmian vb II. *to harm.* I.9.101; 27.79; AppB3.229.

hearpe wk f. *harp, harp-playing*(?). I.22.187.

heawan vb 7. *to cut, cut down* (branches, etc.). I.4.85; 6.194; 14.21, 133. Pret. **heowon;** pp. **geheawen.** Cf **a-.**

Hebær Heber, ancestor of the Hebrews. I.1.227.

hebban vb 6. *to lift up.* I.34.246. Cf **a-, an-, on-, upa-.**

hebreisc see **ebreisc.**

hedan vb I. *to pay heed to.* w. gen. I.23.68; II.8.109, 115; 36.98.

hefe m. *weight.* I.6.202; 20.161, 164; II.11.193; 40.205. [7 ex.]

hefig adj. *heavy.* **hefegum** II.34.54.

gehefian vb II. *to weigh down, burden.* pp. **gehefgode** II.1.290.

hefiglice adv. *severely, gravely*. II.19.231.

hefi(g)tyme adj. *burdensome, grave, severe*. I.3.175; 29.47; II.5.36; 19.184; 23.57. [12 ex.]

hefigtymnyss f. *burden*. I.40.120; II.37.168.

hege m. *hedge*. II.23.18, 100, 104; 30.49.

hehþ see **hon**

hel, hell f. *Hell*. I.praef.73; 1.170, 277, 288; 7.99; II.1.17; 4.233. ns. **hel** 3x, **hell** 2x, **helle** 1x. **helle fyr** *Hell-fire*, II.3.32; 19.147; 39.193. (It is unclear whether such forms, and the following, should be treated as compounds [cf BTA], and practice in the printed texts of CH I and II is not consistent.) [30 ex.]

Helias, Elias Elijah the prophet. I.11.185; 21.196; 25.18; 26.8, 28; II.7.13; 10.105; 14.6; 19.277. ags. **helian**, ds. **heliam**.

hellegeat n. *gate of Hell*. I.15.167–9; 26.13, 72–3. nap. **-gatu**.

hellegrund m. *depths of Hell*. I.9.56; 26.155.

hellesusl n. *torment of Hell*. I.1.292; 8.59; 24.80; 36.245; 40.155; II.37.98 (**helle susle**).

hellewite n. *torment or punishment of Hell*. I.1.44; 6.58; II.1.17; 3.289 (printed as **helle wite** in CH II). [22 ex.]

hellic adj. *hellish, pertaining to Hell*. I.2.96; 23.88; II.4.245; 5.132. [15 ex.]

helm m. *helmet*. II.12.472; 34.54; *crown* II.14.200, 217; 34.230, 236; *top, crown* (of tree) II.10.302. Cf **cyne-**.

(ge)helpan vb 3. *to help*. w. gen. or dat. I.11.212; 31.19; II.1.19; 8.81. Pres.s.3 **hylpþ, gehelpþ**; pret.s. **(ge)heolp**; pp. **geholpen**. [26 ex.]

helwara fp. *inhabitants of Hell*. I.2.120; 25.221; 27.217; 32.65–7, 80, 149; II.22.42 (**hell-**), 47. Cf **burh-** etc.

gehende adj. *close, near*. I.5.175; 22.84; II.20.179; 25.49. [20 ex.]

gehende adv. *near by, at hand*. I.37.72; II.11.61, 122; 34.179, 300–2.

gehende prep. w. dat.(?) *near*. II.34.133.

gehendnyss f. *neighbourhood*. **on gehendnysse**, *in the neighbourhood, near by* I.28.93; II.11.334, 488; 23.103.

hengen f. *cross, rack*. I.29.165, 175; 36.75; II.14.261; 18.90; *hanging* II.2.123. [7 ex.] Cf **rode-**.

Henoh see **Enoh**

heof m. *weeping, grief*. I.28.210.

heofen, heofon, heofonan strong m., strong and wk f. *Heaven, sky, firmament*. Strong m., I.1.9; 2.94; II.1.202; 3.108; strong f., I.19.58, 62; 35.34; II.3.72; 30.31; wk f., I.20.166; 35.29; II.19.288; 20.12; *that part of the sky which contains the sun*? I.19.58, 62; **heofenan rice** *the kingdom of heaven* (106x). (Strong f. marked only in ns., wk f. occurs only in agds.; clear instances of m. occur only in pl. except 2x (**heofenes geat** II.39.181, and possibly **oð heofon** I.22.114). [399 ex.]

heofenlic, heofonlic adj. *heavenly, of or from heaven*. I.praef.105; 1.233; II.1.294; 4.276. [256 ex.]

heofenwaru, heofonwaru f. *heavenly community, inhabitants of heaven*. I.2.119; 30.113, 117; II.22.47. Cf **burh-** etc.

heofian vb II. *to weep, lament*. I.5.153; 11.215; 28.111; II.27.128. [12 ex.]

heofonrice n. *the kingdom of Heaven*. I.10.169.

heofung f. *lamentation, mourning*. I.5.156; 24.74; II.5.260; 9.119. [11 ex.]

heofungtid f. *time of mourning*. II.5.271.

heolstor m. *hiding-place*. II.10.233.

heonon adv. *from here*. I.18.189; 21.78; II.10.92; 30.82 (**heonan**); *from this point of time* II.5.245. [9 ex.]

heononforþ adv. *henceforth, after this time*. I.1.200 (**heonun-**); 6.25; II.11.85; 15.144. [14 ex.]

heorcnian vb II. *to listen to*. I.23.23; 29.89; II.5.36; 6.57. [7 ex.]

heorcnung f. *listening, power of hearing*. I.1.258; 6.104; II.1.185; 39.42.

heord f. *herd*. I.34.11, 16; II.23.163.

heord- see **hyrd-**

heort m. *hart, stag*. II.1.190.

heorte wk f. *heart* (as seat of emotion and thought). I.1.32; 3.166; II.2.169; 6.66. [171 ex.] Cf **clæn-, heard-, lat-, mild-**.

heorþ m. *hearth*. II.15.10.

her adv. *here*. I.1.24; 8.148; II.1.205; 3.64. **her æfter** *after this* II.Expl.10; cf. I.16.103. **her bæftan** *after this* I.35.94; II.5.170. [90 ex.] See also **herwiþufan**.

herbufan adv. *above, before in this text*. II.13.54.

here m. *army*. I.28.42; 32.191; II.12.87; 15.30. gs. **heres**. [24 ex.]

Hereberhtus Northumbrian priest and hermit, friend of St Cuthbert. II.10.309 ff.

her(e)gung f. *ravaging, making war*. I.15.180; II.4.88.

heretoga m. *leader of an army*. I.5.19; 6.44 (Moses); II.18.8; 38.227. [22 ex.]

(ge)hergian vb. II. *to harry, make war*. II.1.225; 4.87; 28.99; *seize, take by force* II.4.244 (**geheregað**); 5.247?; 39.185.

herian vb I/II. *to praise*. I.2.28; 4.269; II.19.265; 28.121. Pres.s.3 **herað, hereð**; pret. **hered-, herod-**; pp. **gehered, -od**. [45 ex.]

heri(g)endlic adj. *praiseworthy*. I.3.194; 14.129–30; II.4.28; 26.55. [9 ex.] Cf **un-**.

herigendlice adv. *laudably*. II.9.20; 11.142; 38.215.

herinne adv. *inside here*. II.18.128.

Hermogenes, Hermoines magician converted by St James the apostle. II.27.7 etc.

Herodes the name of three successive kings in Palestine (cf II.24.42–6). (a) Herod the Great, king of the Jews 37–4BC. I.5.4 etc; 7.35 etc; 31.257; 32.35, 40; II.27.147(2nd ex.); (b) his son, ruling at the time of Christ's death and that of St John the Baptist (= Antipas). I.32.6, 33, 52–3, etc; II.14.170 etc; (c) grandson of the first king Herod, ruling at the time of St James the apostle's death and St Peter's arrest (= Agrippa I). I.35.101; 37.240; II.24.2, etc; 27.147(1st ex.). as. **herodem**; gs. **herodes**; ds. **herode**.

Herodias wife of King Herod II. I.32.7 etc. ads. **herodiaden**.

herto adv. *in addition to this, associated with this*. II.22.71.

herung f. *praise*. I.2.138; 4.55; II.2.163; 10.5. [42 ex.]

herwiþufan adv. *above, earlier in this text*. II.13.75; printed as 2 words, I.40.26, 151.

hete m. *hatred, hostility*. I.24.19.

hetelice adv. *fiercely, violently*. I.5.164; 26.245; 30.249; II.17.120; 34.172.

hetol adj. *hostile, hateful*. II.14.209; 18.22 (**hetelum**).

hextan see **heah**

hider adv. *here, to this place, to this world*. I.25.74; 31.45; II.12.27; 18.128. [12 ex.]

Hieremias the prophet Jeremiah. I.5.51; 26.8, 28; II.1.134, 182; 5.253. gs. **-ias**.

Hiericho the city Jericho. I.5.148; 10.11, etc.; **iericho** II.12.389.

Hieronimus St Jerome, c.345–420. I.praef.15; 30.4 ff; II.18.3, 51; 29.2, 124.

Hierusalem Jerusalem. I.3.14; 5.11; II.1.143; 4.215. **hirus-** I.27.49; **iherus-** I.26.206; 37.158; 38.96; **ihrus-** I.37.179. [55 ex. in 25 texts]

Hiesus see **Iesus**.

higeleas adj. *thoughtless, foolish*. II.12.505.

hi(g)least f. *folly*. I.32.97; II.16.213.

hiht m. *hope*. I.1.219; 6.126; II.1.197; 19.229. **hyht** 1x. [40 ex.]

hihtan vb I. *to hope, trust*. II.19.230.

Hilarius St Hilarius of Poitiers, c.315–67. I.21.148 (app.crit.); II.34.60, 90–92.

hindan adv. *from behind*. I.34.58; II.18.122.

hingrian vb II. *to be hungry*. impers. w. dat. of person. I.11.11, 45; 13.199; II.7.147; 29.27. [10 ex.] Cf **of-**.

hird- see **hyrd-**

hired m. *household, family* (of a king, lord, patriarch). I.praef.119; 4.73; II.5.41; 14.175; *(religious) community* I.22.41, etc; AppB2.51(?); II.40.303, 306. **hiredes ealdor, hiredes hlaford** (= *paterfamilias*) 16x; **hyred-** 5x. [53 ex.]

hiredcniht m. *servant* (in a royal household). I.26.163.

hiredman m. *member of a (military?) community or household, soldier*? II.3.42 (**hiredmenn and cempan** = *milites*).

Hispania Spain. II.2.15; **ispanian** I.37.49.

Hispanienscis Spanish. I.29.193.

historia anglorum Bede's Historia Ecclesiastica. II.9.7; 21.1, 142.

hiþþ(u)? f. *benefit*. as. **hiððe** II.7.44.

hiw n. *appearance, form*. I.1.37, 129; 26.172; II.3.73; 15.153. **hywe** II.12.200. [68 ex.] Cf **scinn-**.

hiwan mp. *members of a family or household*. I.1.187; 29.230, 258, 261; II.2.64; 4.113 (**hiwon**).

hiwere m. *hypocrite, pretender*. II.26.24.

hiwian vb II. *to make (it) appear, to represent*. I.praef.106 (**gehiw-**); 34.175; II.7.85; 26.21; *form, fashion* II.11.551; pp. as adj., *feigned, apparent, simulated* I.28.83; 30.26; II.13.284–5. [16 ex.]

hiwisc n. *household.* I.22.6; 29.106, 252; II.3.80; 10.290.

hiwræden f. *household.* I.29.104; II.5.44; 8.13, 68; 21.5; 36.45.

hiwung f. *dissimulation.* I.7.261; 18.109; II.19.199; 26.29. **hywung** II.12.530. [8 ex.]

hladan vb 6. *to draw up, take up* (water or wine). II.4.16–19; 9.26; 11.438. Pret. **hlod, hlod-.**

hlaf m. *bread, loaf of bread.* I.2.81; 11.206; II.8.16; 11.147. [121 ex.]

hlafhus n. *bread-house.* I.2.81.

hlafmæsse wk f. *Lammas-day* (= 1 August). I.AppB2.11; II.24.52.

hlaford m. *lord, master, owner.* I.1.9; 2.210; II.6.100; 19.216, 221; 35.40–41. (Frequently used to render Biblical masters (*dominus, paterfamilias, etc*) who are types of Christ, but otherwise infrequently used of God or Christ.) [132 ex.]

hlafordscipe m. *lordship* (= Lat. *dominatio*, one of the nine orders of angels). I.24.91, 124, 130; 40.61.

hlænnyss f. *leanness, thinness.* I.35.73.

hleaht- see **leahter**

hleapan vb 7. *to leap, spring.* I.32.118; II.1.190. Cf **æt-.**

hleapung f. *leaping, springing.* I.32.88, 181.

hleor n. *cheek.* II.20.207.

hleotan vb 2. *to cast lots for, gain by lot.* II.12.572.

hleoþrian vb II. *to proclaim.* I.2.136.

hleowþ f. *shelter.* II.10.193; 31.44.

hlid n. *lid.* I.15.85; II.14.345.

hlihan vb 6. *to laugh (at).* I.11.215; 26.166; II.21.48; 33.26, 28. Pres.pl. **hlihgað, hlihað**; pret.pl. **hlogon.** [8 ex.]

hlisa m. *fame.* I.15.81; 25.127–9; II.11.25; 39.77. **hlysan** II.39.74. Cf **woruld-.**

hlisful adj. *famous.* II.10.161; 12.526 (**lisful**); *praise-worthy, bringing fame.* II.16.82.

hlosnian vb II. *to spy on.* w. gen. II.10.76.

hlowan vb 7. *to low, bellow.* I.38.214.

hlud adj. *loud.* I.4.238; 26.119; 29.186; II.4.145. [7 ex.; all **hlud(d)re stemne.**]

hlude adv. *loudly.* I.7.42; II.12.228; 21.48; 34.312.

hludswege adv. *loudly.* II.14.137.

hluttor adj. *pure, clear.* I.4.11; 29.16; 34.116; 36.92; II.20.194; 26.145.

hluttornyss f. *purity.* I.36.21; AppB3.228.

gehlyd m. *noise.* II.14.191; 20.52, 72; 34.156; 37.165.

hlyda m. *March.* I.6.150.

hlyst m. *the sense of hearing.* I.9.69; 36.109; II.23.45; 38.47. [9 ex.]

hlystan vb I. *to listen to.* w. gen. or dat. I.3.155; 26.178; II.6.190; 17.11. [10 ex.]

hlystere m. *listener.* II.4.54.

hlyte m. *portion, lot.* I.24.150. Cf **or-, efenhlytta.**

hlywan vb I. *to cover, clothe.* pp. **gehlywde** II.30.45.

hnappian vb II. *to sleep, doze.* I.5.139; II.13.107; 39.10, 95.

hnecca m. *neck.* II.11.461.

hnesce adj. *soft, delicate.* I.39.37; II.12.502; 23.52.

gehnexian vb II. *to soften.* II.6.104.

gehnipum see **genip**

hnol m. *crown of the head.* II.14.243; 30.118; 32.212; 34.242.

hnutu f. *nut.* ap. **hnyte** II.1.53, 56.

hoc m. *hook.* I.25.214.

gehoforod pp. as adj. *humpbacked.* II.40.197.

hogu f. *care.* as. **hoge** I.8.184; 30.176.

hogian vb II. *to think, consider, take care.* I.2.159; 3.191; II.9.21, 120; 20.185. Cf **for-, ofer-, ymb-.**

hoh n. *heel.* **æt þam hon** *close behind* II.12.93.

hohful adj. *anxious, full of care.* II.10.310, 314.

hol n. *hole.* I.10.146.

hold adj. *loyal, faithful (*of an inferior*); caring, supporting* (of a superior*).* I.11.67; II.4.256; 18.121; 19.102. [10 ex.] Cf **un-.**

holdlice adv. *lovingly, protectively.* II.22.156.

holdræden f. *loyal service.* II.10.301.

holian vb II. *to scoop out, hollow out.* I.34.150; II.10.173; 11.131.

holt nm. *a wood.* I.26.286 (app.crit.); II.18.59; 34.281.

hon vb 7. *to hang.* I.AppB2.12 (pres.s.3 **hehð**); II.14.229 (infl.inf. **honne,** pret. pl. **hengon**); 18.90. Cf **a-, oferhangen.**

hopa m. *hope.* I.24.207; 37.160.

hopian vb II. *to hope.* II.16.13; 27.59; *hope for* I.18.112, 120 (w. gen.); **hopian to** *trust in, hope for* I.18.117; II.29.101; 39.189; **hopian on** *trust in* I.18.201.

hoppestre wk f. *female dancer.* I.32.121.

hoppian vb II. *to leap, jump.* I.13.177.

hordere m. *cellarer, steward.* II.11.419–20, 429.

hordfæt n. *casket, treasure-box.* ap. **-fatu** I.5.29; 7.32, 204.

hordian vb II. *to hoard, amass.* I.4.118–9; II.7.87, 99, 106.

[horh] mn. *stain, defilement.* dp. **hor(e)-wum** II.4.55; 14.34; 30.167.

horig adj. *dirty.* I.31.36, 262; 35.155.

horn m. *horn* (of an animal). I.35.68; II.4.150.

hors n. *horse.* I.29.262; II.10.32 ff; 18.30; 33.220. [7 ex.]

hosp m. *scorn.* I.3.181; 4.35; II.8.4; 13.117. [26 ex.]

hosplic adj. *scornful.* II.13.164.

hospspræc f. *scornful speech.* II.34.250.

hospword n. *scornful comment.* II.13.107, 148.

hraþe adv. *quickly, soon.* I.14.128; 19.113; II.6.88; 14.79; **swa hraþe swa** *as soon as*, I.1.109; II.11.248; etc. **raþe, raþor** 3x. [40 ex.]

hræd adj. *quick.* I.40.182.

hrædlic adj. *quick, premature.* I.5.88.

hrædlice adv. *quickly, soon.* I.1.177; 2.186; II.3.76; 9.200. [38 ex.]

hrædnyss f. *speed, swiftness.* II.11.394, 460.

hrægel n. *clothing.* I.31.262; II.31.71.

hream m. *noise, shouting, calling.* I.18.51; 28.206; II.11.181; 12.44.

hreaw adj. *raw.* II.15.16, 273–5.

hreaw mn. *corpse.* I.26.251; II.20.232.

hreddan vb I. *to rescue.* I.22.16. Cf **a-**.

hredding f. *salvation.* I.13.73; 17.36; 35.247.

gehrefan vb I? *to roof.* I.1.186.

hrem(m) m. *raven.* II.3.184; 10.105, 184 ff; 11.144, 147.

hremman vb I. *to hinder.* I.4.53; 27.146; 38.238; II.33.105 (**gehremman**); *encumber* I.10.70; II.26.77. Pres.s.3 **hremð**; pret.s. **hremde**.

hreod n. *reed.* II.14.201.

hreofla m. *leprosy.* I.8.10, 28, 78; 27.245 (**reoflan**), 247; *a leper* I.8.30, 35; 27.226.

hreoflig adj. *leprous.* I.8.81; 23.140; II.27.19; 34.211. Forms: **hreoflia, hreoflian, hreoflig-, hreofline, hreoflinne, hreoflium; reofl-** (7x). [28 ex.] Cf **un-**.

hreoh adj. *rough, turbulent.* I.12.32.

hreohnyss f. *turbulence, storm.* II.1.210; 23.132; 24.91, 214–5; **reohnys-** I.18.18, 26.

hreosan vb 2. *to fall.* I.26.246; 28.145; II.30.78; 34.172–4. Pres.s.3 **hryst**; pret.s. **hreas**. [7 ex.] Cf **a-, niþer-, of-**.

hreowlic adj. *sorrowful, grievous.* I.21.120; 31.196.

hreowlice adv. *wretchedly, grievously, in a manner causing pain or grief.* I.31.57; 32.41; 35.98; II.21.46.

hreppan vb I. *to touch.* I.1.72; 8.9; II.2.161; 24.84–5; *to mention, refer to, deal with* I.4.176; 10.23; 18.143; II.Ex-Dict.16. Pres.s.3 **hrepað**; pl. **hreppað**; pret. **hrepod-, hreped-, gehrepode** (II.11.411); pp. **gehrepod**. [43 ex.] Cf **unge-**.

hre(p)pung f. *touch, touching.* I.8.33–4; 9.69; II.23.45, 51; 34.214. [15 ex.]

hreþe see **reþe**

hricg m. *back.* I.20.171; II.2.82; 18.122; 27.56.

hridder n. *sieve.* II.11.11, 15, 19.

hring m. *ring.* II.2.82, 87–90, 94. Cf **eag-**.

hriþian vb II. *to be feverish?* I.5.130.

hrof m. *roof.* I.1.206; 8.92; II.10.55; 11.510. [10 ex.]

hrofstan m. *roof-stone (i.e. stone forming a roof).* I.34.115.

hrose see **rose**.

hryman vb I. *to shout, call, cry out.* I.10.14, 78; 18.92; II.3.156; 17.16. [35 ex.]

hryre m. *fall, destruction, ruin.* I.2.57, 62; 3.102; II.1.68; 11.211. [18 ex.]

hryþer n. *ox.* I.28.88–90; 37.207. pl. **-u**.

hryþerhyrde m. *oxherd.* I.22.188.

hu adv. *how.* Modifying adj., adv. or vb. in direct or indirect questions or exclamations. I.1.42; 2.4; II.1.18; 6.189. As interj. alone or with **la**, introducing a question, I.24.8; 29.236; II.1.249; 5.28, 30. [276 ex.]

gehu adv. *in all sorts of ways.* II.15.95.

hulc m. *hut.* I.23.139; 36.107.

Humbre the river Humber. II.9.192.

humeta adv. *how, why.* I.27.42; 32.163; II.16.60; 18.94. [10 ex.]

hund m. *dog.* I.23.8; 26.142; II.8.16; 18.74. [22 ex.]

hund n. *hundred.* w. noun in g., I.1.168; 21.33; II.12.85; 16.124; w. noun taking its case from the context, II.11.299; 30.11, 205; 32.154. [20 ex.]

hundeahtatig num. *eighty*. I.9.10, 190; 32.217; II.9.160; 17.54. [9 ex.]

hundfeald adj. *hundredfold, a hundred times*. I.9.208; 24.25; II.6.32, 132; **be hundfealdum (-on)** *a hundredfold, multiplied by a hundred* I.27.132; II.6.13; etc. [15 ex.]

hundlic adj. *doglike*. I.26.195.

hundnigontig num. *ninety*. Usu. w. g. I.4.244; 6.40; 24.15, 47; II.1.150. [8 ex.]

hundred m. *a troop of hundred soldiers*. **hundredes ealdor** *centurion* I.8.88, etc; II.14.280, 305; 27.111. [12 ex.]

hundseofontig num. *seventy*. Usu. w. g. I.1.252 (**-syfentig**); 30.13; II.4.223; 5.241. [16 ex.]

hundseofontigfeald adj. *seventy-fold*. II.5.242, 249.

hundteontig num. *hundred*. w. g. I.6.40; 24.7 (**hunteontig**), 23, 26; 37.88; II.40.44.

hundtwelftig num. *one hundred and twenty*. II.40.62, 168.

hunger, hungor m. *hunger, famine*. I.4.28; 14.132; II.11.292; 12.31. [22 ex.]

hungergear m. *famine-year, season of famine*. II.11.416.

hungrig adj. *hungry*. I.11.207; 12.49; II.7.153; 11.331. Forms: **hungrian, hungrie, hungrigum, hungrine, hungrinne, hungrium**. [8 ex.]

hunig n. *honey*. I.15.59; II.1.89; 10.69; 12.366. [9 ex.] Cf **wude-**.

hunigswete adj. *sweet as honey*. ds. **-swettre** II.9.27.

hunta m. *huntsman*. I.38.23.

huntian vb II. *to hunt, chase*. I.38.23.

huntoþ m. *meat produced by hunting*. II.40.44.

huru adv. *especially, even, at least*. I.4.217; 11.141; II.1.284; 3.186. [18 ex.]

huruþinga adv. *at least*. I.28.215; II.5.125; 7.32.

hus n. *house, building*. I.4.44; 9.10; II.3.139; 4.298; often used for church or temple, esp. as **godes hus**. [103 ex.] Cf **gebed-, gest-, hlaf-, maþm-**.

Hus the land where Job lived. II.30.7.

husel n. *eucharistic bread*. I.2.84; 19.116; II.11.350; 15.4 etc. [45 ex.]

huselgang m. *going to, or participating in, the eucharist*. I.4.112; 34.108; II.3.231; 11.346. [9 ex.]

huselhalgung f. *attendance at the eucharist*. I.3.165; II.3.229. (Apparently equivalent to **huselgang**; cf. II.3.229–31.)

(ge)huslian vb II. *to administer the eucharistic sacrament to someone*. I.29.229–31; II.11.560; 20.55.

huslung f. *administration of the sacrament*. II.37.193.

huxlic adj. *shameful*. II.3.94; 13.46.

huxlice adv. *shamefully, scornfully*. I.3.72; AppB3.53, 160.

hwa mf., **hwæt** n. inter. pron. *who, what*. I.3.73; 11.40; 17.41–2; II.1.24; 10.100; 21.120; indef. pron. *someone, anyone, something, anything* I.3.141; 27.66; II.12.453; 40.235; **swa hwa swa, swa hwæt swa** *whoever, whatever* I.3.96; 9.61; II.9.182; 15.182; **to hwan** *to what benefit* I.12.15; II.28.91; 40.119; **to hwi** *for what reason* I.14.13; II.5.78; etc. Forms: **hwa, hwam, hwan, hwæne, hwæs, hwæt, hwi**. [c. 405 ex.]

gehwa mf. indef. pron. *everyone*. I.praef.133; 3.181; II.1.108; 13.70. **gehwæt** n. *everything* only at II.23.53. [62 ex.]

hwanon adv. *from where* (in direct or indirect questions). I.1.57, 170; 8.141; II.3.201; 30.22, 33. [10 ex.]

gehwæde adj. *small, slight*. I.5.112; 23.83; 34.138; II.11.127, 420; 35.96.

hwæl m. *whale*. I.18.28; 32.184 (**hweles**).

hwænne adv. *when* (in direct and indirect questions). I.9.42, 91; II.7.152 ff, 167; 11.31; 19.76. [12 ex.]

hwær adv. *where* (in direct and indirect questions). I.4.46; 5.11; II.4.141; 21.118. *somewhere, anywhere* I.11.74; *on some occasion*? I.32.111. **swa hwær swa** *wherever*. I.20 124; II.12.102; etc. [34 ex.]

gehwær adv. *everywhere*. I.9.38; 14.195; II.10.70; 17.41. [31 ex.]

hwærto adv. *to what place*. I.24.119.

hwæt interj. Used as first element (except **La hwæt** II.10.103). (a) introducing a question (usu. as **hwæt la**). I.29.233; 38.323; II.6.189. 11.320. (b) introducing a statement, usu. narrative, esp. as **hwæt þa**. I.6.159; 37.79; II.2.166; 5.187. [c.120 ex.]

hwæte m. *wheat*. I.35.130; II.10.179.

hwæten adj. *wheaten, made of wheat.* II.10.41.

hwæthwega adv. *somewhat, a little.* I.7.237; 24.184; II.2.155; 11.131. [9 ex.]

hwæþer pron. *which of two.* I.15.95; 18.191–3; II.14.187.

hwæþer conj. *whether.* I.11.40; 14.116; II.3.249; 5.109; **hwæþer (þe) . . . þe** *whether . . . or* I.1.170; II.9.62; 23.48; introducing direct question, I.9.43. [32 ex.]

hwæþere adv. *yet, nevertheless, however.* I.1.181; 6.191; II.1.43; 3.135. **hwæþre** 5x. [36 ex.] Cf **þeahhwæþere, swaþeahhwæþere.**

hwearftlian vb II. *to revolve, roam, wander.* I.27.134; 34.209 (**hwyrftlað**); 35.191.

hwelp m. *puppy.* II.3.266; 8.17, 87, 100, 105.

hwem m. *corner.* I.31.179; II.14.244; 28.81; 30.78. **hwemmas, hwemmum**. Cf **hwom.**

gehwemmed adj. *having corners or angles* (Lat. *angulosus*). I.34.101.

hwene adv. *a little.* **hwene ær,** *a little earlier.* I.29.18; 30.263; II.2.165; 6.90. **hwene æror** I.25.150. [9 ex.]

hweol n. *wheel.* II.2.53.

hweorfan vb 3. *to change, sink.* **gehworfen** (= Lat. *devolutum*) I.38.223. Cf **nig-.**

gehwettan vb I. *to urge, incite.* I.1.274.

hwi adv. *why.* I.1.130, 142; 3.60; II.5.14; 7.68. **hwy** II.24.209. For **to hwi** see **hwa, hwæt.** [81 ex.]

hwider adv. *to which place, where (to).* I.10.147; 29.270; II.2.106; 34.75; **swa hwider swa** *wherever, to whichever place* I.5.185; II.27.75; etc. **hweder** I.34.254; **hwyder** 3x. [17 ex.]

hwil f. *time, space of time.* I.1.68; 4.97; II.1.215; 6.25; **þa hwile þe,** conj. *while* I.1.42; 15.43; II.9.126; 12.458. [33 ex.] Cf **hand-, preowt-.**

hwilc, hwylc inter. pron. and adj. *which, what sort of.* pron. I.18.45; 40.103; II.13.16; 23.140; adj. I.3.135; 18.97; II.3.208; 9.60; indef. pron. and adj., *some, any*: pron. I.37.46; II.7.138; adj. I.34.233; II.1.77; 19.281; 34.253; **swa hwilc . . . swa** *whichever* I.6.64; II.32.103; etc. [77 ex.]

gehwilc, gehwylc pron. and adj. *each, every, all.* pron. I.2.71; 39.52; II.20.119; 35.69; adj. I.6.57; 8.60; II.6.3; 12.236. *many* I.30.73(?); II.15.86; 34.82, 278, 305. [96 ex.]

hwilon adv. *once, on one occasion, at times, sometimes.* I.11.144; 12.32–4; II.10.51; 29.1. [40 ex.]

hwiltidum adv. *at times, sometimes.* I.10.44; 28.157; II.12.429; 20.189. **-on** I.12.33. [16 ex.]

hwilwende adj. *transitory.* I.4.103; 32.194; II.35.116.

hwilwendlic adj. *transitory.* I.10.186; 11.32; II.13.282; 15.145. [28 ex.]

hwilwendlice adv. *temporally, fleetingly.* I.4.99; 10.161; 27.209; II.24.91.

gehwiss see **gewis**

hwit adj. *white.* I.5.185; 31.34; II.9.57; 11.551. Used of clothing, skin, hair, snow, lamb, etc. **þæt hwite,** *the white of an egg* I.2.183. [25 ex.] Cf **snaw-.**

hwitel m. *blanket.* II.11.213.

hwitnyss f. *whiteness.* I.30.129; II.14.10; 19.140.

hwom m. *corner.* **hwommas** I.8.160. Cf **hwem.**

hwon adv. *a little, slightly.* I.5.139; 15.148; 31.35; II.30.57; **na to ðæs hwon** *not for so little* II.9.166.

hwonlic adj. *little, slight.* I.2.135; II.36.108.

hwonlice adv. *little, slightly, briefly.* I.24.62; 28.71; II.5.125; 25.118. [11 ex.]

hwosan vb 7. *to cough.* pret.s. **hweos** I.5.130.

hwoþerian vb II. *to grumble, mutter?* II.24.146.

gehwyrfan vb I. *to change, turn.* trans., I.4.90; intrans., I.5.120; 28.149. Cf **hweorfan.**

hwyrftlian see **hwearftlian.**

hyd f. *skin.* II.11.54; 15.307; 30.167.

hydan vb I. *to hide.* II.11.279; 14.94. Cf **be-.**

[hyldu] f. *support, favour.* as. **hylde** I.37.23; II.10.303.

hyll f. *hill.* I.38.24.

hynan vb I. *to injure, afflict, oppress.* II.18.117; 34.164, 195; 37.76.

[hynþu] f. *injury, affliction.* I.24.59; 36.206.

hype wk f. *heap.* I.30.226; II.31.101. Cf **mold-.**

(ge)hypan vb I. *to heap up.* I.28.152.

hyr f. *hiring, wages.* II.5.26.

hyra m. *hireling*. I.17.5, 7 etc. [9 ex.]
gehyran vb I. *to hear, listen to*. I.praef.51; 2.37; II.1.171; 6.81; *to obey* (w. dat.) II.34.123; possibly I.7.43; *to belong* I.2.12, 70. **gehierdon** I.10.3. [239 ex.] Cf **of-**.
hyrde m. *guardian, shepherd*. I.praef.102; 2.21 ff; 34.243; II.13.106; 30.70. [91 ex.] Cf **hryþer-, scep-**.
hyrdeleas adj. *without a shepherd*. I.26.271.
hyrdeman m. *herdsman*. I.2.105; II.10.48, 301; 11.41.
hyrdel m. *iron frame, bed* (= Lat. *craticula*). I.29.224.
hyrdræden f. *guardianship, care*. I.34.248; II.15.311; 16.174; 22.171; 37.123. **heord-** II.6.103; **hird-** II.10.303.
(ge)hyrian vb I/II. *to hire*. II.5.5, 16, 83; w. prefix, II.5.20, 51, 86. Pret.s. **(ge)hyrde**, pp. **gehyred**.
hyrigman m. *hired worker*. II.5.6.
hyrman m. *hired worker*. II.5.9; 30.155.
hyrned adj. *horned*? I.6.180. Cf **eahta-**.
hyrnstan m. *corner-stone*. I.7.60, 69.
gehyrsum adj. *obedient*. I.1.76; 14.163; II.1.28; 11.150. [24 ex.]
gehyrsumian vb II. *to obey*. w. dat. I.1.51; 2.99; II.1.16; 5.193. **hyrsum-** I.24.155; II.22.172. [49 ex.]
gehyrsumnyss f. *obedience*. I.1.126; 3.34 (**-nesse**); II.3.102; 4.131. **hyrsumnysse** II.19.24. [19 ex.] Cf **unge-**.
gehyrtan vb I. *to encourage, hearten*. I.10.28; 15.101; II.1.187; 37.27. [15 ex.] Cf **gehat-**.
hyrwan vb I. *to scorn, revile*. I.29.126; 37.159 (**gehyrwde**); II.28.28; 32.47.
hysecild n. *male child*. I.5.48; 6.21; 9.8; II.12.40. [8 ex.]
hyþ f. *harbour*. II.29.68; 38.227.
[hyþþu] f. *gain, benefit*. agp. **hyþþa** I.17.49; 36.206.

For i- see also under y-
Iacob the patriarch Jacob. I.7.129; 8.99; II.5.186; 12.29; etc. nas. **iacob**; gs. **iacobes**; ds. **iacobe**. [16 ex.]
Iacob, iacobus (a) St James the apostle, son of Zebedee and brother of John the Evangelist (and cousin of Christ? see II.27.3 and note). I.15.17(n); 21.29; 28.27; 35.102; 38.9, 154; II.16.109; 24.4; 27.*passim*; 35.4; 37.138 ff; (b) the other apostle St James, identified with James the Righteous, leader of the church in Jerusalem after Christ's death (see introd. to II.17). I.21.31; 22.102; 28.28, 31; II.17.63, etc; 24.34; 35.5; (c) the author of the epistle of St James, identified by Ælfric with James the Righteous. I.21.140; 36.266; II.19.134. ns. **iacob, iacobus**; as. **iacob, iacobum**; gs. **iacobes**; ds. **iacobe**.
Iafeþ Japhet son of Noah. I.1.184.
ic pron. *I, me, we, us*. I.praef.44; 1.77; II.praef.29; 1.93. as. **me**; gs. **min**; ds. **me**; np. **we**; ap. **us**; gp. **ure**; dp. **us**; dual **wit** (5x), **unc** (5x). we as authorial plural, I.AppA1.1; AppA2.1; II.praef.41; 16.100–3. See also possessive adj. **min** and **ure**. [c.1582 s. + 2037 pl.]
geican, geycan vb I. *to increase, expand, add*. I.2.57–9; 6.34; 28.35; II.22.52; 31.11, 62. Pres.pt. **geyicende** I.2.55; pret. **geiht-, geyht-**; pp. **geyht**. [15 ex.]
Iericho see **Hiericho**
Iesus (a) Christ. I.6.9, 77; 13.53, 113 (**hiesus**); II.4.270; 12.418–20, 557; 35.110. (Ælfric generally treats **Jesus** as a Hebrew word, to be translated as **hælend**, and the examples here are all special cases.) (b) Jeshua, the high-priest who restored the temple in Jerusalem after the Babylonian exile. II.4.226, 268 (**hiesus**). (c) Joshua, leader of the Hebrews. II.12.418, 423. cf **Iosue**.
igdæges, ydæges adv. *on the same day*. II.11.224, 366.
igeoþ m. *island*. I.4.27.
igland n. *island*. II.9.168, 189; 10.164–71, 236, etc; 20.259; 21.2. [11 ex.]
Iherusalem see **Hierus-**
ile, yle m. *sole of the foot*. II.17.73; 30.118.
Iliricum the Roman province of Illyricum on the Adriatic. I.26.206
in, inn adv. *in*. I.5.28; 18.41; II.1.244; 36.10. [33 ex.]
in, inn n. *dwelling, lodging*. I.7.125; 26.136; AppB2.52; II.16.27; 33.142, 179.
in prep. *in*. II.29.28.
inc, incer see **þu**.
incniht m. *servant*. I.34.13.
incoþu f. *inner sickness*. II.38.236.
incund adj. *inner, internal*. I.24.162; 33.60; II.9.243; 12.556. [9 ex.]
India one of three eastern regions of this

name, distinguished at I.31.4–7; I.21.239; II.38.186.

Indisc Indian. I.31.32; 35.105; II.33.8, 31, 42.

infaran vb 6. *to enter*. I.8.92, 109; 30.54; II.6.96.

infær n. *entrance, mode of entry, access*. I.11.175; 26.81; II.9.114; 39.177. **innfær** I.1.288. [12 ex.]

inferan vb I. *to enter*. **inferde** I.3.130; 30.167.

ingan anom. vb. *to enter*. I.34.72, 94; 35.21; 37.111. (treated as 2 words in CH II; cf **inn eodon** II.12.396; **inn eode** II.11.241; 37.187)

ingang m. *entrance, entry*. I.9.9; 34.15, 38, 251.

ingehid, ingehyd f. *understanding, mind, inner thought or consciousness*. I.22.110; 24.139; II.4.54; 15.280. **inngehyd** I.AppB3.183. [34 ex.]

innan adv. *within, inwardly*. I.5.128; 35.164; II.3.56.

inne adv. *inside, within*. I.30.239; 33.87; II.2.140; 3.140. [10 ex.]

innewe(a)rde n. *intestines*. I.20.226; II.15.17, 285, 292.

innewerd, innweard, inwe(a)rd adj. *inward, inmost*. I.8.57; AppB3.244; II.5.225; 9.64. [12 ex.]

inneweardlic, innwerdlic adj. *inward, inner*. I.17.39; 19.153.

geinnian vb II. *to make good, compensate for*. I.1.62; 11.219; 24.58; 36.143; *to provide lodging for* II.32.116.

innon prep. w. dat. *within, inside*. I.15.34; 26.136; 35.127.

innoþ m. *womb*. I.1.175; 2.213; II.1.71; 12.294; *stomach, intestines* I.5.135; 20.228; II.14.165; 32.214. [37 ex.]

geinnsegelian vb II. *to seal shut*. II.14.352.

inra adj. *inner*. I.8.41, 46; 33.19; II.11.56; 24.223. [10 ex.]

insegl n. *seal*. I.15.13.

insiht f. *perception*. I.38.221, 229.

instæpe m. *entrance, threshold*. I.5.100.

instæppan vb 6. *to enter*. II.37.172.

intinga m. *cause, reason, matter, sake*. I.5.96; 13.70; II.2.156; 14.231. [21 ex.]

into prep. w. dat. *into*. I.1.292; 9.33; II.1.240; 3.96; *in amongst?* I.1.188; 16.5, 16, 28; II.18.128 (perhaps better interpreted as 2 words). **innto** II.11.196, 432. [141 ex.]

inwe(a)rdlice adv. *inwardly, from the heart*. I.4.15; 26.216; 37.269; 38.136; II.35.43.

Ioachim father of the Virgin Mary. II.DSM.4.

Iob Job. I.praef.100; 22.160; 31.280–3; 35.204; II.19.253–6; 30.2, etc.

Iohannes (a) St John the Evangelist. I.4.*passim*; 11.123; 30.32 ff; 37.246–8; 38.9, 155; II.14.264 ff; 16.105 ff; 28.69; 37.139. [70 ex.] (b) St John the Baptist. I.13.165 ff; 23.42; 25.*passim*; 32.*passim*; 34.74; II.3.*passim*; 4.313; 11.176. [93 ex.] (c) one of the mission to convert England. II.9.172; (d) one of the seven sleepers. II.27.187. as. **iohannem**; gs. **iohannes**; ds. **iohanne**.

Iohel the prophet Joel. I.22.59.

Ionas the prophet Jonah. I.18.14; 32.184.

Iordanis the river Jordan. I.5.142; 28.32; II.3.27, etc.; 12.386. ds. **iordanen, iordane**.

Iosaphat the vale of Josaphat, site of the Virgin Mary's tomb. I.30.68.

Ioseph (a) husband of the Virgin Mary. I.2.*passim*; 5.33 ff, 167 ff; 9.146, 222; 13.*passim*; (b) Joseph of Arimathia. I.14.185; II.14.336; (c) the historian Josephus. I.32.189. ds. **iosepe, iosephe**.

Iosias a pharisee converted by St James the apostle. II.27.148 ff. as. **iosiam**, ds. **iosian**.

Iosue Joshua, leader of the Hebrews in succession to Moses. I.2.147; II.12.377, etc. See also **Iesus**.

Irtacus king of the Ethiopians. II.32.151, etc.

is see **beon**.

Isaac son of Abraham. I.6.28–31; 8.99, 156; II.4.132 ff; 12.28; etc. [19 ex.]

Isai Jesse, father of king David. II.4.185–6.

Isaias the prophet Isaiah. I.6.108; 31.317; II.1.140, 177, 187, 192; 5.43; etc. ns. **isaias, issaias**; gs. **issaies, yssaie(?)**; ds. **isiam, isaiam**. [19 ex.]

isen n. *iron, iron tool or weapon*. II.11.138; 14.94; 32.102; 34.194. [7 ex.]

isen adj. *iron, made of iron*. I.9.172; 29.131–2; II.23.151; 24.20. [17 ex.]

Ispanian see **Hispania**

Israhel Israel. Used, in sing., as a name for

the people, alone or in apposition with **folc**. I.9.19, 37; 12.81; II.1.136; 5.250. nads. **-hel**, gs. **israheles**. [27 ex.]

Israhela gp. of the Israelites; esp w. **folc** or **þeode**. I.4.278; 27.130; II.1.49; 5.44. [67 ex.]

Italia Italy. I.26.102; II.34.4.

iu see **geu**.

Iudas (a) Judas Iscariot. I.1.267; 27.211; II.14.17; 40.296; [18 ex.] (b) the other apostle Judas. I.21.31; II.33.*passim*; 35.6. (c) Judah, one of the 12 sons of Jacob. I.25.146. agds. **iudan**.

Iudei the Jews. I.3.17, 50; 7.75; II.4.258; 12.20. Used without article in gp., in **iudea land**, the land of the Jews, etc, and occasionally in np. Forms: gp. **iudea**; dp. **iudeum** (no ex. of ap.). [42 ex.]

Iudeisc adj. *Jewish*. I.2.78; 5.9; II.3.33; 32.10. [103 ex.] wk pl. as sb. *the Jews*. I.3.45; 8.168; II.4.69; 13.50. [65 ex.] **iudeiscean** 1x, **iudeisra** 2x, **iudeisre** 1x.

iuguþ see **geogoþ**

Iulianus Julian the apostate. I.30.200 ff; II.34.19, 45.

iungling m. *youth, young man*. II.18.140.

Iustinus a priest in Rome at the time of the martyrdom of St Laurence. I.29.228, 265, 280 ff.

Iustus one of the mission to convert England (later archbishop of Canterbury, d. 627). II.9.172.

katacumbas the Catacombs in Rome. I.26.290.

kycene wk f. *kitchen*. II.11.196–7, 204.

kyþþe see **cyþþ**.

la interj. used to call attention, usu. either to a question, often in association with **hwæt** or **hu**, I.24.8; 34.163; II.1.249; 11.473; or in a direct address, with **leof**, I.10.105; II.3.67; etc. [57 ex.]

lac nf. *gift, offering*. I.5.29; 9.74 ff; II.10.198; 11.144. pl. **lac**; gender mostly indeterminate but fem.s. at I.8.72; 9.12; II.40.171. [100 ex.]

gelacnian vb II. *to heal*. I.8.68; 24.22; II.34.211, 218. **lacnian** II.21.151. [9 ex.]

lacnung f. *healing*. I.37.122.

gelacod pp. *accompanied with gifts*. I.9.16.

lactuca wk f. *lettuce*. II.15.15, 262, 269.

ladian vb II. *to excuse*. II.23.64. Cf **be-**.

ladung f. *excuse, defence*. I.19.172. Cf **be-**.

laf f. *remnant, remainder*. I.12.22; 15.60; II.4.268; 25.16; **to lafe**, *remaining, left* I.1.46; II.12.98; etc. [17 ex.]

lam n. *clay, earth*. I.1.66; 16.119; II.30.170.

lama adj. *lame, crippled*. I.1.257; II.6.201.

lamb n. *lamb*. I.9.77; 22.6; II.3.64; 12.350. [57 ex.]

land n. *land, country*. I.2.11; 5.39; II.11.102; 16.120. [122 ex.] Cf **boc-**, **yrþ-**.

landar f. *landed property*. I.4.96; 22.78; II.12.572.

landfolc n. *inhabitants* (of a particular region). II.11.176, 293; 24.81.

lang adj. *long*. I.1.186; 9.91; II.10.97; 11.270. [16 ex.]

gelang adj. **æt . . . gelang**, *dependent on*. I.18.124.

lange adv. *long*. I.9.188; 32.215; II.10.216; 19.111; **swa lange swa**, *as long as* I.3.153; II.7.157; etc. comp. **leng**. [51 ex.]

langfære adj. *lasting, durable*. comp. I.6.194.

gelangian vb II. *to summon*. I.5.151; 30.234; II.2.38; 18.68. [10 ex.]

langlice adv. *for a long time*. I.4.136; 29.243; II.11.125; 33.138. [10 ex.]

langnyss f. *length*. II.26.93.

langsum adj. *long, long-lasting* (with ref. to time). I.praef.77; 3.35; II.5.147; 9.64. [45 ex.]

langsumlic adj. *lengthy, taking a long time*. I.25.218.

langsumlice adv. *lengthily*. II.14.3.

langsumnyss f. *length*. II.30.6; 32.148; 40.140.

lar f. *knowledge, teaching, doctrine, instruction*. I.praef.50; 1.139; II.1.119; 4.61. [216 ex.]

lareow m. *teacher, scholar*. I.2.103; 3.87; II.3.236 ff; 4.175. [167 ex.]

lareowdom m. *office or role of teacher; teaching, instruction*. I.27.117; 36.174; II.2.187; 6.159. [8 ex.]

larlic adj. *instructive, containing knowledge or doctrine*. I.24.144; II.16.2; 23.83; 25.112.

larspel n. *instructive discourse.* II.19.121; 36.67.

late adv. *slowly, at a later stage.* I.7.207; 15.19; comp. **lator,** *later* I.6.198–9; in adj. function(?), I.20.127.

latestan see **lætt**

latheorte adj. *slow in mind.* II.16.19.

latteow m. *guide.* I.2.79; 7.109; II.12.198; 21.36. **lateow** II.21.32. [13 ex.]

laþ adj. *hateful, unpleasant.* I.AppB3.245; II.16.223; 14.82; 18.103; 19.237; 34.16.

laþ n. *harm.* II.12.498.

laþettan vb I. *to make hateful.* II.40.270.

laþian vb II. *to be hateful or unwelcome.* II.34.130.

gelaþian vb II. *to invite.* I.35.6–8, 16–17; II.4.186; 23.4, 24, etc. **laþ-** 3x. [64 ex.] Cf **unge-**.

laþlic adj. *loathsome, hostile.* I.1.38; 8.44; II.37.32.

gelaþung f. *church, assembly.* (The usual word for the church as a body of believers.) I.2.73; 3.4; II.1.91; 3.234. [148 ex.]

Laurentius (a) St Laurence. I.29.*passim.* (b) one of the mission to convert England (second archbishop of Canterbury, d. 619). II.9.171.

Lazarus (a) brother of Martha and Mary, resurrected by Christ. I.14.26, 32; 16.81, 90; 33.79, 100, 117–8. (b) the poor man in the parable told by Christ. I.23.*passim*; treated as a common noun?, ap. **lazaras** *lepers?* I.23.126. as **-um**; gs. **-es**; voc. **-e**.

gelæccan vb I. *to seize, snatch, catch.* I.10.151; 12.14; II.9.107; 21.52. Pres.s.3 **gelæcþ, gelæhþ**; pret. **gelæht-**; pp. **gelæht.** [47 ex.]

læce m. *doctor.* I.5.136–7; 8.67; II.32.211–3; 37.179. [15 ex.] Cf **woruld-**.

læcecræft m. *skill of doctors, practice of medicine.* I.31.316; II.2.80.

læcedom m. *healing.* I.4.56; 8.69; 33.106; II.7.47; 32.54; 34.260.

læcewyrt f. *medicinal herb.* I.31.319, 322; II.10.38.

(ge)lædan vb I. *to lead, take.* I.1.232; 3.124; II.1.225; 5.138–9. Pres.s.3 **(ge)læt, lætt** (1x). [183 ex.] Cf **a-, be-, for-, forþ-, mis-**.

læfan vb I. *to leave (behind).* I.32.40; II.6.54; 30.88; *remain* II.3.83. Cf **be-**.

læfer f. *metal plate?* II.33.268.

læmen adj. *earthen, made of clay.* I.36.270.

læn f. *loan.* II.11.12–13, 398, 406; 31.96.

læne adj. *transitory.* II.15.334; 34.150, 271.

[læpeldre] f. *dish.* II.14.42.

læran vb I. *to teach, advise.* I.praef.109; 1.260; II.2.81; 5.68. **gelærde** II.2.123. pp. as adj. **gelæred** *learned, educated* I.praef.123; II.30.227; etc. [59 ex.] Cf **for-, samlæred, ungelæred.**

lærestre wk f. *(female) teacher.* II.37.192.

læs adv. *less.* I.21.112; 30.182; II.37.23, 200. **na þe læs** *just as much* I.31.266. As pron., I.35.273. See also **þy læs þe**.

læs f. *pasture.* I.17.65; AppB3.26–7, 189–90. np. **læswa,** dp. **læswum.**

læssa, -e comp. adj., wk. *lesser, inferior, weaker, smaller.* I.9.80; 20.59; II.3.185; 15.150. [26 ex.]

læst sup. adj. *least, smallest, weakest.* II.7.158; 29.35.

læst sup. adv. *least.* II.7.88; 39.109.

gelæstan vb I. *to accomplish, fulfil.* I.19.84; 27.188; II.1.129; 5.173; w.dat., *to serve* I.14.97. [8 ex.]

læswian vb II. *to feed, pasture.* I.17.67; AppB3.11, etc; II.10.302; 16.178. **leswaþ** I.AppB3.205. [14 ex.]

lætan vb 7. *to let, allow, leave.* I.9.245; 11.203; II.21.171; DSM.10. Pres.s.3 **læt**; pret. **let, leton.** [39 ex.] Cf **a-, for-**.

lætt adj. *late.* II.39.183; sup. **latestan,** *last* II.5.30, 32.

læwa m. *betrayer.* II.14.43, 82, 159. Cf **be-**.

læwed adj. *lay, secular, not ordained.* I.6.83; 30.259; II.12.550; 21.47. [35 ex.]

lead n. *lead* (metal). I.18.172; II.27.85.

leaden adj. *leaden, made of lead.* I.29.132, 156; AppB2.13.

leaf n. *leaf.* I.16.122–3.

leaf f. *permission.* I.35.60, 67; AppB3.50; II.11.224, 227; 23.184.

geleafa m. *faith, belief.* I.1.219; 2.73; II.2.169; 3.268. [319 ex.]

geleafful adj. *believing, devout, possessed of the (right) faith.* I.2.104; 3.7; II.4.32–4; 5.42. **leaffulran** II.12.121. [135 ex.] Cf **un-**.

geleaffulnyss f. *belief, credence.* I.16.96. Cf **unge-**.

geleaflæst n. *disbelief.* np. **geleaflæstu** I.15.140. (Possibly the same as **geleafleast** f.)

geleafleas adj. *without faith.* II.24.211.

geleafleast f. *lack of belief, unbelieving state.* I.10.47; 22.149; II.4.108; 8.77. **-leste** I.18.146. [11 ex.]

geleaflic adj. *believable, likely.* I.30.150, 267; 34.272; II.3.117; ExDict.16. Cf **un-**.

geleaflice adv. *credibly, with conviction.* II.14.301.

leahter, leahtor m. *sin, vice.* I.praef.118; 1.121; II.1.280; 12.495 ff. **hleaht-** I.13.123; 14.107. [94 ex.] Cf **fyrn-, heafod-**.

leahterful adj. *sinful.* I.34.213; II.26.43; 29.103.

leahterlic adj. *sinful.* II.23.61.

leahtorlice adv. *with sins.* I.7.241.

(ge)leahtrian II. *to corrupt.* I.praef.131; II.praef.45; 13.52, 66.

lean n. *reward.* I.13.147; 27.126; 30.213; II.12.557. Cf **ed-**.

geleanian vb II. *to reward.* pp. **-nod** I.27.208; 36.221.

leas n. *falsehood.* I.praef.131; II.praef.46.

leas adj. *false, lying.* I.praef.62; 3.20; II.praef.47; 6.43. [68 ex.] Cf **un-**.

leasetan vb I. *to lie, pretend.* II.32.111.

leasgewita m. *a false witness.* np. **leasgewitan** I.3.52. More commonly as two words (6x).

leasgewitnyss f. *false testimony.* II.25.51; 40 280. Printed as ns. **leas gewitnyss** II.12.509; cf also as. **lease gewitnysse** I.32.183.

leaslic adj. *false.* I.28.86; II.11.241.

leaslice adv. *falsely.* II.31.29; 39.159.

leasung f. *lying, lie, falsehood.* I.praef.95; 1.120; II.7.17; 10.115. [23 ex.]

leaswyrcend m. *maker of falsehood.* I.6.176.

lec m. *look, gaze.* II.23.58.

(ge)lecgan vb I. *to lay, place.* I.2.35; 3.53; II.2.34; 14.344. Pret. **(ge)led-, leidon**; pp. **geled**. [26 ex.] Cf **a-, under-**.

leden n. *Latin.* I.praef.54; II.praef.30; 22.190; **on leden** *in Latin* I.30.14; AppB2.25; II.5.273; 13.219 (**læden**); **of leden(e)** *from Latin* I.praef.55; II.9.8; ExDict.8; Expl.6. [19 ex.]

leden adj. *Latin.* I.praef.49; 30.11, 22; II.praef.29, 33; 9.18; 14.232; 22.189.

ledenspræc f. I.30.12. (2 words, I.30.22)

ledenwara f.pl. *people speaking Latin.* I.30.13. Cf **burh-** etc.

lefung f. *lameness?* II.33.84.

leger n. *sickness.* II.6.180; 11.559; 12.377; 34.296.

legerbed n. *sickbed.* I.31.278; II.10.321; 34.197.

gelegered, -od adj. *ill.* II.10.327; 12.116.

legerstow f. *burial-place.* I.29.226.

lencten n. *Spring* (season). I.AppB2.13.

lenctenlic adj. *of Spring.* I.6.134, 147; 30.127; *Lenten, of Lent* II.7.2, 21–5.

gelendan vb I. *to land, disembark.* pret. **gelendon** II.23.147.

gelendan vb I. *to endow (with land).* pret. **gelende** II.9.35.

lendena, lendenu n.pl. *loins (as implied seat of sexual appetite?).* I.7.185; II.12.470; 15.19, 303; 39.61–2.

gelengan vb I. *to lengthen.* I.6.164; II.ExDict.3; 40.37.

gelenge adj. *related, near.* II.19.11.

[leng] f. *length.* II.21.25; 31.63, 66; 40.55–6. See also **lange**.

leo m? *lion.* I.6.179; 37.207 ff; II.15.95 ff; 30.36. gds., np. **leon**, gp. **leona**, dp. **leon, leonum**. [17 ex.]

leodbiscop m. *bishop.* I.4.179; II.10.260, 334; 34.110. [The 3 examples do not appear to show any special function for the **leod-** element.]

[leod] f. *people, nation.* I.5.11; 6.133–5; II.9.90; 19.100. In sing. designates a nation; in plural either a single nation (e.g. **iudeiscra leoda cyning**) or several nations (e.g. **of eallum leodum**), or people more generally (e.g. II.10.131). [48 ex.]

leodscipe m. *nation.* I.13.120; 14.70; II.12.69; 14.103. **-scype** I.17.85. [19 ex.]

leof adj. *beloved, dear.* I.4.17; 7.43; II.4.132; 32.163; in impers. constructions, *pleasing* II.10.230; 32.63–4; as form of address, esp. **la leof**, *sir, lord* I.10.105; II.33.121; etc.; as form of address to a congregration, **men þa leofostan**, etc. I.1.294; II.7.1; etc. [90 ex.]

leof- see **lybban**

leogan vb 2. *to lie, speak falsely.* I.1.118; 11.62; 22.94; 26.198; 36.165, 258. Pres.s.2 **lyhst**; pret.s.2 **luge**; 3 **leah**. Cf **a-, for-**.

leoht n. *light, lamp.* I.1.101; 2.113; II.11.286; 16.218. [99 ex.]

leoht adj. *minor, slight.* I.38.244; 29.37;

II.40.261; **leohtre on mode** *less grievous in heart* I.23.51.

leoht adj. *bright*. I.10.46.

leohtbeamed adj. *having beams or rays of light?* (of comets). I.40.43.

leohtberend m. *light-bearer* (= *Lucifer*). I.1.30.

leohtfæt n. *lamp*. II.11.565; 12.228, 232; 14.81; 32.122; 39.4, etc. nap. **-fatu**; dp. **-fatum, -fætum**. [15 ex.]

leohtleas adj. *devoid of light*. II.34.102.

leohtlic adj. *small, insubstantial, minor, simple*. I.33.107; II.19.291; 40.255.

leohtlice adv. *easily, without effort*. II.11.192; 14.279.

leoma m. *light, radiance, brightness*. I.4.273; 20.102 ff; II.11.527; 14.273. [12 ex.] See also **lim**.

leornere m. *disciple*. II.25.102.

(ge)leornian vb II. *to learn*. I.4.51; 14.89; II.3.287; 10.330; 19.2. [28 ex.]

leorningcild n. *(young) pupil*. II.11.168.

leorningcniht m. *disciple*. I.3.87; 4.17; II.4.5; 36.3. **leorninccniht** 4x, **leornincgcniht** 1x. [113 ex.]

leorningman m. *disciple*. II.25.27; 27.27, 42; 29.23 (= Martha and Mary).

leoþ n. *poem*. II.40.48 (= *carmen*).

leoþcræft m. *poetry, poetic art*. II.1.219.

leoþlic adj. *poetic*. II.10.6.

leoþwise wk f. *poetic form*. II.ExDict.9.

letaniae f.pl. *the greater Litany, or Rogationtide*. I.18.2.

letanias m.pl. *litanies* (i.e. invocations to the saints). II.9.153 (**Lætanias**), 159, 161.

(ge)lettan vb I. *to hinder, impede, detain*. I.26.267; 38.294; II.11.10, 580; 20.65.

Leui the thirteenth tribe of Israel, descendants of Levi son of Jacob. I.27.168.

Libanius officer of the emperor Julian. I.30.245.

Libia queen of the emperor Nero. I.26.161.

lic n. *body, corpse*. I.4.39; 8.45; II.2.19, 83; 9.125. [74 ex.]

gelic adj. *similar, like* (w. dat.), *alike*. I.1.32; 2.42; II.1.253; 23.193. [53 ex.] Cf **un-**.

gelica m. *an equivalent, one like another, a match or parallel*. I.8.175; 18.185–7; II.1.84; 9.24. [13 ex.]

Licaonia region in Anatolia (Asia Minor). I.23.136.

liccetan vb I. *to dissimulate, feign*. I.27.237.

liccetere m. *hypocrite, dissimulator*. I.7.261; 36.259; II.26.31.

geliccian vb II. *to lick*. I.23.9, 61.

liccung f. *licking*. I.23.61.

gelice adv. *alike, equally*. I.16.118; 28.99; II.3.126; 19.222; **swa gelice** *similarly* I.12.20; 27.62; II.1.222; 12.567. [21 ex.]

licgan vb 5. *to lie, lie down*. I.2.211; 23.126; II.1.211; 2.87. Pres.s.3 **liþ**; pret.s.3 **læg, læig** (5x), **lægi** (1x), **gelæg** (2x); pl. **lagon**; subj. **læge**. [88 ex.]

lichama m. *body*. I.1.116; 2.85; II.9.57; 11.570. **lichoma, -an** 6x. [289 ex.]

lichamlic adj. *bodily, physical*. I.6.191; 25.170; II.11.43, 50; 15.120. [29 ex.]

lichamlice adv. *physically, literally*. I.2.45; 6.80; II.1.105; 12.16. **lichomlice** 4x. [51 ex.]

(ge)lician vb II. *to please*. w. dat. I.8.206; 20.12; II.9.85; 39.140. Pres.pl. **liciaþ, licigeaþ**. [40 ex.] Cf **mis-, of-**.

licman m. *one attending on a corpse or dying person*. I.4.131–4; II.6.193; 20.51; 21.8; 37.200.

gelicnyss f. *likeness, similarity, appearance*. I.5.146; 22.129; II.3.151; 4.204. [22 ex.] Cf **an-**.

licþenung f. *obsequies, funeral attendance*. I.5.153; II.2.67.

licþrowere m. *leper*. I.23.7, 138.

lif n. *life*. I.praef.126; 1.248; II.2.66; 3.260; **on life** *while alive* I.23.115; II.21.31; etc. **liif** I.10.60; **lyf-** 5x. [580 ex.] Cf **ancer-, munuc-, mynster-**.

geliffæstan vb I. *to endow with life*. I.1.17; 2.172; II.12.287; 15.133. [13 ex.]

liffæstende adj. *life-bestowing*. I.20.87.

lifi- see **lybban**

lifleas adj. *lifeless*. II.26.50; 34.107; 40.8.

liflic adj. *living, of life*. I.2.82; 4.156; II.1.57; 6.97. [23 ex.]

liflice adv. *with life, giving life*. II.14.47.

lig m. *fire, flame*. I.23.15; 31.190; II.1.243; 17.110. [25 ex.]

ligen adj. *fiery*. II.11.180.

geligenod pp. *belied, guilty of falsehood*. I.3.143.

liget m. or n. *lightning*. I.15.25; 34.54; II.11.503; 12.126. [9 ex.]

gelihtan vb I. *to alight, dismount*. II.10.39. Cf **a-**.

lihting f. *lighting, illumination*. I.7.124; 8.187 (**lyhtinge**); II.39.7. Cf **onlihtan**.

lilie wk f. *lily*. I.30.127–9, 147; II.10.67; 31.13–15, 72; 37.153.

lim n. *limb, part of body, member*. I.5.110; 6.102; II.2.119; 15.230. nap. **lima, leoma, leomu, lyma, lymu**; gp. **lima**; dp. **limum, leomum, lymum**. [67 ex.]

limleas adj. *without limbs or parts of the body*. I.16.131, 135; II.15.134.

gelimp n. *event, experience, fortune*. I.18.132 (*good fortune*); 34.9; 38.13. Cf **unge-**.

gelimpan vb 3. *to happen, occur, befall* (w. noun subject, or **hit**, or none). I.7.133; 32.216; II.2.92; 6.5. Pret. **gelamp, gelumpon**; pp. **gelumpen**. [73 ex.] Cf **be-**.

gelimplic adj. *fitting, appropriate*. I.AppA2.1; II.10.11; 12.177.

gelimplice adv. *fittingly, appropriately*. I.14.192; 38.166; II.5.174.

Lindisfarnea Lindisfarne. II.10.142.

Lindisfarneisc, Lindisfarnensisc of Lindisfarne. II.10.259, 332.

linen adj. *made of linen*. II.14.342.

Linus a bishop ordained in Rome by St Peter. I.37.13.

liss f. *alleviation, relief*. I.23.67; 37.80.

liþ see **licgan**

liþe adj. *gentle, mild*. I.14.89; 15.109; II.3.155; 10.125. [14 ex.] Cf **cum-, un-**.

liþebig adj. *supple*. II.10.337; *bending down*? II.14.31.

liþig adj. *soft, supple*. II.17.73; 34.207.

(ge)liþian vb II. *to soften*. w. dat. I.22.142, 178; II.10.38; *to alleviate* I.40.175. Pres.s.3 **-liþegaþ**; pret. **-liþegod-**; pp. **-liþegod**.

liþelice adv. *gently*. I.38.270.

geliþewæcan vb I. *to soften*. II.36.62.

liþnyss f. *gentleness, softness*. I.15.106; 22.137 (**lyþnysse**), 142; II.3.157, 180; 36.61. Cf **cum-**.

loc n. *lock*. I.37.233.

loca, loce interj. **loca hwæt** *whatever* I.32.17; II.40.22 (**loce**); **loce hu** *however* I.31.309; **loca nu** *behold* I.10.20, 116; 25.137; 30.36.

locc m. *lock (of hair)*. I.31.189; II.11.101; 30.80; 34.242.

locian vb II. *to look*. I.18.128, 130; 20.169; AppB3.38. Cf **on-**.

loddre m. *beggar*. I.18.186.

lof n. *praise*. I.1.26; 3.194; II.5.276; 12.100. [56 ex.]

lofian vb II. *to appraise, value*. I.38.75, 110; II.19.237.

lofsang m. *song of praise* (incl. *canticle, hymn*). I.3.165; 5.187; II.5.256, 283; 16.217. In pl., *liturgy, divine service*? II.1.279; 11.109; 27.1; 40.17, 144. [34 ex.]

lofung f. *valuation*. I.38.75.

gelogian vb II. *to place, put in position*. I.22.82; 30.261; II.7.136; 25.127; *arrange, order, dispose* I.11.38; 20.163; II.3.234; 14.3; *settle* I.36.231; *provide or fill (a place with inhabitants)* I.24.103; AppB1.4; II.34.122; *establish* II.35.87. **up gelogian**, *raise up, disinter* II.10.335. **logiaþ** II.30.149. [26 ex.]

gelome adv. *frequently*. I.2.111; 7.190; II.5.37; 10.39. [32 ex.]

gelomlæcan vb I. *to be or become frequent*. I.40.78.

gelomlæcende adj. *frequent*. I.38.55; 40.120; II.21.37.

gelomlice adv. *frequently*. I.9.107; 15.7; II.2.4; 10.138. [22 ex.]

losian vb II. *to perish*. I.6.24; 12.124; II.3.293; 6.64; *to be lost* I.17.65; 24.9, 77; 28.221; II.15.317. [52 ex.]

losi(g)endlic adj. *perishing, about to perish*. I.28.109, 112.

lotwrenc m. *device, wile*. I.13.8; 19.183; 26.170; 31.102.

Loþ Lot, nephew of Abraham. I.2.147.

Lucas St Luke the evangelist. I.2.8; 4.177; II.13.231; 16.2. gs.**lucas**. [14 ex. (in 14 homilies)]

Lucillus blind man healed by St Laurence. I.29.84, 91.

lufian vb II. *to love*. I.1.28; 3.132; II.1.281; 4.41. [191 ex.]

lufiend m. *lover*. II.24.219 (ap. **-dras**).

lufi(g)endlic adj. *lovable, desirable, attractive*. I.21.119, 219; II.20.22; *friendly, loving* II.20.255.

luftyme adj. *desired*. II.9.165.

lufu f. *love*. I.3.119; 9.209; II.3.125; 4.77. ags. **lufe**; ds. **lufe, lufan** (IX), **lufon**

(14x; only in expression **for godes lufon**, etc, *for God's sake*). Frequently collocated with **soþ** (73x). [206 ex.] Cf **woruld-**.

Lunden London. II.21.168.

lus f. *fly*? **hundes lusum** II.12.59 (see note).

lust m. *pleasure, desire*. I.4.125; 5.129, 141; II.1.78; 10.218. Almost always with negative implications; often collocated with **flæsclic**. [58 ex.] Cf **un-**.

lustbære adj. *pleasant*. I.8.156 (adv?).

lustbære adv. *gladly*. I.35.244; II.10.197; 11.304.

gelustfullian vb II. *to take pleasure, to delight (in)*. I.33.88, 93; *to give pleasure, to please* II.6.39; 9.216; impers. w. dat. *it pleases* I.25.185; AppB3.90.

lustfullung f. *desire, delighting, taking pleasure*. I.11.138–44; II.12.368; 23.94; 24.226; 37.62. **gelust-** 1x.

lustlice adv. *willingly, eagerly, gladly*. I.31.301; 33.33; 36.213; II.13.91; 38.160.

lutan vb 2. *to bow, stoop*. I.2.148; 21.19. Pret. **leat, luton**. Cf **a-**.

lutian vb II. *to hide, lurk*. I.33.92; 36.107; II.32.122. (All pres. part.) Cf **æt-**.

ly- see also **li-**

lybban vb III. *to live*. I.praef.112; 1.93; II.5.117; 6.124. Pres.s.2 **leofast**; 3 **leofaþ**; pl. **lybbaþ, libbaþ** (1x); pres. part. **lybbende**; infl. inf. **lybbenne, libbenne**; pret. **leofod-, lyfod-**. Pres. part. as adj. applied to God, = *the living God/Lord* (cf esp. I.26.47.), **lifi(g)ende, lyfi(g)ende**: I.4.267; II.1.223; etc (28x). [215 ex.] Cf **mis-**.

gelyfan vb I. *to believe*. Alone or with **þæt**: I.1.254; 7.181; II.1.122; 6.25; w. acc. object, I.21.98; II.1.272; w. gen. object, II.12.214; 27.125; w. dat. object, I.25.21; II.27.127; **gelyfan on** *believe in*, w. dat. I.31.221; II.33.96; w. acc. I.20.8; II.1.269; pp. as adj., **gelyfed** *devout, believing* I.1.276; II.1.230; etc. [246 ex.] Cf **rihtge-, unge-**.

lyffetende adj. *flattering*. I.33.41, 52 (**lyffetyndra**).

lyffetere m. *flatterer*. I.33.57; II.39.159, 170.

lyffetung f. *flattery*. I.33.45, 51; II.26.37; 38.223; 39.171; 40.265.

lyft f. *air, sky*. I.26.167, 236, 245; II.6.71; 11.499; 27.45. [10 ex.]

lyften adj. *of the sky* (as distinct from the firmament). I.21.198, 209.

lyre m. *loss*. I.praef.114; 1.62; II.20.171; 30.88. [11 ex.]

lystan vb I, impers. w. dat. or acc. *to please*. I.9.213; 10.181; 16.138; II.12.520; 13.128.

lyt adv. *little*. II.10.118, 126.

lyt n. *few*. I.praef.110.

lytel adj. I.1.82; 9.49 ff; II.3.134; 19.84. [59 ex.] Cf **un-**.

lytle adv. *a little*. **lytle ær** *a little before* I.14.26; 22.109; II.2.164; 14.155. [11 ex.]

lytling m. *little person, child*. I.5.103; 34.142, 144, 179; II.16.95. [10 ex.]

lyþre adj. *wicked*. I.11.34; 19.183; II.14.63; 38.28. [9 ex.]

ma indecl. sb. *more (in number)*. I.5.180; 29.50; II.12.281; 37.76; as adj. II.5.14; as adv., *more, rather* I.28.35; 36.241; **þe ma þe**, conj., *any more than* I.7.157; 14.127; II.3.173; 19.89. [29 ex.]

gemaca m. *mate, spouse*. I.1.87, 188; 9.12, 116, 209; II.4.101. Cf **gemæcca**.

Macherunta a town or fort in Judaea where John the Baptist was imprisoned. I.32.61.

macian vb II. **(hit) macian**, *to fare, act*. I.37.141; II.21.110.

gemacian vb II. *to cause* (w. **þæt**). I.praef.100; II.11.155; 33.119; *cause to be or become* II.5.204; 6.48.

maga, -as see **mæg**

magan pret.pres. vb. (a) *to be able, can* (w. inf., sometimes implied from preceding clause). I.1.12; 2.95; II.1.18; 2.78; w. verb of motion implied, I.23.19. (b) w. **aht, naht**, etc, *to have power* (or perhaps *to be able to do (anything)*) I.26.14, 72; 38.329; II.20.237; 33.118. (c) *to avail, be of use* I.12.16; II.24.49; 28.61(?); 40.119; etc. Pres.s.1 **mæg, mægi, mæig**; 2 **miht**; 3 **mæg, mæig**; pl. **magon**; subj. **mage, mæge; magon, magan**; pret.s. **mihte, myhte** (2x); pl. **mihton**; subj.s.2 **mihtest**. [679 ex.]

Magdalenisc adj. applied to St Mary Magdalen. I.15.17.

mage wk f. *kinswoman*. I.13.59, 161, 170; II.32.152.

Magilros Melrose in Scotland, where Dryhthelm became a monk. II.21.17.

gemaglic adj. *insistent, persistent*. II.9.142, 145; 11.377.

gemaglice adv. *persistently*. **gemahglice** I.10.100; **gemahlice** II.11.46.

gemagnyss f. *persistence*. II.9.143; *complaint, grumbling?* II.12.524.

Malchus one of the Seven Sleepers. II.27.186.

Mamertus bishop of Vienne in Gaul who instituted the Rogationtide fast (d. c475). I.18.9.

Mamortini a prison in Rome (where, according to tradition, St Peter had been imprisoned). I.29.22.

man, mann m. *human being, person, man*. I.1.64; 2.11; II.praef.30; 1.15; used with ref. to a woman, I.1.129; 19.91; II.1.83; 6.148; 7.140; 24.108; as indef. pron., *one* I.7.206; 19.154; II.1.162; 14.223. nas. **man** (410x), **mann** (128x), **mon** (1x, MS K); gs. **mannes**; ds. **men, menn**; nap. **men, menn**; gp. **manna**; dp. **mannum**. [1664 ex.]

man n. *evil, sin*. II.2.120; 34.193.

gemana m. *intercourse, company*. I.1.239; 27.182; II.1.57; 25.71. [7 ex.]

manaþ m. *evil oath*. I.AppB3.246.

manbære adj. *productive of humans*. I.30.218 (= *hominum ferax*).

mancynn n. *mankind*. I.praef.64; 1.151; II.1.17; 4.115. **manncynn-** 5x. [114 ex.]

mandæd f. *evil deeds*. I.praef.72; 1.180; II.4.203; 5.132. [27 ex.]

maneg- see **menig-**

manful adj. *evil, wicked*. I.291; 5.103; II.2.204; 4.266. [27 ex.]

manfullic adj. *wicked*. I.26.39; 32.8; II.2.122; 12.329.

manfullice adv. *wickedly*. I.28.19; 5.165; II.2.117; 9.129.

manfulnyss f. *wickedness*. II.15.264.

mangian vb II. *to trade*. I.28.169.

mangere m. *trader, merchant*. I.18.172.

mangung f. *trading, business*. I.35.86; II.6.151.

manian vb II. *to exhort*. I.21.2; 26.215; II.5.260; 9.162. **geman-** 2x. [33 ex.]

manlic adj. *wicked*. II.13.73.

manlice adv. *wickedly*. II.19.191.

manna n. *manna (i.e. the miraculous food with which the Hebrews were fed in the wilderness)*. I.4.277.

manna m. *person, man*. I.1.63, 66; 33.18; II.3.58; 11.447. as. only. [17 ex.]

manncwealm m. *pestilence*. II.9.89.

manræden f. *allegiance*. I.30.192.

manslaga m. *murderer*. I.3.43, 149 (**mann-**); 8.191; II.12.321; 13.62–4. [15 ex.]

mansliht m. *murder*. I.32.117, 130; AppB3.247 (**-slyhtas**); II.12.513; 14.186. [7 ex.]

mansumung f. *cursing, excommunication*. I.26.88.

manswara m. *perjurer, breaker of promises*. I.32.120.

manþwærnyss f. *mildness, gentleness*. I.25.217; AppB3.250; II.13.44.

mara wk adj. (comp. of **micel**) *greater, larger, more*. I.1.14; 8.130; II.2.115; 5.22. [c.108 ex.]

Marcus St Mark the evangelist. I.4.177; 21.95, 224; 32.5; II.25.2; 28.68.

mare n. *more, a greater amount, a greater thing*. I.4.114; 10.43; II.7.46; 29.119. [c.19 ex.]

mare adv. (comp. of **micle**). *more*. I.9.148(?); 16.95; AppB3.84; II.9.179 (2nd ex.).

Maria (a) the Virgin Mary, mother of Christ. I.1.237; 2.15; II.1.3; 4.4. [117 ex.] (b) Mary Magdalen. I.15.17. (c) Mary 'mother of James' (perhaps identified by Ælfric as sister of the Virgin Mary and wife of Zebedee; see introdn. to I.15 and II.17). I.15.17. (d) Mary, sister of Martha and Lazarus. I.8.147; 33.80; II.29.*passim*. agds. **marian**.

marmanstan m. *marble*. I.34.66, 95; 37.111; **marmstanum** II.33.266.

marmstangedelf n. *quarrying of marble*. I.37.64.

Mars the god Mars. I.29.20, 21, 61. gs. **martis**; ds. **marti**.

Martha sister of Mary and Lazarus. I.8.147; 33.79; II.29.*passim*.

Martialis a pagan healed by St Stephen's relics. II.2.22.

Martinianus one of the Seven Sleepers. II.27.186.

Martinus St Martin of Tours, c316–97. II.34.*passim*. as. **martinum**; gs. **-es**; ds. **-e**.

martir, martyr m. *martyr*. I.3.18; 5.105; II.2.158; 18.153. [49 ex.]

martirdom, martyrdom m. *martyrdom*. I.praef.94; 3.83, 88; II.2.186; 37.132. [38 ex.]

gemartirian, -tyrian vb II. *to martyr*. I.5.60; 9.171, 176; II.17.63; 18.66; 32.187. [17 ex.]

Martirius a monk of Licaonia. I.23.136, 144, 148 (voc. **martiri**).

Martius Latin name for March. I.6.149.

Matheus St Matthew the evangelist. I.4.177; 5.7; II.16.132 ff; 32.*passim*. as. **matheum**; gs. **-ees**; ds. **-eo**. [43 ex.]

Mathias the apostle. II.35.7–9.

maþa m. *worm, maggot*. I.5.133; 31.283; II.30.194. dp. **maþan**.

maþm m. *treasure*. I.29.40, etc; 30.43; 32.159; II.18.45. **madmas** I.29.76. [15 ex.]

maþmfæt n. *precious vessel*. II.4.220 (**madm-**); 28.101, 138, 149. pl. **-fatu, -fatum**.

maþmhus n. *treasury*. I.38.97–8.

Mauricius Roman emperor in the East, 582–602. II.9.97, 105. ds. **mauricium**.

Maurus disciple of St Benedict. II.11.94 ff.

Maxentius Roman emperor 306–12, defeated by Constantine. II.18.8, 21, 23.

Maximianus one of the Seven Sleepers. II.27.186, 220.

Maximus (a) a monk in a story told by Gregory the Great. I.28.206–8. (b) bishop of Ostia in the time of the Emperor Decius. I.29.290. as. **-um**.

gemæcca m. *spouse*. II.34.6.

mæden n. (a) *virgin* (ref. to the Virgin Mary, other religious women, or the parable of the virgins). I.1.237, 241; 30.5; II.1.3, 36, etc; 39, *passim*. (b) *girl, servant*. I.32.15, 88; 33.86–8; II.24.27; 34.152. **medenes** I.25.107. [140 ex.]

mædencild n. *female child*. I.9.9.

mædenlic adj. *of a virgin, of virgins*. I.13.113; 30.19, 22; 31.76.

mædenmann m. *virgin*. I.21.220.

mæg m. *kinsman*. I.4.242; 6.73; II.2.59; 33.170; *friend*? (apparently corresponding to *amicus*) II.10.281; 30.191, 197; cf too II.37.17n. pl. **mag-**. [27 ex.]

mægen n. *virtue*. I.18.114; 31.301; II.6.108; 37.124; *mental power* II.16.205; *strength* II.5.99; 9.96; 28.108; *host, troop* I.24.179. gs. **mæignes**; ds. **mægne, mægene**; nap. **mægenu, mægnu**; gp. **mægena, mægna, mæigna**; dp. **mægnum**. [31 ex.]

mægenfæst adj. *strong*. I.6.192.

mægenleas adj. *weak, without strength*. I.11.56.

mægenleast f. *weakness*. I.23.140; 28.45; II.12.504.

mægenþrym m. *majesty, glory*. I.1.290; 4.89; II.4.287; 7.132. [15 ex.]

mægenþrymnyss f. *majesty, glory*. I.20.33, 138 (**-þrynnysse**); 37.255; II.7.134; 23.143.

mæglic adj. *of kinship*. I.26.57 (**mæig-**); **mæglic sibb** *the bond of kinship* I.4.6; 8.116; 28.44.

mægslaga m. *kin-slayer, murderer of kindred*. II.4.107.

mæ(i)gþ f. *nation*. I.1.222–3; 40.18, 129; II.13.195; 27.143; *family, kindred, line of descent* I.2.15; 5.66; II.9.12; 11.335; *generation* I.6.20; 13.188(?); II.28.122(?); 30.223. [41 ex.]

mæ(i)gþhad m. *virginity*. I.3.151; 4.7 ff; II.1.47, 76 ff; 4.36. **mæiþhad** I.31.81. [46 ex.]

mæl n. *eating-time, meal*. II.12.494; 40.266.

mænan vb I. *to mean*. I.12.66; 40.44; II.15.201–2; 36.73–4; *mention* I.23.69. **gemæn-** 2x. [19 ex.] Cf **be-**.

gemæne adj. *general, common, shared, in common*. I.4.109 ff; 21.128 ff; II.13.175; 19.268. **gemæne had,** *minor orders (of clergy)* II.6.142. [24 ex.]

gemænelic adj. *general, universal*. I.5.113–4; 7.225; II.7.31; 15.298; *communal, living in community* I.36.112. **gemen-** 1x. [22 ex.]

gemænelice adv. *communally, for all, in general, jointly*. I.4.182; 19.217; 20.120; 30.53; 33.131 ff; II.ExDict.5.

gemænged see **gemenged**; **(ge)mæni-** see **(ge)meni-**

gemænscipe m. *community*. I.33.63.

mænsumung f. *participation, communion, acceptance*. I.9.85; II.11.359.

mære adj. *great, glorious*. I.1.57; 3.40–1; II.3.10; 18.58. [82 ex.] Cf **wid-**.

gemære n. *boundary, border, region*. I.5.49; 21.64; II.8.7, 25; 23.146. Pl. **-u**. [10 ex.]

mærlic adj. *glorious, splendid*. I.5.85; 25.60; II.2.5; 4.97. [7 ex.]

mærlice adv. *in splendour, with glory*. I.23.6; II.17.47; 18.110; 21.121. [7 ex.]
mærsian vb II. *to glorify, celebrate*. I.5.3; 12.140; II.9.149; 22.7, etc. **gemærsode** II.22.116. [36 ex.] Cf **(ge)wid-**.
mærsung f. *celebration, glorification*. I.24.44; 32.87, 91; II.7.6; 22.42, etc. [15 ex.]
mærsungtima m. *time of glorification*. II.22.39.
mærþ f. *glory, glorious act*. I.2.113; 3.40; II.3.148; 11.21. [19 ex.]
mæsse wk f. *celebration or sacrament of mass*. I.4.252; 34.89; II.15.41, 102; 21.141. [25 ex.] Cf **hlaf-**.
mæssedæg m. *festival, feast-day*. I.13.157; 25.105; 30.111; II.38.192.
mæssepreost m. *priest (in full orders, qualified to teach and celebrate mass)*. I.praef.44; 26.91; II.6.145–7; 19.104. (Distinguished from **preostas** in lower orders at II.6.142–6.) [27 ex.]
mæssereaf n. *mass-vestment*. II.9.247.
mæssian vb II. *to celebrate mass*. II.11.355; 15.162; 21.170; w. ind. object in dat. (those for whom the mass is celebrated), I.29.229 (**gemæssode**); II.32.181.
mæst adj. *greatest, largest*. I.15.156; 18.113; II.1.286; 8.76. [14 ex.]
mæst adv. **eal mæst**, *almost entirely*. II.DSM.8.
gemæst adj. *fattened*. I.35.9, 53 ff; II.40.45.
mæþ f. *degree, measure*. I.9.100; 13.196; II.35.83; 40.277. The sense *degree of ability* shades into a sense *power, ability*: I.10.173; II.4.315; 16.61. [17 ex.]
mæþleas adj. *rapacious?, cruel?*. II.34.279. Cf **unmæþlic**.
mearcian vb II. *to mark*. I.15.13; 29.48; II.11.125; 15.52. **gemearc-** II.11.127. [12 ex.]
mearcung f. *marking*. II.15.24.
mearu adj. *tender*. np.wk.n. **mearewan** I.39.38.
med f. *reward, payment*. I.3.175; 9.208, 210; II.5.18; 6.163. [43 ex.]
Medas the Medes, subjects of Darius. I.31.5 (**medos**, reproducing the ap. form of the source); II.28.155 (dp. **medum**), 158–9.
medeme adj. *middling*. I.26.209; 31.35; II.19.241.
gemedemian vb II. (a) reflexive, *to humble, subject*. I.2.43; 32.79; II.4.25; 31.61. (b) trans., *to join(?), to place on a level with(?)* I.29.128. (c) intrans., *to condescend, deign* I.3.88; 29.157; 35.145; II.3.95. [16 ex.]
medemlic adj. *well-proportioned(?), moderate*. I.31.34.
medemlice adv. *moderately*. II.32.105.
medgilda m. *hireling*. I.17.56 (ns. **-gilde**); II.30.151.
melda m. *betrayer*. I.3.43.
Meldanus priest in the story of Fursey. II.20.162, 201.
meldere m. *betrayer*. I.AppB3.165.
meldian vb II. *to inform against, accuse*. II.14.136. Cf **a-**.
Mellitus one of the mission to convert England (third archbishop of Canterbury, d. 624). II.9.171.
[melu] n. *flour*. gs. **melowes, meluwes**. II.11.300; 40.42–3.
gemenelic see **gemænelic**
gemengan vb I. *to mix*. I.2.180–3; 32.121; II.12.369–70; 15.249. Pres.s.subj. **gemencge**; infl.inf. **gemencgenne**; pret. **gemengd-**; pp. **gemænged, gemencged, gemengd, gemenged**. [15 ex.]
gemen(c)gednyss f. *mixing, combination, confusion*. I.36.96; 40.8, 30, 51; II.1.45.
menig adj. & pron. *many, many a*. I.14.127; 24.109; II.2.76; 9.213. nsm. **menig, mænig** (1x); asm. **menine**; pl. **manega, mænige** (2x, MS D), **menige**; **manegra**; **manegum**. [133 ex.]
menigfeald adj. *numerous, of many kinds*. I.3.180; 4.116; II.5.203; 9.2; *abundant* I.8.117; 36.166; *complicated, abounding in detail* I.30.185; II.40.133 (1st ex.). **mænig-** 2x; **meni-** 2x. [53 ex.]
menigfealdlice adv. *abundantly*. I.13.36; 36.112; II.1.47; 4.294. **mænig-** 1x. [8 ex.]
gemenigfyldan vb I. *to enrich, increase, multiply*. I.6.16; 39.93; II.1.181; 12.280–2; 292. Pres.s.3 **-fylt**. **gemæn-** 5x. [16 ex.]
meni(g)u f. *crowd, multitude*. I.2.28; 4.76; II.4.34; 27.145. **-u** in all cases. [59 ex.]
mennisc adj. *human*. I.praef.73; 2.172; II.1.59; 15.277. [59 ex.]
mennisc n. *mankind, people, crowd*.

I.praef.66; 1.218; II.9.61; 27.143. **mennyssc** I.1.269. [18 ex.]

mennisclice adv. *in human form.* II.12.419.

menniscnyss f. *humanity, human form* (of Christ's incarnation). I.1.250; 2.177 ff; II.1.2; 4.89. **mennysc-** 4x. [132 ex.]

meolc f. *milk.* I.AppB3.10, 48; II.10.41; 12.46; 34.308 (**meoloc**).

meox n. *dung.* I.7.243; 18.210; II.19.118; 23.189. [9 ex.]

mercels m. *marked place.* II.11.130.

Mercurius a martyr of Cappadocia who, according to legend, after his death killed Julian the apostate. I.30.235–7.

[meregrot] n. *pearl.* dp. **-um** I.38.298.

meri(g)en m. *morning, morrow, next day.* I.6.151; 14.182; II.5.92; 11.368; 15.295; 21.14. ads. **meri(g)en**; gs. **merigenes.** [30 ex.] See also **ærnemerigen, tomerien.**

merigenlic adj. *in or of the morning.* II.5.73; 10.86; **merigenlic dæg** *a following day, a tomorrow* I.32.223.

gemet n. *measure, limit, moderation, extent, way.* I.6.202; 10.173; 34.124; II.19.8; 34.10. nap. **gemetu.** [23 ex.]

gemetan vb I. *to meet, find.* I.2.26; 7.261; II.1.52; 2.118. **mette** I.34.14. **þa gemettan,** *those who have met together* II.15.313, 317. [111 ex.]

gemett pp as adj. *painted.* II.26.25.

mete m. *food, portion of food.* I.1.145; 4.278; II.3.37; 9.45. nap. **mettas,** gp. **metta,** dp. **mettum.** [60 ex.] Cf **est-, flæsc-, for-.**

gemetegian vb II. *to control, moderate, balance, apportion.* I.20.274; 30.156; II.3.176; 10.266. [7 ex.] Cf **unge-.**

gemetegung f. *moderation.* II.12.549. Cf **unge-.**

meteleas adj. *without food.* II.25.4.

meteleast f. *lack of food.* II.25.33.

gemetfæstnyss f. *restraint, self-control.* I.6.117; 25.174; 39.100; II.1.283.

meting f. *picture, painting.* I.12.68–9; 23.112.

metod m. *god, fate?* As (apparently) gp., I.35.285; II.14.208; 23.185; 34.233; as possibly wk noun or adj. in s., I.38.351; II.19.49, 259. (On the uncertain class and sense of this poetic word in Ælfric's usage, see Godden 1980.)

metrumnyss f. *sickness.* I.34.122.

mettrum adj. *sick.* II.34.213.

gemicclian vb II. *to magnify, increase.* II.40.143.

micclum adv. *much, greatly.* I.8.157; 35.224; II.2.88; 11.314; **swa micclum swa,** *as much as* I.5.104; II.4.60; etc (21x). [100 ex.] (**micele/miccle** is more common in CH I, **micclum** in CH II; but both Series use **swa micclum swa** rather than .. **micele** .. .)

micel adj. *great, large.* I.1.177; 2.28; II.1.208; 2.120. Forms: **micel-, miccl-, micl-.** [530 ex.]

micele, miccle adv. *much.* I.8.46; 35.234; II.9.179; 12.489. [38 ex.]

micelnyss f. *size, amount, greatness, abundance.* I.3.121; 24.107; II.3.152; 4.112. [10 ex.]

Michael, Michahel St Michael the archangel. I.34.*passim.*

Micheas the prophet Micah. I.5.17; 7.21; II.1.138. as. **micheam.**

mid prep. w.dat. *with (by means of, in association with, accompanied by, filled with, etc).* I.praef.94; 1.9; II.praef.40; 1.3; **mid ealle** *entirely* I.1.59; 10.130; II.10.193; 12.562; **mid þam,** adv., *thereupon, at that* I.4.144; 15.37; II.8.14; 24.73; **mid þam þe,** conj., *while, when* I.8.108; 33.54; II.6.190; 31.27. [2844 ex.]

mid adj. see **middæg, midniht**

middan see **onmiddan, on . . . middan, ælemidde.**

middan(g)eard m. *the world, the earth.* I.praef.62; 1.210; II.1.18; 3.65. **-eard** 223x, **-geard** 8x (CH II 1x).

middaneardlic adj. *of the world.* I.AppB3.201; II.4.304; 9.208; 12.224. [8 ex.]

middæg m. *middle of the day, noon* (= Lat. *sexta hora*). ns. **middæg** II.5.63, 95; ds. **middæge** I.7.97; 15.177; as. **midne dæg** (after **ofer, on, ymbe**) I.8.124; II.5.11, 52, 95; 14.272.

middeweard adj. *middle.* **on middanweardan cyle** *amid the chill* I.5.106.

middewinter m. *midwinter, Christmas.* gs. **middewintres** I.13.157; **middes wintres** I.25.105.

midl n. *bit (for controlling a horse, etc.).* I.25.177.

midniht f. *midnight.* II.39.107; **on middere**

(midre, middre) nihte I.15.161; 18.46; II.34.321; 39.11, 105 ff.

midspreca m. *advocate*. I.27.68.

midwunung f. *cohabitation, living in company*. I.24.160; AppB3.104.

miht f. *power, might*. I.1.9; 4.199; II.15.114; 17.17; *act of power* I.15.151; 21.185; *virtue* I.15.81; 24.148; II.19.21; 40.242; as a term for an order of angels, I.24.86, 117. np. **miht** I.40.60? [172 ex.] Cf **un-**.

mihtig adj. *mighty, powerful*. I.1.25; 12.147; II.1.236; 14.216. [20 ex.] Cf **æl-, un-**.

mihtiglic adj. II.10.158 (or adv.).

mihtiglice adv. *powerfully, with strength*. I.8.32; 30.254; II.12.563; 15.3. **mihtelice** 3x, **mihtlice** 1x. [10 ex.]

mil f. *mile*. I.2.219; 34.6; II.11.172; 16.5. [9 ex.]

milde adj. *kind*. I.3.155; II.19.220.

mildheort adj. *merciful*. I.2.115; 3.154; II.5.251; 8.65. [31 ex.]

mildheortlice adv. *mercifully*. I.12.49; 31.293; 39.12, 60; AppB3.106; II.2.181.

mildheortnyss f. *mercy, mercifulness*. I.4.166; 7.158; II.1.282; 5.227 ff. [72 ex.]

milts f. *mercy, compassion*. I.37.136; II.18.112.

(ge-)miltsian vb II. w. dat. *to have mercy, to pardon*. I.1.161; 4.166–7; II.2.183; 5.223. **mylts-** 1x; **gemylts-** 1x; **gemildsige** 1x (MS Q). [44 ex.]

miltsung f. *mercy, forgiveness*. I.4.239; 27.28; II.8.36; 9.163. **mildsung** 2x. [24 ex.]

min poss.adj. *my, mine*. I.1.77; 2.42; II.1.1; 2.44. [609 ex.]

gemindig see **gemyndig**

mirre, myrre wk f. (and m.?). *myrrh*. I.5.30; 7.33, 209, 218, etc; AppB2.28; II.14.340. ns. **mirra** I.7.239. [14 ex.]

Misac one of the three Hebrew 'children' punished by Nebuchadnezzar. II.4.251. = **Missahel**.

misbysnian vb II. *to set a bad example*. II.3.241.

misdæd f. *misdeed*. I.16.81; II.3.232; 19.57; 28.38, 51.

misfaran vb 6. *to go wrong, fare badly*. I.6.172; II.19.3.

mishealdan vb 7. *to neglect, mistreat*. I.AppB3.58 (pret. **-heoldon**).

mislædan vb 1. *to lead astray*. Pres.s.3 **mislæt** I.10.184.

mislic adj. *variable, various*. I.5.115; 11.40; II.3.221; 6.56–7. **mys-** 1x. [71 ex.]

mislice adv. *variably, in various ways*. I.11.218; 15.52; II.4.232; 10.227.

mislician vb II. w. dat. *to displease*. I.29.31; 34.192.

mislicnyss f. *variety, variation*. II.5.90.

mislybban vb III. *to live badly*. I.AppB3.67, 218; II.19.180.

misræcan vb I. *to revile, treat roughly (?)* (= Lat. *exasperat*; cf Pope 15.176). II.40.266.

misræd m. *misguidance, ill counselling*. II.19.99.

Mis(s)ahel one of the three Hebrew 'children' punished by Nebuchadnezzar. I.37.191; II.1.231 ff. = **Misac**.

misscryda m. *ill-dressed person*. I.35.175, 182.

mist m. *mist*. I.AppB3.24, 187 ff.

mistæcan vb I. *to teach wrongly*. II.3.241.

misweaxan vb 7. *to grow wrongly*. pres.pt. as adj., **misweaxendan**, II.5.55.

miswendan vb I. *to corrupt, turn to wrong ends*. I.4.145; 7.147.

[mitta] m. *a measure of flour* (= Lat. *modius, corus(?); about 2 gallons?*). II.11.300; 40.42–3.

mixen f. *dung-heap*. II.30.119.

mod n. *mind, heart, spirit, state of mind*. I.praef.48; 3.133; II.1.82; 3.112. **mood, moode** 6x. [208 ex.] Cf **an-, æ-, ead-, eaþ-, forht-, heard-, ofer-, or-, þol-, unforht-, wac-**.

moder, modor f. *mother*. I.1.242; 4.131; II.1.11; 2.54. as. **moder, modor**; gs. **meder, moder, modor**; ds. **meder**; nap. **moddru, modru**; gp. **moddra**; dp. **moddrum**. [156 ex.] Cf **foster-**.

moderlic adj. *of a mother*. I.5.101; II.2.147.

modig adj. *proud, haughty*. I.8.138; 9.53, 57; II.12.60; 28.133. [19 ex.]

modigian vb II. *to exalt oneself, to grow proud*. I.1.31; 9.56–8; 18.201; II.12.537; *to resent out of pride* II.11.287. **modeg-** 5x; pp. **gemodode** I.35.92. [9 ex.]

modignyss f. *pride, haughtiness, self-exalting*. I.praef.104; 7.252; II.12.531 ff; 19.229. [39 ex.]

modrie wk f. *maternal aunt*. I.4.5; II.6.149; 27.3 (**moddrian**).
molde wk f. *earth, ground*. II.10.166; 18.45.
moldhype wk f. *mound of earth*. I.33.46.
mona m. *moon*. I.1.95; 4.110; II.12.428; 33.221 ff. [30 ex.]
monandæg m. *Monday*. I.6.168.
monaþ m. *month*. I.6.145 ff; 13.62; II.9.257; 17.28. gds. **monþe**; nap. **monaþ, monþas**; gp. **monþa**; dp. **monþum**. [23 ex.]
monaþseoc adj. *menstruating*. II.6.122.
monelic adj. *lunar*. I.40.40.
morþdæd f. *act of violence(?)*. I.AppB3.246.
gemot n. *meeting, assembly, council*. I.20.221, 224; II.10.239; 24.37.
motan pret. pres. vb. *to be allowed to, may*. I.praef.100; 1.71; II.3.201; 18.110; *to be obliged to, must*; I.5.126; AppB3.2, 119; II.39.102; 40.259; *to be able to, can(?)* II.10.180; w. vb. of motion implied, I.23.87; II.21.85; 23.164, 172. Pres.s.1 **mote**; 2 **most**; 3 **mot**; pl. **moton**; pret. **moste, moston**. [139 ex.]
motian vb II. *to address a meeting, make a speech*. II.24.38.
moþþe wk f. *moth*. II.7.105, 107.
Moyses Moses. I.2.189; 5.64; AppA1.1; II.1.48; 5.63. as. **moysen**; gs. **moyses**; ds. **moyse, moysen**. [75 ex.]
gemunan pret. pres. vb. *to remember*. w. gen. I.2.210; 24.197; II.5.222; 14.254; *to record* I.3.67. Pres.s.1 **gemune**; 3 **gemanþ** (I.20.204); imper. **gemun**; pret. **gemund-**. [14 ex.]
mund f. *protection*. I.34.46.
(ge)mundian vb II. *to protect*. I.19.235; II.7.48.
mundbora m. *protector*. I.23.65, 130; 24.208; 26.279. Cf **ræd-, swurd-**.
munt m. *mountain*. I.34.53 ff; II.11.119, 124, 572; 12.124 ff, 226 ff; 34.65 (dp. **munton**). [18 ex.]
munuc m. *monk*. I.praef.44; 23.135 ff; II.10.61; 11.28, etc. s. **munec-, munuc-**; pl. **munec-**. [43 ex.] Cf **mynster-**.
munuccild n. *boy-monk, child member of a monastery*. II.11.212, 362.
munuchad m. *monastic order*. I.27.198, 248; 35.220; II.9.157; 11.445.
munuclic adj. *monastic*. I.27.224; 35.253; II.9.51; 11.28; 34.94, 119 (**muneclice**).
munuclif n. *monastery*. I.22.106; II.9.32; 10.60, 141; 11.222. [9 ex.]
murcnian vb II. *to complain, grieve*. I.9.91.
must m. *new wine*. I.22.57.
muþ m. *mouth*. I.3.156; 4.224; II.1.193; 2.42. [82 ex.]
my- see also **mi-**
gemynd n. *memory, memorial, mention, record, festival*. I.2.218; 3.30, 35; II.2.6, 55; 13.4. [40 ex.]
gemyndig adj. *mindful*. I.25.94; *memorable, celebrated* I.25.76; **beon gemyndig** *to remember, keep in mind* I.3.157; 9.14; II.2.213; 28.135. **gemindig** 1x. [29 ex.] Cf **unge-**.
myndleas adj. *inattentive*. II.19.199; **gemyndleas** *witless, mad* II.11.578.
mynecenu, mynecynu f. *nun, woman leading a religious life*. II.2.57; 11.334 ff, 499, 514; 34.313; 37.176.
mynegian vb II. *to warn, exhort*. I.13.146; 15.4; II.3.296; 33.184. Pres. **myneg-, mynig-, myning-**; pp. **gemynegod, gemyngod**. [10 ex.]
mynegung f. *warning, exhortation*. I.praef.116; 25.220; II.9.182; 10.10. **mine-** 1x, **myng-** 2x. [20 ex.]
mynetcypa m. *money-changer*. I.28.177.
mynetere m. *money-changer, minter*. I.28.88, 166; II.38.31, 113, 119.
mynster n. *monastery*. I.praef.46; 22.107; II.10.87; 11.90. nap. **mynstra, mynstru**. [62 ex.]
mynsterlic adj. *monastic*. I.27.217; 34.112; II.10.62; 11.76.
mynsterlif n. *monastery*. II.20.261.
mynsterman m. *monk or nun*. II.20.187.
mynstermunuc m. *monk (a monk of one's own monastery?)*. I.35.223; II.11.385, 430.
gemyntan vb I. *to intend, design*. I.5.46; 28.200; II.2.86; 12.482. [15 ex.]
Myrce Mercians. gp. **myrcena** II.21.144.
myrhþ f. *joy, bliss*. I.praef.90; 4.4; II.1.201; 5.248. **myrcþ** 1x; **myrihþe** 1x; **myrþe** 1x; **myryhþe** 1x. [33 ex.]
myrig adj. *pleasant*. I.10.44; 12.17, 32–3; II.6.189.
myse wk f. *table*. I.12.117; 23.68; II.8.18; 10.293. [15 ex.]

na adv. *not, no.* I.1.111; 2.170; II.1.43; 3.41. [373 ex.]

Naaman Syrian general cured of leprosy by Elisha. I.27.230 ff.

Nabal enemy of David. I.32.114.

nabban vb III (= **ne habban**). *not to have, have not.* I.1.24; 3.113; II.4.7; 6.8. Pres.s.1 **næbbe**; 2 **næfst**; 3 **næfþ**; pl. **nabbaþ**; subj. **næbbe, næbbon**; pret. **næfde, næfdon**. [131 ex.]

Nabochodonosor, Nabuchodonosor Nebuchednezzar king of Babylon c604–562BC. I.37.190 (**nabochodenossor**); II.1.223 ff; 4.214 ff; 18.129; 28.97 ff.

Naboþ Naboth the Jezreelite, killed through the plots of Jezebel (1 Samuel 21). I.32.183.

nacednyss f. *nakedness.* I.27.108 (**næc-**); 29.238.

nacod adj. *naked, bare, lacking (outer) clothes.* I.1.141; 4.109–10; II.2.83; 11.155. **naced-** 4x. [23 ex.]

nagan pret. pres. vb (= **ne agan**). *to have not.* I.23.138; 35.227; II.12.510. Pret.s. **nahte**.

naht indef. pron. *nothing.* I.5.75; 6.187; II.18.92; 28.86; as adv., *not, not at all* I.5.63; 29.144; II.1.244; 6.105; as adj., *worthless* I.19.152; 20.237; II.13.32; 30.171. [48 ex.]

nahwar adv. *nowhere, never, not at all.* I.4.260; 20.111, 175; 35.133; II.12.295; 17.22. **nawar** 1x. [13 ex.]

Naim the town of Nain in Galilee. I.33.4, 16.

nama m. *name.* I.1.68; 2.55; II.1.142; 9.67; **for . . . naman** *on . . . behalf, for the sake of* I.27.130; 38.161; II.28.59; 37.79. [242 ex.]

namcuþ adj. *well-known.* I.23.46; II.20.161.

namcuþlice adv. *by name, individually.* I.37.28; II.4.316.

(ge)namian vb II. *to name, specify, appoint.* I.1.85; 5.158; II.8.63; 12.259. [13 ex.]

nan adj. *none, no.* I.1.13; 2.100; II.1.181; 3.43; as pron., *none, no-one* I.20.125; II.5.205; etc. Forms: **naan, nane, nænne, nanes, nanre, nare** (2x), **nanra, nanum**. [656 ex.]

nast, nat see **nytan**

nateshwon adv. *not at all.* I.5.18; 7.192; II.2.136; 5.161. Cf **na to þæs hwon** II.9.166. [32 ex.]

Nathan the prophet. II.40.12.

Nathanael one of Christ's disciples, sometimes identified with St Bartholomew. II.16.109.

naþor pron. *neither.* I.1.171; 7.144; II.15.252; 22.76; as adv, in construction **naþor (ne) . . . ne,** *neither . . . nor* I.10.106; 20.46; II.1.84; 3.17. **naþer** 3x. [25 ex.]

Nazarenisc adj. of Nazareth. I.5.178; II.16.11.

Nazareth town in Galilee. I.5.176. **nazareþ,** I.2.13; 9.222; 13.43.

næddercynn n. *the kind or genus of serpents (including dragons).* I.32.174. Cf **wyrmcynn**.

næddre wk f. *serpent.* I.1.129; 6.181; II.11.282; 13.239 ff. [44 ex.]

næfre adv. *never.* I.praef.61; 1.151; II.1.238; 3.92. [101 ex.]

nægl m. *nail.* I.9.172; 14.183; II.14.241; 18.50; *finger-nail* I.16.120; II.28.117. nap. **næglas, næiglas**; dp. **nægelum, næglum, næiglum**. [9 ex.] Cf **wer-**.

næglian vb II. *to nail (on the cross).* pp. **genæglod** I.5.86.

nær-, næs see **beon**

næsþyrl n. *nostril.* II.12.60. Cf **nos-**.

ne negative particle. *not.* I.praef.53; 1.13; II.praef.30; 1.33; as conj., *nor* I.16.136 ff; 22.140 ff; II.1.20; 3.156 ff. **næ** 1x; **ny** 1x. [2183 ex.]

(ge)neadian vb II. *to compel, press, urge.* I.praef.76; 1.121; II.9.221; 33.223. [21 ex.]

neadung f. *compulsion, force, pressure.* I.25.152, 159–61; 35.185; II.12.510.

neadunga, -ge adv. *by force, under compulsion.* I.14.168; 37.205; II.5.250; 40.271. [10 ex.]

neadwis adj. *due, requisite.* II.20.108.

neadwislice adv. *of necessity.* I.6.68.

genealæcan vb I. *to approach, draw near, be at hand.* w. dat. or less commonly **to**. I.5.137; 8.88; II.1.255; 4.136; with ref. to marital relations, I.9.12; II.19.182; *to resemble* I.27.226. Pres.s.3 **genealæcþ, -læhþ**; pl. **-læcaþ**; pret. **genealæht-, -lehton** (1x); pp. **-læht**. [90 ex.]

nealæcung f. *approach.* I.5.162; 38.56; 40.91; **genealæcung** II.13.6.

nean adv. *from near by*. I.25.136 (*near in time*); II.2.180 (*from close behind*); 25.59.
Neapolis Naples. as. **neapolim** I.34.58.
Neapolite the people of Naples. I.34.40.
near adv. (or adj.), comp. of **neah**. *nearer*. I.19.165, 168; 39.50; II.19.68; 22.194; 30.62.
nearo, nearu adj. *narrow*. I.2.95; 10.167–9; 35.262, 269; II.11.538, 544. dsf. **nearure**; np. **nearowe**.
nearunyss f. *difficulty, oppressiveness* (= Lat. *angustia*). II.16.59.
neawist f. *vicinity*. I.5.173; 8.77; II.2.3; 11.140. [17 ex.]
neb n. *face*. I.19.61; 20.171; II.7.60–1; 11.46. [12 ex.] Cf **heard-**.
[nebbian] vb II. *to confront? rebuke?* I.18.187.
nebwlitu f. *face*. I.3.27; 31.32; II.26.36; 27.215. Cf **and-**.
nedbrice m. *needs*. II.10.201 (here a euphemism for a privy).
nehgebur m. *neighbour*. I.24.11, 37–9; 25.28, 35; II.37.32. **necheburas** I.34.19.
nehstan see **next**
nellan anom vb (= **ne willan**). *to be unwilling, to refuse, will not*. I.praef.115; 1.50; II.3.31; 5.120. Pres.s.1 **nelle, nylle** (1x); 2 **nelt**; 3 **nele**; pl. **nellaþ**; pret. **nolde, noldest, noldon**. [261 ex.]
(ge)nemnan vb I/II. *to name, mention by name, mention specifically*. I.20.131; 23.47; II.11.230; 16.110. Inf. **nemnan** 1x, **nemnian** 1x (I.AppA1.14); pret.s. **nemde, genemnode**; pp. **genemned, genemnod**. [19 ex.]
neod f. *need, necessity, what is needed*. I.2.194; 5.110; II.3.91; 7.126. [53 ex.]
neodlice adv. *urgently*. I.23.150; II.2.35.
neogoþa see **nigoþa**.
neom see **beon**
neorx(e)nawang m. *Paradise* (as the Garden of Eden or a future place of rest). I.1.69 ff, 131 ff; 7.249–51; II.5.137, 146 (printed as 2 words); 20.3, 12. **neorcsenawang** 3x. [15 ex.]
geneosian vb II. *to visit*. I.2.219; 3.196; II.7.150 ff; 10.309. [43 ex.]
(ge)neosung f. *visitation, visit*. I.4.4; 22.210; II.10.151; 19.35. [13 ex.]
neoþan adv. *beneath, at the bottom*. II.14.277; 32.212.
neoþewerde adv. *below*. II.30.118. **oþ neoþeweardan**, *to bottom* II.33.257.
neoþor adv. *lower*. I.3.86.
neow- see **nyw-**
gener n. *refuge, help*. II.21.149.
Nerfa the Roman emperor Nerva, reigned 96–8AD. I.4.33.
generian vb I/II. *to rescue, liberate*. I.14.204; 15.167; 30.162, 254; II.9.74. Pret.s. **generede, -ode**; pp. **-od**.
Nero Roman emperor, reigned 54–68AD. I.4.22; 26.148, etc; 35.100. ds. **nerone**.
nese interj. *no*. II.16.115; printed **ne se** I.23.24.
nest n. *nest*. I.10.146; AppB2.27; II.10.192.
net n. *net*. I.27.140; 38.8, etc; II.16.115 ff. ds. **nette**; ap. **net**. [19 ex.]
[netel] f. *nettle*. **netelum** II.11.53.
next adj. (from superl. of **neah**). *last*. II.10.312; **æt nextan** *at last, finally* I.1.236; 5.162; II.2.44. **æt nehstan** 3x. [32 ex.] Cf **ende-**.
nexta m. *neighbour*. I.22.220; 38.122; II.5.207; 19.7, 60 ff. **nehsta** 1x. [17 ex.]
Nicanor (a) one of the first seven deacons. I.3.10. (b) kinsman of King Xerxes of Persia, healed by St Simon the apostle. II.33.170.
Nichodemus a Pharisee and leader of the Jews, converted to Christ, and assisting at his burial. I.14.185; II.13.237; 14.340.
Nicolaus one of the first seven deacons. I.3.11.
nigan, nigon num. *nine*. I.1.24; 4.244; II.5.243; 11.256. [17 ex.]
nighworfen adj. *newly converted*. II.9.232.
nigontyne num. *nineteen*. I.29.106, 252.
nigoþa, neogoþa adj. *ninth*. I.36.250, 255; II.5.74; 12.74, 328; 14.273.
niht f. *night*. I.2.122; 4.240; II.7.12; 24.142; **nihtes** *by night* I.4.123; 5.36; II.6.180; 11.498; **on niht** *at night* I.16.36; II.30.168; etc. as., ap. **niht**; ds. **nihte**; gp. **nihta**; dp. **nihtum, nihton** (1x). [113 ex.] Cf **em-, mid-, sæter-, sunnan-**.
nihtlic adj. *nocturnal, in the night*. I.5.140; 7.123; II.12.112; 24.89. [7 ex.]
genihtsum adj. *abundant, abounding*. I.4.101; 17.65; 24.67; 33.5; AppB3.26, 189.
genihtsumian vb II, pers. and impers. *to suffice, to be good enough, to abound*.

I.4.114; 8.68; II.6.66; 38.151; 39.16, 149. [12 ex.]

genihtsumlice adv. *sufficiently, abundantly, in abundance.* I.4.193; 20.167; II.7.67; 20.225. [11 ex.]

genihtsumnyss f. *sufficiency, abundance.* I.4.115; 13.38; II.11.134; 12.110. [11 ex.]

(ge)niman vb 4. *to take.* I.4.95; 5.168; II.3.80; 5.29; *to feel, show, have* (an emotion, virtue, etc) I.9.90; 11.141; II.19.256; etc.; **niman bysne æt** or **be,** *to take as an example* I.9.197; etc. Pres.s.3 **nimþ, nymþ, genimþ**; pl. **nimaþ, nymaþ, genimaþ**; subj. **nime, nyme, genime**; inf. **niman, geniman, genyman**; imper. **nim, genim; nimaþ**; pres.pt. **nimende**; pret.s. **nam, genam, gename**; pl. **namon, genamon**; pp. **genumen**. [155 ex.]

Nineue the city of Nineveh in Assyria. ds. **nineuen** I.18.15, 31; **niniue** I.37.187.

Niniueisc of Nineveh. I.18.12; II.9.137.

genip n. *(gloom of) cloud or mist.* I.34.55 (**gehnipum**); 40.125; AppB3.24, 187, 197. (Renders Lat. **nubila**, *cloudy weather*, at I.40, but **caligo** in I.34—though it is round a mountain top and perhaps therefore cloud rather than mist; in AppB3 **mist and genip** render 3x **nubes et caligo**, in that order, but the interpretation focuses on mist alone, unlike the probable source, and the sense of **genip** may here be the gloom of mist.)

nis see **beon**.

nitenlic adj. *bestial, brutish.* I.35.270 (but perhaps also implying *ignorant, unknowing*, cf **nytenlic**).

niþ m. *hostility, hatred.* I.3.153; 24.20; II.4.194; 11.140. [7 ex.]

niþer, nyþer adv. *down, downwards.* I.3.198; 11.111; II.3.119; 5.146. [13 ex.]

niþer- see also **nyþer-**.

niþerhreosende adj. *falling back.* I.11.111.

geniþerian, genyþerian vb II. *to condemn.* I.4.56; 11.92; II.3.260; 12.487. [10 ex.]

geniþerung, genyþerung f. *damnation.* I.21.81; 23.58; 28.110; II.39.131. [11 ex.]

niþerlic, nyþerlic adj. *lower, low down.* I.35.72; II.11.545; 20.95.

niþful adj. *malicious, full of hatred.* I.39.89, 91; II.11.33, 158; 13.13.

niþfullice adv. *maliciously, out of hatred.* I.3.44; II.13.61.

niwan adv. *recently.* II.11.62; 14.346 (**niwe**); 22.186; 23.11.

niwe adj. *new.* I.6.107 ff; 7.71; II.7.18; 14.52; *recent* I.40.33; as partitive genitive, I.40.44; II.18.86. [42 ex.] Cf **ed-**.

niwerene adj. *small, recently born?* **niwerenan cilde** I.37.129 (= Lat. *filio parvulo*).

geniwian vb II. *to repeat, rehearse.* I.3.35. Cf **geed-, edniwung**.

niwlice adv. *soon.* II.33.207.

Noe the patriarch Noah. I.1.181 ff; 6.14; II.4.113 ff; 5.62 ff. [16 ex.]

genoh adj. and pron. *enough.* I.12.20; 23.55; II.20.136; 26.119. [9 ex.]

genoh adv. *enough, sufficiently.* I.1.134, 273; 9.21; 19.75, 155; II.9.8.

non m. *the ninth hour* (3 hours after mid-day). I.7.97; 15.177; II.5.13, 64; 14.273.

nontid f. *the ninth hour.* I.14.184; II.5.12, 52, 97–8.

norþdæl m. *northern part.* I.1.33; 34.94, 115; II.14.243.

norþduru f. *northern door.* I.34.66.

norþerne adj. *northern* (= here *Northumbrian*). II.21.150.

Norþhymere the Northumbrians. gp. **-era** II.21.4, 144.

nosþyrl n. *nostril.* II.6.194; 21.51. Cf **næs-**.

nosu f. *nose.* I.31.34; 37.180; II.23.49. ads. **-u**.

notian vb II. *to use.* II.26.106 (w. gen.), 114–5 (w. acc.).

notu f. *office, duty.* II.40.303.

nu adv. *now, at this point in time.* I.praef.110; 13.222; II.1.263; 7.34; as a connective introducing a new point, esp. with **cweþan**, I.1.117; 3.172; 30.91; II.3.246; 28.13; as conj., *now that, since* I.6.190; 38.174; II.16.101; 39.146; **nu for feawum dagum** *a few days ago* I.7.3; etc. (but not II.25.6, etc).; **nu on þunresdæig** *this Thursday*; **nu todæg** *today, on this day* I.2.120; II.5.136; etc. [622 ex.]

(ge)nydan vb I. *to compel, attempt to compel.* I.1.54; 11.69; 37.99; II.1.27; 23.18, 100. pp. **genedd** I.1.155. pp. as adj. **genydne,** *enforced* II.33.147. [12 ex.]

nydbehefe adj. *necessary*. I.18.205; 21.156; 31.254; 34.228; II.34.294.

nydbehof adj. *necessary*. II.29.16, 45.

nydþearfnyss f. *necessity, need*. I.30.266; II.10.312.

nyrewet n. *narrowness*. I.2.96.

genyrwian vb II. *to enclose*. I.28.9, 134. pp. **genyr(e)wed** *narrow(ed), crowded* I.2.98; 35.267, 270.

nyt adj. *useful*. I.28.174. Cf **un-**.

nytan pret. pres. vb (= **ne witan**). *not to know*. I.1.209; 6.49; II.2.183; 5.179. pres. part. as adj. w. gen., *ignorant*, II.40.26. Pres. **nast, nat, nyton**; subj. **nyte**; pret. **nyste, nyston**. [61 ex.]

nyten n. *animal* (esp. domestic). I.1.96; 6.98; II.10.85; 12.132. nap. **-nu**. [50 ex.]

nyten adj. *ignorant, unknowing*. I.4.69; II.8.127.

nytencynn n. *species or race of (domestic) animals*. I.1.105.

nytenlic adj. *ignorant, unknowing*. II.10.8. Cf **nitenlic**.

nytennyss f. *ignorance, lack of understanding*. I.2.123; 4.142; II.3.181; 11.581. **nytten-** 1x. [18 ex.]

nyþemest adj. *lowest*. I.35.263; II.4.299.

nyþergan anom. vb. *to go down, descend*. Pret.s. **nyþereode** I.8.6.

nyþerfeallan vb 7. *to fall down*. I.5.28; 7.32.

nyþeweard adj. *lower*. I.35.233; **on nyþeweardan** *at the bottom* I.35.262.

nywelnyss f. *abyss*. I.1.192; 11.133; 31.157; II.21.40 ff. **niwel-** 1x, **neowel-** 1x. [8 ex.]

Octauianus the Roman emperor Augustus, 63BC–14AD. I.2.9, 53.

of prep. w. dat. *from, off, out of, away from*. I.praef.55; 1.18; 2.11; II.praef.31; 1.36; 2.16. Indicating derivation (esp. by birth or descent), separation, construction (**of golde**); motive or prompting emotion: **na of rihtwisnysse ac of niþe**, *not out of righteousness but out of malice* (I.24.20); denoting place in which an action occurs, but relating to a distant object: **þæt fæt of his setle bletsode**, *blessed that vessel from his seat* (II.11.77); *after* a point of time: **of þam andweardan dæge** (II.10.313); partitive (**micel menigu . . . of iudeiscre þeode**); partitive without noun object, implying *some of*, **bringaþ of þam fixum** (II.16.122), *some part of*, **se þe of þam hlafe geet** (I.2.82), or *something from*, **gif ge of þam treowe geetaþ** (I.1.134); as adv., = *off*, II.11.431. [904 ex.]

ofarn see **ofyrnan**

ofaxian vb II. *to learn, discover*. II.9.221; 21.154.

ofæt- see **ofet**

ofbeatan vb 7. *to beat severely(?), beat to death*. I.36.75; II.3.44. pp. **ofbeaten**.

ofcalen pp. as adj. *chilled*. II.14.131. (from **ofcalan** vb 6)

ofclypian vb II. *to summon by calling?* II.11.529.

ofcyrf m. *cutting off, offcut or piece cut off*. I.6.82; II.34.35.

ofdræd adj. (wk pp. of **ofdrædan** vb 7?) *frightened*. I.15.28, 103; II.1.188 (**nan þing ofdrædde,** *frightened in any way*); 24.70, 152; 34.68.

ofelete wk f. *eucharistic wafer*. II.11.355.

ofen m. *oven, furnace*. I.36.87; 37.192 ff; II.1.229 ff; 18.123 ff.

ofer m. *bank, shore*. II.10.107, 209; 12.89.

ofer prep. w. dat. or acc. *over, above, upon, beyond, outside, on top of, throughout, across, after*. I.1.36; 2.102; 5.142; II.1.151; 3.150; 5.13. Expressing location or movement above a point or throughout a space or across a boundary, time after a point or throughout a period, superiority or comparison, action taking effect on something or following on from something or going beyond boundaries, etc. No clear distinctions between usage with dat. and acc.; cf, e.g., I.36.125 and 127. [218 ex.]

oferarn see **oferyrnan**

oferæt m. *over-eating, gluttony*. I.35.191; 39.31, 75.

oferbord see **oforbord**.

oferbrædan vb I. *to cover*. I.34.107; II.2.59.

oferbricgian vb II. *to bridge, make a bridge over*. II.18.23.

oferdon anom. vb. *to overdo, do to excess*. pp. **oferdon** II.36.64.

oferdrenc m. *excessive drinking*. II.1.288; 40.281.

oferdrifan vb 1. *to defeat, overcome*. I.11.152 (pret.s. **-draf**); II.27.124.

ofereaca m. *remainder*. II.4.217; 9.36; 19.232.

oferfaran vb 6. *to pass through or beyond*. pp. **oferfaræn** I.15.92.

oferfæreld n. *passage, crossing over*. I.15.117; II.4.38.

oferfeohtan vb 3. *to conquer*. II.37.129.

oferferan vb I. *to pass over or through*. I.12.26–8; II.10.54.

oferflowedlic adj. *excessive, superfluous*. I.25.172.

oferflowednyss f. *excess, superfluity*. I.11.39; 23.83, 127; II.6.103; 37.61; **oferflowendnysse** II.12.494.

oferfyll f. *surfeit, excessive consumption*. II.1.288–90; 12.495.

ofergan anom vb. *to overrun, cover*. I.5.132–4; 40.144; II.23.146; 40.248. Pres.s.3 **-gæþ**; pret. **ofereod-**. [7 ex.]

ofergægednyss f. *transgression*. II.31.39; 33.92.

ofergeotan vb 2. *to suffuse, drench*. II.20.50 (pp. **-goten**), 239.

ofergeweorc n. *sepulchre*. II.26.25. (cf Pope p. 897)

oferglidan vb 1. *to glide over, pass over*. I.7.75 (pret.s **-glad**).

ofergyld adj. *gilded*. II.40.190.

oferhangen adj. (pp. of **oferhon**). *covered*. I.34.55.

oferheafod adv? *singly*? I.2.11.

oferhogian vb II. *to despise, repudiate*. I.34.11.

oferhydig adj. *haughty, arrogant*. II.11.337.

[**ofermettu**] f. *pride, arrogance*. dp. I.1.45; 13.7.

ofermod adj. *proud, arrogant*. II.28.96.

oferniman vb 4. *to seize, overpower*. pp. **-numen** I.15.57.

oferrædan vb I. *to read over, read through*. I.7.3; 11.7; 39.11; II.21.180; 30.227.

oferrrowan vb 7. *to row across*. II.23.147 (pret. **-reowon**); 24.59. (The refs. seem to be to rowing rather than sailing.)

ofersc(e)adewian vb II. *to cast a shadow upon*. I.13.58, 129–33.

ofersceawian vb II. *to examine, investigate*. II.19.102.

ofersceotan vb 2. *to jump over*. I.32.128 (pres.s.3 **oferscyt**; perhaps better as **þærofer scyt**.)

oferseon vb 5. *to see over*. II.11.526 (pret.s. **-seah**), 537.

oferslege n. *lintel*. I.22.7; II.3.82; 15.13, 53.

oferslype m. *over-garment, surplice(?)*. I.31.36.

oferspece adj. *contentious, disputatious*. I.32.176.

oferstælan vb I. *to reveal, prove*. I.40.93; *to defeat, refute* II.7.18.

ofersteall m. *resistance, standing in opposition*? I.35.241.

oferstigan vb 1. *to surpass, rise above*. I.1.193; 4.184; 38.25; II.9.16; 39.49. **oferstigende**, pres.part. as adj., *superior, surpassing* I.19.62; 24.155; II.26.94. Pres.s.3 **-stihþ**; pret.s. **-stah**. [18 ex.]

oferswiþan, -swyþan vb I. *to overcome, defeat, surpass*. I.3.18; 4.214; II.11.57; 12.362. Pres.s.3 **-swiþ**. [44 ex.]

oferteon vb 2. *to cover*. I.1.198 (pres.s.1 **-teo**).

ofertrahtnian vb II. *to expound thoroughly*. I.13.194.

oferþeccan vb I. *to cover*. pp. **-þe(a)ht** II.21.35; 23.133.

oferþeon vb 2(?). *to excel, surpass*. pp. **oferþogen** I.30.208.

oferweaxan vb 6. *to overgrow*. pp. **oferweaxen** I.34.106.

oferwinnan vb 3. *to defeat, overcome*. I.3.120; 14.206–9; II.12.477 ff; 37.127. Pret. **-wan(n), -wunnon**. [18 ex.]

oferwreon vb 1/2. *to cover, cover over*. I.3.121; II.2.65; 11.430; 12.98, 128; 27.133. Pret.s. **-wreah**; pp. **-wrogen**. Cf **on-, under-**.

oferyrnan vb 3. *to go through, discuss briefly (a text)*. I.7.7; 13.195; 27.65; 38.151; *to overwhelm* II.12.97. Pret. **-arn, -urnon**.

ofet n. *fruit*. I.25.45; 36.115 (ds. **ofæte**); AppB2.2 (np. **ofætu**); II.3.18.

offeallan vb 7. *to fell, destroy by falling*. II.34.174 (pret.s. **offeoll**).

offeran vb I. *to overtake, catch up with*. II.12.87.

offlowan vb 7. *to flow from*. II.15.180 (pret s. **offleow**). (But better as 2 words, **of fleow**.)

(ge)offrian vb II. *to offer* (a gift, sacrifice, etc to God or gods; object sometimes unexpressed). I.3.156, 160 ff; 7.204 ff; II.3.88; 4.133 ff. **ofr-** 6x. [129 ex.]

offringsang m. *hymn sung during the offering*. I.14.202.

offrung f. *offering* (the act of giving something to God, or the object given). I.31.116; 38.130–1; II.4.141 ff; 15.24. [27 ex.]

ofgan anom. vb. *to require, exact, extort*. I.praef.113; 17.62; II.11.449; 20.147; 38.32, 124; *to win, obtain* I.7.258; II.9.146. Pres.s.1 **ofga**; 3 **ofgæþ**; imper. **ofgang** I.29.79 (from next word). [11 ex.]

ofgangan vb 7. *to go out or forth*. pres. part. I.20.80.

ofgeotan vb 2. *to quench, dowse*. II.11.200.

ofhingrod adj. *hungry, afflicted by hunger*. I.13.200; 36.159, 211–2. (pp. of **ofhingrian**?)

ofhreosan vb 2. *to ruin, overwhelm, bury*. Pret.s. **ofhreas** I.40.35 (= Lat. **subruo**); pp. **ofhroren** I.33.46; 36.77 (both = Lat. **obruo**). (Meanings perhaps affected by Latin models.)

ofhreowan vb 2. *to grieve, to sadden*. impers. w. **þæt** clause, I.praef.53; w. dat. of person affected and nom., gen. or dat. of cause, I.13.13–14; 23.140; 38.328; II.25.5, 31–3; pers., w. dat. *to grieve for, feel sorry for* I.4.134. Pres.s.3 **ofhrywþ, ofhreowþ**; pret.s. **ofhreow**.

ofhyran vb I. *to overhear*. II.32.13.

oflangod adj. *afflicted with longing*. II.11.364. (Pp. of **oflangian**?)

oflician vb II. *to displease*. w. dat. II.12.453; 21.97.

oflyst adj. *desirous (of), eager (for)*. I.9.23; 13.200; 18.85.

oforbord adv. *overboard*. I.18.19, 25. (Perhaps better as **ofer bord**, with **bord** = *side of ship*.)

ofost f. *haste*. I.26.233.

ofsc(e)amod adj. *ashamed*. II.10.124; 27.74; 34.327.

ofsceotan vb 2. *to shoot (i.e. kill by shooting)*. I.34.17, 27, 57, 63. pp. **ofscoten**.

ofseon vb 5. *to see*. I.4.46; 28.5; 38.295; II.11.526; 34.155. Pret.s. **ofseah**.

ofsettan vb I. *to oppress, afflict*. I.15.103; 34.58; II.15.247; 26.39. [12 ex.]

ofsittan vb 5. *to oppress, assail, attack*. I.10.70; 12.110; 17.56; 35.59; II.25.75.

ofslean vb 6. *to kill*. I.5.155; 9.171; II.12.442; 14.70. Pres.s.3 **ofslihþ, ofslyhþ**; pl. **ofsleaþ**; imper. **ofslih**; pret. **ofsloh, ofslog-**; pp. **ofslegen**. [66 ex.]

ofsniþan vb 1. *to kill*. I.AppB3.58, 62; II.4.172; 15.38. (Object in all cases is a sheep.) Pres.s.3 **ofsniþ**; pret. **ofsnaþ, ofsnidon**; pp. **ofsniden**.

ofspring m. *offspring, progeny, descendants*. I.1.153; 3.33; II.4.155; 12.20. **ofsprincg** 2x. [28 ex.]

ofstingan vb 3. *to kill (by piercing with a spear)*. Pret.s. **ofstang**. I.30.264. Cf **be-**.

oft adv. *often, frequently*. I.4.257; 6.129; II.3.266; 5.127; **swa oft swa**, *as often as, whenever* I.11.135; II.25.99; etc. comp. **oftor**, sup. **oftost**. [65 ex.]

ofteon vb 2. *to withdraw, take away* (w. dat. of person taken from). I.11.213; 16.10; II.6.155; 7.75–6. Pres.s. **ofteo, oftihst, oftihþ**; pl. **ofteoþ**; pret.pl. **oftugon**; pp. **oftogen**. [20 ex.]

ofthrædlice adv. *frequently*. II.4.195.

oftorfian vb II. *to pelt to death* (with stones), *to stone*. I.2.190; 3.54, 117; 13.85; 28.26.

oftredan vb 5. *to trample, tread down*. I.12.110; II.6.69; 24.146–8. Pres.s.3 **oftret**; pret.s. **oftræd**; pp. **oftreden**. Cf **for-**.

ofþincan vb I. impers., *to regret*. w. dat. of person and *þæt*-clause, I.1.180; II.12.86; and noun in gen., I.5.141; 13.10 (or nom.?); and noun in nom., II.33.141. Pret.s. **ofþuhte**.

ofþriccan vb I. *to crush* (to death). I.33.51; 35.246; II.6.99; 11.164; 30.79. Pres.s.3 **ofþrihþ**; pret.s. **ofþrihte**.

ofþricednyss, ofþryc(c)ednyss f. *pressure, crowding*. I.40.8, 30, 34.

ofþringan vb 3. *to crowd around*. II.24.240 (pres.s.3 **ofþrincþ**).

ofþyrst adj. *afflicted by thirst*. I.36.159, 211–2. (Pp. of **ofþyrstan**?)

ofunnan pret.pres. vb. *to withhold, not grant*. I.26.87.

ofwundrod adj. *amazed*. I.9.147; II.40.158. (Pp. of **ofwundrian**?)

ofyrnan vb 3. *to overtake (by running)*. I.27.236 (pret.s. **ofarn**).

oga m. *terror*. I.15.106; 16.69; II.6.188; 18.124. [21 ex.]

(ge)olæcan vb I. *to flatter, treat well or kindly or obsequiously*. I.32.219; 33.50;

II.6.177; 19.263–4. Pres.s.3 **olæcþ, geolæhþ**; pret. **olæht-**. [8 ex.]

olæcung f. *flattery, seductive charm*. I.32.186; 33.41–2.

olfend m. *camel*. I.23.43; 31.69; II.17.73; 30.11, 73; 34.130. **oluend-** 3x. [13 ex.]

Olifeti, Olíueti the Mount of Olives near Jerusalem. I.14.7; 21.17; 30.69.

oll n. *taunting?* **mid olle,** *triumphantly, tauntingly* II.11.207.

om, omm m. *rust*. II.7.105–7.

on prep. *in, into, on, among, at, with, by means of, against* signifying location in place or time, motion into, condition or situation, form or instrument, object of belief, etc. I.praef.45; 1.12; 2.5; II.praef.33; 1.42; 2.11. Usu. with dat., but w. acc. (a) in sense *into*, I.1.45; 8.169 (cf. app. crit.); II.19.291; 23.131 (though often with dat. instead); (b) after **gelyfan,** *to believe*, (sometimes w. dat.; q.v.); (c) in certain expressions of time, e.g. **on æfen, on ær** (*previously*), **on midne dæg, on sumne timan, on ealra worulda woruld** (= *for eternity*); (d) in certain other expressions, e.g. **on an** *continually*, **on emtwa** *in two*, **on englisc** *in English*, **on idel** *in vain*, **on riht** *rightly*, **on . . . wisan** *in . . . ways*. (For authorial changes of case, see CH I p. 128–31, and CH II p. lxxx.) [4851 ex.]

onælan vb I. *to ignite, kindle, heat* (often figuratively). I.7.237; 38.287; II.1.239; 3.143. [18 ex.]

onbeslagen adj. *inflicted*. II.6.42. Cf **slean**.

onbryrdan vb I. *to inspire, infuse*. II.3.112, 142; pp. as adj., **onbryrd,** *inspired, incited, moved* I.4.14; 9.89; II.2.47; 6.82. [22 ex.]

onbryrdnyss f. *inspiration, zeal, devotion, sincere emotion, stirring*. I.9.32, 88; 16.87; II.28.49; 32.32.

onbugan vb 2. *to submit, yield, give way*. I.praef.90; II.1.207; 17.79 (pres.s.2 **onbihst**); 22.47.

onbutan, onbuton prep. w. dat. *around, about*. I.AppB2.11; II.1.210; 20.243; 32.202. adv. II.30.35.

onbyrian, onbirian vb I. *to taste, partake of*. w. gen. I.1.151; 2.83; II.4.18; 13.28. [27 ex.] Cf **a-**. Pres.s.3 **-rigþ**; pl. **-riaþ, -rigaþ**; pret. **-rigd-**.

oncnawan vb 7. *to recognize, acknowledge*. I.4.69; 9.98; II.20.208; 26.35; *to perceive, discover, learn, come to know, understand* I.17.75 ff; 36.22; II.13.26; 18.46. Pres.s.2 **oncnæwst,** 3 **oncnæwþ**; pret. **oncneow, oncneowon**; subj. **oncneowe, oncneuwe** (1x); pp. **oncnawen**. [117 ex.] (Senses difficult to distinguish, and some tendency to use past tense = *have come to know, have discovered*, to mean *to know*.)

oncnawennyss f. *acknowledgement, understanding, knowledge*. I.28.144; II.16.45; 22.78 ff.

ondrædan vb 7. *to fear, dread, be afraid*. I.38.280; 40.25–6; II.9.112–3; 34.77. w. refl. pronoun, I.16.91; 18.129; II.4.295; 9.241–3. Used absolutely, with noun object or **þæt**-clause. Pres.s.2 **ondrædst, ondrætst,** 3 **ondræt**; pret. **ondred, ondredon**. [62 ex.] Cf **a-**.

ondrædendlic adj. *frightening, to be dreaded*. I.29.60; II.5.183.

ondon anom. vb. *to undo, open*. pret.s. **ondyde** II.1.193.

oneardian vb II. *to inhabit*. I.20.179.

onem, onemm, onemn prep. w. acc. *near, beside*. I.2.22; II.23.163; adv. *near by* II.16.122, 186.

onettan vb I. *to hasten*. I.26.290; 27.109; II.10.324; 21.56. [8 ex.]

onfangennyss f. *receiving, reception, acceptance*. II.5.169; 38.163, 172.

onfon vb 7. *to receive, accept, take*. w. acc. or gen. I.4.219; 8.43; II.2.44; 5.22. Pres.s.1 **onfo**; 3 **onfehþ**; pl. **onfoþ**; imper. **onfoh, onfoþ**; pret. **onfeng**; pp. **onfangen**. [33 ex.] Cf **underfon**.

ongean prep. w. dat. or acc. *against, contrary to, in contrast to*. I.19.118; 35.282; II.4.56, 202; 34.172; *in response to?* I.13.177; *opposite* I.14.8; AppB2.14; II.11.241; 12.404; *towards, to meet* I.4.36. [110 ex.]

ongean adv. *back (returning, responding)*. I.27.62; 31.48; II.11.437; 34.174; *in opposition* II.3.86. **ongeon** I.37.186. [53 ex.]

onginnan vb 3. *to begin*. (a) used absolutely, I.6.138; II.5.243; (b) w. noun object, I.6.132; II.14.65; (c) w. inf., I.4.73; II.17.94; (d) w. **to** + infl. inf., I.9.91; II.5.23. Pres.s. **onginþ, ongynþ**; pl. **onginnaþ, ongynnaþ**; pret.

ongan(n), ongunnon; pp. **ongunnen**. [74 ex.] Cf **be-** etc.

ongytan vb 5. *to perceive, realise*. I.1.125; 38.202; II.6.184; 10.45. Pret.s. **ongeat**. [8 ex.] Cf **be-** etc.

ongyte f. *infusion, inspiration*. I.25.217.

onhagian vb II impers. *to be fitting, appropriate, feasible*. I.11.213; 27.207; 30.186.

onhebban vb 6. *to exalt* (usu. reflexive). I.13.198; 31.298; II.5.175; 19.228. Pres.s.3 **onhæfþ, onhefþ**; pret. **onhofon**. [9 ex.]

onhinder adv. *backwards*. I.11.113.

onhrop m. *persistence*. I.18.52, 88.

onlihtan vb I. *to illuminate*. I.7.115; 10.58; II.10.47; 16.67–8. **onlyht-** 1x. [37 ex.]

onlihting f. *illumination, enlightenment*. I.7.112; 10.64 (**onlihttinge**); 20.154; II.40.178. [7 ex.]

onlocian vb II. *to watch, look at*. Pres.pt. I.21.18; 30.67, 264; 31.198; II.6.18.

onmiddan prep. w. dat. *amid, in the middle of*. I.1.72; 30.233; II.1.251; 10.173; **on . . . middan**, II.10.165; 20.57; **on . . . middum**, II.21.38. [16 ex.]

onsægednyss f. *sacrifice*. I.25.145; 32.99; II.12.346; 40.20. [13 ex.]

onscunian vb II. *to shun, avoid, reject*. I.7.175; 8.56; II.1.280; 4.41. [14 ex.] Cf **a-**.

onscyte m. *attack, onslaught*. II.40.66. Cf **under-, un-**.

onsigan vb 1. *to approach menacingly, impend*. I.18.32; 28.110, 203; II.9.110, 142; 10.219. Pres.s.3 **onsihþ**; pret.pl. **onsigon**.

onstandan vb 6. *to exist, to be contained*. II.27.93 (pret.s. **onstod**).

onsundran, -on adv. *apart, separately*. I.10.4; II.10.31, 310; 34.67; Expl.8.

ontendan vb I. *to kindle, set on fire, incite*. I.17.45; 31.52; II.19.83; 20.96. Pres.s.3 **ontendt, ontent**. [13 ex.] Cf **a-**.

ontendnyss f. *burning, excitement*. II.11.50, 56–9, 448; 27.47, 65, 84.

onuppan adv. *above, on top*. II.16.122, 186. (Or perhaps as next word, with ellipsis of object.)

onuppan prep. w. dat. *upon, on top of*. II.2.19; 12.400; 32.214; 34.200. Printed as **on uppon**, I.16.9; **on uppan** I.27.35. (Occurs only in postposed position after a pronoun object, and could perhaps be analysed as **on uppan**, *on from above*.) Cf **þæronuppan, upon**.

onweg see **aweg**.

onwinnan vb 3. *to attack, invade*. Pres.pt. as adj., II.28.82.

onwreon vb 1/2. *to reveal*. I.praef.122; 12.78; II.22.188; 25.66. Pres.s.3 **onwrihþ**; pl. **onwreoþ**; pret.s. **onwreah**; pp. **onwrigen**. [16 ex.] Cf **ofer-, un-**.

onwrigen(n)yss f. *revelation*. I.4.30; 9.46; II.1.254; 17.43. [11 ex.]

onwunian vb II. *to dwell, reside (in)*. I.5.27; 7.30; II.4.192.

onwunung f. *residing, in-dwelling*. II.19.35; 40.106.

open adj. *open*. I.3.49; 10.127; II.10.49; 28.77. [14 ex.]

geopenian vb II. *to open* (trans. and intrans.), *reveal*. I.1.191; 4.265; II.1.184; 4.102; 27.133. **open-** 3x.

openlic adj. *visible, open*. II.11.178.

openlice adv. *openly, publicly*. I.1.249; 4.13; II.3.47; 14.19. [17 ex.]

geopenung f. *act of opening*. I.36.178.

ord m. *beginning, source, starting-point, point (of sword)*. I.praef.85; 6.139; 21.218; II.12.532; 32.214.

ordfruma m. *source, beginning, starting-point*. I.1.6–7; 3.123; 6.176; 20.10; II.35.81.

orf n. *cattle* (in the narrow sense, or more generally as domestic livestock). I.9.61; 28.91 (**orof**); 34.10; II.10.302; 12.65. [10 ex.]

orfcyn n. *kind of domestic livestock*. I.6.171.

orgelice, orgollice adv. *insolently, arrogantly*. II.14.168; 18.83.

orgelword n. *scornful or arrogant speech*. II.14.126.

orhlyte adj. *devoid of, lacking in*. w. gen. I.24.147; II.12.4; 16.93; 18.119; 25.71; 35.73.

ormæte adj. *great, huge, heavy*. I.praef.92; 34.10; II.11.187; 21.39. [46 ex.]

ormæte adv. *greatly, enormously*. II.18.29; 30.12.

ormætlice adv. *enormously*. I.15.22; II.21.25.

ormætnyss f. *greatness, great extent*. II.11.545.

ormod adj. *despairing, despondent*. I.35.259; II.21.44.

orsorh adj. *carefree, without anxiety.* I.3.127; 4.115; II.27.80; 34.53; w. gen., *free of, unconcerned about* II.10.169; 14.300; etc. (4x). Infl. forms **orsorg-**; comp. **orsorhgre**. [24 ex.]

orsorglice, orsorhlice adv. *securely, without anxiety.* I.22.194; 29.33; II.1.246; 34.301. [8 ex.]

orsorhnyss f. *security, confidence.* I.40.56; II.37.58.

(ge)ortruwian vb II. *to despair, doubt.* I.3.190; 32.78; II.5.207; 19.54, 58; *to despair of,* w. direct object in acc. II.9.136; in gen. I.35.172; uncertain I.18.130 (**geortruaþ**); II.24.208. [12 ex.]

orþian vb II. *to breathe.* I.5.131; 31.27; 35.234; *to aspire* II.9.31.

orþung f. *breathing.* I.40.115; II.32.107; *inspiration,* II.35.54.

orwene adj. *without hope, despairing, despaired of.* I.5.149; 23.94; II.2.57; 10.278. [7 ex.] Cf **unwene**.

orwennyss f. *hopelessness, despair.* I.18.148; 35.243; II.12.517.

Osee the prophet Hosea. II.36.123.

Ostiensis the city of Ostia near Rome. I.29.290.

oþ prep. w. dat. or acc. *until, to, up to.* Expressing extent to a limit of time or space. I.4.280; 11.193; II.4.292; 5.236. (No apparent distinction of sense between dat. and acc.; on Ælfric's revisions, from dat. to acc., see *CH I* pp. 131–2, *CH II* p. lxxx.) **oþþ** 2x. [118 ex.]

oþ þæt conj. *until.* I.2.205; 5.26; II.3.16; 4.197. [111 ex.]

oþer adj. and pron. *other, another, different, second.* I.1.42; 27.159; II.1.61; 3.229; **oþer . . . oþer,** *one . . . other* I.25.156; II.4.242; **swilce oþer,** *like* II.12.92; 33.126 (with **oþer** implying literal difference or analogy?). Used in strong declension only. [633 ex.]

oþfleon vb 2. *to flee from.* w. dat. I.28.143; II.12.400 (pret.pl. **oþflugon**).

oþsceotan vb 2. *to depart, turn aside.* I.26.94 (pres.s.3 **oðscyt**).

oþþe conj. *or.* I.3.152; 4.52; II.praef.39; 2.89; correl., **oþþe . . . oþþe,** *either . . . or* I.36.277; II.12.73. [315 ex.]

oxa m. *ox.* I.2.210–1; 28.165 ff; II.2.82; 23.10. [17 ex.] Cf **feld-**.

Palladia girl cured by St Stephen. II.2.127.

pallium m. *(archiepiscopal) mantle.* II.9.249.

palm m. *palm (-tree, -twig or -leaf).* I.14.202 ff; II.25.125.

palmtwig n. *twig or frond of palm-tree.* I.5.187; 14.196, 200; 36.10; II.25.124 (**-twygum**). nap. **-twigu**.

Pannonia the Roman province south of the Danube. II.34.2.

papa m. *pope.* I.16.27; 37.10; II.9.1; 18.64. [41 ex.]

papanhad m. *papal office, the papacy.* II.9.164.

papolstan m. *pebble.* I.4.89.

paraclitus Greek name for the holy spirit. I.22.176; 36.208.

paralisin Greek name for paralysis. II.37.179.

Parmenen one of the first seven deacons. I.3.10.

pascha Hebrew term for passover. II.15.324.

paternoster n. *the paternoster or Lord's prayer.* I.19.71, 186; 20.2–5; II.19.222. (printed as 2 words in CH I)

Paþmas Patmos, island in the Aegean and site of St John the evangelist's exile. I.4.27.

Paula St Paula, Roman widow and later abbess, follower, patron and correspondent of St Jerome. I.30.6, 18.

Paulus (a) St Paul the apostle, originally Saul. I.26.157 ff; 27.*passim*; II.1.92; 2.191. [106 ex.] (b) man healed by St Stephen, II.2.127.

pæll m. *cloth (of rich material or silk).* I.34.99; AppB2.19; II.11.565.

pællen adj. *of rich material.* I.4.97; 31.69; II.9.39. **pellenum** I.18.186.

pæþ m. *path.* nap. **paþas** I.25.188, 205.

Pelagius Pelagius II, pope and predecessor of Gregory the Great, 579–90. II.9.90.

pening m. *penny.* II.5.7, 23 ff, 138; 11.404, 407. nap. **penegas,** gp. **penega.** (Translating one **denarius** or a twentieth of a **solidus.**)

peningwurþ n. *pennyworth, an amount to the value of a penny.* I.12.13.

pentecostes m. *Pentecost.* I.21.26; 22.3, 21 ff. dat. **-costen**.

Peohtas the Picts. II.10.253.

Pergamum city of Asia Minor. I.4.77.
Perscisc Persian. I.30.206, 221; 34.265, 269; II.28.155.
Persida Persia. II.33.3, 197.
Petrus (a) St Peter the apostle. I.6.116; 26.*passim*; II.14.10, etc; 24.*passim*. [159 ex.] (b) one of the missionaries to England, d. 607 (first abbot of St Augustine's). II.9.172.
Pharao ruler of the Egyptians at the time of Moses (treated as a personal name). I.22.11 ff; 24.127; II.12.37, etc; 15.22 ff. **phareo** 1x; gs. **pharaones**.
Pharisei the Pharisees. II.14.80; 17.74; 27.10. (More commonly translated as **sunderhalgan**.)
Philetus disciple of the sorcerer Hermogenes converted by St James. II.27.8 ff.
Philippus (a) St Philip the apostle. I.12.10, 44–6, 98; 21.30; II.17.1 ff; 32.89; 35.5. (b) Philip the tetrarch, ruler of Judaea, 4BC-34AD. I.26.18; 32.49 ff. (c) one of the first seven deacons. I.3.9.
Philistei the Philistines. I.15.159, 160 (**filistei**), 164.
Pictauienscisce the people of the Poitiers region. II.34.316, 322.
Pilatus Pontius Pilate, procurator of Judaea 26–36AD. I.15.7, 12; 32.34; II.14.168 ff; 24.45.
gepiled adj. *spiked? barbed?* I.29.132, 163.
pinbeam m. *pine-tree*. II.34.162.
pinung f. *torment*. I.10.133; 14.125; II.3.147; 5.153. [17 ex.]
pinungtol n. *instrument of torture, equipment for torture*. I.29.134, 190.
pistol m. *letter, epistle*. I.30.4, 17; 39.94; II.4.255; 9.97. [15 ex.]
pistolræding f. *lesson in church service from Epistles or Acts*. I.21.2; 22.39; 39.26; II.24.1.
Placidus disciple of St Benedict. II.11.93 ff.
plantian vb II. *to plant*. I.8.179 (see app.crit.); 21.158. Cf **a-**.
plega m. *playing, dancing*. I.4.126 (*acting, pageantry?*); 32.16, 97; II.10.12 ff; 11.157; 12.505.
plegian vb II. *to play, dance*. I.32.15, 84; II.2.53; 10.9; 11.156.
pleoh n. *danger*. I.11.202; 23.37; II.16.141; 36.83. ds. **pleo**.
pleolic adj. *dangerous, perilous* (as threatening damnation). I.25.180; 32.117; II.12.331, 522. Cf **un-**.
pluccian vb II. *to pluck, gather*. I.14.135.
pocha m. *bag, pouch*. I.AppB2.12.
Polimius king of India. I.31.55, 68, 198, 237.
port n. *(fortified) city or town*. II.28.80n.
portgeat n. *city gate*. I.33.6, 28.
portic n. *porticus, portico, collonade*. I.34.94, 97; II.40.56 (prob. better treated as a compound, **eastportic**; see note). The structure in I.34 appears to be a kind of transept. The one in II.40 appears to be an entrance area, a porch or vestibule, in the OT.
Possidius bishop of Calama in North Africa, c370–c440. II.2.16.
[potian] vb II. *to gore, strike*. I.35.68.
prafost, profost m. *prior*. II.10.141; 11.310, 313.
preost m. *priest, cleric (not necessarily in priest's, or even deacon's, orders)*. I.29.5 ff, 43; 30.203; 38.347; II.3.284; 6.142; 11.38; in pl., can designate the household of a bishop (= Lat. **clerus**?), e.g. I.29.5, 30.227. [35 ex.] Cf **mæsse-**.
preosthad m. *priest's orders, priesthood*. II.1.164; 9.156; *clerical order, clergy* II.11.444.
preowthwil f. *blinking of an eye, brief moment*. II.39.124.
prician vb II. *to prick*. II.6.39; 18.136.
prica m. *point (of time)*. I.6.198–9.
pricung f. *pricking*. II.6.41.
Procorus one of the first seven deacons. I.3.9.
protomartyr Greek term (= first martyr) applied to St Stephen. I.3.90.
pryte wk f.(?) *arrogance*. II.12.530.
pund n. *pound*. as a sum of money, I.27.239–40 (= **talentum**); II.11.396, 406 (= 24 **solidi**); 38.5, etc. (= **talentum**); as a weight (of gold), II.33.205 (= **libra**).
purpure wk f. *purple clothing, purple cloth*. I.23.5, 39; 31.201; AppB2.19; II.28.145; 34.229, 235. [10 ex.]
pusa m. *bag*. I.18.177; II.27.86; 36.8, 70, 74, 102.
pytt m. *pit*. II.11.127.

Quiriaca Roman widow healed by St Laurence. I.29.45, 226.

[racenteage, -teah] f. *chain, fetter*. I.29.272; 31.26, 60; 34.118; II.23.150–2; 24.12, 16. ds. **-teage**; nap. **-teagan**. [14 ex.]

Rachel wife of patriarch Jacob. I.5.52, 116–7.

racu f. *narrative, discourse, exposition*. I.3.35; 5.183; II.2.150; 5.35. [26 ex.]

gerad n. *wisdom*. I.14.60.

gerad adj. *expert, wise*. I.19.199. Cf **un-**.

ramm m. *ram*. II.4.149–50, 169–72; 12.351; 30.184.

rap m. *rope*. I.14.47; 28.79; 31.154–6; II.2.193.

Raphahel the archangel Raphael. I.34.257; II.10.47.

Rapsacen the Assyrian general Rabsaces. I.37.157.

rarian vb II. *to lament, howl*. I.4.132; 28.111.

raþ- see **hraþe**

ræcan vb I. *to give, offer*. I.32.27 (**ræhte**). Cf **a-, mis-**.

geræcan vb I. *to reach*. I.31.61; 34.103; II.6.173.

ræd m. *purpose, intent*. I.1.34–6, 47; 5.75; II.22.105; *advice* I.8.67; 34.21; II.27.24; 39.156; *advisedness, judgement* II.16.204; 38.110; *council, deliberation* II.14.18; 35.45(?); **to ræde,** *advisable* II.2.28. [29 ex.] Cf **mis-**.

rædan vb I. *to read*. I.21.204; 30.85; II.16.103; 30.227; *interpret* II.28.145; *guess, deduce* II.14.119; *decide, agree* I.26.283; II.3.132 (**geræddon**); 11.72; 27.114; *deliberate, consult* I.29.287. Pres.s.3 **ræt**; pp. **geræd(d), geredd** (1x). [84 ex.] Cf **ofer-**.

rædbora m. *adviser, counsellor*. I.30.223; II.1.179; 35.41.

gerædе n. *trappings, accoutrements (of a horse)*. I.14.87.

ræden f. *condition, provision*. I.3.178.

rædere m. *reader, lector* (as church office). I.34.110.

rædfæst adj. *just, showing good judgement?* I.AppB3.172, 175.

ræding f. *text, lesson, reading (appointed for the day)*. I.3.60; 28.133; II.24.86; 36.16; *(act of) reading* I.AppB3.233; II.11.455, 463. **rædung** 2x. [26 ex.] Cf **pistol-**.

rædlic adj. *wise, prudent, well-advised*. I.AppB2.44; as comp. adv., I.32.112.

ræsan vb I. *to rush*. I.26.191. Cf **a-**.

read adj. *red*. I.3.36; 34.99; II.12.57; 14.203; describing gold, I.4.87, 93; II.9.40; 40.58. [20 ex.] Cf **wolcn-**.

readnyss f. *redness, red colour*. I.30.128.

reaf n. *clothing, garment*. I.1.148; 3.108; II.1.195; 2.63; *winding-sheet?* I.15.111 ff. [64 ex.] Cf **mæsse-**.

reafere m. *robber*. I.23.31; 28.47; 37.276; II.19.286; 26.34; 28.8.

reafian vb II. *to steal, extort*. I.8.174. **reafigende,** *rapacious* II.26.4. Cf **be-**.

reaflac n. *robbery*. I.38.147–8; AppB3.246; II.3.173; 12.326. [12 ex.]

Rebecca wife of the patriarch Isaac. I.7.128.

[rec(c)an] vb I. *to care (for, about)*. w. gen. Pret. **roht-** only, I.10.148; 15.112; II.10.73; 19.206; 39.78.

(ge)reccan vb I. *to narrate, tell*. I.2.3; 30.20; II.1.216; 17.125; *to report to be?* II.9.188; **is gereht,** *is interpreted, means* (used of name-interpretations) I.praef. 79; 2.81; II.1.142; 4.234; etc (18x). Pres.s.3 **recð**; pret. **(ge)reht-**; pp. **gereht**. **recenne** 1x. [89 ex.] Cf **a-**.

gerec(c)ednyss f. *narrative, account, discourse*. I.7.4; 32.189; 38.348; II.praef.34; 4.205. [15 ex.]

reccend m. *ruler*. II.19.97.

reccendom m. *ruling, caring*. II.19.94.

receleas adj. *careless, negligent*. I.22.143; II.36.62.

receleaslice adv. *negligently*. II.19.205.

receleasnyss f. *recklessness*. II.19.206.

recels m. *incense*. I.5.30; 7.33, 205, 213–5.

Redempta a nun living in sixth-century Rome. II.37.185, 192.

gerefa m. *tax-gatherer, public official* (= **publicanus**). I.24.3; II.3.38; 32.8; *officer of king or emperor, governor* I.25.157; 29.81 (**gereua**), 114; II.17.7; 34.214(?). Cf **heah-, tun-, weorc-**.

gerefscir f. *public office (*specif. *tax-collecting?*). II.6.150.

regol m. *rule (for life)*. I.26.133; 35.91; II.6.125; 11.68, 226, 547. [9 ex.]

regollic adj. *according to a rule, of a rule*. I.35.220; II.11.67; 34.124.

regollice adv. *according to rule*. I.27.201; II.9.34.

regolsticca m. *instrument for ruling lines.* I.25.214n.
reliquiae fpl. *relics.* I.31.229, 311; II.2.133; 9.248. ap. **-quias,** dp. **-quium**.
remian vb II. *to mend.* I.38.10.
ren m. *rain.* I.1.191; 28.99; II.7.77; 19.278, 281; 33.182. Pl. 3x.
renboga m. *rainbow.* I.1.199.
renscur m. *rainshower.* I.4.112; 35.65; II.7.76–8; 12.449; 31.102.
reocan vb 2. *to stink, reek.* pres.pt. as adj., I.23.159; II.19.118.
reofl- see **hreofl-**; **reoh-** see **hreoh-**
gereonian vb II. *to deliberate, conspire, devise a plan.* I.27.45.
gereonung f. *conspiracy.* I.26.227.
gereord n. *speech, language.* I.1.204; 21.53; II.5.273; 14.2. [57 ex.]
gereord n. *feast, meal.* I.12.112; 32.14; II.10.295; 32.9. [41 ex.]
gereordian vb II. *to nourish, feed.* I.3.38; 23.133; II.7.24; 25.101; refl., I.21.39; II.16.126; intrans., *to eat* I.12.106; II.16.73. **reordigende** I.21.6. [35 ex.]
gereordung f. *a meal, nourishment.* I.4.43; 39.76; II.29.56.
reps m. *response (in church services).* II.13.8.
rest f. *rest, resting-place.* I.9.92; 18.80; II.12.306; 20.68.
(ge)restan vb I. *to rest* (intrans. or refl.). I.7.42; 8.155; II.11.574; 14.163. [27 ex.]
restendæg m. *day of rest.* I.16.4; II.12.141, 300 ff.
reþe adj. *cruel, fierce.* I.5.31; 14.172; II.3.178; 11.234. **hreþe** 1x. [54 ex.] Cf **un-**.
reþnyss f. *ferocity.* I.3.120; II.11.444, 456, 466.
rewet n. *rowing, sea-journey.* I.10.156 (**reute**); II.16.121; 24.63, 90, 140; 29.67; *boat(?)* II.16.116, 159.
rib n. *rib.* I.1.89.
ric(c)etere n. *power, secular authority.* I.5.83; 8.132; 17.56; II.36.79; 40.301.
rice n. *kingdom.* I.1.44; 4.22; II.4.207; 9.191–3; *rule, authority* I.1.33, 42; 2.49; II.4.223; 28.159?. ap. **ricu**. [308 ex.] Cf **cyne-**.
rice adj. *rich, powerful.* I.4.111; 18.174 ff; II.3.94; 7.67 ff. (The two senses cannot always be distinguished, but the 'rich' sense is dominant; see Godden 1990.) [87 ex.] Cf **woruld-**.
ricene adv. *quickly.* I.5.155; II.10.189; 11.98.
riclice adv. *powerfully.* II.9.191.
rics-, ricx- see **rixian**
ridan vb 1. *to ride.* I.14.16–18, 99; II.10.31; 11.452; 18.27–9. Pret.s. **rad. geridan** I.AppB2.51.
ridda m. *rider.* II.10.32; 12.93, 96–8; 34.29; 40.47.
gerifod adj. *wrinkled?* (cf OE **rifelede**.). I.40.114.
riftere, ryft- m. *reaper.* I.37.210; II.36.5, 33.
Riggo swordbearer of the Gothic king Totilla. II.11.238 ff.
riht n. *what is right, the true or just way.* I.3.186; 36.248; II.2.109; 3.236; **on riht,** *properly, rightly* I.16.76; II.1.115. [15 ex.] Cf **un-**.
riht adj. *proper, just, true.* I.32.53; 6.88; II.4.300; 5.103. [38 ex.] Cf **up-**.
gerihta, -tu n.pl. *religious rites, due services.* II.2.145; 10.144; 18.154.
gerihtan vb I. *to correct, put right.* I.praef.130–1; 25.189, 205, 213; II.praef.44–6; 19.31.
rihte adv. *directly.* I.32.21.
rihtgelyfed adj. *true-believing, orthodox.* I.20.214, 255.
rihtgeþancod adj. *right-minded.* I.2.114.
rihting f. *correction, improvement.* I.37.25; II.12.336; 19.264, 283; 26.87.
gerihtlæcan vb I. *to correct.* I.praef.133; 3.30; II.praef.48; 9.141. pp. **-læced, -læht**. [26 ex.]
rihtlæcung f. *correction.* II.12.156.
rihtlic adj. *right, just.* I.4.201; 6.161; II.3.264. Cf **un-**.
rihtlice adv. *rightly, justly.* I.1.38; 2.121; II.1.132; 5.118. **ryhtlice** 1x. [63 ex.]
rihtwis adj. *virtuous, righteous, just.* I.1.185; 3.189; II.4.105; 16.70–1. **ryht-** 1x. [116 ex.]
gerihtwisian vb II. *to make or proclaim righteous, just or virtuous.* I.3.111; 26.225; II.13.47; 19.146. **rihtwisiað** II.26.23. [10 ex.]
rihtwisnyss f. *justice, righteousness, right living.* I.1.264; 7.144; II.1.154, 159; 4.241. **ryht-** 1x. [83 ex.] Cf **un-**.

gerim n. *number, reckoning*. I.6.136; 35.284. Cf **ungerim**.
geriman vb I. *to count, enumerate*. I.36.8; II.28.51, 54; 33.58; 35.61. (**gerimod,** see **geryman**.)
gerimboc f. *calendar*. I.6.140.
[rind] f. *bark (of tree), crust, rind*. I.16.122; II.1.55; 8.110.
gerinu see **gerynu**
gerip n. *harvest*. I.12.60; II.36.5–6, 33–7.
ripan vb I. *to reap, harvest*. II.31.10, 51; 36.109; 38.27, 30, 102.
(ge)ripian vb II. *to ripen*. II.7.79; 10.183; **geripod,** *ripe* I.5.98; II.2.22. Cf **unge-**.
gerisan vb 1. w. dat. *to befit, be proper*. I.29.36; AppB1.4; II.19.93. Pres.s.3 **gerist**.
[riþe] wk f. *stream*. I.30.126.
rixe wk f. *rush*. II.25.123–4.
rixian vb II. *to reign*. I.1.296; 3.116; II.10.255; 11.257; *to dominate* I.39.80. **ricsað** 2x; **ricxað** 1x. [82 ex.]
rod f. *cross*. I.4.68; 10.158; II.14.204; 18.1, 18, etc. [81 ex.]
Rode Rhoda, girl in the household of Mary mother of Mark in Jerusalem. II.24.28.
rodehengen f. *cross (as instrument of execution)*. I.1.276; 4.18; II.2.182; 5.133. **-hæncgene** 1x, **-hencgene** 1x. [9 ex.]
rodetac(e)n n. *sign of the cross*. I.29.49; 31.185; II.3.82; 11.77–8; as two words, II.13.290. [24 ex.]
rodor m. *firmament* (i.e. the higher region beyond the skies). II.10.81; 14.255.
rodorlic, roderlic adj. *celestial, belonging to the firmament*. I.21.198, 211; II.10.16; 19.288.
Romani the Romans. I.6.132; otherwise in gp. **romana,** I.4.22; 37.51; II.9.23; 17.129. [15 ex.]
Romanisc adj. *Roman*. I.2.9; 6.136; II.9.166; 18.20. [26 ex.]
Romanus (a) St Romanus the martyr, a Roman soldier converted by St Laurence. I.29.169 ff. (b) Italian monk who supported St Benedict. II.11.28 ff.
[Rome] city of Rome. ds. **rome** I.5.42; II.9.229.
Romeburh city of Rome. ds. **romebyrig** I.20.180; 26.103; 38.32; II.6.169; II.11.27, 92, 256.
Romula nun living in sixth-century Rome. II.37.177 ff.
rose wk f. *rose*. I.4.98; 30.127–8, 147 (dp. **rosam**); II.10.68 (**hrosan**); 31.72; 37.154.
rosen adj. *rosy, rose-coloured*. II.20.50 (emended).
rot adj. *fine, noble*. I.19.165; II.31.57–8. Cf **un-**.
rotian vb II. *to rot, decay*. I.7.207, 240; 15.19. Cf **for-**.
rowan vb 7. *to row, to travel on water*. I.12.32; II.10.244; 23.179; 24.80. Pret. **reow, reow-**. Cf **ofer-**.
rum adj. *spacious*. I.2.99; 10.168; 35.266.
rumgifelnyss f. *generosity, liberality*. I.25.165.
rumlic adj. *abundant, plentiful*. I.35.74.
gerunnen see **yrnan**
runstæf m. *runic letter*. II.21.160.
ryman vb I. *to clear, open, extend*. I.2.53 (**gerymde**); 18.75; II.7.93; 20.204; *to make space for*, w. gen. object and dat. of person I.15.86; 35.239; 37.110. pp. **gerimod**. [9 ex.]
rymet n. *space, room, extent*. I.2.19; 19.60; 34.98; II.23.17, 96–8.
rymetleast f. *lack of room*. I.2.87.
ryne m. *course, run, flow*. I.29.37; II.5.96; 11.101; 24.234; 38.231.
gerynu f. *mystery, sacrament, hidden meaning*. I.10.35; 38.188, etc; II.14.2; 15.5, 107, etc. **-nu** is used for all cases, s. and pl., except dp. **-um**; **-no** 2x (as. or ds.); **-ne** 1x (ds.). **gerin-** 2x. Gender always fem. when marked (8x), though recorded as neut. elsewhere. [48 ex.]
gerynelice adv. *as a mystery or sacrament*. II.15.154.
rysl m. *lard, fat*. I.35.76; II.10.199.
ryþþa m. *dog*. I.26.136–7.

Saba given as the name of the Queen of Sheba (= Sabaeans in SW Arabia). II.40.147, 155.
Sabaria city of the Roman province of Pannonia, south of the Danube. II.34.3.
Sabei people who raid Job's fields. II.30.67.
Sabellius heretic, probably 3rd century Roman theologian. I.20.231.
sacerd m. *priest* (often of the Old Law). I.8.13, 61 ff; 30.4; II.4.226; 15.102. (When used of Christians, seems to mean priests in full orders, translating

presbyter or often **sacerdos**; cf **preost.**) [46 ex.]

sacian vb II. *to contend, quarrel.* II.16.216. Cf **wiþersaca, yfelsacung.**

sacu f. *conflict, strife.* I.11.204; 28.126; II.3.156; 37.4, 30. [9 ex.]

(ge)sadelian vb II. *to saddle.* pp. **gesadelod** I.14.102.

[sagol] m. *club, stick.* dp. **saglum** I.29.142, 243; 31.224.

sagu f. *account, prophecy.* II.33.39.

Sale Salah, descendant of Noah and father of Heber. I.1.226.

Salla Zalla, an Arian Goth in 6thC Italy. II.11.443 ff. (On the form of the name, see notes.)

Salome sister of Herod the Great. I.5.151.

Salomon king Solomon; cited also as author of Proverbs, Wisdom, Sirach. I.3.41; 7.229; II.19.192; 40.18, etc. [36 ex.]

Salustium. botl salustii, the **palatium Salustii** in Rome. I.29.184.

Samaria city of Israel. II.13.96; 27.7. (Designated a city by Ælfric, but the sources are perhaps referring to the region in general, bordering on Judaea.)

Samaritanisc belonging to the city or region of Samaria. I.32.109; II.8.48; 13.20, 95 ff.

samcucu adj. *half-dead.* I.34.58; II.10.287; 34.197.

samlæred adj. *having a little learning, partially learned.* II.29.4.

gesamnian vb II. *to assemble, gather together* (trans. and intrans.). I.5.15; 7.18; 28.39; 31.202.

gesamnung f. *assembly, meeting.* II.27.134; 37.10 (**-som-**), 67.

samod adv. *together, as well, at the same time.* I.praef.102; 3.122; II.2.166; 9.248. [94 ex.]

Samson champion of the Israelites against the Philistines. I.15.158 ff; 32.185.

samt- see **sæmt-**

Samuhel the prophet. II.4.182 ff.

sanct m. *saint.* II.34.325.

sanct adj? *saint* (used as epithet before a saint's name). I.30.241, 252; 34.4, 74; 35.219; II.11.175. Forms: **sancta** (gsf., a/dsf.); **sancte** (dsf., dsm., gsm.); **sanctus** (nsm.).

sand f. *sending, mission.* I.13.41; II.9.4; 17.35; 32.81; *dish or supply of food* (specifically sent in first 2 cases). I.37.218; II.10.57; 11.231.

sandceosol m. *(grains of) sand.* I.35.281, 284; II.4.156; 12.33; 35.62; 40.40.

sandcorn n. *(grain of) sand.* II.30.148.

sang m. *singing, song.* I.136; 30.88; II.6.191; 37.195. [20 ex.] Cf **æfen-, lof-, offring-, sealm-, tid-.**

sangere m. *cantor* (as ecclesiastical office). I.14.202; 34.110.

sape wk f. *soap.* I.31.262.

Saphira woman who, with her husband Annanias, deceived the disciples. I.22.88, 96; 27.212, 221.

sar n. *pain.* I.2.197; 16.140; II.4.171; 30.138. [6 ex.]

Sara, Sarai, Sarra Sarah, wife of Abraham. I.6.27, 36–7, 118.

Sarascenisc the Saracen people (probably referring to the Arabs). I.28.59.

sarig adj. *sorrowful.* I.37.133; II.14.116.

sarlic adj. *sorrowful.* I.29.276.

sarlice adv. *sorrowfully, painfully.* I.29.185; II.11.12; 30.119; 34.112.

sarnyss f. *pain, sorrow.* I.4.275; 8.53; II.11.14; 20.240. [19 ex.]

Saul king of Israel. II.4.179 ff;

Saulus original name of St Paul. I.3.54, 107 ff; 27.18, etc; II.5.201. **sauwle** IX.

sawan vb 7. *to sow.* I.27.59; 32.199; II.31.9; 36.108. Pres.s.2 **sæwst**; 3 **sæwð**; pret.s. **seow**; pp. **gesawen.** [15 ex.] Cf **a-, be-, to-.**

sawlian vb II. *to expire.* II.34.300.

sawul f. *soul.* I.praef.115; 1.169–70; II.1.73; 12.294–5. ns. **saul, sawl, sawul**; as. **saule, sawla, sawle**; gds. **saule, sawle**; nagp. **saula, sawla**; dp. **saulum, sawlum.** [279 ex.]

sawulleas adj. *without a soul.* I.10.128; 21.127; II.19.179; 26.50. [7 ex.]

sæ f. (indecl.) *sea.* I.3.36; 6.196; II.16.108; 24.55; without article, I.1.96; 15.174; II.30.149. [97 ex.] Cf **suþ-.**

sæd n. *seed.* I.12.62; 27.59; II.6.5; 10.177; *posterity, semen* I.6.116; II.4.156; 13.202. [29 ex.]

sædere m. *sower.* II.6.58–9.

sægne see **segen**

sægrund m. *sea-depths.* I.37.250.

sæl m. *time, occasion.* **æt sumum (-on) sæle,** I.4.77; 25.9; II.6.156; 9.53. [15 ex.]

sælic adj. *of the sea*. I.38.18; 40.8; II.4.156; 10.79–85. [12 ex.]

gesælig adj. *blessed, fortunate* (used almost exclusively in a religious sense). I.5.95; 13.187; II.10.297; 19.96. [28 ex.] Cf **unge-**.

gesæliglice adv. *blissfully, fortunately, in a state of (spiritual) bliss*. I.5.99; 7.255; II.9.3, 23; 19.50.

gesælþ f. *prosperity, good fortune, bliss*. I.1.162–3; 7.142; II.24.224; 30.237; **sælþ** I.31.94. [12 ex.] Cf **unge-**.

sæmninga adv. *wholly*. II.25.79.

sæmtinges adv. *together, wholly, immediately*. II.12.115 (**samtinges**); 13.117; 27.191; 34.176.

sæp n. *sap*. II.1.55. Cf **unsæpig**.

særwian vb II. *to dissimulate*(?). II.18.69.

sæstrand n. *sea-shore*. I.4.170; 37.104 (but should be **sæ strande**); II.40.40. cf I.4.88.

sæternesdæg m. *Saturday*. II.5.244; 12.276, 300, 304; 21.119, 126. **sæternes** II.14.334.

sæterniht f. *night before Saturday, Friday night*. I.14.187.

scadu, sceadu f. *shadow*. I.22.83; 25.99; II.4.65, 311; 34.142.

scandlic, sceandlic adj. *shameful, vile*. II.4.244; 6.129; 34.210.

scaw- see **sceaw-**

scawungstow f. *place of observation*. I.14.93.

scægan vb I. *to jeer*. II.21.48n (**scegdon**).

scænan vb I. *to break*. II.14.317; 15.318.

scæþ f. *sheath*. I.32.116.

sceacan vb 6. *to depart*. II.11.7 (pret.s. **sceoc**), 389; *depart from, leave* (?) II.19.220 app.crit.(pres.s.3 **scæcð**). Cf **a-, to-**.

gescead n. *account, reckoning*. I.6.101; II.12.528; *understanding, reason, discrimination* I.6.96; 21.126; II.19.175; *meaning, explanation* I.12.66; 7.91; *reason (cause)* I.6.137–9; 13.80. **gescad** 1x. [29 ex.] Cf **to-**.

sceadewung f. *casting a shadow*. I.40.42.

gesceadwis adj. *rational, having understanding*. I.7.52; 35.271; II.15.132; 19.97. **sceadwis** I.38.188. [10 ex.] Cf **unge-**.

gesceadwisnyss f. *rationality, discrimination*. I.9.212.

gesceaft n. *creature, created thing, the created world*. I.1.13; 2.170; II.4.323; 13.215. nap. **-a**. [106 ex.] Cf **frum-**.

sceal anom. vb. *must, ought*. (a) w. inf., *is destined to, ought to, will, shall, must, should* I.13.60; 20.2, 270; II.praef.48; 3.238. (b) with vb. implied, I.18.29; II.21.97. Forms: **sceal, sceall, scealt, sceolon, -un, scolon, sculon, scyolon; sceole, sceule, scole, scule, scyle; sceold-, scold-**. [c.671 ex.]

scealfra m. *cormorant*. II.34.275, 280.

sceamelic adj. *shameful*. I.28.50.

sceamian vb II. impers. w. gen. object and dat. of person. *to be ashamed of, feel shame about*. I.1.142; 23.148–9; 35.153; II.26.118. Cf **of-**.

sceamleast f. *shamelessness*. I.38.271; AppB3.75.

sceamu f. *shame, disgrace*. I.35.154; II.19.180.

sceanca m. *leg*. II.10.31; 14.312, 315–6; 15.319; 34.158.

sceap, scep n. *sheep*. I.17.5 etc; 24.8 etc; II.26.3; 30.10. nas. **scep, sceap**; gs. **scepes**; ds. **sceape**; nap. **scep, sceap**; gp. **sceapa, scapa** (1x); dp. **sceapum**. [105 ex.]

gesceap n. *genitals, penis*. I.5.133; 6.53, 82; II.34.210. nap. **-pu**.

gesceapennyss f. *creation, act of creation*. I.6.156, 170, 191; 19.35–7; II.1.59 ff; 12.291.

scearp adj. *sharp, rough, acute*. I.29.270; 31.188; AppB3.198; II.17.128; 26.88; 34.207.

scearpecged adj. *sharp-edged*. I.6.52.

scearplice adv. *acutely*. I.36.34.

scearpnyss f. *acuteness, roughness*. I.4.28; 25.189, 215.

sceat m. *reward, payment* (often in plural form, with sing. or general meaning). I.5.158; 15.42; II.14.63; 19.146; *treasure, gift* I.30.224, 253; 38.118. **scet** 1x. [18 ex.]

sceaþa m. *criminal, robber*. I.4.230; 28.15; II.5.129; 14.228. [34 ex.]

sceawere m. *observer, watcher*. I.34.32; II.10.93.

sceawian vb II. *to look at, examine, consider*. I.2.182; 3.169–70; II.4.92; 23.8. **scaw-** 2x; **gesceawode** 1x. [43 ex.] Cf **be-, fore-, ofer-**.

scegdon see **scægan**

scencan vb I. *to pour, give drink.* I.23.133; II.4.20, 293; 7.148, 154.

sceocca, scucca m. *demon, devil.* I.1.120; 4.147; II.6.77; 20.116. [21 ex.]

sceofan, scufan vb 2. *to push, thrust.* I.38.231 (inf. **sceofon**); II.17.93, 96; 33.129; 37.105. Pret. **scufon.** Cf **a-, be-.**

sceogan vb I. *to shoe, put on shoes.* II.15.20, 306–7; 24.17. Imper. **sceo**; pp. **gesceod.**

sceoh, scoh m. *shoe.* I.31.37 (np. **scos**); II.10.199 (dp. **scon**); 26.122–4 (ap. **sceos**). Cf **gescy.**

sceort, scort adj. *short.* I.23.78; 29.7; II.5.35; 19.260. comp. **scyrtran** 1x. [23 ex.]

sceortlice, scortlice adv. *briefly.* I.13.195; 20.51; II.12.3; 31.24.

sceortnyss, scortnyss f. *brevity, abbreviation.* I.AppA2.1; II.10.96; 11.285.

gesceot n. *railing, enclosure.* II.2.161.

(ge)sceotan vb 2. *to fall, tumble down.* I.11.170; 25.210; II.12.126; *defer, appeal* II.18.53; 20.122; *rush* I.28.46; II.18.130; 23.166; *shoot (an arrow, etc.)* I.34.18; II.37.26; *fall to, accrue* I.11.197; II.15.150; 33.205. Pres.s.3 **(ge)scyt**; pl. **sceotaþ, (ge)scotaþ**; imper. **sceut**; pret. **(ge)sceat, sceotan, scuton**; pp. **gescoten.** [24 ex.] Cf **a-, be-, for-, of-, ofer-, oþ-, to-, þurh-.**

sceoþwang m. *shoestrap.* II.3.54.

scep see **sceap**

scephyrde m. *shepherd.* II.7.135.

scet see **sceat**

scinan vb 1. *to shine, glow with colour.* I.4.98; 28.98; II.31.73; 39.59. Pret. **scean, scinon. scynend-** 2x. [67 ex.] Cf **be-, ymb-.**

scincræft m. *sorcery, magic.* II.33.6 (**scyncræfton**), 119, 200.

scinnhiw n. *ghost, spectre.* II.24.153.

scip n. *ship.* I.19.163; 27.140; II.18.24, 29; 24.59. nap. **scipu. scyp** 2x. [21 ex.]

gescipe m. *station, rank.* II.3.44.

scipman m. *sailor, ship's crew.* I.18.17 (**scyp-**); II.24.78.

scir f. *region, province.* I.28.196; 31.31; II.9.71; 14.170. **scyre** 1x. [14 ex.] Cf **burh-, geref-, toll-.**

scirman m. *person of a region or province.* II.9.72.

Sciþþia Scythia (vaguely, the region north and east of the Black Sea). II.17.4.

sco- see also **sceo-**

scol f. *school.* I.30.62, 201.

Scolastica St Scholastica, nun and sister of St Benedict, c480–c543. II.11.486 ff.

scorian vb I/II. *to refuse, stand out.* I.4.212 (pret.s. **scorede**); 7.181.

Scotland modern Scotland? II.20.252 (see note to this line in *CHII*, p. 366).

Scottas the inhabitants of Scotland, or its western parts and islands(?). II.10.255; 20.258 (see note to line 252 in *CHII*, p. 366).

scræf n. *cave, pit, den.* I.28.15, etc; 37.223; II.11.40; 27.198 (**screafe**). [20 ex.]

screadian vb II. *to peel, prune, cut away.* I.5.163; II.5.58–9. Cf **a-.**

scrift m. *confessor.* I.10.199; II.6.127; 7.4.

scrin n. *shrine.* = *the ark of the covenant,* II.1.50; 12.432; = *a tomb,* II.27.227 (**scryn**).

scrincan vb 3. *to recoil?* II.28.143 (pret.s. **scranc**). Cf **for-.**

scrud n. *clothing, garment.* I.4.116; 25.150; II.19.242; 26.122. [12 ex.]

scrutnian vb II. *to examine, pay attention to.* I.38.108; II.5.205.

scrydan vb I. *to clothe.* I.11.209; 23.134; II.18.151; 29.84; 31.17. **gescryddon** II.14.219. [26 ex.] Cf **un-, ymb-, wanscryd, misscryda.**

scufan see **sceofan.**

sculdor m. *shoulder.* II.207, 249.

scur m. *shower (of rain).* I.36.47. Cf **ren-.**

gescy npl. *shoes.* I.28.48; II.15.306; 36.8, 70, 74.

scyfe m. *pushing, impulsion.* II.23.167.

scylcen f. *female entertainer? shameless woman?* II.11.157.

scyld m. *offence, sin.* I.28.143; 32.87; 33.152; II.32.65.

scyld m. *shield.* I.37.180; II.12.472; 20.29; 34.54.

gescyldan vb I. *to protect, shield, defend.* I.14.107; 19.104; II.1.81; 9.183. Pres.s. **gescyltst, gescylt.** [21 ex.]

scyldig adj. *guilty.* I.9.153; 16.77; II.14.228; 19.260; **scyldig . . . to,** *guilty and thereby condemned to* II.5.131; 14.127; **deaðes scyldig,** *guilty and thereby condemned to death* II.12.313. [14 ex.] Cf **for-, un-.**

gescyldnyss f. *protection.* I.4.25; 18.124; II.7.9; 10.130. [11 ex.]

scyldung f. *shielding, protection.* II.20.64.
scylf m. *pinnacle, turret.* I.11.16, 59, 171; II.17.80–82.
scylling m. *silver coin* (translating **drachmae argenti, sicli argenti, argenteos**). I.5.158; 9.60, 68; 24.76; II.14.21 (**scilling**).
gescyndan vb I. *to confound, humiliate, shame, rout.* I.3.68, 118; 32.97; II.4.235; 23.90. (Generally translating Lat. **confundere**.) [12 ex.]
gescyndan vb I. *to drive out.* II.32.141. (Or perhaps an example of the preceding word.) Cf **a-**.
gescyndnyss f. *defeat, humiliation, confusion.* I.22.127; 39.82; II.4.233–4. (Translating Lat. **confusio** and sharing its range of senses.)
gescyppan vb 6. *to create.* I.1.57–8; 20.24; II.1.60–61; 12.290 ff; *devise or give (a name)* I.1.85; 6.46, 73–5; 26.20; 32.37. Pret. **gesceop, gescop, gesceop-, gescop-**; pp. **gesceapen, -scapen** (1x). **sceop(-)** 3x, **scyppende** 1x (II.14.328). [121 ex.] Cf **frum-, unge-**.
scyppend m. *Creator.* I.1.28; 2.194; II.1.15; 9.80. [115 ex.]
scyran vb I. *to distinguish.* II.16.157 (but see note *CHII* p. 361). Cf **a-(sciran), be-**.
scyran vb 4. *to shear.* II.1.193. Cf **be-**.
gescyrtan vb I. *to shorten.* I.praef.65–6.
scyrting f. *abbreviation.* II.30.228.
scyte wk f. *sheet.* I.15.34; II.14.342. Cf **wæter-**.
Scyttisc *Irish*? (or pertaining to the Scottas whether in Ireland or Scotland). II.20.19.
se m., **seo** f., **þæt** n. demonstr. and def.art. *the, that, that one.* I.praef.113; II.1.73; 3.22; w. proper names, *this* I.31.29; II.11.453; **þæt is, þæt sind,** *that is, those are* II.1.88, 91; **se þe** (often w. correl. **se** as well), *the one who, he who* I.15.149; II.23.108; without **þe**, as rel. pron., *who* I.13.24; 37.210; II.5.237; 11.173; instr. with comp. adj., *the more, more by virtue of that* I.28.103; II.12.121; **þæs þe**, *after, from the time that* II.12.123; **þæs þe** w. comp. adj., *the more because of that* I.32.38; II.1.268–9. See also **for þam, for þy, to þy**. Forms: **se; þone, þane** (1x), **þæne** (1x); **þæs; þam, þan, þæm** (7x); (instr.) **þe, þi, þy**; **seo; þa; þære, þæræ** (1x), **þare** (1x), **þere** (1x); **þæt, þætte** (1x), **þet** (2x); **þa; þara, þæra; þam, þæm** (1x).
sealf f. *ointment.* I.15.18, 77 ff; II.14.340.
sealm m. *psalm.* II.6.186; 40.17.
sealmboc f. *psalter.* I.39.78.
sealmsang m. *psalm, psalm-singing.* I.12.102 ff; 39.105.
sealmscop, -sceop m. *psalmist, psalmwriter.* I.7.60, 230; 13.75; II.1.271; 5.210, 226. [17 ex.]
sealmwyrhta m. *psalmist, psalmwriter.* I.8.37; 24.173; II.1.170; 3.116. [11 ex.]
sealt n. *salt.* II.12.369–70; 36.133–5.
sealt adj. *salt, salty.* II.10.75, 164, 189, 209.
seam m. *seam, join.* I.1.187; II.14.238.
searocræft m. *wile, trick.* I.13.14.
[searu] n. *device, wile, plot.* dp. **syrwum** II.10.115.
seaþ m. *pit.* I.32.182; 37.206 ff; II.11.136; 12.535. [9 ex.]
seax, see **sex**.
Sebaste the city formerly called Samaria but rebuilt and renamed by Herod the Great. I.32.151.
secan vb I. *to seek, look for, try to obtain.* I.7.260–1; 31.304; II.6.50; 21.149. Pres.s.3 **secð, sehð**; pret. **soht-**; pp. **gesoht**. [84 ex.]
gesecan vb I. *to come to, visit, approach, return to.* I.26.249; 29.48; 37.117; II.10.236; 34.92; *to seek, try to obtain* (or perhaps just *to obtain, fetch*) I.31.312. Pres.s.3 **gesecð, gesehð**; pret. **gesoht-**. [28 ex.]
secgan vb III. *to say, tell, utter, address* (w. dat. of person). I.3.25; 14.111; II.12.3; 30.4; **beon gesæd,** *to be called, termed.* Pres.s.2 **segst**; 3 **segþ, seigþ, seiþ, sægþ**; pl. **secgaþ, sæcgaþ**; pret. **sæd-**; pp. **gesæd**. [389 ex.] Cf **a-, be-, for-, fore-**.
Sedechias king of Israel. II.4.211.
segen f. *speech, speaking, utterance.* I.10.28; 32.155 (**sægne**); II.14.126; 19.127; 25.139. [7 ex.] Cf **soþ-**.
seglian vb II. *to sail, voyage.* II.11.256.
sehtnyss f. *peace, settlement.* II.12.156.
sellic, syllic adj. *strange, wonderful.* I.AppB2.19–20; II.17.108; 31.103n.
sellice adv. *wonderfully.* II.12.389.

selost adj. *best.* I.18.121; 30.223; II.19.85; 29.16, 59.

selra adj. *better.* I.19.173; 34.144, 151; II.14.54; 29.61–2. [18 ex.]

seltcuþ adj. *strange, rare.* I.7.73; 22.116.

Sem Shem son of Noah. I.1.184, 224.

geseman vb I. *to settle (a dispute), to judge.* II.20.90.

Semmeus follower of SS Simon and Jude. II.33.215–7, 253.

sendan vb I. *to send.* I.1.189; 5.22; II.4.213; 9.235; w. object (*message, etc.*) understood, I.35.51; II.11.208. Pres.s.3 **sent. gesend-** I.4.268; 37.49. [99 ex.] Cf **a-, be-, fore-, to-.**

senian vb II. *to bless, consecrate* (with a sign of the hand). II.14.50, 66.

Sennacherib king of the Assyrians 705–681BC. I.37.155 ff.

seo f. *pupil (of the eye).* I.34.240.

seoc adj. *ill.* II.2.31; 34.112, 197. Cf **deofol-, monaþ-, witt-.**

seocnyss f. *illness.* II.2.52; 10.94. Cf **wæter-.**

seofan, seofon num. *seven.* I.3.11; 9.189; II.4.113; 9.35. **syfan** 4x, **syfon** 1x. [70 ex.]

seofonfeald adj. *sevenfold, numbering seven.* I.22.229, 232; II.1.167; 9.153; 25.65 ff; **be seofonfealdan,** *seven times* I.40.164. [12 ex.]

seofoþa adj. *seventh.* I.1.97–8; 19.178; II.9.33; 12.68. [18 ex.]

seol m. *seal* (the animal). II.10.82n.

seolfor n. *silver.* I.1.213; 10.106; II.18.49; 40.231, 240. [18 ex.]

geseon vb 5. *to see.* I.2.28, 33; 3.49; II.1.248, 251; 3.63. Pres.s.1 **geseo;** 2 **gesihst;** 3 **gesihþ, gesyhþ;** pl. **geseoþ;** imper. **geseoh;** pres.pt. **geseonde;** pret. **geseah, geseh; gesaw-;** pp. **gesewen.** [331 ex.] Cf **be-, for-, of-, ofer-, þurh-.**

seoþan vb 2. *to boil.* II.15.274, 278. pp. **gesoden.** Cf **for-.**

Sepontina town in SE Italy. I.34.7. **sepontinisc,** *of Sepontina* I.34.41.

Septuagesima the period of the church year from seventy days before Easter. II.5.240 ff.

Seraphion one of the seven sleepers. II.27.187.

Seruulus Roman paralytic in a story told by Gregory the Great. II.6.170.

setl n. *seat, throne* (often in the sense *office*). I.3.77; 13.190; II.9.49; 11.77. [27 ex.] Cf **ancer-, biscop-, cyne-, heah-, steor-, toll-, þrym-, weard-.**

setlung f. *setting (of sun).* II.5.101; 17.114.

gesetnyss f. *establishment, ordinance, decree, composition.* I.3.44; 4.33; II.4.67; 6.120. [55 ex.]

(ge)settan vb I. *to place, set down, establish, decree, arrange, occupy.* I.1.92; 2.9; II.1.146; 40.17. Pres.s.3 **set;** subj. **sete;** pp. **gesett.** [226 ex.]

geseten see **gesittan**

(ge)seþan vb I. *to testify, affirm.* I.23.155; 27.44; 30.83; 37.24; II.9.218; 27.22.

seþung f. *testimony.* I.37.20; II.2.170; 14.107; 15.169; 27.13–14, 118.

Seueriana wife of the 'emperor' Aurelianus. II.18.144, 150.

Seustius lunatic cured by St Bartholomew. I.31.59.

gesewenlic adj. *visible.* I.praef.75; 8.20; II.1.36; 18.13. [15 ex.] Cf **unge-.**

gesewenlice adv. *visibly.* I.39.13; 40.62; II.6.72.

sex, seax n. *knife, sword.* I.5.163; 6.124; II.10.294; 34.34. Cf **ceorf-, hand-.**

sib f. *peace.* I.2.31, 46 ff; 16.7; II.1.139; 33.29; *relationship, bond (of kinship)* I.4.6; 8.116; 28.44; II.11.363 (all). **syb-** 5x. [99 ex.]

gesibb adj. *related as kin* (?). II.30.130n; *related as friends* II.18.101.

(ge)sibbian vb II. *to reconcile, make peace between.* II.29.85; 34.57, 274; 40.79.

siblic adj. *peaceful.* I.36.90.

sibling m. *close relative, kinsman, member of the family.* I.5.156; 23.97, 102; II.35.108; 37.111. **gesiblingum** I.34.161. [10 ex.]

gesibsum adj. *peaceful.* I.3.166; 36.162; II.3.159; 40.75 ff. [16 ex.]

gesibsumian vb II. *to reconcile.* I.3.159.

gesibsumnyss f. *peacefulness.* I.22.140.

Sibylla treated as name of one of the sybils? II.1.219 (cf *CH II* p. 346).

gesican vb I. *to suckle.* I.5.108.

siccetung f. *sighing, panting, wheezing.* I.5.131 **(sicet-);** 40.114; II.9.64.

[Sicilie] Sicilians. **sicilia lande** Sicily II.9.33.

sid adj. *broad, full.* I.31.34, 188.

side wk f. *side*. I.1.89; 16.6; II.4.102; 6.172. [20 ex.]

side wk f. *silk, silk material*. I.AppB2.9–10.

sideful adj. *chaste, pure*. I.36.133; 38.317.

Sidon town in northern Palestine. II.8.6.

Sidonisc people of Sidon. II.24.37.

Sidrac Shadrach, one of the three 'children of Israel' under Nebuchadnezzar. II.4.251. = **Annanias**.

sigan vb I. *to descend, fall*. pret.s. **sah** II.34.171.

sige m. *victory, triumph*. I.14.208; 25.76; II.12.401; 18.16. [17 ex.]

sigebeacen n. *emblem of victory*. II.25.125.

sigefæst adj. *victorious, triumphant*. I.3.197; 14.205; II.12.189; 22.98. [23 ex.]

Sigeric Archbishop of Canterbury 990–995. I.praef.4, 38; II.praef.2.

sigor m. *victory, triumph*. I.38.280.

sigrian vb II. *to triumph*. I.29.143.

gesihþ f. *sight, vision, gaze, appearance*. I.14.96; 28.217; II.1.154; 38.47. **gesyhþ-** 5x. (Used in pl. with sing. meaning, e.g. I.29.4.) [145 ex.]

Silhearwa an Ethiopian (often implying a negro). I.31.5, 188; II.32.83; 33.5, 151, 249.

Simeon the devout Jew at the presentation of Christ in the temple. I.9.18 (**symeon**), 48, 181.

Simon, Symon (a) Simon Peter the apostle I.26.11; 38.5, 153 ff; II.16.36; 24.165. (b) the other apostle Simon I.21.31; II.33.passim; 35.6; (c) Simon Magus, opponent of SS Peter and Paul I.26.106, etc.

Sinai, Synay Mount Sinai. I.22.19; II.12.125, 226.

singal adj. *continual*. I.5.138; 16.140; II.2.163; 9.206. [10 ex.]

singallic adj. *continual*. I.30.113; II.9.46.

singallice adv. *continually*. I.6.127; 24.38; II.6.134; 23.41. [12 ex.]

singan vb 3. *to sing, chant*. I.9.246–7; 14.198; II.5.262; 9.161; *to perform or celebrate (mass)* I.4.252 (**gesang**); 34.89 (**gesing**); II.21.158; of birds, I.9.118 (**syngað**); II.14.137. Pret. **sang, sungon**. **syng-** 3x; **gesungon** I.38.113. [58 ex.]

sinoþ mn. *synod, council*. II.10.248.

sinscipe m. *marriage*. I.30.180; 32.129; II.6.118; 39.79. **syn-** 1x. [14 ex.]

sinu f. *sinew*. I.16.124; II.15.132.

Sion the hill in Jerusalem. I.14.17, 93–4; 30.68; II.20.36.

Siria the Roman province of Syria. I.2.11.

sittan vb 5. *to sit*. I.3.77; 10.59 ff; II.14.23; 24.38; *to reside* I.1.32; 35.279; **sittan on,** *to afflict* I.40.116. Pres.s.2 **sitst**; 3 **sit, sitt**; imper.s. **site**; pret. **sæt, sæt-**. [93 ex.]

gesittan vb 5. *to sit, sit down*. I.12.39; 38.96; II.29.52; 34.257; *to reside, settle* II.10.325; 30.7; *to occupy* I.22.104; II.9.50; 18.36; *to perch?* II.3.73; 10.107; 20.229(?). **gesitst** 1x (otherwise always in past tense); pret. **gesæt, gesæt-**; pp. **geseten**. [26 ex.]

siþ m. *lot, fate, experience*. I.37.58; II.4.183; 11.181; 21.173; *journey, departure* I.21.117; 27.16; II.10.100; 34.91; *time, occasion* I.16.55; 33.26; II.14.136; 20.243; **siþan,** *'times', multiplied by* I.24.159. [21 ex.] Cf **forþ-, un-, wræc-**.

siþe m. *scythe*. II.11.135.

siþfæt n. *journey, way*. I.6.106; 30.174; II.10.43; 19.151. [9 ex.]

siþian vb II. *to travel*. I.8.127; 29.186; II.10.70; 12.81. [28 ex.]

siþlice adv. *by chance? on an occasion? for the occasion?* II.10.191; 14.109. [Not otherwise found in OE.]

siþþan, syþþan adv. *afterwards, subsequently*. I.praef.96; 1.154; II.1.84; 4.114; conj., *after, since* I.praef.104; 13.62; II.6.160; 9.164. [289 ex.]

six, syx num. *six*. I.1.97; 4.11; II.12.274; 16.120. [32 ex.]

sixta adj. *sixth*. I.3.10; 19.146; II.5.73; 4.90. **syxtan** 1x. [17 ex.]

sixtig num. *sixty*. I.11.191; II.32.131, 219; 40.43, 55.

sixti(g)feald adj. II.6.32, 116, 128; **be sixtigfealdon,** *sixty times* II.6.12.

sixtyne num. *sixteen*. I.28.56 (**syx-**); II.24.7.

Sixtus, Syxtus (a) bishop in Rome in the time of Decius (249–51AD) I.29.4–5, etc. (b) a bishop from the east in the period of Trajan (98–117) II.18.152.

slaga m. *killer*. I.21.88; II.2.185, 211; 8.95. Cf **man-, mæg-**.

slapan vb 7. *to sleep*. I.1.88; 9.226; II.13.106; 39.10. Pres.s.3 **slæpð**; pret.s. **slæp, slep**; pl. **slepon**. [22 ex.]

slapere, slæpere m. *sleeper*. I.AppB2.35; II.27.185.

slapolnyss f. *somnolence*. II.12.523.

slaw adj. *slow*. II.24.184.

slæp m. *sleep*. I.4.44; 5.140; II.2.135; 23.142; **on slæpe,** *asleep* II.23.134; 34.322. [18 ex.] Cf **frum-**.

slæpleast f. *sleeplessness*. I.5.138 (**sl_p-**).

sleac adj. *slack, lethargic, slow*. I.39.40; II.3.177; 5.122; 7.31. [8 ex.] Cf **a-**.

sleacnyss f. *slackness, lethargy*. I.24.200; II.15.314.

(ge)slean vb 6. *to strike, hit*. I.18.125; 35.105; II.12.108; 34.194; *to pitch (a tent)* II.14.10; *to coin (money)* II.38.31, 114, 119; *to become (suddenly)* II.16.117; *to shoot out* (used of light, fire, smell) I.37.195; II.20.164; *to fix, fasten* I.37.180 (**geslea**). Pres.s.3 **slihþ**; imper. **sleh**; pret. **(ge)sloh**; pp. **geslagen, geslegen**. [29 ex.] Cf **be-, of-, onbe-, un-**.

slege m. *slaughter, killing, death*. I.3.118; 5.99; II.1.24; 3.86; *blow, strike* I.18.136; II.34.195, 247. [28 ex.]

slep adj. *asleep*. I.18.20.

sliht m. *slaughter, death*. II.9.117. Cf **man-**.

sliper adj. *slippery, unsteady*. II.6.101.

geslit n. *biting*. II.13.264, 280; 33.137; 37.120.

slyfe wk f. *sleeve*. I.26.188.

Smaragdus abbot of Saint-Mihiel in NE France (fl. 809–19). I.praef.16.

smæte adj. *pure?* II.18.18; 21.118.

smeagan vb II. *to ponder, investigate, consider, plan* (followed by **hu, hwæt** etc, **ymbe,** or direct object). I.1.13, 42, 160, 265, 268; 19.110; II.1.18; 13.43. Pres.s. **smeað**, pl. **smeagað, smeiað**; pret. **smead-**. [76 ex.]

smeagung f. *questioning, pondering, consideration*. I.4.53; 14.160; 15.132; II.38.82. **smeaungum** 1x. [13 ex.]

smealice adv. *wonderingly, inquiringly*. II.11.533.

smeaþancellice, -þanclice adv. *subtly, acutely*. I.28.191; II.11.311.

smeaþancelnyss f. *subtlety, discrimination*. II.5.179.

smed(e)ma m. *fine flour*. I.12.94; II.10.41.

smercian vb II. *to smile*. I.29.233.

smeþe adj. *smooth*. I.10.168, 178, 184; 25.216; II.21.59; 23.52. [8 ex.] Cf **un-**.

gesmeþian vb II. *to make level*. I.25.189; 30.217.

smeþnyss f. *smoothness*. I.1.257.

smic m. *smoke*. I.35.193; 38.242; II.12.236–9 (**smyce**); 27.84.

smiþian vb II. *to forge, to make (as a smith)*. I.26.79; II.18.18.

smiþþe wk f. *smithy, forge*. I.4.91.

smocian vb II. *to smoke, give off smoke*. II.12.229.

smylte adj. *calm*. I.12.31.

smyltnyss f. *calm, peace*. I.40.24; II.20.163; 21.58; 23.139 (**smilt-**). [8 ex.]

smyrels m. *ointment, embrocation*. II.34.153.

(ge)smyrian vb I/II. *to anoint*. I.15.18; II.1.155, 162 ff; 2.8, 68; 10.275. Pres.s.3 **smyraþ**; pret. **gesmyrode**; pp. **gesmyrod**.

snaw m. *snow*. I.15.105–6; II.10.70; 14.9; 19.140. [7 ex.]

snawhwit adj. *snow-white*. I.27.247; II.10.32.

snæd m. *handle* (of a scythe). II.11.135 ff.

snæd f. *piece, segment*. II.15.171.

sniþan vb 1. *to kill (a lamb)*. I.AppB3.10; II.3.81; 12.348; 15.12. Pret.pl. **snidon**. Cf **ymbsnidenyss**.

snod f. *hairband*. II.2.83, 88–90.

snoter adj. *wise, prudent*. I.25.153; 32.115; II.10.4; 19.96; 39.6, etc. **snotor-** 2x. [19 ex.]

snoterlice adv. *wisely, with wisdom*. I.praef.55.

snoternyss f. *wisdom, intelligence, prudence*. I.5.114; 8.106, 110; 22.159, 165; II.40.39. **snotor-** 2x. [10 ex.]

snotorwyrde adj. *clever in speech*. I.5.44.

socn f. *visiting*. II.34.146.

Socrates the Greek philosopher (469–399BC). I.27.143n.

Sodoma the city of Sodom. I.18.38.

Sofar Sophar, one of Job's three comforters. II.30.133, 191.

softe adj. *soft, gentle, easy*. I.10.179; 37.143. Cf **un-**.

softnyss f. *ease, comfort*. I.10.186; 19.175; AppB3.116; II.34.131.

som f. *agreement, harmony?* II.12.155. Cf **unge-**.

gesomnung see **gesamnung**

sona adv. *immediately, forthwith*. I.1.45;

26.139; II.2.56; 9.81. [86 ex., 79 in CH II]

Sophonia the prophet Sophonias or Zephaniah. I.40.168.

sorh f. *sorrow*. I.15.157; 16.140. Cf **be-, or-, unbe-**.

sorhful adj. *sorrowful*. II.10.288.

sorhlice adv. *sorrowfully, with grief*. II.10.229.

soþ adj. *true, genuine, real*. I.praef.73; 4.63; II.1.58; 5.114. [c.452 ex.]

soþ n. *truth* (usu. as object of **secgan** etc). I.8.96; 27.127; II.1.250; 7.120; 13.117; **to soþan, -on** *truly* I.8.98; II.38.35. [c.54 ex.]

soþfæst adj. *true-speaking, reliable*. I.7.262; 27.93; II.I.122; 17.97. [11 ex.]

soþfæstnyss f. *truth*. I.3.71; 6.48; II.4.66; 13.56–8. [62 ex.]

soþlice adv. *truly, with truth, actually, indeed*. I.6.80; 7.183; II.10.7; 30.231; as loose connective, I.38.293; II.29.11; 39.125. [265 ex.]

soþsegen f. *truth-telling*. II.13.116; 14.151.

sparian vb II. *to spare, save*. w. acc. or dat. I.11.210; II.4.165, 292; 5.218; 7.85; 19.194.

spatl, spætl n. *spittle*. I.31.295; II.14.130.

spearca m. *spark*. I.31.190; II.21.41.

specan vb 1. *to speak*. I.38.270 (pret.s. **spæc**).

speda f.pl. *riches, possessions, treasures*. I.4.55; 38.71; II.6.47; 19.72. [16 ex.]

spedig adj. *rich, prosperous*. I.18.206; 37.31. Cf **þurh-, un-, wan-**.

gespelia m. *representative*. II.19.123.

spelian vb II. *to represent, act as substitute for*. II.4.170; 40.302.

spell n. *discourse, sermon?* II.14.357; 19.43; Expl.11. Cf **big-, god-, lar-**.

spellung f. *chatter, talk, tale*. I.9.194; 11.214; 21.167; 33.33; II.20.74.

spendan vb I. *to expend*. I.18.207.

spendung f. *expenditure*. II.38.168.

speowan vb 7. *to prosper*. impers., w. dat. of person and gen. of ref. I.35.120; II.32.112, 200. Pres.s.3 **speowð**; pret.s. **speow**.

speowþa m. *vomiting*. II.16.215.

spere n. *spear*. I.9.173; 14.183; 30.243; II.4.102; 14.318.

spincge wk f. *sponge*. II.14.271.

spinnan vb 3. *to spin* (thread). II.31.14; intrans., *to twist, turn* II.2.122; 34.106. Pret.s. **span**.

spræc f. *speech, talking, prophetic utterance, decree, discourse, language, eloquence, conversation*. I.praef.49; 1.138; 22.180; II.1.149; 10.237; 23.58. [61 ex.] Cf **fore-, gegaf-, hosp-, leden-, sunder-, ymbe-**.

gespreca m. *interlocutor, confidant?* (used of patriarchs who spoke with God). I.6.13; 36.42; II.12.18. Cf **fore-, mid-**.

sprecan vb 5. *to speak, talk*. I.2.150, 163; 3.60; II.2.1; 19.275. Pret. **spræc, spræcon**; pp. **gesprecen**. [158 ex.] Cf **be-, for-, fore-**.

gesprecan vb 5. *to address, speak to*. I.8.74; 29.28; II.10.311; 11.81. Pret. **gespræc, gespræcon**; pp. **gesprecen**. [21 ex.] Cf **un-**.

sprencgan vb I. *to scatter*. I.31.190.

springan vb 3. *to shoot up or out, to grow rapidly, to flourish, to spread*. I.15.155; 21.162; II.6.9; 19.20. Pret. **sprang**. [8 ex.] Cf **a-, of-, to-, upa-**.

spring m. *wound, sore*. I.8.45; 23.159.

spryttan vb I. *to sprout* (intrans.), *to produce (shoots or plants,* trans.*)*. I.40.15, 106, 109–10; II.5.48; 6.67, 79; *to incite* I.14.176.

spurnan vb 3. *to strike against*. I.27.19, 78–9. Pres.s.3 **spyrnþ**. Cf **æt-**.

spylcan vb I. *to bind with splints*. I.AppB3.12, 29, 60, 210. Pret. pl. **spylton, gespylcton**.

spyrte wk f. *basket*. II.25.17, 23, 121–3.

Stacteus young man of Pergamum raised from death by St John. I.4.144, 157.

stafian vb II. *to dictate?* II.13.201.

stalian vb II. *to steal*. II.12.145, 325; 25.88.

[stalu] f. *stealing*. I.AppB3.246; II.12.509; 25.51; 34.143; 40.280. ns. **stale** at I.15.47 in MS A only, others **stalu**.

stalcung f. *stalking, following stealthily*. II.10.77.

stan m. *stone, rock*. I.15.22; 18.56; II.11.187; 24.162. [99 ex.] Cf **cwyrn-, gym-, hagel-, hrof-, hyrn-, marman-, papol-, weorc-**.

stanclud m. *rock, cliff*. II.11.30–32; 12.109; 15.32.

standan vb 6. *to stand, stay still*. I.1.72; 3.50; II.2.148; 5.14; *to exist, be present, be written, be established, continue* I.19.7;

40.163; II.12.142; 27.223; *to come out, to emerge* I.5.136; II.21.51; *to strike* (of fear, w. dat.) I.4.107; II.33.27; (of illness) I.35.231; **standan ongean,** *to resist, prevail against* I.35.250; II.12.467. Pres.s.2 **stenst**; 3 **stent, stænt**; pret. **stod, stod-**; pp. **gestanden**. [175 ex.] Cf **a-, an-, æt-, be-, for-, on-, to-, under-, wiþ-**.

gestandan vb 6. (a) intrans. *to stand, stop*. I.5.26; 7.29; II.11.251, 523; *to remain* II.12.66. (b) trans. *to sustain* II.11.110; *to oppose* I.praef.111; II.20.146; 23.66; *to strike* II.9.90; 11.49; 32.210; *to attend* II.15.161. Pres.s.2 **gestentst**; 3 **gestent**; pret. **gestod, gestod-**.

stangeweorc n. *stonework, building with stone*. I.30.71.

stanig see **stænig**

stanweall m. *wall of stone*. II.12.92.

starian vb II. *to gaze*. I.21.20–22.

staþelfæst, staþol- adj. *firm, firmly established*. I.24.108; II.15.331.

staþelfæstnyss, staþol- f. *stability, firm establishment*. I.24.38; 32.212; II.16.146; 24.92. [8 ex.]

gestaþolfæstan vb I. *to make firm, to establish firmly*. I.1.48.

gestaþolian vb II. *to establish, found, settle*. I.1.195; 27.117; 35.220; II.3.235; 11.118. Cf **geed-**.

stæf m. *letter*. I.6.33–4; 12.65 ff; II.6.176–9; 12.172. pl. **staf-**. Cf **run-**.

stæf m. *staff, rod*. II.15.20, 310; 27.80–2.

stæflic adj. *literal*. II.8.111, 115.

stænan vb I. *to stone*. I.3.52; 13.84; II.2.185; 5.201–2. [8 ex.]

stænen adj. *made of stone*. I.20.184; 26.13; II.14.343; 24.166–9. [21 ex.]

stænig adj. *stony*. II.6.7, 23, 79 (**stanigum**), 85.

stæning f. *stoning*. I.3.108; II.13.230.

stæpe m. *step*. I.8.22; 34.37, 210; II.2.159; 29.114 (gp. **stapa**); *grade, order* I.36.250; II.4.299 ff; 6.133. Cf **in-**.

stæpmælum adv. *by degrees, gradually*. I.34.97, 119.

stæppan vb 6. *to step, advance, pass*. I.7.257; 26.153; II.14.84; 29.114. Pres.s.3 **stæpð**; pres.pt. **stæppende, steppende**; pret. **stop, stopon**. [14 ex.] Cf **be-, fore-, forþ-, in-**.

stæþ n. *river-bank*. II.11.95.

stæþþig adj. *firm, steady*. II.10.12. Cf **un-**.

stæþþignyss f. *stability, steadiness*. II.10.26; 12.361. Cf **un-**.

steal m. *standing*. I.3.78. Cf **fore-, ofer-, wiþer-**.

steam m. *exhalation (of fire or breath)*. I.5.136; II.21.52.

steap adj. *high*. II.12.387; *large* I.31.34.

stearc adj. *strong, severe*. I.25.220; 29.142; II.10.269; 21.108. [6 ex.]

steda m. *horse, stallion*. I.14.86.

stede m. *place*. I.22.248; 31.93; II.13.88; 26.77; *standing still* I.10.87. [11 ex.] Cf **sun-**.

steman vb I. *to steam, exude*. I.30.126.

stemn f. *voice, noise*. I.3.57; 7.54; II.3.114; 5.255. [104 ex.]

stenc m. *smell*. I.7.246; 9.69; II.6.194; 34.238. [15 ex.]

stencan vb I. *to scatter*. I.AppB3.24, 187, 194. Cf **to-**.

steng m. *rod, crowbar*. I.29.180, 245; 31.154; 36.75; II.17.102.

steopbearn n. *orphan*. II.30.41, 46; 33.67.

steopcild n. *orphan*. II.19.137.

steor f. *correction, reproof*. I.12.80; 19.143; II.1.135; 36.63. [9 ex.]

steorfan vb 3. *to die*. I.27.222.

steorman m. *steersman, pilot*. II.38.226.

steorra m. *star*. I.1.95; 5.12; II.4.155; 17.108. [36 ex.] Cf **dæg-**.

steorsetl n. *stern (of a ship)*. II.23.135.

Stephanus (a) St Stephen protomartyr. I.3.passim; 27.12; II.2.passim; 5.201–3. [47 ex.] (b) an exemplary monk. II.37.164. as. **-um**, gs. **-es**, ds. **-e**.

sticce n. *fragment*. I.26.242, 251; II.11.14. nap. **-a, -u**.

stic(c)els m. *goad, prick*. I.31.297–9.

stician vb II. *to inhere, remain in place, to lie hidden*. I.14.173; 31.156; II.11.280; 24.113; 33.10.

sticmælum adv. *piecemeal, in parts*. II.15.145.

sticol adj. *difficult, rough?* I.10.167 ff.

stigan vb 1. *to climb (up or down), embark*. I.12.29; 18.17; 38.83–5; II.5.96. Imper. **stih**; pret.s. **stah**. Cf **a-, ofer-, uppa-**.

gestihtan vb I. *to appoint, predestine*. I.7.167. Cf **fore-**.

gestillan vb I. *to silence, make still, suppress, deter*. I.1.255; 10.75; II.9.163; 12.346;

(intrans.) *to cease* II.24.78. **gestyll-** 1x. [17 ex.]

stille adj. *gentle, quiet, unmoving*. I.38.235; 40.119; II.3.46; 11.498. **styl-** 2x. [9 ex.]

stille adv. *still, quietly*. II.12.566; 29.37, 67.

stilnyss f. *silence, calm, stillness*. I.38.16, 238; II.20.188; 29.103; 33.237. **styl-** 2x. [10 ex.] Cf **un-**.

stincan vb 3. *to smell* (intrans.). I.7.238; 14.27; II.21.52; 34.237. Pret.s. **stanc**. [10 ex.] Cf **to-**.

stiþ adj. *severe, rough, hard*. I.22.143; 29.243; II.14.145; 34.298. [14 ex.]

stiþe adv. *rigorously, austerely*. II.10.211.

gestiþian vb II. *to grow strong or hardy*. II.3.14n.

stiþlic adj. *severe, austere, fierce*. I.25.44, 149; II.1.210; 11.558; 20.153.

stiþlice adv. *severely, sternly*. I.23.43; 40.63; II.3.16; 9.47. [6 ex.]

stiþnyss f. *strictness, austerity*. II.5.259, 272; 10.269; 23.69.

stor m. *incense*. I.7.205, 209, etc; AppB2.28; II.32.123.

storc m. *stork*. I.28.65.

storcylle wk f. *censer, incense-container*. II.17.6.

storm m. *storm*. I.35.131; 40.167; II.11.503; 37.49.

stow f. *place*. I.3.24–5; 10.92–3; II.7.123; 11.125. [115 ex.] Cf **cenning-, cwealm-, eardung-, leger-, scawung-, witnung-**.

stowlic adj. *located in place*. I.24.167–9.

stowlice adv. *in terms of place*. I.7.67–8.

strand n. *shore*. I.4.88; II.4.156; 16.112, 119, etc. Cf **sæ-**.

strang adj. *strong*. I.11.57; 13.76; II.1.179; 19.144; *severe* I.18.37. comp. **strengra**. [48 ex.] Cf **byrþen-, un-**.

gestrangian vb II. *to strengthen*. I.10.30; 12.95; II.32.178; 36.110 (**strangað**). [11 ex.]

stranglic adj. *strong*. I.35.59.

stranglice adv. *strongly*. I.39.65.

strangung f. *strengthening*. I.9.226; 21.44.

stræt f. *market-place, open space in a city*. I.4.46; 22.82; II.5.9; 9.55. ds., ap. **stræt**, dp. **strætum**. [9 ex.] (Translates **forum** and **platea**; latter can mean *street* in classical Latin, but no clear evidence of this sense in CH.)

stream m. *stream, river, current*. I.37.79; II.2.95; 11.95 ff; 12.109. [8 ex.]

streamlic adj. *of a stream or river*. I.30.126.

streamrynes adv. *in the manner of a stream*. II.11.133.

streaw n. *straw, hay*. I.28.48 (**streow**); II.40.232, 251, 254, 268.

strec n. *violence, compulsion*. I.25.161 ff, 182.

strec adj. *severe, rigorous*. I.25.152; 36.105; II.9.121, 153. wk. mgs. **-en** I.38.56. [7 ex.]

streccan vb I. *to stretch, extend*. I.18.127. Cf **a-**.

strecnyss f. *severity*. I.35.178; 40.179.

strencþ f. *strength*. I.3.16; 13.75; II.5.97; 15.97. **strengþ** 2x. [15 ex.]

gestreon n. *treasure, wealth, profit*. I.4.47; 17.54; II.5.112; 25.80; *acquisition* II.31.6, 28; *procreation* I.9.211; 25.22; II.6.121. [26 ex.]

strica m. *stroke, line (of a letter)*. II.12.172.

gestrynan vb I. *to acquire, amass, beget (children)*. I.20.47 ff; 21.214 ff; 27.98; II.1.118; 3.183; 38.9–10. **stryn-** 2x; **gestrendon** 1x; **gestreon-** 2x. [54 ex.] (Senses 'to acquire wealth' and 'to beget children' mostly distinct, but there is a sense 'to acquire people, souls, for God, etc.' which links the two.)

stulor adj. *stealthy*. II.24.216.

stunt adj. *foolish*. I.14.54; 29.238; II.7.97; 30.122. [29 ex.]

stuntlic adj. *foolish*. I.31.285.

stuntlice adv. *foolishly*. II.7.25.

stuntnyss f. *foolishness*. I.14.60; 32.118; 38.223; II.19.204; 38.107.

styman vb I. *to steam, give off odour*. II.10.68.

stypel m. *tower*. I.1.205; 22.113; II.32.95.

styran vb I. *to censure, reprove, restrain*. w. dat. I.22.137; 25.174, 179 (**gestyran**); II.10.10; 19.192; 38.63. **gestyrede** II.19.212. [11 ex.]

styrian vb I/II. *to stir, move*. trans., I.31.155; II.17.65; intrans., I.26.116, 165–7; II.12.77, 114, 403. Pret. **styred-, styrod-**. Cf **a-**.

styrne adj. *stern, severe*. II.38.26, 29, 101.

styrnlic adj. *severe, harsh*. I.12.34.

styrnyss f. *censure, restraint*. I.25.175;

severity, harshness I.AppB3.13, 61. (Possibly 2 words, from **styran** and **styrne**.)

styrung f. *disturbance, commotion, impulse.* I.25.174; 37.132; II.23.132; 39.45. [14 ex.] Cf **eorþ-**.

Suanir city of Persia. II.33.203, 214.

subdiacon m. *subdeacon.* II.11.413, 419, 428.

Sublacus modern Subiaco, 40 miles east of Rome. II.11.26.

sucan vb 2. *to suck.* I.18.35; II.33.133.

sulh, sul fm. *plough.* II.30.66 (np. syll).

sum adj. and pron. *a, a certain (one), one, some, some part.* I.praef.46; 1.76; 6.137; 24.189; II.1.86; 2.8; 5.102; 21.149; qualifying a number, *some, about* II.23.166; with def. art., **sume þa**, etc, *some of the* I.3.17; 7.148; w. pers. pron., **sume hi** etc, *some of them* I.28.47; II.17.75. dsm., dsn. **suman, sumon, sumum**; dsf. **sumere, sumore, sumre**. [625 ex.]

sumerlic adj. *of the summer.* I.6.134; 40.124.

sumorlæcan vb I. *to approach summer.* I.40.16 (**sumur-**), 106.

sund n. *swimming, ability to swim.* I.1.107; *sea* II.10.86.

gesund adj. *sound, whole, healthy.* I.4.255; 8.123; II.2.137; 14.353. [12 ex.] Cf **an-**.

sunderhalga m. *pharisee.* I.24.4; II.12.456; 27.145 ff; 28.6, etc. [15 ex.]

sunderspræc f. *private, separate or secret meeting.* I.5.20, 70; 15.41; II.14.149; 27.4. [7 ex.]

gesundful adj. *whole, healthy.* I.23.56; 37.124; II.10.285; 34.101; *safe?* I.12.33; *prosperous?* II.19.97. [13 ex.]

gesundfullice adv. *safely.* II.9.190.

gesundfulnyss f. *health, prosperity, time of prosperity.* I.6.164; 18.4; II.6.113–4; 23.116. [13 ex.]

sunlic adj. *of the sun.* I.40.41.

sunnandæg m. *Sunday.* I.4.248; 6.169; 14.191; II.5.243; 12.302, 306. [7 ex.]

sunnanniht f. *Saturday night.* I.14.187.

sunnanuhta m. *early hour of Sunday morning (cockcrow).* I.4.251.

sunnbeam m. *sunbeam, rays of sun.* II.10.30.

sunne wk f. *sun.* I.7.96; 40.40; II.5.96–8; 33.236 ff. (Often without article.) [60 ex.]

sunstede m. *solstice.* I.6.134.

sunu m. *son.* I.1.20; 4.5; II.1.10, etc; 11.470 ff. as. **sunu**; gs. **suna**; ds. **suna, sunu**; pl. **suna, sunum**. [326 ex.]

supan vb 2. *to drink.* I.AppB3.10, 48; II.14.51. Pret.pl. **supon**.

susl f. *torment.* I.praef.96; 8.190; 35.111; II.5.132. [12 ex.] See also **cwic-, helle-**.

sutere m. *shoemaker.* II.21.122–4.

suþ adv. *southwards.* II.20.260.

suþdæl m. *southern part, southern region.* I.34.93; II.40.147.

suþduru f. *south door.* I.34.37.

suþerne adj. *southern.* II.40.149–50.

suþsæ f. *the English Channel.* II.9.192.

suþwag m. *south wall.* I.34.99.

suwian vb II. *to be silent.* I.10.16; 17.51; II.1.209; 6.189. [19 ex.] Cf **for-**.

swa adv. *so, thus, in this way.* I.4.70, 89; 9.25; II.2.44; 6.178; conj. *as* I.3.28; 19.163 (1st); II.14.237; 32.157 (fairly rare; more commonly in association with adv. **swa**, as follows); correl., **swa . . . swa**, *as . . . so* I.19.161 ff; II.9.47; 30.202–3; *so . . . as* I.23.157; 30.133; *whether . . . or*, I.1.156–7; 20.265–6; **swa swa**, *just as* I.1.176; 19.145; II.4.323; 5.226; **swa . . . swa swa**, *as . . . as* I.20.227 ff; II.20.83–4; **swa hwa swa**, etc, *whoever*; **swa hraþe swa**, *as soon as*. [2885 ex.]

swalewe wk f. *swallow.* I.28.65.

swan m. *herdsman.* II.23.167.

swangettung f. *turbulence, agitation.* I.38.13.

swatclaþ m. *handkerchief.* II.27.34, 37; 38.25.

swatig adj. *sweaty.* I.29.171.

swaþeahhwæþere adv. *yet, however, nevertheless.* II.18.102; 22.104; 30.113.

swæcc m. *taste, flavour.* I.9.69; 34.121; II.4.310; 10.68. **swæc** 2x. [19 ex.]

swær adj. *heavy, grievous.* I.3.170; 14.110; II.30.148; 40.260. [7 ex.]

swærlic adj. *grievous.* II.11.167.

swærlice adv. *heavily, grievously.* II.19.183; 34.102.

swærnyss f. *weight, heaviness.* I.23.152–3.

geswæs adj. *gentle, soothing, pleasing.* I.4.204; 24.22; II.11.296; 14.36. [11 ex.]

(ge)swæslice adv. *gently.* II.10.34, 289.

swæsnyss f. *flattery, blandishment.* I.33.42.

swætan vb I. *to sweat, exude moisture.* I.28.205; II.11.131.

swearcian vb II. *to darken.* II.14.287.

sweart adj. *dark, black.* I.praef.73; 3.153; II.10.165; 14.288. [27 ex.]

swefen n. *dream.* I.5.30; 34.85; II.11.309; 28.103. [17 ex.]

geswefian vb II. *to put to sleep.* I.1.88; 33.87; II.27.203. [6 ex.]

sweflen adj. *sulphurous.* I.31.190 (**sweflan**; see app.crit.).

sweg m. *sound.* I.22.19; 36.58; II.11.31; 37.186. ns. **swegi** 1x. [10 ex.]

swegan vb I. *to make a noise, resound, roar.* I.7.42; 13.176; II.6.190; 34.181; *signify* II.9.18. [14 ex.]

geswel n. *swelling.* I.8.45; 24.22; II.10.29; 12.67.

sweltan vb 3. *to die.* I.1.132; 17.81; II.22.83; 34.96. Pres.s. **swyltst**; **swelt, swylt**; pres.pt. **sweltende, swyltende**; pret. **swealt**; **swulton**. [40 ex.] Cf **for-**.

geswencan vb I. *to oppress, afflict.* I.23.79; 35.93; II.2.57; 6.100–2. Pret. **geswenct-**. **swencað** II.12.25. [33 ex.]

geswencednyss f. *affliction, oppression.* I.AppB3.119; II.6.104; 12.63; 30.168; 37.203.

sweoster, swuster, -or f. *sister.* I.4.19; 5.151; II.6.148; 10.213; 29.9; *sister in religion* II.37.185. s. indecl., nap. **swustru**. [26 ex.]

gesweostru, geswustra, -u f.pl. *sisters.* I.19.52; 27.131; II.2.101; 29.97. **geswystru** 1x. [9 ex.]

swer m. *column, pillar.* II.12.111.

swerian vb 6. *to swear.* I.29.151; 32.17, 103 ff; II.4.153; 13.193. Pret.s. **swor**; pp. **gesworen**. [15 ex.] Cf **for-**.

swete adj. *sweet.* I.30.89; II.10.68. Cf **hunig-**.

swetnyss f. *sweetness.* II.9.215; 16.195; 37.188.

geswettan vb I. *to sweeten.* II.10.266.

swica m. *deceiver, betrayer.* I.15.7; II.24.216.

geswican vb 1. *to cease, cease from, forsake.* w. gen. I.1.210; 10.72; II.5.254; 10.17. Pret. **geswac, geswic-**. [69 ex.]

swicdom m. *treachery, deceit.* I.1.163; 5.63; 34.219; II.18.23. [6 ex.]

geswicen(n)yss f. *cessation, abstention.* I.19.160; II.3.229; 6.165; 19.299.

swician vb II. *to deceive, cheat.* I.22.94; 27.216, 221; AppB3.230. Cf **æ-, beswican**.

swicol adj. *treacherous, deceitful.* I.5.77; 32.185; II.10.118; 14.78. **swicel-** 4x. [16 ex.] Cf **un-**.

swigdæg m. *day of silence* (when preaching is not permitted). I.14.220 (app.crit.); II.14.357.

swige wk f. *silence.* II.10.91; 11.178; 37.178.

swigen f. *silence.* II.36.55.

swilc, swylc pron. and adj. *such, such a.* I.24.60; 34.229; II.5.154; 19.145; 40.53; correl., **swilc . . . swilc swa,** *such . . . as* I.2.47. [58 ex.]

swilce, swylce conj. *as, like, resembling, as if.* I.30.125; 34.54; II.13.135; 34.209; *as it were, something resembling* I.34.66; 35.73; II.28.140; followed by clause, w. subj., *as if* I.1.76; 11.210; II.4.48; 11.197. See also **eac swilce,** *also.* [181 ex.]

geswinc n. *toil, effort, hardship.* I.1.167; 2.100; II.5.161; 7.73. **geswync-** 2x. [41 ex.]

swincan vb 3. *to toil.* I.6.189; 10.188; II.9.180; 31.13; *to labour, struggle* (of a ship) II.24.134. Pret. **swanc, swunc-**. [20 ex.] Cf **be-**.

geswincful adj. *toilsome, full of hardship.* I.14.212; II.12.184; 16.147, 151; 20.58. [9 ex.]

swincleas adj. *free of toil.* II.22.88.

swingan vb 3. *to beat, scourge, chastise.* I.26.284; 29.126; II.18.78; 19.247. Pret.pl. **swungon**. [8 ex.] Cf **be-**.

swingel f. *blow, affliction, (physical) punishment.* I.31.333; 38.49; II.9.111; 36.65. **swincgelum** 1x. [18 ex.]

[swipe] f. *whip.* I.28.79, 163; 29.132, 156, 164, 245; 36.75. Forms: **swipe** asf.; **swipe** ds.; **swipan** np.; **swipum** dp.

swiþe adv. *very, exceedingly, greatly, widely.* I.1.25; 3.67; II.10.156; 23.175; **swiþor** *more, rather* I.3.104 ff; 7.194; II.4.300; 11.23 **swiþost** *most, most of all* I.2.106; 6.14; II.6.133; 7.30. **swyþ-** 7x. [364 ex.]

swiþlic adj. *great, strong, powerful.* I.5.141; 40.167; II.14.172; 19.144. **swyþ-** 2x. [14 ex.]

swiþlice adv. *greatly, strongly, quickly, urgently, very.* I.35.13; 37.131; II.10.211, 311; 12.393. **swyþ-** 1x. [6 ex.]

swiþra adj. (comp. of **swiþ,** *strong*). *right,*

right-hand. I.21.225; 37.75; II.7.136; 16.116. **swyþ-** 2x. [17 ex.]

swiþra m. *right hand, right-hand side*. I.3.49; 22.63–5; II.14.50; 18.19–20. **swyþ-** 1x. [20 ex.]

geswogen adj. *in a swoon, unconscious*. II.21.147.

swura m. *neck*. I.3.42; 27.99; II.21.104; 34.190. **swyran** 4x. [17 ex.]

swurbeah m. *collar, necklace*. II.28.146, 156. Cf **wuldor-**.

swurd n. *sword*. I.5.109; 9.177; II.4.139, 144; 20.30. **sweordes** 1x. [30 ex.]

swurdbora m. *swordbearer*. II.11.238.

swust- see **sweost-**

swutel, -ol adj. *clear, visible*. I.7.79; 40.38; II.3.262; 40.233. [11 ex.]

geswutelian vb II. *to reveal*. I.praef.124; 2.114; II.4.187; 5.276. **-tol-** 1x, **-tul-** 1x; **swutel-** 3x. [144 ex.]

swutel(l)ice adv. *clearly, openly*. I.2.63; 20.51; II.1.209; 5.123. **swutol-** 2x. [23 ex.]

swutelung f. *revelation, explanation, rubric*. I.32.33; 34.22; II.praef.41; 15.160, 167; 18.46.

swutelungdæg m. *day of revelation, Epiphany*. II.3.1.

swyft, swift adj. *swift, rapid*. I.21.46; 37.218; 40.169, 180; II.11.101, 531.

swyftlice adv. *swiftly*. I.30.263; 38.86; II.11.331.

swyftnyss f. *swiftness*. II.5.198.

swylt- see **swelt-**

swymman vb 3. *to swim, float*. I.20.22; II.4.116; 11.138; 16.120; 34.275; 39.52 (**swimð**). Pret. **swam**.

swyn n. *pig*. II.10.199 (**swines**); 23.163, etc. [11 ex.]

swyþrian vb II. *to be strong, to prevail*. I.27.43.

syf- see **seofon**

syferlice adv. *sincerely, soberly, purely*. II.2.33; 6.143.

syfernyss f. *sobriety, purity*. I.25.165; II.7.25; 12.366; 15.268.

syfling f. *relish, something eaten with bread (apparently referring to fish at II.16.114)*. I.12.105; II.10.57n; 16.114.

syfre adj. *sober, temperate*. I.38.319; II.30.34.

sylen f. *gift*. I.38.130; II.20.121; 28.148; 34.40, 47; 38.165.

sylf pron. *self, himself, etc*. After noun or pron., used for emphasis or in reflexive constructions, I.praef.81–3; 2.44; II.1.71; 24.235; after article, declined weak, for emphasis or = *very* I.38.202; II.7.80. [543 ex.]

sylfren adj. *made of silver*. I.26.41; 34.117; II.4.221; 28.101. [7 ex.]

sylfwilles adv. *willingly, of one's own will*. I.9.237; 38.190 ff; II.5.249; 11.511. **silf-** 1x. [23 ex.]

syll f. *foundation timber*. II.10.202, 207.

syllan vb I. *to give*. I.5.159; 6.28; II.5.10; 7.39–40; **syllan . . . wiþ** *to give in exchange for, to sell for* I.AppB3.51; II.14.60. Pret. **seald-**, pp. **geseald**. **gesylle** 1x, **gesealde** 3x. [222 ex.]

syltan vb I. *to salt*. II.36.134.

gesyman vb I. *to load*. I.31.68.

symbeldæg m. *festival*. I.30.110; II.14.24, 310; 29.115, 120.

symle adv. *always, continually*. I.6.197–9; 9.71–2; II.4.196; 17.122. **simle** 2x. [132 ex.]

syn, synn f. *sin*. I.1.50; 2.143; II.1.152; 3.52. [247 ex.] Cf **unsynnig**.

synderlic adj. *separate, individual*. I.22.77; 24.170; II.32.97; 34.125. [9 ex.]

synderlice adv. *separately, specially, individually*. I.19.59; 30.42; II.8.62; 24.243. **sind-** 4x. [21 ex.]

syndrig adj. *separate, private*. II.9.46.

gesyne adj. *visible*. II.20.250; 33.175.

synful adj. *sinful*. I.15.108; 19.65; II.4.118; 9.134. [92 ex.]

syngian vb II. *to sin*. I.7.174; 19.161; II.14.160; 19.59. [32 ex.] See also **singan**.

synlic adj. *sinful*. II.19.202.

[syrwian] vb I. *to plot, conspire*. I.5.170; 17.24; 26.152; II.8.77. Pres.s.3 **syrwþ**; pl. **-wiaþ**; pret. **syrwd-, syrwed-, syrwod-, syrewyd-**. [9 ex.]

syrwum see **searu**

syrwung, syrewung f. *plotting*. I.5.63; 27.47; II.12.467; 30.128. [11 ex.]

ta wk f. *lot, straw* (in drawing lots). I.18.20–22; II.14.237.

tabele wk f. *tablet*. II.12.137, 142, 255 ff, 336.

tacn, tacen n. *sign*. I.praef.63; 6.53;

II.4.49; 18.14. nap. **tacna, -nu**. [106 ex.] Cf **rode-**.

getacnian vb II. *to signify, symbolise, stand for*. I.8.50; 9.170; II.3.154; 4.53. [175 ex.]

getacnigendlic adj. *signifying, bearing symbolic meaning*. I.7.207; II.15.258.

getacnigendlice adv. *symbolically, with symbolic meaning*. II.8.101.

getacnung f. *signifying, signification, symbol, foreshadowing*. I.6.126; 28.90; II.12.306; 13.191; **habban getacnunge** (w. gen.) *to signify* I.7.58; II.15.188. [85 ex.]

tal n. *reproach, blasphemy*. I.24.20; 33.124–5, 149; II.1.264; 12.541. [12 ex.]

talian vb II. *to account, consider, reckon, ascribe*. I.7.186–7; 28.125; II.7.72; 12.498. [14 ex.]

tallic adj. *abusive, blasphemous*. I.3.20, 24; 33.33 (**talice**), 126.

tallice adv. *reprehensibly, in blameworthy fashion*. I.23.82.

tam adj. *tame*. II.33.187.

tang f. *tongs*. II.21.53, 57.

taper m. *candle*. II.32.123.

tawian vb II. *to afflict*. II.33.98.

tæcan vb I. *to teach*. w. acc. object and dat. of person. I.praef.109; 1.283; II.3.235 ff; 6.127. Pres.s.3 **tæcþ, tæhþ**; pret. **tæht-**; pp. **getæht**. [86 ex.] Cf **be-, mis-**.

tæcung f. *teaching*. I.3.162; 10.200; II.3.227; 40.311. **tæcing** II.6.143. [10 ex.]

tægl m. *tail*. I.18.125–31.

getæl see **getel**.

tælan vb I. *to blame, reproach, censure*. I.3.72; 11.211; II.19.246; 20.127. [11 ex.] Cf **wiþertalu**. For **tælþ** see also **tellan**.

tætteca m? *rag*? **tættecon** I.18.187.

team m. *offspring, brood*. I.16.137; 33.22; II.1.88; 19.173. [7 ex.] Cf **bearn-**.

tear m. *tear* (of weeping). I.4.141; 28.109; II.9.153; 10.21. [9 ex.]

teart adj. *painful, sharp*. II.40.272, 292.

teartlice adv. *sharply, severely*. I.23.71.

teartnyss f. *roughness, sharpness*. I.23.42; 38.50.

Tecla St Thecla of Iconium, 1st century virgin saint. II.34.223.

getel, getæl n. *number, reckoning*. I.3.13; 11.194; II.5.249; 16.184. [41 ex.]

tela adv. *well, good*. I.3.179; 18.134; II.2.215; 12.446. **teala** 1x. [9 ex.]

geteld n. *tent, tabernacle*. II.1.50; 12.159, etc; 14.10.

teldwyrhta m. *tentmaker*. I.27.119.

tellan vb I. *to reckon, enumerate, ascribe, consider, count*. I.6.157; 9.66; II.4.317; 11.231. Pres.s.3 **telþ, tælþ** (I.31.320; 38.71); pret. **teald-**; pp. **geteald**. [83 ex.] Cf **be-**.

getemian vb II. *to tame*. I.14.61–4; II.33.178.

tempel, templ n. *temple*. I.3.41; 4.200 (masc., but cf app. crit.); II.5.265; 40.3, etc. [117 ex.]

getemprian vb II. *to temper, moderate, heal*. I.25.171; 31.317; II.3.177.

tengan vb I. *to hasten*. I.22.11; 26.139 (**getengde**); II.11.151; 12.87. [7 ex.]

getenge adj. *oppressing, afflicting*. II.23.178; 34.263.

geteohian vb II. *to intend, determine*. I.13.126.

teolian vb II. *to procure, toil to obtain*. w. acc. or gen. I.32.200; II.5.118; 23.42; 38.181; without express object, II.38.8; *to labour* I.AppA1.7; *to work on behalf of* (w. dat.) I.28.166, 176; II.5.110; **teolode his** *toiled to obtain his needs* I.27.136. Cf **tilian**.

teolung f. *produce, acquisition, profit*. I.4.124; 28.167; II.5.113; 12.576; *working, labour, occupation* I.19.231; 35.85; II.7.98; 16.136 ff. [21 ex.] Cf **tilung**.

(ge)teon vb 2. *to drag, bring, draw, extend*. I.5.183; 29.263; II.11.112; 16.123; *to educate* I.26.200; 36.57; 38.25; II.9.87; intrans., *to hasten, depart* I.18.27; II.33.134; **him to geteon** *to appropriate, arrogate* I.5.83; II.36.80; 40.301–2. Pres.s. **tihst, tihþ**; pl. **teoþ**; imp. **teoh**; pret. **(ge)teah, (ge)tug-**; pp. **getogen**. [40 ex.] Cf **a-, be-, forþ-, forþa-, of-, ofer-, þurh-, ungetogen**.

teona m. *injury, harm, anger*. I.3.65; 6.173; II.2.112; 8.39. [18 ex.]

teonful adj. *slanderous, reproachful*. II.11.343.

teorian vb II. *to fail, become exhausted*. I.12.44. Cf **a-**.

teorung f. *exhaustion*. II.11.580. Cf **a-**.

teoþa adj. *tenth*. I.1.27; 24.78; II.11.257; 12.78. [11 ex.]

teoþian vb II. *to tithe, take a tenth part of.* I.11.191, 199; II.28.10, 36.

teoþin(c)gdæg m. *tenth-part day, day forming a tenth, tithe-day.* I.11.192, 195, 198.

teoþung f. *tenth part.* I.11.197.

teran vb 4. *to tear, lacerate.* II.10.55, 191; 13.257; 36.60. Pret. **tær, tær-**. Cf **to-**.

Tetradius nobleman converted by St Martin. II.34.198.

Theodolus see **þeodolus**.

Theodosius Theodosius I, Roman emperor 379–95. I.AppB2.36; II.27. 206 ff.

Thomas, þomas the apostle Thomas. I.16.12, etc; 21.30; II.ExDict.7; 38.185. gs. **thomes**; ds. **þome, þoman**. [11 ex.]

Tiberius Roman emperor, 14–37AD. I.26.19; 40.36 (gs. **Tyberies**).

ticcen n. *kid.* II.12.361.

tid f. *time, period, hour, season.* I.6.148; 27.171; II.5.13; 9.160. [129 ex.] Cf **bereowsung-, gebyrd-, easter-, freols-, heofung-, non-, þrowung-, undern-**.

tidsang m. *service of the divine office, lauds.* II.11.110, 114.

(ge)tigan vb I. *to tie.* I.26.135; 29.262; II.4.150; 10.54. [12 ex.] Cf **un-**.

tige m. *dragging.* I.29.263; *signification* I.18.79; II.5.35.

tiger m. *tiger.* np. **tigres** II.33.176, 186.

tihtan vb I. *to urge, incite.* w. acc. and occas. dat. I.3.188; 10.100; II.9.110; 10.8. [41 ex.] Cf **yfeltihtend**.

tihtendlic adj. *encouraging, persuasive, admonitory.* I.37.67; II.40.1.

tihting f. *encouragement, incitement.* I.7.160; 11.138 ff; II.9.169; 19.263. **tyht-** 5x. [27 ex.]

tilia m. *worker, cultivator.* II.5.73.

tilian vb II. *to acquire (by toil), labour to obtain.* w. acc. or gen. I.1.145; 23.124; II.10.177; 16.135; **tylað his sylfes** *labours for himself, to obtain his own good?* I.17.53. **tyl-** 2x. [8 ex.]

getillan vb I. *to touch.* II.30.57.

tilung f. *profit, gain.* II.38.81 (**tyl-**); *activity, action?* I.31.304. Cf **teolung**.

tima m. *time, occasion, period.* I.1.236, 240; 4.246; II.5.141; 6.121. **tym-** 4x. [114 ex.] Cf **mærsung-, þrowung-**.

getimbrian vb II. *to build, construct, strengthen.* I.26.13; 28.195; II.4.272; 40.230. **timb-** 4x. [39 ex.]

getimbrung f. *building, construction (as activity), building work.* I.1.210; 6.194; II.11.187; 33.267. [20 ex.] Cf **antimber**.

getimian vb II. *to happen, occur.* impers. or w. abstract noun as subject, and dat. of person. I.8.102; 9.196; II.10.138; 19.255. [41 ex.]

Timotheus (a) one of the first seven deacons. I.3.10. (b) correspondent and friend of St Paul. I.AppB3.158 (ds. **-theae**).

getinge adj. *eloquent.* I.38.28; II.1.191.

getingelice adv. *eloquently, articulately.* II.33.164.

getingnyss f. *eloquence.* I.1.258 (**getinc-**); 38.31; II.10.133; 40.241.

tintrega mn. *torment, torture.* I.21.120; 23.111; II.11.447 ff; 37.71. ns. **tintrega**; nap. **-gan, -gu**; gp. **-gena**; dp. **-gum**. [40 ex.]

(ge)tintregian vb II. *to torment.* I.19.141; 23.18; II.23.158; 27.195. [8 ex.]

tintregung f. *tormenting.* I.23.22; 29.7.

Tiri the people of Tyre. dp. **tirum** II.24.37. Cf **Tyrus**.

(ge)tirian, (ge)tyr- vb I. *to affront, blame, reproach, vex.* I.37.90; II.2.105, 108; 12.313; 30.141; 36.47. Pres.s.3 **-rigþ**; subj.pl. **-rion**; pret. **-rigd-**. [9 ex.]

Titus Roman emperor, 79–81AD. I.28.38.

tiþ f. *assent, gift.* I.26.294.

tiþa m., **tiþe** wk f. *receiver, beneficiary.* **beon tiþa (tiþe)** *to receive, be granted.* I.32.17; 37.137.

(ge)tiþian vb II. *to grant, permit.* w. acc. or gen. object and dat. of person. I.4.282; 18.93–5; II.10.187; 13.285. [41 ex.]

to prep. w. dat. *to* (after verbs of motion, speaking, changing, etc). I.praef.46; 1.35; II.praef.29; 2.10; *as, for, to be or provide* I.praef.96; 14.113; II.1.14; 10.242; w. infl. inf. I.3.63; II.1.126. [c3784 ex.]

to adv. *too.* I.10.26; AppB3.159; II.5.206; 38.61. [c10 ex.]

to þy þæt, to þy . . . þæt conj. *in order that, to this end . . . that, for the purpose . . . that.* I.1.125; 2.63; 5.84; II.4.98. [30 ex. (only 1x in CH II)]

toarn see **toyrnan**

toberan vb 4. *to carry, carry off.* I.27.32; II.6.65. Pret.pl. **tobæron**.

toberstan vb 3. *to break, shatter* (intrans.). I.26.242; 29.67; II.11.426; 16.165. Pret. **tobærst, toburston**; pp. **toborsten**. [24 ex.]

Tobias subject of the apocryphal book of Tobit. I.34.257; II.10.46. ads. **tobian**.

toblawennyss f. *swollenness*. I.5.135.

tobrecan vb 4. *to break, shatter* (trans.). I.1.82, 142; 4.52; II.4.215; 16.28. Pres.s.3 **tobrecþ, tobrycþ**; pret. **tobræc, tobræc-**; pp. **tobrocen**. [49 ex.]

tobrytan vb I. *to break, destroy*. I.31.220; 32.165; II.6.112; 33.246. [6 ex.]

toceorfan vb 3. *to cut, cut in pieces*. II.34.33 (pret.s. **tocearf**).

toceowan vb 2. *to chew up*. II.15.146 (pp. **tocowen**).

tocinen adj. (pp. of **tocinan**, vb 1). *wounded, scarred*(?). I.23.138.

toclifrod adj. (pp. of **toclifrian**, vb II). *scratched*. II.11.54.

toclofen adj. (pp. of **tocleofan**, vb 2). *split, broken in pieces*. II.11.15.

toclypian vb II. *to address, speak*. II.19.215.

toclypung f. *invocation*. II.3.218.

tocnawan vb 7. *to distinguish, recognise, acknowledge, know*. I.1.75; 4.207; II.4.116; 13.26. Pres.s.3 **tocnæwþ**; pret. **tocneow, tocneow-**; pp. **tocnawen**. [36 ex.]

tocnawennyss f. *recognition, understanding*. II.22.77.

tocwysan vb I. *to crush, destroy*. I.4.48; 31.212; II.2.54; 11.212 ff. [13 ex.]

tocwysednyss f. *crushing, destruction*. I.4.71.

tocyme m. *arrival, coming, advent*. I.2.122; 7.92; II.3.6; 5.152. [99 ex.]

todal n. *separation, distinction*. I.3.82; 27.210; II.1.46.

todæg adv. *today, on this day*. I.3.200; 14.181; II.1.3; 2.2. **todægi** 1x, **todæig** 12x. [46 ex.]

todælan vb I. *to divide, distribute*. I.12.20; 18.169; II.12.248; 28.154. [22 ex.]

todræfan vb I. *to drive out, expel*. I.1.259; 2.122; 9.144; 10.79. [11 ex.] Cf **a-**.

todræfednyss f. *expulsion*. I.28.80.

toeacan prep. w. dat. *in addition to, as well as*. I.9.201; 31.259; II.3.239; 36.2; adv. *as well* II.11.404. Cf also **þærtoeacan**.

tofeallan vb 7. *to fall down, fall apart*. II.12.436 (pret.pl. **tofeollon**).

toferan vb I. *to scatter*. I.1.210; 21.236; 22.102, 118.

toflowan vb 7. *to flow apart*. II.14.165 (pret.s. **tofleow**).

toforan prep. w. dat. *in front of, in advance of, more than, superior to, in addition to*. I.14.54; 23.40; II.3.5; 25.118. [12 ex.]

toforlætennyss f. *intermission*. I.38.304; II.21.28, 30; 24.10.

togan anom. vb. *to separate* (intrans.). II.12.90, 386; 19.165. Pret. **toeode**.

togædere adv. *together, at the same time, without a gap*. I.1.191; 7.61; II.1.43; 12.264. [17 ex.]

togeanes prep. w. dat. *to, towards, to meet, against*. I.1.291; 3.46; II.2.64; 12.469. **togenes** 1x. [59 ex.] Cf also **þærtogeanes**.

togebicnian vb II. *to point towards*. I.37.77 (or two words?).

getogen see **(ge)teon**

toglidan vb 1. *to glide away, depart*. II.14.13 (pret.s. **toglad**).

tol n. *tool, equipment*. I.29.131; II.11.137; 14.314. Cf **pinung-**.

tol, toll n. *tax, tax-gathering*. I.34.157–66; II.16.136; 32.7, 25.

togelaþian vb II. *to invite (to)*. I.33.91 (or two words?).

toliþian vb II. *to dismember*. II.15.164.

tollere m. *tax-collector*. I.22.191; 34.155; II.3.39; 16.133; 32.22.

tollscir f. *office of tax-collecting*. II.32.31.

tollsetl n. *tax-collecting seat or booth*. II.16.134; 32.5.

tolysan vb I. *to undo, untie, loosen*. I.16.82; 31.156; II.2.116; 34.72; *to relax, dissolve, make at ease* I.28.117; II.6.100. Cf **a-**.

tomerien, tomerigen adv. *tomorrow*. I.26.154; 28.215; II.5.197; 31.16. [16 ex.]

tomiddes prep. w. dat. *among, in the midst of*. I.34.139; II.16.52.

toniht adv. *tonight, on this night*. II.7.97.

tor m. *tower*. I.26.229–35; 34.101.

torfian vb II. *to stone*. I.3.96; II.13.40, 221; 17.96, 100. Cf **of-**.

tosawan vb 7. *to sow, scatter, spread*. I.30.26; 33.29. Pres.s.3 **tosæwð**; pp. **tosawen**.

tosceacan vb 6. *to drive away, extinguish*. I.37.195; 39.57. Pret.s. **toscoc**.

toscead n. *distinction*. I.22.182.

tosceadan vb 7. *to divide, distribute, distinguish, reason*. I.8.116; 21.127; II.7.135; 13.123. Pres.s.3 **toscæt**. [12 ex.]

tosceotan vb 2. *to scatter, spring apart* (intrans.). II.18.29; 21.56. Pret.pl. **toscuton**.

tosendan vb I. *to send (in all directions)*. I.28.56; 31.121.

tosigan vb 1. *to wear out*. pp. **tosigen** I.31.37; II.12.117.

toslean vb 6. *to strike (and break apart)*. II.30.77 (pret.s. **tosloh**).

toslitan vb 1. *to tear, bite, lacerate*. I.8.188; II.13.285; 33.124. pp. **tosliten**.

toslupan vb 2. *to become loose*. I.5.146; II.2.89; 34.197. Pret.subj. **toslupe**; pp. **toslopen**.

tosomne adv. *together, without a break*. II.2.110; 10.189; 12.32; 14.148. **tosamne** 1x. [7 ex.]

tosprædan vb I. *to widen, stretch out, extend*. I.35.269; II.11.539.

tospringan vb 3. *to spring apart*. II.11.35; 24.20. Pret.s. **tosprang**.

tostandan vb 6. *to differ*. II.4.310 (pres.s.3 **tostent**).

tostencan vb I. *to scatter, divide* (trans.). I.2.111; 17.6; 22.115; II.14.71. [17 ex.]

tostencednyss f. *destruction, scattering*. I.28.60; II.37.124.

tostincan vb 3. *to smell, distinguish by smell*. II.23.49.

toswollen adj. (pp. of **toswellan**). *swollen*. I.5.134; II.30.194; 34.246.

getot n. *pomp*. II.3.277; 11.241; 12.526.

toteran vb 4. *to tear, tear apart, lacerate*. I.6.180; 26.143; II.6.40; 9.103. Pret. **totær, totæron**; pp **totoren**. [15 ex.]

Totilla Gothic king in 6th C Italy. II.11.234, 247.

totwæman vb I. *to separate, divide*. I.2.160; 17.46; 20.111, 153; 28.179; 33.141.

toþ m. *tooth*. I.3.46 (**tetð**); 26.141; II.15.146; 34.207. nap. **teþ**. [18 ex.]

toþunden adj. (pp. of **toþindan**?). *swollen, inflated* (lit. and fig.), *proud*. I.23.59; 28.199; 30.236; II.10.42. [6 ex.]

toþundennyss f. *swollenness, swelling*. I.23.159; *arrogance* I.36.182.

toweard adj. *impending, approaching* (in time or place), *future, with reference to the future, destined to come*. I.5.35; 12.24; II.2.93; 12.308; with adverbial sense, **towearde** *in advance* I.7.168–70; 38.137; II.37.35. **towerdan** 2x. [87 ex.]

towendan vb I. *to overturn, overthrow, destroy*. I.3.25; 37.170; II.11.174; 24.224. [6 ex.]

toworpennyss f. *destruction*. I.28.18, 81, 106; 40.96.

towritennyss f. *census*. I.2.10, 65.

towurpan vb 3. *to overthrow, destroy*. I.4.199–200; 6.69; II.4.203; 17.14. Pres.s.2 **towyrpst**, 3 **towyrpþ**; pret. **towearp, towurpon**; pp. **toworpen**. [43 ex.]

toyrnan vb 3. *to run together*. II.12.389 (pret.s. **toarn**).

Trahianus the Roman emperor Trajan, 98–117AD. I.37.52–3, 93.

traht m. *exposition*. I.7.5; 11.6; II.4.294; 36.138. [8 ex.] Cf **godspel-**.

trahtboc f. *book of commentary or exposition*. I.30.8, 15; II.9.254.

trahtnere m. *expositor, commentator*. I.15.143; 21.227; II.4.297; 5.187. [13 ex.]

trahtnian vb II. *to expound*. I.7.8; 12.89; II.6.34 (**getrahtnian**), 55; 16.41. [29 ex.] Cf **ofer-**.

trahtnung f. *exposition, commentary*. I.7.200; 8.15; II.praef.32; 3.77. [18 ex.]

trendel n. *orb*. I.20.102; 40.40.

treow n. *tree, beam, wood, wooden object*. I.1.72, 213; 31.313; II.10.204; 13.288 ff. nap. **-a, -u**. [61 ex.] Cf **fic-**.

treowcynn n. *species of tree*. I.AppB2.2; II.40.49.

getreowe, getrywe adj. *faithful*. II.4.255; 20.196; 37.111; 38.17, etc. [9 ex.] See **untrywe**.

treowen adj. *of a tree*. II.10.302; *wooden* I.37.171.

getreowfullice adv. *confidently, with full faith*. I.36.124.

treowleas adj. *faithless, false*. II.19.142.

getreowlice adv. *faithfully*. I.26.219; II.38.149.

Triphonia queen of the emperor Decius. I.29.279, 284.

trucian vb II. *to be lacking*(?). II.3.128.

trum adj. *healthy, sound, firm*. I.37.4; II.12.173; 24.177, etc; 34.166. [7 ex.] See **met-, un-**.

truma m. *troop*. I.30.122. Cf **fyrd-**.

getrumian vb II. *to strengthen, heal.* I.33.113. Cf **geun-**.

trumlice adv. *firmly*. II.28.80.

trumnyss f. *defence, foundation.* I.3.123; II.24.172. Cf **un-**.

Trumwine Northumbrian bishop to the Picts, c680. II.10.245.

truwa m. *faith, confidence, pledge.* I.11.82; 27.134; II.21.172; 24.69. ns. **truwe** I.24.207. [11 ex.]

truwian vb II. *to trust, rely.* I.24.61; 29.137–9; II.2.4; 14.111. **trua** (imp.) 1x; **getruwast** 1x. [20 ex.]

getrymman vb I. *to strengthen.* I.praef.68; 20.4; II.4.323; 10.214. Pres.s.3 **getrymþ**; pret. **getrymd-**. **trymdon** I.AppB3.11. [35 ex.] Cf **ymb-**.

(ge)trymming f. *strengthening.* I.2.3; 15.72; II.23.128; 24.49. [7 ex.] Cf **ymb-**.

trymnyss f. *strengthening, encouragement.* I.21.112.

trywþ f. *loyalty, goodwill.* I.AppB3.163. Cf **unge-**.

tua, tuwa adv. *twice.* I.1.241; 16.54; II.1.5; 19.182. [12 ex.]

(ge)tucian vb II. *to afflict, torment.* II.30.142.

tun m. *farm, small village.* I.35.11, 83–4; II.4.3, 37; 23.8, 38 ff. (Translating **villa** and **viculus**.) Cf **æppel-, ber-, cauer-**.

Tuna priest and abbot, brother of Ymma. II.21.153.

tunece wk f. *tunic.* I.2.93; 4.232, 235; II.2.58; 30.80. (Translating **tuneca**.) [8 ex.]

tunge wk f. *tongue.* I.3.98; 23.15; II.1.191; 2.205. [21 ex.]

tungel m. *star.* I.4.111; 7.73; 11.102; II.34.61. [6 ex.]

tungelcræft m. *astronomy.* I.40.39.

tungelwitega m. *one skilled in the stars, astronomer.* I.5.10, 24, etc; 7.14, 24, etc. [24 ex.]

tungerefa m. *city-governor or -administrator.* I.29.96, 175 (referring to the deputy of the prefect of Rome).

tunman m. *neighbour, inhabitant of the same tun?* II.20.209.

turnian vb II. *to turn.* I.34.211.

Turonisc of the region of Tours in Gaul. II.34.110, 121, 316, 323.

turtle wk f. *turtle-dove.* I.9.77, 80, etc; II.12.363.

twa, twegen num. *two.* I.1.252; 4.47; II.4.239; 2.49. gp. **twegra, tweigra**; dp. **twam**. [229 ex.]

twæming f. *separation, distinction.* I.2.181; 26.35; 34.231; 40.153; II.19.160, 166.

twelf num. *twelve.* I.1.251; 4.210; II.1.49; 11.90. gp. **twelfa**. [54 ex.]

twelffeald adj. *twelve-fold, numbering twelve.* I.12.127; 27.165, 169, 174; 36.55.

twelfta adj. *twelfth.* I.5.54.

twentig num. *twenty.* I.21.33; 26.104; II.3.142; 11.404. [15 ex.]

tweo m. *doubt.* **buton tweon, twyn** *without doubt, undoubtedly* I.7.76; 13.77; II.4.110; 27.222. [13 ex.]

twyfeald adj. *twofold, double.* I.31.265; 36.135; II.4.12; 16.56; *duplicitous* I.27.217; II.26.136; **be, mid twyfealdum** *twice, doubly* I.31.287; II.30.199, 211. [23 ex.]

twyfealdlic adj. *twofold.* I.9.88.

twyfealdlice adv. *twice, in two ways.* I.9.152–3; II.26.57; 28.17.

getwyfyld adj. (pp. of **twyfyldan**?). *doubled.* II.23.54; 38.75, 137; 39.37.

twylic adj. *doubtful, ambiguous.* II.3.260; 10.217.

twyn m. *doubt.* II.29.113.

twynian vb II. *to doubt.* impers., I.4.229; 8.196; II.16.48; 24.77; w. personal subject, II.24.210–11. [20 ex.]

twynung f. *doubt, uncertainty.* I.4.231; 11.37; II.15.6; 16.45. [20 ex.]

twyrednyss f. *dissension, discord.* II.20.101.

getwysa m. *twin.* I.7.129.

twywintre adj. *two-years old.* I.5.49, 73.

Tyberiadis (sea) of Tiberius. I.12.4; II.16.108.

Tyberianum; botl tyberianum the palatium Tyberianum in Rome. I.29.224.

Tyberius see **Tib-**.

tyddernyss f. *weakness, frailty.* I.36.145; II.1.33; 7.22; 28.74. [7 ex.]

tyddre, tydre adj. *weak.* I.18.181–2; 20.158.

getyddrian vb II. *to produce, bear.* II.5.50.

tyman vb I. *to produce (offspring), to reproduce.* I.1.153; 18.109; II.1.86–8; 6.123; 12.382.

getym n. *team* (of oxen). II.23.10, 43–4, 53; 30.11, 205–7. nap. **-a, -e, -u**.

tyn num. *ten.* I.1.22; 24.76; II.9.257; 12.55. [26 ex.]

[getyn] vb I. *to instruct.* pp. **getyd** II.9.22.
tynan vb I. *to anger, insult, slander.* II.2.111, 216; 12.447.
tynfeald adj. *tenfold, of ten.* II.39.38.
getyr- see **getir-**
tyran vb I. *to shed tears, to water (of eyes).* I.8.195; 35.193.
tyrnan vb I. *to turn.* I.34.208; II.12.426; 34.158.
Tyrus region of Tyre in Palestine. II.8.5. Cf **Tiri**.
tyrwa m. (or **tyrwe** f.). *tar, pitch.* I.1.187.

þa adv. *then.* I.1.29; 2.12; II.2.12; 3.15. conj. *when* (usu. in form **þa þa**, and freq. correlated with **þa** *then*). I.1.35; 2.16; II.1.24; 2.67; alone, I.22.67; II.11.367. See also **se**.
geþafian vb II. *to permit, allow.* I.praef.91; 2.153; II.6.96; 9.85. [66 ex.]
geþafung f. *consent, permitting.* I.4.34; 11.139 ff; 33.81; II.12.565. [10 ex.]
þanc m. *will.* **agenes þances** *of his own will* II.1.124.
geþanc n. *thought.* I.1.55; 9.54; II.21.33; 26.136. [17 ex.]
þancful adj. *thankful.* I.39.103.
þancian vb II. *to thank, give thanks.* w. dat. of person and gen. of thing for which thanks are given. I.2.125; 4.269; II.25.97–9; 28.8. **geþanc-** 2x. [38 ex.]
þancung f. *thanks, gratitude.* I.36.14; II.11.277; 40.70.
þancwurþ adj. *acceptable, welcome.* I.38.262; II.32.36.
þanon, þonon adv. *thence, from there, from that person.* I.19.58; 29.52; II.8.5; 21.82. **þonon ðe** conj., *through the fact that, on the grounds that.* II.9.246. [16 ex.]
þæc n. *thatch.* II.10.55.
þær adv. *there.* I.1.46; 2.96; II.1.230; 2.48. conj. *where.* I.7.107; 38.249; II.10.325; 11.580; in form **þær þær** I.5.142; 8.170; II.3.140; 7.105. [465 ex.]
þæradune adv. *downwards.* I.19.227.
þæræfter adv. *after that.* I.19.217.
þærbinnon adv. *within that place.* I.28.13; 30.195; 34.74; II.10.54. conj., *within which.* II.21.59. [8 ex.]
þærinne adv. *inside that place.* II.3.141; 11.424; 40.141.
þærofer adv. *above that place.* I.34.69; II.33.225.
þæron adv. *on, in or into that place or thing.* I.1.216; 4.24; II.1.71; 18.25. (Printed as 2 words I.15.153.) [23 ex.]
þæroninnan adv. *within that place.* I.31.152; II.11.280.
þæronuppon adv. *above, on top of, that place.* I.30.69; II.11.190.
þærrihte adv. *immediately.* I.1.102–3; 4.14; II.1.241; 2.10. **þarrihte** 1x. [114 ex.]
þærto adv. *to that place or object.* I.1.207; 32.46; II.23.4; 31.23; *in addition to or association with that* I.9.247 (printed as two words); II.4.76; 33.222; 38.21, etc. conj., **þær . . . to** *to which place.* II.1.31. [22 ex.]
þærtoeacan adv. *as well, in addition to that.* I.4.122; 27.116; II.5.224; 9.46. [12 ex.]
þærtoge(a)nes adv. *in opposition or response to that.* I.1.192; 16.114; 19.67; 26.168. (I.15.33 should perhaps be **þær togeanes**.)
þæslic adj. *suitable.* I.13.68; 34.111. Cf **un-**.
þæslice adv. *suitably.* II.9.28.
þæslicnyss f. *appropriateness.* II.19.221. Cf **un-**.
þæt conj. *that, so that, in order that.* I.1.30, 32; 2.8–11; II.1.25–7; 2.5, 18. (For demonstr. and relative, see under **se**.)
þe indecl. rel. particle. *who, which, that.* I.1.31, 34; 2.12, 16; II.1.11, 57; 2.2, 42; combined with demonstrative, **se þe** etc., I.1.60; 2.31; II.1.4, 132; 2.13. Also used to form a conjunction with **for þam, for þy, þeah** etc.
þeah adv. *yet, however, nevertheless.* I.2.185; 38.47; II.2.45; 11.537; as **swa þeah**, I.7.102; 8.171; II.1.57; 2.134 (the usu. form in CH II). conj., *although.* I.14.216; 16.128; II.11.540; 19.17; more commonly as **þeah þe**, I.praef.106; 1.269; II.4.180; 5.173. [c400 ex.] See also **þeahhwæþere, swaþeahhwæþere**.
þeahhwæþere adv. *yet, however, nevertheless.* I.9.13; 10.24; 11.98; 13.10. II.3.131; 20.106. [77 ex; only 6 in CH II]
geþeaht n. *design, intention, advice.* I.5.90; 20.138; 25.30; II.2.114; *council, meeting* I.3.23, 27. **þeaht** 1x. [9 ex.]
þeahtian vb II. *to deliberate, discuss in council.* I.37.235.

þearf f. *need.* I.17.70; 24.63; II.9.21; 12.107. [11 ex.] Cf **nydþearfnyss**.

þearfa m. *poor or needy person.* I.18.174 ff; 19.43; II.7.59; 23.15; used adjectivally, I.9.84; 36.188; II.6.170; 9.42. [101 ex.]

þearfleas adj. *without need or necessity.* I.5.81; II.30.108.

þearflice adv. *profitably.* I.36.284.

þearle adv. *greatly, severely, very.* I.2.97; 6.16; II.1.239; 2.15. [53 ex.]

þeaw m. *custom, practice, way of life, behaviour.* I.6.81; 8.85; II.3.183; 5.69. [67 ex.] Cf **un-**.

þeawfæst adj. *well-behaved.* II.19.101.

þeawfæstnyss f. *good behaviour, proper living.* II.1.136; 19.112; 36.53.

geþeawian vb II. *to accustom, discipline, instil with a way of life.* I.26.212; II.4.79.

þeawleas adj. *ill-behaved.* II.23.190.

þeawlic adj. *moral.* **æfter þeawlicum andgite** *according to the moral or tropological sense.* I.7.227; II.8.37; 12.357.

þecen f. *roof.* I.8.109.

þegen m. *follower, supporter, officer, nobleman.* ref. to someone of wealth or high standing, incl. an officer of an emperor or king, I.praef.47; 22.88; 27.239; II.11.302; 21.3, 146; 34.199; ref. to apostles and saints, etc, as thegns of God, I.1.267; 11.200; II.14.141; 34.56. **þeignas** 1x. [49 ex.] Cf **heah-**. See also **þen**.

þegenlic adj. *brave.* I.24.66; 38.154, 163.

þegenlice adv. *bravely.* I.24.64; 38.161.

þen m. *servant.* (Usu. viewed as a variant spelling of **þegn**, but usage in CH seems generally distinct.) I.21.213 (= **famulus**); 26.149, 238; II.3.281; 11.73. [14 ex.] Cf **disc-**.

þencan vb I. *to think, think about, intend.* I.1.56; 15.52; 26.184–8; II.29.29; 30.149. Pret. **þoht-**. [14 ex.] Cf **be-**.

geþencan vb I. *to think.* II.40.153; *to think about, remember* I.20.197; 37.272 (w. gen.). Pret. **geþoht-**.

þenian vb II. *to serve, attend to.* w. dat. I.11.26; 19.226; II.7.170; 29.91–2; *to supply, provide* I.34.196; II.8.102. [38 ex.]

þeningboc f. *service-book.* I.6.138.

þeninggast m. *attending spirit.* I.34.130.

þeningman m. *servant.* I.4.11 (**þeninc-menn**); 35.23; II.4.13–14.

geþensum adj. *serviceable, useful.* I.34.234; II.10.63.

þenung f. *serving, service (incl. religious service or rite).* I.5.103; 39.2; II.2.145; 10.36. [53 ex.]

þeod f. *nation.* I.2.79; 3.33; II.5.45–7; 9.1, 60. [132 ex.]

geþeodan vb I. *to join, unite, attach.* I.2.51; 26.149; II.9.30; 10.18; intrans., I.4.76; II.34.95. Pres.s.3 **geþeot**. [23 ex.] Cf **under-**.

geþeode n. *language.* I.6.7; 13.26; 14.138; II.13.16.

geþeodnyss f. *unity, association.* II.32.180. Cf **under-**.

þeodolus priest martyred with St Alexander. II.18.65, etc. Theodolus 1x.

þeodorus Theodore, archbishop of Canterbury 668–90. II.10.240.

geþeodræden f. *fellowship, company.* I.34.236.

þeodscipe m. *people, nation.* I.26.93, 293.

þeof m. *thief.* I.4.220; II.7.105–7; 14.185; 18.43; 39.111.

þeofilus Theophilus, saved from the devil by the Virgin Mary. I.30.192.

þeoh n. *thigh.* II.13.193–203.

(ge)þeon vb 2. *to thrive, prosper, flourish, grow, grow up.* I.25.41; 37.15; II.9.23; 10.256; **gode geþeon** *to thrive with God, achieve favour with God* I.1.113; II.1.287; etc. Pres.s.3 **geþihþ**; pl. **geþeoþ**; pres.pt. **(ge)þeonde**; pret. **(ge)þeah, (ge)þug-**; pp. **geþogen**. [50 ex.] See also **geþungen**. Cf **fore-, ofer-**.

þeorf adj. *unleavened.* II.12.364; 15.14, 27, 262, 270.

þeorfnyss f. *unleavened state, purity.* II.12.365; 15.268.

þeosterful, þeostorful adj. *dark.* I.4.150; II.20.94; 21.34, 43.

þeosterlic adj. *dark.* I.34.55.

þeostru n.pl. *darkness.* I.8.180–2; 35.182–97; II.12.75; 16.214, 218. nap. **-a, -u**. **þystrum** 1x. [43 ex.] Cf **aþeostrian**.

þeotan vb 2. *to roar, howl.* I.26.144.

þeow, þeowa m. *servant, minister.* I.1.77; 8.32; II.3.233; 19.216. ns. **þeow** (10x), **þeowa** (32x); as. **þeow** (1x), **þeowan** (c10x); gds. **þeowan**; nap. **þeowas** (17x), **þeowan** (c18x); gp. **þeowena** (1x); dp. **þeowum**. Strong forms preferred in phrase **Godes þeow(as)**, *God's minister(s)*. [128 ex.] Cf **efen-**.

þeowcnapa m. *servant*. II.34.199.

þeowdom m. *service, servitude*. I.8.165; 22.25; II.5.248; 35.45. [17 ex.]

þeowe adj. *serving?* In **þeowe men** *servants*. I.26.219; II.4.255; 19.215, 221; 26.121.

þeowian vb I/II. *to serve, be subordinate to*. w. dat. I.4.234; 11.103; II.1.207; 31.3–5. Inf. **-wgean, -wgian, -wian**; pres.s.3 **-waþ**; pl. **-wiaþ**; pret. **þeoud-, þeowd-, þeowod-**. [33 ex.]

[**þeowraca**] m. *threat*. I.30.223 (as. **-ce**); 37.97; II.3.147; 10.167. (Mainly weak, and apparently masc. at I.37.97 but cf app. crit.) [7 ex.]

þeowt m. *servitude, service*. I.7.147; 28.57; II.15.45; 19.224–6. [19 ex.]

þeowtlic adj. *of servitude*. II.12.310.

þeowtling m. *slave*. I.6.24 (**þeowet-**); II.13.78.

þes m., **þeos** f., **þis** n. dem. pron. and adj. *this*. I.praef.49, 58, 70, 77, 78, 123; II.1.1, 8, 14, 62, 134, 149, 150, 184, 218, 275. Forms: **þes, þess; þisne, þysne; þises, þyses; þissum, þisum, þysum; þeos; þas; þisere, þissere, þysre, þysse** (1x), **þyssere, þyssre; þis, þiss; þises, þyses; þysum, þisan, þison, þissum; þas; þissera; þisum, þissum, þysum**.

þicce adj. *thick, dense*. I.AppB3.203; II.11.52; 12.75; 21.35.

þicce adv. *thickly*. II.11.53.

þicgan vb I. *to eat*. I.11.55; 19.121; II.11.267; 15.19. Pret. **þigd-, þygd-** (1x), **þyged-** (1x). **geþicgan** 1x. [32 ex.]

þider, þyder adv. *thither, to that place*. I.9.55; 26.289; II.2.13; 7.94. [22 ex.]

þigen f. *eating*. I.7.251; 19.125; II.7.7; 19.294. **þygene** 1x. [14ex.]

þin poss. adj. *your*. I.2.151; 11.208–9; II.1.183; 3.268. [c.489 ex.]

þincan vb I. *to seem*. I.5.183; 6.84–5; II.5.36; 13.46; *to think?* II.3.94 (cf app. crit. for 93–4); **beon (weorþan) geþuht** *to seem, appear, seem advisable* I.2.134; 5.144; II.2.28; 3.134. Pret. **þuhte**; pp. **geþuht**. [80 ex.] Cf **of-**.

[**geþincþ**] f. *dignity, honour*. I.5.64; 6.159; 24.152; II.1.292; 6.50. as. **-þe**; nap. **-þu**. **geþincgþe** 1x, **geþingcþ-** 5x, **geþingþ-** 6x. [35 ex.]

þinen f. *maidservant*. I.13.63, 142–5, 186; II.6.133; 32.177.

þing n. *thing, possession, matter*. I.1.17; 4.66; II.1.283; 2.16. adverbially, **nan þing** *in no way* II.1.188 (cf Pope on **ænig þing**, under **ænig**). **þinc** 9x, **þincg** 25x. [454 ex.] Cf **woruld-**.

þingere m. *intercessor*. I.23.128; 34.278; 35.251; 38.350; AppA2.6. Cf **fore-**.

(ge)þingian vb II. *to intercede*. I.4.159; 11.121; II.2.182; 19.116. [24 ex.]

þingræden f. *intercession*. I.30.231; 36.140; II.11.463; 16.183. [10 ex.]

þingung f. *intercession, mediation*. I.5.184; 11.120; II.2.46; 8.42. [15 ex.] Cf **fore-**.

þinne adj. *thin, light*. II.31.102.

(ge)þiwan vb I. *to threaten, check*. I.26.194; II.11.360; 18.78 (**þywde**); 23.138.

geþofta m. *companion, confidant*. I.3.33.

(ge)þoftræden f. *fellowship, friendship*. I.6.13; II.27.59.

geþoht m. *thought*. I.6.101; 9.70; II.6.41; 21.88. [29 ex.]

þolian vb II. *to suffer, endure*. I.25.152; 28.127; II.9.212; 11.23; *to suffer the loss of* (w. gen.) I.9.101; II.1.265; 6.150; 11.261. **geþolian** 1x. [26 ex.] Cf **a-**.

þolmod adj. *patient*. II.30.160.

þomas see **Thomas**.

þonne adv. *then, therefore*. I.praef.61; 1.79, 134; II.1.78; 2.212. conj., *when*. I.3.62; 5.23; II.1.77; 2.211; *seeing that, since* II.1.123; 10.222.

þonne conj. *than*. I.1.39–41; 6.98; II.4.29; 10.69.

þorn m. *thorn*. I.1.146; 24.67; II.6.9; 14.213–4. [18 ex.]

þornig adj. *thorny*. I.24.68.

þoterung f. *wailing, howling*. I.4.152; 5.52; II.17.123.

þotorian vb II. *to howl*. II.33.126.

þrafian vb II. *to reprove, reproach*. I.21.37.

þrafung f. *reproach, correction*. I.21.5n; II.30.146.

þrawan vb 7. *to twist, rack*. II.18.91; 34.181 (pret.s. **þreow**). Cf **a-**.

þreagan vb I. *to chastise, reprove, correct*. I.3.127; 31.250; II.8.3; 19.101. Pres.s. **þreaþ**; pret. **þreade**. [38 ex.]

þreal f. *reproval, correction*. I.25.220; AppB3.119; II.28.149.

þreat m. *crowd, host.* I.24.154; 30.123; *threatening* I.28.203.

(ge)þreatian vb II. *to afflict, coerce, press with violence or threats.* I.8.90; 28.222; 29.23, 268; 38.260; II.33.235.

þreatnian vb II. *to coerce.* I.29.117.

þreatung f. *threat, admonition.* I.28.140; 36.98.

þreo, þry num. *three.* I.1.20; 5.20; II.3.127; 9.137. gp. **þreora**; dp. **þrim, þrym**. [193 ex.]

þreottene, -tyne num. *thirteen.* I.40.36; II.9.257.

þreotteoþa adj. *thirteenth.* I.27.167; 29.264; 31.229; II.35.10.

þridda adj. *third.* I.1.280; 3.9; II.1.63; 5.73. [66 ex.]

þringan vb 3. *to crowd, press upon.* II.24.243 (pret.s. **þrang**). Cf **of-**.

þrit(t)ig num. *thirty.* I.1.186; 9.128 (**þriti**); II.3.47; 14.21. **þrytig** 1x. Decl. as adj., I.4.130, 163. [24 ex.]

þritteogoþa adj. *thirtieth.* I.26.274.

þrit(t)igfeald adj. *thirtyfold.* II.6.31, 116–9; **be þrittigfealdon** *thirty times* II.6.12.

þriwa adv. *three times.* I.4.137; 31.299; II.14.75; 16.175.

þrosm m. *gulf?* I.23.18, 85.

þrostle wk f. *blackbird, thrush?* (translates **merola**). II.11.46.

þrote wk f. *throat.* II.6.95; 9.27; 14.155.

þrowend m. *scorpion.* I.18.58, 99, etc.

þrowian vb II. *to suffer, endure.* I.praef.72; 1.271; II.1.28; 2.194. **geþrowian** 5x. [99 ex.]

þrowigendlic adj. *able to suffer, passible.* I.8.20; II.1.37; 14.267; 19.277. Cf **un-**.

þrowung f. *suffering, (Christ's) passion.* I.3.5; 9.170; II.1.22; 37.81. [141 ex.]

þrowungtid f. *time of suffering.* I.37.115.

þrowungtima m. *time of suffering.* II.4.50.

þruh f. *tomb.* I.15.13; 37.111; II.14.343; 33.269. ds. **þrih, þryh, þyrih**. [9 ex.]

þrutian vb II. *to strut?* II.11.242.

þryfeald adj. *threefold.* I.7.39 (dp. **þrimfealdum**), 204; 20.112; 33.80; II.4.13, etc.

þryflere adj. *having three floors.* II.4.298.

geþryl n. *crowding?* I.2.97.

þrym m. *host, military force* I.30.98; 37.158; II.18.9; 29.135; 33.226; *majesty, glory* I.21.79; 36.23; II.20.201; 28.107. (Senses frequently hard to distinguish in individual cases.) [15 ex.] Cf **mægen-**.

þrymsetl n. *throne.* I.5.186; 19.56; 24.92; II.30.31. [17 ex.]

þrymwealdend adj. *glory-ruling.* I.7.150; II.19.32.

þrynnyss f. *threeness, threesome, Trinity.* I.1.18; 20.6, 30, etc; II.3.120; 22.74 ff. [42 ex.]

þrywintre adj. *three-year old.* II.10.11–13.

þu, ge pers.pron. *you.* I.praef.111–5; 2.24–6; 22.97–8; II.11.317–22. Forms: **þu; þe; þin; git, gyt; inc; incre; ge; eow; eower**. See also possessive adj. **þin** and **eower**.

geþungen adj. (pp. of **(ge)þeon**?). *full–grown, mature.* I.32.210; II.5.103; *excellent, accomplished, having prospered* I.24.103, 107; II.praef.31; 3.10; 9.87, 167. [12 ex.]

þunor m. *thunder.* II.11.503; 12.68, 126, 227–30; **þunres** *Thurs(day)* II.14.26 (perhaps to be understood as gen. of *þunor* or *Þunor*).

þunresdæg m. *Thursday.* I.14.158.

þurfan pret.pres. vb. *to need, to have cause.* I.1.150; 11.18; II.3.225; 37.13. Pres.s.3 **þearf**; pret. **þorft-**. [19 ex.] Cf **be-**.

þurh prep. w. dat. or acc. *through* (spatially or causally), *because of, by means of, by, by the agency of.* I.praef.82; 1.16–17; II.praef.45; 20.164. **þuruh** I.10.176. [1201 ex.] (On the variation between dat. and acc., and Æ's changes from former to latter, see *CH I*, pp. 126, 128–32, and *CH II*, pp. xxii and lxxix.)

þurhdrifan vb 1. *to pierce through, drive through.* I.15.54 (pp. **-drifen**).

þurhferan vb I. *to pass through.* I.21.210; 30.145.

þurhgan anom. vb. *to pass through, penetrate, pierce.* I.9.170, 177; II.32.215 (pret.s. **þurheode**); 34.52.

þurhsceotan vb 2. *to shoot through, pierce.* I.4.80 (pp. **-scoten**).

þurhseon vb 5. *to see through, see into.* I.AppB3.199, 204; II.39.154. Pres.s.3 **-sihþ**.

þurhslean vb 6. *to strike through, pierce.* II.2.120 (pp. **-slegen**).

þurhsmeagan vb I. *to explore, examine thoroughly.* II.15.299; 29.130.

þurhspedig adj. *very rich.* I.34.8.

þurhteon vb 2. *to accomplish, achieve, carry through.* I.34.209 (pres.s.3 **þurhtihð**); II.7.22; 19.74; *to be strong or rich enough, to manage (it)* I.4.100; 9.76; *to manage or suffice to produce* I.38.117.

[þurhþydan] vb I. *to pierce.* I.30.250; 36.75; II.1.194; 30.169.

þurhwacol adj. *remaining constantly awake.* I.5.139; II.11.512; 34.297.

þurhwunian vb II. *to remain, continue, persevere.* I.4.8; 7.210; II.1.101; 6.165. [83 ex.]

þurhyrnan vb 3. *to pierce.* I.5.110 (pret.s. **þurharn**).

þurst m. *thirst.* I.27.107; 32.206.

þurstig adj. *thirsty.* I.38.106; II.7.124, 153, 168; 9.26.

þus adv. *thus, so, in this way, in this form.* I.4.137; 5.11; II.7.21; 35.74. [232 ex.]

þusend num. *thousand.* I.2.134; 4.116; II.14.99; 25.134; inflected (11x), I.7.104; 24.158–9; II.14.98; 20.37. [58 ex.]

þusendfeald adj. *thousandfold.* II.40.20.

geþwære adj. *united, in agreement.* I.19.209, 220; 22.120; *gentle, meek* I.14.18.

geþwærian vb II. *to be in agreement with, to accord with.* I.34.197.

geþwærlæcan vb I. *to assent to.* I.4.203; *to be in accordance with, to harmonize with, resemble* I.6.196; 36.55, 150; 40.136; II.11.65; *to agree, conspire* II.24.44; *to reconcile* I.25.18; II.40.79. Pres.s.3 **-læcþ, -læhþ**; pret. **-læht-**. [11 ex.]

geþwærnyss f. *concord.* I.19.219. Cf **man-, unge-**.

þweal n. *washing.* II.14.32; 23.190. Cf **fot-**.

þwean vb 6. *to wash.* I.29.46; II.3.56–7. Pres.s.3 **þwehþ**; pret.s. **þwoh**. Cf **a-**.

þwyr, þweor adj. *perverse, wicked.* I.16.52; 28.100–102; II.6.156; 12.55. **þwyres** adv. *back to back* II.18.126; *backwards* II.34.181. [26 ex.]

þwyrian vb II. *to act in opposition, disagree, resist.* I.26.228; 36.229; 37.46; 38.132; II.14.309; 17.74.

þwyrlic adj. *perverse, opposed, contrary.* I.praef.79; 6.177; II.6.100; 25.54. [14 ex.]

þwyrlice adv. *perversely, adversely.* I.14.70; 34.235; 35.92; II.2.27.

þwyrnyss f. *wickedness, perversity.* I.praef.88; 4.212; II.9.141; 36.82; *adversity* II.30.236. [16 ex.]

þy see **se, for þy, to þy**.

þy læs þe conj. *lest.* I.praef.130; 4.53; II.2.192; 10.115. [41 ex.]

þydan vb I. *to stab, pierce.* I.5.164; 29.209, 213; II.32.186. Cf **þurh-**.

þyderweard adv. *in that direction.* II.2.159.

þyg- see **þicg-, þig-**

geþyld n. *patience.* I.11.85; 26.244; II.1.283; 6.108. [53 ex.] Cf **unge-**.

geþyldelice adv. *patiently.* I.3.183; 9.196; II.3.87; 4.180. [8 ex.]

geþyldig adj. *patient.* I.11.6; 31.263; II.19.252; 34.249. [12 ex.] Cf **forþyldigian**.

þylian vb II. *to cover with planks.* II.18.24.

þyllic adj. *such, of this kind.* I.5.164; 28.91; II.5.126; 25.53. [25 ex.]

þyrih see **þruh**

þyrl n. *hole.* II.11.139. Cf **eh-, næs-, nos-**.

þyrnen adj. *thorny, made of thorns.* I.10.159; II.14.200, 217.

þyrstan vb I. *to thirst.* impers. w. dat. I.23.133; II.7.147, 163; 14.270; 15.182; 29.27.

þywde see **þiwan**

Ualeria province of Italy. I.28.197.

Ualerianus imperial prefect under the emperor Decius (249–51AD). I.29.59, etc.

Ueor king of Ethiopia. II.32.218.

Uespasianus the Roman emperor Vespasian (69–79AD). I.28.37.

ufan adv. *from above.* I.praef.97 ff; 27.18; II.14.276; 32.212. **ufon** 1x. [10 ex.]

ufemesta adj. *highest, uppermost.* I.21.203; II.5.96.

ufenan prep. *upon.* I.13.129.

ufera adj. *higher.* I.24.59.

geuferian vb II. *to raise, exalt.* I.25.209; 30.64; 36.125; II.9.100; 29.135; *defer, delay* I.5.59. [7 ex.]

ufewerd adv. *upwards.* II.30.118; **fram ufweardan** *from the top* II.33.257; **on ufweardan** *at the top* I.35.262.

ufor adv. *further away.* I.4.204; II.2.155; 37.199.

Uigenna Vienne in Gaul. I.18.6.

uigilia m. *vigil, eve.* II.22.28.

Uita patrum the collection of lives and

sayings of the desert fathers. I.36.111; II.15.159.

unabeden adj. *without being asked.* II.23.34.

unaberendlic adj. *unbearable.* I.5.134.

unaberendlice adv. *unbearably.* II.27.58.

unacenned adj. *not born.* I.31.167.

unacumendlic adj. *intolerable.* I.35.194.

unadwæscendlic adj. *inextinguishable.* I.35.125; II.4.266.

unagunnen adj. *without beginning, having no beginning.* II.16.197. Cf **unbegunnen**.

unalyfed adj. *unpermitted, illicit.* I.31.304; II.19.297; 20.108; 23.59; 36.84.

unalyfedlic adj. *unpermitted, illicit.* I.28.145; 31.320; II.11.69; 37.57. [14 ex.]

unalysendlic adj. *unredeemable.* I.33.152.

unamansumod adj. *freed from excommunication.* II.11.356.

unameten adj. *unlimited, boundless.* II.19.9.

unandwerd adj. *not present.* I.8.128.

unaræfniendlic adj. *unattainable, impossible.* I.13.61.

unarwurþian vb II. *to dishonour, show no respect for.* I.30.104; II.13.22, 118.

unascyrigendlice adv. *inseparably.* I.22.242.

unasecgendlic adj. *unspeakable, inexpressible, indescribable.* I.4.151; 5.127; II.11.460; 12.341. [18 ex.]

unasecgendlice adv. *inexpressibly.* I.30.160.

unasmeagendlic adj. *inscrutable.* II.13.138; *beyond conception, unimaginable* I.27.121.

unateorigendlic adj. *undying, unfading, lasting.* I.6.100; 36.97; II.31.56.

unawemmed adj. *unspotted.* I.38.228. Cf **unge-**, **unwemme**.

unawriten adj. *unwritten.* II.ExDict.7.

unæþelboren adj. *lowborn.* I.19.41.

unbefangennlic adj. *unencompassable, unintelligible.* I.20.174.

unbegunnen adj. *not begun, without beginning.* II.12.250. Cf **unagunnen**.

unbehreowsiende adj. *unrepentant.* I.33.150.

unbesorh adj. *not cared about, dispensable? healthy, not injured or handicapped? without anxiety*?. II.33.76n.

unbeswungen adj. *unchastised.* I.AppB3.112, 115.

unbeweddod adj. *unmarried.* I.13.84.

unbiddende adj. *not begging.* I.10.63.

unbindan vb 3. *to unbind, untie, set free.* I.14.118–21; 16.85–9; II.1.245; 3.54. Pres.s.2 **unbinst**; pret.s. **unband**; pp. **unbunden**. [22 ex.]

unbliss f. *misery.* I.12.37.

unbrosniendlic adj. *uncorruptible, not subject to decay.* I.16.40–41; 21.85; 27.162.

unbrosnung f. *state of not decaying, incorruptibility.* I.27.157; II.12.273.

uncarfullice adv. *carelessly, irresponsibly.* I.AppB3.69.

uncer poss.adj. *our (of two).* II.10.237.

unclæne adj. *unclean.* I.9.62, 70; 14.54–6; II.19.38; 23.158–60. [12 ex.]

unclænlice adv. *shamefully, immodestly.* I.29.256.

unclænnyss f. *lack of chastity, foulness.* I.9.72; 14.60; 39.32; II.12.496. [6 ex.]

uncoþu f. *disease, illness.* I.4.105.

uncuþ adj. *unknown.* I.15.121; 21.61; II.5.208; 20.37, 232. [12 ex.]

uncyst f. *lack of generosity, meanness, parsimony.* I.4.117; 9.106; 23.34, 50, 58; *vice* I.24.124.

uncystig adj. *ungenerous, niggardly.* I.23.31; II.7.174.

uncyþþ(u) f. *ignorance.* I.7.68.

undeadlic adj. *immortal.* I.1.150; 2.93; 20.158; II.14.221. [8 ex.]

undeadlicnyss f. *immortality.* I.1.162–4; 15.98; II.15.123; 40.179. [6 ex.]

undeaþlic adj. *immortal.* I.15.88, 122.

undeaþlicnyss f. *immortality.* II.4.286.

undeopþancol adj. *unintelligent.* I.20.176.

under prep. w. dat. *under* (with ref. to location or subjection, etc.). I.1.11; 8.92–3; II.2.53; 8.116; w. acc. I.17.87; II.2.34; 11.440; 13.193 (cf. 203). [51 ex.]

underbæc adv. *behind, back, backwards.* I.11.24, 108–10; 18.128–30; II.4.149; 14.87. [16 ex.]

underbugan vb 2. *to bend under, to suffer.* I.26.256.

undercrammian vb II. *to stuff underneath.* I.29.208.

undercreopan vb 2. *to seize inwardly.* I.27.236 (pp. **-cropen**).

undercyning m. *sub-king.* I.8.118–20.

underfon vb 7. *to receive, accept, take in.* I.1.290; 3.44; II.1.152; 7.8. Pres.s.1 **-fo**, 2 **-fehst**, 3 **-fehþ**, **-fecþ**; pl. **-foþ**; subj. **-fo**, **-fon**; imper. **-foh**; infl.inf. **-fonne**;

pres.pt. **-fonde**; pret. **-feng, -fencg, -feng-, -fencg-**; pp. **-fangen**. [236 ex.]

undergendlic adj. *unharmful*. I.21.52.

undergitan, -gytan vb 5. *to perceive, understand*. I.8.42; 10.119; II.4.77; 10.219. Pres.s.3 **-gyt(t)**; pret. **-geat, -geaton**; pp. **-gyten**. [27 ex.] Cf **be-** etc.

undergynnan vb 3. *to undertake, begin*. I.praef.57 (pret.s. **-gann**); 40.21. Cf **be-** etc.

underhnigan vb 1. *to submit to, bow under, undergo*. w. dat. I.29.72 (pret.s. **-hnah**), 182; II.34.138.

underlecgan vb I. trans., *to underprop, support from beneath*. II.10.203; *to lie beneath* (w. dat.) II.19.117 (pres.s.3 **-liđ**).

undern m. *the third hour, nine a.m.* I.4.252; 34.50; II.5.8, 52, 62; 33.30.

underniman vb 4. *to adopt, receive*. I.16.110 (imper.pl. **-nymađ**); 38.219.

underntid f. *the third hour, nine a.m.* I.22.57; II.5.93; 21.169.

underscyte m. *passing underneath*. I.40.40. Cf **on-, ut-**.

understandan vb 6. *to understand, perceive*. I.1.14; 6.94; II.2.92; 4.161. Pres.s.2 **-stenst, stentst**; 3 **-stent**; pret. **-stod, stodon**; pp. **-standen**. [85 ex.]

underþeodan vb I. *to subject, subordinate*. I.34.61; 38.54; II.10.14; *to serve, be subordinate to* II.33.33; otherwise as pp., *subject (to), subordinated (to)* I.2.49; II.22.63; etc. [23 ex.]

underþeodda m. *subordinate, someone placed in one's charge*. I.2.108; 28.183; 34.185; 35.7; II.2.210. [11 ex.]

underþeodnyss f. *subjection, submission*. I.24.92, 155.

underwryþian vb II. *to support, prop*. I.30.148 (**-wriđ-**); II.10.30 (**-wređ-**); 15.312.

undon anom. vb. *to open, undo*. I.23.143; 36.155; 37.233. Pret.s. **undyde**.

uneaþe adv. *scarcely, with difficulty*. II.11.50.

uneaþelice adv. *with difficulty*. II.10.286.

unforburnen adj. *not consumed by fire*. II.32.208.

unforht adj. *unafraid, fearless*. I.29.111; 37.178; II.14.84; 18.131. [7 ex.]

unforhtigende adj. *unafraid, fearless*. II.10.132.

unforhtlice adv. *fearlessly*. I.21.54; 34.87; II.38.201.

unforhtmod adj. *unafraid*. I.4.219; 29.6.

unformolten adj. *unconsumed*. I.32.184.

unforod adj. *unbroken*. I.19.49.

unforsceawedlice adv. *without pre-ordination*. I.16.93.

unforswæled adj. *unburnt*. II.1.252.

unforwandodlice adv. *without hesitation*. I.38.247.

unfulfremednyss f. *imperfection*. I.35.174.

ungeaxod adj. *unasked*. I.29.181.

ungebeorhlice adv. *without cause?* II.19.154.

ungebletsod adj. *unblessed*. II.33.99.

ungebroced adj. *uninjured*. I.31.144.

ungebrosnod adj. *uncorrupted*. II.39.126.

ungeclænsod adj. *not purged*. I.40.149.

ungecnyrdnyss f. *sloth, lack of zeal*. II.38.105.

ungedafenlic adj. *unfitting, improper*. II.6.129.

ungederod adj. *unharmed*. I.32.178; 37.249; II.20.75.

ungeendod adj. *endless, without end*. I.1.8; 4.269; II.12.250; 21.25. [6 ex.]

ungefoh adj. *excessive, immoderate*. I.28.117, 200; II.23.57.

ungefohlice adv. *greatly, excessively*. I.28.205; 35.88.

ungefullod adj. *unbaptized*. II.3.256; 34.42.

ungehealdsum adj. *unchaste, unrestrained*. I.AppB3.164; II.12.502.

ungehrepod adj. *untouched*. I.1.152.

ungehyrsum adj. *disobedient*. I.1.157–8; AppB3.161; II.4.181; 11.428.

ungehyrsumnyss f. *disobedience*. I.1.82; 7.153; II.11.424; 12.539.

ungelaþod adj. *uninvited*. I.8.129.

ungelæred adj. *unlearned*. I.praef.51; 6.84; II.10.98; Expl.3. [12 ex.]

ungel m. *fat, lard*. I.35.76.

ungeleafful adj. *unbelieving, lacking faith*. I.3.29; 4.194; II.4.127; 40.93. [23 ex.]

ungeleaffulnyss f. *lack of faith*. I.21.111; 39.34; II.12.437; 13.12. [7 ex.]

ungeleaflic adj. *not believable*. II.Ex-Dict.10.

ungelic adj. *unlike*. II.2.166.

ungelimp m. *misfortune*. I.18.132; 38.120; II.6.112–4; 10.149. [17 ex.]

ungelimplice adv. *unseasonably? by* or *bringing ill-fortune?* II.37.49.

ungelyfed adj. *unbelieving, not believing (in the true God)*. I.31.100; II.3.291; 12.397.

ungelyfendlic adj. *incredible*. I.5.135.

ungemetegod adj. *immoderate, excessive, given to excess*. I.39.81; II.12.504; ExDict.3.

ungemetegung f. *lack of moderation, intemperateness*. II.37.46.

ungemetlice adv. *excessively, without moderation*. I.35.85; II.11.364; 23.73; 40.266.

ungemyndig adj. *forgetful*. I.5.74; II.10.206.

ungerad adj. *foolish, misguided*. I.10.185; 21.169; II.29.126.

ungerim adj. *countless*. I.praef.75; 21.240; II.4.220; 11.565. [14 ex.]

ungeriped adj. *premature, untimely*. I.27.97.

ungesælig adj. *wretched, accursed, unfortunate* (but with implications of personal responsibility rather than bad luck). I.4.114; 15.171; 29.134, 214; 32.87; AppB3.77.

ungesælþ f. *misery*. I.28.122.

ungesceadwis adj. *irrational, unintelligent, foolish*. I.14.54; 30.215; II.19.176; 34.105.

ungesceadwislice adv. *unwisely, illadvisedly*. II.35.118. Cf **unsceadwislic**.

ungesceapen adj. *unmade, not having been created*. I.31.294.

ungesewen adj. *unseen*. I.7.106.

ungesewenlic adj. *invisible*. I.2.110; 8.19; II.15.124, 138, etc; 25.132. [30 ex.]

ungesewenlice adv. *invisibly*. I.39.14; II.6.71; 19.33.

ungesom adj. *estranged, at odds*. I.32.51.

ungetemed adj. *untamed*. I.14.63; 29.262.

ungetogen adj. *uneducated*. I.38.24, 39.

ungetrywe adj. *unfaithful*. I.AppB3.62.

ungetrywþ f. *unfaithfulness, treachery*. I.AppB3.173.

ungeþwære adj. *at variance, discordant*. II.29.85; 34.273, 283.

ungeþwærnyss f. *conflict, disharmony, disputatiousness*. I.2.141; 33.29; II.12.530; 19.81. [8 ex.]

ungeþyld n. *impatience*. II.37.124.

ungeþyldig adj. *impatient*. I.21.170; 31.264; II.13.116.

ungewæpnod adj. *unarmed*. II.34.56.

ungewemmed adj. *unspotted*. I.2.101; 4.8; 29.16; II.1.252. [10 ex.] Cf **una-** etc.

ungewiss adj. *uncertain, doubtful*. I.11.150–1; 18.201; II.4.90; 21.44. **ungewis** IX, **ungewisre** IX. [6 ex.]

ungewittig adj. *ignorant, unknowing*. I.5.112; II.3.271.

ungewunelic adj. *unaccustomed, unusual*. I.2.47; 12.59.

ungewunelice adv. *in unaccustomed fashion*. I.40.51n.

ungewyldelic adj. *uncontrollable*. II.6.87.

ungrapiende adj. *not gripping, that cannot hold*. I.26.42.

unhal adj. *unhealthy, unsound*. II.32.52.

unhearmgeorn adj. *unharmfull*. II.3.155.

unherigendlic adj. *undeserving of praise*. II.26.56.

unhold adj. *unfaithful*. II.38.157.

unhreoflig adj. *not leprous*. I.8.76.

unhyhst adj. *least high*. I.32.128.

unleas adj. *true, genuine*. I.38.164; II.20.17.

unleaslice adv. *without lying, not falsely, sincerely*. I.2.214; II.24.105; 37.152.

unliþe adj. *harsh, cruel*. I.AppB3.164.

unlust m. *sinful desire*. I.10.69; 25.178; 33.56; II.6.99; 37.135; with ref. to sexual desire, I.9.216; II.1.81; 11.55. [13 ex.]

unlybba m. *poison*. I.4.221, 224; 21.103; II.11.73; 34.88. [8 ex.]

unlytel adj. *not small*. I.38.259.

unman m. *inhuman or wicked or foolish person*. II.14.100; 19.290.

unmæþlic adj. *excessive, cruel?* II.12.509. Cf **mæþleas**.

unmiht f. *lack of power*. II.3.128.

unmihtig adj. *not powerful, weak*. I.15.188; 20.136.

unmyndlunge adv. *without thinking, unaware*. II.11.100.

unna m. or **unne** f. *permission, favour*. I.34.80.

geunnan pret.pres. vb. *to grant*. w. gen. or acc. I.26.32; 30.253 (**uþon**); II.9.184; 10.132; 14.19; 18.21. Pret. **geuþ-**; pp. **geunnen**. [14 ex.] Cf **of-**.

unnyt adj. *useless*. II.26.56.

unnyt m. *folly, idleness*. II.23.56.

unnytwurþlice adv. *uselessly, unprofitably*. I.23.96; II.12.529.

unofslegen adj. *not killed*. II.37.148.

unpleolic adj. *safe, not harmful*. I.21.191; 31.319; II.16.140.
unpleolice adv. *harmlessly, safely*. I.27.118.
unrædlice adv. *illadvisedly*. I.30.83.
unreþe adj. *not cruel*. II.3.160.
unriht n. *injustice, wrongful behaviour*. I.1.264; 28.79; II.4.42; 5.113; **on unriht** *unjustly* I.8.174. [8 ex.]
unrihthæman vb I. *to commit adultery*. II.12.318; 25.88.
unrihthæmere m. *adulterer*. II.19.163, 170.
unrihtlic adj. *wrongful, unjust*. I.20.242; II.7.27; 20.67.
unrihtlice adv. *wrongly, unjustly*. I.38.95; AppB3.63, 73; II.12.144; 27.138. [7 ex.]
unrihtwis adj. *unrighteous, wicked, unjust*. I.praef.111; 11.34; II.4.260; 7.58. [31 ex.]
unrihtwisdom m. *injustice*. I.38.312.
unrihtwisnyss f. *wickedness, injustice*. I.praef.113; 7.177; II.4.242; 20.147. [26 ex.]
unrot adj. *unhappy, dejected*. I.22.178; 32.141.
unrotnyss f. *unhappiness, misery*. I.31.93; 40.101; II.11.296; 12.514 ff. [10 ex.]
(ge)unrotsian vb II. *to grieve, feel sad*. II.7.59; 12.515, 519; 14.39; **geunrotsod** (pp. as adj.) *sad, dejected* I.9.120; II.30.144.
unsæd adj. *unsaid*. II.DSM.10.
unsæpig adj. *without sap*. I.6.195.
unscæþþig adj. *innocent, blameless, unharmful*. I.5.166; 9.112; II.9.214; 10.196. **unsceþþ-** 2x. [24 ex.]
unscæþþignyss f. *innocence, harmlessness*. I.25.144; 28.187; II.3.189; 12.351. **unsceþþ-** 2x. [27 ex.]
unsceadwislic adj. *foolish, irrational*. II.12.360.
unscrydan vb I. *to unclothe, strip*. I.15.46; 29.126, 236; II.11.51; 14.198, 203. [8 ex.]
unscyldig adj. *guiltless*. I.praef.120, 134; 16.91; II.4.106; 14.151. [18 ex.]
unsiþ m. *misfortune*. II.10.147; *unfortunate or ill-advised expedition* II.10.253.
unsmeþe adj. *rough*. II.23.52; 34.213.
unsoftlice adv. *harshly, cruelly*. I.29.271.
unspedig adj. *poor*. I.9.78; 38.35.
unsprecende adj. *unable to speak*. I.9.126; 25.26; II.3.252, 258; 8.124.
unstaþolfæst adj. *restless, unsettled*. II.11.376.
unstaþolfæstnyss f. *restlessness, instability*. II.11.379.
unstæþþig adj. *restless, wanton, unstable*. I.32.88; II.11.109; 15.331.
unstæþþignyss f. *restlessness, wantonness, instability*. II.6.101; 11.380; 12.496, 505.
unstilnyss f. *restlessness, instability*. II.23.56.
unstrang adj. *weak*. I.10.180; II.14.146; 22.195; 24.176 ff. Comp. **unstrengr-**. [10 ex.]
unswicol adj. *untreacherous, trustworthy*. I.AppB3.171.
unsynnig adj. *sinless*. I.25.56; AppB3.109, 115–8; II.13.46; 19.291; 35.75.
untæle adj. *blameless*. I.7.158.
untællice adv. *blamelessly, without fault*. I.13.162.
untela adv. *badly, ill*. I.18.134.
untigan vb I. *to untie*. I.14.9, 13, etc; 26.137. [8 ex.]
untobrocen adj. *unbroken*. II.19.68.
untodæledlic adj. *indivisible*. I.9.234; 13.96–8; II.3.121; 13.189. [17 ex.]
untodæledlice adv. *indivisibly*. I.20.191, 202, 208; 26.51; 33.149.
untosliten adj. *uncut, undivided*. II.14.238.
untotwæmed adj. *undivided*. I.2.185; II.22.132.
untrum adj. *sick, unhealthy, weak*. I.praef.78; 2.146; II.19.252; 24.177, 187. [57 ex.]
geuntrumian vb II. *to make ill, unsound or weak*. I.praef.80, 83; 31.282; II.30.203; *to become ill or unsound* I.31.103. pp. **geuntrumod** *ill, weak, afflicted with disease* I.21.174; 31.276 ff; II.7.150; 17.9. [20 ex.]
untrumnyss f. *illness, weakness, infirmity*. I.1.259; 21.205; II.2.18; 4.51. [33 ex.]
untwylice adv. *undoubtedly*. I.20.118; 26.197; II.4.273; 5.72. [17 ex.]
untymende adj. *barren*. I.25.8; II.6.129.
unþances adv. *unwillingly, by compulsion*. I.7.99; 9.217; II.11.272; 26.133. [8 ex.]
unþancwurþe adj. *ungrateful, unwelcome, unpleasing*. I.AppB3.162 (**-wyrðe**); II.9.144; 27.102.
unþæslic adj. *unsuitable, unseemly*. I.32.97; II.10.17.
unþæslicnyss f. *unseemliness*. II.19.37.
unþeaw m. *vice*. I.4.58; 9.161; II.3.15; 11.7. [20 ex.]

unþrowi(g)endlic adj. *impassible, incapable of suffering*. I.7.223; 8.19; II.1.35; 4.170; 15.144.

unwær adj. *unwary*. I.1.121; AppB3.71; II.12.487, 537; 27.85. **unwar-** 3x. [8 ex.]

unwærlice adv. *unwarily, imprudently*. I.32.111.

unwærscipe m. *folly*. I.4.149.

unwæstmbære adj. *unfruitful, barren*. I.13.61; 25.102; II.7.77; 26.54 ff. [7 ex.]

unwæstmbærnyss f. *barrenness*. I.25.64; II.37.47.

unweder n. *bad weather*. I.35.132; II.10.52.

unwemme adj. *unblemished, unstained*. I.25.110. Cf **una-** etc.

unwene adj. *despairing*. II.34.247.

geunweorþod adj. *unhonoured*. I.1.221.

unwilles adv. *unwillingly*. I.37.274–5; II.11.511.

unwindan vb 3. *to unwind, unwrap*. I.4.137.

unwis adj. *unwise, foolish*. I.AppB2.49; II.19.98.

unwita m. *fool*. I.AppB3.176.

unwittig adj. *foolish, ignorant*. II.36.64.

unwiþmetenlic adj. *incomparable*. I.30.112, 152.

unwiþmetenlice adv. *incomparably*. I.4.101; 30.110; 38.119; II.13.143.

unwreon vb 1/2. *to uncover, reveal*. I.25.121 (pret.s. **unwreah**); II.20.51 (pret.pl. **unwrugon**). Cf **ofer-, on-**.

unwurþ, unwurþe adj. *unworthy, undeserving, worthless*. II.11.346; 15.248; 26.125; 34.108; 35.121.

unwurþlic adj. *worthless*. I.22.248.

unwynsum adj. *unpleasant*. I.12.35; II.14.286.

up adv. *up, upwards*. I.1.193, 206; 6.30; II.1.201, 243; 2.72. **upp** 2x. [57 ex.]

upahafennyss f. *elevation, being lifted up*. II.13.262.

upahebban vb 6. *to lift up, exalt*. I.28.116; II.28.11, 20. Pp. as adj., *upraised* I.4.136; 21.17; II.13.258; 22.6. pp. **upahafen**. [9 ex.]

upahefednyss f. *arrogance, presumption*. I.1.59, 127; 23.34, 58; II.28.24, 105; 38.224. [8 ex.]

upaspringan vb 3. *to spring up*. I.5.106; 20.180.

upastigan vb 1. *to ascend, climb up, spring up*. II.6.11; 17.95; 21.38; 22.31, 178. Pret.pl., subj.s. **-stig-**.

upfæreld n. or m. *journey upwards*. I.30.118.

upferan vb I. *to go up*. I.21.86.

upflering f. *upper chamber*. I.21.25 (**-ung**); 22.45; *the flooring of an upper chamber?* II.11.162.

upflore f. *upper chamber*. I.22.42; II.11.161, 523 (both ds. **upflora**).

uplendisc adj. *rustic, from the countryside*. II.17.116.

upon, uppon prep. w. dat. *upon, on top of*. I.4.236; 7.41; II.6.29; 16.143; w. acc. I.14.15; II.33.48; 39.51. [57 ex.]

upplic adj. *upper, heavenly*. I.7.235; 24.105; II.7.16; 33.256. **uplic** 2x. [26 ex.]

upriht adj. *upright, erect*. I.20.15.

upspring m. *rising, shooting up*. I.7.85; 40.44; II.6.8.

upstige m. *ascension*. I.4.21; 21.76, etc; II.1.200; 2.179; *upward journey, climb* I.34.6. **upp-** 1x, **upstie**. [36 ex.]

upweard adv. *upwards*. II.37.198.

ure poss.adj. *our*. I.1.246; 2.42; II.1.2; 2.146. [c700 ex.]

ut adv. *out, outside*. I.praef.101; 10.126; II.1.243; 5.8. [63 ex.] Cf **yttra**.

utan adv. *from outside*. I.28.41; II.3.56.

utawegan vb 5. *to carry out*. I.4.254 (2 words?). Cf **awegan**.

ute adv. *out, outside*. I.10.41; II.12.69.

utfaran vb 6. *to go out*. I.30.55.

utfær n. *way out*. I.28.142; 32.126.

utflowan vb 7. *to flow out*. I.37.110; II.14.318–9; 21.68. Pret.s. **utfleow**.

utgang m. *departure, way out*. I.15.85.

utgangan vb 7. *to go out*. II.11.358.

uton vb (pres.pl.1 auxiliary, derived from **witan** *to go*). w. inf. *let us*. I.2.33; 3.131; II.1.299; 4.93. [93 ex.]

utscyte m. *exit-point*. I.35.16, 116–8. Cf **on-, under-**.

uþon see **unnan**

uþwita m. *philosopher*. I.4.46, 54 ff; 27.143; 38.29, 38.

uþwitegung f. *philosophy*. I.30.208–9.

Uuarardah Persian general. II.33.18, 152.

wa interj. *woe, misery*. w. dat. I.6.183; 11.215; II.14.43; 19.142–4; **wa la wa** *alas* II.9.65. [18 ex.]

wac adj. *mean, humble, insignificant, of low*

quality. I.praef.44; 14.87; II.3.220; 31.51. [18 ex.]

wacian vb II. *to keep watch, be vigilant, stay awake*. I.2.21; 30.248; II.34.323; 39.23, 213 ff. [14 ex.]

waclic adj. *mean, insignificant, humble, lowly*. I.2.155, 182; 4.81; II.11.287; 23.28. [12 ex.]

waclice adv. *meanly, poorly*. I.23.43; 35.153.

wacmod adj. *faint-hearted, cowardly*. II.1.187.

wacmodnyss f. *faint-heartedness*. II.12.516; 19.189.

wacnyss f. *meanness, lowly state*. I.4.163; 23.131; II.31.78.

wacol adj. *vigilant*. I.2.110; 12.114; II.9.19; 38.232. **wacel-** 4x. [11 ex.] Cf **ær-, þurh-**.

wacollice adv. *vigilantly*. II.9.20.

wah m. *wall, fence*. I.20.184; 28.212; AppB2.12; II.28.141, 151; 40.121. infl. **wag-**. [7 ex.] Cf **suþwag**.

wahryft n. *curtain, veil*. II.14.276, 295.

wamb f. *belly, stomach*. I.4.116; 39.81; II.19.297; 29.57.

wana m. *lack*. I.19.211; II.25.92.

wandian vb II. *to hesitate, hold back*. I.AppB3.83, 86; II.38.107. Cf **for-**.

wanhal, wannhal adj. *weak, infirm*. I.8.83; 34.149; II.23.15, 81; 34.129. [7 ex.]

(ge)wanian vb II. *to reduce, repress*. I.6.103; 18.178; II.10.121; 31.100; *to wane, diminish* I.10.52–3; 25.122 ff; II.5.99. **heora ðing wanian** *to let blood*? I.6.167n. [25 ex.]

wann adj. *dull, colourless*? II.4.97.

wanscryd adj. *lacking clothes*. II.34.26.

wanspedig adj. *poor, indigent*. I.4.125; 8.133; 9.80; 37.28; II.7.44 (**wann-**).

wanung f. *reduction, diminishing*. I.6.83, 198; 25.131; 35.277; 36.21.

wanung f. *howling, mourning*. I.31.197, 271; 38.246; 40.171; II.33.250.

warnian vb II. intrans., *to take heed*. I.8.11; 23.21; II.2.198; 36.122; trans., *to warn* I.23.25, 117; AppB3.93; II.11.209; 35.124; refl., *to guard oneself* II.1.288; 26.31; 28.148. **gewarn-** 4x. [17 ex.]

[waru] f(?). *article for sale*. I.18.19 (ap. **waru**); II.9.54 (ap. **ware**), 56 (dp. **warum**). For **ware** see also **wærr**.

waru f. *protection, vindication, concern for protection(?)*. I.17.48; 27.75; 38.266; II.20.92.

gewæcan vb I. *to weaken, harrass, oppress*. I.28.121; 35.12; II.37.17, 100; pp. as adj. **gewæht** *troubled, afflicted, scourged, exhausted, weakened* I.32.206–7; 38.212; 40.114; II.19.249; 25.42. Pret. **gewæht-**; pp. **gewæht**. [14 ex.] Cf **geliþe-**.

wæcce wk f. *vigil, period of watch*. I.11.201; 27.108; II.7.4; 24.140–1. [9 ex.]

gewæcednyss f. *weakness*. II.38.99.

wæd f. *garment*. I.29.180; 32.200; II.7.165; 34.42. [6 ex.]

gewæda, -du n.pl. *clothing*. I.27.220; 39.97; II.10.268; 14.9. [10 ex.]

wædla m. *beggar, poor man*. I.22.78; 23.6; II.6.46; 7.70. [18 ex.]

wædlian vb II. *to be poor*. I.4.81, 99; 23.130; II.7.128; 10.229. [6 ex.]

wædlig adj. *poor*. II.34.26.

wædlung f. *poverty*. I.23.79; 37.29–31; II.19.243.

wæfels m. *garment, cloak (perhaps a short cloak)*. I.4.81; II.9.42; 14.117, 199 ff.

wæfersyn f. *spectacle, show*. I.4.49; 26.235; 36.79.

wæge wk f. *scales, balance*. II.28.153; 30.148.

wæig- see **weg-**

wæl n. *slaughter, battlefield*. I.34.62; II.21.155.

wælhreawnyss f. *cruelty*. I.31.257; II.12.324 (**wælreow-**); 32.60; 36.63.

wælhreawlice, -hreow- adv. *cruelly, savagely, in bloodthirsty manner*. I.21.232; 29.126; II.14.196; 19.205. [6 ex.]

wælhreow adj. *cruel, bloodthirsty*. I.praef.105; 5.4; II.2.114; 18.8. **-hræw** 3x, **-hreaw** 1x, **-ræw** 2x, **-reow** 4x, **welhreow-** 2x. [60 ex.]

wæpen n. *weapon*. I.30.240, 262; 34.58; II.13.62; 34.194. nap. **-pna, -pnu**. [18 ex.]

wæpman m. *male person*. I.9.204; 30.88.

gewæpnian vb II. *to arm*. I.4.224; 34.61. pp. as adj., *armed* I.31.206; II.14.81, 88; 20.29; 34.53. [12 ex.] Cf **unge-**.

(ge)wæpnung f. *arms, military equipment*. II.12.467; 14.108; 17.115; 25.132.

wærlice adv. *carefully, warily, prudently*. I.22.90; II.11.279–81; 38.218. See also **werlice**.

wærr adj. *careful, wary, watchful*.

I.AppB3.130 (np. **ware**); II.10.114; 11.278. Cf **un-**.

wærscipe m. *caution, watchfulness.* I.30.82; 40.55; II.28.78. Cf **un-**.

wæstm m. *fruit, crop, produce.* I.1.73; II.1.58; 26.6–9; *growth, stature, maturity* I.31.35; 40.113; II.5.95–7; 31.12. **westm** 2x. [91 ex.] Cf **frum-**.

wæstmbære adj. *fruitful.* I.24.68; 30.47; II.5.60; 9.170. [8 ex.]

wæstmbærnyss f. *fruitfulness.* I.20.167; 30.49–52; II.37.60. Cf **un-**.

wæstmleas adj. *fruitless, unproductive.* II.26.98.

wæt n. *drink, drinking.* I.4.123; 25.171; II.12.495; 40.262. [8 ex.]

wæta m. *liquid, moisture.* I.25.15, 45; 34.118–23; II.6.81, 86; 39.50, 53. [18 ex.]

wæter n. *water.* I.1.107; 4.264; II.1.113; 4.14. [107 ex.] Cf **fant-**.

wæteræddre wk f. *water-source, spring.* I.37.75; II.10.174 (wrongly printed as 2 words).

wæterfæt n. *water-vessel, water-pot.* II.4.11, 68, etc. nap. **-fatu**.

(ge)wæterian vb II. *to water.* I.21.158; II.7.78.

wæterig adj. *watery, damp.* II.25.124.

wæterscipe m. *pool, lake, water-source.* II.11.120–22.

wæterscyte wk f. *towel.* II.14.28.

wæterseocnyss f. *dropsy* (= Lat. *morbus hydropis*). I.5.132.

wæterþeote wk f. *floodgate.* I.1.192.

wæterung f. *watering, fetching water.* I.21.159; II.12.561.

we pron. See **ic**.

wealcan vb 7. *to toss, revolve.* I.18.105; 30.193 (pret.s. **weolc**).

weald conj. *in case, lest*(?). **weald hwa** *whoever* or *in case anyone* I.praef.107; **weald hu** *however* I.22.91. as adv., **weald þeah** *perhaps* II.20.133; 31.104. (See Mitchell, *OES*, esp. 2937–9.)

geweald n. *power, control.* I.praef.98; 23.139; 31.131; II.12.511. Cf **an-**.

(ge)wealdan vb 7. *to control, govern.* w. gen. or acc. I.5.42, 67; 24.124; 28.37; II.9.257; 18.83. Pres. pt. as adj., I.21.194; 23.4; etc. (7x). Pres.s.3 **gewylt**; pret.s. **geweold**; subj. **weolde**. [27 ex.] Cf **eall-, þrym-**.

wealdend m. *ruler* (used only of God). I.4.100; 21.83; II.7.74; 14.219. [25 ex.]

[wealh] m. *slave.* II.19.52 (np. **wealas**).

wealhstod m. *translater, interpreter.* I.30.12 (**wealg-**); II.9.193–4.

weall m. *wall.* I.7.61; 27.48; II.11.211; 40.121. **weal** 2x. [16 ex.] Cf **burh-, grund-, stan-**.

weallan vb 7. *to boil, surge, spring, gush* (of water, fire and bodies, and figuratively). I.5.133; 31.283; II.3.190; 21.26. Pret. **weoll-**. [9 ex.]

weallweorc n. *work on walls, wall-construction.* II.11.206, 217.

weamet f. *anger.* II.12.485, 510, 554.

weard. wiþ . . . weard, prep. with acc. or gen. *towards.* I.3.47; 21.22; II.11.249; 18.11. **to . . . weard**, prep. with dat., *towards.* I.23.141. [10 ex.]

weard m. *guard.* I.15.12; 27.46; II.14.350; 24.13. [8 ex.]

weard fm. *watch, guard.* I.26.251. Cf **cyrc-**.

weardman m. *guard.* I.15.26, 40.

weardsetl n. *detachment of guards, watch-point.* I.30.248, 264; II.24.19.

wearm adj. *warm.* II.10.56.

wearmian vb II. *to become warm.* II.21.105.

wearrig adj. *calloused, knotty*? II.17.73.

weax n. *wax.* II.16.196.

weaxan, wexan vb 7. *to grow, increase.* I.1.193; 4.280; II.6.10; 12.429. Pres.s.3 **weaxst, wehst, wexst, wexþ, wyxt, wyxþ**; pret. **weox, weox-**; pp. **geweaxen, gewexen**. [39 ex.] Cf **mis-, ofer-**.

weaxbred, wex- n. *writing-tablet.* II.12.135, 241, 250. nap. **-bredu**.

wecg m. *bar (of gold), piece (of gold).* I.4.52; 27.144–5; 34.165n.

wed(d) n. *pledge, guarantee (i.e. the visible sign of a promise, and also the promise itself).* I.1.197, 200; 3.135; 6.15, etc; II.15.153–5.

wedan vb I. *to go mad, to rage.* I.3.98; 31.234; II.11.180; 13.164; 24.137. Cf **a-**.

weder n. *weather.* II.11.498. Cf **un-**.

weg, weig m. *way, road.* I.5.32; 10.167; II.2.85–7; 6.6. **be wege** *on the journey, en route* I.27.36; II.25.8; etc. **wæig** 1x, **wegi** 2x. gp. **wega, wegena** (I.35.16, 116–8). [103 ex.]

wegferend m. *traveller, passer-by*. II.6.65; 30.49.
weigfærende adj. *travelling, journeying*. I.18.74, 174 (**wæig-**).
weigferende adj. *travelling, journeying*. I.10.183.
wel adv. *well, thoroughly*. I.praef.89, 110; 7.43; II.2.109; 3.240. **well** IX. [58 ex.]
wela m. (only in pl.) *riches, possessions, wealth*. I.4.59; 11.21; II.5.208; 6.39. [46 ex.]
weldæd f. *good deed, benefit, favour*. I.8.56; 28.222; II.15.337; 17.59. [18 ex.]
weler mf. *lip*. I.37.181; II.30.85, 98 ff.
gewelgian vb II. *to enrich*. I.21.45; 23.80; II.30.160; 36.111. [10 ex.]
welig adj. *rich, prosperous*. I.18.205–6; 23.5; II.6.46–8; 7.99. wk. **weleg-**. [22 ex.]
wellwillendnyss, wel- f. *benevolence, kindness*. I.39.99; AppB3.164.
wellybbende adj. *living properly*. II.34.122.
welwillende, -wyll- adj. *benevolent*. I.3.128; AppB3.216; II.13.111; 16.97. [7 ex.] Cf **yfel-**.
welwyllendlice adv. *benevolently*. I.24.22.
geweman vb I. *to seduce, entice, persuade, lead*. I.19.32; 29.248; II.30.54; 32.161, 200. **weman** II.16.140. [10 ex.]
gewemman vb I. *to defile*. I.2.196; 14.108; 23.83; 33.100; II.1.74; 18.20. Pres.s.3 **gewemþ**; pl. **-mmaþ**; pret. s. **-wemde**.
gewemmedlic adj. *defiling*. II.20.266.
gewemmednyss f. *defilement*. I.5.186; 6.123; II.15.266; 38.94. [6 ex.]
wen mf. *expectation*. II.34.169. **wen is** *I expect* I.6.49; 38.61. Cf **or-, un-**.
wena m. *belief, opinion*. I.7.182, 199; 8.71; 25.131; 26.26.
wenan vb I. *to believe, expect*. I.8.68; 23.36; II.3.200; 24.153; w. noun object in gen., I.36.267; II.39.119; in acc., I.23.103 (**gewende**); II.23.35. [50 ex.]
wencge n. *jaw*? II.11.440.
wendan vb I. intrans., *to turn, go*. I.5.146; 34.17; II.10.255; 11.158; trans., *to turn, change* I.11.47, 136; 19.61; 26.258; 29.218. Pres.s. **wentst, went**. [21 ex.] Cf **a-, be-, mis-, to-**.
gewendan vb I. intrans., *to turn, go*. I.1.169; 5.169, 174; II.9.226; 30.180. Pres.s. **gewentst, gewent**. [48 ex.]
weofod n. *altar*. I.3.157–9; 4.254; II.2.34; 6.144. **weofude** IX. [27 ex.]
weorc n. *act, action, deed, task*. I.1.98; 9.67; II.1.278; 5.71. [204 ex.] Cf **handge-, oferge-, stange-, weall-**.
weorcgerefa m. *overseer*. II.4.252.
weorcstan m. *masonry, building-stone*. I.28.20; II.27.202.
weornian vb II. *to weaken, wither*. I.11.56. Cf **for-**.
weorod see **werod**; **weoruld** see **woruld**
weorp- see **wurpan**
weorþan, wurþan vb 3. *to become*. I.1.157; 3.86; II.3.269; 11.376; *to happen, come to pass* II.14.96; as auxiliary for passive, I.1.158; 2.28; II.2.41; 15.89; **beon (weorþan) geworden** *to become, be made* I.1.102; 2.180; II.4.3; 13.124. Forms: inf. **weorþan**; pres.s.3 **wyrþ**; pl. **wurþaþ**; subj. **wurþe, -on**; pret. **wearþ, wurd-**; pp. **geworden**. [574 ex.] Cf **for-**.
geweorþan, gewurþan vb 3. *to become, come into being*. I.1.243; II.1.27; 13.208–11; 22.102; *to happen, come to pass* I.1.101–2; 26.289; II.11.106; 14.5; impers., *to agree, conspire* (w. dat. of person) I.22.98; II.5.6, 28; 11.83; as auxiliary of passive, I.1.111(?). Pres. **gewyrþ, geweorþ-, gewurþ-**; pret. **gewearþ, gewurd-**. [38 ex.] (pp. counted under **weorþan**)
weorþian see **wurþian**.
wepan vb 7. *to weep*. I.4.147; 11.216; II.10.21; 33.189. Pret. **weop, weop-**. [19 ex.] Cf **be-**.
wer m. *man, husband*. I.5.151; 9.196, 202; 37.7; II.1.64; 3.40; 11.96, etc. [205 ex.]
wered adj. *sweet*. I.34.116; II.23.49.
werhad m. *male gender*. II.37.195; 38.76; 39.40.
werian vb I/II. *to defend*. I.27.77n (pres.s.2 **werast**). Cf **a-, be-**.
werig adj. *weary*. II.12.277.
werignyss f. *weariness*. I.32.214.
werlice adv. *bravely, strongly*. I.12.113–6; 25.172n (**wærlice**); 36.72; 38.162; II.34.47.
wernægel m. *wart, tumour*? II.2.81n.
werod n. *army, host*. I.1.22 ff; 22.239; II.12.481; 21.63. nap. **werod**. Infl. forms **werod-, wered-**; **weorod** IX, **weorede** IX. [77 ex.]

werodnyss f. *sweetness*. II.12.368.
wesan see **beon**.
westdæl m. *western direction, region*. I.8.98; 34.38; II.14.241; 17.117. [14 ex.]
weste adj. *deserted, barren*. II.10.53, 172.
westen n. *wasteland, desert, wilderness, uncultivated or uninhabited territory*. I.3.37; 6.178; II.10.268; 11.86. [50 ex.]
westen adj. *deserted, desolate*. II.11.26.
weþer m. *ram*. II.40.44.
wex- see **weax-**
wic fn. *town*. I.28.32 (translating **oppidum**); *a street or district in a town or city* II.23.14, 79, 102; 24.21 (all translating **vicus**). ds. **to anre wic**; ap. **wic**.
wicce wk f., or **wicca** m. *witch*. II.19.289.
wiccecræft m. *witchcraft*. I.31.305; AppB3.246; II.40.282. (Associated with healing at I.31.)
wice wk f. *office, role, employment*. I.17.63; II.40.301.
wician vb II. *to camp, lodge temporarily*. I.2.17; 30.248; II.2.85; 12.103, 114.
wicnere m. *servant, steward*. II.5.17.
(ge)wicnian vb II. *to serve, attend upon*. II.11.287, 335.
wid adj. *wide*. I.1.186; 35.262; II.21.25; 40.57; **on widdre sæ** *in the open sea?* I.27.145; 36.76.
widcuþ adj. *widely known*. II.2.127.
wide adv. *widely, far and wide*. I.30.26; AppB2.9, 20; II.34.86.
gewideru n.pl. *weather*. I.AppB2.13.
widgil adj. *broad, extensive*. II.12.562.
widgylnyss f. *expanse, breadth*. I.21.47.
widmære adj. *widely known, widely famous*. II.2.99.
(ge)widmærsian vb II. *to publicise, report widely*. I.2.109, 204; 8.56; 25.36; II.10.300; 11.18.
widnyss f. *width*. II.40.55–7.
wif n. *wife, (married) woman*. I.1.130; 7.128; II.1.38; 19.154ff. **wyf** 1x. [162 ex.]
wifhad m. *female gender, order, rank*. I.36.123; II.1.83; 6.148; 37.196. [7 ex.]
wifian vb II. *to marry (a wife)*. I.4.9, 130; 16.136; II.13.192–5; 23.11; **wifian on** *to get married to* I.32.49 (**ge-**); II.19.162.
wiflic adj. *of a (married) woman*. I.13.109.
wifman see **wimman**.
wifung f. *marrying*. II.23.72.
wig n. *warfare*. II.12.383, 433.
wigan vb 1. *to fight, make war*. pres.pt. as adj. **wigendra** I.AppA1.6; II.12.85.
wigelere m. *one who practises sorcery or divination*. II.19.289.
wigelung, wiglung f. *sorcery, witchcraft*. as divination, I.6.162, 184–95; using plants for healing, I.31.320; unspecific, I.AppB3.246.
wiglian vb II. *to prognosticate, observe (auspices or auguries)*. I.6.162.
wilde adj. *wild, untamed*. I.14.62; 18.7; II.11.144; 12.62; 23.104.
wildeor n. *wild animal*. I.32.172 (**wildedeor**), 187; AppB2.7; AppB3.15, 133, 142 (all 3 **wilddeorum**); II.28.112, 116.
[wilige] wk f. *basket*. I.12.23, 122, 127; 27.48, 95; II.25.21 (**wylian**).
will n. *will*. **his (agenes) willes** *voluntarily, by his own will*. I.1.122; II.20.45.
willa m. *will, intent*. I.1.19; 2.31; II.5.230; 20.113. [121 ex.]
[willan] anom. vb. *to will, desire, wish, be willing, intend*. I.praef.110, 134; 1.16, 32, 62–3; II.1.30–31, 214; 26.111. Pres.s.1 **wille, wylle**; 2 **wilt, wylt**; 3 **wile, wyle**; pl. **willaþ, wyllaþ**; pret. **wold-**. [c645 ex.]
(ge)wilnian vb II. *to desire*. w. gen. I.4.58; 23.131; 32.214; II.6.130; 9.48; 10.227. [65 ex.]
gewilnigendlic adj. *desirable*. I.7.229; II.25.75 (or *desiring, greedy*).
gewilnung f. *desire*. I.9.25; 11.165; II.9.31; 12.333. [21 ex.]
wimman, wifman m. *woman*. I.1.90; 2.189; 9.205; II.11.155; 16.17. [20 ex.]
win n. *wine*. I.1.255; 4.10; II.3.17; 4.8, etc. [49 ex.]
[winberige] wk f. *grape*. II.26.5, 42.
winboh m. *vine-shoot*. II.5.50.
wind m. *wind*. I.18.18; 19.164; II.23.133; 24.63. [20 ex.]
(ge)windan vb 3. *to twist, turn*. I.20.226; 23.145; 28.211; II.34.195. Pret. s. **(ge)wand**. Cf **æt-, be-, un-**.
windig adj. *windblown*. II.19.148; *stormy* II.24.138.
windrenc m. *drink of wine*. II.14.224.
wingeard m. *vineyard*. II.5.6, etc; 26.73–5. [22 ex.]
winlic adj. *wine-like*. II.4.110, 206; 10.175.
gewinn n. *conflict, strife*. I.27.80; 29.36–7; II.10.316; 14.110. [22 ex.]

winnan vb 3. *to fight*. I.19.210; 26.154; II.4.241; 14.112. Pres.s.3 **winþ**; pret. **wann, wunnon**. [13 ex.] Cf **ofer-, on-**.
gewinnan vb 3. *to win, conquer*. I.25.76; II.12.411, 433, 546–8. Pres.s. **gewann**; pp. **gewunnen**.
winter m. *winter*. I.25.105; AppB2.6–7, 12; II.10.63; 34.27; *year* I.1.233; 19.4; II.2.22; 3.61. **wynt-** 1x. ds. **wintra** (1x); np. **-tre**. [13 ex.] Cf **midde-**.
winterlic adj. *of winter*. I.36.78; AppB2.1–2; II.21.102; 31.67.
wipian vb II. *to wipe*. I.29.171.
wis adj. *wise*. I.1.83; 9.127; II.2.1; 5.237. [36 ex.] Cf **un-**.
wiscan vb I. *to desire*. w. gen. I.38.280; 40.99 (**ge-**); II.2.192; *to adopt*? I.35.45; *to express a wish* II.18.75, 95.
gewiscendlice adv. *by adoption*. I.19.19.
wisdom m. *wisdom*. I.1.16; 22.180; II.3.144; 19.94. [100 ex.] Cf **unriht-, woruld-**.
wise wk f. *way, manner*. I.9.89, 117; 11.145; II.1.219; 12.22. Only in the form **on .. wisan** (as., ap.), **on . . . wison** (ap.), **on . . . wisun** (dp., 1x). [28 ex.]
wislic adj. *true*. II.12.370, 554.
gewislic adj. *certain*. I.7.163.
wislice adv. *wisely*. I.16.113; 34.25; II.10.12; comp. *wiser* I.praef.107.
gewislice, gewisslice adv. *truly, assuredly, for certain*. I.15.80; 23.38; II.4.119; 5.42. **wislice** II.14.212. [15 ex.]
gewiss, gewis adj. *certain, true, real, sure*. I.24.198; 26.177; 34.84; II.6.36; 15.92; 34.291. **gehwiss** I.AppB2.51. **to gewisson** *truly, as a certainty* I.6.87. Cf **un-**.
gewiss adv. *truly*. II.1.237; 18.43.
(ge)wissian vb II. *to guide*. I.3.125; 22.212–3; II.12.14; 19.95. [39 ex.]
wissung f. *guidance, direction*. I.36.195; II.33.3; 40.299, 310.
gewissung f. *certainty*. I.30.65; 40.127.
wist f. *banquet*. I.4.149, 257.
(ge)wistfullian vb II. *to feast, to attend or enjoy a banquet*. I.4.247; II.7.97; 15.267.
wit, wyt see **ic**.
wita m. *wise man, counsellor, senator*. I.7.229; 32.14, 82; II.10.288; 28.128, 137. [15 ex.] Cf **un-, uþ-**.
gewita m. *witness, testifier*. I.3.20; 5.98; II.9.149; 12.145, 327. [20 ex.] Cf **leasge-**.
witan pret. pres. vb. *to know*. I.praef.107, 123; 1.160; II.4.19; 15.280. Pres. **wast, wat, witon, wite**; pret. **wist-, wyst-**. [111 ex.] Cf **be-**.
witan vb 1. *to accuse, to lay to someone's charge*. II.11.186. Cf **æt-**.
gewitan vb 1. *to depart, die, pass*. I.3.58; 4.126; II.2.45, 59; 11.49. Pret. **gewat, gewit-**. [136 ex.]
wite n. *torment, punishment*. I.4.127; 11.223; II.20.89; 21.33. nap. **wita, witu**; gp. **wita, witena**. [78 ex.] Cf **helle-**.
witega m. *prophet*. I.praef.111; 1.229; II.1.134, etc; 4.182. **witigena** 1x, **wyt-** 2x. [223 ex.] Cf **tungel-**.
witegung f. *prophecy, prophetic saying*. I.2.209; 5.38; II.1.146; 4.312. [41 ex.] Cf **uþ-**.
gewitendlic adj. *transitory*. I.3.182; 10.111; 13.206; 27.212; 28.115.
witiendlic adj. *prophetic*. I.25.62; 36.44.
(ge)witigian vb II. *to prophesy*. w. acc. or **be** or **embe**, or **þæt** clause. I.5.51; 22.61; II.1.138, etc; 4.313. **witeg-, witog-, witighg-, wittigg-**. [44 ex.] Cf **fore-**.
gewitleas adj. *foolish*. I.38.207.
gewitleast f. *foolishness*. I.29.129; II.30.162.
witnere m. *punisher, tormentor*. I.28.161.
(ge)witnian vb II. *to punish*. I.23.32; 40.176; II.9.129; 19.156–7. [14 ex.]
witniendlic adj. *of punishment*. I.28.123; II.20.203, 208; 40.272, 275, 283; *worthy of punishment* II.34.302.
witnung f. *punishment*. I.28.154, 160.
witnungstow f. *place of punishment*. II.21.72, 114.
gewitnyss f. *testimony, evidence*. I.8.13; 32.183; II.1.214; 33.181. [18 ex.] Cf **leas-**.
witodlice adv. *truly, certainly*. I.1.289; 3.113; II.4.192; 5.137. [183 ex.]
gewitt n. *intelligence, sense, sanity*. I.1.259 (**gewyt**); 24.95–6; II.10.152; 28.119; 32.145. [8 ex.]
gewittig adj. *sane, having full senses*. I.25.41; 37.125; II.2.10; 10.154. [9 ex.] Cf **fore-, un-, unge-**.
gewittiglice adv. *sanely, with full senses*. I.31.54.
wittseoc adj. *lunatic*. I.31.56 (**wit-**); II.23.169, 172 (**gewitt-**); 33.156.

wiþ prep. w. dat. or acc. *against, in opposition to*. I.3.136; 20.213; II.1.81; 10.114; *with* (usu. ref. to speech, etc.) I.29.287, 294; II.24.37; *in exchange for* I.27.144; II.5.7; w. acc. or gen., *towards* I.2.148; II.24.65; **wiþ . . . weard** (w. acc. or gen.) *towards, in the direction of* I.3.47; 26.191; II.11.480. [167 ex.]. (For authorial changes from dat. to acc., see *CH I* pp. 128–32, and *CH II* pp. lxxx–lxxxi.)

wiþbredan vb 3. *to withhold*. I.5.159 (pret.pl. **-brudon**).

wiþcweþan vb 5. *to oppose, reject, repudiate, deny, refuse*. w. dat. or occas. acc. I.praef.91; 3.174; II.2.26; 4.168. Pres.s. **-cwyst; -cweþ, -cwyþ**; pret. **-cwæþ, -cwæd-**. [37 ex.]

wiþercora m. *reprobate, sinner, one damned or not elect* (often opposed to **gecorenan**, *the elect*). I.23.87; 31.202; 35.168, 194.

wiþercoren adj. *reprobate, one damned or not elect*. I.23.91; 28.103; 35.134, 282; II.39.135. [10 ex.]

wiþercorennyss f. *apostasy? state of being reprobate or non-elect?* II.16.167.

wiþerian vb II. *to resist, struggle*. I.36.230; II.3.86; 4.240; 9.96; 13.12; 35.27.

wiþerræde adj. *opposed, contrary, rebellious*. I.18.138; II.13.244.

wiþersaca m. *adversary, apostate*. I.26.176, 202; 30.200, 211, etc; II.34.20. [9 ex.]

wiþersæc n. *apostasy*. II.14.139. Cf **and-**.

wiþersteal m. *place of conflict or betrayal?* II.14.109.

wiþertalu f. *speech in defence*. I.35.170.

wiþerweard adj. *resisting, opposing*. II.12.436; 19.279.

wiþerweardlic adj. *contrary, hostile*. I.1.123.

wiþerweardnyss f. *rebelliousness, opposition*. I.1.60.

wiþerwinna m. *adversary*. I.24.64; 26.106; II.18.15; 20.67. **wiþærwinna** IX. [20 ex.]

wiþfeohtan vb 3. *to oppose*. w. dat. II.34.87 (pret.s. **-feaht**).

wiþhabban vb III. *to resist, restrain*. I.33.56 (pres.s.3 **-hæfð**).

wiþinnan adv. *inside, inwardly*. I.8.182; 37.241; II.14.33; 15.104. [30 ex.]

wiþmetan vb 5. *to compare, liken, equate*. **to wiþmetenne** *to be likened to, comparable to* I.32.169, 173; 38.315; II.13.123; pp. **wiþmeten, -mæten** *compared, likened* I.6.94; 10.40; II.12.203; 39.33. [16 ex.]

wiþmetennyss f. *comparison*. I.40.175; II.3.13; 23.82; 28.62, 124.

wiþsacan vb 6. *to renounce, reject, deny*. w. acc. or dat. I.9.154; 14.128; II.3.250; 14.75–7. Pres.s. **-sæcst, -sæcþ**; pret. **-soc, -soc-**. [46 ex.] Cf **for-**.

wiþstandan vb 6. *to resist, oppose*. w. dat. I.1.13; 3.42; II.11.50; 28.125. Pres.s.3 **-stent**; pret. **-stod**. [25 ex.]

wiþþe wk f. *rope*. I.38.289, 310.

wiþufan adv. *above, at the top*. I.29.213; 35.267; 40.26, 151 (see **herwiþufan**).

wiþutan adv. *outwardly, outside*. I.5.127; 8.184; II.3.56; 14.32. prep. w. dat. *outside*. II.30.48. [37 ex.]

[**wlæc**] adj. *warm*. ds. **wlacum** I.5.144.

wlite m. *beauty*. I.13.109; 15.25; II.9.59, 69; 28.108. [10 ex.]

wlitig adj. *beautiful*. I.1.25; 30.115; II.9.61; 31.71. Infl. forms **wlitig-, wliteg-**. [17 ex.]

wlitigian vb II. *to beautify*. I.35.157–8.

wod adj. *mad*. I.20.249; 31.50; II.3.263; 23.148. [24 ex.]

wodlic adj. *mad, insane*. II.11.466.

wodlice adv. *madly*. II.13.110.

wodnesdæg m. *Wednesday*. II.9.158.

wodnyss f. *madness*. I.31.56–9; II.2.115; 10.139; 11.263. [10 ex.]

woh n. *error, falsehood*. ds. **woge** I.praef.133; II.praef.48.

wohnyss f. *crookedness, falsity, irregularity, wickedness*. I.25.189; AppB3.74, 176; II.11.68; 19.31.

wolcn n. *cloud*. I.1.199, 290; 21.19; II.11.498; 12.111. nap. **wolcnu**. [29 ex.]

wolcnread adj. *scarlet* (= Lat. *coccin(e)us*). II.14.199, 211; 19.140.

wolice adv. *wrongly, unjustly*. I.AppB3.78, 154. (From **woh**.)

wom mn. *blemish*. I.16.133; 36.95.

wop m. *weeping*. I.4.41; 5.52; II.2.25; 9.128. [45 ex.]

woplic adj. *tearful*. I.25.78; 28.20.

word n. *word, speech, message, clause*. I.2.33; 25.140; II.1.198; 12.136. [360 ex.] Cf **greting-, hosp-, orgel-**.

wordfæst adj. *true to one's word*. I.AppB3.172.

wordlung f. *idle talk*. II.12.524.

worian vb II. *to wander, roam.* pres.pt. **worigende** I.9.195; 11.39; II.2.125; 11.111, 579.

woruld f. (a) *the world, the earth.* I.praef.59, 70; II.5.49; 24.135. (b) *secular life, worldly terms.* I.4.100; II.9.15; 20.20. (c) *time, age.* II.1.128; in expressions meaning *for ever*, **on ealra worulda woruld** I.2.223; II.6.205; etc.; **a on worulde** I.23.167; **a to worulde** II.38.240. (d) *the next world.* II.1.180; 21.164. **weoruld** 2x. as. **woruld.** [229 ex.]

[woruldcaru] f. *secular or worldly cares, preoccupations, concerns.* II.1.290; 6.94; 11.336.

woruldcræft m. *secular skill or trade.* I.27.119.

woruldhlisa m. *worldly fame.* II.39.77.

woruldlæce m. *earthly physician.* I.31.268.

woruldlic adj. *earthly, worldly, physical.* I.4.49; 10.156; II.9.37; 24.217. **woreld-** 2x; **worold-** 4x. [59 ex.]

woruldlufu f. *love of the world.* I.34.209.

woruldmen m.pl. *ordinary people (as distinct from the learned or perfect or the apostles), the ignorant.* I.12.123; 26.23, 29n; 27.181; II.6.152; 11.7. [9 ex.]

woruldrica m. *person with worldly power or wealth.* II.34.255.

woruldþing n. *earthly possession.* I.27.123, 126; 38.69; II.9.29; 21.16. [16 ex.]

woruldwisdom m. *earthly wisdom.* I.4.50; 38.25 (printed as two words).

worung f. *wandering.* II.12.524.

wracu f. *vengeance.* I.5.125; 11.137; II.2.194; 14.194. [18 ex.]

wræcful adj. *miserable, full of hardship, of exile.* I.5.94; 32.196, 220; II.29.40; 37.62. [7 ex.]

wræcsiþ n. *exile.* I.4.27 ff; 32.45; 37.55 ff; II.9.88. [9 ex.]

wræcsiþian vb II. *to live in exile.* I.37.56.

wrecan vb 5. *to punish, avenge* (w. sin or injury as object). I.7.175; 26.215; II.9.155; 13.117; 20.80; 27.65. Cf **a-**.

gewrecan vb 5. *to avenge* (w. injury or person as object). I.23.100; 26.180; 35.109; II.27.42; ExDict.14. Pret.s. **gewræc**; pp. **gewrecen**.

wregan vb I. *to accuse, lay charges against* (w. person as object); *to report (as a charge)* (w. crime as object). I.31.202; 32.44; 37.200; II.14.150; 26.126. Pret. **wreht-, gewregdon** (1x); pp. **gewreged** 2x, **gewreht** 3x. [11 ex.]

wregere m. *accuser.* II.20.77, 146.

gewrit n. *writing, scripture, letter.* I.praef.54; 2.9; II.9.236; 14.233. nap. **-tu.** [55 ex.] Cf **ærend-, hand-**.

writan vb 1. *to write (as author or scribe), copy.* I.praef.131; II.18.51; 20.6; 34.127. Pret.s. **wrat**; pp. **gewriten.** [10 ex.] Cf **a-**.

writere m. *writer, scribe.* I.praef.130; 12.65; II.praef.45. Cf **wyrd-**.

wriþa m. *thong, loop (for binding).* I.37.180.

gewriþan vb 1. *to bind, tie.* I.14.47; 33.52; II.2.91; 15.305. Pret.s. **gewraþ**; pp. **gewriþen.** [24 ex.]

wroht f. *accusation.* II.14.150.

gewrohton see **(ge)wyrcan**

wucu f. *week.* I.6.168–9; 14.181; II.5.245; 16.208. ns. **wucu**; gds. **wucan;** dp. **wucan, -on.** [10 ex.]

wudehunig n. *wild honey.* I.25.46.

wudewe, wuduwe see **wydewe**.

wudu m. *a wood, grove, woods, wooded area.* I.4.85; 26.285; II.3.19; 11.145; *firewood* II.4.138–40, 167. as. **wudu, wuda**; ds. **wuda**; ap. **wudas.** [12 ex.]

wudung f. *collecting firewood.* II.12.561.

wuht fn. *creature, object.* II.33.111.

wuldor n. *glory.* I.2.30; 4.143; II.4.23; 12.123. **wuldre, wuldres.** [137 ex.]

wuldorbeagian vb II. *to crown with glory.* I.3.93, 129, 199; 5.121 (**to -gienne**, *to be crowned*); 36.82.

wuldorbeah m. *crown (of glory).* I.3.93; 29.9, 33; II.32.179; 33.229, 233. ds. **wulderbeage.** Cf **swur-**.

wuldorful, wulder- adj. *glorious.* I.29.38; 36.38; II.2.75; 31.70. [18 ex.]

wuldorfullice adv. *gloriously, with glory.* I.5.60; 30.66, 167; II.9.256.

wuldrian vb II. *to glorify, celebrate* (trans.). I.2.39; 14.151; II.13.31; 17.89; *live in glory* I.3.201; II.38.95; **wuldrian on** *glory in, rejoice in, celebrate* I.36.262; 38.42–3; II.31.82; 35.65, 86. [35 ex.]

wulf m. *wolf.* I.2.110; 17.6, etc; II.26.4; 36.8. [25 ex.]

[wull] f. *wool.* ds. **wulle** I.AppB3.10, 47.

gewuna m. *custom, habit.* I.6.137; 29.30; II.10.79; 20.87. [31 ex.]

wund f. *wound.* I.3.105; 9.133; II.6.42; 11.54. [18 ex.]

gewundian vb II. *to wound.* I.9.173; 14.183; II.12.218; 15.322. [6 ex.] Cf **for-**.
wundor n. *miracle, wonder, wonderful thing.* I.praef.75; 20.173; II.11.18; 33.49. nap. **wundra, wundru** (1x). [134 ex.]
wundorlic, wunder- adj. *wonderful, miraculous.* I.9.164; 11.83; II.6.192; 11.529. [19 ex.]
wundorlice, wunder- adv. *wonderfully, miraculously.* I.6.196; 24.135; II.10.176; 31.73. [10 ex.]
wundrian vb II. *to wonder, wonder at.* w. gen. I.2.37, 203; 8.95, 139; II.1.259; 33.243; w. acc. I.38.197. [32 ex.]
wundrung f. *amazement, wonder.* I.15.57; 22.52; II.11.19, 323.
gewunelic adj. *customary, usual.* I.2.188; 4.50; II.1.65; 2.135. [19 ex.]
gewunelice adv. *usually, commonly, by custom.* I.2.212; 34.35; II.21.129; 29.19. [8 ex.] Cf **unge-**.
wunian vb II. *to live, dwell, remain.* I.8.78; 9.96; II.1.90; 4.300, 302. [224 ex.] (**Gewuniað** at I.35.140 should probably be **Ge wuniað**.) Cf **on-, þurh-**.
gewunod adj. *accustomed.* I.36.108; II.2.132; 10.74; 11.70, 145. [10 ex.]
wunung f. *dwelling, habitation.* I.1.65; 3.197; II.5.153; 6.147. [49 ex.] Cf **mid-, on-**.
wurpan vb 3. *to throw, cast.* I.3.97; 14.15; II.16.115; 18.123. Pres.s.3 **wyrpþ**; pl. **wurpaþ, weorpaþ**; pret. **wearp, wurp-**. **gewearp** 1x. [34 ex.] Cf **a-, to-**.
wurþ n. *value, price, worth.* I.4.60, 64; 22.79; 38.108; II.14.164. [9 ex.] Cf **pening-**.
wurþan see **weorþan**
wurþe, wyrþe adj. *worthy, deserving.* I.39.17; 9.187; II.19.51; 26.88. [29 ex.] Cf **deor-, un-**.
wurþful adj. *full of honour.* I.13.41; 30.170.
wurþfullice adv. *with honour, worthily.* I.20.159; 30.177, 261.
wurþfulnyss f. *honour.* I.24.156.
wurþian vb II. *to honour.* I.2.156; 8.134; II.1.278; 2.178. Pres. **wurþ-, weorþ-**; pret. **wurþod-, weorþod-**. [81 ex.] Cf **unweorþod, ar-, unar-**.
wurþlice adv. *honourably, fittingly.* I.3.63.
wurþmynt m. *honour.* I.2.112; 17.38; II.10.230; 19.56. **wyrþ-** 3x. [91 ex.]
wurþscipe m. *honour.* I.24.171; 34.247; 36.174; II.6.52. **weorþ-** 1x, **wyrþ-** 1x. [7 ex.]
wydewe wk f. *widow.* I.4.39; 9.182, etc; II.2.101; 7.117. **wudew-** 5x, **wuduw-** 5x. [38 ex.]
wyfan vb I. *to weave?* I.32.200.
gewyht f. *weight.* II.14.341.
gewyldan vb I. *to subdue, overpower.* I.1.287 (w. gen.); 12.111; II.12.62; 37.127–8 (other examples of **gewylt** prob. all from **gewealdan**). pp. **gewyld**; as adj., **gewyldra** *more subdued* I.19.162. [15 ex.] Cf **ungewyldelic**.
gewylde adj. *powerful.* II.12.245.
[wylian] vb I/II. *to roll.* II.11.52. Cf **awilian. For wylian see also wilige.**
wyll m. *spring, well.* II.25.126.
wylm m. *fervour.* II.9.177.
wyln f. *female servant.* I.7.134–5; II.14.132–4.
wylspring m. *spring, water-source.* I.1.192 (**-spryngas**); 3.123 (**-springcg**); 37.71, 79; II.3.97 (**wyll-**); 15.112.
wynn f. *joy.* II.10.182; 34.304; 38.240.
wynstra adj. *left.* I.15.91; II.7.137, 143, 160; 16.160; as noun, *left side or hand* (m.) II.14.242.
wynsum adj. *pleasant.* I.30.154; 34.118; II.10.174; 21.83. [17 ex.] Cf **un-**.
wynsumlice adv. *pleasantly, delightfully.* I.7.237; 30.100.
wynsumnyss f. *pleasantness, sweetness.* I.29.211; AppB3.125; II.10.171; 20.49. [7 ex.]
(ge)wyrcan vb I. *to perform, build, make, do.* I.1.185; 4.262; II.3.28, 31; 19.59. Pres.s.2 **wyrcst**; 3 **wyrcþ, wyrhþ**; pret. **-worht-, wurhton** (1x), **gewrohton** (1x); pp. **geworht**. **wircan** 1x. [262 ex.] Cf **be-, for-**.
gewyrd f. *destiny, fate.* I.7.120 ff (-200); **wyrd** I.7.118.
gewyrdelic adj. *historical.* I.4.8.
wyrdwritere m. *historian.* I.5.40; 31.4; 32.189.
gewyrht fn. *action* (w. ref. to merit). I.AppB2.43; II.1.127; 20.107; 27.122.
wyrhta m. *maker, worker, builder.* I.praef.125; 21.187; II.5.5, etc; 11.188. [30 ex.] Cf **gym-, heafod-, sealm-, teld-**.
wyrian vb I. *to curse.* I.7.193; 36.164; II.2.110, 190 ff; 19.191, 205. Pres.s. **wyr-**

igst, wyrigþ; pret.s. **wyrigde. wirig-** 2x. [20 ex.] Cf **a-**.

wyriung f. *cursing.* I.6.172–4; 36.259–60; II.2.105, 123, etc.

wyrm m. *worm, serpent.* I.8.187–9; 18.58; AppB2.9 ff; II.3.161; 34.246. **wurm-** 3x. [17 ex.]

wyrmcynn n. *kind of serpent.* I.6.179; 32.178 (**wurm-**), 187; 35.139.

wyrms m. *corrupt matter.* II.30.120.

gewyrpan vb I. *to recover, revive.* I.8.123. Cf **a-**.

wyrs adv. *worse.* II.10.139.

wyrsa, -e adj. *worse.* I.1.41; 11.162; II.3.222; 21.108. **wersan** 1x. **wyrsta, -e** *worst, wickedest* I.4.141; 26.281; II.13.77; 14.285. **wyresta** 1x. [25 ex.]

wyrsian vb II. *to deteriorate.* I.8.78.

wyrt f. *plant, herb.* I.21.158; 31.320–3; II.14.342; 15.269; 31.16, 67 ff. [19 ex.] Cf **læce-**.

wyrtbræþ m. *incense, fragrance.* I.AppB2.28; II.40.182, 186.

wyrtruma m. *root.* I.8.179; 16.122; II.6.24; 26.109–10. **wyrttruma** 1x. [14 ex.]

gewyrtrumod pp. as adj. *rooted.* II.26.91.

Xerxes king of Persia in 1st century AD. II.33.7, 71, etc.

For **y-** see also **i-**.

geyc-, geyht(-), geyic- see **geican**

ydæges see **igdæges**.

yddysc n? *property.* II.11.457.

ydel, idel adj. *useless, vain, idle, empty.* I.4.56–7; 31.212; II.5.9, 79; 19.45; **on ydel** *in vain* I.4.118; II.25.116; etc. See also **gylp**. [69 ex.]

ydelnyss, idel- f. *idleness, folly, uselessness.* I.28.221; 38.261; II.4.243; 17.37; **on ydelnysse** *idly, as nothing* II.12.140, 268. [12 ex.]

yfel n. *evil, wickedness, harm.* I.praef.131; 1.136–41; II.19.150; 20.68. nap. **yfelu.** [254 ex. of noun and adj.]

yfel adj. *evil, wicked.* I.1.54; 9.67; II.4.248; 19.160.

yfeldæd f. *evil deed.* I.6.178; 7.138; 28.107; II.27.38.

yfeldæde adj. *wicked, doing evil.* I.1.214.

yfele adv. *wickedly, badly, gravely, wrongly.* I.34.213; AppB2.43; II.3.236; 14.159. [16 ex.]

geyfelian vb II. *to injure, harm.* I.3.163.

yfelnyss f. *wickedness.* I.praef.84–8; 3.189; II.5.217; 13.59. [40 ex.]

yfelsacung f. *wicked strife*(?). II.12.540.

yfeltihtend m. *inciter of evil.* I.6.176; 35.138.

yfelwyllende adj. *wishing evil, malevolent.* II.19.197. Cf **wel-**.

ylca, -e adj. *same.* I.praef.110; 1.171 ff; II.1.14; 2.24, 35. **ilc-** 7x. [174 ex.]

yld f. *age, period of life or history.* I.5.96; 6.122; II.4.83 ff; 34.8; *old age* I.13.60; 40.119; II.19.174; 34.295; *old people* II.34.127. [44 ex.]

yldesta adj. (superl. of **eald**). *oldest, chief, most senior.* I.1.224 (**yltstan**); 4.212; II.12.375; 13.192; 27.220; 30.76.

yldian vb II. *to delay, defer.* I.24.199.

ylding f. *delay.* I.5.124; 15.47; II.5.165; 9.91, 118.

yldra m. (from compar. of **eald**). *parent.* I.4.47; 7.192; 18.197; II.1.90.

ymbclyppan vb I. *to embrace.* I.38.302 (**ymclyp-**). Cf **be-**.

ymbe, embe prep. w. dat. or acc. *about, concerning.* I.1.14; 2.106; II.3.24; 8.113; *at, after (a point of time)* I.14.184; 22.17; II.11.489; 27.142. **embe wolde** *would act concerning him* I.5.79. [161 ex.]

ymbeganges adv. *in circumference.* II.33.266.

ymbespræc f. *comment.* II.9.176.

ymbgedelf n. *digging round.* II.26.103.

ymbgyrdan vb I. *to gird, fasten around.* II.39.61–2. Cf **be-**.

ymbhogian vb II. *to consider, be anxious about.* II.29.43.

ymbhwyrft, ymhwyrft m. *cultivation, attention.* II.5.57n; *orb or circumference of the world* I.5.3; 27.174; II.3.138; 37.55; *circle, circuit, orbit, course* I.20.168; 34.211; 36.12; II.12.391. **imb-** 1x. [20 ex.]

ymbhydignyss, ymhid- f. *anxiety, concern.* I.24.141; 40.57; II.6.98 ff; 31.40. [7 ex.]

ymbren, -ryne m. *course, circuit (esp. of the year).* I.5.62; 37.143 (ns. **ymbren,** but see app. crit.); II.praef.36; 7.1 (ns. **ymryne**). [19 ex.]

ymbscinan vb 1. *to shine on, around.* I.38.336 (pret.s. **-scean**); II.30.27.

ymbscrydan, ym- vb I. *to clothe*. I.14.101; 39.98; II.1.44; 12.466. [19 ex.]

ymbsettan vb I. *to besiege, surround, beset*. I.28.41, 51, 142; 37.160 (**ym-**). (All pp., and possibly used as pp. of next word.)

ymbsittan vb 5. *to besiege, beset*. I.15.161 (**imbsæton**); 28.9, 133.

ymbsniþan, ym- vb 1. *to circumcise*. I.6.9, 12, etc.; II.4.279. Pret. **-snaþ, -snidon**; pp. **-sniden, -snyden**.

ymbsnidenyss f. *circumcision*. I.6.49, 74, etc.; II.4.281 (**ymsnydennys**).

ymbstandende pres.pt. *standing by or near*. as noun, I.29.167; II.38.33 (**ym-**); as adj., II.17.10.

ymbtrymman vb I. *to support, strengthen, enclose*. I.30.123 (**ym-**), 127, 147; II.30.55; 36.81. Pret. **ymbtrymed-**.

ymbtrymming f. *enclosing force or guard*. I.28.9, 134; II.14.352.

ymbwlatung f. *contemplation*. I.24.163.

ym- see also **ymb-**

ymesene adj. *blind*. I.29.47.

ymgang m. *walking round*. II.12.433.

Ymma thegn of Æthelred king of Mercia (but a Northumbrian thegn according to Bede). II.21.147.

Ypolitus deputy of the prefect of Rome under the emperor Decius. I.29.82, etc.

Yponienscis of Hippo in N. Africa. II.2.8.

[Yras] the Irish. **yrum** II.20.258.

yrcþ f. *cowardice*. II.14.142.

yrfenuma m. *heir, inheritor*. I.2.66–8; 3.182–4; II.4.176; 9.125. [10 ex.]

yrfwyrdnyss f. *inheritance*. II.12.574 (**yrf-weard-**); 35.103.

geyrman vb I. *to afflict*. II.2.196.

yrmþ f. *misery, affliction*. I.praef.108; 23.82; II.2.128; 30.147. ap. **yrmþu** I.28.50 (but see app.crit.). [27 ex.]

yrnan vb 3. *to run, move*. I.9.218; 26.138; II.10.108; 12.405. pp. **gerunnen** *mixed, run* I.2.184; II.1.43. Pret. **arn, urne, urnon**. [46 ex.] Cf **be-, fore-, forþ-, of-, ofer-, to-, þurh-**.

yrre n. *anger*. I.40.170; II.20.184.

Yrrland Ireland. II.20.252.

yrsian vb II. *to be or become angry*. I.25.216; 29.235; 35.13; II.12.453; 13.205; 23.13.

geyrsian vb II. *to anger*. II.19.141; *to be angry* II.9.147 (w. ind. obj. **us**). pp. **geyrsod** *angry, angered* I.29.156, 162; II.32.167; 33.119.

yrsung f. *anger, wrath*. I.38.235; 39.93; II.12.511.

yrþland n. *ploughland*. I.30.217.

yrþling m. *ploughman*. I.24.66; 31.159; II.11.470; 19.181. [7 ex.]

[ysl] f. *ember*. II.19.148; 30.170.

ysope wk f. *hyssop tree*. II.40.50.

yting f. *journey*. I.2.79.

yttra, -e adj. *outer*. I.8.100; 35.24; II.9.242; 11.56. [25 ex.]

yþ f. *wave*. I.18.105; 40.8; II.10.79, 164; 24.145. [23 ex.]

yþigende pres.pt. as adj. *surging, wave-tossed, raging*. I.38.15; II.4.117; 11.503; 16.181. [7 ex.]

yþung f. *tossing, fluctuation*. I.33.16.

Zacharias father of John the Baptist. I.9.202; 13.161, 164; 25.5 ff. gds. **-ian**.

Zacheus wealthy disciple of Christ, and taxgatherer. I.8.172; 38.77 ff. ds. **-eo**.

Zaroes sorcerer opposed to St Matthew and SS Simon and Jude. II.32.83, 141; 33.4, 72, 199. as. **-en**.

Zebedeus father of the apostles James and John. I.38.10. ds. **-eo**.

Zebeus Persian disciple of Simon and Jude. II.33.110.